NATURAL RESOURCES LAW

Private Rights and Collective Governance

By

Eric T. Freyfogle
Max L. Rowe Professor of Law
University of Illinois

AMERICAN CASEBOOK SERIES®

THOMSON
WEST™

Mat #40400547

610 Opperman Drive
P.O. Box 64526
St. Paul, MN 55164–0526
1–800–328–9352

Printed in the United States of America

ISBN: 978–0–314–16311–0

TEXT IS PRINTED ON 10% POST CONSUMER RECYCLED PAPER

Preface: The Functional Approach

For many years, natural resources law has been a mainstay of the law school curriculum, and with good reason. The physical things of daily life begin as elements of the natural world. Our food, heat, shelter, clothing, cars, computers—all start as natural resources, which someone, somewhere, has severed from the natural fabric and reshaped for human use. Nature's elements provide recreational opportunities and pleasing surroundings. They sustain the ecological processes upon which all life depends.

The approach typically used in studying resources law is to consider natural resources one by one—minerals, water, timber, wildlife, and the so on. These resources, in turn, are divided between the publicly owned and privately owned. Over the years, public resources have received heightened attention as has federal law generally, particularly the legal questions that reach the United States Supreme Court. With that focus has come a heavy dose of federal administrative law and constitutional jurisprudence.

This book employs a different approach.

At its base, natural resources law is about (i) dividing nature into pieces (use rights); (ii) defining the elements of these use rights; (iii) allocating or making them available to people in some way; (iv) resolving the conflicts that inevitably arise among users; (v) integrating these use rights into landscapes; and (vi) providing mechanisms to adjust the use rights and reallocate them over time. These six tasks are the basic functions that natural resources law performs or makes possible. And it performs them, necessarily, in pretty much every resource setting.

These functions provide the framework for this casebook. The book explores the law of natural resources on a function-by-function basis, assembling and drawing upon legal materials from an unusually wide array of resource settings. With this approach, it's possible to see clearly the tasks that the law is called upon to perform. It is also possible to perceive the similarities that exist in the laws dealing with various specific resources. These similarities are hardly surprising. The law's assigned tasks are largely the same from resource setting to resource setting. So are the practical problems that lawmakers encounter.

Consider, for example, the laws that make resources available to people on a first-in-time basis. First possession (as it is sometimes termed) is used to allocate water, wild animals, mineral deposits, recreational—use rights, and other resources. When we compare cases drawn from these resource settings, we see that first-in-time encounters the same practical difficulties whenever it is used. It also (although not always) yields similar legal resolutions. Armed with these lessons, we can anticipate the problems likely to arise when first-in-time is put to use in a novel resource setting. Similar insights emerge when we examine other basic resource issues: for example, (i) how long use rights endure (chapter 6), and (ii) what powers an owner has to transfer them (chapter 7). Reallocating resources is an important functional task in all resource settings, necessary to accommodate endless economic and social change. How has the law addressed this need to reallocate, and what do we learn by comparing its answers?

One question that arises early in any resource-governance regime is deciding which resources are attached to land (and thus allocated along with land), and which resources are, instead, severed from land and made available for separate acquisition. Chapter 2 takes up this topic. One benefit of addressing the topic so early (and by examining little-known resources such as ice and seaweed) is that we see more readily that land is really just a *bundle* of natural-resource use rights, differing in degree rather than kind from other private rights in nature. In short, the law of land use might rightly be viewed as a subset of the more general topic of natural resources law! To include land use in this study also helps in another way: It provides the beginning point for deciding how an owner of a discrete resource can use what she owns. Laws that govern the uses of discrete resources (chapter 5) build upon, and are largely variants of, the basic rules that govern land use (chapter 4).

Because rights to use nature are the focus of this book, we shall deal at length with the law of private property. We'll thus spend more time examining state law than federal law—and appropriately so, given that state law resolves the vast majority of resource-use disputes. As for the federal law that does appear, it is intermingled with state law according to functional issue. In similar fashion, federal-lands questions are not separated from questions involving private lands.

Indeed, a basic theme of the book is that the categories of public land and private land are far from distinct. The public has legitimate interests in the ways private lands are used, while private actors often possess secure, enduring property rights in public lands. The federal government is indeed a powerful sovereign, but it is also a major landowner. Consequently, the federal government encounters the same problems and opportunities that other landowners face.

As this book's subtitle suggests, another issue shares center stage with private use rights in nature, and that is the whole matter of collective governance. Law comes from lawmaking bodies, which are constantly tinkering with it. Private use rights, moreover, are intermingled and interdependent, so much so that mechanisms are regularly required to coordinate or dovetail the private uses to reduce conflicts and increase overall benefits. The materials here highlight the need for ongoing governance and illustrate how the law has addressed it. On this topic, too, the book pushes readers to rethink assumptions. Just as we're prone to consider private and public land as distinct, so too we readily distinguish private from public governance methods. In truth, these categories also overlap. Looking ahead, perhaps no natural resource topic deserves more careful attention than the need for better-integrated, public-private methods to coordinate resource activities at varying spatial scales.

As we'll see, the inevitable conflicts that arise among land and resource users can be diminished (though not entirely avoided) in various, quite different legal ways. The law can try to define private use rights so precisely that all foreseeable conflicts are resolved in advance (much like drafters of contracts try to foresee problems and resolve them in the contract). Alternatively, the law can define private rights more vaguely and deal with future conflicts by creating governance methods by which the affected parties can get together more readily and work out their differences. American law has tended to favor the first of these approaches (for instance, in dealing with prior appropriation water rights), but the cost of that approach can be high in terms of inflexibility in resource-use patterns. (When rights are defined in great detail it becomes much harder to change patterns of resource use and shift resources to more highly valued uses.) Perhaps the time has come to lessen reliance on that approach and to consider more seriously an approach that relies more on process and structured negotiations rather than on clear substantive rights. As for that possibility, we'll see instances of it in various corners of natural resources law.

In the course of this study we'll have occasion to take backward glances into the law's past. We'll see that today's most contentious issues are little different functionally from legal issues addressed by lawmakers long ago. Indeed, hardly any "new" legal issue is without significant historical precedents. History is also worth studying because the past weighs so heavily upon this legal field, as it does on property law generally. One can hardly understand current law without knowing at least the rough outline of its trajectory to the present. There are some resource-use issues—such as the public's right to use waterways—where the law has become so confused that only an historical inquiry can make sense of it. With regularity courts still turn to old precedents for guidance. Nowhere is this more true than in wildlife law. (Witness one of the Note cases in the materials that follow, a judicial decision from late 2004 that employs an English precedent from the reign of Queen Elizabeth I.) In the law relating to nature, the past remains alive.

When approaching natural resources law in this manner—function by function—particular ideas crop up regularly, much like fictional characters who leave a story's scene only to return repeatedly. Four ideas appear most often: (i) *reasonable use* as an evolving limit on the exercise and scope of private rights (and the tension that reasonable use creates with such competing ideas as first-in-time and nature-as-baseline); (ii) *accommodation*, or the need for one user, when feasible, to adjust her activities for the benefit of another resource user; (iii) *ancillary rights*, or the add-on entitlements required by an owner to make efficient use of a particular resource right; and (iv) *shared governance*, or the need for resource users somehow to work in concert for their mutual benefit. Many of the Notes in the book use sequential titles—Reasonable use I, II, III, and so on—to highlight these issues and help readers track them.

Several of the Notes draw repeated attention to two further issues. These receive prominence, not because of their practical importance, but because they're likely to conflict with the reader's expectations. A common presumption (strengthened by rulings of the United States Supreme Court) is that the preeminent entitlement of land ownership is the *right to exclude* outsiders. As we'll see, however, natural resources law features many instances where this right is curtailed to promote efficient resource exploitation. To study the various limits on the right to exclude is to question how important this particular right really is. (Lawmakers two centuries ago placed greater emphasis on the related but distinct right of quiet enjoyment, which allowed owners to halt actual interferences with their activities.) Natural resources law has long embraced the notion that multiple people can securely use the same tract of land at the same time.

Also highlighted in this text is the long history of *private condemnation* in natural resources law. The widely held presumption on this issue is that condemnation has always been about takings of property for *public* use. Yet, beginning in the colonial era and gaining frequency in the nineteenth century, courts and legislatures authorized resource owners to make use of landed property rights possessed by others—to convey water to a mine or farm, for instance; to carry drainage water away; to flood a field; to gain physical access to a land-locked resource; to construct a transportation corridor; to impose dust or fumes on a neighbor, or in other ways to make resource exploitation more efficient. Sometimes the taking was acknowledged and landowners got paid. Other times (continuing still today—see the 2002 *Park County* case in chapter 2), courts chose to redefine landed property rights without compensation to facilitate the favored resource-use arrangement.

This book's final chapter includes three detailed discussion problems. These problems invite readers to consider resource challenges of the type so prevalent today—not challenges involving single resources on individual parcels, but the knottier challenges that arise when we try to integrate multiple resource uses in fragmented landscapes while sustaining the land ecologically. By the end of this text, students should be able to propose their own resource-use regimes to meet the needs of these landscapes and their fictional residents: defining the appropriate use rights, formulating governance regimes, and providing mechanisms for adjusting resource uses over time. These concluding problems could aid in a course review; they could provide topics for in-class presentations; they could serve as terminal writing assignments.

Two final comments for instructors.

This book is short enough to use in its entirety in a 3-hour, one-semester course, although it is possible, of course, to cut (particularly some of the readings in the final chapter). Because of the book's tight integration, the material is best covered in the order presented and with no major parts completely omitted (although the final chapter can be dealt with quickly if needed).

As for the specific resources studied, students will learn most about the laws governing water (including surface uses), wildlife (including inland fisheries), and subsurface land rights (oil and gas, hardrock mining, and caves). They'll receive also a basic introduction to grazing rights on federal lands and recreational land uses. Necessarily, there are omissions. Uses of federal lands are covered but not federal land planning or relations among the branches of federal government; state wildlife law is covered in its basics but not the many federal statutes; the uses and ownership of minerals are covered but few issues involving leases; and except incidentally, little is said about federal-state relations or Indian tribes, save for a brief comment on tribal reserved water rights.

While this book was in manuscript Michael Blumm was courageous enough to use it in a course and to send detailed comments on it. I'm particularly grateful for his help.

*

Summary of Contents

Table of Contents

*

Table of Cases

The principal cases are in bold type. Cases cited or discussed in the text are roman type. References are to pages. Cases cited in principal cases and within other quoted materials are not included.

*

NATURAL RESOURCES LAW

Private Rights and Collective Governance

*

Chapter One

DIVIDING AND MANAGING NATURE

Imagine a group of people, standing on a mountainside and looking upon a vast, open landscape, lacking human occupants. They are immigrants, and they arrive with the intent to make their homes and stay. The settlement challenges they face will be numerous. High among them is the need to decide how they'll use this land. In what ways should they use it? Who will do the using? And who gets to make decisions?

As the people address these questions they will no doubt consider their needs for food, shelter, clothing, and recreation. They'll also pay attention to nature itself, to the land's varied features and its interdependencies. The groups could simply let individuals wander off, one by one, and use the land however they prefer. But this approach can succeed only if their numbers remain small and only if individuals refrain from stealing or invading one another's privacy. Even if the people are unusually well behaved, resource uses by one person will inevitably conflict with the activities of someone else. What happens when two people want to use the same part of nature at the same time? What happens when one proposed land use conflicts with another one? And what about land uses (for instance, large-scale irrigation) that are possible only if people work together?

What is likely to happen is that our arriving people will come up with formal or informal laws that govern uses of their landscape. In some manner, they'll allocate to individuals and to small groups the right to use nature in particular ways and places. The options they have in doing this are nearly infinite, in terms of the precise ways they might define the use rights and then make them available. The people could retain some use rights for the shared enjoyment of everyone individually. They could reserve other use rights for collective exercise, to provide particular services or benefits for the people as a whole. Other use rights are likely to go to individuals, families, and small groups, rights to build homes, for instance, to plant crops, and to operate stores. As for allocation methods, the assembled people could give these use rights away, sell them, offer them to the first taker, or employ a variety of public-interest considerations. Like the use rights themselves, methods for allocating resources come in a wide variety of shapes and sizes.

The ways the people go about this resource-allocation work will depend to some degree upon the land itself, in terms of its natural features. Methods that make sense in one landscape may make little sense elsewhere. Even more the methods they choose will depend upon the people themselves, their numbers, their values, and their hopes. As these policy determinants change over time, so too change will come in the ways people use nature and in how they resolve their inevitable resource-use squabbles.

And thus our subject: *Natural resources law* is the expansive body of rules and processes governing the ways people interact with nature. At its core are rules that define and protect specific rights to make use of nature. Many use rights will be held by individuals, what we would call *private* property. Other use rights will be held for communal use or to provide shared services, what we would call *public* property. But we'll need to employ this private-public distinction with care, for reasons that will become evident (if they aren't already). Public and private interests—or, as we might term them, shared and individual interests—are present pretty much everywhere in natural resources law. Use rights can't be squeezed into two distinct categories. Both public and private rights are given shape by law; both of them have to do with using nature; and both are aimed at fostering the good of the social whole. Public property is often used by private actors who hold rather secure rights to do so. On the other side, the public has legitimate (albeit contested) interests in the way most private property is used. Public and private are thus complexly mixed, whether we realize it or not.

Another categorization that we'll need to employ carefully is the familiar line between owning *land* and owning some discrete *component of nature*; owning a mineral deposit, for instance, a grazing right, or a stand of trees. As commonly understood, natural resources law deals with the latter; property law covers the former. But "land" as a legal concept is really just a bundle of rights to use the elements of nature that exist in a defined place. It is a compilation of resource-use rights, packaged together and then allocated and traded as a unit. As for what use rights such a bundle might include, lawmakers must decide for themselves: there is no Platonic ideal for "land" that lawmakers can turn to for guidance. Over time and among cultures, the rights of land ownership have varied widely in time and place. To say that a person owns land really tells us almost nothing unless we know something about the surrounding culture and applicable legal regime. When we conceive of land ownership this way—as a package of use rights rather than as a monolithic entity—we are more apt to identify its many details and to spot the ways it changes over time. Making matters more complex is the fact that landowners routinely fragment their bundle of rights, selling off one or more resource-use rights while retaining others. (Though as we'll see the law does not always allow this; some resource-use rights are attached to land and cannot be severed. Why might this be done?) A landowner's bundle often changes shape due to voluntary actions.

And then we have the complexity that arises in natural resources law because one person's activities can readily affect what other people do. Here we confront countless questions about how the rights of one person should fit together with the use rights of someone else. Sometimes the conflict is between two people who are adjacent landowners (as when landowner A's mining operation pollutes neighbor B's groundwater). Instead, one might be a landowner and the other the holder of a right to use a natural resource (for instance, on oil and gas lease) located in the same place. Or they might both possess narrowly tailored rights to use different resources on the same land parcel (for instance, a right to graze livestock and a right to hunt). Whatever the situation, conflict can and will arise. One of the prime tasks of resources law is to define resource-use rights so as to anticipate these conflicts, avoiding them whenever they can be avoided and resolving them when they cannot.

Like all law, natural resources law is dynamic. Its evolution over time will also be part of our story. Nature's parts can gain or lose economic value due to scarcity, to rising human populations, to new technology, and to shifts in ethics and aesthetics. Advances in ecological knowledge also play a guiding role, as we heighten awareness of the ecological ripple effects that a given resource use can stimulate. Over the past century, pressures have risen for more integrated resource management and at larger spatial scales, at the level of the watershed, the ecosystem or the fishery. Moreover, we now perceive, more clearly than in the past, grave costs in allowing individuals to use their separate parts of nature however they see fit. Indeed, according to many observers, important land-use goals can only be achieved when decisions are made or coordinated at relatively large spatial scales. One illustration of this reality appears in the first reading: a Maine lobster fishery, which can remain productive only if the harvesting efforts of all users are coordinated, in timing, amount, and harvest method.

Landscape-scale resource management can succeed fully only if it remains attentive to the inevitable fluctuations in nature itself. How many cattle can a pasture hold, for instance? How many lobsters can be harvested, when, and of what size? The answers vary, from place to place and from time to time, often due to forces that people only dimly understand. Individual users, of course, can and should make many of these decisions. We have good reasons to propose, as an overall policy ideal, that individual users ought to possess as much independent authority over their resources as they can safely exercise. But individual management has its limits, even among individuals who are well-meaning, far-sighted community members. Many land-use goals are attainable only by coordinated action at a scale well above the individual level. And as economists have long pointed out, the good discipline of the market is not strong enough to keep the land healthy for future generations.[1] In

1. The foundation paper on what is now ecological economics offered an overview of the various economic reasons why neither the market nor private property provided

addition to these important points, we need to keep in mind that private property is a morally problematic institution (as our first reading, again, illustrates). Private property depends for it existence upon the willingness of people collectively, acting through their governance mechanisms, to protect and enforce private rights. Private property does not somehow exist in a private sphere of life, apart from the public, governmental sphere. It cannot exist in the absence of communal governance, nor without police and courts that are available to protect it. Take away this public protection—take away the law and government—and we end up with the free-for-all of the unregulated commons—the nightmare of all resource-use arrangements. Private ownership is a messier, more complicated, and more fascinating institution than we might suppose.

With these introductory comments in place we can now identify the two main elements of natural resources law, introduced in the Preface.

First, there are the *resource-use rights*. Natural resources law *prescribes* these use rights, in terms of what they include, how holders can exercise them, and how the rights of one user fit together with the rights of others. The law also *allocates* the resources by explaining how individuals and groups can gain ownership of them. As we'll see, the story of resource use rights in America has a distinct theme to it: the rise of "reasonable use" as the dominant paradigm governing resource activities.

Second, there is the matter of *governance regimes*. Some resource activities are mild enough that individual owners can act in near isolation from other users. But many resource activities require oversight or communal input of some sort, whether to enhance the resource's overall productivity (for instance our Maine lobster fishery or a producing oil and gas field) or to protect the land's lasting health and beauty. Often, governance regimes are erected in nested, hierarchical form, from the local level to ever broader spatial scales. Rules are then needed to specify the proper governance roles at each level.

Just as resource use-rights do not fit neatly into categories of public and private, so too governance regimes come in diverse shapes and sizes. Best known are the law-making engines of constituted civil governments, whether federal, state or local. But natural resource lawyers have always had an element of imagination that other lawyers have lacked(!) Governance regimes can take many other forms, blending private and public. Resource-users in particular settings could create their own governance regimes without consulting outsiders (and have done so, many times). The resulting institutions could look like a typical homeowners' association in a residential subdivision, like a drainage district set up by landowners in a farm landscape, or—to anticipate again our first read-

sufficient incentive for a landowner to use land in an ecologically sound way. L[ewis] C. Gray, *The Economic Possibilities of Conservation*, 27 QUARTERLY J. OF ECON. 497 (1913).

ing—like the communal management regime set up by lobstermen on Monhegan Island, Maine.

Perhaps the most understudied area of natural resources law has to do with these governance regimes and with how best to structure them. A common inclination today is to propose one of two paths: to rely upon voluntary transactions among individuals to get things done, and when this doesn't work to turn to government to remedy the problem. Yet many other possibilities exist, alternative collective management arrangements that are more private than public. The options are many, and our too-frequent inability to appreciate the full range of options has long been a nagging cultural problem. To cite one manifestation of the problem, the American West has long been conflicted over the expansive federally owned lands, in terms of their extent and the ways they are managed. The problem has resisted resolution in part due to the widespread assumption that land comes in only two types—*private* land, which the individual owner can use largely at will and in isolation (including the right, critics say, to degrade it), and *public* land, which government ought to operate for the benefit of all citizens (and to the unfair disadvantage, critics say, of local populations). In fact, these ownership options supply only the poles of a wide continuum of resource-management arrangements. In between are countless other possibilities, mixing private initiative with collective guidance.

Natural resources law is as venerable a field as any part of Anglo–American legal culture. From its first known beginnings, the law has been called upon to resolve disputes over nature. Ever since then, resource law has been on the move, right along with society itself. Hardly any era, though, has seen as much change as the past half century. Today, pressures are strong to create new types of resource-use rights, in parts of nature once deemed valueless; to extend the reach of private property. At the same time, the inherited concept of land as an expansive bundle of use rights is under stress. Bundles are being fragmented so that more resource-use rights are separately held, often in collective or communal hands (for instance, ranch lands subject to conservation easements that prohibit development). Important questions are also being raised about the presumed ability of resource-owners to degrade or destroy what they own. Should the ownership of farmland, for instance, include the power to erode its soils? All the while, new forms of resource governance are bubbling up, albeit with resistance and a good deal of intellectual confusion. Beneath it all are the undercurrents that animate modern society generally—the endless tensions between freedom and control; the individual and the collective; the present versus the future; and humankind versus the larger organic whole.

The materials in this first section introduce these thematic elements: use rights in nature, governance regimes, and legal change over time. Once these characters have made their opening bows on stage, we'll turn to the first main issue in natural resources law: What use-rights does a person acquire by buying land? Which resource-use rights should we place into the bundle that we call land, and which use rights should we make available under separate resource-allocation schemes? To illustrate: should a person who buys land acquire, as part of the package, rights to the minerals beneath the surface, to the water in an adjacent lake, to the wildlife that scampers across fields, or (to look ahead to our first cases) to the ice that congeals on a river and the seaweed deposited on the foreshore? How much control over nature should a landowner get?

As for the importance of the whole subject of natural resources law, we might merely note the brief ruling of the Colorado Supreme Court in Power v. People, 17 Colo. 178, 28 P. 1121 (1892). Mark Power and his sister had been locked in controversy with a neighbor—a Mr. Baer—over an irrigation ditch used by Baer that crossed the Powers' land. The Powers claimed that the ditch interfered their rights as landowners, and also that they had certain water rights themselves in the ditch. Baer denied the claims and continued using the ditch. Negotiations did nothing to reduce the mounting tension. Pledging to those who could hear that he "would settle the ditch controversy with Baer" Mark Power took his rifle and shot Baer "at a short distance, perhaps 40 steps." The attending physician "testified that he found a large gunshot would in Baer's right thigh, caused by a large bullet, ranging upward, coming out back, and doing great damage [and] that there was no pulse in the wrist." Upholding Power's conviction for murder, the court explained the relative importance of natural and human resources in the West:

> Under such evidence, the important question to be determined on the trial was the nature of the homicide, whether justifiable or unlawful, and, if unlawful, the degree of the offense. The [trial] court charged the jury that the mere fact that Baer may have wrongfully or otherwise attempted to operate a ditch through defendant's or his sister's ranch would not justify the defendant in taking Baer's life. The instruction was proper. Human blood is more precious than water, even in this thirsty land.

LOBSTER STEWARDS

Colin Woodard

Orion (November–December 2004).

On December first, at a time of year when most Maine lobstermen have called it quits for the winter, the lobstering community of Monhegan Island, fourteen miles off the coast, is just kicking off its season. Most of Monhegan's seventy-five year-round residents turn out to help the dozen lobstermen haul their traps down to the wharf, onto their boats, and down into the cold, dark seas surrounding the rockbound island.

Once the fishermen have set their traps, they'll continue fishing through the dead of winter, braving heavy seas, high winds, and subzero temperatures—a combination that can leave their twenty-eight-to forty-foot boats entombed in frozen spray. "You go out and it's twenty below zero and it's blowing like hell and you get wondering, 'What the hell am I doing out here?' " says island native Zoe Zanidakis, who lobstered these waters for years. The answer: preserving a livelihood and the resource it depends upon.

In 1907, Monheganers convinced the state legislature to pass a law prohibiting anyone from fishing for lobsters in area waters from July through November. The law, intended to protect the island's lobsters from overfishing, is but one local example of Maine's notable lobster conservation laws, which lobstermen, by and large, enforce themselves through peer pressure and social sanctions. The rules—which include restrictions against taking oversized, undersized, or egg-bearing lobsters or fishing with anything other than a lobster trap—seem to have worked. While most New England fisheries have been decimated by overfishing over the past fifteen years, Maine's annual lobster catch has nearly tripled, with little sign that the population is under stress. And according to a 1996 statewide survey by University of Maine lobster scientist Robert Steneck, the winter-going Monheganers have one of the most productive areas on the entire coast.

Winter-only fishing gives area lobsters a break, but Monhegan's lobstermen also benefit from this conservative approach. Lobsters fetch higher prices in the winter months, when their shells are hard—and more packed with meat—and catching them is even harder. And because nobody has been fishing the island's lobster grounds for many months, the lobstermen can count on several weeks of tremendous catches and lucrative income.

But maintaining this arrangement hasn't been easy. Monheganers have been able to carve out their winter-only fishery because they control their own piece of ocean real estate, extending some two miles out in all directions. In fact, much of the state's lobstering grounds are divided into informal territories, each defended by the lobstermen from one or more nearby harbors. Through custom, peer pressure, and the occasional extra-legal act like cutting a violator's traps, the lobstermen of each harbor have conserved their respective turf, determining who fishes it and, to a certain extent, by what means. Violations of traditional practices or Maine's conservation laws can get somebody in a great deal of trouble, possibly even run out of town.

In the '70s, the Monhegan Islanders imposed a 600–trap limit on themselves at a time when many mainland lobstermen were fishing twice as many. And while there was the usual friction with lobstermen from nearby mainland harbors—with rivals pushing borders between the harbors, for example—things generally went smoothly. "It's just a matter of honoring the other fellow's pasture," explains Sherman Stanley, Sr., a retired lobsterman and onetime patriarch of Monhegan.

But in the fall of 1995, things turned ugly out on the water. Fishermen from the mainland town of Friendship, sixteen miles northeast, launched a full-scale invasion of Monhegan's traditional territory. Friendship, with a winter population nearly twenty times that of Monhegan, had been encroaching on Monhegan since the 1970s, when faster, safer boats made it practical to tend traps farther from the mainland. But now the number of interlopers exploded, triggering an all-out lobster war as Monhegan defended its turf. Traps were cut by both sides and at one point unidentified vandals sank one of the Monhegan lobsterboats. "Guns were being toted around; I thought, this is wrong," recalls Doug Boynton, one of Monhegan's leading lobstermen. "We were pushed to the point where we felt if we didn't do something, we would lose our lobster bottom, and that would be the end of the winter community out here."

State officials tried to negotiate compromises, but they fell apart because of critical gaps between the laws of the state and the laws of the lobstermen. Defying tradition, but with the law on their side, the Friendship lobstermen argued that as holders of state lobster licenses they could fish wherever they pleased. In the fall of 1997, five of them even tried to register as legal members of Monhegan's winter-only fishing fleet, despite their residence on the mainland. If the move had been successful, it would have represented a nearly 50 percent increase in the number of lobstermen fishing Monhegan waters, a crushing blow to the lobster-dependent island.

That's when Monhegan's lobstermen met in the Stanley family's fish house—the work center and informal capital of the island's fishing community—and decided to fight the law with the law. First, the island's lobstermen petitioned then-Governor Angus King, asking him to intervene and overturn the Department of Marine Resource's decision to issue permits to the "Friendship Five." Monhegan lobsterman John Murdock even appeared opposite the governor on a live television call-in program, further imploring him to take action to protect the system of traditional territories. As word of the islanders' plight spread, newspapers published editorials in favor of the Monheganers, and the fishermen of Matinicus, another rugged offshore island, sent in a petition lending their support as well. But while King and DMR Chief Robin Alden were sympathetic to the islanders' position, there was nothing they could do under current law. The lobstermen were told they had to get a new law passed by the state legislature. With the encouragement of state senators Marge Kilkelly and Jill Goldthwait DMR drew up a bill that would effectively recognize tradition by placing the islanders in control of their fishery.

Meanwhile, Friendship boats were preparing to set their traps in Monhegan's waters. The islanders took a massive gamble. Rather than set their own traps, many of the Monheganers packed their families onto their boats and headed to the mainland and the State House in Augusta, where the legislative session had begun. With the advice of Kilkelly and a pro bono lobbyist, the islanders pressed for their bill. "In Maine we've killed every [other] fishery by unlimited entry and greed," Dough Boynton told reporters. "This is a chance to prevent that." John Murdock's family lodged in Augusta for much of the winter. His younger son, Kyle, age eight, proved one of the most effective lobbyists, pigeonholing senators in elevators and paging for members of the House. "They basically moved in," Kilkelly recalls. "Their absolute commitment to their way of life and the fact that the legislature literally controlled whether or not they survived really made an impression."

If it passed the bill endorsing Monhegan's fishing territory, the Maine legislature would be validating a model once prevalent throughout the world. While increasingly rare, such communally managed systems still exist in places like the coral reefs of parts of Micronesia, the high alpine pastures of Switzerland, and the inshore fishing cooperatives of Japan.

In the end, to the surprise of all the lobstermen, the legislature passed the measure by a staggering margin: 29 to 1 in the Senate and 132 to 14 in the House. The law closed Monhegan's grounds to outsiders, giving the islanders control of apprenticeship programs required to become a lobsterman there.

In the five years since, Monhegan lobstermen say the law has worked out well, putting the cycle of trap-cuttings and boat-sinkings into the past. "It's enough work fishing, and if you're continually fighting [with rival harbors] them its bad for both sides," says Boynton. "Before, when things got nasty, it got people involved in unlawful acts and where does that end? They were a necessary evil, but I'm glad they're becoming less necessary."

Notes

1. *Managing the common pool.* The lobster fishery discussed in this article provides a classic example of a common-pool resource that can remain productive over the long-term only if the uses of it are controlled carefully. But how can control take place, when lobster fishing is done by individuals and small groups competing with one another? What must the local lobster fishermen do (and thus wield the power to do) to keep their fishery intact and prevent over-harvesting? They obviously must be able to exclude outsiders or else their internal harvest limits will go for naught. But what else is necessary? More generally, what does it take for a group of individuals acting together to manage a commons successfully over the long-run? After exploring natural resources law in its many manifestations, we'll attempt to answer these questions in the final chapter. The questions are central to the entire field.

2. *Defining use rights.* The focus of this article is on the ability of the lobster fishermen to protect their fishery against invasion by outsiders, and how they needed ultimately to get the state to help them (that is, they didn't possess enough power to get the task done themselves). The story is a classic illustration of how property rights—whether individual or group—exist only to the extent recognized and protected by law. But what about the problems that will inevitably arise on the island among the lobster fishermen themselves, in terms of who gets to harvest, where, how much, and when? Consider, too, the changes that are likely to take place over time, in terms of the families that live on the island. However the harvesting rights of

[margin annotations: "common-pool resource" and "prop. rights exist only to extent recognized/protected by law."]

individual fishermen are defined, whether in terms of number of lobster traps or as geographic territories, what power should the fishermen have to sell their rights? Would their individual harvesting rights be a form of private property that can be bought and sold? Could they sell the rights to other people on the island or even off the island? Alternatively, should the island people who run the fishery be able to screen potential purchasers and prohibit sales to people who aren't long-time island residents? And what about some young person, growing up on the island, who wants to get into the lobster business? Should a young fisherman be entitled to a share of the harvest automatically, simply by virtue of growing up on the island, even if this means that all other shares are modestly diminished to make room? Or should the person instead be obligated to purchase a share from some existing fishermen? Can we imagine, within the island society, arguments over the meaning of a person's "right to fish" (an issue that has arisen in many disputes involving American Indians)? These questions arise regularly, scholars tell us, in real-world situations involving locally controlled, common-pool resources. We'll return to the story of Maine lobsters in chapter 8, when we look in more detail at the challenges of collective governance at the landscape scale and learn more about limits imposed on members of the "lobster gangs."

3. *The fundamental elements of resources law.* Though we learn only a little about this lobster fishery from the article, we can nonetheless see here the fundamental elements of natural resources law. For the fishery to remain successful the islanders somehow must make collective decisions about its use, drawing upon their ecological knowledge and taking into account a wide array of human considerations. This need for collective guidance of the fishery will continue indefinitely—enforcing rules, imposing punishments, re-adjusting quotas somehow, and otherwise dealing with new circumstances. Thus, we have issues here both about individual use rights and about the best methods of collective resource governance. We also can see a dynamic element to this arrangement, given the obvious likelihood that changing circumstances will necessitate alterations in the fisheries regime. Is the best way to facilitate change simply to let the owners negotiate among themselves as individuals, perhaps buying and selling shares and looking for common ground? Instead, should the local governance regime, however it is set up, be given power to impose change through its governance processes? Or perhaps should major change, when it is needed, be imposed from above by state law, particularly when transactions costs among users are comparatively high and local governance regimes are weak?

4. *The coercive side of private rights.* What about outsiders, the people who want to fish in island waters and who now are prohibited by state law from doing so? Isn't this new arrangement unfair to them, perhaps a restriction of their liberty? The answer: indeed it is unfair and an interference with individual liberty, and necessarily so. But that is the way private property in nature always works! One person or group can gain rights over a part of nature only at the expense of other people.

To allow A to take over a piece of land (or a fishery), giving her the power to exclude outsiders, is necessarily to deprive all other people of their liberties to enter and use what A now owns. Here, the effect of the Maine statute was essentially to give the lobster fishermen of Monhegan Island a limited private property right in their lobster territory. Note, however, that this is not an exclusive property right, in terms of *all* uses of the waters around the island. The public presumably remains free to use the same waters for other purposes. What the fishermen collectively own is merely an exclusive right over the lobsters, along with some level of protection in the event their harvesting activities are wrongly disrupted by others. We should also note, though, that the scope of these new, community-owned property right in the island fishery is by no means fully clear (at least to us, based on this reading). Islanders can keep outside fishermen from coming in to harvest lobsters; that much we know. But the statute doesn't anticipate or address other conflicts that could easily arise, especially with regard to outsiders who want to use other natural resources in the same waters. In truth, the statute enacted by the legislature has only begun the process of defining precisely the property rights islanders collectively have in their fishery.

5. *Single-species management.* One of the dangers of a resource-use scheme such as the one described here is that it gives resource users an incentive to manage their territory to maximize production of one particular species. Yet almost inevitably, wildlife managers tell us, an effort to increase the population of one species comes at the expense of other life forms. What is good for the lobster might be bad for other species of aquatic life. Before the state gives the islanders the power to exclude outsiders, it might want to consider the ecological condition of the waters as a whole, leading perhaps to limits on the things islanders can do to increase lobster yields (killing lobster predators or artificial propagation, for instance). On this issue (and in connection with the case below), consider Strahan v. Coxe, 127 F.3d 155 (1st Cir. 1997) (state found guilty of an unlawful take of endangered northern right whale for continuing to issue permits for lobster pot and gillnet fishing when entanglement with such gear was a major source of human-caused injury or death to the whales). The state, then, might wisely give the island people exclusive rights to harvest lobster but limit those rights so as to protect aquatic ecosystem and facilitate other uses of island waters.

As you think about this issue, keep in mind that it also arises on tracts of land, which are inevitably interconnected ecologically to surrounding lands. Consider, for instance, the Midwestern farmer who tills a farm field completely, wards off plants and animals with pesticides, and then devotes the land to a single species: corn. Are the ecological effects of this kind of single-species management less troubling to society than an expanse of ocean managed solely for lobster? If ecological limits are appropriate for the latter, are they appropriate also for the former? Can we imagine, that is, reconceiving landowner rights as a bundle of one or more tailored use rights? (We will read the thoughts of political scientist Lynton Caldwell on this issue at the end of chapter 2.)

6. *Landed property rights in seventeenth-century New England.* By way of comparison—and for another glimpse at the origin of property rights—consider the following summary of land settlement by the English settlers in seventeenth-century Massachusetts. The colonial government in early Boston controlled the colony's settlement expansion by allocating new land only by deliberate legislative act and only to groups of town settlers deemed worthy. Once a new town was approved and a grant made to the town

leaders, these leaders took it upon themselves to divide the land among the initial settlers, reserving much land for later allocation and for communal use. As they did this work, the town founders carried out one of the key functions of natural resources law:

> The first English emigrants to Massachusetts tended to recreate in the New World the land use practices and other traditional, familiar ways of life that they had left behind in English villages. Many settlers arrived with intentions to reform traditional legal structures, but these reforming impulses were overpowered by the settlers' cultural baggage. As a result, the initial settlements in colonial Massachusetts took on the appearance of rural English farm and coastal communities. The distribution of land to residents in the first New England towns, as well as the regulation of the uses of town lands, reflected the primacy of communal, noneconomic goals. In an effort to maintain godly communities, town fathers distributed town lands only to immigrants who passed moral and religious tests. To maintain solidarity, towns generally prohibited land ownership by other than town residents and required town approval of land sales. Deference to social betters was evident in nearly all aspects of town and church life. Land distributions reflected this deference as towns allocated new lands not in equal increments per capita or per family but according to the substantial social class variations that existed among town residents. Land ownership thus played a vital communal role in supporting what was perceived as the natural social structure.
>
> Town land distributions also reflected the considerable variety in land use practices that existed in England, practices that colonists carried with them to the New World. In some English villages individual farmers owned small strips scattered over large village fields that were tilled communally by the village farmers; in other villages, where the enclosure movement had begun earlier, farmers held their lands in the form of single, enclosed farms that were farmed individually. In some areas land had a well-recognized market value and was regularly bought and sold; in other areas, transfers for value were rare and land values were less influenced by proximity to market. Some colonial towns, like Sudbury and Andover, Massachusetts, adopted open-field farming techniques by dividing town lands into several large fields and allocating to each town family one or more discrete strips in each of the fields and by setting aside substantial areas as communal pasturages and woodlots. Farming decisions in these open-field towns were commonly made by the farmers as a group. Because the landholdings of each farmer in open-field towns were widely scattered, farm families naturally lived together in villages, much like their Indian neighbors, rather than dispersed upon individual farms.
>
> Most towns adopted enclosed-field farming practices and allocated to each family one or a small number of larger, more isolated land tracts. Farmers in such towns tilled their lands separately and tended to share fewer items of personal property. Even towns that followed this enclosed-farm practice, however, often tried to force residents to live in a single village and in close proximity to the local church. In an effort to build close-knit, neighborly communities and to preserve religious and

social solidarity, home building was restricted to specified geographic areas near the town centers, even though farm lands, and hence the work sites of town residents, might be far distant. The economic benefits of living closer to farm work sites (and farther from watchful, critical neighbors), however, encouraged families to move onto their separate farms. Within a few decades of settlement, the enclosed-farm towns were characterized by a broad dispersion of the farm families

Not all land was allocated to families, however. Many towns allocated to the first settlers only a small portion of the total town chartered lands and reserved most lands for later distribution as needs dictated, thus retaining the town's power to control development for decades. Some areas were held as commons with specific, limited rights to use the commons allocated to families in the same manner (and often at the same time) as private lands were allocated. Other areas were simply surplus lands, generally more distant from the town center, retained to accommodate later town expansion and owned and managed in the interim by town governments. (Freyfogle, *Land Use and the Study of Early American History,* 94 Yale L. J. 717, 725–27 (1985) (citations omitted))

MARINCOVICH v. TARABOCHIA

114 Wash.2d 271, 787 P.2d 562 (1990).

DOLLIVER, JUSTICE.

Plaintiffs and defendants are commercial gillnet fishermen who make their living on the lower Columbia River. Plaintiffs are members of the Altoona Snag Union, Inc., which pools together funds collected from its members in order to coordinate the yearly removal of snags and debris from areas of the river where gillnet fishing would otherwise be impossible.

Snags are most commonly cleared from drifts, which are expanses of water over which gillnet fishermen set their nets. Certain drifts on the lower Columbia River have long been recognized and maintained according to local custom and usage. The State of Washington Department of Fisheries issues snagging permits to individual fishermen for the purpose of authorizing snag removal.

Membership in the Altoona Snag Union is evidenced by ownership of a "drift right", by which the union gives an exclusive right to fish a particular drift where snags have been removed. Drift rights have traditionally been treated as valuable personal property and have been passed to family members through probate and divorce proceedings. It is undisputed fishermen have paid valuable consideration for their drift rights.

Membership in the union is exclusive. Agreement to help pay for snag clearing does not make one a member; instead, a person interested in joining must locate an already existing right and purchase it with the union's approval. Enforcement of drift rights occurs in a variety of ways, all of which include some degree of intimidation and, in some cases, threats to life and property. The most common form of enforcement is "corking". This entails placing one's fishing net so close to that of the offending fisherman that the offender is forced to remove his net from the water to avoid ripping or tearing.

In October 1985, plaintiffs filed a complaint for damages and injunctive relief against defendants arising from a dispute over an area of the river not clearly controlled under the drift right system. The trial court imposed a permanent injunction against the defendants and ordered them to stop interfering with plaintiffs' fishing operations. Defendants filed a counterclaim challenging the legality of plaintiffs' drift rights. In February 1987, defendants filed a motion for summary judgment on this issue. The trial court concluded that before a material issue of fact can arise, plaintiffs must possess a basic legal right to exclude others from fishing the cleared drifts. Finding no such right existed, the trial court granted defendants' summary judgment motion. The court granted a stay of judgment pending the outcome of plaintiffs' appeal.

The Court of Appeals affirmed the trial court's ruling. Marincovich v. Tarabochia, 53 Wash.App. 633, 769 P.2d 866 (1989). We also affirm.

When reviewing an order of summary judgment, this court engages in the same inquiry as the trial court. *Highline Sch. Dist. 401 v. Port of Seattle,* 87 Wash.2d 6, 15, 548 P.2d 1085 (1976). A summary judgment motion can be granted only when there is no genuine issue as to any material fact, and the moving party is entitled to judgment as a matter of law. *Wilson v. Steinbach,* 98 Wash.2d 434, 437, 656 P.2d 1030 (1982). The court must consider the facts in the light most favorable to the nonmoving party, and the motion should be granted only if, from all the evidence, reasonable persons could reach but one conclusion. *Wilson,* at 437, 656 P.2d 1030.

Plaintiffs argue local custom and usage constitute a sufficient legal basis for recognizing they have a proprietary interest in drift rights; as such, they assert the trial court erred by granting summary judgment in favor of defendants on this issue. Plaintiffs base their position on essentially three separate arguments: analogy to trade use and custom as applied in contract law; reliance on customary water appropriation principles as a means to perfecting a legal right; and the notion that because the Department of Fisheries issues snagging permits, these permits impliedly give the holders the exclusive right to fish the areas they have cleared.

We reject plaintiffs' analogy to contract law under the facts of this case. As the Court of Appeals succinctly stated, the cases plaintiffs cite in support of their argument have to do with applying custom and trade use to interpret contracts or otherwise to flesh out rights already recognized by law. *Marincovich,* 53 Wash.App. at 634, 769 P.2d 866. In this case, neither contracts nor rights previously given legal recognition are at issue. For this reason, the Court of Appeals properly rejected plaintiffs' argument.

Nor do we accept plaintiffs' argument that under customary water appropriation principles, their drift rights should be legally recognized. Article 21, section 1, of the Washington Constitution provides that the use of the waters in this state for irrigation, mining, and manufacturing purposes shall be deemed a public use. In addition, 43 U.S.C. § 661 also recognizes rights to the use of water for mining and other such purposes when the same have been recognized by local custom, laws, and the decisions of courts. Neither of these provisions, nor the case law cited by plaintiffs in support of their argument, convince us this case should be analyzed under this theory. *See Isaacs v. Barber,* 10 Wash. 124, 38 P. 871 (1894); *Thorpe v. Tenem Ditch Co.,* 1 Wash. 566, 20 P. 588 (1889); *Hunter v. United States,* 388 F.2d 148 (9th Cir.1967); *Department of Parks v. Department of Water Admin.,* 96 Idaho 440, 530 P.2d 924 (1974). *See also* Trelease, *Coordination of Riparian and Appropriative Rights to the Use of Water,* 33 Tex.L.Rev. 26 (1954). The appropriated use of water is not analogous to the recognition of drift rights for fishing.

We also reject plaintiffs' argument that the Department of Fisheries, by issuing snag removal permits, has impliedly given permit holders the exclusive right to fish the areas they clear. The Department of Fisheries has been given the duty to promote orderly fisheries and to enhance and improve commercial fishing within the state. RCW 75.08.012. It does this in part by issuing snagging permits since the permits enable it to discern between those persons who are legally clearing snags and those who may be fishing illegally. Nothing in the record or the case law supports plaintiffs' argument that this somehow carries with it the exclusive right to fish the areas covered by the individual permits.

It has long been established in Washington and Oregon that citizens enjoy equal access to the navigable waters of their respective states. *Morris v. Graham,* 16 Wash. 343, 47 P. 752 (1897); *Radich v. Fredrickson,* 139 Or. 378, 10 P.2d 352 (1932); *Driscoll v. Berg,* 137 Or. 499, 293 P. 586, 1 P.2d 611 (1931); *Johnson v. Jeldness,* 85 Or. 657, 167 P. 798 (1917); *Hume v. Rogue River Packing Co.,* 51 Or. 237, 83 P. 391 (1908). In addition, this court has previously held the State, in its sovereign capacity, owns the fish in its waters. *Washington Kelpers Ass'n v. State,* 81 Wash.2d 410, 502 P.2d 1170 (1972), *cert. denied,* 411 U.S. 982, 93 S.Ct. 2274, 36 L.Ed.2d 959 (1973). As such, individual fishermen cannot assert a property right over the fish until they are caught. *Washington Kelpers Ass'n,* 81 Wash.2d at 415, 502 P.2d 1170 (quoting *Vail v. Seaborg,* 120 Wash. 126, 131, 207 P. 15 (1922)). These cases establish the fact plaintiffs do not enjoy a legal right to portions of public waters to the exclusion of other citizens of this state.

In its memorandum opinion, the trial court found *Radich v. Fredrickson,* 139 Or. 378, 10 P.2d 352 (1932) to be analogous to the present case. In *Radich,* gillnet fishermen sued to enjoin other fishermen from erecting a fish trap which would have severely interfered with their ability to fish the river. *Radich,* 139 Or. at 379, 10 P.2d 352. The court held defendants did not have a right to set up fish traps since to do so would interfere with the right to fish the public waters of the state, a right shared equally by all citizens. *Radich,* at 386, 10 P.2d 352.

It is interesting to note the plaintiffs in *Radich* had established an operation similar to the one established by plaintiffs in this case. The fishermen would clear snags from the river and take turns fishing the drifts to the exclusion of fishermen who did not participate in the clearing efforts. *Radich,* at 385, 10 P.2d 352. However, *Radich* is distinguishable from the present case in one important aspect; namely, under the system enjoyed in that case, any fisherman who wanted to help clear snags was invited to fish. *Radich,* at 385, 10 P.2d 352. In the present case, however, the same interest in helping to clear snags is not enough to gain access to the drifts. Instead, the inquiring individual must locate and purchase, with the union's approval, an already existing drift right before he will be allowed to fish the drifts.

The cases cited and discussed above establish that local custom and usage do not support legal recognition of plaintiffs' drift rights. This is true even though drift rights have existed in Oregon and Washington for many years. As the Court of Appeals stated, plaintiffs claim would arrogate to them rights owned in common by all of the people of the state. *Marincovich,* 53 Wash.App. at 635, 769 P.2d 866. We affirm the Court of Appeals.

A final comment: Although not necessary to the disposition of this case, we recognize the trial court's reluctance in ruling against plaintiffs in this case. In the words of the trial court:

> [T]here is no dispute as to the allegation that the denial of the rights asserted by plaintiff would result in, (1) chaos in the use of the drifts; (2) economic detriment to those holders of the drift rights; (3) to avoid overcrowding, no additional fishermen should be used on those drifts.

Clerk's Papers, at 174–75.

We also are sympathetic to these concerns. However, under RCW 75.08, regulation of the particular issues raised in this case is vested within the Department of Fisheries. That Department, by allowing plaintiffs to carry out snag clearing for many years, may have allowed plaintiffs to operate under the impression their drift rights were legally enforceable. By this opinion that impression comes to an end. The problems presented in this case must be resolved by departmental rules and regulations, not by the self help of the Altoona Snag Union. Only the Department is in a position to establish the orderly promotion of gillnet fishing on the Columbia River.

Notes

1. *The true origin of property*? *Marincovich* gives us a useful glimpse into the way property rights emerge. An assertion commonly encountered in basic property-law courses is that private property arises when an individual takes physical possession of an unowned thing; first occupancy, it is said, is

the origin of property. This can be apt from an individual's perspective, but it is true only if (i) a governance regime already exists that recognizes private property rights and (ii) the governance regime allows people to gain ownership by taking things in this way. Unless these conditions are met, we have merely the king-of-the-hill world of might makes right. Property rights come second; a governance regime of some sort, formal or informal, must come first. But how does such a regime of property rights itself first come into existence? The basic answer is simple: somehow, a group of people need to come together and make rules governing uses of nature.

Once a people do create some sort of property-rights regime, what options do they have in terms of making property rights available to individuals? First occupancy is one possibility, but as we'll see it is only one of many resource-allocation methods. At common law, its role in allocating property was in fact quite modest compared with other allocation methods. It had little or no role in allocating land, for instance, or in allocating the many forms of intangible property rights that were so important before the modern age. Rarely, in fact, did private ownership begin with first possession rather than by way of grant from above or other collective action.

As best we can tell, how did the informal (but apparently well-enforced) system of property rights in *Marincovich* come into existence? Many current holders of drift rights apparently acquired their rights by purchase. But how did the first holders gain their rights? Can we imagine the true origin of individual property rights in this fishery?

2. *Shared governance I: restrictions on sale, and who decides?* As best we can tell, how did the Snag Union rule its watery territory and enforce its private rights? And what powers did individual owners of drift rights have to sell them? As for the latter question, the court notes that sales had to be made "with the union's approval." Does this sound like an undue restriction on individual rights, or is this partial restraint on alienation perhaps a necessary fixture of an effective resource-management regime? Would the Maine lobstermen likely come up with a similar restriction governing rights to harvest lobsters?

When a natural resource is a single integrated whole, uses of it must somehow be orchestrated by someone. One way to understand *Marincovich* is as a dispute, not chiefly about private use rights, but about the identity of the governing body. Would it be the Snag Union and its leaders, or would it instead be the state? The Snag Union's governance arose by private action, without any sanction by the state. Apparently, it was efficient, effective, and low cost. The effect of the court's ruling was to undercut the effectiveness of that private governance, thereby replacing private governance with public governance. Was the shift a wise one, in policy terms? We can answer the question, of course, only by undertaking a comparative study of the relative merits and demerits of the two governance regimes. As we do that, we are likely to recognize that the two regimes need not be distinct. Public lawmakers could choose to vest governance powers in the Snag Union, subject perhaps to various limits that turn the Union into a quasi-public body. The Union, that is, could operate as a management intermediary between the state and the individual fishers.

3. *Gaining rights by prescription.* Although the Snag Union presented three legal arguments to the court, only one had much merit: the Union's claim that it ought to control the fishing territory because it was first in time to take possession and because it had used the fishery productively for years. Implicit here was the claim that Union fishermen had mixed their labor with the fishery, adding value to it by removing snags. The addition of this value gave rise to a moral claim to the fishery under the labor theory of property. More explicit was the fishermen's claim that their long-continued use of the fishery was tantamount to the acquisition of an easement by prescription. Why did the court reject the plaintiffs' first-in-time/prescription argument? As a policy matter should it have done so?

At the beginning of the nineteenth century, U.S. courts tended to allow fishermen to take exclusive control of fisheries in navigable waters by reliance upon the law of prescription. *E.g.*, Carson v. Blazer, 2 Binn. 475 (Pa. 1810); Pitkin v. Olmstead, 1 Root 217 (Conn. Super. 1790); Freary v. Cooke, 14 Mass. 488 (1779). *See Acquisition of Title by Prescription*, 19 Am. Jurist 96 (1838). As the century progressed, however, courts turned against the idea, embracing instead the line of reasoning used in *Marincovich*: navigable waters are open to public fishing, and no person can claim exclusive rights in them, no matter how long the use. *E.g.*, Shrunk v. Schuylkill Navigation Co., 14 Serg. & Rawle 71 (Pa. 1826). This new, anti-monopoly reasoning aligned with the economic liberalism that dominated society in the decades before the Civil War.

4. *The power of government to alienate public rights.* Note the appellate court's favorable quotation (from the trial court record) on how a refusal to recognize the plaintiffs' rights in the fishery would bring "chaos in the use of the drifts." Why would this be so? Are other outcomes also possible—such as an end to snag removal and an end to net fishing at the mouth of the river? And could there be environmental benefits to this outcome? This last question would be difficult to answer without knowing the ensuing ecological effects. We'd also need to know the overall effects, if any, on total fish harvests, since an end to fishing in the river's mouth could well produce larger harvests elsewhere. Would snag removal reduce fish spawning and thus overall fish harvests? Would it be better to avoid harvesting the fish at the river's mouth and wait until the migrating fish get nearer to their natal streams where they would be easier to catch?

The resolution of this predicted chaos, the court makes clear, was a matter for administrative rather than judicial action. Only the Department of Fisheries (or the state legislature presumably) had the power "to establish the orderly promotion of gillnet fishing on the Columbia River." But if it is legitimate for a state agency to allow private parties to take over a public fishery, why would it be illegitimate for a court to do so? Wouldn't the public suffer in the same way by being denied access to a valuable fishery? If private rights in fact conflict unduly with the public's rights to fish, how then could an agency fairly create exclusive fishing territories? In terms of its legal jurisdiction, the Department may or may not possess the power to close the fishery to public fishing, and doing so may or may not be consistent with public rights guaranteed by the federal navigation servitude.

5. *What's next?* If a state agency, in a case such as this, were to take action to create a new property system in this public resource (akin to the lobster fishery in Maine), how might it go about doing its work? What steps would be involved in the process?

The agency would need to identify fishing territories, presumably. Then, as in all other resource settings, it must devise a rule that somehow makes the resource available for public acquisition. Realistically, what options are available to allocate territorial fishing rights in a case in which existing users have already "squatted" on the fishery? Is it practical to make the resource available on a first-in-time basis when existing users are already in place without recognizing some form of squatters' rights? But if not first-in-time, what options are there for territorial allocation, particularly if the agency also worries about the second concern mentioned by the trial court in *Marincovich*, the need to avoid "economic detriment" to current holders of drift rights? If existing users, given political realities, are likely to end up with the fishing rights anyway, shouldn't the court have simply recognized their rights in this litigation and saved all the trouble?

6. *The homesteading comparison.* As the American West was settled, eager homesteaders often moved onto federal lands that were not yet surveyed and open to settlement. Squatting did not give the first arrivals an automatic preference, but squatters frequently found ways to gain ownership of their lands once the government did put the lands up for sale. From time to time Congress would validate squatting retroactively by means of "preemption" statutes, while claiming to discourage it prospectively. (The General Preemption Act of 1841 did authorize prospective preemption under certain, much-abused circumstances.) Another method used by initial first settlers to protect their unauthorized claims was to form "claims associations," in which members agreed to respect one another's squatting claims by not bidding for occupied land and by warding off outsider bidders. See George Coggins, Charles Wilkinson & John Leshy, FEDERAL PUBLIC LAND AND RESOURCES LAW 75–76 (5th ed. 2002). The practice held true in the frontier Midwest early in the nineteenth century:

> Not only did settlers mutually acknowledge the rights of squatters to their improvements [on land that they had settled], but they acted together to defend these customary rights against legal encroachments. According to Pascal P. Enos, registrar at the Springfield office in the 1820s, there were no instances "on any person biding more than the Govt. prices, or any persons biding against a person that held by possession." Speculators were probably intimidated in Springfield, as they were elsewhere, by associations of squatters showing up en masse to protect their claims. In Wisconsin in 1835, according to one contemporary report, "if a speculator should bid on a settler's farm, he was knocked down and dragged out of the land office, and if the striker was prosecuted and fined, the settlers paid the expense by common consent among themselves." "A kind of common-law was established by common consent and common necessity," John Reynolds wrote, "that the improvements on congress land shall not be purchased by any person except he who made the improvement."

James Mack Faragher, SUGAR CREEK: LIFE ON THE ILLINOIS PRAIRIE (1986), 55.

Preemption was conceptually distinct from homesteading, which involved more than just taking possession of land. (It differed also, of course, in being an ex post validation of seizing land rather than an ex ante authorization.) Homesteaders typically had to cultivate, irrigate, build upon, or otherwise improve a portion of their homestead before gaining secure title. As an allocation system, therefore, homesteading was not merely a rule of first occupancy. In practice, homestead laws were "liberally applied in favor of the entryman," which brought the system closer to allocation by first possession. Stewart v. Penny, 238 F.Supp. 821 (D. Nev. 1965) (concluding that homesteader had satisfied the 20–acre cultivation requirement on arid land even though crops had entirely failed due to "freezing, depredations by mice, rabbits, and other rodents, and invasions of ranging livestock").

COLUMBIA RIVER FISHERMEN'S PROTECTIVE UNION v. CITY OF ST. HELENS

160 Or. 654, 87 P.2d 195 (1939).

BEAN, JUSTICE.

[Plaintiffs were gillnet fishermen in the Columbia River who fished downstream from the outfall of defendant's city sewers. Their fishing was materially disrupted by reason of that pollution as well as certain industrial pollution, chiefly by pulp and paper companies that discharged directly into the river. According to the complaint, the various defendants deposited] said sewage, chemicals and waste matter in the waters of said Columbia river and the waters of the Willamette Slough, and by reason thereof the said waters are being destroyed for fishing purposes, and the fish and aquatic life are being destroyed, and the nets of plaintiffs are being destroyed, causing said nets to be rotted by the chemicals and foreign matter clinging to said nets, and salmon passing through said waters to the spawning grounds of the Willamette and Columbia rivers are so affected by the aforesaid wrongful acts of defendants in polluting said waters that the said salmon are unable to survive and pass through said waters and are killed . . .

Plaintiffs, as gill net fishermen, have a special interest, distinct from the public in fishing their drift which will be protected in a court of equity against destruction by acts of the defendants, which destroy their nets and interfere with their fishing. . . .

It is stated in the plaintiffs' brief that the lower court sustained the demurrer on the grounds that the complaint shows these plaintiffs have suffered no special and peculiar injury differing in kind from that suffered by the public, and therefore they cannot maintain this suit. The defendants rely largely upon this rule, and cite as authority for sustaining their position the decision in the case of Kuehn v. Milwaukee, 83 Wis. 583, 53 N.W. 912, 18 L.R.A. 553. Suffice it to say that this rule has not been followed in the state of Oregon, but a different rule has been adopted in numerous cases.

To delete the fish from the Columbia and Willamette rivers is to prevent the plaintiffs from pursuing their vocations and earning their livelihood fishing with gill nets in the portions of the rivers where they have been accustomed to fish.

There is a vital distinction between the rights of plaintiffs, who are accustomed to fishing in the river and have a license so to do, and the rights of other citizens of the state, who never fish in the river and do not intend to and are interested only in a general way in the benefit the state receives by the prosecution of a valuable industry, so that surely the plaintiffs have a special interest differing widely from the interest of the public in fishing in the portions of the river mentioned. . . .

Numerous suits have been maintained in the courts of this state to prevent interference with the right of fishing. The difference between this case and the several others cited above is in degree. There is a greater degree of interference in the present case than in the cases heretofore prosecuted.

Enormous quantities of salmon are found in the Columbia and Willamette rivers and are of extensive commercial value. The salmon industry has grown to great proportions and has been one of the principal industries of the state of Oregon for many years. Thousands of citizens of Oregon earn their livelihood by catching salmon, and the business aggregates hundreds of thousands of dollars annually. All the citizens of Oregon have a common right to fish in the waters mentioned in the complaint, and to deprive any one citizen of that right is to violate the state constitution. On its admission to the Union, Oregon was vested with the title to the land under navigable waters within the state, subject to the public right of navigation and to the common right of the citizens of the state to fish. Monroe v. Withycombe, supra. In the latter case, where the opinion was written by Mr. Justice Harris, plaintiffs brought suit to enjoin the interference of fishing rights in the Columbia River. The case, in principle, is like the one at bar.

Fish are classified as *ferae naturae*. While the ownership of the fish in question, before they are taken, is in the state of Oregon, as far as ownership can be established, this suit is not brought for the purpose of obtaining the salmon but to protect the right of fishermen to pursue their vocation of fishing. Monroe v. Withycombe, *supra*.

Strandholm v. Barbey, *supra*, was a case brought to protect the fishing rights of plaintiff in the Columbia river, which had been interfered with by the construction of a wharf and three fish traps by defendant. At page 442 of 145 Or., at page 52 of 26 P.2d we find the language of Mr. Justice Rossman: "We are therefore satisfied that, since the wharf interferes with long-established fishing rights possessed by the plaintiff, he is entitled to a decree enjoining the maintenance of the wharf beyond the line just mentioned." . . .

Radich v. Fredrickson, *supra*, is a case where thirty-three gill net fishermen, as plaintiffs, brought a suit to protect their rights and to restrain the construction of a fish trap and interfering with the rights of plaintiffs to fish. The syllabus reads: "Maintenance of fish traps should be enjoined where it prevented fishing with gill nets in adjacent navigable waters." [139 Or. 378, 10 P.2d 353.]

Section 39–603, Oregon Code Supplement 1935, prohibits the pollution of streams and public waters of the state by depositing any deleterious substance or any substances which do or may render the waters of a stream, or any other body of water, destructive of fish life. Section 40–213, Oregon Code 1930, prohibits depositing deleterious substances, explosives or poisons, or using the same in the waters of the state.

The regulatory power of a state extends not only to the taking of its fish, but also over the waters inhabited by the fish. Its care of the fish would be of no avail if it had no power to protect the waters from pollution. 11 R.C.L. 1047, § 35. See Eagle Cliff Fishing Co. v. McGowan, 70 Or. 1, 137 P. 766. We read in 11 R.C.L. 1039, § 26, as follows: "But, on the other hand, a member of the public who is specially injured by the maintenance of a nuisance, may abate it or maintain an equitable action for relief therefrom. Thus, if one exercising his right to take fish from a common fishery is obstructed by a nuisance, he may abate the obstruction."

The jurisdiction of equity courts to grant relief by injunction in a proper case against a nuisance, either public or private, is undoubted and well-settled, and wherever the circumstances of the case are such that adequate redress cannot be obtained elsewhere, equity will afford relief. 14 Enc. of Pl. & Pr. 1118; 1 Am. & Eng. Enc. of Law, 2d Ed. 64.

The provision for a statutory penalty for polluting a stream is not a bar to prosecuting a suit to prevent the same. 26 C.J. 619, § 36.

Notes

1. *What is the legal right?* Is *Fishermen's Protective Union* consistent with *Marincovich*? If gillnet fishermen have no property rights in their fishing territories, what then is the special legal interest they possess that allows them to sue for interferences with their fishing operations? If not a property right in the resource, then what is it? Are there legal protections that resource-harvesters enjoy that don't amount to property rights?

The legal rule embraced by the court is widely accepted. Fishers in navigable waterways, open to public use, typically can recover for lost profits under a nuisance-like standard when they can show substantial harm unreasonably imposed. *E.g.*, Union Oil Co. v. Oppen, 501 F.2d 558 (9th Cir. 1974). The fact that they engage in fishing and suffer reduced fish catches is sufficient to satisfy the "special injury" standing requirement that applies in public nuisance actions.

2. *Protection in the rush to capture.* As *Marincovich* and *Fishermen's Protective Union* explain, fish and other wildlife are owned by the state in a trust-like capacity; they are owned by the state in a special sovereign capacity, for the benefit of the people collectively. Subject to the substantial limits imposed by state fish and game laws, wild animals are typically available for capture by licensed takers on a first-in-time basis.

Is it useful to think of *Fishermen's Protective Union* as a case dealing, not with property rights, but with the protection a person enjoys while engaged in the process of resource acquisition? When resources are made available to the first taker, the rush to capture can lead to wild, dangerous behavior, as each person tries to be first. To keep the whole process fair and safe, rules of conduct can be necessary. We'll return to the issue of first-in-time resource allocation in a later chapter, where we'll see decisions that involve this policy issue.

3. *Reasonable use I: nature and multiple use.* Another way to consider this decision is to focus not on the plaintiff fishermen but on the polluters. They, too, are using the river, and their use of the river (to carry off pollution) is not per se illegitimate. Thus, we have a conflict between two users of a single natural resource. Which use will take priority? As we resolve this paradigmatic resource-use conflict, should the law aim to produce one winner and one loser, or should it strive instead to find ways that allow both users of the river to co-exist?

Consider the major ways that this conflict, and countless ones like it, might be resolved.

a. We could use *nature as the baseline,* prescribing as the guiding rule that anyone can use the resource so long as its natural conditions remain fundamentally unchanged.

b. Another possibility is to look to *priority in time.* Whichever user is first gets to keep using the river without interference.

c. A third possibility is to assess the competing uses in terms of their *reasonableness,* or how much they promote the common good. The term "reasonable" is notoriously vague, so we'd have to explain what it means. Does it refer just to the type of resource use? To its efficiency? To its suitability for the location where it is conducted? To its value in relation to competing uses of the same resource?

d. Yet another possibility to carve up the resource and then allocate fair shares of it to each interested user, employing a *correlative rights* approach.

e. A fifth possibility is to focus on the ability of the competing users to make alterations in their practices so as to diminish the conflict. That is, we could seek out possibilities for *accommodation,* then press for change by the party that can more easily diminish the conflict.

f. Of course, we could do nothing, and leave the parties to resolve things as they see fit. But note that this approach is by no means a neutral, hands-off approach by government. When the law allows parties to act as they see fit, it has essentially chosen to *favor the party whose resource use is more intensive*. In the case of Columbia River fishing, to allow the parties to act at will is deliberately to favor the polluters over the fishermen (given that the fishing doesn't disrupt the polluters). If we decide to let the market rule—leaving the parties to negotiate an agreement privately—we have chosen this sixth option, deliberately favoring the intensive resource user.

g. Lastly, we could choose a process-oriented solution. Instead of dictating a particular resolution of the dispute, the law could create (or stimulate) a *private governance body of resource users,* which possesses the power to decide which river uses will take place and on what terms.

Keep these options in mind for continued reflection, for they will reappear regularly. Indeed, most of what follows in this book elaborates upon these seven conflict-resolution options, illustrating how they appear in various corners of resource law and how lawmakers over time have chosen (and re-chosen) among them. A central theme of what follows has to do with the rise of option c, reasonable use, which has largely displaced options a and b (although option a has enjoyed a modest resurgence in the context of resources set aside for wildlife and recreation). We'll also see a growing role for the accommodation idea of option e. As for the final option, it has made only cameo appearances to date. Its heyday likely has not yet come.

4. *Accommodation I: a seventeenth-century example.* One way to allow multiple people to use the same land or waterway at the same time, for different and possibly conflicting purposes, is to define use rights in the resource carefully so that the uses conflict as little as possible. The difficulties of performing this task vary greatly, as one would expect, depending upon the nature of the various resource uses and the degree of conflict that can arise among them. On this issue, consider the following summary of a resource-use arrangement quite different from our own. This approach, too, centered around private property rights, but it defined and allocated the rights in ways suited to a much different economy and culture.

This summary considers the land-use patterns and arrangements employed by the seventeenth-century Algonquians, who inhabited much of New England and bordering Canada at the time the first English-speaking settlers arrived. As you read the excerpt take note, not just of the ways use rights were defined and allocated, but of how the use rights were apparently made more productive through tribal land-management efforts (from Freyfogle, Review Essay, *Land Use and the Study of Early American History,* 94 Yale L. J. 717, 719–23 (1985) (citations omitted)):

> The countryside of early New England was divided among numerous Indian villages, each generally inhabited by a couple hundred residents. The leader or sachem of each village held sovereign title as village representative to all of the village lands. Boundaries among villages, although subject to occasional change, were relatively clear and respected. In many instances, sachems owed homage to higher or stronger sachems of the same tribe, and some villages at times had easement-like rights to use or to cross lands held by other villages. But generally, the village was the basic unit of sovereign land ownership with tribal land co-ownership rare or unknown.
>
> The average Indian group that comprised a single village migrated seasonally on the lands it owned. Village groups in northern areas with climates hostile to agriculture were pure hunter-gatherer societies. Villages in areas where agriculture was possible typically lived on their agricultural lands in the warm months; like their northern compatriots, they migrated farther inland during colder months and dispersed themselves for hunting. A village group usually changed its camp locations only after a number of years, when agricultural fertility had declined, firewood had become scarce, or a site had otherwise become undesirable.

Such seasonal migrations were possible because the Indians were content with insubstantial, portable dwellings and possessed few personal belongings. Southern tribes set aside village lands for hunting, burning the land regularly to aid travel and to remove low-level shrubs that hindered the hunter's sighting of animals. . . .

Individual Indian families generally possessed and tilled their own agricultural lands. Such lands were privately owned and used until soil fertility declined or the village changed its camp location, at which point the lands were abandoned without afterthought. Indians commonly mixed several crops—corn, beans and squash, for example—in a single field, a technique that produced fields that seemed messy and overgrown in comparison to the clean, single-crop English fields but that yielded substantial benefits by reducing weeds, preserving soil moisture, and increasing crop yields. . . .

The Indian land tenure system's incorporation of diverse forms of individual and group ownership is particularly worthy of scrutiny. In their use of property, the Indians clearly embraced a system of private ownership, although they carved up property rights much differently than the colonists did and retained more property rights for communal use. Indian families owned exclusively the land on which their wigwams or other dwellings stood. This exclusive right of use continued until the family abandoned the land. Village agricultural lands were divided up and owned by individual families, with each family's ownership rights in the farm lands continuing only so long as the family made actual use of the lands. The family's rights

> did not include many of the privileges Europeans commonly associated with ownership: a user could not (and saw no need to) prevent other village members from trespassing or gathering nonagricultural food on such lands, and had no conception of deriving rent from them. Planting fields were 'possessed' by an Indian family only to the extent that it would return to them the following year. In this, they were not radically different in kind from other village lands. . . .

In short, an Indian who 'owned' agricultural lands simply had a usufruct right—an exclusive right for the period of ownership to use the land for agricultural purposes. Ownership interests in all other Indian lands—the 'clam banks, fishing ponds, berry-picking areas, hunting lands, the great bulk of a village's territory'—were even more clearly limited to usufruct rights and even more distinctly fragmented. Rights to collect edible wild plants and birchbark for canoes, to catch fish and shellfish, to hunt populous roaming animals such as deer and turkeys, and to set snares and traps for less numerous or more sedentary creatures were all viewed as separate land use rights and all subject to different use allocation schemes.

Thus, an Indian who 'owned' land possessed only one or more rights to use the land for a particular purpose. Some uses, such as use of a wigwam site, were exclusive uses, while others, such as the right to take migratory birds from the land, were retained in common by the village and not allocated to individuals. Significantly, some rights that are currently associated with land ownership, such as the right to amass and hold land that is in excess of personal needs and the right to transfer for value unneeded land to another person, were alien to Indian land tenure practices and cultures (until introduced by the colonists) and were not rights that belonged to anyone, individually or communally....

5. *"Resources" as moral agents.* The materials in this chapter have all dealt with disputes among people with respect to parts of nature. But the law has not always had this sharp focus. Consider the ancient common law principle of *deodand*, under which property rights in an object were forfeited to the state if the object was implicated in a human death—for instance, a stack of logs or a horse involved in a fatal accident. J.H. Baker, An Introduction to English Legal History 322 (2d ed., 1979). More alien to modern sensibilities was the practice centuries ago of holding animals morally responsible for harms caused to people and their property.

THE HISTORICAL AND CONTEMPORARY PROSECUTION AND PUNISHMENT OF ANIMALS

Jen Girgen

9 Animal Law 97, 98–99 (2003).

"Once upon a time,"—and we might well begin in that manner because the story is as fantastic as a fairy tale—animals were held to be as liable as men for their criminal acts and torts.

In 1386, in Falaise (France), an alleged female killer mangled the face and arms of a child, thereby causing the child's death. The defendant was brought before the local tribunal, and after a formal trial she was declared guilty of the crime. True to *lex talionis*, or "eye-for-an-eye" justice, the court sentenced the infanticidal malefactor first to be maimed in her head and upper limbs and then to be hanged. A professional hangman carried out the punishment in the public square near the city hall. The executioner, officially decreed to be a "master of high works," was issued a new pair of gloves for the occasion "in order that he might come from the discharge of his duty, metaphorically at least, with clean hands, thus indicating that, as a minister of justice, he incurred no guilt in shedding blood."

This particular trial and execution is interesting both because of the retaliatory nature of the punishment and the fact that the village commemorated the execution with a fresco painted on a wall in the south transept of the local Church of the Holy Trinity. However, the case is especially significant because of the fact that the defendant was a pig.

Today, it would seem peculiar for a community to prosecute and punish an animal for a criminal or other offense. We would like to believe that our present-day criminal justice system is too sophisticated to resort to holding animals accountable for the harms they sometimes cause. Not so long ago, however, animal trials and executions, such as that of the Falaise sow, were a regular part of our Western jurisprudential history....

A. The Two Kinds of Trials

Medieval animal trials are most appropriately thought of as two distinct proceedings, depending upon the transgressing animal's offense and species. If the animal caused a public nuisance (typically involving the destruction of crops intended for human consumption), the transgression was addressed by church officials in an ecclesiastical court. Alternatively, when an animal caused physical injury or death to a human being, the animal was tried and punished by a judge in a secular court....

In spite of their nontraditional defendants, both the ecclesiastical and secular courts took these proceedings very seriously and strictly adhered to the legal customs and formal procedural rules that had been established for human criminal defendants. The community, at its own expense, provided the accused animals with defense counsel, and these lawyers raised complex legal arguments on behalf of the animal defendants. In criminal trials, animal defendants were sometimes detained in jail alongside human prisoners. Evidence was weighed and judgment decreed as though the defendant were human. Finally, in the secular court, when the time came to carry out the punishment (usually lethal), the court procured the services of a professional hangman, who was paid in a like manner as for the other, more traditional, executions he performed.

Chapter Two

WHAT COMES WITH LAND?

When it comes to making resource-use rights available for public acquisition, lawmakers have essentially two options. They can allocate the resources one by one, or they can assemble them into bundles and allocate the bundles. The latter approach is often used, and the best known bundle of resource-use rights is the one known as "land."

Land may seem like an ordinary idea, clear enough in meaning. But culturally derived conceptions can mislead. Numerous questions emerge when a legal system makes land available for acquisition, particularly in terms of the parts of nature that come with a tract of land. This issue can arise *before* any specific natural resources have been allocated, in which case the question is posed in the abstract: what rights does a landowner get, and which rights instead are retained as part of the common pool, available for separate acquisition? Alternatively, the issue can arise at a later point, *after* a government has sold or otherwise allocated specific natural resources as discrete use rights (by selling off mineral rights, for instance), and then decides to bundle the resource rights that are leftover and sell them as land. At that point, the legal question is slightly different: what rights does the later land purchaser get, and what rights are held instead by the person(s) who earlier obtained from the government rights to specific resources on the land?

A. AT WATER'S EDGE

We begin this inquiry into the physical elements of land by turning to one of nature's many components that have fluctuated in market value as human needs and technology have evolved: ice. As you read the case, pay attention to what the court also says about uses of waterways for fishing and travel. But be forewarned: the court's comments on this law are not entirely accurate today.

WASHINGTON ICE COMPANY v. SHORTALL

101 Ill. 46 (1881).

MR. JUSTICE SHELDON delivered the opinion of the Court:

This was an action of trespass *quare clausum fregit,* brought in the circuit court of Cook county by Shortall, against the Washington Ice Company, for cutting, removing and appropriating, in January and February, 1879, a quantity of ice which had formed over the bed of the Calumet river, within the limits of plaintiff's land, in Cook county....

From the evidence it appears that ... the Calumet river, extending from Lake Michigan westward past the plaintiff's premises, where it is between 165 and 200 feet wide, is in fact a navigable river; that the defendant company owned ice-houses on its own property on the next lot east of plaintiff's, and that in operating on the ice it did not go on the plaintiff's land, save as it entered upon the ice; that it first gathered the ice in front of its own land from the river, and then commenced to take the ice opposite the plaintiff's premises.

The court, at plaintiff's request, instructed the jury that the plaintiff was the owner of the whole bed of the river flowing through his premises; that when the water became congealed, the ice attaching to the soil constituted a part thereof, and belonged to the owner of the bed of the stream, and that he could maintain trespass for the wrongful entry and taking the ice ... Defendant ... asked the court to instruct the jury that a riparian owner on the banks of a river, navigable in fact, has no property in the ice formed in the midst of the stream, where he has done nothing to pond or separate it; but that any person might, as against such riparian owner, where he could gain access without passing over the shore or banks of the owner, enter upon the ice and remove the same....

It may be well to inquire, first, whether plaintiff, as riparian proprietor on both sides of the Calumet river, is the owner of the bed of the stream within the limits of his land. By the common law, only arms of the sea, and streams where the tide ebbs and flows, are regarded navigable. The stream above the tide, although it may be navigable in fact, belongs to the riparian proprietors on each side of it to its centre, and the only right the public has therein is an easement for the purpose of navigation. Chancellor Kent, in his Commentaries, declares it as settled that grants of land bounded on rivers or upon their margins, above tide water, carry the exclusive right and title of the grantee to the centre of the stream, subject to the easement of navigation, unless the terms of the grant clearly denote the intention to stop at the edge or margin of the river. If the same person be the owner on both sides of the river, he owns the whole river to the extent of the length of his lands upon it. 3 Comm. 427, 428, Marg. And this title to the middle of the stream includes the water, the bed, and all islands. 2 Hilliard on Real Prop. 92; Angell on Water Courses, sec. 5.

This rule of the common law has been adopted in this State, and is here the settled doctrine. It was so held in *Middleton v. Pritchard,* 3 Scam. 510, and *Houck v. Yates,* 82 Ill. 179, with regard to the Mississippi river where it bounds this State; in *Braxon v. Bressler,* 64 Ill. 488, as to Rock river; *City of Chicago v. Laflin,* 49 Ill. 172, and *City of Chicago v. McGinn,* 51 Ill. 266, in regard to the Chicago river.

The Calumet river then being non-tidal, and plaintiff owning lands on both sides of it, he is the owner of the whole of the bed of the stream to the extent of the length of his lands upon it.

The next question respects the ownership of ice formed over the bed of the river passing through the land. It is objected by defendant that water in a running stream is not the property of any man,—that no proprietor has a property in the water itself, but a simple usufruct while it passes along; but manifestly different considerations apply to water in a running stream when in a liquid state and when frozen.

In *Agawam Canal Co. v. Edwards,* 36 Conn. 497, it is said: "The principle contained in the maxim, '*cujus est solum ejus est usque ad coelum,*' gives to a riparian owner an interest in a stream which runs over his land. But it is not a title to the water,—it is a usufruct[2] merely,—a right to use it while passing over the land. The same right pertains to the land of every other riparian proprietor on the same stream and its tributaries; and as each has a similar and equal usufructuary right, the common interest requires that the right should be exercised and enjoyed by each in such a reasonable manner as not to injure unnecessarily the right of any other owner, above or below."

In *Elliott v. Fitchburg Railroad Co.* 10 Cush. 191, SHAW, Ch. J., says: "The right to flowing water is now well settled to be a right incident to property in the land,—it is a right *publici juris,* of such character that whilst it is common and equal to all through whose land it runs, and no one can obstruct or divert it, yet as one of the beneficial gifts of Providence each proprietor has a right to a just and reasonable use of it as it passes through his land; and so long as it is not wholly obstructed or diverted, or no larger appropriation of the water running through it is made than a just and reasonable use, it can not be said to be wrongful or injurious to a proprietor lower down. * * * Still, the rule is the same, that each proprietor has a right to the reasonable use of it for his own benefit, for domestic use, and for manufacturing and agricultural purposes."

In *Rex v. Wharton,* 12 Mod. 510, HOLT, Ch. J., says: "If a river run contiguously between the land of two persons, each of them is, of common right, owner of that part of the river which is next his land." . . .

2. [Ed. Usufruct literally means a right to use and enjoy the fruits of land or of another physical thing without damaging or diminishing it through use. More generally it refers to a right to use something, separate from any right to consume, degrade or destroy it.]

It will thus be seen that the riparian owner, as such, has rights with respect to water in a running stream,—he has a right of use, which right authorizes the actual taking of a reasonable quantity of the water for his purposes. The limitation in extent of the use of the water is, that it shall not interfere with the public right of navigation, nor in a substantial degree diminish and impair the right of use of the water by a lower or upper proprietor as it passes along his land. The only opposing rights are such rights of the public, and such upper and lower proprietors. But when the water becomes congealed, and is in that state, these opposite rights are in nowise concerned. The ice may be used and appropriated without detriment to the right of navigation by the public, or to other riparian owners' right of use of the water of the stream when flowing over their land. The just and reasonable use of the water which belongs to the riparian proprietor would be, in such case of congealed state of the water, the unlimited use and appropriation of the ice by him, as it would be no interference with rights of others. We are of opinion there is such latter right of use, and that it should be held property, of which the riparian owner can not be deprived by a mere wrongdoer. When water has congealed and become attached to the soil, why should it not, like any other accession,[3] be considered part of the realty? Wherein, in this regard, should the addition of ice formed over the bed of a stream be viewed differently from alluvion, which is the addition made to land by the washing of the sea or rivers? And we do not perceive why there is not as much reason to allow to the riparian owner the same right to take ice as to take fish, which latter is an exclusive right in such owner.

In *McFarlin v. Essex Co.* 10 Cush. 309, SHAW, Ch. J., remarked: "It is now perfectly well established as the law of this Commonwealth, that in all waters not navigable in the common law sense of the term,—that is, in all waters above the flow of the tide,—the right of fishery is in the owner of the soil upon which it is carried on, and in such rivers that the right of soil is in the owner of the land bounding upon it. . . ."

The riparian proprietor has the sole right, unless he has granted it, to fish with *nets* or *seines* in connection with his own land. Angell on Water Courses, sec. 67.

In *Adams v. Pease,* 2 Conn. 481, it was held that the owners of land adjoining the Connecticut river above the flowing and ebbing of the tide, have an exclusive right of fishery opposite to their land, to the middle of the river; and that the public have an easement in the river as a highway, for passing and repassing with every kind of water craft. So, too, sea-weed thrown upon the shore belongs to the owner of the soil upon which it is cast. *Emans v. Turnbull,* 2 Johns. 313.

The exclusive right in the owner to take the ice formed over his land, is an analogous right to those other ones which are acknowledged

3. [Ed.: Accession is a property owner's right to all that is added to the property (esp. land) naturally or by labor, including land left by floods and improvements made by others. As the next sentence of the opinion explains, physical material added to land by flowing water is often referred to more specifically as alluvion.]

to exist in the subjects which have been mentioned, and may with like propriety be recognized. It is connected with and in the nature of an accession to the land, being an increment arising from formation over it, and belonging to the land properly, as being included in it in its indefinite extent upwards.

Ice, from its general use, has come to be a merchantable commodity of value, and the traffic in it a quite important business. It would not be in the interest of peace and good order, nor consist with legal policy, that such an article should be held a thing of common right, and be left the subject of general scramble, leading to acts of force and violence. In reference to the rule which we here adopt, of assigning to the owner of the bed of a stream property in the ice which forms over it, we may well use, as fitly applying, the language of HOSMER, J., in *Adams v. Pease, supra,* in speaking of the common law rule as to the right of fishery, viz: "The doctrine of the common law, as I have stated it, promotes the grand ends of civil society, by pursuing that wise and orderly maxim of assigning to everything capable of ownership a legal and determinate owner."

The views we hold are in accordance with the holding in *The State v. Pottmeyer,* 33 Ind. 402, that when the water of a flowing stream running in its natural channel is congealed, the ice attached to the soil constitutes a part of the land, and belongs to the owner of the bed of the stream, and he has the right to prevent its removal. See further, relative to the subject, *Myer v. Whitaker,* 55 How. Pr. Rep. 376; *Lorman v. Benson,* 8 Mich. 18; *Mill River Woolen Manufacturing Co. v. Smith,* 34 Conn. 462; *Brown v. Brown,* 30 N. Y. 519.

Defendant claims that it committed no trespass in taking the ice, because the ice in the midst of a stream navigable in fact, is naturally an obstruction to navigation, and that any one has the right, having obtained access independent of the riparian owner, to enter upon the ice and remove it. We said in *Braxon v. Bressler,* above cited: "Where the river is navigable, the public have an easement or a right of passage upon it as a highway, but not the right to remove the rock, gravel or soil, except as necessary to the enjoyment of the easement." The same is to be said as to the ice here. But it was not removed as necessary for the enjoyment of the public easement of navigation,—it was for the purpose only of the appropriation of it for defendant's gain. . . .

Notes

1. *Methods of judicial reasoning*. Although ice harvesting is hardly a subject that draws much attention today, it is nonetheless useful to see how courts addressed this once-novel issue. The Illinois court did not look first for other ice cases from other jurisdictions (of which there were few), but instead chose to begin its reasoning elsewhere. One tool it used was to reason by analogy, to liken the resource at issue (ice) with another resource that was legally similar (in this case, fish). Few nonlawyers would think that ice and fish have much in common, but then again (to look ahead to another

analogy), even fewer might see a link between a wild animal and underground oil. Reasoning by analogy has a long history in natural resources law. This is one reason why it is valuable to study the field issue by issue, rather than resource by resource, so that cases involving similar problems are more readily compared. Aside from using this ice-fish analogy, how does the court resolve the issue? After reaching its conclusion the court bolsters it by referring to "that wise and orderly maxim of assigning everything capable of ownership to a legal and determinate owner." Was this maxim (and the reasoning embedded in it) a likely motivating force for the court's ruling, rather than just an afterthought?

Common law courts for generations showed anxiety over the possibility that a valuable item might have no owner. A prominent illustration of this anxiety came in a ruling by the British House of Lords in 1865, Blades v. Higgs, 11 H.L. Cas. 621, 11 Eng. Rep. 1474. The Lords were called upon to decide the ownership of a wild animal killed by a hunter who both spotted and killed the animal while trespassing on private land. The hunter didn't own the carcass because his capture was unlawful. Yet land ownership conferred no property rights in the animal either, at least while it was alive. The Lords could have simply said that the animal once killed was unowned, and thus available for the first person to come along and take it. But this would have left the carcass unowned for a time—precisely the outcome the common law disliked.

The issue was a difficult one for judges, which is why it went unresolved for generations and ultimately required a ruling by the Lords. Feeling compelled to select an owner (and inclined perhaps to favor their fellow landowners over poaching commoners), the Lords decided that the dead animal should go to the landowner. The same rule was soon adopted in the United States, though not without resistance by judges who saw within it the taint of "feudalism and royal prerogative." Sterling v. Jackson, 69 Mich. 488, 37 N.W. 845, 859 (1888) (Campbell, J., dissenting). In both the United States and England, courts reached a different legal result when a hunter started an animal on his own land but made the kill while trespassing; then the hunter was guilty of trespass and liable for trespass damages but nonetheless owned the game.

2. *Bed ownership, fishing rights, and navigability. Washington Ice* relates the legal rule that governs the ownership of river bottoms in roughly the eastern half of the United States: river beds are owned by adjacent landowners, even in the case of the largest navigable rivers (under Illinois law this includes the Mississippi River). For various reasons, states in the western half of the country have largely retained ownership of riverbeds in the state itself, though differing among themselves as to where exactly private property ends and the public's ownership begins. As for the right to fish, the comments in *Washington Ice* should be taken advisedly for they do not represent prevailing law. Notice that the dispute here deals with a *navigable* waterway, but when the court announces that the right to fish is owned by the landowner it relies upon precedents involving *nonnavigable* waterways (a sloppy bit of legal work). We'll return to this issue later in the chapter. We'll also see the practical implications of the well-established rule that water in rivers is owned by the public; riparian landowners (and, in

prior appropriation states, appropriators) hold only a right to make use of the water.

As to navigability, early American law began with the English idea that a waterway was navigable only if it was subject to the ebb and flow of the tides. During the nineteenth century the law largely shifted to a much-different test, under which a waterway was navigable if it was navigable in fact. The issue of navigability arises in many legal settings and the term is defined a bit differently each time it comes up. A given river can thus be navigable for some legal purposes but not others. Deeply embedded in the history of this important issue—so embedded that it is nearly forgotten—is the fact that navigability disputes in England and early America had almost nothing to do with navigability as commonly understood, as the right to use a waterway for travel. Instead, the disputes were largely about rights to fish and, secondarily, to use the submerged land. In navigable waterways the public had fishing rights; in nonnavigable waters only riparian landowners did. We get a glimpse into this history in *Washington Ice* in the court's discussion of *Adams v. Pease*, a prominent Connecticut ruling. That ruling was handed down when navigability was limited to tidal waters. Because the case involved nontidal waters, the riparians involved in the case had "an exclusive right of fishery." Yet, according to the court, the public nonetheless had "an easement in the river as a highway, for passing and repassing with every kind of water craft." The history of navigability and its relation to fishing disputes is considered in Dale D. Goble & Eric T. Freyfogle, WILDLIFE LAW: CASES AND MATERIALS 272–99 (2002).

3. *Ownership in place versus exclusive right to harvest: ice.* Note how the court mixes together two quite different ways of thinking about ice. One idea is that the ice is owned in place by the riparian because it is physically attached to the land. The other is that the ice is unowned until harvest, but the riparian landowner has the exclusive right to harvest it in the part of the river that he owns. These might sound like much different ideas, but how different would they be in practice in this resource setting? The court asserts that ice is like everything else that becomes physically attached to land: it becomes part of the real property of the landowner. Yet, the court also asserts that ice is like fish, which the landowner has the right to harvest but does not actually own until the fish are captured. So which is it? As for the claim that the ice is owned in place, we might consider a hypothetical. What if a large chunk of plaintiff Shortall's ice breaks off and floats onto the river section adjacent to the riparian land of Washington Ice? Would Shortall still own it or is the situation akin to the wild animal that escapes? Would someone who seized the ice be guilty of theft? *See* Haase v. Kingston Co-operative Creamery Assn., 212 Wis. 585, 250 N.W. 444 (1933) (owner of land beneath non-navigable pond open to public use owns in place the ice that forms on the pond). And what if the ice collides with a bridge and damages it?

The majority rule today is that the public has a right to fish in all waterways that are navigable in fact, regardless of bed ownership. Had this rule been recognized in *Washington Ice*, the court would have had to choose between its two lines of reasoning. Its ice-as-physical-accession would have pointed toward ownership by the riparian landowner. The ice-as-fish analogy would instead have favored Washington Ice and others who harvest ice from the river.

We'll return repeatedly to this distinction: ownership in place versus the right to harvest or capture. At times we'll add a third, lesser option, a power to control a natural resource that entails no personal right to harvest the resource but does include the power to keep others from harvesting it.

4. *The technology of ice harvesting and dangers of first-in-time.* In thinking about natural-resource issues it is always wise to consider the practical implications of various alternatives, particularly in economic and technological terms. By way of policy rationale the court in *Washington Ice* cites an obvious concern: If the ice remains unowned, available to the first person to take it, it could become "the subject of general scramble, leading to acts of force and violence." How likely is this outcome? Are people more likely to fight over ice than they are over wild animals or other resources made available on a first-in-time basis?

As for the methods used by ice companies to harvest ice, the court tells us nothing. What if ice harvesting was most economically done, not by dragging blocks of ice directly upon shore, but instead by loading them on a barge that slowly moves up the river? If harvesting from the river is the preferred option, does this cast doubt on the wisdom of the court's conclusion? Is it sensible to require a commercial ice company to gain permission of each landowner on both sides of the river in order to harvest? What if one landowner refuses or demands an extortionate fee? Alternatively, if the law were to side with Washington Ice, allowing any river user to harvest the ice, could a problem arise that the court failed to note? Might competing ice companies, each wanting to be first, be prone to harvest the ice too early, before it had reached ideal thickness, perhaps fearing that a delay could leave the ice for someone else to harvest? Does the rush to be first inevitably lead people to harvest too much too soon?

In all likelihood the ice being harvested in this dispute, from the Calumet River in southern Cook County, Illinois (which includes Chicago), was being used to pack and ship beef or pork from Chicago-area stockyards. The idea of packing meat in iced railcars for long-distance transport was developed by a Detroit meat packer, George H. Hammond, in about 1868. After working the kinks out of his new system, Hammond

> decided to move nearer to the main source of supply for cattle, and so shifted his operations to Chicago. Given his great need for ice, Hammond chose to build his plant on the banks of the Calumet River next door to an already existing ice-harvesting operation. There, in what would become Hammond, Indiana, he began to introduce the nation to this new form of beef. By 1873, he was doing a million dollars worth of business annually.

William Cronon, NATURE'S METROPOLIS: CHICAGO AND THE GREAT WEST (1991), p. 233.

5. *Right to exclude I: navigable rivers.* Note that the landowner in this dispute owns the land beneath the Calumet River, yet the public has the right to enter and use the surface of the river without the landowner's consent. The court refers to the public's right as an easement. It is just as

apt to say that the landowner's right to exclude is limited. We'll see other instances of limits on the right to exclude, crafted by lawmakers to promote more efficient, often multiple uses of natural resources.

6. *Accommodation II: landowner and river user.* Another way to think about this interface between the landowner and the public is to consider that the law in effect requires the landowner to accommodate the needs of other resource users, when it is possible to do so without material interference with the landowner's activities. As the Illinois court thought about rights to the ice, it decided it was best to turn the ice over to the landowner, who perhaps could harvest it as well as anyone else. Might the outcome of the dispute have turned out differently if the clash had involved a member of the public who wanted to use the ice in place while the landowner wanted to harvest it? What if someone wanted to use the frozen surface to travel on skates or by sled, or to engage in ice fishing, and didn't want the ice removed at all? What if local people wanted to use the ice for recreational skating or to play hockey? Could a court somehow accommodate these conflicting desires?

MATHER v. CHAPMAN

40 Conn. 382 (1873).

SEYMOUR, C. J.

The first count of the plaintiffs' declaration is in trespass for the taking and converting to his own use by the defendant of large quantities of sea-weed alleged to be the proper goods and estate of the plaintiffs. This sea-weed was cast upon the shore adjoining the defendant's land,[4] and was there, below high-water mark, taken by the defendant and converted to his own use. The Court of Common Pleas, against the request of the plaintiffs, instructed the jury, in substance, that sea-weed cast and left upon the shore (that is, between ordinary high and low-water mark) *prima facie* belongs to the public and may lawfully be appropriated by the first occupant.

To this charge the plaintiffs object, and the principal question in the case arises upon this objection.

A different question arises under the second count, which will be considered in its proper place.

It is conceded that by the settled law of Connecticut the title of a riparian proprietor terminates at ordinary high-water mark. It is also conceded that though his title in fee thus terminates, yet he has certain privileges in the adjoining waters.

Among the most important of these privileges are—(1.) That of access to the deep sea. (2.) The right to extend his lands into the water

4. [Ed.: It is possible that the court meant the plaintiff's land, since the plaintiff's argument was that the defendant took the seaweed from the foreshore that existing between the plaintiff's land and the water. Apparently, though, the defendant did own nearby land, and in fact the roles of the parties are largely reversed on the second issue in this case: it is the plaintiff, also a seaweed harvester, who seeks to make use of the defendant's land.]

by means of wharves, subject to the qualification that he thereby does no injury to the free navigation of the water by the public. (3.) The right by accretion to whatever lands by natural or artificial means are reclaimed from the sea, subject however to certain qualifications not necessary here to be mentioned.

The plaintiffs claim that among the privileges of the riparian proprietor is also that of the exclusive right to the sea-weed which is cast upon the shore and left there by the receding tide.

— P's arg

In respect to the weed cast by extraordinary floods upon the land of the proprietor and there left above ordinary high-water mark, the law of this state is settled, in conformity with what we understand to be the common law of England. The owner of the soil has it *ratione soli*. No other person can then take it without a trespass upon the owner's land, and as owner of the land he is deemed to be constructively the first occupant.

But below high-water mark the soil does not belong to the owner of the upland. The sea-weed in dispute was not taken from the plaintiffs' land, and their title, if they have a title, is not *ratione soli*. No trespass on the plaintiffs' land was committed by the defendant in taking the weed, for the taking of which recovery is sought in this count.

No trespass in taking sea-weed

Upon what ground then can the plaintiffs sustain the title which they claim to the weed? While it was floating on the tide it was *publici juris*. Why, when it is left on the shore by the receding tide, should it become their property?

In Massachusetts and Maine, by virtue of the Colonial Ordinance of 1641, the individual title of proprietors adjoining navigable water extends to low-water mark. Sea-weed left by the receding tides being then on private property, the owner of the soil has title *ratione soli*, not only to sea-weed but to other articles cast upon and left on the shore. Thus in *Barker v. Bates*, 13 Pick., 255, a stick of timber was thrown up and had lodged on the shore within the old colony of Plymouth. The question is largely discussed by Shaw, Ch. J., whether the ordinance of 1641 extends to the colony of Plymouth. That being settled, the learned judge proceeds to say: "Considering it as thus established that the place upon which this timber was thrown and had lodged was the soil and freehold of the plaintiff, the defendants cannot justify their entry for the purpose of taking away or marking the timber. We are of opinion that such entry was a trespass, and that, as between the plaintiff and defendant, the plaintiff had in virtue of his title to the soil the preferable right of possession, and that the plaintiff has a right to recover the agreed value of the timber."

The cases therefore in Massachusetts and Maine which decide that sea-weed left on the shore belongs to the riparian proprietor have no application here. In New Hampshire the Massachusetts ordinance is adopted as law.

In New York the common law rule is adopted, as with us, in relation to the boundary line between the public and the riparian proprietor, and it is claimed that in *Emans v. Turnbull*, 2 Johns. R., 313, the question before us is decided in conformity with the plaintiffs' claim. The judgment in that case is pronounced by a judge of profound learning, whose opinion upon the point now under discussion, if really given, would be entitled to great weight; but we are inclined to think that the sea-weed in that case was cast upon the land of the plaintiff. The main argument at the bar and on the bench relates to the title to the locus in quo. Chief Justice Kent says:-"If the marine increase be by small and imperceptible degrees, it goes to the owner of the land. The sea-weed must be supposed to have accumulated gradually."

In the case we are called on to decide the sea-weed could not be regarded as a marine increase of the plaintiffs' land, for it had not reached their land and was not attached to it nor connected with it. To be a marine increase it must form part and parcel of the land itself. Being between high and low-water mark, at each returning tide it would be afloat, and even in Massachusetts sea-weed when afloat is *publici juris*, although floating over soil which is private property.

The sea-weed in this suit is not treated as part of the real estate which by small and imperceptible degrees had become part of the plaintiffs' land. It is treated as personal property, and the defendant is sued for taking it as such and converting it to his own use. In the case of *Emans v. Turnbull* the plaintiff's title was held good upon a liberal construction of the *jus alluvionis*, which implies that the weed had then become part and parcel of the plaintiff's land and must therefore have been above or upon ordinary high-water mark. Title to personal property *jure alluvionis* would be a novelty in the law. 2 Black. Com., 262. Title by accretion is substantially the same as by alluvion. Both are modes of acquiring title to real property.

Title however to personal property may be acquired by what in law is called accession, but to acquire title by accession the accessory thing must be united to the principal, so as to constitute part and parcel of it. "Accessio" is defined by Bouvier as "a manner of acquiring the property in a thing which becomes *united* with that which a person already possesses." The plaintiffs therefore seem to us to have no title by alluvion, or by accretion, or by accession, certainly none *ratione soli*, and they cannot be regarded as first occupants by construction merely because of the *propinquity* of their land to the property in dispute.

The question under discussion does not seem to be fully settled in England. The soil of the sea-shore is there, as with us, *prima facie* in the public, but it may become private property, and frequently is so, where the adjoining lands are part of the manor. The authority of Bracton is clearly in favor, (1st,) of the common right *of all* to the *shores* of the sea as *part of the sea itself*. (2d.) In Liber 2, speaking of the right of first occupancy, he says "Item, locum habet eadem species occupationis in iis quae communia sunt, sicut in mare et *littore maris, in lappillis et geminis et ceteris in littore maris inventis.*" Sea-weed must be included within the *et ceteris* of Bracton in this passage, and upon his authority belongs to the first occupant. . . . [Discussion of other English precedents omitted.]

[T]he right of taking sea-weed would seem to stand on the same ground as the right of taking fish. We see no reason for making a distinction between the vegetable and animal products of the ocean. Neither in the state of nature is the property of any one; the title to both depends upon the first occupancy. It is agreed that while afloat both are alike common; why, when the tide recedes and leaves shellfish and sea-weed on the shore, should the sea-weed belong to the riparian proprietor when confessedly the shell-fish remains common property?

We think the charge of the judge in regard to the first count was correct. In respect to the second count a different question arises.

The plaintiffs under that count claimed to recover for the throwing off from the defendant's upland upon the shore a small heap of sea-weed which had been gathered by the plaintiffs and laid there. The plaintiffs claimed the right to pile it on the upland where it was piled, and the defendant denied the right and justified the removal of the heap as a nuisance. The conveyances upon which this question depends are as follows.

Prior to January 7th, 1847, John J. Avery was the owner of a large tract of land in the town of Groton lying contiguous to the waters of Fishers' Island Sound, divided into two farms, and bounding southerly for some distance on "salt water." On that day he conveyed to his son, Albert L. Avery, the south part of the farm, reserving "all the sea-manure privilege of the shore east of the mow lots north of Pine Island, & c., with the privilege of piling up said sea-manure on the shore, and then re-carting to the north farm; for the use of his son Erastus Avery, or whosoever should improve his said north farm."

The plaintiffs claimed title under the foregoing deed to Erastus Avery. . . .

The court charged the jury that, as the plaintiffs are limited by their deeds to piling sea-weed "*on the shore*," they had no right by virtue of their deeds and reservations therein to pile it upon the *upland*. The defendant's argument is that the word "shore" has a definite and inflexible meaning in law, denoting the space between ordinary high and low-water mark. It is true that the word is now generally used in treatises on navigable waters in that sense, but Lord Hale says there be three kinds of shore. (Hale *de Jure Maris*, chap. 6.) One of these three kinds is the space between high and low-water mark. Both the other kinds embrace portions of the land above ordinary high-water mark.

Webster, in his Dictionary, defines shore thus:—"The coast or land adjacent to the ocean, sea or a large lake or river." He says we use the word to express the land near the border of the sea or of a great lake to an indefinite extent, as when we say "a town stands on the shore."

Bouvier defines shore as "land on the side of the sea or a lake or river." He gives to the compound word "sea-shore" the more limited meaning of land between high and low-water mark.

The privilege of piling the manure above high-water mark, on the margin of the land granted, is a valuable privilege and a proper subject of reservation, for it reserves a right in the thing granted, but the land below ordinary high-water mark not belonging to the grantor, the reservation of a right to pile sea-weed there would be the reservation of a right not in nor upon the land granted, but wholly outside of it. The reservation ought to be construed as reserving something which but for the reservation would have passed by the deed; but the right to pile sea-weed between high and low-water mark is a right which, as we have already seen, does not pertain to the riparian proprietor. Besides, such a right would be of small value, if indeed of any value, for each returning tide would probably scatter the pile.

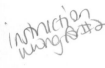

In regard to this count, we think the construction given to the reservation was wrong, and therefore advise a new trial. In this opinion the other judges concurred.

Notes

1. *Transient property rights*. Given the court's conclusion in *Mather*, what is the legal status of seaweed that is floating at high tide above the foreshore (the area of beach between high and low tide)? If the ebbing tide leaves the seaweed on the foreshore, who then owns it? If the next tide picks it up again, who then owns? And if that tide pushes it slightly above the high-tide line and deposits it again, what is the legal status? Should the answers to any of these questions depend upon whether the private land is posted against trespassers?

As for giving the seaweed to the landowner when it is deposited above the usual high-tide line, what did the landowner do to deserve it? If the seaweed grew in public waters and while growing was public property, why should the landowner now get to claim it, simply because ocean waves deposited it on her land? Could we decide instead that it remains public property wherever it is deposited, subject to the rule that a person harvesting it cannot be a trespasser? (Note the similarity of this latter possibility to the legal rule proposed by Washington Ice in the preceding case (*viz* anyone with lawful access has right to harvest).) In a later chapter, we'll see that wild animals that enter private land remain publicly owned, at least so long as they remain alive. Anyone with lawful access to the land can capture them, assuming compliance with hunting regulations. Like wild animals and unlike ice, seaweed really is not affixed to the soil.

2. *Digging worms:* People v. Brennan. A nonresident of Queens County, New York, was arrested for digging sand worms between high-and low-water marks on the shores of Little Neck bay. The village that included the beach required *non*residents to obtain licenses to take "fish bait from shores within or bounding upon the village." In the course of sustaining the

Depression–Era conviction, despite its overt discrimination against nonresidents, the court commented on the law of the foreshore in New York:

> The right of the public to use the foreshore for passing, repassing, fishing, bathing and purposes of navigation is open to no manner of doubt. . . .
>
> The rights of the public in the foreshore are of a restricted nature and include only passing, fishing, bathing, hunting and navigation. In none of these activities is there any disturbance of the soil. Sand worms, however, can be obtained only by digging—oftentimes to a considerable depth. In the case at bar it is claimed that such digging on the shores of Little Neck bay has undermined the sea walls, although there is nothing in this record to substantiate the contention. Does the right of the public go the distance of permitting an actual disturbance of the soil? In Johnson v. May (189 App. Div. 196, a decision by the Second Department) it was held that a bather could not lawfully drive four stakes in the ground for the purpose of erecting a temporary sun shelter. In the strong dissenting opinion of Mr. Justice DAVIS in Stewart v. Turney (203 App. Div. 486) the right of a hunter to erect a temporary blind between high and low-water marks was denied. . . .
>
> It has long been settled law that the public cannot gather seaweed from the foreshore. (Parsons v. Miller, 15 Wend. 561; Nolan v. Rockaway Park Imp. Co., 76 Hun, 458; Emans v. Turnbull, 2 Johns. 313; 45 C. J. 507.) These cases sustain the view that the public right in the foreshore is both qualified and narrowly restricted. . . .
>
> Principles governing the rights of the public in the land between high and low-water marks have their roots in ancient times and primitive conditions. With the improvement of the gasoline engine and the consequent increase of traffic by land and sea, the owner of water front property is now subject to constant attack from both front and rear. To minimize this the Legislature has appropriated vast sums to provide shore front playgrounds which are freely placed at the disposal of all the people. A very substantial part of this burden of expense has fallen upon the inhabitants of Nassau county. Conceivably the Legislature had these conditions in mind in delegating some measure of authority in such matters to the trustees of incorporated villages. As was said by the Court of Appeals in Klein v. Maravelas (219 N.Y. 383): 'The needs of successive generations may make restrictions imperative to-day which were vain and capricious to the vision of times past.'

People v. Brennan, 142 Misc. 225, 255 N.Y.S. 331 (N.Y.Co.Ct. 1931).

3. *Law of the foreshore*. An indication of the former importance of this body of law can be gained simply by looking at the bulk of what was (and still is, though little used) the leading Anglo–American legal treatise on the subject, Stuart A. Moore, A History of the Foreshore and the Law Relating Thereto (3d ed. 1888) (liv & 984 pp.) As the court in *Mather* notes, different legal rules about foreshore ownership are followed in Massachusetts and Maine based on colonial charters. In these states, landowners own to the low-tide mark, not the high-tide mark. A few other Atlantic coast states also follow this rule, though landowner rights are subject to various public uses of the foreshore. Contemporary treatises on property law typically short-

change foreshore issues. Two useful introductions, reflecting differing policy slants, are offered in Comment, 31 Mich. L. Rev. 1134 (1933), and Winthrop Taylor, *The Seashore and the People*, 10 Cornell L. Q. 303 (1925). This once-important, experience-filled body of law is fading from legal memory.

4. Jus publicum *and* jus privatum. Older legal writings (and a few courts still today) make use of the centuries-old legal distinction between *jus publicum* and *jus privatum* when addressing issues about navigable waterways, public-use rights, and private land ownership. *Jus publicum* had to do with the sovereign powers of government and the rights held by the public in various lands. *Jus privatum* had to do with the proprietary or private powers that came with land ownership. The distinction was used in a 1970 New York ruling that upheld the power of a town to order a landowner to remove fill that he had placed upon the foreshore:

> First, there is the *jus publicum*: the right shared by all to navigate upon the waters covering the foreshore at high tide and, at low tide, to have access across the foreshore to the waters for fishing, bathing or any other lawful purpose (Barnes v. Midland R.R. Terminal Co., 193 N.Y. 378, 384, 85 N.E. 1093, 1095). Second, there is the *jus privatum*: the right of the owner of the foreshore. Originally, this right was peculiar to the King of England who, in his individual capacity, held title to all land under navigable water throughout his kingdom as his private property (Commonwealth v. Alger, 7 Cush. 53, 82, 90; Lewis Blue Point Oyster Cultivation Co. v. Briggs, 198 N.Y. 287, 291, 91 N.E. 846, 847). When ownership of this land, as is usually the case, is vested in a governmental authority, it is said to hold title in trust for the public good, with the right to control and regulate commerce and navigation thereon, as well as fishing or bathing, subject to the *jus publicum* (Trustees of Freeholders & Commonalty of Town of Brookhaven v. Smith, 188 N.Y. 74, 78, 80 N.E. 665, 667).

Arnold's Inn, Inc. v. Morgan, 63 Misc.2d 279, 310 N.Y.S.2d 541 (N.Y. Sup. Ct. 1970). According to Stuart Moore, writing late in the nineteenth century, English law was clear that private landowners who gained ownership of the foreshore by royal grant acquired only the *jus privatum*, and held their lands subject to the public use rights protected by the *jus publicum*. Stuart A. Moore, A History of the Foreshore and the Law Relating Thereto 652–55 (3d ed. 1888). Public rights protected by the *jus publicum*, however, did not include the right to gather seaweed. *Id.*, 656.

The Supreme Court of South Carolina drew upon this distinction in a recent ruling involving a landowner who claimed that his ocean-front (and increasingly submerged) land had been unlawfully "taken" by the government without compensation when it barred him from filling his land to raise it above the high tide:

> As a coastal state, South Carolina has a long line of cases regarding the public trust doctrine in the context of land bordering navigable waters. Historically, the State holds presumptive title to land below the high water mark. As stated by this Court in 1884, not only does the State hold title to this land in *jus privatum,* it holds it in *jus publicum,* in trust for the benefit of all the citizens of this State. *State v. Pacific*

Guano Co., 22 S.C. 50, 84 (1884); *see also State v. Hardee,* 259 S.C. 535, 193 S.E.2d 497 (1972); ...

The State has the exclusive right to control land below the high water mark for the public benefit, *Port Royal Mining Co. v. Hagood,* 30 S.C. 519, 9 S.E. 686 (1889), and cannot permit activity that substantially impairs the public interest in marine life, water quality, or public access. *Sierra Club v. Kiawah Resort Assocs.,* 318 S.C. 119, 456 S.E.2d 397 (1995); *see also Heyward v. Farmers' Min. Co.,* 42 S.C. 138, 19 S.E. 963 (1884) (public trust land cannot be placed entirely beyond direction and control of the State); *Cape Romain Land & Improvement Co. v. Georgia–Carolina Canning Co.,* 148 S.C. 428, 146 S.E. 434 (1928) (protected public purposes of trust include navigation and fishery). The State's presumptive title applies to tidelands. *State v. Yelsen Land Co.,* 265 S.C. 78, 216 S.E.2d 876 (1975).

Significantly, under South Carolina law, wetlands created by the encroachment of navigable tidal water belong to the State. *Coburg Dairy, Inc. v. Lesser,* 318 S.C. 510, 458 S.E.2d 547 (1995). Proof that land was highland at the time of grant and tidelands were subsequently created by the rising of tidal water cannot defeat the State's presumptive title to tidelands. *State v. Fain,* 273 S.C. 748, 259 S.E.2d 606 (1979).

As described above, each of McQueen's lots borders a man-made tidal canal. At the time the permits were denied, the lots had reverted to tidelands with only irregular portions of highland remaining. This reversion to tidelands effected a restriction on McQueen's property rights inherent in the ownership of property bordering tidal water.

restriction on rights [handwritten margin note]

The tidelands included on McQueen's lots are public trust property subject to control of the State. McQueen's ownership rights do not include the right to backfill or place bulkheads on public trust land and the State need not compensate him for the denial of permits to do what he cannot otherwise do. *Accord Esplanade Props., Inc. v. City of Seattle,* 307 F.3d 978 (9th Cir.2002) (finding no taking where state public trust doctrine precludes dredging and filling tidelands).

McQueen v. South Carolina Coastal Council, 354 S.C. 142, 580 S.E.2d 116 (2003). Note in *McQueen* that this rule of law makes the landowner's right to exclude dependent in part on the vagaries of nature: as the tidal waters invade private land, the public gains access to that land without regard for the landowner's wishes. Also see Glass v. Goeckel, 473 Mich. 667, 703 N.W.2d 58 (2005), noted after the article below on beach access.

5. *Ancillary rights I: temporary storage.* The second issue in *Mather* seemingly has to do with a rather ordinary issue of deed interpretation, but it is connected to a natural-resources issue of considerable significance. Imagine a person trying to harvest seaweed to use as fertilizer on farm fields. The harvester needs to gather a large quantity of seaweed, far more than he could possibly carry. What is he to do? One possibility is to put the gathered seaweed in piles, then come back later and load the piles onto a wagon. But note the danger here. If the pile is left on the foreshore, the seaweed remains unowned or at least can wash away.

Practically speaking, if a seaweed harvester cannot safely leave the seaweed piled on the foreshore, where is he to put it? Is it reasonable to say that he can place the pile on private land, adjacent to the foreshore, as an adjunct or ancillary right to his right to use the foreshore—something akin to the canoeist who is allowed to step onto private land to portage around a river rapids? Hasn't the court unwittingly diminished the value of the public's harvesting right on the foreshore by failing to think about the practical elements of its exercise? Issues such as this arise repeatedly in natural resource law: what ancillary rights do resource owners require so as to make reasonable use of their resources?

6. *Getting to the resource: beaches*. For the most part, beaches in the United States are open to public use below the high-tide line (Massachusetts and Maine are exceptions, as we've seen, and so are states that give the public broader rights in the upland "dry sand" beach). But getting to the beach can sometimes be a challenge. Through concerted action, private landowners and accommodating local governments can make it hard for the public to exercise its ownership rights. One method of restricting public use is to provide few or no parking places near public access points. Another is to provide parking but make it available only to holders of permits, which are then issued only to local residents. A more ambitious, legally questionable device is to allow only local residents to make use of a public access path. Beach-access problems of this type are considered in the following newspaper account. As you read it, consider how this same issue might play out in other resource settings: Those who control access routes can indirectly control use of the resource itself.

BEACH ACCESS: WHERE DO YOU DRAW THE LINE IN THE SAND?

Jane Costello

THE NEW YORK TIMES, January 21, 2005.

For some, Ponte Vedra Boulevard is the road to paradise. Multimillion-dollar mansions and million-dollar teardowns line the narrow boulevard, which runs parallel to an expansive stretch of white-sand beach on Florida's northeast coast just below Jacksonville. The mansions are large and close together, and as you drive along, the Atlantic Ocean is visible only by peeking through hedges or catching a glimpse of blue through spotless picture windows.

Access to that beach, or lack of it, is what also makes the boulevard in the resort town of Ponte Vedra Beach a battleground of sorts. Over the last two decades, public access to Florida's 1,200 miles of coastline has diminished drastically. Now, as in other coastal states around the country, lines are being drawn in the sand between residents demanding better beach access and oceanfront property owners determined to keep the public off their private land.

Ponte Vedra Boulevard is one of those lines.

According to the Florida Department of Environmental Protection, at least 60 percent of beaches in the state are private and offer little or no access to the public, enabling both developers and homeowners to claim those beaches as their own. But many contend that there is no such thing as a private beach: as in other states, the constitution of Florida recognizes that the beach is publicly owned up to the high-tide mark. In addition, Florida law requires the state to ensure "the public's right to reasonable access to beaches," and various court rulings have affirmed that principle.

Nevertheless, over the last 20 years local governments in Florida have routinely ceded access points to developers. Along both the Atlantic Ocean and the Gulf of Mexico, developers have been granted the right to stake claim on dry sand and build waterfront communities, which then bring in hefty tax revenues to local jurisdictions.

"The question is, what is a beach?" said Graham Ginsburg, a resident of Naples on Florida's gulf coast and a beach access advocate who is also a member of the Collier County Coastal Advisory Committee. "You can say you own a piece of sand, but sand doesn't constitute a beach until it meets the ocean. And when it does, that beach is mine."

For the last two years, this dispute has played itself out in Ponte Vedra Beach. Referred to by some as Jacksonville's Malibu, Ponte Vedra is a barrier island between the Intracoastal Waterway and the Atlantic that is home to approximately 25,000 residents, along with the Association of Tennis Players and the Professional Golfer's Association.

The pristine sandy beach is the third jewel in Ponte Vedra's crown. Until recently, one of the best-kept secrets in town was the existence of 14 public beach access points along Ponte Vedra Boulevard, half of them unmarked and none actively maintained by St. John's County. There is no parking on the seven-mile-long, two-lane thoroughfare, nor are there bicycle racks, boardwalks or public toilets, except at Mickler's Landing, the 15th and very visible public access point, in a county park at the south end of the road.

"You'd be hard pressed to find any of the access points," said Vince Di Viesti, a Ponte Vedra resident who is the founder of a new advocacy group, the Florida Beach Access and Awareness Coalition. "There aren't signs for most of them, and the signs that do exist are either facing the wrong way or point to the road, not the beach. It's basically a private beach for five or six miles, which is great for people who live on the beach but bad for everybody else."

Those who live on or near the boulevard say that the area was never designed to accommodate a large number of beachgoers. But the growth of the community over the last 30 years, as well as others nearby, has residents thinking about how best to preserve their piece of paradise. "When I moved here in 1972, this was a sleepy bedroom community of Jacksonville," said Carl Bloesing, a former president of the Ponte Vedra Community Association, whose home is on the lagoon that runs parallel to the ocean and along the boulevard. "Now Ponte Vedra is just about built out. But west of us, the county is planning huge, huge developments. When it comes time, those people will look for the closest beach, which would be ours."

Mr. Bloesing said that although most residents don't object to the county's opening up existing beach access points, they don't want accommodations made for additional parking. In 2003, residents successfully petitioned the county to vacate a 34–foot-wide, 7,000–foot right of way on the boulevard that advocates for beach access wanted converted to parking.

The county argued that it never owned the land in the first place and claimed rights only for underground utility use. That action left 76 homeowners free to claim a proportional piece of the land as part of their property, which in turn prompted a lawsuit filed by the Jacksonville chapter of the Surfrider Foundation, a nonprofit environmental organization.

Among other charges, the lawsuit claimed the move violated county law requiring that all residents have adequate access to the beaches. The case was dismissed in December, to the relief of Ponte Vedra homeowners who envisioned an influx of inland day-trippers on warm, sunny days.

"This is a hot-button issue that pits constituents against each other," said Bruce Maguire, a St. John's County commissioner. According to Mr. McGuire, the county has added 50,000 residents in the last five years, and an additional 15,000–acre development is expected to provide housing for another 30,000. The county has 42 miles of beach and a total of 170 access points, but 115 of them are closed. "Historically, there was never a need to open them," he said. "But with all this growth, we have to figure out how to do it."

Beach access is a growing concern throughout Florida. North of Ponte Vedra, the town of Fernandina Beach is in a battle over a private beach boardwalk built by a condominium association. The town maintains the boardwalk should be open to the public and has closed it until the dispute is settled. On the gulf coast, residents find themselves fighting for space on the few beaches still accessible to the public. Mr. Ginsburg, the Naples beach-access advocate, said that the problem began as a result of the building boom in the area in 2000. "We had plenty of access up until that point," he said. "Now it's even hard to find a parking space during the week. And on the weekends, the lots are filled by 8 or 9 in the morning."

Perhaps the biggest example, in terms of the sheer amount of beachfront involved, is in the Florida panhandle. There, in 2002, the state gave permission to develop 27 miles of coastline to the St. Joe Company, Florida's largest private landowner and developer. In exchange, the company provided two public beach-access points.

The conflict over beach access has become increasingly contentious—and litigious—around the United States over the last 10 years. In 1995, a Stamford, Conn., resident sued the neighboring town of Greenwich for denying him access to the beach at Greenwich Point. In July 2001, the Connecticut Supreme Court ruled in his favor, opening up the beach park to people who do not live in Greenwich.

Last summer in Malibu, the undisputed capital of coastal access contention, the California Coastal Commission ordered the removal of "No Trespassing" signs at Broad Beach as well as an end to private security patrols on all-terrain vehicles intended to keep visitors off the dry sand. The commission also went a step further, posting detailed information on its Web site describing the public access points.

"What you're seeing is a hemorrhaging of access across the country," said Scott Shine, president of the Jacksonville chapter of the Surfrider Foundation. "People like to blame the developers, but in reality, it's more a question of local governments having abdicated their responsibilities." . . .

Note

Beach access in Michigan. The public's access to beaches along the Great Lakes came before the Michigan Supreme Court only recently, in *Glass v. Goeckel*, 473 Mich. 667, 703 N.W.2d 58 (2005). In a much-discussed ruling the court applied the *jus privatum-jus publicum* distinction in the course of concluding that the public had rights of access to all private land along the Great Lakes below the mean high water mark. The court admitted that the idea of mean high water mark was hard to apply in the case of inland lakes. It clarified the term by borrowing a definition crafted by the Supreme Court of Wisconsin in *Diana Shooting Club v. Husting*, 156 Wis. 261, 145 N.W. 816 (1914): the mean high water mark was "the point on the bank or shore up to which the presence and action of the water is so continuous as to leave a distinct mark either by erosion, destruction of terrestrial vegetation, or other easily recognized characteristic." A dissenting opinion attacked the distinct as excessively difficult to apply and proposed instead that the public be limited to access to lands that at any given moment were submerged.

[margin note: high water mark (inland water)]

B. BENEATH THE GROUND

Our inquiry into the physical attributes of land now shifts to resources that lie beneath the surface. As in the case of resources at water's edge, we have the same foundational issue: which natural resources are part of the land and which are available for separate acquisition? Should we answer this question using an abstract, easily understood ideal of land ownership, or does it make more sense to consider each resource separately, paying attention to its physical attributes and to the practical challenges of putting the resource to effective use? As we go about defining landowner rights, should we aim to accommodate various resource uses in the same place, or simply get nature into private hands as quickly and cleanly as possible?

[margin note: part of land vs. separate acquisition?]

The next case introduces these issues. Again, be forewarned: the court's legal statements are not all true today.

HICKS v. BELL

3 Cal. 219 (1853).

APPEAL from the Tenth Judicial District, for Yuba County.

The complainants, styling themselves members of the National Mining Company, state that, on the 27th of July, 1852, and for two years previous, they were owners of a certain mining claim, situated in the bed of Yuba River, beginning at the mouth of Deer Creek and extending two hundred yards down said river, including the bed of the same, and that said claim was held by the said plaintiffs "according to the rules and customs of miners in the immediate vicinity of said river mining claim," and was worked by them during the mining season of 1851, and also the mining season of 1852, so far as the said season has continued, up to the period of the commencement of this suit. That the defendants as well as H. Hitchcock, Martin, and others, unknown, members of the Rockville Company, did on the 27th of July take possession of and work upon about ninety feet of the upper portion of the said claim; and do now, contrary to the rights of your complainants, after being fully advised of the same, work upon the said claim to the extent of said ninety feet; and complainants say that said ninety feet is worth $5000. That defendants well knew that plaintiffs were the first and lawful owners of said claim, and although repeatedly notified to leave the same, and though possession thereof was demanded by plaintiffs, defendants had refused to surrender the same. The plaintiffs therefore pray for damages, & c., and to be placed in possession of the premises, and for further relief, & c. . . .

HEYDENFELDT, JUSTICE

The objection that the record discloses that there was no actual possession, is not good, because it appears there was actual possession of a portion adjacent to the premises in dispute, and, as I understand it, constructive possession of the latter was claimed by the rules and customs of miners on that part of the river. . . .

The main reliance in this case of the appellants is, that the land in question is the public land of the United States, and therefore the statutes of this State, which recognize the possessions of miners, which provide for their protection, and require mining claims to be decided according to the rules and regulations of bodies of miners, at each particular mining locality, are mere police regulations, and are invalid to confer any right, such as that of possession, or to enable the recovery thereof.

This position involves the decision of the question, to whom do the mines of gold and silver belong? To arrive at a satisfactory solution, it is only necessary to examine a few of the leading authorities.

According to the common law of England, mines of silver and gold are termed royal mines, and are the exclusive property of the Crown. Blackstone says, vol. 1, p. 294: "A twelfth branch of the royal revenue, the right to mines, has its original from the king's prerogative of coinage, in order to supply him with materials, and therefore those mines which are properly royal, and to which the king is entitled, when found, are only those of silver and gold. By the old common law, if gold or silver be found in mines of base metal, according to the opinion of some, the whole was a royal mine, and belonged to the king." And he cites 2 Just. 577.

English cl.—gold/silver = King (coinage)

In the case of The Queen and the Earl of Northumberland, cited from Plowden, it was decided that although the king grant lands and the mines which are in them, yet royal mines will not pass by so general a description. It was further explicitly decided, in the same case, that all mines of gold and silver within the realm, though in the lands of subjects, belong to the crown; and this right is accompanied with full liberty to dig, and carry away the ores, and with all such incidents thereto, as are necessary to be used for getting them.

despite being in hands of others = King

This case has never been overruled, and stands as the accepted exposition of the common law. For although Lord HARDWICKE, in the case of Siddal v. Weston, 2 Atk. 20, seems to confine the royal right of entry to cases where the mine had already been opened, yet he does not question the royal ownership, and seems finally to decide the case upon a different reason. Even, however, his slight departure from the doctrine of the case in Plowden, was subsequently disapproved and doubted as authority by Sir WM. GRANT, Master of the Rolls, in the case of Seaman v. Vaudrey, 16 Vesey, 393. . . .

Blackstone, it will be seen, attributes the origin of the law to the right of coinage. Plowden says, that the reason is because gold and silver are most excellent things, and the law has appointed them to the person who is most excellent, and that was the king. It is, however, immaterial as to the reason for its origin; the law has been settled beyond question, as it is declared by the earliest and most distinguished judges, and to this time has never been disputed. See Bainbridge on the Law of Mines and Minerals, where the authorities are collected.

This doctrine of the law has been acted upon in some, and probably in many, of the States in the Union. In Pennsylvania, it was the subject of legislation as early as 1787. In that year, by an act establishing a land office, she reserves for the use of the Commonwealth, one-fifth of all gold and silver ore. See Dunlap's Laws of Pennsylvania. In New York, as early as 1789, an act of the legislature was passed, exempting the discoverers of gold and silver mines from paying to the people of the State as sovereign thereof, any portion or dividend of the yield, for the space of 21 years from the time of giving notice of the discovery; and forbidding the working of the same after the expiration of that term. See 1 Laws of New York, 124.

Again, in 1827, another act was passed, which declares that all mines of gold and silver discovered, or hereafter to be discovered, within this State, shall be the property of the people of this State, in their right of sovereignty. See 1 Revised Statutes, 281.

CA law—gold/silver prop. of ppl of state (sovereignty)

This was in effect but a re-enactment of the common law, which vested the right in the State government as the successor of the king.

It is hardly necessary at this period of our history, to make an argument to prove that the several States of the Union, in virtue of their respective sovereignties, are entitled to the jura regalia which pertained to the king at common law. . . .

In reference to the ownership of the public lands, the United States only occupied the position of any private proprietor, with the exception of an express exemption from State taxation. The mines of gold and silver on the public lands are as much the property of this State, by virtue of her sovereignty, as are similar mines in the lands of private citizens. She has, therefore, solely the right to authorize them to be worked; to pass laws for their regulation; to license miners; and to affix such terms and conditions as she may deem proper, to the freedom of their use. In her legislation upon this subject, she has established the policy of permitting all who desire it, to work her mines of gold and silver, with or without conditions; and she has wisely provided that their conflicting claims shall be adjudicated by the rules and customs which may be established by bodies of them working in the same vicinity . . .

According to this enactment, the case under consideration has been tried and decided, and for aught that is disclosed by the record, the decision is consonant with right and justice. Judgment is affirmed.

Notes

1. *Prospectors and constructive possession. Hicks v. Bell,* decided not long after California joined the Union, offers a glimpse into life during the gold rush. Miners were piling on top of one another to control the best mining spots—initially in river beds and later, as these were panned out, in ore formations away from the water. Note that the argument here dealt with a single mining claim, staked out on a first-in-time basis in accordance with local custom. The claim extended 200 yards along the Yuba River, a dimension no doubt mandated by local custom. The second-in-time miner encroached upon 90 feet of this claim. This 90–foot section was the entire subject matter of the law suit (and loaded with more than fool's gold, one hopes).

The first paragraph of Justice Heydenfeldt's opinion expresses an important rule that applied in mining territory: a prospector who properly stakes out a claim has the exclusive right to work it. So long as the miner is using *part* of the claim he is deemed to have "constructive possession" of the whole of the claim. If another miner shows up and begins working the same claim, he is deemed to have wrongfully disrupted the possession of the first miner, even though there is no actual physical interference with what the first miner is doing. The idea of constructive possession is, of course, difficult to apply in practice unless it is defined precisely by local custom or agreement.

2. *The twelfth branch of royal revenue.* As the court notes, gold and silver mines in England were claimed by the crown. They were owned by the

King (or Queen), not in a *proprietary* capacity (as the King would own a farm or castle), but in a *sovereign* capacity—the same capacity as the King owned land beneath navigable waterways and wild game. (The terminology here is similar to the *jus publicum-jus privatum* distinction noted after the last case.) These rights passed to the states once Independence was declared or, later, as each state entered the Union. But what was a state to do with its mineral rights, and how did this state ownership relate to land ownership? To the modern reader *Hicks* reaches an unexpected outcome. The common understanding today is that landowners in the United States own all the minerals beneath the surface, gold and silver included. What accounts for the ruling?

Hicks is a surprising case and by no means expresses contemporary law. The ruling is nonetheless useful because it gives good background on the ownership of mines at common law and because it highlights a fundamental policy question that each jurisdiction needs to answer. What minerals go with the surface and which do not? The question could receive widely varied answers. Governments around the world have come up with a variety. (As you might guess from the extreme wealth of various state-run oil companies around the globe, landowners do better in the United States than elsewhere.) The law governing gold and silver is also useful because it illustrates one of the many ways that the United States tailored the inherited common law to suit the circumstances and cultural values of America. Particularly when it came to property, lawmakers paid attention to what England had said but felt free to make even major legal changes.

3. *The law of the mining camp*. In *Hicks* the court decided that certain minerals belonged to the state and were available for separate acquisition. As for how a person could gain ownership of this state-controlled resource, the court was willing to defer to the de facto code that had arisen within the mining camps (largely borrowed from mining regions in Europe): mines go to the first person to discover a valuable deposit and to stake out (or "locate") the claim in accordance with local mining customs. Note that two steps were involved in the court's legal reasoning, and the court could have taken the first step and not the second. The court could have announced that the minerals belonged to the state (step one) but then announced that the first-in-time system was of no legal effect (step two). That is, it could have embraced the reasoning that we saw in the fishery in *Marincovich*, protecting public ownership and yet denying the claims of people who wanted to seize the resource.

The ruling in *Hicks* no doubt made sense to Californians during the gold rush era. The case dealt with land owned by the distant federal government. Fueled by an anti-federal bias, Californians were apparently happy to carve up and carry away minerals on federal lands. The problem that quickly arose concerned the application of *Hicks* to private land. Private owners were not so happy to have outsiders enter their lands, discover gold, and then claim a right to mine it. As it turned out, the rule announced in *Hicks v. Bell* did not survive the decade as a principle of state property law. The California court reversed itself in Moore v. Smaw, 17 Cal. 199, 218 (1861), shifting to the majority American rule that all solid subsurface minerals belong to the owner of the land surface. (An intriguing, half-way step toward reversing *Hicks* was made by the court in 1859 in Boggs v. Merced Mining Co., 14 Cal.

279. The court decided that, while the state owned the minerals underneath private land, it had not granted to the public a general license to enter private lands to engage in mining. In so ruling, the court reaffirmed the public's ownership but then withheld from the public the necessary right of access.)

4. *The progeny of* Hicks. Although the precise holding in *Hicks* would prove short-lived, the ruling played a key role in stimulating two legal developments of immense importance in shaping resource-use in the American West. First, the idea sunk in that the customary law of the mining camp with its first-in-time allocation system applied on federally owned land, and that this law would be viewed chiefly as a component of *state* rather than *federal* law. Mining law was thus subject to variation among the states, even when mining took place on federal land. Congress soon gave its approval to this legal arrangement in statutes enacted over the ensuing decade and a half. That law-making worked culminated in the Mining Law of 1872, which provides the framework for mining today. *Hicks*, in sum, survived in part as the law governing public lands.

The second post-*Hicks* development had to do with a resource that miners soon found essential for their new, hydraulic mining methods: water. If first-in-time made sense among competing miners on federal lands, neither of whom owned the land surface, then it seemed to make equally good sense to allocate water the same way (another example of resource reasoning by analogy). In the case of water, though, the common law was much more clear. Under it, rights to divert and consume water belonged to riparian landowners alone. But with the landowning federal government thousands of miles away and apparently disinterested, the California Supreme Court was left to decide itself between two trespassers. As between trespasser A and trespasser B, which one should get the water? The only rule that made any sense—the rule embedded, for instance, in the law of found property, when a dispute arose between two finders—was to say that the first water user got to keep the water, until the riparian landowner showed up to claim it. Thus was born the prior appropriation system of water allocation, and the key precedent relied upon was *Hicks v. Bell*. See Eric T. Freyfogle, *Lux v. Haggin and the Common Law Burdens of Modern Water Law*, 57 U. Colo. L. Rev. 485 (1986) (arguing that California's embrace of prior appropriation did not involve significant legal innovation, as many commentators have asserted).

5. *Ancillary rights II: minerals, and what else?* Note one problem that quickly arises when we allow one person to acquire rights to minerals underneath land owned by someone else. The miner needs to get access to the minerals, and often needs to alter the land surface significantly in order to extract the minerals. The California court was well aware of this issue. It made specific mention of the fact that, in England, the king's ownership rights in gold and silver was accompanied by "full liberty to dig, and carry away the ores, and with all such incidents thereto as are necessary to be used for getting them." Plainly, this formulation of the king's rights made mining the paramount use of the land surface. The king apparently could disrupt and displace whatever the surface owner was doing, without need to compromise or make reasonable accommodation (what else would we expect, when the king makes the laws?)

Perhaps the California court viewed this arrangement as sensible in California mountains owned by the federal government; after all, what other value did this rocky land have? But the story was quite otherwise in lands that did clearly have other uses. On such lands, it was not so clear that a mining-first policy was socially wise. A policy that favored miners discouraged surface owners from investing in surface-use activities. This conflict over surface uses could be avoided by shifting to the rule in which surface and minerals were combined in a single owner. Then, the surface owner could decide which resource use would take priority. If a surface owner did sell off the mineral rights, the parties could negotiate as to the surface-use rights that the mineral buyer received.

6. *The federal government as proprietor*. A final note on the legal status of federal lands: The court's ruling was made easier because of the then-prevailing assumption among courts that the federal government as landowner "only occupied the position of any private proprietor, with the exception of an express exemption from State taxation." Today the legal understanding is vastly different. Congress holds nearly unlimited lawmaking powers under the Property Clause of the Constitution (Art. IV, section 3, clause 2). Any laws it enacts preempt state law on federally owned lands. Kleppe v. New Mexico, 426 U.S. 529 (1976). State mining law applies on federal lands only because and so long as Congress tolerates it, although a shift in that longstanding policy would plainly need to consider existing property rights.

HAMMONDS v. CENTRAL KENTUCKY NATURAL GAS CO.

255 Ky. 685, 75 S.W.2d 204 (App. 1934).

STANLEY, COMMISSIONER.

The case seems to be one of first impression. About 1919 the appellee exhausted the gas from a field of about 15,000 acres in Menifee and adjoining counties, most of which it had under lease. Thereafter it brought in vast quantities of gas from distant fields and put it by force through its previously drilled wells into the vacated underground reservoir, withdrawing it as desired. In recent rate litigation the company valued these holdings at $2,000,000. See *Central Kentucky Natural Gas Company v. Railroad Commission* (D. C.) 60 F.(2d) 137. The appellant owns 54 acres within this boundary which was never leased to the company. It is not disputed that this geological dome or basin underlies her land. She brought this suit to recover a large sum for use and occupation under the idea of trespass, it being charged that the gas was placed in or under her property without her knowledge or consent. Judgment went for the defendant. The decision must rest upon the character and nature of property in natural gas.

The migratory trait of oil and gas when released from imprisonment in their natural geological reservoirs by decrease of the pressure which confines them when the strata is penetrated, naturally or mechanically—perhaps at a point far removed and where no connection could be suspected—was early judicially recognized. This power, as it were, of self-transmission, or this fleeting nature of oil and gas, soon gave rise to the distinctive rules of law which differentiate these substances from the solid minerals.

In the pioneer case of Hail v. Reed, 54 Ky. (15 B. Mon.) 479 (decided in 1854), suit was filed to recover possession of "three barrels of American oil," valued at $1.25 a gallon, which had been drawn from the plaintiff's salt well in Cumberland county without his license or permission. In the argument the plaintiffs likened the oil to solid minerals, while the defendants suggested the analogies between animals *ferae naturae* and waters of a spring to oil (then a novel product sold as medicine, and stated by the court to be "a peculiar liquid not necessary nor indeed suitable for the common use of man"), and maintained that since the plaintiff had not reduced the oil to possession and as they had done so through their own efforts, they were entitled to retain it. The court passed over the suggested analogies and held that, like water collected, the oil actually in the well, there subject to being taken out, was the property of the owner of the land and belonged to him when drawn out unless it had been done by his licensee. The defendants were regarded as wrongdoers and the oil was restored to the owner of the land. It remained for the Supreme Court of Pennsylvania twelve years later to point out specifically for the first time the distinctions and to lay the predicate for the various rules based upon the fugacious nature of these minerals in Funk v. Haldeman, 53 Pa. 229. In Westmoreland & Cambria Natural Gas Company v. De Witt, 130 Pa. 235, 18 A. 724, 725, 5 L. R. A. 73, that court said:

> "Water and oil, and still more strongly gas, may be classed by themselves, if the analogy be not too fanciful, as minerals *ferae naturae*. In common with animals, and unlike other minerals, they have the power and the tendency to escape without the volition of the owner. Their 'fugitive and wandering existence within the limits of a particular tract was uncertain.' * * * They belong to the owner of the land, and are part of it, so long as they are on or in it, and are subject to his control; but when they escape, and go into other land, or come under another's control, the title of the former owner is gone. Possession of the land, therefore, is not necessarily possession of the gas."

But, as is pointed out in Mills & Willingham on the Law of Oil and Gas, § 13, the doctrine of *ferae naturae* was not carried to its logical conclusion in that state (as it was in Indiana), for Pennsylvania, as in a majority of the oil producing states, has adopted the rule that the owner of land under which oil and gas lie is the absolute owner of them in place in the same manner and to the same extent as is an owner of solid minerals, and that he may create by grant or reservation a separate corporeal estate in oil and gas identical in nature with the estate of the surface, subject, of course, to loss through escape. We so regard it in Kentucky. [citations omitted] Except the easement to explore and develop, the conveyance is in reality the grant of a right in real estate yet to be actually severed or produced, for as to oil and gas not discovered or produced, there is no change of title from the common ownership. Kelly v. Keys, 213 Pa. 295, 62 A. 911, 110 Am. St. Rep. 547; Swiss Oil Corporation v. Hupp, supra.

The conception of absolute ownership can go no further, for beyond that point the wild and migratory nature of oil and gas destroys the theory. They may be here to-day and gone to-morrow. They belong to the owner of the land as a part of it so long as they are on it or in it or subject to his control; when they are gone, his title is gone. Brown v. Spilman, 155 U. S. 665, 15 S. Ct. 245, 39 L. Ed. 304. If they escape into the land of another, they become his property in like degree or manner. So it is declared that oil and gas are not the property of any one until reduced to actual possession by extraction, although by virtue of his proprietorship the owner of the surface, or his grantee of the severed mineral estate, has the exclusive right of seeking to acquire and of appropriating the oil and gas directly beneath. . . .

When gas is thus severed and brought under dominion and into actual possession at the surface, it, of course, becomes the personal property of the one who has extracted it under a right so to do. Willis's Thornton on Oil & Gas, §§ 50 and 60. The appellee acquired such title to the gas here involved. The question is whether that gas, having once been reduced to possession and absolute ownership having vested, was restored to its original wild and natural status by being replaced in a similar reservoir of nature, taking the place of other gas which once occupied that same subterranean chamber. . . .

In seeking for an analogous condition in the law, the courts, since the early Pennsylvania case, have compared natural gas and oil to that of animals *ferae naturae*. The analogy, as we have seen, formed the basis of the all but universal doctrine of property in these wandering minerals. So we may look to that analogous law. From the beginning, wild animals have been regarded as quasi property of the entire human race. It is the recognition of land titles rather than of any individual property in the game that prevents its pursuit, and, barring all questions of trespass, exclusive property in birds and wild animals becomes vested in the person capturing or reducing them to possession. But unless killed, this is a qualified property, for when restored to their natural wild and free state, the dominion and individual proprietorship of any person over them is at an end and they resume their status as common property. 3 C. J. 18, 19. So, too, are fish collective property so long as they remain unconfined in their natural element in a public stream, and not even the owner of the soil over which the stream flows owns the fish therein, although he may have the exclusive right of fishing in the stream where it runs over his land. And, as in the case of wild game, a qualified property in an individual may be acquired by catching and confining fish within a private pond so they cannot escape. If, however, the fish escape and are found at large in their proper element, they again become public property and are subject to appropriation by the first person who takes them. 26 C. J. 597.

If one capture a fox in a forest and turn it loose in another, or if he catch a fish and put it back in the stream at another point, has he not done with that migratory, common property just what the appellee has done with the gas in this case? Did the company not lose its exclusive property in the gas when it restored the substance to its natural habitat?

Another analogue to the moving deposits of oil and gas is subterranean and percolating water which also have a similarity of relation though not of identity, the substantial difference being only that oil and gas are vanishing products while water may be perpetually supplied by nature. One may draw water and it becomes his when placed in his own receptacle. He may appropriate water from a running stream to turn his mill or to irrigate his land and the property therein may be said to exist in him so long as it remains under his control. But once the water is restored to the earth or to the running stream that exclusive, individual title is lost. Willis's Thornton on Oil & Gas, § 42; Hail v. Reed, supra; Rock Creek Ditch & Flume Company v. Miller, 93 Mont. 248, 17 P.(2d) 1074, 89 A. L. R. 200 . . .

We are of opinion, therefore, that if in fact the gas turned loose in the earth wandered into the plaintiff's land, the defendant is not liable to her for the value of the use of her property, for the company ceased to be the exclusive owner of the whole of the gas—it again became mineral *ferae naturae*.

Notes

1. *Who won*? Mrs. Hammonds lost her attempt to collect money damages for the subsurface trespass. If you were her lawyer, what would you advise her to do next? Should the gas company have been more careful in what it asked for, in terms of a rule of law to govern such subterranean disputes? Can gas companies now safely use underground formations for storage when other people own overlying land? (Later in the chapter we'll see this same issue arise with respect to groundwater that is pumped into the ground for storage.)

2. *Ownership in place versus exclusive right to harvest, again*. The court in *Hammonds* faced an issue much like that in *Washington Ice*. Should the landowner own the resource in place or should she merely have an exclusive territorial right to harvest a resource that is unowned prior to harvest? How different are these two approaches in the case of a natural resource like oil and gas that moves underground? And how valuable is privately owned oil under the ground if a neighbor at any time can drill on his own land and pump it out? If in fact oil underground is unowned, would a legal ban on oil drilling take any existing property interest from the landowner?

3. *The wild animal analogy*. Once again we encounter a court reasoning from one type of resource to another. If the court had pressed the wild animal analogy to its fullest extent, where would it have ended up? We'll turn to the law of wild animals in the next section, yet we've seen enough already to get a general answer. If oil is really like a wild animal, then it too

would be owned by the state in its sovereign capacity (as *Hicks v. Bell* asserted with respect to gold). If that is so, the landowner plainly does not own it in place. Equally clear would be the power of the sovereign state (as with wildlife) to assert control over who could take the oil and when, just as it controls hunting. It would not be a foregone conclusion that a surface landowner could take the oil, any more than a surface owner can capture wildlife without the state's consent. Given the low value of nearly all wild animals, it makes sense for the state to allow hunters to capture it for free. But can the same be said of more valuable state property? If the state really owns oil on behalf of the sovereign people, would it be acting responsibly simply to allow landowners to take it for free, without compensating taxpayers? Many states have statutes banning government officials from selling public property at less than fair market value. A law transferring oil and gas from public hands to surface landowners would entail a massive give-away of public property to the great detriment of taxpayers.

4. *Shared governance II: underground oil and gas storage.* It is easy to see that an underground formation, suitable for storing gas, is just as much a common-pool resource as the gas itself or a Maine lobster fishery. Even more than these other common-pool resources, however, an underground formation requires collectively managed use. Because gas freely moves around within the formation, no one can make use of just part of it, nor can two people use the formation (as they could a fishery) without having their gas intermingle (though some types of gas are physically distinguishable). Some sort of collective management is thus essential. But what type? What if the law allowed a person to use the underground formation, perhaps paying a reasonable rental to surface owners but not giving the surface owners a chance to object to the arrangement? This approach may sound sensible; certainly many lawmakers have thought so. But it does raise a troubling issue. According to some, such an arrangement amounts to a taking of private property (the use of the underground formation) by a private party for *private* use—in violation of the constitutional requirement that limits takings to those made for a *public* use. Is it enough to claim that the public-use requirement is satisfied by any activity that makes efficient use of a natural resource, thereby arguably benefitting the public? As we'll see in materials to come, natural resources law offers numerous examples of authorized private condemnation. Indeed, natural resources law, driven by a legislative desire to promote full resource use, offers a good many illustrations of state-sanctioned private takings of property.

5. *The tragedy of fragmentation.* The problem posed by underground formations is a recurring one in natural resources law. When we attach such resources to the land surface and then sell the land off in pieces—thereby dividing the underground formation—we end up in a bind. No one acting alone can use the resource as a whole, which means all landowners must agree on a plan of use. What happens when the landowners can't agree? We end up with what might be termed the *tragedy of resource fragmentation*—a conundrum long familiar to resource lawyers and lawmakers. In recent years, property theorists have taken an interest in this challenge; one commentator has dubbed it the tragedy of the "anticommons." Michael A. Heller, *The Tragedy of the Anticommons: Property in the Transition from Marx to Markets*, 111 Harv. L. Rev. 621 (1998). See Stephen R. Munzer, *The*

Commons and the Anticommons in the Law and Theory of Property, in Martin P. Golding and William A. Edmundson, eds., THE BLACKWELL GUIDE TO THE PHILOSOPHY OF LAW AND LEGAL THEORY 148–62 (2005).

Hammonds implicitly proposes one solution to this tragedy: define (or redefine) the rights of the individual landowners so that they no longer each own a part of the common resource. (Can you see how the court did this?) By doing this, we avoid the fragmented ownership. But there is, of course, a difficulty with this approach. It can throw us back to the opposite problem, the problem of the unowned commons that anyone can use at will, with all the conflicts that result from uncontrolled use. At this point in our study can you identify other possible solutions to the tragedy of fragmented ownership? Do any of the possible solutions steer clear of the accusation that they entail improper takings of private property for private use?

6. Hammonds *curtailed.* In a 1987 ruling, the Supreme Court of Kentucky curtailed the holding in *Hammonds*, after noting that the ruling had been "the subject of violent adverse criticism by many authors and law review writers." The court quoted at length from one source of criticism, a 1962 opinion of the Texas Supreme Court that specifically challenged the wild animal analogy used in *Hammonds*:

> An exegesis of the *Hammonds* opinion, when considered in the light of present day development of the gas industry, is unimpressive. The analogy of wild animals upon which *Hammonds* is founded fails to undergird the ultimate decision of that case. Gas has no similarity to wild animals. Gas is an inanimate, diminishing non-reproductive substance lacking any will of its own, and instead of running wild and roaming at large as animals do, is subject to be moved solely by pressure or mechanical means. It cannot be logically regarded as personal property of the human race as are wild animals, instead of being turned loose in the woods as the fanciful fox or placed in the streams as the fictitious fish, gas, a privately owned commodity, has been stored for use, as required by the consuming public being, as alleged by appellant, subject to its control and withdrawal at any time.

Quoting Lone Star Gas Co. v. Murchison, 353 S.W.2d 870 (Tex. Civ. App. 1962). The Kentucky court decided to limit *Hammonds* to factual situations in which the gas storage reservoir had a "leak," in the sense that the gas company did not fully control access to it:

> In *Hammonds* there was a known "leak" in the gas storage reservoir inasmuch as Mrs. Hammonds' land was, in fact, a part of the natural reservoir, though not controlled by the storage company. In the case at hand, however, it has been stipulated that the gas reservoir has total integrity, and the gas cannot escape nor can it be extracted by anyone except Western. Using the *ferae naturae* analogy, Western has captured the wild fox, hence reducing it to personal property. The fox has not been released in another forest, permitting it to revert to the common property of mankind; but rather, the fox has only been released in a private confinement zoo. The fox is no less under the control of Western than if it were on a leash. . . .
>
> It is therefore the opinion of this court that, in those instances when previously extracted oil or gas is subsequently stored in under-

> ground reservoirs capable of being defined with certainty and the integrity of said reservoirs is capable of being maintained, title to such oil or gas is not lost and said minerals do not become subject to the rights of the owners of the surface above the storage fields.

Texas American Energy Corp. v. Citizens Fidelity Bank & Trust Co., 736 S.W.2d 25 (Ky. 1987).

The issue in the 1987 case had to do with the proper way of perfecting a security interest in the gas and, indeed, with whether underground gas could even be the subject of a security interest. Based on the above reasoning, the court concluded that the underground gas was personal property and thus subject to the security interest provisions of the Uniform Commercial Code. Note, though, that the law of Mrs. Hammonds' case would still govern factual settings such as hers. To keep a reservoir from having any "leaks," a gas company would need to lease all surface lands or otherwise get contractual promises by surface owners not to extract the gas.

WRONSKI v. SUN OIL COMPANY

89 Mich.App. 11, 279 N.W.2d 564 (1979).

HOLBROOK, JUDGE.

Plaintiffs are the owners of 200 acres of land and the attendant mineral rights located in St. Clair County: Plaintiffs Koziara own two twenty-acre tracts (Tracts 1 & 2) and one forty-acre tract (Tract 6). Plaintiffs Wronski own an eighty-acre tract (Tract 7) and a forty-acre tract (Tract 13). These properties overlie the Columbus Section 3 Saline–Niagaran Formation Pool, and Tracts 2, 6 and 7 have producing oil wells. Tracts 6 and 7 are under lease to defendant Sun Oil Company.

The Supervisor of Wells, Michigan Department of Natural Resources, pursuant to the authority granted him by 1939 P.A. 61, as amended, established twenty-acre drilling units for the Columbus 3 pool, and provided for a uniform well spacing pattern. The purpose of this order was to "prevent waste, protect correlative rights and provide for orderly development of the pool". The Supervisor, by a proration order effective February 1, 1970, further limited production in the Columbus 3 pool to a maximum of 75 barrels of oil per day per well. This order remained in effect until June 30, 1974, when Columbus 3 was unitized.

Defendant Sun Oil leases property from H. H. Winn (Tract 9) and from H. H. Winn, *et al.* (Tract 12). Sun Oil has drilled several wells on these tracts in compliance with the uniform well spacing pattern, including well 1–C on Tract 9 and wells 3 and 6 on Tract 12. These three wells were operating during the effective date of the proration order and were subject to its terms. Plaintiffs contend that Sun Oil illegally overproduced more than 180,000 barrels of oil from these three wells, and that the illegally overproduced oil was drained from beneath plaintiffs' lands. They sought rescission *ab initio* of their oil and gas leases with Sun Oil coupled with an accounting, or in the alternative both compensatory and exemplary damages.

After a bench trial the court found that Sun Oil had intentionally and illegally overproduced 150,000 barrels of oil, and that 50,000 barrels of this oil had been drained from plaintiffs' property. The court held that this overproduction and drainage constituted tortious breaches of Sun Oil's contractual obligations under the oil and gas leases entered into with plaintiffs, as well as violating plaintiffs' common-law rights to the oil beneath their property. . . .

The Court determines on the basis of all the testimony and evidence in this case and after considering the matters stated above, that it would be reasonable and proper to assess exemplary damages against Defendant Sun Oil Company in the amount of Fifty (50%) per cent of the compensatory damages previously awarded to the Plaintiffs. . . .

This case involves an action sounding in equity and was tried by the court without a jury. . . . Review of the record discloses sufficient facts upon which the trial court could find that Sun Oil systematically, intentionally and illegally produced the H. H. Winn, et al., No. 3 and No. 6 wells, and the H. H. Winn C–1, well in an amount of 150,000 barrels over that allowed by the proration order. The record also supports the finding that one-third of this illegally produced oil was drained from the property of the plaintiffs. . . . We are not convinced that had this Court been the trier of fact that we would have come to a different result . . .

The trial court found that Sun Oil's actions were intentional tortious breaches of its contractual obligation to both plaintiffs under their respective oil and gas leases. It found breaches of the implied covenant to prevent drainage as well as a failure to comply with the orders of the Supervisor of Wells as required by the provisions of the lease. It also found that:

> Sun Oil Company has violated the common law rights of Plaintiffs Wronski and Koziara by illegally, unlawfully and secretly draining valuable oil from beneath their properties.

The nature of Sun Oil's violation, while not clearly stated by the trial court, was a claim for the conversion of oil.

> " 'Conversion is any distinct act of dominion wrongfully exerted over another's personal property in denial of or inconsistent with his rights therein.' " Thoma v. Tracy Motor Sales Inc., 360 Mich. 434, 438, 104 N.W.2d 360, 362 (1960), quoting Nelson & Witt v. Texas Co., 256 Mich. 65, 70, 239 N.W. 289 (1931).

We only address the finding regarding conversion as it is dispositive of the questions in this appeal.

In Michigan we adhere to the ownership-in-place theory. Attorney General v. Pere Marquette R. Co., 263 Mich. 431, 248 N.W. 860 (1933). Under this theory "the nature of the interest of the landowner in oil and gas contained in his land is the same as his interest in solid minerals". William and Meyers, Oil and Gas Law, § 203.3, p. 44. Solid minerals are a part of the land in or beneath which they are located, Mark v.

Bradford, 315 Mich. 50, 23 N.W.2d 201 (1946), and as a consequence the owner of land is also the owner of the oil and gas in or beneath it.

Oil and gas, unlike other minerals, do not remain constantly in place in the ground, but may migrate across property lines. Because of this migratory tendency the rule of capture evolved. This rule provides:

> " 'The owner of a tract of land acquires title to the oil and gas which he produces from wells drilled thereon, though it may be proved that part of such oil or gas migrated from adjoining lands. Under this rule, absent some state regulation of drilling practices, a landowner * * * is not liable to adjacent landowners whose lands are drained as a result of such operations * * *. The remedy of the injured landowner under such circumstances has generally been said to be that of self-help "go and do likewise".' " William and Meyers, Supra, § 204.4, pp. 55–57 (Emphasis supplied.)

This rule of capture was a harsh rule that could work to deprive an owner of oil and gas underneath his land. To mitigate the harshness of this rule and to protect the landowners' property rights in the oil and gas beneath his land, the "fair share" principle emerged.

> "As early as 1931, the Board of Directors of the American Petroleum Institute expressed this principle by declaring a policy:
>
> > "that it endorses, and believes the petroleum industry endorses the principle that each owner of the surface is entitled only to his equitable and ratable share of the recoverable oil and gas energy in the common pool in the proportion which the recoverable reserves underlying his land bears to the recoverable reserves in the pool." Graham, Fair Share or Fair Game? Great Principle, Good Technology But Pitfalls in Practice, 8 Nat.Res. Law. 61, 64–65 (1975).

The API clarified the principle in 1942 by saying:

> "Within reasonable limits, each operator should have an opportunity equal to that afforded other operators to recover the equivalent of the amount of recoverable oil (and gas) underlying his property. The aim should be to prevent reasonably avoidable drainage of oil and gas across property lines that is not offset by counter drainage." Id. at 65.

This fair-share rule does not do away with the rule of capture, but rather acts to place limits on its proper application.

Texas has adopted both the ownership-in-place doctrine and the fair-share principle. Its courts have addressed the interrelationship between these two principles and the rule of capture.

> "It must be conceded that under the law of capture there is no liability for reasonable and legitimate drainage from the common pool. The landowner is privileged to sink as many wells as he desires upon his tract of land and extract therefrom and appropriate all the oil and gas that he may produce, so long as he operates within the

> spirit and purpose of conservation statutes and orders of the Railroad Commission. These laws and regulations are designed to afford each owner a reasonable opportunity to produce his proportionate part of the oil and gas from the entire pool and to prevent operating practices injurious to the common reservoir. In this manner, if all operators exercise the same degree of skill and diligence, each owner will recover in most instances his fair share of the oil and gas. This reasonable opportunity to produce his fair share of the oil and gas is the landowner's common law right under our theory of absolute ownership of the minerals in place. But from the very nature of this theory the right of each land holder is qualified, and is limited to legitimate operations." Elliff v. Texon Drilling Co., 146 Tex. 575, 582, 210 S.W.2d 558, 562 (1948). (Emphasis supplied.)

The rule of capture is thus modified to exclude operations that are in violation of valid conservation orders.

Michigan recognizes the fair-share principle and its subsequent modifications of the rule of capture. When an adjacent landowner drilled an oil well too close to a property line the Supreme Court said that this:

> "(D)eprived plaintiff of the opportunity of claiming and taking the oil that was rightfully hers; and defendants must respond in damages for such conversion." Ross v. Damm, 278 Mich. 388, 396, 270 N.W. 722, 725 (1936).

The Supervisor of Wells Act also incorporated the fair share principle into Section 13. This section concerns proration orders and states in part that:

> "The rules, regulations, or orders of the supervisor shall, so far as it is practicable to do so, afford the owner of each property in a pool The opportunity to produce his just and equitable share of the oil and gas in the pool, being an amount, so far as can be practicably determined and obtained without waste, and without reducing the bottom hole pressure materially below the average for the pool, substantially in the proportion that the quantity of the recoverable oil and gas under such property bears to the total recoverable oil and gas in the pool, and for this purpose to use his just and equitable share of the reservoir energy." M.C.L. § 319.13; M.S.A. § 13.139(13). (Emphasis supplied.)

This right to have a reasonable opportunity to produce one's just and equitable share of oil in a pool is the common-law right that the trial court found Sun Oil violated. Under the authority of Ross v. Damm, supra, if it can be said that Sun Oil's overproduction deprived plaintiffs of the opportunity to claim and take the oil under their respective properties, then Sun Oil will be liable for a conversion.

Production in the Columbus 3 field was restricted to 75 barrels of oil per well per day. Compulsory pooling was also in effect, limiting the number of oil wells to one per twenty acres, and specifying their location. The purpose behind proration is that the order itself, if obeyed, will protect landowners from drainage and allow each to produce their fair share. A violation of the proration order, especially a secret violation, allows the violator to take more than his fair share and leaves the other landowners unable to protect their rights unless they also violate the proration order. We therefore hold that any violation of a proration order constitutes conversion of oil from the pool, and subjects the violator to liability to all the owners of interests in the pool for conversion of the illegally-obtained oil. See Bolton v. Coates, 533 S.W.2d 914 (Tex., 1975), Ortiz Oil Co. v. Geyer, 138 Tex. 373, 159 S.W.2d 494 (1942). . . .

The rule as to the amount of damages for a conversion of oil was established in Michigan in Robinson v. Gordon Oil Co., 266 Mich. 65, 253 N.W. 218 (1934). The Court stated:

> "The general rule in the United States in actions for the conversion of oil, as in the case of conversion of minerals and other natural products of the soil is that, although a wilful trespasser is liable for the enhanced value of the oil at the time of conversion without deduction for expenses or for improvements by labor, an innocent trespasser is liable only for the value of the oil undisturbed; that is, he is entitled to set off the reasonable cost of production." (Citations omitted.) Robinson, supra, at 69, 253 N.W. at 219. (Emphasis supplied.)

This rule sets the liability of the convertor as the enhanced value of the oil at the time of conversion, but then subdivides this liability into two subrules depending upon the nature of the conversion. These two subrules are a "mild" rule which applies to innocent or nonwilful conversion and a "harsh" rule which applies to bad faith or wilful conversions. [The court decided that the "harsh" rule was appropriate on the facts of this case. It also decided that, because of the application of the harsh rule, it was wrong for the trial court also to assess exemplary damages.]

Notes

1. *Oil and gas production today. Wronski* offers a look at how oil production is managed today in larger fields with multiple overlying landowners. As such, the decision is worth a careful read, looking up terms you may not know. States generally employ one of two rules as to the ownership of oil and gas underground. In some states oil and gas are unowned until capture; what landowners possess is the exclusive right to use the surface of their lands for capture. Other states (such as Michigan in *Wronski*) conclude that oil belongs to the surface owner, but it is subject to being taken by other landowners pursuant to the rule of capture. Owen L. Anderson, et al., Hemingway Oil and Gas Law and Taxation 30–36 (4th ed. 2004). The two approaches differ in only modest ways, and they share the chief defects of the rule of capture. Under both, landowners are prompted to act quickly, seizing as much oil as they can for fear that other landowners will take it. With the resource essentially uncontrolled, no one has the power to delay all

production until oil prices are higher. Other problems have to do with the geologic realities of oil production. When oil is removed quickly, more of it remains in place; a slower, steadier rate of withdrawal can produce more oil. Also, wells too close together can interfere with one another, and it is wasteful to have a large number of wells in a field when one or a few wells in time can extract all of the oil. These realities led to cooperation within the oil business and to the establishment of regulatory agencies that control such matters as well spacing, well construction, and rates of withdrawal. They also led to even greater alterations of common law property rights by way of the pooling and unitization arrangements, under which landowners are placed into collective pumping groups. Landowners can be forced to participate in these collective pumping efforts, even over their objections.

2. *Reasonable use II: the fair share ideal.* Exactly what rights does a landowner have in Michigan when the state DNR establishes drilling units (specifying minimum tract sizes per well), sets well-spacing requirements, and imposes production limits? The court explains that landowners are now limited to their fair share of oil production. Rights are shared under a correlative rights scheme. As best we can tell, however, what is each landowner's share? Is it a share of the oil in place? Is it instead a reasonable chance to extract oil? Or is it, for the most part, merely the benefits that an owner obtains indirectly under conservation orders issued by the relevant state agency?

Note that the various conservation rules in combination keep any landowner from extracting too much oil too quickly. But what happens if one landowner sits back and does nothing for years? Can other landowners end up taking all the oil? Note too that the ideas of "fair share" and "correlative rights" are superficially vague. The landowners here were able to sue successfully because the state agency had imposed precise pumping limits, making it easy to determine whether one landowner was extracting too much. Would any relief have been available in the absence of state administrative action?

EDWARDS v. SIMS

232 Ky. 791, 24 S.W.2d 619 (App. 1929).

STANLEY, C.

This case presents a novel question. [The facts that follow are excerpted from a subsequent opinion in this same dispute, set forth below.]

[[Around 1909] L. P. Edwards discovered a cave under land belonging to him and his wife, Sally Edwards. The entrance to the cave is on the Edwards land. Edwards named it the "Great Onyx Cave," no doubt because of the rock crystal formations within it which are known as onyx. This cave is located in the cavernous area of Kentucky, and is only about three miles distant from the world-famous Mammoth Cave. Its proximity to Mammoth Cave, which for many years has had an international reputation as an underground wonder, as well as its beautiful formations, led Edwards to embark upon a program of advertising and exploitation for the purpose of bringing visitors to his cave. Circulars were printed and distributed, signs were erected along the roads, persons were employed and stationed along the highways to solicit the patronage of passing travelers, and thus the fame of the Great Onyx Cave spread from year to year, until eventually, and before the beginning of the present litigation, it was a well-known and well-patronized cave. Edwards built a hotel near the mouth of the cave to care for travelers. He improved and widened the footpaths and avenues in the cave, and ultimately secured a stream of tourists who paid entrance fees sufficient not only to cover the cost of operation, but also to yield a substantial revenue in addition thereto. The authorities in charge of the development of the Mammoth Cave area as a national park undertook to secure the Great Onyx Cave through condemnation proceedings, and in that suit the value of the cave was fixed by a jury at $396,000. In April, 1928, F. P. Lee, an adjoining landowner, filed this suit against Edwards and the heirs of Sally Edwards, claiming that a portion of the cave was under his land, and praying for damages, for an accounting of the profits which resulted from the operation of the cave, and for an injunction prohibiting Edwards and his associates from further trespassing upon or exhibiting any part of the cave under Lee's land. At the inception of this litigation, Lee undertook to procure a survey of the cave in order that it might be determined what portion of it was on his land. The chancellor ordered that a survey be made, and Edwards prosecuted an appeal from that order to this court. The appeal was dismissed because it was not from a final judgment. Edwards v. Lee, 230 Ky. 375, 19 S.W.(2d) 992. . . .]

[Edwards then filed a separate suit, asking the appellate court to issue a writ of prohibition, preventing the underground survey from taking place. The chief issue in this new case was whether or not Edwards, as owner of the cave entrance, would be harmed by having a survey come upon his land to conduct the survey. That issue in turn depended upon the relative property rights of the parties in the cave.]

There is but little authority of particular and special application to caves and cave rights. In few places, if any, can be found similar works of nature of such grandeur and of such unique and marvelous character as to give to caves a commercial value sufficient to cause litigation as those peculiar to Edmonson and other counties in Kentucky. The reader will find of interest the address on "The Legal Story of Mammoth Cave" by Hon. John B. Rodes, of Bowling Green, before the 1929 Session of the Kentucky State Bar Association, published in its proceedings. In Cox v. Colossal Cavern Co., 210 Ky. 612, 276 S. W. 540, the subject of cave rights was considered, and this court held there may be a severance of the estate in the property, that is, that one may own the surface and another the cave rights, the conditions being quite similar to but not exactly like those of mineral lands. But there is no such severance involved in this case, as it appears that the defendants are the owners of the land and have in it an absolute right.

Cujus est solum, ejus est usque ad coelum ad infernos (to whomsoever the soil belongs, he owns also to the sky and to the depths), is an old maxim and rule. It is that the owner of realty, unless there has been a division of the estate, is entitled to the free and unfettered control of his own land above, upon, and beneath the surface. So whatever is in a direct line between the surface of the land and the center of the earth belongs to the owner of the surface. Ordinarily that ownership cannot be interfered with or infringed by third persons. 17 C. J. 391; 22 R. C. L. 56; Langhorne v. Turman, 141 Ky. 809, 133 S. W. 1008, 34 L. R. A. (N. S.) 211. There are, however, certain limitations on the right of enjoyment of possession of all property, such as its use to the detriment or interference with a neighbor and burdens which it must bear in common with property of a like kind. 22 R. C. L. 77.

With this doctrine of ownership in mind, we approach the question as to whether a court of equity has a transcendent power to invade that right through its agents for the purpose of ascertaining the truth of a matter before it, which fact thus disclosed will determine certainly whether or not the owner is trespassing upon his neighbor's property. Our attention has not been called to any domestic case, nor have we found one, in which the question was determined either directly or by analogy. It seems to the court, however, that there can be little differentiation, so far as the matter now before us is concerned, between caves and mines. And as declared in 40 C. J. 947: "A court of equity, however, has the inherent power, independent of statute, to compel a mine owner to permit an inspection of his works at the suit of a party who can show reasonable ground for suspicion that his lands are being trespassed upon through them, and may issue an injunction to permit such inspection." . . .

We can see no difference in principle between the invasion of a mine on adjoining property to ascertain whether or not the minerals are being extracted from under the applicant's property and an inspection of this respondent's property through his cave to ascertain whether or not he is trespassing under this applicant's property.

It appears that before making this order the court had before him surveys of the surface of both properties and the conflicting opinions of witnesses as to whether or not the Great Onyx Cave extended under the surface of the plaintiff's land. This opinion evidence was of comparatively little value, and as the chancellor (now respondent) suggested, the controversy can be quickly and accurately settled by surveying the cave; and "if defendants are correct in their contention this survey will establish it beyond all doubt and their title to this cave will be forever quieted. If the survey shows the Great Onyx Cave extends under the lands of plaintiffs, defendants should be glad to know this fact and should be just as glad to cease trespassing upon plaintiff's lands, if they are in fact doing so." The peculiar nature of these conditions, it seems to us, makes it imperative and necessary in the administration of justice that the survey should have been ordered and should be made . . .

The writ of prohibition is therefore denied.

Logan, J. (dissenting).

The majority opinion allows that to be done which will prove of incalculable injury to Edwards without benefiting Lee, who is asking that this injury be done. I must dissent from the majority opinion.... It deprives Edwards of rights which are valuable, and perhaps destroys the value of his property, upon the motion of one who may have no interest in that which it takes away, and who could not subject it to his dominion or make any use of it....

It sounds well in the majority opinion to tritely say that he who owns the surface of real estate, without reservation, owns from the center of the earth to the outmost sentinel of the solar system. The age-old statement, adhered to in the majority opinion as the law, in truth and fact, is not true now and never has been. I can subscribe to no doctrine which makes the owner of the surface also the owner of the atmosphere filling illimitable space. Neither can I subscribe to the doctrine that he who owns the surface is also the owner of the vacant spaces in the bowels of the earth.

The rule should be that he who owns the surface is the owner of everything that may be taken from the earth and used for his profit or happiness. Anything which he may take is thereby subjected to his dominion, and it may be well said that it belongs to him. I concede the soundness of that rule, which is supported by the cases cited in the majority opinion; but they have no application to the question before the court in this case. They relate mainly to mining rights; that is, to substances under the surface which the owner may subject to his dominion. But no man can bring up from the depths of the earth the Stygian darkness and make it serve his purposes; neither can he subject to his dominion the bottom of the ways in the caves on which visitors tread, and for these reasons the owner of the surface has no right in such a cave which the law should, or can, protect because he has nothing of value therein, unless, perchance, he owns an entrance into it and has subjected the subterranean passages to his dominion.

A cave or cavern should belong absolutely to him who owns its entrance, and this ownership should extend even to its utmost reaches if he has explored and connected these reaches with the entrance. When the surface owner has discovered a cave and prepared it for purposes of exhibition, no one ought to be allowed to disturb him in his dominion over that which he has conquered and subjected to his uses.

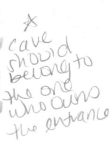

It is well enough to hang to our theories and ideas, but when there is an effort to apply old principles to present-day conditions, and they will not fit, then it becomes necessary for a readjustment, and principles and facts as they exist in this age must be made conformable. For these reasons the old sophistry that the owner of the surface of land is the owner of everything from zenith to nadir must be reformed, and the reason why a reformation is necessary is because the theory was never true in the past, but no occasion arose that required the testing of it. Man had no dominion over the air until recently, and, prior to his conquering the air, no one had any occasion to question the claim of the surface owner that the air above him was subject to his dominion. Naturally the air above him should be subject to his dominion in so far as the use of the space is necessary for his proper enjoyment of the surface, but further than that he has no right in it separate from that of the public at large. The true principle should be announced to the effect that a man who owns the surface, without reservation, owns not only the land itself, but everything upon, above, or under it which he may use for his profit or pleasure, and which he may subject to his dominion and control. But further than this his ownership cannot extend. It should not be held that he owns that which he cannot use and which is of no benefit to him, and which may be of benefit to others.

Shall a man be allowed to stop airplanes flying above his land because he owns the surface? He cannot subject the atmosphere through which they fly to his profit or pleasure; therefore, so long as airplanes do not injure him, or interfere with the use of his property, he should be helpless to prevent their flying above his dominion. Should the waves that transmit intelligible sound through the atmosphere be allowed to pass over the lands of surface-owners? If they take nothing from him and in no way interfere with his profit or pleasure, he should be powerless to prevent their passage? . . .

If he who owns the surface does not own and control the atmosphere above him, he does not own and control vacuity beneath the surface. He owns everything beneath the surface that he can subject to his profit or pleasure, but he owns nothing more. Therefore, let it be written that a man who owns land does, in truth and in fact, own everything from zenith to nadir, but only for the use that he can make of it for his profit or pleasure. He owns nothing which he cannot subject to his dominion.

In the light of these unannounced principles which ought to be the law in this modern age, let us give thought to the petitioner Edwards, his rights and his predicament, if that is done to him which the circuit judge has directed to be done. Edwards owns this cave through right of discovery, exploration, development, advertising, exhibition, and conquest. Men fought their way through the eternal darkness, into the mysterious and abysmal depths of the bowels of a groaning world to discover the theretofore unseen splendors of unknown natural scenic wonders. They were conquerors of fear, although now and then one of them, as did Floyd Collins, paid with his life, for his hardihood in adventuring into the regions where Charon with his boat had never before seen any but the spirits of the departed. They let themselves down by flimsy ropes into pits that seemed bottomless; they clung to scanty handholds as they skirted the brinks of precipices while the flickering flare of their flaming flambeaux disclosed no bottom to the yawning gulf beneath them; they waded through rushing torrents, not knowing what awaited them on the farther side; they climbed slippery steeps to find other levels; they wounded their bodies on stalagmites and stalactites and other curious and weird formations; they found chambers, star-studded and filled with scintillating light reflected by a phantasmagoria revealing fancied phantoms, and tapestry woven by the toiling gods in the dominion of Erebus; hunger and thirst, danger and deprivation could not stop them. Through days, weeks, months, and years—ever linking chamber with chamber, disclosing an underground land of enchantment, they continued their explorations; through the years they toiled connecting these wonders with the outside world through the entrance on the land of Edwards which he had discovered; through the years they toiled finding safe ways for those who might come to view what they had found and placed their seal upon. They knew nothing, and cared less, of who owned the surface above; they were in another world where no law forbade their footsteps. They created an underground kingdom where Gulliver's people may have lived or where Ayesha may have found the revolving column of fire in which to bathe meant eternal youth.

When the wonders were unfolded and the ways were made safe, then Edwards patiently, and again through the years, commenced the advertisement of his cave. First came one to see, then another, then two together, then small groups, then small crowds, then large crowds, and then the multitudes. Edwards had seen his faith justified. The cave was his because he had made it what it was, and without what he had done it was nothing of value. The value is not in the black vacuum that the uninitiated call a cave. That which Edwards owns is something intangible and indefinable. It is his vision translated into a reality.

Then came the horse leach's daughters crying: "Give me," "give me." Then came the "surface men" crying, "I think this cave may run under my lands." They do not know they only "guess," but they seek to discover the secrets of Edwards so that they may harass him and take from him that which he has made his own. They have come to a court of equity and have asked that Edwards be forced to open his doors and his ways to them so that they may go in and despoil him; that they may lay his secrets bare so that others may follow their example and dig into the wonders which Edwards has made his own. What may be the result if they stop his ways? They destroy the cave, because those who visit it are they who give it value, and none will visit it when the ways are barred so that it may not be exhibited as a whole.

It may be that the law is as stated in the majority opinion of the court, but equity, according to my judgment, should not destroy that which belongs to one man when he at whose behest the destruction is visited, although with some legal right, is not benefited thereby. Any ruling by a court which brings great and irreparable injury to a party is erroneous.

For these reasons I dissent from the majority opinion.

[The trial court ordered the survey of the cave, which led in time to the following appellate ruling having to do with Lee's request for compensation for the trespass.]

EDWARDS v. LEE'S ADMINISTRATOR

265 Ky. 418, 96 S.W.2d 1028 (App. 1936).

STITES, JUSTICE.

This is an appeal from a judgment of the Edmonson circuit court sitting in equity. Appellants argue but two points in this court: (1) That the court below applied an improper measure of damages; and (2) even if the measure of damages was correct, the amount was erroneously computed....

A tremendous amount of proof was taken on each side concerning the title of Lee to the land claimed by him; how much, if any, of the cave is under the land of Lee; the length of the exhibited portion of the cave and the amount thereof under the land of Lee; the net earnings of the cave for the years involved; the location of the principal points of interest in the cave and whether they were under the lands of Edwards or of Lee; and whether or not Edwards and his associates had knowledge of the fact that they were trespassing on Lee's property.... [On remand, the trail judge determined that approximately 1/3 of the cave lay beneath Lee's land. Rather than compensate Lee for the nominal injury he suffered, the judge awarded Lee 1/3 of the net proceeds of the cave operation, plus interest. It also enjoined future trespasses.]

Appellants, in their attack here on the measure of damages and its application to the facts adduced, urge: (1) That the appellees had simply a hole in the ground, about 360 feet below the surface, which they could not use and which they could not even enter except by going through the mouth of the cave on Edwards' property; (2) the cave was of no practical use to appellees without an entrance, and there was no one except the appellants on whom they might confer a right of beneficial use; (3) Lee's portion of the cave had no rental value; (4) appellees were not ousted of the physical occupation or use of the property because they did not and could not occupy it; (5) the property has not in any way been injured by the use to which it has been put by appellants ...

Appellees, on the other hand, argue that this was admittedly a case of willful trespass; that it is not analogous to a situation where a trespasser simply walks across the land of another, for here the trespasser actually used the property of Lee to make a profit for himself; that even if nothing tangible was taken or disturbed in the various trips through Lee's portion of the cave, nevertheless there was a taking of esthetic enjoyment which, under ordinary circumstances, would justify a recovery of the reasonable rental value for the use of the cave ...

Appellees brought this suit in equity, and seek an accounting of the profits realized from the operation of the cave, as well as an injunction against future trespass. In substance, therefore, their action is ex contractu and not, as appellants contend, simply an action for damages arising from a tort. Ordinarily, the measure of recovery in assumpsit for the taking and selling of personal property is the value received by the wrongdoer. On the other hand, where the action is based upon a trespass to land, the recovery has almost invariably been measured by the reasonable rental value of the property. Profile Cotton Mills v. Calhoun Water Co., 204 Ala. 243, 85 So. 284.

Strictly speaking, a count for "use and occupation" does not fit the facts before us because, while there has been a recurring use, there has been no continuous occupation of the cave such as might arise from the planting of a crop or the tenancy of a house. Each trespass was a distinct usurpation of the appellees' title and interruption of their right to undisturbed possession. But, even if we apply the analogy of the crop cases or the wayleave cases [Phillips v. Homfray, 24 Ch.Div. 439; Whithem v. Westminster Co., 12 Times L.R. 318; Carmichael v. Old Straight Creek Coal Corporation, 232 Ky. 133, 22 S.W.(2d) 572], it is apparent that rental value has been adopted, either consciously or unconsciously, as a convenient yardstick by which to measure the proportion of profit derived by the trespasser directly from the use of the land itself [9 R.C.L. 942]. In other words, rental value ordinarily indicates the amount of profit realized directly from the land as land, aside from all collateral contracts. . . .

In the leading case of Phillips v. Homfray, 24 Ch.Div. 439, the plaintiffs were the owners of a farm, and the defendants had for some time past been working the minerals underlying lands adjoining plaintiffs' farm. Plaintiffs discovered that the defendants were not only getting minerals from under their farm, but were using roads and passages made by them through the plaintiffs' minerals for the conveyance of minerals gotten by the defendants from their own mines. An action was brought to recover for the minerals taken from under the plaintiffs' property, and also for damages to be paid as wayleave for the use of the roads and passages in transporting the minerals of the defendants across the property. . . . The court held that this defendant's estate was liable in the action for the minerals taken because it had, to that extent, been enriched by the defendant's wrong.

Clearly, the unjust enrichment of the wrongdoer is the gist of the right to bring an action ex contractu. Rental value is merely the most convenient and logical means for ascertaining what proportion of the benefits received may be attributed to the use of the real estate. . . .

Similarly, in illumination of this conclusion, there is a line of cases holding that the plaintiff may at common law bring an action against a trespasser for the recovery of "mesne profits" following the successful termination of an action of ejectment. . . . For example, see Capital Garage Co. v. Powell, 98 Vt. 303, 127 A. 375. Here again, the real basis of recovery is the profits received, rather than rent. . . .

Finally, in the current proposed final draft of the Restatement of Restitution and Unjust Enrichment (March 4, 1936), Part I, § 136, it is stated:

"A person who tortiously uses a trade name, trade secret, profit a prendre, or other similar interest of another, is under a duty of restitution for the value of the benefit thereby received." . . .

Whether we consider the similarity of the case at bar to (1) the ordinary actions in assumpsit to recover for the use and occupation of real estate, or (2) the common-law action for mesne profits, or (3) the action to recover for the tortious use of a trade-name or other similar right, we are led inevitably to the conclusion that the measure of recovery in this case must be the benefits, or net profits, received by the appellants from the use of the property of the appellees. The philosophy of all these decisions is that a wrongdoer shall not be permitted to make a profit from his own wrong. . . .

THOMAS, JUSTICE (concurring).

I concur in the ultimate conclusion reached by my brethren as expressed in the majority opinion, but I differ widely from the reasoning employed therein as a basis for reaching it. . . .

The opinion states the facts, and correctly concludes that "the case is sui generis." It then adds: "Counsel have been unable to give us much assistance in the way of previous decisions of this or other courts. We are left to fundamental principles and analogies." Those excerpts therefrom are undoubtedly true, and some principle must be found by which (1) the involved property (the cave) may be rendered profitable to each of its several owners, and (2) that it may be kept open in its entirety; not only for the purpose of making each owner's portion profitable to him, and all others having proprietary rights therein, but also that the patronizing public might not be deprived of the educational and other benefits to be deprived from visiting the nature made wonder throughout its length, without any obstructing walls by separate segment owners, which under the theory of the opinion they would undoubtedly have the right to construct, provided they could gain entrance into the cave for that purpose.

It is because of the recognition of such segment ownership, as recognized and applied by the opinion, with its following consequences, that has led me to adopt the views hereinafter expressed, and which I am confident will be found to be not only the more practical, but also an assured guarantee is thereby furnished against the possible obstructions, already mentioned, and other potential consequences that lurk in the theory approved and adopted by the court's opinion. . . .

[Thomas urged that the proper measure of damages was not profits from the cave operation, but the reasonable rental value of the cave portion owned by Lee. The trespasser's profit was the appropriate measure, he asserted, only when the profit was equal in value to some physical thing that had been severed from the land.] In all such cases where the trespassing act is willfully done, the measure of recovery of the one trespassed upon is the net value of the substance taken away from the corpus of his property. On the other hand, where no corpus is abstracted and taken away, but only a mere use of the property, with the corpus left intact upon the cessation of the use, the measure of recovery is the reasonable rental value of the property.

I have yet to meet with a case where A would be made to account to B for all of the agricultural profits grown by A on B's land while the grower was an undoubted trespasser. The measure would be the damages that A did to B's land (all of which he would leave intact after the trespassing act ceased) and which is practically universally determined as being the rental value of the land for the use to which it was put....

My theory is this: That the cave in this sui generis case should be treated as a unit of property throughout its entire exhibitable length, including the augmentations of prongs or branches, and that it should be adjudged as owned jointly by all of the surface owners above it, in proportion that the length of their surface ownership bears to the entire length of such exhibitable portion. I realize that herein lies the departure (but which I think is justified from the exigencies of the case) from the ancient rule of, "*Cujus est solum, ejus est usque ad coelum et ad infernos* (to whomsoever the soil belongs, he owns also to the sky and to the depths.)" That maxim literally followed would segmentize ownership both above and below the surface corresponding to boundaries of the latter; and it is the denying of that effect, as applied to property of the nature of a cave, that constitutes the departure from, or exception to the rule that I advocate; whilst the majority opinion not only discards that theory, but advocates other departures equally if not more drastic, and which are necessarily followed by much more impractical and destructive consequences. The same departure has already been made by all courts before which the question has arisen, with reference to ownership "to the sky" by the owner of the surface, in determining aerial navigation rights, and which departure was forced by the necessities of the case. I, therefore, can conceive of no objection to extending it in the opposite direction when the same necessities demand it....

The cave in divided segments according to surface ownership, if the division should be made, would render each segment of little profit producing value. But the theory of the opinion indisputably implies that right which if exercised would render all portions of the cave beyond the Edwards boundary (within which is located its entrance from the surface) absolutely valueless, since it is incontrovertibly established by the evidence in this case that no opening into the cave can be made upon any of the lands of the respective owners extending back from its mouth located, as said, within the Edwards boundary. Nevertheless, as pointed out, the other owners of different segments of the cave (back from its entrance) may prevent, under the theory adopted by the majority opinion, the owners of the Edwards tract from exhibiting any portion of the cave than that which lies under their surface. With the attractiveness of the cave thus curtailed, but a small amount of patronage of inspecting it could be obtained, since the sightseers could penetrate it no farther than the Edwards line. The same consequence would follow as to the other segments, if their owners could make a practical entrance into their separately owned segment, but which as we have seen, they cannot do.

Thus the cave as an entirety, as will be easily seen, could be destroyed as a profit producing property, and also as a pleasing and educating exhibition to the members of the public. But such consequences could not and would not follow the theory herein advanced. Following its adoption, remedies are abundant whereby any joint owner might enforce the continued opening and operation of the cave, even by the appointment of a receiver if necessary, or the employment of some other remedy known to the law.

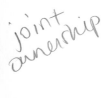

The theory of joint ownership which I conclude is the correct one to adopt and apply under the exigencies of this case does not conflict with the maxim *supra* that the surface owner also owns to the "depths below," except that it applies his ownership—not to the particular segment underlying his surface rights—but to the aliquot part of the entire attractive vacuum made by nature, called "a cave," and that the extent of his joint ownership in the entire property is measured by his surface rights. . . .

For the reasons stated, I concur in the result of the majority opinion, but disagree with the principles or theory upon which it is based.

Notes

1. *The three approaches to cave ownership.* The Edwards/Onyx Cave litigation is a classic in property and natural resources law, in part because of the three ownership approaches proposed by the various judges. As you probe the three approaches, considering their relative merits and demerits, it is useful to keep the following points in mind.

First, to use the cave at all people need access to it, which means crossing someone's private land to get to the entrance. A share in the cave is far less valuable without an ability to make use of it. How do the various approaches handle this practical need?

Second, when the overlying landowners all get along and can work things out themselves, law is hardly needed. Law is most important when the owners don't get along. Thus, in testing the relative appeal of the three approaches we need to imagine the case in which the owners have strong disagreements. How do the various approaches handle these disagreements? What legal remedies does a disgruntled person likely possess?

Finally, as you consider the options, do not look merely to the relative rights of the parties as established by law. Think also of how the landowners are likely to act, given their legal rights, once the rights are established by the court. What negotiations might take place? And what will happen if the negotiations break down?

Sometimes the best approach for natural resources law is not to prescribe the optimal resource-use outcome. It is instead to put the parties in the best position to work out a solution themselves.

2. *Shared governance III: caves.* One problem that arises with the joint ownership option is the need to decide what rights group members have to

get to the cave entrance. That problem is avoided, of course, when the owner of the entrance owns the entire cave. (But how sensible is the entrance-owner-owns-all approach when there are multiple entrances, or when a surface owner cuts a new entrance? Are these problems tractable?) Although Justice Thomas in the second case refers to joint ownership, presumably he has in mind not joint tenancy (with its rights of survivorship) but something like tenancy in common. Recall from your study of basic property the main elements of that form of concurrent ownership: each co-tenant gets to use the whole consistent with the rights of the others to use, and each of them can sell his share without the permission of others. Could the various co-tenants under Thomas's approach each set up cave tour companies and then compete with one another? And what if one landowner simply doesn't want the cave used, perhaps preferring to leave the bats in peace?

Recall that each tenant in common also has the right at any time to seek partition of the property, usually with no questions asked. Would a court likely favor partition of the cave in kind (leading, presumably, to something like the majority's approach of fragmented physical ownership) or would it instead have the cave sold and then divide the money? Finally, what might Justice Thomas say about the ownership of valuable minerals found in a jointly owned cave? Would the joint ownership extend to the minerals, or would it cover only recreational uses of the cave? Finally, what if, under the various approaches, the cave happens to have a flowing river suitable for recreational rafting (cave- or black-water rafting, as it is called in New Zealand and Belize)? Would it make sense to allocate this distinct resource use right separately and perhaps in a different way?

3. *Cujus est solum* ... Like essentially all legal maxims, this one is subject to many exceptions, so much so that one is prompted to ask: was it really the reason for the court's ruling or instead a convenient phrase to deploy in justifying a conclusion reached on other grounds? Is there benefit in having a maxim such as this? Is it merely an elevation of abstraction over sound, practical reasoning, or is there something to be said for a rule of ownership that everyone can readily grasp? The influence of such maxims gained ground in the common law over the centuries, reaching a peak at the end of the nineteenth century (the zenith of abstract thinking about property ownership). Since then courts have viewed them with greater suspicion, using them when helpful, ignoring them when not.

4. *The labor theory of property ownership.* Justice Logan's peroration on the bravery and fortitude of spelunkers contains strong echoes of John Locke's seventeenth-century labor theory of private ownership. The labor theory (which was well known before Locke) justified private property on the ground that its value was *created* by the owner. To recognize private property was thus to give to the owner what he created by his labor. Here, the labor lay not in creating the cave (nature gets credit for that) but instead in preparing it for use and establishing a popular cave-exploration business. Is it fair for other landowners to claim part of this labor, which no doubt accounted for much of the cave's earnings? Would it be for them an unearned economic windfall?

5. *Measuring damages for misuse of resources.* The most important legal decision made by Lee's lawyer was to recognize that Lee would win

virtually nothing if he merely brought a typical trespass suit and asked for damages caused by the trespass. Lee didn't even know that the trespass was occurring, and he suffered no injury because of it. Indeed, he had no access to the cave at all, and thus had no way of using it or even checking it for damages. Had Lee asked for trespass damages, he might well have received an award of $1. Alert to the problem and aware of the existence of alternative remedies, the lawyer decided to waive the tort and to sue in assumpsit, a remedy based on (in this case) a fictional, presumed contract between the parties. The appropriate measure of recovery thus had nothing to do with the injury suffered by Lee. It was instead the amount that Edwards owed under the fictional contract. What the judges could not agree upon was the measure of damages. Was it the rental value of the land used, or was it instead the net profits earned by the trespasser while in the course of the trespass? According to many courts, these measures ought to be the same, but the Kentucky court thought otherwise. Assumpsit and other restitutionary remedies often prove useful to plaintiffs in cases involving misuses of natural resources, particularly when the misuse of the land involves no physical taking from the land and no physical injury to it.

6. *Measuring damages for wrongful drilling.* In light of the Onyx Cave litigation, what measure of monetary recovery should a landowner receive if someone unlawfully drills a well on his land and the well turns up dry, thus providing evidence that no oil underlies the land? The issue arose in Humble Oil & Refining Co. v. Kishi, 276 S.W. 190 (Tex. Com. App. 1925), when the lessee oil company entered the plaintiffs land under a lease that had expired. The plaintiff's 50–acre tract was adjacent to land with a producing oil well. Because of the prospects of finding oil on it, the land had a leasehold value of $1,000 per acre. The trial court award trespass damages of only $1, on the ground that the amount of damages was uncertain and not susceptible of proof. *Held:* The plaintiff's injury was $1,000 per acre, since the plaintiff's land declined in value by this amount due to the dry hole. This was the market value of the leasehold interest that Humble Oil effectively took, and it was appropriate that Humble Oil pay for the resource. Compare Martel v. Hall Oil Co., 36 Wyo. 166, 253 P. 862 (1927) (court awards no damages on similar facts because the trespasser merely made the truth known that the plaintiff's land lacked oil; the plaintiff was merely denied the ability to sell worthless mineral rights to an unsuspecting buyer).

7. *Right to exclude II: subsurface entry.* Note that under the reasoning of both Judges Logan and Thomas, a landowner would have lost his common law ability to exclude outsiders from entering the subsurface of his land. A similar issue arose in Continental Resources, Inc. v. Farrar Oil Co., 559 N.W.2d 841 (N.D. 1997), involving a private land parcel that was included without the landowner's consent into 640–acre oil development unit by the state conservation commission. The proposed well involved horizontal drilling that would penetrate beneath the plaintiff's land. *Held:* The landowner could not recover for the subsurface trespass. Activities undertaken in accordance with force-pooled oil and gas operations were not limited by the law of trespass, which was "necessarily superseded."

8. *Right to exclude III: mining in early Virginia.* Locke's labor theory of property came together with ideas of individual liberty and with memories of the king's rights in valuable mines in an early Virginia statute dealing

with mining. The statute authorized any citizen to enter the unenclosed rural land of another person, in the company of a justice of the peace, and to prospect for minerals. Any minerals found became the property of the finder, who also gained rights to extract the minerals subject only to a requirement that the mine owner compensate the surface owner for damage to the land surface. The statute was one of many indications that early America gave only limited recognition to the landowner's desire to control access to rural, unenclosed lands (an issue taken up in the next section). It was also an indication of the desire of early America to put the continent's natural resources to best use. Ideas about property ownership and the right to property in the late eighteenth century are surveyed in Eric T. Freyfogle, THE LAND WE SHARE: PRIVATE PROPERTY AND THE COMMON GOOD 50–63 (2003).

C. THE LANDOWNER AND WILDLIFE

We turn now to look at another natural resource, wildlife, and to see what rights owners have to it when they acquire land. Earlier cases introduced the law relating to inland fisheries and the general rule that wild animals are owned by the state in its sovereign capacity. Here we explore the issue in more depth, bringing land-based animals into the picture. Granted that landowners do not own the wildlife on their lands, might they nonetheless have exclusive rights to harvest them (by now, for us, a familiar distinction)? And what about the habitat needs of animals and the damage that they can do? Does the state's ownership of wildlife carry with it—as other natural resource rights often do—ancillary rights involving use of the land surface, perhaps by the wildlife itself, perhaps by private citizens who want to view the wildlife?

M'CONICO v. SINGLETON

2 Mill Const. 244, 9 S.C.L. 244 (S.C.Const.App.1818).

This was an action of trespass, *quare clausum fregit*, and to support it the plaintiff proved, that he had warned and ordered the defendant not to hunt on his lands, and that the defendant had, notwithstanding, rode over, and hunted deer on his unenclosed and unimproved lands. The verdict of the jury was, that each party should pay their own costs; and the plaintiff now moves for a new trial on the grounds:

1st. Because the riding over the unenclosed and unimproved lands is in law a trespass, for which an action will lie, when it is contrary to the express orders of the owner.

2d. Because the verdict is in itself a nullity.

JOHNSON, J. delivered the opinion of the court.

Until the bringing of this action, the right to hunt on unenclosed and uncultivated lands has never been disputed, and it is well known that it has been universally exercised from the first settlement of the country up to the present time; and the time has been, when, in all probability, obedient as our ancestors were to the laws of the country, a civil war would have been the consequence of an attempt, even by the legislature, to enforce a restraint on this privilege. It was the source from whence a great portion of them derived their food and raiment, and was, to the devoted huntsman, (disreputable as the life now is,) a source of considerable profit. The forest was regarded as a common, in which they entered at pleasure, and exercised the privilege; and it will not be denied that animals, *ferae naturae*, are common property, and belong to the first taker. If, therefore, usage can make law, none was ever better established.

This usage is also clearly recognized as a right by the several acts of the legislature on the subject; particularly the act of 1769, (Pub. Laws, 276,) which restrains the right to hunt within seven miles of the residence of the hunter. Now if the right to hunt beyond that, did not before exist, this act was nugatory; and it, canuot be believed that it was only intended to apply to such as owned a tract of land, the diameter of which would be fourteen miles.'

It appears to me also, that there is no rule of the English common law, at variance with this principle; but, it is said, that every entry on the lands of another is a trespass, and the least injury, as treading down grass, and the like, will support it. (1 Esp. Dig. Tit. Trespass, 221.) But there must be some actual injury to support the action. Now it will not be pretended that riding over the soil is an injury; and the forest being the common, in which the cattle of all are used to range at large, the grass, if perchance there be any, may also be regarded as common property; and surely no action will lie against a commoner for barely riding over the common.

The right to hunt on unenclosed lands, I think, therefore, clearly established; but if it were doubtful, I should be strongly inclined to support it. Large standing armies are, perhaps, wisely considered as dangerous to our free institutions; the militia, therefore, necessarily constitutes our greatest security against aggression; our forest is the great field in which, in the pursuit of game, they learn the dexterous use and consequent certainty of firearms, the great and decided advantages of which have been seen and felt on too many occasions to be forgotten, or to require a recurrence to.

Having come to the conclusion, that it is the right of the inhabitants to hunt on unenclosed lands, I need not attempt to prove that the dissent or disapprobation of the owner cannot deprive him of it; for I am sure it never yet entered the mind of any man, that a right which the law gives, can be defeated at the mere will and caprice of an individual.

Notes

1. *Right to exclude IV: the right to hunt in early America.* Recent decisions of the United States Supreme Court have referred to the landowner's right to exclude outsiders as perhaps the key piece in the landowner's bundle. *E.g.*, Kaiser Aetna v. United States, 444 U.S. 164 (1979). Early Americans plainly thought otherwise, at least in the case of rural land that

was unenclosed. *M'Conico* gives us a look into that world, now largely lost to legal memory. Look closely at the court's comments about the forest "being the common" and about forage grasses as "common property." One of the great complaints of colonists against mother England were the barbarous hunting rules that applied there. Back in England, they complained, a person had to own land to hunt. Not so in the free country of America, where people could roam the countryside at will, regardless of land boundaries. Although the historical record awaits a careful examination, the understanding in South Carolina was apparently quite widespread. Englishman John Woods, visiting Illinois at about the same time, summarized (mostly for audiences in England) the land-use practices of the settlers he visited:

> The time for sporting lasts from the 1st of January to the last day of December; as every person has a right of sporting, on all unenclosed land, for all sorts of wild animals and game, without any license or qualifications as to property.... Many of the Americans will hardly credit you, if you inform them, there is any country in the world where one order of men are allowed to kill and eat game, to the exclusion of others. But when you tell them that the occupiers of land are frequently among this number, they lose all patience, and declare, they would not submit to be so imposed on.

John Woods, TWO YEARS' RESIDENCE ON THE ENGLISH PRAIRIE OF ILLINOIS (Paul Angle, ed., 1968) (originally published 1822). So valued was this hunting right in Vermont that it was (and still is) expressly incorporated into the state constitution—the right of citizens to hunt on all unenclosed rural land, regardless of land ownership. See Eric T. Freyfogle, THE LAND WE SHARE: PRIVATE PROPERTY AND THE COMMON GOOD 50–55 (2003). At the Pennsylvania convention ratifying the federal constitution, delegates proposed that the federal Bill of Rights include a provision guaranteeing a common right to hunt on all unenclosed land. Thomas A. Lund, AMERICAN WILDLIFE LAW 25 (1980).

A particularly colorful commentary on the subject appears in the most celebrated hunting memoir of the antebellum era, William Elliott's *Carolina Sports by Land and Water*, first published in 1846. Writing as "Venator" and "Piscator" Elliott regaled readers with his exploits of devil-fishing and wildcat hunting. Elliott confirmed that "the right to hunt wild animals" was "held by the great body of the people, whether landholders or otherwise, as one of their franchises." The practical effect of this right, he explained, was that a man's rural land was "no longer his, (except in a qualified sense,) unless he encloses it. In other respects, it is his neighbors' or any bodys.' " So entrenched was the right to hunt, Elliott reported, that some people desired "to extend it to enclosed lands, unconditionally,—or, at least, maintain their right to pursue the game thereon, when started without the enclosure." Even when lands were enclosed owners had trouble halting public users. Proof of trespass was hard to present, juries were "exceedingly benevolent," and the "the penalty insufficient to deter from a repetition of the offence." Though a devout hunter and wanderer, Elliott recognized that things could not continue. Unless laws changed, landowners would be unable to protect and preserve game on their lands and the noble sport of hunting would end. William Elliott, *Carolina Sports by Land & Water, including the Incidents of Devil–Fishing* (Arno Press, facsimile ed. 1967), pp. 166–72.

2. *Right to exclude V: grazing and other land uses.* The right to hunt on unenclosed land was less important economically to early Americans than the similar right to graze livestock, gather firewood, and otherwise forage. In much of the country until the Civil War (and even later in places) landowners had no right to exclude wandering livestock from lands that they had not lawfully enclosed. As the Supreme Court of Alabama generalized in an 1854 ruling, all unenclosed lands of the state by law were "a common pasture for the cattle and stock of every citizen." Nashville & Chattanooga Railroad Co. v. Peacock, 25 Ala. 229 (1854). The high court of Georgia expressed the same legal rule in a case brought by a railroad hoping to avoid liability for killing livestock that had wandered onto its tracks. In rejecting the idea that the livestock was trespassing, the court noted the vast change in landed property rights that the railroad's theory would entail:

> Such Law as this [labeling the horse a trespasser] would require a revolution in our people's habits of thoughts and action. A man could not walk across his neighbor's unenclosed land, nor allow his horse, or his hog, or his cow, to range in the woods nor to graze on the old fields, or the "wire grass," without subjecting himself to damages for a trespass. Our whole people, with their present habits, would be converted into a set of trespassers. We do not think that such is the Law.[5]

The Mississippi court added to the chorus at about the same time, rejecting another proposal by a railroad to change the state's understanding of property ownership. "By the universal understanding and usage of the people," the court explained, all unenclosed lands were "regarded as commons of pasture, for the range of cattle and other stock of the neighborhood." The state's common law of property, as well as various statutes, recognized "the right of any owner of horses, cattle, or other stock, to put them in the range, which means the unfenced wood lands, or other pasture lands in the neighborhood." According to historian John Mack Faragher in his study of early Illinois, this arrangement typified much of antebellum America:

> Sugar Creek [a region in central Illinois] farmers, like their ancestors and counterparts throughout the nation, utilized important rural productive resources in common with their neighbors. Custom allowed farmers, for example, to hunt game for their own use though they might be in woodlands owned by someone else. Hogs running wild in the timber and surviving on the mast paid no heed to property lines. And despite an 1831 prohibition against "stealing" timber from unclaimed congress land, settlers acted as if the resource of these acres belonged to the neighborhood in common and helped themselves, "hooking" whatever timber they needed. . . .

John Mack Faragher, SUGAR CREEK: LIFE ON THE ILLINOIS PRAIRIE (1986), p. 132.

By slow, uneven steps these public rights were curtailed, as the United States became more and more like the country that it broke away from. One chapter in this story is set forth in Richard W. Judd, COMMON LANDS, COMMON

5. Macon & Western Railroad Co. v. Lester, 30 Ga. 911 (1860).

PEOPLE: THE ORIGINS OF CONSERVATION IN NORTHERN NEW ENGLAND 58–120 (1997). It is interesting to note that, as the United States has gradually expanded the landowner's right to exclude, closing off the final vestiges of decisions such as *M'Conico*, Britain has been moving in the opposite direction. Following the lead of Sweden and other European countries it is slowly expanded the public's "right to roam" on certain types of uncultivated rural land regardless of ownership. See Marion Shoard, A RIGHT TO ROAM: SHOULD WE OPEN UP BRITAIN'S COUNTRYSIDE? (1999).

3. *Right to property in early America.* The legal mind today would likely view the demise of *M'Conico* and the strengthening of landowner rights to exclude as an expansion of the right to property. Observers of the late eighteenth century might have viewed it otherwise, although the historical record is scanty and we await a more thorough study. According to one historian, the "right to property" that ranked so high in the late eighteenth century mind was foremost a right to *acquire* property easily, not the right to defend property once it was owned. William B. Scott, IN PURSUIT OF HAPPINESS: AMERICAN CONCEPTIONS OF PROPERTY FROM THE SEVENTEENTH TO THE TWENTIETH CENTURY 36–58 (1977). The homestead laws of the nineteenth century reflected this line of thinking, making land readily available at almost no cost. So did Thomas Jefferson's proposal that his home state of Virginia insert into its constitution a provision entitling each landless white male, 18 years of age or older, to 50 acres of land, provided by the state free of charge. While in France Jefferson complained about the large landholdings of the few while so many men in Paris were unemployed; these massive landholdings, Jefferson asserted, violated the property rights of the landless unemployed. See Eric T. Freyfogle, THE LAND WE SHARE: PRIVATE PROPERTY AND THE COMMON GOOD 50–55 (2003). To many leaders of the late eighteenth century, *M'Conico* would have appeared, not as a limitation on landowner rights, but instead as a recognition and defense of the land-use rights held by the public at large.

4. *Hunting rights in medieval England.* Early American critics of England tended to think of hunting rights as an attribute of land ownership. But that was true in England largely by default and only after a lengthy legal evolution. For centuries the King claimed ownership of all valuable game, even when on private land. His ownership included, not just the right to prohibit landowners from harvesting it, but the power to grant to someone else the right to engage in the harvesting. The recipient of such a hunting right (a franchise of warren) could enter private land and harvest the game, often knocking down fences, scaring livestock, and otherwise causing commotion. Worst of all in the view of many smaller landowners were the fox hunts, which could involve numerous hunters on horseback and cause real damage to the land.

What the King granted to his royal favorites can be likened to the hunting easements of today. Understandably, this royal power was resisted by landowners and gradually fell into disuse, though holders of early grants often retained them tenaciously. Complicating matters further were the British laws that restricted hunting to people possessed of a certain high level of wealth. Many landowners could not hunt on their lands simply because they weren't wealthy enough! By the late nineteenth century, British landowners largely had control over hunting on their lands based on their land ownership (that is, by *ratione soli*—right of the soil—rather than *ratione privilegii*—based on a franchise granted by the crown), subject only to government regulation. See Dale D. Goble & Eric T. Freyfogle, Wildlife Law: Cases and Materials 204–14 (2002).

5. *John Locke, again. M'Conico* is another case that is best understood in the context of the labor theory of property ownership, which justified ownership based on the owner's improvement of it. According to one widely held view, unenclosed rural land was due less respect because it was, in effect, a second-class form of property; it rested on bare legal title, often obtained from a colony or state at little or no cost, and was at most lightly used by the owner. Because the owner hadn't improved the land his moral claim to own it was weak. Indeed, one of the main justifications for taking land from the Indians was precisely because they had not developed the land, European-style, and thus did not really own it. Wilcomb E.Washburn, *The Moral and Legal Justification for Dispossessing the Indians*, in James Morton Smith, ed., Seventeenth-Century America: Essays in Colonial History 15–32 (1972). That same reasoning underlay numerous colonial actions, including the seizure by colonies of plantations that were not properly "planted" or that were left unused.

Well beyond the early federal period writings about property retained an echo of another natural law limit on ownership: the idea, embraced by Locke and others, that a person should not own more land than he needed and could use. Natural law included a firm condemnation of hoarding, at least when others had trouble exercising their property right of fair access. Like the public's right to forage on unenclosed rural land, this natural-law limit on resource ownership faded over time. Eric T. Freyfogle, The Land We Share: Private Property and the Common Good 26, 53–55, 112–15 (2003).

BARRETT v. STATE

220 N.Y. 423, 116 N.E. 99 (1917).

Andrews, J.

At one time beaver were very numerous in this state. So important were they commercially that they were represented upon the seal of the New Netherlands and upon that of the colony as well as upon the seals of New Amsterdam and of New York. Because of their value, they were relentlessly killed, and by the year 1900 they were practically exterminated. But some 15 animals were left scattered through the southern portion of Franklin county. In that year the Legislature undertook to afford them complete protection, and there has been no open season for beaver since the enactment of chapter 20 of the Laws of 1900.

In 1904 it was further provided that:

> 'No person shall molest or disturb any wild beaver or the dams, houses, homes or abiding places of same.' Laws 1904, c. 674, § 1.

This is still the law, although in 1912 the forest, fish, and game commission was authorized to permit protected animals which had become destructive to public or private property to be taken and disposed of. Laws 1912, c. 318.

By the act of 1904, $500 was appropriated for the purchase of wild beaver to restock the Adirondacks, and in 1906 $1,000 more was appropriated for the same purpose. The commission, after purchasing the animals, was authorized to liberate them. Under this authority 21 beaver have been purchased and freed by the commission. Of these 4 were placed upon Eagle creek, an inlet of the Fourth Lake of the Fulton Chain. There they seem to have remained and increased.

Beaver are naturally destructive to certain kinds of forest trees. During the fall and winter they live upon the bark of the twigs and smaller branches of poplar, birch, and alder. To obtain a supply they fell even trees of large size, cut the smaller branches into suitable lengths, and pull or float them to their houses. All this it must be assumed was known by the Legislature as early as 1900.

The claimants own a valuable tract of woodland upon Fourth Lake bounded in the rear by Eagle creek. Their land was held by them for building sites and was suitable for that purpose. Much of its attractiveness depended upon the forest grown upon it. In this forest were a number of poplar trees. In 1912 and during two or three years prior thereto 198 of these poplars were felled by beaver. Others were girdled and destroyed. The Court of Claims has found, upon evidence that fairly justifies the inference, that this destruction was caused by the four beaver liberated on Eagle creek and their descendants, and that by reason thereof the claimants have been damaged in the sum of $1,900. An award was made to them for that sum, and this award has been affirmed by the Appellate Division. To sustain it the respondents rely upon three propositions. It is said: First, that the state may not protect such an animal as the beaver which is known to be destructive; second, that the provision of the law of 1904 with regard to the molestation of beaver prohibits the claimants from protecting their property, and is therefore an unreasonable exercise of the police power; and, third, that the state was in actual physical possession of the beaver placed on Eagle creek, and that its act in freeing them, knowing their natural propensity to destroy trees, makes the state liable for the damage done by them.

We cannot agree with either of these propositions.

As to the first, the general right of the government to protect wild animals is too well established to be now called in question. Their ownership is in the state in its sovereign capacity, for the benefit of all the people. Their preservation is a matter of public interest. They are a species of natural wealth which without special protection would be destroyed. Everywhere and at all times governments have assumed the right to prescribe how and when they may be taken or killed. As early as 1705, New York passed such an act as to deer. Colonial Laws, vol. 1, p. 585. A series of statutes has followed protecting more or less completely game, birds, and fish.

> 'The protection and preservation of game has been secured by law in all civilized countries, and may be justified on many grounds. * * * The measures best adapted to this end are for the Legislature to

> determine, and courts cannot review its discretion. If the regulations operate, in any respect, unjustly or oppressively, the proper remedy must be applied by that body.'

Phelps v. Racey, 60 N. Y. 10, 14, 19 Am. Rep. 140.

Wherever protection is accorded, harm may be done to the individual. Deer or moose may browse on his crops; mink or skunks kill his chickens; robins eat his cherries. In certain cases the Legislature may be mistaken in its belief that more good than harm is occasioned. But this is clearly a matter which is confided to its discretion. It exercises a governmental function for the benefit of the public at large, and no one can complain of the incidental injuries that may result.

It is sought to draw a distinction between such animals and birds as have ordinarily received protection and beaver, on the ground that the latter are unusually destructive and that to preserve them is an unreasonable exercise of the power of the state.

The state may exercise the police power "wherever the public interests demand it, and in this particular a large discretion is necessary vested in the Legislature to determine, not only what the interest of the public require, but what measures are necessary for the protection of such interests. * * * To justify the state in thus interposing its authority in behalf of the public, it must appear, first, that the interests of the public generally, as distinguished from those of a particular class, require such interference; and, second, that the means are reasonably necessary for the accomplishment of the purpose, and not unduly oppressive upon individuals." Lawton v. Steele, 152 U. S. 133, 136, 14 Sup. Ct. 499, 501 (38 L. Ed. 385).

The police power is not to be limited to guarding merely the physical or material interests of the citizen. His moral, intellectual, and spiritual needs may also be considered. The eagle is preserved, not for its use, but for its beauty.

The same thing may be said of the beaver. They are one of the most valuable of the fur-bearing animals of the state. They may be used for food. But apart from these considerations, their habits and customs, their curious instincts and intelligence, place them in a class by themselves. Observation of the animals at work or play is a source of never-failing interest and instruction. If they are to be preserved experience has taught us that protection is required. If they cause more damage than deer or moose, the degree of the mischief done by them is not so much greater or so different as to require the application of a special rule. If the preservation of the former does not unduly oppress individuals, neither does the latter....

We therefore reach the conclusion that in protecting beaver the Legislature did not exceed its powers. Nor did it so do in prohibiting their molestation. It is possible that were the interpretation given by the respondents to this section right a different result might follow. If the claimants, finding beaver destroying their property, might not drive them away, then possibly their rights would be infringed. In Aldrich v. Wright, 53 N. H. 398, 16 Am. Rep. 339, it was said in an elaborate opinion, although this question we do not decide, that a farmer might shoot mink even in the closed season should he find them threatening his geese.

But such an interpretation is too rigid and narrow. The claimants might have fenced their land without violation of the statute. They might have driven the beaver away, were they injuring their property. The prohibition against disturbing dams or houses built on or adjoining water courses is no greater or different exercise of power from that assumed by the Legislature when it prohibits the destruction of the nests and eggs of wild birds even when the latter are found upon private property.

The object is to protect the beaver. That object as we decide is within the power of the state. The destruction of dams and houses will result in driving away the beaver. The prohibition of such acts, being an apt means to the end desired, is not so unreasonable as to be beyond the legislative power.

We hold therefore that the acts referred to are constitutional....

Somewhat different considerations apply to the act of the state in purchasing and liberating beaver. The attempt to introduce life into a new environment does not always result happily. The rabbit in Australia, the mongoose in the West Indies, have become pests. The English sparrow is no longer welcome. Certain of our most troublesome weeds are foreign flowers.

Yet governments have made such experiments in the belief that the public good would be promoted. Sometimes they have been mistaken. Again, the attempt has succeeded. The English pheasant is a valuable addition to our stock of birds. But whether a success or failure, the attempt is well within governmental powers.

If this is so with regard to foreign life, still more is it true with regard to animals native to the state, still existing here, when the intent is to increase the stock upon what the Constitution declares shall remain forever wild forest lands. If the state may provide for the increase of beaver by prohibiting their destruction, it is difficult to see why it may not attain the same result by removing colonies to a more favorable locality or by replacing those destroyed by fresh importations.

Nor are the cases cited by the respondents controlling. It is true that one who keeps wild animals in captivity must see to it at his peril that they do no damage to others. But it is not true that whenever an individual is liable for a certain act the state is liable for the same act. In liberating these beaver the state was acting as a government. As a trustee for the people and as their representative, it was doing what it thought best for the interests of the public at large. Under such circumstances, we cannot hold that the rule of such cases as those cited is applicable.

We reach the conclusion that no recovery can be had under this claim . . . .

Notes

1. *State ownership doctrine. Barrett* provides a typical expression of the state ownership doctrine in wildlife law. As in most such rulings, the doctrine is used to uphold state laws restricting the taking or harming of wildlife. Protective laws and regulations of this type appeared even in the early colonial period in America, as overhunting diminished game populations in occupied areas. Thomas A. Lund, AMERICAN WILDLIFE LAW 19–34 (1980).

In a series of rulings leading up to and including Hughes v. Oklahoma, 441 U.S. 322 (1979), the United States Supreme Court cast doubt on the state ownership doctrine in the course of striking down state wildlife statutes that overtly discriminated against interstate commerce. The Supreme Court's comments, though, need to be understood in the specific context in which they were handed down, as courts have done (but many academic commentators in haste have not). Decisions since *Hughes* have interpreted the Court's rejecting of state-ownership reasoning as applicable only to laws that prohibit the sale of game outside the state or that in some other ways discriminate overtly against interstate commerce. They have not otherwise viewed *Hughes* as altering this foundational doctrine of state wildlife law. E.g., State v. Couch, 196 Or.App. 665, 103 P.3d 671 (2004), *affd.*, 341 Or. 610, 147 P.3d 322 (2006); State v. Fertterer, 255 Mont. 73, 841 P.2d 467 (1992); O'Brien v. State, 711 P.2d 1144 (Wyo. 1986). See Oliver A. Houck, *Why Do We Protect Endangered Species, and What Does That Say About Whether Restrictions on Private Property to Protect Them Constitute "Takings"?*, 80 IOWA L. REV. 297, 311 n. 77 (1995) ("The trust analogy announced in *Geer* was not overruled in *Hughes* and remains the most accurate expression of this state interest: Wildlife belongs to everyone and the state has a special authority, and obligation, to ensure its perpetuation."); Michael C. Blumm & Louis Ritchie, *The Pioneer Spirit and the Public Trust: The American Rule of Capture and State Ownership of Wildlife*, 35 ENVTL. L. 673, 706–717 (2005).

2. *Limits on state ownership.* While it is well established that the public owns and controls wild animals, a line obviously exists between animals that are "wild" and those that are not, just as a line exists between animals in the wild and animals lawfully taken into captivity, which become personal property so long as they remain captive. Litigation involving these lines arises from time to time, usually involving the interpretation of governing state statutes. In an early ruling the New York high court concluded that deer raised in captivity for slaughter and shipment to markets in New York were not covered by the state's game laws, even though the deer roamed in a private deer park of approximately 2,400 acres. Dieterich v. Fargo, 194 N.Y. 359, 87 N.E. 518 (1909). Similarly, the court in Jones v. State, 45 S.W.2d 612 (Tex. Crim. App. 1931) reversed a conviction for violating state fishing regulations in the case of fish removed from a private pond. On the other hand, the court in State v. Couch, 341 Or. 610, 147 P.3d 322 (2006), upheld the application of state game laws to three

species of nonnative wild deer—fallow deer from Europe (made famous, the court noted, by Robin Hood's alleged poaching), axis deer from India, and sika deer from Japan—imported for use on a private ranch, at least so long as the deer were unconfined. In State v. Mierz, 127 Wash.2d 460, 901 P.2d 286 (1995), the court ruled that coyotes are wild animals, even though taken into captivity and treated as pets. When wild animals are taken into captivity in violation of state or local laws they remain wild and subject to state ownership. E.g., Bilida v. McCleod, 211 F.3d 166 (1st Cir. 2000). As for wild animals killed by trespassers, most American jurisdictions seem to follow the lead of the controversial House of Lords ruling in Blades v. Higgs, 11 H.L. Cas. 621, 11 Eng. Rep. 1474 (H.L. 1865), which ruled that the animal once killed belongs to the landowner.

3. *Ancillary rights III: a right to view wildlife? Barrett* makes plain the power of the state, as sovereign owner of wildlife, to protect it against harm. But are there other powers that do or ought to attach to this state ownership? The effect of protecting the beaver in *Barrett* was to restrain the landowner's ability to alter the beaver's occupied habitat. Is this outcome fair to the landowner, particularly given the state's involvement in reintroducing the beaver? On the other side, how meaningful is the state's ownership of wildlife if landowners can freely destroy wildlife habitat, thereby indirectly destroying the wildlife?

If we do take seriously the idea that the state owns wildlife on behalf of the people (and with trust duties to protect them, as courts have regularly asserted), could a member of the public claim an ancillary right to enter private land to view the wildlife—perhaps so long as there is no interference with the landowner's activities? Should a person's co-ownership of wild animals include some minimal ability to enjoy them? If not, why not, at least when the private landowner is not being physically disturbed by the entry?

4. *Accommodation III: a limited right to defend property.* From time to time landowners have gone to court to challenge bans on hunting, claiming that they interfere with the landowner's "right to hunt." Courts have routinely dismissed the arguments, with one stray exception—the ruling of the Florida Supreme Court in Alford v. Finch, 155 So.2d 790 (Fla. 1963). There, the court used "right to hunt" language to strike down a regulation that unfairly distinguished among similarly situated landowners, allowing one landowner to hunt while prohibiting a neighbor from doing so. The nearly universal view is that "the right to hunt wild game upon one's own land is not a property right enforceable against the state." Collopy v. Wildlife Commission, 625 P.2d 994, 999 (Colo. 1981). Landowners, though, have occasionally succeeded in using their property rights as shields when they have violated game laws by killing animals that cause serious property damage. When courts have allowed such defenses, they have typically required landowners to exhaust all nonlethal means of controlling the animals. E.g., Cross v. State, 370 P.2d 371 (Wyo. 1962). More recently, many states have enacted statutes that allow landowners to deal with problem animals, subject to a variety of constraints and notification rules. See Dale D. Goble & Eric T. Freyfogle, WILDLIFE LAW: CASES AND MATERIALS 219–43 (2002).

Note the overriding principle of accommodation that seems to arise when we consider these various wildlife-related rules as a whole—the power of the state to protect wildlife on private land; the ability of landowners to control who can hunt on their lands and where; and the limited ability of landowners to defend their property against wildlife-caused damage. By steps lawmakers are attempting to accommodate two uses of land at the same time, one by the private landowner, the other by the public as owner of the wildlife.

5. *Habitat destruction as a "taking" of wildlife.* The wildlife species that New York sought to protect in *Barrett*, the beaver, has made a spectacular comeback, but other species over the past century have not done as well. The beaver declined because of overharvesting; the bald eagle and other species due to contamination. Most endangered species, however, have declined due to human-induced habitat change. Under the Endangered Species Act, 16 U.S.C. § 1538(a)(1)(B), all persons are banned from engaging in "takes" of animal species listed as endangered or (usually) threatened. The term "take" includes the term "harm." Pursuant to the Act, the U.S. Fish & Wildlife Service has issued regulations including within the definition of take any alteration of habitat that actually kills or injures protected animals (but not habitat alteration that merely frustrates species recovery efforts). The federal regulations were upheld in Babbitt v. Sweet Home Chapter, 515 U.S. 687 (1995). Landowners can gain permission to alter protected habitat, and otherwise engage in takes of listed species, by preparing habitat conservation plans or participating in similar conservation programs.

Similar restrictions on landowner behavior appear in state and local laws. E.g., State v. Sour Mountain Realty, Inc., 276 A.D.2d 8, 714 N.Y.S.2d 78 (2d Dept. 2000) (landowner's erection of 3500–foot long "snake proof fence," intended to exclude migrating timber rattlesnakes, violates state endangered species law); Department of Community Affairs v. Moorman, 664 So.2d 930 (Fla. 1995) (upholding ban on constructing fence on private land that interferes with ability of rare deer to cross land freely).

The next case involves a dispute between a landowner and a state agency. The landowner sought a permit; the agency refused it. The dispute was unusual because the state agency (the appellant) claimed that it lacked the power to issue the requested permit because its issuance would interfere with the public's rights in navigable waterways.

MUNNINGHOFF v. WISCONSIN CONSERVATION COMMISSION

255 Wis. 252, 38 N.W.2d 712 (1949).

. . . .

The respondent, Munninghoff, seeks a muskrat farm license for lands owned and leased by him in Oneida county, which are under the navigable waters of the Wisconsin river. . . . The license was refused by the conservation commission and its director on the ground that sec. 29.575, Stats., does not authorize the granting of a license for navigable waters. . . .

MARTIN, JUSTICE.

. . . .

It is admitted that the lands upon which Munninghoff desires to operate a muskrat farm are his own lands, and are located under the navigable waters of the Wisconsin river. These waters became navigable by the erection by the Rhinelander Paper Company of a dam in the year 1906, which dam flooded the land in question and it has been flooded since that time.

The issues in this case are whether the conservation commission, pursuant to sec. 29.575, Stats., can license privately owned lands lying under navigable waters, and whether such muskrat farming is an incident to navigation.

The muskrat farm law was originally passed in 1919. [As amended, § 29.575(1) provides:] "The owner or lessee of any lands within the state of Wisconsin suitable for the breeding and propagating of muskrats * * * shall have the right upon complying with the provisions of this section to establish, operate and maintain on such lands a muskrat * * * farm, for the purpose of breeding, propagating, trapping and dealing in muskrats." . . .

[Under Wisconsin law, it] is not essential to the public easement that the capacity for navigation be continuous throughout the year to make it navigable or public. It is sufficient that a stream has periods of navigable capacity ordinarily recurrent from year to year and continuing long enough to make the stream usable as a highway. *Willow River Club v. Wade, 1898, 100 Wis. 86, 76 N.W. 273, 42 L.R.A. 305.* The capacity for floating logs to market during the spring freshets which normally lasts six weeks was held to make a stream navigable. *Falls Mfg. Co. v. Oconto River Imp. Co.* et al., 1894, 87 Wis. 134, 58 N.W. 257. . . .

[T]he meaning of [§ 29.575(1) was] construed in *Krenz v. Nichols, 1928, 197 Wis. 394, at page 402, 222 N.W. 300, 303, 62 A.L.R. 466,* wherein it was stated:

> The state, under its police power, and to carry out its trust, passed the statute in question. So far as it affects the public, the statute is reasonable, and is not contrary to any provision of the federal or state Constitution. Nor do we think it is contrary to the decision of this court in *Diana Shooting Club v. Husting, 156 Wis. 261, 145 N.W. 816,* Ann.Cas.1915C, 1148. In that case the court upheld the right of a citizen of the state to hunt from a boat in the navigable inland streams of the state, notwithstanding that the boat should be on the waters over the lands of a private owner. The court there said that was a right incident to the right of navigation, and that the right of navigation was free to all the citizens of the state upon such waters, by virtue of the Ordinance of 1787, the Enabling Act of the state Constitution, and the constitutional provision thereto. . . .

In Wisconsin the owner of the banks of the stream is the owner of the bed, regardless of whether the stream is navigable or non-navigable.

The owner of the submerged soil of a running stream does not own the running water, but he does have certain exclusive rights to make a reasonable use of the water as is passes over or along his land. For instance, he may erect a pier for navigation; he may pump part of the water out of the stream to irrigate his crops; his cattle may be permitted to drink of it; and his muskrats may use it to gather vegetation for the construction of muskrat houses or for food.

It is not within the power of the state to deprive the owner of submerged land of the right to make use of the water which passes over his land, or to grant the use of it to a non-riparian. The riparian's exclusive right to use the water arises directly from the fact that non-riparians have no access to the stream without trespass upon riparian lands.

In the present case the respondent would make use of the water flowing over or past his land in permitting the muskrats to swim in the water, gather feed found in the water or in the bed of the river, build muskrat houses on the bed where the water is shallow, and dig runways in the banks from underneath the surface of the water to their burrows in the banks above the water line.

In general, the rights of the public to the incidents of navigation are boating, bathing, fishing, hunting, and recreation. See *Doemel v. Jantz, 1923, 180 Wis. 225, 193 N.W. 393, 31 A.L.R. 969.* Trapping is not included for it is an incident of land use. See *Johnson v. Burghorn, 1920, 212 Mich. 19, 179 N.W. 225, 228, 11 A.L.R. 234.* Appellant asserts that float trapping does not require the use of the bottom. However, floats for float trapping are always anchored to the bottom and any method of anchoring or securing a float would, of necessity, require the use of the land or the bottom. The right to use the running water of the bed for float trapping is not included in the easement of navigation. To float trap in navigable water constitutes a trespass upon the submerged land for which the trespasser may be prosecuted by the owner of the soil and enjoined from using the public water for that purpose.

The muskrats on a muskrat farm have been bought and paid for by the licensee. They are his personal property whether they are swimming in the waters above his lands or running along on the dry land within the limits of his licensed premises. The presence of the muskrats in a navigable stream covering privately owned lands does not entitle a trespasser to take them any more than a trespasser would be entitled to seize domestic ducks in the same stream. But if a muskrat should leave a licensed area, he becomes *ferae naturae*, and is legitimate prey for a neighboring trapper. See 2, Property Ratione Soli, Am.Jur., p. 699, sec. 12.

Appellant also asserts that the right of navigation includes the incidental use of the bottom. This is true where the use of the bottom is connected with navigation, such as walking as a trout fisherman does in a navigable stream, boating, standing on the bottom while bathing, casting an anchor from a boat in fishing, propelling a duck boat by poling against the bottom, walking on the ice if the river is frozen, etc. These have nothing in common with trapping because the latter involves the exercise of a property right in the land or the bottom.

The conservation department has authority to issue the license applied for.

Notes

1. *Landowner control over navigable waters. Munninghoff* gives a glimpse of the wildlife-related issues that arise with respect to navigable waters. According to Wisconsin law, riparian landowners own the underlying land to the thread of the river, the same rule as Illinois in *Washington Ice*. But of what practical value is that ownership? Does it extend beyond the use of the bed to raise shellfish or to attach traps? Note the relatively fine line that the court draws: public users on waterways can hunt and fish, but they cannot trap because traps must be affixed to the river bottom, which is privately owned.

The court announces that the muskrats raised by Munninghoff would remain his private property even when they are swimming in a navigable river so long as they remain in the area licensed for the muskrat farm. This rule, as we'll see, differs from the normal rule that a wild animal is no longer owned when it is unconfined and has returned to something similar to its wild habitat. Is this rule fair to public users of the river? How are they supposed to know which muskrats are owned and which are unowned? Doesn't the ruling effectively give the landowner an exclusive right to capture muskrats in a section of publicly owned water?

2. *Shared governance IV: inland fisheries.* Overfishing in inland waters is controlled today by state fishing statutes and regulations. These laws, however, only limit harvests, and do little to protect fish populations against other causes of decline, such as pollution, loss of stream-bank vegetation, and alterations of hydrologic flows. Might fish be better served by ending this system and instituting instead a regime of private property rights in waterways? Merely transferring exclusive rights to fish to landowners might not be enough, given that fish are mobile and that individual landowners might have insufficient money at stake to protect a river from degradation. What about, instead, setting up fishery management groups in inland waterways—something akin to the Altoona Snag Union in *Marinkovich*? Could private ownership be authorized but only for a set term of years, with rights to renew if the private managers meet specified management goals related to the health of the fishery and of the river? Is there an opportunity here, that is, for experimenting with new forms of shared governance?

RUTTEN v. WOOD

79 N.D. 436, 57 N.W.2d 112 (1953).

SATHRE, JUDGE

The plaintiff Raymond Rutten owns certain lands in Ramsey County, this State, adjoining both sides of a section line which is also a township line. The section line has been opened for travel and highway purposes pursuant to the laws of the State. During the hunting season of 1951 the plaintiff posted the land on both sides of the section line as provided by law. He brings this action to enjoin the defendant from hunting along said highway.

The complaint alleges in substance that the lands on each side of the section line referred to in the complaint are owned by the plaintiff; that the section line has been opened for highway purposes between plaintiff's two tracts of land for a width of two rods on each side of such line pursuant to statute and that the fee title to such land so used for highway purposes is in the plaintiff; that on the 17th day of October 1951 and at diverse other times the defendant entered upon said highway and parked his car along the right of way and hunted and shot geese flying across plaintiff's land and across the said highway; that such geese fell upon the plaintiff's land and that the defendant thereupon entered upon the plaintiff's fields to take such game; that the plaintiff has caused the lands referred to and described in the complaint to be posted against hunting thereon in accordance with the provisions of law; that the lands were so posted at the time the defendant entered upon said highway and said lands and hunted thereon . . .

He demands judgment enjoining the defendant from entering upon said highway for the purpose of hunting and from engaging in the hunting of game along said highway and from trespassing upon the lands of the plaintiff. . . .

The general rule as to the fee title to highways is stated in 25 Am.Jur. page 426, Highways, Section 132, as follows:

> In the absence of a statute expressly providing for the acquisition of the fee, or of a deed from the owner expressly conveying the fee, when a highway is established by dedication or prescription, or by the direct action of the public authorities, the public acquires merely an easement of passage, the fee title remaining in the landowner.

This is the rule in this state. [citations omitted]

It is admitted that the plaintiff owns the land upon which the highway is located on both sides of the section line and that he posted 'no hunting' signs thereon as provided by law. The statutes of this state do not cover the precise question as to whether the public may legally hunt wild game upon the highways of the state.

Section 20–0119, NDRC 1943, provides that any person may enter upon legally posted land to recover game shot or killed on land where such person had a lawful right to hunt.

Section 20–0117, NDRC 1943 makes it a misdemeanor to hunt or pursue game or enter for the purpose of hunting or pursuing game upon any land belonging to another which has been legally posted, without first having obtained the permission of the person legally entitled to grant the same.

The general law as to the right to hunt on the highways is stated in 24 Am.Jur., Game and Game Laws, Section 5, page 377:

> Since the title to wild game within the boundaries of a state is vested in the people in their sovereign capacity, each of the inhabitants thereof may be said to have an equal right to kill such game. But this equal right is subject to at least two limitations. In the first place, the state may make regulations relative to the killing and marketing of game. Secondly, every landowner has an exclusive common-law right to kill or capture game on his own land, subject to the regulatory action of the state in the preservation of all game for the common use. This right is regarded at common law as property *ratione soli*, or in other words, as property by reason of the ownership of the soil. The state cannot, within constitutional limits, by the issuance of hunting licenses which purport to give a hunter the right to invade the private hunting grounds owned by another person, or by any other means, authorize one to enter another's premises, for the purpose of taking game, without the latter's permission.

This question was considered by the supreme court of Minnesota in the case of L. Realty Co. v. Johnson, 92 Minn. 363, 100 N.W. 94, 95, 66 L.R.A. 439. We quote from the opinion:

> But we may safely assume that the killing of game belonging to the adjacent premises, and found temporarily in the highway, is in no manner connected with or incidental to the public right of passage and transportation. While true that the title to all wild game is in the state, and the owner of premises whereon it is located has only a qualified property interest therein, yet he has the right to exercise exclusive and absolute dominion over his property, and incidentally the unqualified right to control and protect the wild game thereon. In Lamprey v. Danz, supra [86 Minn. 317, 90 N.W. 578] the elementary rule on this subject was stated as follows: 'Every person has exclusive dominion over the soil which he absolutely owns; hence such an owner of land has the exclusive right of hunting and fishing on his land, and the waters covering it.' 'It necessarily follows that, in dedicating the highway in question to the public, respondent reserved to itself all of the other privileges and rights pertaining to the premises, which included the right to foster and protect, for its own use, the wild game thereon, and that such right and privilege were in no manner surrendered to the public in granting the easement. It also follows that the public, including appellant, in accepting the easement thus granted, acquired no right to kill or molest the game inhabiting the property while it was passing to and fro across the highway.'

. . . .

The judgment of the trial court was correct and is affirmed.

Notes

1. *Right to exclude VI: hunting today. Rutten* exemplifies contemporary law on the powers of landowners to exclude public hunters. North Dakota

law authorized landowners to exclude hunters if they posted their lands in accordance with detailed posting laws. Land not properly posed remains open to public use in accordance with longstanding custom. But note the exception for hunters retrieving game—they can enter without the landowner's permission. A growing number of states have taken the final step along the path away from *M'Conico*, entirely banning hunters from entering all private land (or, in some states, all agricultural land) without the prior permission of the owner. What cultural and economic trends explain this significant legal shift? Does it reflect rising selfishness in American culture or merely a decline in the number of hunters who need game to avoid hunger? The law on hunting access today is considered in Mark R. Sigmon, Note, *Hunting and Posting on Private Land in America*, 54 Duke L. J. 549 (2004).

2. *Easement law and the issue of scope.* Many resource-use rights take the legal form of easements, which the law at one time called "incorporeal hereditaments" (meaning, interests in land that were nonpossessory (no exclusive right to possession) and that could pass to heirs and be transferred by will). The parties to an easement agreement have considerable flexibility in defining the easement as they see fit, at least if it is an *affirmative* easement (which allows the recipient of the easement to enter the land of easement grantor) rather than a *negative* easement (which restricts what the grantor can do on or with his land). The common law has long frowned on negative easements, and only specific types are permitted. Affirmative easements, on the other hand, can take almost any form and give to the holder almost any combination of rights to enter the grantor's land (known as the *servient* estate) and do things there.

What the easement holder can do, and when and where she can do it, is determined by the "scope" of the easement. The scope of an easement can be specified with great precision; it can instead be left vague. (We'll see illustrations in Chapter 3.) In *Rutten*, the private land at issue was subject to an easement in favor of the state for a roadway. The legal dispute had to do with the precise scope of that public easement. Did the easement for a public road give to travelers on the road the right to shoot wild game? North Dakota law on the subject was vague; it merely specified that roadways in the state normally took the form of an easement rather than a fee interest, unless a fee interest was clearly specified. But what was that easement? According to the court, it was merely "an easement of passage." Travelers along the Oregon Trail a century earlier might well have needed the right to shoot game as an incident of passage, but highway travelers in the mid-twentieth century apparently do not. A contrary conclusion was reached by neighboring South Dakota in Reis v. Miller, 550 N.W.2d 78 (S.D. 1996), a ruling that stimulated legal conflict that continues (see Benson v. State, 710 N.W.2d 131 (S.D. 2006)) (upholding constitutionality of statute that removed criminal sanction for hunting small game birds along public highways).

Note the similarity of *Rutten* and the argument made by the ice company in *Washington Ice.* The public's right to use navigable waters is a type of easement, akin to a road. The ice company urged that it had the right to harvest ice so long as it was lawfully present on the river—just the argument made by the hunter in *Rutten*. Both arguments, of course, failed. We can note also the similarity with *Munninghoff*: the issue there, indirectly, was whether a public traveler on a navigable waterway did or did not possess the right to trap muskrats.

D. USING THE WATER SURFACE

Navigable waterways are open to use by any member of the public with access to them. But what about all other bodies of water? The right to use their surfaces is itself a natural resource, which the law somehow must allocate. The challenge that arises in defining and allocating this particular resource is similar to the one that arises with respect to caves and underground oil formations. The resource is largely an integrated unit and difficult to divide spatially without greatly diminishing its value. Yet, if the resource is not divided spatially, how will use rights be defined and how can the law avoid overuse? Even if the public has no access to them, water surfaces can still be subject to overuse by the private users who do have access.

THOMPSON v. ENZ

379 Mich. 667, 154 N.W.2d 473 (1967).

KAVANAGH, JUSTICE.

This case concerns certain property rights in and around Gun Lake, which is situated partly in Barry county and partly in Allegan county. The parties agree that this lake has approximately 2,680 acres of surface area and approximately 30 miles of shore line. The defendant corporation is a contract purchaser of a riparian parcel of land having approximately 1,415 feet of frontage on side lake, and the individual defendants are the sole stockholders of the corporation. Plaintiffs are riparian owners of other property abutting Gun Lake. . . .

Defendants are in the process of developing and subdividing their parcel of land into from 144 to 153 lots. Of these lots, approximately 16 will abut on the natural shore line of the lake. The remainder of the lots will front on canals. To give the back lot purchasers access to the lake the defendants' plan calls for excavating across riparian lots Nos 13 and 76. (See plat.) The defendants purport to grant to the purchasers of those lots fronting on the canals riparian rights to the lake and rights of access through the excavation to the lake. The back lots would have frontage on the canals of approximately 11,000 feet.

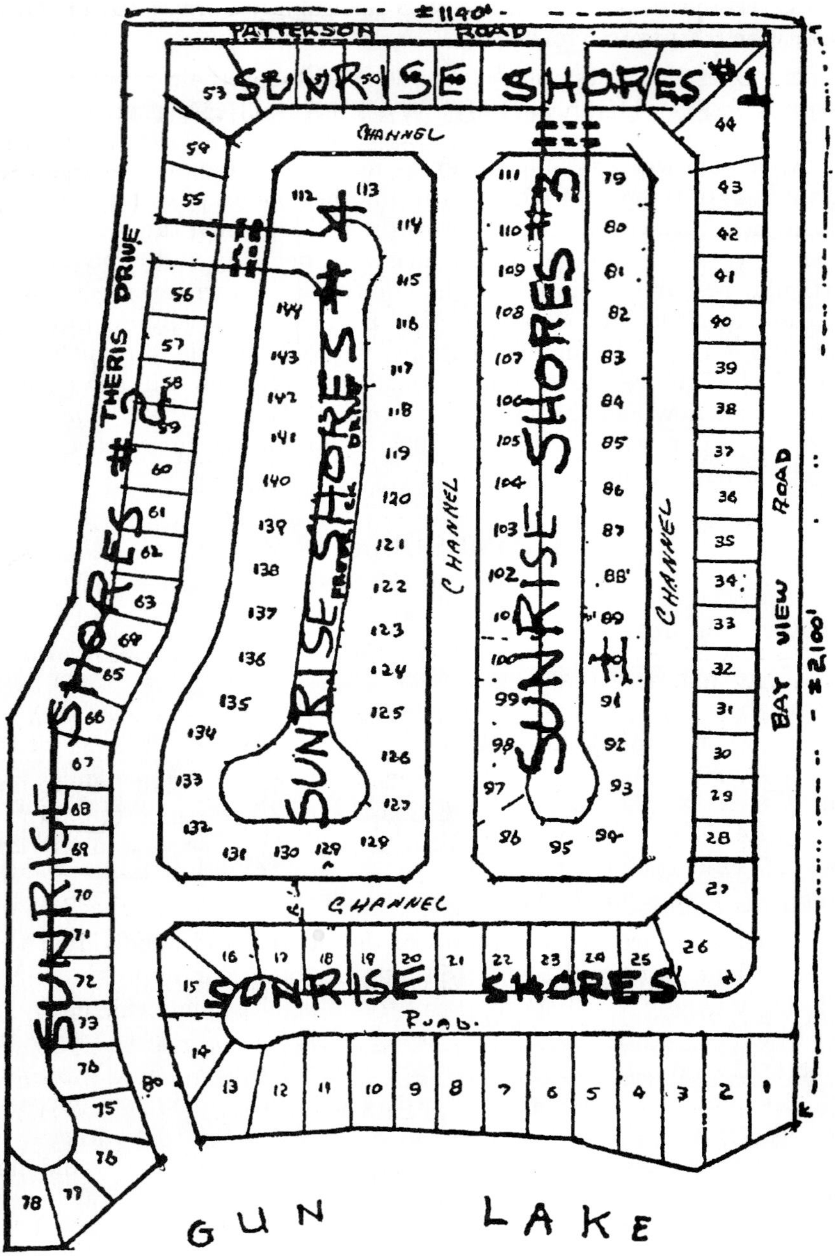

All Lots Front on the
Channel or the Lake.

The following questions are raised on appeal:

1. May a right of access to Gun Lake be created by dredging an artificial canal from the lake through lots having frontage on Gun Lake

to back lots having no frontage thereon, and may ownership of such lots carry with it riparian rights?

2. Does the development by defendants of their property which partially fronts on Gun Lake by the construction of a canal connecting back lots to the lake and granting rights of access to the lake constitute an illegal invasion of the rights of the plaintiffs and an infringement of their riparian rights in and to the surface of Gun Lake and in and to the subaqueous land thereunder?

"Riparian land" is defined as a parcel of land which includes therein a part of or is bounded by a natural watercourse. 4 Restatement, Torts, § 843, p. 326. See, also, Palmer v. Dodd, 64 Mich. 474, 476, 31 N.W. 209; Stark v. Miller, 113 Mich. 465, 71 N.W. 876; Monroe Carp Pond Co. v. River Raisin Paper Co., 240 Mich. 279, 287, 215 N.W. 325. A "riparian proprietor" is a person who is in possession of riparian lands or who owns an estate therein. 4 Restatement, Torts, § 844, p. 331. "The riparian owners have a right to the enjoyment of the natural flow of the stream with no burden or hindrance imposed by artificial means." Koopman v. Blodgett, 70 Mich. 610, 616, 38 N.W. 649, 651; Kennedy v. Niles Water Supply Co., 173 Mich. 474, 139 N.W. 241, 43 L.R.A.,N.S., 836.

As it was stated in Harvey Realty Co. v. Borough of Wallingford, 111 Conn. 352, 358, 150 A. 60, 63:

> 'A riparian proprietor is an owner of land bounded by a water course or lake or through which a stream flows, and riparian rights can be claimed only by such an owner. They are appurtenant only to lands which touch on the water course or through which it flows and which are used as a whole for a common purpose, not to any lands physically separated from the stream and the land bordering on it, although belonging to the same owner.' (Emphasis supplied.)

. . . .

Artificial watercourses are waterways that owe their origin to acts of man, such as canals, drainage and irrigation ditches, aqueducts, flumes, and the like. 4 Restatement, Torts, § 841, subd. h., p. 321. Land abutting on an artificial watercourse has no riparian rights. As is stated in the case of Harrell v. F. H. Vahlsing, Inc., Tex.Civ.App., 248 S.W.2d 762, 769, 770:

> In Kirk v. Hoge, 123 Va. 519, 97 S.E. 116, 120, it was said that:
>
> 'The natural corporeal right in question is possessed by riparian owners of land on natural channels of water courses only. Such right does not exist in the water flowing in an artificial channel. The right of those owning land bordering upon or through which artificial channels pass to the use of the water flowing therein is not a natural right, nor a corporeal right, but an incorporeal right, which can be acquired only by grant, express or implied, or by prescription. Angell on Water Courses, § 90, p. 91; 3 Farnham on Waters and Water Courses, § 820. . . .'

So, too, is the law in Michigan. . . .

We, therefore, conclude that parcels of land to be subdivided from the main tract of land bordering on Gun Lake have no riparian rights as: (1) they neither include therein a part of nor are they bounded by Gun Lake, and (2) the canal itself would be an artificial watercourse giving rise to no riparian rights.

The remaining question for decision is whether or not riparian rights may be conveyed to a grantee or reserved by the grantor in a conveyance which divides a tract of land with riparian rights into more than one parcel, of which parcels only one would remain bounded by the watercourse.

In the case of Harvey Realty Co. v. Borough of Wallingford, *supra*, Justice Hinman, writing for the Court, stated (150 A. p. 63):

> 'It is clear that the grantees or contractees, from the plaintiff, of lots separated from and not bordering on Pine Lake can have, of their own right, no riparian privileges in its waters. And any attempted transfer of the right made by a riparian to a nonriparian proprietor is invalid.'

Defendants direct attention to the statement of Justice Fead in the case of Bauman v. Barendregt, 251 Mich. 67, 69, 231 N.W. 70, 71:

> 'It is a settled rule in this state that, Where there is no reservation of them, riparian rights attach to lots bounded by natural water courses.' (Citing cases.) (Emphasis supplied.)

We hold that what is meant by this 'reservation' of riparian rights is merely the reservation of a right of way for access to the watercourse. . . .

We hold that riparian rights are not alienable, severable, divisible or assignable apart from the land which includes therein or is bounded by a natural watercourse. While riparian rights may not be conveyed or reserved—nor do they exist by virtue of being bounded by an artificial watercourse—easements, licenses and the like for a right of way for access to a watercourse do exist and ofttimes are granted to nonriparian owners.

We will, therefore, treat the proposal here as though easements for rights of way for access are given to the back lot purchasers. We must then consider what right, if any, the owners of the back lots have to use these rights of way. In so doing, attention must be given to the use of riparian rights by the defendants and the remaining proprietors on Gun Lake.

Riparian uses are divided generally into two classes. The first of these is for natural purposes. These uses encompass all those absolutely necessary for the existence of the riparian proprietor and his family, such as to quench thirst and for household purposes. Without these uses both man and beast would perish. Users for natural purposes enjoy a preferred non-proratable position with respect to all other users rather than a correlative one.

The second of these is a use for artificial purposes. Artificial uses are those which merely increase one's comfort and prosperity and do not rank as essential to his existence, such as commercial profit and recreation. Users for artificial purposes occupy a correlative status with the other riparians in exercise of their riparian rights for artificial purposes. Use for an artificial purpose must be (a) only for the benefit of the riparian land and (b) reasonable in light of the correlative rights of the other proprietors. Evans v. Merriweather, 4 Ill. (3 Scam.) 492, 38 Am.Dec. 106. It is clear in the case before us that the use made of the property by the defendants is for a strictly artificial purpose and must meet the test of reasonableness.

In the case of Hoover v. Crane, 362 Mich. 36, pp. 40, 41, 106 N.W.2d 563, 565, Justice Edwards stated:

> 'Michigan has adopted the reasonable use rule in determining the conflicting rights of riparian owners to the use of lake water.'

"In 1874, Justice Cooley said:

> 'It is therefore not a diminution in the quantity of the water alone, or an alteration in its flow, or either or both of these circumstances combined with injury, that will give a right of action, if in view of all the circumstances, and having regard to equality of right in others, that which has been done and which causes the injury is not unreasonable. In other words, the injury that is incidental to a reasonable enjoyment of the common right can demand no redress.' Dumont v. Kellogg, 29 Mich. 420, 425 (18 Am.Rep. 102).

"And in People v. Hulbert, 131 Mich. 156, at page 170, 91 N.W. 211, at page 217, 64 L.R.A. 265 (100 Am.St.Rep. 588), the Court, quoting from Gehlen Bros. v. Knorr, 101 Iowa 700, 70 N.W. 757, 36 L.R.A. 697 (63 Am.St.Rep. 416), said:

> 'No statement can be made as to what is such reasonable use which will, without variation or qualification, apply to the facts of every case. But in determining whether a use is reasonable we must consider what the use is for; its extent, duration, necessity, and its application; the nature and size of the stream, and the several uses to which it is put; the extent of the injury to the one proprietor and of the benefit to the other; and all other facts which may bear upon the reasonableness of the use. Red River Roller Mills v. Wright, 30 Minn. 249, 15 N.W. 167, 44 Am.Rep. 194, and cases cited.' . . .

The trial court made no finding of fact as to the reasonableness of the use. This record is insufficient for us to make a determination as to reasonableness. Therefore, we remand to the trial court for such determination. The trial court should keep in mind the following factors in determining whether the use would be reasonable:

First, attention should be given to the watercourse and its attributes, including its size, character and natural state. In determining the reasonableness of the use in the case at bar, it should be considered that Gun Lake is not a large lake, that it is used primarily for recreational purposes, and that the defendants are changing its natural state by expanding the lake frontage of their property from an actual 1,415 feet to a total inclusive of the canals, of 12,415 feet, being an increase in frontage of approximately 800 per cent.

Second, the trial court should examine the use itself as to its type, extent, necessity, effect on the quantity, quality and level of the water, and the purposes of the users. Factors in this particular case that should be considered include: (a) that this use would permanently add approximately one family without riparian rights to each 18 acres of surface area (or 137 families); (b) the possibility that the level of the lake may be reduced by withdrawing trust waters into over 2 miles of the proposed canals, as is alleged by the Attorney General in his motion to intervene; (c) the possibility that pollution may result; (d) that there is nothing in the record showing any necessity for this use; and (e) the fact that it appears that the purpose of the defendants herein is merely commercial exploitation.

Third, it is necessary to examine the proposed artificial use in relation to the consequential effects, including the benefits obtained and the detriment suffered, on the correlative rights and interests of other riparian proprietors and also on the interests of the State, including fishing, navigation, and conservation. An additional fact to be considered by the trial court in this litigation is whether the benefit to the defendant subdividers would amount merely to a rich financial harvest, while the remaining proprietors—who now possess a tranquil retreat from everyday living—would be forced to endure the annoyances which would come from an enormous increase in lake users.

If, after considering all of these factors and any additional testimony the parties may desire to present, the trial court (as chancellor) concludes the use is unreasonable, that court should retain jurisdiction of the matter for the purpose of granting such further necessary or proper relief as may be necessary to protect the rights and interests of plaintiffs, the public, and riparian owners of property abutting this lake.

Notes

1. *The missing issue.* A curious element of this case is that the court makes no mention of the legal navigability of Lake Gun. Had it been navigable any member of the public with access could use the surface for recreation, with or without riparian rights. Because the back-lot purchasers were interested in using the lake for recreation (not, so far as we can tell, for any other purpose), they could presumably have done so had the lake been navigable, regardless of riparian rights. But what are the rules governing nonnavigable lakes? The court (and both parties, apparently) assumed that only riparians could use the lake surface and that each riparian could use the entire lake surface. It was on this basis that the case was litigated. More on this issue after the next case.

2. *Three lines of argument.* In *Thompson* the court considers three lines of argument that, if successful, could give the owners of the newly created back lots access to and use of the surface of Lake Gun.

First, was the argument that they became riparians themselves and gained riparian rights by means of the construction of the canals; by fronting on the canals, which were connected to the lake, they became lakefront property owners themselves.

Second, was the claim that the landowner(s) who retained actual lakefront property had divided his (or their) riparian rights, severed them from the land, and then transferred a portion of these rights to each back-lot purchaser; each back-lot purchaser thus acquired riparian rights separately from the lot.

Third, was the argument that the riparian landowners who owned the land crossed by the canal to get to the lake (Sunrise Shores #1 lot 13, and Sunrise Shores #2 lot 16, or so it appears) had allowed back-lot purchasers to cross their riparian lands to gain access to the lake; the back-lot purchasers were thus akin to guests visiting the riparian landowners, and they used the lake by making use of the riparian landowners' riparian rights.

How does the court respond to each of these arguments? One further missing piece: The riparian rights of the developer originally attached to the entire riparian tract owned by the developer. Thus, as the back-lots were divided and sold off, the issue was not whether they *gained* riparian rights but whether they could *retain* riparian rights despite being legally severed from the tracts that actually fronted on the lake.

3. *Why riparian landowners only?* Imagine a landscape in which the only reliable water sources are contained in nonnavigable ponds. Is it sensible for the law to announce that only those who acquire riparian (or, to use the more precise term for lakes, littoral) land have rights to use the water? Is it sensible, that is, when dividing a landscape and allocating it to settlers to create an arrangement in which some landowners have no water? Can you imagine a much different approach, offering water to everyone, which could prove feasible? Lawmakers were not obligated to allocate water use-rights only to such landowners; they could have employed a wide variety of other water allocation methods. Why might they have chosen this method? What virtues does it have?

4. *Dividing water from land by private action I.* The court announces that a riparian landowner cannot sever riparian rights from the land and sell them separately. Indeed, the court asserts, "riparian rights are not alienable, severable, divisible or assignable" at all, apart from the riparian land itself. Why might the court have reached this ruling? A landowner can sell trees on his land, grass, minerals, and the like—pretty much all natural parts except the riparian rights. Why the difference? Is the problem a theoretical one, or is the court anticipating grave problems if it allows severance and division to take place? What problems might arise, and are they due more to the *severance* of the water or the *division* of it? If division is the bigger problem, could the court have announced that a riparian landowner can sell riparian rights, but only to one purchaser and once the sale is made the riparian landowner has no remaining rights to use the lake? We'll return to this issue

in the next section, when we consider the rights of landowners to extract water for consumptive use.

5. *Reasonable use III: protecting against overuse.* Ultimately the court decides that true riparian landowners can allow back-lot purchasers to cross their riparian lands and enter the lake, thereby making use of the riparians' lake-use rights. These lake-use rights, possessed by all riparian landowners, are subject in turn to the obligation that each owner's overall use be reasonable. What factors does the court identify as relevant to this factual inquiry? In particular, how much weight should be given to the amount of waterfront land an owner has in relation to the lake as a whole? Does the state supreme court tip its hand, indicating its own views about what is, in the case, chiefly a factual issue for resolution by the trial court? Given the vagueness of the idea of reasonable use, how effective is it likely to be in controlling overuse?

CARNAHAN v. MORIAH PROPERTY OWNERS ASSOCIATION, INC.

716 N.E.2d 437 (Ind. 1999).

SULLIVAN, JUSTICE.

The Moriah Property Owners Association, Inc., which owns approximately 64% of a private lake, seeks to restrict watercraft use on it. The Carnahans, who own a portion of the lake, oppose the restrictions. They contend that they have a prescriptive easement for the recreational use of motorized watercraft on the entire lake. We hold that the Carnahans have failed to establish a prescriptive easement.

BACKGROUND

Lake Julia is an approximately 22–acre lake located in Lake County. Prior to 1972, the lake and all the surrounding property were owned by Charles and Julia Drewry. In November of 1972, the Carnahans purchased a lot from the Drewrys, which was approximately one acre in size and included a portion of the lake bed. From the beginning, the Carnahans engaged in recreational activities including ice skating, fishing, swimming, and the use of various watercraft on portions of the entire lake. In the spring of 1973, the Carnahans placed a houseboat on the lake. They powered the houseboat around the lake, skied behind it, and lived on it intermittently until 1976 when they finished building a lakeside home. Thereafter, they used a ski boat on the lake until 1986, and wave runners and jet skis through the summer of 1993.

On July 26, 1984, the Carnahans purchased an adjacent one acre plot; approximately one-fifth of this new acreage constituted the lake bed. Beginning in 1987, the land around and under Lake Julia was surveyed and an engineering plan prepared which platted various lots comprising the Julia and Lake Additions to Lake County. On December 29, 1987, the Carnahans acquired an additional adjacent 1.2 acres of land; approximately one-eighth of this new acreage included the lake bed. Our calculations suggest that at this point, the Carnahans owned just over half an acre (or 2.5%) of the total 22–acre lake bed.

On December 24, 1991, the current Moriah Property Owner's Association, Inc. ("Moriah") obtained the property rights to a majority of the lake bed including nearly all of the water above it suitable for the operation of watercraft. This property is now legally described as Lot 8, Moriah Addition to Lake County. Lot 8 is 15.6 acres, and 14.1 acres constitutes the lake. Our calculations suggest that this 14.1 acres comprises approximately 64% of the 22–acre lake bed.

In April 1992, Moriah prepared restrictive covenants which included rules intended for the safe use of that portion of Lake Julia described as Lot 8. The relevant restrictive covenant relating to the Carnahans' claimed prescriptive easement for the recreational use of watercraft on Lake Julia states as follows: "No motors are allowed on the lake except electric trolling motors powered by no more than two 12–volt batteries." (R. at 78.) In July 1992, the president of Moriah sent documents to the Carnahans including among other things the restrictive covenants for the use of Lot 8.

On May 21, 1993, the Carnahans filed this lawsuit to establish a prescriptive easement for the use of watercraft on Lake Julia and to quiet title in the easement; they also sought a declaratory judgment regarding their rights in relation to Moriah, and sought to enjoin any interference with their real property, easement, and riparian rights. . . .

I

The Carnahans contend that they have a prescriptive easement over an entire body of water. Prior Indiana decisions adjudicating riparian rights in the context of easements almost exclusively concern land access to the water itself or the construction and use of a dock. *See, e.g., Klotz v. Horn,* 558 N.E.2d 1096 (Ind.1990); . . . These decisions address the riparian rights of lakefront property owners whose land only abuts the water. This case is different and concerns the competing rights of property owners whose real estate is incidentally covered by a relatively small, private lake. Therefore, any decision we make concerning an easement or use right must coincide with our common law as it applies to property underlying an inland, nonnavigable lake.

"A private lake is a body of water on the surface of land within the exclusive dominion and control of the surrounding landowners." *Freiburger v. Fry,* 439 N.E.2d 169, 173 (Ind.Ct.App.1982) (citing 1915–1916 OP.Ind.Att'y Gen. 703; *Patton Park, Inc. v. Pollak,* 115 Ind.App. 32, 55 N.E.2d 328 (1944)). Determinations of riparian rights of inland lakes are based upon whether a lake is navigable or nonnavigable. *Berger Farms, Inc. v. Estes,* 662 N.E.2d 654, 656 (Ind.Ct.App.1996) (citing *Bath v. Courts,* 459 N.E.2d 72, 75 (Ind.Ct.App.1984)). A nonnavigable lake is one "enclosed and bordered by riparian landowners." *Id.* (citing *Bath,* 459 N.E.2d at 75 (citing in turn *Stoner v. Rice,* 121 Ind. 51, 22 N.E. 968 (1889))).

This Court last determined the rights of a lake bed property owner in *Sanders v. De Rose,* 207 Ind. 90, 191 N.E. 331 (1934). Sanders owned approximately twenty acres of land covered by a "non-navigable body of fresh water, known as Center Lake." *Id.* at 90, 191 N.E. at 331. De Rose was a non-property owner who gained access to the lake for fishing via the permission of another riparian owner, whose smaller portion of land both abutted and extended into Center Lake. In reversing the lower court and enjoining De Rose from fishing upon the waters of the lake overlying Sanders's property, this Court emphasized Sanders's rights with respect to other "owners of the bed of such lake." *Id.* at 95, 191 N.E. at 333. It then set forth the common law rule as it applies to an inland, nonnavigable lake: "[E]ach owner has the right to the free and unmolested use and control of his portion of the lake bed and water thereon for boating and fishing." *Id.* . . .

II

Prescriptive easements are not favored in the law, *see* 25 Am.Jur.2d *Easements and Licenses* § 45, at 615 (1996 & Supp.1999), and in Indiana, the party claiming one must meet "stringent requirements," *Fleck v. Hann,* 658 N.E.2d 125, 128 (Ind. Ct. App. 1995) (reversing lower court decision finding prescriptive easement for use of lakefront pier, because testimony was conflicted as to "adverse" or "permissive" use, thus claimants failed to meet the "stringent requirements that an adverse user must prove to acquire a prescriptive easement"). In order to establish the existence of a prescriptive easement, the evidence must show an actual, hostile, open, notorious, continuous, uninterrupted adverse use for twenty years under a claim of right. *Greenco, Inc. v. May,* 506 N.E.2d 42, 45 (Ind.Ct.App.1987). "Each . . . element[ ] . . . must be established as a necessary, independent, ultimate fact, the burden of showing which is on the party asserting the prescriptive title, and the failure to find any one of such elements [is] fatal . . . , for such failure to find is construed as a finding against it." *Monarch Real Estate Co. v. Frye,* 77 Ind.App. 119, 124–25, 133 N.E.156, 158 (1921) (citing *Benedict v. Bushnell,* 65 Ind.App. 365, 117 N.E. 267 (1917)).

Adverse use has been defined as a "use of the property as the owner himself would exercise, disregarding the claims of others entirely, asking permission from no one, and using the property under a claim of right." *Nowlin v. Whipple,* 120 Ind. 596, 598, 22 N.E. 669, 670 (1889). The concept of *adversity* was developed in the context of establishing use rights over static paths or roads that crossed the property of adjoining landowners. The Court of Appeals affirmed the trial court's conclusion as to adversity by citing a prototypical *path or road* case for the proposition that "[a]n unexplained use for 20 years is presumed to be adverse and sufficient to establish title by prescriptive easement." . . .

We agree with the reasoning in the *Mitchell, Fleck,* and *Reder* decisions that "an unexplained use for 20 years" of an obvious path or road for ingress and egress over the lands of another creates a rebuttable presumption that a use was adverse. However, we are unwilling to recognize such a presumption in favor of a party trying to establish a prescriptive easement for the recreational use of a body of water. This is because recreational use (especially of a body of water) is of a very different character from use of a path or road for ingress and egress over land. Recreational use (especially of water which leaves no telltale path or road) seems to us likely to be permissive in accordance with the widely held view in Indiana that if the owner of one land

> sees his neighbor also making use of it, under circumstances that in no way injures the [land] or interferes with [the landowner's] own use of it, [it] does not justify the inference that he is yielding to his neighbor's claim of right or that his neighbor is asserting any right; it signifies only that he is permitting his neighbor to use the [land].

Monarch Real Estate Co., 77 Ind.App. at 127, 133 N.E. at 159 (quoting *Anthony v. Kennard Bldg. Co.,* 188 Mo. 704, 724, 87 S.W. 921, 926 (1905)); . . .

We thus conclude that claimants seeking to establish an easement based on the "recreational" use of another's property must make a special showing that those activities were in fact adverse; they will not be indulged a presumption to that effect. *Kessinger v. Matulevich,* 278 Mont. 450, 925 P.2d 864, 869 (1996) ("Recreational use is insufficient to raise a presumption of adverse use.") (citing *Public Lands Access Ass'n v. Boone & Crockett Club Found., Inc.,* 259 Mont. 279, 856 P.2d 525, 528–29 (1993)); *Ellis v. Municipal Reserve & Bond Co.,* 60 Or.App. 567, 655 P.2d 204, 207 (1982) ("For the public to establish a public recreational easement through prescription, the proof must be clear and positive; vague and general testimony is insufficient.").

We have previously stated that "clear and convincing proof is a standard frequently imposed in civil cases where the wisdom of experience has demonstrated the need for greater certainty." . . . Therefore, we hold that a party seeking to establish a recreational prescriptive easement must show by clear and convincing evidence that their use was adverse. This holding we base on the need for greater certainty in determining the true character of a "recreational" land use, for the recreational use of a neighbor's land will oftentimes be perfectly consistent with that neighbor's (the servient titleholder's) title to the land.

. . . .

The trial court's findings do not address whether the Carnahans' recreational use of the lake was adverse to the Drewrys. They only track the Carnahans' periodic change in the use of recreational equipment over the years. (R. at 206–07; Findings of Fact Nos. 6–12.) Therefore, the findings of fact do not support the court's conclusion that the Carnahans' recreational activities constituted the "adverse seasonal use of Lake Julia." (R. at 210–11; Conclusion of Law No. 3.)

On the other hand, the record does contain ample evidence supporting the inference that the Carnahans' use of the lake was both nonconfrontational and permissive in recognition of the Drewrys' authority as title holders to a majority of the lake bed. For example, Mr. Carnahan testified that Mr. Drewry "would wave" to them as they anchored their houseboat in "plain sight of his house," but that they kept the houseboat "in the middle" as opposed to the "south side of the lake" so as not "to bother anybody." (Suppl. R. at 378.) When asked why they retired their ski boat in 1986, Mr. Carnahan responded that they "didn't want to tick off the neighbors." *Id.* at 382. There are other examples of the Carnahans' non-adversarial use of the Lake, such as Mr. Carnahan's statement that it had "been under [his] driving force that if people were on the lake fishing, [the Carnahans] stayed off," *id.* at 407, and Mrs. Carnahan's statement that "[i]f there are children in the lake, we are either not out there or we are at the opposite end," *id.* at 101.

We find the evidence establishes that the Carnahans' use of Lake Julia was not adverse and was insufficient to overcome the special showing required with respect to establishing a recreational easement....

Notes

1. Beacham v. Lake Zurich Property Owners Association. A similar set of facts involving a nonnavigable lake came to the Illinois Supreme Court in a 1988 case. The lake covered 240 acres, and involved a plan by a landowner who owned "about 15% to 20% of the lake bed" to construct a commercial marina and to rent boats to the public for recreational use on the lake. The Illinois Supreme Court had never ruled on the surface-use rights of landowners around a nonnavigable lake. It thus viewed the issue as one of first impression and felt free to craft a rule that it deemed most appropriate. The court's decision was to reject the common law rule, followed in *Carnahan*, and to apply the much different rule used in the continental European civil law system:

> Under the common law rule, the owner of a part of a lake bed has the right to the exclusive use and control of the waters above that property. This rule is a corollary of the traditional common law view that the ownership of a parcel of land entitles the owner to the exclusive use and enjoyment of anything above or below the property. (See *Smoulter v. Boyd* (1904), 209 Pa. 146, 58 A. 144.) Courts following the common law principle have held that the owner of a part of a lake bed may exclude from the surface of the overlying water all other persons, including those who own other parts of the lake bed....
>
> In those States in which the civil law rule prevails, the owner of a part of a lake bed has a right to the reasonable use and enjoyment of the entire lake surface. (See *Duval v. Thomas* (Fla.1959), 114 So.2d 791; *Beach v. Hayner* (1919), 207 Mich. 93, 173 N.W. 487; *Johnson v. Seifert* (1960), 257 Minn. 159, 100 N.W.2d 689; *Snively v. Jaber* (1956), 48 Wash.2d 815, 296 P.2d 1015.) Those courts rejecting the common law rule have noted the difficulties presented by attempts to establish and obey definite property lines (*Beach,* 207 Mich. at 95–96, 173 N.W. at 488; *Snively,* 48 Wash.2d at 821–22, 296 P.2d at 1019) and certain other impractical consequences of that rule, such as the erection of booms,

fences, or barriers (*Duval,* 114 So.2d at 795). Moreover, application of the civil law approach promotes rather than hinders the recreational use and enjoyment of lakes. (*Duval,* 114 So.2d at 795; *Johnson,* 257 Minn. at 166–67, 100 N.W.2d at 695.) We conclude that the arguments supporting the civil law rule warrant its adoption in Illinois. Restricting the use of a lake to the water overlying the owner's lake bed property can only frustrate the cooperative and mutually beneficial use of that important resource.

We, therefore, affirm the appellate court's holding that where there are multiple owners of the bed of a private, nonnavigable lake, such owners and their licensees have the right to the reasonable use and enjoyment of the surface waters of the entire lake provided they do not unduly interfere with the reasonable use of the waters by other owners and their licensees.

The question remains, however, whether the plaintiffs' use of the lake, including the renting of boats to members of the general public, is a reasonable one that does not unduly interfere with the reasonable use of the lake by other owners and their licensees. (See Comment, *Public Recreation on Nonnavigable Lakes and the Doctrine of Reasonable Use,* 55 Iowa L.Rev. 1064 (1970); see also Maloney & Plager, *Florida's Lakes: Problems in a Water Paradise,* 13 U.Fla.L.Rev. 1, 69–70 (1960) (discussing public use).) Because that question is not before us and remains for consideration by the trial court in the first instance, we express no view on it now.

Beacham v. Lake Zurich Property Owners Assn., 123 Ill.2d 227, 122 Ill.Dec. 14, 526 N.E.2d 154 (1988).

2. Thompson v. Enz, *redux*. As *Carnahan* and *Beacham* make clear, states follow different approaches as to using the surface of nonnavigable lakes. *Thompson* implicitly followed what the Illinois court in *Beacham* refers to as the civil law rule: each riparian can use the whole of the lake surface, subject to the requirement that the riparian's use level be reasonable. Note that the factual issue on remand in *Thompson* is the same as in *Beacham*. In each case, an owner of a small part of the lake wants to allow numerous other people to make use of her riparian rights. The trial court thus must decide whether this use pattern is too much given all the circumstances.

3. *Shared governance V: why unanimity in lake management?* In *Carnahan*, a clear majority of lakefront property owners apparently desired to restrict the use of motorboats on the relatively small lake. Through negotiations and voluntary agreements they were able to restrict uses of most of the lake but not all of it. Given that uses of the lake are inevitably interconnected, and given that the lake is essentially a single natural resource, not easily divided, should the law make it easier for surrounding landowners to come up with a private management scheme? What about a law authorizing some super-majority of landowners to make rules governing the entire lake that would apply to everyone? What problems might arise with this approach, and could they be minimized? (We'll return to this issue in the final chapter.)

4. *Private condemnation I: use of water surface.* Although the Illinois court in *Beacham* claims that the legal issue it confronted was one of first impression, in fact Illinois had adopted the common law wholesale over a century and a half earlier. With the common law came the rule on using nonnavigable waters. If that is so, the effect of the court's ruling was to allow one lakefront owner to enter upon and make use of the private land of another. Is this a violation of the constitutional ban on the taking of private property without just compensation, given that, according to the United States Supreme Court, any permanent physical invasion of a person's land is a *per se* taking? If this does amount to a taking, does it also run afoul of the ban on takings of property for private use? Is there any conceivable claim that a taking designed to improve recreational lake use by a few families is a public use? (On this issue, see also the next note.)

5. *Right to exclude VII:* Parks v. Cooper. What happens when a body of water expands over a period of years, through unusual rainfall or otherwise, and inundates private land? Does the landowner thereby lose his right to exclude outsiders? The issue reached the Supreme Court of South Dakota in Parks v. Cooper, 676 N.W.2d 823 (S.D. 2004). According to the court, all water within the state was owned by the public and managed by the state to promote public interests pursuant to a public trust. The public trust was not limited to lands beneath navigable waterways nor, in the case of waters, to waters located in navigable waterways. Because land titles were set at the time South Dakota entered the Union, the lands involved in the case remained privately owned. Nonetheless, the waters were subject to public trust limitations, which meant the state had the power and duty to manage them for public use notwithstanding the private rights. It was up to the state legislature and appropriate state agencies in the first instance, the court concluded, to decide how to fulfill these trust duties. In so ruling, the South Dakota court noted that several Western states had reached contrary conclusions, limiting public waterway access under state law to waterways that were navigable when the respective states entered the Union.

6. *Prescriptive easements. Carnahan* provides a good review of the elements of acquiring a resource-use easement by prescription. What are the elements, and in what way does the court alter them in the context of easements for recreational use? Can you anticipate problems in applying this new legal test, which apparently governs recreational but not other claimed easements? What of the hunter or fisher who claims an easement to use a nonnavigable lake? Recreational? Does it make a different whether the hunter of fisher needs the game to eat? What if the boat has been rented from a commercial marina?

7. *Common v. civil law.* The Illinois Supreme Court in *Beacham* embraces a body of reasoning similar to that of Justice Logan in the Onyx Cave cases, arguing that shared ownership by all landowners is better than the common law's fragmented ownership approach. Again, we need to ask: Which is likely to work better when the landowners cannot get along?

Under the common law approach, the landowners have an incentive to get together and come to an agreement about lake use. If they don't, each owner is limited to the small water area above his land. Note that, when landowners do set up a lake management association (as in *Carnahan*), they can prescribe lake use rules that are vastly more precise than the vague "reasonable use" rule applied in *Thompson and Beacham*. Note also another defect of the civil law approach: disputes must be taken to court for resolution, which means lengthy delays, expensive litigation, and unpredictable outcomes. Would it not be better to keep such disputes out of court, turning them over to tribunals of property owners? How complex are the legal and factual issues and would the involvement of lawyers really help? Is this a setting in which the law should seek, not to define private rights precisely, but instead to increase the chance that the affected landowners will come to some negotiated agreement governing use?

8. *Other landowner rights in lake surfaces.* Because riparian landowners have rather full rights to enjoy the waters that flow through or beside their lands, they have often recovered damages for various injuries to their nonconsumptive uses of the waters. E.g., Springer v. Joseph Schlitz Brewing Co., 510 F.2d 468 (4th Cir. 1975) (riparian landowner under North Carolina law can recover for pollution of river by upstream landowners, including an injunction); Lee County v. Kiesel, 705 So.2d 1013 (Fla. App. 1998) (landowner can recover for interference with its unobstructed view of the river caused by construction of the public bridge).

E. THE RIGHT TO CONSUME WATER

The legal issues in the last section on uses of water surfaces, important though they are, pale in significance to disputes that arise over consumptive water uses. What rights do landowners get to consume water, either surface water (in rivers and lakes) or groundwater? In contrast, what consumptive water rights does society allocate as discrete resource rights under some other allocation method—by selling to the highest bidder, for instance, or giving them to the first taker? And when the latter approach is used, what problems arise in the legal attempt to sever water—an ecologically integral component of all life systems—from the rest of the natural order?

STRATTON v. MT. HERMON BOYS' SCHOOL

216 Mass. 83, 103 N.E. 87 (1913).

Rugg, C. J.

The plaintiff, the owner of a mill upon a small stream, sues the defendant, an upper riparian proprietor upon the same stream, for wrongful diversion of water therefrom to his injury. The material facts are that the defendant owns a tract of land through which the stream flows and upon which also is a spring confluent to the stream. Upon this land it has established pumping apparatus whereby it diverts about 60,000 gallons of water each day from the spring and stream to another estate belonging to it and not contiguous to its land adjacent to this stream, but located about a mile away in a different watershed, for the domestic and other uses of a boys' school with dormitories, gymnasium and other buildings and a farm. The number of students increased from

363 in 1908 to 525 in 1911, while the number of teachers, employes and other persons on the estate was over 100. During the latter year there were kept on the farm 103 cattle, 28 horses and 90 swine. There was a swimming pool, laundry, canning factory and electric power plant, for the needs of all of which water was supplied from this source. There was evidence tending to show that this diversion caused a substantial diminution in the volume of water which otherwise in the natural flow of the stream would have come to the plaintiff's land and in the power which otherwise might have been developed upon his wheel by the force of the current.

The defendant requested the court to rule in effect that diversion of water to another nonriparian estate owned by it was not conclusive evidence that the defendant was liable, but that the only question was whether it had taken an unreasonable quantity of water under all the circumstances. This request was denied and the instruction given that the defendant's right was confined to a reasonable use of the water for the benefit of its land adjoining the water course, and of persons properly using such land, and did not extend to taking it for use upon other premises, and that if there was such use the plaintiff was entitled to recover at least nominal damages even though he had sustained no actual loss. The exceptions raise the question as to the soundness of the request and of the instruction given.

The common-law rights and obligations of riparian owners upon streams are not open to doubt. Although the right to flowing water is incident to the title to land, there is no right of property in such water in the sense that it can be the subject of exclusive appropriation and dominion. The only property interest in it is usufructuary. The right of each riparian owner is to have the natural flow of the stream come to his land and to make a reasonable and just use of it as it flows through his land, subject, however, to the like right of each upper proprietor to make a reasonable and just use of the water on its course through his land and subject further to the obligation to lower proprietors to permit the water to pass away from his estate unaffected except by such consequences as follow from reasonable and just use by him. This general principle, simple in statement, often gives rise to difficulties in its application. What is a reasonable and just use of flowing water is dependent upon the state of civilization, the development of the mechanical and engineering art, climatic conditions, the customs of the neighborhood and the other varying circumstances of each case. To some extent often the amount and character of the flow may be modified by such use, for which, even though injurious to other proprietors, no action lies. A stream may be so small that its entire flow may be abstracted by the ordinary domestic uses of a farmer. Its bed may be so steep that its reasonable utilization for the generation of power requires its impounding in numerous reservoirs. But whatever the condition, each riparian owner must conduct his operations reasonably in view of like rights and obligations in the owners above and below him. The right of no one is absolute but is qualified by the existence of the same right in all others similarly situated. The use of the water flowing in a stream is common to all riparian owners and each must exercise this common right so as not essentially to interfere with an equally beneficial enjoyment of the common right by his fellow riparian owners. Such use may result in some diminution, obstruction or change in the natural flow of the stream, but such interference cannot exceed that which arises from reasonable conduct in the light of all circumstances, having due regard to the exercise of the common right by other riparian owners. [citations omitted]

In the main, the use by a riparian owner by virtue of his right as such must be within the watershed of the stream, or at least that the current of the stream shall be returned to its original bed before leaving the land of the user. This is implied in the term 'riparian.' It arises from the natural incidents of running water. A brook or river, so far as concerns surface indications, is inseparably connected with its watershed and owes the volume of current to its area. A definite and fixed channel is a part of the conception of a water course. To divert a substantial portion of its flow is the creation of a new and different channel, which to that extent defeats the reasonable and natural expectations of the owners lower down on the old channel. Abstraction for use elsewhere not only diminishes the flow of the parent stream but also increases that which drains the watershed into which the diversion is made, and may injure thereby riparian rights upon it. Damage thus may be occasioned in a double aspect. The precise point whether riparian rights include diversion in reasonable quantities for a proper use on property outside the watershed has never been decided in this commonwealth. There are numerous decisions in other jurisdictions to the effect that the rights of a riparian proprietor do not extend to uses on land outside the watershed. These were made in cases where actual perceptible damages were wrought by the diversion. [citations omitted]

There are numerous expressions to the effect that the rights of riparian ownership extend only to use upon and in connection with an estate which adjoins the stream and cannot be stretched to include uses reasonable in themselves, but upon and in connection with nonriparian estates. See, for example, Lord Cairns in Swindon Water Works Co. v. Wilts & Berks Canal Navigation Co., L. R. 7 H. L. 697, 704, 705. But see, to the contrary, Gillis v. Chase, 67 N. H. 161, 31 Atl. 18, 68 Am. St. Rep. 645, and Lawrie v. Silsby, 76 Vt. 240, 56 Atl. 1106, 104 Am. St. Rep. 927; s. c., 82 Vt. 505, 74 Atl. 94. These principles, however, are subject to the modification that the diversion, if for a use reasonable in itself, must cause actual perceptible damage to the present or potential enjoyment of the property of the lower riparian proprietor before a cause of action arises in his favor. This was settled after an elaborate discussion by Chief Justice Shaw in Elliot v. Fitchburg R. R., 10 Cush. 191, 57 Am. Dec. 85. That case has been widely cited with approval by courts of many states. The soundness of its reasoning never has been questioned. That was a case where an upper riparian proprietor granted to the defendant railroad corporation a right to erect a dam across a stream and conduct water to its depot not on a riparian estate for use in furnishing their locomotive steam engines with water. The plaintiff, a lower riparian proprietor, was denied the right to recover nominal damages in the absence of proof of actual damages, although the principle was fully recognized that an action would lie for any encroachment upon the substantial rights of the lower owner though causing no present damage. See Anderson v. Cincinnati Southern R. R., 86 Ky. 44, 5 S. W. 49, 9 Am. St. Rep. 263. In reason, there seems to be no distinction between diversion of water from a stream for use in the locomotive engines of a railroad, which of necessity consume the water by evaporation on their journeys without perceptible return to any stream, and the diversion of water for any other legitimate use outside the watershed and upon nonriparian land. Whether such a use for locomotive engines is within the rights of riparian proprietorship has been the subject of somewhat varient conclusions as to the fact of reasonable use. See McCartney v. Londonderry & Lough Swilly Ry. [1904] A. C. 301, Garwood v. N. Y. C. & H. R. R. R., 83 N. Y. 400, 38 Am. Rep. 452, and Penna. R. R. v. Miller, 112 Pa. 34, 3 Atl. 780, where recovery has been allowed in favor of a lower proprietor for such use by an upper one. In these cases, however, there was real and perceivable injury to the lower estate. These decisions, while perhaps containing language hard to reconcile with the discussion in Elliot v. Fitchburg R. R., 10 Cuch. 191, 57 Am. Dec. 85, do not appear to conflict with its conclusion. The question in such a case is not whether the diversion, being for a legitimate use, is in quantity such as is reasonable, having regard to all the circumstances, as it is in cases of districtly riparian uses, but only whether it causes actual damage to the person complaining. Any other conclusion, as is pointed out by Chief Justice Shaw, would lead to the absurd result that every lower riparian proprietor from near the source of a river or any of its confluents to the sea could maintain an action and recover nominal damage for an abstraction and diversion so trifling as to be beyond the possibility of ever causing actual injury....

The governing principle of law in a case like the present is this: A proprietor may make any reasonable use of the water of the stream in connection with his riparian estate and for lawful purposes within the watershed, provided he leave the current diminished by no more than is reasonable, having regard for the like right to enjoy the common property by other riparian owners. If he diverts out of the watershed or upon a disconnected estate the only question is whether there is actual injury to the lower estate for any present or future reasonable use. The diversion alone without evidence of such damage does not warrant a recovery even of nominal damages.

The charge of the court below was not in conformity to this principle. It would have permitted the recovery of nominal damages in any event, quite apart from the possibility of real injury to the plaintiff. But the defendant has suffered no harm by this error. The verdict of the jury was for substantial damages and there was ample evidence to support such a conclusion. Exceptions overruled.

Notes

1. *Place of use.* Under the water law rule of riparian rights, the right to use surface water is an attribute of owning and enjoying land over which or beside which the water flows. The water comes with land, as part of the package, when an owner acquires the land. It thus seems logical that the landowner can only use the water on the riparian tract of land itself, and not elsewhere. Yet such a rule raises obvious questions. What is the riparian tract? Can a landowner expand it by acquiring more adjacent land (yes, nearly all states except California say)? If a riparian tract is divided so that one part no longer touches the water, do the water rights on that portion end (yes)? Also, is it entirely impermissible to use water off a riparian tract, or is the law here more of a liability rule: the water can be used elsewhere so long as the use harms no other lawful water user? How does the court in *Stratton* resolve this last issue? Does its holding adequately protect other riparian owners on the river? Does it take into account the legitimate interests of public users of the waterway?

2. *The watershed limit.* Along with the rule that water be used on the riparian tract is the court's concern in *Stratton* about using water within the watershed. A watershed (or, more aptly, a catchment basin) is an area of land that drains into a single waterway. Watersheds, of course, come in various sizes, with smaller ones often nested within larger ones. This physical reality creates problems when it comes to applying a watershed limit on place of use. What is the relevant watershed? Can a water user in, for instance, Missouri, claim that the watershed rule is impossible to violate since all waters in the state flow into the Mississippi? How should we define watershed for this purpose, taking into account (as we should, no doubt) the reason for the rule? And might our answer depend upon the identity and locations of the disputants in a particular case (that is, might the relevant watershed be determined by the location of the downstream user who is complaining)? In any event, what is the point of the watershed rule and why not just phrase the place of use limit in terms of the riparian tract?

3. *Water law and industrialization.* Note the facts of the principal precedent relied upon in *Stratton,* the opinion of the great Massachusetts jurist Lemuel Shaw in *Elliot v. Fitchburg Railroad.* In that case, a steam railroad needed water to run its boilers. It took on more water at particular stops, and then consumed the water as it chugged down the tracks. Obviously, the water was not consumed on the riparian tract from which it came; it was mostly taken away and used elsewhere. The obvious problem: How was a railroad to get the water it needed in a state with a strict place-of-use rule? (As we'll see, a similar place-of-use rule applies in the case of groundwater.) Could a railroad comply with this rule by arguing that it "used" the riparian water when it put the water into the train boilers, rather than when it turned the water into steam (although in *Elliott* even the train depot was off the riparian tract)?

Strict place-of-use rules governing riparian rights meant that the nation's new water-using industrial activities had to be conducted on riparian tracts and within the watershed. If an industry used the water elsewhere it risked the possibility that its water use would be ended by some other water user who could show actual harm. This was a problem, plainly, for states that wanted to promote industrial development. Somehow, water law needed to change to allow water uses by industries not located on riparian tracts. Many courts did so in the way that Massachusetts did, by authorizing off-tract uses subject to a no-harm rule. This particular shift in water law was one of many ways that nineteenth-century property changed to accommodate industrial growth in America—a trend that for the most part authorized more intensive land and resource uses. The larger story is sketched in J. Willard Hurst, Law and the Conditions of Freedom in the Nineteenth Century United States (1956), 6–7; Morton J. Horwitz, The Transformation of American Law 1780–1860 (1977), 31–62. A perceptive study that pays particular attention to the ways railroads influenced the common law is Howard Schweber, The Creation of the Common Law, 1850–1880: Technology, Politics, and the Construction of Citizenship (2004).

4. *What about the public?* Under the rule of law embraced in *Stratton*, the boys' school can use water in a distant location so long as no downstream riparian is harmed in an actual or likely future water use. Does this mean that the last landowner on a river can drain the river dry because there's no one downstream to complain? And what about members of the public who might use the river for boating or fishing, or who are concerned about its ecological condition? Should harm to their interests in the river allow them to challenge water uses that are off tract or out of the watershed?

If we adhere strictly to the reasoning in *Stratton*, it appears that only riparian landowners have water rights and only holders of such rights can complain about what other water users are doing. The public has little or no role. We've seen otherwise, of course, in cases such as the *Columbia River Fishermen*'s case in chapter 1. But the public's interest at common law came mostly under public nuisance law, not because the public had water rights that it could protect.

PYLE v. GILBERT

245 Ga. 403, 265 S.E.2d 584 (1980).

Hill, Justice.

This is a water rights case involving a non-navigable watercourse. It presents a confrontation between the past and the present. Plaintiffs are the owners of a 140–year-old water-powered gristmill. They emphasize the natural flow theory. Defendants are upper riparians using water to irrigate their farms. They emphasize the reasonable use theory of water rights.

The plaintiffs, Willie and Arlene Gilbert, own property commonly known as Howard's Mill located on Kirkland's Creek, a non-navigable stream in Early County which goes into the Chattahoochee River. They acquired a partial interest in the property in 1974. The other interest was acquired at the same time by their daughter and son-in-law. In 1977, they purchased the other interest and now own the fee. Until August 31, 1978, the Gilberts owned and operated a water-powered gristmill on their property. They also rented boats for profit and permitted fishing and swimming in the 40–acre pond. (On August 31, 1978, the mill was destroyed by fire.)

On July 7, 1978, the Gilberts filed a complaint against Sanford Hill, who is an owner of property that is upper riparian in relation to the Gilbert's property, alleging that since 1975 he has been diverting and using water from Kirkland's Creek for irrigation.... The Gilberts [this] diversion ... as both a nuisance and a trespass and sought injunctive relief as well as actual and punitive damages and attorney fees.... Following discovery, the trial court made an extensive examination of our water law and granted the plaintiffs' motions for summary judgment as to liability against all defendants....

1. Over 100 years ago, when this court first considered riparian rights in Hendrick v. Cook, 4 Ga. 241 (1848), several bedrock principles were established. First, the court firmly rejected the doctrine of appropriation and instead applied riparian principles to the dispute. And in stating the principles of riparian rights, the court also adopted the doctrine of reasonable use. As stated by the court (4 Ga. at 256): "Each proprietor of the land on the banks of the creek, has a natural and equal right to the use of the water which flows therein as it was wont to run, without diminution or alteration. Neither party has the right to use the water in the creek, to the prejudice of the other. The plaintiff cannot divert or diminish the quantity of water which would naturally flow in the stream, so as to prejudice the rights of the defendants, without their consent ... Each riparian proprietor is entitled to a reasonable use of the water, for domestic, agricultural and manufacturing purposes; provided, that in making such use, he does not work a material injury to the other proprietors." (Emphasis supplied.) The court also held that an injury to one's riparian rights gave rise to an action for damages for trespass even in the absence of proof of actual damage.[6]

Subsequently, two statutes were enacted and codified in the Code of 1863. Section 2206 of the Code of 1863 appears today almost verbatim at Code § 85–1301: "Running water, while on land, belongs to the owner of the land, but he has no right to divert it from the usual channel, nor may he so use or adulterate it as to interfere with the enjoyment of it by the next owner." (Emphasis supplied.) (See also Code § 85–1305.) Section 2960 of the Code of 1863 now appears at Code § 105–1407: "The owner of land through which nonnavigable watercourses may flow is entitled to have the water in such streams come to his land in its natural and usual flow, subject only to such detention or diminution as may be caused by a reasonable use of it by other riparian proprietors; and the diverting of the stream, wholly or in part, from the same, or the obstructing thereof so as to impede its course or cause it to overflow or injure his land, or any right appurtenant thereto, or the pollution thereof so as to lessen its value to him, shall be a trespass upon his

6. Whether a per se violation will authorize an injunction where water is in short supply, and the lower riparian is not using it, we do not here decide.

property." (Emphasis supplied.) The words "subject only to such detention or diminution as may be caused by a reasonable use of it by other riparian proprietors" first appear in the Code of 1933, § 105–1407, and appear to have been taken from White v. East Lake Land Co., 96 Ga. 415, 416, 23 S.E. 393 (1895). See also Pool v. Lewis, 41 Ga. 162(1) (1870).

Thus it is clear that under both court decisions and statutes, Georgia's law of riparian rights is a natural flow theory modified by a reasonable use provision. Kates, Georgia Water Law 1969, p. 63 (1969); Agnor, Riparian Rights in Georgia, 18 Ga.B.J. 401, 403 (1956). The reasons for the rule and its contradictory reasonable use provision were well stated by the court in Price v. High Shoals Mfg. Co., 132 Ga. 246, 248–249, 64 S.E. 87, 88 (1909): "Under a proper construction (of the pertinent Code sections), every riparian owner is entitled to a reasonable use of the water in the stream. If the general rule that each riparian owner could not in any way interrupt or diminish the flow of the stream were strictly followed, the water would be of but little practical use to any proprietor, and the enforcement of such rule would deny, rather than grant, the use thereof. Every riparian owner is entitled to a reasonable use of the water. Every such proprietor is also entitled to have the stream pass over his land according to its natural flow, subject to such disturbances, interruptions, and diminutions as may be necessary and unavoidable on account of the reasonable and proper use of it by other riparian proprietors. Riparian proprietors have a common right in the waters of the stream, and the necessities of the business of one can not be the standard of the rights of another, but each is entitled to a reasonable use of the water with respect to the rights of others."

In this case, the trial court found that irrigation with modern equipment was a "diversion" which is entirely prohibited by Georgia law, Code §§ 85–1301, 105–1407, *supra*; *i.e.*, the trial court found that irrigation with modern equipment constituted a trespass as a matter of law. We disagree. The use of water for agricultural purposes was recognized as a reasonable use along with domestic use in the first reported Georgia case on riparian rights. Hendrick v. Cook, supra. . . .

The first question, then, is whether the use of water for irrigation is a diversion under our laws and thus is prohibited. We find that it is not. . . . In prohibiting "diversion", Code §§ 85–1301, 105–1407, we do not find that the General Assembly intended to prevent the use of riparian water for irrigation, even though irrigation is accomplished by removing water from its natural watercourse. Rather we think the General Assembly intended to prohibit the diversion of water from a watercourse for other purposes, such as to drain one's own property (see Goodrich v. Ga. R. & Bkg. Co., 115 Ga. 340, 41 S.E. 659 (1902)) or to create a new watercourse on the diverter's property (see McNabb v. Houser, 171 Ga. 744, 156 S.E. 595 (1930)). That this latter use would have been of some concern to the General Assembly is evidenced by the adoption of the natural flow theory, which recognizes that the mere presence of a watercourse on one's property generally enhances it. Rest. Torts 2d, Chapter 41, Topic 3, Introductory Note, p. 212.

Finally, Georgia's Water Quality Control Act (Ga.L.1977, p. 368) exempts farm uses, including irrigation, from its permit requirements. Code Ann. § 17–510.1. This, we think, is a legislative recognition that irrigation is not a prohibited "diversion" but is rather a permitted use where it is reasonable. See Code Ann. § 17–517. Hence we find that irrigation is not per se a diversion of water prohibited by law.

In sum, we find that the right of the lower riparian to receive the natural flow of the water without diversion or diminution is subject to the right of the upper riparian to its reasonable use (Rome R. Co. v. Loeb, 141 Ga. 202, 206, 80 S.E. 785 (1913)), for agricultural purposes, including irrigation. . . .

3. In its detailed analysis of Georgia water law, the trial court had to apply Hendrix v. Roberts Marble Co., 175 Ga. 389, 394, 165 S.E. 223, 226 (1932), to the effect that " . . . riparian rights are appurtenant only to lands which actually touch on the watercourse, or through which it flows, and that a riparian owner or proprietor can not himself lawfully use or convey to another the right to use water flowing along or through his property . . . " Thus Hendrix held water could only be used on riparian lands.[7] Yet four years later, in reversing the denial of an injunction against the use of water on non-riparian land, the court did not rely heavily on Hendrix, *supra*. Instead the court (Russell, C. J., writing the opinion in both cases) based its decision more on general riparian water law principles than on the non-riparian use. Robertson v. Arnold, 182 Ga. 664, 671, 186 S.E. 806 (1936). To the extent that Robertson v. Arnold might reflect ambivalence as to the rule announced in Hendrix, that concern is well-founded.

Not a good rule

A major study of Georgia water law concluded that "Another disadvantage of this doctrine is that it permits the use of stream water only in connection with riparian land." Institute of Law and Government, University of Georgia Law School, A Study of the Riparian and Prior Appropriation Doctrines of Water Law (1955), p. 104. Likewise, the American Law Institute now recommends allowing use of water by riparian owners on non-riparian land, Rest. Torts 2d § 855, as well as allowing non-riparian owners to acquire a right to use water from riparian owners. Id., § 856(2), (see also 7 Clark, Waters and Water Rights 71–72, § 614.1 (1976)). The Restatement relies on two principles: that riparian rights are property rights and as such could normally be transferred, and that water law should be utilitarian and allow the best use of the water. Id., Comment b. Also, the Institute considers the acquisition of water rights by condemnation a "grant of riparian right." Id., comment c. . . .

—property right (should be transferred)
—utilitarian (should be used)

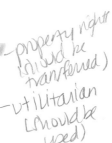

7. It should be noted that the use of water in steam locomotives was a non-riparian use of that water unless the railroad right of way was considered riparian land wherever it went. See, for example, Goodrich v. Ga. R. & Bkg. Co., supra, where such use apparently was approved.

can use on non-riparian land

can be acquired by grant

We agree with the American Law Institute that the right to use water on non-riparian land should be permitted and if that right can be acquired by condemnation, it can also be acquired by grant. Thus we find that the right to the reasonable use of water in a non-navigable watercourse on non-riparian land can be acquired by grant from a riparian owner. The contrary conclusion in Hendrix v. Roberts Marble Co., supra, will not be followed

Judgment reversed.

Notes

1. *From natural flow to reasonable use.* In its original form, riparian rights allowed landowners to make only modest uses of water. They could use it for "domestic purposes"—household drinking and watering barnyard animals. All other uses were subject to the strict-sounding limit that the use cause no alteration of the water's natural flow, either in terms of quantity or quality, at least if the alteration would harm anyone downstream. The rule was stated in an early, influential New Jersey decision, Merritt v. Parker, 1 N.J.L. 460, 1 Coxe 460 (N.J. 1795):

> In general, it may be observed, when a man purchases a piece of land, through which a natural water-course flows, he has a right to make use of it in its natural state, but not to stop or divert it to the prejudice of another. *Aqua currit, et debet currere*, [more fully, *aqua currit et debet currere ut currere solebat*: water runs and ought to run as it is wont to run] is the language of the law. The water flows in its natural channel, and ought always to be permitted to run there, so that all, through whose land it pursues its natural course, may continue to enjoy the privilege of using it for their own purposes. It cannot legally be diverted from its course without the consent of all who have an interest in it. If it should be turned into another channel, or stopped, and this illegal step should be persisted in, I should think a jury right in giving almost any valuation which the party thus injured should think proper to affix to it. This principle lies at the bottom of all the cases which I have met with, and it is so perfectly reasonable in itself, and at the same time so firmly settled as a doctrine of the land, that it should never be abandoned or departed from.

This rule was well-designed to protect family homesteads and other agrarian uses. It protected fish and other aquatic life, and thus the many people whose livelihoods depended upon them. And it embodied the then-strong belief that the key element of private property was the right to halt any interferences with what one was doing; it was not any right to engage in intensive uses of the thing owned, despite harms imposed on others. The natural-flow rule, though, stood as a serious obstacle in the path of industrial development—much as the place-of-use rule did in *Elliot* and *Stratton*. How was a riparian landowner to construct a dam and water wheel to create waterpower to run a new textile mill? And what about the pollution that the textile mill inevitably caused? Could a downstream landowner go to court and get the mill shut down, regardless of economics and community benefit?

The legal answer appeared to be yes—and, given the times, it was the wrong answer politically and culturally.

Disliking this anti-industry answer, courts and other lawmakers got to work, changing the law fundamentally (despite the New Jersey court's wish that the rule "never be abandoned or departed from"). In their usual, conservative writing style courts continued to repeat the natural flow language—each landowner was entitled to it. But slipped in was a major qualification: an owner's right to the natural flow was now subject to the right of upstream owners to make "reasonable use" of the water, even when that use altered the natural flow in quantity or quality. The effect of this shift was potentially profound. Landowners could now use the water more intensively, but as a result they lost much of their legal right to complain when other users caused them harm. The legal shift, that is, did not expand (or contract) property rights overall. Instead, it reconfigured landowner rights, increasing one stick in the bundle of rights (the right to use intensively) while pruning another stick (the right to protection against interferences). This same shift—to allow more intensive resource uses, at the expense of protections against harm—happened in many areas of natural resource law in the nineteenth century.

2. *Place of use in Georgia*. How does *Pyle v. Gilbert* compare with *Thompson v. Enz* and *Stratton* in terms of the riparian landowner's ability to use water off the riparian tract and outside the watershed? (Hint: quite a bit.) What does the court here say about severing water rights from the land for sale as separate resources? If we freely allow uses of water away from riparian tracts, subject only to the reasonable use limit, how successful will the law be in avoiding overuse of the river? Also, if water can be used anywhere, subject only to a reasonable use limit, why then do we retain the allocation rule that allows only riparians to withdraw water? Why not say that anyone with access to a water body can make reasonable use of it? Why is it that riparian landowners should get ownership of all the surface water rights if their water right is not directly linked to and limited by the use of their lands?

A final question to consider as you probe *Pyle v. Gilbert*: Did the court interpret the various state statutes fairly? If not, why not? Might the court have given the statutes less deference because they were enacted in 1863 and displayed a certain anti-Yankee, anti-industrial slant?

COFFIN v. THE LEFT HAND DITCH COMPANY

6 Colo. 443 (1882).

HELM, J.

Appellee, who was plaintiff below, claimed to be the owner of certain water by virtue of an appropriation thereof from the south fork of the St. Vrain creek. It appears that such water, after its diversion, is carried by means of a ditch to the James creek, and thence along the bed of the same to Left Hand creek, where it is again diverted by lateral ditches and used to irrigate lands adjacent to the last named stream. Appellants are the owners of lands lying on the margin and in the neighborhood of the St. Vrain below the mouth of said south fork thereof, and naturally irrigated therefrom.

In 1879 there was not a sufficient quantity of water in the St. Vrain to supply the ditch of appellee and also irrigate the said lands of appellant. A portion of appellee's dam was torn out, and its diversion of water thereby seriously interfered with by appellants. The action is brought for damages arising from the trespass, and for injunctive relief to prevent repetitions thereof in the future....

[The defendants-appellants argued on various grounds that they had superior rights to use this water, and that they therefore did not act wrongly when they used self-help to halt an unlawful interference with the water flowing to them. Their principal arguments were that they had superior rights as riparian water users, and that the plaintiff-appellee's water use was wrongful because it diverted the water outside the watershed of origin for use elsewhere (here, diverting it from St. Vrain creek to James creek and then to Left Hand creek. The trial court and then the Supreme Court rejected the appellants' arguments. In doing so the court surveyed the law of surface water in Colorado):]

It is contended by counsel for appellants that the common law principles of riparian proprietorship prevailed in Colorado until 1876, and that the doctrine of priority of right to water by priority of appropriation thereof was first recognized and adopted in the constitution. But we think the latter doctrine has existed from the date of the earliest appropriations of water within the boundaries of the state. The climate is dry, and the soil, when moistened only by the usual rainfall, is arid and unproductive; except in a few favored sections, artificial irrigation for agriculture is an absolute necessity. Water in the various streams thus acquires a value unknown in moister climates. Instead of being a mere incident to the soil, it rises, when appropriated, to the dignity of a distinct usufructuary estate, or right of property. It has always been the policy of the national, as well as the territorial and state governments, to encourage the diversion and use of water in this country for agriculture; and vast expenditures of time and money have been made in reclaiming and fertilizing by irrigation portions of our unproductive territory. Houses have been built, and permanent improvements made; the soil has been cultivated, and thousands of acres have been rendered immensely valuable, with the understanding that appropriations of water would be protected. Deny the doctrine of priority or superiority of right by priority of appropriation, and a great part of the value of all this property is at once destroyed.

The right to water in this country, by priority of appropriation thereof, we think it is, and has always been, the duty of the national and state governments to protect. The right itself, and the obligation to protect it, existed prior to legislation on the subject of irrigation. It is entitled to protection as well after patent to a third party of the land over which the natural stream flows, as when such land is a part of the public domain; and it is immaterial whether or not it be mentioned in the patent and expressly excluded from the grant.

The act of congress protecting in patents such right in water appropriated, when recognized by local customs and laws, 'was rather a voluntary recognition of a pre-existing right of possession, constituting a valid claim to its continued use, than the establishment of a new one.' Broder v. Notoma W. & M. Co. 11 Otto, 274.

We conclude, then, that the common law doctrine giving the riparian owner a right to the flow of water in its natural channel upon and over his lands, even though he makes no beneficial use thereof, is inapplicable to Colorado. Imperative necessity, unknown to the countries which gave it birth, compels the recognition of another doctrine in conflict therewith. And we hold that, in the absence of express statutes to the contrary, the first appropriator of water from a natural stream for a beneficial purpose has, with the qualifications contained in the constitution, a prior right thereto, to the extent of such appropriation. See Schilling v. Rominger, 4 Col. 103. . . .

It is urged, however, that even if the doctrine of priority or superiority of right by priority of appropriation be conceded, appellee in this case is not benefited thereby. Appellants claim that they have a better right to the water because their lands lie along the margin and in the neighborhood of the St. Vrain. They assert that, as against them, appellee's diversion of said water to irrigate lands adjacent to Left Hand creek, though prior in time, is unlawful.

In the absence of legislation to the contrary, we think that the right to water acquired by priority of appropriation thereof is not in any way dependent upon the locus of its application to the beneficial use designed. And the disastrous consequences of our adoption of the rule contended for, forbid our giving such a construction to the statutes as will concede the same, if they will properly bear a more reasonable and equitable one.

The doctrine of priority of right by priority of appropriation for agriculture is evoked, as we have seen, by the imperative necessity for artificial irrigation of the soil. And it would be an ungenerous and inequitable rule that would deprive one of its benefit simply because he has, by large expenditure of time and money, carried the water from one stream over an intervening watershed and cultivated land in the valley of another. It might be utterly impossible, owing to the topography of the country, to get water upon his farm from the adjacent stream; or if possible, it might be impracticable on account of the distance from the point where the diversion must take place and the attendant expense; or the quantity of water in such stream might be entirely insufficient to supply his wants. It sometimes happens that the most fertile soil is found along the margin or in the neighborhood of the small rivulet, and sandy and barren land beside the larger stream. To apply the rule contended for would prevent the useful and profitable cultivation of the productive soil, and sanction the waste of water upon the more sterile lands. . . .

Affirmed

Notes

1. *Dividing water from land by law I. Coffin v. Left Hand Ditch* was a milestone in natural resources law. The effect of the ruling was to sever water from the land and make it available as a discrete resource. For various reasons, practical and political, the court decided that water law needed to change. By changing the law, the court changed the bundle of rights that landowners obtained. As it engaged in this lawmaking the court contended—as courts are often prone to do—that it was merely applying the law that already existed, but we should not be misled. Like other states, Colorado adopted the common law in full not later than when it entered the Union, riparian rights included. The effect of shifting to prior appropriation was to strip riparian landowners of their water rights—an extraordinary change in an arid land, and one that courts in other jurisdictions (California included) would later view as an unconstitutional interference with private rights.

discrete resource

2. *Why the change?* What prompted the court to decide that riparian rights were ill-suited to circumstances in Colorado? We need to read the case carefully to answer this question, but we can easily surmise the problems simply based upon *Stratton* and *Pyle*. The riparian rights place-of-use limit was apparently a huge problem in both of its forms—its limit to the riparian tract and to the watershed of origin. Also a problem was the requirement to protect a river's natural flow (although this limitation had largely faded by the time of *Coffin*). In too many rivers in the West, one or a few users could drain a waterway dry, the biggest of disruptions of a river's natural flow. It just made little sense in an arid region, especially a booming mining region, to require water users to maintain the natural flow. And so, the Colorado court discarded riparian rights as the governing legal rule. Might the court have done otherwise—maintaining riparian rights—if the riparian rights law that then prevailed had looked something like the more flexible version applied a century later in *Pyle*? Could Colorado, in other words, have dealt with its perceived water problems by modifying riparian rights—allowing more intensive water uses and relaxing the place-of-use limits—rather than abandoning the doctrine wholesale?

In a provocative study of the origins of prior appropriation in Colorado, David B. Schorr argues that courts were motivated by a desire to make resources freely available to ordinary citizens as a way to ensure the wide distribution of property. He links this mentality to the nation's longstanding agrarian traditions. David B. Schorr, *Appropriation as Agrarianism: Distributive Justice in the Creation of Property Rights*, 32 Ecol. L. Q. 3 (2005). Prior appropriation, as earlier noted, began life in California as a way of allocating water rights on federally owned land, a setting in which neither claimant possessed riparian rights. A few years after *Coffin* the California Supreme Court was urged in a major case to abandon riparian rights and shift entirely to prior appropriation, as Colorado had done. The California court rejected the idea (in Lux v. Haggin, 69 Cal. 255, 10 P. 674 (1886), to this day the court's longest decision), thereby retaining riparian rights and making them superior in claim to all prior appropriation rights, regardless of date of original appropriation. The result was a form of legal and economic confusion that lingers to this day. We return to this issue below.

3. *At what cost?* The facts of *Coffin* point out the need for greater legal flexibility in water use than the riparian rights doctrine originally allowed. Change of some sort was plainly required to accommodate social needs. But what costs were involved in the shift from riparian rights to prior appropriation? On this question, consider the effects of transporting water for use miles from the source and outside the watershed. What effects might long-distance water transport have on the ecological functioning and biodiversity of the various waterways involved? Consider also the efficiency of such transport. How much water would be lost along the way? Note that the competing water users in *Coffin* were both irrigators growing crops. As applied here, the first-in-time rule gave the water to the irrigator located far distant from the river (The Left Hand Ditch Co.), instead of to the irrigator who was located along the banks of St. Vrain creek itself. How sensible is this water use pattern? And what if half of the water diverted from the St. Vrain was lost transporting the water to the distant, first-in-time irrigation project? Should this inefficiency not be relevant in deciding who gets the water?

4. *What water?* By severing property rights in water from the land, the Colorado Supreme Court created for itself various legal problems that did not exist under riparian rights. One problem, which the court would be forced to consider repeatedly over the decades, was the need to divide up the hydrologic system. Water, of course, moves in circular flows, beginning as rain, flowing over or percolating through the ground, perhaps reaching the sea but in any event returning through evaporation and transpiration to the sky. When a drop of rain hits the ground, at what point does it enter the river system so that it becomes subject to the first-in-time rule? Surely if the rain is immediately soaked up by plants on a person's land, the landowner has done nothing wrong. But can the landowner also collect rainwater in a cistern and use it, on the theory that he is using rainwater, not water taken from a river? And what about water that flows out of a natural spring on the land? Is this water part of the land, on the theory that it is not yet river water, or is it instead subject to the superior rights of some downstream appropriator the moment it comes from the ground? The possible conflicts are almost countless in terms of their factual permutations, as the following decision illustrates:

SOUTHEASTERN COLORADO WATER CONSERVANCY DISTRICT v. SHELTON FARMS, INC.

187 Colo. 181, 529 P.2d 1321 (1974).

DAY, JUSTICE.

This is an appeal from two judgments and decrees awarding appellees Shelton Farms and Colorado–New Mexico Land Company ("the Company") water rights free from the call of any and all senior decreed water rights on the Arkansas River.

This case, so far as we are advised, is of first impression in the United States, dealing with whether the killing of water-using vegetation and the filling of a marshy area to prevent evaporation can produce a superior water right for the amount of water not transpired or evaporated. The Pueblo district court held it could, and granted both Shelton and the Company such a water right. . . .

Question

I

To comprehend the importance of this lawsuit, it is necessary to understand the Arkansas River and its tributaries.

In 1863 there were virtually no "water-loving" trees along the banks of the river. Their growth was prevented when the great roaming buffalo herds ate the saplings, and the native Indians used most of the timber. In the next 40 years both the buffalo and the Indians were decimated. Phreatophytes (water consuming plants) and cottonwood began to appear along the Arkansas. After the great Pueblo flood of 1921 the river bottom became thickly infested with tamarisk or salt cedar, a highly phreatophytic growth.

Since 1863 all surface flow of the river has been put to beneficial use, until today the Arkansas is greatly over-appropriated. There is not enough flow to satisfy decreed water rights. The phreatophytes have hindered the situation, for they have consumed large quantities of subsurface water which would otherwise have flowed in the stream and been available for decreed use.

In 1940, appellee Shelton bought 500 acres of land on the Arkansas River. Since then, he has cleared two land areas of phreatophytes, and filled in a third marshy area. Shelton claimed he had saved approximately 442 acre-feet of water per year, previously consumed by phreatophytes or lost to evaporation, which is now available for beneficial use. Shelton had 8 previously decreed wells. He asked for the right to augment his previous water rights with the salvaged water, to use during those times when pumping is curtailed by the State Engineer.

asked to augment water rights w/ this new salvaged water

The objectors Southeastern Water Conservancy District, and others, moved to dismiss the augmentation application. The motion was denied and trial was held. The lower court awarded Shelton 181.72 acre-feet of water, free from the call of the river. The lower court analogized to the law of accretion, stating that the capture and use by another of water which ordinarily would be lost is not detrimental to prior holders. The decree contained a comprehensive series of safeguards to protect the prior vested interests. In an amendment to the decree, the trial court held that although 1971 Perm.Supp., C.R.S.1963, 148–21–22 requires that later water rights adjudicated should be junior to prior decreed water rights, the provision did not apply in this case.

Trial ct

Appellee Colorado–New Mexico Land Co., Inc., received a similar award of 181 acre-feet of water, not to exceed 161 acre-feet in any one year, free from the call of the river. . . .

II

The fact in each case are not disputed. Before this Court is totally a question of law. The issue can be stated very simply: May one who cuts down water-consuming vegetation obtain a decree for an equivalent amount of water for his own beneficial use free from the call of the river?

Appellees state that the Water Right Determination and Administration Act ("the Act"), 1969 Perm.Supp., C.R.S.1963, 148–21–1 et seq., permits augmentation or substitution of water captured. Those are flexible terms. Thus, appellees feel that the source of water so provided—whether developed or salvaged—is immaterial, so long as prior vested rights are not injured. They insist that but for their actions the salvaged water would have been available to no one, so now they may receive a water right free from the call of prior appropriators, who are in no way harmed. Appellees conclude that their actions provide maximum utilization of water, protect vested rights, and encourage conservation and waste reduction in the water-scarce Arkansas River Valley.

Also appearing here is the Colorado Water Protection and Development Association, which has filed an amicus brief in support of both judgments below. The Association is presently developing and implementing a plan for augmentation, similar to Shelton's to permit its member wells to continue pumping, allegedly without injury to vested senior rights on the river.

The objectors assert that the lower court's resolution of the issue does violence to Colorado's firm appropriation doctrine of "first in time—first in right" on which the priority of previous decrees is bottomed. They point out that the existing case law in Colorado, which was not changed by statute, limits the doctrine of "free from call" to waters which are Truly developed and were never part of the river system. They argue that appellees' claims were not for developed water, and thus must come under the mandates of the priority system. Furthermore, a priority date free from the call of the river will impinge the entire scheme of adjudication of water decrees as required by the Act.

There is no legal precedent squarely in point for either denying or approving these claims. The answer requires consideration of judicial precedent relating to "developed" and "salvaged" water, as well as consideration of the provisions of the Water Act. Also squarely before us is the equally serious question of whether the granting of such an unique water right will encourage denuding river banks everywhere of trees and shrubs which, like the vegetation destroyed in these cases, also consume the river water.

III

We first consider existing case law. There is no question that one who merely clears out a channel, lines it with concrete or otherwise hastens the flow of water, without adding to the existing water, is not entitled to a decree therefor. [citations omitted]

It is equally true and well established in Colorado that one who adds to an existing water supply is entitled to a decree affirming the use of such water. Strong evidence is required to prove the addition of the water. Leadville Mine Development Co., Supra. There are three important situations, analogous to this case, when these rare decrees have been granted. The first is when one physically transports water from another source, as when the Water Conservancy District transported water from the Frying Pan River basin to the Arkansas River. The second is when one properly captures and stores flood waters. The third is when one finds water within the system, which would never have normally reached the river or its tributaries. An example is trapped water artificially produced by draining a mine. Ripley v. Park Center Land and Water Co., 40 Colo. 129, 90 P. 75 (1907). Another example is trapped water in an independent saucepan-type formation composed of impervious shale which prevents the water from escaping. Pikes Peak v. Kuiper, 169 Colo. 309, 455 P.2d 882 (1969).

A thorough research by all parties, including the amicus, shows no Colorado case where a person has been granted a water right free from the call of the river for water which has always been tributary to a stream. If it is shown that the water would ultimately return to the river, it is said to be part and parcel thereof, and senior consumers are entitled to use it according to their decreed priorities. Even the Pikes Peak case, supra, relied on heavily by appellees, states that "... it is clear that this 240 acre feet of water Never was part of any natural stream...." (Emphasis added.)

Thus, this case law draws a distinction between "developed" and "salvaged" water. Both terms are words of art. Developed implies new waters not previously part of the river system. These waters are free from the river call, and are not junior to prior decrees. Salvaged water implies waters in the river or its tributaries (including the aquifer) which ordinarily would go to waste, but somehow are made available for beneficial use. Salvaged waters are subject to call by prior appropriators. We cannot airily waive aside the traditional language of the river, and draw no distinctions between developed and salvaged water. To do so would be to wreak havoc with our water law. Those terms, and others, evolved specifically to tread softly in this state where water is so precious.

The roots of phreatophytes are like a pump. The trees, which did not have to go to court or seek any right, merely "sucked up" the water from prior appropriators. Appellees now take the water from the trees. Therefore, appellees also are continuing to take from the appropriators, but seek a court decree to approve it. They added nothing new; what was there was merely released and put to a different use. To grant appellees an unconditional water right therefor would be a windfall which cannot be allowed, for thirsty men cannot step into the shoes of a "water thief" (the phreatophytes.) Senior appropriators were powerless to move on the land of others and destroy the "thief"—the trees and phreatophytes—before they took firm root. They are helpless now to move in and destroy them to fulfill their own decrees. The property (the water) must return from whence it comes—the river—and thereon down the line to those the river feeds in turn.

Water returns to river (slt sr. users)

IV

Each appellee decree was assigned an historical priority date. However, each decree was nevertheless to be free from the call of the river. In other words, despite a paper date the decree was to be outside the priority system, in derogation of the "first in time—first in right" water theory normally followed in Colorado.

Appellees argue that there is no injury to prior appropriators by this unusual practice. They assert that the water was unavailable for use anyway, so to grant it to another harms no one, yet benefits the policies of maximum utilization and beneficial conservation. Objectors counter that any decree so granted would found a new system of "last in time—first in right," and make administration of the priority system of the Act impossible.

Appellees would substitute the priority doctrine with a lack of injury doctrine. In Fellhauer v. People, supra, we spoke of the future of water law:

' * * * It is implicit * * * that, along with vested rights, there shall be maximum utilization of the water of this state. As administration of water approaches its second century the curtain is opening upon the new drama of maximum utilization and how constitutionally that doctrine can be integrated into the law of Vested rights. We have known for a long time that the doctrine was lurking in the backstage shadows as a result of the accepted, though oft violated, principle that the right to water does not give the right to waste it.' (Emphasis original.)

The Colorado legislature responded to the Fellhauer decision and its twin mandates of protecting vested rights and achieving maximum utilization by enacting various amendments to the 1963 Water Right Determination and Administration Act. 1969 Perm.Supp., C.R.S.1963, 148—21—2(1) is a declaration of policy that all waters in Colorado have been

' * * * declared to be the property of the public, * * *. As incident thereto, it shall be the policy of this state to integrate the appropriation, use and administration of underground water tributary to a stream with the use of surface water, in such a way as to maximize the beneficial use of all of the waters of this state.'

Section 148—21—2(2) further states that

'(a) * * * it is hereby declared to be the further policy of the state of Colorado that in the determination of water rights, uses and administration of water the following principles shall apply:

'(b) Water rights and uses heretofore vested in any person by virtue of previous or existing laws, including an appropriation from a well, Shall be protected subject to the provisions of this article.

'(c) The existing use of ground water, either independently or in conjunction with surface rights, shall be recognized to the fullest extent possible, Subject to the preservation of other existing vested rights. * * *

We do not read into the enactment of the Post–Fellhauer amendments carte blanche authority to substitute water consumption and raise it to a preferential right.

Beyond question, the Arkansas River is over-appropriated. Water promised has not been water delivered, for there is simply not enough to go around. Thus, the question is not whether prior appropriators are injured today by appellees' actions. The injury occurred long ago, when the water-consuming trees robbed consumers of water which would have naturally flowed for their use. The harm was real and enormous. The logical implication of the injury standard is that until senior consumers have been saturated to fulfillment, any displacement of water from the time and place of their need is harmful to them.

Perhaps most important is the mandate of 1971 Perm.Supp., C.R.S. 1963, 148—21—22. This sets up the priority system of 'first in time—first in right' in Colorado:

'* * * the priority date awarded for water rights * * * adjudged and decreed on applications for a determination of the amount and priority thereof * * * during each calendar year shall establish the relative priority among other water rights * * * awarded on such applications filed in that calendar year; But such water rights * * * shall be junior to all water rights * * * awarded on such applications filed in any previous calendar year * * *.' (Emphasis added.)

This section cannot be ignored, as it is part of the same overall Act. There is nothing in the plain language of the statute to exempt appellees' plans from the priority date system. Thus, we hold that all water decrees of any kind are bound to the call of the river, subject to any specific exemptions found within the law. To hold any other way would be to weaken the priority system, and create a super class of water rights never before in existence.

We arrive at the instant decision with reluctance, as we are loathe to stifle creativity in finding new water supplies, and do wish not to discourage maximized beneficial use of Colorado's water. But there are questions of policy to consider. If new waters can be had by appellees' method, without legislative supervision, there will be perhaps thousands of such super decrees on all the rivers of the state. S. E. Reynolds, State Engineer of New Mexico for many years, pointed out the dangers inherent in this procedure:

'* * * If one ignores the technical difficulty of determining the amount of water salvaged, this proposal, at first blush, might seem reasonable and in the interest of the best use of water and related land resources.

* * *

'On closer scrutiny, it appears that if the water supply of prior existing rights is lost to encroaching phreatophytes and then taken by individuals eradicating the plants the result would be chaos. The doctrine of prior appropriation as we know it would fall—the phreatophytes and then the individual salvaging water would have the best right. Furthermore, if individuals salvaging public water lost to encroaching phreatophytes were permitted to create new water rights where there is no new water, the price of salt cedar jungles would rise sharply. And we could expect to see a thriving, if clandestine, business in salt cedar seed and phreatophyte cultivation.'

If these decrees were affirmed, the use of a power saw or a bulldozer would generate a better water right than the earliest ditch on the river. The planting and harvesting of trees to create water rights superior to the oldest decrees on the Arkansas would result in a harvest of pandemonium. Furthermore, one must be concerned that once all plant life disappears, the soil on the banks of the river will slip away, causing irreparable erosion. . . .

We believe that in this situation unrestrained self-help to a previously untapped water supply would result in a barren wasteland. While we admire the industry and ingenuity of appellees, we cannot condone the removal of water on an ad hoc, farm by farm basis. The withdrawal of water must be orderly, and to be orderly it must come under the priority system. . . .

Judgments reversed and cause remanded to the trial court with directions to vacate the decrees.

GROVES, JUSTICE (specially concurring):

At the conclusion of oral argument I was convinced that I should dissent. I was shocked by the thought that the water emanating through the phreatophytes is being evaporated into the air, robbing decreed rights and being lost to Colorado water users. While I knew that the remedies are properly for the legislature, it then seemed to me that, since the legislature has not acted and has thus permitted this intolerable situation to continue, the judiciary should do what it could.

However, I find myself swayed by Justice Day's opinion, and I am deterred from dissenting. I concur specially for the reason that it preserves the status quo in order to allow the state further time to attempt to rectify an alarming situation. It may pass enabling legislation for the creation of districts, as suggested in the opinion, or conclude to take some other approach. It is earnestly to be hoped that the General Assembly can provide a solution so that this water, now being lost in such large quantities to the phreatophytes may be brought under reasonable control.

Notes

1. *The call of the river.* For water lawyers, the "call of the river" means something quite different from what it meant to Huckleberry Finn. The first-in-time system can work only if an earlier water user who is short of water can look upstream and demand that lower priority water users halt their uses, to the extent physically necessary for the senior water user to get water. (As we'll see in a later chapter, this legal arrangement can be quite inefficient if substantial water is lost getting the water down river to the senior user.) The demands of senior users form the river's call. When water in a river is fully appropriated, someone who wants to use water either needs to acquire it from an existing user or find water that is not yet subject to the river's call, leading to litigation such as this one.

2. *Salvaged water versus developed water.* Note the court's distinction between efforts landowners make to save water from loss (as by lining irrigation ditches) and efforts that actually add new water to a river system (as by importing water from another river system or finding water that would never make it to the river). Is this distinction adequate to resolve all controversies? You should pay particular attention to the examples that the court gives of developed water; this list is nearly exhaustive, rather than illustrative.

3. *Ecological considerations.* One concern motivating the court's holding was its worry about encouraging landowners to destroy streamside vegetation. Such vegetation plays critical ecological roles in riparian ecosystems, sometimes providing habitat for endangered species. According to the majority, both water and land are important and "the elements of water and land must be used in harmony to the maximum *feasible* use of both." If we took this idea seriously, how might it influence the ways we define "permissible" water uses? Traditionally (as we'll see), the beneficial nature of a water use was determined in the abstract, based on the type of use (for irrigation, industry, drinking) with only minimal concerns about water-use efficiency and essentially no concern at all about the ecological disruption of diverting and consuming the water. As for the trees themselves, should the law take into account whether the trees are "native" to the region—that is, whether they existed there when buffalo roamed freely—or is it enough to note their high-valued roles in the altered riparian ecosystems of today?

4. *Dividing water from land by law II.* Aside from the above points, Shelton Farms is a vivid illustration of the problems that arise whenever lawmakers decide to sever one natural "resource" from the land and allocate it separately to someone besides the landowner. No matter what the natural resource, practical problems arise drawing the line between the rights of the landowner and the rights of the owner of the discrete resource. Nature does not come in neat bundles; one valuable resource is ecologically connected to everything around it. Water lawyers for decades have complained about the law's tendency to come up with different rules governing surface water and ground water, as if the hydrological cycle did not exist. The same issue comes up in other settings, for nature's parts are inevitably interdependent. *Shelton Farms* reminds us that plants soak up water. Water is also lost to evaporation and seepage. At the same time, shade trees along rivers can keep

water temperatures down, aiding aquatic life and reducing evaporation. One way, then, to think about *Shelton Farms*—and the reason why it is placed in this chapter, dealing with rights to land—is as a case that articulates the rights of landowners to water on their lands, even in a prior appropriation jurisdiction. According to the court, for instance, a landowner who "finds" water not part of a river system gets to keep it, just as the landowner can usually capture rainfall and keep it. To see this dividing line—between the rights of the landowner and the rights of the owner of the discrete resource—is to identify one of the main functions of natural resources law: it draws this vital line, clarifying the rights of the resource owner and thereby specifying the limits on what a landowner owns.

5. *Water on federal land.* Although Colorado is often credited with establishing the first true prior-appropriation approach to water law, the first-in-time method of water allocation arose in California, as explained in the notes after *Hicks v. Bell*. In California and elsewhere, first-in-time was often used initially to resolve disputes among water users on federal lands, none of whom owned the riparian land. Just as the federal government stood aside on mining issues, allowing state courts to develop laws governing mining on federal lands, it also stood aside on water issues, allowing states to allocate water on federal lands as they saw fit. Many states turned to prior appropriation; others stuck with riparian rights. The federal government's silence, however, could end at any time. Congress clearly has the power to decide for itself how water on federal lands will be used. It need not defer indefinitely to state water law.

So long as the federal government intended to turn its land over to private owners it had little concern about water rights. That inattention changed when the government decided to retain certain lands and devote them to distinct federal uses, many of which required water. In the parts of the country where states allocated water to riparian landowners the federal government possessed water as a riparian owner. But what about in states that embraced prior appropriation? Did the federal government have to appropriate water under state law in order to gain water rights?

UNITED STATES v. NEW MEXICO

438 U.S. 696, 98 S.Ct. 3012, 57 L.Ed.2d 1052 (1978).

JUSTICE REHNQUIST:

The Rio Mimbres rises in the southwestern highlands of New Mexico and flows generally southward, finally disappearing in a desert sink just north of the Mexican border. The river originates in the upper reaches of the Gila National Forest, but during its course it winds more than 50 miles past privately owned lands and provides substantial water for both irrigation and mining. In 1970, a stream adjudication[8] was

8. [Ed.: A stream (or whole stream) adjudication is an unusual, often very complex legal proceeding authorized by various state statutes. A proceeding covers a specified length of a specified river or watershed. Its aim is to identify, quantify, and then prioritize all of the lawful water uses within the specified area. All water users are required to participate and prove their water rights, or risk losing them. Although the federal government normally cannot be sued by private parties who seek to challenge feder-

begun by the State of New Mexico to determine the exact rights of each user to water from the Rio Mimbres. In this adjudication the United States claimed reserved water rights for use in the Gila National Forest. The State District Court held that the United States, in setting aside the Gila National Forest from other public lands, reserved the use of such water "as may be necessary for the purposes for which [the land was] withdrawn," but that these purposes did not include recreation, aesthetics, wildlife preservation, or cattle grazing. The United States appealed unsuccessfully to the Supreme Court of New Mexico. *Mimbres Valley Irrigation Co. v. Salopek,* 90 N.M. 410, 564 P.2d 615 (1977). We granted certiorari to consider whether the Supreme Court of New Mexico had applied the correct principles of federal law in determining petitioner's reserved rights in the Mimbres. 434 U.S. 1008, 98 S.Ct. 716, 54 L.Ed.2d 750. We now affirm.

I

The question posed in this case—what quantity of water, if any, the United States reserved out of the Rio Mimbres when it set aside the Gila National Forest in 1899—is a question of implied intent and not power. In *California v. United States,* 438 U.S. 645, at 653–663, 98 S.Ct. 2985, at 2990–2995, 57 L.Ed.2d 1018, we had occasion to discuss the respective authority of Federal and State Governments over waters in the Western States. The Court has previously concluded that whatever powers the States acquired over their waters as a result of congressional Acts and admission into the Union, however, Congress did not intend thereby to relinquish its authority to reserve unappropriated water in the future for use on appurtenant lands withdrawn from the public domain for specific federal purposes. *Winters v. United States,* 207 U.S. 564, 577, 28 S.Ct. 207, 211, 52 L.Ed. 340 (1908); *Arizona v. California,* 373 U.S. 546, 597–598, 83 S.Ct. 1468, 1496–1497, 10 L.Ed.2d 542 (1963); *Cappaert v. United States,* 426 U.S. 128, 143–146, 96 S.Ct. 2062, 2071–2073, 48 L.Ed.2d 523 (1976).

Recognition of Congress' power to reserve water for land which is itself set apart from the public domain, however, does not answer the question of the amount of water which has been reserved or the purposes for which the water may be used. Substantial portions of the public domain *have* been withdrawn and reserved by the United States for use as Indian reservations, forest reserves, national parks, and national monuments. And water is frequently necessary to achieve the purposes for which these reservations are made. But Congress has seldom expressly reserved water for use on these withdrawn lands. If water were abundant, Congress' silence would pose no problem. In the arid parts of the West, however, claims to water for use on federal reservations inescapably vie with other public and private claims for the limited quantities to be found in the rivers and streams. This competition is compounded by the sheer quantity of reserved lands in the

al water rights, the government can be forced to participate in stream adjudications and prove its rights like other water rights holders.]

Western States, which lands form brightly colored swaths across the maps of these States.[9]

The Court has previously concluded that Congress, in giving the President the power to reserve portions of the federal domain for specific federal purposes, *impliedly* authorized him to reserve "appurtenant water then unappropriated *to the extent needed to accomplish the purpose of the reservation.*" *Cappaert, supra*, at 138, 96 S.Ct., at 2069 (emphasis added). See *Arizona v. California, supra*, 373 U.S., at 595–601, 83 S.Ct., at 1495–1498; *United States v. District Court for Eagle County,* 401 U.S. 520, 522–523, 91 S.Ct. 998, 1000–1001, 28 L.Ed.2d 278 (1971); *Colorado River Water Cons. Dist. v. United States,* 424 U.S. 800, 805, 96 S.Ct. 1236, 1240, 47 L.Ed.2d 483 (1976). While many of the contours of what has come to be called the "implied-reservation-of-water doctrine" remain unspecified, the Court has repeatedly emphasized that Congress reserved "only that amount of water necessary to fulfill the purpose of the reservation, no more." *Cappaert, supra*, at 141, 96 S.Ct., at 2071. See *Arizona v. California, supra*, at 600–601, 83 S.Ct., at 1497–1498; *District Court for Eagle County, supra*, at 523, 91 S.Ct., at 1001. Each time this Court has applied the "implied-reservation-of-water doctrine," it has carefully examined both the asserted water right and the specific purposes for which the land was reserved, and concluded that without the water the purposes of the reservation would be entirely defeated.

This careful examination is required both because the reservation is implied, rather than expressed, and because of the history of congressional intent in the field of federal-state jurisdiction with respect to allocation of water. Where Congress has expressly addressed the question of whether federal entities must abide by state water law, it has almost invariably deferred to the state law. See *California v. United States,* 438 U.S., at 653–670, 678–679, 98 S.Ct., at 2990–2998, 3002–3003. Where water is necessary to fulfill the very purposes for which a federal reservation was created, it is reasonable to conclude, even in the face of Congress' express deference to state water law in other areas, that the United States intended to reserve the necessary water. Where water is only valuable for a secondary use of the reservation, however, there arises the contrary inference that Congress intended, consistent

9. The percentage of federally owned land (*excluding* Indian reservations and other trust properties) in the Western States ranges from 29.5% of the land in the State of Washington to 86.5% of the land in the State of Nevada, an average of about 46%. Of the land in the State of New Mexico, 33.6% is federally owned. General Services Administration, Inventory Report on Real Property Owned by the United States Throughout the World as of June 30, 1974, pp. 17, 34, and App. 1, table 4. Because federal reservations are normally found in the uplands of the Western States rather than the flat lands, the percentage of water flow originating in or flowing through the reservations is even more impressive. More than 60% of the average annual water yield in the 11 Western States is from federal reservations. The percentages of average annual water yield range from a low of 56% in the Columbia–North Pacific water resource region to a high of 96% in the Upper Colorado region. In the Rio Grande water resource region, where the Rio Mimbres lies, 77% of the average runoff originates on federal reservations. C. Wheatley, C. Corker, T. Stetson, & D. Reed, Study of the Development, Management and Use of Water Resources on the Public Lands 402–406, and table 4 (1969).

with its other views, that the United States would acquire water in the same manner as any other public or private appropriator. . . .

The State District Court referred the issues in this case to a Special Master, who found that the United States was diverting 6.9 acre-feet per annum of water for domestic-residential use, 6.5 acre-feet for road-water use, 3.23 acre-feet for domestic-recreational use, and .10 acre-foot for "wildlife" purposes. The Special Master also found that specified amounts of water were being used in the Gila National Forest for stock watering and that an "instream flow" of six cubic feet per second was being "used" for the purposes of fish preservation. The Special Master apparently believed that all of these uses fell within the reservation doctrine, and also concluded that the United States might have reserved rights for future water needs, ordering it to submit a report on future requirements within one year of his decision.

The District Court of Luna County disagreed with many of the Special Master's legal conclusions, but agreed with the Special Master that the Government should prepare within one year a report covering any future water requirements that might support a claim of reserved right in the waters of the Rio Mimbres. . . .

The United States appealed this decision to the Supreme Court of New Mexico. The United States contended that it was entitled to a minimum instream flow for "aesthetic, environmental, recreational and 'fish' purposes." 90 N.M., at 412, 564 P.2d, at 617. The Supreme Court of New Mexico concluded that, at least before the Multiple–Use Sustained–Yield Act of 1960, 74 Stat. 215, 16 U.S.C. § 528 *et seq.* (1976 ed.), national forests could only be created "to insure favorable conditions of water flow and to furnish a continuous supply of timber" and not for the purposes upon which the United States was now basing its asserted reserved rights in a minimum instream flow. 90 N.M., at 412–413, 564 P.2d, at 617–619. The United States also argued that it was entitled to a reserved right for stockwatering purposes. The State Supreme Court again disagreed, holding that stockwatering was not a purpose for which the national forests were created. *Id.*, at 414, 564 P.2d, at 619.

II

A

The quantification of reserved water rights for the national forests is of critical importance to the West, where, as noted earlier, water is scarce and where more than 50% of the available water either originates in or flows through national forests. When, as in the case of the Rio Mimbres, a river is fully appropriated, federal reserved water rights will frequently require a gallon-for-gallon reduction in the amount of water available for water-needy state and private appropriators. This reality has not escaped the attention of Congress and must be weighed in determining what, if any, water Congress reserved for use in the national forests.

The United States contends that Congress intended to reserve minimum instream flows for aesthetic, recreational, and fish-preservation purposes. An examination of the limited purposes for which Congress authorized the creation of national forests, however, provides no support for this claim. In the mid and late 1800's, many of the forests on the public domain were ravaged and the fear arose that the forest lands might soon disappear, leaving the United States with a shortage both of timber and of watersheds with which to encourage stream flows while preventing floods. It was in answer to these fears that in 1891 Congress authorized the President to "set apart and reserve, . . . any State or Territory having public land bearing forests, in any part of the public lands wholly or in part covered with timber or undergrowth, whether of commercial value or not, as public reservations." Creative Act of Mar. 3, 1891, § 24, 26 Stat. 1103, as amended, 16 U.S.C. § 471 (repealed 1976).

The Creative Act of 1891 unfortunately did not solve the forest problems of the expanding Nation. To the dismay of the conservationists, the new national forests were not adequately attended and regulated; fires and indiscriminate timber cutting continued their toll. To the anguish of Western settlers, reservations were frequently made indiscriminately. President Cleveland, in particular, responded to pleas of conservationists for greater protective measures by reserving some 21 million acres of "generally settled" forest land on February 22, 1897. President Cleveland's action drew immediate and strong protest from Western Congressmen who felt that the "hasty and ill considered" reservation might prove disastrous to the settlers living on or near these lands.

Congress' answer to these continuing problems was three-fold. It suspended the President's Executive Order of February 22, 1897; it carefully defined the purposes for which national forests could in the future be reserved; and it provided a charter for forest management and economic uses within the forests. Organic Administration Act of June 4, 1897, 30 Stat. 34, 16 U.S.C. § 473 *et seq.* (1976 ed.). In particular, Congress provided:

> "*No national forest shall be established, except to improve and protect the forest within the boundaries, or for the purpose of securing favorable conditions of water flows, and to furnish a continuous supply of timber for the use and necessities of citizens of the United States*; but it is not the purpose or intent of these provisions, or of [the Creative Act of 1891], to authorize the inclusion therein of lands more valuable for the mineral therein, or for agricultural purposes, than for forest purposes." 30 Stat. 35, as codified, 16 U.S.C. § 475 (1976 ed.) (emphasis added).

The legislative debates surrounding the Organic Administration Act of 1897 and its predecessor bills demonstrate that Congress intended national forests to be reserved for only two purposes—"[t]o conserve the water flows, and to furnish a continuous supply of timber for the people."[10] 30 Cong.Rec. 967 (1897) (Cong. McRae). See *United States v. Grimaud*, 220 U.S. 506, 515, 31 S.Ct. 480, 482, 55 L.Ed. 563 (1911). National forests were not to be reserved for aesthetic, environmental, recreational, or wildlife-preservation purposes.

> "The objects for which the forest reservations should be made are the protection of the forest growth against destruction by fire and ax, and preservation of forest conditions upon which water conditions and water flow are dependent. The purpose, therefore, of this bill is to maintain favorable forest conditions, without excluding the use of these reservations for other purposes. They are not parks set aside for nonuse, but have been established for economic reasons." 30 Cong.Rec. 966 (1897) (Cong. McRae). . . .

As Congressman McRae noted in introducing a predecessor bill to the 1897 Act, Congress was "not dealing with parks, but forest reservations, and there is a vast difference." 25 Cong.Rec. 2375 (1893).

> "fundamental purpose of the said parks, monuments, and reservations . . . is to conserve the scenery and the natural and historic objects and the wild life therein and to provide for the enjoyment of the same . . . unimpaired for the enjoyment of future generations." National Park Service Act of 1916, 39 Stat. 535, § 1, as amended, 16 U.S.C. § 1 (1976 ed.).

When it was Congress' intent to maintain minimum instream flows within the confines of a national forest, it expressly so directed, as it did in the case of the Lake Superior National Forest:

> "In order to preserve the shore lines, rapids, waterfalls, beaches and other natural features of the region in an unmodified state of nature, no further alteration of the natural water level of any lake or stream . . . shall be authorized." 16 U.S.C. § 577b (1976 ed.). . . .

B

Not only is the Government's claim that Congress intended to reserve water for recreation and wildlife preservation inconsistent with Congress' failure to recognize these goals as purposes of the national

10. The Government notes that the Act forbids the establishment of national forests except "*to improve and protect the forest within the boundaries, or* for the purpose of securing favorable conditions of water flows, and to furnish a continuous supply of timber," and argues from this wording that "improvement" and "protection" of the forests form a third and separate purpose of the national forest system. A close examination of the language of the Act, however, reveals that Congress only intended national forests to be established for two purposes. Forests would be created only "to improve and protect the forest within the boundaries," or, *in other words*, "for the purpose of securing favorable conditions of water flows, and to furnish a continuous supply of timber." This reading of the Act is confirmed by its legislative history. Nothing in the legislative history suggests that Congress intended national forests to be established for three purposes, one of which would be extremely broad. Indeed, it is inconceivable that a Congress which was primarily concerned with limiting the President's power to reserve the forest lands of the West would provide for the creation of forests merely "to improve and protect the forest within the boundaries"; forests would be reserved for their improvement and protection, but only to serve the purposes of timber protection and favorable water supply. . . .

forests, it would defeat the very purpose for which Congress did create the national forest system.

> "[F]orests exert a most important regulating influence upon the flow of rivers, reducing floods and increasing the water supply in the low stages. The importance of their conservation on the mountainous watersheds which collect the scanty supply for the arid regions of North America can hardly be overstated. With the natural regimen of the streams replaced by destructive floods in the spring, and by dry beds in the months when the irrigating flow is most needed, the irrigation of wide areas now proposed will be impossible, and regions now supporting prosperous communities will become depopulated." S. Doc. No. 105, 55th Cong., 1st Sess., 10 (1897).

The water that would be "insured" by preservation of the forest was to "be used for domestic, mining, milling, or irrigation purposes, under the laws of the State wherein such national forests are situated, or under the laws of the United States and the rules and regulations established thereunder." Organic Administration Act of 1897, 30 Stat. 36, 16 U.S.C. § 481 (1976 ed.). As this provision and its legislative history evidence, Congress authorized the national forest system principally as a means of enhancing the quantity of water that would be available to the settlers of the arid West. The Government, however, would have us now believe that Congress intended to partially defeat this goal by reserving significant amounts of water for purposes quite inconsistent with this goal.

C

In 1960, Congress passed the Multiple–Use Sustained–Yield Act of 1960, 74 Stat. 215, 16 U.S.C. § 528 *et seq.* (1976 ed.), which provides

> "It is the policy of Congress that the national forests are established and shall be administered for outdoor recreation, range, timber, watershed, and wildlife and fish purposes. The purposes of sections 528 to 531 of this title are declared to be supplemental to, but not in derogation of, the purposes for which the national forests were established as set forth in the [Organic Administration Act of 1897.]"

The Supreme Court of New Mexico concluded that this Act did not give rise to any reserved rights not previously authorized in the Organic Administration Act of 1897. "The Multiple–Use Sustained–Yield Act of 1960 does not have a retroactive effect nor can it broaden the purposes for which the Gila National Forest was established under the Organic Act of 1897." 90 N.M., at 413, 564 P.2d, at 618. While we conclude that the Multiple–Use Sustained–Yield Act of 1960 was intended to broaden the purposes for which national forests had previously been administered, we agree that Congress did not intend to thereby expand the reserved rights of the United States.

The Multiple–Use Sustained–Yield Act of 1960 establishes the purposes for which the national forests "*are* established and *shall* be administered." (Emphasis added.) The Act directs the Secretary of the

Agriculture to administer all forests, including those previously established, on a multiple-use and sustained-yield basis. H.R. 10572, 86th Cong., 2d Sess., 1 (1960). In the administration of the national forests, therefore, Congress intended the Multiple–Use Sustained–Yield Act of 1960 to broaden the benefits accruing from all reserved national forests.

The House Report accompanying the 1960 legislation, however, indicates that recreation, range, and "fish" purposes are "to be supplemental to, but not in derogation of, the purposes for which the national forests were established" in the Organic Administration Act of 1897. . . .

As discussed earlier, the "reserved rights doctrine" is a doctrine built on implication and is an exception to Congress' explicit deference to state water law in other areas. Without legislative history to the contrary, we are led to conclude that Congress did not intend in enacting the Multiple–Use Sustained–Yield Act of 1960 to reserve water for the *secondary* purposes there established. . . .

IV

Congress intended that water would be reserved only where necessary to preserve the timber or to secure favorable water flows for private and public uses under state law. This intent is revealed in the purposes for which the national forest system was created and Congress' principled deference to state water law in the Organic Administration Act of 1897 and other legislation. The decision of the Supreme Court of New Mexico is faithful to this congressional intent and is therefore

Affirmed.

MR. JUSTICE POWELL, with whom MR. JUSTICE BRENNAN, MR. JUSTICE WHITE, and MR. JUSTICE MARSHALL join, dissenting in part.

I agree with the Court that the implied-reservation doctrine should be applied with sensitivity to its impact upon those who have obtained water rights under state law and to Congress' general policy of deference to state water law. See *ante*, at 3013, 3015, 3016–3017. I also agree that the Organic Administration Act of 1897, 30 Stat. 11, cannot fairly be read as evidencing an intent to reserve water for recreational or stockwatering purposes in the national forests.

I do not agree, however, that the forests which Congress intended to "improve and protect" are the still, silent, lifeless places envisioned by the Court. In my view, the forests consist of the birds, animals, and fish—the wildlife—that inhabit them, as well as the trees, flowers, shrubs, and grasses. I therefore would hold that the United States is entitled to so much water as is necessary to sustain the wildlife of the forests, as well as the plants. I also add a word concerning the impact of the Court's holding today on future claims by the United States that the reservation of particular national forests impliedly reserved instream flows. . . .

Notes

1. *Managing federal lands. United States v. New Mexico* usefully introduces the subject of federal lands management, an important element of natural resources law given the vast resources located on them. Lands that are part of the National Forest System are managed today under a multiple-use mandate, which directs the Forest Service to consider and balance a variety of resource uses as it goes about preparing land-use plans. These multiple-use lands differ from those federal lands that are managed for one or two dominant uses (military installations, national parks, etc.) (Wildlife refuges have wildlife protection as a dominant use, but individual refuges often have other specified goals.) What were the two announced reasons for creating the first national forests? Were these likely the only reasons, or might these have been put forward by politicians at the time due to political constraints? In the case of forests created in the eastern part of the country, many political proponents of them, in fact, were far more interested in the lands for recreation and tourism than for timber production, according to Richard W. Judd, COMMON LANDS, COMMON PEOPLE: THE ORIGINS OF CONSERVATION IN NORTHERN NEW ENGLAND (1997). The Supreme Court's rather simplified view of history is usefully compared with the fuller treatment in Samuel P. Hays, CONSERVATION AND THE GOSPEL OF EFFICIENCY: THE PROGRESSIVE CONSERVATION MOVEMENT, 1890–1920 (1959). According to one reading of the federal statutes, Congress essentially meant to divide federal lands into three types—those valuable chiefly as forest, for farming, and for mining; it did not intend to distinguish among types of forest lands depending on their suitability for timber production rather than for hunting, recreation or grazing. Most forest lands, even in National Forests, remained open to homesteading, so there was no reason to worry about reservations of lands suitable for homebuilding.

History aside, how sensible is it for the Court to imply that the Forest Service can manage its lands for timber production (a primary purpose) without taking care to protect its forests as ecological communities? The statute expressly directs the Service to "preserve and protect" the forests. Can it do that without considering the forest as a community of life? On the other hand, if the Forest Service can claim all the water it needs to "preserve" a forest, might it try to claim that it needs everything?

2. *Dividing water from land by law III.* This case is more similar to the previous one, *Shelton Farms*, than might first appear. Indeed, the basic issue, from the perspective of natural resources law, is the same. In each case the court had to draw the line between those parts of nature that belong to the landowner and those parts that are available for separate acquisition under law. As the Court here explains, Congress has largely chosen to allow states, using state law, to allocate waters that are present on federal lands. (As for the vast considerable economic importance of those waters, see the Court's first footnote.) Congress could have done otherwise; it could have chosen to come up with its own water allocation scheme.

In states that embrace prior appropriation, this means severing water flows from the land and making them available to the first appropriator. Appropriations of water on federal lands raise the same issues about dividing water between the landowner and the appropriator as those that arise when land is privately owned. In addition, there are the extra issues that arise when land is federally owned due to the federal government's greater powers over the land and all resources on it. According to the reserved water rights doctrine, explained in this case, Congress implicitly reserves water whenever it officially sets land aside (reserves the land, in legal parlance) for a specified federal purpose. But how much water is reserved by the federal landowner and how much water remains available for acquisition by other people. That was the issue that the Court had to resolve. The question is answered, the Court tells us, by looking to the amount of water physically needed to meet the primary purposes of the land reservation. That answer sounds fair enough on its face, but can prove extremely difficult to apply in practice. Indeed, given the variations among federal reservations the reserved water rights doctrine requires detailed fact-finding and careful decisionmaking on a reservation by reservation basis.

3. *Indian tribal rights.* The federal reserved-water rights doctrine began early in the twentieth century. For decades it seemed to apply only to land set aside by treaty for the use of Indian tribes. In the case above, the Supreme Court embraced a distinction between the primary and secondary purposes of a land reservation. What disputes are likely to arise with respect to the primary purposes of a land reservation for use by Indian tribes? The primary purpose is obviously to support tribal life, but at what population levels and for what modes of life? Is it reasonable for a tribe to contend that it can today use water to supply the needs of a gaming casino? On the other hand, is it fair to insist that tribal water uses remain locked in modes of subsistence living that have little place in the national economy? Most contentious today in many parts of the country: how much water can tribes claim if their original mode of living depended upon fishing and the water is needed to sustain fish populations? Tribal reserved water claims are of heightened importance because they typically have very early priority dates, often predating all other water users.

4. *The nagging problem of vagueness.* As the Supreme Court observes, almost the gravest problem posed by the reserved water rights doctrine is the vagueness of it. Water reserved under the federal law doctrine remains attached to the federal land; only water in excess of primary federal needs is available for allocation as a discrete natural resource under state law. But what happens when, as usual, the amount of federally reserved water is unknown? The main attribute of prior appropriation law, so it is said, is the greater precision it has in relation to riparian rights? Doesn't the reserved water rights doctrine seriously undercut that supposed virtue? Might the doctrine in practice promote negotiation and compromise among water uses, who share the same uncertainties?

5. *The complexity of mixing riparian rights and prior appropriation.* The prior appropriation approach to water allocation, as this case and the previous one illustrate, raises legal problems that did not exist when water rights were firmly attached to land ownership. That complexity is magnified when a state does what California decided to do—to embrace both riparian rights and prior appropriation. In theory, riparian rights hold priority in California; only water not taken by riparians is available for appropriation. The huge problem with this awkward approach is that riparian rights are

not lost by nonuse. That is, a riparian landowner holds rights in perpetuity and can begin using them at any time. It is thus not really possible to know what water in a river, if any, is safely and securely available for appropriators to take. The problem became even more severe when the California Supreme Court originally decided that, while riparian landowners were limited to "reasonable" uses of water as between themselves, the priority of a riparian landowner over an appropriator was total. A riparian thus had priority over an appropriator, even if the riparian's water use was unreasonable under the circumstances. So awkward (and misguided) was this situation that California altered its state constitution to deal with it. It inserted a constitutional provision requiring that all water uses be reasonable. The story of that constitutional amendment, and the effects it has had on California water law, are related in the following lengthy ruling.

Although few states undertake to do what California does—fully mix riparian rights and prior appropriation—California has nonetheless exerted considerable influence in water law. It has handed down influential rulings dealing with both water-law schemes, as well as ruling such as the following one that deal with the intersection of the two. Indeed, pretty much all of the elements of a natural resources law course could be illustrated by drawing upon California's extraordinary water-law experience.

JOSLIN v. MARIN MUNICIPAL WATER DISTRICT

67 Cal.2d 132, 429 P.2d 889, 60 Cal.Rptr. 377 (1967).

SULLIVAN, JUSTICE.

Plaintiffs, owners of lands riparian to Nicasio Creek in Marin County, appeal from a summary judgment for defendant entered in an action in inverse condemnation for damages resulting from defendant's construction of a dam across said creek at a point above plaintiffs' lands.

Plaintiffs' third amended complaint (complaint) alleges that since March 1955 plaintiffs have been, and now are, the owners of a parcel of five acres of land; that a stream (Nicasio Creek) runs through their property; that the normal flow of the waters of the stream carried in suspension rock, sand and gravel which were deposited on plaintiffs' lands; that plaintiffs operated on their property a rock and gravel business in the course of which they sold and used the deposits of rock and gravel; that defendant is a municipal water district organized and existing under the Municipal Water District Act of 1911; that prior to May 1962 defendant constructed a dam across Nicasio Creek; that as a result the normal flow of waters in said stream was obstructed to such an extent that "the normal and usual replenishment of rocks and gravel" upon plaintiffs' lands ceased; that the value of plaintiffs' lands was thereby diminished in the amount of $250,000, and that plaintiffs had been deprived of gravel and rock having an accrued value of $25,000 at the time of filing the complaint. . . .

With some variance in language the parties assert that the principal issue before us is whether defendant, an upstream appropriator of water, is liable in damages to plaintiffs, downstream riparian owners, by reason of having appropriated the waters of the creek under the above-mentioned circumstances.

To bring this appeal into focus, we must first briefly review the growth and development of California water law. In its first stage which began with the "gold rush," this law dealt mainly with those who diverted water from streams in the public domain for mining purposes and sought to adjudicate the competing claims of the parties using such water on the basis of a principle of prior appropriation. Subsequently with the increasing importance of agriculture over mining, the courts became more involved with riparian rights.... This doctrine which had its genesis in the common law of England initially was made to rest in California on the basic principle "that the riparian proprietor is entitled to the full flow of the stream, reduced only by the proper riparian uses which may be made of the water by proprietors above him." (Miller & Lux v. Enterprise C. etc. Co. (1915) 169 Cal. 415, 443, 147 P. 567, 578; see Lux v. Haggin (1886) 69 Cal. 255, 390—394, 4 P. 919, 10 P. 674; Herminghaus v. Southern California Edison Co. (1926) 200 Cal. 81, 94–96, 252 P. 607.) Such riparian rights extended to "the entire flow of the waters of (a) river, considering the same with its seasonal accretions as the usual and ordinary flow of said stream during each and every year." (Herminghaus v. Southern California Edison Co., *supra*, at p. 91, 252 P. at p. 611.)

It was inevitable that the claims of appropriators and riparian owners would collide and that the legal principles upon which they were asserted would appear to be in conflict. Reconciling these principles, this court in the leading case of Lux v. Haggin, *supra*, 69 Cal. 255, 4 P. 919, 10 P. 674, declared "that the rights of the riparian owners to the use of the waters of the abutting stream were paramount to the rights of any other persons thereto; that such rights were parcel of the land and that any diminution of the stream against the will of the riparian owner by other persons was an actionable injury. The question was settled by that case and the riparian right has never since been disputed." (Herminghaus v. Southern California Edison Co., *supra*, 200 Cal. 81, 95, 252 P. 607, 613 quoting from address of Shaw, C.J., see fn. 2 ante.) As a result the principle emerged that an upstream appropriator could not deprive a downstream riparian owner of his right to the use of the full flow of a stream, even though only a small percentage of the flow was utilized the benefit the lands of the downstream riparian. (Herminghaus v. Southern California Edison Co., *supra*, 200 Cal. 81, 94–103, 252 P. 607; see also Tulare Irr. Dist. v. Lindsay–Strathmore Dist. (1935) 3 Cal.2d 489, 523–524, 45 P.2d 972; Miller & Lux v. Madera Canal etc. Co. (1909) 155 Cal. 59, 64, 99 P. 502, 22 L.R.A.,N.S., 391. Lux v. Haggin, *supra*, 69 Cal. 255, 4 P. 919, 10 P. 674.)

Thereafter, and in apparent response to the Herminghaus decision (see Gin S. Chow v. City of Santa Barbara (1933) 217 Cal. 673, 699–700, 22 P.2d 5), the California Constitution was amended in 1928. (Art. XIV,

§ 3.)[11] The amendment was generally construed as applying a rule of reasonable use "to all water rights enjoyed or asserted in this state, whether the same be grounded on the riparian right or the right, analogous to the riparian right, of the overlying land owner, or the percolating water right, or the appropriative right." Peabody v. City of Vallejo (1935) 2 Cal.2d 351, 383, 40 P.2d 486, 499). Thus the rule of reasonableness of use as a measure of the water right which had theretofore been applied as between other contesting claimants but had been denied application as between riparian owners and appropriators was finally extended to include the latter. (Peabody v. City of Vallejo, *supra*, at p. 367, 40 P.2d 486; Gin S. Chow v. City of Santa Barbara, *supra*, at pp. 703–705, 22 P.2d 5; see generally 1 Waters & Water Rights (Clark 1967) § 19.1.)

As epitomized in Peabody, the amendment is said to declare: "1. The right to the use of water is limited to such water as shall be reasonably required for the beneficial use to be served. 2. Such right does not extend to the waste of water. 3. Such right does not extend to unreasonable use or unreasonable method of use or unreasonable method of diversion of water. 4. Riparian rights attach to, but to no more than so much of the flow as may be required or used consistently with this section of the Constitution." (2 Cal.2d 351, 367, 40 P.2d 486, 491.)

It has been long and clearly settled in California that the effect of the passage of article XIV, section 3, "has been to modify the long-standing riparian doctrine * * * and to apply, by constitutional mandate the doctrine of reasonable use between riparian owners and appropriators, and between overlying owners and appropriators." [citations omitted] "The right to the waste of water is not now included in the riparian right." (Peabody v. City of Vallejo, *supra*, at p. 368, 40 P.2d at p. 492.) What is a reasonable use or method of use of water is a question of fact to be determined according to the circumstances in each particular case. (Gin S. Chow v. City of Santa Barbara, *supra*, at p. 706, 22 P.2d 5.)

11. The amendment has not since been modified, altered or changed, and provides: "It is hereby declared that because of the conditions prevailing in this State the general welfare requires that the water resources of the State be put to beneficial use to the fullest extent of which they are capable, and that the waste or unreasonable use or unreasonable method of use of water be prevented, and that the conservation of such waters is to be exercised with a view to the reasonable and beneficial use thereof in the interest of the people and for the public welfare. The right to water or to the use or flow of water in or from any natural stream or water course in this State is and shall be limited to such water as shall be reasonably required for the beneficial use to be served, and such right does not and shall not extend to the waste or unreasonable use or unreasonable method of use or unreasonable method of diversion of water. Riparian rights in a stream or water course attach to, but to no more than so much of the flow thereof as may be required or used consistently with this section, for the purposes for which such lands are, or may be made adaptable, in view of such reasonable and beneficial uses; provided, however, that nothing herein contained shall be construed as depriving any riparian owner of the reasonable use of water of the stream to which his land is riparian under reasonable methods of diversion and use, or of depriving any appropriator of water to which he is lawfully entitled. This section shall be self-executing, and the Legislature may also enact laws in the furtherance of the policy in this section contained."

In Peabody, several lower riparian owners sought to enjoin the City of Vallejo, as an appropriator, from storing the waters of a creek by the construction of a dam and thereafter diverting them to municipal uses. Peabody, one of the plaintiffs, asserted a right to have all the waters flow without interruption since by normally overflowing his land they not only deposited silt thereon but also washed out salt deposits on portions of the land. The court held that "(t)his asserted right does not inhere in the riparian right at common law, and as a natural right cannot be asserted as against the police power of the state in the conservation of its waters. This asserted right involves an unreasonable use or an unreasonable method of use or an unreasonable method of diversion of water as contemplated by the Constitution." (Peabody v. City of Vallejo, *supra*, 2 Cal.2d 351, 369, 40 P.2d 486, 492.)

Although, as we have said, what is a reasonable use of water depends on the circumstances of each case, such an inquiry cannot be resolved *in vacuo* isolated from state-wide considerations of transcendent importance. Paramount among these we see the ever increasing need for the conservation of water in this state, an inescapable reality of life quite apart from its express recognition in the 1928 amendment. On the other hand, unlike the unanimous policy pronouncements relative to the use and conservation of natural waters, we are aware of none relative to the supply and availability of sand, gravel and rock in commercial quantities. Plaintiffs do not urge that the general welfare or public interest requires that particular or exceptional measures be employed to insure that such natural resources be made generally available and should therefore be carefully conserved.

Is it "reasonable." then, that the riches of our streams, which we are charged with conserving in the great public interest, are to be dissipated in the amassing of mere sand and gravel which for aught that appears subserves No public policy? We cannot deem such a use to be in accord with the constitutional mandate that our limited water resources be put only to those beneficial uses "to the fullest extent of which they are capable," that "waste or unreasonable use" be prevented, and that conservation be exercised "in the interest of the people and for the public welfare." (Cal.Const., art. XIV, § 3.) We are satisfied that in the instant case the use of such waters as an agent to expose or to carry and deposit sand, gravel and rock, is as a matter of law unreasonable within the meaning of the constitutional amendment. (See Peabody v. City of Vallejo, *supra*, 2 Cal.2d 351, 369, 40 P.2d 486.) . . . .

Apart from their reliance upon Abbot, plaintiffs have not shown how their claimed use of the stream in the instant case, when measured by the constitutional mandate, is a reasonable one. In essence their position is that such use is a beneficial one encompassed within their riparian rights and that all beneficial uses are reasonable uses. Such a position ignores rather than observes the constitutional mandate. Article XIV, section 3, does not equate "beneficial use" with "reasonable use." Indeed the amendment in plain terms emphasizes that water must be conserved in California "with a view to the reasonable and beneficial use thereof in the interest of the people," that the right to use water "shall be limited to such water as shall be reasonably required for the beneficial use to be served," and that riparian rights "attach to, but to no more than so much of the flow" as may be required "in view of such reasonable and beneficial uses." (Emphasis added.) (Cal.Const., art. XIV, § 3) Thus the mere fact that a use may be beneficial to a riparian's lands is not sufficient if the use is not also reasonable within the meaning of section 3 of article XIV and, as indicated, plaintiffs' use must be deemed unreasonable. Anything to the contrary in Los Angeles Co. F.C. Dist. v. Abbot, *supra*, 24 Cal.App.2d 728, 76 P.2d 188, is disapproved.

Assuming arguendo the unreasonableness of their use of the stream, plaintiffs contend that in any event they are entitled to be compensated for the damage to their property interests. Article XIV, section 3, they say, was only a procedural as opposed to a substantive change in the law and had the effect of merely denying injunctive relief to protect certain riparian uses. Article I, section 14, on the other hand confers on them a cause of action for money damages for the injury to their real property resulting from the district's public improvement....

From the foregoing we arrive at the conclusion that since there was and is no property right in an unreasonable use, there has been no taking or damaging of property by the deprivation of such use and, accordingly, the deprivation is not compensable. (See Peabody v. City of Vallejo, *supra*, 2 Cal.2d 351, 369, 40 P.2d 486; Ivanhoe Irr. Dist. v. All Parties, *supra*, 47 Cal.2d 597, 623, 306 P.2d 824; Crum v. Mt. Shasta Power Corp. (1934) 220 Cal. 295, 307, 30 P.2d 30.)

The judgment is affirmed.

Notes

1. *Reasonable use IV: limits on private rights.* Just as the vagueness of federal reserved water rights has created uncertainty among appropriators, so too riparian rights, where they exist, have caused grave problems. In several Western states the problem was greatly diminished by freezing riparian rights when the state made the shift over to an appropriation system. Riparian landowners who were using water received authority to continue their uses at existing levels, but after a statutorily specified date no new riparian water uses could begin. All new uses had to come under the prior appropriation scheme, which (as we'll see later) specified private water use rights with much greater clarity. California's effort to achieve this same level of predictability in its water system has been long and tortuous.

In *Joslin* the Court made clear that all water rights in the state were legally protected as private property only when and so long as the water was used reasonably. And as the Court also made clear, "reasonable" is a concept that varies over time and that depends upon changing circumstances. As the Joslins learned to their dismay, a water right that is protected property at one time can lose its property status over time. At any time, a court may rule (perhaps based on a jury finding) that a water use is not reasonable, and hence the water user has no property right in it. The idea is a troubling one to many observers of water law—indeed, terrifying to some. But as we'll see in chapter 4, the idea follows rather directly from the longstanding property law doctrine of *sic utere tuo*, which underlies the law of nuisance. Property owners have always been under a duty to use what they own so as to cause no harm to anyone else. That rule has been applied over the centuries in a way that kept it up to date: whether a property use creates "harm" is determined by the ideas of harm that prevail when the case is decided.

2. *Moving the land-water line.* The controversy in California that led to the 1928 constitutional amendment was entirely about line between water attached to land and water that was available for acquisition as a discrete resources. According to the supreme court's early rulings, a riparian landowner could use as much water as she wanted so long as she respected the rights of other riparians. Only water that riparians did not care to use was available for separate acquisition. The constitutional amendment, once interpreted and clarified by the court, moved this line in favor of making more water available as a discrete resource. After the amendment, a riparian was limited to the water that she could devote to a reasonable use. All water beyond reasonable uses was available for appropriators to take.

3. *Property rights and the law. Joslin* is also a useful case in that it gives us a glimpse of the necessary link between property rights and law, a link that was once well understood but has now become somewhat confused. Courts exist to enforce laws, not to apply abstract notions of natural law and justice (though the latter do creep in from time to time; on the general point see William M. Wiecek, Liberty Under Law: The Supreme Court in American Life 44 (1988) (noting the Supreme Court's turning away from natural law as a basis for decision)). In the case of property rights, they are protected only to the extent specified by law. E.g., Board of Regents v. Roth, 408 U.S. 564, 577 (1972) ("property interests ... are not created by the Constitution.") Indeed, as a jurisprudential matter, property is necessarily a product of law, and exists when and to the extent lawmakers provide. (Again, we should note that the Constitution does place minor limits on the ability of governments to redefine the meaning of property rights once in private hands—the "regulatory takings" jurisprudence—and on the taking of property without due process of law.)

But what body or bodies of law specifies the scope of property rights? One tendency is to look to the common law as the source of property rights, and to treat other types of laws as something else: regulations or restrictions on the use of property rights. Yet, how can this be, as a matter of jurisprudence, given that state legislatures have the power to alter the common law by passing statutes (which they frequently do) and given that federal law takes priority over state law? Is it more accurate to say that the content of property rights at any time is determined by looking to the full range of laws that apply in a given time and place? On this issue, *Joslin* provides a partial answer. According to the court, California altered the content of a riparian's property rights when it altered its constitution in the early twentieth century. Thus, a state constitutional amendment had the effect of altering the meaning of landownership, keeping it up to date.

4. *Legal evolution, overt and covert.* For various reasons courts are generally reluctant to make overt changes in the rules governing private

property rights, for fear of disrupting settled expectations and being accused of interfering with the vested rights of individuals. We have seen this reluctance repeatedly in prior cases. In *Beacham* and *Coffin* (and *Pyle*?) courts nonetheless did change fundamental laws, yet claimed in doing so that they really were not. In the Onyx Cave cases, individual court members were willing to consider new legal approaches but the court's majority was not; indeed, the majority's commitment to established property law was sufficiently strong that it saw little need even to respond to the law-reform ideas proposed by Justices Thomas and Logan. Overt legal change makes judges nervous, perhaps no more so than when the laws prescribe the elements of private property rights.

In its prior rulings, particularly *Lux v. Haggin* (1886) and *Herminghaus* (1926), the California Supreme Court showed great hostility to any overt change in the reach and primacy of riparian rights. In *Joslin*, however, we can detect a far different attitude. The reasonable-use rule that the court accepts and applies is, in fact, a mechanism that can bring about substantial long term change in water law, as society changes its ideas about the reasonableness of competing water uses. A water use that is reasonable one day can be unreasonable and thus brought to an end on the next. But there is a big difference in this kind of legal change. When courts apply the reasonable-use doctrine they *appear* to be applying a rule of law that is itself unchanging. In *form* the law stays the same, always banning unreasonable uses; in *application*, though, the content of the restriction can shift greatly as circumstances and prevailing attitudes change. It is little wonder that courts have found it appealing to define private rights in terms of "reasonableness" (or some synonym) so as to allow change to occur without having to change legal norms overtly.

Public appearances aside, is there a virtue to creating a system where legal change must occur covertly? What would the California court say if the California legislature got into the act, enacting a statute proclaiming, for instance, that it is unreasonable to use scarce water to irrigate pastures or to grow farm crops that are overabundant nationally (e.g., corn or cotton)? If a jury could make such a decision as a factual matter, ruling on an issue of reasonableness, why not let the legislature do so?

HIGDAY v. NICKOLAUS

469 S.W.2d 859 (Mo. App. 1971).

SHANGLER, PRESIDING JUDGE.

. . . The facts alleged and in substance shown by the petition of plaintiffs, now appellants, are these: Appellants are the several owners of some 6000 acres of farm land overlying an alluvial water basin in Boone County known as the McBaine Bottom. These lands (projected on Exhibit 'A' appended hereto) extend from Huntsdale at the north to Easley at the south; they are bordered by a line of limestone bluffs on the east and are enclosed by a sweeping bend of the Missouri River on the west. Underlying this entire plain are strata of porous rock, gravel and soil through which water, without apparent or definite channel, filtrates, oozes and percolates as it falls. This water (much of which has originated far upstream within the Missouri River Valley) has been trapped by an underlying stratum of impervious limestone so that the saturated soil has become a huge aquifer or underground reservoir.

Appellants have devoted the overlying lands to agricultural use with excellent resultant yields. They attribute the fertility of the soil to the continuing presence of a high subterranean water level which has unfailingly and directly supplied the moisture needs of the crops whatever the vagaries of the weather. Appellants also use the underground water for personal consumption, for their livestock, and in the near future will require it for the surface irrigation of their crops.

Respondent City of Columbia is a burgeoning municipality of 50,000 inhabitants which has been, since 1948, in quest of a source of water to replenish a dwindling supply. Following the advice of consulting engineers, it settled on a plan for the withdrawal of water by shallow wells from beneath the McBaine Bottom where appellants' farms are located and thence to transport the water to the City some twelve miles away for sale to customers within and without the City. In December of 1966, the electorate approved a revenue bond issue for the development of a municipal water supply by such a system of shallow wells in the McBaine Bottom. Further scientific analysis and measurement of the basin's water resources followed. With the aid of a test well, it was determined that the underground percolating water table, when undisturbed, rises to an average of ten feet below the soil surface. These waters move laterally through the McBaine alluvium at the rate of two feet per day and in so doing displace 10.5 million gallons of water daily.

Respondent City, by threat of condemnation, has acquired from some of these appellants five well sites totalling 17.25 acres. The City now threatens to extract the groundwater at the rate of 11.5 million gallons daily for purposes wholly unrelated to any beneficial use of the overlying land, but instead, intends to transport the water to its corporate boundaries some miles away for purposes of sale. The mining of the water as contemplated will reduce the water table throughout the basin from the present average of ten feet to a new subsurface average of twenty feet. Appellants complain that this reduction of the water table will divert percolating waters normally available and enjoyed by appellants for their crops, livestock and their personal use and will eventually turn their land into an arid and sterile surface.

On the basis of these pleaded allegations, plaintiffs sought (1) a judicial declaration that defendant City is without right to extract the percolating waters for sale away from the premises or for other use not related with any beneficial ownership or enjoyment of the land from which they are taken when to do so will deprive them, the owners of the adjacent land, of the reasonable use of the underground water for the beneficial use of their own land, and (2) that defendant City be enjoined from undertaking to do so. . . .

It is fundamental that injunction will not be granted unless there is some substantial right to be protected. Humphreys v. Dickerson, Mo.,216

S.W.2d 427, 429(5); 43 C.J.S. Injunctions § 19b, p. 430. The indispensable basis for injunctive relief is the wrongful and injurious invasion of some legal right existing in plaintiff. Howe v. Standard Oil Co. of Indiana, Mo.App., 150 S.W.2d 496, 497(1); 42 Am.Jur.2d, Injunctions, Sec. 29, p. 765. The writ will issue also if invasion of that right is threatened by one having the power to do the wrong. Ewing v. Kansas City, Mo., 238 Mo.App. 266, 180 S.W.2d 234, 240(1—3);Sec. 526.030, V.A.M.S. Whether plaintiffs' allegations that the defendant municipality threatens to capture the percolating waters from their subjacent lands for purposes of sale in such quantities as will damage them describe an invasion of legal right which equity will enjoin depends upon whether plaintiffs have a right of property in these waters. The answer to that question, in turn, depends upon the rule to be applied to the ownership and use of subterranean percolating waters.

In legal contemplation, subterranean waters fall into two classifications, either underground streams or percolating waters.[12] An underground stream is defined as water that passes through or under the surface in a definite channel or one that is reasonably ascertainable. Percolating waters include all waters which pass through the ground beneath the surface of the earth without a definite channel and not shown to be supplied by a definite flowing stream. They are waters which ooze, seep, filter and otherwise circulate through the interstices of the subsurface strata without definable channel, or in a course that is not discoverable from surface indications without excavation for that purpose, 93 C.J.S. Waters § 86; 56 Am.Jur., Waters, Secs. 108, 111; Farnham, Water and Water Rights, Sec. 944. The rule is that all underground waters are presumed to be percolating and therefore the burden of proof is on the party claiming that a subterranean stream exists. Maricopa County Municipal Water Conservation Dist. No. 1 v. Southwest Cotton Co., 39 Ariz. 65, 4 P.2d 369, 376(18); C & W Coal Corp. v. Salyer, 200 Va. 18, 104 S.E.2d 50, 53(1); Wilkening v. State, 54 Wash.2d 692, 344 P.2d 204, 206(2).

The law with respect to rights in percolating waters was not developed until a comparatively recent period. Under the English common law rule, percolating waters constitute part and parcel of the land in which they are found and belong absolutely to the owner of such land who may without liability withdraw any quantity of water for any purpose even though the result is to drain all water from beneath the adjoining lands. 93 C.J.S. Waters § 93c(2); 56 Am.Jur., Waters, Sec. 113, 1 R. Clark, Waters and Water Rights, Sec. 52.2(B), and see 55 A.L.R. 1390 and supplementary 109 A.L.R. 397 (both annotations state the

12. These legal classifications have been roundly criticized by hydrologists and legal commentators as without scientific basis both as to the distinction attempted between percolating waters and underground streams and also because they ignore the essential interrelationship between surface and ground waters. See, e.g., Danielson, Ground Water in Nebraska, 35 Neb.L.Rev. 17 (1955); Clark, Groundwater Management: Law and Local Response, 6 Ariz.Law Rev. 188 (1965); 1 R. Clark, Waters and Water Rights, Sec. 3.1, p. 332 (1967). Also, Restatement, Torts, comment a to Sec. 858 (1939); Lauer, Reflections on Riparianism, 35 Mo.L.Rev. 1, 7 (1970).

English rule and list the cases which follow it). Under this rule, a municipality owing land may collect the underlying percolating waters and use them to supply its inhabitants regardless of the effect on adjoining landowners. Warder v. Springfield, 9 Ohio Dec. Reprint 855, 17 Weekly Law Bul. 398 (1887); City of Corpus Christi v. City of Pleasanton, 154 Tex. 289, 276 S.W.2d 798, 802(1); III Farnham, Waters and Water Rights, p. 2717.

The English rule relating to percolating groundwater was generally followed by American courts through the mid-nineteenth century, although not always with the full rigor of the absolute ownership doctrine. At an early day, the courts expressed dissatisfaction with the English common law rule and began applying what has come to be known variously, as the rule of "reasonable use", or of "correlative rights", or the "American rule." By the turn of the century, a steady trend of decisions was discernible away from the English rule to a rule of reasonable use. The trend continues.

Generally, the rule of reasonable use is an expression of the maxim that one must so use his own property as not to injure another.—that each landowner is restricted to a reasonable exercise of his own rights and a reasonable use of his own property, in view of the similar rights of others. 55 A.L.R. 1400; III Farnham, Water and Water Rights, pp. 2718, 2719; 73 C.J.S. Property § 13(b); Clutter v. Blankenship, 346 Mo. 961, 144 S.W.2d 119, 121(3, 4). As it applies to percolating groundwater, the rule of reasonable use recognizes that the overlying owner has a proprietary interest in the water under his lands, but his incidents of ownership are restricted. It recognizes that the nature of the property right is usufructuary rather than absolute as under the English rule. Under the rule of reasonable use, the overlying owner may use the subjacent groundwater freely, and without liability to an adjoining owner, but only if his use is for purposes incident to the beneficial enjoyment of the land from which the water was taken. This rule does not prevent the consumption of such groundwater for agriculture, manufacturing, irrigation, mining or any purpose by which a landowner might legitimately use and enjoy his land, even though in doing so he may divert or drain the groundwater of his neighbor. Kinney on Irrigation (2 ed.) Sec. 1192; 93 C.J.S. Waters § 93(3); 56 Am.Jur., Waters, Sec. 117; 55 A.L.R. 1398(b)(1) and cases there cited.

The principal difficulty in the application of the reasonable use doctrine is in determining what constitutes a reasonable use. What is a reasonable use must depend to a great extent upon many factors, such as the persons involved, their relative positions, the nature of their uses, the comparative value of their uses, the climatic conditions, and all facts and circumstances pertinent to the issues. Bristor v. Cheatham, 75 Ariz. 227, 255 P.2d 173, 179(17) (1953); Bollinger v. Henry, Mo., 375 S.W.2d 161, 166(9, 10) (1964). However, the modern decisions agree that under the rule of reasonable use an overlying owner, including a municipality, may not withdraw percolating water and transport it for sale or other use away from the land from which it was taken if the result is to impair the supply of an adjoining landowner to his injury. Such a use is unreasonable because non-beneficial and "is not for a lawful purpose within the general rule concerning percolating waters, but constitutes an actionable wrong for which damages are recoverable." [citations omitted]

The "reasonable use" rule as developed in the law of ground waters must be distinguished from the "correlative rights' rule. In 1902, the California Supreme Court repudiated the English common law rule in favor of the distinctive correlative rights doctrine which is based on the theory of proportionate sharing of withdrawals among landowners overlying a common basin." Under the doctrine, overlying owners have no proprietary interest in the water under their soil. California remains the only important correlative rights state; Utah has abandoned it, and only Nebraska also applies it to some extent. The administration of such a system of rights has proved extremely difficult in times of water shortage and has tendered towards an "equalitarian rigidity" which does not take into account the relative value of the competing uses. However suitable this doctrine may be for California—the prime consumer of ground water in the country—or any other state which may follow it, the reasonable use rule offers a more flexible legal standard for the just determination of beneficial uses of ground water, particularly under the climatic conditions of Missouri.

Respondent City contends that the English common law rule of absolute ownership of percolating waters governs in Missouri by virtue of statute and judicial decision. The City seems to suggest that since the Territorial Laws of 1816 adopted the common law as the rule of action and decision in this state and present Sec. 1.010 V.A.M.S. continues that legislative policy, we have no power to change or abrogate it. As we have already noted, Acton v. Blundell (marginal reference 3, *supra*), which is generally cited as having established the "English common law" rule of percolating waters, was decided in 1843 long after the Territorial Laws of 1816 were enacted. And not until 1860 was it decided that, without liability to an adjoining owner, an overlying owner might exhaust the groundwater to furnish a municipal water supply. Thus, there was no law of any kind on the subject at the time the common law was adopted by statute in this state. The subsequent English decisions declaring the common law on percolating waters are no more binding on us than the decisions of any court of another state. There is no impediment of inherited doctrine to our determination of the question presented according to the justice of the case.

[The court next considered the ruling of the St. Louis Court of Appeals, in the 1895 case of Springfield Waterworks Co. v. Jenkins, 62 Mo.App. 74, and determined that the ruling did not, as the City contended, firmly embrace the English rule of absolute ownership. The court proceeded to note also that times had changed since 1895:]

The intervening three-quarters of a century since Springfield Waterworks Company v. Jenkins, *supra*, has seen for Missouri a significant urban, industrial and population increase and with it greater demands upon a relatively static water supply. In the past such water disputes as have been brought to our courts usually have arisen "from factual situations pertaining to the existence of too much rather than too little water". Bollinger v. Henry, 375 S.W.2d l. c. 165(7). The controversy between respondent City and plaintiffs over the McBaine Bottom groundwater, however, is prompted by a scarcity, not an excess, of water to supply the vital needs of both. It is a competition which is destined to recur between other municipalities and landowners as present sources of municipal water supplies diminish and the need for them increases. In such circumstances, appeals to a dogma of absolute ownership of groundwater without consideration of the rights of adjoining landowners seem unpersuasive.

Also, since Springfield Waterworks v. Jenkins, *supra*, the science of groundwater hydrology has come into existence and has proven the postulates of the common law rule to be unsound. The premise that the owner of the soil owns all that lies beneath the surface so that he may use the percolating water in any way he chooses without liability to an adjoining owner fails to recognize that the supply of groundwater is limited, and that the first inherent limitation on water rights is the availability of the supply. Another postulate of the common law doctrine ascribes to percolating waters a movement so "secret, changeable and uncontrollable," that no attempt to subject them to fixed legal rules could be successfully made. Chatfield v. Wilson, 28 Vt. 49, 53 (1855); Frazier v. Brown, 12 Ohio St. 294 (1961). Modern knowledge and techniques have discredited this premise also. The movement, supply, rate of evaporation and many other physical characteristics of groundwater are now readily determinable. In fact, respondent City's decision to turn to the McBaine Bottom as the source of its water supply was made only after careful scientific analysis confirmed that this land was particularly adaptable for water production. At the time the City acquired the well and water treatment sites, it had full knowledge of the dimensions of the underlying aquifer, the volume of groundwater it contained, the daily rate of recharge, the direction and rate of flow, the normal water level and, at the rate of capture contemplated by the City, the level to which the groundwater would be lowered. The City cannot be permitted to escape liability by appeals to a doctrine which assumes that the very information the City has acted upon was not available to it. See Forbell v. City of New York, 58 N.E. l.c. 645 (1900).

Recently, in Bollinger v. Henry, *supra*, 375 S.W.2d l.c. 166(9, 10) (1964) the Supreme Court of Missouri applied the rule of reasonable use to determine the rights of riparian owners. Subterranean streams are governed by the rules applying to natural watercourses on the surface, so the rule of reasonable use in now applicable to them also. 93 C.J.S. Waters § 89; 56 Am.Jur., Waters, Sec. 109; Springfield Waterworks Co. v. Jenkins, 62 Mo.App. 80. We believe the same rule should apply to subterranean percolating waters. Jones v. Oz–Ark–Val Poultry Company, 228 Ark. 76, 306 S.W.2d 111, 113 (1957); Wrathall v. Johnson, 86 Utah 50, 40 P.2d 755, 776(13) (1935). It is that legal standard, in absence of a statutory expression of a priority of uses, by which existing water resources may be allocated most equitably and beneficially among competing users, private and public. The application of such a uniform legal standard would also give recognition to the established interrelationship between surface and groundwater and would, therefore, bring into one classification all waters over the use of which controversy may arise.

Under the rule of reasonable use as we have stated it, the fundamental measure of the overlying owner's right to use the groundwater is whether it is for purposes incident to the beneficial enjoyment of the land from which it was taken. Thus, a private owner may not withdraw groundwater for purposes of sale if the adjoining landowner is thereby deprived of water necessary for the beneficial enjoyment of his land. Katz v. Walkinshaw, 141 Cal. 116, 74 P. 766, 64 L.R.A. 236, 99 Am.St. Rep. 35 (1902) Here, the municipality has acquired miniscule plots of earth and by the use of powerful pumps intends to draw into wells on its own land for merchandising groundwater stored in plaintiffs' land, thereby depriving plaintiffs of the beneficial use of the normal water table to their immediate injury and to the eventual impoverishment of their lands. "There is no apparent reason for saying that, because defendant is a municipal corporation, seeking water for the inhabitants of a city, it may therefore do what a private owner of land may not do. The city is a private owner of this land, and the furnishing of water to its inhabitants is its private business. It is imperative that the people of the city have water; it is not imperative that they secure it at the expense of those owning lands adjoining lands owned by the city." Schenk v. City of Ann Arbor, 196 Mich. 75, 163 N.W. 109, 114(2) (1917); Canada v. City of Shawnee, 64 P.2d l.c. 698(4) (1937); see also, 93 C.J.S. Waters p. 765. Under the rule we apply, however, plaintiffs could have no basis for complaint if the City of Columbia's withdrawals of groundwater for municipal purposes from the McBaine Bottom do not interfere with plaintiffs' beneficial use of such water. Jarvis v. State Land Dept., City of Tucson, 104 Ariz. 527, 456 P.2d 385, 7(1) (1969); 93 C.J.S. Waters § 93(3). Under the facts pleaded, the water table could be maintained at its normal level and damage to plaintiffs avoided if the City were to limit its withdrawals to such quantity as would not exceed the daily recharge rate of 10.5 million gallons. If, on the other hand, the City perseveres in its declared intention to mine the water by at least one million gallons per day, it will become accountable to plaintiffs for whatever injury results from such diversion.

We have concluded that the pleaded averments of plaintiffs' petition raise in plaintiffs a property right to the reasonable use of the percolating waters underlying their lands, which right is shown to be threatened with wrongful and injurious invasion by the defendant City.... Plaintiffs' pleadings were sufficient to invoke the trial court's equitable jurisdiction to consider the request for injunctive relief thereby presented.

This is not to suggest that should proof follow upon the pleadings, perforce injunction will issue. Injunctive relief is a matter of grace, not of right. "The writ of injunction is an extraordinary remedy. It does not issue as a matter of course, but somewhat at the discretion of the chancellor. It is his duty to consider its effect upon all parties in interest, and to issue it only in case it is necessary to protect a substantial right, and even then not against great public interest." Smith v. City of Sedalia, 244 Mo. 107, 149 S.W. 597, 601(3); Johnson v. Independent School Dist. No. 1, 239 Mo.App. 749, 199 S.W.2d 421, 424(2); 43 C.J.S. Injunctions § 31. It requires the application of the principles of equity under all the circumstances. "The relative convenience and inconvenience and the comparative injuries to the parties and to the public should be considered in granting or refusing in injunction." Rubinstein v. City of Salem, Mo.App., 210 S.W.2d 382, 386; 42 Am.Jur.2d, Injunctions, Sec. 56. This rule has been applied where "the allowance of an injunction would seriously interfere with or work detriment to public works or works of public benefit, where the issuance of the injunction asked would result in cutting off the water supply" to the public harm. Barber v. School District No. 51, Clay County, 335 S.W.2d 527, 530(3); 43 C.J.S. Injunctions § 31, p. 466. "(A)nd, where the result of such public injury is so great on the one hand as compared to the injury complained of on the other, then it would be unconscionable to grant injunctive relief, and it will be denied." Horine v. People's Sewer Co., 200 Mo.App. 233, 204 S.W. 735, 736(1, 2). And this is so, even though the available remedy at law is not adequate. Johnson v. Independent School Dist. No. 1, 199 S.W.2d 424(2).

The rule of comparative injury suggest that under the facts pleaded and concessions of counsel it may be more equitable to deny injunctive relief than to grant it. The evidence may prompt the trial chancellor to the same conclusion, but that must await the determination of existing circumstances. To be sure, the rights plaintiffs seek to preserve are substantial and may not be treated cavalierly, but they are to be weighed against "the immeasurable value of the health and welfare of the public." Horine v. People's Sewer Co., 204 S.W. 736. Few things are more vital or of such surpassing importance to the public well-being than the assurance of a wholesome water supply. At the time this appeal was submitted, the development of the City's water treatment and distribution system was nearing completion. Perhaps by now it has become operative. The evidence may also disclose, as the pleadings do not, whether the McBaine Bottom is intended to supplement the City's present source of water or to supplant it. Nor do we know the full extent of the City's financial commitment to the project. These and other factors will guide the trial chancellor in deciding whether to impose its restraint upon the City and in doing so, he will be mindful that "the public convenience and public mischief may mark the distinction between sound and unsound discretion in granting an injunction". Johnson v. United Rys. Co. of St. Louis, 227 Mo. 423, 127 S.W. 63, 71.

The City has resisted plaintiffs' requested declaratory and injunctive relief on the theory that the common law rule of absolute ownership of percolating waters has governed its relationship with plaintiffs and, therefore, any damage to them could not be a legal injury. It has not sought to exercise its power of eminent domain to acquire the right to withdraw water from beneath plaintiffs' lands doubtless on the premise that it was under no duty to do so. Should the trial court adjudge that plaintiffs are entitled to the declarations they seek, the rule of reasonable use will apply and defendant City will be answerable to plaintiffs for any damage from its unreasonable use of groundwater. Should the trial court adjudge injunctive relief for plaintiffs appropriate, it would be well within its discretion to condition the imposition of that restraint upon the exercise by the City within a reasonable time, of its power of eminent domain to acquire the water rights it has been violating. Failing that, plaintiffs would still have available to them a remedy in the nature of an inverse condemnation for any damage caused by the City's unreasonable use.

The judgment of the trial court is reversed and the cause is remanded for further proceedings consistent with the views we have expressed.

Notes

1. *Place of use, revisited. Higday* introduces the common law of groundwater allocation. Just as the common law attached surface water to the land, so too did it attach groundwater to the land. Those who acquired land acquired, along with the land, a right to use groundwater. And for similar reasons, too, we see a place-of-use limit on this water right. How does the place-of-use rule in *Higday* compare with that of *Stratton*? With that of *Pyle*? At this point, how secure is the City's water-use right, even to the 10.5 million gallons per day that is the aquifer's apparent recharge rate?

2. *Absolute ownership or no ownership*? One early strand of the common law embraced what was known as the absolute (or English) ownership approach to groundwater law. Under it, a landowner could pump water and use it essentially at will, without limit. The rule was clear enough, but how apt is the name? Under such a regime, does the landowner really own the water absolutely? This rule has obvious parallels with the rule of capture applied in oil and gas law. Yet, recall that in oil and gas law there are two seemingly much different rules that end up in the same place—the ownership in place rule, and the no ownership rule. Is it not just as apt to say that the English rule of groundwater law is the "no ownership" rule? After all, what right does a landowner have to complain if a neighbor drains an aquifer dry? Is this not just a pure rule of capture, with no legal limit on what a person can do with water after capture?

The name given to a legal doctrine may not seem as important as the substance, but names have important connotations. What if a state legislature bans all new groundwater withdrawals? If the governing law is no ownership, who can complain? After all, landowners have lost nothing that they own. If it is absolute ownership, on the other hand, the new law can seem like a significant disruption of existing property rights. As the Missouri court points out, the English rule dated from a time when the subsurface movement of groundwater and the contours of aquifers were largely mysterious. Knowing little about water movement beneath the ground, courts had trouble determining factually whether a withdrawal by one person was adversely affecting withdrawals by another. The absolute ownership (or no ownership) approach avoided any need to figure out who was harming whom. Only with advances in hydrogeology did it become possible to apply a reasonable use rule. Thus we have one of many instances in which the law has changed due to increased knowledge in other fields of inquiry.

What might be the reaction if we used, instead, one of two other ways of describing this legal arrangement: (i) the landowner has an exclusive *right to capture* the groundwater, but does not own it until capture (a verbal formulation, as we've seen, used in some states for oil and gas); or (ii) the landowner has a *right to exclude* others from entering his land to engage in capture (the verbal formulation that applies to wildlife resources located on private land)? Would these alternatives verbal formulations resolve disputes the same way?

3. *Alternative remedies.* The place-of-use rule applied in *Higday* essentially states that off-tract use is permissible unless the water use actually harms another water user who is using water on an overlying tract. Here, the city was pumping water for use miles away, and thus its water use was precarious. At any time an owner of land above the aquifer could show up and claim that the off-tract use was harming his or her own water use. The city, one might think, would be disinclined to rely on such a water source, given the catastrophic effects of having to shut down the city's water system in the event a court issued an injunction halting it. Yet, many cities in the United States do exactly what the City of Columbia has done; they buy up small tracts of land, miles away, install wells and pump the water to the city. The same problem arises, in fact, even if a city's well is located within the city. The water is still being pumped off the tract where the well is located (owned, usually, by a water company) and onto properties throughout the city. Indeed, it would seem like cities everywhere that rely on groundwater are forced to distribute it for use off the overlying tract. How can this arrangement work? Why is there not more pressure to change state laws?

In fact, some state laws have been changed, but the key to the answer lies in the concluding paragraphs in *Higday.* In the court's view, municipal water use is a highly important activity. Even if a city is violating someone's landed property rights, an injunction halting the city's diversion will be issued only if it is equitable to do so. How likely is it that a court would order a city to shut down its water system, given the public health problems? More likely, the city would be given time to find an alternative. Or—perhaps even more likely—the court might refuse the injunction and instead award the plaintiff permanent damages for the invasion of private rights. In *Higday*, the court suggested that the city could exercise eminent domain to condemn the property rights needed to continue its water diversions. Sometimes cities will have this condemnation power, but often they will not because the property involved is outside of, or too far away from, the city's boundaries. Note, though, that a city essentially gains the power to condemn water rights when a court refuses to enjoin an unlawful water use and instead grants the plaintiff permanent damages.

4. Prather v. Eisenmann. The dispute in Prather v. Eisenmann, 200 Neb. 1, 261 N.W.2d 766 (1978), pitted three households, which gained their

domestic water from groundwater wells, against another owner of land over the same aquifer who drilled a deeper well and extracted water for irrigation. The irrigation well was sufficiently close to the household wells that it lowered the surrounding water table, creating an underground "cone of depression." The effect was to render the households unable to pump water unless they drilled their wells deeper while the defendant irrigator kept its well at the same depth. In resolving the dispute the Nebraska court clarified how its groundwater law differed from that of other states, in terms of resolving disputes among landowners all using water on their overlying tracts. The standard American approach to reasonable use, the court (rightly) explained, evaluated the reasonableness of a water use in the abstract, without taking into account competing uses of the same water or the effects of a reasonable use on other water users:

> Under the reasonable use doctrine, two neighboring landowners, each of whom is using water on his own property overlying the common supply, can withdraw all the supply he can put to beneficial and reasonable use. What is reasonable is judged solely in relationship to the purpose of such use on the overlying land. It is not judged in relation to the needs of others. (261 N.W.2d at 770).

Nebraska modified this rule by grafting on to it two other rules. First and as a matter of common law, landowners in Nebraska were each entitled to a "reasonable proportion" of the water contained in a shared aquifer. This shared use rule, the court explained, was similar to, but not as specific as, the correlative rights rule followed in California. Second, Nebraska law included a statute that provided a distinct preference, in case of conflict, for domestic water uses over all competing uses. All domestic users shared in this top priority. Among themselves they were each entitled to a proportionate (or fair) share of the whole. Because the irrigator was not a domestic user, the household users were entitled to a remedy for the invasion of their rights, without regard for whether the irrigator's use was also reasonable. By way of remedy, the court ordered the irrigator to pay the costs of deepening the plaintiffs' wells, and to refrain itself from deepening its own well.

CITY OF BLUE SPRINGS v. CENTRAL DEVELOPMENT ASSOCIATION

831 S.W.2d 655 (Mo. App. 1992).

- underground water not severable from land
- can convey right to use, but not water itself.

Spinden, Judge.

Central Development Association (CDA) and Community Water Company (CWC) appeal a jury's verdict of $100,000 against the City of Blue Springs for the city's taking of property by condemnation. CDA and CWC contend that the trial court erred in excluding their evidence relating to separate values for the surface land and the water beneath it. We affirm the trial court's judgment.

Blue Springs is a fourth class municipal corporation. Until 1990, it purchased water for its citizens from the Missouri Water Company. In 1979 Missouri Water announced that when the existing contract expired in 1990 it would cease supplying water to Blue Springs. Blue Springs seeks a new water source by this condemnation action.

CDA is a Missouri corporation, wholly owned by the Reorganized Church of Jesus Christ of Latter Day Saints. CDA holds title to property for the church, including approximately 6,000 acres of farmland in the Atherton Bottoms area northeast of Independence. Beneath CDA's farmland is an extensive water supply consisting of a deposit of alluvial rocks, gravel and sand, which filters and retains ground water.

After Blue Springs announced its intention to condemn CDA's land in the Atherton Bottoms in 1981, CDA conveyed rights to part of the water under the west 4000 acres by a subsurface water deed to CWC, incorporated in May 1982 as a water company. CDA owns 94 percent of CWC's stock. CDA was to receive one-half of CWC's proceeds from water sales, and CDA reserved the right to use all of the water it needed for farming the land. CWC did not own any wells, pipes, or a water treatment plant.

As CDA expected, Blue Springs did seek to condemn CDA's land on August 6, 1982, but the city wanted only 49.83 acres of CDA's land. The city wanted 34.12 acres for a water treatment plant and transmission lines and 15.71 acres for water wells.

CDA and CWC filed a joint motion to dismiss the condemnation petition. After hearing evidence for three days, the trial court dismissed Blue Springs' condemnation petition, and the city appealed. This court reversed the dismissal in *City of Blue Springs, Missouri v. Central Development Association,* 684 S.W.2d 44 (Mo.App.1984).

On remand, after Blue Springs filed an amended petition, the trial court ordered condemnation and appointed commissioners. . . . The court convened a jury trial on August 6–10, 1990. The jury awarded CDA and CWC $100,000, and on August 28, 1990, the trial court entered judgment consistent with the verdict.

In this appeal, CDA and CWC contend that because CDA conveyed its water rights to CWC, the trial court should have permitted it to present evidence valuing the land and water separately—that judgment should have been entered for the land's value in favor of CDA and for the water rights in favor of CWC. We disagree.

In a condemnation proceeding, the measure of damages is the difference between fair market value of the property before the taking and the fair market value after the taking. Any factor affecting market value is a proper element of damages. *State ex rel. Missouri Highway and Transportation Commission v. Horine,* 776 S.W.2d 6, 12 (Mo. banc 1989). Value of the water certainly was a factor for consideration in this case, but we disagree with CDA's and CWC's contention that the water value should have been separated from the overall land value.

CDA and CWC acknowledge the general rule that mineral deposits are not to be valued separately and are considered only to the extent which they enhance the land's value, but they assert that their case falls within a recognized exception: The values are to be separately stated if the surface and mineral rights have been severed into separate estates. *State ex rel. State Highway Comm'n of Missouri v. Foeller,* 396 S.W.2d 714, 719 (Mo.1965); *A.P. Green Refractories Co. v. Duncan,* 659 S.W.2d 19, 21 (Mo.App.1983). We conclude, however, that the water at issue in this case should be distinguished from mineral deposits generally and that neither the rule nor the exception apply.

water ≠ mineral deposits.

not mineral deposits

In *Higday v. Nickolaus,* 469 S.W.2d 859, 865 (Mo.App.1971), this court recognized two categories of subterranean waters—underground streams and percolating waters:

> An underground stream is defined as water that passes through or under the surface in a definite channel or one that is reasonably ascertainable. Percolating waters include all waters which pass through the ground beneath the surface of the earth without a definite channel and not shown to be supplied by a definite flowing stream. They are waters which ooze, seep, filter and otherwise circulate through the interstices of the subsurface strata without definable channel, or in a course that is not discoverable from surface indications without excavation for that purpose[.]

underground stream
percolating water ∴ presumed.

Underground waters are presumed to be percolating, and if a party claims that a subterranean stream exists, he bears the burden of proof. *Id.* CDA and CWC do not contend that the water at issue is not percolating.

Under the English common law, percolating waters were a part of the land in which they were found and belonged absolutely to the land's owner. A landowner could withdraw any amount of water without liability, no matter what effect his use had on adjoining landowners and the water under their lands. *Id.* Because of dissatisfaction with this rule, many courts, including Missouri, began applying the "reasonable use" rule:

percolating reasonable use

> Generally, the rule of reasonable use is an expression of the maxim that one must so use his own property as not to injure another— that each landowner is restricted to a reasonable exercise of his own rights and a reasonable use of his own property, in view of the similar rights of others.... As it applies to percolating ground water, the rule of reasonable use recognizes that the overlying owner has a proprietary interest in the water under his lands, but his incidents of ownership are restricted. It recognizes that the nature of the property right is usufructuary rather than absolute as under the English rule.

Id. at 866 (citations omitted). Under the reasonable use rule, a landowner may use the underlying ground water freely for any purpose incidental to his beneficial enjoyment of the land. He does not, however, own the water. Because of the wandering and migratory nature of percolating water, a landowner does not own it in the absolute sense.

Not absolute ownership

— can use freely for purpose incidental to enjoyment of the land

— does not own the water

This court finds persuasive the analysis of the Florida Supreme Court, in *Village of Tequesta v. Jupiter Inlet Corp.*, 371 So.2d 663 (1979), in which the court considered whether a landowner had sufficient interest in percolating water to require condemnation. The court held:

> [T]he term "ownership" as applied to percolating water never meant that the overlying owner had a property or proprietary interest in the corpus of the water itself.
>
> This necessarily follows from the physical characteristic of percolating water. It is migratory in nature and is a part of the land only so long as it is in it. There is a right of use as it passes, but there is no ownership in the absolute sense. It belongs to the overlying owner in a limited sense, that is, he has the unqualified right to capture and control it in a reasonable way with an immunity from liability to his neighbors for doing so. When it is reduced to his possession and control, it ceases to be percolating water and becomes his personal property. But if it flows or percolates from his land, he loses all right and interest in it the instant it passes beyond the boundaries of his property, and when it enters the land of his neighbor it belongs to him in the same limited way. The right of the owner to ground water underlying his land is to the usufruct of the water and not to the water itself. The ownership of the land does not carry with it any ownership of vested rights to underlying ground water not actually diverted and applied to beneficial use.

Id. at 667. The court concluded that the user's right to the water was not a private property right requiring condemnation proceedings unless the right was rendered useless for certain purposes.

We conclude that water is not severable from the land through or under which it flows. A landowner may convey his right to use the water, but not the water itself. That distinction alone makes water different from cases dealing generally with minerals and their severance. A further distinction is that mineral deposits typically are finite; once the mineral is removed no new deposits form. Water, on the other hand, is replenished. . . .

We conclude that the trial court properly excluded evidence regarding the separate value of the water. CDA's and CWC's points concerning the issue are denied. . . .

Notes

1. *Dividing water from land by private action II.* Again we see arising our by-now familiar question: When water rights are part and parcel of a tract of land, can the landowner voluntarily sever the water rights and sell them? What result does the court here reach, and based on what considerations? How does its reasoning compare with the reasoning we've seen in cases involving riparian rights (especially *Thompson v. Enz* and *Pyle*)?

To make sense of this ruling, we need to pay careful attention to the distinctions that the court makes. As *Higday* established, landowners in

Missouri can use water off the overlying tract subject to a no-harm rule. That apparently means also that they can convey to other people the right to enter their land and pump water for use on distant tracts—subject again to the no harm rule. Yet, the landowner's right to the water does not include ownership in place of the water. It is merely a use right in the water, a right to capture it so long as the water is there. While that use right, the court tells us, can be sold, such a sale does not involve a sale of the underlying water itself. This means that water is not like minerals that remain in place; it cannot be sold as a separate estate, apart from the land surface. Using this reasoning, the court decides that a city that condemns land to gain access to water need not pay separately for the water estate when the landowner has tried to sever the water estate and sell it to someone else. Thus we see how conflicts over place of use can get intertwined with ideas about the nature of a resource use right, about the ability of landowners to sever a resource right from the land itself, and (finally) about the meaning of reasonable use.

If this all seems confusing and rather artificial, it is. Is it fair to suspect that courts decide such cases based on the facts, practical fairness, and communal needs, and then find ways to incorporate their desired outcome into legal terms? In any event, how satisfying is the court's reasoning in the case? The court admits that CWC acquired a valid water use right from CDA (a right to enter CDA's land to pump and remove water). Isn't this plainly a form of private property? If so, why isn't it something that the City of Blue Springs must condemn in order to gain the right itself to pump water from the land that it is buying? (Hint: As you think about this you should ask: what exactly has CDA given up when it contracted with CWC, and how, if at all, are CWC's rights reduced by the actions of the city? Indeed, if CWC in the future begins using water on overlying land, isn't it the city that will then need to worry about the security of its water rights?)

2. *First in time?* A curious aspect of this ruling is the court's repeated emphasis (in portions of the ruling largely omitted) that the plaintiffs-appellants were not then engaged in a major water-use activity. CWC talked vaguely about starting such an activity—even getting in the water distribution business—but had not initiated any water uses. The court ignored these assertions because they dealt with hypothetical future activities. We might note, though, that a landowner's right to use water is not lost through nonuse. The right exists and can be exercised at any time. (This contrasts, as we'll see, with prior appropriation rights, which can be lost through abandonment or forfeiture, and in any event only arise based on actual, beneficial use.) If the City of Blue Springs has undercut the ability of these landowners to engage in future water-use activities, have not their property rights been diminished? And if we are to ignore this future harm (as the court is prone to do), haven't we essentially altered somewhat the method by which water is allocated in the state by placing more emphasis on being first in time to use the water? Put otherwise, might the case have come out differently if CWC, right before the condemnation, had installed major pumps and begun exercising its water use right?

The next case is factually complex but well worth a careful review given all that is in it. The facts will remind you of several prior cases, particularly Mrs. Hammond's clash with Central Kentucky Gas. It also raises an extraordinary number of the issues we've seen before, including ancillary rights, access to a natural resource, limits on the right to exclude, the possibilities of private condemnation, and the willingness of courts to reshape private rights to serve public needs:

PARK COUNTY BOARD OF COMMISSIONERS v. PARK COUNTY SPORTSMEN'S RANCH, LLP

45 P.3d 693 (Colo. 2002).

JUSTICE HOBBS delivered the Opinion of the Court.

In this appeal from a judgment of the District Court for Water Division No. 1 (Water Court), Plaintiffs–Appellants, the Park County Board of County Commissioners, James B. Gardner, and Amanda Woodbury (Landowners) claimed in a declaratory judgment action that the applicant for a conditional water right, Park County Sportsmen's Ranch, LLP (PCSR) has "no right to occupy the space beneath the lands of the Plaintiffs to store water or other substances on or below the surface of the lands. Any such placement or storage of water on or below the surface constitutes a trespass for which the Defendant may be liable for damages." For this proposition, the Landowners rely upon the common-law property doctrine "Cujus est solum ejus est usque ad coelum et ad inferos"[13] (cujus doctrine). The Landowners also contend that Article XVI, sections 14 and 15, section 37–87–101(1), and other statutes require PCSR to obtain consent or condemn property interests and pay just compensation to them in connection with its conjunctive use project even though PCSR does not propose to drill into or locate any of its project's facilities on or within the Landowners' properties. . . .

I.

The Landowners and PCSR own property in South Park, Colorado, a high mountain valley approximately seventy-five miles southwest of Denver. PCSR filed with the Water Court an application for a conditional water rights decree and plan for augmentation and exchange involving extraction from and recharge of water into the South Park formation for augmentation, storage, and beneficial use. The South Park formation is a natural geological structure containing aquifers PCSR intends to utilize in connection with its project.

PCSR owns 2,307 acres of land in South Park. As part of its conditional water rights application and plan for augmentation and exchange, PCSR claimed the right to occupy saturated and unsaturated portions of the South Park formation for water extraction, augmentation, and storage as part of a water project it calls the South Park Conjunctive Use Project intended for City of Aurora municipal use. Project features would include twenty-six wells to withdraw water from the South Park formation and six surface reservoirs for artificially

13. This phrase translates to mean: "To whomsoever the soil belongs, he owns also to the sky and to the depths." *See* Norman W. Thorson, *Storing Water Underground: What's the Aqui–Fer?,* 57 Neb. L.Rev. 581, 588 (1978).

recharging the aquifers. PCSR's application did not propose to locate any of the project's recharge and extraction features on the Landowners' properties. . . .

The Landowners objected to PCSR's Water Court application. They also filed a complaint for declaratory relief in the Park County District Court seeking a determination that the placement or storage of water above or below the surface of their lands, absent their consent, would constitute a trespass. . . .

The Water Court found that PCSR's project did not include the construction of any facilities on or in the Landowners' properties and the Landowners had not alleged that the use, benefit, and enjoyment of their properties would be invaded or compromised in any way. The Water Court determined as a matter of law that PCSR's project did not require the Landowners' consent or condemnation and payment of just compensation. The Water Court ruled that: (1) the property rights of the Landowners do not include ownership of waters tributary to a natural stream; (2) natural streams crossing the property of another may be utilized, without consent, for the transportation of water by a lawful appropriator; (3) natural stream water includes the water in the aquifers; (4) water is treated differently from a property owner's traditional rights in the land estate; (5) Colorado's eminent domain law applies only if the holder of the water use right constructs facilities on or in a non-consenting landowner's property; (6) Colorado law encourages rather than restrains the efficient utilization of the state's scarce water resources; (7) the General Assembly intended to authorize artificial recharge of natural subsurface formations and conjunctive use of ground water placed therein, as part of its maximum utilization goal for beneficial use of water; and (8) the movement of underground water into, from, or through land underlying another's property, resulting from artificial recharge into an aquifer by the holder of a decreed water right, does not constitute a trespass. At the Landowners' request, the Water Court entered judgment in favor of PCSR so that the Landowners could appeal the court's declaratory judgment ruling to us. . . .

II.

The Water Court determined that: (1) artificial recharge activities involving the movement of underground water into, from, or through aquifers underlying the surface lands of the Landowners would not constitute a trespass; and (2) PCSR's proposed project would not require the Landowners' consent or condemnation and the payment of just compensation under the provisions of Article XVI, sections 14 and 15, section 37–87–101(1), or the other statutes the Landowners invoke, because the project did not involve the construction of any facilities on or in the Landowners' properties. We agree with the Water Court and uphold its judgment. . . .

B. Landowners' Trespass Claim

. . . On appeal, the Landowners take no exception to the passage of augmentation water through the aquifers underlying their lands. They also concede that PCSR's proposed project does not involve the construction of any facilities on or within their properties. However, they contend that use of the aquifers for "storage" of PCSR's artificially recharged water within their properties would constitute a trespass. This novel proposition has attracted several amicus briefs arguing that artificial recharge, augmentation, and storage of water in aquifers are authorized by Colorado law and do not require the consent of overlying landowners, unless the project facilities are located on or within the overlying landowners' properties.

To support their theory, the Landowners invoke our decisions in *Walpole v. State Board of Land Commissioners,* 62 Colo. 554, 163 P. 848 (1917) and *Wolfley v. Lebanon Mining Co.,* 4 Colo. 112 (1878). The Landowners invoke *Walpole* and *Wolfley* for the assertion that their "fee ownership includes the space underneath the land" and therefore they have a right to withhold consent and require compensation for PCSR's project. In *Walpole* . . . we said:

> Land has an indefinite extent upward and downward from the surface of earth, and therefore includes whatever may be erected upon it, and whatever may lie in a direct line between the surface and the center of the earth.

Walpole, 62 Colo. at 557, 163 P. at 849–50. In *Wolfley,* we said: "At common law a grant of land carries with it all that lies beneath the surface down to the center of the earth." *Wolfley,* 4 Colo. at 114.

The Water Court found that "Plaintiffs have not alleged that their use, benefit and enjoyment of the estate will be invaded or compromised in any way." The Landowners simply assert that common-law principles entitle them to control the storage space in aquifers underneath the surface of their lands and grant them a remedy in trespass against migration of PCSR's water laterally into their property. The Ohio Supreme Court has rejected a very similar contention in *Chance v. BP Chemicals, Inc.,* 77 Ohio St.3d 17, 670 N.E.2d 985 (1996). In that case, a property owner claimed that the migration of injected liquid into portions of a very deep aquifer underlying its property constituted a trespass. Determining that the injectate mixed with "waters of the state" in the aquifer, the Ohio Supreme Court rejected the property owner's claim of ownership and trespass based on the cujus doctrine. It stated:

> Our analysis above concerning the native brine illustrates that appellants do not enjoy absolute ownership of waters of the state below their properties, and therefore underscores that their subsurface ownership rights are limited. As the discussion in *Willoughby Hills*[14] makes evident, ownership rights in today's world are not so

14. *See Willoughby Hills v. Corrigan,* 29 Ohio St.2d 39, 278 N.E.2d 658, 664 (1972) (stating that "the doctrine of the common law, that the ownership of land extends to the periphery of the universe, has no place in the modern world") (citing *United States v. Causby,* 328 U.S. 256, 66 S.Ct. 1062, 90 L.Ed. 1206 (1946)).

> clear-cut as they were before the advent of airplanes and injection wells.
>
> Consequently, we do not accept appellants' assertion of absolute ownership of everything below the surface of their properties. Just as a property owner must accept some limitations on the ownership rights extending above the surface of the property, we find that there are also limitations on property owners' subsurface rights. We therefore extend the reasoning of *Willoughby Hills,* that absolute ownership of air rights is a doctrine which "has no place in the modern world," to apply as well to ownership of subsurface rights.

Chance, 670 N.E.2d at 992.

We find the Ohio Supreme Court's discussion of state waters and limitations upon absolute subsurface ownership rights to be of particular significance to the case before us, in light of Colorado's strong constitutional, statutory, and case law holding all water in Colorado to be a public resource and allowing holders of water rights decrees the right of passage for their appropriated water through and within the natural surface and subsurface water-bearing formations. The Arizona Court of Appeals has rejected a claim of property ownership rights very similar to the Landowners' claim in this case. *See W. Maricopa Combine, Inc. v. Ariz. Dep't of Water Resources,* 200 Ariz. 400, 26 P.3d 1171, 1176 (App.2001); *see also Los Angeles v. San Fernando,* 14 Cal.3d 199, 263–64, 123 Cal.Rptr. 1, 537 P.2d 1250, 1297 (1975) (recognizing ground water storage by artificial recharge and stating that the "fact that spread water is commingled with other ground water is no obstacle to the right to recapture the amount by which the available conglomerated ground supply has been augmented by the spreading.") . . .

C. Tributary Aquifer Hydrology

Legislators, administrators, and judges generally have a better understanding of surface water systems than ground water systems. *See* Robert Jerome Glennon & Thomas Maddock, *The Concept of Capture: The Hydrology and Law of Stream/Aquifer Interactions,* Forty–Third Annual Rocky Mountain Mineral Law Institute § 22.02, at 22–7 (1997). Some states that allocate their surface water by the principles of prior appropriation nevertheless allocate ground water by a rule of capture that permits overlying landowners to possess the ground water appearing under their land without regard to the effect of its extraction upon other ground water and surface water users. However, such a rule of capture defies hydrologic reality and impairs the security and reliability of senior water use rights that depend on an interconnected ground and surface water system. Colorado law contains a presumption that all ground water is tributary to the surface stream unless proved or provided by statute otherwise. *Safranek v. Town of Limon,* 123 Colo. 330, 334, 228 P.2d 975, 977 (1951).

An aquifer is a subsurface water bearing formation. Hydrologic continuity exists if there is a hydrologic connection between a surface stream and the water table of an aquifer. Glennon & Maddock, *supra,* at 22–7 to 22–8. The water moves through a shared, permeable layer. Ground water, in an interconnected hydrologic system, provides a base flow for surface streams through the saturated layer of the water bearing formation. Water added to a ground water system can increase the flow of the surface stream; conversely, well pumping that results in lowering the water table can deplete the surface stream.

Aquifers consist of unsaturated and saturated zones. The unsaturated zone contains both air and water in the spaces between the grains of sand, gravel, silt, clay, and cracks within the rock. *See Ground Water and Surface Water, A Single Resource,* U.S. Geological Survey Circular 1139, at 6 (1999) [hereinafter *USGS*]. The movement of water in the unsaturated zone above the water table is controlled by gravity and capillary forces. Georg Matthess, *The Properties of Groundwater* 173 (1982). In the saturated zone, these voids are completely filled with water. *USGS* at 6. The upper surface of the saturated zone is the water table. *Id.* Water that infiltrates the land surface moves vertically downward through unsaturated areas to the water table to become ground water. Once the water has infiltrated the soil, its passage downward to join the ground water depends on the geologic structures and rock composition. *See* Elizabeth M. Shaw, *Hydrology in Practice* 124 (2d. ed.1989). Storativity can be calculated for confined and unconfined aquifers. *Id.* at 128.The ground water typically moves laterally within the ground water system. *USGS* at 7. Well pumping creates a cone of depression, with the point of the inverted cone occurring at the bottom of the well pipe. This causes surrounding water in the aquifer to flow into the cone from all sides. *See Fellhauer v. People,* 167 Colo. 320, 331, 447 P.2d 986, 992 (1968).

The interaction between streams and tributary aquifers occurs in three basic ways: streams gain water from inflow of ground water into the surface stream, streams lose water to the aquifer from outflow from the stream, or do both by gaining water from aquifers in some reaches and losing it to aquifers in other reaches. *USGS* at 9. Without human intervention, the surface/ground water interconnected system "exists in a state of approximate equilibrium" which implies "a long-term balance between natural recharge and discharge processes in a groundwater basin." Glennon & Maddock, *supra,* at 22–10.

"Recharge," whether natural or artificial, is "the accretion of water to the upper surface of the saturated zone." *USGS* at 6. "Discharge" is the contribution of aquifer water that migrates to the surface. *Id.* "Storage" is the retention of ground water in the aquifer for a temporal period. The length of the retention time depends upon the specific characteristics of the aquifer:

> Aquifers have two main functions in the underground phase of the water cycle. They store water for varying periods in the underground reservoir, and they act as pathways or conduits to pass water along through the reservoir. Although some are more efficient as

pipelines (e.g., cavernous limestones) and some are more effective as storage reservoirs (e.g., sandstones), most aquifers perform both functions continuously.

John C. Manning, *Applied Principles of Hydrology* 156 (1987)....

Under the Landowners' property ownership theory, each landowner would have a cause of action against PCSR or any other person attempting to pursue a conditional water rights application for storage of water in the aquifer. However, we determine that the General Assembly, in authorizing the use of aquifers for storage of artificially recharged waters pursuant to decreed conjunctive use projects, has further supplanted the Landowners' common-law property ownership theory.

Conjunctive use projects are water projects that employ the natural water bearing formations—on the land's surface and in the aquifers—in the exercise of decreed water use rights according to their priority vis-à-vis all other decreed water rights. We now discuss the General Assembly's authorization for such projects.

D. *Statutory Authorization for Conjunctive Use Projects*

When parties have use rights to water they have captured, possessed, and controlled, they may place that water into an aquifer by artificial recharge and enjoy the benefit of that water as part of their decreed water use rights, if the aquifer can accommodate the recharged water without injury to decreed senior water rights.

Can recharge & enjoy if no harm to others.

This authority resides in a number of statutory sections that implement the "Colorado Doctrine," which is that all water in the state is a public resource dedicated to the beneficial use of public and private agencies, as prescribed by law. *See Chatfield E. Well Co. v. Chatfield E. Prop. Owners Ass'n*, 956 P.2d 1260, 1268 (Colo.1998).

Sections 37–92–305(9)(b) and (c) provide that the Water Court may issue a conditional decree for storage of water in underground aquifers if the applicant can and will lawfully capture, possess, and control water for beneficial use which it then artificially recharges into the aquifer. Section 37–87–101(1) provides that the right to store water of a natural stream is a right of appropriation in order of priority, and section 37–87–101(2) provides that underground aquifers can be used for storage of water that the applicant artificially recharges into the aquifer pursuant to a decreed right.

The storage definition of section 37–92–103(10.5), 10 C.R.S. (2001), contains a two-part definition. The statute provides:

"Storage" or "store" means the impoundment, possession, and control of water by means of a dam. Waters in underground aquifers are not in storage or stored *except to the extent waters in such aquifers are placed there by other than natural means with water to which the person placing such water in the underground aquifer has a conditional or decreed right.*

Only artificial recharge of aquifer is storage

Id. (emphasis added). The first part defines "storage" as the impoundment, possession, and control of water by means of a dam and describes the typical reservoir, which is a constructed impoundment. The second definition contemplates the artificial recharge of water into the aquifer for "storage" and describes the circumstances under which a decree may be issued for aquifer storage. Thus, the legislature contemplated a two-step process: that a person will capture, possess, and control water and then artificially recharge it into the aquifer for storage and subsequent use, pursuant to a decreed water right....

Construing the General Assembly's wording and intent and effectuating evident legislative purposes, we determine that the General Assembly has authorized the issuance of decrees for artificial recharge and storage of water in an aquifer when the decree holder lawfully captures, possesses, and controls water and then places it into the aquifer for subsequent beneficial use....

We now turn to water use rights and property ownership rights under Colorado law.

E. Water Use Rights and Land Ownership Rights Under Colorado Law

[The court began its discussion of state law by surveying the history of water law, beginning in the early English cases and continuing through the beginnings of Colorado law.]

When first announcing the Colorado Doctrine, we said that "rules respecting the tenure of private property must yield to the physical laws of nature, whenever such laws exert a controlling influence." *Yunker v. Nichols,* 1 Colo. 551, 553 (1872) (Hallett, C.J.).

> When the lands of this territory were derived from the general government, they were subject to the law of nature, which holds them barren until awakened to fertility by nourishing streams of water, and the purchasers could have no benefit from the grant without the right to irrigate them. It may be said, that all lands are held in subordination to the dominant right of others, who must necessarily pass over them to obtain a supply of water to irrigate their own lands, and this servitude arises, not by grant, but by operation of law.

Yunker, 1 Colo. at 555. Commenting on the 1861 Territorial Act, Justice Wells, in *Yunker,* confirmed this principle:

> I conceive that, with us, the right of every proprietor to have a way over the lands intervening between his possessions and the neighboring stream for the passage of water for the irrigation of so much of his land as may be actually cultivated, is well sustained by force of the necessity arising from local peculiarities of climate.... But it appears to me that this right must rest altogether upon the necessity rather than upon the grant which the statute assumes to make.... It seems to me, therefore, that the right springs out of the

> necessity, and existed before the statute was enacted, and would still survive though the statute were repealed.

Id. at 570 (Wells, J., concurring). We followed *Yunker* 's lead with *Coffin v. Left Hand Ditch Co.,* 6 Colo. 443 (1882), holding that an appropriator could capture water from a stream and transport it to another watershed, using streams in both watersheds to convey the appropriated water to its place of beneficial use....

Accordingly, by reason of Colorado's constitution, statutes, and case precedent, neither surface water, nor ground water, nor the use rights thereto, nor the water-bearing capacity of natural formations belong to a landowner as a stick in the property rights bundle. Section 37–87–103, 10 C.R.S. (2001), for example, codifies this longstanding aspect of the Colorado Doctrine. It provides that water appropriated by means of a reservoir impoundment and then released for travel to its place of beneficial use shall enjoy the right of passage through the natural formation in the administration of water use rights....

F. Accommodation of Water Use Rights and Land Ownership Rights

Upon adoption of Colorado's constitution, the state struck an accommodation between two kinds of property interests—water use rights and land rights—by requiring the owners of water use rights to obtain the consent of, or pay just compensation to, owners of land in, upon, or across which the water right holders constructed dams, reservoirs, ditches, canals, flumes, or other manmade facilities for the diversion, conveyance, or storage of water. *See* Colo. Const. art. XVI, § 7; Colo. Const. art. II, §§ 14 & 15; § 37–86–102, 10 C.R.S. (2001).

But, this requirement does not extend to vesting in landowners the right to prevent access to the water source or require compensation for the water use right holder's employment of the natural water bearing surface and subsurface formations on or within the landowners' properties for the movement of its appropriated water. Our decision in *Southwestern,* reaffirming the Colorado Doctrine, is adverse to the Landowners' property right and just compensation claims in this regard....

In deference to the laws of nature, which we held to be foundational in *Yunker v. Nichols,* Colorado law does not recognize a land ownership right by which the Landowners can claim control of the aquifers as part of their bundle of sticks. To the contrary, "[a]s knowledge of the science of hydrology advanced, it became clear that natural streams are surface manifestations of extensive tributary systems, including underground water in stream basins," *Three Bells Ranch Assocs. v. Cache La Poudre Water Users Ass'n,* 758 P.2d 164, 170 (Colo.1988), and passage of appropriated water through the natural streams is part of the Colorado law of water use rights.

However, Article XVI, section 7 does subject the construction of artificial water facilities on another's land to the payment of just compensation and grants a right of private condemnation for the construction of such waterworks:

> All persons and corporations shall have the right of way across public, private and corporate lands for the construction of ditches, canals and flumes for the purpose of conveying water for domestic purposes, for the irrigation of agricultural lands, and for mining and manufacturing purposes, and for drainage, upon payment of just compensation.

Colo. Const. art. XVI, § 7. . . .

In sum, the holders of water use rights may employ underground as well as surface water bearing formations in the state for the placement of water into, occupation of water in, conveyance of water through, and withdrawal of water from the natural water bearing formations in the exercise of water use rights. *See Coffin,* 6 Colo. at 449; *Larimer County Reservoir Co. v. Luthe,* 8 Colo. 614, 616, 9 P. 794, 795–96 (1885) (holding that an appropriator can use the natural non-navigable stream for water storage); *People v. Emmert,* 198 Colo. 137, 142, 597 P.2d 1025, 1028 (1979) (stating that section 5 of Article XVI of the Colorado Constitution "was primarily intended to preserve the historical appropriation system of water rights upon which the irrigation economy in Colorado was founded"); *Danielson v. Vickroy,* 627 P.2d 752, 756 (Colo.1981) (stating that the purpose of the Ground Water Management Act was to permit the full economic development of designated ground water resources); *Bayou Land Co. v. Talley,* 924 P.2d 136, 146 (Colo.1996) (holding that Congress did not grant ownership of water along with land grants and the General Assembly's statutory provisions control); *Chatfield E. Well Co. v. Chatfield E. Prop. Owners Ass'n,* 956 P.2d 1260, 1268 (Colo.1998) (stating that water is a public resource and the "right to use nontributary ground water outside of a designated basin is purely a function of statute and landowners do not have an absolute right to ownership of water underneath their land"); *Park County Sportsmen's Ranch v. Bargas,* 986 P.2d 262, 275 (Colo.1999) (holding that ground water beneath lands in South Park is tributary and is subject to the doctrine of prior appropriation).

We reject the Landowners' claim that the *cujus* doctrine provides them with a property right to require consent for artificial recharge and storage of water in aquifers that extend through their land. Water is not a mineral. *See Andrus v. Charlestone Stone Prods.,* 436 U.S. at 615, 98 S.Ct. 2002. The law of minerals and property ownership we relied on in *Walpole* and *Wolfley* is inapplicable to water and water use rights.[15]

15. We decline to extend principles of mineral law to water law in Colorado for additional reasons. Ownership of oil and gas is a private right closely tied to property ownership; it logically follows that the right to ownership, extraction, and storage of mineral resources would remain sticks in the property owner's bundle of sticks. Water is a public resource, and any rights to it are usufructuary. Mineral law is a special body of law derived from special circumstances. *See Chance v. BP Chems., Inc.,* 77 Ohio St.3d 17, 670 N.E.2d 985, 991 (1996) ("We find the situation before us is not analogous to those present in oil and gas cases, around which a special body of law has arisen based on special circumstances not present here.").

G. Condemnation for Constructed Waterworks

We now address the Landowners' contention that certain statutory provisions, in combination with Article II, sections 14 and 15 of the Colorado Constitution, evidence legislative intent to require consent or the payment of just compensation for the right of storage occupancy in aquifers extending through the Landowners' properties....

The Colorado Constitution prohibits the taking of private property for public or private use without the property owner's consent, but provides five exceptions to this prohibition, four of which pertain to constructed water facilities. Article XVI, section 7: (1) provides for access to the water source across the lands of others, embodying the common-law right-of-way rule for artificial water structures we first articulated in *Yunker v. Nichols;* and (2) requires compensation for the construction of water project features on the land of those who do not consent. Article II, section 14 further recognizes and addresses the private right of condemnation for the construction of waterworks:

> Private property shall not be taken for private use unless by consent of the owner, except for private ways of necessity, and except for reservoirs, drains, flumes, or ditches on or across the lands of others for agricultural, mining, milling, domestic or sanitary purposes.

Colo. Const. art. II, § 14.[16] Article II, section 15 establishes a compensation requirement for such takings:

> Private property shall not be taken or damaged, for public or private use, without just compensation. Such compensation shall be ascertained by a board of commissioners, of not less than three freeholders, or by a jury....

Colo. Const. art II, § 15.

[The court next considered several state statutes, concluding that they did not alter this constitutional rule governing compensation.]

Article XVI, section 7, Article II, sections 14 and 15, and section 37–87–101(1) establish a private right of condemnation of private property through eminent domain for "those interests in real property reasonably necessary for the construction, maintenance, or operation of any water storage projects." Section 37–87–101(1) provides in full:

> The right to store water of a natural stream for later application to beneficial use is recognized as a right of appropriation in order of priority under the Colorado constitution. No water storage facility may be operated in such a manner as to cause material injury to the senior appropriative rights of others. Acquisition of those interests in real property reasonably necessary for the construction, maintenance, or operation of any water storage reservoir, together with

16. We conclude that this provision's reference to condemnation for "reservoirs" on or across the lands of others refers to artificial structures constructed on or in land to hold water in storage, as each of the remaining terms in the provision is an artificial structure and reservoirs are generally understood to be flat water impoundments constructed for the purpose of damming water.

> inlet, outlet, or spillway structures or other facilities necessary to make such reservoir effective to accomplish the beneficial use or uses of water stored or to be stored therein, may be secured under the laws of eminent domain.

§ 37–87–101(1), 10 C.R.S. (2001).

The first two sentences of this subsection clearly provide that storage for subsequent use of natural stream waters is a constitutionally protected appropriative right, the exercise of which must not cause material injury to decreed senior appropriative rights. The third sentence plainly pertains to facilities that the holder of a water use right constructs to divert, store, or convey water in the exercise of decreed rights. *See* Roaring Fork, 36 P.3d at 1232.

In the case before us, the proposed project facilities include constructed wells, dams, recharge reservoirs, and other water works, but the project does not include the location of any artificial features on or in the Landowners' properties. Thus, PCSR would not need the consent of the Landowners or an easement, nor would it have to pay just compensation to them, and no trespass occurs simply as the result of water moving into an aquifer and being contained or migrating in the course of the aquifer's functioning underneath the lands of another. . . .

We agree with the Water Court's holding that artificially recharging an aquifer "is analogous to the use of an unconfined aquifer or natural stream for transport." This comports with longstanding principles of Colorado water law that have allowed passage of the appropriator's water across the lands of another. . . .

The Water Court did not err in concluding that PCSR's recharge, augmentation, and storage activities in aquifers pursuant to a decreed water use right would not constitute a trespass or require condemnation and the payment of just compensation, unless project features are constructed on or in the Landowners' properties. Accordingly, we affirm the Water Court's judgment.

Notes

1. Hammonds, *redux*. This Park County dispute has obvious similarities to Mrs. Hammonds' problems with Central Kentucky Gas (in which she claimed that gas returned to the ground trespassed upon her subsurface rights), as well as with the cases governing ownership and use of the Onyx Cave in Kentucky. How do the rulings compare in terms of outcome, reasoning, and policy slants? How does Colorado law on groundwater seem to avoid the practical problem created by the ruling of the Kentucky Supreme Court in *Hammonds*? Can we explain the different outcomes based on the fact that the state has a particularly strong interest in ensuring the productive use of water in a semi-arid region?

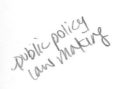

Whatever the reason for the different outcomes, *Park County* displays a distinct willingness by a court over time to shape the common law to promote a distinct public policy (here, the efficient use of water), and to redefine private property rights to achieve that policy goal. We also see a willingness to define private property rights in ways that take nature into account; that is, the rights a landowner has vary based on the land's physical features. Land that is crossed by a physical structure capable of conveying water (on or below the surface) does not have the same rights to exclude as does the owner of different types of land. Differences like this in landowner rights arise regularly in natural resources law, even though the resulting rules conflict with the widely held cultural idea that landed property rights are defined abstractly, in ways that give the same rights to all landowners. Finally, the court's decision here is permeated by a sense that owners of land and valuable resources need to take into account the respective needs of one another. Note the title that the court gives to part II.F. of its opinion: "Accommodation of Water Use Rights and Land Ownership Rights." This obligation to accommodate recurs regularly in natural resources law, and with increasing frequency. Indeed, it is an idea that might well have a considerable future as courts identify new ways in which accommodation can increase resource-use efficiency and decrease ecological degradation.

2. *What this means for the landowner.* This scholarly ruling—by a justice known for his scholarly writings—is highly useful in identifying all the ways that the rights of landowners in Colorado are limited so as to promote the efficient use of water in the state. You might find it useful to make a list of them, starting with the fact that water itself is not attached to the land and considering the many ways that the landowner's control over the land surface and subsurface are curtailed. It's worth including also the landowners' liability to having his land taken through private condemnation.

3. *The complexities of modern water law. Park County* is a challenging decision to read because it presumes a rather advanced knowledge of water law. Three basic points that will help: a *conditional water rights* decree in Colorado is a judicial declaration that a water user is undertaking the steps necessary to gain an appropriative water right; once all the steps are taken (basically, physically diverting the water and applying it to a beneficial use), the new water right will ripen and, in terms of temporal priority, will date back in time to the date of the conditional water rights decree. The decree is conditional on completion of all the steps, and if the steps aren't completed in a timely manner the right ends. A *plan of augmentation and exchange* involves a situation in which a party that wants to use water from one source (typically where water is fully appropriated) can gain the right to do so by replacing the water it is removing with water from elsewhere. The idea may seem strange but in many physical settings makes good sense in terms of reducing the costs of transporting and storing water. As for *conjunctive use*, it is a broad term that covers various arrangements by which surface water is used in conjunction with groundwater.

4. *Law versus nature.* Whenever nature is divided into discrete natural resources, problems arise in defining where one resource ends and the next begins. Water law is no exception. In nature, surface and groundwater are often closely connected hydrologically. A well drilled next to a river can easily draw water out of the river. Disputes are inevitable when surface water is allocated one way and groundwater in another. Even when both forms of water are allocated based on priority in time, we can easily have a holder of a relatively recent groundwater right taking water indirectly from

the holder of a much older surface water right—and legally so, if the temporal priority schemes for the two types of water are entirely separate. Note how Colorado has attempted to address the problem; it "contains a presumption that all ground water is tributary to the surface stream unless proved or provided by statute otherwise."

5. *Ancillary rights IV: the land rights of water users*. One effect of this ruling and preceding ones is that the owners of water rights have, attached to their water rights, the ability to make use of the private land of other people to the extent necessary for them to make good use of their water. They can cross private land to get to the water, and they can convey the water to their place of use employing natural channels and subsurface formations on the land of other people. In a sense, these land-use rights are ancillary and attached to the primary water rights. The law, in other words, bundles legal entitlements together to promote more efficient use: a person who acquires water gets certain land-use rights along with the water. (Keep this reality in mind when you read the next main case.) Another way to phrase this point is to note that, in Colorado, the water user sometimes wins in a clash with an owner of private land. As early Colorado lawmakers saw things, water was the scare commodity, and it was more important that water be used efficiently than it was to use all land efficiently.

6. Central and West Basin Water Replenishment District v. So. Cal. Water Co. The Central Basin in Los Angeles County underlies approximately 277 square miles of land. At the time of the case, rights to extract groundwater from the Basin were held by 148 pumpers. The pumpers claimed that they collectively controlled the unused storage capacity of the Basin (totaling approximately 645,700 acre feet of storage), as part of their acknowledged legal rights to take water from it. (That is, they argued that the storage right was ancillary to their water extraction rights.) *Held:* (i) the right to store water is a separate and distinct right from the right to extract groundwater, even when (as here) groundwater pumpers possess limited rights to leave water in the ground from year to year, thus giving them limited storage rights; (ii) the Central Basin is a public resource that, like other water resources, must be used in the public interest; (iii) allowing the 148 pumpers to control the storage space, even though many of them were public utilities, did not adequately protect the public interest and respect the legislature's expressed priority for domestic water uses, and (iv) the express authority of the state-created Water Replenishment District to store water in the Basin and to manage and control water for persons within the district gave the District the power to control storage in the Basin. No claim was made by any of the litigants that rights to control the Basin were vested in overlying landowners. Central and West Basin Water Replenishment District v. Southern Cal. Water Co., 109 Cal.App.4th 891, 135 Cal.Rptr.2d 486 (2003).

7. *Right to exclude VIII: water in natural channels*. Again, we come across the recurring problem in natural resources law: it doesn't mean much to own a natural resource unless one can gain access to it and put it to use. How does this issue play out in Colorado water law, which allows water users to divert water from a river and use it on land far distant? What rights does a water user have to cross the lands of other private landowners, not just to get to the water but to bring the water to his land? (The water user's right, as the court makes plain, depends upon whether the water is being

transported in a natural channel rather than by way of a human-made structure.) Is this yet another illustration in which natural resources law, in the name of promoting full resource use, revises a landowner's right to exclude? If a state decided to craft such a rule of law today, would it amount to a taking of private property requiring compensation, or would it be a permissible redefinition of what land ownership means?

8. *Private condemnation II: passageways for water flows.* It is a surprise to many students of the law (new and old alike) to learn that many states have statutes that expressly authorize takings of private property for private use, as Colorado does in the context of water. Under what circumstances can a California water user condemn a right to use private land upon payment of just compensation? As for the constitutionality of such takings it may be useful to back up and think first about the property rights that landowners have. If a state from the beginning has reserved the right to reclaim land to devote to particular types of private uses, is the exercise of that reserved right a taking of private property? Could we view it instead as merely taking advantage of a pre-existing limit on the rights that the landowner has always possessed?

F. OTHER RESOURCES ON FEDERAL LANDS

The materials in this chapter have all had to do with a single main issue (with, of course, lots of incidental material): What natural resources are attached to land and allocated along with the land, and what resources are severed from land and available for separate allocation? By way of concluding this section we turn to a few related problems that arise in connection with federally owned lands.

As we've seen, the federal government pursued policies that allowed private parties to gain access to particular resources on federal lands, even while the lands remained in federal ownership. The two chief examples we've seen have had to do with water rights and mining rights. Another example: the federal government has typically allowed states to exercise control over wildlife on federal lands, controlling hunting and thus allocating wildlife resources in accordance with state rather than federal law.

For the most part, states began allocating these resources well before the federal government gave its consent to the arrangement. The private rights that arose on federal lands were based more on custom (the law of the mining camp) than on express state statutes. If we keep these points in mind—and remember, too, the history of the American West, including the long history of squatting—we can make better sense, legally and culturally, of the following decision. It raises a question of considerable importance: What rights did private users of the public domain gain prior to the time when the federal government began actively to protect and manage its lands? In thinking about this question, keep in mind the materials already covered, particularly decisions having to do with ancillary rights and the ways the law often bundles natural-resource rights with land-use rights. The decision also gives a helpful introduction to the law of grazing on federal lands, including a look at the federal government's longstanding insistence that grazing permits are not secure property rights. (We'll consider in a later chapter whether that claim makes much legal sense.)

DIAMOND BAR CATTLE COMPANY v. UNITED STATES

168 F.3d 1209 (10th Cir. 1999).

BRISCOE, CIRCUIT JUDGE.

Plaintiffs Diamond Bar Cattle Company and Laney Cattle Company appeal the district court's entry of summary judgment in favor of the United States. On appeal, plaintiffs contend the district court erred in finding plaintiffs had no private property right to graze their cattle on federal lands without a Forest Service permit, and in finding plaintiffs liable for trespass based on use of federal lands for cattle grazing without a permit. We affirm.

Kit and Sherry Laney are the owners and operators of Diamond Bar Cattle Company and Laney Cattle Company. The Laneys and their predecessors in title have used the lands at issue for cattle grazing since 1883. The companies historically have grazed their cattle on government lands by obtaining grazing permits. The first such permit was issued to plaintiffs' predecessors in title in 1907. More recently, the Forest Service issued a ten-year term grazing permit in 1985 allowing Laney Cattle Company to graze cattle on the 27,926–acre "Laney allotment" within the Apache National Forest. The Forest Service issued a similar permit in 1986 to Diamond Bar Cattle Company for grazing on the 146,470–acre "Diamond Bar allotment" within the Gila National Forest. Although the Forest Service notified the companies several times of upcoming expirations of the permits, neither company renewed its permit and the permits expired by their terms in 1995 and 1996. Each company offered to pay the requested grazing fees and negotiate a permit that recognized the companies' "valid existing rights."

Plaintiffs allege they are the owners of a vested water right that was obtained through prior appropriation before 1899, when the United States withdrew from the public domain the land that became the Gila National Forest and Apache National Forest. Plaintiffs claim this water right includes an inseparable right to graze the lands that comprise their allotments. Plaintiffs do not claim title or other real property interest in the land itself; rather, they assert a private "possessory" property right that entitles them to use of the water and range for the purpose of raising livestock. Plaintiffs contend their long-standing private property right was acquired under New Mexico law, obviating the need for plaintiffs to obtain grazing permits after the land was withdrawn from the public domain. The Forest Service denied any such private property rights existed and advised plaintiffs that refusal to complete permit applications would result in accumulation of unauthorized use fees, removal of plaintiffs' cattle from government property, and initiation of a civil trespass action against plaintiffs.

Plaintiffs initiated this action on April 1, 1996, seeking a declaration that plaintiffs are the valid lawful owners of (1) "sufficient permanent living water for the proper maintenance of the cattle owned by Diamond Bar and Laney," and (2) "valid vested existing rights in the range for cattle raising purposes on the lands upon which Diamond Bar and Laney are located."[17] Appellants' App., Doc. 1 at 4. Plaintiffs also asked the court to declare the Department of Agriculture and the Forest Service had "no jurisdiction over the rights to the water and in the range now held by Diamond Bar and Laney," and to permanently enjoin the Forest Service from "interfering with the valid existing rights to water and in the range for cattle raising purposes." *Id.* at 14. The United States counterclaimed to recover damages from plaintiffs for trespass and unauthorized grazing use and to enjoin plaintiffs "from unauthorized and unlawful use of property owned by the United States for livestock grazing purposes." *Id.*, Doc. 2 at 10.

In entering summary judgment for the United States, the district court held plaintiffs obtained no legal right of possession or use merely because their predecessors historically grazed cattle on the land. Nor did the court find it material that plaintiffs' water rights may have long been vested under New Mexico law, stating: "[W]hether Plaintiffs own certain water rights . . . does not change the fact that such rights do not deprive the Forest Service of its statutory authority and responsibility to regulate the use and occupancy of National Forest System lands for livestock grazing through the issuance of grazing permits." *Id.*, Doc. 9 at 15. The court enjoined plaintiffs from grazing livestock in the Gila and Apache National Forests until they obtained authorization from the Forest Service. . . .

Federal Regulation of United States Lands

Article IV of the United States Constitution provides: "The Congress shall have Power to dispose of and make all needful Rules and Regulations respecting the Territory or other Property belonging to the United States." The Supreme Court has characterized Congress' power under the Property Clause to regulate the public lands as "without limitations." *United States v. City and County of San Francisco,* 310 U.S. 16, 29, 60 S.Ct. 749, 84 L.Ed. 1050 (1940). Pursuant to this expansive grant of authority, Congress passed the Organic Administration Act of 1897, which authorized reservation of lands as national forests and directed the Secretary of Agriculture to issue rules and regulations concerning such forests. *See* 16 U.S.C. § 551. Since then, Congress has passed numerous additional statutes directing that grazing in national forests be by permit only. *See, e.g.,* 16 U.S.C. § 580l ("The Secretary of Agriculture in regulating grazing on the national forests . . . is author-

17. Plaintiffs concede their asserted rights are exclusively for raising livestock, and that ownership of such rights does not impact the rights or privileges of any other user of the national forest system lands.

ized, upon such terms and conditions as he may deem proper, to issue permits for the grazing of livestock for periods not exceeding ten years and renewals thereof.''); 43 U.S.C. § 315b; 43 U.S.C. § 1752.

As early as 1906, the Secretary of Agriculture promulgated a regulation requiring that any person seeking to graze stock on national forest land first obtain a permit from the Forest Service. *See United States v. Grimaud,* 220 U.S. 506, 509, 31 S.Ct. 480, 55 L.Ed. 563 (1911). In upholding the Secretary's authority to issue this regulation, the Supreme Court iterated that an ''implied license'' to graze on public lands existed ''so long as the government did not cancel its tacit consent.'' *Light v. United States,* 220 U.S. 523, 535, 31 S.Ct. 485, 55 L.Ed. 570 (1911). The fact that historically the government may not have objected to use of public lands for grazing was never intended to ''confer any vested right on the complainant, nor did it deprive the United States of the power of recalling any implied license under which the land had been used for private purposes.'' *Id.*

The ''implied license'' theory discussed in *Light* was articulated by the Supreme Court as early as 1890, *see Buford v. Houtz,* 133 U.S. 320, 326, 10 S.Ct. 305, 33 L.Ed. 618 (1890), and has since been cited dominantly in cases reaffirming that use of public lands for grazing is not a right but a privilege. . . .

Current regulations provide that ''all grazing and livestock use on National Forest System lands . . . must be authorized by a grazing or livestock use permit.'' 36 C.F.R. § 222.3. Permits are issued for terms of ten years or less and are issued only after submission and approval by the Forest Service of an appropriate application. *See id.* § 222.3(c)(1). A term permit holder has first priority for a new permit at the end of the term period, provided the holder has fully complied with the terms and conditions of the expiring permit. *See id.* Use of forest service lands for grazing purposes without a permit subjects the offender to unauthorized grazing use fees. *See id.* § 222.50(h). Grazing permits ''convey no right, title, or interest held by the United States in any lands or resources.'' *Id.* § 222.3(b).

Plaintiffs concede the existence of the above law, but contend it does not apply to the specific situation presented here, namely the extent to which a permit is required when the rights were ''appropriated'' pursuant to state law before the federal government removed the land at issue from the public domain. However, plaintiffs misconstrue the law upon which they base their ''vested private property rights.''

New Mexico Law

In New Mexico, water rights are obtained and governed by the doctrine of prior appropriation. *See* N.M. Const. Art. XVI, § 2 (''Priority of appropriation shall give the better right.''). Plaintiffs claim their predecessors in title obtained a valid, vested water right through appropriation. This vested water right allegedly entitled plaintiffs' predecessors, and now entitles them, to an inseparable but distinct right to use for grazing, without a permit, the rangeland known as the Diamond Bar and Laney allotments. *See* Plaintiffs' Br. at 17 ("Diamond Bar and Laney are the owners of the water right and the scope of that right includes possession of the range for the purpose of raising livestock.") . . . .

Plaintiffs premise their alleged rights upon N.M. Stat. Ann. § 19–3–13:

> Any person, company or corporation that may appropriate and stock a range upon the public domain of the United States, or otherwise, with cattle shall be deemed to be in possession thereof: provided, that such person, company or corporation shall lawfully possess or occupy, or be the lawful owner or possessor of sufficient living, permanent water upon such range for the proper maintenance of such cattle.

This section has been in effect since its passage in 1889 by the Territorial Legislature of New Mexico. Plaintiffs read this section as bestowing a private property right to graze cattle on the public domain upon all those with a valid water right. Plaintiffs' interpretation is negated by longstanding New Mexico law.

As early as 1915, the New Mexico Supreme Court rejected the proposition that what is now § 19–3–13 created, or was intended to create, a property right in land in the public domain superior or equal to the federal government's right in such land. In *Hill v. Winkler,* 21 N.M. 5, 151 P. 1014 (1915), two private parties had conflicting claims to grazing land in the public domain. The court was asked to decide which party "had a first and prior right to graze the said tract of government land by reason of prior occupancy thereof, and by reason of the further fact that they had acquired and developed permanent waters in connection therewith for the proper maintenance of such cattle." *Id.* at 1015. The court conceded: "There is a serious question concerning the right of the Legislature to make provision such as is argued was here made." *Id.* The basis for the court's reservation was an 1885 federal statute prohibiting the "assertion of a right to the exclusive use and occupancy of any part of the public lands of the United States in any state or any of the territories of the United States, without claim, color of title." *Id.* In addressing the scope of the New Mexico law in light of the 1885 federal statute, the court stated "it seem[ed] clear . . . that the attempted granting of an exclusive right in the use of the public domain . . . would clearly violate the congressional act, and must therefore be held invalid, if that was the intention of the Legislature." *Id.* The court avoided this conflict by limiting the reach of the New Mexico statute:

> We are of the opinion, however, that the [New Mexico laws at issue] can be construed as not intending to grant any exclusive right in the use of the public domain, but, on the contrary, as attempting to provide that all those who seek to stock a range upon the public domain must, before doing so, lawfully possess, or be the lawful owner of, sufficient permanent water on such

> range for the proper maintenance of such cattle. This would be a sound and proper regulation of the use of the public lands which would be defended. It is clear, however, that any attempt on the part of the Legislature to grant exclusive right or occupancy upon a part of a public domain would be clearly . . . invalid.

Id. at 1015–16. Thus, contrary to plaintiffs' argument, § 19–3–13 has not been interpreted to bestow a private property right to graze upon the public domain if one has a concomitant right to the water upon the proposed grazing range. As *Hill* makes plain, § 19–3–13 purports only to limit access to the public domain for grazing purposes to those individuals who have first obtained a valid water right sufficient to maintain the cattle to be grazed. . . .

Plaintiffs direct our attention to *First State Bank of Alamogordo v. McNew,* 33 N.M. 414, 269 P. 56 (1928), where the New Mexico Supreme Court stated that McNew,

> having appropriated and stocked said range with cattle, and being the owner of permanent water for use upon said range for the maintenance of cattle thereon, had possessory rights in the said public lands, which he could protect as against one forcibly entering thereon without right. Equity would protect him in such possession by enjoining another stock-owner not owning or possessing water from willfully turning his cattle upon such range.

Id. at 59 (internal citations omitted). We do not read *McNew* as contravening *Hill* or *Yates,* but as restating that under § 19–3–13 McNew had a right to exclude from public lands anyone seeking to graze cattle upon those lands who did not have a vested water right. In any event, whatever McNew's rights may have been, they were superior only to those who were seeking to make use of public land "without right." As implicitly acknowledged in *Hill* and *Yates,* the government's right to possess, control, and exclude others from public lands is plenary and may not be negated by contrary state law. At best, McNew had a right to possession sufficient to allow him to exclude certain private parties. His own occupation of public lands for grazing was a privilege subject to withdrawal by the government. . . .

Federal Law

The United States has long recognized the validity of private water rights obtained pursuant to state water law. *See Andrus v. Charlestone Stone Products Co., Inc.,* 436 U.S. 604, 614, 98 S.Ct. 2002, 56 L.Ed.2d 570 (1978) (noting in 1866, 1870, and 1872, Congress affirmed the "view that private water rights on federal lands were to be governed by state and local law and custom"). This recognition was made explicit in the Mining Law of 1866, which provides in relevant part:

> Whenever, by priority of possession, rights to the use of water for mining, agricultural, manufacturing or other purposes, have vested and accrued, and the same are recognized and acknowledged by the

> local customs, laws, and the decisions of courts, the possessors and owners of such vested rights shall be maintained and protected in the same; and the right of way for the construction of ditches and canals for the purposes herein specified is acknowledged and confirmed.

43 U.S.C. § 661. Plaintiffs argue § 661 constitutes governmental recognition not just of their water right, but also of their "inseparable" range right, which they contend is within the scope of their water right and was likewise obtained by "priority of possession." In plaintiffs' words,

> The doctrine of prior appropriation is a doctrine which extends far beyond water. It can apply to any natural resource which can be reduced to the control of man by his own labor....
>
> The doctrine applies to the water which the cattle consume and to the range upon which they forage.

Plaintiffs' Reply Br. at 9.

Plaintiffs' interpretation of the Mining Act is contrary not only to the language of the Act itself, which simply recognizes rights to the use of water, but also to the well-settled body of law holding no private property right exists to graze public rangelands. The Act cannot fairly be read to recognize private property rights in federal lands, regardless of whether proffered as a distinct right or as an inseparable component of a water right.

Only one court has intimated that an interest in federal land, other than a ditch right-of-way or an easement for diversion of water from federal to private land, is obtainable under the Mining Act of 1866. In *Hage v. United States,* 35 Fed.Cl. 147 (1996), Nevada ranch owners brought suit alleging the government, by canceling plaintiffs' grazing permit and thereby denying them access to water to which plaintiffs had a vested right, had taken without just compensation plaintiffs' property interests in water rights, ditch rights-of-way, and rangeland forage. Plaintiffs claimed an interest in public land and water which their predecessors had used for cattle grazing since the 1800's. In 1907, Congress had designated the land as national forest. As relevant here, plaintiffs' complaint was twofold. First, plaintiffs claimed they had a "property interest in the permit because the federal government issued the permit in recognition of rights which existed prior to the creation" of the national forest. *Id.* at 168. This interest purportedly was recognized by the Mining Act of 1866: "Plaintiffs claim that the Act of 1866 merely enacted as federal law the custom and usage of the Western states and territories to recognize the rights of the first appropriator to acquire a priority right to the use and enjoyment of the public land over those who had not expended such labor." *Id.* at 170. Second, plaintiffs alleged that under Nevada law, their water right included the right ("inherently part of the vested stockwater right") to "bring cattle to the water, and for cattle to consume forage adjacent to a private water right." *Id.* at 175.

The court rejected plaintiffs' argument that the Mining Act recognized distinct property interests in public lands. *See id.* at 170 ("The Act does not address property rights in the public lands and the court declines to create such rights contrary to the clear legislative intention of Congress."). However, despite conceding grazing was a revocable privilege and plaintiffs had no property interest in the rangeland, the court denied the government's motion for summary judgment with respect to plaintiffs' claim that the water right included the right to adjacent forage.

> If Nevada law recognized the right to graze cattle near bordering water as part of a vested water right before 1907, when Congress created the Toiyabe National Forest, plaintiffs may have a right to the forage adjacent to the alleged water rights on the rangeland.
>
> . . . .
>
> When the federal government created the Toiyabe National Forest, it could not unilaterally ignore private property rights on the public domain. If Congress wanted to remove all private property interests in the public domain, which were created by the state under state law, the Constitution would have required the federal government to pay just compensation. Just as the federal government could not take private property rights in water or ditch rights-of-way when it created the Toiyabe National Forest, the government could not take any other form of private property right in the public domain. Plaintiffs will have the opportunity at trial to prove property rights in the forage stemming from the property right to make beneficial use of water in the public domain within Nevada originating prior to 1907.

Id. at 175–76. In a subsequent order, the court explicitly recognized plaintiffs had a property interest in their ditch rights-of-way and forage rights appurtenant to their water right. *See Hage v. United States,* 42 Fed.Cl. 249, 251 (1998) ("[I]mplicit in a vested water right based on putting water to beneficial use for livestock purposes was the appurtenant right for those livestock to graze alongside the water."). The court held this forage right encompassed the "ground occupied by the water and fifty feet on each side of the marginal limits of the ditch." *Id. See Store Safe Redlands Assoc. v. United States,* 35 Fed.Cl. 726 (1996).

The circumstances here are appreciably different than in *Hage.* First, it is not the law in New Mexico that a water right includes the right to graze public lands. As noted, the New Mexico Supreme Court has specifically disavowed such an interpretation of N.M. Stat. Ann. § 19–3–13. *See Hill,* 151 P. at 1015. It is irrelevant to the present case that Nevada law may attach a forage right to a water right. Second, the property interest not explicitly recognized by the Mining Act but asserted by plaintiffs and recognized as potentially compensable in *Hage* was a narrow right to forage along the waterfront. Here, plaintiffs do not assert a right to forage only along the waterfront or a right to lead their cattle to water solely to drink, but a right to occupy and possess, without federal authorization, 174,396 acres of federal land for cattle grazing purposes. . . .

At best, plaintiffs possess a valid water right that is protected by the Mining Act. However, the United States has not acted to take plaintiffs' water rights, has not denied access to the water, and has not sought to divert plaintiffs' use to a governmental purpose. In fact, the United States concedes if plaintiffs do hold a valid water right, the government may not usurp that right. Plaintiffs contend their water right is of little utility if their cattle have no place to graze. If true, the fault lies with plaintiffs, who were fully apprized of the consequences of failing to renew their permits. See Hage, 35 Fed.Cl. at 171 ("The court also understands that without a grazing permit, the ranch may become worthless. But the court emphasizes that plaintiffs' investment-backed expectations and reliance on the privilege to graze do not, in themselves, create a property interest in the rangeland or the permit.").

AFFIRMED

Notes

1. *Ancillary rights V: a grazing right attached to a water right?* At first glance the grazers arguments in *Diamond Bar Cattle* may seem frivolous—the idea that a person who gains a water right gains along with it a right to graze cattle. But is the idea so crazy in an arid land where land is worth virtually nothing without water? If water is the dominant resource (as commentators such as Wallace Stegner have long asserted), could not lesser resources be deemed incidental to it? Recall the *Park County* ruling that we just read: the holder of a water right gains incidental rights to cross private lands and to make use of natural water formations on them, all without the landowner's consent and without payment of compensation. The truth is, many natural resources have to be used in combination or not at all. What good is a water right with no way to use it? And what good is a grazing right if the animals have nothing to drink? Doesn't it make sense in arid lands to bundle the two resource rights?

In many resource settings, a person who acquires a natural resource gains the right to cross lands as needed to get to the resource and exploit it. This is commonly true when the person acquiring the resource buys it from the landowner. Yet, as the *Park County* ruling illustrates, a resource owner might be able to use the resource only if he can gain access by using land owned by someone who had no involvement in the resource acquisition. Note, though, that the plaintiffs in *Diamond Bar Cattle* went well beyond that idea. They asked not merely for the right to cross public lands to get to their water, but for the right to graze animals on the federal lands. Compare this request with the ruling by the Claims Court in *Hage v. United States*, discussed in *Diamond Bar Cattle*. The Claims Court recognized a land-use right, ancillary to the water right, but it was a land-use right of much more limited scope.

2. *Transferring land first:* BedRoc Limited, LLC v. United States. The basic issue that's been covered in this chapter often arises when an owner of land that includes a particular resource sells the land (or makes it available

to another person in some other way) but expressly reserves for himself or herself certain resources in the land. When this happen we again face the question: What parts of nature go with the land to the new owner, and what parts do not? In settings such as this it is essential to look to the intentions of the parties, because they are typically free to carve up nature as they see fit, transferring certain rights and retaining others. When the transferor is the government, however, such issues are often resolved not by looking to the parties' intent so much as by looking to the law governing the transaction. This issue arises under several federal laws, because the federal government over time has often transferred lands to private owners while retaining certain rights in the lands. Inevitably, interpretations of these transfers have depended upon the exact language of the statute governing each type of transfer. Even when statutes use similar or identical words, the words can have different meanings based on the statutory context.

In BedRoc Limited, LLC v. United States, 541 U.S. 176 (2004), the Supreme Court considered the rights that a landowner obtained under the Pittman Underground Water Act of 1919. The Act authorized sales of certain "nonmineral lands" in Nevada on which settlers could obtain permits to drill for water. Under the Act, the United States as grantor retained all coal and other "valuable minerals" in the lands, along with the right to enter the lands and remove the minerals. The question at issue was whether the reservation of "valuable minerals" included ordinary sand and gravel. As it confronted this issue, the Court drew upon its earlier ruling in *Watt v. Western Nuclear, Inc.* from 1983, in which it ruled over vigorous dissent that a reservation of "minerals" under the Stock–Raising Homestead Act of 1916 did include a reservation for the United States of sand and gravel. Ample evidence indicated that the statutory terms "valuable minerals" and "minerals" were used interchangeably by Congress, and that the reservation of minerals in the 1919 Pittman Act was meant to duplicate the reservation in the 1916 Stock–Raising Act.

In resolving the dispute, none of the nine Justices believed that the reservation in the Pittman Act covered sand and gravel. The Court's ruling in the case, nonetheless, was badly fragmented. The plurality opinion concluded that the Pittman Act differed from the 1916 Stock–Raising Act because it included the word "valuable"; thus, sand and gravel were reserved in the Stock–Raising Act but not in the Pittman Act. Two justices, concurring, concluded that the two statutes were identical in meaning—neither reserved sand and gravel—but felt that it was inappropriate for prudential reasons to reverse the ruling in *Watt*, covering the 1916 Act, even though the ruling was erroneous. These two justices, thus, thought it best to interpret the two statutes differently, even though Congress intended to have them interpreted the same. The remaining three justices, dissenting, agreed with the concurring justices that the two statutes were identical. They agreed, too, that it was inappropriate for prudential reasons to reverse *Watt* given that many land-use actions had been undertaken based on it. The dissenters concluded, however, that the Court should nonetheless follow *Watt* by interpreting the 1919 Pittman Act in the same erroneous way as the 1916 Stock–Raising Act because so many land-use actions had been taken in reliance on this erroneous interpretation. In support of their view, the dissenters noted the "need for certainty and predictability where land titles are concerned" *quoting* Leo Sheep Co. v. United States, 440 U.S. 668 (1979).

RIGHTS OF OWNERSHIP OR RIGHTS OF USE?—THE NEED FOR A NEW CONCEPTUAL BASIS FOR LAND USE POLICY

Lynton K. Caldwell

15 William & Mary Law Review 759 (1974).

The materials in this chapter have explored the limits of land and noted many instances in which lawmakers have severed particular resources from land and made them available for separate acquisition as use rights. As human uses of landscapes become more varied, the question arises whether the law should shift even further in the direction of separate use rights and away from the notion that nearly all use rights are owned by a single land owner. The following excerpt, advocating a shift in that direction, was written by one of the architects of our nation's environmental laws. In the essay, the author criticizes the conventional concept of land ownership as "detrimental to rational land use, obstructive to the development of related environmental policies, and deceptive to those innocent individuals who would trust it for protection." He calls for "a new conceptual basis for land use" in order "to reconcile the legitimate rights of the users of land with the interest of society in maintaining a high quality environment." His proposed new conceptual basis centers on the following elements, which draw upon largely forgotten writings by leading land economists and land planners from the 1920s and 1930s:

First, rights of ownership should be redefined to apply not to land itself but to specific rights to occupy or use particular parcels of land, or both, in accordance with publicly established criteria. Rights to use might be bought and sold, and could confer possession, but the land itself would cease to be the representative symbol of these rights. The ultimate repository for such rights would be in society, and their administration, while through government, could involve extensive citizen participation.

Second, rights of occupancy would be defined by law, with land classified according to its economic and ecological capabilities, and would be regulated by provisions specifying the obligations of occupancy and governing the acquisition of additional rights. The term "rights" would encompass those activities in relation to the land in which the occupant or user might freely engage, as well as those aspects of privacy and of security from external damage or annoyance which society through government would undertake to defend and protect. Obligations concomitant to custody of land would include, in addition to traditional restriction against public nuisance, measures designed to protect air and water quality, the integrity of ecosystems, and the character of the landscape, whether manmade or natural. The classification system, allocating specific rights to particular areas or parcels of land, would be the product of public planning. For any given piece of land, only those rights allocated to it could be exercised, although not all available right would have to be exercised. Furthermore, a purchaser might buy some but not all of the rights pertaining to a parcel of land; he could, for example, purchase the right to farm without also obtaining the rights to mine or to develop the land. The combination of rights and obligations thus defined could apply to communities and public authorities, as well as individuals and corporation. Such application would be especially important with respect to land used for public works, such as power plants, energy transmission lines, airports, highways, military installations, scientific research, recreation, historic preservation, and natural resources development.

Finally, taxation would apply to the economic value of the rights actually possessed and exercised, not to the land itself or in anticipation of rights that *might* be obtained for the particular piece of land. The tax rate could be adjusted to compensate the public for any burden, such as air pollution, that a particular land use might place upon a community. This system would put an end to the practice of assessing land at its presumed market value regardless of its use. The owner of the right to farm a tract of land, for example, could be taxed only in relation to that right, even though the farm was surrounded by land for which highly taxed development rights had been granted. In addition, since capital gains in land per se would not be obtainable, the owner of the right to farm a piece of land could not follow the present practice of holding land off the market in anticipation of an increase in its value. He could not develop the land or sell development rights to others unless he possessed such rights, and any changes in the use of land not included among the rights already possessed by the user would require purchase of additional rights from the appropriate public authority. . . .

A major objective of these changes in land law would be to assure that publicly created values in land would accrue to the public. Thus, increases in the value of land at newly constructed interchanges on interstate highways would afford no opportunity for profit to the existing land users. Whether development rights or franchises would be granted would depend upon considerations of areal physical planning and public necessity and convenience. . . .

A secondary purpose of the proposed changes would be prevention of socially and ecologically harmful speculation in development. Although a grant of development rights would confer limited authority to change the uses of land in certain ways, major environmental changes, such as development of a shopping center involving public services and transportation, would require an additional franchise. . . .

A virtue of the foregoing approach to land use policy is that decisions affecting the public would in effect become public decisions, a circumstance that occurs imperfectly, if at all, under the laws currently prevailing in most states. The decisional process could be made more open and explicit than generally is the case under the system of private

rights to use approach

land ownership. The "rights to use" approach would direct public action away from litigation and toward planning and administration. . . .

The principal effect of the foregoing propositions would be to take from private persons, individual or corporate, the power to effect significant alterations in the environment without public consent. It does not follow, however, that the power of environmental planning and management would be transferred to public bureaucracy. Use of citizen boards of review and open planning sessions, as well as provision for input from science and the design arts, could result in more socially and ecologically responsible land use decisions than might be expected under the existing technicalities of land use law.

The objectives of these propositions are, in a very fundamental sense, conservative. They are intended to preserve and to conserve, to encourage and to enforce responsibility toward society and posterity, and to reduce the likelihood of rash and destructive uses of land and resources . . .

Chapter Three

ALLOCATING DISCRETE RESOURCES

A. FIRST-IN-TIME ALLOCATIONS

Once a legal system has decided to make parts of nature available as discrete resources, rather than as part of the land bundle, it faces the need to allocate that resource in some manner. Not all resources, of course, will be offered for individual use. Some may be retained and operated as a commons (a public park, for instance). Government will likely retain some natural resources to use in providing services. And some can be simply left alone, helping to sustain the health and beauty of the natural landscape or for future generations to use. As for those resources that will be made available to private takers, the methods of allocation are many. We saw one possible allocation in use among the English settlers of early New England towns. They allocated land based in part on family need and in part on the perceived social status of the each family. The native Indians, in contrast, apparently allocated resources based largely on need, though the historical record is scanty. In this chapter, we'll look at legal issues that arise when lawmaking communities use other allocation methods, whether by deliberate decision or due to happenstance or inaction. We begin with one of the most obvious methods: giving the resource to the first person to seize it and put it to use.

As you consider these materials dealing with first-in-time or capture as a method of allocation, comparing the problems that arise in various resource settings, it may prove useful to focus on three issues:

(i) What is involved in the capture process? Phrased otherwise, first to do what?

(ii) What protections against interference does a person enjoy while attempting to capture; and

(iii) Once the capture is complete, how do we date the capture in time? Is it when the final act of capture is concluded, when the act of capture was begun, or some other time?

PIERSON v. POST

3 Cai. R. 175, 2 Am.Dec. 264 (N.Y. Sup. Ct. 1805).

THIS was an action of trespass on the case commenced in a justice's court, by the present defendant against the now plaintiff.

COA

The declaration stated that *Post,* being in possession of certain dogs and hounds under his command, did, "upon a certain wild and uninhabited, unpossessed and waste land, called the beach, find and start one of those noxious beasts called a fox," and whilst there hunting, chasing and pursuing the same with his dogs and hounds, and when in view thereof, *Pierson,* well knowing the fox was so hunted and pursued, did, in the sight of *Post,* to prevent his catching the same, kill and carry it off. A verdict having been rendered for the plaintiff below, the defendant there sued out a *certiorari,* and now assigned for error, that the declaration and the matters therein contained were not sufficient in law to maintain an action.

TOMPKINS, J.

The question submitted by the counsel in this cause for our determination is, whether *Lodowick Post,* by the pursuit with his hounds in the manner alleged in his declaration, acquired such a right to, or property in, the fox, as will sustain an action against *Pierson* for killing and taking him away? The cause was argued with much ability by the counsel on both sides, and presents for our decision a novel and nice question. It is admitted that a fox is an animal *ferae naturae,* and that property in such animals is acquired by occupancy only. These admissions narrow the discussion to the simple question of what acts amount to occupancy, applied to acquiring right to wild animals?

issue

what amts to occupancy in wild animals?

If we have recourse to the ancient writers upon general principles of law, the judgment below is obviously erroneous. *Justinian's Institutes,* lib. 2. tit. 1. § 13. and *Fleta,* lib. 3. c. 2. p. 175. adopt the principle, that pursuit alone vests no property or right in the huntsman; and that even pursuit, accompanied with wounding, is equally ineffectual for that purpose, unless the animal be actually taken. The same principle is recognised by *Bracton,* lib. 2. c. 1. p. 8. *Puffendorf,* lib. 4. c. 6. § 2. and 10. defines occupancy of beasts *ferae naturae,* to be the actual corporal possession of them, and *Bynkershoek* is cited as coinciding in this definition. It is indeed with hesitation that *Puffendorf* affirms that a wild beast mortally wounded, or greatly maimed, cannot be fairly intercepted by another, whilst the pursuit of the person inflicting the wound continues. The foregoing authorities are decisive to show that mere pursuit gave *Post* no legal right to the fox, but that he became the property of *Pierson,* who intercepted and killed him.

mere pursuit gives no legal right Have to kill

It therefore only remains to inquire whether there are any contrary principles, or authorities, to be found in other books, which ought to induce a different decision. Most of the cases which have occurred in *England,* relating to property in wild animals, have either been discussed and decided upon the principles of their positive statute regulations, or have arisen between the huntsman and the owner of the land upon which beasts *ferae naturae* have been apprehended; the former claiming them by title of occupancy, and the latter *ratione soli.* Little satisfactory aid can, therefore, be derived from the *English* reporters.

Barbeyrac, in his notes on *Puffendorf,* does not accede to the definition of occupancy by the latter, but, on the contrary, affirms, that actual bodily seizure is not, in all cases, necessary to constitute possession of wild animals. He does not, however, *describe* the acts which, according to his ideas, will amount to an appropriation of such animals to private use, so as to exclude the claims of all other persons, by title of occupancy, to the same animals; and he is far from averring that pursuit alone is sufficient for that purpose. To a certain extent, and as far as *Barbeyrac* appears to me to go, his objections to *Puffendorf's* definition of occupancy are reasonable and correct. That is to say, that actual bodily seizure is not indispensable to acquire right to, or possession of, wild beasts; but that, on the contrary, the mortal wounding of such beasts, by one not abandoning his pursuit, may, with the utmost propriety, be deemed possession of him; since, thereby, the pursuer manifests an unequivocal intention of appropriating the animal to his individual use, has deprived him of his natural liberty, and brought him within his certain control. So also, encompassing and securing such animals with nets and toils, or otherwise intercepting them in such a manner as to deprive them of their natural liberty, and render escape impossible, may justly be deemed to give possession of them to those persons who, by their industry and labour, have used such means of apprehending them. ... The case now under consideration is one of mere pursuit, and presents no circumstances or acts which can bring it within the definition of occupancy by *Puffendorf,* or *Grotius,* or the ideas of *Barbeyrac* upon that subject.

The case cited from 11 *Mod.* 74–130. I think clearly distinguishable from the present; inasmuch as there the action was for maliciously hindering and disturbing the plaintiff in the exercise and enjoyment of a private franchise; and in the report of the same case, 3 *Salk.* 9. *Holt,* Ch. J. states, that the ducks were in the plaintiff's decoy pond, and *so in his possession,* from which it is obvious the court laid much stress in their opinion upon the plaintiff's possession of the ducks, *ratione soli.*[1]

We are the more readily inclined to confine possession or occupancy of beasts *ferae naturae,* within the limits prescribed by the learned authors above cited, for the sake of certainty, and preserving peace and order in society. If the first seeing, starting, or pursuing such animals, without having so wounded, circumvented or ensnared them, so as to deprive them of their natural liberty, and subject them to the control of their pursuer, should afford the basis of actions against others for

1. [Ed.: The court here is discussing *Keeble v. Hickeringill,* the next main case in this text. *Keeble* was originally reported in two, quite different forms (hence the New York court's reference to two different reports).]

intercepting and killing them, it would prove a fertile source of quarrels and litigation.

However uncourteous or unkind the conduct of *Pierson* towards *Post,* in this instance, may have been, yet his act was productive of no injury or damage for which a legal remedy can be applied. We are of opinion the judgment below was erroneous, and ought to be reversed.

LIVINGSTON, J. My opinion differs from that of the court. . . .

Whether a person who, with his own hounds, starts and hunts a fox on waste and uninhabited ground, and is on the point of seizing his prey, acquires such an interest in the animal, as to have a right of action against another, who in view of the huntsman and his dogs in full pursuit, and with knowledge of the chase, shall kill and carry him away?

This is a knotty point, and should have been submitted to the arbitration of sportsmen, without poring over *Justinian, Fleta, Bracton, Puffendorf, Locke, Barbeyrac,* or *Blackstone,* all of whom have been cited; they would have had no difficulty in coming to a prompt and correct conclusion. In a court thus constituted, the skin and carcass of poor *reynard* would have been properly disposed of, and a precedent set, interfering with no usage or custom which the experience of ages has sanctioned, and which must be so well known to every votary of *Diana.* But the parties have referred the question to our judgment, and we must dispose of it as well as we can, from the partial lights we possess, leaving to a higher tribunal, the correction of any mistake which we may be so unfortunate as to make.

By the pleadings it is admitted that a fox is a "wild and noxious beast." Both parties have regarded him, as the law of nations does a pirate, "*hostem humani generis,*" and although "*de mortuis nil nisi bonum,*" be a maxim of our profession, the memory of the deceased has not been spared. His depredations on farmers and on barn yards, have not been forgotten; and to put him to death wherever found, is allowed to be meritorious, and of public benefit. Hence it follows, that our decision should have in view the greatest possible encouragement to the destruction of an animal, so cunning and ruthless in his career. But who would keep a pack of hounds; or what gentleman, at the sound of the horn, and at peep of day, would mount his steed, and for hours together, "*sub jove frigido,*" or a vertical sun, pursue the windings of this wily quadruped, if, just as night came on, and his stratagems and strength were nearly exhausted, a saucy intruder, who had not shared in the honours or labours of the chase, were permitted to come in at the death, and bear away in triumph the object of pursuit? Whatever *Justinian* may have thought of the matter, it must be recollected that his code was compiled many hundred years ago, and it would be very hard indeed, at the distance of so many centuries, not to have a right to establish a rule for ourselves. In his day, we read of no order of men who made it a business, in the language of the declaration in this cause, "with hounds and dogs to find, start, pursue, hunt, and chase," these animals, and that, too, without any other motive than the preservation of *Roman* poultry; if this diversion had been then in fashion, the lawyers who composed his institutes, would have taken care not to pass it by, without suitable encouragement. If any thing, therefore, in the digests or pandects shall appear to militate against the defendant in error, who, on this occasion, was the foxhunter, we have only to say *tempora mutantur;* and if men themselves change with the times, why should not laws also undergo an alteration?

It may be expected, however, by the learned counsel, that more particular notice be taken of their authorities. I have examined them all, and feel great difficulty in determining, whether to acquire dominion over a thing, before in common, it be sufficient that we barely see it, or know where it is, or wish for it, or make a declaration of our will respecting it; or whether, in the case of wild beasts, setting a trap, or lying in wait, or starting, or pursuing, be enough; or if an actual wounding, or killing, or bodily tact and occupation be necessary. Writers on general law, who have favoured us with their speculations on these points, differ on them all; but, great as is the diversity of sentiment among them, some conclusion must be adopted on the question immediately before us. After mature deliberation, I embrace that of *Barbeyrac,* as the most rational, and least liable to objection. If at liberty, we might imitate the courtesy of a certain emperor, who, to avoid giving offence to the advocates of any of these different doctrines, adopted a middle course, and by ingenious distinctions, rendered it difficult to say (as often happens after a fierce and angry contest) to whom the palm of victory belonged. He ordained, that if a beast be followed with *large dogs and hounds,* he shall belong to the hunter, not to the chance occupant; and in like manner, if he be killed or wounded with a lance or sword; but if chased with *beagles only,* then he passed to the captor, not to the first pursuer. If slain with a dart, a sling, or a bow, he fell to the hunter, if still in chase, and not to him who might afterwards find and seize him.

Now, as we are without any municipal regulations of our own, and the pursuit here, for aught that appears on the case, being with dogs and hounds of *imperial stature,* we are at liberty to adopt one of the provisions just cited, which comports also with the learned conclusion of *Barbeyrac,* that property in animals *ferae naturae* may be acquired without bodily touch or manucaption, provided the pursuer be within reach, or have a *reasonable* prospect (which certainly existed here) of taking, what he has *thus* discovered an intention of converting to his own use.

When we reflect also that the interest of our husbandmen, the most useful of men in any community, will be advanced by the destruction of a beast so pernicious and incorrigible, we cannot greatly err, in saying, that a pursuit like the present, through waste and unoccupied lands, and which must inevitably and speedily have terminated in corporal possession, or bodily *seisin,* confers such a right to the object of it, as to make any one a wrongdoer, who shall interfere and shoulder the spoil. The *justice's* judgment ought, therefore, in my opinion, to be affirmed.

Judgment of reversal.

Notes

1. *First to do what? Pierson* is a classic of property law, regularly used in introductory classes. From the point of view of Pierson and Post, the legal issue was about how a hunter gained ownership of a fox while hunting on public land. From the point of view of lawmakers, the issue is slightly different: how to allocate the fox, and, in the case of a first-in-time method of allocation, how to decide when the capture is far enough along to award the fox to a hunter. Note that the majority and dissent both apply the rule of first capture. Their disagreement is about its details. Exactly what acts would each judge require before private ownership can arise? What are the policy rationales that the two opinions cite in support of their respective positions? And are they persuasive? Would the majority's rule really reduce conflict among hunters if, as Livingston contends, hunters would perceive the rule as tolerating breaches of hunter ethics? As for Livingston's arguments, would his rule really provide greater encouragement for farmers to get rid of noxious foxes? And is it clear, given the role of foxes in eating rodents, that farmers would really prefer a fox-less countryside?

2. *Blending issues.* One way to distinguish these two opinions is by noting that Livingston in dissent employs a broader view of the dispute. Livingston seeks to answer two questions at once: what must a hunter do to gain ownership, and what protection should a hunter have while engaged in the hunt? As for the first question, Livingston agrees that actual capture is needed, doesn't he? His hunter will gain nothing if, after hot pursuit with intent and ability to capture, the hunter then abandons the hunt and goes home. Thus, Livingston's hunter, while in hot pursuit, doesn't really own the fox, does he? How would we describe his legal rights in the fox at that point, while still in hot pursuit? Livingston would protect Post because Pierson's interference with his hunt was, by hunter standards, immoral and thus illegitimate. The majority, in contrast, seems to focus on only the first issue—what acts are needed to consummate the capture—while overlooking Pierson's unsportsmanlike behavior.

Can we, then, largely sum up the two approaches this way: the majority is concerned about certainty and predictability in the law, while Livingston in dissent is more concerned about fairness?

3. *Pros and cons of first occupancy.* What are the pros and cons of allocating resources based on a first-in-time basis? Are frequent disputes likely to arise about who is first, as well as claims of improper interference in the race to capture? Is hoarding of the resource likely to be a problem? Alternatively, can we argue that it really makes little difference who ends up with the resource so long as it gains an owner and so long as the owner can then sell the resource in the market, thereby allowing market processes to shift the resource to its highest and best use? Should the aim be, as some economists urge, simply to get resources into private hands as quickly as possible?

A much-touted virtue of first-in-time is that it provides an incentive for people to act—to hunt with skill or to find valuable resources. Note also that the act of capture gives at least some cause, morally speaking, to favor the capturer over other people who might also desire the resource. The act of capture doesn't *create* the resource in any sense and may not add much value to it. Thus, mere capture doesn't amount to the kind of moral justification that John Locke relied upon with his labor theory of private property. (Locke presumed that the item of property was so plentiful as to have no value in nature, and that the entire value of it was therefore due to the labor that the putative owner mixed with it. His theory, of course, is readily challenged on the ground that no natural resource is so plentiful as to have no value.) Still, the one who captures the resource has done something, and competing claimants for the same resource, in contrast, might well have done nothing.

4. *Alternative allocation methods*? The court in *Pierson* does not consider the possibility of other methods of allocating wild foxes found on public land open to public hunting. Can you think of any other method that would be feasible? (If not, try a bit harder. Recall that fox hunting in England was an activity for the wealthy; ordinary people not only did not hunt foxes but by law were prohibited from doing so.)

Some observers have claimed that the court was following well-established precedent by giving the fox to the first one to capture it. E.g., Richard Epstein, *Possession as the Root of Title*, 13 GA. L. REV. 1221 (1979); Carol M. Rose, *Possession as the Origin of Property*, 52 U. CHI. L. REV. 73 (1985). If that is true, however, why did the court have no judicial precedents to cite in support of its position, either from the United States or England? Why did it view all English cases as off-point, thus finding it necessary to turn to the philosophic speculations of philosophers and treatise writers? Notes in chapter two give us clues as to the answer. Wild game in England was owned by the King, not unowned. De jure hunting rights came by grant from the King. In the absence of grants and in the case of animals not covered by them de facto hunting rights existed based on land ownership, though poaching probably was common. Thus, under the common law as applied in England, first-in-time as the prime element of allocation had only limited application to wild animals. As for American cases, the lack of available precedents had a more pragmatic explanation. The first published case reporters began appearing sporadically in the final years of the eighteenth century. The court in *Pierson* therefore had very little American precedent to draw upon. In American law, nearly all early cases dealt with the only wildlife resource worth litigating—fish and shellfish. These cases typically addressed claims made by particular fishers (sometimes riparian landowners, sometimes not) that they held exclusive rights to particular fisheries. It is understandable, then, that the New York Supreme Court in *Pierson* could find no precedents with similar facts that applied a first-in-time allocation rule.

5. *The origin of property? Pierson* is commonly used in first-year property law courses, usually described as a case about the origin of property. In the case, a thing with no private owner (a fox) becomes privately owned. From the point of view of Pierson, thus, it is indeed a story of how private property begins. But note that from the point of view of society the case is not about that—it's about how society is going to allocate the resource. The story doesn't really begin with Pierson grabbing the fox

away from Post. It begins well before then. Pierson becomes owner of the fox only because a law exists making the fox available to the first hunter to capture it. A property law must come before the capture. Before the law there has to be some law-making entity, which in turn requires some sort of social order governed by law. The law-making entity could have allocated the resource (as we've seen) in some other way. In the American common law, wild animals are owned by the state as trustee for the people collectively. When Post grabbed the fox, then, he took the item from the stock of commonly owned property and transformed it into individually owned property.

KEEBLE v. HICKERINGILL

11 East 574, 103 Eng. Rep. 1127 (Queen's Bench 1707).

Action upon the case. Plaintiff declares that he was, 8th November in the second year of the queen, lawfully possessed of a close land called Minott's Meadow, *et de quodam vivario, vocato* a decoy pond, to which divers wildfowl used to resort and come: and the plaintiff had at his own costs and charges prepared and procured divers decoy ducks, nets, machines, and other engines for the decoying and taking of the wildfowl, and enjoyed the benefit in taking them: the defendant, knowing which, and intending to damnify the plaintiff in his vivary, and to fright and drive away the wildfowl used to resort thither, and deprive him of his profit, did, on the 8th of November, resort to the head of the said pond and vivary, and did discharge six guns laden with gunpowder, and with the noise and stink of the gunpowder did drive away the wildfowl then being in the pond: and on the 11th and 12th days of November the defendant, with design to damnify the plaintiff and fright away the wildfowl, did place himself with gun near the vivary, and there did discharge the said gun several times that was then charged with the gunpowder against the said decoy pond, whereby the wildfowl was frighted away, and did forsake the said pond. Upon not guilty pleaded a verdict was found for the plaintiff and 20 damages.

HOLT, C.J.:—I am of opinion that this action doth lie. It seems to be new in its instance, but not new in the reason or principle of it. For 1st, this using or making a decoy is lawful. 2dly, this employment of his ground to that use is profitable to the plaintiff, as is the skill and management of that employment. As to the first, every man that hath a property may employ it for his pleasure and profit, as for alluring and procuring decoy ducks to come to his pond. To learn the trade of seducing other ducks to come here in order to be taken is not prohibited either by the law of the land or the moral law; but it is as lawful to use art to seduce them, to catch them, and destroy them for the use of mankind, as to kill and destroy wildfowl or tame cattle. Then when a man useth his art or his skill to take them, to see and dispose of for his profit; this is his trade; and he that hinders another in his trade or livelihood is liable to an action for so hindering him.... [W]here a violent or malicious act is done to a man's occupation, profession, or way of getting a livelihood; there an action lies in all cases. But if a man doth him damage by using the same employment; as if Mr. Hickeringill had set up another decoy on his own ground near the plaintiff's and that had spoiled the custom of the plaintiff, no action would lie because he had as much liberty to make and use a decoy as the plaintiff. This is like the case of 11 H. 4, 47. One schoolmaster sets up a new school to the damage of an antient school, and thereby the scholars are allured from the old school to come to his new. (The action there was held not to lie.) But suppose Mr. Hickeringill should lie in the way with his guns, and fright the boys from going to school, and their parents would let them go thither; sure that schoolmaster might have an action for the loss of his scholars. [ ] A man hath a market, to which he hath toll for horses sold: a man is bringing his horses to market to seel; a stranger hinders and obstructs him from going thither to the market; an action lies because it imports damage.... Now considering the nature of the case, it is not possible to declare of the number [of birds], that were frighted away; because the plaintiff had not possession of them, to count them. Where a man brings trespass for taking his goods, he must declare of the quantity, because he, by having had the possession, may know what he had, and therefore must know what he lost.... And when we do know that of long time in the kingdom these artificial contrivances of decoy ponds and decoy ducks have been used for enticing into those ponds wildfowl, in order to be taken for the profit of the owner of the pond, who is at the expense of servants, engines, and other management, whereby the markets of the nation may be furnished; there is great reason to give encouragement thereunto; that the people who are so instrumental by their skill and industry so to furnish the markets should reap the benefit and have their action. But in short, that which is the true reason, is, that this action is not brought to recover damage for the loss of the fowl, but for the disturbance.... So is the usual and common way of declaring.

Notes

1. *A property case*? Another classic judicial ruling, *Keeble* at first glance may seem to differ in outcome from *Pierson v. Post*. According to the English court, the landowner enjoys legal protection for his duck hunting even though he has not captured the ducks physically. But the ruling, of course, isn't about the *ownership* of wild animals and how someone becomes owner. Instead, it is about the *protection* that a person enjoys while engaged in the process of capture. On the facts, what made Hickeringill's conduct wrongful? Was it his physical behavior? Was it his mental state? Could he have gotten away with what he did by claiming that he was trying to hit the ducks but was simply a bad shot? As for Keeble, did he enjoy protection because he was a hunter or was it important also that he owned the land? Is this a case involving the protection of hunting, or the protection of lawful activities undertaken on private land?

2. Pierson, *redux*. Could Livingston have made use of Keeble to support his position in *Pierson*? Can we distinguish between the behaviors of interlopers Pierson and Hickeringill, or do we need more facts to do so?

3. *Hunter harassment statutes*. Occasionally lawful hunters are disrupted in their hunting activities by citizen-activists who oppose hunting on moral grounds. When protests take place on private land the owner can sometimes resolve the conflict by exercising property rights. On public lands the situation is more difficult. Nearly all states have addressed the issue—always favorably to the hunters, even though animal welfare supporters seem to outnumber them—by enacting statutes that make it an offense to harass hunters engaged in the hunt. A few of the statutes were struck down in part as unconstitutional because the activities viewed as harassment included simply speaking against hunting and trying to convince hunters not to hunt—classic exercises of free speech rights. In a remarkable show of political clout, hunting groups have managed to get laws enacted even in states that have had not a single recorded instance of harassment. The statutes are considered critically in Jacqueline Tresl, *Shoot First, Talk Later: Holes in Freedom of Speech*, 8 Animal L. Rev. 177 (2002); Katherine Hessler, *Where Do We Draw the Line Between Harassment and Free Speech?: An Analysis of Hunter Harassment Law*, 3 Animal L. Rev. 129 (1997). The Illinois statute was partially invalidated on free speech grounds in People v. Sanders, 182 Ill.2d 524, 231 Ill.Dec. 573, 696 N.E.2d 1144 (1998).

4. *Capturing mines*. Under the Mining Law of 1872—a statute still very much on the books—a prospector on federal lands that are open to mining is free to seek out mineral deposits. If he is the first to find one, he gains the exclusive right to exploit it, with no royalties due the United States. The process seems straight-forward, but of course problems arise as with any first-in-time rule. In the case of a captured fox, we have little trouble identifying the thing that has been captured—the fox (though query, what if it is a mother fox, which has immobile young in a den and each fox has a bounty on its head; does capturing the mother give a hunter ownership of the young?). In the case of a mineral deposit, in contrast, the boundaries of the thing captured are far less clear. Where does the deposit start and stop, both on the surface and under the ground? Before getting to that issue, we have the foundational issue: did the prospector actually find a mineral *deposit* rather than, say, merely one or two valuable rocks? If the answer is yes, and if the other required steps are properly taken (locating the mining claim, filing the right papers, working the deposit a bit), then the finder can do what the party in the next case sought to do—go the federal government and ask for a patent on the land. At that point, though, the miner's claim is scrutinized. Did the claimant really find a "valuable mineral deposit"? Did he really complete the act of capture?

UNITED STATES v. COLEMAN

390 U.S. 599, 88 S.Ct. 1327, 20 L.Ed.2d 170 (1968).

Mr. Justice Black

In 1956 respondent Coleman applied to the Department of the Interior for a patent to certain public lands based on his entry onto and exploration of these lands and his discovery there of a variety of stone called quartzite, one of the most common of all solid materials. It was, and still is, respondent Coleman's contention that the quartzite deposits qualify as "valuable mineral deposits" under 30 U.S.C. § 22[2] and make the land "chiefly valuable for building stone" under 30 U.S.C. § 161.[3] The Secretary of the Interior held that to qualify as 'valuable mineral deposits' under 30 U.S.C. § 22 it must be shown that the mineral can be "extracted, removed and marketed at a profit"—the so-called "marketability test." Based on the largely undisputed evidence in the record, the Secretary concluded that the deposits claimed by respondent Coleman did not meet that criterion. As to the alternative "chiefly valuable for building stone" claim, the Secretary held that respondent Coleman's quartzite deposits were a "common variet(y)" of stone within the meaning of 30 U.S.C. § 611,[4] and thus they could not serve as the basis for a valid mining claim under the mining laws. The Secretary denied the patent application, but respondent Coleman remained on the land, forcing the Government to bring this present action in ejectment in the District Court against respondent Coleman and his lessee, respondent McClennan. The respondents filed a counterclaim seeking to have the District Court direct the Secretary to issue a patent to them. The District Court, agreeing with the Secretary, rendered summary judgment for the Government. On appeal the Court of Appeals for the Ninth Circuit reversed, holding specifically that the test of profitable marketability was not a proper standard for determining whether a discovery of "valuable mineral deposits" under 30 U.S.C. § 22 had been made and that building stone could not be deemed a "common variet(y)" of stone under 30 U.S.C. § 611. We granted the Government's petition for certiorari because of the importance of the decision to the utilization of the public lands. 389 U.S. 970, 88 S.Ct. 476, 19 L.Ed.2d 460.

We cannot agree with the Court of Appeals and believe that the rulings of the Secretary of the Interior were proper. The Secretary's determination that the quartzite deposits did not qualify as valuable mineral deposits because the stone could not be marketed at a profit does no violence to the statute. Indeed, the marketability test is an admirable effort to identify with greater precision and objectivity the

2. The cornerstone of federal legislation dealing with mineral lands is the Act of May 10, 1872, 17 Stat. 91, 30 U.S.C. § 22, which provides in § 1 that citizens may enter and explore the public domain and, if they find "valuable mineral deposits," may obtain title to the land on which such deposits are located by application to the Department of the Interior. The Secretary of the Interior is "charged with seeing * * * that valid claims * * * (are) recognized, invalid ones eliminated, and the rights of the public preserved." Cameron v. United States, 252 U.S. 450, 460, 40 S.Ct. 410, 412, 64 L.Ed. 659.

3. The 1872 Act, supra, was supplemented in 1892 by the passage of the Act of August 4, 1892, 27 Stat. 348, 30 U.S.C. § 161, which provides in § 1 in pertinent part: "That any person authorized to enter lands under the mining laws of the United States may enter lands that are chiefly valuable for building stone under the provisions of the law in relation to placer mineral claims * * *."

4. Section 3 of the Act of July 23, 1955, 69 Stat. 368, 30 U.S.C. § 611, provides in pertinent part as follows: 'A deposit of common varieties of sand, stone, gravel, pumice, pumicite, or cinders shall not be deemed a valuable mineral deposit within the meaning of the mining laws of the United States so as to give effective validity to any mining claim hereafter located under such mining laws * * *. 'Common varieties' as used in this Act does not include deposits of such materials which are valuable because the deposit has some property giving it distinct and special value * * *.'

factors relevant to a determination that a mineral deposit is "valuable." It is a logical complement to the "prudent-man test" which the Secretary has been using to interpret the mining laws since 1894. Under this "prudent-man test" in order to qualify as "valuable mineral deposits," the discovered deposits must be of such a character that "a person of ordinary prudence would be justified in the further expenditure of his labor and means, with a reasonable prospect of success, in developing a valuable mine * * *." Castle v. Womble, 19 L.D. 455, 457 (1894). This Court has approved the prudent-man formulation and interpretation on numerous occasions. See, for example, Chrisman v. Miller, 197 U.S. 313, 322, 25 S.Ct. 468, 49 L.Ed. 770; Cameron v. United States, 252 U.S. 450, 459, 40 S.Ct. 410, 64 L.Ed. 659; Best v. Humboldt Placer Mining Co., 371 U.S. 334, 335–336, 83 S.Ct. 379, 9 L.Ed.2d 350. Under the mining laws Congress has made public lands available to people for the purpose of mining valuable mineral deposits and not for other purposes. The obvious intent was to reward and encourage the discovery of minerals that are valuable in an economic sense. Minerals which no prudent man will extract because there is no demand for them at a price higher than the costs of extraction and transportation are hardly economically valuable. Thus, profitability is an important consideration in applying the prudent-man test, and the marketability test which the Secretary has used here merely recognizes this fact.

The marketability test also has the advantage of throwing light on a claimant's intention, a matter which is inextricably bound together with valuableness. For evidence that a mineral deposit is not of economic value and cannot in all likelihood be operated at a profit may well suggest that a claimant seeks the land for other purposes. Indeed, as the Government points out, the facts of this case—the thousands of dollars and hours spent building a home on 720 acres in a highly scenic national forest located two hours from Los Angeles, the lack of an economically feasible market for the stone, and the immense quantities of identical stone found in the area outside the claims—might well be thought to raise a substantial question as to respondent Coleman's real intention.

Finally, we think that the Court of Appeals' objection to the marketability test on the ground that it involves the imposition of a different and more onerous standard on claims for minerals of widespread occurrence than for rarer minerals which have generally been dealt with under the prudent-man test is unwarranted. As we have pointed out above, the prudent-man test and the marketability test are not distinct standards, but are complementary in that the latter is a refinement of the former. While it is true that the marketability test is usually the critical factor in cases involving nonmetallic minerals of widespread occurrence, this is accounted for by the perfectly natural reason that precious metals which are in small supply and for which there is a great demand, sell at a price so high as to leave little room for doubt that they can be extracted and marketed at a profit.

We believe that the Secretary of the Interior was also correct in ruling that "(i)n view of the immense quantities of identical stone found

"common variety" stone (too much)

in the area outside the claims, the stone must be considered a "common variety" and thus must fall within the exclusionary language of § 3 of the 1955 Act, 69 Stat. 368, 30 U.S.C. § 611, which declares that "(a) deposit of common varieties of * * * stone * * * shall (not) be deemed a valuable mineral deposit within the meaning of the mining laws * * *." Respondents rely on the earlier 1892 Act, 30 U.S.C. § 161, which makes the mining laws applicable to "lands that are chiefly valuable for building stone" and contend that the 1955 Act has no application to building stone, since, according to respondents, "(s)tone which is chiefly valuable as building stone is, by that very fact, not a common variety of stone." This was also the reasoning of the Court of Appeals. But this argument completely fails to take into account the reason why Congress felt compelled to pass the 1955 Act with its modification of the mining laws. The legislative history makes clear that this Act (30 U.S.C. § 611) was intended to remove common types of sand, gravel, and stone from the coverage of the mining laws, under which they served as a basis for claims to land patents, and to place the disposition of such materials under the Materials Act of 1947, 61 Stat. 681, 30 U.S.C. § 601 et seq., which provides for the sale of such materials without disposing of the land on which they are found.... Thus we read 30 U.S.C. § 611, passed in 1955, as removing from the coverage of the mining laws "common varieties" of building stone, but leaving 30 U.S.C. § 161, the 1892 Act, entirely effective as to building stone that has 'some property giving it distinct and special value' (expressly excluded under § 611).

Materials Act (not mining Act) removes common varieties from mining Act

For these reasons we hold that the United States is entitled to eject respondents from the land and that respondents' counterclaim for a patent must fail. The case is reversed and remanded to the Court of Appeals for the Ninth Circuit for further proceedings to carry out this decision.

Holding ejected

Notes

1. *The marketability test.* On the facts of *Coleman* it seems clear that the "miner" seeking a land patent had no interest at all in mining and every interest instead in owning a nice home "in a highly scenic national forest." His case may seem audacious except that it builds upon a long history of misuse of public land laws. Indeed, taking advantage of the government was (and for some, perhaps, still is) one of the prime forms of entertainment in the American West. Still, the marketability test as a means for judging the value of mineral deposits is not without its criticisms. A mineral deposit that cannot be exploited today, because the costs of exploitation or transport are too high, might well become usable in the future, when richer mines have been exhausted and more convenient mineral sources are gone. Note the final excerpted sentences of the Court's opinion: the marketability test is used chiefly for "nonmetallic minerals of widespread occurrence." It is used far less in the case of precious metals such as gold and silver, even when ore concentrations are, for the time being, too low to mine at a profit.

2. *Capturing minerals: the other elements.* To complete the capture of a mineral deposit, the claimant must do more than show that the deposit is

"valuable" and "mineral." (As for the issue of "mineral," courts have ruled that it excludes both water and topsoil, even though both are valuable. Statutes enacted since 1872, including the Mineral Leasing Law of 1920, have also excluded from the original act's coverage a variety of specific minerals, including oil, gas, and coal.) The miner must also stake out his claim, properly locating its boundaries. Once these steps are completed the miner gains an "unpatented mining claim," which is a potentially perpetual property interest in the mineral deposit. The task of locating a claim can be complicated because mineral deposits are divided at law into two types—lode claims and placer claims, depending upon whether the valuable mineral is or is not embedded in an ore formation (a lode claim is embedded). A miner who errs on this factual issue, treating a lode claim as a placer claim (or vice versa), has not properly completed the work of capture and thus does not gain an unpatented mining claim. Errors can also be made in establishing the exact dimensions of a claim. Note that the issues of "valuable" and "mineral" in this setting are essentially questions of statutory interpretation as they were in *BedRoc Limited, LLC*, the 2004 Supreme Court ruling dealing with federal lands considered at the end of chapter 2. In other legal settings they can be questions of deed interpretation (as we'll see in chapter 5), as when a landowner transfers land but reserves all minerals. And, of course, the term "mineral" can have widely different meanings in different legal settings.

3. *How much incentive*? The effect of the Mining Law of 1872 is to give valuable resources on federal lands to the person who discovers and develops them. The rationale is that the deposit is a reward for the labor of discovery, and thus an incentive for miners to seek out valuable deposits. When the nation's mineral wealth is exploited, labor is employed and the nation's economy benefits. The question that has loomed for many decades is whether the Mining Law offers too much of a reward or incentive. Would miners work just has diligently if they had to pay a royalty for the minerals that they extracted? In the case of oil and gas production, the federal government shifted long ago to leasing arrangements under which lessees paid royalties if and when they produced. In the most attractive locations for oil production, leases are auctioned off. Potential lessees compete for the leases by bidding on the bonus payments that they make up front to obtain the lease. In general, a first-in-time system appears to make sense when the resource is of too little value to merit a more cumbersome allocation method and when the resource is an adequate reward or incentive for the labor involved in capturing or discovering it. Are there other rationales that might also justify this allocation method?

GEOMET EXPLORATION, LTD. v. LUCKY MC URANIUM CORP.

124 Ariz. 55, 601 P.2d 1339 (1979).

HAYS, JUSTICE.

Geomet appealed from a decision granting exclusive possession of certain unpatented mining claims to Lucky Mc Uranium Corporation....

By use of modern scintillation equipment in September of 1976, plaintiff/appellee, Lucky Mc Uranium Corporation, detected "anomalies" (discontinuities in geologic formations) indicative of possible uranium deposits in the Artillery Peak Mining District in Yuma County, land in the federal public domain. In November, 1976, Lucky proceeded to monument and post 200 claims (4,000 acres), drill a 10–foot hole on each claim, and record notices pursuant to A.R.S. §§ 27–202, 27–203 and 27–204. Subsequently, defendant/appellant, Geomet, peaceably entered some of the areas claimed by Lucky and began drilling operations. Employees of Geomet were aware of Lucky's claims but considered them invalid because there had been no discovery of minerals in place and Lucky was not in actual occupancy of the areas Geomet entered.

Lucky instituted a possessory action seeking damages, exclusive possession and a permanent injunction against trespass by Geomet or its employees. There was insufficient evidence to establish a valid discovery, but the trial court found that Lucky was entitled to exclusive possession and a permanent injunction. Although Geomet pointed out that, prior to discovery of minerals in place, the doctrine of *pedis possessio* requires a prospector to be in actual occupancy of the claim and diligently pursuing discovery, the court based its reasoning on the economic infeasibility of literal adherence to the element of actual occupancy in view of modern mining techniques and the expense involved in exploring large areas.

Additionally, the court found that Geomet had entered the land in bad faith, knowing that Lucky was claiming it.

We must decide a single issue: Should the actual occupancy requirement of Pedis possessio be discarded in favor of constructive possession to afford a potential locator protection of contiguous, unoccupied claims as against one who enters peaceably, openly, and remains in possession searching for minerals?

Pedis Possessio

Mineral deposits in the public domain of the United States are open to all citizens (or those who have expressed an intent to become citizens) who wish to occupy and explore them "under regulations prescribed by law, and according to the local customs or rules of miners in the several mining districts, so far as the same are applicable and not inconsistent with the laws of the United States." 30 U.S.C. § 22 (1970).

The doctrine of *pedis possessio* evolved from customs and usages of miners and has achieved statutory recognition in federal law as the "law of possession," 30 U.S.C. § 53 (1970):

> No possessory action between persons, in any court of the United States, for the recovery of any mining title, or for damages to any such title, shall be affected by the fact that the paramount title to the land in which such mines lie is in the United States; but each case shall be judged by the law of possession.

Regardless of compliance with statutory requisites such as monumenting and notice, one cannot perfect a location, under either federal or state law, without actual discovery of minerals in place. Best v. Humboldt Placer Mining Co., 371 U.S. 334, 83 S.Ct. 379, 9 L.Ed.2d 350 (1963); 30 U.S.C. § 23 (1970); A.R.S. § 27–201. Until discovery, the law of possession determines who has the better right to possession.

The literal meaning of *pedis possessio* is a foothold, actual possession. Black's Law Dictionary 1289 (rev. 4th ed. 1968). This actual occupancy must be distinguished from constructive possession, which is based on color of title and has the effect of enlarging the area actually occupied to the extent of the description in the title. Id. at 1325. A succinct exposition of *pedis possessio* is found in Union Oil Co. v. Smith, 249 U.S. 337, 346–48, 39 S.Ct. 308, 310–11, 63 L.Ed. 635 (1919):

> Those who, being qualified, proceed in good faith to make such explorations and enter peaceably upon vacant lands of the United States for that purpose are not treated as mere trespassers, but as licensees or tenants at will. For since, as a practical matter, exploration must precede the discovery of minerals, and some occupation of the land ordinarily is necessary for adequate and systematic exploration, legal recognition of the *pedis possessio* of a bona fide and qualified prospector is universally regarded as a necessity. It is held that upon the public domain a miner may hold the place in which he may be working against all others having no better right, and while he remains in possession, diligently working towards discovery, is entitled at least for a reasonable time to be protected against forcible, fraudulent, and clandestine intrusions upon his possession.

Whatever the nature and extent of a possessory right before discovery, all authorities agree that Such possession may be maintained only by continued actual occupancy by a qualified locator or his representatives engaged in persistent and diligent prosecution of work looking to the discovery of mineral.

If the first possessor should relax his occupancy or cease working toward discovery, and another enters peaceably, openly, and diligently searches for mineral, the first party forfeits the right to exclusive possession under the requirements of *pedis possessio*. Cole v. Ralph, 252 U.S. 286, 295, 40 S.Ct. 321, 325, 64 L.Ed. 567 (1920); Davis v. Nelson, 329 F.2d 840 (9th Cir. 1964).

Arizona has recognized *pedis possessio* and the concomitant requirement of actual occupancy for a century. Field v. Grey, 1 Ariz. 404, 25 P. 793 (1881). In Bagg v. New Jersey Loan Co., 88 Ariz. 182, 188–89, 354 P.2d 40, 44 (1960), we said: "Location is the foundation of the possessory title, and possession thereunder, As required by law and local rules and customs, keeps the title alive, ... " (Emphasis added.) It is perhaps more proper to speak of a possessory right than a title because, until discovery of mineral and issuance of a patent, absolute title in fee simple remains in the United States. Bagg, *supra*, at 192, 354 P.2d 40; Bowen v. Chemi–Cote Perlite Corp., 102 Ariz. 423, 432 P.2d 435 (1967). Since this is a possessory action, the party with the better right is entitled to prevail. Rundle v. Republic Cement Corp., 86 Ariz. 96, 341 P.2d 226 (1959).

Conceding that actual occupancy is necessary under *pedis possessio*, Lucky urges that the requirement be relaxed in deference to the time and expense that would be involved in actually occupying and drilling on each claim until discovery. Moreover, Lucky points out that the total area claimed 4,000 acres is reasonable in size, similar in geological formation, and that an overall work program for the entire area had been developed. Under these circumstances, Lucky contends, actual drilling on some of the claims should suffice to afford protection as to all contiguous claims. Great reliance is placed on MacGuire v. Sturgis, 347 F.Supp. 580 (D.C.Wyo.1971), in which the federal court accepted arguments similar to those advanced here and extended protection on a group or area basis. Geomet counters that MacGuire, *supra*, is an aberration and contrary to three Wyoming Supreme Court cases upholding the requisite of actual occupancy. Sparks v. Mount, 29 Wyo. 1, 207 P. 1099 (1922); Whiting v. Straup, 17 Wyo. 1, 95 P. 849 (1908); Phillips v. Brill, 17 Wyo. 26, 95 P. 856 (1908).

To adopt the premise urged by Lucky eviscerates the actual occupancy requirement of *pedis possessio* and substitutes for it the theory of constructive possession even though there is no color of title. We are persuaded that the sounder approach is to maintain the doctrine intact. In Union Oil, *supra*, the Court considered the precise question of extending protection to contiguous claims and refused to do so:

> It was and is defendant's contention that by virtue of the act of 1903, one who has acquired the possessory rights of locators before discovery in five contiguous claims . . . may preserve and maintain an inchoate right to all of them by means of a continuous actual occupation of one, coupled with diligent prosecution in good faith of a sufficient amount of discovery work thereon, provided such work tends also to determine the oil-bearing character of the other claims.

In our opinion the act shows no purpose to dispense with discovery as an essential of a valid oil location or to break down in any wise the recognized distinction between the *pedis possessio* of a prospector doing work for the purpose of discovering oil and the more substantial right of possession of one who has made a discovery. . . . Union Oil, 249 U.S. at 343, 353, 39 S.Ct. at 309, 312. (Emphasis added.)

We have canvassed the Western mining jurisdictions and found the requirement of actual occupancy to be the majority view. Davis v. Nelson, *supra*; United Western Minerals Co. v. Hannsen, 147 Colo. 272, 363 P.2d 677 (1961); Adams v. Benedict, 64 N.M. 234, 327 P.2d 308 (1958); McLemore v. Express Oil Co., 158 Cal. 559, 112 P. 59 (1910).

There are always inherent risks in prospecting. The development of *pedis possessio* from the customs of miners argues forcefully against the proposition that exclusive right to possession should encompass claims neither actually occupied nor being explored. We note that the doctrine does not protect on the basis of occupancy alone; the additional requirement of diligent search for minerals must also be satisfied. The reason for these dual elements and for the policy of the United States in making public domain available for exploration and mining is to encourage those prepared to demonstrate their sincerity and tenacity in the pursuit of valuable minerals. If one may, by complying with preliminary formalities of posting and recording notices, secure for himself the exclusive possession of a large area upon only a small portion of which he is actually working, then he may, at his leisure, explore the entire area and exclude all others who stand ready to peaceably and openly enter unoccupied sections for the purpose of discovering minerals. Such a premise is laden with extreme difficulties of determining over how large an area and for how long one might be permitted to exclude others.

We hold that *pedis possessio* protects only those claims actually occupied (provided also that work toward discovery is in progress) and does not extend to contiguous, unoccupied claims on a group or area basis.

Lucky calls our attention to former A.R.S. § 27–203(B), under which a potential locator was allowed 120 days to sink shafts to a specified depth. The contention is that during that period, Lucky should have been granted exclusive possession in order to discover mineral in place, and, since Geomet entered certain claims before the expiration of the 120 days, Lucky did not have the benefit of the full term in which to make discovery.

We point out, however, that the first statute concerning location of claims, A.R.S. § 27–201, reads as follows:

> Upon discovery of mineral in place on the public domain of the United States the mineral may be located as a lode mining claim by the discoverer for himself, or for himself and others, or for others. (Emphasis added.)

Discovery is the *sine qua non* that lends validity to other statutory procedures designed to complete a location. A.R.S. §§ 27–202 Et seq. We have on two occasions held that acts of location confer no right in the absence of discovery. State v. Tracy, 76 Ariz. 7, 10, 257 P.2d 860, 862 (1953); Ponton v. House, 75 Ariz. 303, 306, 256 P.2d 246, 247 (1953). It is certainly true that, even after discovery, one may be held to have abandoned a location or forfeited his rights for failure to comply with additional statutory requirements. A.R.S. § 27–203(E). But prior to discovery, the only right one has to exclude others flows from *pedis possessio* and not from statutory law.

Finally, Lucky asserts that Geomet cannot invoke *pedis possessio* because Geomet, knowing that Lucky claimed the area, entered in bad faith. Lucky relies principally on Bagg v. New Jersey Loan Co., *supra*, and Woolsey v. Lassen, 91 Ariz. 229, 371 P.2d 587 (1962). It is true that a potential locator must enter in good faith. Union Oil Co. v. Smith, *supra*.

There is language in our decisions that appears to indicate that mere knowledge of a prior claim constitutes bad faith. Although we are sure that our holdings were sound in the cases Lucky cites, certain statements may have been an inadvertent oversimplification of the issue of good faith and we take this opportunity to clarify the point.

In general terms, good faith may be defined as honesty of purpose and absence of intent to defraud. People v. Bowman, 156 Cal.App.2d 784, 320 P.2d 70 (1958); Thurmond v. Espalin, 50 N.M. 109, 171 P.2d 325 (1946). Both Bagg and Woolsey, *supra*, dealt with those who had discovered minerals in place and were in actual occupancy when others attempted to usurp their claims. These facts immediately distinguish them from the instant case, in which Lucky had neither made discovery nor was in actual occupancy of the areas Geomet entered.... In summary, both cases differ significantly from this case in their factual framework and did not depend for their resolution solely upon the element of knowledge. We stand by our conclusions in those cases but wish to emphasize that mere knowledge of a previous claim, in and of itself, does not constitute bad faith.... Since Geomet's entry concededly was open and peaceable, we hold that the entry was in good faith.

In conclusion, Lucky was not in actual occupancy of those areas Geomet entered and Pedis possessio affords Lucky no protection as to those particular claims. Geomet is entitled to the exclusive possession of the disputed claims.

We reverse the trial court, order that the injunction be quashed, and remand for proceedings consistent with this opinion.

Notes

1. *The fair chase.* The issue in *Geomet* chiefly has to do with the rules of the hunt, mining style. How close can one prospector get to another, without acting unfairly? Prospectors today, of course, don't often go out with their mules, pick in hand. They more often go out with explosives and highly technical equipment, undertaking expensive seismic tests to look for underground ore formations. Once a likely formation has been found, they then need to go to the site and work on it. It is thus easy enough for other miners simply to watch what the big companies do and where they go, figuring that a company that sets up operation in a particular place must be doing so because its underground tests have turned up promising evidence of valuable deposits. The question here, then, is not simply about physically disturbing another miner. It is about taking advantage of information on underground ore formations that a miner has obtained at considerable expense. Should this contemporary reality have received more weight in the case than it did? On the other hand, note how much land Lucky was attempting to control, even though it had not actually discovered a valuable mineral deposit. As for the issue of Geomet's bad faith, how does the court now define "bad faith"? Under what circumstances might a person exhibit it? Is the issue of good or bad faith simply about whether Geomet is attempting itself to make a discovery, rather than (as in *Keeble*) attempting to disrupt Lucky's prospecting effort?

2. *Discovery, and the hidden evidence.* Note that whether a person has or has not discovered a valuable mineral deposit is based on evidence often known only to the miner. As the law operates, no one asks to see the evidence of discovery, nor is it judged unless one of two things happens: someone (the government most likely) challenges a miner's claim to possess an unpatented mining claim, or (as in *Coleman*) a miner goes to the government and asks for a patent, thus triggering a legal requirement to prove the deposit and satisfaction of the other legal requirements. In the meantime, a person can assert and enjoy exclusive use of mining claims without proving their validity (there is no limit to how many a person can have, so long as each claim is perfected). Note how Lucky goes about conducting its business: once it finds a place where a valuable deposit might exist, it proceeds to locate its claims and file its papers, even though it has not yet discovered, and might never actually discover, a valuable mineral deposit. Lucky is thus doing things a bit out of order, locating claims before the discovery is made. Yet, once Lucky has asserted control over claims and located them, who is to know whether it has discovered valuable minerals, and thus who is to know whether Lucky does or does not have unpatented mining claims?

Is this whole arrangement perhaps unfair, both to other miners and to the public? Is it sensible to allocate a resource based on first-in-time, when only the actor knows whether he really has "captured" the resource?

3. *Capturing air waves.* For a brief period when radio broadcasts first began and before the federal government stepped in to regulate, private companies scrambled with one another to gain control of the air waves. Inevitably broadcasters claimed ownership of particular frequencies based on a rule of capture. At least one broadcaster met early success. The story was briefly related by Samuel Wiel, a prominent writer on natural resources law:

> In 1926 a press notice of a radio ruling in an Illinois county court [Tribune Co. v. Oak Leaves Broadcasting Station, Cook County Circuit Court] stated:
>
>> Judge Wilson, who wrote the opinion, said that it was a case unique in judicial annals and without direct precedent, but that nevertheless under the general principles of the common law relief might be granted. He found authority for this decision *in the water right cases from the Western States, where the rule of first come, first served, has been laid down by the courts* so that today the individual who first appropriates the water of a running stream and puts the water to beneficial use may hold it against any one who later attempts to take it, even though there can be no such thing as absolute ownership in running water.
>
> In 1931 the Supreme Court of the United States remarked:
>
>> Much argument was directed to the proposition that one who first established a broadcasting station in and serves a given area *thereby appropriates that portion of the ether* which he employs or though which the station's radio activity operates; and it was suggested that *in analogy to the doctrine as to appropriation of waters, et id omne genus,* a property right is thus acquired. It was urged that the question presents this proposition; but it clearly fails to do so. We

> are not required to answer it. [White v. Johnson, 282 U.S. 367, 372 (1931)]
>
> In 1932, however, the Supreme Court abandoned any priority idea for radio. The Supreme Court definitely interpreted the Radio Act of Congress in the language of equality (which is the reverse of priority), effectuated by reasonable use and equitable apportionment . . .

Samuel C. Wiel, *Natural Communism: Air, Water, Oil, Sea, and Seashore,* 47 Harv. L. Rev. 425, 429 (1934).

4. *Capturing water.* As we've seen, the rule of capture is widely applied in oil and gas law. There, an actor becomes full owner of oil and gas once it has been taken into actual physical possession; removed from the ground and stored in some way. What, though, about water, when it is made subject to the rule of capture? Water users aren't usually satisfied with just a specific quantity of water. Instead, they want to gain control over a recurring flow of water, day after day, year after year. It is easy to see how a person can capture one gallon of water. But how does one capture a flow? And when it comes to a water flow, what does it mean to be first?

OPHIR SILVER MINING CO. v. CARPENTER

4 Nev. 534 (1869).

Lewis, C. J.:

This action is founded upon an alleged unlawful diversion of water, whereby it is claimed the plaintiff was damaged in the sum of $3,000, for which judgment is asked against the defendants. An injunction is also prayed for to restrain any future diversion. The defendants claim the right to divert the full quantity of water taken by them, by reason of an appropriation prior in point of time to any claim or appropriation by the plaintiff. And thus this controversy may be determined upon its merits by the resolution of the question which of the parties made the first appropriation of the water diverted by the defendants.

We have carefully examined the voluminous record in the case for the purpose of determining this main question, and as our conclusions are in favor of the plaintiff, the consideration of any minor questions is rendered unnecessary. We concede for the purposes of the present discussion (although it is a fact by no means beyond doubt) that the grantors of the defendants made claim to and intended to appropriate the full volume of water now claimed by them long prior to the time when the plaintiff's grantors appropriated what is claimed by it, and place our decision entirely upon the failure on the part of those from whom defendants derive their title to prosecute their claim to consummation with that diligence which is necessary when it is attempted to make the final act of appropriation relate to the time when the first step was taken or the first act done to make it.

We propose to rely solely upon the undisputed facts and uncontradicted evidence to support the conclusion at which we have arrived, the substance of which may be thus stated: In the spring of the year 1858, J.

H. Rose, the grantor of defendants, desiring to convey water to the village of Dayton from the Carson river, constructed for that purpose a ditch about four and a half miles in length, and of dimensions varying at different points. At its immediate head it was sixteen feet wide. For a distance of one-fourth of a mile below it averaged seven and one-half feet wide on top, and two and one-half feet deep. Its general size below that point was three and one-half feet wide at the top, two and one-half feet on the bottom, and two and one-half feet deep. The ditch was thus constructed in the year 1858. In the following year water was run through it to Dayton. And it remained pretty much in this condition until the fall of the year 1862, at which time Rose entered into a contract with Shanklin and McConnell for its enlargement to its present capacity. Work was immediately commenced under that contract, and the present ditch completed early in 1865. Under this contract an entirely new survey was made, and the water was taken from the river at a point one-quarter of a mile above the head of the old ditch, and on the opposite side of the river. The size of this new ditch, which is called the Shanklin and McConnell ditch, is thirteen feet in width at the top, nine feet on the bottom, and four feet deep. Its flumes are six feet by three, with a fall of one-fifth of an inch to the rod. The volume of water which can be run through it is ten times greater than could have been run through the old Rose ditch, its capacity being fifty-seven cubic feet per second, while the old ditch was capable of discharging only about four and a half feet. The grantors of the plaintiff made no claim to any water until the month of July, A.D. 1859. In that year they diverted the water from the river at a point some distance below the head of the Rose ditch, used some quantity of it that year, and in the fall of 1860 completed their ditch to its present capacity; and have ever since used the water thus diverted for motive power. The defendants claim that the ditch as constructed or enlarged by Shanklin and McConnell is in accordance with the original design of Rose, from whom they acquire their right; that such design was manifested by the fact that his first ditch was of as great capacity for a quarter of a mile from its head as the present ditch, and hence that their right to the entire volume of water which the present ditch will carry must relate to the time when Rose did the first act towards appropriating it, which was in the spring of the year 1858.

The plaintiff concedes that the defendants, as the first appropriators, have the right: First. To divert through their ditch so much of the water of the river as would have run through the old ditch. It is then claimed that the plaintiff is entitled to sufficient water to fill its ditch, counsel arguing on its behalf that the grantors of defendants had no right to increase the capacity of the old ditch to its prejudice. Where the right to the use of running water is based upon appropriation, and not upon an ownership in the soil, it is the generally recognized rule here that priority of appropriation gives the superior right. When any work is necessary to be done to complete the appropriation, the law gives the claimant a reasonable time within which to do it, and although the appropriation is not deemed complete until the actual diversion or use of the water, still if such work be prosecuted with reasonable diligence, the right relates to the time when the first step was taken to secure it. If, however, the work be not prosecuted with diligence, the right does not so relate, but generally dates from the time when the work is completed or the appropriation is fully perfected.

As we have already stated, we concede the fact, for the present, that Rose designed, when he constructed his ditch in the year 1858, to enlarge it to the capacity of the present ditch, and if he has shown that the design thus conceived was prosecuted with a reasonable degree of diligence until its completion, then the defendant's right to that quantity of water now claimed by them will relate back to the spring of 1858, and thus antedate the plaintiff's right eighteen months or two years, thereby giving them the superior right. But in our opinion the evidence shows an utter failure on the part of Rose to prosecute his original design with that diligence which the law requires. The manner in which this work was prosecuted we gather from the testimony of Rose himself. In the year 1858 the ditch was constructed, and a great deal of work was necessarily done. In the succeeding year also a considerable amount of work was done in cleaning out the ditch and enlarging it in some places. Some time in the summer of this year the ditch was completed to such an extent that a small quantity of water was run through it to Dayton. It is very doubtful whether any work was done this year towards a systematic enlargement of the ditch for the purpose of increasing its general capacity. Rose himself thus describes the work done: "I was trying to get more water through; so wherever earth or rock slid in from the sides of the ditch, all the men hired by the day were instructed to dig or throw it out, and to throw out all the loose dirt or gravel that was not worked out by the water running through." However this may be, it is certain that in the succeeding year, that is in 1860, nothing whatever was done towards enlargement. Indeed the only thing done during the entire year was the employment of two men, who were engaged for a few days in throwing out rock from the ditch. This is all the work that was done between the fall of 1859 and the month of May, A. D. 1861, a period of more than eighteen months. As counsel for appellant very aptly remarked, "Rose during this time gave to other pursuits his time and industry, and to the vast enterprise of securing all the waters of the Carson river, only a diligent contemplation." The year 1861 is little less barren of results. A few men were employed for a period of three months only, who, Rose says, were engaged in cleaning out and enlarging the ditch. From the fall of 1861 to the summer of 1862 nothing appears to have been done. In the summer from three to twenty men were employed, and continued work for about five months. But it is not pretended that they were employed at enlarging, but only cleaning out the ditch. Rose testifies that he did not know that it was enlarged at all that year; that the heavy rains during the winter had filled it up in many places; that he had it all cleaned out. In September of this year the contract between Rose and Shanklin and McConnell was entered into, and during the years 1863 and 1864 the work progressed, and the present ditch of the defendants was completed. Thus, it appears, that from the fall of 1859 to the summer of 1862, a period of over two years and a half, work was done upon the ditch for about three months only; that was during the year 1861, when Rose testifies that from seventeen to twenty men were employed. During this period of inactivity on the part of Rose, the grantors of the plaintiff prosecuted their work vigorously, and finished their ditch to its present capacity in the year 1860. These facts, it is argued on behalf of defendants, show such diligence on the part of their grantor in the prosecution of his original design as to make their right to the quantity of water now diverted by them relate to the time when Rose in the year 1858 did the first act towards appropriation. We are constrained to differ from counsel upon this proposition.

In our judgment those facts exhibit an utter want of diligence in the prosecution of the design which it is claimed was undertaken by Rose. If the labor of twenty men for three or four months, in a period of two years and a half, constitutes diligence in the prosecution of such a vast enterprise as this, it is difficult, if not impossible, to designate the entire want of diligence. The manner in which this work was prosecuted certainly does not accord with what is generally understood to be reasonable diligence. Diligence is defined to be the "steady application to business of any kind, constant effort to accomplish any undertaking." The law does not require any unusual or extraordinary efforts, but only that which is usual, ordinary, and reasonable. The diligence required in cases of this kind is that constancy or steadiness of purpose or labor which is usual with men engaged in like enterprises, and who desire a speedy accomplishment of their designs. Such assiduity in the prosecution of the enterprise as will manifest to the world a *bona fide* intention to complete it within a reasonable time. It is the doing of an act, or series of acts, with all practical expedition, with no delay, except such as may be incident to the work itself. The law, then, required the grantors of the defendants to prosecute the work necessary to an execution of the design with all practical expedition. But the evidence clearly shows that this was not done. The ditch was of the same general size, and the flumes of the same capacity, at the time when Shanklin and McConnell commenced work, as they were in the spring of 1859. As no great effort is made necessary, so no unreasonable dilatoriness or delay is tolerated. But it is unnecessary for us to determine what would be deemed reasonable diligence on the part of the grantors of the defendants in this case; it is enough to say that the doing of five or six days' work during a period of sixteen months, that is from the fall of 1859 to the month of May, 1861, and only three months' labor during a period of two years and a half, does not exhibit that diligence which the law requires. The weather would not have prevented work upon this ditch ordinarily more than three or four months in the year, hence labor upon it could probably have been prosecuted during eight or nine months out of every twelve. Here, however, there was a period of thirty months, when only about three months' work was done, or one month out of every ten. Rose during this time may have dreamed of his canal completed, seen it with his mind's eye yielding him a great revenue; he may have indulged the hope of providential interposition in his favor; but this cannot be called a diligent prosecution of his enterprise. Surely he could hardly have expected to complete it during his natural life by such efforts as were made through this period.

It is, however, claimed on behalf of the defendants that all the work was done at this time which under the circumstances could be done, and that the law requires no more. Rose's illness for a short time early in the year 1860; his want of means, and considerations of economy, are suggested as circumstances to be considered in determining whether the enterprise was prosecuted with reasonable diligence. Rose testifies that in the spring of the year 1860 he was sick. But it is not shown that that should necessarily interfere with the prosecution of the work. For aught that appears in the record it could have proceeded notwithstanding his illness. If it were admitted, however, that his illness constituted a valid excuse for a want of diligence, it would only excuse it whilst such illness continued, which was only for a short time in the early part of 1860. But we are inclined to believe that his illness is not a circumstance which can be taken into consideration at all. Like the pecuniary condition of a person, it is not one of those matters incident to the enterprise, but rather to the person. The only matters in cases of this kind which can be taken into consideration are such as would affect any person who might be engaged in the same undertaking, such as the state of the weather, the difficulty of obtaining laborers, or something of that character. It would be a most dangerous doctrine to hold that ill-health or pecuniary inability of a claimant of a water privilege will dispense with the necessity of actual appropriation within a reasonable time or the diligence which is usually required in the prosecution of the work necessary for the purpose. . . .

We conclude, therefore, that Rose and his associates did not prosecute the work upon their ditch with that diligence which the law required, and so their right to any quantity of water, beyond what could be taken through the old ditch, is subordinate and subject to the rights of the plaintiff. . . .

Notes

1. *First to do what?* According to *Ophir*, what does a putative appropriator have to do in order to gain a property interest in water? An initial need, of course, is to find water that isn't already claimed. But what else in physical terms? And how does the court's answer to the recurring question compare with the answers that we've seen in other resource settings?

2. *Relation back. Ophir* is chiefly about the relation-back doctrine, which allows an appropriator who completes the act of appropriation to date the appropriation as of the date when work on the diversion commenced. Once the diversion work is fully completed and water is actually applied to a beneficial use, the initiation of that beneficial use relates back in time to the date when the diversion work commenced. A person can take advantage of

this relation-back rule, the court tells us, only when the person uses due diligence in completing the project. What, though, is due diligence in a setting such as this? More aptly, what excuses can an appropriator use to explain delays in completing a project?

Today, appropriators must first get permits to initiate a water use, but the relation-back rule of due-diligence still applies. A water right only ripens into a lasting form of private property when all the elements of appropriation are met. Only when the appropriator uses due diligence in completing them does the appropriation relate back in time to the date of the permit. Can you think of other settings in which a relation-back rule is applied, or might usefully be applied? Presumably if a person's due diligence is interrupted by a competing claimant, the person has an excuse for not completing work in a timely manner. Could this line of argument have helped Lodowick Post in his fox hunt? Lucky Mc Uranium?

3. *When the race gets congested.* What happens under a first-in-time allocation system when the number of people seeking to be first gets too great? What if, as a practical matter, lots of people tie for first, or else the temporal differences among them are trivial? What are lawmakers to do then? On this issue consider the following decision, which was handed down under a since-repealed provision of federal law dealing with oil and gas leases. (The law applied only on lands that were not "within any known geological structure of a producing oil and gas field." Because such leases were not within a producing oil field they were considered less valuable, too low in value to justify auctioning them off to the highest bidder.)

THOR-WESTCLIFFE DEVELOPMENT, INC. v. UDALL

314 F.2d 257 (D.C. Cir. 1963).

J. SKELLY WRIGHT, CIRCUIT JUDGE.

Section 17 of the Mineral Leasing Act of 1920 provides that public lands "not within any known geological structure of a producing oil or gas field" shall be leased "to the person first making application" at not less than fifty cents per acre. In an effort to eliminate the chaos which sometimes resulted from competition among applicants to be literally the "person first making application" for leases having speculative value far in excess of leasing costs, the Secretary of the Interior promulgated a regulation providing for simultaneous filing and a public drawing in the event of multiple applications. Appellant attacks this regulation as unresponsive to the statutory command that the lease be given to the "person first making application." The District Court granted summary judgment in favor of the Secretary. We affirm.

Experience in the administration of the Act has demonstrated that land subject to leasing after expiration or cancellation of a prior lease often has significant speculative value in spite of the fact that it is not actually "within in any known geological structure of a producing oil or gas field." In order "to assure public notice and fuller public participation in the process of reissuing relinquished leases," Regulation

192.43 provides for the posting of descriptions of such expired lease land in each Interior Department land office on the third Monday of each month, together with "a notice stating that the lands in such leases are subject to the simultaneous filings of lease offers from the time of such posting until 10:00 o'clock a.m. on the said fifth working day thereafter." If at 10:00 a.m. on the fifth day more than one offer has been received to lease the same acreage, the priorities are determined by lot.

Prior leases on the lands in suit expired by operation of law on June 30, 1961. Appellant filed its applications for leases on July 3, 1961, the next business day. On July 17, 1961, the lands were posted under the procedure described above and applications for leases were accepted until 10:00 a.m. on the "fifth working day thereafter." Appellant filed no applications during this interval. A drawing was held among those applications filed during this period and intervenor Boyle was the winner. Appellant's applications of July 3, 1961, were rejected as untimely. Having exhausted its remedies within the Department, appellant brought suit for a judgment declaring Regulation 192.43 invalid and granting the leases to it.

Appellant, ignoring Mr. Justice Frankfurter's famous dictum,stands Firmly on the literal language of the statute. It was the "person first making application" after the prior leases expired, it argues, and consequently the Secretary must comply with the statutory mandate. The Secretary relies upon the regulation, which he justifies as necessary to end the mad scrambles, breaches of the peace, damage to tract books, and corruption of land office employees as applicants compete to be the "person first making application." Appellant does not contest the existence of these problems with respect to cancellation or other premature termination of a lease, but asserts (1) that these problems do not exist where leases terminate by expiration, (2) that other methods of meeting these problems are available, and (3) that in any event this regulation on its face conflicts with the statutory requirement and is therefore invalid.

The Secretary has full authority under the Act "to prescribe necessary and proper rules and regulations" to accomplish its purposes. Stripped to its essence, the question presented here simply is: does Regulation 192.43 comport with the Secretary's statutory authority? It is not for us, nor for appellant, to suggest a method for solving the problems which have arisen in the administration of the Mineral Leasing Act. Congress has consigned that function to the Secretary. Our inquiry ends when we determine whether or not the method adopted by the Secretary is "unreasonable and plainly inconsistent" with the statute, having in mind that regulations "constitute contemporaneous constructions by those charged with administration of these statutes which should not be overruled except for weighty reasons." Commissioner v. South Texas Co., 333 U.S. 496, 501, 68 S.Ct. 695, 92 L.Ed. 831 (1948).

In administering the Mineral Leasing Act, the Secretary exercises a discretionary, rather than a ministerial, function. Compare Udall v. States of Wisconsin, Colorado and Minnesota, 113 U.S.App.D.C. 183, 306

F.2d 790 (1962). The provisions of the Act "plainly indicate that Congress held in mind the distinction between a positive mandate to the Secretary and permission to take certain action in his discretion." United States ex rel. McLennan v. Wilbur, 283 U.S. 414, 418, 51 S.Ct. 502, 75 L.Ed. 1148 (1931). This, of course, does not mean that the Secretary is permitted to grant a lease to one other than "the person first making application." It does mean that the Secretary is to determine who that first person is. Hence the provision in the Act authorizing the promulgation of regulations. 41 Stat. 450, 30 U.S.C. § 189. It is likewise clear that the language "person first making application" is not so definite, particularly when prior experience with its application is considered, as to render an interpretative or implementing regulation inappropriate. Compare Helvering v. R. J. Reynolds Co., 306 U.S. 110, 114, 59 S.Ct. 423, 83 L.Ed. 536 (1939); Morrissey v. Commissioner, 296 U.S. 344, 354–355, 56 S.Ct. 289, 80 L.Ed. 263 (1935).

Having recognized the authority in the Secretary to promulgate a regulation implementing the statutory language "person first making application," we must decide whether Regulation 192.43 is consistent with the Act and a reasonable exercise of the Secretary's authority thereunder, or whether the regulation is "in the teeth of the unambiguous mandate of the statute, (is) contradictory of its plain terms, and amounts to an attempt to legislate." Helvering v. Sabine Trans. Co., 318 U.S. 306, 311–312, 63 S.Ct. 569, 87 L.Ed. 773 (1943). We find, considering the language and purpose of the statute, as well as the experience of the Secretary in the implementation thereof, that the regulation is neither unreasonable nor inconsistent with the plain language of the Act.

Appellant does not argue that Regulation 192.43 unfairly favors some applicants for leases at the expense of others or that the procedure provided therein is inconsistent with the legislative purpose to distribute these leases fairly with the opportunity for full participation by the interested public. Its argument seems to be that, because of practical difficulties attendant its administration, the Secretary has rewritten the statute.

It must be owned that the procedure outlined in Regulation 192.43, on superficial examination, bears little resemblance to the "person first making application" language of the statute. But Congress could hardly have supposed that granting $.50 per acre mineral leases can be accomplished as simply as the statutory language seems to indicate. The history of the administration of the statute furnishes compelling proof, familiar to the membership of Congress, that the human animal has not changed, that when you determine to give something away, you are going to draw a crowd. It is the Secretary's job to manage the crowd while complying with the requirement of the Act. Regulation 192.43 is the Secretary's effort in this direction. We cannot say that it is an impermissible implementation of the statutory purpose.

Affirmed.

Notes

1. *Still first in time?* The federal appellate court in *Thor-Westcliffe* upholds the agency's action because it sympathized with the agency's plight. Realistically, what can first mean when floods of people show up at the same time? But is a lottery system merely a variant on first in time—a method of breaking the tie, in a sense? Or is it really an entirely different method of resource allocation, with different pros and cons? Obviously a lottery system requires that people get their names in by some deadline, and those who don't are too late. To that extent it is based on time. But what does the random drawing part of the selection process have to do with temporal priority? More generally, what are the virtues and vices of a lottery system? Are there settings in which it makes sense and settings in which it does not? If we look upon a space in the entering class of a law school as a natural resource (a use right, of a sort), would we be troubled by a law school that used a lottery to decide who gets in? Is this better or worse than auctioning off law school spaces to the highest bidder?

To answer these questions we might recall the two settings in which first-in-time allocation made the most sense: when the resource was of too little value to warrant a more cumbersome allocation process, and when the resource was a suitable reward or incentive for the act of capture. Do either of these apply in the case of a government-run auction?

2. *On the road.* One of the virtues of first-in-time is that it does include a rough element of justice in it—or so Americans of today would say, drawing upon our culture. Even when no law governs and it is, as a legal matter, a world in which might-makes-right, people tend to defer to the person who came first. Yet, even when people are willing to defer to the person who is first-in-time, problems can arise. Consider, for instance, the following tale, paying attention to the issues already considered. Does the law on road-kill deer perhaps need a bit of refinement, to deal with such disputes? If so, how would you alter it?

THE STRANGE-BUT-TRUE STORY OF THE SAW-WIELDING COP, THE ANGRY IRONWORKER AND THE HEADLESS DEER

John Keilman

THE CHICAGO TRIBUNE, February 3, 2005 Copyright (c) 2005, Chicago Tribune.

In the woods, the rule is simple: You kill a deer, you take it with you—hooves, hide and head. But when it happens along a busy suburban road, things can get messy.

A deer struck by an SUV on Golf Road several weeks ago set off a nasty dispute between a cop with an eye for an impressive crown of antlers and an ironworker with a stubborn belief that the code of the forest holds true on the streets.

Their disagreement over the ethics of harvesting roadkill ended with the ironworker, Michael Cox, 30, of Glenview, angrily heaving the deer's headless carcass onto the doorstep of the Des Plaines Police Department.

Though he was promptly charged with littering and ultimately pleaded guilty, Cox remains unrepentant. "I have no regrets," he said. "If that's what it took to get my point across that this was wrong, that's what had to be done."

The drama began about 7:30 a.m. Dec. 13, when a Honda Passport driven by a Skokie man slammed into a 10–point buck—a mature male with antlers branching into 10 tips—near Camp Pine Woods Forest Preserve in Des Plaines. A police officer who arrived shot and killed the mortally wounded animal.

Under Illinois law, a driver who strikes a deer is entitled to the carcass, but the Skokie man didn't want it. That made it a case of "first come, first served," said Jill Willis, a conservation police officer with the Illinois Department of Natural Resources.

Des Plaines police said an officer back at the station heard about the accident and put in the first claim. After getting a supervisor's permission, the officer drove to the scene in his personal car, bringing a saw so he could remove the deer's head and have it mounted. But before the officer arrived, Cox, a bear-sized ironworker with a bristling beard, got a call from a friend who had spotted the buck on the roadside.

Cox, a hunter since his youth, went through the recent deer season without a kill. He said he needed the venison because an injury put him on disability. So when he heard about the buck, he hopped in his Chevy Suburban and roared to Golf Road. After he was told a police officer had already claimed the deer, he said, he backed off—until he learned the cop wanted only the animal's head.

"I was taken aback by that, because being a hunter since I was 12, 13, there's a certain code of ethics between sportsmen," he said. "It's not written down anywhere, it's just how it is. The ethical thing would be to take the animal and use the entire thing, not just cut off the head and leave the rest."

Some hunters agree that that is the preferred protocol for a deer taken in the woods, though many lawfully leave the animal's entrails behind. But Jeff Davis, editor of Whitetails Unlimited magazine in Wisconsin, said the ethics regarding roadkill are muddier. "Internal organs can be struck. [The carcass] can be so broken up that the meat is a little chancy," he said. "I don't think it's unusual when a deer is struck by a car to leave the rest of the carcass."

Roadkill rage

Cox said the officer made a similar argument, though the animal's trunk did not appear damaged. Cox was offered the meat, but said he turned it down because he was angry about the officer's actions. After the officer dragged the deer's body over a berm to remove the head away from public view, Cox drove off, seething.

That night, after attending a Boy Scout meeting as an assistant scoutmaster, Cox returned to see what happened to the body. Police said they normally notify public works staff about carcasses in the road, but the department has no record of a call that day. When Cox arrived, the headless deer was still there.

Cox loaded the remains into his truck, thinking he would use the carcass as evidence of what he saw as the officer's dishonorable conduct. But he said that when he arrived at the Des Plaines Police Department the next morning, he ran into a wall of indifference.

Incensed, he returned to his truck. Though his first thought was to drop the deer's body on the curb as a sign of his disgust, he decided to make a more dramatic gesture. He said he dragged the headless body to the front door of the police station and dumped it, telling bewildered onlookers: "There's a cop inside who got the head. He's missing this part of it."

Cox was quickly surrounded by police cars when he tried to drive away and spent the next five hours in a holding cell, he said. Though a disorderly conduct charge was later dropped, Cox paid a $169 fine after pleading guilty to unlawful littering. . . .

Soon after the clash, Cox gave his side of the story on a local hunting and fishing Web site but got little sympathy. One posting read: "You wanted the meat, they offered the meat and you didn't take the meat? Why are you so ticked?"

Cox is still convinced he did the right thing. Needy though he was, he said, he would never take venison from a mutilated carcass. "I'd rather starve than see this cop get away with something that's not right," he said.

Notes

1. *"Put in a claim"?* According to the story, the police officer "put in a claim" for the deer. But what does this have to do with first-in-time? Again we encounter the question: First to do what? Shouldn't the answer be: first to take possession of the deer, not merely to announce an intent to take possession of it (as Post had done by pursuing his fox)? What problems are there with the application of such a rule, when the first finder of a large animals lacks the tools or truck necessary to cart the animal away (or to cut off the head and antlers)? If the first person leaves to get the right tools and then returns, only to find that a competing claimant has shown up, what happens then? Has the first finder, by leaving, given up any claim to the animal? Should there be some deer-hunting protection equivalent to *pedis possessio*? And should we craft a relation-back rule of some sort, based on due diligence? What if the first finder leaves a tag or note on the carcass claiming it? Should that suffice, and if so for how long?

2. *Meat v. antlers: an alternative allocation method?* Along with raising intriguing questions about the physical application of first-in-time, this tale encourages us to consider alternative allocation schemes for items such as road-kill deer. What policy was the frustrated iron-worker attempting to promote with his argument? Is it sensible for the law, when allocating

animals, to favor a user who will eat the animal over one who will not? Is this a valid expression of public policy, or would it seem to violate some notion of equality among citizens (treating the hungry and the well-fed alike)? Such an allocation approach might still take first-in-time in account, but it would blend priority in time together with intended use of the deer as joint factors. For such a system to work, decisions would need to be made about how the two factors would be merged into a single allocation system. For instance, the user's intent might be used merely to break a tie when two captors arrive at the same time, or perhaps some window of time would be set aside in which the first meat-eater to arrive could get the deer, before it would go to the first taker who did not intend to eat it. (We'll comment later on the difficulties that arise when a first-in-time water allocation system is blended with allocation based on public interest.)

We'll return to hunting and wild animal cases from time to time in this book, for they provide splendid illustrations of resource issues of broad application. As we'll see, many states do penalize hunters for wasting the meat of large animals. We'll also see the way lawmakers allocating wild animals can pay special attention to the subsistence hunters and fishers who depend upon them. At least some lawmakers think that the hungry should get top priority.

3. *Getting the market to help.* One of the prime virtues of the market is its ability to allocate valuable resources to people willing and able to pay the most for them. When a first-in-time system seems to break down (for instance, when the waiting list gets 10 years long), what is a government entity to do? In some settings sale to the highest bidder seems to make sense, and is perhaps fairest to taxpayers. But in other settings this allocation method may give pause. Consider the following case dealing with a particular nonconsumptive resource-use right, the right to boat down the Colorado River. How would we describe the allocation method that the Park Service has implemented for the resource use? Economically, what is going on, and do the economics seem fair to taxpayers and the public?

WILDERNESS PUBLIC RIGHTS FUND v. KLEPPE

608 F.2d 1250 (9th Cir. 1979).

MERRILL, CIRCUIT JUDGE:

These cases involve the manner in which use of the Colorado River for rafting and boating is apportioned between concessioners approved by the National Park Service and noncommercial users. Permits from the National Park Service are required for river use and the dispute here concerns the apportionment made in granting permits.

In December, 1972, the Secretary of the Interior found that the boating and rafting use of the Colorado River in the Grand Canyon National Park had experienced such an increase that it posed a threat to the ecology of the river. A study was initiated for the purpose of ascertaining river capacity and it was decided that until completion of the study use of the river should be frozen at the 1972 level. Accordingly, river use was limited to 96,600 user days per year (a user day being one day spent on the river by one person). This total use was apportioned between two user groups in the ratio of actual 1972 use by each group: 89,000 user days or 92 percent of the total use was allotted to commercial concessioners of the Park Service who, for a fee, make guided trips through the canyon; 7,600 user days or 8 percent of the total was allotted to noncommercial users who apply for permits as private groups. Noncommercial users for the most part are experienced in river running and furnish their own equipment and supplies. Expenses are shared, as is the performance of the necessary duties involved. Permits for river use and the apportionment thereof have remained frozen at the 1972 level.

Appellants are, or represent, noncommercial river runners who, on various grounds, challenge the apportionment between commercial and noncommercial users. They assert that they, or those they represent, have applied for permits from the Park Service which were denied, the Service instead having granted permits to persons who used them for commercial purposes. In January, 1975, a member of Wilderness Public Rights Fund petitioned the Secretary for a change in the allocation system for the issuance of permits. The request was denied .....

A number of statutes and regulations bear on the issues of these actions. 16 U.S.C. § 1 creates the National Park Service (hereinafter NPS) in the Department of the Interior and directs it to "promote and regulate the use of the Federal areas known as national parks, monuments and reservations * * * by such means and measures as conform to the fundamental purpose of said parks, monuments and reservations * * *." That purpose is stated to be "to conserve the scenery and the natural and historic objects and the wild life therein and to provide for the enjoyment of the same in such manner and by such means as will leave them unimpaired for the enjoyment of future generations."

16 U.S.C. § 3 provides in part:

> The Secretary of the Interior shall make and publish such rules and regulations as he may deem necessary or proper for the use and management of the parks, monuments, and reservations under the jurisdiction of the National Park Service * * *. He may also grant privileges, leases, and permits for the use of land for the accommodation of visitors in the various parks, monuments or other reservations (herein provided for) but for periods not exceeding thirty years; and no natural curiosities, wonders, or objects of interest shall be leased, rented, or granted to anyone on such terms as to interfere with free access to them by the public * * *."

Pursuant to this authority the Secretary has promulgated 36 C.F.R. § 7.4(h)(3) as follows:

> (3) No person shall conduct, lead, or guide a river trip unless such person possesses a permit issued by the Superintendent, Grand Canyon National Park. The National Park Service reserves the right to limit the number of such permits issued, or the number of persons travelling on trips authorized by such permits when, in the opinion of the National Park Service, such limitations are necessary

> in the interest of public safety or protection of the ecological and environmental values of the area.

The Concessions Policy Act, 16 U.S.C. § 20 provides in part:

> It is the policy of the Congress that such development (concessions) shall be limited to those that are necessary and appropriate for public use and enjoyment of the national park area in which they are located * * *.

Appellants first attack the failure of the NPS to follow the dictates of the Administrative Procedure Act. They contend that the allocation of user days between commercial and noncommercial users amounted to rule making and that no hearings were held where the noncommercial users could present their views, contrary to the requirements of the Administrative Procedure Act. That Act, 5 U.S.C. § 553(a)(2), excepts from the rule-making procedures "a matter relating * * * to public property, loans, grants, benefits or contracts." The government contends that this exempts the action of the Secretary in freezing the 1972 river use and apportioning that use between the commercial and noncommercial users. We agree. . . .

Appellants contend that allocation between commercial and noncommercial use of the river is not an acceptable method of accomplishing a limitation of river use. They propose that anyone wishing to run the river should apply for a permit, leaving to him, if his application be granted, the choice between joining a guided party or a noncommercial party; that permits then be granted by lottery or on a first-come-first-served basis. They assert that the record establishes that such a method is feasible. They contend that there is no justification for allocating between commercial and noncommercial use, and that to do so amounts to arbitrary action; that it denies them "free access" to the river contrary to 16 U.S.C. § 3 and permits development by concession to a degree in excess of that allowed by the Concessions Policy Act. We disagree.

The Secretary of the Interior, acting through the NPS, has the wide ranging responsibility of managing the national parks. 16 U.S.C. § 3. Universal Interpretive Shuttle Corp. v. WMATC, 393 U.S. 186, 187, 89 S.Ct. 354, 21 L.Ed.2d 334 (1968); Udall v. Washington, Virginia & Maryland Coach Co., 130 U.S.App.D.C. 171, 398 F.2d 765 (D.C.Cir. 1968), Cert. denied, 393 U.S. 1017, 89 S.Ct. 620, 622, 21 L.Ed.2d 561 (1969). Pursuant to this authority, the NPS regulates use of the Colorado River through the permit requirement described in 36 C.F.R. § 7.4(h)(3), *supra*. In issuing permits, the Service has recognized that those who make recreational use of the river fall into two classes: those who have the skills and equipment to run the river without professional guidance and those who do not. The Service recognizes its obligation to protect the interests of both classes of users. It can hardly be faulted for doing so. If the over-all use of the river must, for the river's protection, be limited, and if the rights of all are to be recognized, then the "free access" of any user must be limited to the extent necessary to accommodate the access rights of others. We must confine our review of the permit system to the question whether the NPS has acted within its authority and whether the action taken is arbitrary. Citizens to Preserve Overton Park v. Volpe, 401 U.S. 402, 414, 91 S.Ct. 814, 28 L.Ed.2d 136 (1971). Allocation of the limited use between the two groups is one method of assuring that the rights of each are recognized and, if fairly done pursuant to appropriate standards, is a reasonable method and cannot be said to be arbitrary. It is well within the area of administrative discretion granted to the NPS.

Throughout these proceedings Wilderness Public Rights Fund has persisted in viewing the dispute as one between the recreational users of the river and the commercial operators, whose use is for profit. It asserts that by giving a firm allocation to the commercial operators to the disadvantage of those who wish to run the river on their own the Service is commercializing the park. The Fund ignores the fact that the commercial operators, as concessioners of the Service, undertake a public function to provide services that the NPS deems desirable for those visiting the area. 16 U.S.C. § 20a. See, Universal Interpretive Shuttle Corp. v. WMATC, supra. The basic face-off is not between the commercial operators and the noncommercial users, but between those who can make the run without professional assistance and those who cannot.

While the Concessions Policy Act, 16 U.S.C. § 20, *supra*, expresses the congressional intent that the granting of concessions shall be limited to "those that are necessary and appropriate for public use and enjoyment" of the park involved, the authority for the granting of concessions is given to the Secretary by 16 U.S.C. § 3, and there is no showing here of arbitrary action or abuse of that authority.

Appellants also complain that noncommercial applicants receive unfair and unequal treatment at the hands of the Service. They must apply to the Service for permits and thus must plan their trips well in advance. Deadlines must be met. The names of all in the proposed party (with signatures) must be set forth. Those who make the trip under guide may deal directly with the concessioners and make arrangements at the last minute. This comports with the NPS' right to regulate river trips in the interests of safety. 36 C.F.R. § 7.4(h)(3). We find nothing unreasonable in thus assuring, as matter of safety, that those who make the trip on their own without concessioners' supervision have undertaken the necessary preparation and possess the necessary skill to participate in the activities involved.

We conclude that allocation between the two classes of recreational users is not per se an arbitrary method of recognizing and accommodating the interests of the two classes. The question remaining is whether allocation has been fairly made pursuant to appropriate standards.

There is a judicial presumption favoring the validity of administrative action. See Duesing v. Udall, 121 U.S.App.D.C. 370, 350 F.2d 748 (D.C.Cir.1965), *cert. denied*, 383 U.S. 912, 86 S.Ct. 888, 15 L.Ed.2d 667 (1966). Where several administrative solutions exist for a problem, courts will uphold any one with a rational basis, but the Secretary's balancing of competing uses must not be an arbitrary one. Udall v. Washington, Virginia and Maryland Coach Co., *supra*.

Appellants challenge the method used by the Park Service in determining allocation between the classes of users for the reason that it is founded on 1972 data. It is asserted that since that year there has been a substantial increase in the demand for use by noncommercial users, and that to freeze allocation of use on the basis of seven-year-old data in the face of rapid change is arbitrary and unreasonable.

We are informed, however, that the study initiated by the National Park Service has now been completed and that the interim basis for allocation between the two classes of users freezing at the 1972 level is being abandoned. A proposed management plan for the river and a draft environmental impact statement have been completed and published. The allocation departs from the 1972 level of 92 percent user days for commercial operators and 8 percent user days for noncommercial river runners. Under the plan,70 percent of the user days will be allocated for commercial trips and 30 percent for noncommercial trips. The period assigned for comment has expired and it is anticipated that a final plan will be forthcoming in a matter of weeks.

This renders moot challenges to the specifics of the interim management plan, now about to be superseded by a final plan. The basis for the claim of arbitrariness that the freezing of use and allocation of use at the 1972 levels is, in 1979, unreasonable falls from the case.

Judgment affirmed.

Notes

1. *A sugar coating?* The plaintiffs in this case sought to distinguish between public users of the river and commercial operators, pointing to the fact that the Park Service itself distinguished between the two groups in its quota system: one group got 8 percent of the permits, the other group 92 percent. The court disagreed with this characterization of things, contending instead that the division was been those who could make the river run without professional assistance and those who could not. Which division seems more factually apt? Given how few permits are open directly to the public, might some of the people who use commercial guides be fully able to take a trip without professional help, thus blurring the categories? And as for the people who do get permits directly, has the Park Service in any serious way screened them to determine whether they can make the run alone (further blurring things)? According to the court, members of the public simply needed to send in their names well in advance. Is the ability to plan a trip in advance, however, proof that a person can run rapids safely? What really is going on here as a political matter? Can we guess? Is the court (aided by Park Service lawyers) putting a sugar coating on an allocation method that in fact shows great favoritism to commercial operators? If so, might this be justifiable?

2. *Choosing based on merit.* According to the court, river users come in two types—those who can run the rapids alone and those who cannot. Assuming the accuracy of this crude division and assuming a need to favor one over the other, which might we prefer? And what other factors might we take into account? Should a demonstrated ability to run a river without professional help count for or against a person who seeks the experience? Should a person who has run the river once be put at the bottom of the list? Might other factors seem relevant?

3. *The economics of it all.* Whenever a desired resource gets scarce, people are typically willing to pay money for it. Consider, then, what really takes place economically when the Park Service gives permits to commercial operators who then turn around and charge fees for their services? Can't we expect that patrons who take trip with the outfitter will indirectly be paying for their permits, at perhaps a far higher cost than people pay when getting permits directly from the Park Service? Regardless of how the permits are allocated, why should the government be giving away valuable permits to commercial companies, which essentially then re-sell them for a profit? At the least shouldn't the commercial permits be allocated by auction? Before answering that question, we might consider another one. If we did hold an auction, might we expect the commercial rafters along a particular river to do what so many bidders have done over the generations at government auctions: collude in advance to ensure that the bids stay low?

Before moving on, consider two further questions: What would be wrong with the plaintiffs' proposed approach, that potential visitors get their own permits, and then choose their own rafting companies? Second, what effect is the current system likely to have on the ability of new people to enter the commercial rafting business (that is, does this allocation method operate to *restrain competition* among river rafting companies or does it instead provide *much-needed stability* in the local economy)?

4. *Allocation based on historical use.* Note that the permit system used by the National Park Service was implemented long after commercial rafting companies had begun business. The shift from an unregulated commons to a regulated ones never goes smoothly, and existing users are often at the forefront of those resisting the shift. Or they are, that is, unless the government does what governments have done again and again, and that is to allocate the new permits largely based on historic patterns of use. When that is done, existing resource users can be quieted, and the new system can be more smoothly implemented. Note that such preferences for historic users operate akin to a first-in-time system, by rewarding users who are already on the scene. To the extent they emphasize first-in-time, the references are largely inconsistent with allocation methods that bring in the most money for taxpayers. Thus, they raise again a recurring question: If a publicly owned natural resource is economically valuable, does the government act right when it simply gives the resource out for free?

B. PUBLIC INTEREST ALLOCATIONS

When natural resources are being made available to the public, lawmakers have often found it appropriate to allocate the resource based on the recipient's planned use of it. The basic idea is simple: some resource uses are more socially valuable than others, and the government should favor them. At first glance the idea seems sensible, but there are complications with it. Complications arise immediately when government officials are required to evaluate competing uses in terms of the public interest. The task is harder than it might sound. Another problem is that allocation based on public interest only works effectively if the resource, once allocated, is subject to constraints on how it can be used and whether and how it can be transferred. It makes little sense to allocate a resource to A to use in manner X, if A is free immediately to put it to a far different use or to sell it to B for different use. We can consider, as an example of this problem, the allocation of government housing to low-income families. If the housing is provided at well below market value, it entails the distribution of a valuable resource. Yet, if the low-income recipient can immediately re-sell or re-lease the housing to a person of high income, the government scheme is undercut. (As an aside, how might we best describe such a resource allocation method?)

This practical reality needs to be kept in mind as we turn to allocation schemes based on public interest. In practice, does it appear that, the more carefully we select resource recipients based on the public interest, the more strictly we then must control how they use the resource and when they can transfer it? In no resource setting has this issue drawn more attention than in water allocation (chiefly under prior appropriation schemes but increasingly under riparian rights schemes as well). Consider the following main case. In what ways are the public interest taken into account? What is the public interest, and who decides it? And by public, do we mean the national public, the state public or a public that is far smaller and more local?

SHOKAL v. DUNN

109 Idaho 330, 707 P.2d 441 (1985).

Bistline, Justice.

On December 21, 1978, respondent Trout Co. applied for a permit to appropriate 100 c.f.s. of waters from Billingsley Creek near Hagerman, Idaho. Numerous protests were filed by local residents, property owners, and Billingsley Creek water users. The Department of Water Resources (Water Resources) held a hearing on the application on April 24, 1979, and issued Permit No. 36–7834 on November 14, 1979, pursuant to an order of that same date.... Some of the protestants, including the petitioners and appellants here, sought judicial review in the Fourth Judicial District Court, where the matter came before District Judge Gerald F. Schroeder. On December 22, 1980, Judge Schroeder issued an opinion and order reversing the decision of the Director of Water Resources and remanding the application for further proceedings. Judge Schroeder found Water Resources' consideration of at least two issues inadequate: (1) The financial ability of the applicant, and (2) the local public interest with respect to the proposed water project. Judge Schroeder also found errors of law in assigning the burden of proof. He held that the applicant for a permit had the burden of showing the impact of the project on the public resource, whereas a party who claimed a harm peculiar to himself had the burden of going forward to establish that harm. Judge Schroeder also determined that Water Resources had failed to properly evaluate the question of "local public interest," holding that the applicant had the ultimate burden of proving that a proposed water use was in the local public interest under I.C. § 42–203A. . . .

[The court's discussion of various procedural issues is omitted. It then proceeded to consider the merits of whether the respondent Trout Co. deserved to get the permit for which it had applied.]

II. Financing

Judge Smith held that the Director of Water Resources used an incorrect standard with regard to financing of projects in conjunction with a permit application. I.C. § 42–203A requires the Director to consider as one of several factors the financial resources of the applicant when deciding whether or not to issue a permit. In the instant case the Director, at the first hearing on the matter, determined the applicant had sufficient financial resources. Judge Schroeder disagreed and held the Director's decision was clearly erroneous: "A finding of financial ability to complete a $265,000 to $270,000 project on a $4,500 base is 'clearly erroneous' within the meaning of I.C. 67–515." Judge Schroeder concluded "there is a clear lack of evidence to support the finding of financial ability" and remanded the case to Water Resources for further hearing.

On remand, the Director determined the applicants did have sufficient financial resources. The Director stated:

> The financial ability criterion of I.C. 42–203[A] should not be interpreted as requiring the applicant, at the time of the hearings on the protested application, to have enough cash available to immediately complete the project. The applicant must show that he can obtain the necessary financing to complete the project within five years. At the hearing, the applicant must prove that it is reasonably probable that he can obtain the necessary financing to complete the project within the time constraint of the permit and the Idaho Code.

The Director then stated in Conclusion of Law No. 4: "At a hearing on a protested application, the applicant must prove that it is reasonably probable that he can obtain the necessary financing to complete the project within the time constraints of the permit and the Idaho Code." The Director concluded that the applicant, Trout Co., made the necessary evidentiary showing and had established its financial ability to complete the project. On the second appeal to the district court, Judge Smith disagreed with the Director's analysis.

Judge Smith objected to the "reasonably probable" standard used by the Director. He also concluded that the evidence in the case clearly did not support the Director's conclusions:

> The evidence indicates that at the time of the hearing, the applicant did not have the financial resources to complete the project but would have to obtain financing from others who said they might invest in the project. The evidence did show an increased investment by the applicant from $4500 to $92,000. However, the project was said to require an investment of $127,350 additional to complete it. This Court believes that it was the intent of the legislature in enacting I.C. 42–203[A] that *an applicant was bound to show at the hearing that he then and there had the financial resources* to complete the project within the time allotted—not to exceed five (5) years as provided by I.C. 42–204. (Emphasis added.)

Judge Smith concluded that the Director's actions were "clearly erroneous in view of the reliable, probative, and substantial evidence on the whole record."

We believe Judge Smith was incorrect in his interpretation of the financial showing an applicant must make to comply with I.C. § 42–203A. Judge Smith's requirement that applicants show that they "then and there" have the financial resources is far too restrictive; such a standard may have an excessively chilling effect on water and land development in this state. The ultimate question under the financial resources requirement of I.C. § 42–203A is this: who should bear the risk of failure. Under the district court's "then and there" standard any risk of failure is eliminated at the permit application stage. Yet, opportunities for development of the water resources of the state also are eliminated for those who may not have the cash in the bank, but may be able to secure sufficient resources during the five-year time limitation imposed by I.C. § 42–204 to put the water to beneficial use. The "then and there" standard, while admirably encouraging pecuniary caution, goes beyond a reasonable reading of the statutory requirement of "sufficient financial resources." I.C. § 42–203A(5)(d).

The "reasonably probable" standard used by Water Resources shifts the risk of failure and shows that the state is more willing to take a risk by providing individuals with the opportunity to put water to beneficial use. It indicates a willingness on the part of the state to take a chance that a proposed water use with sound prospects of financing will become a successful venture, thereby benefiting both the water user and the state. We believe this to be a more appropriate standard for the financial resources requirement of I.C. § 42–203A. The water resources of this state are not so limited that they must be safeguarded with permits issued *only* when the applicant has secured all necessary financing prior to the water appropriation permit application. At the same time, the applicant must make a showing that it is reasonably probable he or she will obtain the necessary financing within five years. The extent of the applicant's own investment is a strong factor to be considered.

The financial resources requirement, added in 1935, was clearly intended to prevent the tying up of our water resources by persons unable to complete a project because of financial limitations. The financial requirement provision was added at a time when unscrupulous promoters were obtaining permits and lulling unsuspecting investors into purchasing worthless securities on worthless projects. *See* Eighth Biennial Report of the Department of Reclamation, State of Idaho, 1933–1934, R.W. Faris, Commissioner of Reclamation, pp. 28–29. The legislature has provided Water Resources with the authority to weed out the financially insufficient applications. I.C. § 42–203A. We believe a showing by the applicant that it is "reasonably probable" that financing can be secured to complete the project within five years serves the purpose of screening out undeserving projects without being destructive of growth and development in the state. . . .

III. THE LOCAL PUBLIC INTEREST

Since Water Resources's decisions on financing are reinstated, the only matters for the agency to consider on remand are those which relate generally to the local public interest. I.C. § 42–203A(5)(e). We turn first to the interpretation of this provision, a question of first impression before this Court.[5]

A. *Defining the Local Public Interest.*

Under I.C. § 42–203A(5)(e), if an applicant's appropriation of water "will conflict with the local public interest, where the local public interest is defined as the affairs of the people in the area directly affected by the proposed use," then the Director "may reject such application and refuse issuance of a permit therefor, or may partially approve and grant a permit for a smaller quantity of water than applied for, or may grant a permit upon conditions."

The Utah Supreme Court interpreted a similar provision to authorize the State Engineer "to reject or limit the priority of plaintiff's application [for a permit to appropriate water for a power project] in the interest of the public welfare." *Tanner v. Bacon,* 103 Utah 494, 136 P.2d 957, 964 (1943); *see also People v. Shirokow,* 26 Cal.3d 30, 162 Cal.Rptr. 30, 37, 605 P.2d 859, 866 (1980) (In the public interest, the Water Board may impose the condition that the applicant salvage the water required for his or her project.); *East Bay Municipal Utility District v. Department of Public Works,* 1 Cal.2d 476, 35 P.2d 1027, 1029 (1934) ("Where the

5. The requirement that Water Resources protect the public interest is related to the larger doctrine of the public trust, which Justice Huntley comprehensively discussed in *Kootenai Environmental Alliance v. Panhandle Yacht Club, Inc.,* 105 Idaho 622, 671 P.2d 1085 (1983). The state holds all waters in trust for the benefit of the public, and "does not have the power to abdicate its role as trustee in favor of private parties." *Id.* at 625, 671 P.2d at 1088. Any grant to use the state's waters is "subject to the trust and to action by the State necessary to fulfill its trust responsibilities." *Id.* at 631, 671 P.2d at 1094. Trust interests include property values, "navigation, fish and wildlife habitat, aquatic life, recreation, aesthetic beauty and water quality." *Id.* at 632, 671 P.2d at 1095. Reviewing courts must "take a 'close look' at the action [of the legislature or of agencies such as Water Resources] to determine if it complies with the public trust doctrine and will not act merely as a rubber stamp for agency or legislative action." *Id.* at 629, 671 P.2d at 1092. Justice Huntley concluded, "The public trust at all times forms the outer boundaries of permissible government action with respect to public trust resources." *Id.* at 632, 671 P.2d at 1095.

facts justify the action, the water authority should be allowed to impose [on an application to appropriate water for a power project], in the public interest, the restrictions and conditions provided for in the act," or to reject the application "in its entirety."). Both the Utah and California Supreme Courts have upheld state water agencies which had granted appropriations subject to future appropriations for uses of greater importance—in effect prioritizing among uses according to the public interest. *Tanner, supra,* 136 P.2d at 962–64; *East Bay, supra,* 35 P.2d at 1027–30 (Both cases approved making appropriations for power subject to future appropriations for agricultural or municipal purposes.). The Director of Water Resources has the same considerable flexibility and authority, which he has already implemented in earlier proceedings in this matter, to protect the public interest.

Indeed, I.C. § 42–203A places upon the Director the affirmative *duty* to assess and protect the public interest. In assessing the duty of the state water board imposed by California's "public interest" provision, the California Supreme Court declared, "If the board determines a particular use is not in furtherance of the greatest public benefit, on balance the public interest must prevail." *Shirokow, supra,* 162 Cal.Rptr. at 37, 605 P.2d at 866; *accord, Tanner, supra,* 136 P.2d at 962 (The State has "the *duty* to control the appropriation of the public waters in a manner that will be for the best interests of the public.") (emphasis added).

The authority and duty of the Director to protect the public interest spring naturally from the statute; the more difficult task for us is to define "the local public interest." Public interest provisions appear frequently in the statutes of the prior appropriation states of the West, but are explicated rarely. *See, e.g.,* Cal. Water Code § 1253; *see generally* 1 R. Clark, ed., *Waters and Water Rights,* § 29.3 (1967). I.C. § 42–203A provides little guidance. Fortunately, however, the legislature did provide guidance in a related statute, I.C. § 42–1501. We also derive assistance from our sister states and from the academic community.

In I.C. § 42–1501, the legislature declared it "in the public interest" that:

> the streams of this state and their environments be protected against loss of water supply to preserve the minimum stream flows required for the protection of fish and wildlife habitat, aquatic life, recreation, aesthetic beauty, transportation and navigation values, and water quality.

Not only is the term "public interest" common to both §§ 42–1501 and 42–203A, and the two sections common to the same title 42 (Irrigation and Drainage—Water Rights and Reclamation), but also the legislature approved the term "public interest" in both sections on the *same day,* March 29, 1978. 1978 Idaho Sess. Laws, ch. 306 § 1, pp. 768–69, and ch. 345, § 11, pp. 891–97. Clearly, the legislature in § 42–203A must have intended the public interest on the local scale to include the public interest elements listed in § 42–1501: "fish and wildlife habitat, aquatic life, recreation, aesthetic beauty, transportation and navigation values, and water quality." *Accord,* National Water Commission, *New Directions in U.S. Water Policy* 5 (1973) ("The people of the United States give far greater weight to environmental and aesthetic values than they did when the nation was young and less settled."), *cited in* R. Robie, *The Public Interest in Water Rights Administration,* 23 Rocky Mtn. Min.L.Inst. 917, 933 (1977).

In so intending, the legislature was in good company. Unlike other state public interest statutes, the Alaska statute enumerates the elements of the public interest. The public interest elements of I.C. § 42–1501 are almost precisely duplicated within the Alaska statute, which is set out in the margin.[6] Notably, the principal author of the Alaska statute was the eminent water law scholar, Dean Frank J. Trelease. R. Robie, *supra,* at 940 n. 95. The views of Dean Trelease have been well received.

The Alaska statute contains other elements which common sense argues ought to be considered part of the local public interest. These include the proposed appropriation's benefit to the applicant, its economic effect, its effect "of loss of alternative uses of water that might be made within a reasonable time if not precluded or hindered by the proposed appropriation," its harm to others, its "effect upon access to navigable or public waters," and "the intent and ability of the applicant to complete the appropriation." Alaska Stat. § 46.5.080(b).

Several other public interest elements, though obvious, deserve specific mention. These are: assuring minimum stream flows, as specifically provided in I.C. § 42–1501, discouraging waste, and encouraging conservation. *See Shirokow, supra,* 162 Cal.Rptr. at 37, 605 P.2d at 866 (The California Supreme Court found water salvage to be sufficiently in the public interest to require it of a permittee.).

The above-mentioned elements of the public interest are not intended to be a comprehensive list. As observed long ago by the New Mexico Supreme Court, the "public interest" should be read broadly in order to "secure the greatest possible benefit from [the public waters] for the public." *Young & Norton v. Hinderlider,* 15 N.M. 666, 110 P. 1045, 1050

6. Alaska Stat. § 46.15.080 provides:

(b) In determining the public interest, the commissioner shall consider

(1) the benefit to the applicant resulting from the proposed appropriation;

(2) the effect of the economic activity resulting from the proposed appropriation;

(3) the effect on fish and game resources and on public recreational opportunities;

(4) the effect on public health;

(5) the effect of loss of alternate uses of water that might be made within a reasonable time if not precluded or hindered by the proposed appropriation;

(6) harm to other persons resulting from the proposed appropriation;

(7) the intent and ability of the applicant to complete the appropriation; and

(8) the effect upon access to navigable or public waters.

See also Bank of Am. Nat. Trust & Sav. Assoc. v. State Water Resources Control Bd., 116 Cal.Rptr. 770, 771, 42 Cal.App.3d 198, 201 (1974) (If supported by the record, the state water board can condition a permit for a reservoir on providing for the public interest element of public access for recreation.).

(N.M.1910) (Rejects considering only public health and safety; considers relative costs of two projects.). By using the general term "the local public interest," the legislature intended to include any locally important factor impacted by proposed appropriations.

Of course, not every appropriation will impact every one of the above elements. Nor will the elements have equal weight in every situation. The relevant elements and their relative weights will vary with local needs, circumstances, and interests. For example, in an area heavily dependent on recreation and tourism or specifically devoted to preservation in its natural state, Water Resources may give great consideration to the aesthetic and environmental ramifications of granting a permit which calls for substantial modification of the landscape or the stream.

Those applying for permits and those challenging the application bear the burden of demonstrating which elements of the public interest are impacted and to what degree. As Judge Schroeder correctly noted below, this burden of production lies with the party

> that has knowledge peculiar to himself. For example, the designer of a fish facility has particularized knowledge of the safeguards or their lack concerning the numbers of fish that may escape and the amount of fecal material that will be discharged into the river. As to such information the applicant should have the burden of going forward and ultimately the burden of proof on the impact on the local public interest. On the other hand, a protestant who claims a harm peculiar to himself should have the burden of going forward to establish that harm.

However, the burden of proof in all cases as to where the public interest lies, as Judge Schroeder also correctly noted, rests with the applicant:

> [I]t is not [the] protestant's burden of proof to establish that the project is not in the local public interest. The burden of proof is upon the applicant to show that the project is either in the local public interest or that there are factors that overweigh the local public interest in favor of the project.

The determination of what elements of the public interest are impacted, and what the public interest requires, is committed to Water Resources' sound discretion. *See* 1 R. Clark, ed., *Waters and Water Rights* § 29.3, 170 (1967).

In light of the preceding discussion, the district court admirably established some of the public interest elements which Water Resources must consider in this case. Judge Schroeder observed:

> First, as previously outlined, if the Department gives weight to the economic benefits of the project, it should also give consideration to the economic detriments. The effect of the project on water quality should be considered. It is not clear to what extent that was done in this case. The effect of the project on alternative uses of the

watercourse should be considered—e.g., the impact on recreational and scenic uses. The effect on vegetation, wildlife, and other fish should be considered. This is not a catalogue of all factors that may relate to the public interest element, but is a suggestion of factors to be weighed in determining whether the project will or will not be in the public interest.

Judge Smith provided some specific guidelines, also needful of comment, to which our attention is now drawn.

B. Specific Considerations Raised Below.

1. Finality of Design

In order to be able to assess a project's impact on the public interest, the project's design must be definite enough to reflect its impacts and implications. Judge Smith held that because the applicant has the burden of proof to show a project is worthy of issuance of a permit, "the design of the proposed facility should be final, detailed and not schematic." . . .

In our perception, Judge Smith's language requires an applicant to present "blueprint quality" plans at the outset of seeking a permit, much in the same vein as his "here and now" standard of financing required ready cash. We are not persuaded that blueprint quality plans of a facility are *always* necessary when applying for a permit to appropriate water. Rather, the design plan for a proposed facility depends on the nature of the facility, the complexity of the proposal, and the extent of the proposed appropriation's impact on the local area. In this particular case, the Department will determine at the hearing on the amended application whether blue print quality plans and drawings are a prerequisite to giving approval. In all cases the plans should be sufficient to generally apprise the public of the efficacy of the proposed use in the planned facility, and of its potential impact. . . .

3. Health Hazard

Judge Smith opined that the law will not allow Billingsley Creek to become a nuisance or a health hazard, adding also that "a permit cannot issue which would allow construction of a project contrary to the authority of the Board of Health in policing water for pollution." Hence, Judge Smith concluded that the Director had authority to consider whether the design of any particular facility will meet all environmental requirements.

We believe this to be a correct assessment of the law, but add a word of caution regarding the differing functions of Water Resources and the Department of Health and Welfare. Water Resources must oversee the water resources of the state, insuring that those who have permits and licenses to appropriate water use the water in accordance with the conditions of the permits and licenses and the limits of the law. It is not the primary job of Water Resources to protect the health and welfare of Idaho's citizens and visitors—that role is vested in the Department of

Health and Welfare, including compliance with the water quality regulations and monitoring effluent discharge in our state's waterways. Nevertheless, although these agencies may have separate functions, Water Resources is precluded from issuing a permit for a water appropriation project which, when completed, would violate the water quality standards of the Department of Health and Welfare. It makes no sense whatsoever for Water Resources to blindly grant permit requests without regard to water quality regulations. Hence, Water Resources should condition the issuance of a permit on a showing by the applicant that a proposed facility will meet the mandatory water quality standards. . . .

condition permit

The decision of the district court is reversed in part, affirmed in part, and remanded for further proceedings consonant herewith.

Notes

1. *Reasonable use V: conflict with first-in-time?* Idaho supposedly still embraces the prior appropriation system of water allocation, in which water goes to the first person to divert it. But how relevant is priority in time any more—at least with respect to future appropriations—when the public interest review is as strict as it seems to be in *Shokal*? Isn't allocation based on public interest really quite different from allocation based simply on first-in-time? In the extreme, a state water agency after *Shokal* could apparently decide itself how remaining water ought to be used, and then only make the water available for that identified use. Isn't this, in effect, a complete abandonment of priority in time?

What should be clear here is that first-in-time is a quite different method of allocating a resource from allocation by public interest. The two methods can be combined in various ways, which Idaho apparently does (by giving the water to the first applicant who meets public interest standards). But we should not overlook the distinct tradeoff involved here. The more we emphasize public interest, the less we emphasize priority in time.

2. *Which public? Which interest?* According to the court, how does Idaho law go about identifying the public interest? Don't members of the public in reality have widely differing ideas about how water might best be used? Surely it is one thing to compile a lengthy list of relevant public-interest factors, and quite another to resolve conflicts among them and set priorities. In any event, won't the public interest shift over time, so that a water use that makes sense today may seem less appealing later? Is this a resource setting in which we should allow market mechanisms to govern, given the market's ability to shift resources to the use that brings the most money for the owner? Or are the indirect effects and ecological implications of water uses so great that market mechanisms are inevitably flawed?

3. *Grazing rights and the public interest.* As we saw in *Diamond Bar Cattle* (chapter 2), grazing on federal lands is undertaken by holders of permits or licenses, which are issued for specified terms and subject to renewal if certain conditions are met. Similar schemes apply on lands owned by certain states. For many ranchers in the West, the possession of grazing permits is vital to the economic survival of their livestock operations. The management of public lands for grazing, however, involves obvious trade-

offs. The more grass that is reserved for cattle, the less there is available for wild animals. Predators are a problem for livestock and often must be controlled; wild animals, in contrast, require no predator control. Governments that issue grazing permits inevitably have to decide how to allocate them. But before they get to that issue they must decide how much land (or grass) to devote to livestock and how much will be set aside to secure other interests and needs. Given that grazing is a commercial activity undertaken for economic gain, should not grazing permits be sold to the highest bidder? If so, what if the highest bidder chooses to forgo using the permit, in effect making the grass available for grazing wild animals? Consider the following case:

FOREST GUARDIANS v. WELLS

197 Ariz. 511, 4 P.3d 1054 (App. 2000).

VOSS, JUDGE.

In this appeal from the affirmance of an administrative decision, we consider whether the State Land Department and its Commissioner abused their discretion in denying grazing leases to appellants, who wished to rest the lands from grazing for conservation and recreation purposes. We conclude that the Commissioner acted within the law and his discretion and thus affirm the trial court judgment.

FACTS AND PROCEDURAL HISTORY

In August 1997, appellant Forest Guardians, a non-profit corporation, submitted bids to the Arizona State Land Department ("the Department") on the two grazing leases that are the subject of this appeal. In one, Forest Guardians applied for a ten-year lease on approximately 5,000 acres of state trust land located in Coconino County ("Coconino County land"). This land is bisected by an ephemeral drainage area known as Cataract Creek. The existing lessee of the Coconino County land paid a grazing rental fee of approximately $2,150 per year to graze 85 head of cattle on the land. In its application, Forest Guardians offered to pay twice the amount paid by the existing lessee. It stated on the application that it did not intend to stock the land with cattle; it contended that nongrazing would increase the value of the land to conservationists, prospective livestock interests, and trust beneficiaries. The existing lessee also applied to renew its grazing lease.

In its second application, Forest Guardians applied for a ten-year lease on approximately 162 acres of state trust land in Santa Cruz County ("Santa Cruz County land"). It was interested in this lease because a segment of the Babocomari River runs through the parcel. The existing lessee, who applied to renew the lease, paid $50.16 per year for the grazing lease. Forest Guardians offered to pay five times that amount, also indicating that it would not stock the land with livestock.

In a cover letter accompanying the applications, Forest Guardians requested, pursuant to A.A.C. R12–5–705(O), that the State Land Commissioner ("the Commissioner") authorize the use of the land "for purposes other than domestic livestock grazing.'' Forest Guardians noted that, based on its higher-than-minimum bids and the important recreational and biological values of the areas, allowing grazing non-use for ten years would enhance the corpus of the trust while also meeting the Department's legal obligation to maximize revenue from school trust lands.

In July 1997, appellant Jonathan Tate also applied for a ten-year lease on approximately 16,000 acres of state trust land in Pinal County. In his application, Tate offered to pay $4.20 per animal unit month, which was approximately twice the amount paid by the existing lessee. Tate also indicated that he did not intend to use the land for livestock grazing.

By letters to Forest Guardians and Tate, the Department advised them that their applications were subject to rejection because they did not intend to put the lands to the use for which they were classified. The Department informed them that, if they wished to lease trust land for habitat preservation or riparian restoration, they should apply for commercial leases, which would require reclassification of the lands to commercial use . . .

The Department denied the lease applications submitted by Forest Guardians and Tate. The Department noted that the applicants' objective of preventing grazing on the properties directly contradicted the intent, policy, and language of the statutes and rules concerning grazing leases. Such an objective, stated the Department, would be consistent with a commercial lease, not a grazing lease, and nonconformance to the classification scheme might prevent the Department from receiving the full appraised value and compensation for the higher use. Thus, the Department concluded, it was ''not in the best interests of the State Trust'' to approve the applications.

Discussion

. . . .

B. Review of Grazing Lease Denial

In 1910, the United States Congress passed the Arizona–New Mexico Enabling Act (''the Enabling Act''), which authorized citizens of the territories of Arizona and New Mexico to form state governments. *See Kadish v. Arizona State Land Dep't,* 155 Ariz. 484, 486, 747 P.2d 1183, 1185 (1987), *aff'd, ASARCO, Inc. v. Kadish,* 490 U.S. 605, 109 S.Ct. 2037, 104 L.Ed.2d 696 (1989). Under the Enabling Act, the United States granted almost ten million acres of land to Arizona; this land could be used only for the support of the common schools of the state (school trust lands) and for internal improvements to the state. *See id.* Voters in Arizona accepted the land grants by ratifying article 10, section 1 of the Arizona Constitution. *See id.*

The Enabling Act is one of the fundamental laws of Arizona and is superior to our state constitution. *See Gladden Farms, Inc. v. State,* 129

Ariz. 516, 518, 633 P.2d 325, 327 (1981) (citing *Murphy v. State,* 65 Ariz. 338, 181 P.2d 336 (1947)). Thus, neither the Arizona Constitution nor laws may conflict with the Enabling Act or alter or amend the trust provisions in it without congressional approval. *See id.; Kadish,* 155 Ariz. at 486, 747 P.2d at 1185.

Section 28 of the Enabling Act requires Arizona to hold the lands in trust for the beneficiaries and specifies that the property can be disposed of only as authorized in the Act. This section further provides that the trust lands may not be sold or leased "except to the highest and best bidder at a public auction" after notice by advertisement. However, pursuant to a 1936 act of Congress, the legislature may prescribe procedures for leases of ten years or less. *See Kadish,* 155 Ariz. at 491, 747 P.2d at 1190, *citing* Act of June 5, 1936, Pub.L. No. 658 (ch. 517), 49 Stat. 1477. The 1936 act "gives the legislature power to regulate the overall manner of the making of the lease, and the general terms of the lease, so long as there is substantial conformity to the restrictions of § 28." *Id.*

Given the restrictions on dealing with school trust lands, it is clear that "[t]he duties imposed upon the state were the duties of a trustee and not simply the duties of a good manager." *Id.; see also State ex rel. Ebke v. Bd. of Educ. Lands and Funds,* 154 Neb. 244, 154 Neb. 596, 47 N.W.2d 520, 525 (1951); *County of Skamania v. State,* 102 Wash.2d 127, 685 P.2d 576, 580 (1984). Among the fiduciary duties of a trustee is the obligation to obtain the highest possible return for the benefit of the trust....

Mindful of this law, appellants argue that the Department has violated its fiduciary duty by denying their offers to lease the Coconino, Santa Cruz, and Pinal County lands. They assert that their offers would not only provide more income for the trust than the minimum grazing rental being collected, but would also increase the forage capacity of the lands to produce a greater return to the trust once the lands were returned to grazing ...

Appellees respond that the Commissioner did not abuse his discretion in denying appellants' applications for grazing leases because, under Arizona statutes, he may not issue a grazing lease to a party who does not intend to use the leased land for grazing. They argue that this prohibition is part of a statutory scheme that governs leases of Arizona trust land and is consistent with the Enabling Act in that it requires lessees to pay rental rates that are consistent with the appraised value of the land under the classification that reflects the highest and best use of the land. The legislature has directed the Commissioner to classify and appraise all state lands for the purpose of leasing. A.R.S. § 37–132(A)(5). The classifications of lands listed in A.R.S. section 37–212 include "lands suitable for grazing purposes" and "lands suitable for commercial purposes." A.R.S. § 37–212(B)(2) and (4). "Grazing lands" are statutorily defined as "lands which can be used only for the ranging of livestock." A.R.S. § 37–101(7). " 'Commercial lands' means lands which can be used principally for business, institutional, religious, charitable, governmental or recreational purposes, or any general purpose other than agricultural, grazing, mining, oil, homesite or rights-of-way." A.R.S. § 37–101(3).

State lands are subject to lease for grazing purposes without public auction if the term is not more than ten years. A.R.S. § 37–281.01(A). Such leases are granted under the Arizona constitution and laws and the rules of the Department. *Id.* Pursuant to these laws and rules, the lessee must use the leased land for the purpose for which the land is leased. A.R.S. § 37–281(D). Pursuant to A.A.C. R12–5–502:

> All state lands . . . shall be classified by the Commissioner prior to the lease thereof and shall be leased only under the classification fixed by the Commissioner, unless such land is reclassified as provided by law. The Commissioner shall have the power to reclassify such lands from time to time when he deems such reclassification to be for the best interests of the state, and all leases and permits shall be subject to such reclassification.

See also A.R.S. § 37–212(C) (Commissioner may reclassify lands if he determines that reclassification is in the best interest of the trust and of the state). Any person who wishes to have any state land reclassified must apply to the Commissioner and submit an application to lease the lands for the reclassified purpose. A.A.C. R12–5–530. The Commissioner's discretion to reclassify lands will not be disturbed absent an abuse of discretion. *See Havasu Heights Ranch & Dev. Corp. v. State Land Dep't,* 158 Ariz. 552, 557, 764 P.2d 37, 42 (App.1988).

In light of this statutory scheme, we conclude that the Department was justified in rejecting appellants' applications to lease grazing land for nongrazing purposes. As noted above, the legislature has defined "grazing lands" as "lands which can be used only for the ranging of livestock." A.R.S. § 37–101(7). Because of this limitation on the use of grazing lands, acquisition of a grazing lease with the intent to prevent grazing in order to promote conservation and restoration is not permitted.

The issuance of a lease for conservation use is not precluded under the relevant statutes; the statutes preclude only the issuance of a grazing lease for conservation or recreation purposes. The legislature has provided categories for leases other than grazing; conservation and recreational use as proposed by appellants fall within the commercial classification.

Applying federal law, the court in *Public Lands Council v. Babbitt,* 154 F.3d 1160 (10th Cir.1998), reached a similar conclusion. There, the United States Interior Secretary allowed the issuance of ten-year permits to use public lands for conservation purposes to the exclusion of livestock grazing. Pursuant to 43 U.S.C. section 315b, the Secretary was authorized "to issue or cause to be issued permits to graze livestock" on public lands. In regulations adopted in 1995, the Secretary authorized the issuance of grazing permits or leases for "livestock grazing, suspended use, and conservation use." 43 C.F.R. § 4130.2(a) (1995). The effect of the regulation was that a grazing permit could be issued to an individual or group that would not graze livestock for the entire duration of a permit. *Id.* at 1180.

The issue posed to the court was whether the Secretary had the authority to issue a grazing permit that excluded livestock grazing for the entire term of the permit. *See id.* at 1181. The court held that he did not have such authority. *Id.* It noted that 43 U.S.C. section 315b does not authorize permits for any type of use other than grazing on lands in the grazing districts. The court found that neither that statute nor two other similar statutes at 43 U.S.C. sections 1702(p) and 1902(c) authorized permits intended exclusively for conservation use. It rejected as "simply untenable" the Secretary's assertion that grazing permits for use of land in grazing districts need not involve an intent to graze livestock. *Id.* In summary, the court stated that Congress intended that once the Secretary established a grazing district under the statute, the primary use of that land should be grazing and could be changed only if the Secretary withdrew the land from grazing use in accordance with statutory withdrawal provisions. *Id.* We agree with this reasoning and apply it to the issue before us.[7]

Appellants argue that the Commissioner may authorize their intended conservation use under A.R.S. section 37–285(H), which provides:

> The department may authorize non-use for part or all of the grazing use upon request of the lessee at least sixty days prior to the beginning of the billing date. The rental fee shall be based on the animal unit months use, but the total rental fee for partial or full non-use shall not be less than five cents per acre per annum.

The Department takes the position that this provision applies only to the request of a lessee who has been grazing livestock and cannot be construed to allow appellants to obtain a grazing lease for a nongrazing purpose. . . .

Appellants' proposed use of the lands falls within the commercial classification, because "recreational purposes" is stated as a use of commercial lands and conservation purposes fall within uses for either charitable or "any other general purpose other than agricultural, grazing, mining, oil, homesite or rights-of-way." A.R.S. § 37–101(3). The Department advised appellants to pursue commercial leases but they declined to do so. John Horning, representing Forest Guardians, testified at the administrative hearing that Forest Guardians was interested in a grazing lease and was not interested in reclassification to commercial or anything else. He indicated that Forest Guardians was not engaged in commercial activity and was not interested in paying commercial lease rates. Forest Guardians was concerned that a commercial lease would

7. The dissent attempts to distinguish *Babbitt* on the basis that the federal government was not a trustee in that case, with the attendant fiduciary duties that are imposed in this case by the trust. However, this case does not involve the question whether a fiduciary duty to the trust was breached by a discretionary decision; rather, it involves only a narrow determination by the Commissioner that he had no legal authority to issue a grazing lease for a nongrazing purpose.

have rates that were more than it could pay. No evidence of what a commercial lease rate would be for these parcels was presented.

We conclude that the reclassification provisions further the goals of the Enabling Act and benefit the school lands trust; therefore, applicants for leases must adhere to those provisions. Appellants' belief that a commercial lease rate would be considerably more than they had offered for the leases and more than they could afford is mere speculation. Only after an application for reclassification and appraisal would they know the rate to be charged. Appellants unreasonably sought to limit the rental amount by insisting on a grazing lease with its low rental rate, even though appellants offered to pay more than the minimum rate.

If the Commissioner had accepted appellants' offers, he would have given them the benefit of grazing appraisals without any appraisal for the actual intended conservation and recreation uses. As stated by the ALJ, "the value of [appellants'] proposed conservation and recreational uses cannot properly be established solely by an offer to pay more than the estimate of forage usage, which is the basis for annual grazing lease rentals." The Enabling Act requires appraisal of the leased lands. If nongrazing uses are treated as grazing uses, leases potentially could be obtained for less than the fair market value of the actual use of the leased lands. This result would be detrimental to the trust. If in fact the land is suitable for a use that is defined by statute as commercial, the trust is entitled to benefit from the increased value of the land.

Appellants assert that the commissioner's obligation to achieve the "highest and best use" of these lands required acceptance of the applications because appellants have offered more money than other applicants and have offered to rest the land. Thus, appellants contend that, because the applications were rejected, "the state violates its fiduciary duty to the trust to maximize both revenue and land welfare." The dissent agrees with this assertion.

The factual record before us on appeal simply does not support this legal conclusion. The condition of these lands was neither litigated nor adjudicated. Other than a reference to a small portion of the land having been overgrazed to a "moonscape" condition, the record before this court simply does not contain evidentiary support to reach a legal conclusion that nongrazing constitutes the "best use" of the land at this point . . . . .

Additionally, the "highest use" of the land, in terms of economic revenue, cannot be ascertained from this record. Although appellants argue that they offered to pay a rental rate higher than that of any other current grazing applicant, they conceded at oral argument they did not know what the commercial lease rate would be because neither an application to reclassify nor an appraisal to determine such a rate has been pursued in this case. Whether they cannot "afford" the commercial rate—another factual issue that cannot be determined from this record—is simply irrelevant. Therefore, it is speculative at the very least to conclude that these applicants provided the greatest potential revenue from the use of these lands to the trust. Furthermore, as we have recently pointed out, "maximizing short-term lease income is not the Department's only concern" when deciding how to serve the best interests of the trust. *Jeffries v. Hassell,* 310 Ariz. Adv. Rep. 3, ¶ 10, 197 Ariz. 151, ¶ 10, 3 P.3d 1071, ¶ 10 (App.1999). Thus, the "highest bidder" is not necessarily granted a lease to state trust lands.

Appellants argue that, due to the Commissioner's statutory and fiduciary duties, he should have initiated reclassification of the lands if it would have resulted in increased revenues to the trust. Appellees respond that the failure of the Commissioner to consider reclassification is not an appealable agency decision. The trial court apparently considered appellants' argument and we do so as well inasmuch as the ALJ concluded that the Commissioner did not breach his statutory and fiduciary duties by not reclassifying the tracts to commercial lands because appellants had indicated that they would not accept a commercial lease.

As noted above, the Commissioner's decision regarding reclassifying leased lands will not be disturbed absent an abuse of discretion. The evidence in this case supports the conclusion that the Commissioner did not abuse his discretion in failing to reclassify the parcels sought by appellants . . . . .

GERBER, JUDGE, Dissenting.

I respectfully disagree with the majority. In my view, the Department's rejection of the appellants' grazing lease applications frustrated the Enabling Act's mandate that trust land leases go only to the "highest and best bidder." *See Lassen,* 385 U.S. at 461–62, 87 S.Ct. 584 (Enabling Act restrictions are "few and simple," referring to the highest and best bidder requirement).

Who is the "highest and best bidder" continues to be a two-part inquiry. *See Keith v. Johnson,* 109 Ky. 421, 59 S.W. 487, 488 (1900) ("force is to be given to both the controlling words 'highest' and 'best' " when interpreting the phrase "highest and best bidder"). The "highest" bidder offers the most money. *See Brown v. City of Phoenix,* 77 Ariz. 368, 375, 272 P.2d 358, 363 (1954). Here, the appellants, who bid two and five times as much as their competitors, were clearly the highest monetary bidders.

The "best" prong requires the Department to determine which lessee would best serve pecuniary and non-pecuniary interests, which include the welfare of the land itself. *See Havasu Heights Ranch & Dev. Corp. v. Desert Valley Wood Products,* 167 Ariz. 383, 392, 807 P.2d 1119, 1128 (App.1990) (maximizing revenue is not the sole consideration for leases). If the highest monetary bid does not serve the interests of the trust, the Department should accept the next highest bid that does.

Appellants' applications more than satisfied the highest and best bidder requirement. The monetary advantage of their bids is undisputed. As to the "best interests," our own court has noted that "factors such as

. . . environmental considerations may be significant." *Jeffries v. Hassell*, 310 Ariz. Adv. Rep. 3, 5 n. 1, 197 Ariz. 151, 154 n. 1, 3 P.3d 1071, 1074 n. 1 (App.1999). Ceasing further damage to the land's resources, coupled with their regeneration, serves the best interests of the trust because resting overgrazed land restores its value. . . .

On this record, the Department seems to care little about its fiduciary responsibility. It did not inspect or evaluate the conditions of these lands before denying appellants' applications. It even argued that it was "irrelevant" that overgrazing had rendered some of its land a "moonscape," surprising insensitivity for a trustee. . . .

Nothing in the Enabling Act prefers grazing over conservation or ranchers over conservationists. The nostalgia and myth of pioneer history are irrelevant. *See County of Skamania v. State*, 102 Wash.2d 127, 685 P.2d 576, 580 (1984). Appellants' willingness both to pay more money and to rest depleted land would maximize trust revenues and preserve trust assets for both short-and long-term uses. The Department's devotion to its internal policies and statutes frustrates its primary fealty to the Enabling Act. A court which respected the Enabling Act's precedence over lesser laws would order the Department to issue the leases in question.

Notes

1. *Gifts with strings.* When it comes to allocating land, whether as patents or leases, governments in the United States have regularly succumbed to political considerations, giving land to interests favored by those in power. Sometimes the favoritism has appeared directly in the laws. Other times it has come through biased administration if not outright fraud. Although given its own record the federal government was hardly in a position to criticize the states on this issue, Congress during the nineteenth century did show increasing concern about the land-distribution practices of states. As states entered the Union, Congress granted them vast tracts of federal land, usually to support schools or government bodies (often specified sections of each square mile). States often disposed of the lands at far below fair market value. As time went buy, Congress became more clear and strict in the legal limits placed on the lands granted to the states, to halt below-market transfers.

As one of the final states to the enter the Union, Arizona received particularly strict limits on its lands. As the court notes, Arizona was obligated as a matter of federal law (section 28 of the Arizona Enabling Act) to dispose of land by sale or lease only "to the highest and best bidder at a public auction." Note that this rule was later weakened to allow greater state control so long as any state action was in "substantial conformity" with section 28. Here we see Arizona turning down an offer to lease lands at a rental five times what it was receiving. We also see it offering leases, not a public auction, but through means that excluded all bidders except grazers and at rates of about 50 cents per acre per year.

2. *Politics as usual?* Putting law to one side, is it not clear what is going on here? Arizona strongly favors grazers in the allocation of resources,

and for the moment at least Arizona courts are willing to allow the state to get away with it. The particular legal steps Arizona took to protect grazers are of only local importance but worth noting nonetheless. Arizona began by classifying its lands, claiming that classification was a useful step in ensuring that the lands were put to their best uses. The court was willing to allow the land classification, subject to review only for abuse of discretion—a highly deferential standard that in effect removed the court from providing real oversight of the state in its trustee role. Once the lands were classified the state was home free, because the lands involved in the case were classified solely for grazing. All other uses were unlawful. Note that the court never bothers to interpret the meaning of "high and best bidder" under the federal statute (as the dissenting judge does), nor does it decide whether, as a matter of federal law, existing grazers fit the definition. Note also that the prime beneficiaries of the trust—the state schools—are hardly mentioned, much less asked for advice on how their income sources ought to be managed.

3. *"Highest and best bidder."* The conflict here, at bottom, was about the best method of allocating resources. Should state lawmakers decide on policy grounds what land uses (and thus land users) they prefer? Or should the market play a bigger role, with the land going to potential users willing to pay the most money? If the Arizona court had taken the federal statute seriously, how might it have interpreted the critical phrase, "highest and best bidder"? Are bidders at an auction necessarily rated strictly based on how much the pay? Alternatively, could highest and best be viewed as a public interest calculation in which money is only one of several factors?

In any event, should an allocation statute such as this override normal state powers to regulate land use? After all, a state has legitimate interests in the ways all lands within its borders are used. Could the state simply have zoned the relevant land for agricultural purposes only, and then offered it for sale at public auction to anyone who cared to bid? If so, would this have helped keep out the environmental bidders? On this issue, consider the following, more complex resource-allocation dispute:

MADISON v. ALASKA DEPARTMENT OF FISH AND GAME

696 P.2d 168 (Alaska 1985).

MOORE, JUSTICE.

This case arises as a consolidated appeal of two cases. It concerns the validity of a Board of Fisheries' (hereafter board) regulation designed to identify eligibility for subsistence fishing in the Cook Inlet region.

Appellants (hereafter Madison and Gjosund) are two groups of Alaskan residents who live along the Kenai coastline and near Homer. For many years, they have fished with set nets for salmon for their personal and family use. Nonetheless, the board denied subsistence permits to Madison and Gjosund because their use of salmon did not meet the board's regulatory definition of subsistence. Both Madison and Gjosund challenged the regulation as exceeding the scope of the state's subsistence law. In both cases, the trial courts upheld the regulation as consistent with the statutory grant of authority. We hold the regulation invalid since it is inconsistent with AS 16.05.251(b), AS 16.05.940(22) and AS 16.05.940(23) and contrary to the legislature's intent in enacting the 1978 subsistence law.

I. Summary of Facts

Records indicate that subsistence fishing in Cook Inlet was minimal through the mid–1970s.[8] However, a core group of residents of each Cook Inlet community has traditionally fished for Cook Inlet salmon for subsistence. Participation in the subsistence salmon fishery is most visible in the smaller, more isolated villages, where the subsistence group represents a larger percentage of the population.

In 1977 the board established a comprehensive management policy for Cook Inlet, 5 AAC 21.363, which essentially allocated specific salmon stocks to sports fishermen and commercial fishermen on the basis of seasonal fish movements. *See Kenai Peninsula Fisherman's Cooperative Ass'n v. State,* 628 P.2d 897 (Alaska 1981). Although the policy did not specifically refer to subsistence uses of salmon in Cook Inlet, it had a substantial impact on subsistence fishing. Commercial fishermen, accustomed to taking subsistence salmon from their commercial catch, instead obtained subsistence salmon fishing permits in order to fish for their personal and family use after the commercial season was over.

Before 1978, subsistence fishing was defined in AS 16.05.940(17) as fishing for "personal use and not for sale or barter." In 1978, the Alaska State Legislature enacted ch. 151 SLA 1978 (hereafter the 1978 subsistence law). Subsistence fishing was redefined as fishing for "subsistence uses." Subsistence uses were defined as "customary and traditional uses . . . for direct personal or family consumption, and for the customary trade, barter or sharing. . . ." AS 16.05.940(23). Furthermore, the legislation required the board to adopt regulations permitting "subsistence uses" of fish stocks, absent a showing that this use would jeopardize the sustained yield principle. AS 16.05.251(b). Under AS 16.05.251(b), subsistence uses have priority over sport and commercial uses if the board finds it necessary to restrict the taking of fish to assure the maintenance of fish stocks or to assure the continuation of subsistence uses. If further restrictions are necessary after giving priority to all subsistence uses, the legislature established specific criteria to restrict subsistence uses based on the subsistence user's customary and direct dependence on the resource, local residency and availability of alternative resources. *Id.* As a result, the board could no longer allocate for subsistence uses at its discretion pursuant to AS 16.05.251(a). The legislature mandated in AS

8. From 1971 to 1977, the average number of subsistence permits issued annually for the Upper Cook Inlet was 87 and the average catch was 405 salmon. Commercial harvest averaged about two million fish per year. However, this statistical data does not necessarily reveal the total subsistence use since many people did not obtain permits and some commercially caught salmon were used for subsistence.

16.05.251(b) that the board regulate for the protection of subsistence uses as the priority use of fish and game.

The passage of the 1978 subsistence law, combined with adoption of the board's 1977 management policy, heightened public awareness of the state's subsistence fishing provisions. This public interest resulted in a substantial increase in the demand for subsistence permits and a corresponding increase in total catch.[9] The board responded to the permit increase by restricting subsistence fishing; it limited areas open to subsistence fishing, length of fishing periods and maximum length of gill nets. Several lawsuits were filed, all of which resulted in decisions unfavorable to the board.

In December 1980, the board held hearings to respond to the 1978 subsistence law and received a considerable amount of testimony on subsistence uses in Cook Inlet. The meeting resulted in the establishment of characteristics for identification of "customary and traditional uses" of Cook Inlet salmon.[10] In addition, the board decided to "adopt a

9. This chart reflects the trend in Upper Cook Inlet:

	Subsistence Use		Commercial Harvest
	Permits Issued	Salmon Caught	
1978	323	3,735	5,118,041
1979	1,161	9,923	1,923,229
1980	1,331	14,775	4,138,648

In 1980, household permits were issued instead of individual permits.

10. With some modification, these characteristics became the basis of 5 AAC 01.597, which states:

CHARACTERISTICS OF SUBSISTENCE FISHERIES

(a) The Board of Fisheries finds that certain customary and traditional practices and procedures associated with the utilization of fish in the Cook Inlet Area can be used to identify subsistence uses. Based on testimony to the board, the following characteristics are those that should be evaluated in the identification of subsistence fisheries:

(1) a long-term, stable, reliable pattern of use and dependency, excluding interruption generated by outside circumstances, e.g., regulatory action or fluctuations in resource abundance;

(2) a use pattern established by an identified community, subcommunity or group having preponderant concentrations of persons showing past use;

(3) a use pattern associated with specific stocks and seasons;

(4) a use pattern based on the most efficient and productive gear and economical use of time, energy and money;

(5) a use pattern occurring in reasonable geographic proximity to the primary residence of the community, group or individual;

(6) a use pattern occurring in locations with easiest and most direct access to the resources;

(7) a use pattern which includes a history of traditional modes of handling, preparing and storing the product without precluding recent technological advances;

(8) a use pattern which includes the intergenerational transmission of activities and skills;

(9) a use pattern in which the effort and products are distributed on a community and family basis including trade, bartering, sharing and gift-giving; and

(10) a use pattern which includes reliance on subsistence taking of a range of wild resources in proximity to the commu-

set of criteria drawn from the characteristics ... and apply [them] to communities, subcommunities, groups and individuals who wish to continue to participate in an established customary and traditional fishing effort in Cook Inlet."

At its March 1981 meeting, the board received written testimony from the public about subsistence uses of Cook Inlet salmon stock. Subsequently, it decided to apply all of the ten criteria to determine "customary and traditional uses" eligible for the subsistence priority. When the board applied the ten criteria, it determined that no group or community in the Cook Inlet region other than Tyonek, English Bay and Port Graham satisfied all ten of the criteria. The board limited the 1981 subsistence catch to these three communities. As a result, the board eliminated from the protection of the state's subsistence statute the majority of Cook Inlet fishermen who formerly fished under subsistence regulations.

Madison and Gjosund challenged the validity of the board's subsistence criteria (now 5 AAC 01.597) on several grounds. They claimed that: (1) the criteria were inconsistent with the statutory language and legislative intent of the 1978 subsistence law; (2) the board failed to comply with the Administrative Procedure Act in adopting the criteria; and (3) their equal protection and due process rights were violated by the board's action. Both courts issued preliminary injunctions compelling the board to authorize personal use fishing for Madison and Gjosund similar to that allowed in the previous year. The board moved for summary judgment on the plaintiffs' first claim. Both trial courts granted summary judgment to the board, after finding the subsistence criteria consistent with the legislative intent "to provide for and protect personal use ... by persons who reside in rural communities.... "

On appeal, Madison and Gjosund seek reversal of the two trial court decisions. They claim that the board did not act within the legislative authority granted by AS 16.05.251(b) and AS 16.05.940(22) and (23) when it adopted the ten characteristics ultimately codified as 5 AAC 01.597....

III. Legislative History of the 1978 Subsistence Law

Before 1978, subsistence fishing was defined as fishing for "personal use and not for sale or barter." Formerly AS 16.05.940(17). The 1978 subsistence law redefined subsistence fishing as fishing for "subsistence uses." AS 16.05.940(22). "Subsistence uses" were defined as "the customary and traditional uses in Alaska of wild, renewable resources for

nity or primary residency. (b) The board will identify established geographic communities which may be participating in a subsistence system. The board will then apply all of the characteristics in (a) of this section to the communities and to subcommunities, groups and individuals within the communities to determine which uses are customary and traditional and therefore, which communities are eligible for the subsistence priority.

(c) For purposes of this section, a "community" is generally considered to be several households of full-time residents who all reside in a specific geographic area because of common interests.

direct personal or family consumption ... and for the customary trade, barter or sharing...." AS 16.05.940(23). The board argues that the legislature intended to narrow the scope of subsistence fishing to mean fishing by individuals residing in those rural communities that have historically depended on subsistence hunting and fishing. Under this interpretation, the board asserts that its criteria are consistent with the legislature's intent.

The board's argument reveals a fundamental misconception about the structure of the 1978 subsistence law. There are potentially two tiers of subsistence users under AS 16.05.251(b). The first tier includes *all* subsistence users. Under the statute, all subsistence uses have priority over sport and commercial uses "whenever it is necessary to restrict the taking of fish to assure the maintenance of fish stocks on a sustained-yield basis, or to assure the continuation of subsistence uses of such resources.... " AS 16.05.251(b). If the statutory priority given all subsistence users over commercial and sport users still results in too few fish for all subsistence uses, then the board is authorized to establish a second tier of preferred subsistence users based on the legislative criteria expressed in AS 16.05.251(b), namely, customary and direct dependence on the resource, local residency, and availability of alternative resources.

Criteria like the ten criteria of 5 AAC 01.597(a) could be used to distinguish first-tier general subsistence users from second-tier preferred subsistence users, since most of the criteria relate to either "customary and direct dependence" or "local residency," two of the three criteria set out in AS 16.05.251(b). However, before there is any occasion to restrict subsistence fishing to second-tier preferred subsistence users as distinct from all subsistence users, the board must make two findings. It must find: (1) that it is necessary to restrict the taking of fish for sustained-yield purposes; and (2) that eliminating sport and commercial uses will not assure the maintenance of fish stocks on a sustained-yield basis and, thus, establishing a priority among subsistence users is also necessary. The board erred because it applied the ten criteria without making these findings.

The board argues that the words "customary and traditional" in AS 16.05.940(23) authorize it to define first-tier subsistence users by their area of residence. We reject this argument for several reasons. First, the argument ignores the two-tier structure of AS 16.05.251(b) that defines only the second-tier subsistence users in terms of residency. If the legislature had intended to define the class of first-tier general subsistence users by area of residence, it would not have expressed that factor with respect to only the second tier of preferred subsistence users. Moreover, the phrase "customary and traditional" modifies the word "uses" in AS 16.05.940(23). It does not refer to users. The 1978 subsistence law refers to "customary users" at only one point, when it defines the preferred subsistence users of the second tier with the three statutory criteria in AS 16.05.251(b)....

The board based its restrictive regulation 5 AAC 01.597, on the words "customary and traditional." The legislature did not define these words in the 1978 subsistence law. In such a case, reference to legislative history may provide an insight into the legislature's intent and a statute's meaning. *North Slope Borough v. Sohio Petroleum Corp.,* 585 P.2d 534, 540 (Alaska 1978). In the House floor debate on House Bill 960, Representative Cotton introduced an amendment to delete the words "customary and traditional" from the statute. The floor manager of the bill, Representative Anderson, opposed the amendment in the following speech:

> The two words are used in this context to put some guidelines around the uses of Alaska's freedom of resources. *What we were afraid of,* it was brought to our attention by people who were concerned that this would leave the field of the definition wide open. *That newcomers just coming to the State of Alaska would* automatically be able to establish not only residency in 30 days, but *be able to go out and state that they have a customary and traditional use of Alaska's fish and game resources.* The use of customary and traditional also is in recognition of a *historical use* of fish and game for food, shelter, fuel, clothing, tools, transportation, etc. This is *not only* in conformance with the *aboriginal uses, but also* those that have come in, those people who have come in later.... [T]he *nonnative* people in the State of Alaska have established customary and traditional uses of Alaska's fish and game resources for subsistence purposes. And in order to give the Board of Fish and Game more clarification in the area, we have come up with the (inaudible) of customary and traditional rather than leaving that section wide open. *The design is not to be restrictive but to provide guidelines* and that is basically what I feel and many ... members felt it was necessary in ... adding or retaining those two words "customary and traditional."

(Emphasis added).

We consider statements made by a bill's sponsor in the course of legislative deliberations to be relevant evidence when a court is trying to determine legislative intent. *Alaska Public Employees Association v. State,* 525 P.2d 12, 16 (Alaska 1974). Anderson argued for the retention of "customary and traditional" for use as a guideline. His major concern focused on the potential pressure put on resources by newcomers. In his view, the words "customary and traditional" recognized and protected a historical subsistence use by both native and non-native Alaskans. The words were not intended to restrict subsistence use....

The legislative history indicates that the legislature intended to protect subsistence use, not limit it. The words "customary and traditional" serve as a guideline to recognize historical subsistence use by individuals, both native and non-native Alaskans. In addition, subsistence use is not strictly limited to rural communities. For these reasons, the board's interpretation of "customary and traditional" as a restrictive term conflicts squarely with the legislative intent.

IV. The Board's Adoption and Application of 5 AAC 01.597

We now turn to the board's interpretation of the 1978 subsistence law. In December 1980, the board met to examine the uses of salmon in Cook Inlet and to determine which uses would qualify for the subsistence use priority. Tom Lonner, the director of the subsistence section of the Alaska Department of Fish and Game, presented the department's recommendations on the subsistence statute. He suggested that the board begin its analysis of customary and traditional uses with an assessment of user profiles and use patterns on a case by case basis. Lonner noted that such information was most lacking in the major Cook Inlet subsistence fishery because of the rapid growth of subsistence uses in recent years, and that obtaining such information would be expensive.

The board did not follow Lonner's suggested approach. After the board heard extensive testimony on subsistence use, its chairman appointed a committee, consisting of board members and staff, to identify subsistence uses of salmon in Cook Inlet. The committee drafted ten criteria to identify subsistence uses and presented them to the board.

Lonner worked with the committee to develop the ten criteria and explained them to the board. He stated: "These tenets here are ... based on ... the evidence about four relatively self-contained communities.... If, however, you have individual applicants, ... this might not suffice as a test." Therefore, the board was fully aware of the limitations of the proposed criteria.

At its March 1981 meeting, the board received further testimony on uses of Cook Inlet salmon from the area advisory committees and several individual witnesses. After deliberation, the board decided to apply all of the ten criteria "to determine which uses are customary and traditional and therefore are eligible for the subsistence priority." Only the fisheries associated with Tyonek, English Bay and Port Graham met all ten criteria.

In its findings of fact, the board applied the ten criteria to individuals such as Madison and Gjosund. In particular, the individuals failed to meet the second criterion: "A use pattern established by an identified community, subcommunity or group having preponderant concentrations of persons showing past use." The board found:

> Although some users have shown the existence of a community of interest (e.g., the Kenaitze Tribe and the Kachemak Bay Subsistence Group), these persons either are too widely dispersed or are too heterogeneous to be considered an identifiable community, subcommunity or group. On the evidence presented, the Board cannot conclude either that activities are conducted in common or that sharing or other group interchange occurs in relation to the resource.

In other words, an individual subsistence user (such as Madison or Gjosund) would not qualify for a subsistence use priority from the board unless he were part of an identifiable subsistence community or group. Under the board's regulation, many individual users who have historically depended on subsistence fishing are eliminated from subsistence use at the outset.

The board's regulation, 5 AAC 01.597, is inconsistent with the legislative intent to provide guidelines for the protection of subsistence fishing. The regulation exceeds the authority delegated to the board because it operates too restrictively in its initial differentiation between subsistence and non-subsistence uses. Under a statute designed to protect subsistence uses, the board has devised a regulation to disenfranchise many subsistence users whose interests the statute was designed to protect.

The decision of the two trial courts that 5 AAC 01.597 is consistent with AS 16.05.251(b) and AS 16.05.940(22) and (23) is REVERSED.

Notes

1. *Allocation, public interest, and private rights. Madison* is a good case to ponder because it shows how critical elements of natural resources sometimes are inevitably mixed, causing no small amount of confusion. The statute at issue in the case had to do with resource allocation, and it expressed a strong preference for subsistence fishers over other fishers. (Thus, when fish were too few to satisfy all subsistence fishers, certain fishers—rural communities and fishers dependent upon the fish for survival—took priority.) But this allocation issue was closely linked with another issue—the actual legal rights that fishers obtained in the fish, particularly the rights they had to sell the fish that they caught. Note that the 1978 statute allowed fishers to transfer fish to any family members (broadly defined) and also to transfer them in customary trade and barter. Thus, by expanding the legal rights that fishers obtained, it increased the amount of fish that they could use, thereby giving them an economic incentive to catch more fish. Adding complexity to all this was the public interest element. State lawmakers showed a willingness to support historical patterns of subsistence fishing but not to invite all manner of fishers from the entire country to come to Alaska and take up subsistence living. The Alaska scheme, therefore, includes an element familiar throughout resource law: a tendency when allocating a resource to favor historical users of the resource over newcomers, and to favor existing state residents over outsiders. Note in *Madison* the distinct conflict between the state legislature, with its sympathies for subsistence fishers, and the state administrative agency, which slanted strongly toward commercial fishers. Industrial users of land are often more successful in capturing state agencies than they are in influencing the state legislature.

2. *Allocation by regulating harvesting equipment.* In the case of fish and other wildlife, states have long engaged in indirect allocation of resources by means of regulations specifying the lawful methods of catching them. Bans on nets and other commercially essential fishing methods can

effectively allocate resources to sport fishermen, the only ones with the time and inclination to catch fish one at a time. The same result can be achieved by regulating place of harvest. For instance, bans on fishing along inland rivers while allowing fishing in the ocean can effectively exclude those fishers who cannot afford ocean-worthy fishing vessels, such as native tribes that use fish wheels. Such indirect allocation methods are hardly new. In many places, bans on hunting at night and when ordinary workers would be off work were used to reserve wild game for more wealthy hunters with ample leisure time.

3. *Limiting use to state residents:* Conservation Force, Inc. v. Manning. The Supreme Court has made clear that states have substantial but not unlimited power to allocate natural resources in ways that put out-of-state residents at a disadvantage. They can charge higher license fees to out of state hunters, for instance, in recognition of the fact that hunters in-state hunters pay taxes that support highways and police within the state. But what about quota systems, which have been widely used by states for years, in part on a tit-for-tat basis. In Conservation Force, Inc. v. Manning, 301 F.3d 985 (9th Cir. 2002), the court considered an Arizona system that put a 10% cap on the permits issued to out-of-state hunters for bull elk throughout the state and for antlered deer in the portion of the state north and west of the Colorado River. A hunter needed a tag to hunt the animals, and tags were awarded by means of a complicated "bonus point" lottery system, which the court described as follows:

> A bonus point is earned for each year in which the applicant purchased an Arizona hunting license and unsuccessfully applied for a tag, with one additional point awarded for the completing of an approved hunter education course. In the tag lottery, hunters indicate their desired hunts and each is assigned a random number by a computer, plus an additional number for each bonus point. The lowest numbers in the pool for each hunt obtain the available tags, with the exception that higher-number-holding residents may bypass the higher-number-holding nonresidents once the 10% cap on nonresidents is reached for the hunt. In addition, the first 10% of tags for each hunt are awarded to the applicants with the most bonus points, regardless of the random number drawn.

In practice, nonresidents received only 6 to 10% of the hunting tags. The court held that the tag allocation system was subject to scrutiny under the Dormant Commerce Clause, even though recreational hunting did not implicate any fundamental right protected by the Privileges and Immunities Clause. Under prevailing commerce clause analysis, the Arizona scheme was subject to the more strict scrutiny applicable to state laws that discriminated overtly against interstate commerce. Under that analysis, Arizona succeeded in showing that it had a legitimate state interest in preserving the health of its game-animal populations and in maintaining recreational hunting opportunities for its citizens. The state had failed to show, however, that it had narrowly tailored its statute to achieve its conservation interest. To withstand scrutiny, the regulatory scheme had to qualify as the "least discriminatory alternative." The case was returned to the district court for more evidence on whether Arizona could meet this constitutional test.

Essay: Public Interest Allocation and the Market

The idea of allocating resources to the most socially worthy uses has intuitive appeal to many people. This is particularly true when the resource is one that has a value that transcends the monetary or that gives to the recipient an opportunity to develop as an individual. Consider on this point a spot in the entering class of a public law school as a resource right. These spots are allocated by means of methods that combine money (tuition payments) and merit (undergraduate grades, test scores, and so on). It would offend most people if law schools allocated the spots based entirely on money (to the highest bidder) or based on chance (by lottery). Why, though, do these allocation methods seem offensive? Can we put a finger on our concerns? If we can think clearly about this question we might well learn something about the proper uses of many allocation methods.

One of the challenges of public interest allocation, as we've seen, is the difficulty of identifying the public interest. Over the generations, ideas of public interest have shifted considerably. Many governments have given out benefits based on political cronyism or to political machines that keep a particular political party in power. Other resources are given out on humanitarian grounds to relieve suffering. Spots in public schools are made available to all young people who live in a district (that is, they're allocated based on age and place of residence). At various times, rights to cut timber in the National Forests have been allocated by methods that favor local timber harvesters and local timber mills so as to provide stability for the economies of the small nearby communities. Public lands have gone to railroads as incentives to build new rails lines, to former military members as rewards for service, and to landless families to help promote homesteads.

As noted above, allocations intended to serve the public interest typically succeed only if the resource remains devoted to the particular use that promotes the public interest. For instance, if government gives water to a municipality to meet household needs, that public interest is undercut if the municipality immediately sells the water to an irrigator. Similarly, if water is given to an individual family because of a perceived social benefit in promoting small homestead farms, that public interest is undercut if the water is promptly sold to a factory that uses the water to make computer chips. Finally, consider a scarce permit to engage in climbing a mountain, which is allocated to a person who demonstrates great skill in mountain climbing. This allocation system would be frustrated if the climber could then sell the permit on E-bay. (It might be frustrated in a different way if the climber sought to use the permit to climb a different mountain.)

What these hypotheticals illustrate is the reality that government can ensure the public's interest in particular resource uses only if it imposes limits on how the recipients use their resource and on their transferability. Public interest allocation, that is, goes hand in hand with legal definitions of resource rights that limit the owner's options to use the resource and sell it.

As you consider these issues, look back at the three main cases in this section. In *Shokal* the court says that the state agency has broad powers to allocate water and set priorities among new water users based on a rather finely tuned calculation of the public interest. That system might work fine—setting aside questions about whether government will make good decisions—but only if any shift of water to a new use is subject to a similar public-interest review requirements. The state need not insist that the initial water use continue indefinitely; the system doesn't have to be that inflexible. But the state would likely want to insist that any new use of the water also promote the public interest. Otherwise the whole scheme can fall apart.

The facts of *Forest Guardians* raise a related concern. What if the grazers who received the state grazing permits in that case were free to sell the permits on the open market, and what if the appellants in the case—Forest Guardians and Jonathan Tate—were the purchasers, buying the permits at a price well above the price the grazers paid? The permits would end up with the appellants, who would have paid the higher price. But the price differential would have gone to the grazers, not to the state's schools. And if we can believe the state agency and the court in their assessments of the public's interest, the final result would be a pattern of resource use that clashed with public welfare.

Then there is the Alaska fishing dispute, where we see even more starkly the link between public interest allocation and transferability. The local subsistence fishers want enough fish not just to feed themselves and their families but to use for traditional barter. Barter, though, is a form of sale, and fishers who engage in barter do so for purposes of personal gain. The lawmakers who revised the Alaska statute obviously saw clearly the clash here. They wanted to sustain the subsistence fishers in their lifestyles, which required some allowance of barter. On the other hand, they didn't want to allow the fishers to increase their catches significantly and engage in commercial sales of their catches. Fishers who wanted to do that, the lawmakers stated, need to get in line with all other commercial fishers. Thus, to keep the subsistence-fishing program within bounds, the lawmakers had to restrict resale of the fish. In revising the statute they essentially relaxed a near total ban on resale to allow limited transfers.

One complication of all of this is that when resource use rights are restricted to particular uses and users, some mechanism is then needed to ensure that the legal limits are followed. Somebody needs to watch the resource uses to ensure that the public interest considerations are sustained. This might be done by other resource users, who would like to get their own hands on the resources at issue. Alternatively it could be done by the state. Someone, though, needs to perform the function. And it is a function, we should note, that arises only because of the original public interest allocation. If a resource is simply offered based on first in time, or is sold to the highest bidder, then we might not care how the resource is used or who uses it.

Related to this last point is the reality that public-interest limits on using resources have immediate and sometimes grave effects on the existence of a secondary market in the resource. A resource holder who cannot sell the resource, or who can sell only to purchasers who are carefully screened through legal processes, is not really a "willing seller" in the jargon of economists. Markets work best when commodities are relatively fungible and when market prices alone move them to new uses. The market works less well as a reallocation method—and perhaps not at all—when public-interest considerations constrain who can buy the resource and how it can be used. We'll turn to this issue in chapter 7, where we'll consider the transferability of resources and other mechanisms for promoting resource reallocation over time so as to take into account inevitably shifting needs, values, and ecological understandings.

What's important to note here is that reallocation methods cannot be talked about in the abstract, particularly the much-heard claims that we can deal with resource reallocation merely by unleashing the market. Markets do reallocate resources, and they're often the best way to do it. But before embracing the market for reallocation we need to consider the full ramifications of doing so, on the public interest and (as we'll see below) on the interests of other resource uses. We cannot fully unleash the market without undercutting the benefits the public gets from resource allocations schemes such as those considered in the three main cases here. And when we do unleash the market by making resource rights fully transferable, we need to realize that we might well be granting to the current resource holder a huge economic benefit. Consider again the grazing rights in *Forest Guardians*. The grazers in that case stand to make money if they can sell their grazing rights to the appellants or to other potential purchasers. Consider the even more stark case of the farm family that long ago received for free an irrigation right to promote a farm homestead (perhaps subject to the original rule that no irrigator could claim water for more than 160 acres). Is it right now for the farm family to sell the water to a big city at huge profit? If the water is no longer sensibly used for irrigation, should the water right perhaps revert to the government for reallocation? Or if the farm family can sell the water, should the economic gain go to the taxpayers rather than the farm family? On the other hand, if the farm family cannot get at least part of the economic gain, what incentive does it have to terminate its water use?

Questions and challenges such as these permeate the modern law of natural resources, yet they are hardly new. Indeed, they relate to the core functions that natural resources law has addressed for literally centuries. In early feudal England, not long after the Norman Conquest, the issue arose as to whether landed property rights could be transferred. The lands were originally allocated based on loyalty to the king, on oaths of fealty, and on various obligations to sustain the king with knights in times of warfare. From the king's perspective, this was no doubt a public interest allocation! Needless to say, the king was reluctant to allow transfers of land to purchasers who were not loyal or not fully able to supply the needed knights. We can jump ahead to early Puritan New England, where a number of early towns were especially concerned about ensuring that only good people lived in them. Some town leaders exercised vetoes over sales of town lands to outsiders. The lands were originally given only to godly people, and town leaders wanted to ensure that any purchasers who bought the lands and joined the towns were similarly godly. In all such cases, restrictions on transfer inhibited the emergence of open markets in land. Landowners who sought to sell for the highest price, regardless of communal consequences, rose up to challenge them.

Chapter Four

USING LAND-BASED RESOURCES

A. *SIC UTERE TUO*

Having looked at the two initial questions of resource allocation—does a given natural resource attach to land or is it available for separate acquisition, and if the latter, how is the resource initially allocated—we now turn to the core questions about resource use. What rights does an owner have to use a resource? Or to phrase the question a bit differently: what is the scope of the natural resource right, in terms of the particular uses that it authorizes? Necessarily this question is linked to another: how do the rights of one resource owner fit together with those of other owners, given the existence of competing private rights and given the use-conflicts that inevitably arise among them?

As we look into these questions, what we find is what we might well expect, that the law defining a particular resource use right becomes more detailed and fine-tuned as the resource becomes scarce and conflicts over it become more frequent and severe. A resource-law regime that outlines private rights in sketchy, vague terms might work well enough so long as conflicts are infrequent but it causes troubles as scarcity sets in.

The best example of a detailed legal scheme is provided by prior appropriation law on arid-land rivers where water rights are carefully fit together and where water is reused multiple times as it works its way downstream. A scheme that defines legal rights with precision, carefully tailoring competing rights so that they fit together snugly, can allow multiple users to co-exist without much conflict. That is its virtue. But such a scheme comes at a high cost, as the prior appropriation regime again illustrates. When rights are precisely defined the users become tightly bound to existing uses. One user cannot change what she is doing without violating the rights of other users. The whole system thus becomes rigid. It cannot respond to changing circumstances and public values. As time goes on it gets out of date. What is needed, plainly, is some mechanism for adjusting patterns of resource use over time, allowing users to shift to uses deemed more important. But how can this happen when private users are frozen into the legal equivalent of traffic gridlock? Hardly any resource challenge is more pressing, and the answers are by no means clear. The answer for some observers, as we'll see, is to unleash the market, allowing market forces to move resources to more highly valued uses. But markets can move resources around only if the resources are defined so as to allow transfer, and to redefine resource rights at this point to allow transfer would alter significantly the finely tuned regime of interlocked private rights.

We begin the subject of this chapter by returning to cases involving land and the natural resources that they include. Later we'll see that the basic rules applicable to discrete natural resources (water, grazing, timber, mines) are essentially variants on the legal principles crafted to govern uses of land. The basic story line, which we see when we stand back from things, is about the rise of "reasonable use" as a limit on what owners can do with the things they own. But that simple term, of course, means very little unless we see how it operates in practice.

The following treatise excerpt from nearly a century ago highlights the fundamental issue in this chapter. An owner has legal rights to use what she owns, but she can't use it so as to harm neighbors. It is a simple enough idea, do-no-harm, but confusing and frustrating in application. Indeed, you might conclude (as an author below concludes) that the do-no-harm rule is essentially meaningless, either a tautology or else a principle that one can apply only *after* a dispute is resolved. In any event, it should become clear that the basic issue here—whether to allow an intensive resource use or instead to protect more sensitive activities—is very much a question of social policy. It cannot be resolved by applying neutral principles of any sort, nor by turning to the true meaning of words such as "ordinary," "natural," "common," or even "reasonable." A more wide-ranging inquiry is required into the types of land-and resource-uses that are most beneficial to us today.

A TREATISE ON THE LAW OF LIGHT 1 (1911)

R.G. Nicholson Combe.

Our law bestows upon the owner of land, divers right and privileges. It protects him in the enjoyment of those rights and privileges, and affords him assistance if any one infringe them. He is entitled to enjoy that which nature has bestowed as incidents of the subject-matter of his ownership. The physical benefits, such as water air and light are his, because he owns the land and they are incidents of the land. He does not own them as separate subjects of ownership, but because they are necessarily incidents of that one subject—the land.

As every right or privilege in favour of one person necessarily involves an obligation upon others, the landowner's right involves an obligation upon the world at large, and upon his neighbor in particular, to refrain from molesting him in the enjoyment of his land, and in the enjoyment of the natural benefits flowing from his ownership. As every owner of land enjoys equal rights in respect of his land and the incidents attached thereto, it follows that there are limits placed upon the extent and mode of the user and enjoyment of land by an individual owner; for each landowner must perforce have regard to the result of his user and enjoyment of his own land upon the user and enjoyment of the land of his neighbors. There is, in other words, a mutuality of benefit and obligation.

The policy of the law is embodied in the maxim, *sic utere tuo ut alienum non lædas* [so use your own [property] as not to injure another's property].

BRYANT v. LEFEVER

4 C.P.Div. 172, 48 L.J. 380 (Common Pleas, Court of Appeals, 1879).

BRAMWELL, L.J.:

The plaintiff says that he is possessed of a house, that for more than twenty years this house and its occupants have had the wind blow to, over and from it, and that he has, as so possessed, the right that it should continue to do so. That the defendants have interfered with this right and prevented the free access and departure of the wind. He adds that they have committed a nuisance to him as so possessed. He has proved that he is possessed of a house more than twenty years old, that the wind had access to it and passage over it for twenty years without the hindrance recently caused by the defendants; that the defendants have caused a hindrance by putting on the roof of their house (which is as old as the plaintiff's), timber to a considerable height, thereby preventing the wind blowing to and over the plaintiff's house when in some directions, and passing away from it when in others; that this causes his chimneys to smoke as they did not before, to the extent of being a nuisance. The question is if this shews a cause of action. First, what is the right of the occupier of a house in relation to air, independently of length of enjoyment? It is the same as that which land and its owner or occupier have, it is not greater because a house has been built. That puts no greater burthen or disability on adjoining owners. What then is the right of land and its owner or occupier? It is to have all natural incidents and advantages as nature would produce them. There is a right to all the light and heat that would come, to all the rain that would fall, to all the wind that would blow; a right that the rain which would pass over the land should not be stopped and made to fall on it, a right that the heat from the sun should not be stopped and reflected on it, a right that the wind should not be checked, but should be able to escape freely; and if it were possible that these rights were interfered with by one having no right, no doubt an action would lie. But these natural rights are subject to the right of adjoining owners, who for the benefit of the community have and must have rights in relation to that use and enjoyment of their property that qualify and interfere with those of their neighbours; right to use their property in the various ways in which property is commonly and lawfully used. A hedge, a wall, a fruit tree, would each affect the land next to which it was planted or built.

They would keep off some light, some air, some heat, some rain when coming from one direction, and prevent the escape of air, of heat, of wind, of rain when coming from the other. But nobody could doubt that in such case no action would lie. Nor will it in the case of a house being built and having such consequences. That is an ordinary and lawful use of property as much so as the building of a wall or planting of a fence, or an orchard. Of course the same reasoning applies to the putting of timber on the top of a house which, if not a common, is a perfectly lawful act, and it would be absurd to suppose that the defendants could lawfully put another storey to their house with the consequences to the plaintiff of which he complains, but cannot put an equal height of timber. These are elementary and obvious considerations, but if borne in mind will assist very materially in the decision of this case.

* * *

But it is said, and the jury have found, that the defendants have done that which has caused a nuisance to the plaintiff's house. We think there is no evidence of this. No doubt there is a nuisance, but it is not of the defendants' causing. They have done nothing in causing the nuisance. Their house and their timber are harmless enough. It is the plaintiff who causes the nuisance by lighting a coal fire in a place the chimney of which is placed so near the defendants' wall that the smoke does not escape, but comes into the house. Let the plaintiff cease to light his fire; let him move his chimney; let him carry it higher, and there would be no nuisance. Who, then, causes it? It would be very clear that the plaintiff did, if he had built the house or chimney after the defendants had put the timber on their roof; and it is really the same though he did so before the timber was there. But (what is in truth the same answer) if the defendants cause the nuisance, they have a right to do so. If the plaintiff has not the right to the passage of air, except subject to the defendants' right to build or put timber on their house, then his right is subject to their right, and though a nuisance followed from the exercise of their right, they are not liable. *Sic utere two ut alienum no laedas* is a good maxim. But, in our opinion, the defendants do not infringe it. The plaintiff would, if he succeeded. We are of opinion that judgment should be for the defendants on the cause of action the subject of this appeal.

Notes

1. *The causation conundrum.* The foundational principle of all property use is the familiar legal rule of *sic utere tuo*: use your own so as to do no harm to others. This do-no-harm rule sounds clear enough on its face, but as *Bryant* vividly illustrates, it is often hard to decide who is harming whom when two land uses clash. Without the chimney and the fire, no problem would arise. Without the timbers on the roof, no problem would arise. So who has caused the conflict? If we can't come up with an answer, then how do we apply the do-no-harm rule? When causation is unclear, how do we decide which land use will enjoy legal protection and which will not? Note

that, in some manner, the law must resolve this land-use dispute. Either it allows the landowner to place his timbers on the roof (and protects him if his neighbor knocks them down), or it protects the landowner with the smoking chimney. Either way, one landowner wins and one loses. There is no neutral position to take; no way for the state to stand back and act like it is disinterested.

As we've already seen, disputes such as this cannot be resolved by resort to some ideal of land ownership because, pragmatically speaking, land ownership means whatever lawmakers want it to mean. In this case, lawmakers could protect either landowner. There is no pro-property position that can be taken here, nor is there a pro-liberty position. We might say that protecting the right to install timbers promotes individual liberty, but what about the homeowner with the smoking chimney? Hasn't his liberty been disrupted if we fail to protect him? Indeed, isn't the very essence of private property the idea that the law will protect you when outsiders interfere with what you are doing? Unless the law offers some level of protection there really is no private property.

2. *"All natural incidents."* Recall how the law of riparian water rights evolved from the natural-flow ideal to that of reasonable use. Do we see a similar evolution taking place in the law of land use? The shift in water law took place to accommodate more intensive water uses, thus paving the way for industrialization. Much the same process seems present in this case involving urban land parcels. Instead of the ideal of natural flow as the law's starting point we have a similar ideal of landownership as the right to the "natural incidents" of the land, including sunlight and air flow. If the court had stopped at this point in its analysis of the dispute, the plaintiff would have won the case because the natural incidents of his land were disrupted by his neighbor. Yet, just as in the reasonable-use water rulings, the court doesn't stop there. One landowner's right to the natural incidents of the land, the court announces, is subject to the right of his neighbor to use his land more intensively. And what more intensive land uses does the court here seem to allow? How does it decide which intensive land uses are permissible despite the resulting harm and which are not? The court talks about landowners possessing the "right to use their property in the various ways in which property is commonly and lawfully used." How helpful is this phrasing? Does it provide more or less guidance than the phrase used in riparian rights (and elsewhere, as we'll see): "reasonable use"?

Another way to raise this foundational issue is by drawing on older legal language, phrased in Latin. In older parlance, the question would be which harms or losses (*damnum*) does the law recognize and remedy (*injuria*—meaning, roughly, against the law) and which does it not. Thus we have the common phrase *damnum sine injuria* (or *damnum absque injuria*), meaning an actual loss that does not violate any law and is thus not subject to legal remedy. This phrase, of course, is a conclusory one, a label put on a particular loss or harm after a court has decided that no remedy is available. It sheds no light on how we go about deciding which *damnum* amounts to *injuria* and which does not.

3. *The need for a baseline.* The court rules that the land-use problem here was caused by plaintiff and his fireplace fire. The defendant's conduct,

the court asserts, was harmless. But what could be more peacefully domestic and orderly than what the plaintiff was doing? If the court had started with the plaintiff's behavior and passed judgment on it, would it then have pointed a condemning finger at the defendant? Is the court just playing games?

To understand what's going on, we need to follow carefully the court's syllogism, which goes like this:

Ordinary uses of land are lawful.

The defendant's activity was ordinary.

Therefore defendant's activity was lawful.

The logic is unassailable, because the conclusion lies in the premise. But why is the defendant's activity lawful when it results in a houseful of smoke? What the court has done, in effect, is to establish a *baseline* of acceptable landowner behavior. It has decided, at least in cases such as this, what types of landowner behavior are legally acceptable and what types are not. Once such a baseline is established, then it becomes possible to decide who is harming whom. Without such a baseline, though, the do-no-harm rule is logically useless. And of course the do-no-harm principle does not help at all in establishing the baseline, does it?

Note, though, how vaguely the court expresses this all-important baseline of landowner conduct: landowners can engage in activities that are "ordinary and lawful"; activities, that is, in which other landowners "commonly and lawfully" engage. To say that lawful activities are lawful is, of course, a useless tautology that clarifies nothing. So we are left with the words "ordinary" and "common" by way of guidance in deciding what landowners can and cannot do. Are these words helpful? Are they in practice likely to be synonyms of "reasonable use," recognizing that what is "reasonable" might well be determined by referring to what other landowners commonly and ordinarily do? Going further, though, surely the plaintiff's activities are also ordinary and common, so we're left with the question: When two ordinary and common land uses conflict, which will the law favor? The court here decides that the law should take a hands-off approach, allowing both land uses to continue. The effect, of course, is that the more intensive land use is preferred and the more sensitive one is left without legal protection. The law's stance, that is, is to favor the intensive land use.

4. *The demise of first in time?* As best we can tell (given the scanty historical record) the do-no-harm common law rule in the pre-industrial era typically operated to favor the land use that was earlier in time. If landowner A undertakes a land use in isolation and then B shows up nearby, initiating a land use that creates a land-use conflict, then we can simply point the accusative finger at B. B caused the harm because B's arrival led to the conflict; until B arrived, no problem existed. Had the court in *Bryant* retained this simple approach, favoring the first landowner in time, the plaintiff would have won his case. Temporal priority, then, can serve the same function as a land-use baseline of acceptable conduct; it can give us a starting point for deciding which landowner is causing the harm. So why might the court in *Bryant* have chosen to ignore priority in time?

According to historians who have studied the shift, temporal priority tended to disadvantage the newer industrial, urban land uses. To make way for them, the law simply had to withdraw this temporal preference. After all, how could a major city rise to the sky if landowners such as the plaintiff could effectively prohibit high-rise buildings? Beyond this problem, there is the reality that a first-in-time method of resolving disputes can itself seem unfair. What happens if the second landowner on the scene initiates a land use that is identical with the first, and the two simply can't get along? Where is the justice in favoring one landowner over another? On this issue, consider the facts of the prominent ruling from the beginning era of industrialization, the New York ruling in *Palmer v. Mulligan*, 3 Cai. R. 307, 2 Am. Dec. 270 (N.Y. Sup. 1805). While New York was still a colony Palmer constructed a sawmill on a river, with an associated dam that partially blocked the river. The dam raised a head of water to supply power for the sawmill and also helped to collect and store logs being floated to the mill. Later, an upstream landowner constructed essentially an identical dam and mill. The effect was to interfere with Palmer's use of his property. Under the existing law, Palmer deserved to win his case because the new user was causing him harm. The conservative judges on the bench—including the great James Kent, later known for his treatises—voted to uphold that law and the system of private rights based on it. Palmer was wronged and deserved relief, they stated. The majority, led by Brockholst Livingston (who would dissent in *Pierson v. Post*, a contemporaneous ruling) decided to deviate from the old way of determining harm. The old way essentially gave Palmer a monopoly on using the river and thus stifled competition, Livingston explained. To favor Palmer was to undercut the ability of the upstream landowner to do what Palmer had done, when the upstream owner held identical property rights. In time, historians would view Palmer's case as a sign that property law was on the move, shifting from an agrarian system that favored existing uses to one that paved the way for more intensive, industrial activities. See Morton J. Horwitz, THE TRANSFORMATION OF AMERICAN LAW, 1780–1860 31–42 (1977).

As for the unfairness of first in time, we should keep in mind that it routinely has this defect. In truth, being first in time may not count for much in any moral sense, though protection for the first person in time can enhance the stability of property rights. Keep this issue in mind as you consider the next two main cases.

5. *What goes up ...* The rush to embrace industrialization and urbanization lost steam late in the nineteenth century, as Americans began to see vividly some of its downsides. Land-use regulation, long a feature in American law, took on new forms with the rise of city-wide zoning schemes. To no surprise, landowners troubled by the ill effects of factories and mines turned to the do-no-harm rule to challenge the industrial activities. By then, the main remedy available to private landowners was the law of private nuisance. Nuisance law, though, had come a long way during the nineteenth century, in terms of the protections that it offered (or failed to offer) to a landowner. The original do-no-harm rule had become much relaxed, so that it now permitted landowners to engage in more intensive, industrial activities. By late in the century a landowner-plaintiff could obtain relief from the harm that he suffered only if the harm was "substantial" and only if the

harm was imposed under circumstances that were "unreasonable." These vague terms, needless to say, were deeply infused with policy judgments and many harmed landowners left court without a remedy. Juries and judges often viewed industrial pollution simply as the necessary "price of progress." Given the needs of industry it appeared socially reasonable to many to spew pollution onto neighboring land, rendering it uninhabitable.

The times, though, were changing, as the following case illustrates. The harms of industrialization encountered more resistance. In the following case the industrial landowner, for the time being, was able still to prevail and avoid liability (the harm was deemed *damnum sine injuria*). But the case included a stinging dissent, which provided a look at the new age already underway. It was an age that would, in important ways, swing the pendulum back toward the landowners being harmed by industry, giving them more protection and imposing greater liability on those causing the harm. As the law shifted—erratically and evenly—it began vaguely to resemble the legal landscape in place when the nineteenth century began, when the law tended to protect sensitive land uses and expressed suspicion about intensive ones.

WASCHAK v. MOFFAT

379 Pa. 441, 109 A.2d 310 (1954).

Allen M. Stearne, Justice.

The appeal is from a judgment of the Superior Court refusing to enter judgment *non obstante veredicto* for defendants in an action in trespass and affirming the judgment of the Court of Common Pleas of Lackawanna County in favor of plaintiffs.

Gas or fumes from culm banks, the refuse of a coal breaker, damaged the paint on plaintiffs' dwelling. In this action for damages the applicable legal principles are technical and controversial. Considerable confusion appears in the many cases. The field is that of *liability without fault for escape of substances from land.*

Plaintiffs are owners of a dwelling in the Borough of Taylor which is in the center of Pennsylvania's anthracite coal lands. An action in trespass was instituted against two partners, operators of a coal breaker in that Borough. Without fault on the part of defendants, gas known as *hydrogen sulfide* was emitted from two of defendants' culm banks. This caused discoloration of the white paint (with lead base) which had been used in painting plaintiffs' dwelling. The painted surface became dark or black. The sole proven damage was the cost of restoring the surface with a white paint, having a titanium and zinc base, which will not discolor. There was no other injury either to the building or occupants. The verdict was for $1,250.

While the verdict is in a relatively modest amount, the principles of law involved, and their application, are extremely important and far reaching. Twenty-five other cases are at issue awaiting the decision in this case. The impact of this decision will affect the entire coal interests—anthracite and bituminous—as well as other industries. Application of appropriate legal principles is of vital concern to coal miners and to other labor.

The pivotal facts are undisputed. To mine anthracite coal, either by deep or strip mining, requires processing in a coal breaker before marketing. Usable coal, broken to various sizes, must first be separated from its by-products of minerals, rock, etc. The by-products are deposited in piles known as culm banks, portions of which may be reclaimed, while other parts are presently regarded as waste. The mining and processing in the present case are conceded to have been conducted by defendants without fault. Fires frequently appear in the culm banks long after the accumulation. Defendants neither committed any negligent act nor omitted any known method to prevent combustion, fires or the emission of gases. In addition to *hydrogen sulfide* two other gases, *carbon monoxide* and *sulfur dioxide* were shown to have also been emitted, but it is not contended that either of these two gases affected the paint in question. *Hydrogen sulfide* was conceded to have been the gas which caused the damage. The emission of this gas is not ordinarily found in the operation of coal mining and processing. *Defendants did not know and had no reason to anticipate the emission of this gas and the results which might follow*. Of the five culm banks only two of them, the Washington Street bank and the settling basin were shown to have emitted *hydrogen sulfide*.

In the court below the case was tried on the theory of *absolute liability* for the maintenance of a nuisance. The jury was instructed that it should determine, as a *matter of fact*, whether or not what the defendants did and the conditions resulting therefrom constituted a "reasonable and natural use" of defendants' land. The Superior Court declined to adopt the rule of *absolute liability*. That court followed Restatement, Torts, Chapter 40 which relates to "*liability without fault*". The verdict was affirmed, however, because, as stated in the opinion, "[a] vast quantity of coal was brought * * * from lands *outside the borough* * * *" and

> "* * * the fact that *hydrogen sulphide* gas had not been generated in any of the existing * * * culm banks, made up wholly of wastes from coal mined in the borough, it was a fair inference for the jury that a *different chemical content in the foreign coal* which defendants hauled to the borough and processed there, accounted for the presence of the gas in the atmosphere. * * *" (Italics supplied.)

The measure of liability for the escape of substances from land has been a controversial subject in the law. Much learning has been expended in this field. Unquestionably there is confusion in the host of cases on the subject. Judge Robinson tried the case in the court below with care. His charge and opinion reflect scholarly thought and effort. Judge Hirt, with his accustomed learning and acumen, reviewed the facts and the law. Both opinions merit great respect. Legal articles, extensively documented, have been published on the subject. An informative treatise titled "The Absolute Nuisance Theory in Pennsylvania" is found in 95

U. of Pa.L.Rev. 781. Hon. Charles E. Kenworthey, formerly a Judge in the Superior Court, has written an article titled "The Private Nuisance Concept in Pennsylvania: A Comparison With The Restatement" reported in 54 Dick.L.Rev. 109. The Restatement of the Law, Chapter 40 of Torts, sections 822 to 840, with scope and introductory note, on the "Invasions of Interests in the Private Use of Land (Private Nuisance)" with Pennsylvania Annotations in the 1953 Pocket Supplement, restates the law.

From the multitude of cases there appear to have been promulgated three rules of law where there has been an invasion of interests in the private use of land. They arise most frequently where, without negligence or fault, material escapes to the land of another causing damage. The rules may be thus stated:

(1) English rule of Rylands v. Fletcher, L.R. 3 H.L. 330 (a leading case which is frequently cited)

(2) Absolute Nuisance Doctrine

(3) Restatement Rules.

(1) *Rylands v. Fletcher*

The English rule, supra, is concisely expressed by Lord Cranworth as follows (p. 340):

> "* * * If a person brings, or accumulates, on his land anything which, if it should escape, may cause damage to his neighbour, he does so at his peril. If it does escape, and cause damage, he is responsible, however careful he may have been, and whatever precautions he may have taken to prevent the damage."

The strict doctrine of Rylands v. Fletcher, supra, has not been followed by this Court. Pennsylvania Coal Company v. Sanderson, 113 Pa. 126, 6 A. 453; Householder v. Quemahoning Coal Co., 272 Pa. 78, 116 A. 40; Venzel v. Valley Camp Coal Co., 304 Pa. 583, 156 A. 240.

(2) Absolute Nuisance Doctrine

Instead of the English doctrine, ordinarily this Court has heretofore applied what has been termed the Absolute Nuisance Doctrine. As pointed out by Judge Kenworthey, much of the confusion in this field is due largely to the diversification in defining the word "*nuisance*". There is a nuisance *per se* and a nuisance *in fact*. Thus a gas station in a residential neighborhood may be a nuisance *per se*, but a retail grocery supermarket while not a nuisance *per se* may become a nuisance *in fact* if improperly conducted. Essick v. Shillam, 347 Pa. 373, 32 A.2d 416, 146 A.L.R. 1399. There is also confusion respecting failure to distinguish between trespass and nuisance. Many of the cases have used the phrase "*it is not a question of negligence, but of nuisance*". Pottstown Gas Company v. Murphy, 39 Pa. 257; Gavigan v. Atlantic Refining Company, 186 Pa. 604, 40 A. 834; Stokes v. Pennsylvania Railroad Company, 214 Pa. 415, 63 A. 1028. In Kramer v. Pittsburgh Coal Company, 341 Pa.

379, at page 381, 19 A.2d 362, at page 363, when defining nuisance, Chief Justice Schaffer said:

> "* * * In legal phraseology, the term 'nuisance' is applied to that class of wrongs that arise from the unreasonable, unwarrantable, or unlawful use by a person of his own property, real or personal, or from his own improper, indecent, or unlawful personal conduct, working an obstruction or injury to a right of another, or of the public, and producing such material annoyance, inconvenience, discomfort or hurt that the law will presume a consequent damage.' 46 C.J. 645, 646. 'Nuisance is distinguishable from negligence.' Id., 650. 'The distinction between trespass and nuisance consists in the former being a direct infringement of one's right of property, while, in the latter, the infringement is the result of an act which is not wrongful in itself, but only in the consequences which may flow from it.' Id., 651. As we stated in Summit Hotel Co. v. National Broadcasting Co., 336 Pa. 182, 189, 8 A.2d 302, 305, 124 A.L.R. 968: 'In cases of trespass for nuisance, the person responsible may be unable, no matter how careful, to avoid injury to the lands of another, but, again, he knows that injury may result from the nature of his activities regardless of care. Under such circumstances he also assumes the risk. The responsibility for injury lies in creating or maintaining the harmful condition.' "

An invasion of an interest may be *intentional* or *unintentional*. If an owner of land erects a factory upon it, which he operates, his act is, of course, *intentional* when he ignites fires under the boilers which emit smoke or fumes and operate noisy machinery. Such intentional operations *may* become a nuisance and cause damage to an adjoining property, depending upon the method of operation, location of the premises and surrounding circumstances. Under varying conditions the harm caused by the emission of offensive odors, noises, fumes, violations, etc., must be weighed against the utility of the operation. And even where the invasion of property rights is unintentional, and without negligence, if the activity is *ultrahazardous* there will be imposed an absolute liability for damages. Thus in a blasting operation, recovery was had where the damage was due solely to vibration and concussion: Federoff v. Harrison Construction Co., 362 Pa. 181, 66 A.2d 817.

To attempt to cite the host of cases and analyze them would be a Herculean task and prove uneffective. Many of the cases are cited in the Pennsylvania Annotations to the Restatement of the Law of Torts, *supra*.

(3) Restatement Rules

The Rule of the Restatement, which unquestionably is accurate and most comprehensive, is as follows:

Section 822. General Rule.

The actor is liable in an action for damages for a non-trespassory invasion of another's interest in the private use and enjoyment of land if,

(a) the other has property rights and privileges in respect to the use or enjoyment interfered with; And

(b) the invasion is substantial; and

(c) the actor's conduct is a legal cause of the invasion; and

(d) the invasion is either

(i) intentional and unreasonable; or

(ii) unintentional and otherwise actionable under the rules governing liability for negligent, reckless or ultrahazardous conduct.

Rest

RULE

This rule we adopt. We agree that the adoption will obviate the difficulty and confusion in attempting to reconcile or distinguish the great mass of cases. We are not violating precedent and are not conflicting, in major degree, with the principles of *stare decisis*.

We must apply the principles of law enunciated by the Restatement to the facts of this case. Judge Hirt, in his opinion, has ably summarized the principal facts as follows [173 Pa.Super. 209, 96 A.2d 165]:

"In the light of the verdict, based upon testimony in which there is little dispute, these material facts appear: For more than 50 years coal mining has been the most important industry in the Borough of Taylor. Glen Alden Coal Company owned large tracts of land in the borough extending into the township on which it had conducted extensive mining operations during that period. It processed the coal at a large breaker in the borough, located within a few hundred feet of the property now owned by the plaintiffs. In accordance with the general practice, and with the consent of the borough, Glen Alden deposited the by-products of mining, consisting of waste material and coal which could be made saleable by reprocessing, in a culm bank as close to the breaker as possible without interfering with its operation. Glen Alden ceased operating the mines in 1932 and there was then a large refuse dump near the breaker. In 1937 the defendants undertook to reopen the mines and among the lands then leased to them by Glen Alden, were two large tracts, one fronting 2,500 feet on Washington Street in the borough, and the other ear the breaker extending along Main Street for about one-half mile. Defendants from 1937 to 1944 by means of a conveyor line from the breaker, built up an extensive bank of culm or reclaimable sulphurous coal adjacent to the existing Glen Alden bank, referred to as the Main Street dump. This bank was abandoned in 1944 when it started to burn. In the years that followed defendants, from necessity, turned to other locations for their culm banks. In 1944 they started to deposit culm on Washington Street, within the borough, which ultimately developed into a bank 10 to 60 feet high extending 800 feet along Washington Street and 750 feet along an alley in the rear of Union Street. This bank began to burn in 1948 and further dumping was then discontinued. Defendants then began the construction of a large settling basin near their Main Street dump. The walls of the so-called 'silt dam' were 25 feet high and were constructed principally of breaker refuse. The function of the structure was to separate silt from the water used in processing coal at the breaker, to comply with the Act of June 22, 1937, P.L. 1987, 35 P.S. § 691.1 et seq., before discharging it into natural streams. Still another culm bank was started in 1949 on Fourth Street in the borough and defendants continued to deposit wastes from the mine at that location until May, 1951, when this dump also began to burn. The Fourth Street bank was 500 feet in length, 500 feet wide and 40 feet high. Extensive ramps to the dump were also made of breaker refuse material. Defendants are now using a new location as a dumping ground, between the Washington and the Fourth Street culm banks.

"The complaint in this case charged defendants with the creation of a nuisance resulting from the release of poisonous and obnxious gases. Sulphur dioxide was discharged from the burning dumps but the proofs relate to damages caused by hydrogen sulphide alone. Hydrogen sulphide may be generated in culm banks without fire and the evidence is that the gas in the atmosphere in the borough was emitted from two of defendants' waste dumps, beginning in 1948, viz: the Washington Street bank and the silt dam around the settling basin. * * * [U]nder the proofs, there was no intentional invasion of plaintiffs' use and enjoyment of their land and the defendants' conduct in the operation of their collieries was not negligent, reckless or ultrahazardous. * * * [D]efendants' mining operations did not create an 'absolute nuisance' in a legal sense and their liability therefore is not absolute, regardless of fault."

Prior to the year 1934 the Glen Alden Coal Company, owners, had ceased to mine coal in this area. The colliery in question was idle, the breaker was dismantled and minors in Taylor Borough were out of work. A committee of citizens of the Borough called upon the Glen Alden Coal Company requesting that the mines be reopened in order to aid the citizens. The Glen Alden Company agreed to this and leased coal lands comprising a continuous area of coal veins running from Taylor to Dickson City. When the defendants, in 1934, first began to operate the breaker a large culm bank close to the breaker was in existence and was then burning. In 1937 a new culm bank was started because of the fire in the old one and a conveyor was used to carry the culm to the new location. This was the Main Street bank and was used from 1937 to 1944. A new bank was then started known as the Washington Street bank, which was used from 1944 until October 1948. This bank was the same distance from the breaker as the Main Street bank, but in the opposite direction. In 1948 defendants commenced the construction of a settling basin in compliance with the State law concerning pollution of streams. During the construction the State inspectors approved. In 1949, six months after the Washington Street culm bank was discontinued, fire was discovered and defendants ceased using this breaker material for the settling basin. In the spring of 1949 walls in the settling basin ignited.

It is significant that plaintiffs purchased their home on June 23, 1948. It was close to the breaker, near the Washington Street bank.

Of the various gases emitted from the five culm banks, *hydrogen sulfide* was the gas which caused the damage. The record shows that this was emitted only from the Washington Street bank and the settling basin and from no others. Defendants did not know, and had no reason to be aware, that this particular gas would be so emitted and would have the effect upon the painted house. The record shows that the defendants were guilty of no negligence and used every known means to prevent damage or injury to adjoining properties.

Even if the reasonableness of the defendants' use of their property had been the *sole* consideration, there could be no recovery here. Chief Justice Frazer, in Harris v. Susquehanna Collieries Co., 304 Pa. 550, at page 558, 156 A. 159, at page 162, quoting from a previous case, said:

> "* * * As said in Pennsylvania Coal Co. v. Sanderson, 113 Pa. 126, 158, 6 A. 453, 464: 'The plaintiffs knew, when they purchased their property, that they were in a mining region. They were in a (district) born of mining operations, and which had become rich and populous as a result thereof.' * * * '

This statement has peculiar application here. The dwelling in question had been formerly used by a mine inspector who doubtless desired to be close to the breaker. When plaintiffs purchased the dwelling they were fully aware of the surrounding situation.

In Versailles Borough v. McKeesport Coal & Coke Co., 83 Pittsb. Leg.J. 379, Mr. Justice Musmanno, when a county judge, accurately encompassed the problem when he said:

> The plaintiffs are subject to an annoyance. This we accept, but it is an annoyance they have freely assumed. Because they desired and needed a residential proximity to their places of employment, they chose to found their abode here. It is not for them to repine; and it is probable that upon reflection they will, in spite of the annoyance which they suffer, still conclude that, after all, one's bread is more important than landscape or clear skies.
>
> Without smoke, Pittsburgh would have remained a very pretty *village*.

In Pregrad v. Ocean Coal Company, 14 Pa.Dist. & Co.R. 438, the syllabus reads:

> "A coal mining company is not responsible in trespass for damage caused to plaintiff's property by smoke, dust and gases from a burning 'slate dump' on defendant's property, the material having been placed on the dump in the course of operation of defendant's mine and the fire having originated from spontaneous combustion, if there is no known method by which such fires can be extinguished."

In Lauff v. Pittsburgh Coal Co., 10 Wash. Co. 161, Judge Cummins, in a unanimous opinion, in which Judge Howard W. Hughes (later a Justice of this Court) joined, held:

> "The general rule that one must use his own land so as not to injure that of another,—otherwise he is liable in damages, is subject to the exception that every man has the right to the natural use and enjoyment of his own property, and if whilst lawfully in such use and enjoyment, without negligence or malice on his part, an unavoidable loss occurs to his neighbor, it is *damnum absque injuria*, for the rightful use of one's own land may cause damage to another, without any legal wrong."

Chief Justice Maxey said in Hannum v. Gruber, 346 Pa. 417, 423, 31 A.2d 99, 102, "What is reasonable is sometimes a question of law, and at other times, a question of fact." Under the undisputed facts in this case the question is one of law.

The learned court below was in error when it ruled that this case was one of *absolute nuisance*. To compound the error it was ruled that it was "unreasonable and unwarranted" to process coal which was not connected with, or necessary to, the mining of coal "*underlying the surface [the coal breaker] occupies*". The coal leases to defendants did not limit the operation to coal under the breaker. On the contrary, the leases covered coal veins extending from the owner's land in Taylor through that borough to Dickson City. As the coal in this entire area is grnated we see no reason why it cannot be *processed on any portion of the land leased*.

The Superior Court correctly refused to adopt the doctrine of *absolute nuisance*. It cited the Restatement. Judge Hirt said: "* * * Section 822 of the Restatement, Torts, sets forth *some* of the tests for determining liability resulting from a private nuisance. * * *" (Italics supplied.)

It is our view that Section 822 comprehensively encompasses the *entire* statement of principles of liability and is not restricted merely to *some* of them....

In applying the rule of the Restatement, Torts, Sec. 822(d), it is evident the invasion of plaintiffs' land was clearly *not intentional*. And even if it were, for the reasons above stated, it was not unreasonable. On the contrary, since the emission of gases was not caused by any act of defendants and arose merely from the normal and customary use of their land without negligence, recklessness or ultrahazardous conduct, it was wholly *unintentional*, and no liability may therefore be imposed upon defendants.

The judgment is reversed and is here entered in favor of defendants *non obstante veredicto*.

JONES, JUSTICE.

I dissent. The majority opinion works a denial of the plaintiffs' right to a day in court on a material and crucial issue of fact. On the majority's *ratio decidendi* (which was broached for the first time by defendants' counsel in the Superior Court and which that court rejected), the plaintiffs are at least entitled to an opportunity to litigate what has now become an essentially controlling issue of fact as to whether the defendants' conduct which caused the damage was intentional.

MUSMANNO, JUSTICE (dissenting).

The plaintiffs in this case, Joseph J. Waschak and Agnes Waschak, brother and sister, own a modest home in Taylor, Pennsylvania, a town of 7,000 inhabitants in the anthracite region of the northeastern part of the State. The defendants, Robert Y. Moffat and W. K. Moffat, co-partners trading as Moffat Coal Company, lease and operate a coal breaker in this town. They also have under lease coal properties in Taylor, Scranton, Dickson City and Lackawanna Township. The coal obtained from these properties is processed and made ready for marketing at the Taylor breaker.

In the preparation process the coal undergoes a cleansing process known as the Menzies treatment. A specific gravity is built up with pumps or pressure whereby the lighter material floats on the surface and is drawn off as marketable coal. The impurities—slate, rock and coal with sulphur—being of heavier weight, sink to the bottom and become waste or refuse. This refuse is hauled away and, when piled in one location, the resulting heap is known as a culm pile or bank. These banks sometimes attain mountainous proportions. In time the accumulated refuse undergoes a mysterious transformation and it generates various types of gases, mostly of a foul, insidious and pervasive nature. One of these gases, the culprit in this case, is hydrogen sulfide. It is an odoriferous gas. One of the consulting chemists testified at the trial:

> Hydrogen sulfide gas is a very odoriferous gas. It can be detected by the nose in a concentration of less than one part per million. It is also a very poisonous gas. A concentration of hydrogen sulfide as permitted by state labor departments is of the same order as that permitted by those departments for hydrocyanic gases. The effects are dependent on the concentration. That is, in high concentration the one part per thousand say, it is almost instantly fatal. Lower concentrations cause chronic poisoning, and continuous exposure to very low concentrations causes malaise, nausea, headaches. In some cases it causes shortness of breath.'

In 1948 the plaintiffs painted their house with a white paint. Some time later the paint began to turn to a light colored brown, then it changed to a grayish tint, once it burst into a silvery sheen, and then, as if this were its last dying gasp, the house suddenly assumed a blackish cast, the blackness deepened and intensified until now it is a "scorched black." The plaintiffs attribute this chameleon performance of their house to the hydrogen sulfide emanating from the defendants' culm deposits in the town—all in residential areas. The hydrogen sulfide, according to the plaintiffs, not only assaults the paint of the house but it snipes at the silverware, bath tub fixtures and the bronze handles of the doors, forcing them, respectively, into black, yellowish-brown and "tarnished-looking" tints.

Because of these and other complaints, the plaintiffs have charged the defendants with maintaining a nuisance. They sued the defendants in trespass, the case was tried before a court and jury, and on October 9, 1951, the jury returned a verdict in favor of the plaintiffs in the sum of $1,250. The defendants moved for a new trial and judgment n.o.v. The lower Court refused both motions and entered judgment on the verdict. The defendants appealed to the Superior Court which affirmed the judgment, and the case came to us because of the important legal questions involved. It appears that 25 other cases are at issue awaiting this decision.

The Majority of this Court has now reversed the decision of the Superior Court and set at naught the verdict of the jury with the declaration that the defendants are not liable because the emission of gases from the various culm banks "was not caused by any act of defendants and arose merely from the normal and customary use of their land without negligence, recklessness or ultrahazardous conduct," that "it was wholly unintentional, and no liability may therefore be imposed". But it is not necessary in these cases to prove recklessness....

The evidence here does not show any *necessity* on the part of the defendants to locate the culm banks in the very midst of the residential areas of Taylor.

The Majority Opinion explores the law of nuisance ably but does not indicate whether the circumstances here make out a case of nuisance, although it does say that the lower Court erred in ruling that this case was one of absolute nuisance. My opinion is that there can be no doubt that the defendants were operating an actionable nuisance. The record which consists of 600 printed pages, overwhelmingly establishes this fact. The poisonous gases lifting from the defendant's culm banks were destructive of property, detrimental to health and disruptive of the social life of the town.

There was evidence that the poisonous hydrogen sulfide was of such intensity that the inhabitants compelled to breathe it suffered from headaches, throat irritation, inability to sleep, coughing, lightheadedness, nausea and stomach ailments. These grave effects of the escaping gas reached such proportions that the citizens of Taylor held protest meetings and demanded that the municipal authorities take positive action to curb the gaseous invasion.

Did the release of the gases from the defendants' culm banks constitute under the law a nuisance? Nearly every witness testifying for the plaintiff as to the nature of the gas rising from the culm banks declared that it had the odor of rotten eggs. Otto John Zang, the town druggist, testified that the gas was like a nocturnal prowler that would come to his window while he was sleeping and wake him up in the middle of the night:

"Q. When did you first notice the existence of this odor to any appreciable degree? A. The summer of 1949.

"Q. And will you describe what the odor smelled like? Describe the odor. A. It smells of rotten eggs.

"Q. And was it a light odor? A. A very heavy odor.

"Q. And did it seem to be noticeable or only slightly noticeable? A. So noticeable that it will give you a headache.

* * *

"Q. After you had been exposed to this particular odor in Taylor for an evening, let's say, what effect if any does it have on you? A. It made me sick to my stomach and gave me a headache which is very hard to relieve. Unless you get into fresh air the headache persists.

"Q. And what experience have you had at night with reference to sleep. A. It wakes me up."

Gretchen Houser, high school principal, was asked how the odors affected her and she replied:

"Why, they give me a headache very often when it is particularly bad on a rainy day or a foggy day or if the wind is just in the right direction to point it at me. I cough and have a terrible headache, and morning after morning I get awake with a headache."

Miss Houser was asked what she observed and she replied:

"Well, on rainy days it was a very much worse odor. At all times it was like rotten eggs. At night it is usually worse, and frequently we have to get up and close the windows and sleep in an air-tight room."

Rev. G. Wesley Pippen, minister in the town, was asked to describe the odor in the air. He described it as follows:

"It has a smell of sulphur, and I think probably the rotten egg smell would correctly describe it."

Several of the witnesses testified that because of the rotten egg smell which entered their parlors and sitting rooms, it was difficult to entertain visitors. This statement could well qualify as the prize understatement of the case.

It must always be kept in mind that these culm banks were not mole hills. The Main Street dump measured 1,100 feet in length, 650 feet in width and 40 feet in height. If these dimensions were applied to a ship, one can visualize the size of the vessel and what would be the state of its odoriferousness if it was loaded stem to stern with rotten eggs. And that is only one of the dumps. There is another dump at Washington Street and, consequently, another ship of rotten eggs. Its dimensions are 800 feet by 750 feet by 50 feet. A third dump measures 500 feet by 500 feet by 40 feet. Then the defendants constructed a silt dam with the same rotten-egg-smelling materials.

I do not think that there can be any doubt that the constant smell of rotten eggs constitutes a nuisance. If such a condition is not recognized by the law, then the law is the only body that does not so recognize it. . . .

This Court well defined legal nuisance in Kramer v. Pittsburgh Coal Co., 341 Pa. 379, 380, 19 A.2d 362, 363:

> The term (nuisance) signifies in law such a use of property or such a course of conduct as, irrespective of actual trespass against others or of malicious or actual criminal intent, transgresses the just restrictions upon use or conduct which the proximity of other persons or property in civilized communities imposes upon what would otherwise be rightful freedom. In legal phraseology, the term 'nuisance' is applied to *that class of wrongs that arise from the unreasonable, unwarrantable, or unlawful use by a person of his own property*, real or personal, or from his own improper, indecent, or unlawful personal conduct, working an obstruction or injury to a right of another, or of the public, *and producing such material annoyance, inconvenience, discomfort or hurt that the law will* presume a consequent damage."

Whether the facts in the case at bar constitute an actionable nuisance is not a question of law. It is one of fact for a jury to determine. In Gavigan v. Atlantic Refining Co., 186 Pa. 604, 612, 40 A. 834, 835, we said:

> Whether it was a nuisance, and the damage therefrom real and substantial, the court could do no other than submit, on the evidence, to the jury. The defendant's plant was not a nuisance per se. Whether it was a nuisance at all depended wholly on the proof. Whether plaintiff's evidence established the fact could not be determined by the court. To establish that fact it was not necessary he should prove the business of defendant was carried on recklessly, or was not properly managed. *It was sufficient to show that defendant selfishly carried on a lawful business in a populous neighborhood greatly to plaintiff's injury*. It comes under that line of cases commencing with [Pottstown] Gas Co. v. Murphy, 39 Pa. 257, where it was held that the question was not one of negligence or no negligence, but of nuisance or no nuisance.'

There is a golden rule in law as well as in morals and it reads: '*Sic utere tuo ut alienum non laedas*.' The defendants oppose this maxim with the one that every person has the right to a lawful, reasonable and natural use of his land. But it is entirely possible and in fact desirable that these two maxims live together in peace and harmony. The plaintiffs in this case do not question that the defendants have the right to mine coal and process it, but is it a natural and reasonable use of land to deposit poisonous refuse in residential areas when it can be deposited elsewhere? Certainly the defendants may lawfully operate a breaker in Taylor, and whatever noises, dust and commotion result from the breaker operation are inconveniences which the plaintiff and other

Taylor inhabitants must accept as part of the life of a mining community. But the disposition of the poisonous refuse of a mining operation does not fall within the definition of lawful and normal use of land. Nor is the offending debris in this case a byproduct alone of the coal mined in Taylor. Much of the refuse results from coal brought in from distant areas. The cleansing of *that* coal puts the defendants in the category of mills and factories which are unquestionably liable for nuisances created by their operation.

The Majority states that the "emission of offensive odors, noises, fumes, violations, etc., must be weighed against the utility of the operation." In this respect, the Majority Opinion does me the honor of quoting from an Opinion I wrote when I was a member of the distinguished Court of Common Pleas of Allegheny County. Versailles Borough v. McKeesport Coal & Coke Co., 83 Pittsb.Leg.J. 379. That was an equity case where the plaintiffs sought an injunction against the defendant coal company for maintaining a burning gob pile which emitted smoke. The coal mine was located in the very heart of an industrialized area which contained factories, mills, garbage dumps, incinerators and railroads, all producing their own individualized smoke and vapors so that it could not be said that the discomforts of the inhabitants were due exclusively to the operation of the coal mine. Furthermore, after hearings lasting one month I found that the operation of the mine in no way jeopardized the health of the inhabitants:

> Of course, if the continued operation of this mine were a serious menace to the health or lives of those who reside in its vicinity, there would be another question before us, but there is no evidence in this case to warrant the assumption that the health of anyone is being imperiled."

In the instant case the exact contrary is true. The health of the town of Taylor *is* being imperiled. And then also, as well stated by the lower Court in the present litigation, "Many factors may lead a chancellor to grant or deny injunctive relief which are not properly involved in an action brought to recompense one for injury to his land * * * A denial of relief by a court of equity is not always precedent for denying redress by way of damages."

Even so, there is a vast difference between smoke which beclouds the skies and gas which is so strong that it peels the paint from houses. I did say in the Versailles case, "One's bread is more important than landscape or clear skies." But in the preservation of human life, even bread is preceded by water, and even water must give way to breathable air. Experimentation and observation reveal that one can live as long as 60 or 70 days without food; one can keep the lamp of life burning 3 or 4 days without water, but the wick is snuffed out in a minute or two in the absence of breathable air. For decades Pittsburgh was known as the "Smoky City" and without that smoke in its early days Pittsburgh indeed would have remained a "pretty village." But with scientific progress in the development of smoke-consuming devices, added to the use of smokeless fuel, Pittsburgh's skies have cleared, its progress has been phenomenal and the bread of its workers is whiter, cleaner, and sweeter.

On September 8, 1939, this Court, speaking through Chief Justice Kephart, handed down the monumental decision in the case of Summit Hotel Co. v. National Broadcasting Co., 336 Pa. 182, 8 A.2d 302, 124 A.L.R. 968. Chief Justice Kephart there said: 336 Pa. at page 189, 8 A.2d at page 305.

> In cases of trespass for nuisance, the person responsible may be unable, no matter how careful, to avoid injury to the lands of another but, again, he knows that injury may result from the nature of his activities regardless of care. *Under such circumstances he also assumes the risk*. The responsibility for injury lies in creating or maintaining the harmful condition.
>
> In all of these illustrations, the person responsible has, or should have, *prior knowledge of the probable consequences, where the act done, or the instrumentality employed, possesses potentialities of serious harm*.

There can be no doubt that the defendants were thoroughly aware of the probable consequences of their discarding operations before the plaintiffs suffered the damage of which they complain in this litigation. Mrs. Waschak testified that the Washington–Church Street dump was giving off poisonous fumes before the defendants began the erection of the silt dam:

> Q. Now then, at that time when you bought this property on Main Street in Taylor in June, 1948, had the Moffatt Coal Company constructed this silt dam? A. No, sir.
>
> Q. Did you notice anything with reference to that at the time you purchased the property? A. They were just starting to excavate it. * * *
>
> Q. And at that time the Washington Street dump was giving off the fumes, was it? A. Yes, sir.

All of the defendants' refuse dumps have turned into burning mountains. The Main Street dump began to burn in 1944, the Washington–Church Street dump caught fire in 1948, the Fourth Street dump broke into flame in May, 1951, and the silt dam ignited shortly after its construction, and is still burning. It would be difficult to imagine a more effective and continuing notice to the defendants of the nuisance they were creating than the appearance of these volcanic torches, each pouring out hydrogen sulfide of promised disaster to the town.

Even if the rights of the plaintiffs were to be considered by Restatement Rules they would still be entitled to recover under the proposition that the defendants were so well informed of the probable harmful effects of their operation that their actions could only be regarded as an intentional invasion of the rights of the plaintiff. Section 825 of the Restatement of Torts declares:

An invasion of another's interest in the use and enjoyment of land is intentional when the actor

(a) acts for the purpose of causing it; or

(b) knows that it is resulting or is substantially certain to result from his conduct."

The record amply proves that the defendants were at least "substantially certain" that their burning culm deposits would invade the plaintiffs' interest in the use and enjoyment of their land.

If there were *no* other way of disposing of the coal refuse, a different question might have been presented here, but the defendants produced no evidence that they could not have deposited the debris in places removed from the residential districts in Taylor. Certainly, many of the strip-mining craters which uglify the countryside in the areas close to Taylor could have been utilized by the defendants. They chose, however, to use the residential sections of Taylor because it was cheaper to pile the culm there than to haul it away into less populous territory.

This was certainly an unreasonable and selfish act in no way indispensably associated with the operation of the breaker. It brought greater profits to the defendants but at the expense of the health and the comfort of the other landowners in the town who are also entitled to the pursuit of happiness.

Practically every one who writes on the subject of indirect invasion of property rights expatiates on the confusion in the cases, the uncertainty of the authorities, the variation of the precedents and the farrago of the dicta. But in this land of supposed chaos a polestar guides the way, and that is the test of reasonableness. Law is intended to be the distillation of reason applied to the world of realities. No formalistic dicta or involved formula convinces like pragmatic proof. In Hannum v. Gruber, 346 Pa. 417, 423, 31 A.2d 99, 102, this Court said:

> It has been said that a 'fair test as to whether a business lawful in itself, or a particular use of property, constitutes a nuisance, is the reasonableness or unreasonableness of conducting the business or making the use of the property complained of in the particular locality an in the manner and under the circumstances of the case.' 46 C.J. 655. It has also been said: 'Whether the use is reasonable generally depends upon many and varied facts. No hard and fast rule controls the subject. A use that would be reasonable under one set of facts might be unreasonable under another. What is reasonable is sometimes a question of law, and at other times, a question of fact. No one particular fact is conclusive, but the inference is to be drawn from all the facts proved whether the controlling fact exists that the use is unreasonable.' 46 C.J. 656.

It is because of the many fluctuating factors in the cases themselves that the decisions do not seem to be uniform. In point of juridical history, however, they do follow a pattern of wisdom and justice. No one will deny that the defendants are entitled to earn profits in the operation of their breaker, but is it reasonable that they shall so conduct that business as to poison the very lifestream of existence? Is it not reasonable to suppose that if hydrogen sulfide emanating from culm banks can strip paint from wood and steel that it will also deleteriously affect the delicate membranes of the throat and lungs? . . .

I would affirm the decision of the Superior Court.

Notes

1. *Nuisance law. Waschak* provides a summary of nuisance law as it now exists on the books, along with the related law of strict liability for particularly hazardous activities. Why exactly was the defendant's conduct here not a nuisance, given the harm that ensued? Compare this ruling with *Bryant*. What weight does the court seem give to priority in time in deciding which land use to favor? Ultimately (and as best we can tell), what sort of land-use baseline does the court establish for determining causation?

The issue of priority in time—which landowner began operations first—continues to arise in nuisance law. The general rule today is that priority in time is one of many factors to take into account in determining the reasonableness of any particular land use. The factor takes on greater weight when both of the land uses appear reasonable and neither party can reduce the conflict by making relatively easy land-use changes. The majority in *Waschak*, of course, was inclined to give temporal priority greater weight since the mining operation came first. One wonders, though, whether the court with its pro-mining sentiments might have taken a different view if the homeowner had been first on the scene.

2. *The many meanings of intent*. A new legal element that arises in this ruling has to do with the defendant's intent. In nuisance law generally, a defendant is said to act intentionally simply if he intended to do what he did and his conduct was not accidental. It is not necessary to show that the defendant intended to harm the plaintiff. How does the court here apply the idea of intent? According to the court in *Waschak,* what must a landowner intend before his conduct is deemed intentional? In order to answer, you'll need to pay close attention to the court's comments about the defendants' knowledge of the likely harm, and also whether or not the harm was avoidable. Some of the relevant facts are disputed between the majority and the dissent, but the basic facts are shared. The question at issue for the justices was how the court ought to define intent. Should it be enough that the defendant acted volitionally rather than by accident? Must the defendant have known or had reason to know about the ensuing harm? Does a defendant act with intent when there are no feasible alternatives? And when deciding whether the harm was avoidable, how widely do we view the defendant's land-use options? Note that the dissent considered the possibility that the mining company could have put its wastes somewhere else; in his view the harm was avoidable. The majority accepted the fact that the wastes were located where they were, and merely considered whether the mining company could have halted the gas emissions from the existing waste piles. For the majority the harms were unavoidable. On this point, recall the opinion in *Bryant v. Lefever*, where the court said the plaintiff could have

avoided the harm by putting his chimney in a different location, even though the chimney was built long before the land-use conflict arose.

3. *Who decides: law versus fact.* A telling feature of this prominent ruling was the court's conclusion that the ultimate issue in the case was one of law, not fact. The court, accordingly, proceeded to make its own decision about liability and to substitute it for the trial court's ruling. The practical effect of this conclusion was to remove the jury as finder of fact and substitute judges instead. The jury was plainly sympathetic to the landowner plaintiffs; the judges, in contrast, sympathized more with the defendant mining companies. By redefining the issue as law rather than fact the outcome of the case changed; process was more important that substantive law.

This maneuver by the court was a rather common one in the nineteenth century, as the law made way for industrialization. According to historians, one of the legal shifts that allowed more intensive activities to take place on landscapes was the decision by many courts to take power away from juries—first by confining juries to issues of fact (they formerly also resolved issue of law), and then by turning key issues into questions of law for the court to resolve. These steps put key land-use disputes into the safer (though still somewhat unpredictable) hands of industry-leaning judges.

An extreme example of this power shift from jury to judge, taking place mostly in the twentieth century, unfolded in the coal regions of Kentucky. The Kentucky Supreme Court, strongly linked with the coal industry, essentially eliminated all roles of local juries in passing upon the legitimacy of surface-damaging activities done by strip miners. Both the interpretation of mining deeds and their application in particular cases became issues of law for judges to decide—and thus subject to being overturned by higher courts should a local judge fail to decide a case the right way. The story can be followed in Akers v. Baldwin, 736 S.W.2d 294 (Ky. 1987) and Ward v. Harding, 860 S.W.2d 280 (Ky. 1993).

According to most courts today, it is up to the finder of fact to decide whether a given activity is or is not a nuisance. Still, the issue of law-versus-fact looms large in natural resources law. Particularly in states with governments that strongly favor particular local industries, lawmakers often protect their home industries by shifting key liability issues into the "law" category, thereby diminishing the chance that a sympathetic jury will impose liability on the industry. Note that the court in *Bryant v. Lefever* also overturned a jury decision in favor of the plaintiff, but it did so in a slightly different manner: It viewed the liability issue as an issue of fact but then overturned the ruling on the debatable ground that no evidence supported the jury's factual finding.

4. *Reasonable use VI: the conflict with* sic utere. The do-no-harm rule of property law is often viewed as a limit on what property owners can do; as a curtailment of their use rights. And of course it is, in effect. But the rule is also the foundation of property rights. Without it, private property would hardly exist. Landowner A owns property only to the extent that he can draw upon police and courts to keep other people from bothering him. Thus, in a pragmatic sense, A's property rights are determined by the legal remedies available to him to halt harmful disruptions. One legal remedy is

the law of trespass, which protects against physical invasions. Another is the amorphous, shifting body of nuisance law (the word nuisance comes from old French, and merely means "harm"). Nuisance law protects a landowner against indirect interferences with her activities. Without nuisance law a landowner's rights would be much less.

We might be inclined to view a decision such as *Waschak* as pro-property in that it allows the landowner-defendant to engage in intensive land uses, subject only to minimal constraint. But notice the effect the ruling has on the landowning plaintiff: it diminishes the owner's ability to complain about interferences. If we view the *right to use* land intensively as the key attribute of ownership (as many pro-industry people are inclined to do), then *Waschak* does enhance property rights. If instead we view the *right to remain undisturbed* in domestic activities as the key attribute of ownership (as many observers are inclined to do, following the lead of lawmakers late in the eighteenth century), then *Waschak* represents just the opposite—a grave abridgment of property rights. This latter interpretation was the one embraced by the dissenting judges in the 1805 ruling in *Palmer v. Mulligan*, noted above.

The basic issue for lawmakers at all times is to decide what land- and resource-uses will be deemed acceptable and which will not. The issue is necessarily one of public policy and cannot be determined by logic alone. Presumably the issue is best resolved by thinking about the good of society generally. Courts have phrased the issue in many ways: What lands uses are ordinary and common? Which ones cause harm and which ones do not? What is reasonable use? Even when we have a sense of what is reasonable we run into another big challenge. Ideas about reasonableness change over time. How should we accommodate this evolution in the case of longstanding land uses? In *Waschak* the miners' activities might well have appeared socially reasonable when begun but they were not reasonable in the minds of many people years later when the law suit was commenced. Is it fair to judge the miners' decision to locate their waste piles where they did using standards that emerged years later?

A final note: Many students are likely to agree with Judge Musmanno's dissent in *Waschak* rather than the majority opinion. Note, though, that Musmanno does little other than apply the basic ideas set forth in *Bryant v. Lefever* using different values. He, too, makes use of a "definition of lawful and normal use of land," as if the words had some objective meaning. He goes on to assert that the "polestar" is "the test of reasonableness," again on the assumption that the word had some magic content.

5. *Lateral and subjacent support.* Landowners have a legal right to object if excavation or other activities by a neighbor removes support laterally from land so as to cause the land to collapse or leave it unable to support structures. Viewed from the other side, a landowner has no right to excavate or use land in ways that cause cave-ins of adjacent land. The liability is typically absolute and requires no showing of negligence. The protection, though, only extends to land in its natural condition. It does not protect land that caves in only because of structures on it. In addition, a landowner can excavate if neighboring land is protected by a retaining wall. Beyond this strict liability, landowners in most states can be liable if they act

negligently in excavating in a way that harms neighboring structures. These common law rules are often changed in urban areas to require lateral support for adjacent buildings. As for subjacent support, the issue typically arises only when ownership of the surface is severed from ownership of the subsurface. Typically, owners of the subsurface are obligated to maintain support of the surface in its natural condition. The rule is often changed by deeds and mineral leases and by state statutes regulating mining activities. In many states, landowners who pump groundwater can be liable also in negligence if their pumping causes land subsidence on neighboring lands. The issue is considered in Joseph William Singer, INTRODUCTION TO PROPERTY 128–31 (2001).

B. REASONABLE USE

We turn now to dig a bit further into the idea of reasonable use as a "polestar" to use in adjudicating disputes among landowners. The idea, as we've already seen, is very much at the heart of natural resources law generally, and applies to discrete natural resource rights as well as to land itself.

Recall that when the reasonable use doctrine (and its verbal synonyms) arose, it was created by courts so as to authorize more intensive land use practices, ones that the doctrine in effect allowed landowners to continue, even though the practices harmed other landowners and perhaps communities at large. Reasonable use, that is, was offered essentially as a *defense* when a landowner was sued for imposing harm on a neighbor. The following article excerpt dates from the era when legal scholars focused directly on this issue and probed its fundamentals (as shall we). Scholars at the time could see clearly that property rights existed on both sides of this issue. At least some of them knew that disputes could not be resolved without making important decisions about the kinds of landscapes that society wanted.

The following article, though dated, usefully probes this idea of reasonable use and the various ways we might define it. The author also considers such terms as "ordinary" and "natural" uses of land, to test whether these terms are more useful in resolving conflicts. The author, as you will detect, is a strong supporter of the reasonable use idea, and is prone to defend it against the various alternatives.

REASONABLE USE OF ONE'S OWN PROPERTY AS A JUSTIFICATION FOR DAMAGE TO A NEIGHBOR

Jeremiah Smith

17 COLUM. L. REV. 383 (1917).

Suppose that a landowner, by acts done on his own land, has inflicted damage on his neighbor's land, or has substantially impaired the latter's beneficial use of his land. Suppose also that the landowner, when made a defendant in a suit at law by his neighbor to recover damages, justifies on the ground that he has only been making a reasonable use of his own land. This defense involves two points: 1. That defendant has a right, within reasonable limitations, to use his own land in a manner which may inflict actual damage on his neighbor. 2. That defendant, in the case at bar, has not exceeded the limits of this right.[1]

It is common to speak of a landowner's right as "absolute". "But his right to the use of his land is not absolute. It is qualified by the right of adjacent owners to the beneficial use and enjoyment of their property." Professor Freund says: "The nature of real estate as a subject of property makes it impossible that the ownership of it should be as absolute as that of many kinds of personal property. The enjoyment of land is in many respects dependent upon the condition of other and especially neighboring estates. The common law recognizes in consequences of this dependence certain natural rights which landowners have against each other, relating to the purity of the air, to lateral and subjacent support, and to the benefit of natural waters." A landowner's "so-called absolute legal control of his own soil" is "far from being unlimited." It is obvious that unless the rights of individual landowners are modified and limited they must be frequently in conflict one with another. No landowner can always do as he pleases, except by preventing other landowners from doing as they please. "The rule governing the rights of adjacent landowners in the use of their property, seeks an adjustment of conflicting interests through a reconciliation by compromise, each surrendering something of his absolute freedom so that both may live." "The convenience of such a rule may be indicated by calling it a rule of give and take, live and let live."

The question of legal regulation of conflicting rights is not confined to rights in regard to the use of land, but extends to all cases of conflicting rights as to other matters or subjects. An able writer has said: "The due regulation and subordination of conflicting rights constitute the chief part of the science of law." And the author adds: "It is impossible to give any rule applicable to all cases which may arise except the general one that, whenever damage is caused to one man by another, the law, in deciding which shall bear the loss, is governed by principles of expediency modified by public sentiment."

What use is reasonable, as between neighboring landowners in any particular case, is said to be ordinarily a question of fact; to be submitted to a jury, unless the case is so clear that only one decision can be reached by twelve honest and reasonable men. As to the considerations which should be weighed by the jury in passing upon the question of fact, the

1. Does the discussion of the right of reasonable user of land fall under "property" or "torts"?

The question is "whether a particular act * * * constitutes a violation of the obligations of vicinage". Andrews, C. J., Booth v. Rome etc. R. R. (1893) 140 N. Y. 267, at p. 276, 35 N. E. 592.

"* * * the limitations imposed on the use of land * * * are all resolvable into the law of neighborhood." Rankine, Law of Land—Ownership in Scotland (3rd ed.) 327.

"The detailed illustration of the rule in Rylands v. Fletcher, as governing the mutual claims and duties of adjacent landowners, belongs to the law of property rather than to the subject of this work." Pollock, Torts (10th ed.) 509. See 1 Bohlen's Cases on Torts, Preface III.

judge will probably give instructions in very general terms, in substance like one of the three following statements:

1. "In determining the question of reasonableness, the effect of the use upon the interests of both parties, the benefits derived from it by one, the injury caused by it to the other, and all the circumstances affecting either of them, are to be considered."

2. All the circumstances must be taken into consideration, "the importance of the use to the owner as well as the extent of the damage to be inflicted upon his neighbor, and the rights of the parties are to be adjusted in a practical way, the question being whether or not the proposed use is a reasonable use under all circumstances."

3. The cause of action, if any, lies in the excess of the damage beyond what is considered reasonable, after taking into account the circumstances of time and place, and quantity of annoyance, and the relation of adjoining properties to each other."

It is generally admitted that it is impossible to frame a rule so definite that its application will instantly solve all cases of conflicting rights. No rule of law can be laid down which "will furnish a standard so definite and certain that by it every state of facts will be automatically settled." "The respective rights and liabilities of adjoining landowners cannot be determined in advance by a mathematical line or a general formula." As was said in regard to so-called "private nuisances.": "No hard and fast rule controls the subject, for a use that is reasonable under one set of facts would be unreasonable under another." "Whether a given use is reasonable or not is a question of fact depending on many and varied facts."

But, conceding the impossibility of framing a definite and universally applicable rule, still there are some propositions as to specific points which are generally recognized as correct, whether you call them propositions of law, or of fact, or of "curial fact." Mr. Rankine says that "certain rules have been gathered by experience to aid in attaining a consistent and equitable reconciliation between the seemingly conflicting and really identical interests of neighboring landholders." Mr. Wiel, speaking of interference with a stream, says: "What is such unreasonable interference has become defined by repeated decisions of particular cases, crystallizing into some rules." Moreover, "the questions of fact which arise in determining whether a use is reasonable are limited by certain rules of law." Thus, as to the use of a stream by an upper riparian proprietor, "a permanent diversion of a substantial portion of the water, to the detriment of an owner below, cannot be found to be reasonable, although it may be convenient and profitable for the diverter. It is an invasion of a legal right.

[The author next turned to various sources of confusion on this issue, including the confusion arising from the words "damage" and "injury," which were commonly used in ways that differed from the legal definitions of *damnum* and *injuria*.]

Another, and a prolific, source of confusion consists in assuming that the maxim *sic utere tuo ut alienum non lædas* furnishes, *per se*, a solution to all legal problems respecting reasonable user. It is not uncommon for judges to decide important cases without practically giving any reason save the quotation of this maxim, which is evidently regarded by the court as affording, by its very terms, a satisfactory *ration decidendi*. Yet in the vast majority of cases this use of the phrase is utterly fallacious. And its use, being mistaken for a solution, has the effect of preventing a thorough investigation.

Obviously, the maxim cannot be applied without first ascertaining the meaning of *tuo, alienum*, and *loedas*.

If by *lædas* be meant damage, the maximum is untrue as a legal proposition; since the legal exercise of a right is often accompanied with the infliction of positive harm upon another. If by *lædas* be meant injury in the literal sense of an unlawful act (*in* and *jus*), an act in violation of another's legal right, then the maxim is a mere truism or identical proposition. It does not tell us what is a legal right or what constitutes a violation of a legal right. "This maxim paraphrased means no more than: 'Thou shalt not interfere with the legal rights of another by the commission of an unlawful act;' or 'Injury from an unlawful act is actionable.' This affords no aid in this case in determining whether the act complained of is actionable, that is, unlawful. It amounts to no more than the truism: An unlawful act is unlawful. This is a mere begging of the question; it assumes the very point in controversy, and cannot be taken as a *ratio decidendi.*"

"The maxim, *Sic utere tuo ut alienum non lædas*, is mere verbiage. A party may damage the property of another where the law permits; and he may not where the law prohibits; so that the maxim can never be applied till the law is ascertained; and, when it is, the maxim is superfluous." "The maxim, * * * is no help to decision, as it cannot be applied till the decision is made."

"While, therefore, *sic utere tuo etc.*, may be a very good moral precept, it is utterly useless as a legal maxim. It determines no right; it defines no obligation." "Such a maxim can be of no assistance in determining the primary question of liability." "Inasmuch as the exercise of any right of property by the owner may injure another, the Latin maxim does not help to a solution; the real question is what injury to another is, and what is not permissible."

Judge Holmes says: "Decisions * * * often are presented as hollow deductions from empty general propositions like *sic utere tuo ut alienum non lædas*, which teaches nothing but a benevolent yearning." In 1879, a correspondent of the Solicitor's Journal went so far as to call this maxim "an ancient and solemn imposter." . . .

A third source of confusion consists in the employment of the word "reasonable" in two different meanings.

Reasonable user may mean (1) reasonable from the defendant's point of view, i.e., reasonable if the interest of the defendant alone is to be regarded, without reference to the damage thereby caused to adjacent owners. Or, it may mean (2) reasonable, not solely in view of defendant's interest and convenience, but if considered also in view of the interest of surrounding landowners.

The second meaning is the correct one when applied to a case where a defendant attempts to justify a *prima facie* tort on the ground that he was making a reasonable use of his own property; *i.e.*, where defendant alleges that, in doing the act which resulted in damage to plaintiff, he was not acting in excess of his right to make a reasonable use of his own property.

"For the purpose of ascertaining what is reasonable, both sides of the question must be looked at." It is not enough to ask: Is the defendant using his property in what would be a reasonable manner if he had no neighbor, *i.e.*, if he were the only person whose interest could be affected? "The question is, is he using it reasonably, having regard to the fact that he has a neighbor?" A use is not reasonable, if it unreasonably prejudices the rights of others. "In determining the question of reasonableness, the effect of the use upon the interests of both parties, the benefits derived from it by one, the injury caused by it to the other, and all the circumstances affecting either of them, are to be considered." "We concede", said Loomis, J., "that the law will not interfere with a use that is reasonable. But the question of reasonable use is to be determined in view of the rights of others." . . .

. . .

It will be asked, what are the tests or modes of distinguishing superior rights. As in regard to some other topics, specific instances can be given, but it is not easy to generalize. It is, however, possible to assert (negatively) that certain circumstances do *not* furnish a legal test of superiority or inferiority. Thus, the fact that *A's* tract of land is of larger size, or of greater absolute value, or produces a larger rental, than *B's* adjoining tract, does not *per se* confer upon *A* a right of user superior to *B's* right. Still less does it confer on *A* a right to make such use of his land as will practically prevent any beneficial user whatever on the part of *B*.

The above question as to the test of a superior right is, in reality, a part or branch of the larger question as to the general tests of reasonable or unreasonable user. And, as has been said on an earlier page, it does not seem possible to formulate a definite rule or test of universal application, a rule that will automatically solve all cases. Moreover, the answer to the larger question is complicated (made specially difficult) by the fact that the same special considerations do not carry the same weight in all states alike. In some states, a particular mode of user will be preferred to other modes; while, in some other states, the latter modes would be deemed paramount to the former. Some tests have been suggested which are claimed to be applicable in all states alike. Other tests or preferences are suggested, which it is admitted prevail in only a part of the states.

Two tests have been prominently suggested, as applicable in all states alike, *viz.*: ordinary or common user; natural user.

As to the test of "natural" user. The prominence of this term in the present connection is largely due to its use by Lord Cairns, in *Rylands v. Fletcher*. The precise question decided in that case was whether the defendant, in building a reservoir and allowing water to accumulate therein, was acting at his own peril and hence was absolutely liable, irrespective of negligence, for damage caused by the escape of the water. In the first paragraph where Lord Cairns employs the term "natural user", it might be possible to argue that it should be interpreted as synonymous with ordinary user. But in a later paragraph the term is obviously employed in a sense different from "ordinary". Lord Cairns there says: "On the other hand if the Defendants, not stopping at the natural use of their close, had desired to use it for any purpose which I may term a non-natural use, for the purpose of introducing into the close that which in its natural condition was not in or upon it, for the purpose of introducing water either above or below ground in quantities and in a manner not the result of any work or operation on or under the land,—" then the defendants were acting at their own peril and would be liable for damaging results.

The employment of the term "natural" in this connection, with the interpretation thus given it by Lord Cairns, has not met with universal approval.

In *Brown v. Collins*, Doe, J., states specific objections to it (as well as to the so-called Blackburn rule, which is endorsed by Lord Cairns).

Under the "natural" test, as interpreted by Lord Cairns, the erection of a wooden building on land where there were no trees, would be a non-natural use, undertaken at the peril of the owner.

We think that the term "natural" as defined by Lord Cairns is not a satisfactory test of the reasonableness of the use of land. And, if the term "natural" is not employed in Lord Cairns' meaning, it would often, if not generally, be regarded as synonymous with "ordinary".

As to the suggested test of "ordinary" user. This is better than "natural"; but it is not infallible. A mode of user which, if viewed as a single isolated fact, might generally be spoken of as "ordinary", would frequently be deemed "reasonable". But a particular mode of user (*e.g.* a man digging in his own land) is not to be looked at as a single isolated fact. No fact is ever "presented *in vacuo*." The environment is to be regarded.

"Ordinarily, * * * the owner of land has a perfect right to use and remove the earth, gravel and clay of which the soil is composed, as his own interest or convenience may require. But can he do this when the same materials form the natural embankment of a watercourse? He may say, perhaps, that he merely intends to make use of materials which are his own, and to which he has a right, and for which he has other uses. But we think the law will admit of no such excuse; he knows that, when these materials are removed, the water, by the law of gravitation, will rush out, and all the mischievous consequences of diverting the water-course will follow." . . .

PRAH v. MARETTI

108 Wis.2d 223, 321 N.W.2d 182 (1982).

ABRAHAMSON, JUSTICE.

This appeal from a judgment of the circuit court for Waukesha county, Max Raskin, circuit judge, was certified to this court by the court of appeals, sec. (Rule) 809.61, Stats.1979–80, as presenting an issue of first impression, namely, whether an owner of a solar-heated residence states a claim upon which relief can be granted when he asserts that his neighbor's proposed construction of a residence (which conforms to existing deed restrictions and local ordinances) interferes with his access to an unobstructed path for sunlight across the neighbor's property. This case thus involves a conflict between one landowner (Glenn Prah, the plaintiff) interested in unobstructed access to sunlight across adjoining property as a natural source of energy and an adjoining landowner (Richard D. Maretti, the defendant) interested in the development of his land.

The circuit court concluded that the plaintiff presented no claim upon which relief could be granted and granted summary judgment for the defendant. We reverse the judgment of the circuit court and remand the cause to the circuit court for further proceedings.

I.

According to the complaint, the plaintiff is the owner of a residence which was constructed during the years 1978–1979. The complaint alleges that the residence has a solar system which includes collectors on the roof to supply energy for heat and hot water and that after the plaintiff built his solar-heated house, the defendant purchased the lot adjacent to and immediately to the south of the plaintiff's lot and commenced planning construction of a home. The complaint further states that when the plaintiff learned of defendant's plans to build the house he advised the defendant that if the house were built at the proposed location, defendant's house would substantially and adversely affect the integrity of plaintiff's solar system and could cause plaintiff other damage. Nevertheless, the defendant began construction. The complaint further alleges that the plaintiff is entitled to "unrestricted use of the sun and its solar power" and demands judgment for injunctive relief and damages.

After filing his complaint, the plaintiff moved for a temporary injunction to restrain and enjoin construction by the defendant. In ruling on that motion the circuit court heard testimony, received affidavits and viewed the site.

The record made on the motion reveals the following additional facts: Plaintiff's home was the first residence built in the subdivision, and although plaintiff did not build his house in the center of the lot it was built in accordance with applicable restrictions. Plaintiff advised defendant that if the defendant's home were built at the proposed site it would cause a shadowing effect on the solar collectors which would reduce the efficiency of the system and possibly damage the system. To avoid these adverse effects, plaintiff requested defendant to locate his home an additional several feet away from the plaintiff's lot line, the exact number being disputed. Plaintiff and defendant failed to reach an agreement on the location of defendant's home before defendant started construction. The Architectural Control Committee and the Planning Commission of the City of Muskego approved the defendant's plans for his home, including its location on the lot. After such approval, the defendant apparently changed the grade of the property without prior notice to the Architectural Control Committee. The problem with defendant's proposed construction, as far as the plaintiff's interests are concerned, arises from a combination of the grade and the distance of defendant's home from the defendant's lot line.

The circuit court denied plaintiff's motion for injunctive relief, declared it would entertain a motion for summary judgment and thereafter entered judgment in favor of the defendant. . . .

III.

The plaintiff presents three legal theories to support his claim that the defendant's continued construction of a home justifies granting him relief: (1) the construction constitutes a common law private nuisance; (2) the construction is prohibited by sec. 844.01, Stats.1979–80; and (3) the construction interferes with the solar easement plaintiff acquired under the doctrine of prior appropriation.[2] . . .

We consider first whether the complaint states a claim for relief based on common law private nuisance. This state has long recognized that an owner of land does not have an absolute or unlimited right to use the land in a way which injures the rights of others. The rights of neighboring landowners are relative; the uses by one must not unreasonably impair the uses or enjoyment of the other. VI–A *American Law of Property* sec. 28.22, pp. 64–65 (1954). When one landowner's use of his or her property unreasonably interferes with another's enjoyment of his or her property, that use is said to be a private nuisance. *Hoene v.*

2. Under the doctrine of prior appropriation the first user to appropriate the resource has the right of continued use to the exclusion of others. The doctrine of prior appropriation has been used by several western states to allocate water, *Paug Vik v. Wards Cove,* 633 P.2d 1015 (Alaska 1981), and by the New Mexico legislature to allocate solar access, secs. 47–3–1 to 47–3–5, N.M.Stats.1978. See also Note, *The Allocation of Sunlight: Solar Rights and the Prior Appropriation Doctrine*, 47 Colo.L.Rev. 421 (1976).

Milwaukee, 17 Wis.2d 209, 214, 116 N.W.2d 112 (1962); *Metzger v. Hochrein*, 107 Wis. 267, 269, 83 N.W. 308 (1900). See also Prosser, *Law of Torts* sec. 89, p. 591 (2d ed. 1971).

The private nuisance doctrine has traditionally been employed in this state to balance the rights of landowners, and this court has recently adopted the analysis of private nuisance set forth in the Restatement (Second) of Torts. *CEW Mgmt. Corp. v. First Federal Savings & Loan Association*, 88 Wis.2d 631, 633, 277 N.W.2d 766 (1979). The Restatement defines private nuisance as "a nontrespassory invasion of another's interest in the private use and enjoyment of land." Restatement (Second) of Torts sec. 821D (1977).The phrase "interest in the private use and enjoyment of land" as used in sec. 821D is broadly defined to include any disturbance of the enjoyment of property. The comment in the Restatement describes the landowner's interest protected by private nuisance law as follows:

> "The phrase 'interest in the use and enjoyment of land' is used in this Restatement in a broad sense. It comprehends not only the interests that a person may have in the actual present use of land for residential, agricultural, commercial, industrial and other purposes, but also his interests in having the present use value of the land unimpaired by changes in its physical condition. Thus the destruction of trees on vacant land is as much an invasion of the owner's interest in its use and enjoyment as is the destruction of crops or flowers that he is growing on the land for his present use. 'Interest in use and enjoyment' also comprehends the pleasure, comfort and enjoyment that a person normally derives from the occupancy of land. Freedom from discomfort and annoyance while using land is often as important to a person as freedom from physical interruption with his use or freedom from detrimental change in the physical condition of the land itself." Restatement (Second) of Torts, Sec. 821D, Comment *b*, p. 101 (1977)

Although the defendant's obstruction of the plaintiff's access to sunlight appears to fall within the Restatement's broad concept of a private nuisance as a nontrespassory invasion of another's interest in the private use and enjoyment of land, the defendant asserts that he has a right to develop his property in compliance with statutes, ordinances and private covenants without regard to the effect of such development upon the plaintiff's access to sunlight. In essence, the defendant is asking this court to hold that the private nuisance doctrine is not applicable in the instant case and that his right to develop his land is a right which is *per se* superior to his neighbor's interest in access to sunlight. This position is expressed in the maxim "*cujus est solum, ejus est usque ad coelum et ad infernos*," that is, the owner of land owns up to the sky and down to the center of the earth. The rights of the surface owner are, however, not unlimited. *U. S. v. Causby*, 328 U.S. 256, 260–1, 66 S.Ct. 1062, 1065, 90 L.Ed. 1206 (1946). See also 114.03, Stats. 1979–80.

The defendant is not completely correct in asserting that the common law did not protect a landowner's access to sunlight across adjoining property. At English common law a landowner could acquire a right to receive sunlight across adjoining land by both express agreement and under the judge-made doctrine of "ancient lights." Under the doctrine of ancient lights if the landowner had received sunlight across adjoining property for a specified period of time, the landowner was entitled to continue to receive unobstructed access to sunlight across the adjoining property. Under the doctrine the landowner acquired a negative prescriptive easement and could prevent the adjoining landowner from obstructing access to light.

Although American courts have not been as receptive to protecting a landowner's access to sunlight as the English courts, American courts have afforded some protection to a landowner's interest in access to sunlight. American courts honor express easements to sunlight. American courts initially enforced the English common law doctrine of ancient lights, but later every state which considered the doctrine repudiated it as inconsistent with the needs of a developing country. Indeed, for just that reason this court concluded that an easement to light and air over adjacent property could not be created or acquired by prescription and has been unwilling to recognize such an easement by implication. *Depner v. United States National Bank*, 202 Wis. 405, 408, 232 N.W. 851 (1930); *Miller v. Hoeschler*, 126 Wis. 263, 268–69, 105 N.W. 790 (1905).

Many jurisdictions in this country have protected a landowner from malicious obstruction of access to light (the spite fence cases) under the common law private nuisance doctrine. If an activity is motivated by malice it lacks utility and the harm it causes others outweighs any social values. VI–A Law of Property sec. 28.28, p. 79 (1954) This court was reluctant to protect a landowner's interest in sunlight even against a spite fence, only to be overruled by the legislature. Shortly after this court upheld a landowner's right to erect a useless and unsightly sixteen-foot spite fence four feet from his neighbor's windows, *Metzger v. Hochrein*, 107 Wis. 267, 83 N.W. 308 (1900), the legislature enacted a law specifically defining a spite fence as an actionable private nuisance. Thus a landowner's interest in sunlight has been protected in this country by common law private nuisance law at least in the narrow context of the modern American rule invalidating spite fences. See, *e.g.*, *Sundowner, Inc. v. King*, 95 Idaho 367, 509 P.2d 785 (1973); Restatement (Second) of Torts, sec. 829 (1977).

This court's reluctance in the nineteenth and early part of the twentieth century to provide broader protection for a landowner's access to sunlight was premised on three policy considerations. First, the right of landowners to use their property as they wished, as long as they did not cause physical damage to a neighbor, was jealously guarded. *Metzger v. Hochrein*, 107 Wis. 267, 272, 83 N.W. 308 (1900).

Second, sunlight was valued only for aesthetic enjoyment or as illumination. Since artificial light could be used for illumination, loss of sunlight was at most a personal annoyance which was given little, if any, weight by society.

Third, society had a significant interest in not restricting or impeding land development. *Dillman v. Hoffman*, 38 Wis. 559, 574 (1875). This court repeatedly emphasized that in the growth period of the nineteenth and early twentieth centuries change is to be expected and is essential to property and that recognition of a right to sunlight would hinder property development. The court expressed this concept as follows:

> "As the city grows, large grounds appurtenant to residences must be cut up to supply more residences.... The cistern, the outhouse, the cesspool, and the private drain must disappear in deference to the public waterworks and sewer; the terrace and the garden, to the need for more complete occupancy.... Strict limitation [on the recognition of easements of light and air over adjacent premises is] in accord with the popular conception upon which real estate has been and is daily being conveyed in Wisconsin and to be essential to easy and rapid development at least of our municipalities." *Miller v. Hoeschler, supra*, 126 Wis. at 268, 270, 105 N.W. 790; quoted with approval in *Depner, supra*, 202 Wis. at 409, 232 N.W. 851.

Considering these three policies, this court concluded that in the absence of an express agreement granting access to sunlight, a landowner's obstruction of another's access to sunlight was not actionable. *Miller v. Hoeschler, supra*, 126 Wis. at 271, 105 N.W. 790; *Depner v. United States National Bank, supra*, 202 Wis. at 410, 232 N.W. 851. These three policies are no longer fully accepted or applicable. They reflect factual circumstances and social priorities that are now obsolete.

First, society has increasingly regulated the use of land by the landowner for the general welfare. *Euclid v. Ambler Realty Co.*, 272 U.S. 365, 47 S.Ct. 114, 71 L.Ed. 303 (1926); *Just v. Marinette*, 56 Wis.2d 7, 201 N.W.2d 761 (1972).

Second, access to sunlight has taken on a new significance in recent years. In this case the plaintiff seeks to protect access to sunlight, not for aesthetic reasons or as a source of illumination but as a source of energy. Access to sunlight as an energy source is of significance both to the landowner who invests in solar collectors and to a society which has an interest in developing alternative sources of energy.

Third, the policy of favoring unhindered private development in an expanding economy is no longer in harmony with the realities of our society. *State v. Deetz*, 66 Wis.2d 1, 224 N.W.2d 407 (1974). The need for easy and rapid development is not as great today as it once was, while our perception of the value of sunlight as a source of energy has increased significantly.

Courts should not implement obsolete policies that have lost their vigor over the course of the years. The law of private nuisance is better suited to resolve landowners' disputes about property development in the 1980's than is a rigid rule which does not recognize a landowner's interest in access to sunlight. As we said in *Ballstadt v. Pagel*, 202 Wis. 484, 489, 232 N.W. 862 (1930), "What is regarded in law as constituting a nuisance in modern times would no doubt have been tolerated without question in former times." We read *State v. Deetz*, 66 Wis.2d 1, 224 N.W.2d 407 (1974), as an endorsement of the application of common law nuisance to situations involving the conflicting interests of landowners and as rejecting *per se* exclusions to the nuisance law reasonable use doctrine.

In *Deetz* the court abandoned the rigid common law common enemy rule with respect to surface water and adopted the private nuisance reasonable use rule, namely that the landowner is subject to liability if his or her interference with the flow of surface waters unreasonably invades a neighbor's interest in the use and enjoyment of land. Restatement (Second) of Torts, sec. 822, 826, 829 (1977) This court concluded that the common enemy rule which served society "well in the days of burgeoning national expansion of the mid-nineteenth and early-twentieth centuries" should be abandoned because it was no longer "in harmony with the realities of our society." *Deetz, supra*, 66 Wis.2d at 14–15, 224 N.W.2d 407. We recognized in *Deetz* that common law rules adapt to changing social values and conditions.[3]

Yet the defendant would have us ignore the flexible private nuisance law as a means of resolving the dispute between the landowners in this case and would have us adopt an approach, already abandoned in *Deetz*, of favoring the unrestricted development of land and of applying a rigid and inflexible rule protecting his right to build on his land and disregarding any interest of the plaintiff in the use and enjoyment of his land. This we refuse to do.

Private nuisance law, the law traditionally used to adjudicate conflicts between private landowners, has the flexibility to protect both a landowner's right of access to sunlight and another landowner's right to develop land. Private nuisance law is better suited to regulate access to sunlight in modern society and is more in harmony with legislative policy and the prior decisions of this court than is an inflexible doctrine

3. This court has recognized "that the common law is susceptible of growth and adaptation to new circumstances and situations, and that courts have power to declare and effectuate what is the present rule in respect of a given subject without regard to the old rule.... The common law is not immutable, but flexible, and upon its own principles adapts itself to varying conditions." *Dimick v. Schiedt*, 293 U.S. 474, 487, 55 S.Ct. 296, 301, 79 L.Ed. 603 (1935), quoted with approval in *Schwanke v. Garlt*, 219 Wis. 367, 371, 263 N.W. 176 (1935). In *Bielski v. Schulze*, 16 Wis.2d 1, 11, 114 N.W.2d 105 (1962), this court said: "Inherent in the common law is a dynamic principle which allows it to grow and to tailor itself to meet changing needs within the doctrine of *stare decisis*, which, if correctly understood, was not static and did not forever prevent the courts from reversing themselves or from applying principles of common law to new situations as the need arose. If this were not so, we must succumb to a rule that a judge should let others 'long dead and unaware of the problems of the age in which he lives, do his thinking for him.' Mr. Justice Douglas, Stare Decisis, 49 Columbia Law Review (1949). 735, 736." "The genius of the common law is its ability to adapt itself to the changing needs of society." *Moran v. Quality Aluminum Casting Co.*, 34 Wis.2d 542, 551, 150 N.W.2d 137 (1967). See also *State v. Esser*, 16 Wis.2d 567, 581, 115 N.W.2d 505 (1962).

of non-recognition of any interest in access to sunlight across adjoining land.

We therefore hold that private nuisance law, that is, the reasonable use doctrine as set forth in the Restatement, is applicable to the instant case. Recognition of a nuisance claim for unreasonable obstruction of access to sunlight will not prevent land development or unduly hinder the use of adjoining land. It will promote the reasonable use and enjoyment of land in a manner suitable to the 1980's. That obstruction of access to light might be found to constitute a nuisance in certain circumstances does not mean that it will be or must be found to constitute a nuisance under all circumstances. The result in each case depends on whether the conduct complained of is unreasonable.

Accordingly we hold that the plaintiff in this case has stated a claim under which relief can be granted. Nonetheless we do not determine whether the plaintiff in this case is entitled to relief. In order to be entitled to relief the plaintiff must prove the elements required to establish actionable nuisance, and the conduct of the defendant herein must be judged by the reasonable use doctrine. . . .

Because the plaintiff has stated a claim of common law private nuisance upon which relief can be granted, the judgment of the circuit court must be reversed. We need not, and do not, reach the question of whether the complaint states a claim under sec. 844.01, Stats.1979–80, or under the doctrine of prior appropriation. *Attoe v. Madison Professional Policemen's Assoc.*, 79 Wis.2d 199, 205, 255 N.W.2d 489 (1977).

For the reasons set forth, we reverse the judgment of the circuit court dismissing the complaint and remand the matter to circuit court for further proceedings not inconsistent with this opinion.

CALLOW, JUSTICE (dissenting).

The majority has adopted the Restatement's reasonable use doctrine to grant an owner of a solar heated home a cause of action against his neighbor who, in acting entirely within the applicable ordinances and statutes, seeks to design and build his home in such a location that it may, at various times during the day, shade the plaintiff's solar collector, thereby impeding the efficiency of his heating system during several months of the year. Because I believe the facts of this case clearly reveal that a cause of action for private nuisance will not lie, I dissent.

The majority arrives at its conclusion that the common law private nuisance doctrine is applicable by analogizing this situation with the spite fence cases which protect a landowner from *malicious* obstruction of access to light. *Supra*, at 188 and 189. *See Piccirilli v. Groccia*, 114 R.I. 36, 39, 327 A.2d 834, 837 (1974) (plaintiff must prove allegedly objectionable fence was erected *solely* for the avowed purpose of damaging the abutting neighbor and not for the advantage of the person who constructed the fence); *Schorck v. Epperson*, 74 Wyo. 286, 287–88, 287 P.2d 467 (1955) (doctrine of private nuisance founded on maxim that no one should have a legal right to make a malicious use of his property for no benefit to himself but merely to injure another). *Accord* Daniel v. Birmingham Dental Mfg. Co., 207 Ala. 659, 661, 93 So. 652 (1922); *Green v. Schick*, 194 Okl. 491, 492, 153 P.2d 821 (1944). *See also* Comment, *Obstruction of Sunlight as a Private Nuisance*, 65 Calif.L.Rev. 94, 99–102 (1977) ("the ironclad rule has been that the obstruction of a neighbor's light and air is not a nuisance if it serves *any* useful purpose"). *Id.* at 101 (emphasis in original). Courts have likewise refused to limit interference with television reception and other broadcast signals. *The People ex rel. Hoogasian v. Sears, Roebuck and Co.*, 52 Ill.2d 301, 305, 287 N.E.2d 677 (1972), *cert. denied*, 409 U.S. 1001, 93 S.Ct. 323, 34 L.Ed.2d 262. Clearly, the spite fence cases, as their name implies, require malice which is not claimed in this case.

The majority then concludes that this court's past reluctance to extend protection to a landowner's access to sunlight beyond the spite fence cases is based on obsolete policies which have lost their vigor over the course of the years. *Supra*, at 189. The three obsolete policies cited by the majority are: (1) Right of landowners to use their property as they desire as long as no physical damage is done to a neighbor; (2) In the past, sunlight was valued only for aesthetic value, not a source of energy; and (3) Society has a significant interest in not impeding land development. *Supra*, at 189. *See* Comment, *Obstruction of Sunlight as a Private Nuisance, supra* at 105–12. The majority has failed to convince me that these policies are obsolete.

It is a fundamental principle of law that a "landowner owns at least as much of the space above the ground as he can occupy or use in connection with the land." *United States v. Causby*, 328 U.S. 256, 264, 66 S.Ct. 1062, 1067, 90 L.Ed. 1206 (1946); *In Re Honolulu Rapid Transit Co.*, 54 Hawaii 402, 408, 507 P.2d 755 (1973); *Granberry v. Jones, et al.*, 188 Tenn. 51, 54–55, 216 S.W.2d 721 (1949). As stated in the frequently cited and followed case of *Fontainebleau Hotel Corp. v. Forty–Five Twenty–Five, Inc.*, 114 So.2d 357 (Fla.Dist.Ct.App.1959), *cert. denied*, 117 So.2d 842 (Fla.1960):

> "There being, then, no legal right to the free flow of light and air from the adjoining land, it is universally held that where a structure serves a useful and beneficial purpose, it does not give rise to a cause of action, either for damages or for an injunction under the maxim *sic utere tuo ut alienum non laedas*, even though it causes injury to another by cutting off the light and air and interfering with the view that would otherwise be available over adjoining land in its natural state, regardless of the fact that the structure may have been erected partly for spite." *Id.* at 359 (emphasis in original).

See Venuto v. Owens–Corning Fiberglas Corp., 22 Cal.App.3d 116, 127, 99 Cal.Rptr. 350, 357 (1971). I firmly believe that a landowner's right to use his property within the limits of ordinances, statutes, and restrictions of record where such use is necessary to serve his legitimate needs is a fundamental precept of a free society which this court should strive to uphold.

legal / legitimate needs should trump

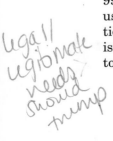

As one commentator has suggested:

> "It is fashionable to dismiss such values as deriving from a bygone era in which people valued development as a 'goal in itself,' but current market prices for real estate, and more particularly the premiums paid for land whose zoning permits intensive use, suggest that people still place very high values on such rights."

Williams, *Solar Access and Property Rights: A Maverick Analysis*, 11 Conn.L.Rev. 430, 443 (1979) (footnote omitted). *Cf.* Goble, *Solar Access and Property Rights: Reply to a "Maverick" Analysis*, 12 Conn.L.Rev. 270 (1980). . . .

I know of no cases repudiating policies favoring the right of a landowner to use his property as he lawfully desires or which declare such policies are "no longer fully accepted or applicable" in this context. *Supra*, at 189. The right of a property owner to lawful enjoyment of his property should be vigorously protected, particularly in those cases where the adjacent property owner could have insulated himself from the alleged problem by acquiring the land as a defense to the potential problem or by provident use of his own property. . . .

I would submit that any policy decisions in this area are best left for the legislature. "What is 'desirable' or 'advisable' or 'ought to be' is a question of policy, not a question of fact. What is 'necessary' or what is 'in the best interest' is not a fact and its determination by the judiciary is an exercise of legislative power when each involves political considerations." *In re City of Beloit*, 37 Wis.2d 637, 644, 155 N.W.2d 633 (1968). *See generally Holifield v. Setco Industries, Inc.*, 42 Wis.2d 750, 758, 168 N.W.2d 177 (1969); Comment, *Solar Rights: Guaranteeing a Place in the Sun*, 57 Or.L.Rev. 94, 126–27 (1977) (litigation is a slow, costly, and uncertain method of reform). I would concur with these observations of the trial judge: "While temptation lingers for the court to declare by judicial fiat what is right and what should be done, under the facts in this case, such action under our form of constitutional government where the three branches each have their defined jurisdiction and power, would be an intrusion of judicial egoism over legislative passivity." . . .

Notes

1. *Reasonable use VII: drainage*: Prendergrast v. Aiken. Perhaps in no area of land-use law did courts experience greater trouble coming up with a baseline of acceptable land use than in the context of drainage (or the law of diffuse surface waters, as it is often termed). Land parcels are interconnected by the water that flows over and through them, including rainwater runoff. Should a landowner have the right to alter the natural runoff to get the water to drain more quickly or to drain in a different place? And should a landowner be authorized to take steps to keep water that flows from adjacent land from entering her land, and otherwise alter an incoming flow to the detriment of adjacent landowners? Changes in natural drainage can easily harm other landowners. When did this harm shift from being mere *damnum* to being *injuria*?

In Prendergrast v. Aiken, 293 N.C. 201, 236 S.E.2d 787 (1977), the North Carolina Supreme Court took up this issue in a case involving an upstream landowner who complained that the conduct of a downstream landowner was causing flooding on his property. The downstream owner filled his land and converted an open waterway into a pipe-enclosed ditch. The capacity of the pipe was too small to handle the waterflow after rainfalls, and the blockage led to the flooding of the plaintiff's ground and building. As it resolved the dispute the North Carolina court altered state law by embracing a reasonable use rule (though, as usual, it largely denied it was doing so). Along the way, the court offered a scholarly survey of the law on the subject and explained what it viewed as the benefits of the reasonable use approach:

> American courts have developed three distinct doctrines governing the disposal of surface waters. The first, the common enemy rule, states substantially that "(s)urface water is recognized as a common enemy, which each proprietor may fight off or control as he will or is able, either by retention, diversion, repulsion, or altered transmission; so that no cause of action arises from such interference, even if some injury occurs, causing damage." Borchsenius v. Chicago, St. P., M. & O. Ry. Co., 96 Wis. 448, 71 N.W. 884 (1897) ... Grounded in the maxim *cujus est solum, ejus est usque ad coelum et ad inferos* (whose is the soil, his is even to the skies and to the depths below), the doctrine is based on two concepts: "(1) the necessity for improving lands with the recognition that some injury results from even minor improvements, and (2) philosophical preference for freedom of each landowner to deal with his own land essentially as he sees fit." Clark, *supra* § 451.1. Despite these laudable goals the rule created many problems. In the words of one commentator: " ... landowners are encouraged to engage in contests of hydraulic engineering in which might makes right, and breach of the peace is often inevitable." Maloney and Plager, *Diffused Surface Water: Scourge or Bounty?*, 8 Nat.Res.J. 73 (1968); *accord*, Butler v. Bruno, 115 R.I. 264, 341 A.2d 735 (1975). The extreme consequences occasioned by strict application of the common enemy rule soon led many courts to adopt modifications based upon concepts of reasonable use or negligence. Note, *Disposition of Diffused Surface Waters in North Carolina*, 47 N.C.L.Rev. 205 (1968); *e. g.*, Stacy v. Walker, 222 Ark. 819, 262 S.W.2d 889 (1953); Mason v. Lamb, 189 Va. 348, 53 S.E.2d 7 (1949). While courts have couched modifications of the common enemy rule in different language, the principle in substance is that a landowner is privileged to use and improve his land for proper purposes even though the natural flow of surface water is thereby altered so long as he uses reasonable care to avoid causing unnecessary harm to others. Kinyon and McClure, *Interferences with Surface Waters*, 24 Minn.L.Rev. 891 (1940), and cases cited.
>
> The second doctrine, commonly called the civil law rule, is, in its purest form, opposed to the common enemy rule. Based on the quoted maxim *aqua currit et debet currere, ut currere solebat* (water flows and as it flows so it ought to flow), the civil law rule subjects a landowner to liability whenever he interferes with the natural flow of surface waters to the detriment of another in the use and enjoyment of his land.

Kinyon and McClure, *supra*. Various rationales have been advanced in support of this rule. Many courts have simply felt that, as it was necessary to have some rule establishing rights and duties in regard to surface water disputes, it was reasonable and just to follow the law of nature....

Nevertheless, since almost any use of land involves some change in drainage and water flow, courts have found that a strict application of civil law principles discourages proper improvement and utilization of land. Thus courts have modified the rule to permit the reasonable use of land. See Annot., 59 A.L.R.2d 421 (1958). For the most part such changes have been piecemeal responses to specialized situations....

The third doctrine of surface water disposition is known as the reasonable use rule. Briefly, this rule allows each landowner to make reasonable use of his land even though, by doing so, he alters is some way the flow of surface water thereby harming other landowners. Liability is incurred only when this harmful interference is found to be unreasonable. City of Franklin v. Durgee, 71 N.H. 186, 51 A. 911 (1901); Armstrong v. Francis Corp., 20 N.J. 320, 120 A.2d 4 (1956); Enderson v. Kelehan, 226 Minn. 163, 32 N.W.2d 286 (1948); see generally, Clark, *supra* § 453. Reasonableness is a question of fact for the jury. Kinyon and McClure, *supra*.

Although sometimes denominated as a "new" or "emerging" doctrine, the rule of reasonable use traces its origin to the mid-nineteenth century. In Basset v. Company, 43 N.H. 569 (1862), the New Hampshire Supreme Court first took note of conflicts inherent in any rigid inflexible system of rules applied to drainage issues. The court there said:

> No land-owner has an absolute and unqualified right to the unaltered natural drainage or percolation to or from his neighbor's land. In general it would be impossible for a land-owner to avoid disturbing the natural percolation or drainage, without a practical abandonment of all improvement or beneficial enjoyment of his land. Any doctrine that would forbid all action of a landowner, affecting the relations as to percolation or drainage between his own and his neighbors' land, would in effect deprive him of his property ...

For this reason the court held that " ... in the drainage a man may exercise his own right on his own land as he pleases, provided he does not interfere with the rights of others. The rights are correlative, and, from the necessity of the case, the right of each is only to a reasonable user or management."

After considerable struggle the Minnesota court adopted a similar rule. See Sheehan v. Flynn, 59 Minn. 436, 61 N.W. 462 (1894); Enderson v. Kelehan, *supra*. Although these jurisdictions were for many years the sole adherents to the reasonable use rule, a growing number have recently adopted the rule fully [citations omitted]....

The rising prominence of the reasonable use rule is seemingly attributable to the increasing industrialization and urbanization of the nation. Where people are forced by social and demographic pressures to live in close proximity with each other and with commercial and industrial development, there will be, of necessity, increased conflict over the proper utilization of land. Long and Long, *Surface Waters and the Civil Law Rule*, 23 Emory L.J. 1015 (1974). It is no longer simply a matter of balancing the interests of individual landowners; the interests of society must be considered. On the whole the rigid solutions offered by the common enemy and civil law rules no longer provide an adequate vehicle by which drainage problems may be properly resolved. For this reason courts have responded, first with modifications of existing rules and then, when those proved unwieldy, by the adoption of the rule of reasonable use. . . .

We believe the reasonable use doctrine affords a sounder approach to the problems presented by surface water drainage. It can be applied effectively, fairly and consistently in any factual setting, Butler v. Bruno, *supra*, and thus has the capacity to accommodate changing social needs without occasioning the unpredictable disruptions in the law associated with our civil law rule.

Other advantages of the reasonable use rule, particularly those relating to evidentiary aspects, are less obvious though no less important. Under the civil law rule it is crucial to determine the "natural flow" of the surface water. The continual process of construction and reconstruction, a hallmark of our age, has made it increasingly difficult to determine accurately how surface waters flowed "when untouched and undirected by the hand of man." City of Houston v. Renault, Inc., *supra*. Adoption of the reasonable use rule obviates the necessity of making such a finding. See Comment, *The Application of Surface Water Rules in Urban Areas*, 42 Mo.L.Rev. 76 (1977). In sum, we think the reasonable use rule is more in line with the realities of modern life and that consistency, fairness and justice are better served through the flexibility afforded by that rule.

Accordingly, we now formally adopt the rule of reasonable use with respect to surface water drainage. That rule is expressed as follows: Each possessor is legally privileged to make a reasonable use of his land, even though the flow of surface water is altered thereby and causes some harm to others, but liability is incurred when his harmful interference with the flow of surface waters is unreasonable and causes substantial damage. Armstrong v. Francis Corp., *supra*; *accord*, Weinberg v. Northern Alaska Development Corp., *supra*.

Analytically, a cause of action for unreasonable interference with the flow of surface water causing substantial damage is a private nuisance action, with liability arising where the conduct of the landowner making the alterations in the flow of surface water is either (1) intentional and unreasonable or (2) negligent, reckless or in the course of an abnormally dangerous activity. . . .

Reasonableness is a question of fact to be determined in each case by weighing the gravity of the harm to the plaintiff against the utility of the conduct of the defendant. Armstrong v. Francis Corp., *supra*; State v. Deetz, *supra*; Restatement (Second) of Torts § 826 (Tent.Draft No. 18, 1972). Determination of the gravity of the harm involves consideration of the extent and character of the harm to the plaintiff, the social

> value which the law attaches to the type of use which is invaded, the suitability of the locality for that use, the burden on plaintiff to minimize the harm, and other relevant considerations arising upon the evidence. Determination of the utility of the conduct of the defendant involves consideration of the purpose of the defendant's conduct, the social value which the law attaches to that purpose, the suitability of the locality for the use defendant makes of the property, and other relevant considerations arising upon the evidence. Rodrigues v. State, *supra*; Armstrong v. Francis Corp., *supra*; Watts v. Manufacturing Co., *supra*; Jones v. Boeing, *supra*; Restatement of Torts ss 829–831 (1939); Restatement (Second) of Torts §§ 827, 828 (Tent.Draft No. 17, 1971); Restatement (Second) of Torts § 829A (Tent.Draft No. 18, 1972); Note, 50 Ky.L.J. 254 (1961–62).
>
> We emphasize that, even should alteration of the water flow by the defendant be "reasonable" in the sense that the social utility arising from the alteration outweighs the harm to the plaintiff, defendant may nevertheless be liable for damages for a private nuisance "if the resulting interference with another's use and enjoyment of land is greater than it is reasonable to require the other to bear under the circumstances without compensation." See Restatement (Second) of Torts (Tent.Draft No. 17, 1971); Restatement (Second) of Torts §§ 826, 829A (Tent.Draft No. 18, 1972). The gravity of the harm may be found to be so significant that it requires compensation regardless of the utility of the conduct of the defendant.

2. *Reasonable use VIII: unpacking reasonableness. Prah* and *Prendergrast* illustrate the tendency of some courts to shift from the law's old linguistic forms (Latin, or even Law French) to newer phrasings, based on plain English. It also shows the greater willingness of many courts to engage overtly in assessing competing policy considerations when they undertake to keep the common law up to date. In *Prah* the court announces that the property rights of landowners extend only to uses and activities that are reasonable, at least when their activities cause noticeable harm. By implication, a law that prohibits an unreasonable land use does not diminish a landowner's property rights. Instead, it merely confirms a limit that already exists. *Prendergrast* does something quite similar in the specific context of drainage by defining landowner rights in terms of practices that are reasonable in light of conditions on the land and on surrounding lands.

Reading these rulings we face the same question as before: How does the court go about deciding what activities are reasonable? More precisely, what guidance do the courts give to the ultimate fact finders who are to make determinations of reasonableness? On this issue in *Prah*, how relevant are the defendant's mental state and his knowledge of the facts? How relevant is the issue of priority in time? And how relevant is it that one party could have avoided the conflict by making modest adjustments to his land use? If we conclude that the court's guidance really is too vague to apply with any predictability, where are we left? Is reasonable use a rule of substantive law, or is it in practice something else—perhaps a rule of procedure that specifies the people (a group of jurors usually) who get to decide on their own whether a given land use will or will not be allowed?

These basic questions—about mental state, knowledge, priority in time, and ability to accommodate—will arise in the following materials, again and again. They are the necessary stuff of any reasonable-use determination. Also relevant, of course, is the central policy issue: What types of land and resource uses strike us appropriate for our shared landscapes? What types of landscapes do we want to inhabit? The law in the end is simply a tool that we use to promote shared goals. What, then, are our land-use goals, and can we pursue them collectively consistent with our desire also to respect individual liberty? (We return to these questions in the final chapter.)

3. *Prior appropriation?* An issue in *Prah* raised by the plaintiffs but not addressed by the court was the claim that Prah gained a right to continued access to sunlight for his solar panels by reason of being first-in-time to make use of the sunlight. The argument at first glance might seem frivolous, and legally it probably was. But the underlying idea is not. Prah no doubt put forth this argument because the quite similar argument based on prescription would not have succeeded. Had Prah claimed that his use of the light gave rise to an easement by prescription across neighboring land he would have lost on several grounds, most plainly because the time period of use was too short and because his use was not adverse to the neighbor. Prior appropriation, if taken seriously, avoids these elements of proof. An appropriation is valid the moment it occurs, and no adversity to any other user is required. Note that prior appropriation is really just a variant on the idea of protecting the first user in time. Prah was first, and he claimed that his earlier use of the sunlight gave him protection against later interferences. Again, the claim may seem weak, but doesn't the court ultimately give Prah at least half of what he wants? Prior appropriation essentially resolves resource-use disputes based on priority in time. The reasonable-use rule that the court employs does not give priority quite so much emphasis—other factors are also relevant—but priority in time does carry weight.

On this issue we might note that the earlier, do-no-harm approach to resolving disputes did operate something like a prior appropriation system. Prah was making use of his land, the neighbor came along and acted in a way that harmed Prah, and thus Prah might have had a remedy based on his priority in time (or prior appropriation, we might say).

4. *Considering the dissent.* How valid are the arguments presented by Justice Callow in his dissent? The points he makes are certainly familiar enough. Callow claims that the legislature should be the one to keep the law of land ownership up to date. Yet is this true? The legislature, of course, has the power to do so. But could not the majority note that the elements of property are judicial creations, and that courts have shouldered the duty to keep them up to date for centuries—even while legislators plied their trade. Why should courts abandon this traditional lawmaking job? (More on this below.) Callow also asserts that the majority's ruling represents a sharp break from prior understandings about landownership. But how true is this, given what we have seen? What does Callow do with the longstanding doctrine of *sic utere tuo* and its more modern incarnation, the reasonable-use limit on landowner activities? Indeed, might Callow himself be accused of deviation from longstanding property norms by ignoring the reasonable-use limit?

These points aside, Callow claims that Prah could have avoided the problem by buying the adjacent land so as to keep anything from being built there. Would this be a good approach for the law to take? (On this point, you might withhold judgment until we've probed more deeply the important principle of accommodation that weaves throughout natural resources law.) He also asserts that citizens attach a high value to land development, as shown by the higher prices they pay for land open for development. Of what value is this fact? Does it represent the views citizens hold on issues of public policy, or does it represent something else? Finally, are there perhaps other, stronger arguments that Callow might have made to support his claim that Prah's suit should be tossed out by the trial judge and not submitted to a jury for a factual determination on reasonableness?

C. REASONABLENESS AND REGULATION

The cases considered so far in this chapter have largely dealt with the elements of private property under the common law. At common law, an owner can use what he owns only in ways consistent with the law of nuisance, and perhaps with the more general, *sic utere tuo*, reasonable-use limit that nuisance law implements. For centuries, courts refined, applied, and gradually changed this limit. As they tinkered with the limit, keeping the common law up to date, they defined both the landowner's (limited) right to use land and the landowner's (limited) reciprocal right to complain about interferences by neighbors.

What happens, though, when lawmakers other than courts get involved in this task of tinkering with the elements of private ownership? What happens when a legislature decides that a particular land use is undesired, and then bans it by statute? How is such a law best understood and its validity determined? Indeed, what really is the legal effect of the statute, if it effectively does what judicial lawmakers have long done: give specific content to *sic utere tuo*?

Statutes and regulations that restrict the uses of private property are typically talked about as exercises of the police power. But how do exercises of the police power fit together with the longstanding limits on private property rights at common law? Is it simply a case of statutes taking precedence over common law rules, as in any other field of law? Or are police power regulations something different, some different type of lawmaking that might interfere with property rights but that does not really alter the meaning of ownership? We turn to these questions next.

STATE v. DEXTER

32 Wash.2d 551, 202 P.2d 906 (1949).

HILL, JUSTICE.

Respondent Avery Dexter and Hazel Dexter, his wife, had since September, 1945, held title in fee simple to three hundred twenty acres of marketable second-growth timber in Pend Oreille county. Beginning in November, 1945, and continuing into 1946, Dexter cut approximately one hundred fifty thousand board feet, log measure, of fir, larch, and white pine on that property; from November, 1945, until a restraining order issued in this action in October, 1947, he cut hemlock suitable for pulpwood.

In 1947 the state forester became aware that the respondent was cutting and removing timber, and directed him to shut down his operations until a permit was obtained. The respondent refused to apply for a permit, and proceedings were instituted by the state enjoining further timber-cutting operations until such time as the respondent should apply for and receive a permit from the state forester, which permit he could not obtain without giving satisfactory assurance that he would comply with chapter 193, Laws of 1945, as amended by chapter 218, Laws of 1947, being Rem.Supp.1945, §§ 5823–10, 5823–16, 5823–18, and Rem. Supp.1947, §§ 5823–11 to 5823–15, inclusive, and § 5823–17. . . .

The trial court, being convinced that the statutes above referred to, under which the state forester had proceeded and the state had brought its action, are unconstitutional, then sustained the demurrer to the complaint, . . . and dismissed the action. The state has appealed.

The act which was held to be unconstitutional by the trial court contains an expression of its purposes and policy in its first section, which reads as follows: "Keeping the forest land of this state continuously and fully productive is one of the most important steps toward perpetuation and conservation of its forest resources. One of the most important means of effectuating such public policy is to keep timber lands productive by seeking to maintain continuous growth of timber on all lands suitable for such purposes, and in order to accomplish this end it is necessary, and in the public interest, to prescribe certain rules of forest practices to be observed in the harvesting of timber." Laws of 1945, chapter 193, § 1, p. 556.

It provides that every owner or operator shall leave reserve trees of commercial species in a quantity deemed adequate under normal conditions to maintain continuous forest growth, or provide adequate restocking to insure future forest protection. Different minimum standards of compliance are provided for operations east and west of the summit of the Cascade mountains. Every owner or operator conducting logging operations (with exceptions not here material) is required to secure a permit from the state forester, to secure which he has to agree to abide by the provisions of the act.

There is just one question before us, i. e., Is the statute constitutional? Or, stated more specifically, Does the state have the right, under its police power, to require those who engage in commercial logging operations to make provision for reforesting the area logged by leaving a certain number of trees for reseeding purposes or by restocking?

The police power of a state is declared "* * * to include all those regulations designed to promote the public convenience, the general welfare, the general prosperity, and extends to all great public needs, as well as regulations designed to promote the public health, the public morals, or the public safety.'' State v. Pitney, 79 Wash. 608, 611, 140 P. 918, 919, Ann.Cas.1916A, 209.

And in Campbell v. State, 12 Wash.2d 459, 122 P.2d 458, we approved the following statement from Shea v. Olson, 185 Wash. 143, 153, 53 P.2d 615, 619, 111 A.L.R. 998: ''However difficult it may be to give a precise or satisfactory definition of 'police power,' there is no doubt that the state, in the exercise of such power, may prescribe laws tending to promote the health, peace, morals, education, good order, and welfare of the people. Police power is an attribute of sovereignty, an essential element of the power to govern, and a function that cannot be surrendered. It exists without express declaration, and the only limitation upon it is that it must reasonably tend to correct some evil or promote some interest of the state, and not violate any direct or positive mandate of the constitution. [Citing cases.]''

The trial court in its ''Memorandum Opinion'' very ably champions the rights of private property and of private enterprise, and pictures graphically the effect of bureaucratic controls on farms and other lawful business in the state. We are in accord with much that is said therein, but it must be realized that private enterprise must utilize its private property in ways that are not inconsistent with the public welfare. . . .

Unfortunately for the respondent's plea for the unrestricted right of the owner of timberland to do as he pleases with his own, the record of such unrestricted use has been one of ''cut out and get out,'' the logged-off lands (having no economic value) being left to revert to the county for unpaid taxes. Denuded hillsides have made possible the rapid runoff of surface waters, thus increasing the dangers from floods and contributing to costly soil erosion.

Fifteen years ago we commented upon the problem of our vanishing forests and the problems of reforestation of the vast areas of our state from which the timber had already been removed, and the necessity of planting ''denuded areas, to remedy, in part at least, the wasteful practices of the past.'' State ex rel. Mason County Logging Co. v. Wiley, 177 Wash. 65, 71, 31 P.2d 539, 542. And now respondent, while personally disclaiming any wasteful practices, says in effect that individuals must be lift free to continue such practices because they have a vested right so to do.

We do not think that the state is required by the constitution of the United States to stand idly by while its natural resources are depleted, and higher authority supports our view. Walls v. Midland Carbon Co., 254 U.S. 300, 41 S.Ct. 118, 65 L.Ed. 276.

Today many companies, faced with the rapid diminution of stands of timber once deemed inexhaustible, have developed effective reforestation programs; the Federal and state governments have for many years carried out such programs at public expense. The issue, then, is, Can the state compel participation in a reforestation program on land for which no other beneficial use is contemplated? . . .

Edmund Burke once said that a great unwritten compact exists between the dead, the living, and the unborn. We leave to the unborn a colossal financial debt, perhaps inescapable, but incurred, none the less, in our time and for our immediate benefit. Such an unwritten compact requires that we leave to the unborn something more than debts and depleted natural resources. Surely, where natural resources can be utilized and at the same time perpetuated for future generations, what has been called "constitutional morality" requires that we do so....

There is ample and sound authority to sustain our conclusion that the challenged legislation is for the general or public welfare and is a proper exercise of the police power:

'* * * the amount of land being incapable of increase, if the owners of large tracts can waste them at will without state restriction, the state and its people may be helplessly impoverished and one great purpose of government defeated.' Opinion of the Justices, 103 Me. 506, 511, 69 A. 627, 629, 19 L.R.A.,N.S., 422, 13 Ann.Cas. 745.

That the protection and conservation of the natural resources of the state is in the general welfare and serve a public purpose, and so constitute a reasonable exercise of the police power, is now so well settled that no further citation of authority is necessary.' Tulare Irr. Dist. v. Lindsay–Strathmore Irr. Dist., 3 Cal.2d 489, 529, 45 P.2d 972, 988.

'One of the inherent powers of the State is to conserve her natural resources and to regulate the severance thereof.' State v. Standard Oil Co. of Louisiana, 188 La. 978, 1007, 178 So. 601, 610.

'The state, in the exercise of its power to enact laws for the general welfare of its people, may enact laws designed to increase the industries of the state, to develop its resources, and to add to its wealth. The majority of the authorities, moreover, support the rule that not only adjoining landowners, but the public at large, have an interest in the preservation of the natural resources of the country sufficient to justify appropriate legislation to prevent exploitation or waste of such resources by the owners of the land on which they are round. This rule finds specific expression in laws forbidding any waste of natural gas, oil, or mineral waters and subterranean flows and in laws forbidding the cutting of standing trees or the removal of stone, gravel, and sand from the seashore.' 11 Am.Jur. 1034, Constitutional Law, § 276....

Respondent develops four arguments in support of the judgment, two of which may be considered together, i. e.: (1) The act authorizes what amounts to the taking of private property without compensation and establishes an unreasonable exercise of the police power; and (2) it destroys private property rights and impairs the obligation of contracts as guaranteed by the Constitution of the United States.

Respondent urges, and the trial court principally relied upon, the proposition that the act in question impairs the obligation of contracts, in contravention of art. I, § 10, of the Constitution of the United States. It is also strenuously urged that it provides for the taking of property without due process of law, in contravention of Amendment 14 of the Constitution of the United States, and art. I, § 3, of the Constitution of the State of Washington. These arguments are bottomed upon the proposition that there are no restrictive reservations in the patent from the United States preventing the cutting of timber on respondent's property or requiring reforestation, and that, having a fee-simple title, respondent is entitled to do as he pleases with his own property.

D's argp

The answer to this argument is admirably expressed in the oft-quoted words of Chief Justice Shaw of the supreme judicial court of Massachusetts (quoted in part, with approval, via Story on the Constitution, Vol. 2 (5th Ed.), 701, § 1954, in State v. Van Vlack, supra):

> 'We think it is a settled principle, growing out of the nature of well ordered civil society, that every holder of property, however absolute and unqualified may be his title, holds it under the implied liability that his use of it may be so regulated, that it shall not be injurious to the equal enjoyment of others having an equal right to the enjoyment of their property, nor injurious to the rights of the community. All property in this commonwealth, as well that in the interior as that bordering on tide waters, is derived directly or indirectly from the government, and held subject to those general regulations, which are necessary to the common good and general welfare. Rights of property, like all other social and conventional rights, are subject to such reasonable limitations in their enjoyment, as shall prevent them from being injurious, and to such reasonable restraints and regulations established by law, as the legislature, under the governing and controlling power vested in them by the constitution, may think necessary and expedient.

can be regulated s/t others + publics rights

> 'This is very different from the right of eminent domain, the right of a government to take and appropriate private property to public use, whenever the public exigency requires it; which can be done only on condition of providing a reasonable compensation therefor. The power we allude to is rather the police power, the power vested in the legislature by the constitution, to make, ordain and establish all manner of wholesome and reasonable laws, statutes and ordinances, either with penalties or without, not repugnant to the constitution, as they shall judge to be for the good and welfare of the commonwealth, and of the subjects of the same.' Commonwealth v. Alger, 7 Cush. 53, 84, 61 Mass. 53, 84.

Not eminent domain—police power

... On the facts as stipulated, the appellant was entitled to prevail and the trial court erred in dismissing the action. The cause is remanded, with instructions to enter an order enjoining the defendant from further timber-cutting operations within the purview of chapter 193 of the Laws of 1945, as amended by chapter 218 of the Laws of 1947, until he shall have obtained a permit from the state forester and given

Holding -enjoined until permit

satisfactory assurances that he will, in his timber-cutting operations, comply with chapter 193 of the Laws of 1945, as amended.

SIMPSON, JUSTICE (dissenting).

Because the majority opinion approves a law which takes from the people of this state another of their constitutional rights, I dissent.

The development of the doctrine of "the police power" has passed all constitutional barriers, so that now all that is necessary to introduce and enforce any repressive measure is to use a high-sounding, plausible preamble, and the courts will then approve, regardless of the fact that personal liberties are taken from the individual....

True, it is of importance that we preserve our natural resources, but they should not be preserved at the expense of the liberties of the people of this state and nation, and that is the thing the present act proposes to do. I call attention to certain provisions of the law which either encroach upon, or take away, an individual's right to do with his property as he pleases. I shall point out later that an individual has a right to sell his own property in any way he sees fit, and to use his property as he desires....

The Supreme Court of Montana announced the proper rule in Gas Products Co. v. Rankin, 63 Mont. 372, 207 P. 993, 998, 24 A.L.R. 294. That decision concerned a statute which declared that the burning of natural gas without utilizing all the heat therein contained for other manufacturing or domestic purposes, was wasteful and unlawful and prohibited that act. In holding the act unconstitutional, the court said:

> Were we to sustain the constitutionality of the act, there would be no limit to which the Legislature might go in depriving persons of the use of private property under the guise of the police power. If it may constitutionally prohibit the use of natural gas taken from privately owned property for use in one industrial or manufacturing business, why not in another? If the rule contended for is given sanction, the use of natural gas in blast furnaces, smelters, factories, or for cooking, heating or lighting is equally a proper subject for such prohibitory legislation. Under this rule there is no limit to which the Legislature may not go. The owner of coal or minerals in the ground may thus by legislative control have his property rights so limited and restricted that he would be compelled to abandon mining although the owner of the fee in the land. The same rule would be applicable to percolating waters, oil, growing trees, and agricultural crops grown upon the land. The landowner would be subject to regulation as to the number, kind, and character of trees he might cut on his own land, and the conditions for cutting imposed. In short, all recognized principles of property rights would thus be destroyed. If the Legislature may prohibit the burning of natural gas in the manufacture of carbon black because of the loss of heat units, why may it not as reasonably condemn its use for fuel on account of the fact that the carbon black contained therein is wasted? We are living in a free government, with definite guaranties

of property rights, not under the rule of an emperor or czar. Such legislation is paternalistic in character and conflicts with the guaranties of the national and state Constitution and is contrary to the theory upon which our government was formed. The paternal theory of government is odious, and we should not treat lightly or disregard the sacred rights of property recognized and guaranteed by the government.'

13 A.L.R.2d 1081

WOODBURY COUNTY SOIL CONSERVATION DISTRICT v. ORTNER

279 N.W.2d 276 (Iowa 1979).

LeGrand, Justice.

This appeal involves a dispute concerning the obligation of landowners to comply with the provisions of ch. 467A, The Code, 1975, commonly referred to as the Soil Conservation Districts Law. The trial court found § 467A.44 of the act, and the section fixing the rules and regulations under which the soil conservation district operates, unconstitutional. We reverse the trial court and remand the case for further proceedings.

The defendants Ortner and Schrank each own farm land in Woodbury County. In 1974, an adjacent landowner, John C. Matt, filed a complaint with the soil conservation district alleging that his farm was suffering damage from water and soil erosion from defendants' land. This complaint was settled by private agreement among the parties, and no formal action was taken by the district.

The following year Matt filed another complaint, alleging similar damage. An investigation made under § 467A.47 resulted in a finding that the soil loss on the Ortner and Schrank farms was in excess of the established statutory limits. The district issued an administrative order finding defendants in violation of the district soil erosion control regulations and requiring them to remedy the situation within six months.

The order offered defendants two alternatives to bring the soil within acceptable limits. They were directed to either seed the land to permanent pasture or hay or to terrace it. Defendants failed to do either within the time allowed by the commission's order and the district brought this action as authorized by § 467A.49, The Code.

Even with state grants which were available through the Department of Soil Conservation to defray part of the cost, terracing would cost the Ortners more than $12,000.00 and the Schranks approximately $1,500.00. There was also testimony that this process would render a number of acres of each farm untillable. The other alternative pasture or hay seeding would be less expensive but would also remove some of each farm from active production. The defendants introduced evidence that either alternative would decrease the value of their land, although there was considerable evidence to the contrary.

The trial court held that § 467A.44, The Code, 1975, is unconstitutional. The court hold that this section places an unreasonable burden on the defendants and that it is unduly oppressive. The trial court concluded that the section in question (§ 467A.44) therefore "deprives (defendants) of rights granted by the Fifth and Fourteenth Amendments of the Constitution of the United States and comparable provisions of the state of Iowa."

The two specific issues raised on this appeal are: Did the trial court err in holding § 467A.44 unconstitutional and did the trial court err in finding that the acceptable soil loss limit on the property is ten tons per acre per year? The second of these may be disregarded because the parties admit there is no support in the record for the trial court's finding that the acceptable soil loss is ten tons per acre per year. Actually the testimony shows without dispute that the acceptable loss limit is five tons per acre per year. The Ortners and Schranks concede as much and we give this no further consideration. The only question before us, therefore, is the constitutional one involving both federal and state constitutional provisions.

In considering the constitutionality of legislative enactments, we accord them every presumption of validity and find them unconstitutional only upon a showing that they clearly infringe on constitutional rights and only if every reasonable basis for support is negated. Bryan v. City of Des Moines, 261 N.W.2d 685, 687–88 (Iowa 1978); Chicago Title Insurance Co. v. Huff, 256 N.W.2d 17, 25 (Iowa 1977); John R. Grubb, Inc. v. Iowa Housing Finance, 255 N.W.2d 89, 92–93 (Iowa 1977).

Important to our decision here is a determination as to whether the restrictions and conditions imposed by ch. 467A, The Code, amount to a taking of property under eminent domain or simply a regulation under the police power of the state. The latter entitles the property owner to no compensation; the former requires that he be paid for the appropriation of his property for public use.

We recognized this distinction in Hinrichs v. Iowa State Highway Commission, 260 Iowa 1115, 1126, 152 N.W.2d 248, 255 (1967) as follows:

> 'Eminent domain' is the taking of private property for a public use for which compensation must be given. On the other hand 'Police Power' controls and regulates the use of property for the public good for which no compensation need be made.

Even the exercise of police power, however, may amount to a taking if it deprives a property owner of the substantial use and enjoyment of his property. See Phelps v. Board of Supervisors, 211 N.W.2d 274, 276 (Iowa 1973). The point at which police power regulation becomes so oppressive that it results in a taking is impossible of general definition and must be determined on the circumstances of each case. Penn Central Transportation Co. v. City of New York, 438 U.S. 104, 124, 98 S.Ct. 2646, 2659, 57 L.Ed.2d 631, 648 (1978); Iowa Natural Resources Council v. Van Zee, 261 Iowa 1287, 1294, 158 N.W.2d 111, 116 (1968); Benschoter v. Hakes, 232 Iowa 1354, 1361, 8 N.W.2d 481, 485–86 (1943). See also 16 Am.Jur.2d, Constitutional Law, § 290 (1964).

In *Van Zee* and *Hakes* we stated that the test is whether the "collective benefits (to the public) outweigh the specific restraints imposed (on the individual)." Factors of particular importance include the "economic impact of the regulation on the claimant and, particularly, the extent to which the regulation has interfered with distinct investment backed expectations." To be considered also is the "character of the governmental action." See Penn Central, 437 U.S. at 124, 98 S.Ct. at 2659, 57 L.Ed.2d at 648. It is important therefore to consider the nature of the public interest involved and the impact of the restrictions placed on defendants' use of their land by ch. 467A, The Code.

It should take no extended discussion to demonstrate that agriculture is important to the welfare and prosperity of this state. It has been judicially recognized as our leading industry. See Benschoter v. Hakes, 232 Iowa at 1360, 8 N.W.2d at 486.

The state has a vital interest in protecting its soil as the greatest of its natural resources, and it has a right to do so. Iowa Natural Resources Council v. Van Zee, 261 Iowa at 1297, 158 N.W.2d at 118. This is the purpose of ch. 467A as is apparent from this declaration of purpose contained in § 467A.2:

> It is hereby declared to be the policy of the legislature to provide for the restoration and conservation of the soil and soil resources of this state and for the control and prevention of soil erosion and for the prevention of erosion, floodwater, and sediment damages, and thereby to preserve natural resources, control floods, prevent impairment of dams and reservoirs, assist and maintain the navigability of rivers and harbors, preserve wild life, protect the tax base, protect public lands and promote the health, safety and public welfare of the people of this state.

This same subject receives further legislative treatment in § 467A.43 as follows:

> To conserve the fertility, general usefulness, and value of the soil and soil resources of this state, and to prevent the injurious effects of soil erosion, it is hereby made the duty of the owners of real property in this state to establish and maintain soil and water conservation practices or erosion control practices, as required by the regulations of the commissioners of the respective soil conservation districts.

Defendants' argument is two-fold. They assert first that the statute amounts to a taking of private property without just compensation. Next, they say the statute is an unreasonable and illegal exercise of the state's police power.

We hold defendants have failed to establish § 467A.44 is unconstitutional. Its provisions are reasonably related to carrying out the announced legislative purpose of soil control, admittedly a proper exercise of police power.

While this imposes an extra financial burden on defendants, it is one the state has a right to exact. The importance of soil conservation is best illustrated by the state's willingness to pay three-fourths of the cost. In Ortner's case, the state's share is $36,760.50 and in Schrank's it is $4,413.00. The remainder to be paid by defendants ($12,253.50 by Ortner and $1,471.00 by Schrank) is still substantial, but not unreasonably so. A law does not become unconstitutional because it works a hardship. Chicago Title Insurance Co., 256 N.W.2d at 25; Diamond Auto Sales, Inc. v. Erbe, 251 Iowa 1330, 1335–36, 105 N.W.2d 650, 652 (1960). The argument that one must make substantial expenditures to comply with regulatory statutes does not raise constitutional barriers. See Northwestern Laundry v. City of Des Moines, 239 U.S. 486, 491–92, 36 S.Ct. 206, 208–09, 60 L.Ed. 396, 400–01 (1916).

There is conflicting testimony concerning the effect which either proposal permanent seeding or terracing will have on future farming operations, the necessity for additional equipment, the possibility of other alternatives, diminution in farm income, and decrease in value of the land. This is not the kind of clear and compelling evidence necessary as a premise for holding a statute unconstitutional.

What we have already said is relevant, too, on defendants' claim the regulations established by the soil conservation district amount to a taking of their property without compensation in violation of the federal and state constitutions.

As we have already pointed out, an exercise of police power may be so sweeping in its scope and so all inclusive in its operation that it becomes a taking rather than a regulation. However, this did not happen here. Defendants still have the use and enjoyment of their property, limited only by the necessity to prevent soil erosion beyond allowable standards.

Each case must be determined on its own facts. Our conclusion on the facts here is that the record does not support the trial court's finding of unconstitutionality. We have reviewed the authorities relied on by defendants and have given particular attention to Penn Central Transportation Co. v. City of New York, 437 U.S. at 124, 98 S.Ct. at 2659, 57 L.Ed.2d at 648, where the factors important to deciding if there has been a taking without compensation are discussed. We are unable to agree they help defendants' position.

Defendants raise one other objection. They say the statute is invalid because it is designed "solely as a means of furthering the purely private property interests of a very limited class of landowners" rather than for the benefit of the public generally. This is based on § 467A.47 which, they allege, provides for action by the soil conservation district upon the complaint of one damaged by erosion, rather than upon the initiative of the district itself. We believe this argument ignores other sections of the act under which the soil conservation district is authorized to act. See

§ 467A. 44(3), under which the commissioners may require owners to act, and § 467A.52, under which, in limited circumstances, they may take independent action. See also Miller v. Schoene, 276 U.S. 272, 281, 48 S.Ct. 246, 248, 72 L.Ed. 568, 572 (1928), where a similar provision was held unobjectionable. We find no merit to this complaint.

The judgment of the trial court is reversed and the case is remanded for such other proceedings as may be appropriate.

Notes

1. *Assessing the effects of regulation: where to start?* In thinking about land-use regulations and the reasonableness of them, the first step is to determine how the regulations affect private property rights. We need to identify how particular regulations have altered landowner rights (if at all), and how grave the change has been. The normal inclination of many people (such as Justice Simpson, dissenting in *Dexter*) is to begin with the assumption that landowners can rather freely do whatever they please unless they are causing obvious, grave harm. When a statute or regulation comes along to ban a land-use activity, its effect is thus to take away from the landowner the legal right to engage in that activity. This could well be true, but is it necessarily and always true? What baseline of property rights should be used when judging the effects of some new law on them? And how do we decide whether a new law is simply a normal updating of ownership norms, the type of legal change that lawmakers (courts mostly) have undertaken for generations, and whether instead it actually takes away property? To make a before-and-after comparison of the regulation, we need to know the "before" part.

How would we think about the above two decisions if the legal restrictions on landowners had come, not by statute or regulation, but by court decision under the common law? What if a court decided that avoidable soil erosion was an unreasonable use of land, and thus not a lawful activity? Similarly, what if a court decided that clearcutting a forest caused harm to other landowners (private nuisance) or to the public at large (public nuisance)? Would our interpretation of the legal actions perhaps then shift? Might we then be inclined to say that the court was merely implementing a pre-existing limit on private property rights rather than taking anything away? We could retort, of course, that such activities are not common law nuisances, and that the court therefore could not ban them. But keep in mind that nuisance has always been an evolving idea, and that "harm" has shifted meaning from generation to generation. The history of nuisance is replete with illustrations of land uses that were once harmful and later deemed benign, or that were benign and later deemed harmful. Indeed, if we were to look for a background principle of property law, it might well be the constancy of gradual change.

Note the considerable difference in these two ways of thinking about legal change, based on which branch of government does it. The difference, of course, stems from the starting point of the inquiry into a law's effects. Do we start with the assumption that landowners can do as they please, or do we start with the assumption that private rights extend only to uses that cause no substantial harm? Recall that the requirement of "substantial" harm was itself a legal change in the nineteenth century; before then, a plaintiff could apparently win by pointing to any harm that wasn't trivial (though, as noted, the historical record is very spotty). When the requirement of "substantial" harm was grafted onto the law of nuisance it had the effect of materially reconfiguring property rights. It *increased* the rights of landowners to use land intensively, despite insubstantial harms, while at the same time *decreasing* the protections landowners enjoyed against interferences. A law today that held landowners accountable for lesser forms of harm would have the opposite effect on property rights; it too would reconfigure rights by raising one element of ownership while depressing another. In natural resources law today (as always), both types of changes are going on, and we need to be alert to them.

2. *Shared governance VI: who makes the rules?* When it comes to specifying the elements of owning nature, whether land or some particular resource, what component(s) of government should do the lawmaking work? Like all other bodies of law, property law can get out of date and need amendment. In many states, courts have stepped aside and decided that the legislature or an administrative agency ought to perform this important work. But is this wise? Are there settings where courts ought to continue the lawmaking function that their judicial predecessors performed for centuries? And if, in fact, legislatures are better able to keep the law up to date, is there a reason why statutory change would be viewed with greater suspicion than common law change? If we do view statutes with heightened suspicion—as interferences with private rights rather than needed updating of them—then why are we deferring to the legislatures at all? If courts are more trustworthy in this work, if their rulings need less scrutiny, then why not encourage courts to keep doing what they have long done?

As we think about this issue, we should keep in mind that legislatures are no new institutions; they've been around for centuries. Courts in England and nineteenth-century America did their work right alongside the legislatures. What has changed are the ways courts understand their roles. Courts in the past were more aware that the common law was itself a judicial creation. They were jealous of their turf, sometimes to the point of viewing statutes with grave suspicion when they altered the common law. Today that suspicion is largely gone and many courts have shifted to the opposite end, giving up their time-honored role almost entirely. Is it right for them to do so? As courts routinely say, it is not right to read too much into inaction by legislatures. There are lots of reasons (including simply being overworked) that lead legislatures to do nothing about a problem. What then? Is it fair to litigants to resolve a dispute based on rules of common law that are no longer consistent with public policy? And the problem gets worse as time passes and the common law gets more out of date. Today's environmental and land-use regulations could appear far differently, in terms of their legal effects, if courts had revised the common law throughout the twentieth century, by (for instance) redefining land use "harms" to take into account ecological degradation.

3. *The expansive police power.* In any event, as these cases illustrate, courts for many decades have been highly deferential to legislatures and administrative bodies when called upon to assess the constitutionality of new

laws governing land and resource uses. A new law is likely to run afoul of the constitutional ban on the taking of private property without just compensation only if it (i) deprives a landowner of all economic use of the property or (ii) permits a "permanent physical occupation" of private land by someone else. *See* Michael C. Blumm & Lucus Ritchie, *Lucas's Unlikely Legacy: The Rise of Background Principles as Categorical Takings Defenses*, 29 Harv. Envtl. L. Rev. 321 (2005). Thus, for instance, a statute that prohibits mining in a region is unlikely to run afoul of constitutional limits unless the land has literally no value for any other purpose. What happens, though, when mining rights to the land have been severed and sold, and then a new law bans all mining? The effect of such a law then is to deprive the mining rights of all value (at least if the market views the law as an enduring, unchangeable limit). Is a ban on mining *illegitimate* as applied to a person who only holds mining rights because it deprives the property right of all economic value while at the same time *legitimate* for a neighboring landowner who holds both surface and subsurface rights? We'll take up this issue in the next chapter.

4. *Forestry practices regulation, state and local.* Many states, particularly in West, regulate forestry practices on private lands, often requiring timber management and harvesting plans for timber operations that cover more than a certain acreage. The rising tendency has been to prohibit clear-cutting and to push where possible for the management of forests to promote multiple species while reducing erosion, protecting waterways, and improving wildlife habitat. In a recent dispute, the California Supreme Court ruled that the extensive state statutes and regulates did not entirely preempt the power of local governments also to get involved in regulating forest operations. Local governments were limited in their abilities to control how timber harvesting took place but they could, in the exercise of local zoning powers, identify specific areas off-limits to harvesting and could control the places where helicopters could operate. Big Creek Lumber Co. v. County of Santa Cruz, 38 Cal.4th 1139, 45 Cal.Rptr.3d 21, 136 P.3d 821 (2006)

5. *A right to degrade*? In the past, the do-no-harm rule has largely applied to harms that cross boundary lines—harms that a landowner imposes on neighbors or on the public at large. Do these two cases, however, suggest that the idea of harm is heading in a new direction? Could the concept of harm also include harm that an owner imposes on his own land, in the form, for instance, of soil erosion? Might we view such degradation as harm to the community as such or as harm to future generations? Or to rephrase these questions: is it necessarily the case that private owners of nature should possess the right to degrade what they own in ecological terms (admitting, of course, the difficulty of deciding what is and is not degradation)? Presumably an owner of nonrenewable resources must have a right to consume them (otherwise, of what value are they?). But what about renewable resources that, if well tended, could last essentially forever in human time-frames? Could an owner's property rights in such resources include merely the right to use the resources, not the right to over-use or degrade them? Note that Congress sought to do something like this in the case of Arizona's school lands in *Forest Guardians*. Further illustrations appear below.

On this issue, consider the Montana decision quoted at length by Justice Simpson in his dissent in *Dexter*. The ruling, *Gas Products v. Rankin,* struck down a regulation that essentially banned the flaring off of natural gas at wellheads, just to get rid of it (a practice, unfortunately, that continues to this day in parts of the world, contributing heavily to global climate change). The Montana court viewed the regulation as an improper interference with the landowner's right to "use" what he owned—which is to say his right to waste what he owned. No one today would seriously dispute the legitimacy of such a conservation measure (assuming it was properly adopted by an agency authorized to do so). Was the Montana court then simply wrong in striking down the regulation, or perhaps were the times then different enough that the regulation did unduly interfere with what people of the day viewed as a reasonable land use?

6. *Paying to halt erosion.* In recent decades, the federal government has adopted various farm programs that pay farmers to take land out of agricultural production so as to reduce soil erosion, protect waterways, and otherwise diminish the sometimes grave environmental harms generation by today's methods of industrial farming. We can put to one side whether such payments are wise from the point of view of sustaining farmers economically, given persistently low crop prices and the nation's need to maintain a secure farm base. What, though, are the effects of such payments on ideas about land ownership? What messages do they convey, and how might they be influencing the ways we think about owning land generally?

To judge from the materials covered so far, many of the payment schemes compensate farmers to halt activities that society views as harmful or unreasonable. They are activities that could be banned by regulation and sometimes even by courts applying common law principles. When that is the case, what happens when farmers get paid to stop the bad practices? After all, we do not pay motorists to drive safely; we do not pay factories to halt their air pollution. Why pay farmers to halt similarly bad or dangerous activities? The danger here, of course, is that the payments implicitly validate the landowner's ability to engage in the unwanted activities in the absence of payments. Landowners are being paid, that is, to halt activities that lawmakers believe they could otherwise undertake. Is there a problem here? Might the payments be undercutting the longstanding limit of reasonable use, and substituting a vision of ownership akin to the one used by Justice Simpson in *Dexter*? Is it fair to expect taxpayers to fund payments programs that halt communally damaging land uses? Payment programs are often touted as "voluntary" conservation—better than mandatory, some say—but we might remember that taxpayers are not volunteers. (On these issues, see the final reading in chapter eight by John Echeverria.)

7. *Varieties of liberty.* One of the key issues in serious thought about private property, especially private land, has to do with the connections between land ownership and liberty. America is preeminently a land of liberty, and places a high value on the protection of liberty. In his dissent in *Dexter*, Justice Simpson contends that the natural gas regulation reduced liberty and was thus invalid. But how complete was Simpson's appraisal of the situation? To be sure, the regulation limited the liberty of the landowner to waste the natural gas if he liked. But is that the end of the inquiry?

Most Americans today think of liberty in the same way that Justice Simpson did, as negative in content (freedom from) and individual in scope (freedom at the individual level). Liberty, though, has many meanings, positive as well as negative, and collective as well as individual. At the time of the Declaration of Independence, probably the most important type of liberty—the type that the signers sought to protect—was the positive power of colonists to get together collectively to make rules governing their activities. Joyce Appleby, CAPITALISM AND THE NEW SOCIAL ORDER: THE REPUBLICAN VISION OF THE 1790S 16–17 (1984); Michael Kammen, SPHERES OF LIBERTY: CHANGING PERCEPTIONS OF LIBERTY IN AMERICAN CULTURE 33–38 (1986). Wasn't the regulation at issue in *Dexter* itself an exercise in liberty, and didn't the court, by striking down the regulation, curtail the liberty of Montana citizens to decide collectively how they would live? Consider, too, the liberties of neighbors, who might not like the gas burning. Aren't their liberties also at issue? On this last question, consider the next case:

MOON v. NORTH IDAHO FARMERS ASSOCIATION

140 Idaho 536, 96 P.3d 637 (2004).

BURDICK, JUSTICE.

The defendant-seed growers are appealing the district court's decision holding the amendments to I.C. § 22–4801 et seq., which were passed by the 2003 Legislature, unconstitutional. This Court granted a permissive appeal of this interlocutory order. For the reasons outlined below, we hold the recently enacted amendments to be in conformity with the Idaho and United States Constitutions.

FACTUAL AND PROCEDURAL BACKGROUND

The plaintiffs are individuals claiming sensitivity to grass smoke, who filed an action against various seed growers in north Idaho who traditionally burn the post-harvest straw and stubble in their fields as part of their farming activities. The plaintiffs' complaint, filed in June of 2002, asserted among others, claims of nuisance and trespass. The plaintiffs filed for a preliminary injunction in July of 2002, seeking to enjoin the defendant-seed growers from burning their Kentucky bluegrass fields. The district court, in August 2002 took testimony from the plaintiffs' medical experts, State officials from Washington and Idaho, class members and grass farmers. The district court issued findings of fact and conclusions of law and ultimately granted the preliminary injunction to abate the injury caused by the field burning of the grass farmers and required the posting of a bond.

In September of 2002, however, the Idaho Supreme Court granted the defendant-seed growers' request for a writ of prohibition, after concluding that the injunction exceeded in some respects the district court's jurisdiction. The Court enjoined the district court from enforcing the terms of the preliminary injunction against the grass burners.

The plaintiffs sought and were granted certification as a class and were granted leave to amend their complaint to assert a punitive damage claim. Thereafter, in the early spring of 2003, several bills related to field burning were under consideration by the Idaho legislature. The district court held a hearing on April 11, 2003, where the impact of the various bills was discussed with respect to the plaintiffs' property and their statutory rights to abate the nuisance and/or enjoin the trespass caused by the grass burners' smoke.

In April 2003, after Governor Kempthorne signed House Bill 391 into law, the plaintiffs filed a motion to the district court to declare the law unconstitutional as applied to the facts of this case. HB 391, which was passed as an emergency measure, amended the Smoke Management and Crop Residue Disposal Act of 1999, I.C. § 22–4801 et seq., and effectively extinguished liability for all North Idaho grass farmers that burn in compliance with its provisions. Of particular significance, HB 391 amended portions of I.C. § 22–4803 and added a new statute, I.C. § 22–4803A.

The district court heard the motion of the plaintiffs, arguing the unconstitutionality of I.C. § 22–4803A(6), which reads as follows:

> (6) Crop residue burning conducted in accordance with section 22–4803 Idaho Code, shall not constitute a private or public nuisance or constitute trespass. Nothing in this chapter shall be construed to create a private cause of action against any person who engages in or allows crop residue burning of a field or fields required to be registered pursuant to section 22–4803(3) Idaho Code, provided such activities are conducted in accordance with chapter 49, title 22, Idaho Code, and rules promulgated thereunder.

On June 4, 2003, the district court issued an order holding HB 391 unconstitutional. The district court held: (1) that HB 391 effects an unconstitutional taking of property without prior compensation or due process; (2) that HB 391 imposes a limitation that is not in the interests of the common welfare and thus violative of Article I, § 1 of the Idaho Constitution; and (3) that HB 391 is a "local or special law" in violation of Article III, § 19 of the Idaho Constitution. The district court concluded that for two months of the year, August and September, "the burning invades and destroys two of the three fundamental aspects of the plaintiffs' property rights ... possession and use." The district court also ruled that by affirmatively granting the grass burners the right to maintain the nuisance on the plaintiffs' property, the State imposed an easement on the plaintiffs' land....

Issues on Appeal

1. Did the district court err in finding HB 391 is an unconstitutional "taking" of private property under both the Idaho and United States Constitutions?

2. Did the district court err in finding that HB 391 is a violation of Article I, § 1 of the Idaho Constitution, because the "limitation" imposed by the amendments were not in the "interests of the common welfare"? . . .

Discussion

HB 391 affected amendments to portions of I.C. §§ 22–4801, –4803 and –4804 and added an entirely new section, I.C. § 22–4803A. The plaintiffs' motion dated April 30, 2003, challenged the constitutionality of HB 391 in several respects.

In asserting their challenge to the statute, the plaintiffs contended that the immunity conferred by I.C. § 22–4803A(6) to the grass farmers who burn their fields results in a taking of private property without the payment of compensation in violation of federal and state constitutional provisions. The statute at issue provides in relevant part: "Crop residue burning conducted in accordance with section 22–4803, Idaho Code, shall not constitute a private or public nuisance or constitute a trespass." The district court determined that I.C. § 22–4803A(6) is unconstitutional because it takes property without prior compensation in violation of the Fifth Amendment to the federal Constitution.

The just compensation clause of the Fifth Amendment of the United States Constitution provides that no person shall "be deprived of life, liberty, or property, without due process of law, nor shall private property be taken for public use, without just compensation." The Idaho Constitution also guarantees its citizens the right of due process if private property is taken for a public use, pursuant to Article I, § 13, and provides for just compensation for such a taking, pursuant to Article I, § 14. The question this Court must answer, then, is whether the grant of immunity to the grass farmers can be deemed a "taking" from the plaintiffs. In other words, have the plaintiffs been deprived, by the statute, of their common law right to bring a nuisance action and/or a trespass action, without remuneration.

Idaho case law has defined "trespass" to apply to the wrongful interference with the right of exclusive possession of real property, while the tort of private "nuisance" applies to the wrongful interference with the use and enjoyment of real property. *Mock v. Potlatch Corp.,* 786 F.Supp. 1545 (D.Idaho 1992). *See also Carpenter v. Double R Cattle Co., Inc.,* 105 Idaho 320, 669 P.2d 643 (Ct.App.1983) ("But where an invasion of property is merely incidental to the use of adjoining property, and does not physically interfere with possession of the property invaded, it generally has been classified as a nuisance rather than a trespass."); I.C. § 52–101 (defining nuisance as "anything which is injurious to health [. . .]or an obstruction to the free use of property, so as to interfere with the comfortable enjoyment of life or property."). A useful differentiation between trespass and nuisance is found in a case that the district court found to be squarely on point, in which the Iowa Supreme Court noted: "Trespass comprehends an actual physical invasion by tangible matter. An invasion which constitutes a nuisance is usually by intangible substances, such as noises or odors." *Bormann v. Board of Supervisors,* 584 N.W.2d 309 (Iowa 1998), *cert. den. sub nom., Girres v. Bormann,* 525 U.S. 1172, 119 S.Ct. 1096, 143 L.Ed.2d 96 (1999), *citing Ryan v. City of Emmetsburg,* 232 Iowa 600, 603, 4 N.W.2d 435, 439 (1942). Thus, in the plaintiffs' situation, an action could be said to lie in nuisance and in trespass, respectively, given the invasion of the thick, oppressive smoke generated by the farmers' burning and the particulates emitted from the smoke onto the plaintiffs' land.

In *Covington v. Jefferson County,* 137 Idaho 777, 53 P.3d 828 (2002), the increased noises, offensive odors, dust, flies, and litter caused by the operation of the landfill near the Covingtons' property formed the basis of their claim of inverse condemnation. In their amended complaint, they alleged that their property was impaired by the operation of the landfill by an amount in excess of 25% of the property's total value, which they claimed amounted to a taking for which they were entitled to compensation. The Court analyzed the elements of the claim, including whether the Covingtons' property was invaded or appropriated to the extent of a taking, and determined as a matter of law that the Covingtons had failed to allege a taking under either the state or the federal constitution. *Id.* at 780, 53 P.3d at 831.

According to the *Covington* court, before an owner is entitled to compensation for a violation of Article I, § 14 of the Idaho Constitution, his property must be "taken" and not merely "damaged." *Id.* at 781, 53 P.2d at 832, *citing Powell v. McKelvey,* 56 Idaho 291, 307, 53 P.2d 626, 632–33 (1935). This conclusion was based on the language of the constitutional provision that contains only the word "taken" and which has not authorized the collection of damages where there is no actual physical taking of the property. *Id.* at 780, 53 P.3d at 831, *citing Idaho–Western Ry. Co. v. Columbia Conference of Evangelical Lutheran Augustana Synod,* 20 Idaho 568, 584–85, 119 P. 60, 65 (1911). The Court also held that under the United States Constitution, a physical invasion or a regulatory taking, which permanently deprives the owner of "all economically beneficial uses" of his land, requires compensation. *Id., citing Lucas v. South Carolina Coastal Council,* 505 U.S. 1003, 112 S.Ct. 2886, 120 L.Ed.2d 798 (1992).

The case presently before the Court is not an inverse condemnation case but as in *Covington,* deals with a regulatory taking. *Covington,* 137 Idaho at 781, 53 P.3d at 832. Although a footnote in *Covington* indicates that "[t]his activity may constitute a nuisance claim which is not before this court," the opinion does not address whether the elimination of such a nuisance claim by act of the legislature could or could not be deemed a taking. The determination of whether or not there was a taking is a matter of law to be resolved by the trial court. *Rueth v. State,* 100 Idaho 203, 596 P.2d 75 (1979). The trial court should also determine the nature of the property interest so taken. *Tibbs v. City of Sandpoint,* 100 Idaho 667, 670, 603 P.2d 1001, 1004 (1979).

The taking asserted by the plaintiffs is not a physical taking because the plaintiffs' land is not appropriated and because the smoke complained of does not result in a loss of access or of any complete use of the property. *See Hughes v. State of Idaho,* 80 Idaho 286, 328 P.2d 397 (1958) (impairment of a right of access constituted a 'taking of property'). *See also Covington, supra* (where there has been no loss of access to or denial of any use of the Covingtons' property). The taking asserted then, is in the nature of a regulatory taking, but the plaintiffs have not claimed a permanent deprivation of all economically beneficial uses of their land. As such, under the Idaho Constitution, which does not allow less than a total deprivation of use or denial of access, and under *Lucas,* 505 U.S. 1003, 112 S.Ct. 2886, 120 L.Ed.2d 798, there is no taking in violation of the state or the federal constitution. *See also Tahoe–Sierra Preservation Council, Inc. v. Tahoe Regional Planning Agency, et al.,* 535 U.S. 302, 122 S.Ct. 1465, 152 L.Ed.2d 517 (2002) (holding no categorical taking had occurred because the regulations had only a temporary impact on the petitioners' fee interest in the properties); *cf. Renninger v. State, et al.,* 70 Idaho 170, 213 P.2d 911 (1950) (a taking requiring just compensation occurs when the state inflicts permanent and irreparable injury on land).

The district court, in analyzing the extent of the taking, concluded that "[a]ny destruction, interruption, or deprivation by the common, usual and ordinary use of property is by the weight of authority a taking of one's property in violation of the constitutional guaranty." *Knowles v. New Sweden Irr. Dist.,* 16 Idaho 217, 231, 101 P. 81, 86 (1908), *as cited in Hughes v. State,* 80 Idaho 286, 294, 328 P.2d 397, 401 (1958). As noted above, the destruction of access and deprivation of the use of property may be compensable, but the mere interruption of the use of one's property, as it is less than a permanent (complete) deprivation, does not mandate compensation. This Idaho authority relied upon by the district court has since been overruled by the Supreme Court's interpretation of the scope of a taking. *Covington, supra.*

The district court also relied on *Renninger v. State,* 70 Idaho 170, 213 P.2d 911 (1950), for the proposition that just compensation is warranted even when the taking is intermittent. This proposition is derived from cases cited in *Renninger* holding that where a *structure* causes 'permanent liability to *intermittent* but inevitably recurring overflows' it is taking. *Id., citing Sanguinetti v. United States,* 264 U.S. 146, 44 S.Ct. 264, 68 L.Ed. 608 (1924). The physical structure in *Sanguinetti* was a dam, and the servitude created by reason of the intermittent overflow was held to be a partial taking. *See id.* In *Renninger,* the structure that led to injury to the land was a bridge—distinguishing it from the smoke created by the field burning in the case at hand.

Another proposition cited by the district court, which is not the holding of *Renninger,* is a quote from *Pumpelly v. Green Bay & Mississippi Canal Co.,* 13 Wall. 166, 80 U.S. 166, 20 L.Ed. 557 (1871):

> where real estate is actually invaded by superinduced additions of water, earth, sand or other material . . . so as to effectually destroy or impair its usefulness, it is a taking, within the meaning of the Constitution, and that this proposition is not in conflict with the weight of judicial authority in this country, and certainly not with sound principle.

Id. at 181, 20 L.Ed. at 561. Rather, in *Renninger,* where the plaintiff sought to recover damages in inverse condemnation for the injury caused by the bridge built by the State, the Court held that when the state inflicts permanent and irreparable injury on the land without making any compensation, there is a violation of Article I, § 14 of the Idaho Constitution. The district court's reading of *Renninger* is inaccurate.

Next, the district court concluded that the right to maintain a nuisance is an easement, citing the Restatement of Property § 451, at 2912 (1944), which provides: "An affirmative easement entitles the owner thereof to use the land subject to the easement by doing acts which, were it not for the easement, he would not be privileged to do." As explained by the comments to § 451:

> In many cases, the use an owner of an affirmative easement is entitled to make enables him to intrude upon the land subject to the easement in ways which, were it not for the easement, would make him a trespasser upon the land. On the other hand, it may entitle him to do acts on his own land which, were it not for the easement, would constitute a nuisance.

Id. cmt. (1944). Idaho, however, has not adopted the Restatement; moreover, in the case before the Court, the smoke created by the burning of the fields is the "nuisance or trespass" immunized by the statute, I.C. § 22–4803A(6). This immunity thus entitles the grass farmers to invade the property of the plaintiffs' with the smoke from their burning fields, while preventing the plaintiff landowners from full possession, use, and quiet enjoyment of their land and denying them a remedy from the invasion from the farmers' smoke.

The district court followed the reasoning of the court in *Bormann v. Board of Supervisors.* In *Bormann,* the Iowa Supreme Court recalled long-standing law that the right to maintain a nuisance is an easement, 584 N.W.2d at 315–16, *citing Churchill v. Burlington Water Co.,* 94 Iowa 89, 62 N.W. 646, 647 (Iowa 1895), which holding is consistent with the Restatement of Property § 451. The court characterized the nuisance immunity provision in section 352.11(1)(a) of the Iowa Code as creating an easement in the property affected by the nuisance (the servient tenement) in favor of the applicants' land (the dominant tenement). *Id.* at 316. Concluding that easements are property interests subject to the just compensation requirements of the Iowa and the Federal Constitutions, the court ruled that the approval of the application for an agricultural area pursuant to 352.11(1)(a) conferred immunity, which resulted in the Board's taking of easements in the neighbors' properties for the benefit of the applicants. *Id.* at 321. The court concluded that the legislature had exceeded its authority by authorizing the use of property in such a way as to infringe on the rights of others by allowing the creation of a nuisance without the payment of compensation, compelling the court to hold "that portion of Iowa Code section 352.11(1)(a) that provides for immunity against nuisances unconstitutional and without any force and effect." *Id.* at 321–322.

There is no direct authority in Idaho holding that the right to maintain a nuisance is an easement....

The challenge in *Bormann* was one of inverse condemnation by the landowners when the Board of Supervisors failed to seek condemnation in court. 584 N.W.2d at 311–12. The landowners claimed an invasion of their property by the Board's approval of an application for an agricultural area designation, the effect of which was an immediate interference with the plaintiffs' enjoyment and use of their land and a corresponding, measurable loss of the property's value. The *Bormann* court found historical support for allowing compensation for interferences short of a physical taking or touching of the land in *Pennsylvania Coal Co. v. Mahon,* 260 U.S. 393, 43 S.Ct. 158, 67 L.Ed. 322 (1922)(statute that was an attempt to condemn property and deny the owner coal company the occupancy and right to mine his property viewed as a taking of an interest without any physical intrusion) and *Richards v. Washington Terminal Co.,* 233 U.S. 546, 34 S.Ct. 654, 58 L.Ed. 1088 (1914) (recognizing the taking of a property interest or right to be free from 'special and peculiar' governmental interference with enjoyment and eliminating the requirement of a physical taking or touching). The *Bormann* court looked to more recent United States Supreme Court cases drawing a distinction between *per se* takings as outlined in *Lucas v. South Carolina Coastal Council,* 505 U.S. 1003, 112 S.Ct. 2886, 120 L.Ed.2d 798 (1992), and all other cases involving regulatory takings, which are to be examined on a case-by-case basis, calling for a balancing test that is one of reasonableness, to determine at which point the exercise of police power becomes a taking. *Bormann,* 584 N.W.2d at 316–17, *citing Penn Cent. Transp. Co. v. New York City,* 438 U.S. 104, 124, 98 S.Ct. 2646, 2659, 57 L.Ed.2d 631, 648 (1978).

The district court in deciding whether the farmers' grass burning effected a taking also relied on *Richards v. Washington Terminal Co.,* 233 U.S. 546, 34 S.Ct. 654, 58 L.Ed. 1088 (1914), as cited in *Bormann,* 584 N.W.2d at 319, which awarded compensation for the gases and smoke emitted from engines in the tunnel, which constituted "special and peculiar" damage resulting in diminution of the value of the plaintiff's property. *Richards,* 233 U.S. at 557, 34 S.Ct. at 658, 58 L.Ed. at 1093. The grass farmers correctly argue here, that the plaintiffs have not alleged any "special and peculiar" damage so as to bring themselves within the scope of a private nuisance as contemplated by *Richards,* but only such damages as naturally and unavoidably result from the field burning and are shared generally by property owners whose lands lie within the range of the inconveniences necessarily incident to proximity to the fields being burned....

The grass farmers argue that the plaintiffs have failed to identify Idaho authority for the proposition that the Legislature is foreclosed from abolishing nuisance or trespass causes of action that have not yet accrued. Article XXI, § 2 of the Idaho Constitution provides that the legislature has the power to modify or repeal common law causes of action. It is well established that "it is the province of the Legislature,

[margin note: legislation gets to modify common law rules.]

and not the court, to modify the rules of the common law." *Moon v. Bullock,* 65 Idaho 594, 607, 151 P.2d 765, 771 (1944). The Court has held that the Legislature can abolish common law causes of action entirely or impose statutes of limitation without violating Article I, § 18. *Hawley v. Green,* 117 Idaho 498, 788 P.2d 1321 (1990). More recently, the Court determined that no one has a vested right to a particular common law or necessarily, to a statutory cause of action. *Osmunson v. State,* 135 Idaho 292, 295, 17 P.3d 236, 239 (2000)....

[margin note: Holding –]

Accordingly, we hold that that the provision of Idaho Code § 22–3806A(6) granting immunity to the grass farmers does not represent an unconstitutional taking under either the state or federal constitution.

II.

The district court ruled that HB 391 violates Article I, § 1 of the Idaho Constitution. The district court applied the test of *Newland v. Child,* 73 Idaho 530, 537, 254 P.2d 1066, 1069 (1953) to analyze whether I.C. § 22–4803A(6) promoted the common welfare and placed a reasonable limitation on the plaintiffs' inalienable right "to possess and protect property" conferred by Article I, § 1. Disagreeing with the Legislature's findings and making an independent finding that Kentucky bluegrass can be grown without burning, as is done in Oregon and Washington, the district court determined that the limitation imposed by the statute was not "in the interests of the common welfare."

The plaintiffs' challenge to the statute is a facial challenge, invoking a standard requiring the challenger to establish that no set of circumstances exist under which the Act would be valid. *United States v. Salerno,* 481 U.S. 739, 745, 107 S.Ct. 2095, 2100, 95 L.Ed.2d 697, 707 (1987); *see also Village of Hoffman Estates v. Flipside, Hoffman Estates, Inc.,* 455 U.S. 489, 498, 102 S.Ct. 1186, 1193, 71 L.Ed.2d 362, 371 (1982); *State v. Newman,* 108 Idaho 5, 12, 696 P.2d 856, 863 (1985), *citing Steffel v. Thompson,* 415 U.S. 452, 94 S.Ct. 1209, 39 L.Ed.2d 505 (1974). Because there clearly are some interests of the common welfare being protected by the Legislature's action in allowing field burning, we cannot say that the plaintiffs have met their burden to show no conceivable constitutional application for this legislation. There were no facts presented at this stage of the case, and accordingly, an "as applied" challenge is not available to the plaintiffs....

The district court erred in holding I.C. § 22–4803A(6) unconstitutional because it violated Article I, § 1 of the Idaho Constitution.

Notes

1. *Property rights and remedies.* What is the relationship between private property *rights* and the *remedies* that the law provides to protect them? *Moon* seems to provide a clear answer, from the point of view of the law.

Practically speaking, property rights exist only to the extent of the legal remedies that exist to vindicate them. Alter the remedies, and the property rights themselves necessarily change. As the old legal adage puts it (with some overstatement), no right without a remedy. To see this reality is to understand why, for centuries, students of the common law centered their studies around the various legal remedies, not on bodies of substantive law as students do today. Even at the end of the nineteenth century, legal study centered on what we would call *causes of action*—what were then called *forms of action*, and what earlier lawyers talked about as *writs*. A study of property law would thus center around the study of trespass, nuisance, and other less familiar remedies for invasions of private rights. As for the remedies themselves, the court in *Moon* is particularly clear in upholding the power of state lawmakers to alter them. "[N]o one has a vested right to a particular common law or necessarily, to a statutory cause of action." To change remedies is to change the underlying rights. Thus, *Moon* effectively recognizes the broad powers of lawmakers to redefine what private property means, in terms of the rights and responsibilities of property owners. The two main pillars of land ownership are trespass and nuisance. To revise these remedies, as the Idaho legislature did, is to alter land ownership at its core.

In terms of the policy rationale behind the Idaho grass-burning statute at issue in *Moon*, we see a strong echo of the kinds of legal change that took place in American law during the nineteenth century, as lawmakers allowed more intensive land uses while concurrently contracting the ability of neighboring landowners to complain about land-use harm. The right to use land intensively has again gone up, while the right to quiet enjoyment has again gone down.

2. *A future interests analogy?* Did the Idaho statute protecting grass burners have the effect of cutting off or taking away the property rights of neighboring landowners (as the plaintiffs alleged), or did it operate in some other way? The question would seem easy: of course it cut off landowner rights. Yet the court's reasoning gives cause to consider the issue more carefully.

In *Moon*, the court employs a distinctly positivist view of property rights by implying that property rights exist only to the extent protected by law. Take away the law, and the property rights disappear. To see the significance of this jurisprudential approach, we can use an analogy borrowed from future interests law—the distinction between a fee simple determinable, which automatically comes to an end upon the occurrence of some specified event, and a fee simple on a condition subsequent, in which a third party possesses the power to terminate a property right (perhaps by going to court). Which analogy is more apt, given the court's reasoning in *Moon*?

On this issue, review note 1, above, following the decisions in *Dexter* and *Ortner*. When a court applying the *common law* rules that a particular land-use is unduly harmful, it essentially announces that the landowner's activities are not legally authorized; the landowner is doing something that the law does not allow. Thus, a finding that a land use amounts to a nuisance does not cut short or take away any landowner rights, it merely identifies and applies a limit on those the rights. Similarly, a plaintiff (as in *Bryant v. Lefever*) who is unsuccessful in a nuisance suit is told (as Bryant was told) that he has no right to the remedy he seeks; his property rights simply do not extend that far. This result holds true, even when—as often happened in the nineteenth century—the court's ruling represents a change in the scope of private property rights. It would thus seem, then, that *common law* change takes the form of the fee simple determinable, as courts announce the built-in limits on private property rights. *Statutory change*, however, typically appears otherwise, as something that cuts short or takes away private property rights.

Might this difference explain why common law limits on property rights typically cause fewer complaints than statutory changes? The Idaho statute evaluated in *Moon* triggered a strong challenge to its constitutionality. Would a similar complaint have been raised if the trial court had ruled that the defendants' conduct did not amount to a nuisance or trespass? Would the effect on the property rights of the plaintiffs have been any less? Presumably the trial court ruling would be accepted as a statement of existing law (even if people didn't like it). The statute, in contrast, comes across as an obvious change in the law. But the truth might be quite otherwise. If these guesses are correct, what does it say about the relative wisdom of having courts versus legislatures keep property law up to date? Given the way legal change in property rights makes most citizens very nervous, would it be better if we left courts in charge, allowing them to make changes in ways that conceal the change?

3. *Other limits on regulation.* The preceding cases have largely involved claims by landowners that regulatory restrictions on their land, or other statutory or regulatory actions, have amounted to unconstitutional takings of their property without the payment of just compensation. When the restrictions are imposed by *local* governments of some type, rather than at the state level, landowners have another broad avenue of attack available to them: They can assert that the local government has exceeded the authority granted to it by the state to impose land-use controls. The possible claims here are many. Local governments can fail to follow the processes mandated by state law (for instance, by failing to hold the right public hearings, or to give due notice and public zoning maps). They can fail to prepare or act in accordance with a comprehensive land-use plan. Or they could impose restrictions that entail either unlawful regulatory means or unlawful ends (for instance, zoning to restrict fair economic competition). On all of these legal issues (which are the stuff of courses on land use law), legal restrictions on using natural resources are typically subject to the same legal requirements as all other local land-use rules.The entire field of land-use law is thus relevant to the practice of natural resources law.

As the following case illustrates, however, locally imposed limits on resource uses can sometimes be subject to special legal rules or requirements, reflecting peculiar state policies relating to natural resources:

SILVA v. TOWNSHIP OF ADA

416 Mich. 153, 330 N.W.2d 663 (1982).

LEVIN, JUSTICE.

These cases, consolidated on appeal, concern the standard for determining the validity of zoning which prevents the extraction of natural resources. In both cases, the Court of Appeals upheld zoning regulations which would prevent the extraction of natural resources without considering whether "very serious consequences" would result from the extraction. We reaffirm the rule of *Certain-teed Products Corp. v. Paris Twp.*, 351 Mich. 434, 88 N.W.2d 705 (1958), that zoning regulations which prevent the extraction of natural resources are invalid unless "very serious consequences" will result from the proposed extraction.

I

A. Clare Silva and Karen J. Silva purchased an 80–acre parcel in an area zoned for specialized farming and single-family residences. The Silvas intended to use this property to strip mine for gravel. The Silvas' property is surrounded by agricultural, residential, and undeveloped property.

The Silvas filed two applications for rezoning with the township zoning authorities, but their applications were denied. In their second application, the Silvas proposed several ways in which they would attempt to minimize any adverse effects of their operations, including limiting mining to ten years, regrading and recontouring the property at the conclusion of the mining operations to make it suitable for farming or home development, fencing, using stockpiles as visual and sound buffers, and restricting the extraction to a 46–acre area.

After their unsuccessful efforts to obtain rezoning, the Silvas filed an action in the Kent Circuit Court. Judgment was entered in favor of the township, and the Court of Appeals affirmed.

The Ottawa Silica Company, intending to mine silica sand, purchased 31 acres in an area zoned for residential use, adjacent to land which it already mines. The south end of Brownstown Township, where this property is located, remains basically rural and undeveloped except for one large subdivision. Two or three homes are directly across from the property.

The township denied a request for reclassification. Ottawa Silica then commenced this action in the circuit court. The court found that:

> The resource to be mined is a unique type of silica sand, which, because of its qualities of being both round and white, is particularly valuable for foundry use and the manufacturing of fine crystal. There is no other deposit of such sand in this country at this relatively shallow level underground, which means that it can be mined more economically than if it were deeper under the ground, and hence can be sold at a most competitive price.

Approximately 49% of the parcel is within a flood plain and cannot legally be built upon. The court ruled the zoning unconstitutional insofar as it applied to the portion of the land west of a stream bisecting it. The Court of Appeals reversed.

II

This Court has recently reaffirmed that a zoning ordinance must be reasonable to comport with the requirements of substantive due process. Zoning ordinances are presumed to be reasonable, and a person challenging the ordinance has the burden of proving otherwise. These appeals concern the standard to be employed in determining reasonableness where the zoning would prevent the extraction of natural resources.

A

Zoning regulations seek to achieve a land use which serves the interests of the community as a whole. Because of the important public interest in extracting and using natural resources, this Court has applied a more rigorous standard of reasonableness when the zoning would prevent the extraction of natural resources.

This Court first noted that zoning which prevents the extraction of natural resources involves different considerations than zoning regulations generally in *North Muskegon v. Miller,* 249 Mich. 52, 57, 227 N.W. 743 (1929), which concerned a zoning ordinance preventing the drilling of oil wells:

> The courts have particularly stressed the importance of not destroying or withholding the right to secure oil, gravel, or mineral from one's property, through zoning ordinances, unless some *very serious consequences* will follow therefrom.''

In *Certain-teed Products, supra,* 351 Mich. at p. 467, 88 N.W.2d 705, this Court reaffirmed that zoning would not be sustained unless very serious consequences would result from the mining operations:

> ''To sustain the ordinance in such case there must be some dire need which, if denied the ordained protection, will result in 'very serious consequences.' ''

We again reaffirm the ''very serious consequences'' rule of *Miller* and *Certain-teed.*

Natural resources can only be extracted from the place where they are located and found. Preventing the mining of natural resources located at a particular site prevents all use of those natural resources. As the United States Court of Appeals for the Sixth Circuit said in *Village of Terrace Park v. Errett,* 12 F.2d 240, 243 (CA 6, 1926):

> There is * * * a substantial difference between an ordinance prohibiting manufacturing or commercial business in a residential district that may be conducted in another locality with equal profit and advantage, and an ordinance that wholly deprives the owner of land of its valuable mineral content.''

Preventing the extraction of natural resources harms the interests of the public as well as those of the property owner by making natural resources more expensive. Because the cost of transporting some natural resources (*e.g.,* gravel) may be a significant factor, locally obtained resources may be less expensive than those which must be transported long distances. It appears that the silica sand involved in one of the cases here on appeal is unique in quality and location.

In most cases, where natural resources are found the land will be suited for some other use and can reasonably be devoted to that use. Unless a higher standard is required, natural resources could be extracted only with the consent of local authorities or in the rare case where the land cannot be reasonably used in some other manner. The public interest of the citizens of this state who do not reside in the community where natural resources are located in the development and use of natural resources requires closer scrutiny of local zoning regulations which prevent development. In this connection, we note that extraction of natural resources is frequently a temporary use of the land and that the land can often be restored for other uses and appropriate assurances with adequate security can properly be demanded as a precondition to the commencement of extraction operations....

C

Our reaffirmance of the "very serious consequences" rule does not imply that zoning which prevents the extraction of natural resources is unreasonable. Zoning regulations are presumed to be reasonable and a person challenging zoning has the burden of proving otherwise. The party challenging the zoning has the burden of showing that there are valuable natural resources and that no "very serious consequences" would result from the extraction of those resources.

The Court of Appeals failed to apply the "very serious consequences" standard in determining the validity of the zoning in the instant cases. We reverse and remand both cases to the Court of Appeals for further consideration.

RYAN, JUSTICE (concurring in part and dissenting in part).

These two cases, consolidated for appeal, involve challenges to zoning ordinances which effectively prevented the strip mining operations contemplated by the plaintiffs. The Ottawa Silica Company wants to remove silica sand from an area in Brownstown Township zoned single-family residential; the Silvas would like to mine gravel in an area of Ada Township zoned for specialized farming and single-family residences. Upon failing in their efforts to obtain rezoning, the landowners filed suit challenging the constitutionality of the respective zoning ordinances. While the circuit courts upheld the Ada Township ordinance and partially invalidated the Brownstown ordinance, the Court of Appeals upheld the validity of both zoning ordinances.

The applicable standard for judicial review is clearly set forth in a number of fairly recent decisions by this Court. *Ed Zaagman, Inc. v. City of Kentwood,* 406 Mich. 137, 277 N.W.2d 475 (1979); *Kirk v. Tyrone Twp.,* 398 Mich. 429, 247 N.W.2d 848 (197); and *Kropf v. Sterling Heights,* 391 Mich. 139, 215 N.W.2d 179 (1974). In a successful challenge to the validity of a zoning ordinance, the plaintiff has the burden of proving:

> "[F]irst, that there is no reasonable governmental interest being advanced by the present zoning classification itself * * * or secondly, that an ordinance may be unreasonable because of the purely arbitrary, capricious and unfounded exclusion of other types of legitimate land use from the area in question." *Kropf, supra,* 391 Mich. at p. 158, 215 N.W.2d 179.

The four rules for applying these principles were also outlined in *Kropf, supra:*

> 1. " '[T]he ordinance comes to us clothed with every presumption of validity.' " *Kropf,* 391 Mich. at p. 162, 215 N.W.2d 179, *quoting Brae Burn, Inc. v. Bloomfield Hills,* 350 Mich. 425, 86 N.W.2d 166 (1957).
>
> 2. " '[I]t is the burden of the party attacking to prove affirmatively that the ordinance is an arbitrary and unreasonable restriction upon the owner's use of his property. * * * It must appear that the clause attacked is an arbitrary fiat, a whimsical *ipse dixit,* and that there is no room for a legitimate difference of opinion concerning its reasonableness.' " *Id.*
>
> 3. "Michigan has adopted the view that to sustain an attack on a zoning ordinance, an aggrieved property owner must show that if the ordinance is enforced the consequent restrictions on his property preclude its use for any purposes to which it is reasonably adapted." *Kropf,* 391 Mich. at pp. 162–163, 215 N.W.2d 179.
>
> 4. " 'This Court, however, is inclined to give considerable weight to the findings of the trial judge in equity cases.' " *Kropf,* 391 Mich. at p. 163, 215 N.W.2d 179, quoting *Christine Building Co. v. City of Troy,* 367 Mich. 508, 518, 116 N.W.2d 816 (1962).

While not purporting to overrule the above-cited cases, my brother's opinion effectively does so by holding, for the first time, "that zoning regulations which prevent the extraction of natural resources are invalid unless 'very serious consequences' will result from the proposed extraction". This holding reverses the presumption of validity accorded zoning ordinances and creates a "preferred use" doctrine in favor of removing natural resources, contrary to our decision in *Kropf, supra,* which specifically abolished the preferred use doctrine. Therefore, I cannot join my brother's opinion.

Even a cursory examination of this Court's opinions in *Certain-teed Products Corp. v. Paris Twp.,* 351 Mich. 434, 88 N.W.2d 705 (1958), and *City of North Muskegon v. Miller,* 249 Mich. 52, 227 N.W. 743 (1929), reveals that the supposed "rule" favoring the removal of natural resources unless "very serious consequences" would result was merely obiter dictum in each case. In Miller, *supra*, the Court affirmed an injunction against oil drilling under a city ordinance requiring a drilling permit; therefore, the supposed policy in favor of exploiting natural resources was not followed in that case. In *Certain-teed* the Court reversed the law case based on the zoning ordinance, but remanded the chancery case in contemplation of continuing judicial supervision and control over the mining project; the plaintiffs in that suit were not given *carte blanche* to develop natural resources, and the Court's opinion explicitly contemplated that in the future an injunction shutting down the mining operation might be proper.

It is particularly inappropriate to elevate dictum to holding when the dictum embodies the public policy of 1929 and 1958, not 1982. We have long since abandoned the illusion that our scarce natural resources are infinite and renewable and therefore should be quickly exploited to the fullest extent. See *Michigan Oil Co. v. Natural Resources Comm.*, 406 Mich. 1, 276 N.W.2d 141 (1979); M.C.L. § 691.1201 *et seq.;* M.S.A. § 14.528(201) *et seq.*

If there was error in either of these cases, it was the failure of the Court of Appeals in *Ottawa* to give adequate deference to the factual findings of the trial judge in this equity case. On this basis, I agree with the remand in that case but would affirm in the *Silva* case.

Notes

1. *Shared governance VII: deference and burdens of proof. Silva* is an unusual ruling, worth reading not because it sets forth a widely prevailing view but because of the opposite: because it alerts us to the quirks of natural resources law and to the possible existence of legal rules, usually crafted long ago, that promote intensive resource utilization. In this dispute, the Michigan court considers a challenge to a zoning ordinance that restricts mining. Zoning ordinances in general are typically accorded great deference, as Justice Ryan explains in his separate opinion. Michigan courts, though, have carved out a special rule for ordinances that restrict the extraction of natural resources. These ordinances are treated with far greater suspicion. What exactly is the Michigan rule, and what can we infer from it about the priority given to natural resource extraction in Michigan? Is this rule based on the importance of natural resources to the state's economy? Are there other possible explanations for the peculiar rule?

This rule protecting natural resource extraction is obviously of judicial creation, a bit of lawmaking by judges to protect resource-related activities at the expense of local governments that want to restrict it. The rule plainly rests on policy considerations specific to natural resources, rather than land-use concerns of greater applicability. How legitimate is it for courts to go out of the way to protect specific industries of their choosing? Does it make a difference whether the views of the court are widely shared by people in the state generally (as, for example, Westerners have been concerned about full water usage)? And even if the special protection made sense when it was incorporated into law, how long should it last, and should courts be the ones to change it? On its face the issue is about zoning law, but the issue quickly becomes one dealing with governance and the allocation of lawmaking power. The Michigan law in effect reduces the power of local governments to control mining, thus giving miners greater ability to resist the local will.

2. *Applying the Michigan rule.* Whenever the law divides human activities into categories, problems arise drawing the lines between the categories. Michigan has divided the universe of zoning ordinances into two categories: those that "prevent" the "extraction" of "natural resources," and those that do not. What problems might we expect in applying this special, resource-extraction rule? What about a regulation, for instance, that does not prohibit mining but makes it so expensive that a miner halts operations? Has the ordinance *prevented* the mining, or has it merely *regulated* the mining? As for extraction, does this include, for instance, cutting trees, or are they harvested rather than extracted? (And if the rule covers harvesting rows of trees, how about harvesting rows of corn or litters of hogs?) Finally, how expansive is the category of "natural resources"? In this book the category is defined broadly to include recreational and aesthetic uses of nature. Would the Michigan rule apply to municipal bans on recreational hunting and fishing within city limits?

These questions would seem difficult enough, but they do not exhaust the difficulties that arise in applying this special rule. Consider two further uncertainties. First, when a local government makes a decision about whether a proposed mining operation will have very serious consequences, how much deference should its determination receive by courts? Would a reviewing court reconsider the factual issue *de novo,* substituting its own judgment for that of local officials? Would it, on the other hand, uphold the trial court ruling so long as it is supported by substantial evidence (or based on some other deferential standard of review)? What does the court intimate? Second, there is the question of burden of proof. Must the local government prove that the very serious consequences will occur, or can they merely make an initial showing on the issue with the landowner then required to prove that the consequences will not take place? What about a 10% chance over 20 years that a given mining operation will leach toxic chemicals that could contaminate a city's water supply?

3. *An alternative view:* Goldblatt v. Town of Hempstead. *Silva* is usefully compared with the ruling of the U.S. Supreme Court in Goldblatt v. Town of Hempstead, 369 U.S. 590 (1962), a case involving a municipal regulation of mining that was sufficiently onerous in its economic effect that it put out of business a longstanding mining operation within the town's limits. The municipal ordinance prohibited any mining excavation below the water table, imposed an affirmative duty on the mining company to refill any excavation already below that level, and made various berm, slope, and fencing requirements more stringent. The mining company challenged the regulation as a taking of their property without just compensation. In the course of rejecting the argument, the Court considered the limits of police power regulation in the context of natural resources:

> Concededly the ordinance completely prohibits a beneficial use to which the property has previously been devoted. However, such a characterization does not tell us whether or not the ordinance is unconstitutional. It is an oft-repeated truism that every regulation necessarily speaks as a prohibition. If this ordinance is otherwise a valid exercise of the town's police powers, the fact that it deprives the property of its most beneficial use does not render it unconstitutional. Walls v. Midland Carbon Co., 254 U.S. 300, 41 S.Ct. 118, 65 L.Ed. 276

(1920); Hadacheck v. Sebastian, 239 U.S. 394, 36 S.Ct. 143, 60 L.Ed. 348 (1915); Reinman v. Little Rock, 237 U.S. 171, 35 S.Ct. 511, 59 L.Ed. 900 (1915); Mugler v. Kansas, 123 U.S. 623, 8 S.Ct. 273, 31 L.Ed. 205 (1887); see Laurel Hill Cemetery v. San Francisco, 216 U.S. 358, 30 S.Ct. 301, 54 L.Ed. 515 (1910). As pointed out in Mugler v. Kansas, *supra*, 123 U.S. at 668–669, 8 S.Ct. at 301:

> '(T)he present case must be governed by principles that do not involve the power of eminent domain, in the exercise of which property may not be taken for public use without compensation. A prohibition simply upon the use of property for purposes that are declared, by valid legislation, to be injurious to the health, morals, or safety of the community, cannot, in any just sense, be deemed a taking or an appropriation of property for the public benefit. *Such legislation does not disturb the owner in the control or use of his property for lawful purposes, nor restrict his right to dispose of it, but is only a declaration by the state that its use by any one, for certain forbidden purposes, is prejudicial to the public interests.* * * * The power which the states have of prohibiting such use by individuals of their property, as will be prejudicial to the health, the morals, or the safety of the public, is not, and, consistently with the existence and safety of organized society, cannot be, burdened with the condition that the state must compensate such individual owners for pecuniary losses they may sustain, by reason of their not being permitted, by a noxious use of their property, to inflict injury upon the community.' [Ed: emphasis added]

Nor is it of controlling significance that the 'use' prohibited here is of the soil itself as opposed to a 'use' upon the soil, cf. United States v. Central Eureka Mining Co., 357 U.S. 155, 78 S.Ct. 1097, 2 L.Ed.2d 1228 (1958), or that the use prohibited is arguably not a common-law nuisance, e.g., Reinman v. Little Rock, *supra*.

This is not to say, however, that governmental action in the form of regulation cannot be so onerous as to constitute a taking which constitutionally requires compensation. Pennsylvania Coal Co. v. Mahon, 260 U.S. 393, 43 S.Ct. 158, 67 L.Ed. 322 (1922); see United States v. Central Eureka Mining Co., supra. There is no set formula to determine where regulation ends and taking begins. Although a comparison of values before and after is relevant, see Pennsylvania Coal Co. v. Mahon, *supra*, it is by no means conclusive, see Hadacheck v. Sebastian, supra, where a diminution in value from $800,000 to $60,000 was upheld. How far regulation may go before it becomes a taking we need not now decide, for there is no evidence in the present record which even remotely suggests that prohibition of further mining will reduce the value of the lot in question. Indulging in the usual presumption of constitutionality, infra, 369 U.S., p. 596, 82 S.Ct., p. 991, we find no indication that the prohibitory effect of Ordinance No. 16 is sufficient to render it an unconstitutional taking if it is otherwise a valid police regulation.

It is worth reading carefully the court's quotation from the important early ruling, *Mugler v. Kansas* (1887), to note the rather different approach that then prevailed among courts as they went about assessing the effects of regulations. The Court in *Mugler* did not uphold the statute challenged in the case on the ground that the statute failed to cut deeply enough into landowner rights to render the statute invalid. Instead, the Court ruled that the "legislation [did] not disturb the owner in the control or use of his property for lawful purposes, nor restrict his right to dispose of it, but is only a declaration by the state that its use by any one, for certain forbidden purposes, is prejudicial to the public interests." In effect, the court concluded that the statute had no effect on the landowner's rights. The landowner only had the right to use the land for lawful purposes—that is, for purposes not "prejudicial to the public interests." Because the challenged statute prohibited activities that did prejudice the public interest, it merely clarified the content of an existing limit on landowner rights; it took away nothing from the landowner. As we have seen and will see again, a common tendency today is to begin the constitutional analysis in a much different place; to start with the assumption that landowners can use their lands as they see fit rather than only in ways that are reasonable. The common effect of this shift, of course, is to portray regulations as altering landowner rights more substantially.

4. *Accommodation IV:* Citizens Organized Against Longwalling v. Division of Reclamation. A group of landowners in a region came together to challenge a state permit that allowed mining to take place on nearby private land. The mining entailed the removal of subsurface coal using a longwall mining machine, which extracts the coal from a 5–foot high seam and allows the ceiling to collapse after the machine has passed through, resulting in immediate land subsidence. Under the state's regulatory regime, the mining company was required to mitigate various harms caused by the mining, including harms to hydrologic systems. Plaintiff landowners challenged the permit on various grounds. The court rejected most of the claims, but did agree that the mining company had failed, as regulations required, to develop an adequate plan to provide substitute water sources for any neighboring landowner whose groundwater supply was contaminated by the mining. The miners' plan, approved by the state, merely spoke of negotiating with landowners to resolve any problems. According to the court neighbors had a right to insist on new, substitute water sources, even if they could not halt the mining activities that would likely ruin their existing water supplies. (The state regulations, that is, effectively allowed the private condemnation of private water supplies to promote private mining activities.) Judge Grey of the court offered the following observations in a concurring opinion:

> As noted in the intervenor's and *amicus* 'briefs', there is an enormous investment in this coal seam. In a like manner, however, there is proportionately a substantial investment by the surface owners in the properties that they hold. The economics in this case are relatively simple. Longwall mining, which is more efficient and more economical, causes some damage because of the subsidence. The cost of this damage does not go away. It must be borne by someone. The landowner whose water supply is de-watered should not be forced to bear the entire economic cost of the effects of longwall mining. Since society as a whole and the permit holder in particular benefit from the granting of the permit, the costs of de-watering equitably, and legally under R.C. 1513.162, ought to be borne by the permit holder. The expense neces-

sary to replace the loss of surface water supplies to any homeowner is just another cost of doing the longwall mining. This expense will increase the cost of coal, and ultimately the cost of electricity, but it is only reasonable that it be paid by electricity users in proportional shares rather than by affected landowners in disproportionate shares.

The board of review found that the overall effect of granting this longwall mining permit would be minimal. I believe the record amply justifies the board's conclusion. However, one might as easily say that when a foul ball is tapped into the stands at a baseball game, the effect of the ball on the crowd is minimal. To the individual fan who catches a hard fast one in the face, the effect is not minimal, but is, as appellant notes, devastating. The board of review, in my opinion, while fully justified in concluding that the overall effects of the permit on the population in general would be minimal, has failed to adequately provide for the individual who is singly and devastatedly affected. The water replacement plan simply does not provide any sort of reasonable protection or remedy for a person whose water supply has been affected by the longwall mining operation....

This plan really provides no protection or enforceable rights for the affected landowner, nor does it impose any duty on the permit holder with any degree of specificity. The duties imposed on the permit holder where there has been a disruption of the water supply is particularly defective because it has no framework by which an affected landowner can establish and enforce his right to an adequate water supply. A right without a remedy is useless. The plan simply talks about "negotiations," and "case by case analysis." The board clearly failed to establish a reasonable plan for guaranteeing surface owners an enforceable right to a continuous and regular source of water. Negotiation is hardly a remedy at all. Indeed a siege is nothing more than negotiation for the surrender of the city, while its inhabitants' water supply dwindles.

It seems clear from the record based on all the exhibits and testimony that not many people will be affected by a loss of water supply. Some of the losses will be self-healing, and some of the disruptions will be only temporary, and only a few will be adversely affected. However, those few individuals will be severely affected. One asks, hypothetically, how long can a homeowner go without a glass of water or a clean shirt or shower? It is an abuse of discretion for the board not to require that those few have a timely, definite, specific and enforceable remedy to compel the permit holder to resupply them with an adequate water supply. The board, for example, speaks of "reasonable time," yet reasonable time is left undefined. Is forty-eight hours a reasonable time? To a family without water anything longer might seem unreasonable.

It is in this area where I believe the board has abused its discretion and has failed to apply the relevant statutes. In order for a permit to be granted, the operator must replace a water supply and reimburse the owner. Since the board found that this will in fact happen to a few people, the board must order very specifically and very definitely procedures to be followed when this happens.

The Ohio regulatory scheme at issue in this case sought to accommodate conflicting interests of property owners. On the one hand, it allowed mining to continue even when it imposed significant harm on particular neighboring landowners who might otherwise have had the right under state nuisance law to halt the mining. In that regard the statutory regime was similar to the new law enacted in Idaho to protect grass growers from nuisance and trespass liability. On the other side, it imposed a specific duty on the mining company to correct any significant harm that it imposed on other landowners, without need of any lawsuit and, as importantly, without any judicial balancing of the social benefits of the competing land uses. Recall that under the reasonableness rule courts often consider the relative values of the land-use activities of the conflicting owners. In this setting, it would appear that the mining operation was more socially valuable than the few residences affected by it. Nonetheless, the court insists that the few affected landowners be made whole for the damage to their water flows. The effect is to allow two land uses to continue side by side based on a principle of accommodation—a principle that the common law often had difficulty implementing.

5. *Federal limits on state regulation:* California Coastal Commission v. Granite Rock Co. The effect of the special Michigan rule on extracting natural resources was to limit the ability of local governments to control extraction activities. A similar issue arises with respect to resource extraction on federally owned lands. Can the state in which federal lands are located impose regulatory limits on resource extractions without running afoul of federal law?

In California Coastal Commission v. Granite Rock Co., 480 U.S. 572 (1987), the U.S. Forest Service granted a permit for limestone mining on federal lands in California. The permit was subject to conditions that took into account the environmental effects of the mining on federal lands but did not consider environmental effects on adjacent nonfederal lands. California demanded that the private mining company also comply with state laws designed to protect the California coastal zone generally. The mining company contended that the state regulatory scheme as applied to federal lands was entirely preempted by federal law and the federal regulatory scheme. In a 5–4 ruling, the Supreme Court disagreed and upheld the state permit program. In its unusual ruling the Court presumed that state laws would be invalid if they *prohibited* mining or if they took the form of zoning or similar *land-use planning* controls. On the other hand, state laws were permissible if they merely *regulated* mining and were aimed at *environmental protection*. Because the California scheme was a regulation rather than prohibition, and because it was an environmental regulation rather than land-use planning, it remained valid. The ruling drew criticism from commentators, who asserted that the Court's two distinctions—prohibition versus regulation and land use planning versus environmental rule—were both unworkable and not based on any law. John D. Leshy, Granite Rock *and the State's Influence Over Federal Land Use*, 18 ENVTL. L. 99 (1987); Eric T. Freyfogle, Granite Rock: *Institutional Competence and the State Role in Federal Land Planning*, 59 U. COLO. L. REV. 465 (1988).

D. ECOLOGICALLY SENSITIVE LANDS

The cases so far in this chapter have all involved limitations on the ways people can use their lands free of disruption. In some of the instances (*Ortner*, *Dexter*, and perhaps *Prah*, depending on what the jury decided on remand), property law constrained the *intensive* land uses. In the other cases (*Bryant, Waschak, Moon*), property law left the more *sensitive* land uses legally unprotected. If we look closely at the facts of these cases, we might well conclude that the rulings in the latter category—involving sensitive land uses that went unprotected—entailed the more severe limitations on property rights. For instance, what was the homeowner in *Bryant* to do if he could not heat his home? What were the homeowners in *Waschak* to do in the face of the on-going deterioration of their homes (and, no doubt, their lungs)? And what about the *Moon* landowners who really could not tolerate the smoke?

Perhaps the most controversial property cases in recent decades have involved, not cases such as *Bryant* and *Waschak* that entail disruptions of a landowner's quiet enjoyment, but rather laws that directly limit how landowners can use their lands. And among these disputes, none have engendered more spirited debate than restrictions on the uses of ecologically sensitive lands. Many particular lands perform important ecological functions and are so easily degraded by alteration that lawmakers have severely limited the ways landowners can reshape their natural features. New laws and regulations have prescribed that landowners can use such ecologically sensitive lands only lightly, sometimes with no development of any type permitted. To no surprise, landowners have sometimes complained loudly. As to the fairness and legality of such laws, consider the following two rulings:

STATE v. JOHNSON

265 A.2d 711 (Maine 1970).

MARDEN, JUSTICE

On appeal from an injunction granted under the provisions of 12 M.R.S.A. 4701–4709, inclusive, the Wetlands Act (Act), originating in Chapter 348 P.L. 1967, which places restrictions upon the alteration and use of wetlands, as therein defined, without permission from the municipal officers concerned and the State Wetlands Control Board (Board). The Act is a conservation measure under the police power of the State to protect the ecology of areas bordering coastal waters. The 1967 Act has been amended in no way pertinent to the present issue except by Section 8 of Chapter 379 of the Public Laws of 1969, which authorized alternatively a mandatory injunction for the restoration of any wetlands previously altered in violation of the Act.

Wetlands Act

The appellants own a tract of land about 220 feet wide and 700 feet long extending across salt water marshes between Atlantic Avenue on the east and the Webhannet River on the west in the Town of Wells.

Westerly of the lots fronting on Atlantic Avenue the strip has been subdivided into lots for sale. The easterly 260 feet approximately of the strip has been filled and bears seasonal dwellings. Westerly of this 260 foot development is marsh-land flooded at high tide and drained, upon receding tide, into the River by a network of what our Maine historical novelist Kenneth E. Roberts called 'eel runs,' but referred to in the record as creeks. Similar marsh-land, undeveloped, lies to the north and south of appellants' strip, and westerly of the River, all of which makes up a substantial acreage (the extent not given in testimony, but of which we take judicial notice) of marshland known as the Wells Marshes. Appellants' land, by raising the grade above high water by the addition of fill, is adaptable to development for building purposes.

Following the effective date of the Act, an application to the municipal officers, with notice to the Wetlands Control Board, for permission to fill a portion of this land was denied by the Board, an administrative appeal was taken and the case reported to this Court, which appears sub nom. Johnson v. Maine Wetlands Control Board, Me., 250 A.2d 825 (Case No. 1) and in which the constitutionality of the Act was challenged. We held, by decision filed March 11, 1969, that absent a record of evidence as to the nature of the land involved and the benefits or harm to be expected from the denial of the permit, the case would have to be remanded.

Subsequent to March 11, 1969 fill was deposited on the land in question, as the result of which the State sought an injunction, the granting of which brings this case before us on appeal (Case No. 2). It is stipulated that the evidence in this case should be accepted as the evidence lacking in (Case No. 1) and that the two cases be consolidated for final determination of both.

The record establishes that the land which the appellants propose to build up by fill and build upon for sale, or to be offered for sale to be built upon, are coastal wetlands within the definition of the Act and that the refusal by the Board to permit the deposit of such fill prevents the development as proposed. The single Justice found that the property is a portion of a salt marsh area, a valuable natural resource of the State, that the highest and best use for the land, so filled, is for housing, and that unfilled it has no commercial value.

The issue is the same in both, namely, whether the denial of permit (Case No. 1) and the injunction (Case No. 2) so limit the use to plaintiffs of their land that such deprivation of use amounts to a taking of their property without constitutional due process and just compensation.

Due Process

Due process of law has a dual aspect, procedural and substantive. 16 Am.Jur.2d, Constitutional Law § 548.

Procedurally, "notice and opportunity for hearing are of the essence" Randall v. Patch, 118 Me. 303, 305, 108 A. 97, 98, and as attributed to Daniel Webster in the Dartmouth College case it is "a law which hears before it condemns, which proceeds upon inquiry; and renders judgment only after trial." Trustees of Dartmouth College v. Woodward, 4 Wheat (U.S.) 518, 4 L.Ed. 629, and see York Harbor Village Corporation v. Libby, 126 Me. 537, 539, 140 A. 382.

The guaranty of procedural due process requires no particular form of procedure. 16 Am.Jur. Constitutional Law § 549, and Green v. State, Me., 247 A.2d 117, (9) 121. The Act meets all requirements of procedural due process.

Substantively, "the terms 'law of the land' and 'due process of law' * * * are identical in meaning." Michaud v. City of Bangor, 159 Me. 491, 493, 196 A.2d 106, 108.

It is "the constitutional guaranty that no person shall be deprived of * * * property for arbitrary reasons, such a deprivation being constitutionally supportable only if the conduct from which the deprivation flows is proscribed by reasonable legislation (that is, legislation the enactment of which is within the scope of legislative authority) reasonably applied (that is, for a purpose consonant with the purpose of the legislation itself)." 16 Am.Jur.2d, Constitutional Law § 550.

It is this substantive due process which is challenged in the Act. In this connection it must be noted that § 4704 (Footnote 1) by its terms equates a deprivation "of the reasonable use" of an owner's property with "an unreasonable exercise of police power."

The constitutional aspect of the current problem is to be determined by consideration of the extent to which appellants are deprived of their usual incidents of ownership,—for the conduct of the public authorities with relation to appellants' land is not a "taking" in the traditional sense. Our State has applied a strict construction of the constitutional provisions as to land. See Opinion of the Justices, 103 Me. 506, 511, 69 A. 627, and State v. McKinnon, 153 Me. 15, 20, 133 A.2d 885.

We find no constitutional definition of the word "deprive," Munn v. Illinois, 94 U.S. 113, 123, 24 L.Ed. 77, since the constitutionally protected right of property is not unlimited. It is subject to reasonable restraints and regulations in the public interest by means of the legitimate exercise of police power. 16 Am.Jur.2d, Constitutional Law § 363. The exercise of this police power may properly regulate the use of property and if the owner suffers injury "it is either *damnum absque injuria*, or, in the theory of the law, he is compensated for it by sharing in the general benefits which the regulations are intended * * * to secure." State v. Robb, 100 Me. 180, 186, 60 A. 874, 876. The determination of unconstitutional deprivation is difficult and judicial decisions are diverse. Broadly speaking, deprivation of property contrary to constitutional guaranty occurs "if it deprives an owner of one of its essential attributes, destroys its value, restricts or interrupts its common necessary, or profitable use, hampers the owner in the application of it to the purposes of trade, or imposes conditions upon the right to hold or use it and thereby seriously impairs its value." 16 Am.Jur.2d Constitutional Law

§ 367. See also State v. Union Oil Company, 151 Me. 438, 446, 120 A.2d 708.

Conditions so burdensome may be imposed that they are equivalent to an outright taking, although the title to the property and some vestiges of its uses remain in the owner. East Coast Lumber Terminal, Inc. v. Town of Babylon, 174 F.2d 106, (5–7) 110 (2 CCA, 1949).

A guiding principle appears in the frequently cited case of Pennsylvania Coal Company v. Mahon et al., 260 U.S. 393, 413, 43 S.Ct. 158, 159–160, 67 L.Ed. 322 (1922) where Mr. Justice Holmes declared:

> 'Government hardly could go on if to some extent values incident to property could not be diminished without paying for every such change in the general law. As long recognized some values are enjoyed under an implied limitation and must yield to the police power. But obviously the implied limitation must have its limits or the contract and due process clauses are gone. One fact for consideration in determining such limits is the extent of the diminution. When it reaches a certain magnitude, in most if not in all cases there must be an exercise of eminent domain and compensation to sustain the act. So the question depends upon the particular facts.'
>
> 'We are in danger of forgetting that a strong public desire to improve the public condition is not enough to warrant achieving the desire by a shorter cut than the constitutional way of paying for the change. As we already have said this is a question of degree-and therefore cannot be disposed of by general propositions.' At page 416.

See also Pumpelly v. Green Bay Company, 13 Wall. (U.S.) 166, 177–178, 20 L.Ed. 557 (1871).

Confrontation between public interests and private interests is common in the application of zoning laws, with which the Wetlands Act may be analogized, and the great majority of which, upon their facts, are held to be reasonable exercise of the police power. There are, however, zoning restrictions which have been recognized as equivalent to taking of the property restricted. See Frankel v. City of Baltimore, 223 Md. 97, 162 A.2d 447, (2) 451 (1960); City of Plainfield v. Borough of Middlesex, 69 N.J.Super. 136, 173 A.2d 785, 788 (1961), and Arverne Bay Const. Co. v. Thatcher, 278 N.Y. 222, 15 N.E.2d 587, (10–13) 591 (N.Y.1938).

The same result has been reached as to zoning laws which identify their purposes as ones of conservation. See Dooley v. Town Plan and Zoning Commission of Town of Fairfield, 151 Conn. 304, 197 A.2d 770, (5, 6) 773 (1964, flood control); and Morris County Land Improvement Company v. Township of Parsippany–Troy Hills et al., 40 N.J. 539, 193 A.2d 232, (6, 7) 241 (1963, swampland preservation), and the rationale expressed in Commissioner of Natural Resources et al. v. S. Volpe & Co., Inc., 349 Mass. 104, 206 N.E.2d 666 (1965, involving "dredge and fill" Act); and MacGibbon et al. v. Board of Appeals of Duxbury, 347 Mass. 690, 200 N.E.2d 254 (1964) and 255 N.E.2d 347 (Mass.1970).

There has, as well, been restrictive conservation legislation which has been held not equivalent to taking. See Patterson v. Stanolind Oil & Gas Co., 182 Okl. 155, 77 P.2d 83, (1–3) 89 (1938, oil and gas "well spacing" Act); Iowa Natural Resources Council v. Van Zee, 158 N.W.2d 111, (10), (11) 117 (Iowa 1968, flood control Act), and Swisher v. Brown, 157 Colo. 378, 402 P.2d 621 (1965, marketing control Act). See also Greenleaf–Johnson Lumber Company v. Garrison, 237 U.S. 251, 260, 35 S.Ct. 551, 59 L.Ed. 939 (1914, directing removal of docks in navigable waters, with dissent), and Miami Beach Jockey Club, Inc. v. Dern, 66 App.D.C. 254, 86 F.2d 135 (1936, legislative prohibition of filling submerged land).

Of the above, the Massachusetts cases are of particular significance inasmuch as the "dredge and fill" Act discussed in *Volpe* is expressed in terms closely parallel to our Wetlands Act and the zoning ordinance in *MacGibbon* deals with facts closely akin to those before us.

Between the public interest in braking and eventually stopping the insidious despoliation of our natural resources which have for so long been taken for granted, on the one hand, and the protection of appellants' property rights on the other, the issue is cast.

Here the single Justice has found that the area of which appellants' land is a part "is a valuable natural resource of the State of Maine and plays an important role in the conservation and development of aquatic and marine life, game birds and waterfowl," which bespeaks the public interest involved and the protection of which is sought by Section 4702 of the Act. With relation to appellants' interest the single Justice found that appellants' land absent the addition of fill "has no commercial value whatever." These findings are supported by the evidence and are conclusive. Danby v. Hanscom, 156 Me. 189, 191, 163 A.2d 372.

As distinguished from conventional zoning for town protection, the area of wetlands representing a "valuable natural resource of the State," of which appellants' holdings are but a minute part, is of statewide concern. The benefits from its preservation extend beyond town limits and are state-wide. The cost of its preservation should be publicly borne. To leave appellants with commercially valueless land in upholding the restriction presently imposed, is to change them with more than their just share of the cost of this state-wide conservation program, granting fully its commendable purpose. In the phrasing of *Robb, supra*, their compensation by sharing in the benefits which this restriction is intended to secure is so disproportionate to their deprivation of reasonable use that such exercise of the State's police power is unreasonable.

The application of the wetlands restriction in the terms of the denial of appellants' proposal to fill, and enjoining them from so doing deprives them of the reasonable use of their property and within Section 4704 is both an unreasonable exercise of police power and equivalent to taking within constitutional considerations. . . .

Holding, as we do, that the prohibition against the filling of appellants' land, upon the facts peculiar to the case, is an unreasonable exercise of police power, it does not follow that the restriction as to draining sanitary sewage into coastal wetland is subject to the same infirmity. Additional considerations of health and pollution which are "separable from and independent of" the "fill" restriction may well support validity of the Act in those areas of concern. See Hamilton et als. v. Portland Pier Site District et als., 120 Me. 15, 24, 112 A. 836, and La Fleur ex rel. Anderson v. Frost et als., 146 Me. 270, 289, 80 A.2d 407.

Within the provisions of Section 4704, the denial of the permit to fill (Case No. 1) and the injunction (Case No. 2) are "set aside."

Appeal sustained in both cases.

Notes

1. *Land as abstraction, land as nature. Johnson* is typical of a number of judicial decisions handed down in the late 1960s and early 1970s, when environmental land-use restrictions were first appearing with regularity. The new laws raised serious questions about what it meant to own land. How should the legal system respond to the growing recognition that some lands are simply not ecologically suited for intensive land use? In the legal (and, even more, the popular) mind, landowners held a certain bundle of entitlements. These entitlements existed in the abstract, and did not depend upon the land's natural features. Land was land, and property rights in it were the same as to all land parcels. Thus, the question arose: Would the law define landowner rights in the abstract, or would the rights of ownership instead depend far more upon nature?

This clash was at the heart of the mounting "private property rights" movement at the end of the twentieth century. Although advocates of the "private property" position contended that they were out to protect private rights, a more apt description was that they sought to protect the rights of landowners to use their lands intensively, even at the expense of the rights of their property-owning neighbors to complain about the resulting harms. They were out to protect and defend an abstract ideal of land ownership, and to ward off attempts to define landowner rights in ways that depended upon the land's natural features. In the lore of abstraction, every Greenacre and Blackacre is appropriate for development. When it comes to real lands, however, the story is different.

2. *Positivism versus culture. Johnson* is usefully contrasted with *Moon*, in terms of the way the court talks about property rights. In *Moon* the court employed a distinctly positivist view of them: property rights are defined by law, and when the law changes the property rights change. (In the positivist view, simply stated, law is the command of a sovereign and is thus determined by looking at what the sovereign has said.) What clues does the court in *Johnson* give as to its much-different view of property? Note the court's framing of the dispute: did the regulation deprive of the landowners "of their usual incidents of ownership"? What does the court mean by "usual incidents"? Do we determine them by looking to the law (and if so what law), or does the court have in mind instead a cultural understanding of what it means to own land? Note also the court's conclusion that the statute deprived landowners of their "reasonable use" of land. Again, who decides

what land uses are reasonable, and is this a cultural question or a legal one? Is reasonable use decided by looking at the benefits received by the landowner alone, or are the effects on other lands and landowners also considered?

Recall the statement by the court in *Moon* that it is the province of the legislature to change the common law. Didn't the Maine legislature do just that, when it decided that the filling of a coastal wetlands was harmful? Doesn't the Maine statute essentially amount to an authoritative declaration that the proposed land uses are unreasonable? Does our answer depend upon our willingness (or unwillingness) to take nature into account (note 1, above)? That is, should we determine the reasonableness of a land use in the abstract (as the court in *Johnson* seems to do) or is reasonableness determined based on the land's natural features, and thus subject to variation among land parcels (the legislature's apparent answer)? Thus, we return again to the recurring issue of lawmaking power: who gets to decide what property ownership means?

3. *The missing neighbors.* A prime reason why lawmakers restrict development on ecologically sensitive lands is because development can often interfere with other private landowners. Filling in wetlands, for instance, can increase flooding of other private lands elsewhere. Thus, bans on using ecologically sensitive lands often work the same way as most land-use laws—they benefit some landowners at the expense of others, increasing property rights in one way and decreasing them in other ways. Note, though, that neighboring landowners (as well as public fishers, etc.) are left out of the drama that the court in *Johnson* recounts. Might the case have appeared differently to the court if the case had been, not a dispute between a regulated landowner and the state, but instead a dispute between a regulated landowner and a group of neighboring landowners, with the state called upon to resolve the conflict?

As we get to the bottom of *Johnson*, it is useful to consider the court's phrasing of the dispute. The case involved a clash, the court tell us, between *private* and *public* interests. Is this an accurate portrayal? Isn't their a public interest in protecting private property rights? (Surely the court would agree.) Indeed, isn't the main reason why the law recognizes property rights, allowing landowners to draw upon public law-enforcement mechanisms, precisely because well-crafted property rights do promote the common good? On the other side, doesn't this wetlands-protection law protect the quiet enjoyment of other private landowners? Indeed, is it not more apt to say that public and private interests lie on *both* sides of the dispute, just as property rights lie on *both* sides of the dispute?

4. *The harm-benefit test.* When courts consider claims that statutes and regulations amount to unlawful takings of private property without compensation, they have often used (as the court in *Johnson* does) what is termed the harm-benefit test. That is, they have asked, when reviewing a statute, whether it effectively halts a harmful activity or whether instead it requires a property owner to use his property in a way that confers a benefit on the public. Laws halting harms are largely lawful; laws that require landowners to confer benefits are more likely unconstitutional unless landowners are paid.

Note how the court here has little trouble deciding where this dispute falls. Wetlands preservation, the court explains, benefits the entire state. Since the benefits spread state-wide, then state taxpayers should foot the bill. Yet, could not the court have just as easily focused on the harms caused by filling in the wetlands? Certainly the lawmakers believed that they were halting harmful conduct. So which is it? Does the statute halt a harm or does it extract a benefit?

To answer the question, of course, we need to return to *Bryant v. Lefever* and to the age-old *sic utere tuo* doctrine, discussed earlier. Just as the court in *Bryant* found it necessary to craft a baseline of acceptable landowner conduct—only then could it decide which landowner was causing the harm—so too the harm-benefit test for regulatory takings is only useful once we set a baseline of permissible conduct. A law that prohibits permissible conduct extracts a benefit; a law that prohibits impermissible conduct instead halts a harm. We are thus, are we not, thrown back to where we started? How do we distinguish between acceptable and unacceptable landowner behavior? And who gets to decide—courts, legislatures, the public at large?

In Johnson, the *judges* began with the unstated assumption that it was fair and reasonable for a landowner to fill a coastal wetland. Its ultimate ruling flowed logically from this implicit assumption. The *legislature*, having (presumably) studied the issue as a policy matter, came to a different conclusion.

ZEALY v. CITY OF WAUKESHA

201 Wis.2d 365, 548 N.W.2d 528 (1996).

ROLAND B. DAY, CHIEF JUSTICE.

. . . The issue before this court is whether the zoning of certain land owned by Plaintiff—Appellant Alfred A. Zealy (Zealy) as a conservancy district in order to protect wetlands constitutes a constructive taking of property by the government for which a landowner should be compensated. We conclude that the conservancy zoning placed on Zealy's land did not effect a constructive taking. We therefore reverse the court of appeals.

The parcel of land here at issue consists of approximately 10.4 contiguous acres. The parcel was originally part of an approximately 250–acre parcel annexed from the Town of Waukesha to the City of Waukesha (City) in 1967. Prior to annexation, the property was zoned A–3 by the Town of Waukesha. This zoning permitted agricultural use, and Zealy's parents used the property to grow crops in a truck farming operation. After annexation, the City zoned the land R–1, a zoning permitting, among other uses, residential use. Later, a small portion of the land was rezoned B–4, allowing business use. The property continued to be used for farming until approximately 1981. The other lands in the 250–acre parcel were sold off until only the 10.4–acre parcel at issue in this case remained in Zealy's possession. As of the time he commenced this action, Zealy used the land for peat mining.

On March 16, 1982, Zealy, his mother, and his brother, all of whom at that time shared interests in the property, executed an easement granting the City the right to construct, maintain, and operate sanitary and storm sewers on Zealy's land. Prior to the execution of the easement, Zealy had met with the City's Director of Public Works and City Engineer. The Director of Public Works presented Zealy with a drawing showing proposed future development of the property as a residential area. The easement provided that the City would not levy any special assessments for the storm or sewer mains installed on the property. Zealy alleges that the representations made by the City's officials led him to grant the easement. The City eventually constructed a sanitary and storm sewer on a portion of the property.

On July 3, 1985, the City changed the zoning on approximately 28.6 acres of land in the City from R–1 to C–1, creating a conservancy district. Included in the conservancy district were 8.2 acres of Zealy's parcel. These 8.2 acres may not be used for residential use; the remaining land in the parcel, approximately 2.1 acres, is zoned for residential (1.57 acres) and business (.57acres) use. The C–1 zoning allows agricultural use of the property.

Zealy has filed a motion with this court asking that we take judicial notice of the minutes of the City's Plan Commission meeting of November 14, 1984, and the City's rezoning ordinance. We hereby grant Zealy's motion.

Prior to the rezoning, the City's assessor had valued the entire 10.4–acre parcel at approximately $81,000.00; after the rezoning, the City assessed the value of the property at approximately $57,000.00. Zealy claims that the fair market value of the 8.2 acres, if developed for residential use as allowed under R–1 zoning, would be approximately $200,000.00. Zealy has never submitted an application for a building permit or plans to the City for residential construction on the land, nor has Zealy shown that he has made any expenditures toward such construction. Zealy claims that the value of the 8.2–acre parcel under the present C–1 zoning is approximately $4,000.

Zealy brought an inverse condemnation action against the City, claiming that its rezoning of his land constituted a regulatory taking without compensation, and that the City should be equitably estopped from enforcing the rezoning because of Zealy's reliance on its representations. . . .

The issue in this case is whether the City's ordinance constituted a taking of Zealy's property without compensation. This is a question of law, and thus we undertake our review without deference to the decisions of the courts below. *Ball v. Dist. No. 4, Area Bd.*, 117 Wis.2d 529, 537, 345 N.W.2d 389 (Ct.App.1984). The Fifth Amendment to the United States Constitution, made applicable to the states by the Fourteenth Amendment, provides in part that private property shall not "be taken for public use, without just compensation." Article I, § 13 of the Wisconsin Constitution states:

> Private property for public use. Section 13. The property of no person shall be taken for public use without just compensation therefor.

Takings jurisprudence has developed from two competing principles: on one hand, respect for the property rights of individuals; on the other, recognition that the government retains the ability, in furtherance of the interests of all citizens, to regulate an owner's potential uses of land. Thus, in *Euclid v. Ambler Realty Co.,* 272 U.S. 365, 47 S.Ct. 114, 71 L.Ed. 303 (1926), the United States Supreme Court held municipal zoning to be a permissible exercise of the police power, while in *Pennsylvania Coal Co. v. Mahon,* 260 U.S. 393, 415, 43 S.Ct. 158, 159–60, 67 L.Ed. 322 (1922), the Court held that "while property may be regulated to a certain extent, if regulation goes too far it will be recognized as a taking." Such takings are described as "constructive" or "regulatory" takings.

In cases decided since *Mahon,* the United States Supreme Court has established a rough framework for determining when a regulatory taking has occurred: "In 70–odd years of succeeding 'regulatory takings' jurisprudence, we have generally eschewed any 'set formula' for determining how far is too far, preferring to 'engag[e] in . . . essentially ad hoc, factual inquiries.'" *Lucas v. South Carolina Coastal Council,* 505 U.S. 1003, 1015, 112 S.Ct. 2886, 2893, 120 L.Ed.2d 798 (1992) (quoting *Penn Central Transp. Co. v. New York City,* 438 U.S. 104, 124, 98 S.Ct. 2646, 2659, 57 L.Ed.2d 631 (1978)). This court has adopted a similar method of inquiry. *See Noranda Exploration, Inc. v. Ostrom,* 113 Wis.2d 612, 624, 335 N.W.2d 596 (1983). The United States Supreme Court has identified several factors particularly relevant to the inquiry in cases alleging a regulatory taking: "[T]he Fifth Amendment is violated when land-use regulation 'does not substantially advance legitimate state interests or denies an owner economically viable use of his land.'" *Lucas,* 505 U.S. at 1016, 112 S.Ct. at 2893–94 (quoting *Agins v. City of Tiburon,* 447 U.S. 255, 260, 100 S.Ct. 2138, 2141, 65 L.Ed.2d 106 (1980)). When a landowner alleges that a regulation effects a taking as applied to a particular piece of property, the factors courts should examine are described as "the character of the governmental action," "the economic impact of the regulation on the claimant," and "the extent to which the regulation has interfered with distinct investment-backed expectations." *Penn Central,* 438 U.S. at 124, 98 S.Ct. at 2659 (quoted in *Lucas,* 505 U.S. at 1019 n. 8, 112 S.Ct. at 2895 n. 8).

Although phrased in slightly differing terms in the cases, the rule emerging from opinions of our state courts and the United States Supreme Court is that a regulation must deny the landowner all or substantially all practical uses of a property in order to be considered a taking for which compensation is required. *See Lucas,* 505 U.S. at 1015, 112 S.Ct. at 2893 (regulatory taking occurs when regulation "denies all economically beneficial or productive use of land"); *Dolan v. City of Tigard,* 512 U.S. 374, ___, 114 S.Ct. 2309, 2316, 129 L.Ed.2d 304 (1994) (regulatory taking occurs if it denies an owner "economically viable use of his land'') (quoting *Agins,* 447 U.S. at 260, 100 S.Ct. at 2141); *Zinn v. State,* 112 Wis.2d 417, 424, 334 N.W.2d 67 (1983) (regulatory taking occurs "when the government restriction placed on the property 'practically or substantially renders the property useless for all reasonable purposes' '') (quoted sources omitted); *Reel Enters. v. City of La Crosse,* 146 Wis.2d 662, 674, 431 N.W.2d 743 (Ct.App.1988), *review denied,* 147 Wis.2d 887, 436 N.W.2d 29 (1988) (regulatory taking occurs if it "deprives the owner of all, or practically all, of the use''). Thus, for example, the United States Supreme Court in *Lucas* held that a landowner who purchased two residential lots at a combined price of nearly one million dollars and was subsequently barred from building residential structures by a state beachfront preservation law, rendering the lots without value, may be entitled to compensation for his loss. *See Lucas,* 505 U.S. at 1006–07, 1019–32, 112 S.Ct. at 2888–89, 2895–2902.

However, before reaching this determination, a court must first determine what, precisely, *is* the property at issue:

> Because our test for regulatory taking requires us to compare the value that has been taken from the property with the value that remains in the property, one of the critical questions is determining how to define the unit of property "whose value is to furnish the denominator of the fraction.''

Keystone Bituminous Coal Ass'n v. DeBenedictis, 480 U.S. 470, 497, 107 S.Ct. 1232, 1248, 94 L.Ed.2d 472 (1987) (quoting Frank I. Michelman, *Property, Utility, and Fairness: Comments on the Ethical Foundations of "Just Compensation'' Law,* 80 Harv.L.Rev. 1165, 1192 (1967)). The court of appeals in this case held that a landowner's anticipated investment opportunities should be examined in order to determine what the parcel at issue should be. In this, the court of appeals was in error. We conclude that the United States Supreme Court has never endorsed a test that "segments'' a contiguous property to determine the relevant parcel; rather, the Court has consistently held that a landowner's property in such a case should be considered as a whole.

> Taking jurisprudence does not divide a single parcel into discrete segments and attempt to determine whether rights in a particular segment have been entirely abrogated. In deciding whether a particular governmental action has effected a taking, this Court focuses rather both on the character of the action and on the nature and extent of the interference with rights in the parcel as a whole....

Penn Central, 438 U.S. at 130–31, 98 S.Ct. at 2662–63. Similarly, in *Keystone,* 480 U.S. at 498, 107 S.Ct. at 1248–49, the Court noted practical arguments against allowing the segmentation of the property at issue:

> Many zoning ordinances place limits on the property owner's right to make profitable use of some segments of his property. A requirement that a building occupy no more than a specified percentage of the lot on which it is located could be characterized as a taking of the vacant area.... [O]ne could always argue that a setback ordi-

nance requiring that no structure be built within a certain distance from the property line constitutes a taking because the footage represents a distinct segment of property for takings law purposes.

The court of appeals in this case cited *Lucas,* 505 U.S. at 1016–17 n. 7, 112 S.Ct. at 2893–94 n. 7, for the proposition that courts should use a flexible approach in deciding when to segment the property at issue in takings cases. *See Zealy,* 194 Wis.2d at 716–17 & n. 6, 534 N.W.2d 917. However, we note that this issue was not before the *Lucas* Court. The Court did not have to consider whether the property in that case might require segmentation because the trial court had found that the entirety of the property at issue was rendered valueless by the contested regulation. *See Lucas,* 505 U.S. at 1016–17 n. 7, 112 S.Ct. at 2893–94 n. 7. Justice Scalia's comments on this point were therefore dicta. Furthermore, in *Concrete Pipe and Prods. v. Construction Laborers Pension Trust,* 508 U.S. 602, 642–44, 113 S.Ct. 2264, 2290, 124 L.Ed.2d 539 (1993), Justice Souter, writing for the majority of the Court, replied in the following manner to an argument that the property at issue should be segmented:

> [W]e rejected this analysis years ago in *Penn Central* . . . where we held that a claimant's parcel of property could not first be divided into what was taken and what was left for the purpose of demonstrating the taking of the former to be complete and hence compensable. To the extent that any portion of property is taken, that portion is always taken in its entirety; the relevant question, however, is whether the property taken is all, or only a portion of the parcel in question.

We note that this opinion was written subsequent to *Lucas,* and that Justice Scalia joined the opinion. We conclude, therefore, that the cases of the United States Supreme Court do not support the proposition that a contiguous property should be divided into discrete segments for purposes of evaluating a takings claim.

We also note a possible difficulty in the application of the rule proposed by the court of appeals in the present case. Looking to a landowner's anticipated use of various parcels and sub-parcels of land in order to determine the extent of the parcel at issue would require ascertaining a landowner's subjective intent before being able to evaluate a possible takings claim. This would confuse both the agencies responsible for zoning and the courts called on to adjudicate such claims, and increase the difficulty of an already complex inquiry.

The court of appeals also cited *Ciampitti v. United States,* 22 Cl.Ct. 310 (1991), and *Loveladies Harbor, Inc. v. United States,* 28 F.3d 1171 (Fed.Cir.1994), for its rule allowing segmentation of property. These precedents, which in any event are merely persuasive, *see Thompson v. Village of Hales Corners,* 115 Wis.2d 289, 307, 340 N.W.2d 704 (1983), do not alter our view of the rule we apply in this case. First, we note that the court in *Ciampitti* had to determine what the extent of the property at issue was after a lengthy series of purchases, *see Ciampitti,* 22 Cl.Ct.

at 311–17, and ultimately decided against segmentation of the property, *id.* at 320. The case thus bears little relation to the instant case, in which the property is part of a single purchase. Second, in *Loveladies,* 28 F.3d at 1180, the court of appeals excluded from the parcel at issue lands that had already been developed and/or sold, as well as lands for which the development rights had been dedicated to the state in return for a building permit on the remaining lands. No such concerns are present in the instant case, in which we consider only the 10.4 undeveloped acres owned by Zealy at the time of its rezoning.

We thus conclude that the property at issue in this case is Zealy's entire 10.4–acre parcel, and now examine the facts in the record to determine whether the City's C–1 zoning effected a taking. First, we note that after the rezoning, Zealy still retains approximately 2.1 acres zoned for business and/or residential use. The City's assessor has valued the property at nearly three-fourths of its former value. Zealy presented the circuit court with an assessment valuing the 8.2–acre parcel at approximately $200,000, presuming residential use was allowed, but as this court stated in *Just v. Marinette County,* 56 Wis.2d 7, 23, 201 N.W.2d 761 (1972):

> [The landowners] argue their property has been severely depreciated in value. But this depreciation of value is not based on the use of the land in its natural state but on what the land would be worth if it could be filled and used for the location of a dwelling. While loss of value is to be considered in determining whether a restriction is a constructive taking, value based upon changing the character of the land at the expense of harm to public rights is not an essential factor or controlling.

Finally, we note that under the City's current zoning ordinance, the 8.2 acres of land zoned C–1 may still be used for its historical use, farming. Viewed as a whole, the parcel retains a combination of residential, commercial, and agricultural uses.

It may be true that in some cases, as Justice Scalia stated in *Lucas,* that "the rhetorical force of [the] 'deprivation of all economically feasible use' rule is greater than its precision," *Lucas,* 505 U.S. at 1016 n. 7, 112 S.Ct. at 2893–94 n. 7 but this is not such a case. The extent of the parcel at issue in this case is clearly identified, and just as clearly the parcel retains substantial uses. Under these facts, we cannot conclude that the City's rezoning deprived Zealy of all or substantially all of the use of his land. Without any such loss to the landowner, a taking cannot occur. We therefore conclude that the circuit court correctly granted summary judgment against Zealy on this issue.

Two further points are raised by the takings issue in this case. First, our conclusion that the City's ordinance did not effect a taking was compelled by our holding that Zealy did not suffer the loss of substantially all of the beneficial uses of his land. We therefore need not consider another factor we may look to in takings cases, whether the regulation did not advance a legitimate state interest. Zealy only contested the interests served by the City's ordinance to the extent that he claimed the City's regulation served the improper purpose of allowing the City to "take" his land rather than purchase it outright, an argument we reject. Second, we also do not reach the issue of the continuing validity of this court's analysis in *Just* in view of the Supreme Court's majority opinion in *Lucas,* which expressed disagreement with the South Carolina Supreme Court's conclusion that the regulation at issue could be justified as an exercise of the police power in order to prevent the harm to the public interest resulting from residential development of wetlands. *See Lucas,* 505 U.S. at 1020–32, 112 S.Ct. at 2896–2902. Such an evaluation would be required only in a case in which, as in *Lucas,* the value of the land at issue is "wholly eliminated." *Lucas*, 505 U.S. at 1026, 112 S.Ct. at 2899 For the same reason, we need not here consider the argument, raised by several amici curiae in this case, that *Just* is a "background principle[ ] of the State's law of property," *see Lucas,* 505 U.S. at 1029, 112 S.Ct. at 2900–01, that would justify even a total regulatory taking. Nothing in this opinion limits our holding in *Just* and cases following its rule. . . .

Wisconsin has a long history of protecting its water resources, its lakes, rivers, and streams, which depend on wetlands for their proper survival. As stated in *Just,* 56 Wis.2d at 17, 201 N.W.2d 761:

> Swamps and wetlands were once considered wasteland, undesirable, and not picturesque. But as the people became more sophisticated, an appreciation was acquired that swamps and wetlands serve a vital role in nature, are part of the balance of nature and are essential to the purity of the water in our lakes and streams. Swamps and wetlands are a necessary part of the ecological creation and now, even to the uninitiated, possess their own beauty in nature.

Our review of the relevant law of this court and the United States Supreme Court leads us to the conclusion that the circuit court correctly dismissed Zealy's claims. We therefore reverse the decision of the court of appeals and reinstate the circuit court's judgment and order.

Notes

1. *Shared governance VII: avoiding the issues, or let the legislature decide? Zealy* is illustrative of contemporary judicial approaches toward laws protecting ecologically sensitive lands. Laws are routinely upheld unless they deprive landowners of all economic value to their lands (assuming no permanent physical invasions of the land). In deciding whether a land parcel retains value, courts look to the parcel as a whole, not just to the portion of it subject to the regulatory restriction. Does this approach resolve the issue raised in the notes after *Johnson*, or does it essentially avoid them? Is the effect of these rulings largely to let legislatures set the baseline for acceptable land-use behavior? That is, are courts presuming that, when the legislature prohibits a landowner from engaging in a particular activity, the legislature has determined that the activity is unreasonable and thus not properly part of the rights that a landowner possesses?

2. *A subtle reaffirmation of* Just. A peculiar feature of this carefully written judicial opinion is the way the court used its earlier, much-cited opinion in *Just v. Marinette County*, 56 Wis.2d 7, 201 N.W.2d 761 (1972). Ever since it appeared, *Just* has been lauded and criticized for asserting that a landowner's protected rights are limited to those land uses consistent with the maintenance of the land in its natural condition. Amicus briefs in *Zealy* urged the court to use the property law principles in *Just* to state plainly that Zealy simply had no property right to fill wetlands, and thus the statute took nothing from him (the line of reasoning highlighted in *Mugler*). The court in *Zealy* was apparently unwilling to take this stark approach, yet it did not ignore *Just*. The court decided that Zealy did retain economic value in their land, and thus his land had not been taken by the government. Having reached that legal conclusion, disposing of the takings claim, the court then considered Zealy's assertion that his land with full development rights would be worth $200,000. It was on this factual issue of valuation that the court made use *Just*. It did so by noting that Zealy's appraisal was based on the erroneous belief that the owner had the right to alter the land's natural condition. Implicit in this factual assertion, which the court offered briefly and without comment, was the conclusion that Zealy in fact had no legal right to develop his wetland as a matter of state property law. But if that was the case, why didn't the court say so earlier in the ruling? The court did expressly assert that the starting point of any takings analysis is to decide what property interest the plaintiff really had. Wasn't this the appropriate place to take note of whether Zealy did or did not have any right to alter his land's natural character? If he had no such right to begin with, then the statute had little or no economic effect on him and the case was therefore a very easy one.

3. *Again, the missing neighbors*. Just as the court did in *Johnson*, the court here also recounts its legal drama without paying attention to neighboring landowners. In *Johnson*, an awareness of neighboring landowners might have prompted the court see how the wetlands-protection statute helped private landowners and fostered other private interests. It might have prompted the court, that is, to consider more carefully the presumed tradeoff between public and private interests. But what about in *Zealy*? Might the neighbors have also helped in a case in which the court was inclined to uphold the law?

To answer this question we can return (once again) to the doctrine of *sic utere tuo*, to its more modern manifestation (reasonable use), and to the unavoidable need to set a baseline for acceptable land use. Recall that, in *Bryant* and *Waschak*, juries decided that the defendants' land uses were unreasonable; in each case the court disagreed, substituting its own contrary judgment. In *Johnson*, the court essentially substituted its own judgment, drawing upon cultural norms, for the judgment of the legislature. In *Moon* and *Zealy*, in contrast, the courts appear to have done the opposite: deferring to their respective legislature's judgment. Yet, when a court does defer to the judgment of a legislative body, should it do more to ensure that, in fact, the legislature has made a settled determination about the reasonableness of a given land use? Can we be sure that a legislature has deemed a particular land use harmful just by looking at the legal treatment of a single parcel of land?

The particular danger that comes when we let legislative bodies re-write property laws is that they can single out one or a few landowners for special burdens. This can happen when a law prohibits one landowner from developing while allowing owners of essentially similar land to develop. When a law operates in this way, what has the legislature really decided? That a given type of land use is harmful generally? Or instead that it wants specific lands left undeveloped? If the latter, the new law may deserve far less judicial deference. Would it therefore help if courts took into account in their inquiry, not just the plight of the landowner challenging a new law, but also at the plight of other owners of ecologically similar lands? If a legislature really concludes that filling wetlands is harmful, it ought to express that conclusion by banning the practice essentially everywhere. If instead it bans the land development only on some lands and not others, what message does this send? Has the baseline of reasonable land use really shifted? Or is something else going on, something less legitimate? To put the issue otherwise: can a court fairly decide what rights a landowner possesses, and whether those rights have been unfairly taken by government, without paying attention to the plight of landowners as a class?

4. *Lands affected by a public trust:* State of Vermont v. Central Vermont Railway. Lands underneath navigable waterways have long drawn legal attention—as we've seen, particularly in *Munninghoff v. Dept. of Conservation* (chapter 2). As states entered the Union (aside from the original 13) they gained immediate ownership of legal title to this land—title that was expanded thereafter when the Supreme Court interpreted navigability to reach beyond tidal waters to include all waters navigable in fact. While states gained ownership of that land (but not the surrounding dry lands!), they took it subject to a peculiar obligation to manage it on behalf of the public subject to a public trust intended to further certain public values or uses—navigability and fishing, above all. The resulting public trust doctrine has evolved as a matter of state law, rather than federal law, and states have given the doctrine more or less force as a constraint on the powers of state government to alienate the land free of public trust limitations. A few states have expanded the doctrine to apply to other categories of land—to dryland beaches, for instance—but the common interpretation is that it only touches lands beneath waterways that are or were navigable in fact. The doctrine was applied in State of Vermont v. Central Vermont Railway, Inc., 153 Vt. 337, 571 A.2d 1128 (1989), which dealt with the legal rights held by a railway in a 1.1 mile strip of land along the waterfront in Burlington, Vermont, largely created by depositing fill. The railroad company no longer needed the land for railroad purposes and sought to sell it to a developer for waterfront development, including retail shops and restaurants open to the public. *Held:* Government grants of land subject to the public trust are strongly construed so as to protect public trust values. Here, although the grant of land appeared to convey a fee simple interest the court construed the grant as conveying only a fee simple subject to a condition subsequent. The railway could use the land only for railroad, wharf, and storage purposes, with the state retaining the right of reentry in the event the condition was breached. "Lands held subject to the public trust," the

court ruled, could "be used only for purposes approved by the legislature as public uses." Only the legislature could therefore authorize alternative uses of the waterfront land.

5. *Common law, statutes, and retroactivity*. Legal change over time inevitably causes problems for people who don't see the change coming or who are otherwise affected by it. When change can operate prospectively only, the conflict can be less, especially when people have enough notice of the change to prepare for it. In the case of private property rights in land and natural resources, however, fully prospective change is often not possible. A new law can apply only to those developments or resource activities begun after a certain date, but even then the law is not fully prospective. Legal changes inevitably affect the market values of things, and thus can take owners by surprise. When legal change imposes costs, people complain.

On this subject, notice how different common law decisions and statutes often appear, especially when courts handing down common law rulings write opinions that minimize the change. The common law has changed radically from where it was centuries ago. And common law change comes about in only one way—it applies retroactively. Some plaintiff brings a law suit based on events that have already occurred or at least already begun. The case works its way through the courts. It reaches some high court, which hands down a new rule of law and applies the law to the case at bar. The new law is applied to events that occurred in the past. Contrast this method of legal change with a statute that applies only to events taking place over its effective date, some time in the future. As between the two, the statute seems more fair. Yet the common reaction to these two legal approaches is much different.

When common law change comes about the court essentially states what the law supposedly has long been. Courts have dropped the pretext that they merely "find" the law, but they nonetheless tend to minimize the degree of change. In any event, we've long accepted common law change, and rarely question it. Statutory change, though, is more visible—often traceable to a specific date when a law is enacted or takes effect. It is easier to see how the statute has changed the law, and to calculate its effect. Thus we have the repeated claims that new statutes and regulations amount to disruptions of private property rights—even unconstitutional takings of them—while the same claim is rarely made about judicial decisions.

This differential treatment raises intriguing questions that are rarely confronted. Should we be more suspicious than we are about legal change brought about by judges? (On this, see Barton H. Thompson, *Judicial Takings*, 76 VA. L. REV. 1449 (1990)). Should we instead be much less suspicious of statutory and regulatory change, at least when it accomplishes something that common law courts could have accomplished without problem? What if the Maine or Wisconsin Supreme Court were to announce that filling a wetland was an unreasonable land use and thus outside the scope of any property rights held by landowners? A problem?

GARDNER v. NEW JERSEY PINELANDS COMMISSION

125 N.J. 193, 593 A.2d 251 (1991).

HANDLER, J.

The central issue in this case is whether the application of state regulations that limit the use of land in an environmentally-sensitive area constitutes an unconstitutional taking of private property. The regulations strictly limit residential development on such land and require that all remaining undeveloped acreage be subject to a recorded deed restriction limiting it to agriculture and related uses. A farmer contends that the application of this regulatory scheme to his farm effects a partial taking of his property without compensation.

Hobart Gardner lived and worked for almost seventy years on a 217—acre farm that had been owned by his family since 1902. The farm is located in Shamong Township, Burlington County, a part of the pinelands region subject to the regulations. Gardner, now deceased, and his son, who lives on the farm today, cultivated sod and grain. The farm includes a two-family house, barns, and out-buildings.

When confronted with the regulations, Gardner sought compensation, claiming that the land-use restrictions resulted in an unlawful taking of his property. After the State refused payment, Gardner, on February 7, 1988, initiated this action for inverse condemnation against the Commissioner of the Department of Environmental Protection and the New Jersey Pinelands Commission (Commission), which had promulgated the regulations. Gardner also contended that the regulations constituted an unlawful exaction and a denial of equal protection. He did not assert that the Pinelands Protection Act and the regulations otherwise are unconstitutional or invalid in terms of whether they constitute an impermissible or unreasonable exercise of the police powers in general or the zoning powers specifically. Moreover, the constitutional claims that he did assert are based exclusively on the New Jersey Constitution. . . .

I

The value of the unique ecological, economic, and cultural features of the New Jersey Pine Barrens, or Pinelands, has been recognized for decades. *E.g., L.* 1971, *c.* 417 (creating Pinelands Environmental Council; repealed by *L.* 1979, c. 111). Protection of the area, however, did not begin in earnest until Congress enacted the National Parks and Recreation Act of 1978, Pub.L. No. 95–625, 92 Stat. 3492 (codified at 16 *U.S.C.A.* § 471i), establishing over one-million acres as the Pinelands National Reserve. The Pinelands were the first natural resource to be protected by the innovative "national reserve" program. Designed to conserve areas of ecological sensitivity, natural beauty, and cultural importance, the national reserve concept combines limited public acquisition of property with land-use controls in a cooperative framework involving federal, state, and local governments, as well as concerned private groups and persons. *Senate Energy and Environment Committee Statement,* reprinted at *N.J.S.A.* 13:18A–1 (*Senate Committee Statement*). Governor Byrne promptly issued an Executive Order restricting development in the Pinelands until appropriate state legislation could be enacted. See *Orleans Builders & Developers v. Byrne,* 186 *N.J.Super.* 432, 434–35, 453 *A.*2d 200 (App.Div.1982).

Congress chose the Pinelands as the first protected site with good reason. New Jersey is the most densely populated state in the nation and lies at the midpoint of the emerging megalopolis that extends from Boston to Richmond. *Statistical Abstracts of the United States, 1990* at 21; J. McPhee, *The Pine Barrens* 4–5 (1981). The central corridor of the state between New York and Philadelphia has been described as "one great compression of industrial shapes, industrial sounds, industrial air, and thousands and thousands of houses webbing over the spaces between the factories." J. McPhee, *supra,* at 4. Astride that corridor in central and southern New Jersey is the Pinelands.

The pristine nature of the Pinelands sharply contrasts with its contiguous, dense urban and industrial surroundings. A "wilderness" of pine-oak forests and wild and scenic rivers, the Pinelands harbors a "wide variety of rare, threatened and endangered plant and animal species," and encompasses "many other significant and unique ecological, historical, recreational, and other resources." *Senate Committee Statement, supra;* J. McPhee, *supra,* at 4–5. The region overlies the vast, seventeen-trillion gallon Cohansey aquifer, "one of the largest virtually untapped sources of pure water in the world." *Senate Committee Statement, supra*; see J. McPhee, *supra,* at 13–16. There has been very little development within the Pinelands; there are no major retail centers, and developed property comprises only one to two percent of the land in most areas. New Jersey Pinelands Commission, *New Jersey Pinelands: Comprehensive Management Plan* 128–29 (1980) (*Comprehensive Management Plan*). Agriculture in the Pinelands, especially the cultivation of cranberries and blueberries, is particularly important both nationally and locally. New Jersey Department of Agriculture, *Annual Report—Ag Statistics* 38, 72–73 (1990).

In recent years, anxiety over the loss of farming and the fragile ecology of the Pinelands has produced increasingly stringent federal and state regulation. Both the federal and the implementing state legislation make clear that conservation, preservation, and protection are the principal ends of governmental regulation of land use in the Pinelands. The federal statute states its purpose is "to protect, preserve and enhance the significant values of the land and water resources of the Pinelands area." 16 *U.S.C.A.* § 471i(b)(1). Similarly, the New Jersey Pinelands Protection Act (Act), *L.* 1979, *c.* 111; *N.J.S.A.* 13:18A–1 to 29, declares that its goals are, among others, to protect, preserve, continue, and expand agriculture and horticulture and to discourage piecemeal and scattered development within the Pinelands. *N.J.S.A.* 13:18A–9b. The Act stresses preservation of the region:

> [T]he continued viability of [the Pinelands] area and resources is threatened by pressures for residential, commercial and industrial development * * * [T]he protection of such area and resources is in the interests of the people of this State and of the Nation * * *.
>
> * * *
>
> The Legislature further finds and declares that the current pace of random and uncoordinated development and construction in the pinelands area poses an immediate threat to the resources thereof, especially to the survival of rare, threatened, and endangered plant and animal species and the habitat thereof, and to the maintenance of the existing high quality of surface and ground waters; that such development and construction increase the risk and extent of destruction of life and property which could be caused by the natural cycle of forest fires in this unique area * * *. [*N.J.S.A.* 13:18A–2.]

The Act authorizes the designation of "protection areas" for promotion of agriculture, horticulture, and "appropriate patterns of compatible residential, commercial and industrial development in or adjacent to areas already utilized for such purposes." *N.J.S.A.* 13:18A–9b. It also calls for the establishment of an extensive "preservation area" to protect especially sensitive land in its natural state and to promote compatible agricultural, horticultural, and recreational uses. *N.J.S.A.* 13:18A–9c.

In keeping with the paramount objective of both federal and state governments, *i.e.,* protecting the Pinelands from overdevelopment and consequent ecological degradation, the plan for the Pinelands National Reserve calls for the full participation of federal, state, county, and municipal authorities. 16 *U.S.C.A.* § 471i(b), (d), (f)(4), (g), (h). To ensure that pressures for development do not overwhelm the need for preservation, actions of the lower levels of government that do not conform to that objective can be pre-empted by a higher authority.

The federal statute directs the Governor of New Jersey to create a planning commission. 16 *U.S.C.A.* § 471i(d). The New Jersey Pinelands Commission (the "Commission") is the instrumentality envisaged by federal and state law as having primary responsibility for planning in the Pinelands. *N.J.S.A.* 13:18A–4. Its charge is to develop a "comprehensive management plan" (CMP) to serve as the land-use blueprint for the region, subject to the approval of the federal Secretary of the Interior. 16 *U.S.C.A.* § 471i(d), (f), and (g); *N.J.S.A.* 13:18A–4,–5,–8,–9. To assist the State's efforts, the federal government provides funds for planning and land acquisition, which are subject to repayment if the State does not properly implement a preservation program. 16 *U.S.C.A.* § 471i(g)(5), (g)(6), (k).

A similar system of incentives to cooperate, reinforced by the power to pre-empt, characterizes the relations between the State and local governments under the Act. Initially, the Commission assumed all power to exercise traditional zoning functions within the Pinelands, promulgating minimum land-use standards under the CMP. *N.J.S.A.* 13:18A–8,–10. Thereafter, counties and municipalities were required to conform their master plans and zoning ordinances to the CMP and to have such plans and ordinances approved by the Commission. *N.J.S.A.* 13:18A–12(a), (b). If a county or municipality fails to conform to the CMP, the Commission will continue to exercise direct control over local land use. *N.J.S.A.* 13:18–12(c).

In developing the CMP, the Commission has been directed to "[r]ecognize existing economic activities within the area and provide for protection and enhancement of such activities as farming, forestry, proprietary recreational facilities, and those indigenous industries and commercial and residential developments which are consistent with such purposes and provisions." *N.J.S.A.* 13:18A–8(d)(3). To those ends, the Commission has been given broad authority to invoke

> a variety of land and water protection and management techniques, including but not limited to, zoning and regulation derived from State and local police powers, development and use standards, permit systems, acquisition of conservation easements and other interest [sic] in land, * * * transfer of development rights, dedication of private lands for recreation or conservation purposes and any other appropriate method of land and water protection and management which will help meet the goals and carry out the policies of the management plan. [*N.J.S.A.* 13:18A–8(d)(1).]

Reflecting the aims of the federal and state statutes, the goals of the CMP include the "continuation and expansion of agricultural and horticultural uses." *N.J.S.A.* 13:18A–9(b)(3). The original CMP, adopted by the Commission in November 1980, stressed that agriculture contributes both to the unique characteristics of the Pinelands and to the environment "by creating open space, terrestrial and aquatic habitats, and wildlife feeding areas." *Comprehensive Management Plan, supra,* at 242. It also stated that suburban development contributes to "an unfavorable economic environment for farmers through escalating taxes, enactment of inhibiting local ordinances, and increased trespassing and vandalism." *Ibid.* Consequently, the original CMP called for several programs to accomplish the objective of agricultural preservation. It identified eight "Pinelands Management Areas" of varying ecological sensitivity, including a Preservation Area District, Forest Areas, Agricultural Production Areas, and Regional Growth Areas. *N.J.A.C.* 7:50–5.12(a).

The original CMP restricted residential development in Agricultural Production Areas, reserving them primarily for farm and farm-related purposes. Section 5–304 of the plan allowed residential units on lots with 3.2 acres as long as the applicant met certain stringent conditions. The original CMP also permitted ten-acre residential zoning, that is, one residential unit per ten acres, "provided that the dwelling unit is accessory to an active agricultural operation, and is intended for the use of the owners or employees of the agricultural operation."

The Commission further created a development-rights transfer program, under which it would award Pinelands Development Credits (PDCs) to landowners for recording permanent deed restrictions on their property limiting the land to specific uses set forth in the CMP. *See Comprehensive Management Plan, supra,* at 210–12 and sections 5–401 to–407; *N.J.A.C.* 7:50–5.41 to –5.47 (current version). The PDC program seeks to channel development by permitting holders of PDCs to transfer them to owners who wish to increase densities in specially-designated Regional Growth Areas. *N.J.S.A.* 13:18A–31; *N.J.A.C.* 7:50–5.41, –5.45. PDCs may be sold privately at market prices; according to the Assistant Director for Development Review at the Commission, Burlington County has a PDC bank that routinely pays $10,000 per credit. A landowner in an Uplands Agricultural Production Area—the designation that apparently includes the Gardner farm—receives two PDCs per thirty-nine acres. *N.J.A.C.* 7:50–5.43(b)(2)(i).

In the fall of 1987, Gardner explored the possibility of subdividing his property into fourteen to seventeen ten-acre "farmettes" in accordance with the CMP option allowing one farm-related residential unit per ten acres of land. Before the application was submitted, the Commission completed a periodic revision and amendment of the CMP, as required by the Act. *N.J.S.A.* 13:18A–8. The Commission determined, according to an affidavit submitted by its Assistant Director for Development Review, that the ten-acre farm option had deteriorated into a ten-acre subdivision requirement with no guarantee that the land actually would be used for farming, and had led in some situations "to the cessation of agricultural operations," "effectively eliminating existing agricultural uses, and threatening significant agricultural use of adjoining areas."

The revised CMP permits only three options for residential development of farmland in Agricultural Production Areas: (1) second-generation Pinelands residents or persons whose livelihood depends on traditional Pinelands economic activities may build homes on 3.2–acre lots, *N.J.A.C* 7:50–5.24(a)(1),—5.32; (2) a home may be constructed on a ten-acre lot for an operator or employee of the farm, but that option may be exercised only once every five years, *N.J.A.C.* 7:50–5.24(a)(2) or (3) homes may be constructed at a density of one unit per forty acres, but only if the residences are clustered on one-acre lots and the remaining thirty-nine acres allocated to each residence are permanently dedicated to agricultural use by a recorded deed restriction, *N.J.A.C.* 7:50–5.24(a)(3),–5.24(c). The restriction of residential development to forty-acre tracts prompted the filing of Gardner's complaint.

II

Land use regulations span a wide spectrum, from conventional zoning, *e.g., Village of Euclid v. Ambler Realty,* 272 *U.S.* 365, 47 *S.Ct.* 114, 71 *L.Ed.* 303 (1926); *Cobble Close Farm v. Board of Adjustment,* 10 *N.J.* 442, 92 *A.*2d 4 (1952), to particularized restrictions on property with special characteristics, *e.g., Penn Cent. Transp. Co. v. City of New*

York, 438 *U.S.* 104, 98 *S.Ct.* 2646, 57 *L.Ed.*2d 631 (1978) (*Penn Central*). The Pinelands Protection Act virtually fills the entire spectrum. It imposes comprehensive and complex regulatory land-use controls over an extensive geographic region with distinctive natural, economic, cultural, and historic characteristics.

Because the Pinelands scheme is fundamentally a regime of zoning, takings doctrine dealing with zoning is particularly relevant. In its most general formulation, takings analysis makes two fundamental demands of any zoning scheme: it must substantially advance legitimate state interests, and it cannot deny an owner all economically viable use of the land. *Agins v. Tiburon,* 447 *U.S.* 255, 260, 100 *S.Ct.* 2138, 2141, 65 *L.Ed.*2d 106, 112 (1980). Those demands may become more elaborate when takings analysis is applied to complex, special-purpose regulations. . . .

A

There is not the slightest quarrel that the Act substantially advances several interrelated legitimate and important public purposes. We need refer only to the Legislature's declaration of the Act's objective: to protect the Pinelands, an area providing "a unique habitat for a wide variety of rare, threatened and endangered plant and animal species" and containing "significant and unique * * * resources." Protection of the Pinelands "is in the interests of the people of this State and of the Nation." *N.J.S.A.* 13:18A–2. The CMP reiterates that purpose, recognizing especially the importance of agriculture because of its capacity to contribute to the special character of the Pinelands and to the environment "by creating open space, terrestrial and aquatic habitats, and wildlife feeding areas," as well as adding "to the cultural, historical, social, visual, and economic characteristics of the Pinelands." *Comprehensive Management Plan, supra,* at 242. That protection of the Pinelands serves the public interest is underscored by the congressional dedication of the region as the Pinelands Natural Reserve. 16 *U.S.C.A.* § 471i.

The preservation of agriculture and farmland constitutes a valid governmental goal. . . . The Act and the land-use regulations directly advance agricultural preservation, particularly through the limitation of residential development by large-tract requirements and complementary deed restrictions on undeveloped, nonresidential land. . . .

The Act further advances a valid public purpose by preventing or reducing harm to the public. That is exemplified most dramatically by its measures to safeguard the environment and protect the water supply by severely limiting development. The Legislature specifically determined that "pressures for residential, commercial and industrial development" and the "current pace of random and uncoordinated development" pose an "immediate threat" to a region of vital public importance. *N.J.S.A.* 13:18A–2. . . .

That land itself is a diminishing resource cannot be overemphasized. *See Holmdel Builders v. Township of Holmdel,* 121 *N.J.* 550, 565–66, 583 *A.*2d 277 (1990). Environmentally-sensitive land is all the more precious. Hence, a proposed development that may constitute only a small insult to the environment does not lessen the need to avoid such an offense. The cumulative detrimental impact of many small projects can be devastating. *See, e.g., Barancik, supra,* 872 *F.*2d 834; *cf. Gilbert v. State,* 218 *Cal.App.*3d 234, 266 *Cal.Rptr.* 891 (1990) (water connections prohibited to preserve water supply). "If exemptions should be granted because development on individual tracts would impair only minutely the entire resources of the Pinelands, the cumulative effect of such exemptions would defeat the legislative goals of the Pinelands Protection Act." *Orleans Builders & Developers, supra,* 186 *N.J.Super.* at 444, 453 *A.*2d 200; *see Lom–Ran Corp. v. Department of Envtl. Protection,* 163 *N.J.Super.* 376, 388, 394 *A.*2d 1233 (App.Div.1978).

Plaintiff argues that the regulatory scheme does not fulfill its public purposes in a lawful manner, relying heavily on the Supreme Court's 1987 decision in *Nollan v. California Coastal Commission,* 483 *U.S.* 825, 107 *S.Ct.* 3141, 97 *L.Ed.*2d 677. There, owners of a beachfront property with a small bungalow applied to the California Coastal Commission for a permit to tear down the bungalow and replace it with a much larger house. Because the larger structure would increase blockage of the ocean view and private use of the shorefront, that Commission conditioned the permit on the owners granting the public a right-of-way easement along the shoreline of their property. *Id.* at 827–29, 107 *S.Ct.* at 3143–44, 97 *L.Ed.*2d at 683–84. The Supreme Court determined first that the easement was tantamount to a permanent physical invasion of the property; hence, had the Commission wished to appropriate a right of way by direct regulation, it would have had to exercise the state's eminent domain power and pay for it. *Id.* at 831–34, 107 *S.Ct.* at 3145–47, 97 *L.Ed.*2d at 686–87. The Court further concluded that preserving visual access to the ocean from the street side of the Nollans' house served a wholly different purpose from creating a right-of-way along the shore, and for that reason the easement was not a reasonable and acceptable exercise of the police powers but a taking of property requiring just compensation. *Id.* at 836–40, 107 *S.Ct.* at 3148–50, 97 *L.Ed.*2d at 688–91.

The restriction in *Nollan* was in the nature of a classic easement or servitude. By authorizing physical access to the beach, it sought to advance a goal collateral to the underlying governmental purpose of preserving visual access to the beach. Here, the underlying regulation limiting residential development on forty-acre tracts restricted predominantly to agriculture directly furthers the central purposes of the Act. The required deed restriction is a constituent part of the regulatory scheme, imposing use limitations substantially identical to the underlying regulation; it does not constitute a burden that is unrelated to the essential purposes of the regulatory scheme. [citations omitted]

We are satisfied that the Act and the regulations implementing it substantially advance legitimate and important governmental objectives.

B

The critical remaining question is whether the regulations impair to an impermissible degree valuable property rights and interests. Diminution of land value itself does not constitute a taking. *E.g., Village of Euclid, supra,* 272 *U.S.* 365, 47 *S.Ct.* 114, 71 *L.Ed.* 303. Similarly, impairment of the marketability of land alone does not effect a taking. *Littman, supra,* 115 *N.J.* at 163, 557 *A.*2d 314; *see Kirby Forest Indus. v. United States,* 467 *U.S.* 1, 15, 104 *S.Ct.* 2187, 2196, 81 *L.Ed.*2d 1, 14 (1984). Also, restrictions on uses do not necessarily result in takings even though they reduce income or profits. *Southern Burlington County NAACP v. Township of Mount Laurel,* 92 *N.J.* 158, 273 n. 34, 456 *A.*2d 390 (1983). A regulatory scheme will be upheld unless it denies "all practical use" of property, *Harrington Glen, Inc. v. Municipal Bd. of Adjustment,* 52 *N.J.* 22, 29, 243 *A.*2d 233 (1968); or "substantially destroys the beneficial use of private property," *Schiavone Constr. Co. v. Hackensack Meadowlands Dev. Comm'n,* 98 *N.J.* 258, 263, 486 *A.*2d 330 (1985), or does not allow an "adequate" or "just and reasonable" return on investment, *Holmdel Builders Ass'n, supra,* 121 *N.J.* at 581–82, 583 *A.*2d 277 (citing *Mount Laurel, supra,* 92 *N.J.* at 268, 456 *A.*2d 390); *In re Egg Harbor Assocs.,* 94 *N.J.* 358, 373, 464 *A.*2d 1115 (1983). Significantly, our courts have applied the standard that focuses on the beneficial or economic uses allowed to a property owner in the context of particularized restraints designed to preserve the special status of distinctive property and sensitive environmental regions, such as the Pinelands. [citations omitted]

Plaintiff acknowledges that preserving agriculture is a legitimate governmental objective that can be achieved through land-use regulation. He contends, nonetheless, that the land-use regulations, including the required deed restrictions of the revised CMP, interfere to an intolerable degree with his right and freedom to use and enjoy his farmland property. The response to that contention is found in *Penn Central, supra,* 438 *U.S.* 104, 98 *S.Ct.* at 2649, 57 *L.Ed.*2d 631, which amplified the takings principles applicable to specialized regulations seeking to preserve the status of distinctive property.

In *Penn Central,* New York City had enacted a landmarks preservation ordinance, requiring approval from the Landmarks Preservation Commission for exterior alterations. *Id.* at 109–12, 98 *S.Ct.* at 2651–54, 57 *L.Ed.*2d at 639–42. Owners of affected buildings could transfer development rights from a landmark parcel to proximate lots. *Id.* at 113–14, 98 *S.Ct.* at 2654–55, 57 *L.Ed.*2d at 642. Penn Central sued when that Commission refused to approve construction of a multi-story building atop Grand Central Terminal, a designated landmark. *Id.* at 116–19, 98 *S.Ct.* at 2655–57, 57 *L.Ed.*2d at 643–45. It contended that New York had "taken" its air space and that the law had both significantly diminished the value of the site as a whole and unfairly singled out people who owned landmark properties to bear the public burden. *Id.* at 130–35, 98 S.Ct. at 2662–65, 57 *L.Ed.*2d at 652–55. The Supreme Court rejected those arguments. It explained that takings jurisprudence focused on the nature and extent of interference with rights in the whole parcel, not discrete segments; that when laws are reasonably related to the general welfare even severe diminution in value will not effect a taking if viable uses remain; and that, far from being discriminatory, the law embodied a comprehensive plan to preserve structures of historic and aesthetic interest throughout the city. *Id.* at 129–35, 98 *S.Ct.* at 2661–65, 57 *L.Ed.*2d at 651–55. Moreover, Penn Central could continue to use the parcel in a gainful fashion and could offset its loss by transferring valuable development rights to other parcels, even though such transfers did not fully compensate it. *Id.* at 137, 98 *S.Ct.* 2666, 57 *L.Ed.*2d at 656–57.

Plaintiff's claim fails under the *Penn Central* analysis. The CMP does not change or prohibit an existing use of the land when applied to plaintiff's farm. *See id.* at 129, 98 *S.Ct.* at 2661, 57 *L.Ed.*2d at 651–52. Like Penn Central, plaintiff may continue the existing, admittedly beneficial use of the property. Further, although whether Penn Central could again make use of all of its property, particularly the airspace over its terminal, was unclear, plaintiff may gainfully use all of his property, including the right to build five homes clustered together on the restricted land. There also is no showing that the economic impact of the regulations interferes with distinct investment-backed expectations. In addition, Penn Central could offset its loss by transferring valuable property rights to other properties, even if such transfers did not fully compensate it. Plaintiff possesses the similar right to offsetting benefits; it may receive Pinelands Development Credits in return for recording the deed restrictions. Finally, there is no invidious or arbitrary unfairness in the application of the regulatory scheme. Gardner's neighbors in Uplands Agricultural Areas are burdened by exactly the same restrictions, and other landowners in the Pinelands must abide by comparable regulations as part of an integrated comprehensive plan designed to benefit both the region and the public. *See Agins, supra,* 447 *U.S.* at 262, 100 *S.Ct.* at 2142, 65 *L.Ed.*2d at 113; *cf. Penn Central, supra,* 438 *U.S.* at 138–53, 98 *S.Ct.* at 2666–74, 57 *L.Ed.*2d at 657–66 (Rehnquist, J., dissenting) (New York scheme singled out specific individual properties and did not impose uniform restrictions)....

In sum, plaintiff retains several viable, economically-beneficial uses of his land under the revised CMP. That those uses do not equal the former maximum value of the land in a less-or un-regulated state is not dispositive, for there exists no constitutional right to the most profitable use of property. We conclude that the restriction on lands to farmland and related uses, given the distinctive and special characteristics of the Pinelands, does not deprive plaintiff of the economic or beneficial use of all or most of his property, sufficiently diminish the value or profitability of his land, or otherwise interfere with his ownership interest to constitute a taking of property without just compensation....

The judgment below is affirmed.

Notes

1. *Again, what is the baseline? Gardner* is another ruling considering the validity of regulations restricting natural resource activities. The ruling tells us more about the leading U.S. Supreme Court cases that set the outer limits for the ability of governments to restrict land-use activities, especially the important *Penn Central* case that announced a multi-factor analysis for evaluating restrictions. Where does the court begin when measuring the effects of the Pinelands regulatory scheme on landowner rights? Does the court take into account the longstanding principles that landowner cannot use their lands in ways that cause harm, including harm to the surrounding community, or does it start with an abstract cultural ideal of ownership?

The Pinelands scheme is a highly unusual one yet could serve over time as a model for similar efforts elsewhere, especially in ecologically sensitive regions. We can see from the facts of the case that changes were made to the scheme as regulatory measures were tried and did not seem to work. Note, for instance, the original plan to allow 10–acre "farmettes," an idea that was dropped when the scheme seemed to do little more than promote large-scale development with 10–acre lots. Notice, also, the allocation of power between federal, state, and local governments. Local governments can wield considerable power over land use, but only so long as they abide by guidelines set forth by the state Pinelands Commission. For a ruling involving a somewhat similar land-conservation scheme applicable to portions of Long Island, see *W.J.F. Realty Corp. v. State*, 672 N.Y.S.2d 1007, 176 Misc.2d 763 (1998); see also Julian Conrad Juergensmeyer, et al., *Transferable Development Rights and Alternatives After* Suitum, 30 Urb. Law. 441 (1998).

2. *Henry George and the economics of development. Gardner* is one of many rulings dealing at its base with the conflict between landowners who want to develop their lands and governments that want to halt the development. Many lands rise in market value due to their development potential, and landowners can only capture this rise in value if they develop or sell at market price to someone else who develops. So routine is it to assume that landowners have and perhaps should have the right to develop that we rarely take time to think about the economics of development, and thus the fairness elements of the situation. This omission is curious, because a century and more ago millions of Americans viewed the issue as a critical one and it remains a fundamental issue in land (and, more recently, ecological) economics.

When John Locke in the seventeenth century sought to justify private property as a natural right he did so by spinning a tale in which people mixed their labor with land to create value. They became owners of the land because of the value that their labors created. Locke recognized that his theory could not justify the ownership of value that arose in any way other than through human labor. By the nineteenth century it was widely understood that land often had vast value that the landowner did not recreate, and that this value came not from landowner labor but from the accumulated activities of surrounding landowners. When a land parcel lay vacant and a city arose around it, the increase in land value was due to the city and the efforts of city members, not to anything the landowner had done. In

America, the political economist most associated with the idea was Henry George, whose books were read by millions. George viewed this rise in land value as something that the community created and thus could claim. The value should not go, he said, to the landowner. See Henry George, PROGRESS AND POVERTY: AN INQUIRY INTO THE CAUSE OF INDUSTRIAL DEPRESSIONS AND OF INCREASE OF WANT WITH INCREASE OF WEALTH (Mod. Lib. ed. 1929); Henry George, A PERPLEXED PHILOSOPHER (R. Schakkenack ed., 1946).

George's ideas, though widely popular, had little legal effect in the United States save to make real estate taxes seem more legitimate. And George himself turned his economic analysis into a "single tax" scheme for funding government that proved highly impractical. Yet George's analysis was economically sound (for a discussion see Herman E. Daly & Joshua Farley, ECOLOGICAL ECONOMICS: PRINCIPLES AND APPLICATIONS 198–200 (2004)), and various countries around the world have used it to justify near total bans on the right to develop land. If the development value of land is a communal creation, where is the unfairness when the community bans development or, when it does permit development, effectively captures the development value on behalf of the public? Americans tend to view the claim as surprising if not outrageous; many other countries, in contrast, accept the reasoning as sound and morally legitimate. (Britain did so to a large degree in 1947 when it enacted its Town and Country Planning Act.) On the issue of Henry George and development rights, see Eric T. Freyfogle, THE LAND WE SHARE: PRIVATE PROPERTY AND THE COMMON GOOD (2003), pp. 126–30; 241–48. The same policy issue arises in the instance of rights to exploit particular natural resources, when the economic value of the resources is not based on labor mixed with the land.

3. *Reasonable use IX: TDR's and the redefinition of development rights.* Henry George aside, the rights of landowners to develop or undertake new intensive uses are defined in the first instance by property law, mostly state law. Few Americans are willing to consider the possibility of curtailing development rights completely, and regulatory takings law, as we have seen, is hostile to it except when the ban on development effectively implements a background principle of property law (such as, one assumes, the do-no-harm or reasonable use rule). Yet, many states and local governments have in fact curtailed development rights so severely as to come close to eliminating them. In this regard, *Gardner* is an illustration. Note that the development rights scheme covering part of the region limited development to one structure per 40 acres, with requirements that the construction be clustered. Plainly this is a severe, though not total, limit on the right to develop.

What is the best way to think about the effect of this legal regime on the rights on landowners in the Pinelands? The temptation is to view the scheme as somehow cutting into landowner rights; that is, the laws (to return to the future interests analogy offered after *Moon*) have disrupted or cut short development rights, maybe even suppressed them until the day when the regulations are removed and the development rights are allowed to spring back. But is it just as apt, maybe more so, to view them as a redefinitions of landowner rights? Could we say that they have, in effect, turned the vague reasonable-use limit on landowner activities into a limit that is more specific and useful—not so much changing landowner rights as bringing them into sharper focus? Obviously, the landowner who wants to develop will see things differently, as a taking of property rights. But what about from the much different point of view of lawmakers who have largely taken over the lawmaking work of common law courts?

4. *Nature as lawmaker.* A key issue that arises in *Gardner*, as in several of the earlier rulings (*Woodbury, Dexter, Johnson, Zealy*) is whether and to what extent the rights of landowners to use land ought to depend upon the natural features of the land itself. Prior cases have presented the issue mostly in the context of particular parcels of land and we have largely considered it at that scale. *Gardner*, though, presses us to consider the issue at broader spatial scales and to consider larger ecological processes and interactions. If, as many conservation writers assert, good land use entails respect for fundamental ecological processes, might lawmakers properly redefine landowner rights to take the processes into account? Should "reasonable use" increasingly take nature and its basic processes into account? The issue is directly relevant to all natural resources, not just the bundle of rights commonly known as land. For claims that nature should play a bigger role in ideas about land ownership see Lynda L. Butler, *The Pathology of Property Norms: Living Within Nature's Boundaries*, 73 S. Cal. L. Rev. 927 (2000); Myrl Duncan, *Reconceiving the "Bundle of Sticks: Land as a Community–Based Resource*, 32 Envtl. L. 32 (2002); Terry W. Frazier, *Protecting Ecological Integrity Within the Balancing Function of Property Law*, 28 Envt. L. 53 (1998).

Chapter Five

OWNING AND USING DISCRETE RESOURCES

The materials in the last chapter introduced the subject of use rights in land and land-based resources. At the core of that law is the vague but nonetheless essential *sic utere tuo*, do-no-harm or reasonable use rule, which underlies both nuisance law and a wide-variety of legislative and regulatory enactments. We saw how property rights typically reside on both sides of land-use disputes, and how lawmakers inevitably must make policy decisions when resolving these disputes. We saw, too, how the idea of land use "harm" has shifted over time—and shows no inclination to end its on-going social evolution. We noted the complex relationships between courts and other lawmaking bodies, openly asking: Whose job is it to keep property law up to date, and how much deference should be afforded any given lawmaker's determinations? And within courts, should juries decide the reasonableness of land uses as questions of fact or are judges better suited to do so? Then there were the uneasy roles applied to both priority in time among land uses and to the vast natural differences that exist among land parcels. Should a landowner's rights to use land as he chooses be greater if he is the first to arrive in an area? And should they depend on the land's natural features, so that a person who wants to engage in a particular land use needs to find lands that are ecologically well suited for the use?

This background on land provides the foundation for the issues in this chapter. Here we go beyond land to talk about the various property rights held by owners of discrete natural resources. That ownership, as we've seen, could take the form of *owning the resource in place*; instead it could entail a *right (exclusive or nonexclusive) to harvest or capture* an unowned resource that is present in a given place. Exactly what rights does a resource owner possess, both to use the resource and to complain about interferences with her use? How do these rights fit together with the rights of the owner of the land where the resource is located? And how do they fit together with the rights of other resource owners, when the activities of competing owners produce conflict? In this setting, too, we'll pay attention to how the law's answers have evolved over time. And we'll revisit the institutional questions about how legal changes take place, to see how they unfold.

As we proceed through these materials (and go on to later chapters), we will repeatedly encounter one of the overriding issues in all of natural resources law. Conflicts among resource users are inevitable, and lawmakers are required to resolve them somehow. We've seen several methods of doing so—favoring the first user on the scene; using some sort of natural-use or natural-incidents background rule for judging land uses; or evaluating the competing uses to see if they are in some sense reasonable. The options, really, are rather few, in terms of distinct types. (You might at this point re-read note 1 on page 23.) Rising above these possibilities is another fundamental choice that lawmakers face, even if they don't expressly realize it, between reliance on property rules and/or on dispute resolution processes.

One way to avoid or reduce resource-use conflicts is to define use rights with great precision in advance, *ex ante*, so resource users know exactly where they stand (or as exactly as possible). When a conflict then arises, existing law with any luck can provide an answer. A rather different approach is to define resource-use rights more vaguely, and then set up some sort of mechanism—akin perhaps to a lake-management or lobster-harvesting association or an irrigation district—that has the power to adjust resource-use practices over time and to resolve conflicts *ex post*, as they arise.

The first of these two approaches might be termed a "substance approach" in that it resolves conflicts by looking to the exact prescribed rights that each user has. The latter approach might be termed a "process approach" in that it relies on user-led processes to deal with problems as they come up. Off to the side we might put the important approach that relies on market forces to resolve conflicts, perhaps by facilitating the buying and selling of resource rights to clear up conflicts. As we'll see, these three approaches are rather different. They require us to define resource use rights in different ways and to vest varying amounts of managerial power in user associations. Lawyers trained in the common law are prone to assume that the first of these approaches is better. Practicing lawyers routinely use it when they draft contractual agreements governing resource uses, foreseeing potential conflicts and trying to resolve them in advance. Today, the market-based approach enjoys considerable popularity, particularly among people suspicious of government. Less familiar and perhaps deserving of greater attention is the process approach. Various scholars today see real benefit in it, particularly for dealing with common pool resources. What many people are now concluding is that a human-occupied landscape, even when divided into private tracts and private use rights, remains in many ways a natural commons, given ecological interconnections and the countless ways private activities affect one another. A fair prediction is that natural resources law in decades to come will rely more and more on user-dominated mechanisms to adjust resource uses over time—on collective governance regimes—and less on the other two dispute-resolution mechanisms.

A. INTERPRETING AMBIGUOUS DEEDS

Many times, a natural resource starts off being owned by the owner of the land where the resource is located. At some point, the landowner transfers the resource to someone else. What rights does the transferee obtain? The place to begin looking for an answer, of course, is in the deed or other instrument by which the resource-right was transferred. Deeds, though, are often ambiguous, and no small part of natural resources law has to do with their interpretation. What problems typically arise under them, and how are they resolved? In particular, what resource use rights must be set forth expressly in a deed, and what rights might transfer by implication?

SAVE OUR LITTLE VERMILLION ENVIRONMENT, INC. v. ILLINOIS CEMENT COMPANY

311 Ill.App.3d 747, 244 Ill.Dec. 275, 725 N.E.2d 386 (2000).

JUSTICE SLATER delivered the opinion of the court:

Plaintiff, Save Our Little Vermillion Environment, Inc. (SOLVE), a nonprofit corporation, filed a complaint for declaratory and injunctive relief against defendant Illinois Cement Company. SOLVE sought to prevent Illinois Cement from mining limestone on a parcel of land (the property) adjacent to Illinois Cement's existing quarrying operation. The trial court granted summary judgment in favor of SOLVE, finding that SOLVE's ownership interest in the "coal and other minerals" underlying the property included the limestone. We reverse.

FACTS

The property at issue, consisting of approximately 34 acres, was conveyed by George Colling to John Fabricki in 1907, "[r]eserving the coal and other minerals underlying the same." SOLVE subsequently acquired an undivided three-fifths interest in the rights reserved by Colling. Illinois Cement is the successor to the rights of Fabricki, which it acquired by deed in 1993. Illinois Cement is a manufacturer of cement; a major component of cement is limestone. In October of 1997, the Illinois Department of Natural Resources issued a surface mining permit to Illinois Cement to engage in the mining of limestone on the property. In July of 1998, SOLVE filed a complaint seeking to be declared the owner of the limestone and to enjoin Illinois Cement from mining.

At the hearing on SOLVE's motion for a preliminary injunction, James Kirk, a quarry foreman for Illinois Cement, testified that the overburden, or surface material covering the limestone, varied from 3 feet to 60 feet. According to Kirk, the only way to mine the limestone was by removing the surface material. H. John Head, a mining engineer, similarly testified to the depth of the overburden and that the limestone could not be removed without disturbing the surface. According to Head, quarrying was the only feasible way to mine the limestone.

SOLVE's motion for a preliminary injunction was denied. Thereafter, both SOLVE and Illinois Cement filed cross motions for summary judgment. The trial court granted summary judgment in favor of SOLVE and this appeal followed.

ANALYSIS

. . . .

In general, an owner of land is entitled to the surface and all that is below it. *Miller v. Ridgley,* 2 Ill.2d 223, 117 N.E.2d 759 (1954). However, it is clear that the mineral estate may be severed from the surface estate by granting the minerals and reserving the surface, or by granting the surface and reserving the minerals. *Failoni v. Chicago & North Western Ry. Co.,* 30 Ill.2d 258, 195 N.E.2d 619 (1964). In this case the grantor reserved "the coal and other minerals underlying" the property. At issue is whether such a reservation includes limestone, or whether limestone is part of the surface estate.

The parties recognize that *Kinder v. La Salle County Carbon Coal Co.,* 310 Ill. 126, 141 N.E. 537 (1923), is the leading case in this area, but they disagree about its application to the facts presented here. In *Kinder,* James Cowey conveyed, in 1867, "all the bituminous or stone coal, together with the right to mine the same" (*Kinder,* 310 Ill. at 127, 141 N.E. at 537) as well as "the oil and minerals, of every description," (*Kinder,* 310 Ill. at 127–28, 141 N.E. at 538) underlying a parcel of land less than one mile from the property at issue in this case. In 1869, Cowey conveyed his remaining interest in the property, reserving "all bituminous or stone coal and other minerals, as well as all petroleum oil, in, upon or underlying said premises above described, together with the right to mine and raise the same." *Kinder,* 310 Ill. at 128, 141 N.E. at 538.

At issue in *Kinder* was whether the limestone on the property belonged to the owner of the mineral estate or the owner of the surface estate. The *Kinder* court rejected the argument that the technical definition of the term "minerals" was controlling (see *Kinder,* 310 Ill. at 132–33, 141 N.E. at 539–40), finding instead that the rule for interpreting grants of minerals was " 'that each case must be decided upon the language of the grant or reservation, the surrounding circumstances, and the intention of the grantor if it can be ascertained.' " *Kinder,* 310 Ill. at 134, 141 N.E. at 540. Because of the obvious similarities between *Kinder* and the instant case, we set forth what we deem to be the most significant portion of the court's analysis at some length:

> When Cowey conveyed to the Chicago Coal Company he was engaged in mining coal in the immediate vicinity of appellees' land, then owned by him. Coal was the only known mineral under the surface which had any commercial value. Cowey knew appellees' land was underlaid with some gravel and limestone. On parts of the

land the limestone was on the surface, and on the rest of it was covered with loam, sand and gravel from a few inches in depth to a depth, in places, of fifty or sixty feet. Where the loam was of sufficient depth the land was available for cultivation in crops and was productive. Cowey knew the limestone was so near the surface that it could not be mined by underground methods without the practical destruction of the agricultural surface. To our minds it would be unreasonable to say his intention was to reserve only the agricultural surface above the limestone and convey to the grantee the limestone, with the right to remove it, and thereby destroy all he had reserved. The granting clause of the deed conveys only the coal, "together with the right to mine the same," and the quit-claim clause of 'all minerals of every description' underlying the land described cannot reasonably be construed to embrace minerals other than such as could be removed by mining operations underground, which would not destroy the surface for agricultural purposes. It is altogether reasonable to presume that Cowey and his grantee had no thought of limestone, sand and gravel as minerals. They knew those were on or near the surface and were of an entirely different nature from coal and oil,—the minerals specifically mentioned in the deed and which could be mined by underground methods.... *Kinder,* 310 Ill. at 134–35, 141 N.E. at 540.

While *Kinder* would appear to favor Illinois Cement's position that they own the limestone, SOLVE argues, and the trial court found, that *Kinder* is distinguishable from the instant case. SOLVE asserts that the following differences between *Kinder* and the case at bar favor a result contrary to *Kinder:* (1) the *Kinder* deeds contained the language "the right to mine and raise the same"; (2) substantial amounts of limestone were visible on the surface of the land in *Kinder;* and (3) because limestone was not a commercially valuable commodity in 1867, the grantor presumably did not consider limestone a mineral.

SOLVE contends that the language "the right to mine and raise the same" evidenced an intent by the grantor to limit the grant to minerals that could be mined and raised by underground mining without destruction of the surface. SOLVE argues that because no such limitation is present in the instant case, there is no basis not to interpret "other minerals" as including *all* minerals, including limestone.

We agree that the *Kinder* court relied on the "right to mine and raise" language as a factor supporting its decision. However, we do not believe such language was critical to the court's decision, nor do we find the absence of such language particularly significant. While SOLVE characterizes the language as a "limitation," it could be seen simply as recognition of the rights of the owner of the mineral estate to enjoy that which he has acquired (see *Jilek v. Chicago, Wilmington & Franklin Coal Co.,* 382 Ill. 241, 47 N.E.2d 96 (1943) (when a mineral estate is severed from a surface estate, the means of obtaining the minerals pass with the grant by implication; no express covenant is necessary)) or as an expansion of those implied rights. On the other hand, one could argue that leaving out such language is evidence of an intent to limit the mineral owner's rights and protect the surface estate to the maximum extent possible. Thus, we find that the presence or absence of such language is not dispositive of the grantor's intent.

SOLVE further argues that because limestone was visible on the surface in *Kinder,* it was obvious that mining the limestone would destroy the surface. This led the supreme court to conclude that the grantor could not have reasonably intended to convey the limestone, thereby destroying the surface which he had reserved. Conversely, in this case the limestone was covered by overburden ranging from 3 to 60 feet. However, the absence or presence of limestone on the surface is relevant only to the extent that aids in discerning the grantor's intent. While the presence of limestone on the surface allowed the *Kinder* court to surmise that Cowey did not intend to convey the limestone, its absence in this case does not support the opposite conclusion. . . .

SOLVE also maintains that the *Kinder* court's conclusion that Cowey and his grantee did not consider limestone a mineral was based on the fact limestone had no commercial value in 1867. However, by 1907 limestone was being used extensively in the manufacture of Portland cement. See *Kinder,* 310 Ill. at 129–30, 141 N.E. at 538. While that may be true, it is of little help in determining Colling's intent. First, it cannot be ascertained if Colling knew of the existence of the limestone. Second, if he knew of it, was aware of its value, and intended to keep it, why did Colling fail to specifically reserve the limestone, as he did the coal?

In summary, while it is true that the instant case is distinguishable from *Kinder,* those differences do not dictate a contrary result. Rather, *Kinder* requires each case to be decided upon the language of the grant or reservation, the surrounding circumstances, and the intention of the grantor, if it can be ascertained. *Kinder,* 310 Ill. at 134, 141 N.E. at 540. In this case there is no evidence of Colling's intent beyond the language of the reservation, "coal and other minerals." That language is ambiguous, and the "surrounding circumstances" are not helpful in resolving that ambiguity.

Illinois Cement asserts that established principles of contract construction support its position. We agree. Under the doctrine of *ejusdem generis,* where general words follow an enumeration of specific things of a particular class, the general words are to be construed as applying only to things of the same general class as those enumerated. *New Hampshire Insurance Co. v. Hanover Insurance Co.,* 296 Ill.App.3d 701, 231 Ill.Dec. 293, 696 N.E.2d 22 (1998). In *Kinder* the court stated that limestone, sand and gravel "were of an entirely different nature from coal and oil." *Kinder,* 310 Ill. at 134, 141 N.E. at 540. Coal is a source of energy that can be mined without disturbing the surface. Limestone is not combustible and cannot be mined without destroying the surface. Moreover, decisions of other jurisdictions that have considered the question have held that a grant or reservation of "minerals" does not include limestone. See, *e.g., Holland v. Dolese Co.,* 540 P.2d 549 (Okla.1975); *Little v. Carter,* 408 S.W.2d 207 (Ky.1966); see also *Downstate Stone Co. v. United States,* 712 F.2d 1215 (7th Cir.1983) (reservation of "all minerals" did not include limestone); 58 C.J.S. *Mines and Minerals* § 175, at 161 (1998) (limestone is not ordinarily included in a grant or reservation of minerals; language of reservation should be clear and specific to justify inclusion of limestone). Indeed, SOLVE has not cited, nor has our research disclosed, a single case from *any* jurisdiction construing the term "minerals" as including limestone.

In addition, "where there is doubt as to the construction of a deed it is to be interpreted most favorably for the grantee." *Patton v. Vining,* 14 Ill.2d 11, 14, 150 N.E.2d 606, 608 (1958); see *A.S. & W. Club v. Drobnick,* 26 Ill.2d 521, 187 N.E.2d 247 (1962) (in case of ambiguity, deed is construed most strongly against its author). In this case SOLVE's interest in the property is derived from the grantor, Colling, and Illinois Cement is successor to the rights of Fabricki, the grantee. Accordingly, any ambiguity should be resolved in favor of Illinois Cement.

We find, therefore, that Illinois Cement is the owner of the limestone on the property.

Notes

1. *Discerning private intent.* How does the court go about interpreting the term "minerals" in this grant? Note that in its reliance on the earlier ruling in *Kinder* the court rejects the idea that "minerals" is a technical term of art in the mining industry, possessing a uniform meaning whenever used. Instead, the term is defined case by case based on what the parties to the original deed intended. What might be wrong with an interpretation that gives the term a uniform meaning in all deeds? Would it not be better and easier to embrace than a definition that requires courts to look into the facts of each transaction? As for the latter approach, which obviously gives greater deference to the parties' intent, what are the problems with it? As you think about this keep in mind that the original parties to deeds do disappear and die, and it is left to newcomers (and title searchers) to interpret deeds. When the parties are long gone, how are we to know what they intended? How is a lawyer or title searcher, knowing nothing about a transaction except what can be gleaned from a deed, to know what the term minerals might mean in a particular deed?

As for the parties' intent in this case, what evidence does the court consider in its effort to interpret the deed? Ultimately, the court decides that the term "minerals" is ambiguous, and that the circumstances surrounding the grant are unhelpful in illuminating the term's meaning. (Is this perhaps a common outcome?) In the earlier *Kinder* decision, the Illinois Supreme Court paid attention to the desire of the surface landowner to continue farming; limestone mining, plainly, would have disrupted that farming. Here, the court reaches the same conclusion—that the owner of the minerals did not own the limestone. This meant that the surface owner could continue using the surface as it wanted. It was mere happenstance that the surface owner wanted to undertake limestone mining. Is there perhaps a policy slant embedded in these cases, some bias in favor of mining?

Note the court's reliance on the interpretive principle *ejusdem generis*. Might the case have come out differently if the original deed had not mentioned coal specifically but had instead simply reserved "all minerals"? As for the tendency to interpret deeds to favor the grantee (another interpretive principle), would the case have come out differently if the parties had been reversed; if the grantor had sold the mineral rights and retained the land surface? In any event, is it not anomalous here that a landowner who possesses no mineral rights is nonetheless engaged in mining the land?

2. *Private intent versus public policy.* In this case the conservation group SOLVE, which sought to claim the limestone, likely had no interest in mining the stone but instead wanted to halt the mining so as to protect a local river. To decide that SOLVE owned the limestone would likely have brought the mining to a halt. The facts thus raise a question of policy: Should courts interpret mineral deeds in such a way as to make mining feasible, when an alternative interpretation might frustrate the mining? Should courts, for instance, look to the surrounding community and attempt to discern what land use would be best for it? We have seen in earlier cases numerous instances of judicial rulings that reflect a distinct policy slant in favor of efficient resource exploitation. Would it be right for a court to embrace such a slant when it goes about deciding what private parties meant when they wrote a particular deed or contract?

JILEK v. CHICAGO, WILMINGTON & FRANKLIN COAL CO.

382 Ill. 241, 47 N.E.2d 96 (1943).

GUNN, JUSTICE.

The circuit court of Franklin county dismissed for want of equity the complaint of John Jilek *et al.*, to quiet title to certain real estate, and for other relief. The issue involved is the ownership of the oil and gas purporting to be conveyed by a certain mineral deed delivered to one J. T. Chenault, and by mesne conveyance to appellees. . . .

It is stipulated that on July 12, 1905, R. Q. Simpson was the owner in fee simple of the land involved. On that date, by warranty deed, he and his wife conveyed to J. T. Chenault

> "all the coal, oil, gas and other minerals in or underlying the following described Real Estate, to-wit: [property description omitted] absolutely and specifically granting the rights to mine and remove all the coal and other minerals underlying said land without any liability for surface subsidence caused by mining out of the coal or other minerals and from not leaving pillars or artificial supports under said land and the further right to make under ground passages or entries through, to and from other mines and lands adjacent thereto, and with the right to the perpetual use of the same for mining purposes. It is also covenanted and agreed that the

grantee herein, his heirs and assigns shall have the right to take and use as much of the surface of the said land as may be deemed necessary for the purposes of erecting, maintaining and operating hoisting, air, pumping, and escape shafts, ditches and reservoirs and the necessary roadways and railroad tracks to and from the same, with the right of way for any railroad necessary or required to carry said coal to market; but all land, the surface of which is so taken, shall, when occupied, be paid for at the rate of Fifty Dollars per acre. If the surface of any land that is occupied by buildings or other permanent improvements is taken, the full cash value of all such permanent improvements shall be paid."

[Later, Simpson sold his rights in the land surface, which passed through several hands before ending up with the plaintiffs, the Jileks.]

Plaintiffs-appellants first contend the deed to Chenault of the mineral rights conveyed no title to oil and gas, or any right to use the surface to explore for or produce oil or gas, and that said oil and gas underlying said premises, because of its being incapable of being so conveyed, passed by Simpson's deed of the surface to appellants. This claim raises squarely the issue of whether the owner of land in fee simple may convey and grant to another the right to take or own oil and gas in the ground in and by a mineral deed without at the same time conveying the superimposed surface of the land.

It has long been recognized in this State that mineral rights may be severed from the surface rights and conveyed separately, and that two estates are thus created in the land, each of which is distinct, and each of which may be conveyed or devised, and each is subject to taxation.... The severance of the underlying mineral estate from the surface estate in the land is effected by the deed which conveys one alone without conveying the other. Kinder v. La Salle County Carbon Coal Co., 301 Ill. 362, 133 N.E. 772; Uphoff v. Trustees of Tufts College, 351 Ill. 146, 184 N.E. 213, 93 A.L.R. 1224. Both the mineral estate and the surface estate in the land, when thus severed, are real estate. Catlin Coal Co. v. Lloyd, *supra*; Renfro v. Hanon, *supra*; Transcontinental Oil Co. v. Emmerson, supra. When the mineral estate is severed from the surface estate the means of obtaining or enjoying it are also granted, and pass with the grant of the minerals, without an express covenant for such purpose....

The principles set forth are firmly fixed with respect to surface and mineral estates in the land, so far as solid minerals are concerned, but it is said a different rule applies to fluid or nonsolid minerals, such as oil and gas, and that because of their supposed fugacious and wandering character a rule should be applied which permits the owner of the land in fee to convey, by deed, rights involving solid minerals, but denies him the power of conveying oil and gas rights, or the right to take them, and as a necessary corollary such rights remain affixed to the surface estate, and will pass by conveyance as a part thereof.

Oil and gas, by the overwhelming weight of authority, are minerals, ... and belong to the owner of the land so long as they remain in the land.... Oil and gas are parts of the land, and though in their natural state, *i.e.*, "in place," they are considered of an impermanent or fugitive character, still they are things which by surface operations may be reduced to possession, and therefore their presence in the land, with their capability of being possessed, is a valuable property right growing out of ownership of land.

Oil and gas leases granting the right to search for and take oil and gas are freehold estates in the land. Triger v. Carter Oil Co. supra; Carter Oil Co. v. Liggett, 371 Ill. 482, 21 N.E.2d 569; Greer v. Carter Oil Co., 373 Ill. 168, 25 N.E.2d 805. Appellants rely almost wholly upon Watford Oil & Gas Co. v. Shipman, *supra*, wherein we said:

> A lease of land to enter and prospect for oil or gas is a grant of a privilege to enter and prospect, but does not give a title to the oil or gas until such products are found. In the eye of the law oil and natural gas are treated as minerals, but they possess certain peculiar attributes not common to other minerals which have a fixed and permanent situs. Owing to their liability to escape, these minerals are not capable of distinct ownership in place. Oil and gas, while in the earth, unlike solid minerals, cannot be the subject of a distinct ownership from the soil....

It is to be observed this language was used in connection with an oil and gas lease by which the owner of land granted the lessee the whole of the premises for the purpose of drilling and operating for oil and gas. It did not involve a severance of the surface and mineral estate in the land.... There is nothing in the statement contained in the *Watford* case that bars the owner of the fee from conveying to another the part of the real estate, viz., the mineral estate, in which oil and gas are most likely to be found.

In the *Watford* case it is to be noticed the court said that executing an oil and gas lease, that is, a right to extract oil, was not a conveyance of the interest of one cotenant in the given property; it was a mere right to explore and prospect. It matters not that a mineral deed actually severs from the surface the strata of sand, rock or gravel in which oil is found, or whether it conveys the incorporeal right to search and reduce to possession a portion of the underlying mineral. In either event, as pointed out above, real estate is conveyed. The *Watford* case, and others using substantially the same language, involved oil and gas leases in which there was no severance of title by which the mineral estate was in one person and the surface estate in another, but in each instance the lessor owned the entire land in fee simple. The question of what passed by a conveyance of the mineral estate was not involved....

Considering oil and gas and the right to prospect for and produce them as parts of the mineral estate, they can be no part of the surface estate, and hence the right to prospect and recapture must come from a grant of the owner of the whole fee-simple estate or from the owner of the mineral estate. A mineral deed executed by the owner of the fee carries not only title to solid minerals, but also to what is necessary to acquire title to or possession of fluid or fugacious minerals, that is, the right to enter, explore and reduce the same to possession.... We know of no authority that holds a freehold estate in land is not subject to transfer.

The true relationship of oil and gas in the earth and the owner of the estate containing it is aptly set forth in Gray–Mellon Oil Co. v. Fairchild, 219 Ky. 143, 292 S.W. 743, 745:

> Oil and gas in the earth stand much as water percolating under the earth. The owner in fee owns to the center of the earth. But he does not own a specific cubic foot of water, oil, or gas under the earth until he reduces it to possession. The reason is, these substances are fugitive, and the water, oil, or gas which is under his land today may be elsewhere tomorrow. He is only entitled to hold as his own the water, oil, or gas which he finds under his land and reduces to possession. But the right to explore for these substances and to reduce them to possession, if found, is a valuable part of his property. It is an interest in the land springing out of his ownership of everything above and below the surface....

No authority from any jurisdiction is cited by appellants (except one overruled case) as sustaining the proposition that the grantee of the entire mineral estate in the land does not acquire the same rights to oil and gas, or the right to explore for, and take oil and gas, as has the owner of the entire fee....

We entertain no doubt of the right of a land owner to convey minerals by deed, and we hold that the mineral deed of July 12, 1905, vested in J. T. Chenault and his grantees the right to such oil and gas under the real estate in question as they might reduce to possession as a part of the mineral estate so conveyed;....

There appears to be little doubt when the mineral estate is severed from the surface estate that with the mineral estate all means to attain it are also granted for the purpose of enjoying it. This is because it is presumed the grantor intended to convey, and the grantee expected to receive, the full benefit of the mineral estate, and therefore the grantor not only conveyed the thing specifically described, but all other rights and privileges necessary to the enjoyment of the thing granted. Threlkeld v. Inglett, *supra*; Ewing v. Sandoval Coal & Mining Co., *supra*; Rhomberg v. Texas Co., 379 Ill. 430, 40 N.E.2d 526; Chicago, Wilmington & Franklin Coal Co. v. Minier, 7 Cir., 127 F.2d 1006.

It is said, however, by appellants, that the rule that the expression of a particular subject implies the exclusion of subjects not enumerated is applicable here, because the specific reservation in the conveyance granting the mineral interest of (a) the right of subsidence without damage; (b) the use of passage ways and entries to move coal from other land; and (c) the right to take surface land for other mining purposes at a certain price, excludes any right to enter the mineral estate from the surface, which might otherwise be implied. If the rights reserved in the mineral deed were, in fact, opposed to the implied right to enter upon the land for the purpose of drilling and exploring for oil, there would be force to this suggestion. However, the rights just enumerated in the mineral deed are not ones which are implied by a grant of the mineral estate. The law requires the owner of the mineral estate to extract minerals without damaging the surface, and, unless there is a specific exemption of liability, the owner of the surface can recover for damages caused by sinking or subsidence caused by mining. Wilms v. Jess, 94 Ill. 464, 34 Am.Rep. 242; Lloyd v. Catlin Coal Co., 210 Ill. 460, 71 N.E. 335.

It requires no citation of authority to sustain the proposition that the surface of the land could not be covered with railway tracks, reservoirs, structures and manufacturing equipment upon the bare license to enter the mineral estate for the purpose of removing the mineral therefrom. These rights necessarily must be covered by an express contract or covenant or they will not exist, and are therefore rights in addition to the implied right to enter, and an extension thereof and not in opposition thereto. . . .

It has been held that the implied right to occupy so much of the surface as may be needed to open and work the mineral estate is not limited by the special grant or reservation of privileges, which would not be implied. Williams v. Gibson, 84 Ala. 228, 4 So. 350 . . .

It is finally contended that the rights of the appellees were lost by adverse possession or by abandonment. As pointed out above, there was a complete severance of the mineral estate from the surface estate, and in such event the law is well settled there can be no adverse possession of the mineral estate by the owner of the surface estate, even though the latter hold an instrument which purports to constitute color of title to the whole estate in the land. Possession of the surface does not carry possession of the minerals. Uphoff v. Trustees of Tufts College, *supra*; Renfro v. Hanon, *supra*; Kinder v. LaSalle County Carbon Coal Co., *supra*. Nor does nonuser or abandonment of the mineral interest terminate the estate. Uphoff v. Trustees of Tufts College, supra; Scott v. Laws, 185 Ky. 440, 215 S.W. 81, 13 A.L.R. 369; Gill v. Fletcher, 74 Ohio St. 295, 78 N.E. 433, 113 Am.St.Rep. 962.

From a careful perusal of the record and the briefs of counsel we find no error in the proceedings of the circuit court, and its decree is accordingly affirmed.

Notes

1. *Private intent v. public policy II.* Note that the original deed in *Jilek* expressly mentioned oil and gas as part of the mineral estate being conveyed. That being so, why did this litigation even arise? The critical issue, presumably, had to do not with private intent but with public policy, and whether the law should or should not allow landowners to transfer their oil and gas rights to someone else. Although the court does not make use of the analogy, we might recall the elements of water law on this point, especially groundwater law. Many states (as we've seen) prohibit landowners from severing

their water rights from the land and selling them separately; they can allow outsiders to come on to their lands and make use of the water, but cannot transfer the water permanently. If that policy makes sense with respect to groundwater, why not also with oil and gas, given the physical similarities between them? Are there reasons why a court might say that a transfer by deed of oil and gas rights is acceptable, but a complete severance and sale of water rights is not? (On this question, does it seem important that the oil and gas is likely a single fixed quantity, while groundwater might be a continuing flow? That people on the land surface might need the groundwater in order to live but not the oil and gas?)

2. *Ancillary rights VI: what comes with the minerals? Jilek* usefully raises an issue that we have seen before in other settings and will see again: When a grantee receives a resource-use right, what ancillary rights come along with it? What rights does the grantee receive to gain access to the resource and to exploit it fully, particularly when the exploitation efforts will likely conflict with the activities or plans of the surface owner?

You should take note of the court's many useful comments on this subject, as well as the extensive language in the original deed that addresses the issue. The original parties obviously thought intently about the issue, and specified a number of surface-use rights (and subsurface rights) that the mining company wanted to obtain. In approaching the subject, it is useful to isolate three issues that courts routinely face: (i) what does the deed say, and how should it be interpreted (the primary issue in *Jilek*); (ii) what back-up rule should the law provide, when the parties themselves have not expressly addressed a particular issue (an issue on which the court comments); and (iii) are there public policy issues present that might limit what the original parties can do when they specify rights or that might influence how a court interprets a deed? These are critical questions, and you should keep them in mind as you read the following materials.

3. *The law's back-up rules.* Note what the court says about the law's back-up rule on surface-use rights, which applies when a deed is silent as to a particular question (the second of the three issues in the above note). When the mineral estate is transferred, the court tells us, "the means of obtaining or enjoying it are also granted, and pass with the grant of the minerals, without an express covenant for such purpose." A mineral deed "carries not only title to solid minerals, but also to what is necessary to acquire title to or possession of fluid or fugacious minerals, that is, the right to enter, explore and reduce the same to possession." Why might courts be so quick to imply such ancillary rights in the case of mineral deeds? Can't those who buy mineral estates look out for themselves when they negotiate contracts? Cannot they identify in advance, and set forth in the deed, those ancillary rights that they will need in order to mine? Before answering these questions (which we'll return to in the next section), consider the following two non-mining cases.

Before leaving *Jilek*, you should record also the three particular ancillary use rights that, under Illinois law, do *not* come with the minerals and that a grantee thus must bargain for separately: the "right of subsidence without damage," the right to use passage ways and entries to move coal from other land, and the right to take surface land for other mining purposes at a price. The original grantee viewed these rights as important, and included them in the original grant.

4. *Adverse possession of minerals.* Also worth noting in *Jilek* are the court's final comments denying the surface owner's claim to have extinguished the oil and gas rights by adverse possession. On the facts the court's conclusion is correct, though its summary of the law is perhaps misleading.

A person who gains title to land through adverse possession gains any mineral rights attached to the land, without any need to engage in mining. The adverse possessor, that is, gets the whole fee interest if that's what the surface owner possesses. When the mineral rights are held separately, however, a person who acquires the surface through adverse possession does not thereby acquire the minerals. The reason: the use of the surface is not adverse or hostile to the mineral estate owner. To gain title to severed mineral rights an adverse possessor must either refuse to allow the mineral estate owner to gain access to the minerals or engage in mining himself. Only then has the surface possessor acted adversely to the mineral estate owner in the sense of interfering with her legal rights.

5. *A timber comparison.* Over the years courts have developed rather complex bodies of common law rules governing particular resources on land. Predictably, common law rules often take into account local conditions, local resource-harvesting methods, and the economic value of various parts of nature. For an illustration we can turn to the laws governing trees and tree harvesting in England. By the late nineteenth century a complex array of rules governed the subject. One foundational distinction, used to interpret deeds, leases, and contracts alike, was between timber trees and other trees:

> Trees are distinguishable in law as timber trees and trees which do not bear timber, that is, wood fit for building. By general custom oak, ash, and elm are timber trees, provided they are of sufficient age, and provided they are not too old to bear a reasonable quantity of useful wood; beech, willow, birch, aspen, maple, and other trees of life kind are not generally timber. By special local custom, beech, willow, and other trees may also be considered timber trees; and they will then pass under that description. Fir and larch which are usually planted for profit by thinning until the whole plantation is cut; or for the protection of plantations of timber trees, are not generally timber trees. By a general rule of law trees which are of the description to bear timber become timber trees at twenty years' growth, whether they are timber trees by general or by local custom; no customary variation of this rule being admissible.

S.M. Leake, A Digest of the Law of Uses and Profits of Land 32–33 (1888). English law anticipated that a landowner could create various types of specific resource rights in the trees growing on his land, whether by grant, by lease or by reservation, and for periods of time based upon someone's life (or a tree's life!), for a definite term of years, or in perpetuity. The separate interest thus created could entail ownership of trees in place (or even a single tree), they could entail additional rights to the soil itself, or they could involve merely the right to enter the land and harvest the trees:

> A grant, or an exception from a grant, of the trees growing in certain land, creates a property in the trees, separate from the property in the

> soil; but with the right of having them grow and subsist upon it. An estate of inheritance in a tree may thus be created; which would be technically described as a fee conditional upon the life of the tree. Also there may be a grant or exception of trees thereafter to grow on the soil.... A grant or exception of trees apart from the soil implies a right to enter upon the land for the purpose of cutting and taking the trees, as a necessary incident of the property in the trees. A license to enter upon land and to cut down trees and take them away may be granted by the owner of the land without conveying to the grantee any property in the soil, or in the trees until cut down and taken by him. Such right would be in the nature of a *profit à prendre* or profit to be taken from the land of another.

Id. 30. A landowner at common law could sell or lease land while excepting some or all of the trees from the transaction, with the result that the purchaser or tenant gained no rights to the trees or their fruit and could not molest them. In the case of a lease for life or for years that did not specifically mention trees, the tenant had no right to cut timber trees even though they were "ripe for cutting or going to decay." Timber harvesting by a tenant was allowed only in the case of " 'timber estates' or land cultivated specially for the growth of timber, in which the timber is considered as an ordinary profit, like annual or other periodical crops; and tenant for life is entitled to cut and take the timber coming to maturity from time to time during his tenancy, subject to the obligation of maintaining the plantations." On the other hand, a tenant for life could "cut and take trees not being timber trees; but subject to impeachment of waste if the cutting is injurious to the inheritance. Cutting of any trees of any kind that are beneficial to the property, for protection, ornament or other permanent purpose is waste." *Id.*, 33–34.

WECHSLER v. PEOPLE

147 A.D.2d 755, 537 N.Y.S.2d 900 (3d Dept. 1989).

CASEY, JUSTICE PRESIDING.

Cross appeals from a judgment of the Supreme Court (Williams, J.), entered March 7, 1988 in Sullivan County, which dismissed plaintiff's complaint and defendant's counterclaims and declared the rights of the parties in certain real property.

Plaintiff commenced this action to enforce and to restrain interference with his hunting and fishing easement over certain lands owned by the State. The easement was created in 1923 when William A. Bradford conveyed a portion of his lands on both sides of the Neversink River in Sullivan County to Alfred J. Crane. The specific language creating the easement recites:

> Reserving, however, to the said William A. Bradford, his heirs, licensees and assigns * * * the exclusive right of fishing and taking away the fish caught, and of shooting and trapping and taking away the game caught, the grantee by the acceptance hereof agreeing that it, its successors and assigns, shall never fish, hunt or trap game on the premises hereby conveyed * * *.

> Reserving, further to said William A. Bradford, his heirs, licensees and assigns, forever, the right to enter upon and make such use of the premises hereby conveyed as may be necessary for the proper enjoyment of the fishing and hunting privileges hereby reserved.

Bradford's deed to Crane also included a covenant restricting the use of the land on the west bank of the river to the erection of a hydroelectric plant and facilities. Crane subsequently conveyed his holdings to Rockland Light and Power Company, predecessor of Orange and Rockland Utilities. Through various mesne conveyances and transactions, plaintiff became the owner of the exclusive hunting and fishing rights originally reserved by Bradford. In the late 1970s, the restrictive covenant on the lands on the west bank of the river was extinguished by court action; plaintiff appeared in opposition to the extinguishment of the restriction upon the ground that it would impair the value of his hunting and fishing easement (*Orange & Rockland Utils. v. Philwold Estates,* 70 A.D.2d 338, 421 N.Y.S.2d 640, *mod.* 52 N.Y.2d 253, 437 N.Y.S.2d 291, 418 N.E.2d 1310). In 1981, the land on the east bank of the river was conveyed to defendant, subject to plaintiff's hunting and fishing easement.

Plaintiff's complaint in this action alleges that two senior employees of the Department of Environmental Conservation (hereinafter DEC) had violated the covenant by fishing and taking away fish upon lands in which plaintiff has those exclusive rights. Defendant has denied the allegations, filed counterclaims and requested a declaration of the rights of the parties. In March 1988, Supreme Court, after hearing testimony, dismissed the complaint and the counterclaims. Supreme Court declared, however, that plaintiff possessed exclusive rights to hunt, fish and trap upon the subject property owned by defendant and that defendant, its successors and assigns "shall never fish, hunt or trap game" on that property. Additionally, Supreme Court found that the maintenance, construction and use of certain permanent structures and the posting of signs on the subject property by plaintiff are "reasonably appurtenant to the exercise of the plaintiff's reserved rights". Supreme Court also exempted plaintiff and his invitees, tenants and licensees while on the subject premises from compliance with DEC's rules and regulations applicable to unique areas. Supreme Court further declared that "defendant, its agents, employees, licensees, and specifically members of the general public may not enter upon the subject property, may not undertake any activities upon the subject property of any kind or nature whatsoever" except that defendant may enter to fight fires, enforce laws or render emergency assistance. The parties have cross-appealed.

Initially, we note that Supreme Court properly denied injunctive relief to plaintiff. Plaintiff's claim was based on a contention that two employees of DEC, on one occasion, fished at the invitation of the owner of the land in violation of plaintiff's easement. Although their fishing is admitted, it is at least doubtful that the fishing was on land subject to plaintiff's easement. The land was not posted and the fishing was done at the express invitation of the owner of the land on only one occasion.

Thus, there is an insufficient basis for the grant of injunctive relief (*see, Buegler v. Walsh,* 111 A.D.2d 206, 489 N.Y.S.2d 241, *appeal dismissed* 65 N.Y.2d 609, 494 N.Y.S.2d 1028, 484 N.E.2d 671).

In regard to the extent of plaintiff's easement, we believe that Supreme Court erred in improperly expanding it beyond its intended scope. Plaintiff has authorized persons to construct permanent structures on the land subject to his easement. This authorization interferes with defendant's right of ownership. Our previous decision characterized plaintiff's easement as "incorporeal or nonpossessory in nature" (*Orange & Rockland Utils. v. Philwold Estates, supra,* 70 A.D.2d at 342, 421 N.Y.S.2d 640). The nonpossessory characterization of plaintiff's interest accords with the legal nature of the easement (*see, Matter of Sierra Club v. Palisades Interstate Park Commn.,* 99 A.D.2d 548, 549, 471 N.Y.S.2d 633, *lv. denied* 63 N.Y.2d 604, 480 N.Y.S.2d 1026, 469 N.E.2d 531) and does not give the holder of the easement a right to maintain or construct permanent structures (*Spring v. Conklin,* 173 App.Div. 719, 720–721, 159 N.Y.S. 1027). However, Supreme Court's decision permitting plaintiff to erect signs to protect his exclusive rights was proper as reasonably appurtenant to the protection and enjoyment of the easement, despite the violation of the regulation regarding unique areas that resulted from the posting of the signs (*see,* 6 NYCRR 190.8[i]).

Finally in our view, Supreme Court improperly limited defendant's access to the subject property. Real Property Law § 240(3) provides, *inter alia,* that an instrument creating an interest in real property "must be construed according to the intent of the parties, so far as such intent can be gathered from the whole instrument, and is consistent with the rules of law". The deed here is silent as to defendant's rights with respect to activities other than that defendant shall "never fish, hunt or trap game" on the subject property. As the holder of an affirmative easement to hunt and fish, plaintiff has no right to prohibit general use or enjoyment of the property by defendant, the landowner (*see, Rahabi v. Morrison,* 81 A.D.2d 434, 440, 440 N.Y.S.2d 941). Burdened by an easement which is not from the wording of its grant an exclusive one, defendant has the right to use its land in any manner that does not unreasonably interfere with the rights of the owner of the easement (*see, Hurd v. Lis,* 92 A.D.2d 653, 654, 460 N.Y.S.2d 173, *appeal dismissed* 70 N.Y.2d 872, 523 N.Y.S.2d 497, 518 N.E.2d 8). Supreme Court's barring of defendant from all activities regarding its land constitutes an impermissible prohibition of the fee owner's right to use and enjoy its property. Granting plaintiff the broad right to bar defendant from virtually all uses of its land was, therefore, error.

Judgment modified, on the law, without costs, by reversing so much thereof as (1) permitted plaintiff to maintain and construct permanent structures, (2) restricted defendant's access to its land, and (3) exempted plaintiff from those provisions of 6 NYCRR part 190 which do not deal with the posting or erecting of signs pursuant to 6 NYCRR 190.8(i), and, as so modified, affirmed.

Notes

1. *Easement scope and private intent versus public policy III.* How does *Wechsler* compare with the above two mining cases, in terms of the rights acquired by the grantee? Both hunters and mineral-estate purchasers acquire rights to enter the land of another and remove a valuable natural resource (a type of easement often termed a profit or profit à prendre). Should the law treat such purchasers similarly, in terms of the ways deeds are interpreted and the back-up rules that the law provides? Here, the court rules that the holder of the hunting easement can erect signs but not erect any structures. As the court considers the issue, it rather surprisingly makes no mention of the particular deed language that would seem most pertinent—the deed provision reserving "the right to enter upon and make such use of the premises hereby conveyed as may be necessary for the proper enjoyment of the fishing and hunting privileges hereby reserved." Does not this clause clearly envision the reservation of additional rights—beyond the express fishing and hunting provisions? Should the court at least have viewed this as a debatable factual issue, whether the structures erected here were "necessary for the proper enjoyment" of the hunting rights? Is the court tipping us off to how seriously it views hunting rights relative to other land uses?

2. *The landowner's use rights.* As the court explains, the holder of an easement cannot exceed its scope, and the landowner-grantor of an easement retains the right to make all other uses of the land affected by the easement (the "servient estate," as it is termed). But what happens when an easement holder, acting within the scope of his easement, is nonetheless disrupted in some way by the activities of the servient estate owner? Who gets priority when the two activities—by the servient estate owner and the easement owner—conflict? Note how the court in *Wechsler* phrases the governing legal rule: The servient estate owner can use the land "in any manner that does not unreasonably interfere with the rights of the owner of the easement." Does this language suggest that some level of interference is permissible? And who decides when an interference is unreasonable? Consider the following case:

MIKESH v. PETERS

284 N.W.2d 215 (Iowa 1979).

REYNOLDSON, CHIEF JUSTICE

This controversy centers around plaintiff Leonard Mikesh's "recreational rights" which he reserved in a deed. Plaintiff sued a successor owner of the land, defendant Corliss Peters, for damages, alleging these rights were lost when defendant "clear-cut" the timber from the land conveyed. Following entry of judgment on a $5500 jury verdict, defendant appeals. . . .

In 1963 plaintiff acquired 27 1/2 acres of timbered real estate located in a bend of the Upper Iowa River in Winneshiek County. The following year he conveyed this real estate to his two sons, reserving a life estate. August 14, 1974, plaintiff and his sons quitclaimed the property to Eugene Carolan, a logger. This deed contained the following reservation:

deed

(S)ubject to exclusive recreational rights in the grantor, Leonard Mikesh; said recreational rights are not limited to but do include rights in Leonard Mikesh to hunt, fish, canoe, camp and trap on the premises or directly adjacent thereto. Said recreational rights to be for a period of twelve years from the date of this deed.

The land was described in the conveyance as "timberland." However, plaintiff testified the transaction envisioned that "we sell him (Carolan) the land, and he got to cut the logable trees, and I would retain the recreational rights in it." The evidence disclosed the boundary lines were obscure and plaintiff wanted to avoid "watching" the logging operation to keep it on his own property.

Carolan testified, "He (plaintiff) knew the land was going to be cleared." Carolan logged the 27 1/2 acres as well as approximately 50 additional surrounding acres, removing all trees with diameters greater than 10 to 12 inches at the top end, save some hollow trees. Carolan testified that, "As you drop the big trees, you smash the little trees (or) scar them all up or they die." Plaintiff admitted he left it up to Carolan to determine which trees were to be cut.

In September 1975 Carolan deeded the property to defendant in consideration for defendant's timber on surrounding land which the latter owned. The deed from Carolan to defendant stated the conveyance was "subject to the exclusive recreational rights as set out in a certain Quit Claim Deed recorded in Book 298 of Deeds, on Page 118 of the Winneshiek County Records."

Plaintiff produced evidence that beginning in 1975 defendant bulldozed trees and brush into piles around the 27 1/2 acres, and into a small pond where plaintiff had previously turtled. Apparently plaintiff unsuccessfully sought to stop the bulldozing on one occasion. Defendant testified he bulldozed only brush, stumps and treetops, and that the trees were already gone. When he acquired the property after it was logged "(t)here was no way you could walk through that timber because they cut every log that was over a foot in diameter. . . . "

Defendant owned the surrounding land. He also bulldozed it after it was logged and planted the whole tract to corn. Photograph exhibits show trees were left standing along the river. There was no evidence defendant had ever denied plaintiff access to the 27 1/2 acres for recreational purposes and his testimony he had offered plaintiff hunting rights on his other land stood undenied. Neither did plaintiff seriously dispute that there was game on the premises, including deer, after it was put into corn. . . .

still access could still hunt still deer

A basic rule relating to such grants is that they must be strictly construed and cannot be extended beyond the terms of the instrument itself. Bland Lake, 311 S.W.2d at 715. Thompson, *supra*, § 140 at 527 (citing cases). Also applicable here is our long-standing concept that "exceptions and reservations in conveyances are to be construed most strongly against the grantor." Wiley v. Sirdorus, 41 Iowa 224, 226 (1875); See generally 23 Am.Jur.2d Deeds § 273 (1965).

strictly construed against grtor

Seeking helpful authority to guide us, we find no recent applicable cases, nor have the parties. We assume this is because in modern practice the grant and the respective duties and rights ordinarily are detailed enough to avoid litigation. But there are several older decisions which reach the issue before us and resolve it against grantees who do not bargain for and obtain restrictions against changes in the servient property.

The decision most on point is Isherwood v. Salene, 61 Or. 572, 123 P. 49 (1912). In *Isherwood* the owners of "the sole and exclusive right, privilege and easement, to shoot, take and kill any and all wild duck and other wild fowl upon and in any and all lakes, sloughs and waters situate, lying or being upon (designated) land" sued the landowner to enjoin her from draining certain lakes and sloughs upon her farmland and also from cutting and burning brush and timber bordering the lakes. The Oregon Supreme Court held that plaintiffs "must exercise the right in the condition it may be at the time," Id. at 575, 123 P. at 50, adding that, "If she (defendant owner of servient estate) is systematically clearing her land, evidencing a bona fide intention to improve it, no complaint can be made against her." Id. at 579, 123 P. at 51. As for draining the lakes, the court said, "If they can be, then surely, in the interest of good farming, she should be permitted to do it, and it is not for the court to say whether she can or cannot." Id. at 579–80, 123 P. at 52. The court observed it was not justified in implying more than was expressed in the deed. Id. at 579, 123 P. at 51. However, the court indicated that "(f)or cutting and burning brush in bad faith, in a manner to injure the hunting, defendant would be liable to plaintiffs in damages. . . . " *Id.* at 580, 123 P. at 52.

Because there was little relevant American authority, the Isherwood court relied heavily upon English cases. We find these cases are analogous.

In Jeffryes v. Evans, 19 C.B. (N.S.) 246, 144 Eng. Rep. 781 (C.P. 1865), plaintiff held, through a lease from defendant, the "exclusive shooting, fishing and sporting" privileges over some land, those privileges having been reserved when defendant leased the land to one Rees. The lessee, Rees, "cut all the underwood and grubbed up the furze-covers (spiny shrubs), thus driving away the game, so as almost entirely to destroy the shooting. . . . " *Id.* at 252, 144 Eng.Rep. at 784. Plaintiff sued his lessor for damages. The court found the issue to be whether the reserved and assigned right implied a covenant not to cut down the brush and underwood, so as to deprive the game of natural cover, even though the cutting was done in the ordinary and reasonable cultivation and use of the land. In deciding the case, Erle, C. J., noted, "There has been no eviction. The plaintiff has just as much right to shoot and sport over the . . . land . . . as he had before: and that is all the plaintiff covenanted that he should have." *Id.* at 265, 144 Eng.Rep. at 789. In the same case, Montague Smith, J., stated,

> (T)he cutting of the furze and underwood, which may have been done in the ordinary course of good management of the farm, was not an interruption of the enjoyment of the incorporeal hereditament granted to the plaintiff. He had the same right to sport over the land as before. If he wished to have the condition of the land as to furze and underwood preserved, he should have expressly stipulated that the present mode of cultivation of the land should not be altered.

Id. at 268, 144 Eng.Rep. at 790.

A similar holding is found in Boyle v. Holcroft, (1905) I.R. 245, 249–50 (Ch.Div.), where the court ruled,

> The right of fishing must be exercised in view of the occupying tenant's (landowner's) right to use all proper and reasonable means which may be necessary from time to time for the management and cultivation of his farm. . . . (A)s a general rule, so long as the tenant is Bona fide and reasonably managing and using the lands, the owner of the fishing rights must be content to exercise his right upon the lands in the condition in which they may happen to be from time to time.

In Fetherstonhaugh v. Hagarty, 3 L.R.Ir. 150 (Ch. 1878), an exclusive Profit a prendre (hunting privilege) was reserved to a landowner under a lease. The court held the tenant was not answerable for acts done in the ordinary cultivation of his farm, despite the fact that the game was destroyed as a result.

Plaintiff does not cite any decision involving analogous facts to support his position.

We hold as a matter of law that "recreational rights," when as here so nearly equated with hunting rights, do not limit the landowner in his or her use of the affected land absent an express covenant to the contrary or a malicious bad faith destruction of the clearly designated object (*i.e.* game or its habitat) of the right. . . .

Although we regret in this instance the destruction of a portion of Iowa's limited timberland, we believe the rule we adopt here is preferred in the context of long-term public policy. We judicially note the permissive "open range" concept of hunting and recreational activities on private land is passing from our scene. The future likely will bring hunting and recreational grants obtained by counsel-protected organizations from individual landowners who, under the rule advanced by plaintiff, might not visualize the range of implied restrictions on what would otherwise be appropriate activities on, and uses of, the land. Such recreational activities may be only a potential incidental use of the property. To say such limited purposes should dictate by implication the remaining uses, permitting the tail to wag the dog, would generate unnecessary uncertainties and needless litigation.

The party reserving or obtaining a grant of such rights may reserve or contract for the preservation of present conditions as well. Here plaintiff neglected to do this. In fact, at the time he made the reservation and sold the land he knew it would be subjected to extensive logging. There was no evidence defendant denied him access or denied him the right to carry on any of the activities delineated in the reservation. . . .

The issue here was one of law for the trial court, absent any showing defendant acted maliciously and in bad faith in clearing the remaining trees and debris and planting his land to corn. There was no evidence of this. Defendant testified he acquired the land with the intent to plant it to corn. He also testified he told plaintiff he could hunt, fish, or do anything else on the land, and on other land defendant owned. Plaintiff does not dispute this testimony. We find no evidence to justify submitting a bad-faith issue to the jury.

Notes

1. *Strictly construed?* According to the court, what is the law's back-up rule governing conflicts between the easement holder and the owner of the servient estate? The basic rule "relating to such grants," the court relates, is that a grant or reservation of an easement "must be strictly construed and cannot be extended beyond the terms of the instrument itself." The law also provides, we're told, that such easements "do not limit the landowner in his or her use of the affected land absent an express covenant to the contrary or a malicious bad faith destruction of the clearly designated object (*i.e.* game or its habitat) of the right." This approach, plainly, is slanted against the hunter and in favor of the servient estate owner. In that regard, it differs greatly from the approach followed in the two mining cases above. Recall the corresponding language from *Jilek*, where the court presumed as a matter of law that "the grantor intended to convey, and the grantee expected to receive, the full benefit of the mineral estate, and therefore the grantor not only conveyed the thing specifically described, but all other rights and privileges necessary to the enjoyment of the thing granted." What accounts for this vast difference in judicial attitudes toward these two resource-use arrangements? Is it that the court deems mining important and hunting unimportant? Or does the favoritism instead have to do with farming over hunting?

The court in *Mikesh* observes that the easement holder anticipated that logging would take place. But isn't there a vast difference between logging mature trees and what the servient estate owner did here: stripping away everything, filling in the pond, and planting the land in corn? Is it a relevant fact that deer and many other game species strongly favor cut-over lands with downed trees and brush, more so than dense stands of timber?

The Supreme Court of Wyoming showed more sympathy for hunters in a recent dispute involving the ability of holders of a hunting easement to use motorized access on the servient estate and to use their easement to cross the servient estate to get access to adjacent public lands. The court asserted the hunting activities under an easement should ordinarily be limited to "the usual and reasonable methods" of hunting "generally used in the vicinity at the time of the execution of the deed." On the other hand, there was the normal rule of interpretation that an easement "carries with it the right of doing whatever is reasonably necessary for the full enjoyment of the easement itself." The court concluded that the easement allowed for motorized activities even though motorized hunting and fishing activities were just beginning at the time the particular deeds were executed. As for access to the public lands, the easement holders could enter and leave public lands from the servient estate while hunting and fishing, but could not use the servient estate merely as a right of way to make use of the public lands. Seven Lakes Development Co. v. Maxson, 144 P.3d 1239 (Wyo. 2006).

2. *Private intent or rule of law?* Another intriguing aspect of *Mikesh* is the court's decision that the term "recreational rights" in the deed had a specific legal meaning. Its interpretation was "a matter of law," apparently having nothing to do with the parties' intentions. Can we imagine why the court took this approach, when terms in private instruments are almost always viewed as factual issues based on actual or presumed intent? Is the term "recreational rights" so often used, and so commonly understood, that it can have only one meaning? On this question the court's ruling invites comparison with the two mineral cases above, in which the courts viewed deed interpretation as a factual issue.

3. *Protecting the little guy.* The court here reiterates the common interpretive rule that deeds will be construed in favor of the grantee. This rule arose long ago because grantors are typically the ones who prepare deeds and because grantors usually know more about the property being sold than do grantees. But does it make sense to apply this interpretive preference in all settings, without regard for actual circumstances—for who wrote the deed, for instance, who knew the most, and who had the upper hand in negotiations? What about mineral leases that are on pre-printed forms prepared by grantee mining companies and signed by landowners who know almost nothing? Should the interpretive presumption in such cases be the reverse, favoring the grantor?

Note the court's particular policy worry in this case: "The future likely will bring hunting and recreational grants obtained by counsel-protected organizations from individual landowners who, under the rule advanced by plaintiff, might not visualize the range of implied restrictions on what would otherwise be appropriate activities on, and uses of, the land." What is the court saying? Are hunters really more likely to be represented by legal counsel than landowners? Are hunters in a position to take advantage of ordinary farmer-landowners (who might well be hunters themselves)? In any event, should a court entertain such a factual assumption without any evidence on the record?

4. *The purpose of a hunting right.* The court in *Mikesh* notes that the holder of the hunting easement was not denied access to the property to hunt. It also notes that deer inhabit open-fields with corn stubble. Does this mean, though, that the hunter in the case can still enjoy his easement despite what the landowner has done? What exactly is the purpose of such a recreational easement? To gain meat, or something else? What if the landowner had turned the land into a manicured golf course rather than a corn field? Is it still hunting to shoot a deer on a golf green?

5. *Accommodation V: hunting by the landowner:* Hunker v. Whitacre–Greer. The hunting easements in the two prior cases were both exclusive

ones by their express terms. If they are not exclusive, the landowner retains the right to hunt and can grant hunting rights to others as well. Is there, however, a limit to what the landowner can do in the case of a nonexclusive easement without interfering with the rights of the easement holder?

In *Hunker v. Whitacre–Greer Fireproofing Company,* 155 Ohio App.3d 325, 801 N.E.2d 469 (2003), the Gully Ridge Hounds hunting club received a deed that granted to it "the non-exclusiveright, privilege, and permission ('the Easement'), to enter upon and use the real property of Grantors ... for the sole purpose of horseback riding, fox hunting with horses and hounds, and hill topping with horses and horse-drawn vehicles and four-wheel vehicles (or motor vehicles)." The court concluded that, because the easement was expressly nonexclusive, the landowner could also engage in fox hunting on the same land. In a concurring opinion, Presiding Judge Waite elaborated on the idea of shared use, explaining how the rights of the easement holder fit together with the retained rights of the landowner:

> Although I agree with most of the reasoning used in the majority opinion, I believe that we must also resolve whether there has been an unreasonable interference with appellees' nonexclusive right to hunt on appellants' property. In so doing, it is important to review the differences between an exclusive and nonexclusive easement....
>
> Unless the easement agreement states otherwise, the servient owner may make any use of the property that does not unreasonably interfere with the enjoyment of the servitude. 1 Restatement of the Law 3d, Property (2000) 581, Section 4.9. "All residual rights remain in the possessory estate—the servient estate." *Id.* at 582; see, also, 1 Thompson on Real Property (1980) 472, Section 135.
>
> > In the absence of detailed arrangements between them, it is assumed that the owner of the servitude and the holder of the servient estate are intended to exercise their respective rights and privileges in a spirit of mutual accommodation. *Id.*
>
> The terms of the fox hunting easement in the instant case must be interpreted with an understanding of the aforementioned commonly accepted legal principles. Based on these principles, there is no ambiguity in the language of the easement agreement. Appellants granted a nonexclusive easement for the purpose of fox hunting (among other things), and there were no restrictions placed on appellants' residual rights except for the promise not to "unreasonably interfere with the rights granted to" appellees. This latter provision is already implied in the very grant of the easement in the first place, and does not materially change the nature of the easement. Seeing that the easement agreement does not place any other restrictions on appellants' use of their property, the law presumes that appellants, as the grantors of the easement, have reserved the right to fox hunt on their property or to issue other nonexclusive easements for fox hunting, within reasonable limits....
>
> Once we have determined that the agreement does not contain an exclusive easement, our review is not ended, because there remains an open question as to whether appellants have unreasonably interfered with appellees' right to fox hunt. The trial court determined, as an alternative legal basis for his decision, that appellants unreasonably

interfered with appellees' right to fox hunt. Whether a person's actions are reasonable or unreasonable is generally a question of fact to be determined by the trier of fact....

The trial court found that it was physically impossible for two groups to regularly fox hunt on appellants' property because it would "diminish, or totally eliminate, the quarry being hunted." On this basis, the trial court held that it would be unreasonable for anyone other than appellees to fox hunt on appellants' property. The trial court has fundamentally misunderstood what the parties actually agreed in their easement. Appellants did not agree to supply live foxes or well-rested foxes or, for that matter, any foxes at all. The easement agreement merely allows appellees the right to hunt for any foxes that happen to be on appellants' property.

The holder of a servient estate generally has no duty to the beneficiary of an easement or profit to maintain the condition of the servient estate. 1 Restatement of the Law 3d, Property (2000) 631, Section 4.13. There is nothing in the easement language that created a duty for appellants to maintain foxes on their property, or to keep the foxes in prime condition for the enjoyment of the hunters. There is nothing in the easement language guaranteeing that appellees would find any foxes on the property....

Appellees' allegation that appellants unreasonably interfered with their right to hunt presumes that some right was actually curtailed by appellants. Appellees must prove at trial that appellants prevented them from hunting on their property. There is nothing in the record indicating that appellants prevented appellees from entering the property at any time for the purpose of fox hunting ...

Once again, we see the language that a servient estate owner may not interfere "unreasonably" with the activities of the easement holder. Yet, what are we to make of the generalization that "the owner of the servitude and the holder of the servient estate are intended to exercise their respective rights and privileges in a spirit of mutual accommodation." Did the corn-planting farmer in *Mikesh* engage in mutual accommodation?

6. *A "license to sport."* Easements to enter land for hunting can be drafted with nearly infinite variations in the terms of the rights that they convey to enter land and hunt. They can be limited to specific times of the year (or the day), to specific game animals and methods of hunting, to specific locations on the land, to specific hunters or hunting methods, and the like. In nineteenth century Britain, Parliament enacted a statute—The Ground Game Act of 1880, 43 & 44 Vict. c. 47—which restricted the ability of landowners to sever game from the land and transfer it to another person. Only "resident members of the household," "ordinary servants," and one outside person paying for the privilege could hunt on the land. The statute did not affect a rather similar contractual arrangement, known as the license to sport. This license allowed a person to enter private land to hunt and kill game but gave no right to take away the game killed. It was "a license of sporting or pleasure only, and not a license of profit; it is therefore strictly personal to the licensee, and not assignable; and it is not any interest in land

within the Statute of Frauds." S.M. Leake, A Digest of the Law of Uses and Profits of Land 80 (1888). Thus the cleverness of natural resources lawyers!

7. *The scope of railroad easements:* Kershaw Sunnyside Ranches, Inc. v. Yakima Interurban. Few resource-related easements have engendered more litigation in recent years then rights of way held by railroad corporations. Two fact patterns have been common. One recurring dispute has dealt with conversions of railroad rights-of-way to recreational trails. Are recreational uses of such an easement within the scope, or do such uses amount to trespass on the servient estate? Decisions from various states have differed widely. Rulings are sometimes based on the precise language in the original deeds but more often reflect judgment calls by the courts themselves, which tend to view the issue more as a matter of law than of fact. *Compare* Toews v. United States, 53 Fed.Cl. 58 (2002) (trail use outside of easement scope; applying California law) *with* Chevy Chase Land Co. v. United States, 355 Md. 110, 733 A.2d 1055 (1999) (trail use within scope). The second recurring dispute has addressed the ability of railroads to authorize the installation of fiber optics cables above or beneath rail lines, with the compensation from the cable company going to the railroad as easement holder rather than to the owner of the underlying fee. On this issue, consider Kershaw Sunnyside Ranches, Inc. v. Yakima Interurban Lines Assn., 156 Wash.2d 253, 126 P.3d 16 (2006), in which the court interpreted a 1905 deed providing as follows:

> NOW THEREFORE, KNOW ALL MEN BY THESE PRESENTS, That we, the said E.A. Kershaw and Ora A. Kershaw . . . for and in consideration of the sum of [$1,000.00] . . . and other good and valuable considerations including the covenants of the [Railway] . . . do hereby give, grant, sell, confirm and convey to the said . . . NORTH YAKIMA & VALLEY RAILWAY COMPANY, a Corporation, its successors or assigns, a strip of land seventy five feet wide, in, along, over and through the hereinafter described land in Yakima County, Washington . . . to be used by [the Railway] as a right of way for a railway forever, together with the perpetual right to construct, maintain and operate a railway or railways over and across the same. Said strip of land being a certain strip of land seventy five feet wide across [setting forth location and referencing as already "staked out."]

The issue on appeal was whether or not the railroad could authorize installation of cables, even though the cables had nothing to do with railroad activities:

> Finally, we determine whether the underground cable on the Kershaw Sunnyside Ranches property constitutes a trespass. The parties expend much energy disputing the application of the incidental use doctrine. The incidental use doctrine "states that a railroad may use its easement to conduct not only railroad-related activities, but also any other incidental activities that are not inconsistent and do not interfere with the operation of the railroad." Danaya C. Wright & Jeffrey M. Hester, *Pipes, Wires, and Bicycles: Rails-to-Trails, Utility Licenses, and the Shifting Scope of Railroad Easements from the Nineteenth to the Twenty–First Centuries,* 27 ECOLOGY L.Q. 351, 421 (2000) (Wright & Hester). The doctrine's underpinning lies in the unique nature of railroad right of

way easements, which often are deemed to include " 'exclusive control of all the land within the lines.' " *Id.* (quoting *Grand Trunk R.R. Co. v. Richardson,* 91 U.S. (1 Otto) 454, 468, 23 L.Ed. 356 (1875)).

The trial court rejected Level 3's contention that the fiber optic lines were an incidental use. Centering its analysis on whether the "incidental use" is reasonably necessary to the operation of the railroad, and finding that "[i]ncidental rights should be limited to facilitating construction, maintenance and operation of the railroad," CP at 18, the trial court determined that the buried fiber optic line here is not an incidental use. *Id.* at 974. It thus concluded that Level 3's line constituted a trespass. *Id.* at 19, 974.

The Court of Appeals found no trespass and rejected the trial court's strict reliance on the relationship between the alleged incidental use and railroad operations. Rather, it held that the incidental use doctrine applies so long as "the use is 'not . . . inconsistent with the public use to which the highways are dedicated,' " *Kershaw Sunnyside Ranches,* 121 Wash.App. at 733, 91 P.3d 104 (quoting *State ex rel. York v. Bd. of County Comm'rs,* 28 Wash.2d 891, 905, 184 P.2d 577 (1947)), and further that revenue from such placement "indirectly serves a railroad purpose." *Id.* The focus of the Court of Appeals decision then was whether the incidental use created an additional burden on the servient estate; it concluded it did not. *Id.* at 733–37, 91 P.3d 104. In sum, the trial court and Court of Appeals conducted very different analyses in determining whether a trespass occurred; the trial court framed the issue as whether the cable was within the scope of the original easement as reasonably necessary to further a railroad purpose while the Court of Appeals framed the issue as whether the cable created an additional burden on the servient fee owner.

Drawing upon various statutes that authorized private condemnation to install such cables, the supreme court ruled that the cables exceeded the scope of the easement and thus amounted to a trespass. From that ruling Justice Madsen and two other court members dissented. Madsen urged that the original deed conveyed a fee simple interest rather than merely an easement. Nonetheless, he proceeded to comment on the scope of the ultimate easement:

> Even if, however, one assumes that an easement was conveyed instead, Level 3's installation of underground fiber optics cables along the railroad right of way is a permitted use under the incidental use doctrine. The majority, however, misapplies RCW.80.36.040 to preclude the cable installation absent Level 3's exercise of the right of eminent domain. The problem with the majority's approach is that it mixes up the rights of telecommunications companies and the separate rights of railroad companies.
>
> Under article XII, section 19 of the Washington Constitution a telecommunications company has the right to construct and maintain telegraph and telephone lines within the state through the power of eminent domain. RCW 80.36.010 implements this constitutional grant of eminent domain power. RCW 80.36.030 provides that telecommunications companies may appropriate land necessary for its telecommunica-

tions lines, including portions of railroad companies' rights of way. RCW 80.36.040 provides that telecommunications companies have the right to construct and maintain telecommunications lines for public traffic on any public road, street or highway and along any railroad corporations' rights of way. RCW 80.36.050 declares that every railroad operating in the state is a "post road" and the corporation or company owning the railroad must allow telephone and telegraph companies to construct and maintain lines along the right of way. The proviso in RCW 80.36.040 relied on by the majority provides, however, that if the grant of a right of way to the railroad was not a public grant, the right to construct and maintain lines along the railroad right of way can be obtained only through exercise of the power of eminent domain.

In contrast, the incidental use doctrine concerns the right of a railroad company to use its easement to conduct not only railroad related activities, but also any other incidental activities that are not inconsistent with and do not interfere with the operation of the railroad. DANAYA C. WRIGHT & JEFFREY M. HESTER, *Pipes, Wires, and Bicycles: Rails-to-Trails, Utility Licenses, and the Shifting Scope of Railroad Easements from the Nineteenth to the Twenty–First Centuries,* 27 ECOLOGY L.Q. 351, 421 (2000). Thus, where a railroad company enters an agreement with a third party telecommunications company to install fiber optic cable along the railroad's right of way, the question is not whether the telecommunications company has lawfully exercised its right to install the cable, but rather whether the railroad company has lawfully exercised its right as holder of the easement to permit an incidental use of its right of way. . . .

As a result of confusing the two distinct rights, the majority has applied a statutory proviso that does not apply in this case at all.

Because the proviso in RCW 80.36.040 does not apply, the question remains whether installation of fiber optic cable is a use that is permitted under the incidental use doctrine. . . .

In *State ex rel. York v. Board of County Commissioners,* 28 Wash.2d 891, 903, 184 P.2d 577 (1947), the incidental use doctrine was applied in this state to public highway rights of way. There, fee owners over whose property certain streets and roads ran as easements sought a writ of mandamus compelling a county board to rescind franchise agreements that allowed an electric company to install power lines on the public roads. The court held that highways are dedicated to the public use, and "[s]ubject to this primary use, highways may be put to any of the numerous incidental uses suitable to public thoroughfares, and with those uses the owner of the abutting land has no right to interfere." *Id.* at 903, 184 P.2d 577. The court explained that for the incidental use doctrine to apply, the use "must have some element of public benefit, and must not be inconsistent with the public use to which the highways are dedicated." *Id.* at 905, 184 P.2d 577. The landowners are entitled to compensation only if the incidental use creates an "unreasonable encroachment" on their interests. *Id.* at 903, 184 P.2d 577.

B. SURFACE USE RIGHTS

The above cases dealing with ambiguous deeds raise questions about the surface use rights that a resource-owner has, when one person owns the land (the servient estate) and another person has an easement or profit to enter the land. In no setting has the conflict been greater than in cases involving mining. The following important case and accompanying notes explain the law on this subject in the context of oil and gas production. Following that is a case that addresses the same issue in the context of hard-rock mining rights on federal lands.

HUNT OIL COMPANY v. KERBAUGH

283 N.W.2d 131 (N.D. 1979).

SAND, JUSTICE.

Ivan and Shirley Kerbaugh appealed from an order of the district court enjoining them from interfering with geophysical explorations carried on over their property by the plaintiffs, Hunt Oil Co. and Williams Oil Co. The Kerbaughs asserted the oil companies do not have an unlimited right to conduct seismic exploration over their property and also that the record in this case was inadequate to grant the oil companies injunctive relief. We conditionally affirm.

This case involves geophysical exploration for oil and gas over approximately 1000 acres of land located in Williams County and owned by the Kerbaughs. The Kerbaughs acquired about 480 acres of this land in 1966 by way of a warranty deed which reserved in the grantor " . . . ALL of the minerals, including oil and gas, in and under or that may be produced and saved from said lands, together with the right of ingress and egress." The Kerbaughs own the remaining land under a 1972 contract for deed which also reserved in the grantor all the minerals under the land, together "with such easement for ingress, egress and use of the surface which may be incidental or necessary to use such rights."

The owners of the mineral estates in this case leased their oil and gas interests to Edward Mike Davis for a period of five years in 1974 and 1975, respectively.[1] Davis then conducted seismic exploration over the property in the early part of 1976. Ivan Kerbaugh testified that after the 1976 seismic activity, the flow from a spring which supplied water to his home and livestock, gradually decreased until it stopped in November 1976. Kerbaugh said he restored the flow of the spring, although at a reduced rate, at his own expense. Ivan also testified, that as a result of the 1976 exploration, open holes were left in his property, along with various types of debris.

1. The lease to Davis of the first tract of land was a form lease which provided: "Lessee shall pay for damages caused by his operation to growing crops on said lands." The leases covering the remaining lands were on what appear to be identical forms, although the above provision was altered to read: "Lessee shall pay for damages caused by his operation to growing crops on said lands. & all surface & underground water"

In 1977, Davis assigned the oil and gas leases to Williams Exploration Co., who subsequently assigned a share of the same leases to Hunt Oil Co. The following summer the oil companies contracted with Pacific West Exploration Co. to conduct seismic exploration activities over certain lands in Williams County, including the Kerbaugh property. Pacific West Exploration contacted Ivan Kerbaugh for permission to conduct the exploration, offering to pay $50 per hole plus additional amounts for damages to growing crops. Kerbaugh rejected the offer and counteroffered with a request of $200 per hole, plus $1 per rod of tracks on the land, a commitment to cement shut any holes, and a guarantee of continued water supply. Although Kerbaugh later reduced his requests, they were rejected by Pacific.

When surveying for the exploration started, Kerbaugh requested the surveyors to leave until an agreement was reached as to compensation for damages to his surface rights. The oil companies then filed a summons and complaint seeking temporary and permanent injunctive relief restraining the Kerbaughs from interfering with the oil companies in the exercise of their rights under the oil and gas lease. [The trial court issued a temporary injunction and Pacific West Exploration then commenced the seismic activities. Later the trial court issued a permanent injunction against the Kerbaughs.]

The Kerbaughs argued the oil companies did not have an unlimited right to conduct seismic exploration over the Kerbaugh property. This court in Christman v. Emineth, 212 N.W.2d 543, 550, 70 A.L.R.3d 366 (N.D.1973), adopted the general rule set forth in 58 C.J.S. Mines and Minerals § 159b as to the implied rights of the mineral estate owner:

> * * * unless the language of the conveyance repels such a construction, as a general rule a grant of mines or minerals gives to the owner of the minerals the incidental right of entering, occupying, and making such use of the surface lands as is reasonably necessary in exploring, mining, removing, and marketing the minerals * * *. The incidental right of entering, occupying, and making such use of the surface lands as is reasonably necessary exists in the case of a reservation of mineral rights as well as a grant.

Rule - implied rights of mineral estate owner

We have also considered the rights of the lessee under the usual oil and gas lease. In Feland v. Placid Oil Co., 171 N.W.2d 829, 834 (N.D.1969), Chief Justice Teigen, speaking for the court, stated:

> Under a usual oil and gas lease, the lessee, in developing the leased premises, is entitled to use of the land reasonably necessary in producing the oil....
>
> Whether the express uses are set out or not, the mere granting of the lease creates and vests in the lessee the dominant estate in the surface of the land for the purposes of the lease; by implication it grants the lessee the use of the surface to the extent necessary to a full enjoyment of the grant. Without such use, the mineral estate obtained under the lease would be worthless.... Texaco, Inc. v. Faris, 413 S.W.2d 147, 149 (Tex.Civ.App.1967).

The above cases recognize the well-settled rule that where the mineral estate is severed from the surface estate, the mineral estate is dominant. See Annot., 53 A.L.R.3d 16; 4 Summers, Oil and Gas, § 652; 58 C.J.S. Mines and Minerals § 159b. The mineral estate is dominant in that the law implies, where it is not granted, a legitimate area within which mineral ownership of necessity carries with it inherent surface rights to find and develop the minerals, which rights must and do involve the surface estate. Without such rights the mineral estate would be meaningless and worthless. Thus, the surface estate is servient in the sense it is charged with the servitude for those essential rights of the mineral estate.

In the absence of other rights expressly granted or reserved, the rights of the owner of the mineral estate are limited to so much of the surface and such use thereof as are reasonably necessary to explore, develop, and transport the minerals. See, Union Producing Co. v. Pittman, 245 Miss. 427, 146 So.2d 553 (1962); 58 C.J.S. Mines and Minerals § 159c; Annot., 53 A.L.R.3d 16 § 3(a). In addition to, or underlying the question of what constitutes reasonable use of the surface in the development of oil and gas rights, is the concept that the owner of the mineral estate must have due regard for the rights of the surface owner and is required to exercise that degree of care and use which is a just consideration for the rights of the surface owner. Getty Oil Co. v. Jones, 470 S.W.2d 618, 621, 53 A.L.R.3d 1 (Tex.1971). Union Producing Co. v. Pittman, *supra*; 58 C.J.S. Mines and Minerals § 159c; Annot., 59 A.L.R.3d 16 § 3(c). Therefore, the mineral estate owner has no right to use more of, or do more to, the surface estate than is reasonably necessary to explore, develop, and transport the minerals. Union Producing Co. v. Pittman, *supra*; 58 C.J.S. Mines and Minerals § 159c. Nor does the mineral estate owner have the right to negligently or wantonly use the surface owner's estate.[2] See, Union Producing Co. v. Pittman, *supra*; 4 Summers, Oil and Gas, § 652.

2. This case does not present, nor does this opinion decide, the issue of whether or not the owner or lessee of the mineral estate is liable for damages arising from the reasonably necessary use of the surface incident to the exploration, development, and transportation of the minerals. The authorities which have considered the issue appear to be in agreement that such damages are *Damnum absque injuria* and no recovery can be had against the mineral estate owner or lessee. See, Getty Oil Co. v. Jones, *supra*; Frankfort Oil Co. v. Abrams, 159 Colo. 535, 413 P.2d 190 (1966); Union Producing Co. v. Pittman, *supra*; 4 Summers, Oil and Gas, § 652; Browder, *The Dominant Oil and Gas Estate Master or Servant of the Servient Estate*, 17 S.W.L.J. 25 (1963). This conclusion seems to rest on a principle that injury necessarily inflicted in the exercise of a lawful right does not create a liability, but rather, the injury must be the direct result of the commission of a wrong. See 10A Thompson on Real Property (1957 Replacement) § 5325. We question, however, the social desirability of a rule which potentially allows the damage or destruction of a surface estate equal or greater in value than the value of the mineral being extracted.

Future mineral exploration and development can be expected to expand as our demands for energy sources grow. Equity requires a closer examination of whether or not the cost of surface damage and destruction arising from mineral development should be borne by the owner of a severed surface estate or by the developer and consumer of the minerals. Although we do not doubt the mineral estate owner's right to use the surface estate to explore, develop and transport the minerals, we specifically do not decide if the right of reasonable use

The requirement that due regard be given to the rights of the surface owner, defines, to a certain extent, a consideration in determining if the mineral owner's use of the surface is reasonably necessary. In Getty Oil Co. v. Jones, *supra*, the Texas Supreme Court set forth what has become known as the "accommodation doctrine":

> There may be only one manner of use of the surface whereby the minerals can be produced. The lessee has the right to pursue this use, regardless of surface damage. (Citations omitted.) And there may be necessitous temporary use governed by the same principle. But under the circumstances indicated here; i. e., where there is an existing use by the surface owner which would otherwise be precluded or impaired, and where under the established practices in the industry there are alternatives available to the lessee whereby the minerals can be recovered, the rules of reasonable usage of the surface may require the adoption of an alternative by the lessee. 470 S.W.2d at 622.

The Utah Supreme Court adopted the opinion of the Texas court in Flying Diamond Corporation v. Rust, 551 P.2d 509 (Utah 1976), where it said, at page 511:

> . . . wherever there exist separate ownerships of interests in the same land, each should have the right to the use and enjoyment of his interest in the property to the highest degree possible not inconsistent with the rights of the other. We do not mean to be understood as saying that such a lessee must use any possible alternative. But he is obliged to pursue one which is reasonable and practical under the circumstances.

We join with the Utah court in adopting the accommodation doctrine set forth in *Getty*:

> The reasonableness of a surface use by the lessee is to be determined by a consideration of the circumstances of both and, as stated, the surface owner is under the burden of establishing the unreasonableness of the lessee's surface use in this light. The reasonableness of the method and manner of using the dominant mineral estate may be measured by what are usual, customary and reasonable practices in the industry under like circumstances of time, place and servient estate uses. What may be a reasonable use of the surface by the mineral lessee on a bald prairie used only for grazing by the servient surface owner could be unreasonable within an existing residential area of the City of Houston, or on the campus of the University of Texas, or in the middle of an irrigated farm. What we have said is that in determining the issue of whether a particular manner of use in the dominant estate is reasonable or unreasonable, we cannot ignore the condition of the surface itself and the uses then being

also implies the right to damage and destroy without compensation. But cf., Bell v. Cardinal Drilling Co., 85 N.W.2d 246 (N.D. 1957). (Under the terms of the oil and gas lease, lessee had the right to use so much of the land as was reasonably necessary in the operation of drilling the test well.)

> made by the servient surface owner.... (I)f the manner of use selected by the dominant mineral lessee is the only reasonable, usual and customary method that is available for developing and producing the minerals on the particular land then the owner of the servient estate must yield. However, if there are other usual, customary and reasonable methods practiced in the industry on similar lands put to similar uses which would not interfere with the existing uses being made by the servient surface owner, it could be unreasonable for the lessee to employ an interfering method or manner of use. These (conditions) involve questions to be resolved by the trier of the facts. 470 S.W.2d at 627–628.

In this case the Kerbaughs sought to prevent the oil companies from conducting seismic exploration activities on their property. The oil companies, on the other hand, sought an injunction prohibiting the Kerbaughs from interfering with such exploration.

The Kerbaughs, in support of their argument for denial of injunctive relief, offered affidavits and testimony indicating the damages they had sustained as the result of prior seismic exploration; that the present seismic activity was causing damage to their grain crop, pasture, and other farmland; and that they fear additional damage to property from further seismic activity.

Whether or not the use of the surface estate by the mineral estate owner is reasonably necessary is a question of fact for the trier of facts. Slope County Board of County Commissioners v. Consolidation Coal Co., 277 N.W.2d 124 (N.D.1979); Getty Oil Co. v. Jones, *supra*. In addition, the burden of proof in such a determination is upon the servient estate owner. Getty Oil Co. v. Jones, *supra*.

The Kerbaughs presented evidence establishing the damage to their property that arose or was likely to arise as a result of seismic activity. They offered, however, no evidence of reasonable alternatives available to the oil companies to explore the properties. They offered no evidence that the same information could be obtained from the prior geophysical exploration; they offered no evidence that the same information could be obtained without transversing over cropland; and the record does not indicate that they offered evidence that the tests could be conducted in another manner which would cause less damage to the Kerbaughs. Although the Kerbaughs did offer evidence suggesting some damage could have been avoided by having the oil companies conduct the operations a few weeks later, the affidavits filed by the oil companies indicate this was not a reasonable alternative. On the basis of the evidence presented by the parties, the Kerbaughs failed to meet their burden of proof that the proposed activities of the oil companies were not reasonably necessary for the exploration of the leased mineral estate. Accordingly, the conclusion by the district court that the oil companies were entitled to injunctive relief was not in error.

It is important to note that the Texas Supreme Court in *Getty* concluded the accommodation doctrine is not a balancing type test weighing the harm or inconvenience to the owner of one type of interest against the benefit to the other. Rather the court said the test is the availability of alternative non-conflicting uses of the two types of owners. Inconvenience to the surface owner is not the controlling element where no reasonable alternatives are available to the mineral owner or lessee. The surface owner must show that under the circumstances, the use of the surface under attack is not reasonably necessary. Getty Oil Co. v. Jones, *supra* at 623.

We agree a pure balancing test is not involved under the accommodation doctrine where no reasonable alternatives are available. Where alternatives do exist, however, the concepts of due regard and reasonable necessity do require a weighing of the different alternatives against the inconveniences to the surface owner. Therefore, once alternatives are shown to exist a balancing of the mineral and surface owner's interest does occur.

Kerbaugh argued and urged this court to adopt a rule of correlative rights and reasonableness, as discussed in Pennington v. Colonial Pipeline Company, 260 F.Supp. 643, 25 Oil and Gas Rptr. 514 (E.D.La.1966) *affirmed* 5 Cir., 387 F.2d 903. In that case the district court said the rights of the holder of a mineral lease, and the rights of the owner of the surface "are correlative rights, neither being superior to nor inferior to the other, and the rights of each party can only be exercised in such a manner as not to unreasonably interfere with the rights of the other. (Citations omitted.)" Be that as it may, it does not change the basic rule that a servitude exists in favor of the oil and gas estate and thus it is the dominant estate and the surface the servient estate. Although the rights implied in favor of the mineral estate can be exercised only by giving due regard to the rights of the surface owner, the mineral estate still remains dominant in the traditional real property sense. The district court in *Pennington*, although applying the right test of reasonableness, made an unfortunate use of the term "correlative rights" which is more appropriately used in referring to rights among various owners of mineral interests. See, Arnstad v. North Dakota State Industrial Commission, 122 N.W.2d 857 (N.D.1963); 1 Kuntz, Oil and Gas § 43. . . .

The order of the district court is affirmed.

Notes

1. *Ancillary rights VII: reasonably necessary surface uses.* The court in *Kerbaugh* sets forth the general rules about the relative rights of the surface landowner and the mineral lessee. The mineral lessee's rights are dominant to the extent that the lessee needs to use the surface for mining purpose, at least so long as the surface use is reasonably necessary. What is reasonably necessary in a given situation will depend greatly upon the facts. According to the court, the issue is one of fact, and thus for resolution by the jury or other fact finder. What is reasonably necessary in one case may not be necessary in another. The standard, as we've seen in other settings, is a vague one—hardly more than a general idea rather than a clear standard.

On this point we might consider the similarity between the mining law rule applied in *Kerbaugh* and the California water law system we saw applied in *Joslin v. Marin Municipal Water District.* In California, riparian water uses are similarly dominant over prior appropriators, but that dominance extends only to the extent that the riparian's use is reasonable. The priority is not absolute.

2. *Accommodation VI: mineral lessees and the virtue of vagueness.* *Kerbaugh* has been a visible, influential ruling in oil and gas law, embracing and extending the accommodation doctrine prominently announced by the Texas Supreme Court in the *Getty Oil* case. The accommodation doctrine is plainly a variant or refinement of the "reasonably necessary" test that has long applied. What exactly are the elements of this new accommodation doctrine? When does it require a lessee to make changes in surface-use practices so as to avoid unnecessarily harming existing surface uses? As the court makes clear, a lessee is not obligated to implement exceptional oil-production methods. It must only consider and, if feasible, adopt other "usual, customary and reasonable methods practiced in the industry on similar lands put to similar uses." It must only give "due regard" for the rights of the surface owner. Note that the doctrine only seems to apply in the case of surface uses by the landowner that are pre-existing, not those that the surface owner begins later. It is also important that the surface owner has the burden of showing that reasonable accommodation was possible.

A marked characteristic of the accommodation doctrine is its vagueness. Is this a defect in the rule, or might it in some way be a virtue? Vagueness affects both sides of a transaction in that neither side knows where it stands and both might be prone to compromise due to the uncertainty. Might the vagueness of the doctrine make it more effective in getting surface owners and mineral lessees to talk to one another; that is, can we think of it not as a substantive limit on the rights of miners but more as a process method of stimulating resource-users to try to get along?

3. *Paying for surface damages.* The court in *Kerbaugh* went out of its way, in footnote 2, to consider whether state law ought to change to require mineral lessees to pay for the surface damage that they cause. The issue is a complex one, often (though not always) covered in the applicable mineral lease. In general, legislatures (and less often courts) in recent decades have shown increasing willingness to compel lessees and other mineral rights holders to pay for surface damage. Statutes in several states protect agricultural and ranching activities from disruption by oil and gas activities. Surface damage does not include simply the rental value of using the surface; lessees can use the surface as a matter of right. Nor does the new liability rule give to surface owners any right to deny the surface use; the lessee again can use the surface as of right. The sole duty is to pay for physical damage or in some other way to make amends.

4. *Specific surface use rights.* How does *Kerbaugh* compare with the Illinois decisions in *SOLVE v. Illinois Cement* and *Jilek* in terms of surface use rights that the mining company possesses? *Kerbaugh* presents the mineral lessee's rights in broad, vague terms. The Illinois courts offered more clear guidance on what mining companies could and could not do. State

law on this issue varies somewhat, but the many judicial rulings on the subject over the past century have articulated a variety of specific rights that lessees typically have implied in their leases, unless expressly excluded. The main right, expressed in *Kerbaugh*, is the right to use and occupy the land surface insofar as reasonably necessary to discover, develop, and exploit the resource. Uses of the surface can involve altering or even destroying parts of the surface when reasonably necessary. They can also include a right to consume water on the premises, or even timber or clay (according to older rulings), as needed to conduct mining operations. These surface use rights, though, are subject to rather clear limits, in addition to the "reasonably necessary" rule and accommodation doctrine. The chief limit is that surface uses must relate exclusively to the extraction of minerals from the servient estate itself. The surface cannot be used to support mining operations on other tracts. Various limits (considered below) apply to mining activities that cause subsidence of the surface, particularly structural damage to buildings. Many states have police-power regulations that apply as well, including requirements that mining companies provide advance notice of planned activities. *See, e.g.*, Murphy v. Amoco Production Co., 729 F.2d 552 (8th Cir. 1984) (upholding the constitutionality of North Dakota statute imposing liability on oil companies).

UNITED STATES v. RIZZINELLI

182 F. 675 (D. Idaho 1910).

DIETRICH, DISTRICT JUDGE.

The defendants are charged with the maintenance of saloons upon mining claims within the limits of the Coeur d'Alene National Forest without a permit, and in violation of the rules and regulations of the Secretary of Agriculture. The claims were duly located, subsequent to the creation of the forest reserve, and they are possessory only, no application for patent ever having been made. The technical sufficiency of the indictment is not called into question, but it is urged: First, that the provision of the statute upon which the rules referred to are founded is unconstitutional, and the rules, therefore, void, because the statute itself does not sufficiently define the acts to be punished, and because it attempts to delegate to an executive officer legislative power; and, second, that, even if the statute be held to be valid, it cannot properly be construed as conferring authority upon the Secretary of Agriculture to make rules applicable to the lands embraced in valid mining claims, whether the same were located before or after the creation of the forest reserve.

The Act of June 4, 1897 (chapter 2, 30 Stat. 34 (U.S. Comp. St. 1901, p. 1538)), to which the charge is primarily referred, and the validity of which the defendants attack, provides for the setting apart and maintenance of forest reservations for the purpose of protecting the forests, and securing favorable conditions of water flow, and to furnish a continual supply of timber for the use and necessities of citizens of the United States. It is declared that:

> The Secretary of the Interior shall make provisions for the protection against destruction by fire and depredations upon the public forests and forest reservations which may have been set aside or which may be hereafter set aside under the said act of March third, eighteen hundred and ninety-one, and which may be continued; and he may make such rules and regulations and establish such service as will insure the objects of such reservations, namely, to regulate their occupancy and use and to preserve the forests thereon from destruction; and any violation of the provisions of this act or such rules and regulations shall be punished as is provided for in the act of June fourth, eighteen hundred and eighty-eight, amending section fifty-three hundred and eighty-eight of the Revised Statutes of the United States.

And it is further provided as follows:

> Nothing herein shall be construed as prohibiting the egress or ingress of actual settlers residing within the boundaries of such reservations, or from crossing the same to and from their property or homes; and such wagon roads and other improvements may be constructed thereon as may be necessary to reach their homes and to utilize their property under such rules and regulations as may be prescribed by the Secretary of the Interior. Nor shall anything herein prohibit any person from entering upon such forest reservations for all proper and lawful purposes, including that of prospecting, locating, and developing the mineral resources thereof: Provided, that such persons comply with the rules and regulations covering such forest reservations. . . .

Subsequently, jurisdiction over forest reserves was transferred to the Secretary of Agriculture, who formulated an elaborate set of regulations, published in what is known as the "Use Book." The particular rules alleged to have been ignored by the defendants (Use Book, pp. 54, 67) are as follows:

> Reg. 6. Permits are necessary for all occupancy, uses, operations or enterprises of any kind within national forests, whether begun before or after the national forest was established, except: (a) Upon patented lands (b) upon valid claims for purposes necessary to their actual development and consistent with their character; (c) upon rights of way amounting to easements for the purposes named in the grants; (d) prospecting for minerals, transient camping, hunting, fishing, and surveying for lawful projects.

> Reg. 19. The following acts within national forests are hereby forbidden: * * * (c) Erecting or conducting telephone, telegraph, or power lines, hotels, stores, sawmills, power plants, or other structures, or manufacturing or business enterprises, or carrying on any kind of work, except as allowed by law and national forest regulations, and except upon patented lands or upon a valid claim for the actual development of such claim, consistent with the purposes for which it was initiated.

. . . .

Concretely stated, the second question is whether or not, assuming that the maintenance of a saloon upon public lands within a national forest to which no previous claim of any kind has attached constitutes a criminal offense, a like offense is committed when such a saloon is maintained upon forest reserve lands, embraced within a valid mining claim, located after the creation of the reserve.

By referring to the extracts above quoted from the statute, it will be noted that the authority conferred upon the secretary to make rules is confined to the purpose of regulating the occupancy and use of, and the preservation of the forests upon, the reservations. Congress contemplated that settlers within the boundaries of the reservations should have the right of egress and ingress, and should be permitted to construct and maintain such roads and other improvements as are reasonably necessary for such purpose, and it was further contemplated that persons should, subject to the reasonable rules and regulations of the secretary, have the right to go upon the reserve for all proper and lawful purposes, including that of "prospecting, locating, and developing the mineral resources thereof." . . . The only express reference in the act to the location of mining claims is found in the last sentence of the second paragraph above quoted, which in full is:

> Nor shall anything herein prohibit any person from entering upon such forest reservations for all proper and lawful purposes, including that of prospecting, locating and developing the mineral resources thereof: Provided, that such persons comply with the rules and regulations covering such forest reservations.

And the last sentence of the last paragraph above quoted, namely:

> And any mineral lands in any forest reservation which have been, or which may be shown to be such, and subject to entry under the existing mining laws of the United States and the rules and regulations applying thereto, shall continue to be subject to such location and entry, notwithstanding any provisions herein contained.

It is the contention of defendants that the valid location of a mining claim *ipso facto* withdraws the land embraced therein from the jurisdiction of the Secretary of Agriculture, and that therefore the rules under consideration are wholly inapplicable. Upon the other hand, the government points to the fact that while qualified persons are authorized to locate claims upon lands containing valuable mineral deposits, within as well as without the boundaries of a reservation, there is no language in the act justifying the conclusion that by the location of a mining claim the lands embraced therein are withdrawn from the reservation, and much significance is attached to the clause which provides that the right to go upon reservations for "all proper and lawful purposes, including that of prospecting, locating, and developing the mineral resources," is expressly conditioned upon a compliance with the rules and regulations covering forest reservations.

For a definition of the rights of the locator upon public lands, both parties refer to section 2322 of the Revised Statutes of the United States (U.S. Comp. St. 1901, p. 1425), where it is declared that:

> The claimant shall have the exclusive right of possession, and enjoyment of all the surface (of the claim), and of all veins, lodes, and ledges, throughout their entire depth, the top or apex of which lies inside of such surface lines, extended downward vertically, etc.

It is conceded by the government that by the forest reserve act of June 4, 1897, Congress did not intend to, and did not, limit or qualify the rights of a locator, or confer any authority upon the Secretary of Agriculture, by regulation or otherwise, to limit or qualify such rights, or to intrude upon the exclusive possession or infringe upon the exclusive 'enjoyment' guaranteed to the locator under section 2322; in short, that the rights of a locator of a mining claim within the boundaries of a forest reserve are substantially the same as those of one who locates such a claim upon the public domain. It is also conceded that the right of exclusive possession runs against the government, as well as against third persons. Obviously, therefore, the controversy is primarily confined to a consideration of the purpose to which the locator may ordinarily and under general law properly devote the surface possession of his mining claim; the defendants contending that they may use the same "for any purpose, whether the same be consistent with mining or not," and, upon the other hand, the government asserting that a locator is, under section 2322, authorized to use the surface of his mining claim only for purposes connected with or incident to the exploration and recovery of the mineral therein contained.

It is familiar law that the citizen may acquire any one of three possible estates in mineral lands upon the public domain. He may content himself with locating a claim in compliance with the statutes and rules and regulations, in which case he acquires a possessory title only, both the equitable and legal title remaining in the United States; or, in the second place, after making such location, he may comply with the further requirements of the law, and pay the required purchase price, thus acquiring the equitable title, the legal title still remaining in the United States; or he may proceed one step further, and obtain patent, thus divesting the government of all interest, both legal and equitable.

The defendants here have the possessory title only. They have a distinct but qualified property right, and, even if we assume that their interest is vested, it is one which may be abandoned at any moment, or forfeited. The primary title, the paramount ownership, is in the government, and upon abandonment by the locator, or his failure to comply with the conditions upon which his continuing right of possession depends, the entire estate reverts to the government; all the time, it retains the title, with a valuable residuary and reversionary interest. This interest, whatever it may be, it has the right to protect and obviously the interest which it retains is the entire estate, less that which is granted by the terms of section 2322, providing that locators shall have "the exclusive right of possession and enjoyment of all the surface of their locations." . . . The government is not seeking to qualify or limit the possession of the defendants or in any respect to intrude thereon, but only to restrict the uses to which such possession shall be devoted. The defendants have a right to the exclusive enjoyment of the surface of their claims, and our task is to determine what is meant by the word "enjoyment" as the name is used in the statute. It is not self-explanatory, or unequivocal, and must be interpreted in the light of the general purpose of the law in which it is found, and in harmony with other provisions thereof. Consciously or unconsciously we necessarily read something into the statute which is not therein expressed. We may differ as to what should be interpolated, but that there must be some interpolation may not be doubted.

The government inserts, after the word "enjoyment," the phrase "for mining purposes," and the defendants the phrase "for all purposes." No other language is suggested, and, indeed, no middle ground appears to be possible; the "enjoyment" is either for mining purposes alone, or for all purposes without qualification or restriction. Under a familiar rule of statutory construction, the necessity of reading into the statute one or the other of these two phrases to make it complete, and its adaptability to either of them, of itself operates strongly to determine the question in favor of the government, for it is well settled that in public grants nothing passes except that which is clearly and specifically granted, and all doubts are to be resolved in favor of the government. Oregon R. & N. Co. v. Oregonian Ry. Co., 130 U.S. 1, 9 Sup.Ct. 409, 32 L.Ed. 837; Coosaw M. Co. v. South Carolina, 144 U.S. 550, 12 Sup.Ct. 689, 36 L.Ed. 537. But, independent of this rule, considerations pertinent to the construction of private grants and contracts clearly lead to the conclusion that the right of enjoyment which Congress intended to grant extends only to mining uses. The general purpose of the mineral laws is well understood; it was to encourage citizens to assume the hazards of searching for and extracting the valuable minerals deposited in our public lands. In form the grant is a mere gratuity; but, in considering the propriety of such legislation, it may well have been thought that by reason of the stimulus thus given to the production of mineral wealth, and rendering the same available for commerce and the arts, the public would indirectly receive a consideration commensurate with the value of the grant. In that view doubtless the legislation has for a generation been generally approved as embodying a wise public policy. But under what theory should the public gratuitously bestow upon the individual the right to devote mineral lands any more than any other public lands to valuable uses having no relation to mining, and for what reason should we read into the statute such a surprising and unexpressed legislative intent?

With much earnestness the consideration is urged that it has become more or less customary to erect valuable buildings upon lands embraced in mineral claims to be used for purposes having no necessary relation to mining operations, and that great hardship would ensue and important property rights would be confiscated if the locator's "enjoyment" of the surface be limited to uses incident to mining. But even if it be true, as suggested, that in many localities sites for dwelling houses and business structures could not be conveniently obtained except upon lands containing valuable mineral deposits and embraced in located claims, the fact is without significance and lends no support to the defendants' contention. If we assume that Congress was cognizant of or anticipated such conditions, we may further reasonably assume that it was thought that ample protection against embarrassment to the mining industry from such a source was furnished in other provisions of the law. At the same time the government confers upon the locator the right to possess and enjoy the surface of a mining claim for mining purposes without the payment of any consideration therefor, it offers for a small consideration to convey to him the entire estate. The government gives the mineral to him who finds it, and, for purposes incident to the extraction thereof, permits him to possess and use the ground in which it is found....

Holding, therefore, that the right of a locator of a mining claim to the "enjoyment" of the surface thereof is limited to uses incident to mining operations, no serious difficulty is encountered in reaching the further conclusion that forest reserve lands embraced in a mining claim continue to constitute a part of the reserve, notwithstanding the mineral location, subject, of course, to all the legal rights and privileges of the locator. The paramount ownership being in the government, and it also having a reversionary interest in the possessory right of the locator, clearly it has a valuable estate which it is entitled to protect against waste and unlawful use. It is scarcely necessary to say that it is the substantial property right of the government, and not the extent to which such right may be infringed in the present case, that challenges our consideration. The burden imposed upon the principal estate by the construction and maintenance of a little saloon building may be trivial, and the damage wholly unappreciable. But that is not to the point. If a worthless shrub may as a matter of legal right be destroyed in the location of a saloon, the entire claim may be stripped of its timber, however valuable, to give place for other saloons and other structures having no connection with the operation of the mine. To concede any such right at all is necessarily to concede a right without limit; there is no middle ground....

For the reasons stated, the demurrer will be overruled.

Notes

1. *How necessary is a saloon?* Like *Kerbaugh*, *Rizzinelli* has to do with the surface use rights of a mining operation. It deals with an unpatented mining claim on federal lands, which entails (as we saw in *U.S. v. Coleman* and *Geomet Exploration* in chapter 3) a secure, exclusive private right to exploit a valuable mineral deposit on federal lands. Along with the right to

mine comes the right to use the land surface subject to reasonable regulations imposed by the federal agency in charge of managing the surface. What standard does the court apply in articulating these surface use rights, and how does it compare with the standard applied in *Kerbaugh*? How did the court determine that a saloon was not reasonably incident to mining? Can we imagine a situation in which it makes sense for a mining company to construct accommodations, dining halls—and, who knows, maybe places of entertainment—for miners working in exceedingly remote locations?

2. *Accommodation VII:* U.S. v. Curtis–Nevada Mines. Certain forms of surface mining can be so intensive in use and sufficiently dangerous (due to blasting, open pits, and other dangers) that no other surface uses can take place. But how far can a miner go, in using the risk of physical danger, to keep other people off the land entirely, particularly on federal lands where the other surface users are members of the public?

In *United State v. Curtis–Nevada Mines, Inc.*, 611 F.2d 1277 (9th Cir. 1980), Curtis asserted title to 203 unpatented mining claims on federal lands, covering some thirteen square miles. Although he asserted that the mining claims were worth "trillions," no mining was taking place and the only employee on the site was charged chiefly with keeping outsiders away. Curtis posted no trespassing signs around the area and excluded hunters, hikers, campers, and other recreational visitors. Under section 4(b) of the Surface Resources Act of 1955, the rights of mining claimants are subject to "the right of the United States, its permittees, and licensees, to use so much of the surface thereof as may be necessary for such purposes," so long as such alternative uses do not "endanger or materially interfere with prospecting, mining or processing operations or uses reasonably incident thereto." *Held*: This statute applied to recreational uses of the surface as well as to other consumptive land uses. The expression "permittees and licensees" included casual recreational visitors; it was not limited to individuals who held specific written permits or licenses to use the same land. Curtis therefore had to let them make free recreational use of the unpatented mining claims.

3. *Extralateral rights*: Swoboda v. Pala Mining, Inc. One of the unusual features of unpatented mining claims on federal lands is the fact that lode claims extend underground as far as the lode-bearing ore formation extends, even if it runs beneath the surface of other land. This rule was applied in Swoboda v. Pala Mining, Inc., 844 F.2d 654 (9th Cir. 1988), which involved a dispute between a miner, Swoboda, and an Indian tribe that owned nearby land. The mine was located in 1898 and the adjacent Pala Indian Reservation in 1920. In 1949, Swoboda's predecessor in interest, Stewart Mine, obtained a patent to the mineral land:

> Within the boundaries of the Stewart Mine is the apex of a pegmatite dike. Swoboda and his predecessors-in-interest have excavated tunnels in the central part of the dike. A segment of the tunnel network within the pegmatite dike runs below the surface of the Pala Indian Reservation adjacent to the western boundary of the Stewart Mine. On October 5 and 9, 1980, appellant Pala Mining, Inc. ("PMI") excavated and removed earth from the surface of the reservation land directly above Swoboda's tunnel network.

The excavation by the tribal mining company interfered with the mining operations of Swoboda beneath the surface of tribal lands. The court explained Swoboda's rights:

> Under 30 U.S.C. § 26, the owner of a mining claim has the exclusive right of possession and enjoyment not only of the land within the boundary lines of the claim, but also of "all veins, lodges and ledges throughout their entire depth, the top or apex of which lies" within the boundary lines extended downward vertically—even though the veins, lodes or ledges extend outside the boundaries of the claim. *See, e.g., Del Monte Mining and Milling Co. v. Last Chance Mining and Milling Co.,* 171 U.S. 55, 88, 18 S.Ct. 895, 908, 43 L.Ed. 72 (1898); *Silver Surprize, Inc. v. Sunshine Mining Co.,* 15 Wash.App. 1, 547 P.2d 1240, 1244 (1976), *aff'd,* 88 Wash.2d 64, 558 P.2d 186 (1977) ("extralateral right" is right to follow vein past boundaries of one's own claim). The parties stipulated that the apex of the pegmatite dike is contained within the Stewart Mine's surface boundary lines and that the dike runs below the surface of the Pala Reservation. Therefore, in this case, if the pegmatite dike constitutes a "vein" under § 26, Swoboda has the extralateral right to follow the vein outside the boundaries of the Stewart Mine.

On the facts the court decided that the ore format did qualify as a "vein." It then considered whether the tribal lands were exempt from the application of the normal mining rules:

> PMI contends that Indian tribal lands are exempt from the assertion of extralateral rights, but does not supply citations for this precise principle. The Mission Indians Relief Act which gave the Pala Mission Indians the land patent to their reservation provided in part "that no patent shall embrace any tract or tracts to which existing valid rights have attached in favor of any person under any of the United States laws providing for the disposition of the public domain." Act of January 12, 1891, 26 Stat. 712. Swoboda's predecessors-in-interest located the Stewart Mine in 1898; the Pala Indians did not receive the patent for the reservation land until 1920. Swoboda's grant conveyed to his predecessors-in interest:
>
> > [T]he said mining premises hereinbefore described ... and all that portion of the said vein, lode, or ledge, and all other veins, lodes, and ledges throughout their entire depth, the tops or apexes of which lie inside the surface boundary lines of said granted premises in said survey extended downward vertically, although such veins, lodes, or ledges in their downward course may so far depart from a perpendicular as to extend outside the vertical lines of said premises....
>
> The Indian trust patent of February 4, 1920, conveyed the land to the Pala Band "subject to all the restrictions and conditions contained in the said Act of Congress of January 12, 1891." *Supp. ER,* Tab 121, Exh. B at 3. Hence, the land patent itself incorporated by reference the condition that "no patent shall embrace any tract or tracts to which existing valid rights have attached in favor of any person under any of the United States laws providing for the disposition of the public domain.... " Consequently, the district court correctly determined that

the trust patent for the Pala Indian Reservation does not preclude ownership by Swoboda of extralateral rights in the pegmatite dike vein within the surface of the reservation. The general principle that Indians own the mineral rights to their reservation land does not change this result.

4. *Surface rights and regulatory restrictions.* In the case of mining disputes between two private parties, surface-use disputes are decided by private agreement and by the background law. When minerals are located on public land, however, the situation is different. Now one party is in a position to change the law. In the context of mining on federal lands, what powers does the government have by means of regulation to alter the surface use rights of miners who already hold unpatented mining claims? Consider the following case:

UNITED STATES v. WEISS

642 F.2d 296 (9th Cir. 1981).

ANDERSON, CIRCUIT JUDGE:

Appellants contend that the district court erred in granting summary judgment to the United States and in enjoining them from conducting any mining activity which could result in the disturbance of surface resources until they had complied with regulations under 36 CFR 252. We affirm the judgment of the district court.

roa

BACKGROUND

The appellants are owners of unpatented placer mining claims located within the St. Joe National Forest in Idaho. They were informed by the Forest Service that regulations had been promulgated which required that they file an operating plan for their mining operations. While the appellants had been in contact with the Forest Service regarding their operations, they had not signed and filed a final plan of operations nor had they submitted a bond which the Forest Service required pursuant to the regulations.

The United States filed a complaint in district court to enjoin the appellants until an approved plan of operations had been filed, and a $2,000 bond was posted. Finding no genuine issue of material fact, the district court granted summary judgment to the United States and enjoined the appellants as requested.

The regulations in question are 36 CFR § 252, which were promulgated by the Secretary of Agriculture on August 28, 1974. 36 CFR § 252 sets forth rules and procedures which are intended to regulate the use of the surface of national forest land used in connection with mining operations authorized by the United States mining laws. 36 CFR § 252.1. The purpose of the regulations is "to minimize adverse environmental impacts on National Forest System surface resources" that can be caused by mining, while, at the same time, not interfering with the rights conferred by the mining laws. *Id.* Under the regulations, the Forest Service must be notified of any mining-related operation that is

Regs

likely to cause a disturbance of surface resources. The initiation or continuation of such an operation is subject to the approval of the Forest Service.

Appellants' contention on appeal is that the regulations have not been promulgated pursuant to adequate statutory authority. They argue that the Organic Administration Act of 1897, 30 Stat. 36 and 35, 16 U.S.C. §§ 478 and 551, do not authorize the adoption of these regulations. Therefore, they argue that the regulations have no force and effect.

DISCUSSION

36 CFR § 252 has been promulgated by the Secretary of Agriculture under the authority of the Organic Administration Act of June 4, 1897, specifically, 30 Stat. 36 and 35, 16 U.S.C. §§ 478 and 551. These provisions are part of the statutory scheme which covers the national forests and which confers administration of the national forests upon the Secretary of Agriculture.

Under §§ 478 and 551, the Secretary may make rules and regulations for the protection and preservation of the national forests, and persons entering upon national forest land must comply with those rules and regulations. The authority of the Secretary to regulate activity on national forest land pursuant to these sections has been upheld in a variety of non-mining instances. See United States v. Grimaud, 220 U.S. 506, 31 S.Ct. 480, 55 L.Ed. 563 (1910) (regulations concerning sheep grazing in national forests); McMichael v. United States, 355 F.2d 283 (9th Cir. 1965) (regulations prohibiting motorized vehicles in certain areas of national forest); Mountain States Telephone & Telegraph Co. v. United States, 204 Ct.Cl. 521, 499 F.2d 611 (1974) (regulations requiring special use permit and payment of fees for a microwave relay facility within a national forest). Sabin v. Butz, 515 F.2d 1061 (10th Cir. 1975) (regulations setting up a permit system for ski operations and instructions on national forest land). That authority has also been sustained to prohibit non-mining activity upon unpatented mining claims. United States v. Rizzinelli, 182 F. 675 (D. Idaho 1910). However, the precise issue of whether these statutory provisions empower the Secretary to regulate mining operations on national forest land does not appear to have been decided before. See United States v. Richardson, 599 F.2d 290, 293 (9th Cir.), cert. denied, 444 U.S. 1014, 100 S.Ct. 663, 62 L.Ed.2d 643 (1980).

We believe that the Act of 1897, 16 U.S.C. §§ 478 and 551, granted to the Secretary the power to adopt reasonable rules and regulations regarding mining operations within the national forests.

The national forests are to be open for entry "for all proper and lawful purposes, including that of prospecting, locating, and developing the mineral resources thereof." 16 U.S.C. § 478. However, "(s)uch persons must comply with the rules and regulations covering such national forests." *Id.* Thus it is clear that persons entering the national forests to prospect, locate, and develop mineral resources therein are subject to and must comply with the rules and regulations covering the national forests.

The Act of 1897, 30 Stat. 35, 16 U.S.C. § 551, as amended, grants authority to the Secretary to make "rules and regulations and (to) establish such service as will insure the objects of such reservations, namely, to regulate their occupancy and use and to preserve the forests thereon from destruction; ... " The section specifically states that the Secretary shall make provision for the protection of the national forests against destruction by fire and depredation. Thus the Secretary has been given the authority to promulgate reasonable rules and regulations which will protect the national forests and which will help to carry out the purposes for which the national forests were created.

The regulations in question, 36 CFR 252, were designed to minimize adverse environmental impacts on the surface resources of the national forests. Such regulations were authorized by the Act of 1897.

The fact that these regulations have been promulgated many years after the enactment of their statutory authority does not destroy the Congressional authorization given. The failure of an executive agency to act does not forfeit or surrender governmental property or rights. United States v. California, 332 U.S. 19, 39–40, 67 S.Ct. 1658, 1668–1669, 91 L.Ed. 1889 (1947); United States v. Southern Pacific Transp. Co., 543 F.2d 676, 697 (9th Cir. 1976). In this situation, a mining claimant may not claim any sort of prescriptive right which would prevent the government from protecting its superior vested property rights.

In analyzing the issue before us, we are keenly aware of the important and competing interests involved. Mining has been accorded a special place in our laws relating to public lands. The basic mining law of May 10, 1872, 17 Stat. 91, 30 U.S.C. §§ 21–54, encouraged the prospecting, exploring, and development of mineral resources on public lands. "The system envisaged by the mining laws was that the prospector could go out into the public domain, search for minerals and upon discovery establish a claim to land upon which the discovery was made." United States v. Curtis–Nevada Mines, Inc., 611 F.2d 1277, 1281 (9th Cir. 1980). So long as they complied with the laws of the United States and applicable state and local laws, locators of mining locations were given "the exclusive right of possession and enjoyment of all the surface included within the lines of their location," along with the subsurface rights. 30 U.S.C. § 26.

On the other hand, our national forests have also been a fundamental part of the use of our public lands. National forests were established to improve and protect our forest land, to secure "favorable conditions of water flows, and to furnish a continuous supply of timber for the use and necessities of citizens of the United States; ... " 16 U.S.C. § 475. The object of the Organic Administration Act of 1897 was "to maintain favorable forest conditions, without excluding the use of reservations for other purposes. They are not parks set aside for nonuse, but have been established for economic reasons. 30 Cong.Rec. 966 (1897) (Cong. McRae)." United States v. New Mexico, 438 U.S. 696, 708, 98 S.Ct. 3012, 3018, 57 L.Ed.2d 1052 (1978).

Moreover, while locators were accorded the right of possession and enjoyment of all the surface resources within their claim, the "primary title, the paramount ownership is in the government ... it retains the title, with a valuable residuary and reversionary interest." United States v. Rizzinelli, et al., 182 F. at 681 (D. Idaho, 1910). "The paramount ownership being in the government, and it also having a reversionary interest in the possessory right of the locator, clearly it has a valuable estate which it is entitled to protect against waste and unlawful use." *Id.* at 684.

We believe that the important interests involved here were intended to and can coexist. The Secretary of Agriculture has been given the responsibility and the power to maintain and protect our national forests and the lands therein. While prospecting, locating, and developing of mineral resources in the national forests may not be prohibited nor so unreasonably circumscribed as to amount to a prohibition, the Secretary may adopt reasonable rules and regulations which do not impermissibly encroach upon the right to the use and enjoyment of placer claims for mining purposes.

The judgment of the district court is AFFIRMED.

Notes

1. *Government as proprietor* and *sovereign.* In the case of mining claims and mineral leases on federal lands, the federal government's role is more expansive than that of the ordinary landowner. Private landowners can enforce their property rights but otherwise cannot compel miners on their lands to change their mining practices. On federal lands the government wears two hats—that of landowner and that of regulatory sovereign. What the government cannot do as landowner it might well be able to do by imposing regulatory restrictions on the private mining or mineral development companies. The situation might well seem unfair. To be sure, mining on private lands is also subject to regulatory controls, promulgated by various levels of government, and landowners can run to government officials and seek protection. But the case of federal lands is still different in that the landowning agency itself wields great regulatory power. What can we learn from *Weiss* in terms of how far the government can go in regulating? Is the court giving us, rapid-fire, a summary of governmental powers in the final paragraph of its ruling?

2. *Getting to the site, multiple agencies, and private rights*: Clouser v. Espy. As we've seen, one of the main needs of resource users is to get access to the resource in a reasonable manner. What happens, though, when a mining claim is surrounded by designated federal wilderness in which roads and vehicles of all types are excluded? What is a miner to do then? The issue arose in Clouser v. Espy, 42 F.3d 1522 (9th Cir. 1994). Mining claimants needed to cross National Forest wilderness areas and were told by the U.S.

Forest Service that they could only use pack animals or other nonmotorized means of ingress and egress. The miners challenged the Forest Service's action on various grounds. An important one had to do with whether the Forest Service (located in the Department of Agriculture) was the right agency to make the decision or whether the Department of Interior (the Bureau of Land Management) should do so, given that the ruling related to a mining claim. The miners presumably wanted to get the BLM involved because of its greater willingness to favor mining over competing land uses. The issue was particularly complicated because unpatented mining claims of the type at issue are legally valid only if they are commercially viable, and the commercial viability of mining depends on how costly it is to gain ingress and egress. The use of pack animals would boost costs, perhaps so much to make mining unprofitable, thereby invalidating the unpatented mining claims. The court rejected this claim about agency power, concluding that the Forest Service was the rightful agency to decide access issues, even though their rulings indirectly affected the validity of the mining claims:

> As to these two claims located in wilderness areas, there can be no doubt whatsoever that the Forest Service enjoys the authority to regulate means of access, for the Department of Agriculture has expressly been granted statutory authority to do so. 16 U.S.C. § 1134(b) provides that
>
> > In any case where valid mining claims or other valid occupancies are wholly within a designated national forest wilderness area, the Secretary of Agriculture shall by reasonable regulations consistent with the preservation of the area as wilderness, permit ingress and egress to such surrounded areas by means which have been or are being customarily enjoyed with respect to other such areas similarly situated.
>
> This provision's unambiguous instruction to the Secretary of Agriculture to permit ingress and egress to such areas "by means which have been or are being customarily enjoyed with respect to other such areas similarly situated" clearly implies an authority and duty to determine what means are being or have been "customarily enjoyed" in like areas. Indeed, the provision expressly empowers the Secretary to promulgate "reasonable regulations" implementing the statutory mandate....

The miners also challenged the access limits on the ground that they were inconsistent with the governing statutes:

> Plaintiffs challenge the above rulings on various grounds. First, they challenge the fact-finding on the basis of which the Service concluded that motorized access was neither "essential" to the operation of the claim under 36 C.F.R. § 228.15(b), nor "customarily used with respect to other such claims" under 36 C.F.R. § 228.15(c). However, federal court review of agency fact-finding—other than fact-finding made in the course of formal adjudications which the instant proceedings are not—is conducted under the deferential "arbitrary and capricious" standard, pursuant to 706(2)(A) of the APA. ...
>
> As explained above, the Forest Service concluded, based on the fact that the Service's own examiner had carried in a five-inch dredge by pack horse when evaluating the claim, and the fact that the operation

proposed was a small one for which plaintiffs also planned to use a five-inch dredge, that motorized access was not "essential" to the mining operation under 36 C.F.R. § 228.15(b). Regarding the "customarily used" standard of 36 C.F.R. § 228.15(c), the record also shows that the access trails plaintiffs proposed using have been blocked by a gate and closed to traffic since 1984. Since that date the trails have not been maintained by the Forest Service, and consequently they are returning to a natural condition. *See* ER at 172–73.

Moreover, plaintiffs have pointed to no evidence in the administrative record that would tend to show motorized access is, in fact, "essential" to the operation of this claim or is "customarily used with respect to other such claims." . . .

Plaintiffs also argued in the district court that the Forest Service acted improperly in ruling that the trails in question do not qualify as public highways under R.S. § 2477 [a longstanding federal statute authorizing continued uses of "public highways"]. Plaintiffs assert that authority to decide whether roads qualify as public highways under R.S. § 2477 is vested in the Department of the Interior. The district court rejected that contention, ruling the Forest Service may properly rule on such issues in the course of carrying out its duty to review and approve plans of operations. . . .

Finally, plaintiffs challenge the Forest Service ruling as violating certain provisions of the mining laws. . . . Plaintiffs cite 30 U.S.C. § 612(b), which provides, in pertinent part

> Rights under any mining claim . . . shall be subject, prior to issuance of patent therefor, to the right of the United States to manage and dispose of the vegetative surface resources thereof and to manage other surface resources thereof. . . . Any such mining claim shall also be subject, prior to issuance of patent therefor, to the right of the United States, its permittees, and licensees, to use so much of the surface thereof as may be necessary for such purposes or for access to adjacent land: *Provided, however, That any use of the surface or any such mining claim by the United States, its permittees or licensees, shall be such as not to endanger or materially interfere with prospecting, mining or processing operations or uses reasonably incidental thereto* . . . .

(Emphasis added). Plaintiffs argue that motorized access to the claim is "[a] use[] reasonably incidental [to mining]" and that the Service's ruling "materially interfere[s] with" that use in violation of this provision. Plaintiffs' position seems to be that Forest Service actions regulating access to claims located within national forest lands must comply not only with the "means . . . customarily enjoyed" standard of 16 U.S.C. § 1134(b) and 36 C.F.R. § 228.15(c), and the "where essential" standard of 36 C.F.R. § 228.15(b), but also with the "materially interfere" standard of 30 U.S.C. § 612.

It is true our circuit has held that Forest Service regulation of activities on mining claims must comport with the standard set out in 30 U.S.C. § 612. *See United States v. Doremus,* 888 F.2d 630, 633 (9th Cir.1989) (upholding Forest Service requirement that claim holders obtain permit before beginning operations on grounds that such Forest Service regulation did not "materially interfere" with mining operation), *cert. denied,* 498 U.S. 1046, 111 S.Ct. 751, 112 L.Ed.2d 772 (1991). However, by its terms, 30 U.S.C. § 612 addresses only "use of *the surface of any ... mining claim* by the United States" (emphasis added). We see no basis for construing the statute as limiting Forest Service regulation of activities on national forest lands outside of the boundaries of the mining claim....

As you consider these excerpts, identify clearly the limits on the Forest Service's ability to restrict access to the mining sites and to regulate surface activities by the miners. Do you sense here something akin to a federal accommodation doctrine in the requirements that miners retain access to "essential" access routes and to those "customarily used"? And note the similarity of the "materially interferes" test with the test we saw applied to surface owner-resource user conflicts in *Mikesh v. Peters.*

3. *Severed minerals on federal lands: Duncan Energy Co. v. Forest Service.* The rights of mineral claimants on federal lands are perhaps greatest when the federal government buys land after the mineral rights have already been severed. What rights then does the government have, as proprietor and sovereign, to restrict use of the surface? The issue appeared in Duncan Energy v. U.S. Forest Service, 50 F.3d 584 (8th Cir. 1995). The dispute arose in North Dakota, where the governing precedent on property rights was supplied by *Kerbaugh, supra.* As a North Dakota landowner the Forest Service only had the right to insist that surface uses be "reasonably necessary" to the mining operation. The mining company asserted that these were the Service's only rights. The Forest Service insisted rather ambiguously that it had the power to regulate the land surface to the same extent as on other Forest lands, yet conceded "that it cannot deny access to or prohibit mineral development" and only had "the authority to determine the reasonable use of the federal surface." The court upheld the Forest Service's regulatory powers and required the mining company to follow Service permitting processes. The federal statutes that empowered the Forest Service to regulate preempted North Dakota property law, which gave miners unrestricted access to the land surface, subject to the "reasonably necessary" standard, once they have given the landowner twenty days' notice.

C. THE REASONABLE AND BENEFICIAL USE OF WATER

Our inquiry into the private ownership of discrete natural resources now turns to private rights in water under those legal systems in which water is allocated separately from land. What rights do water holders possess? How much protection do they enjoy against conflicting water users, given the interconnections of the hydrologic system? And what happens when private water owners collectively are overusing a water source?

The place to begin these questions is with the requirement that all water uses be "beneficial," and the similar rule applicable in many states that they also be "reasonable." Recall that a water user under the prior appropriation system gains a water right only if the water is actually diverted and applied to a beneficial use. If the water is not used beneficially, the water right never arises. And if a beneficial use is not maintained, then the water right is lost through abandonment or forfeiture. The requirement of a beneficial use, therefore, is a defining limit on the private right. What then does beneficial use mean, and does its meaning vary in place and time? To get to the heart of this system we also need to pay attention to the rights that come by being earlier in time. To what extent is it true, as the old saying goes, that first in time is first in right?

The following excerpt on water law comes from *Empire Lodge Homeowner's Association v. Moyer*, a 2001 ruling by the Colorado Supreme Court. It provides a useful background to the materials that follow and is worth reading with care:

> Prior appropriation water law is a property rights-based allocation and administration system that promotes multiple use of a finite resource for beneficial purposes. Accordingly, it fosters optimum use, efficient water management, and priority administration. *See* Santa Fe Trail Ranches Prop. Owners Ass'n v. Simpson, 990 P.2d 46, 54 (Colo.1999). The objective of the water law system is to guarantee security, assure reliability, and cultivate flexibility in the public and private use of this scarce and valuable resource. Security resides in the system's ability to identify and obtain protection for the right of water use. Reliability springs from the system's assurance that the right of water use will continue to be recognized and enforced over time. Flexibility emanates from the fact that the right of water use can be changed, subject to quantification of the appropriation's historic beneficial consumptive use and prevention of injury to other water rights.
>
> Colorado's prior appropriation system centers on three fundamental principles: (1) that waters of the natural stream, including surface water and groundwater tributary thereto, are a public resource subject to the establishment of public agency or private use rights in unappropriated water for beneficial purposes; (2) that water courts adjudicate the water rights and their priorities; and (3) that the State Engineer, Division Engineers, and Water Commissioners administer the waters of the natural stream in accordance with the judicial decrees and statutory provisions governing administration. *Santa Fe Trail Ranches,* 990 P.2d at 53–54, 58. . . .
>
> The property right we recognize as a Colorado water right is a right to use beneficially a specified amount of water, from the available supply of surface water or tributary groundwater, that can be captured, possessed, and controlled in priority under a decree, to the exclusion of all others not then in priority under a decreed water right. *Santa Fe Trail Ranches,* 990 P.2d at 53. "Water right" means a right to use in accordance with its priority a certain portion of the

waters of the state by reason of the appropriation of the same. § 37–92–103(12), 10 C.R.S. (2001). A water right is created when a person appropriates or initiates an appropriation of unappropriated water of a natural stream of the state. *Shirola v. Turkey Canon Ranch Ltd. Liab. Co.,* 937 P.2d 739, 748 (Colo.1997).

A right to use water of the natural stream arises from placing the unappropriated water to beneficial use; a conditional water right holds a place in the priority system to which the water right antedates in the event the appropriator places the unappropriated water to beneficial use. *Dallas Creek Water Co. v. Huey,* 933 P.2d 27, 35 (Colo.1997). Conditional water rights are subject to a requirement of reasonable diligence in actualizing the intended appropriation, and the applicant must file a diligence application six years after the entry of the prior conditional decree or diligence decree for an examination of reasonable diligence in completing the appropriation. § 37–92–304(4)(a)(I) & (III), 10 C.R.S. (2001); *Mun. Subdist. v. Chevron Shale Oil Co.,* 986 P.2d 918, 921 (Colo.1999). A decree for an absolute water right confirms that an appropriative right has vested and identifies the right's priority and amount. *Williams v. Midway Ranches Prop. Owners Ass'n,* 938 P.2d 515, 521 (Colo.1997).

Appropriation of natural stream waters is subject to administration in priority in accordance with judicial decrees determining the existence of water rights. *Aspen Wilderness Workshop, Inc. v. Hines Highlands Ltd. P'ship,* 929 P.2d 718, 724 (Colo.1996). A water right adjudication is a proceeding to determine the respective priorities of water rights on the stream system for purposes of administration. *City of Lafayette v. New Anderson Ditch Co.,* 962 P.2d 955, 960 (Colo.1998). Direct flow water rights and storage water rights are entitled to administration based on their priority, regardless of the type of beneficial use for which the appropriation was made. *People ex rel. Park Reservoir Co. v. Hinderlider,* 98 Colo. 505, 515, 57 P.2d 894, 898–99 (1936) (Butler, J., concurring). The applicant for issuance of a conditional decree bears the burden of demonstrating that there is unappropriated water available for the appropriation, taking into account the historic exercise of decreed water rights. *Bd. of County Comm'rs v. Crystal Creek Homeowners' Ass'n,* 14 P.3d 325, 333 (Colo.2000). In order to perfect the conditional right and obtain an absolute decree, the applicant must have: (1) captured, possessed, and controlled unappropriated water; and (2) placed the water to beneficial use. *City of Lafayette,* 962 P.2d at 961.

Water rights are decreed to structures and points of diversion. *Dallas Creek Water Co.,* 933 P.2d at 38. *But see Colo. River Water Conservation Dist. v. Colo. Water Conservation Bd.,* 197 Colo. 469, 475, 594 P.2d 570, 574 (1979) (establishing that, instead of identifying diversion points and structures, instream flow or lake level water rights identify stream segments or lakes for preservation of the environment to a reasonable degree). Priority, location of diversion at the source of supply, and amount of water for application to

elements of Ap water right

beneficial uses are the essential elements of the appropriative water right. *People ex rel. Simpson v. Highland Irrigation Co.,* 917 P.2d 1242, 1252 n. 17 (Colo.1996)....

This excerpt (written by Justice Hobbs, who also wrote the 2002 opinion in *Park County Commissioners v. Sportsmen's Ranch,* in chapter 2) presents the Colorado water law regime as a coherent, well-functioning whole. We have reason to wonder, though, whether the regime is not being oversold in the sense that its limits and internal conflicts are hidden from view.

In the first paragraph, Hobbs identifies the three goals of the system: security, reliability, and flexibility. We might wonder whether security and flexibility sometimes clash: security might well be greatest in a system that is highly inflexible. In the next paragraph we learn that water is "a public resource" yet is subject to "private use rights." Again, do we have a tension here that is glossed over? And is this related to the tension between secure private rights and the requirement that all water uses be beneficial? According to Hobbs, temporal priority is critical when shortages develop and not all water users can get water. Yet we can't be sure, can we, that the most senior uses will be the ones that promote the goal of "optimum use"? What if a junior water rights holder is engaged in a far more socially valuable water use than a senior one? Doesn't the temporal priority system in such a case interfere with optimum use?

Colorado is unusual in that it gets special water courts involved in adjudicating water rights claims and issuing decrees specifying the terms of valid rights. In other states this work is typically done by a state agency. Colorado also has (as we've seen quickly) a special "conditional water rights" category that allows a water user to lay claim of a water flow without actually applying it to a beneficial use—a bit like the pedis possessio rights of hardrock miners on federal lands. The water claimant must return to court from time to time to demonstrate that it is moving ahead with its diversion project with "reasonable diligence." If it fails to use reasonable diligence its conditional water right can end.

DEPARTMENT OF ECOLOGY v. GRIMES

121 Wash.2d 459, 852 P.2d 1044 (1993).

SMITH, JUSTICE

This matter is before the court upon direct review after we accepted certification from the Court of Appeals, Division Three, pursuant to RCW 2.06.030(d), raising the question of the legal definition of "reasonable use" of water as an element of "beneficial use" under the Water Code of 1917, RCW 90.03, the Water Resources Act of 1971, RCW 90.54, and other related statutes....

In September 1981, the Department of Ecology filed a petition in the Pend Oreille County Superior Court for clarification of existing rights to divert, withdraw, or otherwise make beneficial use of the surface and ground waters of the Marshall Lake and Marshall Creek drainage basin

(Marshall Lake basin). Ecology investigated the Marshall Lake basin and the locality served by it and found that the interests of the public and users of the surface and ground waters would be served by an adjudication and determination of the relative rights of all claimants to the use of these waters....

The Grimeses submitted five claims for water rights, only the first of which is at issue in this appeal. This claim was for the use of waters for domestic supply, irrigation and recreational purposes. The Grimeses requested an instantaneous flow rate of 3 cubic feet per second (c.f.s.) for irrigation purposes, and a storage right of 1,520 acre feet of water in the Marshall Lake reservoir. The referee recommended that this claim be confirmed, but limited it to an instantaneous flow of 1.5 c.f.s. during irrigation season, and a storage right of 183 acre feet plus 737 acre feet for evaporative loss, for a total storage right of 920 acre feet.... [Summary of lower court proceedings omitted.]

General Adjudication

A general adjudication is a special form of quiet title action to determine all existing rights to the use of water from a specific body of water. In Washington, the adjudication procedure is set forth in RCW 90.03.110 *et seq.* The provisions for adjudication in the Water Code, RCW 90.03.110–.245, may not be used to lessen, enlarge or modify existing water rights. An adjudication of water rights is only for the purpose of determining and confirming those rights. The surface water rights of the Grimeses in this case are pre–1917 rights, established 11 years before adoption of the Water Code of 1917 and 65 years before adoption of the Water Resources Act of 1971. Subsequent amendments to the 1917 Water Code have clearly stated that nothing in the act "shall affect or operate to impair any existing water rights." To confirm existing rights, the referee must determine two primary elements of a water right: (1) the amount of water that has been put to beneficial use and (2) the priority of water rights relative to each other....

The Doctrine of Prior Appropriation

The law of prior appropriation was established in this state by the Territorial Legislature in 1873 and recognized by this court in 1897. This court in *Neubert v. Yakima–Tieton Irrig. Dist.* said that "[t]he appropriated water right is perpetual and operates to the exclusion of subsequent claimants." In that case we said appropriative water rights require that:

> Once appropriated, the right to use a given quantity of water becomes appurtenant to the land. The appropriated water right is perpetual and operates to the exclusion of subsequent claimants. The key to determining the extent of plaintiffs' vested water rights is the concept of "beneficial use".... An appropriated water right is established and maintained by the purposeful application of a given quantity of water to a beneficial use upon the land. (Citations omitted.) *Neubert,* 117 Wash.2d at 237, 814 P.2d 199.

Beneficial use refers to the quantity of water diverted by the appropriator, not to its availability in the source of supply. "The underlying reason for all this constitutional, legislative and judicial emphasis on beneficial use of water lies in the relation of available water resources to the ever-increasing demands made upon them." "Beneficial use" is a term of art in water law, and encompasses two principal elements of a water right.

First, it refers to the purposes, or type of activities, for which water may be used. Use of water for the purposes of irrigated agriculture is a beneficial use. The Grimeses' use of water to irrigate alfalfa fields is not at issue in this case.

Second, beneficial use determines the measure of a water right. The owner of a water right is entitled to the amount of water necessary for the purpose to which it has been put, provided that purpose constitutes a beneficial use. To determine the amount of water necessary for a beneficial use, courts have developed the principle of "reasonable use". Reasonable use of water is determined by analysis of the factors of water duty and waste.

In his findings establishing the measure of the Grimeses' water right, the referee stated that:

> [A] valid right for irrigation purposes only exists for the benefit of these claimants and such right is derived from the original 1906 Linsley notice. It is, therefore, recommended that a right be confirmed to these defendants, with a July 13, 1906 priority for the irrigation of 73 acres from Marshall Lake. Quantification of the amount of water to which this right is entitled creates somewhat of a problem in that there has been no direct testimony regarding the amount of water placed to beneficial use other than a reference in the state's investigatory report that 56 sprinklers are utilized in the system.... Therefore, the Referee will allow the standard duty of water which would be 1.2 cubic feet per second plus an additional 25 percent for transportation loss, thus making an aggregate amount of 1.5 cubic feet per second identified with this right....

A second element concerning this right is the amount of storage of water to which these claimants are entitled.... [T]hese waters also have recreational benefits, not only to the riparian owners around the lake but also to the general public through the use of resort facilities located on the lake.... Therefore, the Referee recommends that a related but separate right be confirmed to these defendants for the storage of 920 acre-feet in Marshall Lake for irrigation and recreation purposes. The priority shall be fixed as of July 13, 1906. The period during which waters may be stored shall be identified as those periods of the year which do not include the April 1 to October 31 irrigation season.

The Grimeses challenge the referee's "consideration of the evidence" and his application of the law in making these findings. We first consider the evidence used by the referee in establishing the factors of water duty and waste. We then consider the test of "reasonable efficiency'' employed by the referee, and adopted by the Superior Court, to evaluate these factors.

Water Duty

"[Water duty] is that measure of water, which, by careful management and use, without wastage, is reasonably required to be applied to any given tract of land for such period of time as may be adequate to produce therefrom a maximum amount of such crops as ordinarily are grown thereon. It is not a hard and fast unit of measurement, but is variable according to conditions."

The referee based his determination of the volume of water necessary for irrigation in the Marshall Lake basin on a Washington State University Research Bulletin entitled "Irrigation Requirements for Washington—Estimates and Methodology" (Irrigation Report), and on the expert testimony of Jim Lyerla, the District Supervisor for seven Eastern Washington counties, including Pend Oreille County, in the Water Resources Program of the Department of Ecology. Mr. Lyerla testified that as a part of his work in assigning water quantities to new water permittees, he relied on the Irrigation Report to determine the "water duty" for a proposed use of water. The Irrigation Report provides information for water requirements for specific crops, given in inches per acre per irrigation season, in 40 locations around the state, including Newport, Washington, 5 miles south of Marshall Lake.

Based on the testimony of Mr. Lyerla and the Irrigation Report, the referee determined that an irrigated alfalfa crop grown in the Marshall Lake area requires 21 inches or 1.75 acre feet of water per acre during the irrigation season. The referee then applied an efficiency factor and increased this water duty to 2.5 acre feet per acre per year. The referee found this water duty to be "approximately commensurate with the duty utilized by the Department of Ecology in its quantity allocations in this geographic area under the water right permit system."

Because water rights are characterized in both total yearly allowance and instantaneous flow, the referee also established the maximum rate of diversion at 0.0166 c.f.s. per acre under irrigation. The referee first calculated a standard flow of 1 c.f.s. of water per 60 acres as a reasonable instantaneous flow for alfalfa irrigation in the Marshall Lake basin. In considering the Grimeses' claim, he determined that the Grimeses were entitled to sufficient flow to irrigate 73 acres, or a minimum of 1.21 c.f.s. He then calculated in an efficiency factor to increase this flow by 25 percent and awarded the Grimeses an instantaneous flow of 1.5 c.f.s.

The referee observed that a larger water duty could be awarded to any claimant with specific information proving a right to a larger amount. The 2.5 acre feet/0.0166 c.f.s. water duty was applied when "quantitative evidence of the rate and volume of a right was neither submitted nor made clear during testimony." The referee also observed that "the use of water under all irrigation rights is, however, limited to the amount of water that can be beneficially applied to that number of acres identified in the water right." The referee did not indiscriminately award this water duty to any claim for an irrigation right, but required claimants to prove the number of acres historically irrigated.

In water rights adjudications, the establishment of a water duty must not be disturbed in "the absence of very conclusive evidence contrary to the ... adjudication, showing arbitrariness on [the] part [of the adjudicator].... " The referee's determination of a generic water duty for irrigation of alfalfa in the Marshall Lake basin is supported by a preponderance of the evidence and will not be disturbed by this court.

Waste

From an early date, courts announced the rule that no appropriation of water was valid where the water simply went to waste. Those courts held that the appropriator who diverted more than was needed for the appropriator's actual requirements and allowed the excess to go to waste acquired no right to the excess. A particular use must not only be of benefit to the appropriator, but it must also be a reasonable and economical use of the water in view of other present and future demands upon the source of supply. The difference between absolute waste and economical use has been said to be one of degree only.

Appellant Clarence E. Grimes acknowledged in his testimony that his existing irrigation system required a water flow of up to 3 cubic feet per second in order to deliver 1 cubic foot per second to the field, and that this system was highly inefficient, causing one-half to two-thirds loss of water. Mr. Grimes also testified that uncertainties and ongoing litigation concerning the stability and safety of the irrigation dam had prevented continuous irrigation of his alfalfa acreage. Other claimants testified concerning their use of the water claimed.

While an appropriator's use of water must be reasonably efficient, absolute efficiency is not required. The referee determined that, pursuant to RCW 90.14.160, the uncertainties concerning the irrigation dam constituted sufficient cause not to find a complete abandonment of the Grimeses' water right. He resolved the conflicting testimony by limiting the irrigable acreage to the 73 acres recommended by Ecology. Relying on a standard efficiency factor for irrigation sprinkler systems found in the irrigation report, he confirmed in the Grimeses a water right with one-fourth conveyance loss for a total of 1.5 cubic feet per second. There was at least sufficient evidence for the referee to determine the maximum acreage to which the Grimeses' water right applied, and in limiting the allowable loss for system inefficiency in establishing their instantaneous flow.

The Reasonable Efficiency Test

In limiting the Grimeses' vested water right, the referee balanced several factors, including the water duty for the geographical area and crop under irrigation, the claimants' actual diversion, and sound irrigation practices. In his report, the referee described his method of calculating the Grimeses' water right as a "reasonable efficiency" test.

Amici curiae argue that this test is contrary to judicial decisions which have recognized that the standard of reasonable beneficial use of water for irrigation is limited to consideration of the use of the established means of diversion and application according to the reasonable custom of the locality. Respondent Ecology argues that the 3–part "reasonable efficiency" test cited by the referee provides "the balance sought by the courts between the competing needs of efficiency and maximum utilization of the water, and the existing physical and economic limitations in each situation." Ecology asserts that local custom in irrigation practices is but one of several factors the court must consider in deciding whether a given use of water is reasonable, and, therefore, beneficial.

While the referee stated that he relied on this test, and while he did in fact consider some of its elements, he did not actually utilize the test in its entirety. Therefore, we will review the factors he did consider to determine whether his analysis remained within the boundaries of prior appropriation law. In his discussion of the basis for his recommendation concerning the Grimeses' claim, the referee stated that he would "balance [the water duty] against not only the actual amount of water diverted from the lake for irrigation purposes but also against the concepts of beneficial use of water and sound irrigation practices."

Amici curiae urge this court to hold that only "the established means of diversion and application according to the reasonable custom of the locality" may be considered in defining reasonable use. This argument is based on the eminent domain provision of the state Water Code, which prohibits condemnation of a water right when the owner of that right is using the water:

> for the irrigation of his land then under irrigation to the full extent of the soil, by the most economical method of artificial irrigation applicable to such land according to the usual methods of artificial irrigation employed in the vicinity where such land is situated. In any case, the court shall determine what is the most economical method of irrigation.

This court has consistently held that rights of users of water for irrigation purposes are vested rights in real property. Amici curiae assert that the "local custom" test has been employed historically to determine whether given applications of water are wasteful, within the meaning of beneficial use, and that courts should now apply it in the setting of general adjudications. This is the established law in this state.

Decisions of courts throughout the western states provide a basis for defining "reasonable efficiency" with respect to irrigation practices. While customary irrigation practices common to the locality are a factor for consideration, they do not justify waste of water. As this court stated in a case predating the Water Code of 1917:

> [W]hen rights in such an important element as water is in the arid regions are to be measured by the courts, we cannot lay down a rule that would give to the user an arbitrary right to use water at will. [An irrigator's] rights are to be measured by his necessities . . . and not by any fanciful notion of his own. . . .
>
> . . . .
>
> . . . [C]ustom can fix the manner of use of water for irrigation only when it is founded on necessity . . . [and] an irrigator is entitled to use only so much as he can put to a beneficial use, for the public policy of the people of the United States will not tolerate waste of water in the arid regions.

Local custom and the relative efficiency of irrigation systems in common use are important elements, but must be considered in connection with other statutorily mandated factors, such as the costs and benefits of improvements to irrigation systems, including the use of public and private funds to facilitate improvements.

In limiting the Grimeses' water use by a requirement of reasonable efficiency, the referee properly considered the irrigation report, the Grimeses' actual water use, and their existing irrigation system. The referee alluded to a test incorporating factors that consider impacts to the water source and its flora and fauna. While consideration of these impacts is consonant with the State's obligations under RCW 90.03.005 and 90.54.010(1)(a) and (2), these factors cannot operate to impair existing water rights. Other laws may, however, operate to define existing rights in light of environmental values.

There is some confusion in the record as to the legal standard used by the referee in determining beneficial use. In his original report, the referee discussed determination of water duty. His proposed volume and rates of water were based upon exhibit 5 and expert testimony, when quantitative evidence of the rate and volume of a right was neither submitted nor made clear during testimony. There is no discussion in the original report of any "reasonable efficiency" test.

However, the referee rendered a supplemental report in response to exceptions taken by the Grimeses. In it he considered a storage right and made it clear that that right should not be confused with the diversion right of 1.5 c.f.s. But in a footnote the referee set forth a detailed "test of reasonable efficiency" which he purportedly used in determining beneficial use. That "test" is stated as follows:

> (1) [C]ustomary delivery and application practices in the area, (2) technology and "practices" improvements feasible and available to reduce water consumptions and financial needs associated with implementation thereof, and (3) impacts of improvements of existing facilities and practices, if initiated, upon (a) the water source from which the diversion takes place, (b) the existing flora and fauna within the area of diversion, conveyancy and actual uses, (c) other

water rights from said water source, and (d) other water users on other water sources.

There is nothing in the record to support the referee's statement that he employed the reasonable efficiency test. Nowhere in the record does he discuss application of the elements of the so-called "test". If he had in fact applied the "test", it would be necessary for this court to reverse and remand. That test is without statutory authorization in an adjudication proceeding which relates exclusively to confirmation of water rights established or created under "other provisions of state law or under federal laws."

Adjudication proceedings cannot be used "to lessen, enlarge, or modify the existing rights of any riparian owner, or any existing right acquired by appropriation, or otherwise." The suggested test would be contrary to the vested rights of water users. "It has long been settled in this state that property owners have a vested interest in their water rights to the extent that the water is beneficially used on the land." Included in the vested rights is the right to diversion, delivery and application "according to the usual methods of artificial irrigation employed in the vicinity where such land is situated." The Legislature sets a standard clearly contradictory to the suggested test in RCW 90.03.040, which relates to eminent domain over water rights. The test is contrary also to long established principles of Western water law.

While we reject use of the specific test suggested by the referee, we affirm because (1) there is no indication in the record that he in fact applied the factors stated in the "test", and (2) he applied the actual beneficial use made by Grimes, taking into account the actual needs and use and the methods of delivery and application in the vicinity. The adjudication and confirmation of a water right in an amount less than claimed by Grimes does not result from application of the so-called test. Rather, as the referee makes clear:

> Quantification of the amount of water to which this right is entitled creates somewhat of a problem in that there has been no direct testimony regarding the amount of water placed to beneficial use other than a reference in the state's investigatory report that 56 sprinklers are utilized in the system.

In the absence of such proof, the referee nevertheless confirmed the right by using a normal duty of water for the type of crops raised and specifically added 25 percent for transportation loss. Making the best of inadequate proof by the claimant, it appears from the record that the referee applied the usual methods of irrigation employed in the vicinity where the Grimeses' land is located.

The Takings Argument

Appellants Grimes argue that diminishment of their prior appropriation in any way is a "taking" of their property right for which they must be compensated or have the decision of the trial court set aside. A vested water right is a type of private property that is subject to the Fifth

Amendment prohibition on takings without just compensation. Nevertheless, the concept of "beneficial use," as developed in the common law and as described earlier in this opinion, operates as a permissible limitation on water rights.

RCW 90.14.160 provides for relinquishment of unused water rights. The statute provides that:

> Any person entitled to divert or withdraw waters of the state through any appropriation authorized by enactments of the legislature prior to enactment of chapter 117, Laws of 1917, or by custom, or by general adjudication, who abandons the same, or who voluntarily fails, without sufficient cause, to beneficially use all or any part of said right to divert or withdraw for any period of five successive years after the effective date of this act, shall relinquish such right or portion thereof, and said right or portion thereof shall revert to the state, and the waters affected by said right shall become available for appropriation in accordance with RCW 90.03.250.

Pursuant to RCW 90.14.160, Appellants Grimes were entitled to "divert or withdraw" the subject water. However, the referee's finding, which we will not disturb, that their voluntary failure, "without sufficient cause", to beneficially use all of the waters diverted requires that those waters "revert to the state . . . and . . . become available for appropriation". The Grimeses' claim that their water right has been partially "taken" without just compensation necessarily fails.

Conclusion

Although we agree with the conclusion reached by the referee in this case, we expressly reject the test he purportedly used.

Applying the concepts of "beneficial use" to water rights in this state, we rule on the merits and affirm the decision of the Pend Oreille County Superior Court, dated January 5, 1990, which substantially approved the conclusion of the referee relating to the water rights of Appellants Clarence E. and Peggy V. Grimes.

Notes

1. *The elements of a private water right. Grimes* together with the excerpts from *Empire Lodge* set forth the basic elements of a discrete water right under prior appropriation law. A water right is limited by actual use and further limited by the requirement that the water use be beneficial. Note carefully the various elements that make up the beneficial use limit on a water right in Washington:

   a. First, we are told, the term relates to the *type of use*—in this case agriculture. Apparently no one in the litigation claimed that the use of water to irrigate alfalfa (a hay crop) was not beneficial. In arid and semi-arid parts of the West, the vast bulk of all water is used for agriculture, much of it for low-valued crops such as alfalfa. The economic value of such uses is trivial compared with the value of water devoted to municipal and many industrial uses. Agricultural water uses vary greatly among themselves in terms of the economic value produced by the water use. Is it sensible for lawmakers to continue to sweep all agricultural uses into a single category and label them all beneficial, or has the time come to look at individual agricultural activities more closely and decide which ones are beneficial? Is it beneficial to use water to grow corn or cotton, both of which are in overabundant supply in the nation (and, indeed, a federal conservation program essentially pays landowners in the Midwest not to grow corn!)? To answer this question we need to grapple with another one: is beneficial determined by looking at the type of activity overall (growing corn, which is certainly beneficial) or do we examine particular land uses as instances of producers at the margin (that is, asking whether the extra amount of corn or hay produced by irrigators is beneficial, given the massive supply that comes from landowners who do not have to irrigate)?

b. Beneficial use, we're told, also refers to the *amount of water* "necessary" for the particular purpose. The amount necessary is limited by the idea of reasonable use, which in the case of irrigation is based on the "water duty" and the prohibition on "waste." How does the court define these two terms? Note that, in the case of water duty, the court looks to expert opinion as to the amount of water that ought to be necessary, not to the amount that the landowner actually used. As for waste, the court defines it based on the "reasonable and economical use of the water in view of other present and future demands upon the source of supply." Does this language propose a comparison among various possible uses of the same water? The language seems to suggest that it does, but we see no evidence of the court actually paying attention to other possible uses of this particular water. What factors does the court ultimately view as relevant, and how restrictive are they? How much deference does it give to local custom?

2. *General adjudication and the need to prove*. *Grimes* involved a special type of water litigation known as a general adjudication, which is a proceeding in which all parties claiming water from a particular water source are obligated to show up in court and prove their water rights. It is a day of reckoning for users who have shaky titles or who otherwise are claiming more water than they deserve based upon actual beneficial use. So long as a water use goes unchallenged, a user need not prove what she really owns. General adjudications can become extremely complex, and consume years of time, when they involve dozens or hundreds of water users and when junior users, anxious to move up in priority, are intent on challenging the factual claims made by senior users.

3. *The reasonable efficiency test*. A contentious issue in *Grimes* was whether a water user was obligated to use reasonable efficiency in the methods of water use. Why did this issue arouse the passions of the amicus parties in the case, and what was their objection to it? Is there something inherently dangerous about the idea that the law might require water users to pass such a test? The court makes clear that Washington law contains no such test, and thus water users need not abide by it. But why is this so?

4. *The issue in the closet.* Lurking behind the scenes in *Grimes* was an issue that the court seemed unwilling to express and address directly: Is beneficial use an evolving requirement that applies to existing water users as well as to newly initiated uses? Put otherwise, might a water use qualify as beneficial when it is begun, but later fail the test as the standard of beneficial use changes? If beneficial use is at all like the do-no-harm, reasonable use tests that we have seen applied to landed property rights, the question is easy to answer: yes, the test does change over time, and yes, property owners need to abide by it or risk having their property uses halted. Note that in some ways the test as applied in *Grimes* clearly does evolve over time. The definition of waste clearly looks to current irrigation methods, not irrigation methods used when the appellants' water uses began in 1906. But what the type of water use? Might a water use that seems socially useful at one time become socially wasteful a century later? Then, too, we have the court's express statement that waste is linked to "other present and future demands upon the source of supply." Can this factor receive weight without forcing water users to change their ways over time?

IMPERIAL IRRIGATION DISTRICT v. STATE WATER RESOURCES CONTROL BOARD

225 Cal.App.3d 548, 275 Cal.Rptr. 250 (1990).

FROEHLICH, ASSOCIATE JUSTICE.

This is an appeal from a judgment denying the petition for writ of mandate brought by Imperial Irrigation District (IID) to overturn a decision of the State Water Resources Control Board (Board).

PROCEDURAL BACKGROUND AND STANDARDS FOR REVIEW

In 1980 a private citizen requested the Department of Water Resources to investigate alleged misuse of water by IID which had resulted in a rise in the level of the Salton Sea, flooding the citizen's farmland. After an investigation, an initial conclusion of water waste, and unproductive communications with IID, the Department of Water Resources referred the matter to the Board for investigation and action. The Board held a hearing which encompassed a period of six days late in 1983, taking testimony and receiving evidence from a number of sources including the original complaining citizen, the Department of Water Resources, IID, a number of other governmental agencies, and the intervener herein, the Environmental Defense Fund, Inc.

On June 21, 1984, the Board issued its Decision Regarding Misuse of Water by Imperial Irrigation District, designated Decision 1600 (hereafter sometimes referred to as "Board Decision") which consisted of a 71–page review of the history of the proceedings, the evidence taken by the Board, the Board's findings and conclusions, and an order requiring certain action be taken by IID. The Board gave reconsideration to its decision upon the request of several parties, including IID. By order dated September 20, 1984, all modifications sought were denied and the previous decision was affirmed....

Posture of Appeal

As IID concedes in its brief, the essential facts of this case are not in dispute. The experts on any particular issue were never in complete agreement, but their differences were of degree, not kind. For instance, estimates of water lost through "canal spill" ranged from 53,000 to 135,000 acre feet per annum; and water lost through excessive "tailwater" ranged from 312,000 to 559,000 acre feet per annum. There was no dispute, however, that very large quantities of water in each case were being lost. The dispute is whether such loss (and this is but one example of such decisions made by the Board) was or was not reasonable....

IID's assertions principally attack the conclusions of law made by the Board, as the same were approved by the trial court. We are therefore required to consider whether the Board's determinations, contained in Decision 1600, are sustainable in terms of its jurisdiction, its interpretation of statutes and regulations, and its legal conclusions.

In this regard we note that the very same Decision 1600 was before this court previously, in *Imperial I, supra,* 186 Cal.App.3d 1160, 231 Cal.Rptr. 283. Our court at that time, citing existing statutory and judicial precedent, ruled that the Board had full authority to exercise adjudicatory and regulatory functions in the field of water law (*id.* at p. 1165, 231 Cal.Rptr. 283); that it had "broad authority to control and condition water use, insuring utilization consistent with public interest" (*id.* at p. 1166, 231 Cal.Rptr. 283); that in such adjudication the Board could consider the interests of concerned persons who might not be parties to court action (*id.* at p. 1167, 231 Cal.Rptr. 283); that article X, section 2 of the Constitution requires that all uses of water conform to a standard of reasonable use, and that the Board has a duty to ensure this mandate (*id.* at p. 1168, 231 Cal.Rptr. 283); that the Board's adjudicatory authority is "all-encompassing" (*id.* at p. 1169, 231 Cal.Rptr. 283); and that the Board *shall* take all necessary action in executive, legislative and judicial forums to prevent waste and unreasonable water use. (*Ibid.*)

Our effort to summarize the contentions [in this appeal] results in the following outline of issues:

1. Did the Board err in the definition and exercise of its jurisdiction? Specifically:

(a) Since the Legislature has never set standards for the reasonableness of use of irrigation water, but has left the same for the determination of local agencies, does the Board have the power to establish standards of reasonableness?

(b) Does the Board have power to interfere with vested water rights?

(c) Is the Board's action a violation of the separation of powers doctrine?

2. Assuming the Board acted within its jurisdiction, did it err in the exercise and application of its adjudicatory powers? Specifically:

(d) Did the Board apply the correct measure of deference to the determinations of IID, considering that IID acted in a legislative capacity and its determinations should be reversed only upon a finding of abuse of discretion?

(e) Assuming the Board can adjudicate controversies between disputant water users, does it have any right to investigate and regulate water use of a user when no controversy with any other user is evident, for the benefit of unidentified and undetermined future users who are not within the IID district?

(f) Is the Board's conclusion that IID's water use is beneficial, and reasonable, consistent with its finding of water waste?

(g) Is there anything in the specific order contained in Decision 1600 which exceeds reason or the bounds of the Board's discretion?

DISCUSSION

1. *Jurisdiction*

(a) *Power to Establish Standards of Reasonableness*

Decision 1600 constitutes a comprehensive in-depth study of the water use practices of IID and its customers, and reaches the conclusion that certain practices of IID are wasteful of water and hence unreasonable and a misuse of water in violation of article X, section 2 of the California Constitution and section 100 of the California Water Code.[3] Relying on its own administrative regulations (Cal.Code Regs., tit. 23, § 4000 et seq.) the Board concluded it had the power to conduct hearings and to determine whether IID's water use was reasonable or wasteful.

IID challenges the Board's basic assertion of jurisdiction. IID admits that water use by Constitution and statute must be reasonable, but contends that insofar as use of water for irrigation purposes is concerned the Legislature either expressly or impliedly has left the decision as to what is reasonable to local agencies, such as IID, thus precluding the Board from entering this decision-making field. IID's argument is largely reliant on absence from statutes of any specific delegation of this power to the Board, and is bolstered by the citing of miscellaneous examples of the Legislature's handling of related issues.... [The court concluded that IID's citations were not on point, and that the Board did have the jurisdiction it asserted. The court proceeded to reiterate the conclusions

3. Article X, section 2 provides: "It is hereby declared that because of the conditions prevailing in this State the general welfare requires that the water resources of the State be put to beneficial use to the fullest extent of which they are capable, and that the waste or unreasonable use or unreasonable method of use of water be prevented, and that the conservation of such waters is to be exercised with a view to the reasonable and beneficial use thereof in the interest of the people and for the public welfare. The right to water or to the use or flow of water in or from any natural stream or water course in this State is and shall be limited to such water as shall be reasonably required for the beneficial use to be served, and such right does not and shall not extend to the waste or unreasonable use or unreasonable method of use or unreasonable method of diversion of water...."

about jurisdiction set forth in its earlier ruling.] We repeat in very summary form that:

> (1) By statute (§ 174) the Board "shall exercise the adjudicatory and regulatory functions of the state in the field of water resources."
>
> (2) The Board " 'has been granted broad authority to control and condition water use ... [extending] to regulation of water quality and prevention of waste.' " (Citing *Environmental Defense Fund, Inc. v. East Bay Mun. Utility Dist.* (1977) 20 Cal.3d 327, 341–342, 142 Cal.Rptr. 904, 572 P.2d 1128.)
>
> (3) The Board's duties and rights include ensuring compliance with the mandate of article X, section 2 of the Constitution, which requires that "*All* uses of water ... must now conform to the standard of reasonable use." (Citing *National Audubon Society v. Superior Court* (1983) 33 Cal.3d 419, 443, 189 Cal.Rptr. 346, 658 P.2d 709.)
>
> (4) It was the intent of the Legislature to grant the Board broad, open-ended, expansive authority to undertake comprehensive planning and allocation of water resources. (Citing and quoting *In re Waters of Long Valley Creek Stream System* (1979) 25 Cal.3d 339, 348–349, 158 Cal.Rptr. 350, 599 P.2d 656.) . .

We conclude the Board had jurisdiction to rule on the question whether irrigation practices of IID were reasonable or wasteful.

(b) Interference With Vested Rights

Water used by IID and its customers is diverted from the Colorado River. Diversion instrumentalities, including dams, power plants and the All–American Canal, which brings water from the river to the Imperial Valley, were authorized by the Boulder Canyon Project Act, enacted December 21, 1928. (43 U.S.C., § 617 et seq.) The Boulder Canyon Project Act vested in the Secretary of the Interior the power to enter into contracts for the delivery and allocation of water to users in the southwestern United States. The several interested states were unable to come to an agreement as to water allocation, and their entitlements were finally resolved by the United States Supreme Court in 1963. (*Arizona v. California* (1963) 373 U.S. 546, 83 S.Ct. 1468, 10 L.Ed.2d 542.) Allocation of Colorado River water among users in Southern California was achieved through mutual agreement, however. The agreement, termed the "California Seven–Party Agreement," was executed on August 18, 1931, and remains in effect. Amount of entitlement and priority of distribution to IID are established in this agreement.

IID's water rights, therefore, are the result of federal statute, U.S. Supreme Court decision, and a seven-party agreement allocating water among Southern California users. Water rights within the state of California traditionally were derived from riparian rights or entitlement based upon prior appropriation. (See historical discussion in *United States v. State Water Resources Control Bd.* (1986) 182 Cal.App.3d 82,

100–102, 227 Cal.Rptr. 161.) It is conceivable that IID's water rights, based as they are upon a unique blend of statutory and contractual origins, could be characterized as somehow more stable or securely vested than water rights from traditional sources. IID does not, however, make this claim. It simply contends that a right to use water, no matter how derived, once vested, becomes a property right which cannot be undermined without due compensation.

Illustrative of IID's broad contention is the following quote from *United States v. State Water Resources Control Bd., supra,* at page 101, 227 Cal.Rptr. 161: "It is . . . axiomatic that once rights to use water are acquired, they become vested property rights. As such, they cannot be infringed by others or taken by governmental action without due process and just compensation." The essence of IID's contention, therefore, is that the Board was without power to deprive IID of its discretionary power of determination of water use without providing compensation (which the Board admittedly has no power to provide).

As a preliminary matter we should note exactly what the Board did require of IID. The principal mandate contained in the Board Decision was an injunction that IID develop and present a water conservation plan. The trial court in its memorandum of decision noted that "except for requiring the District to repair defective tailwater structures, Decision 1600 itself requires no specific conservation measures, nor does it compel IID to sell, transfer, or otherwise convey water to the Metropolitan Water District or any other party. Decision 1600 simply requires the District to prepare plans to remedy its misuse of water, while retaining jurisdiction to review the adequacy of IID's plans."

We are unable, however, to agree that Decision 1600 did not substantially erode IID's otherwise virtually complete control over its water use. IID was required within a period of eight months to submit a plan for reservoir construction and to affirm its intent to construct one reservoir per year. Once a general plan of water conservation was achieved, IID was required to submit progress reports every six months "until the objectives have been achieved." The board reserved jurisdiction to monitor IID progress and to "take such other action" as might be required to assure compliance with an approved plan. There can be no doubt that the Board's intrusion into IID's previously untrammeled administration of the use of water in its district was substantial. As often stated in water law cases, "what is meant by a water right is the right to *use* the water. . . . " (*Id.* at p. 100, 227 Cal.Rptr. 161.) While the Board's decision in no way interfered with IID's contractual and statutory entitlement to Colorado River water, it most certainly presaged an interference with IID's utilization of that water once it traversed the All–American Canal.

Our conclusion that the Board Decision substantially impacted the practical use and administration by IID of its water does not, however, result in our acceptance of IID's contention of unconstitutional interference with "vested" rights. Historic concepts of water "rights" in California were dramatically altered by the adoption in 1928 of the above referenced constitutional amendment. (*Id.* at pp. 105, 106, 227 Cal.Rptr. 161.) Our Supreme Court, in *Gin S. Chow v. City of Santa Barbara* (1933) 217 Cal. 673, 22 P.2d 5, acknowledged that the new provision altered previously vested rights.

> "As already observed the amendment purports only to regulate the use and enjoyment of a property right for the public benefit, for which reason the vested right theory cannot stand in the way of the operation of the amendment as a police measure. A vested right cannot be asserted against it because of conditions once obtaining. [Citation.] It has been long established that all property is held subject to the reasonable exercise of the police power and that constitutional provisions declaring that property shall not be taken without due process of law have no application in such cases" (*Id.* at p.703, 22 P.2d 5.) . . .

Put simply, IID does not have the vested rights which it alleges. It has only vested rights to the "reasonable" use of water. It has no right to waste or misuse water. The interference by the Board with IID's misuse (this finding of fact by the Board being accepted for purposes of the present issue) does not constitute a transgression on a vested right.

Only right to reasonable use of water not waste or misuse of it

(c) Violation of Separation of Powers Doctrine

IID argues that its administration of its district's water use, including regulations governing tailwater management, canal spills, etc., is legislative in nature. Apparently presuming that the actions of the Board were adjudicatory and hence "judicial" in nature, IID claims a breach of the separation of powers doctrine.

> "The separation of powers doctrine establishes that none of the coordinate branches of our tripartite government may exercise power vested in another branch. Article III, section 3, of the California Constitution provides: 'The powers of state government are legislative, executive, and judicial. Persons charged with the exercise of one power may not exercise either of the others except as permitted by this Constitution.' " (*Estate of Cirone* (1987) 189 Cal.App.3d 1280, 1286, 234 Cal.Rptr. 749.)

separation of powers doctrine

IID contends that the decisions related to its administration of water use in its district are discretionary legislative decisions reserved by law to its board of directors. IID admits that the Board, as an adjudicatory body, has the power to resolve disputes in California relating to water rights. It contends, however, that the Board here has gone far beyond dispute resolution. In its Decision 1600 (as well as its subsequent Order WR 88–20, which IID asks us to notice although it is subsequent to the decision giving rise to this appeal), the Board has gone well beyond the adjudication of any controversy. It has in fact, IID claims, engaged in the adoption of injunctive-type relief imposing upon IID the obligation of construction of capital improvements, adoption of new water use regulations, and probably the assessment of additional charges to its users. . . .

Claim — gone beyond adjudication

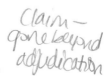

The separation of powers doctrine has also been applied to restrict judicial tampering with the legislative prerogatives of administrative agencies.... [The court concluded that the Board's conduct did not violate separation of powers.]

did not violate sep. of powers

CONCLUSION AND DISPOSITION

We note from IID's brief that it has "engaged for three decades in costly and critical litigation about its water rights." It asks that we reverse all the lengthy deliberations that have preceded our hearing and requests even again an "opportunity to more extensively brief the issue."

All things must end, even in the field of water law. It is time to recognize that this law is in flux and that its evolution has passed beyond traditional concepts of vested and immutable rights. In his review of our Supreme Court's recent water rights decision in *In re Water of Hallett Creek Stream System* (1988) 44 Cal.3d 448, 243 Cal. Rptr. 887, 749 P.2d 324, Professor Freyfogle explains that California is engaged in an evolving process of governmental redefinition of water rights. He concludes that "California has regained for the public much of the power to prescribe water use practices, to limit waste, and to sanction water transfers." He asserts that the concept that "water use entitlements are clearly and permanently defined," and are "neutral [and] rule-driven," is a pretense to be discarded. It is a fundamental truth, he writes, that "everything is in the process of changing or becoming" in water law....

In affirming this specific instance of far-reaching change, imposed upon traditional uses by what some claim to be revolutionary exercise of adjudicatory power, we but recognize this evolutionary process, and urge reception and recognition of same upon those whose work in the practical administration of water distribution makes such change understandably difficult to accept.

Notes

1. *Issue of law or fact?* A highly practical consideration in litigation involving the beneficial-use and reasonable-use limits of water law is whether they are issues of fact, issues of law or some mixture of both. The answer to this question can greatly affect how much deference a trial court finding receives when it is subject to appellate review. The issue arose in *In re Drainage Area of Utah Lake v. Pinecrest Pipeline*, 98 P.3d 1 (Utah 2004). The court analyzed beneficial use, as a trial court determination, under the three-part test it had announced in a 1998 ruling, *State v. Pena*. As it applied the *Pena* three-factor test to determine how much deference a trial-court ruling was due, the court also commented on the nature of the beneficial-use limit:

> We begin with the first *Pena* consideration, which requires us to evaluate the complexity and variety of possible factual issues. In this regard, we note that beneficial use determinations rely heavily on the

facts and circumstances of each case, with the underlying facts varying significantly in each dispute. This variety of factual scenarios supports a broad, rather than narrow, grant of discretion to the finder of fact. *See Dep't of Human Servs. ex rel. Parker v. Irizarry,* 945 P.2d 676, 678 (Utah 1997) ("The variety of fact-intensive circumstances involved [in equitable estoppel cases] weighs heavily against lightly substituting our judgment for that of the trial court. Therefore, we properly grant the trial court's decision a fair degree of deference when we review the mixed question of whether the requirements of the law of estoppel have been satisfied in any given factual situation."); *Kohler v. Martin,* 916 P.2d 910, 912 (Utah Ct.App.1996) ("When the decisions are more fact-dependent, or when the credibility of the witnesses has a strong bearing on the decision, broader discretion is generally granted to the trial court.").

In addition, we note that the concept of beneficial use is not static. Rather, it is susceptible to change over time in response to changes in science and values associated with water use. Janet C. Neuman, *Beneficial Use, Waste, and Forfeiture: The Inefficient Search for Efficiency in Western Water Use,* 28 Envtl. L. 919, 942 (1998) (" 'What is a beneficial use, of course, depends upon the facts and circumstances of each case. What may be a reasonable beneficial use, where water is present in excess of all needs, would not be a reasonable beneficial use in an area of great scarcity and great need. What is a beneficial use at one time may, because of changed conditions, become a waste of water at a later time.' " (quoting *Imperial Irrigation Dist. v. State Water Res. Control Bd.,* 225 Cal.App.3d 548, 570, 275 Cal.Rptr. 250 (1990) (further citation omitted))); *id.* at 946 ("Beneficial use is a somewhat flexible concept, changing over time to accommodate developments in thinking about water use, such as changes in science and values."). Accordingly, beneficial use "must remain a flexible and workable doctrine." *Jeffs,* 970 P.2d at 1245 (applying the *Pena* considerations to unjust enrichment rulings and granting trial courts broad discretion).

The second *Pena* consideration requires us to evaluate the relative novelty of the applicable legal principle. In examining this consideration, we note that the doctrine of beneficial use has roots dating back to the turn of the last century. *See* Neuman, 28 Envtl. L. at 920–21. However, our cases and statutes addressing beneficial use have generally used the term without defining it and have failed to identify any standard factors to be considered in evaluating whether a particular use is beneficial. Stated in terms of the *Pena* metaphor, trial judges in this state confront a pasture that has yet to be narrowly fenced in individual determinations of beneficial use. *See Pena,* 869 P.2d at 937–38 (analogizing the extent of a trial judge's discretion to a pasture that diminishes in size as it is "fenced" by existing laws and clarifications by appellate courts). Consequently, this consideration also supports a relatively broad grant of discretion to the trial court. *See Carrier,* 944 P.2d at 352 (granting limited discretion to a trial court's rule 47(c) decisions because, in part, this court had already "fenced off many scenarios that might arise in such cases," and few possible scenarios remained).

The third *Pena* consideration emphasizes the special ability of trial courts to weigh contradictory evidence from witnesses, assess credibility and demeanor, and make factual findings. 869 P.2d at 939; *Jeffs,* 970 P.2d at 1245. As previously mentioned, beneficial use determinations are generally dependent on the trial court's findings of fact. The same is true in the case now before us, and this consideration thus weighs in favor of our granting broad discretion to the trial judge in determining whether BCWDC put its water to beneficial use.

While the first three *Pena* considerations suggest that the trial court's determination of beneficial use is entitled to broad discretion, we must also consider whether any countervailing policy reason dictates a contrary result. Such a policy reason exists in this case. We have repeatedly recognized the importance of insuring that the waters of our state are put to beneficial use. *See, e.g., Eskelsen v. Town of Perry,* 819 P.2d 770, 775–76 (Utah 1991) ("[T]he state is . . . vitally interested in seeing that none of the waters are allowed to run to waste or go without being applied to a beneficial use for any great number of years." (quotation and citation omitted)); *Wayman v. Murray City Corp.,* 23 Utah 2d 97, 458 P.2d 861, 863 (1969) ("Because of the vital importance of water in this arid region both our statutory and decisional law have been fashioned in recognition of the desirability and of the necessity of insuring the highest possible development and of the most continuous beneficial use of all available water with as little waste as possible.").

In view of the importance of beneficial use determinations in this state, we hold that the discretion afforded to the trial court should be somewhat narrowed. In *Pena,* we described a "spectrum of discretion . . . running from 'de novo' on the one hand to 'broad discretion' on the other." 869 P.2d at 937. In beneficial use determinations, the appropriate degree of deference to the trial court falls somewhere between the two ends of the spectrum. Accordingly, in reviewing the trial court's ruling on beneficial use, we will afford the trial court significant, though not broad, discretion.

2. *Dynamic right v. redefinition v. taking.* How can we best describe in functional terms what the state water board is doing in this case? The IID took the view that the board was depriving it of a secure property right. By insisting that it change its water use practices, in ways that would save water (enough water, we might note, to meet the household needs of some 2 million people!), the board was taking away a right vested under state law and protected by the Constitution. How else might we characterize the board's actions?

One possibility is to say that the board is redefining the property right, exercising a functioning that common law courts exercised for generations. Just as courts kept the common law up to date by tinkering with the elements of private rights, so too the board is performing that function in the case of private rights in water.

Another possibility is to say that the property right that the IID possessed had a dynamic element built into it. The property right limited uses of water to those that were both reasonable and beneficial. As we saw in the last chapter, we can apply such vague terms only by looking to the ideas and values that prevail in the present. The law has long defined private rights in terms of reasonable use, and reasonable has always drawn its content by looking to circumstances and understandings at the time of the adjudication. Thus, whether a water right is reasonable in 1991 is properly determined in light of values and understandings widely shared in 1991, not values and understandings that prevailed generations ago. This perspective is well entrenched in property law generally. Is there a reason why a different understanding should prevail in the case of water rights? Does the fact that water rights are defined precisely, and often quite narrowly in terms of place and nature of use, give cause to adopt a different understanding?

3. *Is a more moderate remedy needed*? The beneficial-use limit is, of course, a specific application of the reasonable-use principle that applies to private property generally. Yet, as courts explain, water is no ordinary resource. It is exceptionally important in parts of the country that are arid or semi-arid. All life depends on it. There is thus a greater social interest in ensuring that water is not wasted or applied to uses that are less then socially optimal. In the case of most resources, we rely upon the market to shift the resources to more highly valued uses. In the case of water, however, the market is less able to bring about such shifts (as we'll see in chapter 7). The problem is that the water rights of one person are often tightly squeezed into a water-use regime in such a way that a user cannot readily make changes in either the place or nature of a water use without harming other people. When water is very short in supply, a water user may have only limited ability to shift water to a new use. The problem is heightened when the new use will take place elsewhere and when it involves diverting water from another location along the river. Changing the place and nature of a water use can greatly affect other water users and can easily and wrongfully interfere with their rights.

What happens, then, when a court (or, as in the above case, a state agency) decides that a given water use is wasteful or otherwise not beneficial? What happens to the water right? Under the literal elements of water law, a water user has no right to use water in a non-beneficial way (or, in California, a non-reasonable way). A non-beneficial water use can therefore be halted immediately. In addition, a water rights holder who goes five years without using water beneficially (the time period varies among states) can lose it under forfeiture statutes or common law abandonment (considered in the next chapter). Note that in this case, however, the state agency is vastly more lenient toward the IID. It could have asserted aggressively that the IID has already lost its rights in the water it was wasting. Instead, the agency merely demanded that the IID come up with a conservation plan. On the surface the board might seem to act boldly, but in fact it pulled its punches—it questioned the reasonableness of the water use, but then did not propose to impose the harsh penalty for forfeiture that normally goes along with that conclusion.

Why might the IID have acted so cautiously? Political realities, no doubt, were important, plus the board likely wanted the IID to have time to make needed changes. Might these considerations, though, apply in the case of many other water disputes? Courts have been highly reluctant to conclude that particular water uses are unreasonable or nonbeneficial, perhaps because the penalty of forfeiture is so harsh. Would they be more likely to do so if a less harsh remedy were available—if they could, for instance, do something akin to what the board did with the IID? Courts might challenge inefficient water uses more regularly if they could, by way of remedy, give the water rights holder a certain period of time in which to improve the water use to make it lawful or sell the water to someone who can use it properly.

4. *Protections for senior users.* A basic element of prior appropriation is that junior users cannot take water if a senior user is not getting his fill. As to the practical application of that rule, consider the following case:

STATE EX REL. CARY v. COCHRAN

138 Neb. 163, 292 N.W. 239 (1940).

CARTER, JUSTICE

This is an action of mandamus brought by a number of irrigators under the Kearney canal, on behalf of themselves and others similarly situated, and by the Central Power Company, which, with the exception of one small user of water, is the owner of the oldest water appropriation on the Platte river and its tributaries. The respondents are the governor, the state engineer, and the chief of the bureau of irrigation and his subordinates. The petition prays for the issuance of a writ of mandamus compelling the proper administration and enforcement of the irrigation laws of the state for the purpose of protecting the irrigation and power rights of the relators from alleged unlawful diversions of water above relators' canal by junior appropriators. . . .

It is not disputed that the waters of the Platte river and its tributaries are subject to appropriation for irrigation and power purposes upon the principle that priority of time bestows priority of right, and that pursuant to such principle the Central Power Company, through its predecessors in interest, was adjudicated and given a priority upon the Platte river, as of September 10, 1882, of 140 cubic feet per second of flow of water for power purposes, and a further appropriation, as of February 12, 1920, of 485 cubic feet per second for the same purposes. It is also admitted by the pleadings that 22 second-feet of water have been adjudicated to certain lands in Buffalo county for irrigation purposes with a priority dating of September 10, 1882, and which, for the purposes of this suit, will be treated as the property of certain of the relators claiming to be the owners thereof in this litigation. The forego-ing appropriations of water, bearing the priority dating of September 10, 1882, are prior in time to all appropriations on the Platte river and its tributaries in Nebraska, except an appropriation to the Nelson Radcliffe canal in Morrill county with a priority dating of June 1, 1882, for 2.77 cubic feet of water per second of time.

The Central Power Company, in reliance upon its adjudicated water rights, reconstructed and rebuilt its power plant and diversion dam, and installed new machinery, appliances and equipment at a cost of $225,000 or more, to make it of sufficient capacity to beneficially use water to which it was entitled under its appropriations adjudicated and allowed as of September 10, 1882, and February 12, 1920. The remaining relators are owners of land in Buffalo county, which is irrigable and irrigated from the waters carried in the Central Power Company canal during the irrigation season, said water being the 22 second-feet adjudicated to certain lands in Buffalo county under the priority dating of September 10, 1882, and appurtenant to said lands subject only to the payment of a carrying charge to the Central Power Company. That relators have constructed laterals leading to and upon their respective lands, and made beneficial use of all of the 22 cubic feet per second of flow under their appropriation whenever it was available in the river, is alleged in the petition. For the purposes of this suit only, this allegation will be considered as true.

The respondents, as officers, agents and employees of the bureau of irrigation, are charged by law with the duty of the administration and enforcement of the irrigation laws of the state and the distribution of the waters of the Platte river and its tributaries within the state in accordance with adjudicated priorities. It is the contention of relators that respondents, in administering and enforcing the irrigation laws of the state and in the distribution of water for irrigation, have continuously permitted and allowed junior appropriators, situated above the headgate of the Central Power Company, to take and use water for irrigation, storage, and other purposes, without regard to priority and to the prejudice and damage of the relators. . . .

It will be noted that the priority date of the appropriation of 140 cubic feet per second of flow for power purposes is September 10, 1882. The appropriation of 22 cubic feet per second for irrigation purposes bears the same priority date. Under the holdings of this court, these water rights became vested as of that date. . . . For all practical purposes, relators have an appropriation of 162 second-feet of water with a priority dating of September 10, 1882, as against all junior appropriators on the stream whether for irrigation or power purposes.

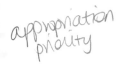

The North Platte river is a nonnavigable stream which has its source in the mountains of Colorado and flows across a part of Wyoming and Nebraska to a point approximately 200 miles from the Wyoming–Nebraska line, where it joins the South Platte river to form the Platte river. The present case involves the administration of irrigation and power rights on the North Platte and Platte rivers from the Wyoming–Nebraska line to the headgate of the Kearney canal located 13 miles west of Kearney, Nebraska. The water discharged into the Platte river from the South Platte river also has its place in the problem before us, but it does not appear to have been treated as of major importance by the parties in the present suit. The North Platte and Platte rivers will therefore be treated as the primary subject of the litigation. For the purposes of this suit, the upper end of the river is at the Wyoming–Nebraska line and the lower end at the headgate of the Kearney canal, it being the last point of diversion for irrigation and power purposes on the river.

The flow of the river even in the summer months is affected by the amount of snow falling in the mountains of Colorado within its drainage basin. The river passes through parts of Colorado and Wyoming, both of which states require irrigation water in excess of the available supply. Storage and control dams under the control of the federal government also exist along the river west of the point where the river enters Nebraska. Water rights, both senior and junior to existing rights and priorities in Nebraska, coupled with the uncertainty of their accurate administration, add to the indefiniteness of the amount of water that passes at any given time across the state line and under the control of the administrative officers of this state.

Losses from evaporation and transpiration are heavy, due to the wide and shallow character of the river. Changes of temperature and varying types of wind add to the uncertainty of the losses resulting from these changing conditions. Losses from percolation vary along the various sectors of the river. The evidence shows that the river valley from the Wyoming–Nebraska line to North Platte or thereabouts is underlaid with impervious formations which do not permit losses of subterranean waters into other watersheds. At some unknown point between North Platte and Gothenburg, the river cuts through the impervious formations and runs into the sheets of sand and gravel with which the territory is underlaid. Losses begin to occur at this point due to the percolation of river water through this sand and gravel formation, in a southeasterly direction into the basin of the Republican river. It was estimated by Professor A. L. Lugn, an expert on geology, stratigraphy and ground-water hydrology, that the loss of the Republican river basin would be from 50,000 to 100,000 acrefeet of water each year. It is true that a large part of this loss occurs below the headgate of relators' canal. This estimate is recited for the purpose of giving some idea of the nature and degree of the loss, without any hope of accurately measuring such losses occurring above the headgate of the Kearney canal. Experts with experience on the river estimate that the loss in delivering water from North Platte to the headgate of the Kearney canal with a wet river bed amounts to three times the amount of delivery, and with a dry river bed that it is almost impossible to get water through without a flood or a large sustained flow. In other words, it requires approximately 700 second-feet of water at North Platte to deliver 162 second-feet at the headgate of the Kearney canal when the river bed is wet. The underlying sand and gravel beds thicken as the river moves east. With the bed of the river on the surface of these sand and gravel deposits, it requires a huge amount of water to recharge the river channel and surrounding water table after the river bed once becomes dry. Until the water table is built up to the surface of the river bed, the river channel will not support a continuous flow. It is also shown that the water table has been affected materially by pump irrigation. It was estimated that there are 500 irrigation pumps in Dawson county alone, which pump as much as 40,000 acre-feet of water in a single season. The evidence bears out the statement that the Platte river east of Gothenburg is a very inefficient carrier of water. In addition to the subterranean losses noted, the river spreads out, causing a broad surface of water and channel bed to be subjected to large evaporation losses. It is further established by early settlers along the river that it was not unusual for the river to go dry in July and August before irrigation was generally practiced along the river. That the river is generally considered a gaining stream, and can be so established by an examination of the statistical records of the mean flow for the calendar year, is borne out by the record. But it is just as clearly shown that the river is ordinarily a losing stream during the months of July and August, when the mean flow for that period is considered. These conditions and activities establish the cause of the huge losses of water between Gothenburg and the Kearney canal. They are important only as factors that must be considered by the officers of the state in distributing an insufficient supply of water to appropriators in the proper order of priority.

Appropriations of water are made throughout the length of the river. The priority dates of these appropriations have no relation whatever to their location on the stream. Hence, very early appropriations may be found at the upper and lower ends of the stream, while very late appropriations are likewise found at both ends. In times of water shortage, the later appropriators are the first to be deprived of water. The closing of canals in accordance with the inverse order of their priority dates necessarily requires certain canals to close their headgates all along the stream at the same time. Water moves down the stream at approximately 25 miles per day with the result that it requires approximately ten days to deliver water from the state line to the Kearney headgate under normal conditions. The resulting lag therefore becomes an important factor to be considered. During the lag period, conditions over which the administrator of the river has no control may change or disrupt all calculations. Excessive heat, continued drouth, and unusual winds may greatly reduce estimated quantities of river-flow, or, on the other hand, low temperatures, rains and floods in the lower river basin may relieve immediate demands. These elements of uncertainty must be considered in protecting the rights of all on the stream. The position of relators at the lower end of the stream is in itself a recognized condition, and while they have the second oldest priority on the river, it is inescapable that their location subjects them to unfavorable conditions which are practically impossible to eliminate.

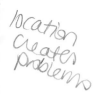

It must also be borne in mind that the amount of flow in the river at any given time during the irrigation season is nothing more than an estimate based on spot measurements. Accurate figures are not obtainable until several weeks after the immediate problem has been determined. The best available basis for the determination of the facts therefore is often very uncertain. The effect of the use of the river as a carrier of storage water also enters into the calculations. The best estimates of the administrator are often affected by unlawful diversions by junior appropriators, injunctions and restraining orders issued by the courts, errors of judgment by the administrator and his subordinates, dilatory compliance with closing orders, and inaccurate reports of rains, floods and weather conditions generally. All of the factors hereinbefore mentioned contribute to the uncertainty of an efficient and accurate distribution of water in accordance with adjudicated appropriations in the order of their priority.

The use of water for irrigation in this state is a natural want. The inadequacy of supply to meet the demands of the public requires strict administration to prevent waste. It is therefore the policy of the law that junior appropriators may use available water within the limits of their own appropriations so long as the rights of senior appropriators are not injured or damaged. And so, in the instant case, junior appropriators may lawfully apply water to their lands within the limits of their adjudicated appropriations until the Kearney canal fails to receive its full appropriation of 162 second-feet. Until the senior appropriator is injured, there is the ever-present possibility of changed weather conditions, precipitation, or other sources of water supply which might alleviate the situation and supply the needs of the Kearney canal. To pursue any other rule would greatly add to the loss by waste of the public waters of this state. We conclude therefore that the use of water by a junior appropriator does not become adverse to or injure a senior appropriator until it results in a deprivation of his allotted amount, or some part thereof. This rule is supported, we think, by our decisions as well as the decisions of other states.

The real question to be decided, however, is the determination of the duty imposed upon the officers of the state in administering the waters of the stream when the available supply of water at the headgate of the Kearney canal is reduced to an amount less than the 162 second-feet to which the relators are entitled. The rights of relators to the use of this water as against all appropriators subsequent to September 10, 1882, cannot be questioned. It is the duty of the administrative officers of the state to recognize this right and to give force to relators' priority. This requires that junior appropriators be restrained from taking water from the stream so long as such water can be delivered in usable quantities at the headgate of the Kearney canal. If it appear that all the available water in the stream would be lost before its arrival at the headgate of the Kearney canal, it would, of course, be an unjustified waste of water to attempt delivery. Whether a definite quantity of water passing a given point on the stream would, if not diverted or interrupted in its course, reach the headgate of the Kearney canal in a usable quantity creates a very complicated question of fact. It therefore is the duty of the administrative officers of the state to determine from all available means, including the factors hereinbefore discussed, whether or not a usable quantity of water can be delivered at the headgate of the Kearney canal. It necessarily follows that this finding of fact must be determined in the first instance by the officers charged with the administration of the stream....

After determination that a given quantity of water passing a certain point on the river would not, even if uninterrupted, reach the headgate of the Kearney canal in usable quantities, the administrative officers of the state may lawfully permit junior appropriators to divert it for irrigation purposes. This results ofttimes in having junior appropriators receiving a head of water at a time when an appropriator farther downstream is getting none, though he is prior in time. Such situations are not therefore conclusive evidence of unlawful diversions.

Amici curiae urge that the doctrine of reasonable use is in force in this state and that it should be applied to the case at bar. We recognize the principle that the public has an interest in the public waters of the state and it is the use thereof only that may be appropriated. Even though an adjudicated appropriation may be vested, it may be subjected to regulation and control by the state by virtue of its police power. It may likewise be circumscribed to the extent that a limited diversion for a specified purpose will not permit of an undue interference with the rights of other appropriators on the stream. But we cannot agree that the doctrine of reasonable use can be applied in a case where delivery of a usable quantity of water can be made, although the losses suffered in so doing are great. To permit the officers of the state the right to say whether prospective losses would or would not justify the delivery of usable quantities of water would clothe such officers with a discretion incompatible with the vested interests of the relators, and destroy the very purpose of the doctrine of appropriation existent in this state. When upstream appropriators applied for and received adjudicated priorities, they did so with the knowledge that there was an earlier appropriator at the lower end of the stream whose rights had to be recognized. When the relators applied for and received their adjudications, they are likewise presumed to have known that other appropriators would obtain inferior rights above them that would have to be recognized. Each is required to respect the vested rights of the others, even though some hardships may be thereby imposed. We therefore hold that the doctrine of reasonable use does not extend so far as to authorize the administrator of the waters of the stream to refrain from delivering a usable quantity of water to a senior appropriator because it might appear to him that excessive losses would result. The duty of the administrator, in administering the waters of the stream by virtue of the police power of the state, is to enforce existing priorities, not to determine, change or amend them . . . . .

[The court held that the senior appropriators were entitled to the water but the trial court properly denied relief because they were too slow in filing their request for mandamus.]

Notes

1. *A wasteful protection?* To understand this case we need to pay particularly close attention to the facts, especially the numbers. How much water had to stay in the river in order to supply water to the senior user? What happened to the water that didn't make it down to the senior use? Was this water essentially wasted? (In answering this question pay attention to

the court's comments on the hydrologic functioning of the river and associated groundwater.) If you were an ardent environmentalist, concerned mostly about the ecological health of the river, what might you say about this ruling?

We also need to note carefully the timing of the senior user's ability to shut down an upstream junior user. What legal rule does the court announce, and does the rule fully protect the senior user? Has the court in some small way reduced the protection enjoyed by senior users?

2. *Water quality:* Farmers Irrigation v Game and Fish Commn. Senior water users are protected not just from diversions by junior users but also by degradations in water quality. Consider Farmers Irrigation v. Game and Fish Commission, 149 Colo. 318, 369 P.2d 557 (1962). Farmers Irrigation Company operated on East Rifle Creek an extensive ditch and reservoir system used for domestic and irrigation purposes. In 1954 the state Game and Fish Commission constructed a fish hatchery on the creek. According to the plaintiffs, the state

> diverted practically all of the water of East Rifle Creek from its natural channel and into said fish hatchery, and into the various divisions and ponds therein; that defendants, in their operations, have placed large quantities of ground liver, flesh, and similar substances and other protein matter used for fish feed in the water diverted into and through said hatchery. Said feed becomes putrid and causes the odor of said water to become offensive, and likewise causes said water to become unwholesome and unfit to use for domestic purposes. Said water is turned back into the channel of Rifle Creek without the impurities, putrid flesh, and foreign matter being removed therefrom.

As a result of the pollution "the water diverted by the Farmers Irrigation Company for use and benefit of its stockholders has acquired a bad and offensive odor and has become noxious, offensive, and unfit for human consumption [so] that plaintiffs are now unable to use said water for domestic purposes because of the unwholesome matter placed therein by defendants; that plaintiffs have no other source of supply for domestic uses and are compelled to haul water a considerable distance for such uses . . . " *Held:* The state hatchery, by seriously polluting the water, damaged the plaintiffs' property rights. The state action amounted to an unconstitutional taking of private property without the payment of just compensation.

3. *Protections for groundwater users.* In the case of water in a river, excessive diversions can leave the river dry. Once it's dry, no more water can be removed. In the case of groundwater the situation is different. Most aquifers are recharged with surface water, yet pumpers can remove water faster than the recharge rate, thereby lowering water tables and requiring pumpers to drill wells deeper. In a prior appropriation groundwater jurisdiction, what protections does a senior pumper have? Can junior users force a senior user from time to time to drill deeper, thereby incurring higher "lift" expenses to get the water to the surface, or are senior users entitled to the continuance of "historic" pumping levels? And what happens when a state decides that it wants to halt the "mining" of aquifers by limiting withdrawals to the estimated aquifer recharge rate? Consider the following decision and the note case accompanying it:

BAKER v. ORE–IDA FOODS, INC.

95 Idaho 575, 513 P.2d 627 (1973).

SHEPARD, JUSTICE.

This is an appeal from a judgment for plaintiffs enjoining defendants from operating their irrigation wells. Defendants' wells pumped from a ground water aquifer underlying both plaintiffs' and defendants' land. This Court must for the first time, interpret our Ground Water Act (I.C. § 42–226 et seq.) as it relates to withdrawals of water from an underground aquifer in excess of the annual recharge rate. We are also called upon to construe our Ground Water Act's policies of promoting "full economic development" of ground water resources and maintaining "reasonable pumping levels."

This case focuses on approximately 20 irrigation wells developed during the late 1950's and early 1960's in the Cottonwood Creek–Buckhorn Creek area of Cassia County in southern Idaho. The parties to this suit were engaged in farming operations in that area. Underlying this area is a limestone aquifer of unknown depth. This aquifer is recharged primarily by means of precipitation. There is not enough annual recharge water to satisfy the needs of all the well owners during the summer irrigation season.

Plaintiffs-respondents Baker, et al., originally brought this action in July 1965 seeking to enjoin defendants-appellants Ore–Ida Foods, et al. from pumping irrigation water from their wells until such time as plaintiffs' wells resumed normal production. In February, 1969 the case was tried to the district court sitting without a jury. The trial was essentially a battle between three hydrology experts presented respectively by the plaintiffs-respondents, defendants-respondents and defendants-appellants. The record in the case in voluminous including prolix water records extending back more than 20 years. The district court entered its amended decree October 5, 1971.

The district court found that the parties and their predecessors in interest had developed irrigation wells having a certain order of priority. The district court also found that all of the wells drew water from a common aquifer underlying the area. The aquifer was of unknown depth but was capable of a metes and bounds description. The court further found that the aquifer is recharged primarily by precipitation, at an average rate of 5,500 acre ft. per year. The court concluded that during the period 1961 though 1968 the parties had withdrawn water from the aquifer far in excess of the annual recharge rate causing a 20 ft. per year drop in the aquifer's water level. In other words the parties were apparently 'mining' the aquifer, *i. e.* perennially withdrawing ground water at rates beyond the recharge rate. Bagley, E. S., *Water Rights Law and Public Policies Relating to Ground Water 'Mining' in the Southwestern States*, 4 J. Law & Econ. 144, 145 (1961).

The court calculated that one cubic foot per second of water flowing for 24 hours would produce 1.983 acre ft. and held that the average annual natural recharge could be pumped entirely by the four senior wells. The court enjoined pumping from all other wells and assigned further administration of its decree to the Idaho Department of Water Administration (IDWA), (formerly the Department of Reclamation, see I.C. § 42–1801a). The decree granted the IDWA full power to expand or limit the amounts of available water for pumping so long as the pumping never exceeded the annual rate of recharge. The amended decree also granted the IDWA the authority to modify its determination of the annual recharge rate. . . .

Appellants assert that Idaho's Ground Water Cat, I.C. §§ 42–226 et seq., has superseded Idaho's common law rules relating to ground water. Appellants argue that, although they are junior, they are nevertheless entitled, under the doctrine of correlative rights, to a mutual pro rata share of the water in the aquifer. Appellants further assert that pursuant to the Ground Water Act senior appropriators may only enjoin junior appropriators from pumping by showing that the juniors' pumping has exceeded reasonable pumping levels.

We must examine the evolution and development of water law to place these important ground water issues in their proper perspective. While the earliest origins of water law are obscure, the Code of Hammurabi and the Roman law contained provisions concerning irrigation and water rights. In U.S. v. Gerlach Live Stock Co., 339 U.S. 725, 744–745, 70 S.Ct. 955, 94 L.Ed. 1231 (1950) Mr. Justice Jackson summarized the development of water law as follows:

> In the middle of the Eighteenth Century, English common law included a body of water doctrine known as riparian rights. That also was the general Mexican law, if it had any lingering authority there * * * except for a peculiar concession to 'pueblos.' Indeed, riparian-rights doctrines prevailed through western civilization.
>
> As long ago as the Institutes of Justinian, running waters, like the air and the sea, were res communes-things common to all and property of none. Such was the doctrine spread by civil-law commentators and embodied in the Napoleonic Code and in Spanish law. From these sources, but largely from civil-law sources, the inquisitive and powerful minds of Chancellor Kent and Mr. Justice Story drew in generating the basic doctrines of American water law.

The law of surface water has evolved along two divergent paths of riparianism and prior appropriation. The origins of the riparian doctrine are disputed and obscure. The riparianism theory came into prominence in both England and the eastern United States during the early 19th Century. Its fundamental precept is that usufructuary rights in a stream's water are created as an incident of ownership of riparian land. Each riparian owner had a co-equal right to the stream's natural flow without any significant alterations of either its quality or its quantity and, therefore, the riparian user must return the water to the stream channel. 1 Clark, Water and Water Rights, § 16 (1967); 1 Hutchins, W. A., Water Rights Laws in the Nineteen Western States, 154–156 (1971).

Riparianism has two distinct allocation theories: natural flow and reasonable use. Under the natural flow theory each riparian owner has an absolute right to the undiminished flow of the stream as it flowed in its natural state. The natural flow theory was harsh and unworkable and the courts evolved the reasonable use theory, i. e., under all the circumstances involved, a determination is made of the reasonability of the use considering the needs of all other riparians. Sax, J. L., Water Law, Planning & Policy, 1–3 (1968); Restatement (Second) of Torts, § 850A (Tent.Draft No. 17, 1971).

Nine western states, plus Alaska and Hawaii have accepted limited forms of riparianism. 1 Clark, Water and Water Rights, §§ 4.3, 15.2 (1967). Eight of the more arid western states (Colorado, Nevada, Arizona, Idaho, Utah, New Mexico, Wyoming and Montana) rejected riparianism and adopted the prior appropriation system. 1 Hutchins, W. A., Water Rights in the Nineteen Western States, 154–156 (1971).

The prior appropriation system was used in both 19th Century Mexico and in the early Mormon settlements in Utah, but it is generally agreed that prior appropriation stems primarily from the customs of the pioneer western miners. 1 Weil, E. C. Water Rights in the Western States, §§ 71 through 81 (3d ed. 1911). Under the prior appropriation doctrine, water rights are created by beneficial use rather than land ownership. The right may be lost by abandonment or nonuse. The water may be beneficially used on nonriparian lands. Disputes between competing appropriators are largely resolved on a seniority basis so that the appropriator with the earliest date of application to a beneficial use will prevail over junior appropriators. 1 Clark, *supra*; see also I.C. §§ 42–101 to 42–112. In Drake v. Earhart, 2 Hasb. 750, 23 P. 541 (1890) Idaho emphasized its allegiance to prior appropriation.

We have heretofore discussed only surface water. The early ground water decisions mirror the riparian doctrine by holding that ground water rights depend on land ownership. The oldest and most rigid theory of ground water allocation is the common law rule of absolute ownership under which a landowner has an unqualified right to remove unlimited amounts of the water underlying his land. Greenleaf v. Francis, 35 Mass. 117 (1836). American courts followed the absolute ownership doctrine until 1862 when the Supreme Court of New Hampshire modified the doctrine by adopting the rule of reasonable use as to percolating ground waters. Bassett v. Salisbury Mfg. Co., 43 N.H. 569, 577–579 (1862). Under reasonable use a landowner could withdraw percolating waters under his land to the extent that such withdrawals were reasonably consistent with the similar rights of other neighboring landowners. However, the reasonable use doctrine prohibited the transportation of ground water for use in areas other than the overlying land. Bassett v. Salisbury Mfg. Co., *supra*. Note, *State Management of Ground Water Mining*, 6 Land & Water L. Rev. 569 (1971).

California altered the reasonable use theory by creating its unique doctrine of correlative rights which requires that a common but insufficient water supply be divided among competing overlying landowners so that each receives an amount of the available water proportionate to his ownership of the overlying land. When there is more than enough water to meet the needs of the overlying owners surplus water may be used on non-overlying lands. However, such transportation is forbidden when there is not enough water to fill the pro rata shares of overlying owners. Katz v. Walkinshaw, 141 Cal. 116, 70 P. 663 (1902); Pasadena v. Alhambra, 33 Cal.2d 908, 207 P.2d 17 (1949); Hutchins, W. A., the California Law of Water Rights, 431–454 (1956); 1 Clark, Water and Water Rights, § 52.2(B)(1967).

In summary, American courts apply one of the following doctrines to ground water:

1. Absolute ownership;
2. Absolute ownership as modified by reasonable use;
3. Correlative rights;
4. Prior appropriation.

The courts and legislatures have drawn further distinctions in applying these doctrines depending on whether the ground water lies in a rechargeable or a non-rechargeable aquifer. In a non-rechargeable aquifer the water is simply a stock resource and it can reasonably be determined when it will be totally exhausted. Decisions must be made as to whether to use it, when to use it and how to use it. New Mexico pioneered this area by imposing strict controls on withdrawals from its numerous non-rechargeable aquifers. Bagley, E. S., *Water Rights Law and Public Policies Relating to Ground Water "Mining" in the Southwestern States*, 4 J.Law & Econ. 144 (1961); Mathers v. Texaco, Inc., 77 N.M. 239, 421 P.2d 771 (1966).

A rechargeable aquifer, however, is a flow resource and the real problem is how best to utilize the annual supply without overdrafting the stock which maintains the aquifer's water level. In the years since World War II, most western states have enacted legislation establishing administrative controls over ground water withdrawals. Clark, R. E., *Ground Water Legislation in the Light of Experience in the Western States*, 22 Mont. L. Rev. 42 (1960). Idaho was in the vanguard of this movement when we enacted our Ground Water Act in 1951; I.C. §§ 42–226 et seq.

The instant case requires construction of the Ground Water Act against the backdrop of the uneven development of our common law concerning ground water. Idaho has vacillated on the question of the appropriability of ground water. As early as 1899 our statutes listed "subterranean waters" as among those subject to appropriation. S.L.1899, p. 380 § 2. In Bower v. Moorman, 27 Idaho 162, 147 P. 496 (1915) the Court repudiated the absolute ownership doctrine and held that percolating waters may be appropriated. Seven years later the court apparently reversed itself in Public Utilities Commission v. Natatorium Co., 36 Idaho 287, 211 P. 533 (1922), and held that percolating waters underlying private land were not subject to appropriation. That case, however, suggested that waters in an underground stream might be appropriated.

In Hinton v. Little, 50 Idaho 371, 296 P. 582 (1931) the court eradicated the questionable historical distinction between underground streams and percolating waters and stated that all underground waters are percolating waters. *Hinton* again rejected the absolute ownership doctrine and held that the litigants could appropriate a common body of artesian water under their land. See also I.L.J. 190 (1931); Union Central Life Ins. Co. v. Albrethsen, 50 Idaho 196, 294 P. 842 (1930).

Silkey v. Tiegs, 51 Idaho 344, 5 P.2d 1049 (1931) further expanded *Hinton* and ruled that percolating waters may be appropriated by diversion and application to a beneficial use. *Silkey* suggested that percolating waters may be appropriated by either the constitutional method or the statutory permit method.

In 1963 amendments to the Ground Water Act, I.C. § 42–229 (S.L.1963, ch. 216, § 1, p. 624), altered the traditional assumption that ground water in Idaho could be appropriated by either the constitutional method or the permit method. We construed that amendment in State ex rel. Tappan v. Smith, 92 Idaho 451, 456, 444 P.2d 412, 417 (1968) and held:

> This section of the statute does not deny the right to appropriate ground water, but regulates the method and means by which one may perfect a right to the use of such water. The regulation is in accord with Article 15, Sections 1 and 3, of Idaho's Constitution, and with I.C. §§ 42–103 and 42–226. Thereby the legislature prescribed that from the effective date of the act which precedes the present action, the statutory method of appropriation would be the sole method of appropriating ground water. The trial court did not err in finding that our laws require an appropriator of ground water to follow the application, permit and license procedure of the Department of Reclamation.

Smith says the state may regulate appropriations of ground water without violating our constitutionally mandated prior appropriation system. See Harvey, L. K., *Mandatory Permit System for the Acquisition of Water Rights in Idaho*, 2 Idaho L. Rev. 42 (1965); Paine, *The Effect of Bonnie and Clyde Upon the Acquisition of Water Rights in Idaho*, 6 Idaho L.Rev. 105 (1969).

We turn now to problems concerning the maintenance of water table levels. An early Idaho case dealing with assessments by an irrigation district set forth the following remarks concerning ground water:

> We conclude, however, that he had no right to insist the water table be kept at the existing level in order to permit him to use the underground waters. There is no proof that he secured water from a natural subterranean stream. The evidence tends to show that he secured it from water collected beneath the surface of the ground

> due to seepage and percolation. To hold that any land owner has a legal right to have such a water table remain at a given height would absolutely defeat drainage in any case, and is not required by either the letter or spirit of our constitutional and statutory provisions in regard to water rights. Nampa & Meridian Irr. Dist. v. Petrie, 37 Idaho 45, 51, 223 P. 531, 532 (1923).

In a subsequent water table case, Noh v. Stoner, 53 Idaho 651, 657, 26 P.2d 1112, 1114 (1933) the Court upheld an injunction forbidding a junior well owner from interfering with a senior's appropriation of ground water. The Court stated:

> If subsequent appropriators desire to engage in such a contest (a race for the bottom of the aquifer) the financial burden must rest on them and with no injury to the prior appropriators or loss of their water. Otherwise, if the users (seniors) go below the appellants (juniors) and respondents were to go below them appellants would in turn, according to their theory, be deprived of their water with no redress.

Noh suggests that a senior appropriator of ground water is forever protected from any interference with his method of diversion. Under *Noh* the only way that a junior can draw on the same aquifer is to hold the senior harmless for any loss incurred as a result of the junior's pumping. If the costs of reimbursing the senior became excessive, junior appropriators could not afford to pump from the aquifer. See Colorado Springs v. Bender, 148 Colo. 458, 366 P.2d 552 (1961). *Noh* was inconsistent with the full economic development of our ground water resources. See Hutchins, W. A., Selected Problems in the Law of Water Rights in the West, at 179 (U.S. Dept. Agric. Misc. Pub. 418, 1942); Comment, *Who Pays When the Well Runs Dry?*, 37 U. Colo. L. Rev. 402 (1965); Sax, J. L., Water Law Planning and Policy, 469 (1968), Note, *Rights to Underground Water in Oregon: Past, Present and Future*, 3 Willamette L.J. 317 (1965); Hutchins, W. A., *The Idaho Law of Water Rights*, 5 Idaho L.Rev. 1 (1968).

Apparently our Ground Water Act was intended to eliminate the harsh doctrine of *Noh*:

> It is hereby declared that the traditional policy of the state of Idaho, requiring the water resources of this state to be devoted to beneficial use in reasonable amounts through appropriation, is affirmed with respect to the ground water resources of this state as said term is hereinafter defined: and, while the doctrine of "first in time is first in right" is recognized, a reasonable exercise of this right shall not block full economic development of underground water resources, but early appropriators of underground water shall be protected in the maintenance of reasonable ground water pumping levels as may be established by the state reclamation engineer (director of the department of water administration) as herein provided. All ground waters in this state are declared to be the property of the state,

whose duty it shall be to supervise their appropriation and allotment to those diverting the same for beneficial use. . . .

* * *

In the administration and enforcement of this act and in the effectuation of the policy of this state to conserve its ground water resources, the state reclamation (director of the department of water administration) is empowered: (Emphasis in original) I.C. 42–237a.

g. To supervise and control the exercise and administration of all rights hereafter acquired to the use of ground waters and in the exercise of this power he may by summary order, prohibit or limit the withdrawal of water from any well during any period that he determines that water to fill any water right in said well is not there available. To assist the state reclamation engineer (director of the department of water administration) in the administration and enforcement of this act, and in making determinations upon which said orders shall be based, he may establish a ground water pumping level or levels in an area or areas having a common ground water supply as determined by him as hereinafter provided. Water in a well shall not be deemed available to fill a water right therein if withdrawal therefrom of the amount called for by such right would affect, contrary to the declared policy of this act, the present or future use of any prior surface or ground water right or result in the withdrawing the ground water supply at a rate beyond the reasonably anticipated average rate of future natural recharge. (Emphasis supplied) I.C. 42–237a, subd. g.

. . . .

Where the clear implication of a legislative act is to change the common law rule we recognize the modification because the legislature has the power to abrogate the common law. Meade v. Freeman, 93 Idaho 389, 462 P.2d 54 (1969); Swayne v. Dept. of Employment, 93 Idaho 101, 456 P.2d 268 (1969). We hold *Noh* to be inconsistent with the constitutionally enunciated policy of optimum development of water resources in the public interest. *Noh* is further inconsistent with the Ground Water Act. . . .

Appellant argues in essence that mutual pro rata rights in the aquifer should be established. This argument is based upon the doctrine of correlative rights. The correlative rights doctrine is based upon the riparian principle of land ownership. See Pasadena v. Alhambra, 33 Cal.2d 908, 207 P.2d 17 (1949), *cert. den. sub nom.* California–Michigan Land and Water Co. v. Pasadena, 339 U.S. 937, 70 S.Ct. 671, 97 L.Ed. 1354 (1950). The doctrine of correlative rights is repugnant to our constitutionally mandated prior appropriation doctrine. . . .

We now hold that Idaho's Ground Water Act forbids "mining" of an aquifer. The evidence herein clearly shows that the pumping by all parties was steadily drawing down the water in the aquifer at the rate of 20 ft. per year. Since our statute explicitly forbids such pumping, the district court did not err in enjoining pumping beyond the "reasonably anticipated average rate of future natural recharge." . . .

Appellants contend that our Act's use of the phrase "reasonable pumping levels" means that senior appropriators are not necessarily entitled to maintenance of historic pumping levels. We agree with appellants in this regard. However, our agreement avails appellants nothing because the trial court found the aquifer's water supply inadequate to meet the needs of all appropriators.

A senior appropriator is only entitled to be protected to the extent of the "reasonable ground water pumping levels" as established by the IDWA. I.C. § 42–226. A senior appropriator is not absolutely protected in either his historic water level or his historic means of diversion. Our Ground Water Act contemplates that in some situations senior appropriators may have to accept some modification of their rights in order to achieve the goal of full economic development. See Piper and Thomas, *Hydrology and Water Law: What is Their Future Common Ground?* Water Resources and the Law 7 (1958); Hutchins, W. A., *Ground Water Legislation*, 30 Rocky Mtn.L.Rev. 416 (1958); Note, *State Management of Ground Water Mining*, 6 Land & Water L.Rev. 569 (1971); Comment, *Appropriation and Colorado's Ground Water: A Continuing Dilemma*, 40 Colo. L. Rev. 133 (1967); cf., Martz, C.O., *The Law of Underground Waters*, 11 Okla.L.Rev. 26 (1958).

In the enactment of the Ground Water Act, the Idaho legislature decided, as a matter of public policy, that it may sometimes be necessary to modify private property rights in ground water in order to promote full economic development of the resource. The legislature has said that when private property rights clash with the public interest regarding our limited ground water supplies, in some instances at least, the private interests must recognize that the ultimate goal is the promotion of the welfare of all our citizens. See Clark, 5 Water and Water Rights, § 446 at 474 (1972). We conclude that our legislature attempted to protect historic water rights while at the same time promoting full development of ground water. Priority rights in ground water are and will be protected insofar as they comply with reasonable pumping levels. Put otherwise, although a senior may have a prior right to ground water, if his means of appropriation demands an unreasonable pumping level his historic means of appropriation will not be protected. . . .

In the case at bar it is apparent under our Ground Water Act that the senior appropriators may enjoin pumping by the junior appropriators to the extent that the additional pumping of the juniors' wells will exceed the "reasonably anticipated average rate of future recharge." The seniors may also enjoin such pumping to the extent that pumping by the juniors may force seniors to go below the "reasonable pumping levels" set by the IDWA.

A necessary concomitant of this statutory matrix is that the senior appropriators are not entitled to relief if the junior appropriators, by pumping from their wells, force seniors to lower their pumps from historic levels to reasonable pumping levels. It should also be noted that those reasonable pumping levels are subject to later modification by the IDWA.

The judgment of the district court is affirmed. Costs to Respondents.

Notes

1. *The twists and turns of legal evolution.* Baker is a useful decision to consider carefully from various angles and its insights extend beyond water law. The court takes the time to review the history of water law over the centuries. Why might it do this? Surely one reason is that it wants to emphasize how even the fundamental elements of private rights in water can change over time in response to physical circumstances, shifting human needs, and differing policy choices. The shift from riparianism and its groundwater equivalents (absolute ownership and reasonable use) was, of course, a very big redefinition of property rights. Idaho made the transition awkwardly in the case of groundwater, apparently shifting to prior appropriation, then pulling back, then shifting again. Appropriation at one time took place in accordance with the simple terms of the state constitution, then was done under both the constitution and a statutory permit system, then shifted so that the statutory method became exclusive. A fundamental element of prior appropriation is the protection senior users enjoy against withdrawals by junior users. On this issue also we see a wandering course by Idaho lawmakers, shifting between absolute protection for senior users (adopted in the now-overruled decision in *Noh*), then protection for reasonable pumping levels, and then to a ban on groundwater mining. Perhaps the court assumed that present and future legal change appear more reasonable when seen as merely the latest installment of an on-going pattern of change.

2. *Reasonable pumping levels and the ban on mining.* The central challenge of the court in *Baker* was to make sense of two seeming inconsistent statements in the new state groundwater statute. On the one hand, the statute repudiated any protection of historic pumping levels and stated that senior users were entitled to the maintenance only of reasonable levels. A pumping level can be reasonable even if the water table declines somewhat and pumpers are forced to drill their wells deeper, and a reasonable pumping level can be maintained even as an aquifer is slowly being mined. On the other hand, the statute bans groundwater mining, which is the withdrawal of water faster than the apparent recharge rate (which is often not well known). The ban on mining would seem to support maintenance of historic pumping levels, but as a matter of hydrology this is not always true. The court in *Baker* chose to blend the two ideas. The stronger protection for the senior users is undoubtedly the ban on mining. While this ban on mining does not fully ensure the maintenance of historic levels, it probably comes close to doing so. On this issue Idaho law differs from that of many states that allocate groundwater by prior appropriation. In them, senior users are entitled to reasonable pumping levels but not to a total ban on withdrawals that exceed recharge.

3. *Accommodation VIII: the conflict with priority in time and correlative rights.* The Idaho statute at issue in *Baker* was intended to promote the

full "beneficial use in reasonable amounts" of the state's groundwater. Will it accomplish that goal, as interpreted in *Baker*? The end result in this litigation was that all of the water in the aquifer was turned over to the four senior-most appropriators. All others had to halt their uses entirely. How else might the law have dealt with this situation of groundwater mining? Might other methods of dispute resolution have worked better?

The problem in this case is that the four senior-most users might be using water for purposes less socially worthy, or in ways less efficient, than the junior users. Another problem is that rather minor changes in the water-use practices of the senior users could well save enough water to allow some of the junior users to continue pumping. Given the court's ruling, the four senior users have no legal obligation to change their practices at all. Perhaps junior users could approach them, offering to pay for conservation measures that would save enough water to allow more pumpers to use the aquifer. But if history is much guide such transactions are unlikely to occur. Could the law, though, somehow encourage them by creating opportunities for discussions to take place? If the aquifer had in place an aquifer management team of some sort that could consider the practices and needs of all pumpers might different outcomes be possible?

The junior users in *Baker* chiefly urged the court to interpret the state statute so as to embrace the correlative rights approach to groundwater. The basic idea of correlative rights is one of equal sharing, with equality variously defined (perhaps based on amount of land ownership, but perhaps based on other factors). Would correlative rights be an improvement on the method embraced by the court, in terms of ensuring that water goes to the most socially valuable and efficient water uses? Yet another option would be to impose on all water users a duty of accommodation, somewhat akin to the duty we saw applied in the oil and gas context in *Kerbaugh*. When water is short all users could be required to adopt reasonable available methods to conserve water; only after that took place and circumstances were reassessed would the court then curtail water uses by junior users. Such an accommodation approach could look a lot like the reasonable use approach employed in riparian rights law to allocate scare water among riparian landowners. In any event, it is important to see clearly the rather stark conflict between two basic ways of dealing with scarcity: giving water to the senior-most users or reviewing all existing uses and then giving the water to the uses that are the most socially beneficial and efficient. The Idaho statute embraces the former approach, even as the legislature announced that it wanted to promote the most beneficial use of state waters.

4. *Senior rights in a fossil aquifer:* Mathers v. Texaco. What rights does a senior groundwater appropriator have in the case of an aquifer that has essentially no natural recharge? In such a case, any water withdrawal reduces the pool of water. Any water that a second or later appropriator pumps from the aquifer inevitably shortens the time period during which the first appropriator can pump. Is this *per se* a violation of the first appropriator's rights? Also, does it make sense to apply a ban on mining to such an aquifer, when the effect would be to leave the water completely untouched?

These issues arose in Mathers v. Texaco, Inc., 77 N.M. 239, 421 P.2d 771 (1966), in which an oil company, Texaco, applied to the state for a permit to withdraw water from a non-recharging aquifer and to use the water to recover additional oil from an underlying oil formation. Under state law a new appropriator could gain a permit only by proving that the additional withdrawal would not impair existing water rights. The parties agreed that the additional withdrawal in this instance would force senior users to deepen their wills more rapidly and would lead to the quicker exhaustion of the aquifer. To promote full water use the state engineer nonetheless decided to allow pumping from the aquifer up to the point where two-thirds of the aquifer's water would be gone in 40 years. Despite the legal requirement that new withdrawals respect existing rights, the state supreme court upheld the decision. To rule otherwise, the court announced, would be to allow only one user of the aquifer, since even a second user would lead to the more rapid depletion of it:

> The administration of a non-rechargeable basin, if the waters therein are to be applied to a beneficial use, requires giving to the stock or supply of water a time dimension, or, to state it otherwise, requires the fixing of a rate of withdrawal which will result in a determination of the economic life of the basin at a selected time.
>
> The very nature of the finite stock of water in a non-rechargeable basin compels a modification of the traditional concept of appropriable supply under the appropriation doctrine. Each appropriation from a limited supply of non-replaceable water of necessity reduces the supply in quantity and shortens the time of use to something less than perpetuity. Each appropriator, subsequent to the initial appropriation, reduces in amount, and in time of use, the supply of water available to all prior appropriators, with the consequent decline of the water table, higher pumping costs, and lower yields.... In fact, if the position of protestants be correct, then each and all of the many permits to withdraw waters from this basin issued by the State Engineer, subsequent to the initial permit, have been issued wrongfully and unlawfully, because each withdrawal, to some degree, has caused a lowering of the water level, and thus an impairment of the rights of the initial appropriator....
>
> The only premise upon which the position of protestants can be logically supported is that "existing rights" embraces the element of perpetuity. As above stated, the beneficial use by the public of the waters in a closed or non-rechargeable basin requires giving to the use of such waters a time limitation. In the case of the Lea County Underground Water Basin, that time limitation was fixed by the State Engineer in 1952 at forty years, after having first made extensive studies and calculations. There is nothing before us to prompt a feeling that this method of administration and operation does not secure to the public the maximum beneficial use of the waters in this basin.
>
> The rights of the protestants to appropriate water from this basin are subject to this time limitation, just as are the rights of all other appropriators. A lowering of the water level in the wells of protestants, together with the resulting increase in pumping costs and the lowering of pumping yields, does not constitute an impairment of the rights of

protestants as a matter of law. These are inevitable results of the beneficial use by the public of these waters.

5. *The hydrologic system.* What happens when the holder of a discrete right to use water (in the following case, an appropriative right to use stream water) comes in conflict with a landowner using a hydrologically connected resource (here, a landowner using groundwater rights that attach to the land)? The materials so far should allow us to anticipate the issues that are likely come up: (i) how much weight do we give to first in time; (ii) are *some resources more important* than others, in the sense that we prefer users of them (as we saw in the case of mining); (iii) do we insist that all uses be *reasonable*, and if so how do we define reasonableness; and (iv) how far do we go in insisting that people adjust their activities so as to *accommodate* the needs of others? Keep these options and issues in mind as you consider the following conflict:

SPEAR T RANCH, INC. v. KNAUB

269 Neb. 177, 691 N.W.2d 116 (2005).

CONNOLLY, J.

ISSUE

issue

This appeal presents the question whether a surface water appropriator has a claim against a ground water user for interference with a surface water users' appropriation . . .

I. BACKGROUND

Spear T filed a complaint alleging that it has surface water appropriations on Pumpkin Creek, which runs through Banner and Morrill Counties. The appellees [Knaub and others] own real property in the Pumpkin Creek basin and have irrigation wells within the boundaries of the basin. The complaint alleged that the ground water irrigation wells are hydrologically connected to Pumpkin Creek. According to Spear T, the appellees' pumping of ground water over the 4 years preceding the complaint drained water from Pumpkin Creek and deprived Spear T of its surface water appropriations; the complaint alleged that the appellees have continued to pump ground water and that Spear T has been unable to irrigate crops and provide water for livestock . . . .

IV. ANALYSIS

The term "surface water" encompasses all waters found on the earth's surface. Richard S. Harnsberger & Norman W. Thorson, Nebraska Water Law & Administration § 1.04 at 9–10 (Butterworth Legal Publishers 1984). Here, the surface water is the stream on which Spear T has water appropriations. In contrast, ground water is defined as " 'that water which occurs or moves, seeps, filters, or percolates through the ground under the surface of the land.' " *Id.* at 12. Accord Neb.Rev. Stat. § 46–635 (Reissue 2004).

Hydrologically, ground water and surface water are inextricably related. Ground water pumping can cause diminished streamflows. Streamflow can support the potential for subirrigation. Seepage from surface water supplies canals, and deep percolation of applied irrigation water from surface projects can recharge ground water aquifers. Harnsberger & Thorson, *supra,* § 5.30. Water law commentators have colorfully described this phenomenon: "[A]ll water is interrelated and interdependent. If groundwater were red, most streams would be various shades of pink; if groundwater were poisoned, the streams would also be poisoned." Richard S. Harnsberger et al., *Groundwater: From Windmills to Comprehensive Public Management,* 52 Neb. L.Rev. 179, 183 (1973).

But Nebraska water law ignores the hydrological fact that ground water and surface water are inextricably linked. Instead of an integrated system, we have two separate systems, one allocating streamflows and the other allocating ground water. Under constitutional and statutory provisions, streamflows are allocated by priority in time. See Neb. Const. art. XV, § 6. Ground water, in contrast, is governed by a common-law rule of reasonableness and the GWMPA [Ground Water Management and Protection Act]. Moreover, the lack of an integrated system is reinforced by the fact that different agencies regulate ground water and surface water. The Department of Natural Resources regulates surface water appropriations. See Neb.Rev.Stat. § 61–201 et seq. (Reissue 2003 & Cum.Supp.2004). In contrast, under the GWMPA, ground water is statutorily regulated by each Natural Resources District (NRD).

The tension between the two systems has long been recognized by commentators. See Harnsberger et al., *supra* at 182 ("[g]round and stream diverters in Nebraska are on a collision course which may occur sooner than most people think"). That day has arrived.

1. Does Spear T Have Common—Law Claim Against Appellees?

We begin by determining whether Spear T has stated a claim. Spear T argues that it has stated a claim based either on the statutory rule of prior appropriation of surface water or on the tort of conversion; we reject these arguments. But as we explain below, we determine that the common law does recognize a tort claim by a surface water appropriator against a ground water user and that Spear T's complaint could be amended to state a claim.

(a) Prior Appropriation

As noted, under constitutional and statutory provisions, streamflows are allocated by priority in time. In its first attempt to state a claim, Spear T relies on prior appropriation. Spear T argues that because the water is hydrologically connected and because it has a prior surface water appropriation, it has priority to the water. According to Spear T, the water is all one "stream" and, as such, Spear T's prior appropriation takes priority over other users of the water, including those who withdraw the water from under its lands. Thus, Spear T essentially asks this court to apply legislatively created surface water priorities to ground water use without considering existing common-law rules. We decline to adopt this approach for several reasons.

First, an application of surface water priorities to ground water requires this court to agree with a legal fiction that considers the ground water to be an "underground stream." We take as true that the water is hydrologically connected, but water rarely runs in a true underground stream. See Richard S. Harnsberger & Norman W. Thorson, Nebraska Water Law & Administration § 1.07 at 13–14 (Butterworth Legal Publishers 1984). Adherence to such a view ignores reality.

Second, no statutory or case law authority supports applying surface water appropriations to ground water. We recognize that most legislatures in western states have developed comprehensive appropriation systems overseen by administrative agencies. See Restatement (Second) of Torts, ch. 41, topic 4 (1979). But in Nebraska, the Legislature has not developed an appropriation system that addresses direct conflicts between users of surface and ground water that is hydrologically connected.

Finally, the prior appropriation rule that Spear T advocates would give first-in-time surface water appropriators the right to use whatever water they want to the exclusion of later-in-time ground water users. This could have the effect of shutting down all wells in any area where surface water appropriations are hydrologically connected to ground water. Richard S. Harnsberger et al., *Groundwater: From Windmills to Comprehensive Public Management,* 52 Neb. L.Rev. 179, 248 (1973) ("[i]f the doctrine of prior appropriation [was] carried to [its] logical conclusion, all Nebraska wells would be shut down"). This would unreasonably deprive many ground water users. Accordingly, we decline to apply the statutory surface water appropriation rules to conflicts between surface and ground water users.

(b) Conversion

Next, Spear T contends that it has stated a claim for conversion. Tortious conversion is any distinct act of dominion wrongfully asserted over another's property in denial of or inconsistent with that person's rights. *Baye v. Airlite Plastics Co.,* 260 Neb. 385, 618 N.W.2d 145 (2000).

A right to appropriate surface water however, is not an ownership of property. Instead, the water is viewed as a public want and the appropriation is a right to use the water. As one article has stated in reference to ground water: "Trespass is unavailable in a typical well interference case because a physical invasion of the plaintiff's property is lacking. Similarly, an action in conversion is unavailable, since the plaintiff has no private property interest in groundwater, at least not prior to capture." Harnsberger & Thorson, *supra,* § 5.27 at 266–67, citing *State ex rel. Douglas v. Sporhase,* 208 Neb. 703, 305 N.W.2d 614 (1981), *reversed on other grounds* 458 U.S. 941, 102 S.Ct. 3456, 73 L.Ed.2d 1254 (1982). Because Spear T does not have a property interest in its surface water appropriation and only has a right to use, it cannot state a claim for conversion or trespass.

(c) Has Spear T Stated Claim Under Other Common–Law Doctrines or, Alternatively, Should It Be Given Leave to Amend?

Although Spear T cannot state a claim under the statutory surface water appropriation rules or for the tort of conversion, this does not end our analysis. The question remains whether it has stated a claim under other common-law principles or if it should be allowed leave to amend to state such a claim.

(i) Review of Common–Law Rules

We begin by reviewing common-law rules that courts have employed to adjudicate disputes between water users.

a. English Rule

Under the English rule of water law—also referred to as the absolute ownership rule—a landowner had absolute ownership of the waters under his or her land. Therefore, the owner could withdraw any quantity of water for any purpose without liability, even though the result was to drain water from beneath surrounding lands. *Prather v. Eisenmann,* 200 Neb. 1, 261 N.W.2d 766 (1978). See, also, *Cline v. American Aggregates,* 15 Ohio St.3d 384, 474 N.E.2d 324 (1984)....

Most American courts, however, have criticized the English rule, recognizing that the rule protected landowners from liability even when water was diverted for malicious purposes. *Maerz v. U.S. Steel Corp.,* 116 Mich.App. 710, 323 N.W.2d 524 (1982), citing *Huber v. Merkel,* 117 Wis. 355, 94 N.W. 354 (1903). The rule has also been criticized because, although a landowner theoretically had a property right in waters beneath his or her land, the overlying owner with the deepest well or largest pump could control water that would otherwise be available to all. *Maerz v. U.S. Steel Corp, supra.* See, also, *Cline v. American Aggregates, supra; Meeker v. East Orange,* 77 N.J.L. 623, 74 A. 379 (1909).

An extreme minority of jurisdictions still adhere to the English rule or a rule that has the same effect as the English rule. See, *Maddocks v. Giles,* 728 A.2d 150 (Me.1999); *Sipriano v. Great Spring Waters of America,* 1 S.W.3d 75 (Tex.1999)....

b. American Rule

Because of disagreement with the English rule, American courts have modified it in different ways. Under what is termed the "American rule" of water law, the owner of the land is entitled to appropriate subterranean or other waters accumulating on the land, but cannot extract and appropriate them in excess of a reasonable and beneficial use of land, especially if the exercise of such use is injurious to others. *Prather v. Eisenmann, supra.*

Under the American rule, the term "reasonable use" relates to the manner in which water is used upon the appropriator's land. The adjacent landowners' interests are in issue only when the appropriator uses water in excess of the reasonable and beneficial use of it upon his or her land and that excess use is injurious to the adjacent landowner. *Prather v. Eisenmann,* 200 Neb. 1, 261 N.W.2d 766 (1978). The American rule has at times also been referred to as a rule of "reasonable use," although it does not consider a balancing of the parties' interests....

Under the American rule, a person who is deprived of surface water because of the use of ground water by a nearby landowner will recover only when the water was not used for a beneficial purpose on the ground water user's land.

c. Correlative Rights

The correlative rights rule of water law originated in California and provides that the rights of all landowners over a common aquifer are coequal or correlative and that one cannot extract more than his or her share of the water even for use on his or her own land if other's rights are injured by the withdrawal. *Prather v. Eisenmann, supra.* The rule first arose in *Katz v. Walkinshaw,* 141 Cal. 116, 70 P. 663 (1902). Under the rule, the overlying landowners have no proprietary interest in the water under their ground and each owner over a common pool has a correlative right to make a beneficial use of the water on his or her land. Priority of use is irrelevant because in times of shortage, the common supply is apportioned among the landowners based on their reasonable needs. Richard S. Harnsberger et al., *Groundwater: From Windmills to Comprehensive Public Management,* 52 Neb. L.Rev. 179 (1973) (describing correlative rights rule)....

d. Restatement

The Restatement (Second) of Torts § 858 (1979) essentially adopts a correlative rights rule that allows for a balancing of many factors to determine reasonableness. Although the rule is initially stated in terms of "reasonable use" similar to the American rule, it adds exceptions that draw on principles of correlative rights. The Restatement rule finds its support in principles of nuisance law and has been suggested as the basic framework for well interference cases. See Richard S. Harnsberger & Norman W. Thorson, Nebraska Water Law & Administration § 5.27 (Butterworth Legal Publishers 1984).

The Restatement, § 858 at 258, states in part as follows:

(1) A proprietor of land or his grantee who withdraws ground water from the land and uses it for a beneficial purpose is not subject to liability for interference with the use of water by another, unless

(a) the withdrawal of ground water unreasonably causes harm to a proprietor of neighboring land through lowering the water table or reducing artesian pressure,

(b) the withdrawal of ground water exceeds the proprietor's reasonable share of the annual supply or total store of ground water, or

> (c) the withdrawal of the ground water has a direct and substantial effect upon a watercourse or lake and unreasonably causes harm to a person entitled to the use of its water.

Although § 858 is under chapter 41, topic 4, entitled "Interference With the Use of Water," *id.* at 253, 217 N.W.2d 339, a note on that topic's scope shows that it is intended to apply to water that is hydrologically connected to ground water. The note states in part: "This Topic covers the rights and liabilities of possessors of land and others withdrawing ground water. It also states the rules governing the rights and liabilities of persons using water where ground water is interconnected with the water of watercourses and lakes." *Id.* Several courts have adopted the Restatement approach. *Cline v. American Aggregates,* 15 Ohio St.3d 384, 474 N.E.2d 324 (1984); *State v. Michels Pipeline Construction, Inc., supra; Maerz v. U.S. Steel Corp.,* 116 Mich.App. 710, 323 N.W.2d 524 (1982).

In addition, the Restatement keeps older definitions of ground water and surface water, but abandons any common-law distinctions between underground watercourses and percolating water. Ground water is defined as "water that naturally lies or flows under the surface of the earth." Restatement, *supra,* § 845 at 198. See, also, *Maddocks v. Giles,* 728 A.2d 150 (Me.1999). Comment *b.* of the Restatement, *supra,* recognizes that ground water may be connected to other forms of water. The comment states: "Most ground water is moving in the hydrologic cycle. It originates from infiltration of precipitation and inflow of streams; it discharges into springs, streams, lakes and oceans. Some ground water is sidetracked from the cycle in closed basins where geologic formations isolate it from recharge or discharge." *Id.* at 199.

Although the Restatement rule is derived from principles of reasonable use, the rule differs from the American rule because it balances the equities and hardships between competing users. *Maddocks v. Giles, supra.* The Restatement (Second) of Torts § 858, comment *b.* at 259 (1979), notes in part:

> The general rule is phrased in terms of nonliability in order to carry forward the policy of encouraging ground water use by permitting more or less unrestricted development of the resource by those who have access to it. The policy and the rule are justified by the fact that since most ground water basins are very large and contain vast quantities of water, it is usually impossible for a single water user to capture the entire supply and leave no water for others.

Comment *c.* at 259–60 provides:

> Exceptions to the general rule are stated in Clauses (a), (b), and (c) of Subsection (1). They incorporate all grounds of liability for use of ground water recognized by the common law but remove some of the restrictions contained in those rules of liability. The majority "American rule of reasonable use" . . . was phrased in terms of the overlying landowner's right to capture ground water, limited by restrictions on the place of use of the water. In operation this

protected small wells for domestic and agricultural uses from the harmful effects of large wells for municipal and industrial supply. The first exception to nonliability, contained in Clause (1)(a), continues this protection but follows a modern tendency to extend similar protection to cases of harm done by unreasonably large withdrawals for operations conducted on overlying lands.

The second exception, Clause (1)(b), imposes liability upon a landowner who withdraws more than his reasonable share of the common supply. This has always been a possible outcome of a controversy concerning ground water if the source could be classified as an underground stream or if the rule of correlative rights were applied. The concept of underground streams was unscientific and its application could be quite arbitrary and the applicability of the rule of correlative rights was in doubt in many states. This exception merges the two rules and makes it possible to apportion shares of the water in the source to the owners of overlying land whenever total withdrawals reach such magnitude that it is necessary to protect the share of an individual landowner from appropriation by others.

The last exception, Clause (1)(c), restates the conditions for recognizing that ground water and surface water are often closely interrelated and should be treated as a single source. In the past this took many forms. Withdrawals of ground water have been called unreasonable when they reduced the flow of springs. A variant of the underground stream concept has enabled the courts to regulate some ground water as the underground segment of a surface stream. The part of an aquifer in contact with the bed and banks of a stream has been called the underflow of the stream and treated as part of it. This Section substitutes a pragmatic test for determining the interconnection instead of employing these doubtful and unscientific categorizations.

Thus, under the Restatement, reasonableness of use is determined on a case-by-case basis and many factors can be considered; the test is flexible. The test for reasonableness is provided in the Restatement:

> The determination of the reasonableness of a use of water depends upon a consideration of the interests of the riparian proprietor making the use, of any riparian proprietor harmed by it and of society as a whole. Factors that affect the determination include the following:
>
> (a) The purpose of the use,
>
> (b) the suitability of the use to the watercourse or lake,
>
> (c) the economic value of the use,
>
> (d) the social value of the use,
>
> (e) the extent and amount of harm it causes,
>
> (f) the practicality of avoiding the harm by adjusting the use or method of use of one proprietor or the other,

> (g) the practicality of adjusting the quantity of water used by each proprietor,
>
> (h) the protection of existing values of water uses, land, investments and enterprises, and
>
> (i) the justice of requiring the user causing harm to bear the loss.

Restatement (Second) of Torts § 850A at 220 (1979).

e. Common–Law Claims in Disputes Between Ground Water Users in Nebraska

We have never been confronted with whether a surface water appropriator may bring a common-law claim against the user of hydrologically connected ground water. We have, however, recognized that a ground water user may bring a common-law claim against another ground water user. We generally have stated the common law in a manner consistent with the American rule blended with a rule of correlative rights. For example, we have stated:

> [T]he owner of land is entitled to appropriate subterranean waters found under his land, but he cannot extract and appropriate them in excess of a reasonable and beneficial use upon the land which he owns, especially if such use is injurious to others who have substantial rights to the waters, and if the natural underground supply is insufficient for all owners, each is entitled to a reasonable proportion of the whole, and while a lesser number of states have adopted this rule, it is in our opinion, supported by the better reasoning.

Olson v. City of Wahoo, 124 Neb. 802, 811, 248 N.W. 304, 308 (1933). [Other citations omitted.]

(ii) Adoption of Restatement for Disputes Between Surface Water Users and Ground Water Users

Having reviewed the common-law rules, we now consider whether we will recognize a common-law claim for interference with surface water by the user of hydrologically connected ground water. Initially, we reject a rule that would bar a surface water appropriator from recovering in all situations. Such a rule would ignore the hydrological fact that a ground water user's actions may have significant, negative consequences for surface water appropriators.

Instead, the common law should acknowledge and attempt to balance the competing equities of ground water users and surface water appropriators; the Restatement approach best accomplishes this. The Restatement recognizes that ground water and surface water are interconnected and that in determining the rights and liabilities of competing users, the fact finder needs broad discretion. Thus, when applying the Restatement, the fact finder has flexibility to consider many factors such as those listed in § 850A, along with other factors that could affect a determination of reasonable use.

Adoption of the Restatement is the modern trend. See, *Cline v. American Aggregates,* 15 Ohio St.3d 384, 474 N.E.2d 324 (1984); *State v. Michels Pipeline Construction, Inc.,* 63 Wis.2d 278, 217 N.W.2d 339 (1974); *Maerz v. U.S. Steel Corp.,* 116 Mich.App. 710, 323 N.W.2d 524 (1982). . . .

Accordingly, we adopt the Restatement to govern conflicts between users of hydrologically connected surface water and ground water. Specifically, we hold:

> A proprietor of land or his [or her] grantee who withdraws ground water from the land and uses it for a beneficial purpose is not subject to liability for interference with the use of water of another, unless . . . the withdrawal of the ground water has a direct and substantial effect upon a watercourse or lake and unreasonably causes harm to a person entitled to the use of its water.

Restatement (Second) of Torts § 858(1)(c) at 258 (1979). Whether a ground water user has unreasonably caused harm to a surface water user is decided on a case-by-case basis. In making the reasonableness determination, the Restatement, *supra,* § 850A, provides a valuable guide, but we emphasize that the test is flexible and that a trial court should consider any factors it deems relevant.

We digress momentarily to offer a word of caution. Although the issue of available remedies is not yet before us, courts should be cautious when considering remedies for interference with surface water. For example, because the recharge of a stream that has dried up because of well pumping could take years, an injunction against pumping might only serve to deprive everyone in a water basin. Such a remedy would be unreasonable and inequitable. Likewise, a court can consider a surface water appropriator's ability to obtain an exception to stays on drilling new wells, or any additional programs that might provide relief.

(iii) Has Spear T Stated Claim Under Restatement?

Having adopted the Restatement approach, we next consider whether Spear T has stated a claim upon which relief can be granted. Our review of Spear T's complaint shows that it did allege—although not precisely—that the appellees' withdraw of ground water has directly and substantially affected Pumpkin Creek. However, although Spear T alleged that it has suffered harm, it did not allege that the appellees have unreasonably caused that harm. Thus, Spear T has failed to state a claim upon which relief can be granted.

We determine, however, that Spear T should be allowed to amend its complaint. Leave to amend should be granted liberally when justice so requires. *Frey v. City of Herculaneum,* 44 F.3d 667 (8th Cir.1995). Accordingly, we determine that the district court erred when it dismissed Spear T's complaint with prejudice for failure to state a claim.

2. *Abrogation*

Having concluded that a common-law claim exists and that Spear T could amend its claim, we turn to the appellees' contention that by passing the GWMPA, the Legislature has abrogated the common-law claim. We have also asked the parties to brief whether 2004 Neb. Laws, L.B. 962, has abrogated any common-law claim. [The court concluded that these statutes had not altered common law remedies.]

V. Conclusion

We adopt Restatement (Second) of Torts §§ 858 and 850A (1979) for resolving disputes between users of hydrologically connected ground water and surface water. Because we adopt the Restatement, we determine that the district court erred when it dismissed the complaint with prejudice for failure to state a claim. . . .

Notes

1. *Reasonable use X: the various options in groundwater. Spear T* is a good decision to read carefully on a number of natural resources issues. It appears here because it tells us more about the types of legal protections enjoyed by the owners of discrete rights to appropriate water. What level of protection does an appropriator have as against a groundwater pumper who is taking water from a hydrologically connected source? The decision is also valuable in clarifying further a rule of law that we have already seen: the reasonable use rule as it applies among groundwater users themselves. The court usefully distinguishes between the reasonable use rule as applied to groundwater by most American jurisdictions and the reasonable use rule as proposed in the Restatement of Torts. What exactly is the difference and how important might it be in actual litigation? One rule looks at the reasonableness of the landowner's activities largely in the abstract, taking account of larger social needs and notions of reasonableness. The other goes further and looks to the particular needs and activities of other users and potential users of the same aquifer.

At first glance it seems appropriate for a court to consider as many facts as possible, to make the best judgment about how water should be used. But is there a down side to litigation that makes more facts and factual issues relevant? Who is supposed to gather this information, particularly if (as is true in many states) it is not publicly available in any way? Many water users are disinclined to tell other people what they are doing, even in terms of how much water they are pumping. Can we criticize the court in *Spear T* for not thinking more about the costs and difficulty of litigation? (Keep this last point in mind in connection with the essay that concludes this chapter.)

2. *Priority in time versus reasonableness. Spear T* follows logically after *Cary v. Cochran* and *Baker v. Ore–Ida* in that it gives us another piece of the story about the protections that an appropriator of water enjoys as against competing users of the water. *Cary* told us about conflicts among surface appropriators; *Baker* about conflicts among groundwater appropriators. Here we see a conflict between a surface appropriator and a groundwater user. What options did the court consider as it framed a rule of law to deal with this particular type of dispute? The conflict was especially hard in Nebraska because surface water was allocated by temporal priority and groundwater based on land ownership and reasonable use. The case thus posed a direct

conflict between two quite different methods of allocating a resource. How does the court resolve this conflict? Which allocation method ends up receiving greater weight? Going further, how much protection does the water appropriator end up getting, and has the court's ruling weakened the idea that first-in-time is first-in-right?

As between a groundwater user and a surface appropriator, the court decides that priority in time is irrelevant; a reasonable use rule will now govern. But if that makes sense in groundwater-surface user conflicts, and in groundwater user v. groundwater user conflicts, then why not shift to this approach in dealing with conflicts among surface users? That is, why not scrap the prior appropriation system entirely and shift to a reasonable use rule among appropriators?

3. *Reasonableness v. correlative rights v. accommodation.* In the course of its analysis, the court gives us raw materials to extend our comparison between three related but distinguishable methods of resolving resource conflicts: reasonable use, correlative rights, and accommodation. Consider the reasonable use rule as it applies in the standard American version of groundwater law—that is, reasonableness determined in the abstract, without concern for competing uses of the same groundwater. Consider next the correlative rights approach, which involves sharing among resource users on some sort of fair-share or pro-rata basis, largely without regard for whose use is more valuable, economically or socially. And finally there is the idea of accommodation, which can be framed in terms of whether one resource user could have avoided harming another by making relatively easy changes in his activities.

What are the relative strengths and weaknesses of these approaches? As you compare them, keep in mind that these are private property rights that we are talking about, and that private property is a valuable institution in American society. It can serve particular social goals, but only if it is well structured. Think, too, about who makes decisions, and how much weight is being given to what decision-making mechanisms. And what about the role of the market: does one of these approaches do a better job than the others in harnessing market strengths and avoiding market weaknesses?

D. RECREATION AND WILDLIFE

Natural resources law is full of detailed rules that prescribe the contours of various types of private use rights in nature. So far in this chapter we've looked at a few common types—mineral rights (on private and public land), oil and gas leases, hunting easements, and appropriative water rights. The basic issues that arise in defining these particular use rights also tend to arise in connection with other types of resource rights.

We conclude this survey in this final section by thinking about recreational use rights on public lands, both state and federal. These use rights are made available to the public, sometimes for a small fee, sometimes for free. Recreational use rights are not typically defined directly as private property interests that members of the public possess (though we might usefully think of them that way). Instead, they are defined by law indirectly, usually in the form of legal limits on the ways public land-management agencies can manage lands. Directly or indirectly legislatures instruct agencies to manage public lands for recreational purposes. To the extent that the agencies are obligated to follow these instructions, the public has use rights in the public lands. As agency flexibility increases, the public's rights become less secure.

As the materials here make clear, recreational uses of public lands tend to go hand in hand with wildlife issues. Lands good for recreation, particularly primitive forms of recreation, often provide good wildlife habitat. And of course many forms of human recreation involve interactions with wildlife.

SIERRA CLUB v. KENNEY

88 Ill.2d 110, 57 Ill.Dec. 851, 429 N.E.2d 1214 (1981).

Simon, Justice:

The local chapter of the Sierra Club brought suit in the circuit court of Jersey County to enjoin the Illinois Department of Conservation from logging or inviting bids for logging a portion of Pere Marquette State Park. The circuit court refused to issue the injunction but held up the Department's proposal for logging pending a review of the plans of the successful bidder. A divided appellate court reversed, holding that there was no statutory authority for the proposal; it enjoined the cutting of trees in State parks. (90 Ill.App.3d 230, 45 Ill.Dec. 388, 412 N.E.2d 970.) This court granted leave to appeal under Rule 315 (73 Ill.2d R. 315). The appellate court's analysis was correct, but the result it reached must be modified.

Pere Marquette State Park was established in 1932 near the confluence of the Illinois and Mississippi rivers. At the time the action was started, the park's 7,743 acres made it the largest State park in Illinois. The area the Department proposed logging is in the Camden Hollow section of the park. The main recreational feature of that area is hiking and equestrian trails.

Camden Hollow, like much of the park, has been subject to many wildfires in the past. In 1974, an accidental man-made fire partially burned 345 acres of Camden Hollow. The terrain is rugged, and the fire damage was heavier higher up on the ridges. No immediate steps were taken in the burn area, and the natural process of regeneration began. The burn area, like much of the park, consists of oak and hickory trees, with a scattering of other species like maple, ash and elm. By the time the suit was heard, a rich new growth of young trees and other vegetation had joined the trees that survived the fire to fill the burn area.

In 1978, following a change in Department of Conservation policy, the Division of Forestry proposed that, for the first time in any Illinois State park, a commercial timber harvest and sale be carried out in the burn area. The Master Management Plan that was developed for Pere Marquette State Park at the same time labels the burn area as part of the Natural Resource Zone of the park. The plan calls for developing that zone by rehabilitating areas damaged by fire (with emphasis on the 1974 burn area), by grazing and by intensive logging.

The logging proposal had four listed purposes: salvage (of dead or injured trees to permit the use of wood fiber in the form of lumber or firewood that might otherwise go to waste), sanitation (to remove fire-damaged trees that are more susceptible to insects or disease), rehabilitation (to create conditions favorable for the growth and regeneration of the oak-hickory climax forest) and wildlife habitat/improvement (to create small openings and cover for game and to increase the eventual output from the remaining trees).

The proposal noted that delay in cutting would result in a substantial loss of wood fiber and the inherent revenue. It postulated that giving the remaining trees more light would increase their growth rate, that increased growth could be obtained through selective harvesting, and that this was desirable for healthy forest development.

The proposed logging was to be carried out by a commercial operator, who would bid for the right to remove trees marked in advance by the Department. In a marking guide drawn up to facilitate the selection of trees to be cut down, the listed objectives of the Department were salvage, sanitation and rehabilitation. The marking guide stated that wood-fiber production was not a management objective on the site. Trees that were injured by fire, insects or disease, or were susceptible to such injury, were to be marked for logging, provided they were merchantable. But, unsalvageable trees were to be left standing because of the potential value to wildlife. The Department proposal foresaw further cutting of timber that had no commercial value by an organization like the Youth Conservation Corps.

Initially marked for cutting were 1,973 trees, or 1% of the trees in the burn area. Of these, 18% were dead; another 60% were live trees to be removed because of damage from the 1974 fire. The remaining 22% were to be logged because they were "economically mature," although three-fourths of these had also suffered slight damage in the fire.

Three hundred forty-eight dead trees were marked for logging in the burn area; 862 dead trees were left unmarked because they were unmerchantable. Of the 1,625 live trees marked, only 1.7% would die each year. If not logged under the Department's plan, though, only 7.1% of those living trees could be salvaged after they died. Ninety additional dead standing trees were later marked for cutting as well.

On August 28, 1978, the Division of Forestry announced a timber sale of the 2,063 trees. The sale was by sealed bid only; specifications for the maintenance of logging and park roads, for firebreaks and for erosion control were mandated. The bids were scheduled to be accepted on October 18, 1978, but the Sierra Club brought this suit before the bid date.

A hearing was held in which photographs of the area were presented by both sides. The trial judge also personally toured the area to be logged. At the hearing, David Kenney, the Director of the Department of Conservation, testified that the purpose of the operation was salvage, sanitation, the safety of those using the park, and the improvement of the park by hastening the regenerative process. The logging was to be handled by commercial sale because the Department did not have the manpower to do the job itself. The successful bidder would pay the Department for the right to log the park and then could sell the wood to recover costs. Kenney was unaware of plans to log any other State parks....

Protection for the delicate ecosystem of the burn area was built into the contract for the logging. Water bars were required on skid trails, skidding of logs could only be uphill, and rubber-tired, not tracked, vehicles were required. Mickleson admitted that some of the smaller growth in the area would have to be taken out to accommodate equipment and to build staging yards to store the logs before they were driven out of the park. He did not anticipate excessive compacting of the soil or the widening of any roads for the logging machinery.

Mickleson had been State Forester under a prior administration and had been witness to several policy shifts within the Department of Conservation. He characterized the decision to log as a change from emphasis on preservation or recreation with little emphasis on conservation to one of total balance, dedicated to multiple use of the State parks. Multiple use, he said, could be a combination of productive and "nature conservation concerns." The Department believed in conserving natural resources; Mickleson noted that because of the energy shortage there was a commercial demand for the logs being removed.

The Sierra Club presented testimony of two witnesses who had observed the area to be logged. One, a veteran hiker, said that the effects of the fire varied throughout the area, with some trees completely dead, others showing some foliage along with scars from the fire, and still others showing complete foliage despite minor fire damage. After a similar fire in Georgia whose effects he had observed, the area was not logged, but left to natural regeneration.

Edmund Woodbury, chairman of the Sierra Club's Great Lakes Chapter, testified that a lay person would not notice that there had been a fire in the burn area. Once he learned that there had been a fire, however, its effects became clear. It seemed to him that most of the trees marked for cutting had a full canopy of leaves. He saw extensive new growth of vegetation and trees sprouting from stumps in the burn area. A site he had seen in Canada after a forest fire had been turned into a wasteland by the combined effect of a ravaging fire and man's cleanup. [The court's summary of the testimony of other witnesses is omitted.]

The trial judge found that the 345–acre burn area had not been devastated, and that the tract had shown the ability to regenerate itself through natural processes, but that the Department's plan to log could not be said to be against good forestry management. However, the circuit court judge found that the logging of trees as proposed posed great dangers to the environmental well-being of the area in question. He cited increased dangers of fire, erosion and injury to young trees not designated for cutting. He expressed the fear that a poorly handled logging operation would cause permanent and widespread injury to the area, and that the operation would deny access by the public to the area for two years.

Although he refused to enjoin the logging proposal, the trial judge required that the Department furnish proof that the contractor chosen was a reliable and responsible operator and that there would be no permanent injury because of the logging.

The Department's proposal to log the Camden Hollow section of Pere Marquette State Park was apparently a good-faith attempt to exercise its discretion in the management of the park consistent with advanced and scientific forestry practices. However, Pere Marquette is a State park, not a State forest, and the techniques developed to encourage productivity and growth in State forests or privately owned timberlands are inappropriate in State parks. The production of commercially valuable timber and forests is subordinated in parks to preservation and recreation. The decision is not left to the discretion of the Department; the policy has been mandated by statute. To the extent that the decision to log reflected a policy change in the Department, it was a change in policy the legislature had not authorized the Department to make.

The Department of Conservation's responsibility is to manage all State parks, including Pere Marquette, in keeping with the policies established by the legislature. (Ill.Rev.Stat.1977, ch. 105, par. 465.) The Department is to fulfill this task, as it fulfills its other statutory tasks, through the use of the statutory powers granted it (Ill.Rev.Stat.1977, ch. 127, par. 63a et seq.). The Department is directed to keep the State parks "open to and * * * for the benefit and enjoyment of all the people" of the State. Ill. Rev. Stat. 1977, ch. 105, par. 465.

In addition to State parks, the legislature has established State forests (Ill.Rev.Stat.1977, ch. 961/2, par. 5901) and State nature preserves (Ill.Rev.Stat.1977, ch. 105, par. 466a). Each was similarly placed under the Department's control. Different interests are at stake in the management of each type of resource. The options are to develop the land for the commercial value of its timber, to use the land for recreation, or to preserve the land in its natural splendor for its aesthetic and cultural value. These uses are not necessarily conflicting, but are not perfectly reconcilable. The statutes governing the management of State forests, State parks and nature preserves reflect a legislative balancing of interests to allow a mix of different uses at each type of resource.

In State forests, the legislature has chosen to give priority to the production of continuous crops of timber for the use of the people and industries of the State. (Ill.Rev.Stat.1977, ch. 961/2, par. 5905.) The Department is authorized to sell the timber, but is restricted to cutting and removing forest products in keeping with the best forestry practices. (Ill.Rev.Stat.1977, ch. 961/2, par. 5906.) Commercial timber forests are also suitable for recreation and provide scenic beauty; thus, as a second priority the legislature has decreed that the Department must also make State forests accessible to the general public for recreation by providing improved highways through the forests. (Ill.Rev.Stat.1977, ch. 961/2, par. 5906.) Residual uses are contemplated by the legislature as well-State forests protect watersheds and maintain the purity of streams and springs. Ill.Rev.Stat.1977, ch. 961/2, par. 5902.

At the other end of the spectrum, nature preserves are established by the legislature to preserve and protect areas "against modification resulting from occupation or development which would destroy their natural condition." These lands have been set aside for research, teaching, natural and historic interest, and as "living illustrations of our original heritage wherein one may experience or envision primeval conditions in a wilderness type environment." (Ill.Rev.Stat.1977, ch. 105, par. 466a.) In maintaining nature preserves, the legislature has commended the Department to conserve the "original character as distinguished from the artificial landscaping" of the land. (Ill.Rev.Stat.1977, ch. 105, par. 467.) In a nature preserve, then, the interest in the preservation of aesthetic and cultural values takes first priority, to the exclusion, if necessary, of conflicting commercial or recreational uses.

State parks strike a third balance; but while they are different from state forests they bear many similarities to nature preserves. They place the major emphasis on recreation but are also dedicated to preservation. State parks are established to preserve large forested areas and marginal lands near waters for recreation. But the types of recreation to be offered are limited. The legislature mandates that a State park offer recreation opportunities "different from that given by the typical city park." (Ill.Rev.Stat.1977, ch. 105, par. 466(3).) But recreation is not the sole priority; the parks are also preserved by legislative directive for their aesthetic and cultural value so that they "may remain unchanged by civilization, so far as possible, and be kept for future generations." Ill.Rev.Stat.1977, ch. 105, par. 466(3).

In addition, State parks are established to preserve the most important historical sites, to set aside areas of scenic and scientific interest, and to connect parks through a system of scenic parkways. (Ill.Rev.Stat. 1977, ch. 105, pars. 466(1), (2), (4).) Notably lacking from the purposes of a State park is any mention of improving or selling the timber grown in them.

To serve the prime recreational purpose of the State park the legislature allows some improvements, but these alterations of the park's original character are limited to those which aid recreation-roads, bridges, trails, camping sites, picnic areas, and the like. (Ill.Rev.Stat. 1977, ch. 105, par. 468(3).) If natural plant areas in a park are devastated, the Department is authorized to replant, increase or supplement those areas. (Ill.Rev.Stat.1977, ch. 105, par. 468(4).) But the statutory authority for improving the parks is narrow-in maintaining a State park the Department is barred from artificial landscaping. As in a nature preserve, the mandate of the legislature is to conserve the original character of the park. Ill. Rev. Stat.1977, ch. 105, par. 467.

In summary, the scheme adopted by the legislature reserves State forests for commercial development and recreation, State parks for recreation and preservation, and nature preserves for preservation and recreation. In State forests there is little place for preservation of the forest in its natural state-improvement of the stand is the order of the legislature. In State parks and nature preserves there is little place for improvement of the forest for commercial development-preservation, for recreation or aesthetic or cultural values, and recreation are what the legislature has ordered.

When the question is the management of forested lands, the distinction between State parks and nature preserves, on the one hand, and State forests, on the other, crystallizes in the criminal penalty provisions of the statutes controlling each. It is a misdemeanor to remove individual trees or timber in a State park or nature preserve. (Ill.Rev.Stat.1977, ch. 105, par. 468b(1).) By contrast, only removing trees is a misdemeanor in a State forest. (Ill.Rev.Stat.1977, ch. 961/2, par. 5911(2).) The difference in wording can be readily explained by the differing legislative intent on the use to which parks, preserves and forest are to be put. State forests exist to grow trees for timber, and thus it is illegal to remove trees before their time but not illegal to harvest them as timber. State parks and preserves are not meant to provide commercial timber, and thus it is illegal to remove both trees and timber from them.

This interpretation of the statutes unifies both the general grants of power to the Department and the specific instructions given to the Department on how to manage the areas under its control. It does not defer to the interpretation adopted by the Department, the administrative agency delegated to carry out the statutes, because the Department does not have a long experience with its interpretation or the policy it now proposes to pursue which has lent credence to it. (See American Oil Co. v. Mahin (1971), 49 Ill.2d 199, 205, 273 N.E.2d 818.) This is, in fact, the first time the Department's interpretation has been put to the test.

The objectives stated by the Department's witnesses bear little relationship to the recreational, aesthetic or cultural uses of a State park. Salvaging timber before it rots is equivalent to the production of a crop of timber. Sanitation of a forest can protect it from disease or infestation that would threaten the proper uses of a State park, but no evidence here indicates any unusual threat of insect infestation or disease. Likewise, the safety of those in a park can be imperiled by dead or injured trees, especially near trails or campsites, but there is no evidence of such threats from the trees marked for logging. The evidence shows no need to rehabilitate the burn area; all that is required for the forest to regain its original vigor is time. By selective harvesting of trees in the burn area the productivity of the forest can be more than doubled, but stimulating forest growth in this manner is the work of civilization from which the legislature tells us the State parks are to be, so far as possible, immune.

The goals of the Department in embarking in good faith on a logging program in a burn area may be laudable, and a sound exercise of discretion, when applied to a State or privately owned forest. But careful and prudent exercises of discretion are to no avail if the result is beyond the goals mandated by the statutes granting the Department the authority to manage State lands. (Village of Lombard v. Pollution Control Board (1977), 66 Ill.2d 503, 6 Ill.Dec. 867, 363 N.E.2d 814 (Board without the power to require regional sewage facilities because not authorized to take such action by statute).) The Department's discretion is harnessed within the policies adopted by the legislature. In a State forest, it is to manage the trees to produce the most and best timber available. In a State park, it is to leave the trees be. . . .

The plan to log in Pere Marquette State Park is not authorized by statute. In addition, it runs afoul of several statutory provisions. Fires and their effects are part of the original character of Pere Marquette State Park. The source of a fire (natural or man-made) does not change its natural effect. However characterized, the Department's program constitutes artificial landscaping. The legislature has chosen not to permit this. Ill.Rev.Stat.1977, ch. 105, par. 467.

The effort to attenuate the effects of the fire by logging to speed regrowth does not leave the park unchanged by civilization, as the legislature intended. (Ill.Rev.Stat.1977, ch. 105, par. 466(3).) Even though the plan may be conservative forestry, there is no showing that any of the techniques of civilization are necessary to serve the recreational purpose of the park. It should be noted that by leaving the burn area alone, the Department would serve one park purpose-providing an area of scientific interest, a living laboratory in which the process of regeneration could be studied. In addition, the loss of two years of public access to the burn area of the park violates the legislative decree that State parks be kept open for the benefit of all the people. Ill.Rev.Stat. 1977, ch. 105, par. 465. . . .

Pere Marquette State Park in its present state is an irreplaceable natural resource. It is held in trust by the State, a holding designed by the legislature to serve the enjoyment and benefit of all the people of the State as a whole. Its future should not be charted by the Department's strained interpretation of guidelines the legislature has given to the agency entrusted with the management of this resource. Where the authority for the Department's irrevocable plan is at best ambiguous, and at worst nonexistent, it is prudent to adopt a "fail-safe" interpretation of the statutes governing the Department and the parks. If the legislature, when presented with the problem, should approve the logging proposal, the trees will still be there to cut. If this court allowed the logging despite our view that the legislature had not intended such a result, it would take decades for the area to regain its original character as a forest untouched by the improvements of man.

Accordingly, we find the logging proposal inconsistent with the legislative purpose for a State park. The Department should therefore be enjoined from proceeding with its logging proposal without more concise legislative directives. The circuit court was incorrect in finding statutory authorization for the logging proposal. The appellate court correctly reversed that portion of the circuit court's judgment.

The appellate court, however, went too far. In ordering the circuit court to enter an injunction as sought in the complaint, the court mandated the Department to "keep from cutting down, harvesting, and logging trees in state parks and conservation areas or from inviting and/or accepting bids, and/or making or entering into contracts or other arrangements, or from in any way authorizing any person to cut down, harvest, and log trees located in or on state parks or conservation areas." This injunction is too broad. While the proposed logging does not comply with the statutes, another selective removal of trees might. An area might have to be opened up for a hiking trail, picnic area or campground, and in such a case the recreational use of the park would take priority over the desire for preservation. It is only when the logging does not serve the recreational or preservation purposes of the park that it must be enjoined.

Instead of the broad injunction entered by the appellate court, the circuit court's injunction should be limited to the Department's proposed timber sale in Pere Marquette State Park. The Department should be left free to carry on its statutory duties in the future in keeping with the views expressed in this opinion and the careful exercise of the Department's discretion.

Accordingly, the judgments of the appellate and circuit courts are vacated and the cause is remanded to the circuit court for entry of an injunction that is in accordance with the views expressed herein.

Vacated and remanded, with directions

Notes

1. *Recreational use rights. Kenney* is useful in explaining the three basic management philosophies that apply on lands open to public recreational use. Nature preserves or wilderness areas are managed so as to ban or keep to an absolute minimum all human alterations. Parks are open for more active recreation. Developments (including roads, structures, and clearings) are permitted in them to the extent they promote recreation. Forests (and other multiple use lands) are managed actively for the production of particular natural resources with recreation allowed as an equal or (in Illinois) secondary land use.

The typical way to think about these land-use options is in just this way—as philosophies of land management, considered from the point of view of the land management agency. But we can also consider them from the point of view of public visitors who possess and use recreational use rights in the lands. How might we define the public's use rights in these three categories of lands? What are the main elements of the rights, and how do they differ among the land types? Might it even help our thinking about public lands management to approach the issue from this unusual direction? A key issue, as we know, in the case of any natural resource use right is the right to halt interferences with the right. What legal enforcement powers do members of the public have, and are they adequate to protect the public's use rights?

It is worth noting that the original justification for protecting wilderness areas on federal lands, articulated by Aldo Leopold (then of the U.S. Forest Service) in the early 1920s, was as places set aside to promote particular forms of primitive recreation that were disappearing elsewhere, mostly due to the good roads movement. (That story is told in Paul S. Sutter, DRIVEN WILD: HOW THE FIGHT AGAINST AUTOMOBILES LAUNCHED THE MODERN WILDERNESS MOVEMENT (2002), and in Julianne Lutz Newton, ALDO LEOPOLD'S ODYSSEY (2006).)

2. *Back to "natural incidents"?* The court tells us that the duty of the Department of Conservation (now the Department of Natural Resources) is to manage lands so as to leave them "unchanged by civilization," except as necessary to promote and enhance recreation. This standard, of course, is similar to the "natural incidents" line of thinking that we saw in various cases involving private rights: landowners were entitled to the natural incidents of their lands, free of interference by other landowners. Once again, nature is providing a baseline for determining good from bad land use practices (as it does, as we've seen, in situations involving legal protections of wetlands, barrier islands, unstable slopes, and critical wildlife habitat). Recreational visitors to natural areas are entitled to enjoy the land's natural incidents. What difficulties, though, can we imagine in implementing this standard? Is it enough that an agency simply leave lands alone?

One problem with the hands-off approach is that it ignores how human activities in other places can alter the natural conditions within parks and nature reserves. Ecological "disturbance regimes" are a key component of nature's functioning. When humans develop surrounding lands they can easily alter such regimes—disrupting forest and prairie fires and routine flooding, for instance—in ways that significantly change the biological composition of the nature reserves. Land managers now know that active human intervention (for instance, burning prairies) is often required in order to keep lands in something close to the condition they were in before Europeans arrived on the scene. Has the court in *Kenney* shown adequate recognition of this ecological reality? Take note of the court's comment that the Department of Conservation can engage in timber harvesting and other actions in parks to the extent necessary for "preservation purposes" as well as recreation. Could the Department after this ruling return to court and assert that its logging plan is essentially an effort at preservation? Keep in mind, on this question, that the fire in the park was apparently human caused.

3. *Challenging agency inaction*: Norton v. Southern Utah Wilderness Alliance. *Kenney* illustrates how a citizen group can successfully challenge

the actions of a land management agency that impair recreational uses of lands in violation of statutes. But what about impairment that takes place while an agency sits and does nothing? Can that be challenged, and if not is the inability to bring suit a significant limit on public rights?

In Norton v. Southern Utah Wilderness Alliance, 542 U.S. 55 (2004), an environmental group seeking to promote wilderness designations in Utah sued the federal Bureau of Land Management for failing to monitor and curtail increased off-road-vehicle use in an area set aside for study as a potential wilderness area under a study process mandated by Congress. The applicable federal statute obligated the agency to manage the lands so as "not to impair the suitability of such areas for preservation as wilderness." Under the BLM land plan applicable to the larger region—a plan expressly carrying the force of law—the BLM stated that it would monitor ORV use and, if warranted, close an area to ORVs. Plaintiff environmental group brought an action to compel the agency to monitor the lands more carefully and otherwise to take steps to protect them against impairment of their wilderness characteristics. *Held*: The BLM's alleged failure to protect the lands against impairment, even if true, did not amount to an "agency action" that the plaintiffs could challenge under the federal Administrative Procedure Act. The failure to act was an "inaction" that was not subject to judicial review. In addition, the agency's pledge in its land-use plan to use "supervision and monitoring" in designated areas did not create "a legally binding commitment" that the plaintiffs could enforce. It was instead a mere prediction of actions the agency would take in the future if resources were available and if the predicted action made sense then in accordance with prevailing agency priorities.

Essay: Specific Use Rights or Good Governance?

Having seen some of the issues that commonly arise in defining and protecting private rights in discrete resources we can return to a question posed in the introduction to this chapter. How might we best define resource use rights so as to accommodate the inevitability of conflicts over resource uses in the future? Should we try to define resource use rights with great precision so that people know where they stand when conflicts arise? If the conflict is between a landowner and a resource user, or two resource users, the law can then supply the answer and the parties can, if they like, negotiate around it. Alternatively, should we define use rights more vaguely and then consider ways of constructing management or dispute resolution mechanisms that can resolve conflicts based on circumstances then in effect? Finally, might we define rights so as to maximize the ability of parties to buy and sell what they own, on the thought that the market can then help resolve conflicts?

As we think about these options, it is useful to begin with a few observations that seem to hold true:

1. Social change is unending—change in populations, technology, ecological understandings, social values, and the like.

2. Conflict among resource uses is inevitable. Some conflicts are foreseeable, others are not.

3. Legal change also seems inevitable, or at least it's taken place for many generations. To the extent that law is based on evolving social factors it can get out of date and will require change.

4. In part based on the above, we simply cannot define resource use-rights precisely in ways that will meet the needs of future generations. Rights defined precisely to meet today's needs will become poorly defined as years go by.

As we think back over the materials in this chapter and the preceding ones, we see numerous examples of legal change that was intended to deal with resource conflicts. Sometimes the precise elements of resource rights have changed to accommodate new resource uses that were not theretofore allowed. Perhaps the best example of this is the emergence of the prior appropriation system of water allocation. Sometimes courts have altered rather precisely defined resource rights so as to make them more vague. The examples of this in the above materials are numerous—the shift in water law from natural flow to reasonable use (and the flexible relaxation of place-of-use rules), the decline of the once apparently strict *sic utere tuo* doctrine, the lessened influence of temporal priority in prior appropriation law, the rise of the duty of accommodation in mineral leases, the flexible powers of the agencies to regulate the surface activities of hardrock miners, the vague limits on the rights of easement holders versus surface landowners, the shift in lake-surface use rights from the common law to the civil law, reasonableness rule, and others. A further trend has been the revival of interest in the land's natural conditions, and the tendency to take nature into account when defining use rights—in wetlands, in wildlife habitat, and on public lands set aside for recreation and preservation.

These changes have not all been in a single direction, but certainly many of them reflect an overriding judicial tendency to embrace vague notions of reasonableness or public interest and to define the rights of private owners based on them. We'll see additional illustrations of this tendency in later chapters, when talking about duration limits on private rights and about the ability of resource owners to transfer what they own.

One big problem with vaguely defined rights is that they leave resource owners uncertain as to where they stand, while leaving the law unable to resolve conflicts quickly and predictably. As we observed earlier, a reasonable use rule is often little more than a rule that tells us *who* gets to resolve a conflict. If the jury decides the reasonableness of a particular resource use, and if the guidance to the jury (as it often does) takes the form of a long list of factors to consider, then the jury is essentially left to do as it pleases. The rule is thus as much a process rule as it is a rule that defines substantive entitlements.

What these considerations point to is the possibility of improving natural resources law by giving greater thought to the mechanisms used to resolve conflicts as they arise. Would the law work better if it focused more on crafting such mechanisms rather than trying to define rights with great precision? Recall the materials on the Maine lobster fishery and on the Altoona Snag Union. Recall also the mining camps in the West and how miners got together to craft rules and resolve conflicts (a matter we only saw briefly). In fact, user groups given half a chance can often find ways to resolve their conflicts, and even to set up mechanisms that exert power over one another. From the academic literature we can get useful guidance from studies of common property regimes that have sometimes operated successfully for centuries in ecologically challenging landscapes. More recently, we have the examples of homeowners' and condominium associations.

In the cases we have seen and in countless cases like them, courts have shown a distinct willingness to define use rights vaguely with the thought that users can resolve the resulting disputes by coming to court. But judicial actions are expensive and time consuming. And they become more expensive and time consuming when courts do what the court in *Spear T* did: increase the facts that are relevant to the resolution of a suit. How much money would need to be at stake in a surface water-groundwater conflict before a party would take the trouble to gather the massive amounts of information and expert testimony needed to launch and prosecute a law suit? Have we not set the cost of litigation too high? Should we not be coming up with quicker, less expensive dispute resolution mechanisms? Irrigators realized the necessity of getting prompt answers when water shortages developed. New institutions arose that gave irrigation-district officials the power to make immediate decisions about who got water and when so as to preserve the entitlements of senior users. It simply makes no sense for a senior user to file a normal civil law suit when she is deprived of water by an upstream junior user. The litigation would take much too long and the water is needed immediately.

We shall return to these questions in the final chapter, after studying two more important functions that natural resources law performs. We will then take time to imagine the types of governance methods that might be developed to add flexibility to resource use patterns and to resolve conflicts more expeditiously and at lower cost.

Chapter Six

DURATION OF RESOURCE RIGHTS

One of the fundamental terms of any resource right is the time period that it lasts—its duration. A fee simple absolute in land is permanent, unless the duration is shortened by private agreement or the land is taken by government through eminent domain or for nonpayment of taxes. Virtually all other rights to use nature are limited in duration, by design or in practice. Sometimes the limit is express and intended. Sometimes it is implicit or comes about because of something the resource owner did or failed to do.

Because many resource use-rights are created through the agreement of private parties, they can include a wide variety of terms relating to duration, including provisions that authorize renewals or that allow resource-use rights to continue for more extended periods if particular actions are taken. As one would expect, many appellate decisions dealing with duration deal with the interpretation of ambiguous provisions in private agreements. Other decisions look to the circumstances surrounding a transaction and attempt to discern the parties' intent from external evidence. Ultimately, though, courts find it necessary to provide back-up rules of law that specify the duration of resource-use rights when the parties have failed to do so, including (as we'll see) rules dealing with abandonment. Legislatures have also gotten into the act, often to enact statutes that promote particular public policies, including the policy of ensuring that natural resources are put to good use. Duration issues thus present the same tensions that we have seen elsewhere in natural resources law, between the *private intent* of the parties and *public policy*.

The materials in this chapter give glimpses of the subject of duration. They are merely illustrative because so many legal rights in nature are affected by private agreements, which are endlessly varied. A fuller inquiry would also make more clear the customs that have arisen in various resource-use areas. Oil and gas leases, for instance, often include nearly identical terms covering duration, even though contracting parties could be as imaginative as they like when negotiating agreements.

TATUM v. GREEN

535 So.2d 87 (Ala. 1988).

ALMON, JUSTICE.

The appellants, Luther T. Tatum and his wife Shelba Tatum and Don Swain and his wife Ray Deena Swain, brought a declaratory judgment action against Margaret Green, seeking to have the trial court declare that Green had no easement across their property . . .

In December 1963, Green's father purchased from the U.S. Government a parcel of property situated in St. Clair County. As part of the transaction, Mr. Green also purchased a "perpetual road right-of-way easement" over the adjoining land. In 1967 and 1968 a portion of Mr. Green's property was flooded by the creation of Neeley Lake. Part of the property that was flooded was that portion of Mr. Green's land to which the easement connected. This portion of the land is still covered with water and the easement no longer touches the property above the water line.

On May 1, 1981, the appellants purchased the property over which the easement purchased by Mr. Green runs. On November 11, 1981, Margaret Green became the owner of her father's property by inheritance.

The appellants brought this action for declaratory judgment to have the right-of-way extinguished and to receive monetary damages from Green for trespass and nuisance. The trial court entered judgment in favor of Green; appellants contend that the trial court erred in finding that Green has a right-of-way over their property.

The general rule is that an easement given for a specific purpose terminates as soon as the purpose ceases to exist, is abandoned, or is rendered impossible of accomplishment. *Sasser v. Spartan Food Systems, Inc.*, 452 So.2d 475 (Ala.1984). Thus, if the easement was granted to Green's father solely for the purpose of access by land to his property, the easement would be extinguished, since the easement no longer reaches the property. *Sasser, supra.*

The Court must look to the written instrument to determine the scope of the grant. *City of Montgomery v. Maull,* 344 So.2d 492 (Ala. 1977).

The deed from the U.S. Government to Green's father did not specify the purpose for which the easement was given but simply granted "a perpetual road right-of-way easement."

If the language is ambiguous or uncertain in any respect, the surrounding circumstances, including the construction placed on the language by the parties, are taken into consideration so as to carry out the intention of the parties. *Maull, supra.* Furthermore, if subject to interpretation, the extent of the easement depends on the intention of the parties as gathered from the terms of the deed and the situation of the land. *Cobb v. Allen,* 460 So.2d 1261 (Ala.1984).

Evidence presented at trial shows that at the time of the grant of the easement engineers from Alabama Power Company had already conducted surveys to determine which lands would be flooded by the construction of Neeley Lake. This evidence tends to show that the parties to the deed were aware of the fact that the easement would cease to be connected to Mr. Green's property due to the construction of the lake. The trial court could have reasonably determined under these circumstances that the easement was also granted to provide Mr. Green access to the lake after its construction. Since access to the lake is a purpose that is still in existence, the easement is also still in existence.

The judgment of the trial court is affirmed.

Notes

The life cycle of resource-use rights. Tatum provides a quick introduction to some of the basic rules governing the duration of resource use rights. The opinion is brief, but there is much to learn from it. As you consider the case, keep in mind the tension between two approaches that the court could take on this issue: implementing the intent of the parties, and pursuing a public interest goal or goals that could override what the parties intended. Discerning private intent is often a difficult job, particular where, as here, the original parties to the written document are no longer around and cannot testify to their designs. Here, the deed governing the easement specifically stated that the easement would be perpetual. Why did this express statement not resolve the dispute immediately? Why did the court go on to probe the likely intentions of the parties as to how the easement would be used? Why, in other words, is the intended purpose of the easement related to the issue of duration when the agreement expressly covered the issue?

The court tells us that an easement "given for a specific purpose" can come to an end in several ways—by abandonment (that is, the owner intentionally gives it up), when the purpose can no longer be fulfilled (impossibility), and when the purpose ceases to exist. Note that the second and third of these causes of termination are related. In the case of each rationale we need to know the chief purpose of the easement. How does the court in *Tatum* figure out the purpose of the easement? What facts does it view as relevant?

Pause for a moment to think about the rules of law that the court sets forth. Land ownership is a perpetual property right (unless expressly limited) and cannot be abandoned. Given this rule, why might the law allow for abandonment of a resource-use easement? Keep in mind that a landowner who buys a fee simple absolute for a specific purpose does not lose her rights simply because her initial intended purpose has come to an end or cannot be fulfilled. A fee simple absolute is perpetual, and the owner can use the land for any lawful purpose. Why then do courts treat easements differently? Put otherwise, why don't we simply look at *what* the purchaser bought (here, a "perpetual" easement) instead of wondering *why* the purchaser bought what she did? The answer, clearly, has something to do with public policies. But what?

Tatum does not give clear answers to these questions, but we can likely surmise them from the materials in prior chapters. Lawmakers (courts included) have long favored the full use of land and resources as a matter of public policy. If the owner of this easement can no longer use it, why not let someone else take it over? Perhaps the more pertinent consideration relates to the owner of the servient estate. The easement restricts what that landowner can do on his land. If the easement remains alive and unused, the owner of the servient estate is restricted unnecessarily, and the public loses whatever indirect benefits might come from a full use of the servient estate. This reality could motivate courts to bring resource-use rights to an end when they are no longer being used. Yet, even if we agree with this reasoning, why not let the parties work things out for themselves? If the easement is largely worthless to its owner, why not let the landowner come forward and offer to buy the easement back, thereby (as a matter of property law) automatically extinguishing it?

A. RESOURCES AFTER CAPTURE: WILD ANIMALS

The main issue in this chapter has to do with the duration of resource-use rights and with the policy considerations that underlie the issue. Occasionally, however, a related legal question arises: What is the duration of the rights that a person gains in the specific items that are taken from the land? As the following case and notes illustrate, the issue comes up vividly in the setting of wild animals. In general, resources severed from land become personal property, and property law allows an owner to abandon personal property at any time. In the case of animals, however, the situation is more complicated. As we've already seen, rights in living wild animals last only so long as the animal remains captive or until it returns to something like a native habitat. But even rights in captive and dead animals, it turns out, can terminate in other ways.

MAGNER v. STATE OF ILLINOIS

97 Ill. 320 (1881).

APPEAL from the Criminal Court of Cook county; the Hon. JOHN A. JAMESON, Judge, presiding.

This is a prosecution for an alleged violation of sections 1, 2 and 6 of what is known as the Game law of this State, entitled "An act to revise and consolidate the several acts relating to the protection of game, and for the protection of deer, wild fowl and birds," approved May 14, 1879.

Section 1 is as follows: "That it shall be unlawful for any person or persons to hunt or pursue, kill or trap, net or ensnare, or otherwise destroy, any wild buck, doe or fawn, or wild turkey, between the fifteenth day of January and the first day of September of each and every year; or any pinnated grouse or prairie chicken between the first day of

December and the fifteenth day of August of the succeeding year; or any quail or ruffed grouse between the first day of January and the first day of October of each and every year; or any wild goose, duck, brant or other water fowl between the first day of May and the fifteenth day of August of each and every year. And it shall further be unlawful to shoot, kill or destroy, or attempt to shoot, kill or destroy, any wild goose, duck, brant or other wild fowl during the night time, at any season of the year; or any woodcock between the first day of January and the fourth day of July in each and every year . . . . ."

Section 2 is as follows: "It shall be unlawful for any person to buy, sell or have in possession any of the animals, wild fowls or birds mentioned in section one of this act, at any time when the trapping, netting or ensnaring of such animals, wild fowls or birds shall be unlawful, which shall have been entrapped, netted or ensnared contrary to the provisions of this act; . . ."

Section 6 is as follows: "No person or persons shall sell, or expose for sale, or have in his or their possession for the purpose of selling or exposing for sale, any of the animals, wild fowls or birds mentioned in section one of this act, after the expiration of five days next succeeding the first day of the period in which it shall be unlawful to kill, trap or ensnare such animals, wild fowls or birds. Any person so offending shall, on conviction, be fined and dealt with as specified in section one of this act; and selling, exposing for sale, or having the same in possession for the purpose of selling or exposing for sale, any of the animals or birds after the expiration of the time mentioned in this section, shall be *prima facie* evidence of the violation of this act: *Provided,* that the provisions of this act shall not apply to the killing of birds by or for the use of taxidermists for preservation, either in public or private collections, if so preserved." . . .

And the 7th section is as follows: "The provisions of this act shall not be construed as applicable to any express company or common carriers into whose possession any of the animals, wild fowl or birds herein mentioned shall come in the regular course of their business for transportation, whilst they are in transit through this State from any place without this State where the killing of said animals, wild fowl or birds shall be lawful. But notwithstanding this provision, the having or being in possession of any such animals, wild fowl or birds as are mentioned in section one, upon any of the days upon which the killing, entrapping, ensnaring, netting, buying, selling or having in possession any such animals, wild fowl or birds, shall be unlawful by the provisions of this act, shall be deemed and taken as prima facie evidence that the same was ensnared, trapped, netted or killed in violation of this act."

The facts are embodied in the following statement of agreed case: . . .

1. That James Magner is a retail dealer in game, and keeps a game market at 76 Adams street, in the city of Chicago, in said Cook county; that on January 14, 1880, said James Magner bought on South Water

street, in said city of Chicago, of a certain dealer, one box of quail, containing 144 quail; that said Magner took said box of quail to his said market, and sold said quail at retail, in different amounts; that on the 15th day of January, 1880, said Magner sold to one James J. Gore, twelve quail, being part of said box of 144 quail, at said market, said Magner and Gore both being citizens of the State of Illinois; that said quail were bought in the State of Illinois, on January 14, 1880, and sold in the State of Illinois, on January 15, 1880.

2. That said James Magner, a citizen of Illinois, bought of William Johnson, of Leavenworth, in the State of Kansas, at said Leavenworth, one box of quail, containing 144 quail, on December 20, 1879; that said box of quail, at said date, was shipped directly to said Magner, at his said market, and, on December 23, received by him; that said Magner sold said box of quail at said market, to said James J. Gore, on January 15, 1880, said Gore being a citizen of the State of Illinois.

3. That said James Magner bought a box of quail, in Leavenworth aforesaid, on January 10, 1880, and sold the same at said city of Chicago, on January 15, 1880, to said James J. Gore, said Gore and Magner being citizens of the State of Illinois.

4. That said James Magner bought said box of quail, containing 144 quail, in Leavenworth, as aforesaid, on January 10, 1880, and retailed, (not sold in bulk or original package,) said quail, and sold twelve of said quail to said James J. Gore, on January 15, 1880, at said city of Chicago, both said Magner and Gore being citizens of the State of Illinois.

[Other similar evidence omitted.]

11. It is also agreed, that game, in large quantities, killed in other States, is shipped to, and sold in, the city of Chicago; that a large trade of that character has grown up in said city of Chicago, amounting to at least $200,000 per year; and also a large amount of game from the State of Illinois is sold in said city of Chicago.

12. It is also agreed, that the game covered by this case, was in entirely fit condition for use as food, as far as game can be during the season the game law of the State has forbidden the killing or sale of the same....

MR. JUSTICE SCHOLFIELD delivered the opinion of the Court:

The grounds upon which it is argued the judgment below should be reversed, are—

1st. Because the statute does not condemn the possession or sale of quail taken and killed beyond the limits of the State, which is subsequently shipped into the State for sale. [Other grounds omitted]

First.—The first section of the statute under consideration makes it unlawful for any person to hunt, pursue, kill or trap, net or ensnare, or otherwise destroy, any quail or ruffed grouse between the 1st day of January and the 1st day of October of each and every year. The second section makes it unlawful for any person to buy, sell or have in possession any of the wild fowls, birds, etc., mentioned in section one, at any time when the trapping, netting or ensnaring of such wild fowls, birds, etc., shall be unlawful, which shall have been entrapped, netted or ensnared contrary to the provisions of the act. This is manifestly but equivalent to saying that it shall be unlawful to buy, sell or have in possession between the 1st day of January and the 1st day of October in each and every year, any of the wild fowls, birds, etc., specified in section one, which shall have been entrapped, netted or ensnared contrary to the provisions of that section. Very clearly this section has reference only to wild fowls, birds, etc., within this State.

But section six is more comprehensive in its language than either section one or section two. It is: "No person or persons shall sell or expose for sale, or have in his or their possession for the purpose of selling or exposing for sale, any of the animals, wild fowls or birds mentioned in section one of this act, after the expiration of five days next succeeding the first day of the period in which it shall be unlawful to kill, trap or ensnare such animals, wild fowls or birds," etc. No exception whatever is made with reference to the time when or place where such "animals, wild fowls or birds" shall have been killed, trapped or ensnared, but the language, as plainly as language can, includes *all* animals, wild fowls and birds.

That this was intended, is further manifest from the language of the seventh section, which declares: "The provisions of this act shall not be construed as applicable to any express company or common carrier in whose possession any of the animals, wild fowls or birds herein mentioned shall come in the regular course of their business for transportation, whilst they are in transit through this State from any place without this State where the killing of said animals, wild fowls or birds shall be lawful," thus, in effect, declaring that but for this qualification the provisions of the act, in such cases, would be applicable to such express companies and common carriers.

But, it is argued this can not be the correct construction, because such a prohibition does not tend to protect the game of this State. To this there seem to be two answers: First, the language is clear and free of ambiguity, and, in such case, there is no room for construction,—the language must be held to mean just what it says. Second, it can not be said to be within judicial cognizance that such a prohibition does not tend to protect the game of this State. It being conceded, as it tacitly is, by the argument, that preventing the entrapping, netting, ensnaring, etc., of wild fowls, birds, etc., during certain seasons of the year, tends to the protection of wild fowls, birds, etc., we think it obvious that the prohibition of *all* possession and sales of such wild fowls or birds during the prohibited seasons would tend to their protection, in excluding the opportunity for the evasion of such law by clandestinely taking them, when secretly killed or captured here, beyond the State and afterwards bringing them into the State for sale, or by other subterfuges and evasions.

It is quite true that the mere act of allowing a quail netted in Kansas to be sold here does not injure or in anywise affect the game here; but a law which renders all sales and all possession unlawful, will more certainly prevent any possession or any sale of the game within the State, than will a law allowing possession or sales here of the game taken in other States. This is but one among many instances to be found in the law where acts, which in and of themselves alone are harmless enough, are condemned because of the facility they otherwise offer for a cover or disguise for the doing of that which is harmful....

In *Phelps v. Racey,* 60 N. Y. 10, the language of the statute was substantially the same as that of the 6th section. The defence there was that the bird—a quail—had been killed in the proper season, but had been kept by a process for preserving game, until after the season expired, and then offered for sale. The court said: "The penalty is denounced against the selling or possession after that time, irrespective of the time or place of killing. The additional fact alleged, that the defendant had invented a process of keeping game from one lawful period to another, is not provided for in the act, and is immaterial." ...

Third.—No one has a property in the animals and fowls denominated "game," until they are reduced to possession. 2 Kent's Com. (8th ed.) 416, *et seq.*; Cooley on Torts, 435. Whilst they are untamed and at large, the ownership is said to be in the sovereign authority,—in Great Britain, the king,—2 Blackstone's Com. (Sharswood's ed.) 409–10,—but, with us, in the people of the State. The policy of the common law was to regulate and control the hunting and killing of game, for its better preservation; and such regulation and control, according to Blackstone, belong to the police power of the government. 4 Com. (Sharswood's ed.) 174....

The ownership being in the people of the State—the repository of the sovereign authority—and no individual having any property rights to be affected, it necessarily results, that the legislature, as the representative of the people of the State, may withhold or grant to individuals the right to hunt and kill game, or qualify and restrict it, as, in the opinion of its members, will best subserve the public welfare.

Stated in other language, to hunt and kill game, is a boon or privilege granted, either expressly or impliedly, by the sovereign authority—not a right inhering in each individual; and, consequently, nothing is taken away from the individual when he is denied the privilege, at stated seasons, of hunting and killing game. It is, perhaps, accurate to say that the ownership of the sovereign authority is *in trust* for all the people of the State, and hence, by implication, it is the duty of the legislature to enact such laws as will best preserve the subject of the trust and secure its beneficial use, in the future, to the people of the State. But in any view, the question of individual enjoyment is one of public policy, and not of private right....

The judgment is affirmed.

Notes

1. *Limits on property rights. Magner* is a ringing endorsement of the power of states to regulate the taking of wildlife, but it is more than that. It is also an endorsement of the power of states to define the extent of private property rights that a person acquires in a resource severed from the land. What limits on wildlife did the court recognize in the case (paying attention to more than just durational limits)? Did the court give adequate attention here to the differences between wildlife caught within Illinois and wildlife acquired elsewhere? In terms of the property rights that a person has in wildlife acquired elsewhere, what law should govern—the law of the state of capture or of the state to which the wildlife is taken? Does it seem legitimate for the Illinois legislature to redefine the private rights that a person has in wildlife acquired in another state (in effect, then, altering property rights that arose under the law of another state)? Is that what it has done?

2. *Banning out-of-state sales.* A state plainly has the power to ban all sales of wild animals and game meat as a matter of state property law. That is, it can define the private rights that an owner obtains so as to give the owner no right to sell. Given this power, though, can a state take an intermediate stance, allowing an owner to sell animals or game within the state while prohibiting any sales out of state?

The Supreme Court said yes to this issue in the important wildlife ruling, Geer v. Connecticut, 161 U.S. 519 (1896). It did so based on the state's original ownership of the wildlife and by viewing a limited right to sell (sale within the state) as a lesser included exercise of the state's power to ban all sales. In Hughes v. Oklahoma, 441 U.S. 322 (1979), however, the Court reversed itself. It held that a limit on sale based on state boundaries ran afoul of the dormant commerce clause and was thus void under the Constitution. In ruling as it did, the Court seemed to call into question the entire idea that states own wildlife as trustees for the people. Lower courts, though, have interpreted this language in the specific factual and legal context of *Hughes*. The ruling only restricts the ability of states to define private rights in captured wildlife based on state boundaries. It has not seemed to affect the many other aspects of the state ownership doctrine. Michael C. Blumm & Lucus Ritchie, *The Pioneer Spirit and the Public Trust: The American Rule of Capture and State Ownership of Wildlife*, 35 ENVTL. L. 673, 706–13 (2005).

3. *Other limits on rights in animals.* Wildlife statutes and regulations often work indirectly to limit the kinds of property rights that owners obtain in the animals that they capture. One common type of statute prohibits hunters from "wasting" the meat of game animals. Such a statute was applied in State v. Huebner, 252 Mont. 184, 827 P.2d 1260 (1992), to a hunter who shot a mountain goat and took only the head, horns, and cape of the animal. The court upheld the hunter's criminal conviction against a claim that the definition of waste was unconstitutionally vague. It also ruled that the statute required no showing of intent but rather imposed absolute liability.

4. *Applying new rules to existing property.* As *Magner* explains, the property rights a person acquires in wild animals need not be, and often are

not, perpetual in duration. Indeed, the property rights might be quite short in duration, as in the case of wildlife caught at the end of a hunting season under laws that ban possession of game out of season.

State law can also limit the owner's right to sell the property, even when possession is lawful. So long as hunters know about these limits in advance they can presumably plan (and eat!) accordingly. But what happens when new rules go into effect that apply to property already in private hands? Is it fair for lawmakers to redefine private property rights in an item (a living or dead animal) when the property rights were essentially perpetual at the time the owner gained possession? Consider the following two rulings. As you read the summaries, keep in mind that the most economically valuable right is often the power to sell the animals or animal parts. What is an owner to do when he ends up with hundreds of deer, elk, zebras or eagle feathers that cannot be sold? What good is the right to possess animals and animal parts that the owner cannot personally use?

a. In Graves v. Dunlap, 87 Wash. 648, 152 P. 532 (1915), the court considered the applicability of a 1913 game statute to a landowner who had previously taken wild deer and pheasants into possession and who kept them largely as pets in enclosed areas. The 1913 statute banned possession of the animals during closed hunting seasons, and prohibited any killing or selling of the animals during the same time periods. The court viewed the statute as constitutionally suspect to the extent it banned continued possession of the animals, given the existing property rights in them. To avoid the constitutional issue, the court construed the state statute so that it did not apply retroactively to the possession of animals that began before the statute took effect; it applied only to animals thereafter acquired. On the other hand, the court understood the difficulties posed to game-law enforcement if the owner could kill or sell the animals out of hunting season. The landowner apparently had no plans to kill or sell any of the animals except for deer that became crippled or injured. Given the landowner's stated intent, the appellate court charted a middle course. It allowed continued possession of the animals and allowed the landowner to kill injured or crippled deer as needed. But in deference to state needs it otherwise enforced the bans on both killing and selling the animals out of season.

b. In Andrus v. Allard, 444 U.S. 51 (1979), the U.S. Supreme Court considered a restriction on selling wildlife products in a dispute involving Department of Interior regulations that banned the sale of feathers and other parts of eagles. The ban applied to eagle parts already held in private hands, including parts incorporated into jewelry intended for sale. After upholding the Secretary's power to issue the regulations under applicable statutes, the Court in a unanimous judgment turned aside the claim that the ban effected a taking of private property without just compensation:

> The regulations challenged here do not compel the surrender of the artifacts, and there is no physical invasion or restraint upon them. Rather, a significant restriction has been imposed on one means of disposing of the artifacts. But the denial of one traditional property right does not always amount to a taking. At least where an owner possesses a full "bundle" of property rights, the destruction of one "strand" of the bundle is not a taking, because the aggregate must be

viewed in its entirety. [citations omitted] In this case, it is crucial that appellees retain the rights to possess and transport their property, and to donate or devise the protected birds.

It is, to be sure, undeniable that the regulations here prevent the most profitable use of appellees' property. Again, however, that is not dispositive. When we review regulation, a reduction in the value of property is not necessarily equated with a taking. Compare *Goldblatt v. Hempstead, supra,* 369 U.S., at 594, 82 S.Ct., at 990, and *Hadacheck v. Sebastian,* 239 U.S. 394, 36 S.Ct. 143, 60 L.Ed. 348 (1915), with Pennsylvania Coal Co. v. Mahon, *supra.* In the instant case, it is not clear that appellees will be unable to derive economic benefit from the artifacts; for example, they might exhibit the artifacts for an admissions charge. At any rate, loss of future profits—unaccompanied by any physical property restriction—provides a slender reed upon which to rest a takings claim. Prediction of profitability is essentially a matter of reasoned speculation that courts are not especially competent to perform. Further, perhaps because of its very uncertainty, the interest in anticipated gains has traditionally been viewed as less compelling than other property-related interests. Cf., *e. g.,* Fuller & Perdue, *The Reliance Interest in Contract Damages (pt. 1),* 46 YALE L.J. 52 (1936).

In *Allard*, the Court construed the legal ban on selling eagle parts as a "regulation" of private property rights. Is it more apt, though, to view the ban as a redefinition of the property rights held by owners? Under the Supremacy Clause, federal take takes precedence over conflicting state law—in this case the state law prescribing private rights in personal property. If the effect of the federal action is to displace the state law authorizing sale, has the federal law not redefined the fundamental elements of ownership in eagle parts, in much the same way (for instance) as the Idaho legislature did for land in the grass-burning ruling, *Moon v. North Idaho Farmers Association*?

B. RENEWAL RIGHTS: GRAZING

In many settings, resource-use rights are created for definite terms of years, with specified rights of renewal. The duration of the right, and indeed whether the right really has much economic value, can depend upon the terms of renewal. Is renewal automatic as long as the resource user asks for it and is willing to continue abiding by the applicable terms of the use right? Instead, is the renewal right more conditional? On the other side, can the owner of land where the resource is located exercise discretion to deny the renewal, either turning the use right over to someone else or devoting the land to a much different purpose? The factual possibilities are nearly endless.

One setting in which renewal rights figure prominently is the case of grazing rights on federal lands (mostly on lands managed by the Bureau of Land Management, though the U.S. Forest Service is also in the grazing business). The legal problems that arise here typify those that arise in other resource settings involving the use of renewable permits.

As you read the following case and accompanying notes, think about the grazing rights from the point of view of a person who wants to acquire or invest in them. How secure are these rights, in terms of duration? What are the risks that the holder of a right will be unable to renew it? And—going further—what dangers are there that permit terms will be altered while an existing permit is in effect?

PUBLIC LANDS COUNCIL v. BABBITT

529 U.S. 728, 120 S.Ct. 1815, 146 L.Ed.2d 753 (2000).

JUSTICE BREYER delivered the opinion of the Court.

This case requires us to interpret several provisions of the 1934 Taylor Grazing Act, 48 Stat. 1269, 43 U.S.C. § 315 et seq. The petitioners claim that each of three grazing regulations, 43 CFR §§ 4100.0–5, 4110.1(a), and 4120.3–2 (1998), exceeds the authority that this statute grants the Secretary of the Interior. We disagree and hold that the three regulations do not violate the Act.

I

We begin with a brief description of the Act's background, provisions, and related administrative practice.

A

The Taylor Grazing Act's enactment in 1934 marked a turning point in the history of the western rangelands, the vast, dry grasslands and desert that stretch from western Nebraska, Kansas, and Texas to the Sierra Nevada. Ranchers once freely grazed livestock on the publicly owned range as their herds moved from place to place, searching for grass and water. But the population growth that followed the Civil War eventually doomed that unregulated economic freedom.

A new era began in 1867 with the first successful long drive of cattle north from Texas. Cowboys began regularly driving large herds of grazing cattle each year through thousands of miles of federal lands to railheads like Abilene, Kansas. From there or other towns along the rail line, trains carried live cattle to newly opened eastern markets. The long drives initially brought high profits, which attracted more ranchers and more cattle to the land once home only to Indian tribes and buffalo. Indeed, an early–1880's boom in the cattle market saw the number of cattle grazing the Great Plains grow well beyond 7 million. See R. White, "It's Your Misfortune and None of My Own": A History of the American West 223 (1991); see generally E. Osgood, The Day of the Cattleman 83–113 (1929); W. Webb, The Great Plains 205–268 (1931).

But more cattle meant more competition for ever-scarcer water and grass. And that competition was intensified by the arrival of sheep in the 1870's. Many believed that sheep were destroying the range, killing fragile grass plants by cropping them too closely. The increased competition for forage, along with droughts, blizzards, and growth in homesteading, all aggravated natural forage scarcity. This led, in turn, to overgrazing, diminished profits, and hostility among forage competitors—to the point where violence and "wars" broke out, between cattle and sheep ranchers, between ranchers and homesteaders, and between those who fenced and those who cut fences to protect an open range. See W. Gard, Frontier Justice 81–149 (1949). These circumstances led to calls for a law to regulate the land that once was free.

The calls began as early as 1878 when the legendary southwestern explorer, Major John Wesley Powell, fearing water monopoly, wrote that ordinary homesteading laws would not work and pressed Congress to enact "a general law . . . to provide for the organization of pasturage districts." Report on the Lands of the Arid Region of the United States, H. Exec. Doc. No. 73, 45th Cong., 2d Sess., 28 (1878). From the end of the 19th century on, Members of Congress regularly introduced legislation of this kind, often with Presidential support. In 1907, President Theodore Roosevelt reiterated Powell's request and urged Congress to pass laws that would "provide for Government control of the public pasture lands of the West." S. Doc. No. 310, 59th Cong., 2d Sess., 5 (1907). But political opposition to federal regulation was strong. President Roosevelt attributed that opposition to "those who do not make their homes on the land, but who own wandering bands of sheep that are driven hither and thither to eat out the land and render it worthless for the real home maker"; along with "the men who have already obtained control of great areas of the public land . . . who object . . . because it will break the control that these few big men now have over the lands which they do not actually own." *Ibid.* Whatever the opposition's source, bills reflecting Powell's approach did not become law until 1934.

By the 1930's, opposition to federal regulation of the federal range had significantly diminished. Population growth, forage competition, and inadequate range control all began to have consequences both serious and apparent. With a horrifying drought came 'dawns without day' as dust storms swept the range. The devastating storms of the Dust Bowl were in the words of one Senator "the most tragic, the most impressive lobbyist, that ha[s] ever come to this Capitol." 79 Cong. Rec. 6013 (1935). Congress acted; and on June 28, 1934, President Franklin Roosevelt signed the Taylor Grazing Act into law.

B

The Taylor Act seeks to "promote the highest use of the public lands." 43 U.S.C. § 315. Its specific goals are to "stop injury" to the lands from "overgrazing and soil deterioration," to "provide for their use, improvement and development," and "to stabilize the livestock industry dependent on the public range." 48 Stat. 1269. The Act grants the Secretary of the Interior authority to divide the public range-lands into grazing districts, to specify the amount of grazing permitted in each district, to issue leases or permits "to graze livestock," and to charge "reasonable fees" for use of the land. 43 U.S.C. §§ 315, 315a, 315b. It specifies that preference in respect to grazing permits "shall be given . . .

to those within or near" a grazing district "who are landowners engaged in the livestock business, bona fide occupants or settlers, or owners of water or water rights." § 315b. And, as particularly relevant here, it adds:

> So far as consistent with the purposes and provisions of this subchapter, grazing privileges recognized and acknowledged shall be adequately safeguarded, but the creation of a grazing district or the issuance of a permit . . . shall not create any right, title, interest, or estate in or to the lands. *Ibid.*

C

The Taylor Act delegated to the Interior Department an enormous administrative task. To administer the Act, the Department needed to determine the bounds of the public range, create grazing districts, determine their grazing capacity, and divide that capacity among applicants. It soon set bounds encompassing more than 140 million acres, and by 1936 the Department had created 37 grazing districts, see Department of Interior Ann. Rep. 15 (1935); W. Calef, Private Grazing and Public Lands 58–59 (1960). The Secretary then created district advisory boards made up of local ranchers and called on them for further help. See 2 App. 809–811 (Rules for Administration of Grazing Districts (Mar. 2, 1936)). Limited department resources and the enormity of the administrative task made the boards "the effective governing and administrative body of each grazing district." Calef, *supra,* at 60; accord, P. Foss, Politics and Grass 199–200 (1960).

By 1937 the Department had set the basic rules for allocation of grazing privileges. Those rules recognized that many ranchers had long maintained herds on their own private lands during part of the year, while allowing their herds to graze farther afield on public land at other times. The rules consequently gave a first preference to owners of stock who also owned "base property," *i.e.,* private land (or water rights) sufficient to support their herds, *and* who had grazed the public range during the five years just prior to the Taylor Act's enactment. See 2 App. 818–819 (Rules for Administration of Grazing Districts (June 14, 1937)). They gave a second preference to other owners of nearby "base" property lacking prior use. *Ibid.* And they gave a third preference to stock owners without base property, like the nomadic sheep herder. *Ibid.* Since lower preference categories divided capacity left over after satisfaction of all higher preference claims, this system, in effect, awarded grazing privileges to owners of land or water. See Foss, *supra,* at 63 (quoting Grazing Division Director F.R. Carpenter's remarks that grazing privileges are given to ranchers "not as individuals, nor as owners of livestock," but to "build up [the] lands and give them stability and value").

As grazing allocations were determined, the Department would issue a permit measuring grazing privileges in terms of "animal unit months" (AUMs), *i.e.,* the right to obtain the forage needed to sustain one cow (or five sheep) for one month. Permits were valid for up to 10 years and usually renewed, as suggested by the Act. See 43 U.S.C. § 315b; Public Land Law Review Commission, One Third of the Nation's Land 109 (1970). But the conditions placed on permits reflected the leasehold nature of grazing privileges, consistent with the fact that Congress had made the Secretary the landlord of the public range and basically made the grant of grazing privileges discretionary. The grazing regulations in effect from 1938 to the present day made clear that the Department retained the power to modify, fail to renew, or cancel a permit or lease for various reasons.

First, the Secretary could cancel permits if, for example, the permit holder persistently overgrazed the public lands, lost control of the base property, failed to use the permit, or failed to comply with the Range Code. [citations omitted] Second, the Secretary, consistent first with 43 U.S.C. § 315f, and later the land use planning mandated by 43 U.S.C. § 1712 (discussed *infra,* at 1821–1822), was authorized to reclassify and withdraw land from grazing altogether and devote it to a more valuable or suitable use. [citations omitted] Third, in the event of range depletion, the Secretary maintained a separate authority, not to take areas of land out of grazing use altogether as above, but to reduce the amount of grazing allowed on that land, by suspending AUMs of grazing privileges "in whole or in part," and "for such time as necessary." [citations omitted]

Indeed, the Department so often reduced individual permit AUM allocations under this last authority that by 1964 the regulations had introduced the notion of "active AUMs," *i.e.,* the AUMs that a permit *initially* granted *minus* the AUMs that the department had "suspended" due to diminished range capacity. . . .

Despite the reductions in grazing, and some improvements following the passage of the Taylor Act, see App. 374–379 (Department of Interior, 50 Years of Public Land Management 1934–1984), the range remained in what many considered an unsatisfactory condition. In 1962, a congressionally mandated survey found only 16.6% of the range in excellent or good condition, 53.1% in fair condition, and 30.3% in poor condition. Department of Interior Ann. Rep. 62 (1962). And in 1978 Congress itself determined that "vast segments of the public rangelands are . . . in an unsatisfactory condition." 92 Stat. 1803 (codified as 43 U.S.C. § 1901(a)(1)).

D

In the 1960's, as the range failed to recover, the Secretary of the Interior increased grazing fees by more than 50% (from 19 cents to 30 cents per AUM/year), thereby helping to capture a little more of the economic costs that grazing imposed upon the land. Department of Interior Ann. Rep. 66 (1963). And in 1976, Congress enacted a new law, the Federal Land Policy and Management Act of 1976 (FLPMA), 90 Stat. 2744, 43 U.S.C. § 1701 *et seq.,* which instructed the Interior Department to develop districtwide land use plans based upon concepts of "multiple use" (use for various purposes, such as recreation, range, timber, minerals, watershed, wildlife and fish, and natural and scenic, scientific, and historical usage), § 1702(c), and "sustained yield" (regular renewable resource output maintained in perpetuity), § 1702(h). The FLPMA strengthened the Department's existing authority to remove or add land from grazing use, allowing such modification pursuant to a land use plan, §§ 1712, 1714, while specifying that existing grazing permit holders would retain a "first priority" for renewal so long as the land use plan continued to make land "available for domestic livestock grazing," § 1752(c).

In 1978, the Department's grazing regulations were, in turn, substantially amended to comply with the new law. See 43 Fed.Reg. 29067. As relevant here, the 1978 regulations tied permit renewal and validity to the land use planning process, giving the Secretary the power to cancel, suspend, or modify grazing permits due to increases or decreases in grazing forage or acreage made available pursuant to land planning. . . .

E

This case arises out of a 1995 set of Interior Department amendments to the federal grazing regulations. 60 Fed.Reg. 9894 (1995) (Final Rule). The amendments represent a stated effort to "accelerate restoration" of the rangeland, make the rangeland management program "more compatible with ecosystem management," "streamline certain administrative functions," and "obtain for the public fair and reasonable compensation for the grazing of livestock on public lands." 58 Fed.Reg. 43208 (1993) (Proposed Rule). The amendments in final form emphasize individual "stewardship" of the public land by increasing the accountability of grazing permit holders; broaden membership on the district advisory boards; change certain title rules; and change administrative rules and practice of the Bureau of Land Management to bring them into closer conformity with related Forest Service management practices. See 60 Fed.Reg. 9900–9906 (1995).

Petitioners Public Lands Council and other nonprofit ranching-related organizations with members who hold grazing permits brought this lawsuit against the Secretary and other defendants in Federal District Court, challenging 10 of the new regulations. [As the case was submitted to the Supreme Court, it dealt with the affirmance by the Court of Appeals of three regulations.] Those three (which we shall describe further below) (1) change the definition of "grazing preference"; (2) permit those who are not "engaged in the livestock business" to qualify for grazing permits; and (3) grant the United States title to all future "permanent" range improvements. . . .

II

A

The ranchers attack the new "grazing preference" regulations first and foremost. Their attack relies upon the provision in the Taylor Act stating that "grazing privileges recognized and acknowledged shall be adequately safeguarded.... " 43 U.S.C. § 315b. Before 1995 the regulations defined the term "grazing preference" in terms of the *AUM-denominated amount* of grazing privileges that a permit granted. The regulations then defined "grazing preference" as

> the total number of animal unit months of livestock grazing on public lands apportioned and attached to base property owned or controlled by a permittee or lessee. 43 CFR § 4100.0–5 (1994).

The 1995 regulations changed this definition, however, so that it now no longer refers to grazing privileges "apportioned," nor does it speak in terms of AUMs. The new definition defines "grazing preference" as

> a superior or priority position against others for the purpose of receiving a grazing permit or lease. This priority is attached to base property owned or controlled by the permittee or lessee. 43 CFR § 4100.0–5 (1995).

The new definition "omits reference to a specified quantity of forage." 60 Fed.Reg. 9921 (1995). It refers only to a priority, not to a specific number of AUMs attached to a base property. But at the same time the new regulations add a new term, "permitted use," which the Secretary defines as

> the forage allocated by, or under the guidance of, an applicable land use plan for livestock grazing in an allotment under a permit or lease and is expressed in AUMs. 43 CFR § 4100.0–5 (1995).

This new "permitted use," like the old "grazing preference," is defined in terms of allocated rights, and it refers to AUMs. But this new term as defined refers, not to a rancher's forage priority, but to forage "allocated by, or under the guidance of *an applicable land use plan.*" *Ibid.* (emphasis added). And therein lies the ranchers' concern.

The ranchers refer us to the administrative history of Taylor Act regulations, much of which we set forth in Part I. In the ranchers' view, history has created expectations in respect to the security of "grazing privileges"; they have relied upon those expectations; and the statute requires the Secretary to "safeguar[d]" that reliance. Supported by various farm credit associations, they argue that defining their privileges in relation to land use plans will undermine that security. They say that the content of land use plans is difficult to predict and easily changed. Fearing that the resulting uncertainty will discourage lenders from taking mortgages on ranches as security for their loans, they conclude that the new regulations threaten the stability, and possibly the economic viability, of their ranches, and thus fail to "safeguard" the "grazing privileges" that Department regulations previously "recognized and acknowledged." Brief for Petitioners 22–23.

We are not persuaded by the ranchers' argument for three basic reasons. First, the statute qualifies the duty to "safeguard" by referring directly to the Act's various goals and the Secretary's efforts to implement them. The full subsection says:

> *So far as consistent with the purposes and provisions of this subchapter,* grazing privileges recognized and acknowledged shall be adequately safeguarded, *but* the creation of a grazing district or the issuance of a permit pursuant to the provisions of this subchapter shall *not* create any right, title, interest or estate in or to the lands. 43 U.S.C. § 315b (emphasis added).

The words "so far as consistent with the purposes ... of this subchapter" and the warning that "issuance of a permit" creates no "right, title, interest or estate" make clear that the ranchers' interest in permit stability cannot be absolute; and that the Secretary is free reasonably to determine just how, and the extent to which, "grazing privileges" shall be safeguarded, in light of the Act's basic purposes. Of course, those purposes include "stabiliz[ing] the livestock industry," but they also include "stop[ping] injury to the public grazing lands by preventing overgrazing and soil deterioration," and "provid[ing] for th[e] orderly use, improvement, and development" of the public range. 48 Stat. 1269; see *supra,* at 1819.

Moreover, Congress itself has directed development of land use plans, and their use in the allocation process, in order to preserve, improve, and develop the public rangelands. See 43 U.S.C. §§ 1701(a)(2), 1712. That being so, it is difficult to see how a definitional change that simply refers to the use of such plans could violate the Taylor Act by itself, without more. Given the broad discretionary powers that the Taylor Act grants the Secretary, we must read that Act as here granting the Secretary at least ordinary administrative leeway to assess "safeguard[ing]" in terms of the Act's other purposes and provisions....

Second, the pre–1995 AUM system that the ranchers seek to "safeguard" did not offer them anything like absolute security—not even in respect to the proportionate shares of grazing land privileges that the "active/suspended" system suggested. As discussed above, the Secretary has long had the power to reduce an individual permit's AUMs or cancel the permit if the permit holder did not use the grazing privileges, did not use the base property, or violated the Range Code. See *supra,* at 1820 (collecting CFR citations 1938–1998). And the Secretary has always had the statutory authority under the Taylor Act and later FLPMA to reclassify and withdraw rangeland from grazing use, see 43 U.S.C. § 315f (authorizing Secretary, "in his discretion, to examine and classify any lands ... which are more valuable or suitable for the production of agricultural crops ... or any other use than [grazing]"); §§ 1712, 1752(c) (authorizing renewal of permits "so long as the lands ... remain available for domestic livestock grazing *in accordance with land use plans*" (emphasis added)). The Secretary has consistently reserved the authority to cancel or modify grazing permits accordingly. See *supra,* at 1820–1821 (collecting CFR citations). Given these well-established pre–1995 Secretarial powers to cancel, modify, or decline to renew individual permits, *including the power to do so pursuant to the adoption of a land use plan,* the ranchers' diminishment-of-security point is at best a matter of degree....

B

The ranchers' second challenge focuses upon a provision of the Taylor Act that limits issuance of permits to "settlers, residents, and other *stock owners*.... " 43 U.S.C. § 315b (emphasis added). In 1936, the Secretary, following this requirement, issued a regulation that limited eligibility to those who "ow[n] livestock." 2 App. 808 (Rules for Administration of Grazing Districts (Mar. 2, 1936)). But in 1942, the Secretary changed the regulation's wording to limit eligibility to those "engaged in the livestock business," 1942 Range Code § 3(a), and so it remained until 1994. The new regulation eliminates the words "engaged in the livestock business," thereby seeming to make eligible otherwise qualified applicants even if they do not engage in the livestock business. See 43 CFR § 4110.1(a) (1995).

The new change is not as radical as the text of the new regulation suggests. The new rule deletes the entire phrase "engaged in the livestock business" from § 4110.1, and seems to require only that an applicant "own or control land or water base property.... " *Ibid.* But the omission, standing alone, does not render the regulation facially invalid, for the regulation cannot change the statute, and a regulation promulgated to guide the Secretary's discretion in exercising his authority under the Act need not also restate all related statutory language. Ultimately it is *both* the Taylor Act and the regulations promulgated thereunder that constrain the Secretary's discretion in issuing permits. The statute continues to limit the Secretary's authorization to issue permits to "bona fide settlers, residents, and *other stock owners.*" 43 U.S.C. § 315b (emphasis added).

Nor will the change necessarily lead to widespread issuance of grazing permits to "stock owners" who are not in the livestock business. Those in the business continue to enjoy a preference in the issuance of grazing permits. The same section of the Taylor Act mandates that the Secretary accord a preference to "landowners engaged in the livestock business, bona fide occupants or settlers." *Ibid.* And this statutory language has been extremely important in practice. See *supra,* at 1819–1820.

The ranchers nonetheless contend that the deletion of the term "engaged in the livestock business" violates the statutory limitation to "stock owners" in § 315b. The words "stock owner," they say, meant "commercial stock owner" in 1934, and a commercial stock owner is not simply one who owns livestock, but one who engages in the business. Hence, they argue, the Secretary lacks the authority to allow those who are not engaged in the business to apply for permits.

The words "stock owner" and "stock owner engaged in the livestock business," however, are not obvious synonyms. And we have found no convincing indication that Congress intended that we treat them as such....

The ranchers' underlying concern is that the qualifications amendment is part of a scheme to end livestock grazing on the public lands. They say that "individuals or organizations owning small quantities of stock [will] acquire grazing permits, even though they intend not to graze at all or to graze only a nominal number of livestock—all the while excluding others from using the public range for grazing." Brief for Petitioners 47–48. The new regulations, they charge, will allow individuals to "acquire a few livestock, ... obtain a permit for what amounts to a conservation purpose and then effectively mothball the permit." *Id.,* at 48, 112 S.Ct. 1011.

But the regulations do not allow this. The regulations specify that regular grazing permits will be issued for livestock grazing or suspended use. See 43 CFR §§ 4130.2(a), 4130.2(g) (1998). New regulations allowing issuance of permits for conservation use were held unlawful by the Court of Appeals, see 167 F.3d, at 1307–1308, and the Secretary did not seek review of that decision.

Neither livestock grazing use nor suspended use encompasses the situation that the ranchers describe. With regard to the former, the regulations state that permitted livestock grazing "*shall be based* upon the amount of forage available for livestock grazing as established in the land use plan.... " 43 CFR § 4110.2–2(a) (1998) (emphasis added). Permitted livestock use is not simply a symbolic upper limit. Under the regulations, a permit holder is expected to make substantial use of the permitted use set forth in the grazing permit. For example, the regulations prohibit a permit holder from "[f]ailing to make substantial grazing use as authorized for 2 consecutive fee years." § 4140.1(a)(2). If a permit holder does fail to make substantial use as authorized in his permit for two consecutive years, the Secretary is authorized to cancel from the grazing permit that portion of permitted use that the permit holder has failed to use....

C

The ranchers' final challenge focuses upon a change in the way the new rules allocate ownership of range improvements, such as fencing, well drilling, or spraying for weeds on the public lands. The Taylor Act provides that permit holders may undertake range improvements pursuant to (1) a cooperative agreement with the United States, or (2) a range improvement permit. 43 U.S.C. § 315c; see 43 CFR §§ 4120.3–2, 4120.3–3 (1998).... The 1995 regulations change the title rules for range improvements made pursuant to a cooperative agreement ... [by] specify[ing] that "title to permanent range improvements" (authorized in the future) "such as fences, wells, and pipelines ... shall be in the name of the United States." [The Court proceeded to uphold the validity of the regulation ...] In short, we find nothing in the statute that denies the Secretary authority reasonably to decide when or whether to grant title to those who make improvements. And any such person remains free to negotiate the terms upon which he will make those improvements irrespective of where title formally lies, including how he might be compensated in the future for the work he had done, either by the Government directly or by those to whom the Government later grants a permit. Cf. 43 U.S.C. § 1752(g) (requiring the United States to pay compensation to a permittee for his "interest" in range improvements if it cancels a permit).

The judgment of the Court of Appeals is *Affirmed.*

Notes

1. *Rights at risk. Public Lands Council* is a veritable catalog of the many ways that a grazing right on federal lands can come to an end, in whole or in part and either permanently or temporarily. The ruling is worth reading closely to make sure you understand the exact terms of these grazing rights. The governing federal statute provides that grazing rights will be "adequately safeguarded." But this statutory protection, as we see, does not override any of the many limits on how long grazing rights will last.

For starters, the Court tells us that a grazing right can be lost through non-use. That is, a holder of a permit must actually put livestock on the range that will eat the forage or else risk permit cancellation. The underlying policy, of course, is familiar to us already: Lawmakers want to see natural resources used, and not left unused. In this setting, though, the forage would not go unused—it would be eaten by wild animals. Note that this use-it-or-lose it rule (which, as we'll soon see, is common in natural resources law) effectively prohibits conservation groups from acquiring grazing permits and then allowing wild animals to graze (we saw the same prohibition under Arizona law in *Forest Guardians v. Wells*, chapter 3). Could a conservation group, though, fight back by litigating the definition of "livestock"? Given that many wild species (elk included) are captive-raised for meat, could a group claim that certain wild species qualify as livestock? What about wild species that are economically valuable because visitors come to view them? Can they be livestock, much like riding horses?

2. *Nonrenewal, cancellation, suspension, and redefinition.* As you read *Public Lands Council* and try to get straight on the exact legal status of grazing rights, it may prove useful to consider four ways that a grazing right might come to an end, partly or wholly.

Grazing permits are issued originally for 10–year terms, so they automatically end if they are not renewed. Permit holders have rights to renew, but they are qualified rights. What dangers are there that a permit will not be renewed? As you answer, consider *nonrenewal* that is caused by the permit holders behavior (or misbehavior) and nonrenewal that is caused instead by decisions and preferences of the BLM. As for the latter, note particularly the ability of the BLM to rewrite land use plans and to decide that particular lands might be better used if withdrawn from grazing and applied to other purposes. One of the key provisions in federal rangeland plans is the provision allocating forage between livestock and wild animals. For decades the BLM routinely allocated nearly all of the forage on ranges to domesticated livestock, and was roundly criticized by conservation groups for doing so. (On nonrenewal, see more in the next note.)

As for *cancellation*, this would take place during the term of a permit, mostly for misconduct by the permit holder. What actions could trigger cancellation, and how is cancellation related to physical conditions on the range itself—conditions that could be caused as much by drought or other weather patterns as by any grazing done by the permit holder?

Then there is the power of the BLM to *suspend* grazing rights to deal with drought, pest problems, and other ecological factors. Pay attention on this issue, not just to the grounds for which the BLM might suspend rights, but how the suspensions are implemented (as best we can tell). We saw, in the case of prior appropriation water rights, that shortages of water are dealt with by terminating the water rights of the most junior water users; only in particular settings (often within organized irrigation districts) is there an effort to force all users to cut back pro-rata. In the case of grazing rights, suspensions take place within regions that are excessively grazed in relation to the land's carrying capacity. Within overgrazed regions, reductions are sometimes made among grazers pro-rata, rather than using a system of temporal priority.

Finally, there is the danger that the terms of a permit will *change in mid-stream* (during the 10–year term) due to changes in applicable land use plans. The specter of this risk underlay *Public Lands Council*, even though the Court did not highlight it. Permits now typically contain express clauses that allow agencies to order grazers to reduce livestock on a range due to poor range conditions. Reductions ordered pursuant to reserved rights are not alterations of the terms of permits, given the reserved agency powers. From the grazer's point of view, however, they nonetheless entail reductions that can prove costly.

3. *Nonrenewal and the Constitution:* Federal Lands Legal Consortium v. United States. Occasionally grazers have challenged agency reductions in their permits on constitutional grounds, contending that permit reductions or nonrenewals amount to takings of property without compensation or denials of due process. In Federal Lands Legal Consortium v. United States, 195 F.3d 1190 (10th Cir. 1999), the court considered charges that the Forest Service violated the Constitution when it amended the terms of grazing permits, both during the middle of a permit term and at the time of permit renewal. The court concluded that the grazing permits were licenses rather than true property rights, but they were nonetheless entitled to constitutional protection. In the court's view, however, the Forest Service retained the right to do what it had done, and thus the Constitution was not violated:

> FLLC argues that the federal government has limited the Forest Service's discretion to change the terms or conditions from previous Gila Forest permits during the permit-renewal process. *See* Appellants' Reply Br. at 3–15. FLLC bases their argument, in part, on the fact that they have a priority for renewal. *See* Appellants' Reply Br. at 12–13; 43 U.S.C. § 1752(c) (providing for priority rights); 36 C.F.R. § 222.3(c)(1)(ii) (same). Although FLLC may have a priority during renewal, this court has repeatedly held that the decision whether to issue or deny a permit is a discretionary one: "[T]he very determina-

tions of whether to renew grazing permits and whether public lands should even be designated for grazing purposes [, *see* 36 C.F.R. § 219.20,] are matters completely within the Secretary of Interior's discretion." [citations omitted]

More importantly, during the permit renewal process, an applicant has a priority for a permit only "[s]o long as ... the permittee ... accepts the terms or conditions to be included by the Secretary ... " 43 U.S.C. § 1752(c)(3); *see also* 16 U.S.C. § 580l ("The Secretary of Agriculture in regulating grazing on the national forest ... is authorized, upon such terms and conditions as he may deem proper, to issue permits for the grazing of livestock.... "). The Forest Service, in turn, has discretion to require any change it deems necessary, *see* 16 U.S.C. § 580l; 43 U.S.C. § 1752(e); 36 C.F.R. § 222.3(c)(1)(vi), including discretion to set the "numbers of animals to be grazed and the seasons of use," 43 U.S.C. § 1752(e); 36 C.F.R. § 222.3(c)(1)(i), which are, in essence, the permit changes at issue in this action....

FLLC next argues that, historically, the Forest Service has renewed the permits without any changes in the permits' terms or conditions. *See* Appellants' Reply Br. at 15; *see also Shufflebarger v. Commissioner,* 24 T.C. 980, 991–92, 997, 1955 WL 643 (1955) (noting the historical practices of the Forest Service). According to FLLC, the Forest Service's practice thereby creates a legitimate entitlement to the terms and conditions of the previous permits. *See* Appellants' Reply Br. at 15; *see also Perry,* 408 U.S. at 602–03, 92 S.Ct. 2694 (holding that a mutually implicit understanding may create a property right).

As an initial matter, it is not apparent that those historical practices survived the enactment of the Federal Land Policy and Management Act in 1976. Under that Act, "future adjudications of grazing use would be based on criteria vastly different than those provided" under the prior acts ..... This court has therefore concluded that "[a]lthough it may well be the case that there were long periods in which the Secretary did not exercise his authority to change the permitted number ... in new permits, this practice did not rise to the level of regulatory mandate." *Public Lands Council,* 167 F.3d at 1297–98 (footnote omitted).

Regardless, "in the absence of a statutory or contractual right to renewal, a person ... can claim no property interest in the indefinite renewal of his or her contract." *Durant v. Independent Sch. Dist. No. 16,* 990 F.2d 560, 563 (10th Cir.1993) ... *Martin v. Unified Sch. Dist. No. 434,* 728 F.2d 453, 454–55 (10th Cir.1984) (holding that a teacher whose one-year contract had been renewed every year for ten years did not have a protected property interest in renewal during the eleventh year) ...

As noted above, the statutory scheme gives the Forest Service discretion to change the terms and conditions during the permit renewal process. That the Forest Service customarily did not exercise that discretion creates, at best, a unilateral expectation that the Forest Service would continue that practice. That expectation is insufficient to establish a property right. *See Roth,* 408 U.S. at 577, 92 S.Ct. 2701 ("To have a property interest in a benefit, a person ... must have more than a unilateral expectation of it."); ...

4. *Contract extensions: a timber illustration:* Louisiana Pacific Corp. v. United States. In the case of timber on federal lands, the government typically sells standing timber under multi-year contracts, which often contain detailed terms that the purchaser must fulfill. Contracts often require that timber be cut by a certain date but leave open the possibility that the contract term will be extended by the Forest Service, with or without imposing additional burdens on the purchaser. In Louisiana Pacific Corp. v. United States, 15 Cl.Ct. 413 (1988), the court considered a claim by a timber purchaser that the Forest Service had waived its ability to alter contract terms by routinely approving contract extensions in the past without changing any material terms. In the case, the Forest Service extended a timber contract but eliminated 88% of the remaining timber from the sale while imposing "new, more efficient, but costly, stream course protection requirements." Due to the alleged waiver of its power to change the terms, the timber company argued, the Forest Service's action amounted to a breach of contract. The court disagreed:

> Plaintiff's argument of breach of contract under Count II of the complaint was based upon an alleged, long-standing, nationwide Forest Service policy of regularly granting timber sale contract extensions without requiring the purchaser to agree to extensive modifications or undertake significant new obligations. That policy was not expressly stated in the contract, but was arguably derived from custom and two sections of the Forest Service Manual; sections 2433.11 and 2433.12, both of which were in effect on the date of execution of the contract with Northern Timber Company.
>
> FSM § 2433.12 (1970) stated: "Ordinarily, the timber sale contract is written on the basis that time is not of the essence." That section noted further, "an extension of time may be granted ... unless [it would be] disadvantageous to the United States." Section 2433.11 permitted the Forest Service to modify extended contracts as "necessary to bring the contract [terms and conditions] up to date with other comparable contracts being issued at the time of the extension." FSM § 2433.11 (1970). Section 2433.11 also specified that to qualify for an extension the contractor must have harvested at least fifty percent of the timber and constructed necessary roads to reach at least sixty percent of the remaining timber. It is clear from the record that plaintiff and its predecessor in interest, Northern Timber Company, had not cut fifty percent of the timber nor had plaintiff constructed roads to reach sixty percent of the remaining timber. At trial, however, there emerged a consensus that the cutting and road construction percentage requirements were often ignored by the Forest Service in reaching its decision whether or not to grant a requested extension of time for contract completion. The court, therefore, does not consider plaintiffs failure to cut timber or construct roads as dispositive of the issue in dispute....

Both parties cite *Everett Plywood Corp. v. United States,* 206 Ct.Cl. 244, 512 F.2d 1082 (1975), in support of their respective positions. *Everett Plywood* involved a government logging contract to which the

Forest Service refused to grant an extension after having granted eight successive extensions of the same contract. The court held that defendant's refusal constituted a breach of contract and awarded damages to plaintiff because the Forest Service applied the wrong standard in determining whether the extension should have been granted. *Id.* at 260, 512 F.2d at 1092. The *Everett Plywood* court described the Forest Service extension policy as very liberal. *Id.* at 255, 512 F.2d at 1089. It found that:

> Extensions were regularly granted for a variety of reasons ranging from bad weather to poor economic conditions. Forest Service personnel testifying at trial could recall no specific instance where, prior to 1969 an extension had been denied.... The fact is that Forest Service extensions of contracts were granted by the Forest Service with very little urging.

Id. at 250, 512 F.2d at 1086. Plaintiff argued that the automatic contractual extension proposition stated in *Everett Plywood* was reaffirmed in *Cape Fox Corp. v. United States, 4 Cl.Ct. 223 (1983)*. In *Cape Fox,* the court found that:

> Forest Service policy applicable to an extension of a timber sale contract in existence at the time the contract was issued, is a part of the contract. The Forest Service is liable for breach of the contract commitment if it erroneously refuses to extend a timber sale eligible for extension.

Id. at 235.

Everett Plywood, as interpreted by plaintiff, is inapplicable to the issues now before the court. In that case the Forest Service was found to have acted in an arbitrary and capricious manner because it failed to evaluate the extension request in accordance with the policy, practice and custom in effect at the time the contract was executed. That court found that defendant improperly used a more onerous "extraordinary conditions" standard instead of the "disadvantageous to the United States" standard and that the imposition of the "extraordinary conditions" standard constituted a breach of contract. *Everett Plywood,* 206 Ct.Cl. at 257–58, 512 F.2d at 1090. This court reads *Everett Plywood* to stand for the proposition that the Forest Service had the discretionary authority to refuse to extend any contract that would be disadvantageous to the United States. *Everett Plywood,* 206 Ct.Cl. at 256, 512 F.2d at 1089. The exercise of that discretion had to be fair and reasonable, not arbitrary and capricious. *Id.* Forest Service policy, old and new, allowed an extension without significant changes from the terms of the original contract if the Service determined that the United States would not be disadvantaged, environmentally or otherwise. The converse is just as true....

In the case at bar the Forest Service exercised its discretion by determining that an extension of plaintiff's contract under the same or similar terms as the original contract would be "disadvantageous to the United States" because of harm to the environment and, thus, would accept only a significantly modified extension responsive to its concerns. The court finds that the Forest Service was reasonable and fair in making that determination. The modifications involved measures to protect wildlife and unstable soils, and required a change in plaintiff's logging procedures; actions that were intended to protect National Forest land from further environmental degradation.

On this issue, consider also the note on *Fanning v. Oregon Division of State Lands* (Or. App. 1997), after the following main case, in which the court allowed a party contracting with the government to resist contract termination by asserting its reasonable reliance upon a longstanding pattern of agency forbearance in exercising its powers.

C. A DUTY TO EXPLOIT

One of the requirements of a federal grazing lease, as we've just seen, is the duty of the permit holder or lessee to use the permit to graze livestock. This use-it-or-lose it rule is common in natural resources law. As a further illustration, we turn here to the illustration of oil and gas leases. Leases are commonly executed by landowners and lessees for a prescribed term of years. Typically, the lease provides for an automatic extension of the lease if, at the end of the initial term, oil or gas is discovered in paying quantities and steps are taken to begin production. When that happens, the lease continues in duration thereafter (into the secondary term) "so long as" production continues. (The "so long as" or "so long thereafter" clause is commonly termed the "habendum clause.") Some leases include further clauses allowing a lessee to discontinue production, without having the lease come to an end, if fixed payments are made (shut-in royalties) during the period of nonproduction. By paying shut-in royalties, the lessee can avoid losing the lease due to nonproduction. Numerous legal issues arise under such leases. For instance, what if a lessee ceases production for a time but then resumes production before the landowner complains (perhaps with the landowner accepting royalty payments)? What if instead the lessee has no right to pay shut-in royalties in lieu of production, but tenders payment anyway and the landowner accepts? Is the lease still valid? (A similar issue arises when payment is late and the landowner nonetheless accepts it.) Related to these issues is the problem that arises when a lease contains an express or implied covenant by the lessee to market oil and gas from a well. What happens when the lessee breaches this covenant to market? And, again, what if marketing resumes before the landowner complains?

The following case raises a number of these issues. If you read it carefully you can learn a great deal about the practical elements of oil and gas law:

DANNE v. TEXACO EXPLORATION AND PRODUCTION, INC.

883 P.2d 210 (Ok. App.1994).

BOUDREAU, PRESIDING JUDGE.

Herbert J. Danne, Richard Danne, Arthur Danne, Florence Wetting, Eloise M. Flint, and William F. Lohmeyer Living Trust, Plaintiffs (lessors), brought this action to cancel oil and gas leases in section 35–17N–8W, Kingfisher County, Oklahoma, leased to Texaco, Inc., Defendant (lessee). Texaco appeals a trial court judgment in favor of all lessors terminating the leases for failure to produce in paying quantities and for failure to exercise due diligence to market the product. Four questions are presented on appeal: (1) whether a lease can expire automatically, according to its own terms, in the secondary lease term; (2) whether a lease can expire automatically for failure to pay shut-in royalties in a timely fashion; (3) whether the acceptance of shut-in royalty and royalty payments estops a lessor from asserting that a lease is terminated; and (4) whether a lessee violates the implied covenant to market by failing to produce gas for over four years from a well that is capable of production.

Factual History

[The case involved chiefly three leases, all of which pertained to a single drilling and spacing unit—which meant that a single well produced gas on behalf of all of the landowner-lessors. A producing gas well was opened, and the three leases covering it were all extended beyond their primary terms into the secondary terms as production continued. For over four years, however, the lessee (Texaco) halted production. It then resumed.

The leases contained a shut-in royalty clause under which Texaco had to make annual royalty payments to keep the leases from terminating. Texaco tendered the royalties only at the end of the four-year period. Lessor Danne refused the payments; lessors Lohmeyer and Flint accepted them. When product resumed, Danne refused production royalty payments while Lohmeyer and Flint accepted them. All three lessors then sought to cancel the lease due to the four-year gap in production. Danne argued that the leases terminated automatically due to the cessation. Lohmeyer and Flint argued the same, and stated further that the acceptance of further payments did not revive the leases. The court began its legal analysis by asking whether the leases ended automatically due to the halt in production, or whether instead the lessors had to take affirmative action to terminate the leases—a distinction that will be familiar to students of the law of estates in land and future interests.]

Automatic Termination of a Lease for Failure to Satisfy the Habendum Clause

Lessors assert, and the trial court agreed, that Texaco's lease terminated automatically, according to the terms of its habendum clause, for failure to produce gas in paying quantities. The question of automatic lease termination is significant in this action; if automatic termination can occur, no action of the lessors (even acceptance of royalty benefits) will have the effect of maintaining the lease in full force and effect. Since the facts relating to the terms of these leases are stipulated, the issue presented is one of law. . . .

We first consider the habendum clauses in the Danne, Lohmeyer, and Flint leases. Each states: "It is agreed that this lease shall remain in force for a period of ____ years from date (herein called primary term) and *as long thereafter* as oil or gas, or either of them, is produced from said land by the lessee." (Emphasis added.) In Oklahoma, "[t]he term 'produced,' when used in a 'thereafter' provision of the habendum clause, denotes in law production in paying quantities." *Stewart v. Amerada Hess Corp.,* 604 P.2d 854, 857 (Okla.1979). *See also Pack v. Santa Fe Minerals, A Div. of Santa Fe Int'l Corp.,* 869 P.2d 323, 326 (Okla.1994) (a typical habendum clause which extends the lease past its primary term as long as oil or gas is produced is interpreted to mean "produced in paying quantities").

Most jurisdictions view habendum clauses using a "thereafter" provision as "conveying an interest subject to a special limitation rather than as conveying an interest subject to a condition, power of termination or right of re-entry." 3 Howard R. Williams, Oil and Gas Law § 604 (1991). In these jurisdictions, the habendum clause may be likened to a determinable estate, which automatically ends upon the happening of a condition, with no action required by the grantor. Oklahoma does not, however, take the view that habendum clauses are special limitations; rather, Oklahoma views the habendum clause as an estate on condition subsequent creating only a right of entry in the grantor. With such an estate, the grantor must bring an action to cause forfeiture of the estate. For example, in *Stewart,* the court held that "[t]he occurrence of the limiting event or condition *does not automatically effect an end to the right.*" *Stewart,* 604 P.2d at 858 (emphasis added). The court further commented that:

> Our law is firmly settled that the result in each case [with regard to cessation of production] must depend upon the circumstances that surround cessation. Our view is no doubt influenced in part by the strong policy of our statutory law against forfeiture of estates. The terms of 23 O.S.1971 § 2 clearly mandate that courts avoid the effect of forfeiture by giving due consideration to compelling equitable circumstances.

Id. This view was confirmed in a recent decision where mineral owners brought an action to cancel a lease for failure to produce in paying quantities during a temporary shut in of gas. The court held that "under *no* circumstances will cessation of production in paying quantities *ipso facto* deprive the lessee of his extended-term estate." *Pack,* 869 P.2d at 327 (quoting *Stewart,* 604 P.2d at 858) (emphasis original).

The view of the supreme court in *Pack* is fully consistent with previous Oklahoma law regarding habendum clauses, but may appear confusing because Oklahoma has also recognized automatic termination of oil and gas leases in some circumstances. However, an examination of the cases indicates that, for the purposes of lease termination, Oklahoma makes a distinction between clauses of the primary term and clauses of the secondary term of the lease *See Duer v. Hoover & Bracken Energies, Inc.,* 753 P.2d 395, 398 (Okla.Ct.App.1986) . . .

In the primary term, before hydrocarbons are discovered, the lessee has the right to explore for a fixed period of time. If he fails to discover hydrocarbons within the enumerated period, he must either buy more time (through payment of something like a delay rental) or lose the lease when the term has expired. When the time runs out on the primary term, the estate is not forfeited, it simply ceases to exist by its own terms, a simple terminable estate. Automatic termination of the lease at this stage of exploration does not divest the lessee of valuable assets, since no assets have yet been proved. *See Duer,* 753 P.2d at 398; *Petroleum Eng'rs,* 350 P.2d at 604; *Ellison,* 244 P.2d at 835.

Occurrences of limiting conditions in the secondary lease term are treated differently. The habendum clause enumerates the conditions of continuation of the lease from the primary fixed term into a secondary term of indefinite duration. It directs continuation of the lease so long as production is maintained for the mutual benefit of the lessee and lessor. No automatic termination of the lessee's estate can be tolerated at this stage in the life of the lease, because the lessee has proved a valuable asset and has established a right to develop that asset. The interest the lessee has, after drilling and proving hydrocarbons, can be likened to a vested estate, the loss of which can only be effected through an action for forfeiture. Consequently, at law, the lessee in the secondary term must be given a reasonable opportunity to develop the asset without unreasonable fear of forfeiture.

Therefore, in the case at bar, since production from the Helen Danne No. 1 well has moved the lease into its secondary term, we hold that Texaco's lease can not be terminated automatically.

II

Automatic Termination of Lease for Failure to Make Timely Payment of Shut-in Royalties

Texaco tendered shut-in royalties to lessors Lohmeyer and Flint four years after the Helen Danne No. 1 well was shut in. The terms of their leases require that shut-in royalties be paid annually to the lessors when a producing well is shut in. . . . By tendering payments four years after the well was shut in, Texaco failed to make timely payment of the shut-in royalties as directed by the terms of the lease. Lessors cite a recent Oklahoma Court of Appeals, Division 3, case as a similar fact situation where the court of appeals affirmed a trial court grant of judgment, in part, on the grounds that "the lease expired under its own terms for failure to pay shut-in royalties in the manner provided by the lease." *Christian v. Texaco,* Appeal No. 79,590 (Okla.Ct.App., June 22, 1993, unpublished opinion). To the extent that lessors rely on *Christian* for the proposition that failure to pay shut-in royalties results in automatic lease termination, we believe they are misguided. Unless a lease clearly provides for forfeiture of the lessee's estate upon failure to make timely payment, the lessor's grounds for relief lay only in contract law. [citations omitted] Similarly, in a case where a lessee failed to pay shut-in royalties promptly the court held that "failure to pay shut-in royalties in and of itself does not operate to cause a termination of the lease." *Pack,* 869 P.2d at 330. We therefore hold that Texaco's failure to timely tender shut-in royalties does not cause automatic forfeiture of Texaco's lease, because the Lohmeyer and Flint leases do not expressly state that such forfeiture is mandated.

III

Estoppel by Acceptance of Benefits

It has been held in Oklahoma that acceptance of royalties does not estop the lessor from asserting lease cancellation, if the lease has already automatically expired, by its own terms, prior to acceptance of royalties. *Woodruff v. Brady,* 181 Okla. 105, 72 P.2d 709, 711–12 (1937). "[I]f a lessee should continue to make royalty payments to the lessor after the lease has terminated according to its own terms, the receipt of such payments will not work an estoppel against the lessor, and such lessor may nevertheless assert that the lease has terminated." 3 E. Kuntz, Oil and Gas § 43.2 (1989).

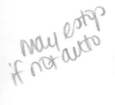

When a lease does not expire automatically, however, the lessor's acceptance of benefits may estop the lessor from asserting lease termination. Even in a case where an express covenant to drill wells was breached by the lessee, the lessor has been estopped from asserting termination of the lease on grounds of acceptance of royalties from lessee. *Anderson v. Talley,* 199 Okla. 491, 187 P.2d 206 (1947). The court ruled that "[b]y the receipt of the [royalty] payments, the lessor clearly and definitely recognized the existence of the lease long after the breach. We conclude the lessor waived the breach of the lease which the lessees had committed and that plaintiff is not entitled to cancellation of the lease therefor." *Id.* 187 P.2d at 208.

Similarly, the court has held that it is "[a] long recognized rule ... that acquiescence in a lease and acceptance of royalty constitutes waiver of any objection the lessor could have taken regarding alteration and estops the lessor from denying the lessee's title." [citations omitted]

It is undisputed that Texaco tendered and lessors, Lohmeyer and Flint, accepted shut-in royalties dated June 3, 1991 (for the period April 14, 1989, to April 13, 1992) and also accepted shut-in royalties dated February 21, 1992 (for annual shut-in royalties dated April 18, 1992). Lohmeyer and Flint also accepted monthly production royalty checks from Texaco from February 24, 1992, to January 23, 1993. Since these leases were held by production in the secondary term, these leases could not expire automatically by their terms; rather, they could only terminate through an action against Texaco. However, before bringing such action, Lohmeyer and Flint accepted the benefits of shut-in royalties tendered expressly for the purpose of continuing the lease in the absence of production. Lohmeyer and Flint also accepted production royalties both before and after this law suit was filed. We find that the conduct of Lohmeyer and Flint affirmed the existence of their leases with Texaco and that they are now estopped from denying Texaco's claim of title. We, therefore, reverse the trial court's grant of lease cancellation to Lohmeyer and Flint.

IV

Termination of the Lease for Failure to Produce in Paying Quantities and Breach of Implied Covenant to Market

Since lessor Danne did not accept benefits in the form of royalties from Texaco after the Helen Danne No. 1 well was shut-in, Danne is not estopped from asserting cancellation of the lease for failure to produce in paying quantities or for failure to exercise due diligence to market the product. It is, therefore, necessary to further consider these issues.

Though we have held that a lease cannot terminate automatically in the secondary term of the lease, this holding should not be construed to imply that failure to satisfy the terms of the habendum clause can never result in forfeiture of the lease. Rather, such forfeiture can result if an action is brought and it is demonstrated that the lessee either failed to produce in paying quantities or failed to market the product with due diligence in breach of the implied covenant to market the product.

In the case at bar, lessors contend that the Helen Danne No. 1 well's capability of producing in paying quantities cannot satisfy the terms of a "thereafter" habendum clause. This issue has been previously considered in Oklahoma in a case where a discovery was made in the primary term of the lease, but a market had not yet been found for the product before expiration of the primary term. *McVicker v. Horn, Robinson & Nathan,* 322 P.2d 410 (Okla.1958). The court in *McVicker* held that with the exercise of due diligence, capability to produce could hold the lease into the secondary term within the meaning of production in the habendum clause. *Id.* The court, however, limited this holding by stating that "[o]il and gas lessees should not be allowed to hold their leases indefinitely, while no product therefrom is being marketed and diligent efforts are not being made to accomplish this." *Id.* at 416. . . .

Most persuasively, in a fact situation nearly identical to the case at bar, where the lessors attempted a lease cancellation because a well that was capable of production had been shut in, the supreme court clarified that capability of production satisfies the terms of the habendum clause. *James Energy Co. v. HCG Energy Corp.,* 847 P.2d 333, 339 (Okla.1992). The plaintiffs admitted that the well was capable of producing in paying quantities. Therefore, the court held that the leases were held by production and did not expire by their own terms. *Id.* We, therefore, hold that a well that is capable of production in the secondary term of the lease can satisfy the requirement of "production" in a "thereafter" habendum clause, subject to satisfaction of other covenants in the lease.

Capability of production alone, however, without a significant attempt to market the product, will not suffice to hold the lease because there is a covenant to market the product with due diligence implied in each oil and gas lease. *See Pack,* 869 P.2d at 330 ("typical oil and gas leases contain an implied covenant to market oil and gas from the subject wells"). The efforts to secure a market for production must be assessed according to the facts and circumstances of each case. *See Flag Oil Corp. of Delaware v. King Resources Co.,* 494 P.2d 322, 325 (Okla. 1972) ("[I]n the absence of ... an express requirement [to market the product], the lessee's duty to market is based on an implied covenant.... [T]he diligence of the lessee's efforts, and the reasonable probability of their [*sic*] success, are factors to be taken into consideration in determining what constitutes a 'reasonable time' under this rule.") An action for lease cancellation, brought for failure to market the product with due diligence, is an action of equitable cognizance, and we will affirm the judgment of the trial court unless it is clearly against the weight of the evidence. *Barby v. Singer,* 648 P.2d 14, 17 (Okla.1982).

Texaco operates a well that is capable of production, but was shut in for over four years. Texaco asserts that the well was shut in by mistake, but acknowledges that during the first two years of shut in, Phillips had a gas meter at the well and could have taken the gas at spot-market prices. Under these facts and circumstances, the trial court took the view that Texaco failed to exercise due diligence to market the product to a readily-available gas purchaser. The trial court's view is neither inconsistent with the facts presented, nor unsupported by previous decisions.

.... Absent any clear evidence undermining the trial court's view that Texaco lacked sufficient cause to justify the shut in, and absent circumstances estopping the claim of lease cancellation (such as affect lessors Lohmeyer and Flint), the trial court's view that this lease is terminated for failure to market the product with due diligence must be upheld. We therefore affirm the trial court's grant of lease cancellation to lessor Danne.

CONCLUSION

In summary, we hold that a lease cannot terminate automatically for lessee's failure to produce in paying quantities within the meaning of the habendum clause or to make timely payment of shut-in royalties. In the secondary term of the lease, when the lease is capable of production, an action for lease termination must be brought in order to cause forfeiture of the lessee's estate. Because Lohmeyer and Flint accepted benefits from Texaco before bringing such action, they are now estopped from denying Texaco's title. We, therefore, reverse the trial court's grant of lease termination to Lohmeyer and Flint. Danne, however, has accepted no benefits from Texaco since bringing this action and is thus not estopped from denying Texaco's title.

Though we hold that, in the secondary term, a well that is capable of production can hold the lease within the meaning of the habendum clause, we find that the weight of evidence supports the trial court's holding that Texaco failed to act with due diligence to market the product. We therefore affirm the trial court's grant of lease cancellation to Danne on grounds that Texaco forfeited the lease for breach of the implied covenant to market.

Notes

1. *Oil and gas leases.* The *Danne* decision gives a good overview of the various lease provisions commonly used in the oil and gas industry to specify the duration of private rights. It may prove useful to identify all of them and then go through the list with the following question in mind: Which provisions are included to protect or promote the interests of the landowner, and which are included instead to protect or aid the lessee-producer? Is the ultimate effect, considering all the provisions, a fair balance between the two parties? When leases are ambiguous, are there particular public policies that ought to kick in? That is, does the state care one way or another whether a lessee produces oil from a given location?

The particular rules of law that the court in *Danne* sets forth invite questions. Automatic termination of a lease occurs due to nonproduction during the primary term but not during the secondary term. Why is that, as a policy matter? Here, Texaco not only failed to produce gas for four years it failed to make timely payments. Acceptance of the payments, the court tells us, waives the delay in payment. Is this a fair rule, particularly in the case of small landowners who may know nothing about oil and gas law and who, with little thought, might cash a check that arrives in the mail? (On this issue, compare Freeman v. Magnolia Petroleum Co., 141 Tex. 274, 171 S.W.2d 339 (1943) (failure to pay shut-in royalty on time results in automatic termination of lease).)

Perhaps the biggest surprise in this opinion is the court's conclusion that a gas well produces gas in paying quantities, even when shut in, so long as the lessee is making reasonable efforts to find someone to buy the gas. (On this issue, it helps to know that above-ground storage of gas is costly and dangerous. Gas is therefore usually not produced from a well unless a buyer is willing to take the gas immediately.) What policy considerations might explain this rule? Note that the rule does operate in tandem with the covenant, implied in all leases, that the lessee must make reasonable efforts to market the gas. The effect of the two provisions is to retain a use-it-or-lose it element in the lease (the lessee must either produce or actively market), while at the same time acknowledging that production might sometimes halt due to the lack of a buyer.

2. *What is production?* A critical issue in many leases that link lease continuance to production has to do with the definition of production. As this case highlights, the definition is not always obvious. Here, the ability to produce matched with marketing efforts is enough. Nearly all states take the view that production must be in "paying quantities" in order to qualify. A leading court defined this phrase as follows:

> The term "paying quantities" involves not only the amount of production, but also the ability to market the product (gas) at a profit. Whether there is a reasonable basis for the expectation of profitable returns from the well is the test. If the quantity be sufficient to warrant the use of the gas in the market, and the income therefrom is in excess of the

actual marketing cost, and operating costs, the production satisfies the term "in paying quantities."

Clifton v. Koontz, 160 Tex. 82, 325 S.W.2d 684 (1959). When deciding profit for this purpose the calculation looks only at marginal costs. The initial costs of drilling and equipping the well are not considered, since these are sunk costs that do not affect decisions about whether to continue production. Complications arise as to overriding royalties (sometimes included in expenses, sometimes not) and as to the cost of plugging wells and other "clean up" expenses. A further issue that has nagged courts has to do with depreciation on well equipment. The tendency is to exclude depreciation on original drilling costs but to include depreciation on production-related equipment that diminishes in value through continued use. E.g., Stewart v. Amerada Hess Corp., 604 P.2d 854 (Okl. 1979).

3. *A mining analogy:* Vulcan Materials Co. v. Holzhauer. In Vulcan Materials, 234 Ill.App.3d 444, 174 Ill.Dec. 665, 599 N.E.2d 449 (1992), a lease covering a rock quarry obligated the lessee to "proceed to mine and quarry the sand, gravel, and/or limestone there contained in a good and economical manner so as to take out the greatest amount of sand, gravel or limestone ... Lessee shall work and mine said premises as aforesaid as steadily and continuously as the market ... and the weather will permit." The lease called for royalty payments based on the tonnage and selling prices of substances removed. It also provided for minimum royalties of $5,000 per quarter. In the event the lessee "abandoned" the premises for one year the lessor could cancel the lease. After mining on the site for several years, the lessee ceased mining for ten years while paying the minimum royalty. At that point, the lessee announced a plan to resume mining. The lessor promptly canceled the lease for abandonment, but then accepted a further check for the minimum royalty. *Held:* While acceptance of the royalties over the ten-year period had no effect on the lessor's rights, the lessor waived his right to cancel the lease when he accepted a further royalty payment after sending notice of termination.

4. *A sea kelp comparison.* In Fanning v. Oregon Division of State Lands, 950 P.2d 353 (Or. App. 1997), plaintiffs leased coastal land from the Oregon Division of State Lands to harvest sea kelp. The lease extended for four and one-half years with an option to renew for an additional ten years so long as the plaintiffs complied with the lease terms. Included among the terms was an obligation to harvest at least 1,000 tons of sea kelp annually. In the event the harvesting duty was violated the Division had the discretionary authority to cancel the lease. During the initial term the plaintiffs breached the harvesting duty every year and the Division refrained from declaring a lease forfeiture. When the plaintiffs sought to renew the lease the Division asserted that the option to renew was forfeited by the breach. The court held that the specific facts related to the Division's behavior—allowing continued breaches of the 1000–ton harvesting obligation—presented a prima facie case that the Division had waived its right to declare forfeiture. Plaintiffs alleged further that the Division committed fraud by advising them that they could renew the release despite the breaches. The Division responded that the plaintiffs did not actually rely on the statements and that, if they did, their reliance was not reasonable under the circumstances. On this issue also the court ruled that the alleged facts presented a valid

case for fraud and that disputes over material facts made summary judgment inappropriate.

D. ABANDONMENT AND FORFEITURE

Except in the case of resource rights that involve corporeal interests in real estate—rather than easements or profits, which are considered incorporeal—private rights can come to an end through abandonment or its statutory variant, forfeiture. Abandonment takes place when the owner of a thing intentionally gives up rights in it. Mere nonuse of an interest does not lead to abandonment, although nonuse can provide strong evidence of intent to relinquish. When the intent to abandon is clear (as when a person throws trash into a waste basket) abandonment can take place in an instant. Forfeiture is usually prescribed by statute and is based on nonuse of a thing for a specified period of time. No intent is required, but the passage of time is normally necessary. Although the terms abandonment and forfeiture are typically used with some precision a reader must always be alert. The terms are sometimes mixed up or even used as synonyms. With some regularity statute drafters use the term abandonment when drafting what are better described as forfeiture provisions.

It may seem strange to think of abandonment and forfeiture as limits on the duration of a resource-use right, but they operate in that way. Sooner or later resource use rights come to an end. Often abandonment and forfeiture occur when a resource right is no longer economically valuable, whether due to exhaustion of it, shifting market forces or other reasons. The doctrines, then, perform a kind of clean-up role. They get rid of legal rights that are no longer of much value.

WHEATLAND IRRIGATION DISTRICT v. LARAMIE RIVERS CO.

659 P.2d 561 (Wyo. 1983).

ROSE, JUSTICE.

The appellant, Wheatland Irrigation District (sometimes referred to as Wheatland), filed a petition with the Board of Control seeking abandonment of 41,100 of the 68,500 acre feet of water appropriated under two reservoir permits issued to the appellee Laramie Rivers Company (sometimes referred to as Laramie Rivers) for the Lake Hattie reservoir near Laramie, Wyoming. The sources of supply for Lake Hattie are the Laramie and the Little Laramie Rivers and, if the petition were to be granted and the Board of Control's order upheld by the courts, appellee Laramie Rivers would be left with a 27,400 acre-foot capacity in the reservoir. The appellant, owner of Wheatland Reservoir No. 3 which receives water from the same water sources as does Lake Hattie, holds a permit junior to those of the appellee Laramie Rivers. It is the appellant's theory that the 41,100 acre feet should be declared abandoned by reason of the directives contained in § 41–3–401(a), W.S.1977, on the ground that the appellee had failed "to use the water therefrom for the beneficial purposes for which it was appropriated * * * during any five (5) successive years * * *." § 41–3–401(a), W.S.1977.

[T]his section of the statute goes on to provide that if the holder of the appropriation has not used the water for this period of time, " * * * he is considered as having abandoned the water right and shall forfeit all water rights and privileges appurtenant thereto."

[The Board of Control denied the petition seeking a declaration of abandonment on the ground that Laramie Rivers had done substantial work repairing the reservoir before the petition was filed, even though more than five years had gone by without use of the reservoir-storage permit covering 41,400 acre feet of water. Because this repair work had started, the petition seeking abandonment was untimely. The issue before the state supreme court was whether the Board of Control could properly deny a petition that was filed after repair work on a reservoir was commenced but before the water was returned to a beneficial use (in this instance, stored in the repaired reservoir.)]

The record in this case shows that a restriction to 27,400 feet of storage has been in effect at Lake Hattie since April 5, 1972 when it was imposed by the State Engineer because of infirmities in the dam. In March of 1980, the state of Wyoming approved a loan to Laramie Rivers so that the dam could be repaired, after which, on May 16, 1980, Laramie Rivers publicly announced its intentions with respect to dam repair and future water storage plans. This was the first Wheatland knew of Laramie Rivers' loan approval and dam improvement plans. One week later, on May 23, the abandonment petition was filed. Two days before the filing of the petition, soil compaction tests had been made and the construction company hired for the repair work was placing fill and proceeding with the construction. By July 7, 1980 the work was substantially complete.

According to the record that is available to this court, the Laramie Rivers Company had not stored water in Lake Hattie, and had not beneficially used any water therefrom in excess of the 27,400 acre-foot limitation from April, 1972 until the time the petition for abandonment was filed on May 23, 1980. In fact, no water was stored or beneficially used above the limitation up to the time of hearing before the Board of Control on February 17, 18 and 19, 1981, nor had any water been stored or used above the limitation when the parties were before the district court on July 1, 1982. . . .

These things being so, we must look to the statute to see whether or not the Board of Control was possessed of the authority to deny Wheatland's petition for partial abandonment on the ground that, at the time of its filing, "substantial work had been undertaken to repair the dam," (¶ 7 of Board's findings of fact) and therefore the petition was not "promptly asserted" (¶ 6 of conclusions of law).

THE LAW

Statutory Construction

There are no innuendos or double entendres to be found in § 41–3–401(a). The intention of the legislature is there expressed in plain English, leaving no room whatever for our seeking out any rules of statutory construction except those which direct us to apply the statute according to the plain, ordinary meaning of the words to be found therein. *Board of County Commissioners of the County of Campbell v. Ridenour,* Wyo., 623 P.2d 1174, reh. denied 627 P.2d 163 (1981).

What does the statute say? It says that where the holder of an appropriation of water for a reservoir water source "* * * *fails* * * * *to use the water therefrom for the beneficial purposes for which it was appropriated* * * *" (emphasis added) for a period of five successive years "*he is considered as having abandoned the water right and SHALL forfeit all water rights and privileges appurtenant thereto.*" (All emphasis added.)

This legislative directive amounts to a forfeiture by statute if the facts fit the mandate. It leaves the Board of Control and the courts no room to save an appropriator from an abandonment petition where his water has not been used for the beneficial purposes for which it was appropriated for the "five (5) successive years" contemplated by the statute. The statute says that the appropriation "SHALL" (emphasis added) be declared abandoned in circumstances where the five-year nonuse showing is made even where the failure to make beneficial application of the water is unintentional. The applicable legislative enactments do not envision authority in the Board of Control or the courts to relieve an appropriator from the abandonment statute's violent impact for any of the reasons that the Board utilized in denying Wheatland's petition.

The Board denied the petition on the grounds that contestee, Laramie Rivers, had undertaken "substantial work" (¶ 6 of conclusions of law, *supra*) to repair the dam when the petition was filed and therefore it was not asserted "promptly." (¶ 6 of conclusions of law, *supra*). But where in the statute can language be found which permits the Board such leeway as will countenance this holding? It simply is not there. The only thing that will save the contestee from the harshness of the abandonment statute's dictate is for Laramie Rivers to be able to show—once nonuse for the statutory period has been established by the contestant—that the water in contest here was not available for application to a beneficial use within the five-year period contemplated by the statute. See § 41–3–401(b), W.S.1977. *State Board of Control v. Johnson Ranches, Inc.,* Wyo., 605 P.2d 367 (1980).

It is clear to this court that the Board of Control did not apply the appropriate rules of law in coming to its conclusions of law, and thus reached an erroneous ultimate decision.

In ¶ 4 of its conclusions of law, the Board's order says:

> THAT abandonment and forfeiture of water rights are not favored. *Sturgeon v. Brooks,* 73 Wyo. 436, 281 P.2d 675 (1955). Forfeitures must be promptly asserted, and if not asserted they are waived. *Sturgeon v. Brooks,* supra.

And ¶ 5 says:

> THAT water rights will not be set aside unless it is justified by clear and convincing evidence. *Wheatland Irrigation District v. Pioneer Canal Co.,* 464 P.2d 533 (Wyo.1970). The contestant has the burden of proving the abandonment by clear and convincing evidence. *Ramsey v. Gottsche,* 51 Wyo. 516, 69 P.2d 535 (1937).

Referring to ¶ 4 above, where the Board cites *Sturgeon v. Brooks,* 73 Wyo. 436, 281 P.2d 675 (1955), to the effect that forfeitures are not favored in the law, we can only say that this proposition is hardly applicable here. Our concern in this appeal necessarily focuses upon a statutory interpretation question—not whether the court abhors forfeiture. We cannot call up the abhorrence-of-forfeiture rule in order to rescue Laramie Rivers from an abandonment of a water right in lieu of requiring that the applicable statute pertaining to abandonment be applied and given its plain English-language meaning. We are not the legislature. Indeed, we do abhor forfeitures, but it is the legislature that has established this rule for forfeiting water rights—not the court!

The Board of Control has also misapplied the rule of Sturgeon v. Brooks, supra, where, in conclusion of law ¶ 4, it cites that authority for the proposition that "[f]orfeitures must be promptly asserted and if not asserted they are waived."

We find no language in § 41–3–401 or any other applicable statute which suggests that a petitioner's lack of promptness will become grounds for penalty at any time before the appropriator's water has been applied to a beneficial use. In any case, it hardly seems that this rule could come into play to deny *this* appellant its statutory right to file a petition for abandonment when it is remembered that the filing was made within a week or ten days from the date the announcement that the improvements would be undertaken—two days after the commencement of the work at the site and in all events prior to the assignment of the contested water to the reservoir or to any other authorized use contemplated by Laramie Rivers' appropriation certificates. . . .

In *Wheatland Irrigation District v. Pioneer Canal Co.,* Wyo., 464 P.2d 533 (1970), we were later confronted with a fact situation (like the case before the court here) where a forfeiture petition was filed *before* the water had been applied to its beneficial use. There, both the Board of Control and the district court found that the Pioneer Canal Company should have a reasonable period of time to enlarge their reservoir to its appropriated size rather than abandoning the right as to any excess over its present capacity. This court reversed the district court's affirmance of the Board of Control's order and declared the excess of the right to be abandoned. Commenting on *Sturgeon v. Brooks,* we said:

> * * * One of the questions dealt with in the case was whether or not the owner had abandoned his storage right because of the prolonged disuse of the reservoir. We held he had not for the reason no formal declaration of abandonment had theretofore been obtained from the board or the district court. It was said, however, 'that if the action for forfeiture had been *brought before Brooks* [defendant] *put the reservoir again into use,* the court would have been justified, if not constrained, to declare a forfeiture,' 281 P.2d at 684. Inasmuch as there has been no change in the statute relating to the matter since that time, see § 41–47, W.S.1957, the rationale of the case is particularly persuasive here, and as indicated above we hold the board and the district court erred in granting Pioneer additional time within which to enlarge its reservoir. (Emphasis added.) 464 P.2d at 540–541.

We subscribe to the rule of *Wheatland Irrigation District v. Pioneer Canal Co.,* supra, as suggested in *Sturgeon v. Brooks,* supra, to the effect that § 41–3–401(a) requires forfeiture to be declared where the nonuse is shown for the statutory period and the only use which will rescue contestees from the gnashing teeth of that statute is *the use of the water* "* * * for the beneficial purposes for which it was appropriated * * *."

Undertaking repairs before filing a petition does not prevent forfeiture. Only the use of the water will prevent a forfeiture. § 41–3–401(a), W.S.1977. . . .

CONCLUSION

We hold that the Wheatland Irrigation District's petition was timely filed, and the Board of Control may not, as was done in this case, circumvent the clear language of § 41–3–401(a), which provides that a forfeiture may only be avoided by application of water to beneficial use . . .

Notes

1. *Why forfeiture?* According to the facts, Laramie Rivers partially drained its reservoir because it had to. The reservoir was unsafe, and repairs were needed. Before making repairs, inspections were needed, engineering work had to take place, and owners needed to arrange financing. All of this can take time. Why does the law impose such a strict, five-year time requirement for getting the work done and refilling the reservoir? Can we imagine a different rule—some sort of flexible, due-diligence rule like those we have seen in other corners of the law (in the relation-back rule for obtaining an appropriative water right and the rule applied in Colorado to retain a conditional water right)? What are the pros and cons of a forfeiture rule that has a strict deadline?

To answer that question, we presumably need to dig even deeper. Why do we have forfeiture rules to begin with? Presumably Wheatland Irrigation District stands to gain if Laramie Rivers has abandoned its storage permit. (We don't know in what way it will gain, but we can presume it has a water right next in line or will otherwise be able to use the water storage right that Laramie Rivers has now lost.) Could the law simply allow the parties to work things out through negotiation? Does the forfeiture rule in operation promote the most efficient and socially beneficial use of water? The underlying idea is a use-it-or-lose it rule, intended to get people to use their resources. But why press a resource-owner to use a resource if use under the circumstances makes little sense? Cannot a use-it-or-lose it mentality sometimes promote wasteful practices by resource uses who want to avoid losing their rights? For instance, why press an irrigator to use more water during unusually wet years, just to avoid any possibility of forfeiture? Why force an oil and gas lessee to continue production when market prices are low and it makes more sense to halt production until prices rise?

2. *A literal application of law?* The court in this ruling chastises the Board of Control for failing to apply the state forfeiture statute in accordance with its literal terms. But did the court sin in the same way? The Board of Control wanted to protect Laramie Rivers from forfeiture if it began repairing the reservoir before any junior water user filed a petition of forfeiture. Note, though, what the court decides. It tell us that Laramie Rivers can avoid forfeiture if it resumes its actual beneficial use of the water. The language on this possibility is dictum, given that Laramie Rivers did not resume beneficial use. But where did the court get this rule of law? If forfeiture is automatic, then how can Laramie Rivers regain its old water right by resuming its beneficial use? Is the issue here essentially the same one that we just saw in *Danne v. Texaco Exploration?* That is, do we have here a distinction between forfeiture that is automatic (akin to a determinable fee), and forfeiture that requires affirmative action by a junior water user to terminate the unused water right (akin to a fee simple on a condition subsequent)?

Putting to one side the statutory language, which of these approaches would be better? Is it wise to have a right that terminates on its own, without any legal action, or is it better to require that a junior user step forward and take legal action to declare a forfeiture? In the case of a large water right of considerable value, a legal action might make sense. But what about a rather modest water right, not worth enough economically to justify legal expenses? Keep in mind, as you consider this issue, the reality that many water disputes are not as publicly visible as this one. Presumably any person could see that Laramie Rivers had largely drained its reservoir and was not fully using its storage permit. But what about water uses that are more private? How is another water user supposed to know that an irrigator has used only three-quarters of his water right for a period in excess of five years? Going further, would it be possible under this ruling for a person to try to revive a water right that has not been used for 50 or even 100 years, just by quietly resuming beneficial use before anyone takes legal action?

3. *The costs of uncertainty.* As you consider this case, pay attention to the awkward positions of the two parties in light of the court's ruling. Laramie Rivers wants to repair its reservoir but the five-year period has run out. Should it risk beginning repair work if, at any moment prior to completion, a junior user could file a petition of forfeiture? On the other side, if you represented Wheatland Irrigation would you think it worth the effort and money to file a forfeiture action if it seemed highly unlikely that

Laramie Rivers would ever try to repair the reservoir? Why incur the legal costs? Might both sides (and everyone else) be better off with a mechanical rule of automatic forfeiture after five years?

4. *Use in the wrong place:* Hannigan v. Hinton. When we think of nonuse we typically think about a complete failure to use a resource. But what if the resource is used, but in the wrong way or in the wrong place?

Hannigan v. Hinton, 97 P.3d 1256, 195 Or.App. 345 (2004), involved a ruling by the Oregon Water Resources Department cancelling a water right on the ground that the rights holder used the water in an unauthorized place. Use in the wrong place, the Department ruled, amounted to nonuse within the forfeiture statute, just as did use of the water for an impermissible purpose. On appeal, the court agreed:

> As we have already noted, ORS 540.610(1) provides that "[b]eneficial use shall be the basis, the measure and the limit of all rights to the use of water * * *." Rights are forfeited when the certificate holder "fails to *use* all or part of the water appropriated for a period of five successive years." *Id.* (emphasis added). Accordingly, our task is to determine whether use of water on land other than that specified in the certificate constitutes "use" for purposes of ORS 540.610.
>
> In *Hennings v. Water Resources Dept.,* 50 Or.App. 121, 124, 622 P.2d 333 (1981), we held that water use for a *purpose* other than that set forth in the certificate did not constitute "use" that could avoid forfeiture of water rights under a prior version of ORS 540.610. The petitioner in *Hennings* had used the water to wet ground for plowing but not for "irrigation" as designated in the certificate. 50 Or.App. at 123–24, 622 P.2d 333. We noted that "[t]he statutory scheme as a whole illustrates that the use contemplated must be that of the perfected water right and not some other use." *Id.* at 124, 622 P.2d 333. . . .
>
> By contrast, in *Russell-Smith v. Water Resources Dept.,* 152 Or.App. 88, 96, 952 P.2d 104, *rev den,* 327 Or. 173, 966 P.2d 217 (1998), we held that the same forfeiture penalty does not apply to unauthorized changes in *point of diversion;* rather, such actions are subject only to injunctive relief, or civil or criminal penalties. *Id.* at 98, 952 P.2d 104. Our conclusion was based on the recognition that Oregon water rights law treats "use" and "point of diversion" as distinct concepts and the forfeiture statute is addressed only to "use." *See id.* at 96, 952 P.2d 104. . . .
>
> We conclude that "place of use" likewise is a component of "use" for purposes of forfeiture. As discussed with regard to "type of use" in *Hennings,* the statutory scheme as a whole illustrates that the place of use contemplated must be that of the perfected water right and not some other place of use. *Cf. Hennings,* 50 Or.App. at 124, 622 P.2d 333. A critical part of that statutory scheme is ORS 540.510(1), which provides, in part:
>
> > Except as provided in subsections (2) to (8) of this section, all water used in this state for any purpose shall remain appurtenant to the premises upon which it is used and no change in use or place of use

of any water for any purpose may be made without compliance with the provisions of ORS 540.520 and 540.530.

Water rights are appurtenant to specific parcels of land; the right to use water is tied to the location on which the water right was perfected ("the premises upon which it is used"), which necessarily is also the location named in the water right certificate. *See* ORS 537.250. ORS 540.510, ORS 540.520, and ORS 540.530 set forth a procedure by which a certificate holder may apply to the department for a change in place of use, but petitioners have not received department approval for such a change, nor do they argue that they are subject to any other exception to ORS 540.510(1) (as set forth in ORS 540.510(2) to (8)). . . .

[Our] interpretation also comports with common-law understandings of "use" and "beneficial use" that existed during the early development of the Oregon Water Code. *See State v. Tarpley,* 157 Or.App. 693, 700, 972 P.2d 1201 (1998), *rev den,* 328 Or. 465, 987 P.2d 514 (1999) (recognizing that context, under the *PGE* analysis, includes "the preexisting common law and statutory framework within which the law was enacted"). The Oregon Supreme Court has held that use of water on premises other than those specified in the certificate is waste. In *Squaw Creek Irr. Dist. v. Mamero et al.,* 107 Or. 291, 295, 214 P. 889 (1923), the state ordered a water district, which had rights to use water on a particular tract, to discontinue using the water on a different tract. The district refused and sought a declaratory judgment of its right to use the water in other locations. *Id.* at 295–96, 214 P. 889. The court agreed with the state that failure to use the water on the land to which it was appurtenant, without prior approval of the state water board, "was unlawful and constituted waste." *Id.* at 304, 214 P. 889.

Waste is the antithesis of "use." *In re Waters of Deschutes River,* 134 Or. 623, 665, 286 P. 563, *on reh'g,* 134 Or. 623, 294 P. 1049 (1930), *appeal dismissed,* 290 U.S. 590, 54 S.Ct. 83, 78 L.Ed. 520 (1933) ("wasteful application of water, even though a useful project, * * * is not included in the term 'use' as contemplated by the law of waters"); *Hennings,* 50 Or.App. at 125, 622 P.2d 333 ("unreasonable waste of all or part of the water constitutes 'non-beneficial use' "). Accordingly, unless the statutory procedure for change of place of use is followed, failure to use a water right for five successive years in the certificated place of use constitutes nonuse and results in forfeiture of the right under ORS 540.610.

TEXACO v. SHORT

454 U.S. 516, 102 S.Ct. 781, 70 L.Ed.2d 738 (1982).

JUSTICE STEVENS delivered the opinion of the Court.

In 1971 the Indiana Legislature enacted a statute providing that a severed mineral interest that is not used for a period of 20 years automatically lapses and reverts to the current surface owner of the property, unless the mineral owner files a statement of claim in the local county recorder's office. The Indiana Supreme Court rejected a challenge to the constitutionality of the statute. Ind., 406 N.E.2d 625 (1980). We noted probable jurisdiction, 450 U.S. 993, 101 S.Ct. 1693, 68 L.Ed.2d 192, and now affirm.

As the Indiana Supreme Court explained, the Mineral Lapse Act "puts an end to interests in coal, oil, gas or other minerals which have not been used for twenty years." The statute provides that the unused interest shall be "extinguished" and that its "ownership shall revert to the then owner of the interest out of which it was carved."[1] The statute, which became effective on September 2, 1971, contained a 2–year grace period in which owners of mineral interests that were then unused and subject to lapse could preserve those interests by filing a claim in the recorder's office.

The "use" of a mineral interest that is sufficient to preclude its extinction includes the actual or attempted production of minerals, the payment of rents or royalties, and any payment of taxes; a mineral owner may also protect his interest by filing a statement of claim with the local recorder of deeds. The statute contains one exception to this general rule: if an owner of 10 or more interests in the same county files a statement of claim that inadvertently omits some of those interests, the omitted interests may be preserved by a supplemental filing made within 60 days of receiving actual notice of the lapse.

The statute does not require that any specific notice be given to a mineral owner prior to a statutory lapse of a mineral estate. The Act does set forth a procedure, however, by which a surface owner who has succeeded to the ownership of a mineral estate pursuant to the statute may give notice that the mineral interest has lapsed. . . .

At all stages of the proceedings, appellants [whose mineral rights lapsed under the statute] challenged the constitutionality of the Dormant Mineral Interests Act. Appellants claimed that the lack of prior notice of the lapse of their mineral rights deprived them of property without due process of law, that the statute effected a taking of private property for public use without just compensation, and that the exception contained in the Act for owners of 10 or more mineral interests denied them the equal protection of the law; appellants based these arguments on the Fourteenth Amendment of the United States Constitution. Appellants also contended that the statute constituted an impairment of contracts in violation of Art. 1, § 10, of the Constitution.[2] The state trial court held that the statute deprived appellants of property without due process of law, and effected a taking of property without just compensation.

On appeal, the Indiana Supreme Court reversed. The court first explained the purpose of the Mineral Lapse Act:

1. "Any interest in coal, oil and gas, and other minerals, shall, if unused for a period of 20 years, be extinguished, unless a statement of claim is filed in accordance with section five hereof [*sic*], and the ownership shall revert to the then owner of the interest out of which it was carved." Ind.Code § 32–5–11–1 (1976).

2. "No State shall . . . pass any Bill of Attainder, ex post facto law, or Law impairing the Obligations of Contracts, or grant any Title of Nobility."

> "The Act reflects the legislative belief that the existence of a mineral interest about which there has been no display of activity or interest by the owners thereof for a period of twenty years or more is mischievous and contrary to the economic interests and welfare of the public. The existence of such stale and abandoned interests creates uncertainties in titles and constitutes an impediment to the development of the mineral interests that may be present and to the development of the surface rights as well. The Act removes this impediment by returning the severed mineral estate to the surface rights owner. There is a decided public interest to be served when this occurs. The extinguishment of such an interest makes the entire productive potential of the property again available for human use." Ind., 406 N.E.2d, at 627.

The court rejected the argument that a lapse of a vested mineral interest could not occur without affording the mineral owner prior notice and an opportunity to be heard. The court noted that "[p]rior to any extinguishment the owner of an interest will have had notice by reason of the enactment itself of the conditions which would give rise to an extinguishment and at a minimum a two-year opportunity to prevent those conditions from occurring by filing a statement of claim." The Indiana Supreme Court also rejected the argument that the statute effected a taking without just compensation....

Appellants raise several specific challenges to the constitutionality of the Mineral Lapse Act. Before addressing these arguments, however, it is appropriate to consider whether the State has the power to provide that property rights of this character shall be extinguished if their owners do not take the affirmative action required by the State.

In *Board of Regents v. Roth*, 408 U.S. 564, 577, 92 S.Ct. 2701, 2709, 33 L.Ed.2d 548, the Court stated:

> Property interests, of course, are not created by the Constitution. Rather, they are created and their dimensions are defined by existing rules or understandings that stem from an independent source such as state law—rules or understandings that secure certain benefits and that support claims of entitlement to those benefits.

The State of Indiana has defined a severed mineral estate as a "vested property interest," entitled to "the same protection as are fee simple titles." Through its Dormant Mineral Interests Act, however, the State has declared that this property interest is of less than absolute duration; retention is conditioned on the performance of at least one of the actions required by the Act. We have no doubt that, just as a State may create a property interest that is entitled to constitutional protection, the State has the power to condition the permanent retention of that property right on the performance of reasonable conditions that indicate a present intention to retain the interest.

From an early time, this Court has recognized that States have the power to permit unused or abandoned interests in property to revert to another after the passage of time. In *Hawkins v. Barney's Lessee*, 5 Pet.

457, 8 L.Ed. 190, the Court upheld a Kentucky statute that prevented a landowner from recovering property on which the defendant had resided for more than seven years under a claim of right. The Court stated:

> "Such laws have frequently passed in review before this Court; and occasions have occurred, in which they have been particularly noticed as laws not to be impeached on the ground of violating private right. What right has any one to complain, when a reasonable time has been given him, if he has not been vigilant in asserting his rights?" *Id.*, at 466.

Similarly, in *Wilson v. Iseminger*, 185 U.S. 55, 22 S.Ct. 573, 46 L.Ed. 804, the Court upheld a Pennsylvania statute that provided for the extinguishment of a reserved interest in ground rent if the owner collected no rent and made no demand for payment for a period of 21 years. Though the effect of the Pennsylvania statute was to extinguish a fee simple estate of permanent duration, the Court held that the legislation was valid.

In these early cases, the Court often emphasized that the statutory "extinguishment" properly could be viewed as the withdrawal of a remedy rather than the destruction of a right. We have subsequently made clear, however, that, when the practical consequences of extinguishing a right are identical to the consequences of eliminating a remedy, the constitutional analysis is the same. *El Paso v. Simmons*, 379 U.S. 497, 506–507, 85 S.Ct. 577, 582–83, 13 L.Ed.2d 446. The extinguishment of the property owners' "remedy" in *Hawkins* and *Iseminger* placed them in precisely the same position as that held by the mineral owners in the instant cases after their interests had lapsed.

The Indiana statute is similar in operation to a typical recording statute. Such statutes provide that a valid transfer of property may be defeated by a subsequent purported transfer if the earlier transfer is not properly recorded. In *Jackson v. Lamphire*, 3 Pet. 280, 7 L.Ed. 679, the Court upheld such a statute, even as retroactively applied to a deed that need not have been recorded at the time delivered. . . .

These decisions clearly establish that the State of Indiana has the power to enact the kind of legislation at issue. In each case, the Court upheld the power of the State to condition the retention of a property right upon the performance of an act within a limited period of time. In each instance, as a result of the failure of the property owner to perform the statutory condition, an interest in fee was deemed as a matter of law to be abandoned and to lapse.

It is also clear that the State has not exercised this power in an arbitrary manner. The Indiana statute provides that a severed mineral interest shall not terminate if its owner takes any one of three steps to establish his continuing interest in the property. If the owner engages in actual production, or collects rents or royalties from another person who does or proposes to do so, his interest is protected. If the owner pays taxes, no matter how small, the interest is secure. If the owner files a written statement of claim in the county recorder's office, the interest remains viable. Only if none of these actions is taken for a period of 20 years does a mineral interest lapse and revert to the surface owner. . . .

In ruling that private property may be deemed to be abandoned and to lapse upon the failure of its owner to take reasonable actions imposed by law, this Court has never required the State to compensate the owner for the consequences of his own neglect. We have concluded that the State may treat a mineral interest that has not been used for 20 years and for which no statement of claim has been filed as abandoned; it follows that, after abandonment, the former owner retains no interest for which he may claim compensation. It is the owner's failure to make any use of the property—and not the action of the State—that causes the lapse of the property right; there is no "taking" that requires compensation. The requirement that an owner of a property interest that has not been used for 20 years must come forward and file a current statement of claim is not itself a "taking."

Nor does the Mineral Lapse Act unconstitutionally impair the obligation of contracts. In the specific cases under review, the mineral owners did not execute the coal and oil leases in question until after the statutory lapse of their mineral rights. The statute cannot be said to impair a contract that did not exist at the time of its enactment. Appellants' right to enter such an agreement of course has been impaired by the statute; this right, however, is a property right and not a contract right. In any event, a mineral owner may safeguard any contractual obligations or rights by filing a statement of claim in the county recorder's office. Such a minimal "burden" on contractual obligations is not beyond the scope of permissible state action.

[The Court also rejected the appellants' claims that they were denied due process because they were not given personal advance notice that their mineral rights were about to lapse.]

Notes

1. *Cleaning-up land titles.* A grave practical problem arises when mineral rights in a parcel of land are fragmented among many owners and it is difficult if not impossible for a potential purchaser or lessee to track down all the owners to negotiate a deal. The problem is most severe when mineral rights are severed from the land surface and separately owned by a person who does not use them. That person dies, perhaps forgetting about the mineral rights. Another generation comes along, and perhaps another after that, with mineral rights increasing fragmented among heirs who may be entirely unaware of them. Mining companies often hire genealogists or private investigators to track down missing heirs so that they can buy or lease rights. The Indiana statute upheld in Texaco v. Short was enacted to help with the problem.

2. *Regulation or redefinition?* Notice that the Court treats the new statute as if it were a regulation of mineral rights. But could we not view it (to use a by-now familiar distinction) as simply a redefinition of the property rights that a person holds in minerals? Private rights in minerals are defined

chiefly by state law and extend only so far as state law provides. Has not Indiana merely exercised its right to recalibrate the duration of private rights in minerals? Just as the state can redefine the rights a landowner has to use property and to complain about interferences, should it also be able to redefine the duration of private rights, making them less than perpetual?

3. *Duration limits on easements and covenants.* Many states have statutes that limit the time period during which an easement or covenant can be enforced—similar to the lapsed mineral rights statute upheld in *Texaco v. Short.* These statutes (sometimes called marketable title acts) can be more restrictive than the mineral rights statutes in that use of the easement may be insufficient to keep it alive. An owner can extend an easement only by periodically filing a notice of intent to extend. Wisconsin's statute was considered in Figuliuzzi v. Carcajou Shooting Club of Lake Koshkonong, 184 Wis.2d 572, 516 N.W.2d 410 (1994), a dispute involving an 1896 grant of rights to hunt and fish.

4. *Maintaining unpatented mining claims:* U.S. v. Locke. One of the challenges that long faced the federal government in managing lands was its difficulty in knowing which lands were subject to unpatented mining claims under the Mining Law of 1872. By 1975, literally millions of mining claims covered federal lands, many of them invalid for lack of adequate discoveries of valuable mineral deposits, failures to locate claims properly, and failures to perform the minimum work required to keep claims alive. Claims were recorded under state rather than federal law, typically in county recorders' offices. A 1976 federal statute instituted a new federal reporting requirement, under which a mining claimant had to file with the Bureau of Land Management, "prior to December 31" of each year, a notice of intention to hold the claim. The Act provided that a failure to comply with the reporting requirement "shall be deemed conclusively to constitute an abandonment of the mining claim." The Act was challenged in United States v. Locke, 471 U.S. 84 (1985). *Held:* Congress has the power to condition ownership of mining claims on the compliance with such annual filing requirements and the Constitution did not require individual notice to mineral claimants whose rights were about to expire. The statute was valid even as applied to mineral claimants who filed on December 31 and who were arguably misled by federal officers to think that the deadline was simply the end of the calendar year.

RIVERSIDE DRAINAGE DISTRICT OF SEDGWICK COUNTY v. HUNT

33 Kan.App.2d 225, 99 P.3d 1135 (2004).

McAnany, J.

[This dispute involved the alleged abandonment of a drainage easement created in 1964 in favor of the public in a small, platted subdivision. The easement was not used prior to 2001, when they governmental drainage district board realized that the easement existed. By then, lot owners had constructed mobile homes, flag poles, two signs, and various fences within the easement area. The owner of one lot, Hunt, removed his fencing and certain other property from the easement area when requested to do so but refused to remove other property. In response to a declaratory judgment action seeking an order requiring removal of the property Hunt raised various defenses: the easement had been abandoned; Hunt had obtained unobstructed title through adverse possession; and the parties by implicit mutual consent had agreed to establish a new boundary line.]

The general rule regarding abandonment of property is set forth in *Botkin v. Kickapoo, Inc.,* 211 Kan. 107, 109–10, 505 P.2d 749 (1973):

> "The law respecting abandonment as applied to property and property rights is well established. Generally, abandonment is the act of intentionally relinquishing a known right absolutely and without reference to any particular person or for any particular purpose. Abandoned property is that to which the owner has voluntarily relinquished all right, title, claim and possession, with the intention of terminating his ownership, but without vesting it in any other person and with the intention of not reclaiming future possession or resuming its ownership, possession or enjoyment. In order to establish an abandonment of property, actual relinquishment accompanied by intention to abandon must be shown. The primary elements are the intention to abandon and the external act by which that intention is carried into effect. Although an abandonment may arise from a single act or from a series of acts the intent to abandon and the act of abandonment must conjoin and operate together, or in the very nature of things there can be no abandonment. The intention to abandon is considered the first and paramount inquiry, and actual intent to abandon must be shown; it is not enough that the owner's acts give reasonable cause to others to believe that the property has been abandoned. Mere relinquishment of the possession of a thing is not an abandonment in a legal sense, for such an act is not wholly inconsistent with the idea of continuing ownership; the act of abandonment must be an overt act or some failure to act which carries the implication that the owner neither claims nor retains any interest in the subject matter of the abandonment. It is not necessary to prove intention to abandon by express declarations or by other direct evidence; intent to abandon property or rights in property is to be determined from all the surrounding facts and circumstances. It may be inferred from the acts and conduct of the owner and from the nature and situation of the property. Mere nonuse of property, lapse of time without claiming or using property, or the temporary absence of the owner, unaccompanied by any other evidence showing intention, generally are not enough to constitute an abandonment. However, such facts are competent evidence of an intent to abandon and as such are entitled to weight when considered with other circumstances. [Citations omitted.]"

The drainage district claims, however, that a different rule applies when the land is an easement dedicated for public use. When land is dedicated for a specific purpose, " 'neither the legislature, a municipality, or its successor, nor the general public has any power to use the property for any other purpose than the one designated....' [Citation omitted.]" The *State, ex rel., v. City of Manhattan,* 115 Kan. 794, 795, 225 P. 85 (1924) (quoting 18 C.J. [Dedication] 127, § 167). The court in *City of Manhattan* went on to state:

> Inasmuch as there are three parties interested in every dedication—the dedicator and his representative, the general public, and the property owners with special interests, such as owners of lots abutting on streets—no one of them without the consent of the others can change or destroy the use. [Citation omitted.] 115 Kan. at 795, 225 P. 85.

The drainage district argues that the easement in question was dedicated for a public use and that Hunt cannot unilaterally change or destroy the use. The drainage district relies upon *Matlack v. City of Wichita,* 195 Kan. 484, 407 P.2d 510 (1965), in which the City acquired property through condemnation for street purposes. A strip of the condemned land was not used and was unoccupied for over 10 years and the plaintiff, who purchased the property, claimed that the City lost the easement by not using it for its intended purposes. The court stated:

> An easement on land dedicated to or condemned for a public use does not revert to the fee owner unless its use for the dedicated or condemned purpose has become impossible, or so highly improbable as to be practically impossible. [Citation omitted.] 195 Kan. at 486, 407 P.2d 510.

The drainage district argues that the purpose for which its maintenance easement was dedicated has not become impossible or so highly improbable as to be practically impossible. The purpose of the easement is to facilitate maintenance of the existing drainage ditch. The drainage ditch exists and will need maintenance from time to time. Thus, the drainage district argues, the district court erred in finding that it abandoned the easement.

Hunt relies on *Pratt v. Griese,* 196 Kan. 182, 409 P.2d 777 (1966), in which the federal government condemned an easement in 1943 during World War II to construct and operate a railroad line to an airfield. Tracks were laid and used for rail access to the airfield. In 1945 at the end of the war, the airfield was shut down, the tracks were removed, and the airfield was eventually sold. In finding that the federal government had abandoned its easement, our Supreme Court held that "[h]owever created, an easement for a railroad right of way is limited by the use for which the easement is acquired, and when that use is abandoned the easement is terminated and the property reverts to the owner of the servient estate. [Citation omitted.]" 196 Kan. at 185, 409 P.2d 777. The court went on to state:

> The general rule is that the right and title to a *mere* easement in land acquired by a *quasi*-public corporation, either by purchase, condemnation or prescription, for a public purpose is dependent upon the continued use of the property for that purpose, and when such public use is abandoned the right to hold the land ceases, and

the property reverts to its original owner or his successors in title. See *Canton Co. v. Baltimore & O.R. Co.,* 99 Md. 202, 57 A. 637 (1904), where it was said at p. 218 (quoting in part from *Vogler v. Geiss,* 51 Md. 407 [1879]): "A cesser of the use, coupled with any act clearly indicative of an intention to abandon the right, would have the same effect as an express release of the easement, without any reference whatever to time." *Pratt,* 196 Kan. at 186, 409 P.2d 777 (quoting *Ma. & Pa. RR. Co. v. Mer.-Safe, Etc., Co.,* 224 Md. 34, 39, 166 A.2d 247 [1960]).

Of particular note in *Pratt* is the specific finding that the government's acts "conclusively rendered it impossible for the easement to be used for the purpose for which it was taken, viz, any military purpose, thereby constituting an abandonment of the easement and causing defendant's land to be relieved of it." 196 Kan. at 187, 409 P.2d 777. This is consistent with the court's reasoning in *Matlack.* Accordingly, Hunt was required to satisfy the "impossible, or so highly improbable as to be practically impossible" rule of *Matlack* in order to prevail. See 195 Kan. at 486, 407 P.2d 510. This he failed to do. . . .

The district court erred in finding that the drainage district had abandoned the easement. In oral argument, the drainage district concedes that in order to preserve its easement Hunt need not be required to remove from the easement area the existing pavement or underground utility lines. Their presence will not interfere with the drainage district's future use of the easement area. Further, Hunt may continue to park vehicles or mobile homes on the easement area, so long as they can be moved whenever the drainage district needs access to the easement area to maintain the drainage ditch.

Adverse Possession—Hunt's Cross-appeal

Hunt's cross-appeal challenges the district court's determination that since the drainage district is a quasi-municipal corporation, its property is not subject to adverse possession by an individual or private entity.

In *Gauger v. State,* 249 Kan. 86, 92, 815 P.2d 501 (1991), our Supreme Court reaffirmed the rule that "[r]ights cannot be acquired in public lands by adverse possession or any statute of limitation. [Citations omitted.]" Hunt, however, points to *Wichita Boeing Employees Assoc.* for support that the rule in *Gauger* does not apply to easements. The court found in *Wichita Boeing Employees Assoc.* that the association could claim the land by adverse possession after the drainage district abandoned the easement and title reverted to the fee owner. These are not our circumstances. The drainage district did not abandon its easement so as to make it subject to adverse possession against the private property owner to whom it reverted. Hence, *Wichita Boeing Employees Assoc.* does not apply. The rule in *Gauger* stands: Hunt could not acquire the drainage district's maintenance easement by adverse possession.

Finally, Hunt argues that a new boundary line was established by agreement or custom of the parties, as was the case in *Moore v. Bayless,* 215 Kan. 297, 524 P.2d 721 (1974). In *Moore,* the court stated:

> [W]here parties by mutual agreement fix a boundary line between their properties, acquiesce in the line so fixed and thereafter occupy their properties according to the line agreed upon, it must be considered as the true boundary line between them and will be binding upon the parties and their grantees. The line becomes the true dividing line between the lands in question by virtue of such an agreement, even though a subsequent survey should establish a different boundary line. [Citations omitted.] 215 Kan. at 300, 524 P.2d 721.

The boundary line between Hunt's land and the drainage right-of-way is not in dispute. When the drainage district's survey of the property disclosed that the fence encroached on the drainage right-of-way, Hunt removed the fence from the right-of-way. This suit arose when Hunt refused to remove his other property from the easement area. Hunt testified that he believed the north boundary of the land was the existing fence line, which included the maintenance access easement area. In truth, Hunt owns the property to its northern boundary, but it is subject to the maintenance easement. There is no dispute as to the dimensions or location of the maintenance easement. It is the very existence of the easement that is in dispute, not its boundary. The reasoning in *Moore* does not apply.

Notes

1. *Abandonment of public resources. Riverside Drainage* gives us a glimpse of some of the special rules that apply in the case of resource use rights owned by the government. It is commonly said that adverse possession does not run against the public or governments. We also see a special rule that diminishes the possibility that the public would abandon property. What might account for this special rule? Does it reflect a special judicial interest in protecting the public? Does it reflect the fact that the "public" as a whole really has no way of forming any intent, and thus it is awkward to figure out whether the public did or did not intend to abandon? Here we have the additional awkward element that arises because government officials may rarely have need to use the drainage easement. Drainage ditches sometimes require maintenance only once every several decades. If that is the case, nonuse of an easement for 20 years may give no evidence of an intent to abandon.

2. *A dislike of railroad easements?* The rails-to-trails movement of the past few decades has stimulated numerous judicial rulings having to do with the duration of railroad easements, particularly abandonment. While the law of abandonment nominally is the same for such easements as for other resource use rights, many court display a distinct, usually unexplained hostility toward such easements. Even railroads that overtly announce an intent to retain easements after rail service is terminated can nonetheless find that they have lost their property rights. E.g. Chatham v. Blount

County, 789 So.2d 235 (Ala. 2001) (removal of tracks and other steps that render rail service impossible results in abandonment, even though railroad moved immediately to sell the easement for recreational purposes and otherwise made clear its intent to retain the easement); Toews v. United States, 53 Fed.Cl. 58 (2002) (same; applying California law). Other courts, however, have taken sharply different views, finding abandonment only when the railroad evidences an intent to do so. *E.g.*, Chevy Chase Land Co. v. United States, 355 Md. 110, 733 A.2d 1055 (1999). A careful reading of the cases suggests that courts might be conflating two issues that are better kept separate: What is the scope of the easement (can a railroad easement be used for hiking and biking) and was the easement abandoned? Courts finding abandonment have sometimes expressed concern that it is unfair to servient estate owners to subject them to public hiking and biking when they never agreed to it.

E. REGULATORY TERMINATION

CAWSEY v. BRICKEY

82 Wash. 653, 144 P. 938 (1914).

ELLIS, J.

Action to enjoin the enforcement of an order creating a game preserve in Skagit county. The plaintiffs constitute a gun club, and have leased for a term of years certain lands as a shooting preserve, including lands of the interveners, and have for a long time maintained thereon a gun club, and have expended considerable sums in equipment. The defendants are the sheriff, prosecuting attorney, game warden, and the three members of the game commission, of Skagit county, appointed under the Game Code (chapter 120, Laws of 1913, p. 356 et seq.). Acting under section 4 of that law, the game commission selected certain lands as a game preserve, including the lands covered by the plaintiffs' lease as well as those owned by the interveners. The injunction was denied. The plaintiffs and interveners have appealed.

The appellants attack the law of 1913, and particularly subdivision 7, of section 4, claiming that it is unconstitutional: . . . (2) because that subdivision deprives the appellants of valuable property rights and privileges without due process of law, bears unequally on different persons and communities, and is class legislation; . . .

(2) Subdivision 7, section 4, of the act reads as follows:

> 'The county game commission in their respective counties shall have the power and authority by giving notice thereof by publication for three successive weeks in a newspaper published at the county seat of such county describing such lands to be set aside as a game preserve, to set aside certain parts or portions of their respective counties as game preserves wherein no game bird or game animal or game fish can be caught or killed within the boundaries thereof, for such time and so long as they may see fit and proper . . .' Laws of 1913, page 359.

Do these provisions tend to deprive any one of property rights or vested privileges? We think not. Under the common law of England all property right in animals *ferae naturae* was in the sovereign for the use and benefit of the people. The killing, taking, and use of game was subject to absolute governmental control for the common good. This absolute power to control and regulate was vested in the colonial governments as a part of the common law. It passed with the title to game to the several states as an incident of their sovereignty, and was retained by the states for the use and benefit of the people of the states, subject only to any applicable provisions of the federal Constitution. [citations omitted] There is no private right in the citizen to take fish or game, except as either expressly given or inferentially suffered by the state. State v. Tice, 69 Wash. 403, 125 Pac. 168, 41 L. R. A. (N. S.) 469.

Section 21 of the Game Code provides:

> No person shall at any time or in any manner acquire any property in, or subject to his dominion or control, any of the game birds, game animals, or game fish, or any parts thereof, of the game birds, game animals or game fish herein mentioned, but they shall always and under all circumstances be and remain the property of the state. Laws of 1913, p. 365.

This is but declaratory of the common law. Whatever special or qualified rights or, more correctly speaking, privileges, a landowner may have as to game, while it is on his own land, though protected by the laws of trespass as against other persons, have no protection, because they have no existence, as against the state. Since the title to game is in the state for the common good, the state's right to control, regulate, or prohibit the taking of game wheresoever found and on whosesoever land is an inherent incident of the police power of the state. Tiedeman's Limitations of Police Power, § 121f. It may be exercised ad libitum so long as the regulation or prohibition bears equally on all persons similarly situated with reference to the subject-matter and purpose to be served by the regulation. Portland Fish Co. v. Benson, 56 Or. 147, 108 Pac. 122.

Does the act here in question bear unequally on persons similarly situated so as to be obnoxious to the constitutional inhibition against class legislation? We think not. It is the universality of the operation of a law on all persons of the state similarly situated with reference to the subject-matter that determines its validity as a general and uniform law, not the extent of territory in which it operates. That its operation may not be at all times coextensive with the territorial limits of the state is usually an immaterial circumstance. State ex rel. Lindsey v. Derbyshire, 79 Wash. 227, 237, 140 Pac. 540. The owner of land which from its location and character is peculiarly suited for a game preserve is not situated similarly to other landowners with reference to the subject-matter and purpose of a law creating a preserve. The subject-matter and purpose is protection and preservation of game. It is so declared in the title of the act. One whose land is thus peculiarly suited to meet those purposes obviously occupies a different relation to the purpose of the law from that occupied by one whose land is not so suited. When, therefore, the state authorizes the setting apart of his land for a game preserve and deprives him and all others of the privilege of taking game thereon, the law operates equally on all persons similarly situated, and is a proper exercise of the police power.

In this phase the case here is not distinguishable from Hayes v. Territory, 2 Wash. T. 286, 5 Pac. 927, where a territorial law restricted hunting in only five counties. Obviously owners of land in those counties were subjected to restricted hunting on their own land, while owners of land in other counties could hunt on their own land without restriction. The law was assailed as invalid on the ground that it granted special privileges. The Territorial Supreme Court, through Greene, C. J., tersely and soundly disposed of the question as follows:

> The game law in question restricted hunting in five counties only. It is contended that, for this reason, it is inconsistent with that inhibition in the Organic Act, which forbids the Legislature from granting special privileges. But the provisions of this game law fall without distinction upon all inhabitants of the territory. All are forbidden to hunt at certain seasons within the counties named. There is no special privilege, unless it be in favor of the brute life of the specified area, or those of human kind who are so happy as to be alive at the hunting season.

In both the *Hayes* case and this case the circumscribed geographical operation of the law makes the difference in the relation of those owning land within and those owning land without the circumscribed area. Barring this difference, the law is absolutely uniform in its operation on all persons. No one can hunt or take game or fish within that area. . . .

The judgment is affirmed.

Notes

1. *Sudden termination.* It is important to realize that the plaintiffs in *Cawsey* were not the owners of the land affected by the ban on hunting. They were members of a gun club that held only the right to use the land to maintain a gun club and engage in hunting. When the state banned hunting, it reduced, perhaps to zero, the value of the natural resource use right that the gun club held. (We can only guess whether the land remained useful to support a gun club even though hunting was impermissible.) Had the landowner retained hunting rights, the state regulation would have left the owner with alternative land uses. But when a distinct resource use right is separately owned, and the law then bans the resource activity, the resource owner is left with no alternative uses. (On this issue, more after the next case.)

2. *Reasonable use XI: taking nature into account. Cawsey* is an intriguing case because of the court's comments on how nature can affect private property rights—a point taken up earlier. The plaintiffs alleged that the

state regulatory scheme was improper because it affected landowners unequally. Some landowners were allowed to hunt, while others could not. The court responds, in essence, by stating that equality is about treating *people* the same, not treating *land parcels* the same. The law can properly prescribe differing rules for differing land parcels based on their natural features. Because land parcels differ, the owners of them can possess differing legal rights:

> The owner of land which from its location and character is peculiarly suited for a game preserve is not situated similarly to other landowners with reference to the subject-matter and purpose of a law creating a preserve. The subject-matter and purpose is protection and preservation of game. It is so declared in the title of the act. One whose land is thus peculiarly suited to meet those purposes obviously occupies a different relation to the purpose of the law from that occupied by one whose land is not so suited.

PENNSYLVANIA COAL CO. v. MAHON

260 U.S. 393, 43 S.Ct. 158, 67 L.Ed. 322 (1922).

Mr. Justice Holmes delivered the opinion of the Court.

This is a bill in equity brought by the defendants in error to prevent the Pennsylvania Coal Company from mining under their property in such way as to remove the supports and cause a subsidence of the surface and of their house. The bill sets out a deed executed by the Coal Company in 1878, under which the plaintiffs claim. The deed conveys the surface but in express terms reserves the right to remove all the coal under the same and the grantee takes the premises with the risk and waives all claim for damages that may arise from mining out the coal. But the plaintiffs say that whatever may have been the Coal Company's rights, they were taken away by an Act of Pennsylvania, approved May 27, 1921 (P. L. 1198), commonly known there as the Kohler Act. . . .

The statute forbids the mining of anthracite coal in such way as to cause the subsidence of, among other things, any structure used as a human habitation, with certain exceptions, including among them land where the surface is owned by the owner of the underlying coal and is distant more than one hundred and fifty feet from any improved property belonging to any other person. As applied to this case the statute is admitted to destroy previously existing rights of property and contract. The question is whether the police power can be stretched so far.

Government hardly could go on if to some extent values incident to property could not be diminished without paying for every such change in the general law. As long recognized some values are enjoyed under an implied limitation and must yield to the police power. But obviously the implied limitation must have its limits or the contract and due process clauses are gone. One fact for consideration in determining such limits is the extent of the diminution. When it reaches a certain magnitude, in most if not in all cases there must be an exercise of eminent domain and compensation to sustain the act. So the question depends upon the particular facts. The greatest weight is given to the judgment of the legislature but it always is open to interested parties to contend that the legislature has gone beyond its constitutional power.

This is the case of a single private house. No doubt there is a public interest even in this, as there is in every purchase and sale and in all that happens within the commonwealth. Some existing rights may be modified even in such a case. Rideout v. Knox, 148 Mass. 368, 19 N. E. 390, 2 L. R. A. 81, 12 Am. St. Rep. 560. But usually in ordinary private affairs the public interest does not warrant much of this kind of interference. A source of damage to such a house is not a public nuisance even if similar damage is inflicted on others in different places. The damage is not common or public. Wesson v. Washburn Iron Co., 13 Allen (Mass.) 96, 103, 90 Am. Dec. 181. The extent of the public interest is shown by the statute to be limited, since the statute ordinarily does not apply to land when the surface is owned by the owner of the coal. Furthermore, it is not justified as a protection of personal safety. That could be provided for by notice. Indeed the very foundation of this bill is that the defendant gave timely notice of its intent to mine under the house. On the other hand the extent of the taking is great. It purports to abolish what is recognized in Pennsylvania as an estate in land—a very valuable estate—and what is declared by the Court below to be a contract hitherto binding the plaintiffs. If we were called upon to deal with the plaintiffs' position alone we should think it clear that the statute does not disclose a public interest sufficient to warrant so extensive a destruction of the defendant's constitutionally protected rights....

It is our opinion that the act cannot be sustained as an exercise of the police power, so far as it affects the mining of coal under streets or cities in places where the right to mine such coal has been reserved. As said in a Pennsylvania case, "For practical purposes, the right to coal consists in the right to mine it." Commonwealth v. Clearview Coal Co., 256 Pa. 328, 331, 100 Atl. 820, L. R. A. 1917E, 672. What makes the right to mine coal valuable is that it can be exercised with profit. To make it commercially impracticable to mine certain coal has very nearly the same effect for constitutional purposes as appropriating or destroying it. This we think that we are warranted in assuming that the statute does....

The general rule at least is that while property may be regulated to a certain extent, if regulation goes too far it will be recognized as a taking. It may be doubted how far exceptional cases, like the blowing up of a house to stop a conflagration, go—and if they go beyond the general rule, whether they do not stand as much upon tradition as upon principle. Bowditch v. Boston, 101 U.S. 16, 25 L. Ed. 980. In general it is not plain that a man's misfortunes or necessities will justify his shifting the damages to his neighbor's shoulders. Spade v. Lynn & Boston Ry. Co., 172 Mass. 488, 489, 52 N.E. 747, 43 L. R. A. 832, 70 Am. St. Rep. 298. We are in danger of forgetting that a strong public desire to improve the public condition is not enough to warrant achieving the desire by a shorter cut than the constitutional way of paying for the change. As we already have said this is a question of degree—and therefore cannot be disposed of by general propositions. But we regard this as going beyond any of the cases decided by this Court. . . .

We assume, of course, that the statute was passed upon the conviction that an exigency existed that would warrant it, and we assume that an exigency exists that would warrant the exercise of eminent domain. But the question at bottom is upon whom the loss of the changes desired should fall. So far as private persons or communities have seen fit to take the risk of acquiring only surface rights, we cannot see that the fact that their risk has become a danger warrants the giving to them greater rights than they bought.

Mr. Justice Brandeis dissenting.

The Kohler Act prohibits, under certain conditions, the mining of anthracite coal within the limits of a city in such a manner or to such an extent 'as to cause the subsidence of * * * any dwelling or other structure used as a human habitation, or any factory, store, or other industrial or mercantile establishment in which human labor is employed.' Act Pa. May 27, 1921, § 1 (P. L. 1198). Coal in place is land, and the right of the owner to use his land is not absolute. He may not so use it as to create a public nuisance, and uses, once harmless, may, owing to changed conditions, seriously threaten the public welfare. Whenever they do, the Legislature has power to prohibit such uses without paying compensation; and the power to prohibit extends alike to the manner, the character and the purpose of the use. Are we justified in declaring that the Legislature of Pennsylvania has, in restricting the right to mine anthracite, exercised this power so arbitrarily as to violate the Fourteenth Amendment?

Every restriction upon the use of property imposed in the exercise of the police power deprives the owner of some right theretofore enjoyed, and is, in that sense, an abridgment by the state of rights in property without making compensation. But restriction imposed to protect the public health, safety or morals from dangers threatended is not a taking. The restriction here in question is merely the prohibition of a noxious use. The property so restricted remains in the possession of its owner. The state does not appropriate it or make any use of it. The state merely prevents the owner from making a use which interferes with paramount rights of the public. Whenever the use prohibited ceases to be noxious—as it may because of further change in local or social conditions—the restriction will have to be removed and the owner will again be free to enjoy his property as heretofore.

The restriction upon the use of this property cannot, of course, be lawfully imposed, unless its purpose is to protect the public. But the purpose of a restriction does not cease to be public, because incidentally some private persons may thereby receive gratuitously valuable special benefits. Thus, owners of low buildings may obtain, through statutory restrictions upon the height of neighboring structures, benefits equivalent to an easement of light and air. Welch v. Swasey, 214 U. S. 91, 29

Sup. Ct. 567, 53 L. Ed. 923. Compare Lindsley v. Natural Carbonic Gas Co., 220 U.S. 61, 31 Sup. Ct. 337, 55 L. Ed. 369, Ann. Cas. 1912C, 160; Walls v. Midland Carbon Co., 254 U. S. 300, 41 Sup. Ct. 118, 65 L. Ed. 276. Furthermore, a restriction, though imposed for a public purpose, will not be lawful, unless the restriction is an appropriate means to the public end. But to keep coal in place is surely an appropriate means of preventing subsidence of the surface; and ordinarily it is the only available means. Restriction upon use does not become inappropriate as a means, merely because it deprives the owner of the only use to which the property can then be profitably put.... If by mining anthracite coal the owner would necessarily unloose poisonous gases, I suppose no one would doubt the power of the state to prevent the mining, without buying his coal fields. And why may not the state, likewise, without paying compensation, prohibit one from digging so deep or excavating so near the surface, as to expose the community to like dangers? In the latter case, as in the former, carrying on the business would be a public nuisance.

It is said that one fact for consideration in determining whether the limits of the police power have been exceeded is the extent of the resulting diminution in value, and that here the restriction destroys existing rights of property and contract. But values are relative. If we are to consider the value of the coal kept in place by the restriction, we should compare it with the value of all other parts of the land. That is, with the value not of the coal alone, but with the value of the whole property. The rights of an owner as against the public are not increased by dividing the interests in his property into surface and subsoil. The sum of the rights in the parts can not be greater than the rights in the whole. The estate of an owner in land is grandiloquently described as extending ab orco usque ad coelum. But I suppose no one would contend that by selling his interest above 100 feet from the surface he could prevent the state from limiting, by the police power, the height of structures in a city. And why should a sale of underground rights bar the state's power? For aught that appears the value of the coal kept in place by the restriction may be negligible as compared with the value of the whole property, or even as compared with that part of it which is represented by the coal remaining in place and which may be extracted despite the statute. Ordinarily a police regulation, general in operation, will not be held void as to a particular property, although proof is offered that owing to conditions peculiar to it the restriction could not reasonably be applied. See Powell v. Pennsylvania, 127 U.S. 678, 681, 684, 8 Sup. Ct. 992, 1257, 32 L. Ed. 253; Murphy v. California, 225 U. S. 623, 629, 32 Sup. Ct. 697, 56 L. Ed. 1229, 41 L. R. A. (N. S.) 153. But even if the particular facts are to govern, the statute should, in my opinion be upheld in this case. For the defendant has failed to adduce any evidence from which it appears that to restrict its mining operations was an unreasonable exercise of the police power. Compare Reinman v. Little Rock, 237 U.S. 171, 177, 180, 35 Sup. Ct. 511, 59 L. Ed. 900; Pierce Oil Corporation v. City of Hope, 248 U. S. 498, 500, 39 Sup. Ct. 172, 63 L.

Ed. 381. Where the surface and the coal belong to the same person, self-interest would ordinarily prevent mining to such an extent as to cause a subsidence. It was, doubtless, for this reason that the Legislature, estimating the degrees of danger, deemed statutory restriction unnecessary for the public safety under such conditions. . . .

Notes

1. *Police power and regulation that "goes too far." Mahon* is often viewed as the initial decision in what is now called the regulatory takings doctrine—the idea that a regulation limiting private property rights can be so severe as to amount to confiscation of the property requiring compensation. The doctrine has appeared several times in earlier chapters. While *Mahon* may have begun this body of law, the opinion by Justice Holmes did little to clarify the line between legitimate regulation and illegitimate takings. The Court merely stated that a regulation was invalid, thus triggering a duty to pay compensation, when it went "too far" in cutting into private rights.

In brief, a taking occurs today when a regulation authorizes a "permanent physical invasion" of private land or when it deprives an owner of all economically valuable uses of the property, unless the regulation essentially implements a background limit on private rights. When neither of these "per se" takings rules apply, the regulation is assessed under the multi-factor takings test set forth in Penn. Central Transpo. Co. v. City of New York, 438 U.S. 104 (1978). A detailed survey of the law is offered in David A. Dana & Thomas A. Merrill, PROPERTY: TAKINGS (2002). Although *Mahon* has not been overruled, its vague holding has been much clarified and the Supreme Court upheld the constitutionality of a nearly identical state mineral-use statute in Keystone Bituminous Coal Assn. v. DeBenedictis, 480 U.S. 470 (1987).

2. *The whole parcel rule.* Many landowners, seeking to resist a regulation, have asserted that a regulation amounts to a total taking of a distinct property interest in their bundle of private rights. The issue was prominently presented in Penn Central Transpo. Co. v. City of New York, 438 U.S. 104 (1978), where Penn Central claimed that an historic preservation ordinance in effect took its air rights above its rail terminal. The Court rejected the argument, insisting that takings law required an assessment of the economic effect of a regulation on the land parcel as a whole. The Court refused to apply takings law to the air rights separately. In decisions since then the Court has consistently adhered to the whole parcel rule. E.g., Palazzolo v. Rhode Island, 533 U.S. 606 (2001) (in applying takings rule court looks to entire parcel of land, and not merely to portion of land on which development is completely banned).

While the "whole parcel" rule is thus firmly established, the Supreme Court has yet to make clear how takings law applies to a distinct resource use right that is severed from land and separately owned at the time a new law takes effect—the fact pattern posed in *Cawsey v. Bricker*. The issue was raised by Justice Brandeis, dissenting in *Mahon,* and remains open today. Brandeis took the view that a ban on mining that was valid when applied to a fee simple owner was equally valid when applied to a party that only owned the mineral rights to the land, even though the economic effect on the mineral rights holder could be a total loss in property value. Brandeis's argument was that a private transaction between two parties, severing and selling part of the land, should not diminish the regulatory powers of government. Also relevant are the unequal results that arise when a regulatory limit is deemed valid when applied to a landowner holding a fee simple interest (under the whole parcel rule) but invalid when applied to an identical, neighboring land parcel in which mineral rights are separately held. The economic effect on both parcels could be the same, as is the public interest underlying the regulation. On the other side, the expectations of the mineral rights holder are more plainly and completely frustrated.

3. *Ending a grazing right:* United States v. Fuller. Earlier in this chapter we considered various powers the federal government has to alter, refuse to renew or otherwise curtail a right to graze livestock on federal lands. A further hazard for permit holders, relating to termination by government action, was illustrated in United States v. Fuller, 409 U.S. 488 (1973). In that case, the federal government condemned 920 acres of private ranch land, paying just compensation. Attached to the ranch were rights to graze livestock on 31,461 acres of federal land. In the market, a buyer of the private ranch would have paid far more for the private land because of the attached grazing permits. The landowner's argument was that just compensation for the 920 acres should take into account the considerable extra value of the land due to the grazing permits, even though the grazing permits were revocable by the government. *Held:* The government under the just compensation clause need not compensate for the extra value attributable to revocable grazing permits:

> [T]he general principle [is] that the Government as condemnor may not be required to compensate a condemnee for elements of value that the Government has created, or that it might have destroyed under the exercise of governmental authority other than the power of eminent domain. If ... Government need not pay for value that it could have acquired by exercise of a servitude arising under the commerce power [the navigation servitude], it would seem *a fortiori* that it need not compensate for value that it could remove by revocation of a permit for the use of lands that it owned outright.

4. *When the government contracts.* In earlier cases we saw the complications that arise when the government wears two hats: it is private landowner possessing proprietary powers, and also a regulatory entity possessing sovereign governmental powers. Similar complications arise when the government is both contracting party and regulatory entity. In Mobil Oil Exploration and Producing Southeast, Inc. v. United States, 530 U.S. 604 (2000), the Court considered a claim by two oil companies that the federal government had breached contracts governing the leasing of offshore oil lands. For $158 million in up-front bonuses and promises to pay production royalties the oil companies obtained 10–year renewable leases for certain lands. Rights to explore for oil and to engage in production were expressly subject to compliance by the oil companies with various statutes and regulations, including provisions designed to minimize environmental harms. Some years later, when the oil companies had nearly completed the various regulatory review processes, Congress enacted a new statute designed to

enhance environmental protections. The Interior Department insisted that the oil companies comply with it. *Held:* The government's action breached the contract. While the oil companies were obligated by contract to comply with laws and regulations in effect at the time the leases began, they did not agree to comply with any future laws. Here, compliance with future laws imposed substantial burdens, and the government's breach was sufficiently material to allow the oil companies to terminate the leases and recover their payments.

For a comparable ruling involving timber contracts, see Everett Plywood Corp. v. United States, 227 Ct.Cl. 415, 651 F.2d 723 (1981), in which the court found that the Forest Service had breached a timber contract when it insisted on changing contract terms in mid-stream to take into account unexpected environmental damage. The risk of environmental harm was clearly foreseeable at the time the contract was signed. The Forest Service nonetheless specified in detail exactly what the timber purchaser could and could not do, without retaining any reserved rights to impose additional constraints.

F. WHEN THE USE ENDS

HODEL v. VIRGINIA SURFACE MINING & RECLAMATION ASSN., INC.

452 U.S. 264, 101 S.Ct. 2352, 69 L.Ed.2d 1 (1981).

JUSTICE MARSHALL, delivered the opinion of the Court.

These cases arise out of a pre-enforcement challenge to the constitutionality of the Surface Mining Control and Reclamation Act of 1977 (Surface Mining Act or Act), 91 Stat. 447, 30 U.S.C. § 1201 *et seq.* (1976 ed., Supp.III). The United States District Court for the Western District of Virginia declared several central provisions of the Act unconstitutional and permanently enjoined their enforcement. 483 F.Supp. 425 (1980). In these appeals, we consider whether Congress, in adopting the Act, exceeded its powers under the Commerce Clause of the Constitution, or transgressed affirmative limitations on the exercise of that power contained in the Fifth and Tenth Amendments. We conclude that in the context of a facial challenge, the Surface Mining Act does not suffer from any of these alleged constitutional defects, and we uphold the Act as constitutional.

I

A

The Surface Mining Act is a comprehensive statute designed to "establish a nationwide program to protect society and the environment from the adverse effects of surface coal mining operations." § 102(a), 30 U.S.C. § 1202(a) (1976 ed., Supp.III). Title II of the Act, 30 U.S.C. § 1211 (1976 ed., Supp.III), creates the Office of Surface Mining Reclamation and Enforcement (OSM), within the Department of the Interior, and the Secretary of the Interior (Secretary) acting through OSM, is charged with primary responsibility for administering and implementing the Act by promulgating regulations and enforcing its provisions. § 201(c), 30 U.S.C. § 1211(c) (1976 ed., Supp.III). The principal regulatory and enforcement provisions are contained in Title V of the Act, 91 Stat. 467–514, 30 U.S.C. §§ 1251–1279 (1976 ed., Supp.III). Section 501, 30 U.S.C. § 1251 (1976 ed., Supp.III), establishes a two-stage program for the regulation of surface coal mining: an initial, or interim regulatory phase, and a subsequent, permanent phase. The interim program mandates immediate promulgation and federal enforcement of some of the Act's environmental protection performance standards, complemented by continuing state regulation. Under the permanent phase, a regulatory program is to be adopted for each State, mandating compliance with the full panoply of federal performance standards, with enforcement responsibility lying with either the State or Federal Government.

Section 501(a) directs the Secretary to promulgate regulations establishing an interim regulatory program during which mine operators will be required to comply with some of the Act's performance standards, as specified by § 502(c), 30 U.S.C. § 1252(c) (1976 ed., Supp.III). Included among those selected standards are requirements governing: (a) restoration of land after mining to its prior condition; (b) restoration of land to its approximate original contour; (c) segregation and preservation of topsoil; (d) minimization of disturbance to the hydrologic balance; (e) construction of coal mine waste piles used as dams and embankments; (f) revegetation of mined areas; and (g) spoil disposal. § 515(b), 30 U.S.C. § 1265(b) (1976 ed., Supp.III). The interim regulations were published on December 13, 1977, see 42 Fed.Reg. 62639, and they are currently in effect in most States, including Virginia.[3] . . .

B

On October 23, 1978, the Virginia Surface Mining and Reclamation Association, Inc., an association of coal producers engaged in surface coal mining operations in Virginia, 63 of its member coal companies, and 4 individuals landowners filed suit in Federal District Court seeking declaratory and injunctive relief against various provisions of the Act. The Commonwealth of Virginia and the town of Wise, Va., intervened as plaintiffs. Plaintiffs' challenge was primarily directed at Title V's performance standards. Because the permanent regulatory program was not scheduled to become effective until June 3, 1980, plaintiffs' challenge was directed at the sections of the Act establishing the interim regulatory program. Plaintiffs alleged that these provisions violate the Commerce Clause, the equal protection and due process guarantees of the Due

3. New surface mining operations, excluding those on "Federal lands" or "Indian lands," commencing on or after February 3, 1978, must comply with the performance standards established by the interim regulatory program at the start of operations. And, with certain limited exceptions, surface mining operations begun prior to February 3, 1978, were required to be in compliance with the interim regulations as of May 3, 1978. §§ 502(b), (c), and 701(11), 30 U.S.C. §§ 1252(b), (c) and 1291(11) (1976 ed., Supp. III).

Process Clause of the Fifth Amendment,[4] the Tenth Amendment,[5] and the Just Compensation Clause of the Fifth Amendment.[6] . . .

II

On cross-appeal, appellees argue that the District Court erred in rejecting their challenge to the Act as beyond the scope of congressional power under the Commerce Clause. They insist that the Act's principal goal is regulating the use of private lands within the borders of the States and not, as the District Court found, regulating the interstate commerce effects of surface coal mining. Consequently, appellees contend that the ultimate issue presented is "whether land *as such* is subject to regulation under the Commerce Clause, *i.e.* whether land can be regarded as 'in commerce.'" Brief for Virginia Surface Mining & Reclamation Association, Inc., et al. 12 (emphasis in original). In urging us to answer "no" to this question, appellees emphasize that the Court has recognized that land-use regulation is within the inherent police powers of the States and their political subdivisions, and argue that Congress may regulate land use only insofar as the Property Clause grants it control over federal lands.

We do not accept either appellees' framing of the question or the answer they would have us supply. The task of a court that is asked to determine whether a particular exercise of congressional power is valid under the Commerce Clause is relatively narrow. The court must defer to a congressional finding that a regulated activity affects interstate commerce, if there is any rational basis for such a finding. *Heart of Atlanta Motel, Inc. v. United States*, 379 U.S. 241, 258, 85 S.Ct. 348, 358, 13 L.Ed.2d 258 (1964); *Katzenbach v. McClung*, 379 U.S. 294, 303–304, 85 S.Ct. 377, 383, 13 L.Ed.2d 290 (1964). This established, the only remaining question for judicial inquiry is whether "the means chosen by [Congress] must be reasonably adapted to the end permitted by the Constitution." *Heart of Atlanta Motel, Inc. v. United States, supra*, at 262, 85 S.Ct., at 360. See *United States v. Darby*, 312 U.S. 100, 121, 61 S.Ct. 451, 460, 85 L.Ed. 609 (1941); *Katzenbach v. McClung,* 379 U.S., at 304, 85 S.Ct., at 383. The judicial task is at an end once the court determines that Congress acted rationally in adopting a particular regulatory scheme. *Ibid.*

Judicial review in this area is influenced above all by the fact that the Commerce Clause is a grant of plenary authority to Congress. See *National League of Cities v. Usery, supra*, at 840, 96 S.Ct., at 2468; *Cleveland v. United States*, 329 U.S. 14, 19, 67 S.Ct. 13, 15, 91 L.Ed. 12 (1946); *NLRB v. Jones & Laughlin Steel Corp.*, 301 U.S. 1, 37, 57 S.Ct. 615, 624, 81 L.Ed. 893 (1937). This power is "complete in itself, may be

4. The Due Process Clause of the Fifth Amendment states that no person shall "be deprived of life, liberty, or property, without due process of law."

5. Under the Tenth Amendment, "[t]he powers not delegated to the United States by the Constitution, nor prohibited by it to the States, are reserved to the States respectively, or to the people."

6. The Compensation Clause prohibits the taking of private property "for public use, without just compensation."

exercised to its utmost extent, and acknowledges no limitations other than are prescribed in the constitution." *Gibbons v. Ogden*, 9 Wheat. 1, 196, 6 L.Ed. 23 (1824). Moreover, this Court has made clear that the commerce power extends not only to "the use of channels of interstate or foreign commerce" and to "protection of the instrumentalities of interstate commerce ... or persons or things in commerce," but also to "activities affecting commerce." *Perez v. United States*, 402 U.S. 146, 150, 91 S.Ct. 1357, 1359, 28 L.Ed.2d 686 (1971). As we explained in *Fry v. United States*, 421 U.S. 542, 547, 95 S.Ct. 1792, 1795, 44 L.Ed.2d 363 (1975), "[e]ven activity that is purely intrastate in character may be regulated by Congress, where the activity, combined with like conduct by others similarly situated, affects commerce among the States or with foreign nations." [citations omitted]

Thus, when Congress has determined that an activity affects interstate commerce, the courts need inquire only whether the finding is rational. Here, the District Court properly deferred to Congress' express findings, set out in the Act itself, about the effects of surface coal mining on interstate commerce. Section 101(c), 30 U.S.C. § 1201(c) (1976 ed., Supp. III), recites the congressional finding that

> "many surface mining operations result in disturbances of surface areas that burden and adversely affect commerce and the public welfare by destroying or diminishing the utility of land for commercial, industrial, residential, recreational, agricultural, and forestry purposes, by causing erosion and landslides, by contributing to floods, by polluting the water, by destroying fish and wildlife habitats, by impairing natural beauty, by damaging the property of citizens, by creating hazards dangerous to life and property by degrading the quality of life in local communities, and by counteracting governmental programs and efforts to conserve soil, water, and other natural resources."

The legislative record provides ample support for these statutory findings. The Surface Mining Act became law only after six years of the most thorough legislative consideration. Committees of both Houses of Congress held extended hearings during which vast amounts of testimony and documentary evidence about the effects of surface mining on our Nation's environment and economy were brought to Congress' attention. Both Committees made detailed findings about these effects and the urgent need for federal legislation to address the problem....

The Committees also explained that inadequacies in existing state laws and the need for uniform minimum nationwide standards made federal regulations imperative. See S.Rep.No. 95–128, at 49; H.R.Rep.No. 95–218, at 58. In light of the evidence available to Congress and the detailed consideration that the legislation received, we cannot say that Congress did not have a rational basis for concluding that surface coal mining has substantial effects on interstate commerce.

Appellees do not, in general, dispute the validity of the congressional findings. Rather, appellees' contention is that the "rational basis" test should not apply in this case because the Act regulates land use, a local activity not affecting interstate commerce. But even assuming that appellees correctly characterize the land use regulated by the Act as a "local" activity, their argument is unpersuasive.

The denomination of an activity as a "local" or "intrastate" activity does not resolve the question whether Congress may regulate it under the Commerce Clause. As previously noted, the commerce power "extends to those activities intrastate which so affect interstate commerce, or the exertion of the power of Congress over it, as to make regulation of them appropriate means to the attainment of a legitimate end, the effective execution of the granted power to regulate interstate commerce." *United States v. Wrightwood Dairy Co.,* 315 U.S., at 119, 62 S.Ct., at 526. See *Fry v. United States,* 421 U.S., at 547, 95 S.Ct., at 1795; *NLRB v. Jones & Laughlin Steel Corp.,* 301 U.S., at 37, 57 S.Ct., at 624. This Court has long held that Congress may regulate the conditions under which goods shipped in interstate commerce are produced where the "local" activity of producing these goods itself affects interstate commerce. See, *e. g., United States v. Darby,* 312 U.S. 100, 61 S.Ct. 451, 85 L.Ed. 609 (1941); *Wickard v. Filburn,* 317 U.S. 111, 63 S.Ct. 82, 87 L.Ed. 122 (1942); *NLRB v. Jones & Laughlin Steel Corp., supra; Kirschbaum Co. v. Walling,* 316 U.S. 517, 62 S.Ct. 1116, 86 L.Ed. 1638 (1942). Cf. *Katzenbach v. McClung,* 379 U.S. 294, 85 S.Ct. 377, 13 L.Ed.2d 290 (1964). Appellees do not dispute that coal is a commodity that moves in interstate commerce. Here, Congress rationally determined that regulation of surface coal mining is necessary to protect interstate commerce from adverse effects that may result from that activity. This congressional finding is sufficient to sustain the Act as a valid exercise of Congress' power under the Commerce Clause.

Moreover, the Act responds to a congressional finding that nationwide "surface mining and reclamation standards are essential in order to insure that competition in interstate commerce among sellers of coal produced in different States will not be used to undermine the ability of the several States to improve and maintain adequate standards on coal mining operations within their borders." 30 U.S.C. § 1201(g) (1976 ed., Supp. III). The prevention of this sort of destructive interstate competition is a traditional role for congressional action under the Commerce Clause....

III

The District Court invalidated §§ 515(d) and (e) of the Act, which prescribe performance standards for surface coal mining on "steep slopes," on the ground that they violate a constitutional limitation on the commerce power imposed by the Tenth Amendment. These provisions require "steep-slope" operators: (i) to reclaim the ined area by completely covering the highwall and returning the site to its "approximate original contour"; (ii) to refrain from dumping spoil material on the downslope below the bench or mining cut; and (iii) to refrain from disturbing land above the highwall unless permitted to do so by the regulatory authority. § 515(d), 30 U.S.C. § 1265(d) (1976 ed., Supp. III). Under § 515(e), a "steep-slope" operator may obtain a variance from the approximate-original-contour requirement by showing that it will allow a postreclamation use that is "deemed to constitute an equal or better economic or public use" than would otherwise be possible. 30 U.S.C. § 1265(e)(3)(A) (1976 ed., Supp. III).

The District Court's ruling relied heavily on our decision in *National League of Cities v. Usery,* 426 U.S. 833, 96 S.Ct. 2465, 49 L.Ed.2d 245 (1976). The District Court viewed the central issue as whether the Act governs the activities of private individuals, or whether it instead regulates the governmental decisions of the States.... [The Court's discussion of *National League of Cities* is omitted]

It should be apparent from this discussion that in order to succeed, a claim that congressional commerce power legislation is invalid under the reasoning of *National League of Cities* must satisfy *each* of three requirements. First, there must be a showing that the challenged statute regulates the "States as States." *Id.*, at 854, 96 S.Ct., at 2475. Second, the federal regulation must address matters that are indisputably "attribute[s] of state sovereignty." *Id.*, at 845, 96 S.Ct., at 2471. And, third, it must be apparent that the States' compliance with the federal law would directly impair their ability "to structure integral operations in areas of traditional governmental functions." *Id.*, at 852, 96 S.Ct., at 2472. When the Surface Mining Act is examined in light of these principles, it is clear that appellees' Tenth Amendment challenge must fail because the first of the three requirements is not satisfied. The District Court's holding to the contrary rests on an unwarranted extension of the decision in *National League of Cities*.

As the District Court itself acknowledged, the steep-slope provisions of the Surface Mining Act govern only the activities of coal mine operators who are private individuals and businesses. Moreover, the States are not compelled to enforce the steep-slope standards, to expend any state funds, or to participate in the federal regulatory program in any manner whatsoever. If a State does not wish to submit a proposed permanent program that complies with the Act and implementing regulations, the full regulatory burden will be borne by the Federal Government. Thus, there can be no suggestion that the Act commandeers the legislative processes of the States by directly compelling them to enact and enforce a federal regulatory program....

Appellees' claims accurately characterize the Act insofar as it prescribes federal minimum standards governing surface coal mining, which a State may either implement itself or else yield to a federally administered regulatory program. To object to this scheme, however, appellees must assume that the Tenth Amendment limits congressional power to pre-empt or displace state regulation of private activities affecting interstate commerce. This assumption is incorrect.

pre-empt

A wealth of precedent attests to congressional authority to displace or pre-empt state laws regulating private activity affecting interstate commerce when these laws conflict with federal law. [citations omitted] Moreover, it is clear that the Commerce Clause empowers Congress to prohibit all—and not just inconsistent—state regulation of such activities. [citations omitted] Although such congressional enactments obviously curtail or prohibit the States' prerogatives to make legislative choices respecting subjects the States may consider important, the Supremacy Clause permits no other result. [citations omitted] As the Court long ago stated: "It is elementary and well settled that there can be no divided authority over interstate commerce, and that the acts of Congress on that subject are supreme and exclusive." *Missouri Pacific R. Co. v. Stroud*, 267 U.S. 404, 408, 45 S.Ct. 243, 245, 69 L.Ed. 683 (1925).

Thus, Congress could constitutionally have enacted a statute prohibiting any state regulation of surface coal mining. We fail to see why the Surface Mining Act should become constitutionally suspect simply because Congress chose to allow the States a regulatory role. . . .

IV

The District Court held that two of the Act's provisions violate the Just Compensation Clause of the Fifth Amendment. First, the court found that the steep-slope provisions discussed above effect an uncompensated taking of private property by requiring operators to perform the "economically and physically impossible" task of restoring steep-slope surface mines to their approximate original contour. 483 F.Supp., at 437. The court further held that, even if steep-slope surface mines could be restored to their approximate original contour, the value of the mined land after such restoration would have "been diminished to practically nothing." *Ibid.* Second, the court found that § 522 of the Act effects an unconstitutional taking because it expressly prohibits mining in certain locations and "clearly prevent[s] a person from mining his own land or having it mined." *Id.*, at 441. Relying on this Court's decision in *Pennsylvania Coal Co. v. Mahon*, 260 U.S. 393, 43 S.Ct. 158, 67 L.Ed. 322 (1922), the District Court held that both of these provisions are unconstitutional because they "depriv[e] [coal mine operators] of any use of [their] land, not only the most profitable. . . . " 483 F.Supp., at 441.

We conclude that the District Court's ruling on the "taking" issue suffers from a fatal deficiency: neither appellees nor the court identified any property in which appellees have an interest that has allegedly been taken by operation of the Act. By proceeding in this fashion, the court below ignored this Court's oft-repeated admonition that the constitutionality of statutes ought not be decided except in an actual factual setting that makes such a decision necessary. [citations omitted] Adherence to this rule is particularly important in cases raising allegations of an unconstitutional taking of private property. Just last Term, we reaffirmed that

> "this Court has generally 'been unable to develop any "set formula" for determining when "justice and fairness" require that economic

injuries caused by public action be compensated by the government, rather than remain disproportionately concentrated on a few persons.' Rather, it has examined the 'taking' question by engaging in essentially ad hoc, factual inquiries that have identified several factors—such as the economic impact of the regulation, its interference with reasonable investment backed expectations, and the character of the government action—that have particular significance." *Kaiser Aetna v. United States*, 444 U.S. 164, 175, 100 S.Ct. 383, 390, 62 L.Ed.2d 332 (1979) (citations omitted).

These "ad hoc, factual inquiries" must be conducted with respect to specific property, and the particular estimates of economic impact and ultimate valuation relevant in the unique circumstances.

Because appellees' taking claim arose in the context of a facial challenge, it presented no concrete controversy concerning either application of the Act to particular surface mining operations or its effect on specific parcels of land. Thus, the only issue properly before the District Court and, in turn, this Court, is whether the "mere enactment" of the Surface Mining Act constitutes a taking. See *Agins v. Tiburon*, 447 U.S. 255, 260, 100 S.Ct. 2138, 2141, 65 L.Ed.2d 106 (1980). The test to be applied in considering this facial challenge is fairly straightforward. A statute regulating the uses that can be made of property effects a taking if it "denies an owner economically viable use of his land. . . . " *Agins v. Tiburon, supra*, at 260, 100 S.Ct., at 2141. See *Penn Central Transp. Co. v. New York City*, 438 U.S. 104, 98 S.Ct. 2646, 57 L.Ed.2d 631 (1978). The Surface Mining Act easily survives scrutiny under this test.

First, the Act does not, on its face, prevent beneficial use of coal-bearing lands. Except for the proscription of mining near certain locations by § 522(e), the Act does not categorically prohibit surface coal mining; it merely regulates the conditions under which such operations may be conducted. The Act does not purport to regulate alternative uses to which coal-bearing lands may be put. Thus, in the posture in which these cases comes before us, there is no reason to suppose that "mere enactment" of the Surface Mining Act has deprived appellees of economically viable use of their property.

Moreover, appellees cannot at this juncture legitimately raise complaints in this Court about the manner in which the challenged provisions of the Act have been or will be applied in specific circumstances, or about their effect on particular coal mining operations. There is no indication in the record that appellees have availed themselves of the opportunities provided by the Act to obtain administrative relief by requesting either a variance from the approximate-original-contour requirement of § 515(d) or a waiver from the surface mining restrictions in § 522(e). If appellees were to seek administrative relief under these procedures, a mutually acceptable solution might well be reached with regard to individual properties, thereby obviating any need to address the constitutional questions. The potential for such administrative solutions confirms the conclusion that the taking issue decided by the District Court simply is not ripe for judicial resolution.[7]

Notes

1. *Cleaning up the mess.* The strip-mining statute upheld in *Hodel* is illustrative of statutes and regulations that require resource users to take steps, once they have finished operations, to clean up the messes they have made. (Similar obligations are routinely included in private contracts and leases.) Mineral lessees are routinely required to close wells properly by plugging them, often with concrete to reduce the chance that oil can leak into groundwater supplies. Timber companies are often required to replant the trees that they cut and take other steps to reduce erosion or environmental damage from their harvesting and road-building efforts. Sometimes resource users know about these obligations in advance so they can calculate the costs of compliance in their business plans. In other settings the obligations are imposed by law on ongoing operations. Among the most contentious burdens imposed after-the-fact have been liabilities incurred by mining companies for mining operations ceased decades earlier, particularly for mining tailings that pollute waterways.

2. *Reasonable use XII: repairing the surface.* Many clean-up duties are prescribed by statutes and regulations or set forth expressly in leases and contracts. But the limited property rights held by resource users can also include implicit bounds on their ability to leave a mess behind. In Tenneco Oil Co. v. Allen, 515 P.2d 1391 (Okl. 1973), an oil and gas lessee was authorized to use the land surface only to the extent reasonably necessary for the conduct of production operations. The land had been previously leased, and earlier lessees had left abandoned wells, equipment, and concrete foundations. *Held:* the lessee was obligated, when terminating production, to fill and level the abandoned wells and to remove the equipment and cement foundations. Failure to do so amounted to a use of the land surface that was not reasonably necessary and thus interfered with the landowner's surface use rights.

7. Although we conclude that "mere enactment" of the Act did not effect a taking of private property, this holding does not preclude appellees or other coal mine operators from attempting to show that as applied to particular parcels of land, the Act and the Secretary's regulations effect a taking. Even then, such an alleged taking is not unconstitutional unless just compensation is unavailable. . . .

Chapter Seven

REALLOCATION OVER TIME

Another critical issue in the definition of a use right is the owner's power to transfer it. From the owner's perspective, transfer is vital to capture the resource's market value in the event the owner no longer wants to use it. From society's perspective, the issue appears a bit different. Society commonly desires that resources be put to their highest and best uses. One mechanism for doing that is to facilitate a market in the resource, allowing people to buy and sell it. But the market is hardly the only means of moving resources to new uses. Indeed, reallocation methods are numerous.

The issue of transfer or reallocation is closely tie to the issues considered in earlier chapters, particularly to legal questions relating to the duration of rights (chapter 6) and to the limits on use rights (chapters 4 and 5). To see how these issues are related is to become aware of some of the nonmarket ways that the law brings one resource use to an end to make way for another.

One common means of resource reallocation is for a present use right to end, making the resource then available to someone else. This happens when leases or permits terminate and the owner of the land decides upon a new user and perhaps new use. When rights are abandoned or forfeited, reallocation can also take place. Adverse possession and its easement equivalent, prescription, are further means by which one resource use (or nonuse) can give way to another.

Courts and other lawmakers get involved in resource reallocation when they tinker with the legal elements of private rights. We have seen numerous illustrations of this form of reallocation. Consider *Bryant v. Lefever*, where the English court revised property law to allow more intensive resource uses while withdrawing protection for sensitive ones, thereby allowing one land use to give way to another. In *Moon v. North Idaho Farmers Association* the Idaho legislature rewrote trespass and nuisance law to allow soot-producing grass burning. *Prah v. Maretti* was about allocating sunlight to a solar panel, while *Zealy v. City of Waukesha* involved laws that protected wetlands, thereby promoting the various resource uses dependent upon healthy hydrologic systems. In *Hunt v. Kerbaugh* the North Dakota court reallocated resources when it adopted the accommodation doctrine in the context of oil and gas leases. And the list goes on. Indeed, a chief means of reallocating resources over time has been for lawmakers to tinker with natural resource laws so as to curtail one resource activity and promote another. Much of this legal work has taken place quietly in the context of evolving definitions of reasonable use. The definition of reasonable use over time has changed considerably, in ways that have materially altered resource-use practices.

In this chapter, we look mostly at the legal rules governing market transfers of resources. After surveying the basic common law rules on transfer (and glancing quickly at alternative reallocation methods), we turn to the particular instance of water rights in prior appropriation jurisdictions, one setting in which resource reallocation is much needed. Can the market bring about the needed water reallocations or could other reallocation methods work as well or better? We will look at academic commentary on this question as well as case law. The chapter concludes by examining yet another form of resource reallocation that has figured prominently in the history of natural resources law: private condemnation.

A. THE COMMON LAW

GOSS v. C.A.N. WILDLIFE TRUST, INC.

157 Md.App. 447, 852 A.2d 996 (2004).

KRAUSER, J.

We are asked to decide whether the right to hunt and fish on an adjoining property owner's land, when that right has been acquired by deed, is a "license" or a "profit a prendre." In this instance, we conclude it is a profit a prendre. . . .

Approximately thirty years ago, Charles F. Deffinbaugh sold two of his 380 acres of land to Charles R. Goss and Geraldine E. Goss as tenants by the entireties for the sum of $10.00. In the deed transferring the property, Deffinbaugh "grant[ed] to the [Gosses] . . . and to those invited guests at their camp all hunting and fishing rights and the use of the creek waters on the whole tract of land" that he owned. The Gosses then erected a hunting camp on the two acres so that Mr. Goss, an avid hunter, could hunt on Deffinbaugh's land.

In the years that followed that transaction, Deffinbaugh conveyed several other small portions of his property; seven of those conveyances included a grant of the right to hunt and fish on his land. On February 11, 1977, Deffinbaugh sold the rest of his property, which then consisted of 323 acres, to Carl C. Benson and Charlotte A. Benson. [The property was then acquired by C.A.N. Wildlife Trust, Inc., a closely held family corporation formed by Donald H. Nixon and his two sons largely for the purpose of acquiring title to the Deffinbaugh property. When Mr. Goss died, his widow transferred the 2 acres with hunting rights to herself and her daughter, Christine Franklin. In 2001, Goss and Franklin, who were not interested in hunting, purported to assign the hunting rights to the Cooks, who used the rights and gave permission to a friend, Jacob Kasecamp, to hunt as well. Although not relevant to the dispute, the Cooks were in the process of purchasing the two acres from Goss and Franklin. The Trust then filed to suit, contending that the hunting rights were no longer valid. According to the court, the single issue in the case was as follows: "Did the deed granting hunting and fishing rights on an adjoining property to Charles and Geraldine Goss create a profit a prendre or a license, and, if it created a profit a prendre, does the profit a prendre run with the land?"]

Discussion

Appellants claim that the Goss deed created, not a license, but a profit a prendre to hunt and fish on the Deffinbaugh property, which is now owned by the Trust. That profit, appellant maintains, was assignable to others, such as the Cooks. The circuit court disagreed. Observing that the language of the deed conferring hunting and fishing rights on the Gosses "did not use terms such as heirs or assigns that would suggest an intention to make [those rights] assignable" in the granting clause, the court found that Goss and her invited guests "were given the personal privilege to hunt or fish on the [Trust's] adjoining acreage" and nothing more. The Goss deed, it declared, "created a license, not an easement or profit a prendre" and the "purported assignment of July 18, 2001," to the Cooks was accordingly a "nullity."

To understand how the circuit court reached that conclusion, we must first define the terms central to its analysis: "license," "easement," and "profit a prendre." To define the first two terms, we need look no further than Maryland caselaw, but to define the third term—profit a prendre—we must look further afield and delve into the caselaw of other jurisdictions and the works of respected authorities.

The difference between a "license," on the one hand, and an easement (and, by implication, a profit a prendre), on the other, is that "a license is merely a personal privilege to do some particular act or series of acts on [another's] land without possessing any estate or interest therein," while an easement is "an interest in land" that grants the right to use that land for a specific purpose. *Griffith v. Montgomery County,* 57 Md.App. 472, 485, 470 A.2d 840 (1984); *see* Black's Law Dictionary 527 (7th ed.1999). Moreover, a license, as a "mere personal privilege," ceases upon the death of the grantor or grantee, while an easement, as an interest in land, may be both transferable and inheritable. *Griffith,* 57 Md.App. at 485, 470 A.2d 840.

A profit a prendre ("profit"), like an easement, is an incorporeal interest in land. But, while an easement confers a right to use another's land for a specific limited purpose, a profit a prendre confers the right to enter upon another's land and remove something of value from the soil or the products of the soil, *see Chester Emery Co. v. Lucas,* 112 Mass. 424

(1873); *Hanson v. Fergus Falls Nat'l Bank,* 242 Minn. 498, 65 N.W.2d 857 (1954); *Anderson v. Gipson,* 144 S.W.2d 948 (Tex.Civ.App., 1940); *see also* 25 Am.Jur.2d *Easements & Licenses* § 4, at 573–74 (1996), something which an easement impliedly forbids. *See Anderson,* 144 S.W.2d at 950 ("[A]n easement implies that the owner thereof shall take no profit from the soil.... "). Moreover, unlike an easement, "it is within the statute of frauds and requires a writing for its creation." *Id.; see also Hanson,* 65 N.W.2d at 861.

Since "the right of hunting on premises is an incorporeal right growing out of the soil," *Hanson,* 65 N.W.2d at 863, that right, when conveyed by a deed, constitutes a profit a prendre. *See Fairbrother v. Adams,* 135 Vt. 428, 378 A.2d 102, 104 (1977); *see also Hanson,* 65 N.W.2d at 860; *Anderson,* 144 S.W.2d at 950. The Gosses, having received from Deffinbaugh by deed two acres of land and "all hunting and fishing rights" on Deffinbaugh's adjoining property, obtained a "profit a prendre" to hunt and fish upon Deffinbaugh's property. *See Fairbrother,* 378 A.2d at 104; *see also* Hanson, 65 N.W.2d at 860; *Anderson,* 144 S.W.2d at 950. But that does not end our inquiry. The next question is what type of profit a prendre did the Gosses receive from Deffinbaugh.

Like an easement, a profit can be either appurtenant to land or in gross. *See Hanson,* 65 N.W.2d at 860–61. Once we have determined which of these two types of profits the Gosses received from Deffinbaugh, we shall know whether they could have transferred the profit to the Cooks without also transferring their land. If the profit exists to serve a dominant estate, the profit is appurtenant to that estate and can only be transferred or alienated along with the dominant estate. *See* 25 Am.Jur.2d, *supra,* at 574; *see also Hanson,* 65 N.W.2d at 861; *Hopper v. Herring,* 75 N.J.L. 212, 67 A. 714, 715–16 (1907). Conversely, if the profit does not exist to serve a dominant estate, it is a profit in gross, and may be transferred or alienated separate and apart from the dominant estate. *See* 28A C.J.S. *Easements* § 9, at 179–80; *see also Hanson,* 65 N.W.2d at 861, 863; *Beckwith v. Rossi,* 157 Me. 532, 534, 175 A.2d 732 (1961).

That feature—the transferability of a profit a prendre in gross—distinguishes it from an easement in gross. In short, an easement in gross cannot be transferred while a profit in gross can. *See* 28A C.J.S., *supra,* at 180, 184; *see also Hanson,* 65 N.W.2d at 861. That is because a profit in gross "has the character of an estate in the land" itself that exists independent of ownership of land. *Hanson,* 65 N.W.2d at 863; *see* 28A C.J.S., *supra,* at 180; *see also Hanson,* 65 N.W.2d at 861. In sum, a profit a prendre is closely related to an easement, but, unlike an easement, it affords the grantee an opportunity to share in the products or profits of the grantor's land and a profit in gross can be transferred apart from the dominant estate. *See* 28A C.J.S., *supra,* at 171–85; *see also Hanson,* 65 N.W.2d at 861–62; *Anderson,* 144 S.W.2d at 950.

To determine what type of profit the Gosses received, we look to the deed which granted the profit. *See Hanson,* 65 N.W.2d at 861–62. As we do, we note that the "cardinal rule in the construction of deeds" is that the intention of the parties governs the transaction. *Calvert Joint Venture #140 v. Snider,* 373 Md. 18, 38, 816 A.2d 854 (2003). To determine that intent, we must consider the language of the deed in light of the facts and circumstances surrounding the transaction. *See id.* at 38–39, 816 A.2d 854. The "true test" of what was meant by the language of the deed is "what a reasonable person in the position of the parties would have thought it meant." *Chesapeake Isle, Inc. v. Rolling Hills Dev. Co.,* 248 Md. 449, 453, 237 A.2d 1 (1968); *see also James v. Goldberg,* 256 Md. 520, 527, 261 A.2d 753 (1970).

Where the grant or reservation is for an exclusive right to the products of the soil, such as minerals or game, the grant reflects a general intent of the parties to sever the estate in the products of the land from the surface estate, allowing the severed estate to be freely transferred or assigned. *See Calvert Joint Venture,* 373 Md. at 50, 816 A.2d 854; *see also Chester Emery Co.,* 112 Mass. at 435 (holding that the grant of "all the iron ore, metals, and minerals in and upon the tract" was a "grant of an estate in the mines and minerals"). But, where the grant is nonexclusive, it reflects an intent to create an incorporeal hereditament that cannot be severed from or further transferred without the dominant estate. *See Johnstown Iron Co. v. Cambria Iron Co.,* 32 Pa. 241, 246 (1858)(finding that a grant of a privilege to mine on the grantor's lands in common with him was an incorporeal hereditament to mine); *Gloninger v. Franklin Coal Co.,* 55 Pa. 9, 16 (1867)(noting that where the grantor reserves a right to mine along with the grantee, the grantee receives an incorporeal hereditament to mine).

When the profit is created in conjunction with the transfer of a particular parcel of land for its benefit, the profit is appurtenant to that parcel. *See Council v. Sanderlin,* 183 N.C. 253, 111 S.E. 365, 368 (1922)(holding that where the grantee received a tract of land and a profit to hunt, the profit could only be transferred along with ownership of the premises conveyed); *see also Hopper,* 67 A. at 716 (holding that where the grantee received a sawmill and the right to take gravel from the grantor's property to maintain the mill's dam, the profit to remove gravel was appurtenant to the sawmill); *Grubb v. Grubb,* 74 Pa. 25, 33–34 (1873)(holding that the right to take coal from one tract of land to benefit another tract was appurtenant to the second tract because the right added value to that land). *See generally Clayton v. Jensen,* 240 Md. 337, 346, 214 A.2d 154 (1965)(stating that an easement established for benefit of a particular tract of land is an "appurtenant right" that passes with ownership of the benefited tract). And, the profit may not be transferred without also conveying the land to which it is appurtenant. *See id.; see also Grubb,* 74 Pa. at 33–34.

The Gosses' profit was appurtenant to the two acres they received from Deffinbaugh. Because the profit was granted in the same deed that transferred the two acres of land, the profit to hunt and fish on

Deffinbaugh property was part and parcel of that transaction and inseparable from it. *See Sanderlin,* 111 S.E. at 368; *see also Grubb,* 74 Pa. at 33–34. Indeed, the two acre tract was purchased by the Gosses for a hunting camp. It was of little or no value to them without the attendant right to hunt and fish on Deffinbaugh's property. Moreover, the deed did not convey to them an exclusive right to hunt and fish on that property. As noted, Deffinbaugh conveyed that same right to the purchasers of seven other pieces of his land. Thus, the Gosses' profit a prendre was appurtenant to the land they purchased from Deffinbaugh.

And, like all profits appurtenant, the Gosses' hunting and fishing rights could not be transferred without conveying the land to which they are appurtenant. *See Sanderlin,* 111 S.E. at 368; *see also Hanson,* 65 N.W.2d at 861; *Grubb,* 74 Pa. at 33–34. Thus, the 1997 transfer of those rights from Goss to herself and Franklin was valid because the rights were in fact conveyed with the title to the two acres of land. On the other hand, the 2001 purported assignment of the hunting and fishing rights to the Cooks was not valid because Goss and Franklin did not also convey, with that assignment, ownership of the two acres. Accordingly, we shall affirm the judgment of the circuit court, but not without noting that, in doing so, we do not address the import or impact of the December 2001 lease agreement.

Notes

1. *Common law background. Goss* introduces us to the various common law rules on transfer, mostly drawn from the law of easements, profits, and licenses. How many rules does the court articulate, and can we figure out the policy rationales for them? Obviously, contracting parties are free to set terms that differ from the law's back-up rules. Are the common law rules largely based on the presumed intent of parties, or do they instead promote public policies that are unrelated to private intent?

As the court notes, licenses are presumed to be personal and nontransferable, unless coupled with some larger property interest. The latter possibility arises rather frequently in natural resources law. A buyer of standing timber, for instance, may have an implicit license to enter the land to cut and remove the timber. That license attaches to the timber and can be transferred along with it.

The court's comments in *Goss* about easements and profits are also reasonable statements of current law, although rules among the states do differ slightly. Appurtenant easements and profits—those that attach to land—are transferable only with the land; they cannot be severed and sold separately. Generally, easements in gross are not transferable unless the parties expressly provide otherwise. Profits, on the other hand, are typically transferable unless the parties prohibit it. Some states have largely done away with the easements-profits distinction, and view profits as merely a type of easement. When that is done, the distinction is drawn between easements in gross that are and are not *commercial* in nature; the former (but not the latter) are viewed as transferable unless the parties say otherwise.

Closely related to transfer is the ability of a resource user to *divide* the resource use rights into smaller pieces for allocation to multiple buyers. Typically that can be done when the resource use right is exclusive but not when it is nonexclusive. (Even when the right is exclusive, the total usage under the original easement or profit cannot exceed overall use limits on it.)

What *Goss* does not cover, in its summary of the common law of transfer, are the rules governing leases and transactions that entail the transfer of actual title to resources in place. A lease is a legal arrangement in which the lessee gains exclusive physical possession over some part of the land; it is a possessory (corporeal) interest rather than, like an easement, a nonpossessory (incorporeal) interest. Mineral lessees, for instance, gain exclusive rights to possess the minerals covered by their leases. Under basic landlord-tenant law, leases are freely transferable (by assignment or sub-lease) unless lease agreements provide otherwise. And like exclusive profits, they are subject to division so long as overall usage does not exceed the lease terms.

As for transfers of resources in place, we have seen this issue in earlier chapters. States typically allow the transfer of hardrock minerals in place (the most common transaction), and may or may not allow transfers in place of oil and gas. Precedents dating back many generations also allow the transfer in place of standing timber (or even, as we briefly saw, individual scenic trees). These resource rights are treated as real property and subject to the normal rules allowing free transfer and division (as well as rules governing deeds and title recordation).

2. *A personal right to hunt:* Maw v. Weber Basin Water Conservancy District. In a deed transferring a right of way to a duck hunting club, a landowner reserved the right for each of her four named sons to hunt on the club's grounds. Each son had the right to designate one of his own sons to exercise the rights instead. *Held:* these hunting rights were "noncommercial easements in gross" and were limited by their terms to the exact people named. As "a mere personal interest in the property" the rights were not assignable or inheritable. When one of the original four sons died the right of that son ended and could not be exercised by the sons of the deceased son. Maw v. Weber Basin Water Conservancy District, 20 Utah 2d 195, 436 P.2d 230 (1968).

3. *Interpreting confused language:* Seven Lakes Development Co. v. Maxson. As courts go about interpreting deeds they often pay little attention to the technical legal terms used by the parties. In Seven Lakes Development Co. v. Maxson, 144 P.3d 1239 (Wyo. 2006), a deed transferring land contained the following language "Hunting and fishing privileges are extended to all lands now owned by grantor, or hereafter acquired by grantor in said Sections 22 and 27, but said privileges must not be commercialized by grantees herein;" and "These covenants are to run with the land and shall be binding on grantors and grantees and all persons claiming under them." *Held:* Despite the parties' use of the terms "privileges" and "covenants," the transaction transferred to the grantees profits a prendre that were appurtenant to their lands and that could be transferred along with the lands. The transaction did not create, as grantor's successor in interest argued, a

revocable, nontransferable license that was personal to the original grantor and grantees.

ARKANSAS RIVER RIGHTS COMMITTEE v. ECHUBBY LAKE HUNTING CLUB

83 Ark.App. 276, 126 S.W.3d 738 (2003).

JOHN F. STROUD, JR., CHIEF JUDGE.

This case involves the public's right of access to the following water-covered areas off the west bank of the Arkansas River in Desha and Lincoln Counties: 1) a narrow passage of water called the Echubby Chute, which may be entered from the Arkansas River; 2) a body of water located west of the Chute, called the Echubby Lake; 3) a ditch that connects the Chute and the lake; and 4) another small lake situated farther south in the Coal Pile area (collectively, "the Echubby areas"). Appellant, Arkansas River Rights Committee, a nonprofit group of hunters and fishermen, contends that, despite appellee's record ownership of the Echubby areas, the public has a right to access them because they are navigable and because they have been used by the public for more than seven years, such that a prescriptive right of use has been acquired....

Although the Echubby areas are now covered by water, that has not always been the case. In the 1960s, the Corps of Engineers constructed Lock and Dam No. 2 on the Arkansas River in southeast Arkansas as part of the McClellan–Kerr Navigation project. The project, using a system of locks and dams, rendered the Arkansas River navigable between Tulsa, Oklahoma, and the Mississippi River. Lock and Dam No. 2 was completed in 1968 and, as a result, the river level rose in the area. This caused the Echubby Chute and the connecting ditch to become filled with water, thus making the Echubby areas accessible from the river where they had not been before....

[The evidence largely showed that the Echubby areas were not accessible to the public until 1968. Thereafter the public gained physical access due to construction changes to the Arkansas River. Boaters and hunters used the area until 2001, when the appellee hunting club bought the land and sought to cut off public use of it. The case posed two legal issues: Did the public gain rights to use the water surface by prescription (based on open and notorious use for seven years), and/or did the public have rights to use the water surface by operation of law as soon as it became attached to existing bodies of navigable water.]

PRESCRIPTIVE USE

Although incursions on the land of another for the purpose of hunting and fishing do not signify an intention to appropriate lands for one's own use, *State ex rel. Thompson v. Parker,* 132 Ark. 316, 200 S.W. 1014 (1917), the State's inundation of another's lands may, in some circumstances, put the State in possession of those lands and thus allow access by the public. *Id.* Appellant relies on *Thompson v. Parker* to support its argument that a fact question remains as to whether the public acquired a prescriptive right to use the Echubby areas.

Thompson involved certain areas of Horseshoe Lake, a large body of water in Crittenden County. The lake, as its name suggests, is shaped like a horseshoe with a large peninsula of land in its center. A hunting club owned property on this peninsula. In 1905, the St. Francis Levee District built a levee across an outlet of the lake and, as a result, the lake's waters rose and covered approximately 1,000 acres of the club's land. The club contended that it still owned that water-covered land and tried to exclude the public's access. The supreme court recognized that, although the newly-covered land was not part of the lake bed prior to the levee being built, when the levee was built and the land was inundated by water, a new situation was created:

> When the waters of natural navigable lakes in this State are *extended by artificial means so as to cause the land of riparian owners to be flooded, without their consent,* and this condition is not merely temporary but is *continued for a sufficient length of time for the standing waters to produce a distinctive new high-water mark* for the waters of the lake bed, *this gives the State, as the owner of such lake bed, the possession of the lands so covered by the high-water mark.... The State has acquired title by prescription* or limitation.... The inundation of [the club's] lands, under the circumstances, put the State in possession and as effectually foreclosed any private ownership and dominion in the [club]....

132 Ark. at 321–23, 200 S.W. at 1016 (emphasis added). The court held that, after the levee was constructed and water from a navigable body inundated the riparian owner's land without the owners's consent for a sufficient length of time, the public acquired the right to use the lands so covered.

The facts in *Thompson* bear a similarity to the facts in the case at bar. Here, after the lock and dam were constructed in 1968, water rose and covered previously dry land, creating a connection to and access from the Arkansas River. Under the holding in *Thompson,* if the encroachment of river water into the Echubby areas was for a sufficient length of time to produce a new high-water mark and was without the landowner's consent, the public may have acquired a prescriptive right of usage of the areas.

[The appellee argued that *Thompson* was inapplicable because of alleged factual differences in the two cases, but the court disagreed. The court also turned aside a claim that *Thompson* had been curtailed by a later judicial ruling. On the issue of public rights gained by prescription, the court ruled that prescription was possible and that factual disputes made summary judgment inappropriate.]

Navigability

Determining the navigability of a stream is essentially a matter of deciding if it is public or private property. *State v. McIlroy,* 268 Ark. 227,

595 S.W.2d 659 (1980), *cert. denied,* 449 U.S. 843, 101 S.Ct. 124, 66 L.Ed.2d 51 (1980). If a body of water is navigable, it is considered to be held by the State in trust for the public. *See Hayes v. State,* 254 Ark. 680, 496 S.W.2d 372 (1973); 9 *Powell on Real Property* § 65.11[2][a] (2003). Navigability is a question of fact. *Goforth v. Wilson,* 208 Ark. 35, 184 S.W.2d 814 (1945).

Arkansas law has defined navigability as follows:

> The true criterion is the dictate of sound business common sense, and depends on the usefulness of the stream to the population of its banks, as a means of carrying off the products of their fields and forests, or bringing to them articles of merchandise. If, in its natural state, without artificial improvements, it may be prudently relied upon and used for that purpose at some seasons of the year, recurring with tolerable regularity, then in the American sense, it is navigable....

McIlroy, 268 Ark. at 234–35, 595 S.W.2d at 663 (quoting *Lutesville Sand & Gravel Co. v. McLaughlin,* 181 Ark. 574, 26 S.W.2d 892 (1930)). In 1980, this definition was expanded by the supreme court to include consideration of the water's recreational use as well as its commercial use in determining navigability. *McIlroy, supra.* In *McIlroy,* the court was asked to determine whether a stream that had considerable recreational value for boating and fishing was navigable, even though it lacked the commercial adaptability that was the hallmark of traditional navigability. The case involved the Mulberry River, described in the opinion as an intermediate stream at least 100 feet wide at some points, that for fifty to fifty-five miles of its length could be and often was floated by canoes or flat-bottomed boats. The Mulberry was designated by the state Department of Parks and Tourism as Arkansas's finest whitewater float stream. In 1838, it was "meandered" by surveyors, which is prima facie evidence of navigability. Based on these facts, the supreme court held that "there is no doubt that the segment of the Mulberry River that is involved in this lawsuit can be used for a substantial portion of the year for recreational purposes. Consequently, we hold that it is navigable.... " *McIlroy,* 268 Ark. at 237, 595 S.W.2d at 665.

Under *McIlroy,* it is apparent that navigability may be established by recreational usefulness as well as commercial usefulness. In the present case, the Selvey affidavit filed by appellant shows that the Echubby areas have at least some recreational usefulness. Selvey stated that, in the past seven years, he and other fishermen have boated over the entire surface of Pool 2, which includes the Echubby areas, and further that water covers the areas year round. Admittedly, there is nothing in the record at this point to show that the level of recreational use in the Echubby areas compares with the extensive use of the Mulberry River in *McIlroy,* and obviously, the occasional foray by a fisherman into an area does not render it navigable; if that were so, every creek and pond in the state would be navigable. However, we believe that the Selvey affidavit is sufficient to create a fact question as to the Echubby areas' navigability. Therefore, summary judgment was improper on this issue.

Appellee contends that the areas' present-day navigability is not relevant; rather, navigability must solely be determined as of the date of Arkansas's statehood because each state, upon entry into the union, took title to the navigable waters within its borders. *See generally Utah v. United States,* 403 U.S. 9, 91 S.Ct. 1775, 29 L.Ed.2d 279 (1971); *Anderson v. Reames,* 204 Ark. 216, 161 S.W.2d 957 (1942). We disagree that the concept of navigability for the purpose of determining the public's right to use water is that static. Although navigability to fix ownership of a river bed or riparian rights is determined as of the date of the state's entry into the union, navigability for other purposes may arise later. *See, e.g., United States v. Appalachian Elec. Power Co.,* 311 U.S. 377, 408, 61 S.Ct. 291, 85 L.Ed. 243 (1940); *Hitchings v. Del Rio Woods Recreation & Park Dist.,* 55 Cal.App.3d 560, 568, 127 Cal.Rptr. 830, 835 (1976) ("navigability for purposes of a public navigational easement need not be evaluated as of the date of statehood; it may later arise"); *Bohn v. Albertson,* 107 Cal.App.2d 738, 743, 238 P.2d 128, 132 (1951) ("if the evidence showed the creation of a new channel of the river, the fact that there was no such channel [at statehood] would not prevent the assertion by proper public authority of the right to use that channel for navigation and fishing"); 65 C.J.S. *Navigable Waters* § 12 at 68 (2000). This point can be illustrated by the fact that, in the following cases, the Arkansas Supreme Court did not address navigability for the purpose of public usage in terms of whether the water was navigable at the time of statehood but whether the water was currently navigable. *See State v. McIlroy, supra; Hayes v. State, supra; Five Lakes Outing Club, Inc. v. Horseshoe Lake Protective Ass'n,* 226 Ark. 136, 288 S.W.2d 942 (1956); *McGahhey v. McCollum,* 207 Ark. 180, 179 S.W.2d 661 (1944). One case phrased the question of navigability as "whether the lake is susceptible of public servitude as a means of transportation *either now or within the foreseeable future. . . .* " *Parker v. Moore,* 222 Ark. 811, 814, 262 S.W.2d 891, 893 (1953). Thus, we do not believe that an area's navigability, in the sense that the public may use it, is conclusively established by that area's status in 1836.

Appellee also contends that navigability should be determined by the condition of the area in its natural state, without improvements. It bases its argument on the oft-repeated adage that a waterway is navigable "if, in its natural state, without artificial improvements, it may be prudently relied upon and used for that purpose." *See Lutesville Sand & Gravel Co. v. McLaughlin,* 181 Ark. 574, 577, 26 S.W.2d 892, 893 (1930). Appellee claims that, because the level of the water in the Echubby areas was artificially raised by the lock and dam, the areas cannot be navigable. First of all, there were no improvements made to the Echubby areas themselves; the inundation of water occurred as the result of improvements on another waterway, the Arkansas River. Second, we have found no Arkansas case, and appellee has cited none, in which the courts have held that a body of water should be closed to the public simply because it was rendered navigable through improvements made to another body of water. We therefore decline to affirm the summary judgment on this basis.

Notes

1. *Prescription, physical change, and redefinition. Arkansas River Rights* illustrates three further ways that resource reallocation can take place. One possibility is that a new user can gain rights by engaging in open and notorious, hostile use of land for the specified period of prescription. As we saw in chapter two (in *Carnahan v. Moriah Property Owners Assn.*), courts are reluctant to allow recreational use rights to arise by prescription, but the possibility does exist—as this case illustrates.

Another way reallocation can take place is by means of physical changes that occur in nature itself. When rivers meander, for instance, the boundaries of land parcels can change through the operation of legal rules governing accretion and reliction. Here, changes in the physical navigability of a waterway, however they come about, automatically change the legal rights Arkansas residents have in the waterway.

Then there is the possibility of a change in the law that rearranges use rights. Arkansas changed its legal definition of navigability in State v. McIlroy, 268 Ark. 227, 595 S.W.2d 659 (1980), expanding the definition so as to allow public uses of all waterways suitable for regular recreational use. The legal change expanded public access while restricting the ability of private owners to deny access. Various states did the same thing in earlier decades to accommodate state industries. Thus, various northern states in the nineteenth adopted a "log floating" test of navigability to open waterways for use by timber companies desirous of floating logs to their mills.

2. *Right to exclude VIII: shifting navigability.* Note that *Arkansas River Rights* illustrates two ways that a landowner can lose the right to exclude the public from using a private waterway. One way is for lawmakers to redefine navigability in a way that expands public rights and diminishes the right to exclude. The Arkansas Supreme Court did that with its ruling in *McIlroy.* An entirely different way is when a body of water for the first time becomes connected to a navigable waterway—as apparently happened in this case. The moment that happens, the public gains rights to the body of water under Arkansas law because the water body is now navigable in fact. That rule of law apparently has long applied in Arkansas and is a defining term of the rights held by private landowners. Put otherwise, Arkansas property law only vests landowners with the right to exclude the public from nonnavigable waterways—a category of waters that varies over time.

B. WATER TRANSFERS

Perhaps no body of resource law has developed more complex rules governing transfers than water law. The reasons are not hard to identify. A holder of a water right who wants to sell his water will likely encounter no difficulties so long as the sale involves the entire water-using operation and the new owner wants to continue using water in the same place and in the same way. The change in owners poses no threat to anyone else. Problems arise, though, as soon as the purchaser of the water wants to use the water in a new way or, even more disruptive, wants to use the water in a new place, perhaps diverting the water from a new location along the river. Water uses generate distinct patterns of return flow. A change in the nature or place of a water use can greatly affect the return flow and thus other water users downstream. Similar effects can arise from changes in the point of diversion of a water use, whether moving it upstream or downstream. Because of these "third party effects" (as they are termed), proposed water transfers can be highly contentious. At the same time, water is scarce in much of the country and a big need exists to shift water from low-valued uses (often agriculture) to ones that are more highly valued. Reallocation is very much needed. Some mechanism is needed to help bring it about. But which one or ones?

Our first look at water transfers introduces us to the general rule that transfers can take place only to the extent that no material injury is imposed on other water users, senior or junior. Given the physical interconnection of water uses, this rule can be difficult to apply. Its application can require a careful analysis of the exact details of the water right being transferred. The following case highlights the complexity of the market option.

GREEN v. CHAFFEE DITCH COMPANY

150 Colo. 91, 371 P.2d 775 (1962).

MOORE, JUSTICE.

Lydia Hoffman Morrison and her brother Milton Coy Hoffman are the owners of seventy-two acres of land along the bank of the river. In the water adjudication of April 11, 1882, under priority No. 13, the Coy Ditch was awarded 31.63 c. f. s. from the stream. One-half of this water right, or approximately 16 c. f. s., is owned by Morrison and Hoffman. They entered into a contract to sell to the city of Fort Collins 8 c. f. s. of this water, and the city requests permission to change the point of diversion thirteen miles upstream. Numerous protests were filed to the requested change. These protests contain the assertion that Morrison and Hoffman did not own 16 c. f. s., and that if any such water rights had ever existed they had been abandoned.

The trial court entered findings which, in pertinent part, contain the following:

"That the land owned by said petitioners, Milton Coy Hoffman and Lydia Hoffman Morrison, irrigated by said water is seventy-two acres along the river bottom, the Cache La Poudre River dividing said land. That the top soil is a sandy loam and varies in thickness from about five feet to a few inches and is underlain with coarse gravel, which in some places comes to the surface. That because of the soil conditions and the proximity to the river, all water applied to said land, not consumed by plant life and evaporation, returns to the river within a very short time and again becomes a part of the river and available to other appropriators. That the amount of water necessarily consumed by plant life to produce a maximum crop, in addition to natural rainfall, is 15 inches of water or one and one-fourth acre feet of water for each acre irrigated, thus requiring 90 acre feet of water each year for the proper irrigation of said land. That the efficiency of water on this particular land is 25%, requiring the application to this land of 360 acre feet of water during each irrigating season to produce maximum crops. That in addition to the 90 acre feet of water consumed on this land, five acre feet are lost by evaporation and seepage while the water is in transit from the headgate of the Coy Ditch to the Hoffman–Morrison farm, making a total consumptive use of 95 acre feet of water each year. That the only domestic use of this water has been a small amount for the watering of livestock. That the irrigating season on this land has been from April 15th to October 15th of each year.

"That the City of Fort Collins, during the period from April 15th and October 15th of each year has an average return flow through its sewage disposal plant, storm sewers and other sources of 50% of the water taken in at its intake pipeline.

"That for many years last past, and ever since the entry of the original adjudication Decree, the petitioners Milton Coy Hoffman and Lydia Hoffman Morrison and their predecessors in title and interest have never beneficially used at any one time more than eight cubic feet of water per second of time for the irrigation of the lands now owned by them. Any diversions by petitioners or others in excess of that amount were a subterfuge and not made in good faith.

"That any diversion of water from said priority from October 16th of any year to April 14th, inclusive, of the following year, except for livestock purposes, would injuriously affect the storage rights of protestants, or some one or more of them, as they have historically depended upon the filling of their storage decrees during said time."

The court decreed inter alia that:

"No diversion from Priority No. 13 awarded to the Coy Ditch can be transferred without injury to junior appropriators, except under the conditions herein set forth, and any transfer of water, heretofore beneficially used, must be upon condition that the land heretofore irrigated must be forever deprived of irrigation water from this Decree, and cannot be a transfer of water not needed or beneficially used.

"That there can be diverted from the headgate of the Coy Ditch to the headgate of the City of Fort Collins pipeline without injury to the protestants, that amount of water which, when the return flow from the City sewage plant and other sources is considered, permits the City to consumptively use 95 acre feet of water during the irrigating season. Therefore, under the foregoing findings, the City should be permitted to divert 190 acre feet of water during each irrigation season under the conditions that the City at no time shall divert more than eight cubic feet of water per second of time, and the City shall divert no water under said Decree after October 15th or before April 15th of each year, and that no diversion be made under said Priority No. 13 by Milton Coy Hoffman and Lydia Hoffman Morrison, or either of them, or by their agents, heirs, administrators, grantees or assigns for use on the lands now owned by them, except for stock water after October 15th and prior to April 15th of any year.

"Since all diversions by petitioners and their predecessors in excess of eight cubic feet of water per second of time were a subterfuge and not in good faith, and since not more than eight cubic feet of water per second of time could be beneficially used, all water in excess of said eight cubic feet of water per second of time has been totally and completely abandoned.

"Junior appropriators, who appropriated this excess water have a vested right to have the conditions on the river remain as they were when their appropriations were made.

"The Court is aware that as the City of Fort Collins continues to grow, additional water will be needed for its inhabitants. However, need is not the matter to be considered in a change of point of diversion. The element to be considered under the statutes is injury to junior appropriators. No change may be allowed unless injury can be obviated by the imposition of conditions. In this case, the conditions listed are essential to protect junior appropriators against substantial injury.

"To prevent injury to junior appropriators, no call for water under said priority may be made at the new point of diversion during any period from October 16th to April 14th, inclusive. No call for water under said priority for use on the farm lands of petitioners or elsewhere may be made, except allowed at the new point of diversion, except water for livestock purposes from October 16th to April 14th, inclusive. If any one or more of said conditions is not imposed there will be injury to junior appropriators on the river, and this is the controlling factor."

There is competent evidence in the record before us to sustain all the findings of fact entered by the trial court. . . .

The grounds on which plaintiffs seek reversal are variously stated by their attorneys. In the briefs of counsel for Morrison and Hoffman it is argued that:

> *First:* "There is no evidence to support the court's finding that ever since the entry of the original adjudication decree the owners thereof have not beneficially used in excess of eight cfs." and
>
> *Second:* "The trial court was without jurisdiction to decree abandonment of waters other than those transferred."

There is an abundance of evidence establishing the fact that at no time has an amount of water in excess of 8 c. f. s. been applied to beneficial use on the seventy-two acres of land involved. We doubt that it would be possible to apply even as much as 8 c. f. s. to beneficial use in agricultural pursuits on seventy-two acres of land. There is no merit to the first contention.

With reference to the second contention that the court lacked jurisdiction to decree abandonment of waters other than those sought to be transferred, we direct attention to the fact that from the very beginning no more than 8 c. f. s. was actually acquired by anyone for use on the Morrison–Hoffman land. The decree under which a priority of 31 c. f. s. was "adjudicated" to the Coy Ditch could only afford protection to the extent that said water, or fraction thereof, was actually applied to beneficial use. That adjudication decree in 1882 specifically provided:

> No part of this decree shall be taken or held as adjudging to any claimant * * * any right to take * * * any water from any natural stream except to be applied to the use for which said appropriation has been made, nor to allow any excessive user of water whatsoever, nor to allow any diversion of water except for lawful and beneficial uses.

The trial court authorized transfer of the point of diversion of 8 c. f. s. Under specific findings made on competent evidence this volume of water was all that had ever ripened into a water right owned by Morrison and Hoffman. Actually they had contracted to sell to the city all the water which they could lawfully have used at any time. Under the specific findings of the trial court that no more than 8 c. f. s. was ever applied to beneficial use, that volume of water was the full measure of the water right acquired. All asserted water right which never came into being cannot be "abandoned", and the reference to "abandonment" in the trial court's judgment is an erroneous concept the result of which is harmless in this case.

No good purpose would be served in lengthening this opinion by detailed analyses of other contentions advanced by plaintiffs. Applicable and controlling rules concerning these contentions are to be found in the opinion of this court in Farmers Highline Canal and Reservoir Company et al. v. City of Golden et al., 129 Colo. 575, 272 P.2d 629. From that opinion we re-state basic concepts which require an affirmance of the judgment in the instant action. The case cited was one involving an application for change in the point of diversion of water. It was there held:

> (1) Where the proceeding is conducted pursuant to statutory direction, ' * * * all users of water affected by said proceeding were, in effect, parties and had full right to protect their rights had they so desired. * * * '
>
> (2) 'It is recognized that water is a property right, subject to sale and conveyance, and that under proper conditions not only may the point of diversion be changed, but likewise the manner of use. It further is recognized that such change may be permitted, by proper court decree, only in such instances as it is specifically shown that the rights of other users from the same source are not injuriously

affected by such change, and that the burden of proof thereof rests upon petitioner.

* * *

(3) 'There is absolutely no question that a decreed water right is valuable property; that it may be used, its use changed, its point of diversion relocated; and that a municipal corporation is not precluded from purchasing water rights previously used for agricultural purposes and thereafter devoting them to municipal uses, provided that no adverse affect be suffered by other users from the same stream, particularly those holding junior priorities.

(4) 'Equally well established, as we have repeatedly held, is the principle that junior appropriators have vested rights in the continuation of stream conditions as they existed at the time of their respective appropriations, and that subsequent to such appropriations they may successfully resist all proposed changes in points of diversion and use of water from that source which in any way materially injuries or adversely affects their rights. * * *

(5) 'All appropriations of water, and all decrees determining the respective rights of users, regardless of whether specific mention be made therein, are subject to all constitutional and statutory provisions and restrictions designed for the protection of junior appropriators from the same stream. * * * '

We think the following language contained in the opinion in the case cited is pertinent to the issues in the instant case:

> Petitioner contends, however, that it is entirely within the right of an appropriator of water to enlarge upon his use, and now that the City of Golden is the owner, it may enlarge upon the use to the extent of the entire decree. Counsel for petitioner here confuse two altogether different principles. This doctrine even on behalf of an original appropriator, may be applied only to the extent of use contemplated at the time of appropriation. It has no application whatever to a situation where a decree is sought for change of point of diversion or use. There the right is strictly limited to the extent of former actual usage. 'The right to change the point of diversion is, of course, nonetheless a qualified right because petitioner acquired it by purchase.' Fort Lyon Canal Co. v. Rocky Ford, etc., Co., 79 Colo. 511, 515, 246 P. 781.
>
> * * *
>
> ' * * * Where the entire amount fixed by the decree was reasonably required in the proper irrigation of the lands to which first applied, then the whole priority properly may be changed for similar usage; but where such irrigation did not require the entire volume of the decree, then only that portion may be changed which previously had been necessary for proper irrigation. It is not a question of whether the amount of water decreed was adequate, but whether it was

excessive. The extent of needed use in original location is the criterion in considering change of point of diversion. This, of course, is premised upon the assumption that whatever of the decreed water was not properly used remained in the stream.

* * *

'Where it appears that the change sought to be made will result in depletion to the source of supply and result in injury to junior appropriators therefrom, the decree should contain such conditions as are proper to counteract the loss, and should be denied only in such instances as where it is impossible to impose reasonable conditions to effectuate this purpose.'

We conclude that the trial court determined the issues in the instant case in a manner consistent with the foregoing principles, and find no error requiring a reversal of the judgment. There was no abuse of discretion in the assessment of costs.

The judgment accordingly is affirmed.

Notes

1. *Interlocking rights. Green* is a splendid decision in terms of the vivid illustration it gives of interlocking water rights and of the way the law looks to actual water-use practices to define the extent of private rights. Hoffman and Morrison, the court tells us, only own the right to use the precise amount of water that they have been using consistently over the years. And their right is limited by all the particulars of their pattern of use. They can only use the water during the precise times when they have been using it (here, during the irrigation season of April 15 to October 15). The cannot at any time divert more water than they have diverted in the past (here, a maximum of 8 cubic feet per second). And the total diversions during the year cannot exceed the amount they have been diverting annually (here, a total of 365 c.f.s.). It is the actual pattern of beneficial use that sets the terms of a water right, not the number written on a decree or permit.

The reason why water rights are so carefully limited, as we see, is to protect the junior users on the river who rely upon this pattern of use to establish their own water uses. Note the general rule that the court announces: "Junior appropriators, who appropriated this excess water, have a vested right to have the conditions on the river remain as they were when their appropriations were made." This is a bedrock principle of prior appropriation law, and has both high benefits and high costs. The main benefit of protecting the expectations of junior users is that these users can begin their water using activities with a fairly high degree of confidence that they will have water available (natural fluctuations aside, of course). The rule, that is, encourages junior users to take advantage of return flows, and thus encourages the full, multiple use of water before it finally ends up in the ocean. The down side is that it makes water uses rather inflexible. To protect the junior users is to restrict greatly the ability of senior users to alter where and how they use their water flows. They can make changes in the nature and place of their water uses and their points of diversion only so long as the changes cause no harm to anyone else.

Pay attention to how this do-no-harm rule plays out on the facts of this case. (It may help to draw a picture of the river and to go over the court's arithmetic calculations.) The court decides that Hoffman and Morrison have been consuming 95 acre feet of water per year. That water is lost to the river, and is thus not available for use by water users downstream. If Hoffman and Morrison transferred 95 acre feet to Fort Collins and halted their own irrigation uses, no one downstream would be worse off. But note that Fort Collins does not consume all of the water that it diverts. About half of its diverted water returns to the river and is available for downstream users. The court takes this return flow into account in deciding how much water Fort Collins can divert. So far as we can tell, it makes little difference that Fort Collins plans to divert the water from a location thirteen miles upstream. Had intervening water users been harmed by the switch we presumably would have heard about it.

2. *The dangers and inefficiencies of water transfers.* One of the dangers for a water user in stepping forward to propose a water transfer is that the transfer process draws scrutiny to the user's actual pattern of behavior. Has the use consistently been beneficial? Has there been a gap in use that can raise claims of forfeiture? What exactly are the limits on water-use practices, and how much of a water right has been lost through nonuse? Many water users would rather not have these questions asked, and are therefore reluctant to consider water transfers. The effect is to inhibit water markets. But what can be done about this situation, short of changing the legal protections enjoyed by junior users?

Consider also the economic effect of the transfer rules. Hoffman and Morrison were diverting 365 acre feet of water per year. They were able to transfer to Fort Collins only the right to divert 190 acre feet per year. Any right to divert more than that quantity was lost. This transaction will make economic sense to the parties, then, only if 190 acre feet is worth more to Fort Collins than 365 acre feet was to Hoffman and Morrison. If the water is worth, on a per-acre-foot basis, only 50% more to Fort Collins than to Hoffman and Morrison, the transfer would not take place. Indeed, given the high transaction costs involved in these transfers the transfer is likely to occur only if the water to Fort Collins is worth at least three or four times more than it is to Hoffman and Morrison. Water transfers, that is, do not move water to slightly more valuable uses. They move water only to water uses that are considerably more valuable. In economic terms, the market is decidedly inefficient.

One way to describe this situation is to highlight the tension between protecting junior users and promoting a well-functioning market. The law can do one or the other but cannot do both. Protecting junior users promotes the full use of water before it gets to the ocean. Promoting the market, on the other side, leaves junior users at great risk but allows for more ready transfers of senior water rights to higher and better uses. This tradeoff is at the heart of the water predicament today in arid parts of the American West. Market advocates (as we'll see below) call for "streamlining" transfers so as to facilitate markets. Too often they shortchange the cost of doing that—

diminished protections for junior water users. Imagine if Hoffman and Morrison were allowed to transfer to Fort Collins the full amount of water that they wanted to transfer—8 cubic feet per second of water year round. The harm to downstream users could have been considerable as Fort Collins diverted far more water than Hoffman and Morrison ever did. (The harm would have been even greater if Hoffman and Morrison had continued their own water diversion, as they proposed.) To give Hoffman and Morrison that right would be to redefine radically the property rights long held by downstream junior uses. On the other side, defenders of the current, protective regime can sometimes fail to see the high cost of it. Current water uses are hard to change when junior users are fully protected. The system overall experiences gridlock. Water is devoted to low-valued uses while higher-valued needs go unmet.

BONHAM v. MORGAN

788 P.2d 497 (Utah 1989).

PER CURIAM:

. . . Plaintiff Stanley B. Bonham, who is not a water user, protested against a permanent change application filed under Utah Code Ann. § 73–3–3 (1980) in the office of the defendant state engineer (state engineer) in June of 1984 by defendants Salt Lake County Water Conservancy District and Draper Irrigation Company (applicants). Applicants sought to change the point of diversion, place, and nature of use of certain water rights in Bell Canyon, Dry Creek, Rocky Mouth Creek, and Big Willow Creek. At a subsequent hearing, Bonham produced evidence of substantial flooding and damage to plaintiffs' properties and adjacent public lands during 1983 and 1984. Bonham informed the state engineer that the flooding was the result of applicants' construction of a screw gate, pipeline, and diversion works after they obtained preliminary approval of their change application. According to Bonham, the flooding had occurred and would recur on a yearly basis whenever the applicants closed their screw gate, allowing the waters to be diverted down the hillside onto plaintiffs' properties and nearby property contemplated for use as a public park. Bonham objected that the proposed structures and improvements contemplated after final approval would detrimentally impact the public welfare.

The state engineer conducted on-site inspections but eventually issued his memorandum decision in which he concluded that he was without authority to address Bonham's claims in ruling on the permanent change application, as Bonham was not a water user, that the state engineer's authority was limited to investigating impairments of vested water rights, and that there was no evidence before him to indicate that the implementation of the change application would impair those rights. The state engineer then granted the permanent change application. . . .

Utah Code Ann. § 73–3–3 (1980) [the statute governing changes in water uses], at the time the state engineer rendered his decision, read in pertinent part:

> Any person entitled to the use of water may change the place of diversion or use and may use the water for other purposes than those for which it was originally appropriated, but no such change shall be made if it impairs any vested right without just compensation. Such changes may be permanent or temporary. Changes for an indefinite length of time with an intention to relinquish the original point of diversion, place or purpose of use are defined as *permanent changes. Temporary changes* include and are limited to all changes for definitely fixed periods of not exceeding one year. Both permanent and temporary changes of point of diversion, place or purpose of use of water including water involved in general adjudication or other suits, shall be made in the manner provided herein and not otherwise.
>
> No permanent change shall be made except on the approval of an application therefor by the state engineer.... *The procedure in the state engineer's office and rights and duties of the applicants with respect to applications for permanent changes of point of diversion, place or purpose of use shall be the same as provided in this title for applications to appropriate water;* but the state engineer may, in connection with applications for permanent change involving only a change in point of diversion of 660 feet or less, waive the necessity for publishing notice of such applications. No temporary change shall be made except upon an application filed in duplicate with the state engineer.... The state engineer shall make an investigation and *if such temporary change does not impair any vested rights of others he shall make an order authorizing the change.*

(Emphasis added.)

Section 73–3–8 (1985) [the statute governing issuance of permits for new appropriations], at the time the state engineer rendered his decision, read in pertinent part:

> (1) It shall be the duty of the state engineer to approve an application if: (a) there is unappropriated water in the proposed source; (b) the proposed use will not impair existing rights or interfere with the more beneficial use of the water; (c) the proposed plan is physically and economically feasible, unless the application is filed by the United States Bureau of Reclamation, and would not prove detrimental to the public welfare; (d) the applicant has the financial ability to complete the proposed works; and (e) the application was filed in good faith and not for purposes of speculation or monopoly. *If the state engineer, because of information in his possession obtained either by his own investigation or otherwise, has reason to believe that an application to appropriate water will interfere with its more beneficial use for irrigation, domestic or culinary, stock watering, power or mining development or manufacturing, or will unreasonably affect public recreation or the natural stream environment, or will prove detrimental to the public welfare, it is his duty to withhold his approval or rejection of the application until he has investigated*

> *the matter. If an application does not meet the requirements of this section, it shall be rejected.*

(Emphasis added.) . . .

We agree with the position taken by plaintiffs and the NPCA that both statutory purposes and a reasonable textual interpretation of water allocation statutes support the application of appropriation criteria to permanent change applications. The language critical to our determination was added to section 100–3–3, R.S. Utah 1933, in 1937. *See* L.1937, ch. 130, § 1. The amendment removed provisions addressing notice requirements and added for the first time language defining permanent and temporary changes. After setting out procedures relating to applications for permanent changes, the 1937 amendment continued:

> The procedure in the state engineer's office *and the rights and duties of the applicant with respect to application for permanent changes* of point of diversion, place, or purpose of use *shall be the same as provided in this title for applications to appropriate water.*

(Emphasis added.)

The remaining amendments to section 100–3–3 dealt with procedures relating to temporary changes, criteria for rejecting applications for both permanent and temporary changes, procedures with respect to types of changes, and finality of the state engineer's decision and penalties for changes without following statutory prescriptions. In essence, the substantive provisions enacted in 1937 remain unchanged to date.

> The appropriations statute, section 100–3–8, R.S. Utah 1933, to which the amendment made cross-reference, contained then, as section 73–3–8 does now, a specification on the duties of the state engineer when acting on appropriation applications. These were to be granted if, and only if, they did not interfere with more beneficial use, public recreation, the natural stream environment, or the public welfare, as more specifically set out in the statute. In contrast to the cross-reference between *permanent change* applications and appropriations, the 1937 amendments prescribed different and very summary procedures for *temporary changes,* under which the state engineer "shall make an investigation and *if such temporary change does not impair any vested rights of others, he shall make an order authorizing the change.*" *See also* § 73–3–3 (1980). From these contrasting references and procedures, we draw the rational inference that in temporary change applications the review criteria (now contained in section73–3–8) did not apply, but in considerations of permanent change applications they did. . . .

Even were we convinced, which we are not, by the state engineer's argument that the "procedure in the state engineer's office" in section 73–3–3 refers only to his ministerial duties, the lack of precision in the cross-reference is of little avail to the state engineer. The further mention in that section of the "rights and duties" of the applicants and the reference to section 73–3–8 are sufficient by themselves to show that the legislature meant to require more than similar procedures alone. The only reasonable meaning to read into section 73–3–3 is that the state engineer must investigate and reject the application for either appropriation or permanent change of use or place of use if approval would interfere with more beneficial use, public recreation, the natural stream environment, or the public welfare. It is unreasonable to assume that the legislature would require the state engineer to investigate matters of public concern in water appropriations and yet restrict him from undertaking those duties in permanent change applications. Carried to its logical conclusion, such an interpretation would eviscerate the duties of the state engineer under section 73–3–8 and allow an applicant to accomplish in a two-step process what the statute proscribes in a one-step process. For all that an applicant would need to do to achieve a disapproved purpose under section 73–3–8 would be to appropriate for an approved purpose and then to file a change application under section 73–3–3. . . .

We hold that the state engineer is required to undertake the same investigation in permanent change applications that the statute mandates in applications for water appropriations and that plaintiffs are aggrieved persons who have standing to sue him pursuant to Utah Code Ann. § 73–3–14 (1980) for a review of his decision approving the subject change application. The summary judgment in favor of the state engineer is vacated, and plaintiffs' complaint against him reinstated for trial on the merits.

Notes

1. *Broader protections, and more gridlock?* In Utah as in most Western states, changes in the nature and place of a water use (very minor changes aside) typically require approval in an administrative or even judicial proceeding. Anyone who would suffer legal injury from the change can step forward to block it, in whole or in part. Note the extensive review that Utah provides. The change can be made only if it will not impair existing rights, interfere with the "more beneficial" use of water or prove detrimental to the public welfare. The statute goes on to mention protection for public recreation and natural stream conditions. In combination the statutory provisions would seem to embrace a strict do-no-harm rule, barring any material changes in water use practices that could cause noticeable harm of any sort, including (as here) harm to landowners who are not themselves water uses. As you consider the statute you might imagine the difficulties that would arise applying it. How much diminution in a water flow would be enough to interfere with public recreation? And what rivers have anything close to "natural stream conditions"?

Has the Utah statute perhaps gone too far in limiting transfers, given the resulting difficulties water owners will have selling to new, possibly more valuable uses? Would it make better sense to allow transfers to take place while requiring the transferee to pay damages to anyone specifically harmed by the transfer—without allowing the injured party to halt the transaction?

(A thoughtful proposal to that effect is offered in Megan Hennessey, Note, *Colorado River Water Rights: Property Rights in Transition,* 71 U. Chi. L. Rev. 1661 (2004).) Perhaps most significantly, can we fault lawmakers for not taking a broader view of the situation? What about a water transfer that produces a more desirable water use pattern overall, even though it causes some harm? Would it make more sense to have courts undertake an overall, before-versus-after comparison, to decide whether the transfer makes good sense as a whole, despite the ensuing harm?

2. *Permanent versus temporary changes.* Note the different, easier rules that govern when a water user seeks to make a temporary change in water use practices. The easier rules do pose dangers to public interests, but the possible benefits are evident. A water user who can temporarily avoid using water is given an easier way to make it available to someone else. Overall water uses are more efficient, and the water owner does not have to worry about losing the water right through abandonment or forfeiture. Temporary changes also facilitate deal-making to address times of drought. One water user can temporarily sell water to another as a way to address a water emergency.

3. *Public interest allocation and restrictions on transfer.* A comment made by the court in *Bonham* highlights a problem that we have seen before. The court explains that a transfer of water to a new use needs to comply with the criteria for initial water appropriation, because if it did not, a water user then could circumvent the limits on original appropriation. "For all the applicant would need to do to achieve a disapproved [water use], would be to appropriate for an approved purpose and then to file a change of application." Put simply, if lawmakers want water used in particular ways, then they need to limit transfers of the water to make sure that new uses of it (by the same or another owner) are consistent the same use limits. Phrased more broadly, when allocation of a natural resource is based on public-interest criteria, the same criteria have to be applied later, when the resource is transferred, to avoid giving resource users a two-step process for devoting the resource to a disapproved use. When subsequent transfers are limited in this way, though, markets are impaired and reallocation becomes harder. The market works on the assumption that resources should go to the highest bidder—an allocation system quite contrary to allocation based on merit or public interest. (On this issue, you might re-read the essay that concludes chapter three.)

4. *Farm water for farmers alone*: City of West Richland v. Dept. of Ecology. A state statute, the Family Farm Water Act, gave farmers a special opportunity to gain water for use on "family farms." The statute allowed some flexibility in shifting irrigation water to other agricultural uses and to certain uses in "urbanizing areas" consistent with "adopted land use plans." *Held*: Given the clear public-interest limits imposed by the statute, a family farmer was prohibited from leasing his water rights for 50 years to City of West Richland. The city's use did not qualify for the special treatment accorded family farms. City of West Richland v. Department of Ecology, 124 Wash.App. 683, 103 P.3d 818 (2004).

5. *Interstate commerce in water.* Although a state can impose severe restrictions on where water can be used and on water transfers—prohibiting

them entirely if it wants—it faces constitutional limits when it defines transfer options in ways that discriminate against interstate commerce. In Sporhase v. Nebraska ex rel. Douglas, 458 U.S. 941 (1982), the Court struck down, as a violation of the dormant commerce clause, a Nebraska statute that authorized the transport of groundwater to another state only if that state similarly allowed the export of its own water into Nebraska. The Court recognized that Nebraska might preserve its water for use by state residents as a way of dealing with scarcity and promoting conservation. The challenged provision, however, was not carefully tailored to promote conservation: it authorized export of water in a discriminatory way.

* * *

The above two cases and accompanying notes explain the basic rules on water transfers in prior appropriation jurisdictions. Transfers are possible but transaction costs are high. Moreover, the basic, do-no-harm rule operates in many jurisdictions to ban water transfers except to the extent of a water user's consumptive use. Water that is used consumptively is entirely lost to a river system and thus can be diverted for use elsewhere, for any purpose, without causing harm to the river system of origin and to downstream water users. But when water owners desire to transfer more of their water, problems arise—as we've seen. The law tends to limit transfers in the interest of protecting junior users and thus the stability of the entire water-use regime. But how, then, are we to facilitate shifts of water to higher-valued uses, particularly to urban uses where thirsty water users are willing and easily able to outbid agricultural users?

One possible answer to this problem is for states to redefine reasonable and beneficial water use so as to prohibit water uses that no longer make economic and social sense. If urban areas need water (as they do), and if lawmakers view municipal water uses as high in social priority (as they do), then why should massive amounts of water be used for low-valued agricultural purposes, particularly to irrigate crops (such as corn and cotton) that are overabundant, to pasture livestock (also abundant), and to produce hay (of little value except in local markets)? And why should irrigators be allowed to continue using irrigation methods that are vastly less efficient than technological options that are readily available and widely used outside the United States?

What if a court, legislature or regulatory agency decided that a water use was not reasonable or even beneficial when it entailed irrigating low-valued crops or entailed the use of inefficient distribution systems—as the California State Water Resources Control Board did in the *Imperial Irrigation District* dispute? What would the effect of such a ruling be, particularly if the irrigators affected by it were given a period of time in which to shift to a more beneficial use or to sell the water to someone else? Could a new definition of reasonable and beneficial use not only curtail socially undesirable water uses but stimulate a more active market in water rights? Alternatively, as the first article below by now-Judge Stephen Williams argues, should we move in precisely the opposite direction, getting rid of the beneficial use limit and doing all we can to stimulate markets? Is that option, however disruptive to junior users in the short run, more likely (given American culture) to bring long-term benefits?

A MARKET–BASED APPROACH TO WATER RIGHTS: EVALUATING COLORADO'S WATER SYSTEM

Stephen F. Williams.

in TRADITION, INNOVATION AND CONFLICT: PERSPECTIVES ON COLORADO WATER LAW (Lawrence J. Macdonnell, ed. 1986)

INTRODUCTION

Continuation of Colorado's prosperity obviously requires water. Its availability depends on facilitating transfers and on minimizing waste. Fortunately, Colorado's current agricultural usage provides a generous pool from which underused or wasted water can be drawn. As of 1980, for example, agriculture was responsible for 87% of Colorado's consumptive water use. Fairly trivial savings in the agricultural sector could, therefore, provide for a doubling or tripling of industrial and municipal consumption. How can these savings best be brought about?

The current system is a mix of market and government control, with the market element dominant. However, many support increasing the regulatory component, in the form, for example, of using the "beneficial use" doctrine to mandate water saving. These suggestions seem ill-conceived. The interest in getting the most value out of our water would best be served by moving in the opposite direction—by diminishing the current fetters on the market.

The arguments for reliance on the market are familiar ones. Above all, the market is an extraordinary system for generating information. Individuals and firms, buying and selling in a market, generate prices. Those prices, coupled with individual ingenuity, in turn enable people to make sensible decisions on how much to consume, how much to produce, and how to go about production. Thus a wheat farmer is able to decide how much and what kind of fertilizer he will use without knowing anything about how the fertilizer is made. His and millions of others' decisions on how much to buy give fertilizer manufacturers critical information about how much fertilizer to produce. No government agency could ever pull together the information needed to make these decisions.

Before discussing Colorado water law itself, let me respond in advance to the most common attack on reliance on the market in water—"Water is essential to life itself and should not be left to allocation by market forces." First, if the market is a good instrument for allocating non-essential resources, one might think that it makes even more sense to use it for allocating an essential one. Second, quite a few other resources are essential for life. Have you ever tried growing wheat without land? Yet generally we allow the allocation of land to be market-determined. There is no apparent reason why water must be treated differently. Third, none of the institutions discussed here will ever jeopardize—or even seriously affect—the supply of water for the purposes that make us call it essential. Somewhere out in the great western desert there may be a person or two about to expire for want of water, but that will be because of an extremely local problem—for example, he may have inadequately prepared for a camping trip or for a journey across a long barren stretch of road. In this discussion, by contrast, we are talking of water as an input to agriculture, or to industry, or to non-vital domestic uses. Suppose, for example, the domestic price of water were to double. Lawns might shrink, cars might be cleaned less often (or more efficiently), but no one would die of thirst, or have to go about dirty, or even have to alter his cooking methods.

There is a great western tradition of proclaiming water essential—and then adopting institutions that guarantee its waste. We could perhaps do better by simply focusing on the issue of how to nurture institutions that will diminish waste....

A Market System

The key to preventing waste in the allocation of water resources is to give the holders of water rights conventional market incentives to avoid waste. Conditions that would establish market incentives are as follows: A) Owners of water rights will not waste water if they bear the cost[1] of such waste; B) Owners of water rights will bear the opportunity cost of waste if their rights are readily transferable; and C) Water rights meet the above test of ready transferability if (1) administrative/adjudicative costs are kept low, (2) water rights are clearly defined, (3) transfer is restricted only in the interest of projecting junior appropriators, and (4) the adjustments made in the interest of protecting juniors are the minimum consistent with that protection. This section will elaborate on these criteria.

Owners of Water Rights Will Not Waste Water If They Bear the Cost of Such Waste

Suppose a farmer could save[2] 1000 acre-feet of water (annually) by using a device that he can install for $5000. (To keep matters simple, assume the device has no operating costs and has a perpetual life.) The opportunity cost of *not* installing the device is the value of the water saved, less the cost of installation. If the water saved is worth $20,000, then the opportunity cost of the farmer's inaction—the farmer's waste—is $15,000.

There are various ways of making the farmer "bear" that cost. The state could fine him; it could penalize him by taking the water away from him; it could install the device and insist on payment from the farmer. These methods are inconsistent with our dominant institutions and are very inefficient. All of them require that the state snoop around,

1. For the purposes of the above statement, "cost" means "opportunity cost." "Opportunity cost" is further defined as the monetary or other advantage surrendered (or foregone) for something in order to acquire (or retain) it in competition with other potential users.

2. "Save" refers to real savings, i.e., to water otherwise lost through evaportranspiration. It does not refer to return flow or water that seeps out of a ditch and is put to use by downstream users.

determine that the particular waste reduction is feasible, and bring the weight of its bureaucracy to bear on the farmer. Who is in a better position to determine what action is most efficient for the farmer, a bureaucrat or the farmer himself? The answer is obvious.

More basically, determination that a particular practice is wasteful requires some device for valuing the water saved. Unless we know that value, we cannot determine whether the extra water is worth the expense. Determining a value for water essentially requires the existence of a reliable water market to generate prices.

Defects in the water market drive a wedge between a farmer's and a bureaucrat's view of sensible water saving methods. The bureaucrat may well value water at its incremental cost—the cost of adding new water supplies through dam building, etc. This might amount to, say, $500 per acre-foot. But if the farmer is unable to realize that amount for water that is saved, he will clearly compare the cost of the savings against a much lower value. In the extreme case, where he cannot sell it and he cannot increase the yield from his land by increasing water use, he would value the extra water at zero.

For precisely this reason, a recent report for the Environmental Defense Fund takes a skeptical view of bureaucratic enforcement of the concept of "reasonable and beneficial use." It points to a proceeding by the State Water Resources Control Board in California, in which the agency was valuing water at $200 an acre-foot (a very conservative estimate of the cost of new water supplies), while the farmers in the Imperial Irrigation District were valuing it at the $9 cost per acre-foot that the district paid. In such a case, the opposing parties will be talking at cross-purposes. Farmers will fight enforcement of water conservation measures with bitterness and at great cost, and in all probability only the most egregious waste will be ended (if any). The EDF Report concluded that the episode "illustrated the difficulty of this approach, clearly only second best when compared to the establishment of a market for water transfers."

Because of the difficulty of agreeing on values for purposes of comparing expenses with water saved, a regulatory system for preventing waste cannot work unless accompanied by an adequate market. With such a market, the farmer can quickly recognize that by failing to install the device, he is foregoing the benefit that the saved water is worth. In our example, he is foregoing the difference between the $20,000 the saved water is worth minus the $5000 cost of the device, or a net gain of $15,000. His opportunity cost is $15,000. Recognizing this cost should give him ample incentive to install the device and avoid the need for regulatory intervention.

Owners of Water Rights Will Bear the Opportunity Cost of Waste if Their Rights Are Readily Transferable

With very limited exceptions, the state does not go around demanding that a landowner apply his or her land to specific uses. It imposes limitations on what he may do (zoning), but it does not affirmatively demand that he do anything very much. It does not, for example, insist that the owner of any parcel of downtown Denver real estate build on it. Why does the state evidently feel free to allow urban landowners to "neglect" their land (in the sense of underusing it, of failing to apply it to a beneficial use)? Is it because urban landowners are smart and the owners of water rights are not? Probably not.

My explanation would be this: Real property law implicitly recognizes that the owner of urban real estate is disciplined by the market. It assumes that if he fails to apply his property to the most productive use, there are plenty of people who would like to make productive use of the land and who will bring their bids to the owner's attention. He can indulge in the luxury of underuse of the land only at the cost of foregoing those bids.

While Colorado real property law has developed on the implicit premise that the land transfer market works well enough to discipline the neglectful landowners, Colorado water law has developed largely on the opposite premise—that the water rights market cannot adequately discipline neglectful water rights owners. Three principles of Colorado water law reflect this more pessimistic premise: (1) the requirement of beneficial use; (2) the doctrine of abandonment; and (3) the concept that an appropriator does not ordinarily have a property interest in the return flow from his use (e.g., he cannot prevent a downstream junior from using his return flow).

A variety of rationales are likely to be invoked in favor of these rules. First, it may be said that they prevent anyone from being a "dog in the manger"—that is, preventing benefits to others for no good reason. Second, they might be defended on the ground that, since water is a uniquely precious resource, the public interest in efficient water use requires state supervision. Thus, in the case of beneficial use, the public interest requires that water is not wasted and that no one use water unless it is used for some useful purpose. In the case of abandonment, anyone who has failed to use his water over an extended period might be said to have established by his behavior that his use is not for a useful purpose and thus the public interest requires its termination. In the case of return flow, it may be argued that allowing the owner to veto downstream use of his return flow by someone else, would lead simply to waste of water.

All of these arguments, however, imply that the market is not developed well enough to put adequate pressure on people either to use their water efficiently, or to sell it to one who can. But, so long as the market enables those with good ideas for the use of water to bid it away from current owners, there is no reason to believe that any of the abovementioned doctrines is needed to assure efficient water use. In fact, the present system of Colorado water rights fails to take full advantage of the market system and presents many opportunities for improvement. The following section addresses the criteria that must be met if water rights are to be transferable enough so that the market can discipline those inclined to waste.

Criteria for Reasonable Transferability of Water Rights

Water rights meet the test of reasonable transferability if: 1) administrative and adjudicative costs are kept low; 2) water rights are clearly defined; 3) transfer is restricted only in the interest of protecting the junior appropriators; and 4) the adjustments made in the interest of protecting juniors are the minimum consistent with that protection. Below I will review each of the four subparts of these conditions for adequate transferability.

Administrative and adjudicative costs are kept low. In a critique of the present approach of administering Colorado's water, Clyde Martz has suggested a number of procedures which would improve the current system of water rights administration in Colorado.“ Central to his theme is a greater reliance upon the technical and managerial capabilities of the Office of the State Engineer in administering surface and ground water rights, and less reliance on court adjudications to establish and protect water rights by water users. His arguments that such a system would be more efficient, less costly, and less time-consuming appear persuasive.

Water rights are clearly defined. Each of the doctrines discussed in the first part of this paper tends to undermine the clear definition of water rights. The concept of beneficial use, for example, means that the vendor and vendee of water rights will be uncertain, at least in some cases, weather the would-be transferor has any rights to transfer. The same effect is found with the doctrine of abandonment, and the rule that an appropriator has no absolute right to his return flow. Again, let me draw the contrast to the urban land market. If "A" owns a tract that he has used only as a parking lot for 15 years, he can clearly sell the area to which he initially acquired title, without anxiety that his use in that period may be deemed not "beneficial" and thus expose him to a claim that he had abandoned his right. Nor will the quantity available for sale be reduced on the ground that his "historic use" was less than his paper title. But Colorado water law creates precisely such gaps between paper title and legally transferable right.

Transfer is restricted only in the interest of protecting junior appropriators. On this point, Colorado law confirms to the principles I've set out. Unlike some other states, Colorado does not mandate an open-ended inquiry into whether the transfer serves the public interest. In my judgment, the Colorado rule is entirely correct. Any broadening of the inquiry would increase the risk of disapproval; anything that increases the risk of disapproval makes the owner's expectations of revenues from a sale more uncertain and anything that makes that expectation more uncertain will dull the market's incentives. . . .

The adjustments made in the interest of protecting juniors are the minimum consistent with that protection. Here is an area where Colorado law could be improved. It is a well established rule that an appropriator does not have a property right in his return flow. He cannot, for example, prevent a downstream junior from using his return flow. Reasonable transferability of water requires modification of this concept in the context of water transfers. When transfer occurs, the new right (or newly reconstituted right) should be defined so that the owner has a property right in any return flow that would otherwise be a windfall to downstream users.

Let me illustrate. Suppose "A" has a right to divert 10 cfs and his use is 50% consumptive. He proposes to transfer the right downstream. Suppose it is determined that, in order to protect juniors located between the two points of diversion, the water right must be cut in half, say from 10 cfs to 5 cfs. Further suppose that the new use is also 50% consumptive. Juniors downstream of the new use will, under current law, enjoy a windfall. As the new use might have been 100% consumptive, they are getting extra security for their rights in the form of the 2.5 cfs that the transferor could have used himself, but doesn't. When the law reduces the right from 10 to 5 cfs this transfer is effectively taxed at a rate of 50%. Enabling the transferor to enjoy a property right in the return flow (which his action has conferred upon downstream juniors) would offset that penalty. It would thus reduce the negative effects on transferability that flow from the protection of juniors....

In the absence of a water market, direct government action to monitor and prohibit waste is doomed. It will generate antagonism between farmers and the enforcement agency, with prolonged and expensive proceedings before agency and court. Only on very rare occasions, where extreme waste is involved, would it likely save any water. With a reasonably efficient water transfer market, no such direct governmental action would be necessary. Water users, with an eye to resale of any water savings, would adopt economical water saving devices on their own....

Conclusion

The key to minimizing waste of any water resource is to have that resource freely transferable between private owners in a free market and to place the owners of the resource in a position to bear the opportunity cost of resource waste. Transferability is aided when administrative and adjudicative costs are kept low and the dimensions of the water rights are defined with certainty. Restrictions on transferability are justified only when protecting vested rights of other users and must be limited so as not to interfere with transferability for any other purpose....

Notes

1. *Criticizing beneficial use.* Before getting to Judge Williams's affirmative touting of the market, pay attention to his criticisms of beneficial use, particularly as an evolving limit on existing water use practices. Keep in mind, too, that the beneficial-use requirement is linked to forfeiture rules;

water is forfeited if the owner fails to use it beneficially for a specified period of time. By doing away with beneficial use we would largely do away with forfeiture rules. Has Williams adequately considered the consequences of that move? The beneficial-use rule is what effectively limits property rights in water to actual patterns of use, which are often vastly less than paper rights. If, as Williams proposes, we began honoring paper rights starting with the most senior—without regard for actual use—what disruptions might ensue? If the main complaint against beneficial use is that it is a vague limit, could we deal with the problem by having a regulatory agency issue regulations giving the term more precise meaning? What if an agency specified irrigation methods and prohibited irrigation of certain low-valued crops? If the rules were clear enough would they avoid the problems that Williams raises or might they instead create even greater problems?

2. *Public uses and ecological health.* Can we imagine the effects of Williams's ideas on public uses of waterways and on the ecological health of river systems? In his comments about water being essential to life Williams only talks about human life and about the need to drink; he makes no mention of other life forms or of the water needs of the ecological systems that sustain all life, humans included. How would his proposed system protect the ecological functioning and public uses of waters? Is he assuming that taxpayers and public interest groups would buy water rights for these communal purposes? Could this system work and be reasonably fair?

3. *Reducing protections for junior users.* The most immediate effect of Judge Williams's proposal would be to enhance the rights of senior users at the expenses of junior uses, although we would need to hear more details to know how much change he has in mind. Certainly any proposal to respect paper rights, rather than actual patterns of use, would deprive countless current water users of their water rights. (His approach in that regard is hardly pro-private property.) Williams opposes anything like the public-interest review process that we saw Utah using in the *Bonham* case. He would curtail water transfers only to the minimum extent necessary to protect junior users. But what would this mean? Would his reasoning lead to a different outcome, for instance, in *Green v. Chaffee Ditch*? Would minimum protection for junior users have allowed Hoffman and Morrison to transfer more of their paper rights or of their actual diversion?

THE IMPORTANCE OF GETTING NAMES RIGHT: THE MYTH OF MARKETS FOR WATER

Joseph W. Dellapenna

25 Wm. and Mary Envtl. L. & Poly. Rev. 317 (2000).

D. Why Private Property Systems Fail for Water Resources

Ronald Coase demonstrated, in The Problem of Social Cost, that a private-property market system is the most efficient mechanism for allocating resources to particular uses when it does work, but that the system fails if there are significant barriers to the functioning of a market. The fact is that markets in water as such have never actually played much of a role even in such a paradigmatic private property system as appropriative rights. This itself constitutes evidence that markets do not work well for ambient resources like water. . . .

The explanation for this phenomenon goes under the rather straightforward name of "externalities"—a use by one person affects the uses by many others, perhaps all others, and hence a significant change in any use infringes upon the interests of many other users. While it might theoretically be possible for a properly structured market to cope with all of these concerns, in any economically large or complex hydrologic system the difficulty and expense of structuring transactions (the problem of transaction costs) are a sufficient explanation of why real markets simply have never developed in practice, and do not appear likely to develop. Only if the law chooses to disregard all such externalities could markets become a possibility.

Under appropriative rights, water rights are defined in terms of an authorization to commit a specific quantity of water at a specific point at specific times for specific uses on specific land and with a specific (time-based) priority; the regime comes as close as one might hope to a true private property system of water rights. One might expect that such externalities would be less of a problem under appropriative rights because senior appropriators (those whose appropriations began earlier in time) have superior rights to junior appropriators. Strongly enforcing temporal priorities among water uses might lead one to expect that the law would routinely ignore externalities in appropriative rights states when the transfer is undertaken by a senior appropriator and any externalities affects only junior appropriators. The law of appropriative rights, however, consistently prohibits even a senior appropriator from changing the time, place, or manner of use if the change would produce a significant injury to a junior appropriator. Generally the burden of proving that there will be no injury to other users of water is on the one seeking to make the change, rather than on the one objecting to the change. Thus, if the evidence is inconclusive, a court will prohibit the change.

Precisely such uncertainty, however, is usually the case if the question is what portion of the water diverted from the stream (the usual measure of the appropriative right) was consumptively used by the senior appropriator and what portion constituted a return flow to the benefit of junior appropriators. Indeed, placing a burden on the applicant for a change of proving a negative—that there would be "no injury" to any other water user—often is a practical impossibility. While we can easily obtain exact measurements of return flows through "point sources" of discharge that characterize return flows from municipalities or industries, measuring return flows through "non-point sources"—as is characteristic of agriculture—is far from easy and nearly always uncertain. Yet it is from agriculture that the proponents of markets seek to move water, not the other way around.

The result of the third party rule is that a sale (or lease) of a water right can be blocked by any affected third party—including a junior appropriator—who is willing to sue for an injunction against the modification of the water right. The consequence is that the transaction cannot take place unless all potentially affected holders of water rights have consented. Obtaining such consents will require contracts and compensation to be paid to all such third parties. On even a moderately sized water source, the costs of identifying each affected water right holder and then securing the necessary consents will be prohibitively expensive....

The law of appropriative rights does not go as far as it might in inhibiting transfers of water to new uses. For one thing, only the rights of other appropriators are protected. Generalized social costs, such as the loss of tax revenues to a community, are not protected from the effects of transfers. Concern over generalized social costs have generated enough political pressure to bring about the enactment of "area-of-origin" statutes. Area-of-origin statutes have not appeared to be significant barriers to market transactions only because the law protecting the rights of junior appropriators provides sufficient deterrence to market transactions that it really does not matter much whether social costs are ignored or considered.

Economists and others who champion the free play of the market have insisted that the protection of third-party rights represents only an overly rigid legal regime. If only such requirements were removed, markets would flourish. This mischaracterizes the situation. Area-of-origin statutes are regulations that have the potential to interfere with or to prevent market transactions. The protection of third-party rights operates differently. Such protections prevent market-generated externalities from destroying the property rights of third parties. Rather than representing government intervention that prevents or distorts markets, such protections are the minimum that is necessary to assure that property rights—each person's property rights—are transferred only through markets....

Once one realizes how the law affects the possibility of sales of water rights, one readily grasps why small-scale transfers of water rights among farmers or ranchers—all of whom are making roughly similar uses at more or less the same place—are the only ones that regularly occurred without state intervention. For these small-scale, like-kind transactions, there is little likelihood of effects on third parties. The only large-scale transactions involving a significant change in the place or manner of use and achieved purely by market transactions have been in situations where the transferor was the last beneficial user of the water. The prime example could well be the transfer of water from the Imperial Irrigation District in southern California to the Metropolitan Water District or the San Diego County Water Authority serving the urban conglomerates of southern California. In that context, if the transferred water was not conserved by the irrigation district and conveyed to the water district, it would have passed into the increasingly saline and increasingly polluted Salton Sea which increasingly will not even sustain wildlife. Even so, the transactions evoked strong, but unavailing resistance from local communities that feared the ensuing fallowing of land would injure their economic base and from other irrigation districts who contended that the salved water should have gone to them without charge notwithstanding that they did not benefit from any relevant return flow.

WATER RIGHTS AND THE COMMON WEALTH

Eric T. Freyfogle
26 Envtl. L. 27 (1996).

The water-rights system so debated today is part of a larger private-property regime, created over many centuries and handed down within our culture, generation to generation. Private ownership is a form of state-sanctioned private power; by owning something, we gain rights that offer power, not just over the thing itself, but over other people whose lives are linked to the thing. The main justification for this system, really its only defensible justification, is that it is useful; it provides benefits that exceed its costs. . . .

For a private property regime to fulfill its functions and retain its moral legitimacy, it needs to be kept up to date, to bend and take on new shapes as communal values and circumstances evolve. Sometimes that happens smoothly, as it largely did in the nineteenth century when cultural values shifted to emphasize economic development and geographic expansion at the expense of sensitive land uses and settled agrarian culture. Sometimes, though, change does not come smoothly. Sometimes property regimes get out of date, a prospect that becomes both more likely and more ominous when holders of private rights are politically powerful enough to resist change. When change is halted, a property regime begins to lose its legitimacy. Step by step, people come to view it as unfair, as an illegitimate exercise of state-sanctioned power, as an enemy that divides and destroys the community rather than as a tool that supports and sustains it. Sometimes it is the allocation of property within the society that causes the problems. More commonly it is the way ownership rights are defined, it is the elements or attributes of what private ownership entails. Private property yields its legitimacy when, in the eyes of community members, it vests owners with the power to impose harm without consequence; when it allows them to dominate others unfairly; when it allows them to abuse and undermine things that the community has come to treasure.

In the 1960s, Congress passed laws banning racial discrimination in public accommodations, restaurants, and motels. Affected property owners claimed their property rights were being altered, and they were right. Before the new laws, landowners had the right to discriminate; after the laws they no longer had that power. They lost the power to discriminate, and for just this reason: In the evolving culture of the day, the power to discriminate had become an unfair form of power, a cruel and hurtful form of domination.

Consider a second scene, from the hills of eastern Kentucky, a landscape of badly polluted rivers and degraded communities. During the first half of this century, holders of mineral interests in Kentucky had the right to destroy the surface of the land and every structure on it in their race to stripmine the coal. They caused grave damage, and paid no compensation. By the 1960s, that form of private ownership had lost public favor, and the push for change gained strength. By the 1980s, disfavor had become so strong and so angry that, for many Kentuckians, the very legitimacy of the state was in question. For far too long the government had bent to the wishes of the coal mining industry. Change came slowly in Kentucky, but come it did. Today, mining companies still can destroy the land surface without bothering to seek permission. But at least they have to pay for what they destroy. Sooner or later, one day, they will need to ask consent.

Since prior appropriation was born in the 1850s, it has undergone a continuing evolution in the elements that define private rights. Yet even with this evolution, people are increasingly offended by it. As critics see it, water law gives owners too much power to dominate and cause harm. What is noteworthy about this otherwise unexceptional evolution is that the underlying harm is not to other people, at least not directly. It is harm to the land and water itself. Restaurants that discriminated by race caused human harm. Strip miners did destroy land, but the harm that moved Kentucky citizens to react was less the environmental degradation than it was the human drama, the farm houses slipping down hillsides, the towns being literally uprooted, the poor people ejected as so much trash. Cultural values, circumstances, definitions of harm, and aesthetic appraisals—all of them change. If water law is going to retain its legitimacy, it too needs to change, far more than it has done.

The water rights advocate, of course, has a ready response to all of this. Are not we simply talking about the need to shift water uses? Cannot the market accommodate this fluctuation in preferences? Cannot tax dollars be used to purchase the water flows now needed to promote ecosystem health and other new public values?

The answer is yes, the market can help alleviate this problem; and yes, tax money can end the most affronting and damaging water uses. But moving money around does not address the core concern of morality and legitimacy. Market transfers shift rights among owners and bring about resource reallocations, but they do not alter the nature of those rights. In the case of water law, as with the 1960s restaurants and the Kentucky stripminers, the complaint is not about the distribution of property rights. It is about the meaning of ownership itself, about the power that private ownership entails. For the law to remain legitimate it needs to ban harmful activities, which is to say activities the community has come to view today as wrong and illegitimate. It is not enough for the law to furnish mechanisms to pay property owners to stop the harm. We could have paid motel owners to stop discriminating, and perhaps there was a moment in time when payment appeared sensible. By the 1960s, that solution was no longer just. And it was not simply a matter of saving tax money. Racial discrimination had come to be wrong. It was no longer legitimate for state-sanctioned power to stand ready to aid landowners who chose to discriminate. . . .

Western water law faces a crisis of legitimacy because of the way it defines water rights, because it allows water uses that now seem wrong. Some permitted uses, in fact, now seem so wrong that it would be an affront to communal values, as well as a distasteful reaffirmation of a flawed property regime, to expect taxpayers to pay owners to change their hurtful ways. To expect the market to remedy this situation is to misunderstand the law's unavoidable role in expressing communal values, particularly our shared, evolving senses of community and lasting health.

* * *

How then might the law of prior appropriation change in order to regain its legitimacy, to respond to the mounting claim that it empowers private owners to use their property in ways that unjustly harm and oppress?

One obvious target for change is the rule that a water right is obtainable only if a user diverts the water from the streambed. By requiring diversion, water law discredits water uses that promote in-stream-flow values, particularly the natural health of the waterways themselves. . . .

A second target for reform is the long-standing, much-modified rule that water is available for appropriation so long as a single drop remains in the stream or aquifer. Total consumption, draining a river dry, is the apotheosis of shortsighted, anthropocentric hubris. A more sensible rule must be found.

These two matters, and several others like them, would improve prior appropriation law. But if we are to cut to the root of the problem, we need to get serious about the long-standing yet ineffectual requirement that all water uses be beneficial. As too often now applied, beneficial use is out of date, not the least because it ignores water quality.

Beneficial use too often means beneficial based on circumstances in effect in the late nineteenth century when almost any type of mining, agricultural, or commercial use of water seemed beneficial, without regard for environmental consequences or foreseeable shortages. Beneficial use as it stands today is an affront to attentive citizens who know stupidity when they see it, who know, for instance, that no public benefit arises when a river is fully drained so that its waters might flow luxuriously through unlined, open ditches onto desert soil to grow surplus cotton and pollute the water severely. People know better than this, and if the law does not soon learn better, the clamor for change will become more angry and disruptive.

Beneficial use must expressly come to mean beneficial by the standards of today's culture, not by the standards of some culture long-eclipsed by changing values and circumstances. It must come to mean beneficial to the community, not just to the individual user, particularly a user whose calculation of gain ignores resulting ecological harms. Bank robbery, after all, is beneficial to the robber....

To bring Western water law up-to-date, bold changes are needed. Whether operating in legislative or judicial arenas, lawmakers must openly state that many current water uses are simply not appropriate—unlined irrigation ditches running through desert lands, irrigation to grow pasture grasses and hay crops, diversions that yield substantial salinization and other pollution, diversions to grow cotton or rice in the desert, and unmetered municipal water systems, to name a few. In many settings, perhaps all such water uses simply do not promote the common good, which surely ought to be the pre-eminent legal standard. And the time has come to say so.

When weighing the utility of particular water uses, lawmakers need to fashion and apply new standards of harm, ones that embrace a longer time frame and that recognize humans' inextricable dependence on surrounding natural communities. Harm must register and weigh in the balance even when it is widespread or far downstream, even when it is hard to trace and its causes are many. Harm to ecological communities deserves attention, even if no human today can demonstrate pecuniary loss. Given that our knowledge of nature is so frightfully limited and is likely to remain that way, there is abundant need for caution on this point. Because we cannot fully predict the effects of particular water diversions and pollutants, we would be wise to err on the side of caution when passing judgment on individual cases. We should err on the side of mimicking natural water flows more closely and reducing pollutant loads as far as possible, so as to reduce the nasty surprises that so often jump out at us when we tinker arrogantly with the natural order.

Notes

1. *Political feasibility.* The above two readings propose that lawmakers give greater force to the beneficial/reasonable use limit on water rights and push water users to change their ways. If the law worked in that way—more than it already does—it would approximate the reasonable use rule that we have seen operating in the context of riparian rights, in nuisance law, and in resource law generally. Is there a reason why courts have been so reluctant to conclude that particular, low-valued water uses are no longer reasonable or beneficial by today's standards? On this point we might recall the California Supreme Court's ruling in *Joslin v. Marin Municipal Water District* (chapter 2), in which the court ruled that a riparian landowner acted unreasonably by using water to carry gravel and sand to his land. The court did not hesitate to end this use after deciding that it was much less socially useful than municipal water uses. The same, of course, could be said about uses of water to irrigate low-valued crops, or irrigation that produces significant water pollution. Why the differing treatment?

In thinking about this issue, consider the effect of a ruling of unreasonableness. In *Joslin*, the landowner could still use his land for other purposes. Moreover, the landowner retained his riparian water rights; he simply could not use the water for this particular purpose. In the context of prior appropriation water rights the situation, as we have seen, is different. The water right is considered in isolation, not as part of a package of landowner rights. The effect of a finding of unreasonableness is that the water right comes to an end. Aside from these differences there are the political realities in the arid and semi-arid West. Though relatively few in number, irrigators retain considerable political clout. Moreover, a ruling that a particular agricultural activity is no longer socially beneficial is a rather stiff condemnation of an entire way of life. It can call into question generations of hard work on the land. Is it any wonder that Western states are reluctant, politically and culturally, to claim that irrigation to sustain cattle (and thus the cowboy culture) is a wasteful resource practice?

The "stick" approach of threatening water users with loss of water rights so far has shown little promise. Can we thus rule it out on political grounds, as inconsistent with prevailing cultural values? Does it seem to clash too directly with popular support for private property rights?

2. *Working in tandem?* The two approaches to water reallocation—stimulating transfers and tightening the beneficial-use limit—are often presented as alternatives. But are they? Might they work in tandem, in a form of carrot and stick motivation or like the good-cop/bad-cop interrogation method? Water markets have largely failed to provide sufficient incentive to move irrigation water to higher-valued uses. Could the threat of losing the water provide the needed prod to stimulate seller action, leading to more successful markets? On the other side, could opportunities to sell water soften the political resistance to tighter beneficial-use limits? That is, if irrigators had ample opportunities to sell their water and thus retain much of its economic value, might they soften their resistance to judicial or administrative actions that criticize longstanding water-use activities?

3. *A third alternative?* Particularly in the newer, statutorily controlled riparian systems in the Eastern states, water users receive permits that are limited in duration. Rights to renew are conditioned, at least on paper, on a showing that a water use remains consistent with overall social needs. The effect of this approach is to create a governance structure that possesses power to facilitate the reallocation of water to higher and better uses. The governance structure does not itself decide new water uses: market forces are more influential on that issue. Instead, the governance structure helps bring old uses to an end via a process that allows society to pass judgment on the continued value of existing resource-use practices. Governance structures, of course, can be more or less responsive to the popular will and more or less able to consider the full implications of alternative resource uses.

Can we imagine new institutional arrangements in the West that might allow residents of a region or watershed to exercise more direct control over water uses, allowing them a similar role in bringing outdated uses to an end and promoting shifts to higher and better water uses? That is, could water rights be defined, not in terms of a legal limit such as beneficial use, but in terms of whether a given water use continues to enjoy support from a particular governance regime? This latter approach would replace a substantive legal limit on a private use right with a limit that is more overtly process based. Thus, the holder of a water use right would have the legal power to use the water only in ways deemed socially appropriate by the governing body, with the body expressly possessing the power to revise its views from time to time and to apply new standards to existing water users. (You might, on this issue, re-read the essay that ends chapter five.) Could such a system work, in practice, or would it (as Judge Williams contends) produce too much instability in water rights, thereby undercutting many sound water-use practices? If such a governance structure were set up, how much influence should local water users have in it, and how much power should be vested in outsiders who pay attention to larger communal concerns? The question is by no means easy to answer. We'll return to it in the final chapter.

C. PRIVATE CONDEMNATION

The power of eminent domain is essentially the power of government to reclaim land or other resources for reallocation to a new use or user, public or private. Almost always, the new use is known in advance, so the condemnation serves as a preliminary step to the reallocation. In many natural resource settings, governments have frequently used their eminent domain power out of a desire to promote particular resource uses that are deemed consistent with, if not essential to, the common good. The condemnations, that is, paved the way for new allocations of land and resources to promote the public interest. The following excerpt by a prominent legal historian considers the uses of condemnation in the nineteenth century, with particular reference to the way courts interpreted the requirement that condemnations be undertaken only for public uses. Indirectly it tells us much about the role of government in reallocating natural resources to promote then-prevailing social goals.

PROPERTY LAW, EXPROPRIATION, AND RESOURCE ALLOCATION BY GOVERNMENT, 1789–1910

Harry N. Scheiber

33 J. of Econ. Hist. 232 (1973), *reprinted in* L. Friedman & H. Sheiber, eds, American Law and the Constitutional Order (1978).

In many states, because of the importance of gristmills to a farming community the legislatures had extended special privileges to millers. Among these privileges was the power to overflow neighboring lands in order to create a millpond or reservoir for waterpower. To compensate owners of the land overflowed, the milldam statutes had provided for either annual assessment by commissioners of the income loss incurred or else a once-for-all damage judgement.

Beginning in the mid–1830s and continuing through the next three decades, numerous states greatly extended the milldam principle by devolving the expropriation power upon manufacturing firms in quest of water-power sites for purposes other than grinding grain. The New Jersey court was the first to adjudicate a case challenging this dramatic enlargement of eminent-domain doctrines. When that state's legislature authorized a private corporation to expropriate land for the development of some seventy mill sites along a six-mile stretch of the Delaware River, lawyers resisting the project termed it a blatant attempt to "take private property for private use"—a legal innovation that would render worthless the "public use" limitation on the eminent-domain power. But the court upheld the statute. Even though the corporation's primary purpose was private profit, the court said, "The ever varying condition of society is constantly presenting new objects of public importance and utility; and what shall be considered a public use or benefit, must depend somewhat on the situation and wants of the community for the time being."

Massachusetts followed suit soon afterward, its high court ruling that a tide-dam corporation given the expropriation power, "although commenced with a view to the private advantage of the stockholders, promised to be of immense and certain utility to the state." Although New York, Georgia, and Alabama courts refused to permit expansion of the "public use" concept to validate expropriation for general manufacturing purposes, the enthusiasm spread widely to other states. By 1870 such laws had been upheld in Maine, Connecticut, New Hampshire, Wisconsin, Indiana, and Tennessee. The most pragmatic sort of validating doctrine was adopted in all these states: that if water-power development "would largely conduct to the prosperity of the state," as one critic phrased it, then expropriation of land at dam sites was constitutional.

. . . .

The heyday of expropriation as an instrument of public policy designed to subsidize private enterprise can probably be dated as beginning in the 1870s and lasting until about 1910. During that era of alleged laissez faire (which in fact was a period of broad-ranging public subsidies for business), all the constitutional stops were pulled out.

No longer did judges or framers of state constitution rely so much upon sophistries about "public use." Instead, they now merely paused to assert prescriptively that one private interest or another—mining, irrigation, lumbering, or manufacturing—was so vitally necessary to the commonweal as to be a public use by inference. In some of the western states, they went beyond that; without verbal evasion, they simply declared certain types of private enterprises to be "public" in their constitutions. All this was done, moreover, despite the availability of the Fourteenth Amendment—an instrument which the courts readily used when they decided to invalidate state laws to regulate private enterprise.

. . . .

Colorado blazed the path of eminent-domain law for the West. That state's constitutional convention of 1875–76 adopted a provision that private property might be taken for private use "for private ways of necessity, . . . reservoirs, drains, flumes, or ditches on or across the lands of others, for mining, milling, domestic, or sanitary purposes." Other Rocky Mountain states followed this model closely. In the Idaho constitutional convention of 1889, the debate over expropriation produced a sharp clash of farming interests against miners. Neither interest group stood for an abstraction that can be termed "vested rights"; rather, each wanted the upper hand in the rivalry to exploit common resources. The bitter debate over what one delegate termed "a doctrine that is anti-republican in very respect, ... contrary to the right to hold property ... or to pursue happiness" ended in a compromise. Idaho's constitution thus declared as a public use all uses of land for irrigation and drainage purposes, for the draining and working of mines including "the working thereof, by means of roads, railroad, tramways, cuts, tunnels, ,shafts, hoisting works, dumps or other necessary means to their complete development, or any other use necessary to the complete development of the material resources of the state." For these purposes might private property be expropriated upon payment of compensation.

. . . .

In Idaho the legislature enacted a law in 1887 for devolution of the eminent-domain power which, after revision in 1903, embraced the following: "Wharves, docks, piers, chutes, booms, ferries; bridges, toll-roads, by-roads, plank and turnpike roads; steam, electric, and horse railroads; reservoirs, canals, ditches, flumes, aqueducts, and pipes; [projects] for public transportation, supplying mines and farming neighborhoods with water, and draining and reclaiming lands," and for storing logs. Reviewing this statute in 1906, the Idaho court found little in the state's constitution that could fault such a law, for unless the eminent-domain power was as broad as this, "a complete development of the material resources of our young state could not be made." On similar grounds, the courts in Nevada, Montana, Colorado, Idaho, Washington, New Mexico, and Arizona upheld laws permitting expropriation of property when necessary for purposes of running an irrigation canal or ditch across private land. For, as the Arizona territorial court insisted, a legislature must be permitted to use (or devolve) the power of eminent domain so that local "advantages and resources may receive the fullest development or the general welfare." Elsewhere the public-utilities doctrine was invoked to validate takings for private irrigated farming: so long as water companies could be regulated, they could be vested with eminent-domain power.

A vital part of the constitutional context was, of course, the response of the Supreme Court when the western states' doctrines were challenged. In a word, the Supreme Court largely upheld local practices.... In 1897 the Court expressly ruled that the Fourteenth Amendment in effect applied the Fifth Amendment's "just compensation" requirement to all state-sanctioned eminent-domain proceedings. But when the legitimacy of the broad expropriation power for explicitly "private use" in the western states came before the Court, there was no comparable will to intervene. California's laws permitting water companies to condemn private land for irrigation purposes were tested before the Court in 1896 and were upheld. Eight years later, in the case of *Clark v. Nash*, the Court validated a Utah statute authorizing an individual to condemn a neighbor's land in order to convey water to his own. If the taking "be essential or material for the prosperity of the community," the Court declared, it was valid. Such statutes must be adjudged by a standard of constitutionality, said that Court, that takes account of "peculiar condition[s] of the soil or climate".

> The validity ... may sometimes depend upon many different facts, the existence of which would make a public use, even by an individual, where, in the absence of such facts, the use would clearly be private ... [The State's own courts] understand the situation which led to the demand for the enactment of the statute, and they also appreciate the results upon the growth and prosperity of the State ... The Court must recognize the difference of climate and soil, which render necessary these different laws in the States so situated.

No doubt the Supreme Court may well have been moved to leave such broad discretion with the arid-land states out of sympathy, too, for efforts to prevent "water monopoly" from blocking new settlement or leaving latecomers at the mercy of men who had already established title to lands along the region's streams. But its solicitude reached beyond the concerns of small farmers to embrace mining corporations, lumber companies, and railroad interests as well, and in 1907 the Court upheld an eastern railroad's taking of property to construct a spur track which would serve the factory warehouse of a large shipper and relieve congestion at the company's existing terminal and yards. The Court recalled that it had consistently upheld state courts' positions on what constituted a "public use" in expropriation cases, and it reaffirmed that it would give sympathetic consideration not only to evidence as to "the resources" and "the capacity of the soil" but also as to "the relative importance of industries to the general public welfare, and the long-established methods and habits of the people."

Notes

1. *Indirect condemnation.* Private condemnation essentially allows a buyer of property to take it from the seller without the seller's permission, paying fair market value of the item rather than an agreed-upon price. Sometimes this occurs expressly. It can also, though, occur indirectly when legal rules change and an owner of property can no longer turn to the courts to protect what she owns. Consider the legal options when one riparian landowner constructs a dam, backing up the water flow and flooding the land of an upstream neighbor. The activity is plainly a violation of the property rights of the upstream owner. But what legal remedies are available? If a court stands ready to enjoin the flooding, the upstream owner can halt the trespass. But a court might instead—as many courts did in eighteenth and nineteenth century America—refuse to halt the flooding and instead merely award permanent damages for the flooding. The effect is to authorize a private condemnation—taking the seller's property without her permission. Injunctions, of course, are equitable remedies, and courts have long conditioned their availability on assessments of all relevant factors. The relevant factors could well include consideration of the public interest, and whether the public would benefit by allowing the flooding to take place.

Note that indirect condemnation of this type can appear less disruptive of private property rights than overt exercises of eminent domain. A court that refuses an injunction still upholds the landowner's property rights, declares a trespass, and grants a legal remedy. The upstream landowner wins, even as the private condemnation is allowed to take place.

2. *Public use as an evolving concept, and who decides?* One of the many values of good legal history is that it allows us to see legal change over time and to track that change along with other social developments. The nineteenth century was plainly an era when people valued economic development and the law evolved in many ways to facilitate it. The public use rulings that Professor Scheiber surveys were part of this legal evolution. The just compensation clause, however, is meant to be a constitutional check on the power of majoritarian government—on the power of people collectively to redistribute property without due regard for individual rights. Should "public use," therefore, be a term of fixed meaning that is immune from shifting public sentiment? Should the courts define it so that its meaning stays constant over the generations, even as the public changes its ideas about the kinds of resource uses that would promote the common good? Embedded in this question is another one: Which component of government should make decisions about public use? Constitutional limits are ordinarily interpreted by courts, especially the United States Supreme Court. But the entire idea of "public use" calls for an assessment of public needs, which is a task that seems to play to the strengths of legislatures and other majoritarian institutions. Should courts, then, defer to legislative determinations of public use, or would such a practice excessively weaken the just compensation clause as a limit on the power of the majority to ignore private rights?

* * *

The "public use" requirement governing condemnations rose to high public visibility in 2005 with the following Supreme Court ruling. As you read it, consider its implications for natural resources law, particularly for provisions such as the one in Colorado law that allows a water-rights holder to condemn an easement across a neighbor's land to construct a water transport route. Although the Supreme Court in the following ruling upheld a condemnation undertaken to promote economic development, it limited its ruling in ways that call into question many longstanding practices used to promote efficient resource uses. As you read excerpts from the various opinions, also consider how faithful the Justices are to the nation's legal history as described by Scheiber.

KELO v. CITY OF NEW LONDON, CONNECTICUT

545 U.S. 469, 125 S.Ct. 2655, 162 L.Ed.2d 439 (2005).

JUSTICE STEVENS delivered the opinion of the Court.

In 2000, the city of New London approved a development plan that, in the words of the Supreme Court of Connecticut, was "projected to create in excess of 1,000 jobs, to increase tax and other revenues, and to revitalize an economically distressed city, including its downtown and waterfront areas." 268 Conn. 1, 5, 843 A.2d 500, 507 (2004). In assembling the land needed for this project, the city's development agent has purchased property from willing sellers and proposes to use the power of eminent domain to acquire the remainder of the property from unwilling owners in exchange for just compensation. The question presented is whether the city's proposed disposition of this property qualifies as a "public use" within the meaning of the Takings Clause of the Fifth Amendment to the Constitution.

I

The city of New London (hereinafter City) sits at the junction of the Thames River and the Long Island Sound in southeastern Connecticut. Decades of economic decline led a state agency in 1990 to designate the City a "distressed municipality." In 1996, the Federal Government closed the Naval Undersea Warfare Center, which had been located in the Fort Trumbull area of the City and had employed over 1,500 people. In 1998, the City's unemployment rate was nearly double that of the State, and its population of just under 24,000 residents was at its lowest since 1920.

These conditions prompted state and local officials to target New London, and particularly its Fort Trumbull area, for economic revitalization. To this end, respondent New London Development Corporation (NLDC), a private nonprofit entity established some years earlier to assist the City in planning economic development, was reactivated. In January 1998, the State authorized a $5.35 million bond issue to support the NLDC's planning activities and a $10 million bond issue toward the creation of a Fort Trumbull State Park. In February, the pharmaceutical company Pfizer Inc. announced that it would build a $300 million research facility on a site immediately adjacent to Fort Trumbull; local planners hoped that Pfizer would draw new business to the area, thereby serving as a catalyst to the area's rejuvenation. After receiving initial approval from the city council, the NLDC continued its planning activities and held a series of neighborhood meetings to educate the public about the process. In May, the city council authorized the NLDC to formally submit its plans to the relevant state agencies for review. Upon obtaining state-level approval, the NLDC finalized an integrated development plan focused on 90 acres of the Fort Trumbull area.

The Fort Trumbull area is situated on a peninsula that juts into the Thames River. The area comprises approximately 115 privately owned properties, as well as the 32 acres of land formerly occupied by the naval facility (Trumbull State Park now occupies 18 of those 32 acres). The development plan encompasses seven parcels. Parcel 1 is designated for a waterfront conference hotel at the center of a "small urban village" that will include restaurants and shopping. This parcel will also have marinas for both recreational and commercial uses. A pedestrian "riverwalk" will originate here and continue down the coast, connecting the waterfront areas of the development. Parcel 2 will be the site of approximately 80 new residences organized into an urban neighborhood and linked by public walkway to the remainder of the development, including the state park. This parcel also includes space reserved for a new U.S. Coast

Guard Museum. Parcel 3, which is located immediately north of the Pfizer facility, will contain at least 90,000 square feet of research and development office space. Parcel 4A is a 2.4–acre site that will be used either to support the adjacent state park, by providing parking or retail services for visitors, or to support the nearby marina. Parcel 4B will include a renovated marina, as well as the final stretch of the riverwalk. Parcels 5, 6, and 7 will provide land for office and retail space, parking, and water-dependent commercial uses. 1 App. 109–113.

The NLDC intended the development plan to capitalize on the arrival of the Pfizer facility and the new commerce it was expected to attract. In addition to creating jobs, generating tax revenue, and helping to "build momentum for the revitalization of downtown New London," *id.*, at 92, the plan was also designed to make the City more attractive and to create leisure and recreational opportunities on the waterfront and in the park.

The city council approved the plan in January 2000, and designated the NLDC as its development agent in charge of implementation. See Conn. Gen.Stat. § 8–188 (2005). The city council also authorized the NLDC to purchase property or to acquire property by exercising eminent domain in the City's name. § 8–193. The NLDC successfully negotiated the purchase of most of the real estate in the 90–acre area, but its negotiations with petitioners failed. As a consequence, in November 2000, the NLDC initiated the condemnation proceedings that gave rise to this case.

II

Petitioner Susette Kelo has lived in the Fort Trumbull area since 1997. She has made extensive improvements to her house, which she prizes for its water view. Petitioner Wilhelmina Dery was born in her Fort Trumbull house in 1918 and has lived there her entire life. Her husband Charles (also a petitioner) has lived in the house since they married some 60 years ago. In all, the nine petitioners own 15 properties in Fort Trumbull—4 in parcel 3 of the development plan and 11 in parcel 4A. Ten of the parcels are occupied by the owner or a family member; the other five are held as investment properties. There is no allegation that any of these properties is blighted or otherwise in poor condition; rather, they were condemned only because they happen to be located in the development area. . . .

III

Two polar propositions are perfectly clear. On the one hand, it has long been accepted that the sovereign may not take the property of *A* for the sole purpose of transferring it to another private party *B,* even though *A* is paid just compensation. On the other hand, it is equally clear that a State may transfer property from one private party to another if future "use by the public" is the purpose of the taking; the condemnation of land for a railroad with common-carrier duties is a familiar example. Neither of these propositions, however, determines the disposition of this case.

As for the first proposition, the City would no doubt be forbidden from taking petitioners' land for the purpose of conferring a private benefit on a particular private party. See *Midkiff,* 467 U.S., at 245, 104 S.Ct. 2321 ("A purely private taking could not withstand the scrutiny of the public use requirement; it would serve no legitimate purpose of government and would thus be void"); *Missouri Pacific R. Co. v. Nebraska,* 164 U.S. 403, 17 S.Ct. 130, 41 L.Ed. 489 (1896). Nor would the City be allowed to take property under the mere pretext of a public purpose, when its actual purpose was to bestow a private benefit. The takings before us, however, would be executed pursuant to a "carefully considered" development plan. 268 Conn., at 54, 843 A.2d, at 536. The trial judge and all the members of the Supreme Court of Connecticut agreed that there was no evidence of an illegitimate purpose in this case. Therefore, as was true of the statute challenged in *Midkiff,* 467 U.S., at 245, 104 S.Ct. 2321, the City's development plan was not adopted "to benefit a particular class of identifiable individuals."

On the other hand, this is not a case in which the City is planning to open the condemned land—at least not in its entirety—to use by the general public. Nor will the private lessees of the land in any sense be required to operate like common carriers, making their services available to all comers. But although such a projected use would be sufficient to satisfy the public use requirement, this "Court long ago rejected any literal requirement that condemned property be put into use for the general public." *Id.,* at 244, 104 S.Ct. 2321. Indeed, while many state courts in the mid–19th century endorsed "use by the public" as the proper definition of public use, that narrow view steadily eroded over time. Not only was the "use by the public" test difficult to administer (*e.g.,* what proportion of the public need have access to the property? at what price?), but it proved to be impractical given the diverse and always evolving needs of society. Accordingly, when this Court began applying the Fifth Amendment to the States at the close of the 19th century, it embraced the broader and more natural interpretation of public use as "public purpose." See, *e.g., Fallbrook Irrigation Dist. v. Bradley,* 164 U.S. 112, 158–164, 17 S.Ct. 56, 41 L.Ed. 369 (1896). Thus, in a case upholding a mining company's use of an aerial bucket line to transport ore over property it did not own, Justice Holmes' opinion for the Court stressed "the inadequacy of use by the general public as a universal test." *Strickley v. Highland Boy Gold Mining Co.,* 200 U.S. 527, 531, 26 S.Ct. 301, 50 L.Ed. 581 (1906). We have repeatedly and consistently rejected that narrow test ever since.

The disposition of this case therefore turns on the question whether the City's development plan serves a "public purpose." Without exception, our cases have defined that concept broadly, reflecting our longstanding policy of deference to legislative judgments in this field....

Viewed as a whole, our jurisprudence has recognized that the needs of society have varied between different parts of the Nation, just as they have evolved over time in response to changed circumstances. Our earliest cases in particular embodied a strong theme of federalism, emphasizing the "great respect" that we owe to state legislatures and state courts in discerning local public needs. See *Hairston v. Danville & Western R. Co.,* 208 U.S. 598, 606–607, 28 S.Ct. 331, 52 L.Ed. 637 (1908) (noting that these needs were likely to vary depending on a State's "resources, the capacity of the soil, the relative importance of industries to the general public welfare, and the long-established methods and habits of the people"). For more than a century, our public use jurisprudence has wisely eschewed rigid formulas and intrusive scrutiny in favor of affording legislatures broad latitude in determining what public needs justify the use of the takings power.

IV

Those who govern the City were not confronted with the need to remove blight in the Fort Trumbull area, but their determination that the area was sufficiently distressed to justify a program of economic rejuvenation is entitled to our deference. The City has carefully formulated an economic development plan that it believes will provide appreciable benefits to the community, including—but by no means limited to—new jobs and increased tax revenue. As with other exercises in urban planning and development, the City is endeavoring to coordinate a variety of commercial, residential, and recreational uses of land, with the hope that they will form a whole greater than the sum of its parts. To effectuate this plan, the City has invoked a state statute that specifically authorizes the use of eminent domain to promote economic development. Given the comprehensive character of the plan, the thorough deliberation that preceded its adoption, and the limited scope of our review, it is appropriate for us, as it was in *Berman,* to resolve the challenges of the individual owners, not on a piecemeal basis, but rather in light of the entire plan. Because that plan unquestionably serves a public purpose, the takings challenged here satisfy the public use requirement of the Fifth Amendment.

To avoid this result, petitioners urge us to adopt a new bright-line rule that economic development does not qualify as a public use. Putting aside the unpersuasive suggestion that the City's plan will provide only purely economic benefits, neither precedent nor logic supports petitioners' proposal. Promoting economic development is a traditional and long accepted function of government. There is, moreover, no principled way of distinguishing economic development from the other public purposes that we have recognized. In our cases upholding takings that facilitated agriculture and mining, for example, we emphasized the importance of those industries to the welfare of the States in question, see, e.g., *Strickley,* 200 U.S. 527, 26 S.Ct. 301; in *Berman,* we endorsed the purpose of transforming a blighted area into a "well-balanced" community through redevelopment, 348 U.S., at 33, 75 S.Ct. 98; in *Midkiff,* we upheld the interest in breaking up a land oligopoly that "created artificial deterrents to the normal functioning of the State's residential land market," 467 U.S., at 242, 104 S.Ct. 2321; and in *Monsanto*, we accepted Congress' purpose of eliminating a "significant barrier to entry in the pesticide market," 467 U.S., at 1014–1015, 104 S.Ct. 2862. It would be incongruous to hold that the City's interest in the economic benefits to be derived from the development of the Fort Trumbull area has less of a public character than any of those other interests. Clearly, there is no basis for exempting economic development from our traditionally broad understanding of public purpose.

Petitioners contend that using eminent domain for economic development impermissibly blurs the boundary between public and private takings. Again, our cases foreclose this objection. Quite simply, the government's pursuit of a public purpose will often benefit individual private parties. For example, in *Midkiff,* the forced transfer of property conferred a direct and significant benefit on those lessees who were previously unable to purchase their homes. In *Monsanto,* we recognized that the "most direct beneficiaries" of the data-sharing provisions were the subsequent pesticide applicants, but benefiting them in this way was necessary to promoting competition in the pesticide market. 467 U.S., at 1014, 104 S.Ct. 2862. The owner of the department store in *Berman* objected to "taking from one businessman for the benefit of another businessman," 348 U.S., at 33, 75 S.Ct. 98, referring to the fact that under the redevelopment plan land would be leased or sold to private developers for redevelopment. Our rejection of that contention has particular relevance to the instant case: "The public end may be as well or better served through an agency of private enterprise than through a department of government—or so the Congress might conclude. We cannot say that public ownership is the sole method of promoting the public purposes of community redevelopment projects." *Id.,* at 34, 75 S.Ct. 98. . . .

JUSTICE O'CONNOR, with whom THE CHIEF JUSTICE, JUSTICE SCALIA, and JUSTICE THOMAS join, dissenting.

Over two centuries ago, just after the Bill of Rights was ratified, Justice Chase wrote:

> "An ACT of the Legislature (for I cannot call it a law) contrary to the great first principles of the social compact, cannot be considered a rightful exercise of legislative authority. . . . A few instances will suffice to explain what I mean. . . . [A] law that takes property from A. and gives it to B: It is against all reason and justice, for a people to entrust a Legislature with SUCH powers; and, therefore, it cannot be presumed that they have done it." *Calder v. Bull,* 3 Dall. 386, 388, 1 L.Ed. 648 (1798) (emphasis deleted).

Today the Court abandons this long-held, basic limitation on government power. Under the banner of economic development, all private property is now vulnerable to being taken and transferred to another private owner, so long as it might be upgraded—*i.e.,* given to an owner who will use it in a way that the legislature deems more beneficial to the public—in the process. To reason, as the Court does, that the incidental public benefits resulting from the subsequent ordinary use of private property render economic development takings "for public use" is to wash out any distinction between private and public use of property—and thereby effectively to delete the words "for public use" from the Takings Clause of the Fifth Amendment. Accordingly I respectfully dissent.

[O'Connor and the other dissenting Justices would have struck down all exercises of eminent domain undertaken for purposes of economic development, while holding open the possibility that property might be condemned by government and turned over to a developer for another purpose, such as eliminating blight.]

JUSTICE THOMAS, dissenting.

Long ago, William Blackstone wrote that "the law of the land ... postpone[s] even public necessity to the sacred and inviolable rights of private property." 1 Commentaries on the Laws of England 134–135 (1765) (hereinafter Blackstone). The Framers embodied that principle in the Constitution, allowing the government to take property not for "public necessity," but instead for "public use." Amdt. 5. Defying this understanding, the Court replaces the Public Use Clause with a " '[P]ublic [P]urpose' " Clause, *ante,* at 2662–2663 (or perhaps the "Diverse and Always Evolving Needs of Society" Clause, *ante,* at 2662 (capitalization added)), a restriction that is satisfied, the Court instructs, so long as the purpose is "legitimate" and the means "not irrational," *ante,* at 2667 (internal quotation marks omitted). This deferential shift in phraseology enables the Court to hold, against all common sense, that a costly urban-renewal project whose stated purpose is a vague promise of new jobs and increased tax revenue, but which is also suspiciously agreeable to the Pfizer Corporation, is for a "public use."

I cannot agree. If such "economic development" takings are for a "public use," any taking is, and the Court has erased the Public Use Clause from our Constitution, as Justice O'Connor powerfully argues in dissent. *Ante,* at 2671, 2674–2677. I do not believe that this Court can eliminate liberties expressly enumerated in the Constitution and therefore join her dissenting opinion. Regrettably, however, the Court's error runs deeper than this. Today's decision is simply the latest in a string of our cases construing the Public Use Clause to be a virtual nullity, without the slightest nod to its original meaning. In my view, the Public Use Clause, originally understood, is a meaningful limit on the government's eminent domain power. Our cases have strayed from the Clause's original meaning, and I would reconsider them....

Though one component of the protection provided by the Takings Clause is that the government can take private property only if it provides "just compensation" for the taking, the Takings Clause also prohibits the government from taking property except "for public use." Were it otherwise, the Takings Clause would either be meaningless or empty. If the Public Use Clause served no function other than to state that the government may take property through its eminent domain power—for public or private uses—then it would be surplusage. See *ante,* at 2672 (O'Connor, J., dissenting); see also *Marbury v. Madison,* 1 Cranch 137, 174, 2 L.Ed. 60 (1803) ("It cannot be presumed that any clause in the constitution is intended to be without effect"); *Myers v. United States,* 272 U.S. 52, 151, 47 S.Ct. 21, 71 L.Ed. 160 (1926). Alternatively, the Clause could distinguish those takings that require compensation from those that do not. That interpretation, however, "would permit private property to be taken or appropriated for private use without any compensation whatever." *Cole v. La Grange,* 113 U.S. 1, 8, 5 S.Ct. 416, 28 L.Ed. 896 (1885) (interpreting same language in the Missouri Public Use Clause). In other words, the Clause would require the government to compensate for takings done "for public use," leaving it free to take property for purely private uses without the payment of compensation. This would contradict a bedrock principle well established by the time of the founding: that all takings required the payment of compensation. 1 Blackstone 135; 2 J. Kent, Commentaries on American Law 275 (1827) (hereinafter Kent); J. Madison, for the National Property Gazette, (Mar. 27, 1792), in 14 Papers of James Madison 266, 267 (R. Rutland et al. eds.1983) (arguing that no property "shall be taken *directly* even for public use without indemnification to the owner"). The Public Use Clause, like the Just Compensation Clause, is therefore an express limit on the government's power of eminent domain.

[Justice Thomas urged the Court to overrule an extensive series of precedents and return to the long-discredited view that property is taken for a public use only if used by government or open to the public.]

Notes

1. *Private benefit versus public purpose.* The majority in *Kelo* distinguishes between takings that are intended to confer a private benefit and those that are designed to promote a public purpose. How meaningful and useful is this distinction? Can we imagine condemnations of property that the Court would strike down as purely private? Does the answer mostly have to do with how we evaluate the public's interest in private land-use activities generally? The key question might well be this: Does the public benefit when land is well used or is the public's interest more limited—merely in avoiding land uses that are affirmatively harmful? What if the owner of a large tract of suburban land simply leaves it vacant for decades, allowing development to proceed around it? The effect might be to promote sprawl, to increase infrastructure costs (roads, sewers, etc.), and to lengthen daily commutes of many people. Could government condemn this vacant private land and turn it over to a willing developer so as to reduce further sprawl, or would such an action merely promote a private benefit? And what about the longstanding practice of allowing an owner of a land-locked parcel to use condemnation to gain physical access to it or allowing a farmer to condemn a drainage easement across a neighbor's land? Are these practices still constitutional in light of *Kelo*?

How does the majority seem to decide that the proposed condemnation here promotes a public benefit? The Court obviously pays attention to the judgment on the issue of state lawmakers, and to the processes of decision-making. How important was it that the state legislature got directly involved, instead of leaving the matter to local authorities? How important was it that the plan emerged out of a lengthy planning process?

In operation, is the public purpose requirement perhaps less a substantive limit on what government can do and more of a process rule—a rule that government cannot take private property to promote economic development unless it carefully and openly studies the entire situation and gives thought to the public implications? In that regard, we might compare the public use limit with the longstanding requirement that local zoning be undertaken only in conformity with a "comprehensive plan." In many jurisdictions, courts that enforce the comprehensive plan requirement are less interested in ensuring that local governments actually prepare an overall land-use plan than they are in ensuring that governments consider the larger spatial contexts of land-use decisionmaking and avoid making decisions on a parcel-by-parcel basis that ignore spillover effects. (We'll take up the issue in the next chapter.)

2. *The implications of the dissents.* Justice O'Connor's dissent would bar all condemnations undertaken to promote economic development. If the majority embraced this rule, however, how workable would it be? Does a condemnation promote economic development when it aims to increase inner-city jobs, thereby promoting the welfare of workers and their families while sustaining the ability of local government to provide services? What about condemnation that aims to restrain sprawl, thereby reducing public infrastructure costs? When is economic development the aim and when is it merely a desirable side effect?

Were the majority to embrace O'Connor's view, it would soon need to confront factual disputes such as the much-cited *Boomer v. Atlantic Cement* nuisance ruling and *Moon v. North Idaho Farmer's Association.* In *Boomer*, the court refused to enjoin air pollution by a cement factory, despite the violation of property rights of neighbors, on the ground that the cement factor was too important economically to the community to shut down. A dissenting justice in the case complained that the ruling effectively authorized private condemnation—as it did. How would such a ruling stand up to the public use test proposed by Justice O'Connor? We can ask the same question about the Idaho statute described in *Moon.* The legislature revised the state's laws of trespass and nuisance to allow more intensive grass burning. The statute had the same effect as the nuisance denial in *Boomer* (save for the lack of damage payments)—essentially allowing one private party (the grass grower) to condemn an easement for smoke and soot on neighboring lands. Would this type of legal change now be unconstitutional as a violation of the public use requirement?

3. *A missed interpretive possibility?* In his separate dissent Justice Thomas purports to consider all of the possible interpretations of the Fifth Amendment provision prohibiting the taking of private property for public use without the payment of just compensation. Read literally, as Thomas notes, the phrase does not limit takings to situations involving public uses. It

states merely that takings for public use require compensation. Could this mean that takings for private use can be done without compensation? That result, Thomas contends, would be patently absurd, which means that the public use limit applies to all takings. Has Justice Thomas, though, perhaps overlooked an interpretive possibility? In fact, takings for private use were not unknown at the time of the Bill of Rights. The uniform practice of the day, apparently, was that compensation was always paid in such cases by the private party acquiring the property. Compensation was not always paid, however, when takings took place for public use. Could we thus interpret the just compensation clause as follows: Takings of property always require just compensation, *even when* the taking is for a public use. To read the clause this way is to assume that it was precisely tailored to deal with the problem of the day—takings of private property for public use without compensation. (It is perhaps also to credit James Madison with greater clarity as a writer than the prevailing interpretation of the clause seems to admit.) According to historians, the original meaning of the clause is hard to discern, given that the clause elicited little discussion and did not respond to widely discussed concerns of the day. E.g., William Michael Treanor, *The Original Understanding of the Takings Clause and the Political Process*, 95 Colum. L. Rev. 782 (1995).

BRIDLE BIT RANCH COMPANY v. BASIN ELECTRIC POWER COOPERATIVE

118 P.3d 996 (Wyo. 2005).

Hill, Chief Justice

Employing its powers of eminent domain, the Respondent, Basin Electric Power Cooperative (Basin), sought to condemn a right-of-way through a portion of Campbell County in order to build a 230–kilovolt (kV) power transmission line. Basin asserted that the transmission line was necessary so as to provide additional electrical power to areas of Campbell County where coal bed methane (CBM) is being developed and to otherwise enhance the availability and reliability of electrical service to that area. Basin is a regional wholesale electric generation and transmission cooperative that supplies wholesale electricity to its distribution cooperatives. Powder River Energy Corporation (PRECorp) is a Wyoming non-profit corporation and is one of Basin's distribution cooperative members. PRECorp provides electricity at retail to its customers in Northeastern Wyoming, including Campbell County.

Basin was able to reach settlements with approximately 82% of the private landowners affected by the transmission line, as well as with the United States Forest Service. At the time of the hearing on this stage of the condemnation action (the "taking"), Basin had not yet reached agreements with two groups of landowners, nor with The State of Wyoming, Office of State Land and Investments (State Lands), or the Bureau of Land Management (BLM). Case No. 04–134 is a challenge to the district court's order granting Basin immediate possession of the lands owned by a group of landowners to whom we will refer collectively as "the Bridle Bit Group." Case No. 04–136 is a similar challenge to that same order by another group of landowners to whom we will refer as "the Roush Group." . . .

Issues

The Bridle Bit Group raises these issues:

A. Did the district court commit clear error in finding Basin located the transmission line in the manner most compatible with greatest public good and least private injury?

B. Did the district court err in finding that a perpetual easement for transmission lines is permitted under Wyoming law? . . .

Facts and Proceedings

During the winter of 2000, Basin began looking at selecting a route for an additional power transmission line in Campbell County. By letter dated December 21, 2000, Basin submitted the following inquiry to PSC:

> Basin Electric Power Cooperative (Basin Electric) is currently reviewing its resources for supplying wholesale power to its member Powder River Energy Corporation (PRECORP). PRECORP has experienced a sudden and rather substantial increase in its membership load because of the development of coal bed methane in the Powder River Basin.
>
> While Basin Electric is considering several options for power supply, the first phase of an overall program needs to move forward expeditiously so that Basin Electric can meet its power supply obligations. Our studies show that Basin Electric needs approximately 40–50 MW [megawatt] of capacity in place in the PRECORP service territory on or before May of 2002. . . .

[To supply this power to its various members, Basin needed to construct further transmission lines, which would cross both private and federal land.] . . .

[Basin applied to the state for a certificate of public convenience and necessity to support its proposed project, which was necessary if it was a public utility. The applicable state commission decided, however, that Basin was not a public utility because it did not serve the public directly.]

During 2001, Basin began the process of obtaining easements from landowners and public entities. As a part of this process, Basin had a consultant prepare an environmental assessment as required by the U.S. Forest Service and a 25–year, renewable easement was obtained from that federal agency in 2003. The record is unclear as to what, if any, compensation was paid for that easement, although it appears that the only cost associated with that easement is an application fee. The easement may be renewed. Basin was able to obtain easements from about 82% of the affected landowners, but had not as yet obtained firm commitments for easements from State Lands or the BLM. With respect to State Lands, an application for an easement had been submitted, but such an easement is not acted upon until the applicant for the easement has obtained access from all necessary private landowners. When such easements are approved by State Lands, they are generally for a period of 35 years, but may be for longer periods of time, including perpetuity. With respect to the BLM, Basin had been offered a 30–year easement that could be renewed and that easement could be for as long as 50 years. The BLM does not require the payment of compensation for the easement, nor is there a fee for the renewal process.

On January 30, 2004, Basin filed a complaint for condemnation seeking to take the lands of those private landowners who had not yet settled with Basin. . . .

Discussion

[The court first agreed with the state commission that Basin was not a public utility because it did not serve the public directly. In the course of that discussion it included comments about the power of eminent domain in the state.]

With respect to condemnation of private land, the Wyoming Constitution provides, at art. 1, § 32:

> § 32. Eminent domain. Private property shall not be taken for private use unless by consent of the owner, except for private ways of necessity, and for reservoirs, drains, flumes or ditches on or across the lands of others for agricultural, mining, milling, domestic or sanitary purposes, nor in any case without due compensation.
>
> . . . .
>
> Wyo. Stat. Ann. § 1–26–815 (LexisNexis 2005) provides:
>
> § 1–26–815. Right of eminent domain granted; ways of necessity for authorized businesses; purposes; extent.
>
> (a) *Any person, association, company or corporation authorized to do business in this state may appropriate by condemnation a way of necessity over, across or on so much of the lands or real property of others as necessary for the location, construction, maintenance and use of* reservoirs, drains, flumes, ditches including return flow and wastewater ditches, underground water pipelines, pumping stations and other necessary appurtenances, canals, *electric power transmission lines and distribution systems,* railroad trackage, sidings, spur tracks, tramways, roads or mine truck haul roads required in the course of their business for agricultural, mining, exploration drilling and production of oil and gas, milling, electric power transmission and distribution, domestic, municipal or sanitary purposes, or for the transportation of coal from any coal mine or railroad line or for the transportation of oil and gas from any well.
>
> (b) The right of condemnation may be exercised for the purpose of:
>
> (i) Acquiring, enlarging or relocating ways of necessity; and

(ii) Acquiring easements or rights-of-way over adjacent lands sufficient to enable the owner of the way of necessity to construct, repair, maintain and use the structures, roads or facilities for which the way of necessity is acquired.

(c) A way of necessity acquired hereunder shall not exceed one hundred (100) feet in width on each side of the outer sides or marginal lines of the reservoir, drain, ditch, underground water pipeline, canal, flume, power transmission line or distribution system, railroad trackage, siding or tramway unless a greater width is necessary for excavation, embankment or deposit of waste from excavation. In no case may the area appropriated exceed that actually necessary for the purpose of use for which a way of necessity is authorized.

. . . .

As a private corporation, Basin may condemn private property to obtain a right-of-way (way of necessity) across the lands of other private persons and entities. Wyo. Stat. Ann. § 1–26–815. The landowners argue here that Basin cannot be pursuing a private interest and, at the same time, argue that its business is vested with a public interest. However, the statute does not appear to preclude such a circumstance. The Wyoming Constitution does not prohibit such a "taking," and the landowners involved in this litigation do not make such an argument. . . .

Did Basin Comply With Condemnation Statutes

The condemnation process is governed by statute. . . . Wyo. Stat. Ann. § 1–26–504 (LexisNexis 2005) provides:

§ 1–26–504. Requirements to exercise eminent domain.

(a) Except as otherwise provided by law, the power of eminent domain may be exercised to acquire property for a proposed use only if all of the following are established:

(i) The public interest and necessity require the project or the use of eminent domain is authorized by the Wyoming Constitution;

(ii) The project is planned or located in the manner that will be most compatible with the greatest public good and the least private injury; and

(iii) The property sought to be acquired is necessary for the project.

(b) Findings of the public service commission, the interstate commerce commission and other federal and state agencies with appropriate jurisdiction are prima facie valid relative to determinations under subsection (a) of this section if the findings were made in accordance with law with notice to condemnees who are parties to the condemnation action and are final with no appeals from the determinations pending.

Wyo. Stat. Ann § 1–26–509 (LexisNexis 2005) provides:

§ 1–26–509. Negotiations; scope of efforts to purchase.

(a) A condemnor shall make reasonable and diligent efforts to acquire property by good faith negotiation. . . .

The Bridle Bit Group contends that Basin did not locate the transmission line in a manner most compatible with the greatest public good and the least private injury. Wyo. Stat Ann. § 1–26–504(a)(ii) This is based on Basin's admitted decision to avoid public lands in favor of private lands as one factor used in selecting the route ultimately chosen. Other routes were available to Basin that used somewhat more public land, but Basin chose a route that included only a small amount of public land. The Bridle Bit Group asserts that this decision by Basin was arbitrary and capricious, as well as an act made in bad faith and constituted an abuse of its discretion with respect to the location of the transmission line.

The Roush Group contends that Basin failed to demonstrate that public interest and necessity require the project at issue and that Basin's proposed route does not comply with the requirement that the project be located so as to do the greatest public good and the least private harm. Wyo. Stat. Ann. § 1–26–504(a)(i) and (ii). Those landowners contend that the project is designed solely for the benefit of PRECorp so that it can provide electricity for CBM development, but that there is no evidence that the public interest and necessity require the project. . . . Further, the Roush Group asserts that Basin failed to negotiate in good faith as required by Wyo. Stat. Ann. § 1–26–509. . . .

Basin contends that the route was chosen after considerable thought and study, and that it listened to the concerns of landowners. Basin considered the following factors in selecting the route now at issue: (a) Tie-in or connections to the existing electrical system infrastructure; (b) physical limitations, such as topography, railroad crossings, existing improvements, and dry lakebeds; (c) landowner concerns; (d) costs of construction; (e) reliability and safety matters (e.g., avoiding paralleling existing high power transmission lines); (f) minimizing the number of landowners being crossed; (g) minimizing impact to government property; (h) minimization of visual impact; (i) environmental concerns; (j) avoidance of archeological sites; and (k) avoidance of cultivated property. Basin ascertained that, given that the transmission line was necessary, the proposed route (and the bottom line is that it had to pick a route) was the most compatible with the greatest public good and the least private injury. Basin asserts that no evidence to the contrary was brought to bear by the landowners. Furthermore, Basin contends that its evidence establishes that public interest and necessity do require the transmission line project. Without it, Basin asserts, it cannot meet its projected demands from its users (including mineral developers, farmers and ranchers). Basin also maintains that it enjoys considerable discretion in selecting an appropriate route.... Finally, Basin claims that it negotiated in good faith with all landowners.

The standard of review applicable to these arguments has been articulated with clarity. In the case, *Conner v. Board of County Commissioners, Natrona County,* 2002 WY 148, ¶ 8, 54 P.3d 1274, 1278–79 (Wyo.2002) we set out that standard:

> Eminent domain proceedings are authorized by constitutional and statutory provisions and governed by W.R.C.P. 71.1. The district court determines all issues arising on the complaint for condemnation including notice, the plaintiff's right to make the appropriation, plaintiff's inability to agree with the owner, the necessity for the appropriation, and the regularity of the proceedings. W.R.C.P. 71.1(e)(2)(A). Only the issue of compensation may be tried before a jury. W.R.C.P. 71.1(j).

When we review the district court's determination of issues required by Rule 71.1(e)(2), "we uphold the judgment if there is evidence to support it, and in doing so we look only to the evidence submitted by the prevailing party and give to it every favorable inference which may be drawn therefrom, without considering any contrary evidence." ...

The *Conner* case also iterated:

> When a condemnor seeks to establish the requirement of necessity in an eminent domain proceeding, it need only show a reasonable necessity for the project. As explained by one court, the term "necessity," when used in the context of an eminent domain proceeding, means "reasonably convenient or useful to the public." *City of Dayton v. Keys,* 21 Ohio Misc. 105, 252 N.E.2d 655, 659 (1969). A showing that the project will increase public safety is sufficient. *See Greasy Creek Mineral Company v. Ely Jellico Coal Company,* 132 Ky. 692, 116 S.W. 1189 (1909).

Board of County Commissioners of Johnson County v. Atter, 734 P.2d 549, 553 (Wyo.1987). And further:

> To comply with W.S. [§]1–26–504(a)(ii), the [board] needs to present evidence that it has planned or located the project in a manner most compatible with the greatest public good and the least private injury. The district court then reviews the evidence and decides whether the [board] has met its burden. Once W.S. [§]1–26–504(a)(ii) has been complied with and the landowners still wish to contest the action, the burden shifts to them to show that the condemnor acted in bad faith or abused its discretion as to that particular determination.

Town of Wheatland v. Bellis Farms, Inc., 806 P.2d 281, 283 (Wyo.1991) (footnotes omitted). Before filing an eminent domain complaint, a condemnor must make reasonable, diligent, and good faith efforts to negotiate with the condemnee. Wyo. Stat. Ann. § 1–26–509 (LexisNexis 2001). Efforts made in compliance with the statutes constitute prima facie evidence of the condemnor's good faith. Wyo. Stat. Ann. § 1–26–510 (LexisNexis 2001).

54 P.3d at 1282–83.

In *Wyoming Resources Corporation v. T–Chair Land Company,* 2002 WY 104, ¶ ¶ 13–14, 49 P.3d 999, 1003–04 (Wyo.2002) we held:

> The taking of private property for a private way of necessity is recognized as valid in Wyoming because "[t]here is a public interest in giving access by individuals to the road and highway network of the state as a part and an extension thereof for economic reasons and the development of land as a resource for the common good, whether residential or otherwise." *Hulse v. First American Title Co. of Crook County,* 2001 WY 95, ¶ 30, 33 P.3d 122, ¶ 30 (Wyo.2001). "[T]he right to condemn a way of necessity under constitutional and statutory provisions is an expression of public policy against landlocking property and rendering it useless." Id.; see Coronado Oil Co., 603 P.2d at 410.

The legislature has enacted the eminent domain and private road establishment acts so that access will be available to permit mineral estate owners to realize the full benefit of their property ownership and landlocked property will not be rendered useless.

Did Basin Demonstrate Public Interest and Necessity

It is evident from the above-described standard of review that this Court has ascribed a broad meaning to the phrase "public interest and necessity," and that is consistent with the overall tenor of Wyoming's eminent domain statutes. *See* 2A *Nichols on Eminent Domain,* § 7.02[3] at 7–29—7–35 (3rd ed.2004); and 29A C.J.S. *Eminent Domain* § 29 (1992). *Nichols* identifies three core criteria for this analysis: "(1) That the taking affect a community as distinguished from a single individual; (2) That the use to which the taken property is applied is authorized by law; (3) That the title taken not be invested in a person or corporation as private property to be used and controlled as private property unless the public receives some public benefit as a result of the private possession." 2A *Nichols,* § 7.02[3] at 7–35.

The evidence presented by Basin plainly demonstrated the need for additional electric power to PRECorp's service territory and that additional power would inure to the benefit of the public in that locality, both in terms of the additional power itself and the reliability of service in the area. The landowners presented no evidence to contradict Basin's comprehensive studies that established the ever-increasing demand for more electric power. The district court's findings that Basin demonstrated that the project was necessary and in the public interest is unassailable and we affirm it here.

Did Basin Demonstrate That the Project Was Most Compatible With the Greatest Public Good and Least Private Harm

The landowners' argument in this regard focuses almost entirely on Basin's decision to avoid public lands. However, the record is replete with evidence that Basin considered many alternative routes and finally settled on the one at issue here for a variety reasons, one of which was the avoidance of public lands .....

Again, the record amply demonstrates that Basin did examine several alternate routes, but ultimately had to make a decision as to which one best fulfilled all of the various criteria that went into making a decision to move forward with the project and begin the process of acquiring the necessary rights-of-way and access easements. Several years have been devoted to that effort....

We conclude that the district court's determination that the transmission line was located in such a manner so as to be the most compatible with the greatest public good and the least private harm is correct.

Did Basin Negotiate in Good Faith

The landowners contend that Basin did not negotiate in good faith as required by the statute. There is little, if any, dispute that Basin negotiated in good faith with respect to the amount of money to be paid for the easements and accesses.... Basin negotiated with all landowners over a period in excess of a year (in some instances longer), and those negotiations continued up until the day of trial. Indeed, several additional landowners settled just before trial.

The sticking points in the final negotiation process were the location of the transmission line, as well as the term for the easements and accesses, i.e., that they were to be perpetual or for as long as they were needed for the transmission line. The record establishes that just prior to trial, Basin agreed to settle for easements with a duration of 99 years, rather than perpetuity.

We have held above that Basin had great discretion with respect to the location of the transmission line. In addition, we note that Basin attempted to accommodate owner concerns about location, especially early on in the negotiation process. As Basin settled with more and more landowners, it became ever more difficult to accommodate the concerns of the remaining landowners without then making alterations to other settled portions of the route. The record contains seven voluminous exhibits that detail the contacts Basin had with each of the landowners involved in these appeals. We note that those exhibits amply demonstrate Basin's good faith efforts to negotiate with all landowners, to the extent that was practicable....

We will further discuss the issue of the perpetual term for the easements in the final section of this opinion.

Should the Easements Be Perpetual

We embark on this discussion with a reference to Wyo. Stat. Ann. § 1–26–515, which provides for the termination of condemned easements, such as those at issue here, because of nonuse, upon certain transfers or attempted transfers of the easement by the condemnor, and where a new use is not identical to the original use. The landowners contend that since the Forest Service will give only a 25–year easement, the State a 35–year easement, and the BLM a 30–year easement, their property should not be saddled with perpetual easements. Although the circumstances with the State are somewhat different, with both the Forest Service and the BLM renewal of the easement is a matter of formality and does not require the payment of additional compensation. It is the goal of the landowners (who apparently might settle for a 50–year term) to require that compensation be renegotiated after, e.g., 50 years, so that future generations will derive benefit from the land as well.

The district court did not characterize the easements as perpetual. Rather it found that the easements would be required for "an unlimited length of time." Evidence adduced at trial showed that existing electrical transmission infrastructure had been in place for over 50 years and would continue to be needed for the indefinite future. As a general rule, easements may be perpetual, or for an indefinite duration, or for so long as they are needed for their intended purpose or so long as the necessity continues. 4 *Powell on Real Property* § 34.19, at 34–179—34–184 (2001); 25 Am.Jur.2d *Easements and Licenses* § 94 (2004).

The landowners have not cited pertinent authority that convinces us that the district court erred in determining that the easements were for an indefinite period of time, although they are, of course, limited by a use consistent with Wyo. Stat. Ann. § 1–26–515.

[The court affirmed the trial court in all respects, upholding the private condemnation.]

Notes

1. *Consistent with* Kelo? Although handed down several months after the Supreme Court's ruling in *Kelo*, *Bridle Bit Ranch* makes no reference to the ruling and does not raise expressly the public use limit on condemnations. Had the issue been raised would the condemnation have been allowed? Are the "public interest" and "greatest public good" determinations under state law essentially the same as the "public purpose" test that *Kelo* uses to interpret the public use requirement? Note the court's various references to the public interest in promoting full access to private land. The public has an interest, the court contends, in the "the development of land as a resource for the common good, whether residential or otherwise." Does this language go too far in authorizing private condemnations?

Imagine how the various Justices of the Supreme Court might have ruled on the public use issue if the case reaching the Court had been *Bridle Bit Ranch* rather than *Kelo*? Justice O'Connor, a former state legislator from the West, often displayed in her rulings a willingness to defer to state legislatures, particular from her part of the country. Other dissenters in *Kelo* have often shown a willingness to take constitutional positions that favor intensive land use activities such as mining and timber harvesting. What if condemnation in this case were disallowed, leaving Basin Electric Power with no way to locate its transmission lines and thus no way to deliver power to PRECORP? Should the legitimacy of the condemnation turn on the seemingly minor issue of whether Basin Electric Power sells its power at wholesale or retail? Does the public "use" the transmission lines in one case and not the other?

2. *Private condemnation III: pros and cons.* Underlying these various disputes is the larger policy question about whether legislatures should be able to authorize private condemnations when they believe that the public would benefit from them. The question is not an easy one to probe, and would seem to call for serious thought about the entire institution of private property rights in nature. Property is a creature of law, as we have seen, with private rights defined and redefined over time by legal action. Landowners, that is, only have those rights authorized by widely applicable common law and statutory rules. The governing legal rules set forth not just what landowners can and cannot do but the remedies available to them to assert their rights. Changes in the applicable laws (as in *Moon*) or in the availability of remedies (as in *Boomer*) do not seem to differ much from statutes that authorize private condemnations under specified circumstances. Where, then, do we draw the line when it comes to legal actions that reallocate private property? What types of legal reallocations should be permissible and which should be banned?

Should the answer to these questions depend on whether we can rely upon the market to bring about resource reallocation? That is, should we pay close attention to the sources and varieties of market failures to decide when condemnation is proper? One possibility is to authorize private condemnation under conditions of monopoly–that is, when a prospective buyer is forced to deal with a single seller under circumstances that allow the seller to overcharge for the property involved (as when, for instance, a farmer must acquire a drainage easement over neighboring land, and is forced by physical realities to buy the easement from a particular neighbor). If we followed this reasoning, what would the outcomes be in *Kelo* and in *Bridle Bit Ranch*? Did these disputes involve situations of monopoly? Can we even answer that question without getting clear first on what the prospective buyer is trying to accomplish by buying the property (that is, can we know whether there is more than one seller without questioning what the buyer wants (or really needs) to buy)?

3. *Tighter state limits.* Many states limit the power of eminent domain more than does the federal constitution. A number of states essentially embrace the position of Justice O'Connor in *Kelo,* concluding that condemnation to promote economic development is not a public use. E.g., Board of County Commissioners of Muskogee County v. Lowery, 136 P.3d 639 (Ok. 2006) (concluding that government could not condemn right of way for water lines to serve a new gas-powered electric generating facility that was privately owned); City of Norwood v. Horney, 110 Ohio St.3d 353, 853 N.E.2d 1115 (2006) (concluding that economic or financial benefit alone is not enough to satisfy the public use requirement, even in a "deteriorating area"). Compare Hoffman Family L.L.C. v. City of Alexandria, 272 Va. 274, 634 S.E.2d 722 (2006) (public use is furthered by condemnation to acquire land for stormwater box culvert that serves a single private landowner but that is part of larger regional stormwater system).

In the aftermath of *Kelo*, virtually every state legislature considered bills or constitutional amendments addressing the exercise of eminent domain to promote economic development. By September of 2006, some 24 states had enacted measures of one type of another. According to one legislative tracking service (www.ncsl.org/programs/natres/emindomainleg06.htm) the new laws have fallen generally into distinct categories, chiefly:

— prohibiting (or temporarily halting) eminent domain either for economic development purposes or to increase the tax base, except when responding to blighted conditions,

— defining "public use" in ways that largely limit it to the possession, occupation or enjoyment of property by the public at large or a public entity or utility,

— requiring greater public notice or more public hearings before condemnation occurs, and

— requiring higher compensation for the taking of a primary residence.

Chapter Eight

GOVERNING THE COMMONS

A. TAILORING USE RIGHTS

Chapter one began with a vision of people standing on a mountainside, looking out upon a vast open landscape and wondering how they might inhabit it. How would they use the land? What types of private rights would they create and allocate? In what ways would private rights remain responsive to collective needs and the collective will? How could the people arrange their affairs so as to stimulate enterprise and creativity? Natural resources law, we noted at that point, "is the expansive body of rules and processes governing the ways people interact with nature." A major portion of natural resources law sets the terms of use rights in nature and prescribes the ways people can create, terminate, and transfer them. The other component of natural resources law embeds these use rights in governance regimes and provides mechanisms over time to alter their terms and control their exercise. Basically, we noted, natural resources law performs six major *functions*: (i) dividing nature into use rights, whether for individual or collective ownership; (ii) defining the elements of these use rights; (iii) allocating or making them available to people in some way; (iv) resolving the conflicts that inevitably arise among users; (v) integrating these use rights into landscapes; and (vi) providing mechanisms to adjust the use rights and reallocate them over time. These are the functions natural resources law performs or makes possible. And it necessarily performs them, as we have seen, in pretty much every resource setting.

We are now in a position to elaborate upon theses tasks, and to comment about some of the problems that arise in performing them.

1. *Bundling resource rights, and what attaches to land?* As we've seen, a big issue in any legal regime is to decide what resource use rights will be packaged together and allocated as a bundle, particularly the bundle of rights known as land. To what extent should we divide the landscape into precisely bounded parcels and allocate extensive private rights in the parcels, and to what extent is it wiser to allocate more limited use rights in landscapes—particularly under regimes that allocate multiple use rights in the same lands? What parts of nature should

attach to land and be part of the land and what parts should be kept legally separate—either for separate allocation or for continued public ownership? And in the case of resources allocated separately, when should we bundle two or more of them together?

Two issues here merit separate attention. First, what rights should the landowner have to exclude other resource users? (In answering this question we'll want to distinguish the right to exclude from the right to halt interferences with the owner's resource-related activities.) Second, when we decide to sever a resource from the land we need to realize the challenges that inevitably arise in the process of legal severance—illustrated by our numerous decisions dealing with the prior appropriation and with severed mineral rights. When a resource is allocated separately, exactly what physical parts of the land go to the separate resource owner and what physical parts remain part of the land? When is a drop of water part of the river? What physical substances are minerals?

2. *Allocating resources.* We have seen various methods by which the law might make parts of nature available for use. Sale to the highest bidder is one obvious approach—or simply sale to the public after setting the asking price. Allocation based on first-in-time capture is another approach, and we have seen the issues that routinely arise when that method is used: First to do what? What protections does the capturer enjoy while attempting the capture? and How do we date the capture when the act of capture extends over a period of time? Lottery allocation is another possibility, as are various public-interest or merit-based allocations. As for the latter, we have seen the challenges that arise in attempting to screen potential uses and users based on public-interest considerations. We have seen also how it becomes necessary, typically, to limit secondary transfers of resource rights allocated based on public interest to avoid undercutting the public-interest values that the allocation method is designed to achieve. Finally, we have seen possibilities for shared resource ownership—as in the case of the Kentucky cave and the ownership of surface-use rights in nonnavigable lakes. Resources can be allocated to groups of users who possess shared rights, perhaps linked to some formal or informal mode of shared resource management.

3. *Defining use rights.* Certainly one of the law's main jobs is to define the various rights that users have in particular resources, including land. In what ways can the owner make use of the resource? Where can the use take place? How intensive can the use be, and does it include the right to consume or degrade nature itself? And what rights, in particular, should landowners have to develop? At bottom, does the use right entail ownership of the resource in place or is it instead an exclusive or nonexclusive right to capture, harvest or otherwise exploit the resource? In the case of publicly held resources (water, wildlife, navigable rivers), does the title-holding body (some governmental unit, probably) bear trustee duties of some sort to manage and protect the resource in the public interest?

A big issue in defining use rights is whether nature itself—the natural features of a landscape—ought to influence the ways the law defines private rights. Should nature play a role in the scope of private rights in the sense that the rights an owner possesses will vary based upon the land's natural features? Another big issue has to do with the overriding idea of do-no-harm or reasonable use. How will this limit appear in the law and who will make the decisions (legislature or courts; judge or jury; lawmakers or ordinary citizens)?

4. *Resolving resource-use conflicts.* As we define resource-use rights we necessarily pay attention to the various methods of resolving conflicts among users, either ex ante or ex post. When two or more resource uses conflict, how might we resolve the conflict? The issue is of special importance. Recall the alternatives sketched in chapter one after the *Columbia River Fishermen's* case dealing with conflicting uses of a river–alternatives that we thereafter saw in action in various factual settings:

a. We could use *nature as the baseline,* prescribing as the guiding rule that anyone can use the resource so long as its natural conditions remain fundamentally unchanged.

b. Another possibility is to look to *priority in time.* Whichever user is first gets to keep using the resource without interference.

c. A third possibility is to assess the competing uses in terms of their *reasonableness,* or how much they promote the common good. The term "reasonable" is notoriously vague, so we'd have to explain what it means. Does it refer just to the type of resource use? To its efficiency? To its suitability for the location where it is conducted? To its value in relation to competing uses of the same resource?

d. Yet another possibility is to carve up the resource and then allocate fair shares of it to each interested user, employing a *correlative rights* approach.

e. A fifth possibility is to focus on the ability of the competing users to make alterations in their practices so as to diminish the conflict. That is, we could seek out possibilities for *accommodation,* then press for change by the party that can more easily diminish the conflict (and approach often used in dispute among riparian water users).

f. Of course, we could do nothing, and leave the parties to resolve things as they see fit. But this approach, we have seen, is by no means a neutral, hands-off approach by government. When the law allows parties to act as they see fit, it has essentially chosen to *favor the party whose resource use is more intensive.* In the case of Columbia River fishing, to allow the parties to act at will was deliberately to favor the polluters over the fishermen (given that the fishing did not disrupt the polluters). In the case of *Bryant v. Lefever* it meant favoring the landowner who put timbers on the roof; in *Moon* it meant favoring the grass growers; in *Prah v. Maretti* it would have meant favoring the new home builder over the existing homeowner with the solar panels. If we decide to let the market rule—leaving the parties to negotiate an agreement privately—we have chosen this sixth option, deliberately favoring the intensive resource user.

g. Lastly, we could choose a process-oriented solution. Instead of dictating a particular resolution of the dispute, the law could create (or stimulate) a *private governance body of resource users,* which possesses the power to decide which resources uses will take place and on what terms.

5. *Access and ancillary rights.* Of particular interest, as we go about defining use rights, is a consideration of the issue of access: what rights does the resource user have to gain physical access to the resource. This issue has come up in many settings–including materials dealing with private condemnation and with the regulatory powers of government (recall the mining company that was forced to resort to pack animals to gain access to a federal mining site). Access rights are a part of the larger package of ancillary use rights that a resource owner is likely to need to make reasonable use of a particular resource, including, in many instances, surface or subsurface use rights of various sorts. What ancillary rights should various resource owners receive in the original allocation process? When interpreting deeds or other private agreements, what rights should transfer by implication and which should transfer only by express language?

6. *Duration.* As we've seen, we cannot define a use right, whether in land or in some particular resource, without considering its duration. The options are many: renewable term permits; use rights defined based on some intent or purpose and its fulfillment; rules governing abandonment and forfeiture; and regulatory powers that bring unwanted resource uses to an end. Will a resource user face a use-it-or-lose-it burden of some sort? And what about when the resource use ends? Will the user have some obligation to restore nature to a pre-use condition or otherwise clean up messes it has made? Resource uses have life cycles—beginnings, middles, and endings—and the ending deserves just as much attention from lawmakers as the beginning.

7. *Transfer and other reallocation.* Important also is the question of resource reallocation over time and the role of the market in performing this vital task. How can we ensure that resource uses vary over time in response to shifting conditions and values? As we have seen, markets work well to move resources around only when the resources are originally defined so as to facilitate transfer, which means the reallocation issue needs to be taken into account when we define the resource use rights initially. Recall that in many resource settings transfers are subject to approval by some governing body, which could screen potential purchasers based on who they are (residents of a island of lobster fishers) or on how they intend to use the resource (public interest review in prior appropriation law). Recall also that some resource rights attach

to land and cannot be severed and sold separately (various water rights and appurtenant easements). What about condemnation as a method of reallocation? And what powers might governing bodies possess, either to recall and reallocate resources or to redefine use rights in ways that push users to shift to new and better resource uses? On this last issue—redefining use rights over time—should legal change be undertaken in overt ways that people can see and discuss (as by legislative or regulatory action) or is it better to have legal change take place more covertly, as when use rights are defined in terms of evolving social values such as reasonable use?

8. *Clear entitlements versus governance processes.* Running through several of these issues is the rather fundamental tradeoff between two basic approaches to resource management: defining use rights with great precision so people know where they stand (the ex ante conflict-resolution approach), and defining them more vaguely and leaving it to some governing body (including, perhaps, a civil jury) to resolve conflicts ex post. As we have seen, the law often makes use of vague standards (especially "reasonable use") in ways that essentially leave it to decision-makers and to private negotiations to resolve conflicts as they arise. But are better conflict-resolution methods possible? We could, for instance, simply say that lakefront landowners each have the right to make reasonable use of the lake surface (as the Illinois Supreme Court did in *Beacham*). But might it be better to go further and construct some sort of lake-management group that helps users come together to talk and make collective decisions about their shared resource? That is, if we decide to leave use rights defined in vague ways, would it help to make improvements in the conflict-management processes? (As for lake management, we will return to that in one of the discussion problems below.)

9. *Public enforcement powers.* Inevitably the public will have interests in the ways many if not all natural resources are used. The public itself will no doubt retain certain use rights in landscapes or land parcels. The public will likely also need to have powers to ensure that resource users abide by the legal limits on what they can do, particularly limits that are crafted (i) to protect the land's ecological functioning, (ii) to promote other communal interests, and (iii) to keep land productive for future generations. What mechanisms should exist for the public to protect its interests? Should government be left to perform this work? Should private groups (not-for-profit entities, perhaps) be enlisted to do some of it?

10. *Allocating governance powers.* Finally, there is a constellation of issues that arise having to do with the allocation of governing power among various levels of government (using the term government here broadly, to include entities that are only quasi-public). What powers should reside at each level of governance, and what accountability should one level of government have to another? What functions are best performed at each level? And how might civic governing bodies make use of more private or quasi-public bodies to assist in the overall governance process?

Readings later in this chapter will help you think more deeply about these fundamental issues, which are at the forefront of resources law today.

The challenges of crafting use rights and governance regimes are all the more difficult due to the ways that lands and human activities on land are interconnected and interdependent. Land uses do not take place in isolation. What one land- or resource-owner does inevitably affects other people and other activities. Ecological interdependence is particularly important in this field of law. To divert water from a river and transport it over a watershed is inevitably to affect not just other water users but hydrologic systems and the many life forms dependent upon them. To keep a river healthy requires coordinated action throughout the catchment basin that feeds the river. To protect wildlife often requires coordinated action to protect widespread habitat, to control invasive species, and to maintain balanced biotic communities that keep species populations in rough counterpoise.

As ecologists have made clear (and human experience has verified), landscapes have carrying capacities, in terms of the maximum levels of human use they can sustain. Human flourishing depends upon the continued ability of ecosystems to provide "services" to us, and overuse of landscapes can undercut nature's provision of these services. Issues get even more complex when humans living today sense duties to protect nature for future generations and when citizens see moral and prudential reasons to treat nature with caution, given our limited understanding of how nature works and how our actions are affecting it. Our dominant legal tradition presupposes that moral value resides in humans alone and that humans are best understood as autonomous individual beings. Yet, more and more evidence casts doubt on these assumptions. Indeed, serious conservation thought, first and foremost, has posed a wide-ranging challenge to the dominant social and intellectual assumptions of the day. To the extent these critiques gain support, natural resources law will require change.

Interconnection and interdependence become all the more important as human populations rise and people use nature more thoroughly. Rising populations and resource demands create pressures to use nature more efficiently, which means, in many settings, promoting multiple uses of particular tracts of land by differing people. Particularly in urban and suburban area, private lands are already subject to multiple use rights or other private claims, typically in the forms of easements and covenants. The multiple-use ideal that was crafted to govern federal lands—though much maligned for its vagueness—has nonetheless supplied a guiding ideal for use on private lands as well, and arguably needs to become even more important. In many ways, today's dominant land-use trajectory is toward landscapes that blend multiple use rights, subject to overall governance by one or more (often quite a few!) governing bodies. To see this trajectory is to pose obvious questions: how can we define use rights better, and what governance structures would serve best to resolve resource-use disputes while shifting resources to new uses that serve evolving values and circumstances?

* * *

The materials in this chapter follow up on these questions. They draw together the previous seven chapters and attend particularly to some of the challenges and possibilities for landscape governance. Before proceeding, it may help to consider the following questions (which were prepared for use on exams!). They offer opportunities to synthesize the materials in chapters one through seven dealing with use rights. They thus set the stage for further discussions of governing the commons. The first question includes extensive notes that help identify the relevant legal issues. With respect to the other questions you are on your own.

Question 1: Your client, Ann Baxter (AB), has come to you with the following problem. AB owns a 120–acre tract of land that borders on Lake Forbes, which is used for boating and swimming. AB's family has long had a cabin on this land and used it as a weekend retreat. Now, she is thinking about building a year-round home and perhaps selling off parts of the land to other people to construct additional homes. Her particular problem is the following.

Long ago AB's father gave permission to the local boy scouts to use the 120–tract in connection with occasional camping activities conducted on neighboring land that the boy scout region owned, which did not front on the lake. In a letter written to the boy scout regional head, AB's father expressly granted permission for scout troops to (i) pump water from the lake across the tract for use on the boy scouts' neighboring land and (ii) to cross the tract to get access to the lake for "boating and other recreational purposes." In return, the boy scouts expressly granted to AB's father permission to use the scout lands for "all recreational purposes ... whenever the scouts were not present on campouts."

For many years during the summer months scout troops made regular use of AB's tract, crossing the land to get to the lake and leaving their canoes and rowboats on the lake shore. They also constructed temporary water lines to pump lake water to containers on the scout land, used for various purposes (other than drinking). Use by scout troops diminished about 20 years ago, AB says, and came to halt around 15 years ago. AB's father died around the same time, and neither CD nor any other family member since then has made use of the scout land.

In 2004, the boy scout region that owned the land sold it to Columbia Daredevil Explorers (CDE), a motorcycle group that has begun using the land for motorcycle rallies and sundry other outdoor activities. AB's concerns are several. CDE apparently has "sold" its right to pump lake water to another adjacent landowner, an industrial firm that has begun pumping water year-round for industrial use and has announced its plan to install, across AB's tract, a permanent pipe to transport the water. The planned pipeline location would interfere with AB's plans to divide the land and sell parts of it. Also, CDE members have begun bringing jet-skis to the lake, which they park on AB's water front. They are also using the lake surface for hunting of ducks and other waterfowl. At times during CDE rallies literally dozens of people are using the lake surface at once, causing AB to receive complaints from other landowners around the lake.

AB has come to you for advice. She wants to know whether she can object to anything that CDE is doing. What legal issues are raised by these facts, and where does AB stand legally with respect to CDE and to the industrial firm that wants to pump water?

Some hints in answering this question:

1. *What sort of interest* does CDE have? A license? Easement? Is it appurtenant to the boy scout land? In gross? Was it instead personal to the boy scouts organization?

2. What is the *scope* of the interest that CDE obtained? Does it cover use of jet-skis on the lake? Is hunting a "recreational purpose" in light of the boy scout context of the original letter? Does it include, as an ancillary right, the incidental use of the lakefront for boat storage? Further, has CDE exceeded the scope of the interest in terms of the overall intensity of use, and would the industrial firm exceed the scope by installing the pipeline and pumping more water for non-scouting purposes? (As you answer the questions, consider the (conflicting) legal principles of interpreting ambiguous instruments.)

3. *Duration*: On this issue, consider possible abandonment or termination because the original purpose can no longer be fulfilled. Also, was CDE's interest somehow linked to the life of CD's father so that it ended upon his death?

4. Questions about the *water extraction*. Is this a riparian rights or prior appropriation jurisdiction? Consider particularly the place of use and whether water rights can be severed from land as well as the reasonable/beneficial use of the water. What about abandonment and forfeiture and the industrial firm's plan to alter the historic pattern and place of the boy scouts' water use? Is a new appropriation needed?

5. Questions about usage of the lake surface. Is this a navigable or nonnavigable lake, and what difference does that make? If nonnavigable, is the governing law the common law or the civil law rule? Is the usage of the lake surface reasonable overall, in light of how much waterfront AB owns (if this issue is relevant)? If the lake is navigable, do public rights to use the lake surface include the right to engage in waterfowl hunting? Using jet-skis? If this is a navigable waterway the public has rights to use it (assuming lawful access). But again what are the public's rights to use the surface? Do they include hunting? Using jet skis?

6. If AB sells part of the land, will it be encumbered by CDE's interest? Can AB invoke a doctrine of accommodation to compel

CDE to confine its activities (including the location of any pipeline) to the lands that AB retains?

7. Might overuse of the lake surface amount to a nuisance (public? private?), particularly due to water pollution and noise?

Question 2: An Atlantic coast state desires to promote its coastal oyster industry, and has identified a number of coastal areas that are suitable for planting oyster beds. Oysters once planted are relatively sedentary, unlike fin fish, and thus stay in place. State leaders are uncertain how to go about making these beds available to commercial oyster producers, who would need to plant specific beds with oyster breeding stock, take care of them, and in time harvest the mature oysters. Some of the potential beds are more attractive and easier to use than others, of course. State leaders have come to you for help in addressing three specific issues and one more general one:

a. Could they make these oyster beds available to users on a first-in-time system, and if so what problems might they anticipate in doing so?

b. One alternative possibility is to make the beds available to people with longstanding ties to the local coast area, particularly people from families that have relied on the ocean for sustenance. What problems might they anticipate in allocating the beds on this basis?

c. State leaders are uncertain how long the use rights should last, assuming that the bed rights are incorporated into some sort of permit or leasing system. What are the major possibilities, and what advice would you give?

d. Finally, are there other considerations that leaders ought to take into account as they develop a resource-use scheme for these new beds, other than obvious questions about where the beds are and how long the use rights will last?

Question 3: A problem has come up in a state along the Ohio River dealing with groundwater irrigation and its effects on caves. An area near the River is underlain with limestone formations that have fractured and eroded over the millennia to form underground structures, some of which open above ground. Some of the caves provide habitat for rare forms of aquatic life that live in shallow, dark pools—life forms that are often blind. The problem deals with one of these caves.

A corn farmer in the area has begun pumping groundwater from a central well and distributing the water by pipes to various farm fields in a region (the fields are not quite contiguous). The water is used for irrigation. Much of the water seeps into the ground, and works its way into the limestone formations. In the case of one cave, the extra water is distorting ecological conditions in the cave, both by increasing water flows (thereby altering the ponds) and by adding pollution in the form of various farm chemicals. Wildlife ecologists have expressed concerns about the altered cave conditions, and would like to challenge the water usage.

The cave most in danger underlies land that is owned by a wildlife ecologist, although the only cave entrance is on land owned by someone else. The ecologist has asked whether she or a local conservation group can take action to halt or slow the groundwater usage.

What legal issues are raised by these facts and what causes of action might be brought to challenge this water usage? Consider actions that might be brought by the local conservation group as well as by the ecologist as landowner, including actions against the state. Are there steps that either the group or the landowner-ecologist might take to increase the chances of succeeding in any of their challenges?

Question 4: State lawmakers are concerned about the continuing problem of soil erosion, especially on farmlands. A major cause of erosion is the annual tilling of sloping lands, even lands on which the slope is as slight as a 2 or 3 percent grade. Various programs have pushed farmers to install filter strips along waterways to trap soil that is carried into waterways, and the continuing problem of silt in waterways is not particularly major. But erosion continues to degrade lands, even when there are no spillover harms from one land parcel to the next.

State leaders would like to impose limits on tilling slopes, but they are concerned about the likely arguments that such laws would interfere with private property rights. They have turned to you for help in responding to this argument. What ideas might you offer them, to explain how and why such laws could be consistent with private ownership?

B. MIXING PUBLIC AND PRIVATE

When thinking about using landscapes it is helpful to keep in mind some of the classic dangers that human experience has revealed. Perhaps none is more visible today, particularly in academic writing about the environment, then the danger known as the "tragedy of the commons"—the tragedy that arises when too many people use a shared natural resource under uncontrolled circumstances. That tragedy, though, is not the only one that needs to draw our attention. Moreover, the solutions to the tragedy of the commons are more complex and interwoven than typically understood. We will need to move beyond simplistic answers to think clearly about the particular challenges of coordinating resource uses at the landscape scale to achieve good overall results.

The essay that propelled the "tragedy of the commons" into such prominent as an explanatory theory was written in 1968 by biologist Garrett Hardin.[1] In his essay of that title, Hardin considered why people

1. 162 Science 1243 (1968). Much of the text in this paragraph and several that follow is adapted from THE LAND WE SHARE:

who used a shared natural resource tended to overuse it, and ultimately degrade it, when their activities were unrestrained. Hardin employed the example of an unregulated pasture to illustrate his argument, which went something like this. When an individual grazer is free to add more livestock to the communal pasture, he will do so. He will add the livestock because the benefit of doing so—the extra forage eaten by the animals—is pure gain for the grazer. The extra animals are by no means costless: adding an animal means less forage available for animals already in the pasture, and the pasture's overall productivity declines when too many animals are put on it (that is, once its biological carrying capacity is exceeded). But these various costs do not fall just on the individual grazer who added the animal; they are spread among all users of the commons. The grazer who adds the animal, that is, enjoys all the gain while bearing only a portion of the total costs. Even when the total costs vastly exceed the grazer's gain, the grazer has an incentive to keep adding. What is true for one grazer is also true for others: each has an incentive to drag down the pasture as a whole.

Hardin was not the first to comment on unrestrained common ownership as a cause of land degradation. Writings about it go back at least as far as Aristotle.[2] Sir Thomas Smith, a leading critic of land enclosures in England, noted the problem in his important work from 1549, *A Discourse on the Common Weal*: "That which is possessed of many in common is neglected of all," he wrote. "Tenants in common be not so good husbands as when every man has his part in severality."[3] Hardin added to this old wisdom the catchy phrase of his essay's title, and his phrase quickly caught on. The unregulated commons gave rise to a tragedy, he asserted, a tragedy not just in the sense of a bad outcome but in the sense that ancient Greek dramatists and Shakespeare used the term: a bad outcome caused by the inexorable working of forces that dragged people down, an outcome that flowed from a human character trait and that was the predictable consequence of that trait. In the case of the tragedy of the commons, the human trait was the penchant of people to promote their separate interests over the good of the whole. And what allowed this to happen was their individual freedom. "Ruin is the destination toward which all men rush," Hardin asserted, "each pursuing his own best interest in a society that believes in the freedom of the commons."

Modern air and water pollution, Hardin asserted, presented natural tragedies along analogous lines. The individual who could freely pollute stood to gain by avoiding the economic costs of pollution control. The pollution itself caused harm, of course, but other people largely bore that harm, the people downstream or downwind. Once again, benefits and

PRIVATE PROPERTY AND THE COMMON GOOD (2003), pp. 158–161.

2. Elinor Ostrom, GOVERNING THE COMMONS: THE EVOLUTION OF INSTITUTIONS FOR COLLECTIVE ACTION 2 (1990) ("what is common to the greatest number has the least care bestowed upon it," *quoting* Aristotle, POLITICS, Book II, ch. 3).

3. *Quoted in* James A. Montmarquet, THE IDEA OF AGRARIANISM: FROM HUNTER-GATHERER TO AGRARIAN RADICAL IN WESTERN CULTURE 73–74 (1989).

costs were out of alignment. A polluter might rationally go ahead and pollute, even when, at the societal level, the costs of the harm caused by the pollution vastly exceeded the costs of halting it.

At this point, Hardin could have turned his narrative into a simple morality tale. The root of his tragedy was the selfish human nature displayed by the grazer and the polluter; their tendencies, not just to favor themselves over others, but to do so even when their conduct harmed others more than it benefitted themselves. This was a destructive form of egotism, which Hardin might have condemned under any well-grounded ethical scheme.

Rather than take that route, though, Hardin looked for institutional arrangements that could channel or contain this resource tragedy. As he saw matters, two arrangements offered promise. One approach was for group members to get together and impose restraints on themselves: "Mutual coercion, mutually agreed upon," as Hardin would phrase it. If users of the commons limited one another in what they each could do, they could reduce the tragedy. If they used good science and sound virtue when doing so, they might even so moderate use of the commons that it would remain healthy in perpetuity.

The second approach to avoid the tragedy was to divide the commons into private shares and assign an individual owner for each. When that was done, he argued, costs and benefits came into better alignment. The individual grazer now had complete control of a single parcel. The grazer was still free to add another animal and get the gain from it, but this time the costs would all be borne by that grazer, or so Hardin assumed. Human selfishness would then no longer lead to tragedy, Hardin theorized; it would normally lead to an economically sound decision on animal-stocking levels.

Hardin's analysis met pointed criticism when it came out, largely because of its title. Other scholars had spent time studying actual common-property regimes, including common grazing lands, and they knew full well that common-property arrangements sometimes worked just fine, with nothing like the tragedy that Hardin predicted.[4] What Hardin had described was essentially an open-access commons, one in which outsiders could show up at any time and start using it or in which existing users could increase their use at will. In truth, scholars have pointed out, long-term grazing arrangements do not work this way. They are highly controlled affairs in which usage is carefully restricted by one form or another of Hardin's mutual coercion mutually agreed upon.[5]

4. Much of the scholarly writing through 1990 is drawn upon in Elinor Ostrom's now classic work, GOVERNING THE COMMONS: THE EVOLUTION OF INSTITUTIONS FOR COLLECTIVE ACTION (1990). As Ostrom notes, some observers so strongly favor privatization as to deny that any other option can solve Hardin's tragedy. *Id.* at 12–13.

5. Differing perspectives on how commons might successfully be managed are offered in Robert Constanza, et al., eds., INSTITUTIONS, ECOSYSTEMS, AND SUSTAINABILITY (2000); John A. Baden & Douglas S. Noonan, eds., MANAGING THE COMMONS (2d ed. 1998); Bonnie J. McCay & James M. Acheson, eds., QUESTIONS OF THE COMMONS: THE CULTURE AND ECOLOGY OF COMMUNAL RESOURCES (1990).

Hardin's analysis, at least once properly limited to open-access types of commons, seemed to many readers to offer great insights, both into the fundamental nature of America's environmental predicament and into how a nation devoted to individualism and private enterprise might best deal with it. If resource-use problems were caused by the tragedy of the commons and if privatization was a solution, then the best environmental policy was one that put resources into private hands. If a resource could be divided, it should be. Only resources that could not be divided, such as flowing air or migratory birds, needed to remain commonly owned and called for some form of mutual coercion.

What Hardin failed to note, and what scholars since have made clear, is that private property and the discipline of the market are not always strong enough to get landowners to take care of what they own in any ecological sense. Landowners can easily consume or degrade lands in pursuit of wealth maximization, and it is too easy for landowners to ignore the external effects of their land practices. These points were made clear in a 1913 article by land economist Lewis Cecil Gray—one of the first articles in the field now known as environmental or ecological economics. *The Economic Possibilities of Conservation,* 27 QUARTERLY J. OF ECON. 497 (1913). Gray worked in Wisconsin and had first-hand experience with landscapes degraded by private owners. He undertook to figure out exactly why this degradation occurred—why economic forces were not strong enough to encourage landowners to use their lands in ecologically sound ways. Economists since then have added to his analysis, pointing out the many ways that private ownership can reduce the problems of the open-access commons but does not guarantee good land use. *See* Herman E. Daly & Joshua Farley, ECOLOGICAL ECONOMICS: PRINCIPLES AND APPLICATIONS (2004), 157–219.

The following excerpt comments on Hardin's two proposed solutions to the tragedy of the commons, to their substantial overlaps, and to the related problem or tragedy of natural landscapes that are fragmented too thoroughly, leaving insufficient managerial power to coordinate activities at the landscape level.

THE LURE OF PRIVATIZATION

Eric T. Freyfogle

in THE LAND WE SHARE: PRIVATE PROPERTY AND THE COMMON GOOD (2003).

No matter what standard one uses in measuring the health of landscapes, there is little doubt that many [private land] owners fall below it. Somewhere, Hardin's privatization analysis contains flaws. To get at them, we need to return to the beginning of Hardin's story and look again at the process of dividing land into private shares. What does it mean to transform a commons into privately owned pieces? If we start with a common landscape and fragment it into individual parcels, in what way have we divided the commons?

First, assuming we have not erected fences or other barriers, we must recognize that privatization does nothing to the commons in any physical sense. The animals that scampered across it are still free to do so. The wind that blew across it still does, too. The groundwater percolating beneath the surface, the birds that fly through, the insect populations that ebb and flow—none are affected by this intangible action called privatization. Nature is an integrated whole, and it remains integrated before privatization and after. Cattle will likely respect property lines (at least when bounded by barbed wire or electric fences), and so might other large mammals. But as for the latter, in what useful sense have they been privatized?

What has been divided, of course, is not the land but authority over the land, particularly the power to make decisions about it. Privatization is not chiefly a physical act but instead a matter of fragmenting rights and responsibilities among people. When a commons is intact and uncontrolled, no one has management power over it; it is an unmanaged free-for-all, precisely the kind of place that Hardin condemned. On the other hand, when a commons is well managed by all users collectively, rights and responsibilities are vested in the group as a whole. The users collectively have the power, if not to avoid the tragedy entirely, at least to diminish it considerably.

When Hardin proposed privatization as a solution, he assumed that what private owners did within their tracts would stay within those tracts. Harms associated with an owner's land use would be shouldered by the owner alone, perhaps not completely but to such a high degree that harms imposed on neighbors could be ignored. Privatizing solved the tragedy of the commons by bringing mismatched costs and benefits into alignment.

But is this so? What does happen, in terms of costs and benefits, when a natural commons is broken up?

The most obvious effect is that the scale of management shifts to a physically smaller one. Instead of having a single management regime over a large scale there are lots of management regimes over smaller scales. And many consequences could flow from this change—some good but some definitely not so good. One not-so-good consequence is that the problem of management boundaries increases significantly. If boundaries provide incentive for land managers to ignore the effects that spill over onto neighbors, a vast increase in boundaries exacerbates the problem. When the grazing commons is intact, an effect that spreads from one part of the commons to another part remains within the same commons, and those who manage the commons are affected by it. But when the commons is divided into private shares, a boundary line might intervene between the one causing the harm and the one affected by it.

Related to this problem of harms that spill across property lines is a second problem exacerbated by the fragmentation brought on by privatization: the increased difficulty of addressing ecological challenges that require planning at the landscape level. When a sound land-use plan is possible only over large spatial scales, successful planning becomes less and less likely as the land is divided into ever-smaller pieces.

Consider the case of downstream flooding caused by excessive upstream drainage. When an entire watershed is managed as a single commons, the group that drains is the group that suffers the flooding; costs and benefits are matched. When the commons is divided, however, with upstream and downstream lands separately owned, a mismatch is created. The upstream owner now has little incentive to reduce drainage. The downstream owner has reason to act but not the power; decisions about upstream drainage are not his or hers to make. The only recourse may be to file suit against the upstream owner and hope that law offers relief.

The problem here is not only a matter of dividing land into private parcels. It is also a problem of dividing landscapes into smaller political units. Here, urban sprawl offers evidence. When a single governing unit controls all land planning around an urban area, it can control the rate and forms of expansion. When the political commons is divided into smaller legal entities, in contrast, externalities increase, and no person or group has the power to coordinate the whole. Division worsens the problem.

One might consider also the case of wildlife habitat, perhaps along a riparian corridor. To make the case realistic pick one of the 99 percent of all species that lack market value. Most species today are declining in population because of habitat loss. When sufficient habitat exists within a single parcel, a parcel manager theoretically could prepare and execute a habitat-protection plan. But nearly always, critical habitat will be spread over many parcels. No single owner is able develop a conservation plan. Once again, fragmentation of the whole gives rise to a crisis of management.

In these instances, fragmentation does not undercut all chance of cooperative management. Managers acting together can still make joint plans to remedy problems that transcend human-drawn lines on the map. But negotiations are costly, and many people balk at them for social and cultural reasons. They often do not occur, even when only two parties are involved. As the numbers increase above two, the chances of agreement fall quickly.

When Garrett Hardin and others viewed privatization as a solution to the tragedy of the commons, they implicitly embraced three assumptions that are critical to their reasoning. They assumed that what a landowner did on his or her parcel would pretty much stay within the bounds of that property; spillover effects or externalities, that is, would be minor or easily remedied. They assumed that the power of the market was sufficient to encourage owners within the bounds of their parcels to conserve what they owned. And they assumed that landowners were able, acting alone or through easily arranged private transactions, to use their lands in ways that amounted to good land use. It is now clear, or at least ought to be, that these assumptions are wrong to significant degrees.

It is clear, ecologically, that spillover effects are numerous, vital, and often hard to trace. Harms and benefits, that is, remain poorly matched, even when pollution laws curtail the obvious forms of air and water pollution. It is equally clear that, even within land boundaries, the power of the market is not strong enough to promote sound, long-term land practices—as the widespread soil-erosion problem illustrates. Indeed, the competitive pressures of the market can push (or pull) landowners to embrace practices that are distinctly unwise. Finally, it is clear that much conservation work requires coordination of land uses on large spatial scales. Problems such as urban sprawl, excessive drainage, and wildlife habitat degradation are simply not matters that individual owners acting alone can handle.

If Hardin's privatization alternative has significant limitations, what of his other solution to the commons tragedy: mutual coercion mutually agreed upon? What does it entail, and can it shed further light on the benefits and limits of privatization?

In the mutual coercion option, landowners collectively impose limits on the ways that they each can use the commons. They might do so unwisely, of course, embracing rules that lead to the early destruction of the commons. But if they did their work well, what steps would they undertake? What work is needed to craft a coercive regime that successfully protects the land's vigor?

An indispensable first step is to settle upon the desired long-term condition of the land—to made a decision, that is, about what it means to take care. Once selected, this goal would set the overall limits on land use. In the case of a grazing pasture that can handle only a particular number of animals, overall uses would need to stay below that number. If parts of the pasture could handle more animals, if animals needed shifting from time to time, or if animal numbers required adjusting because of changed conditions, these matters too would go into the mix, affecting the total rights that users possessed.

Once overall limits were put in place, users of the commons could proceed in several ways. They could decide to use the commons together, perhaps managing their animals in communal herds or flocks. Alternatively, they could assign each user a share, allowing the user to pasture a specific number of animals, perhaps in specified locations and during specified seasons. Such rights could well be created as secure private property rights, and made fully transferable. Or the group could restrict the transfer of rights in the name of protecting the good of the whole. However this is done, private rights would be specifically designed to sustain the common good.

In all likelihood, the group of commons users would want to make their schemes more complex than this. In the real world, commons-management regimes tend to be highly sophisticated, whether they are grazing commons (which still exist), forests, or fisheries. Successful regimes provide for on-going changes in the ways people can use the commons, mostly to respond to changes in the land itself and its capacity to withstand use. Provision also needs to be made to bring in the next generation of users, and to accommodate shifting needs of current users. One fundamental precept: a commons regime can work only if the vast majority of local residents view it as fair, and only if they sense that they have voices in its management.

We can now get finally to the bottom Hardin's privatization alternative. What would it take for privatization to achieve the good results that commons management at its best can bring about? The overriding answer is straightforward. For privatization to work well, it needs to deal successfully with all of the challenges that the common-property regime is forced to address. In a divided landscape as in a shared one, users need to tailor their actions to respect the well being of the whole. In a divided landscape as in a shared one, uses need to be sensitive to nature's fluctuations. When private landowners are allowed to overuse their lands or to ignore the external effects of what they do, the private landscape can slide downward, ecologically and socially, just as an open-access commons can. Dividing the commons does not reduce the challenges of good land use; it merely divides up responsibility for achieving that goal. The challenges remain, and if information-gathering and administrative costs sometimes decline with privatization, other problems worsen—the trans-boundary problems, the costs of boundary enforcement, and the problems requiring landscape-scale coordination.

At root, perhaps the chief flaw in Garrett Hardin's reasoning was his failure to see that his two solutions were, in fact, variants on a single solution. He failed to note that private property itself, considered as a legal institution, is a form of mutual coercion mutually agreed upon. When property law recognizes one person as owner, it prescribes limits on how the person can use what she owns. It sets even stricter limits on the ways that other people can use the owner's tract. Landowners agree to respect the rights of one another, and nonowners accept the system's coercive limits because it benefits them as well: Mutual coercion, mutually agreed upon.

With little difficulty, one could create a private property regime and a common-property regime that are essentially identical. In a common-property regime as in a private-property one, a user could hold the exclusive right to graze animals on some designated part of the grazing commons. The right could be transferable and even perpetual, though subject to the rights of the group as a whole to impose cutbacks (or increases) in usages when deemed necessary. In the common-property setting the group typically has overt powers to limit uses patterns. But a similar law-making power is held in the private property setting by courts, legislatures, and city councils. In both instances, private rights evolve over time.

Centuries ago—back when land was relatively plentiful, land-uses were not intensive, and actions on one parcel had few spillover effects—the categories of private versus common property were more distinctly different. In such a world, private landowners could use their parcels as they saw fit; few overt problems arose, and hence there was little need for coercion. But when landscapes became more congested, when land-uses intensified, when spillover effects multiplied, and when social values shifted so that the public began to worry about subtle signs of long-term decline, the gap between the two options narrowed rapidly. Indeed, if the land community of the future is to remain healthy, the private-property approach will need to take on even more of the trappings of a successful common-property regime. Landscapes everywhere will be made up, not of two types of land—private and commons—but of a wide array of variants that blend the two....

When all is said and done, privatization of a landscape is no silver bullet. It is no magic mechanism to turn land degraded by private greed into a healthy, beautiful place for people to live. A people who want to live in a place well, in high numbers, and with modern technology, have no choice but to study the nature around them, to identify its limits, and to shape their activities to fit within those limits. Individual landowners could do some of this work, but many of them do not, and when they do not they drag others down with them. Moreover, even well-meaning landowners cannot alone address landscape-scale problems such as from urban sprawl and wildlife habitat protection.

Garrett Hardin was fundamentally right in his analysis of the unregulated commons. The open-access commons is a prescription for tragedy. But probably more important than the tragedy of the commons in terms of the environmental predicament in present-day United States is the *tragedy of fragmentation*: the tragedy that comes when landscapes are divided into small pieces without effective mechanisms to correct market failures and to achieve landscape-scale goals. The more fragmented a landscape becomes, the harder it is to make sensible, large-scale plans. Externalities increase. Market imperfections rise. Transaction costs escalate. It becomes ever harder to identify sources of problems and to trace their ripple effects. It becomes infeasible if not impossible for people to pursue goals that require coordinated action.

In the land-use arena, America's problem is not chiefly one of the commons that needs dividing; it is that the natural commons has been overly divided in terms of decision-making powers. Rather than needing stronger or clearer powers to act individually, landowners collectively need greater control over the landscapes that they share. Without that control, their landscapes are tragically doomed.

* * *

The above excerpt introduces indirectly some of the literature produced by scholars who have studied longstanding, successful common property regimes, attempting to identify the elements of them that account for their success. Why does one commons get overused to degradation while another is carefully controlled by users to protect its continued productivity?

Out of this research has come rather clear answers to the success of common property regimes. Regimes work best when the population of users is relatively stable and socially and ethnically homogeneous. When users interact in various spheres of life, particularly in settings in which their reputations are important, they are more likely to cooperate in the management of shared resources and respect communal rules. An essential requirement is that a commons have rather clear boundaries and that users of it have mechanisms to exclude outsiders. So long as outsiders can enter, overuse will happen. Sometimes local users can set and monitor boundaries themselves. More often they need assistance from higher levels of governance, particularly civil government, to police boundaries and punish outside violators. Just as important is the need to tailor the use rights of users to the natural features of the commons, taking into account essentially all relevant factors. The principle identified above—letting nature play a role in lawmaking—has proven essential in common property regimes. Only in that way can the overall use of the commons stay within its carrying capacity. For users to shape and reshape use rights in this manner they need to have the power to govern their internal affairs to a rather large extent, which is to say a power to organize and manage the commons and uses of it, including power to punish violators. This power overlaps considerably with powers in the United States that are reserved for civil government. A successful common property regime, then, needs to assume governmental powers, partially displacing other units of governance. For users of the commons to accept its activities and limits, they must participate in its governance, particularly in the processes of modifying the rules over time. It is important also that they have access to rapid, low-cost mechanisms for resolving conflicts as they arise. Finally, it is essential that the activities of users be monitored, preferably by the users themselves, and that sanctions be imposed for violations. The standard pattern, it turns out, is for successful regimes to impose relatively modest sanctions for first-time violators, and to increase the penalties for recurring violations.

In chapter one we looked briefly at the lobster fishery on Monhegan Island off the coast of Maine. We saw how island fishers were unable to maintain boundaries around the island and to ward off outsider lobster fishers. They thus had to turn to the state legislature, getting it to authorize a geographic zone in which the Monhegan fishers could exercise exclusive control over lobster fishing. The following article gives two more glimpses of the intriguing lobster fishing arrangements in Maine. It considers the same issue of boundaries and boundary protection for the coast generally, noting the tendency of various lobster "gangs" to try to expand their exclusive territories over time. The reading concludes with a few sentences about a different issue—the need to impose overall harvesting limits on individual lobster fishers. As the authors explain, even well-maintained territories are susceptible of having outsider fishers join the local community and begin fishing in the territory, thereby increasing overall harvesting rates. One tool used to keep overall harvests in check is to prescribe maximum limits on the number of traps an individual fisher can set.

CHANGES IN THE TERRITORIAL SYSTEM OF THE MAINE LOBSTER INDUSTRY

James M. Acheson and Jennifer F. Brewer
in N. Dolsăk & E. Ostrom, eds., The Commons in the New Millennium: Challenges and Adaptations (2003).

Over the course of the past several decades, all local lobster fishing boundaries in Maine have moved somewhat, but some have moved surprisingly slowly. Whether boundaries remain stable or move is the result of a political process involving competition and conflict between groups of fishermen. Boundaries move when a group of fishermen—usually a small group from one harbor—successfully place traps in the area occupied by another harbor gang and are able to keep them there. Not all attempts to expand the amount of fishing space are successful, however, and some gangs have been very successful in defending their fishing territories for decades.

Movement of local-level boundaries is rarely the result of actions by a single individual. A single person who attempts to move into an area occupied by a group or to defend a boundary against a group of invaders may lose so much gear that he is forced to retreat in defeat. A successful defense against invaders or a successful invasion against opposition depends on the ability to organize an effective and coordinated team. Usually such teams are composed of a small group (three to eight people) whose forays are coordinated by one or two leaders. Their activities are usually kept quiet. In many cases, but not all, the fishermen involved are quite young.

Although teams are composed of more than one person, entire gangs are not involved. One older fisherman from an island that has been very successful in defending its boundaries explained the situation in these words: "You never attempt to defend lines by yourself. If you do, you will become a target. We just get the number of people it takes to do the job. If two or three people can hold the lines, fine. But if it takes more, we get them."

The major impediment to organizing such teams is overcoming a strong inclination among those affected to be a free rider. It is very tempting to let others do the dirty work of invading or defending boundaries while getting the benefits of their activities. After all, everyone in the harbor benefits when boundaries are defended, and it is only those involved in the defense who are generally in serious danger of prosecution or retaliation. Some harbors have been much more successful in organizing such teams than others.

A decision to defend one's own lines against invasion or invade the area of others depends on the costs and benefits involved. Maintaining a local territory reduces the numbers of fishermen in that territory. This can result in two kinds of benefits: fewer snarls and increased catches per unit of effort. The primary costs of defending a territory are the threat of prosecution, the potential to lose some of one's own gear, and the psychic costs of being involved in conflict (not to be discounted). The fact that in mainland harbors a sense of territorial ownership is very strong near shore and nonexistent in offshore fishing areas can be explained in terms of the competition for productive fishing bottom and the way this affects the costs and benefits involved. Lobsters are concentrated in inshore areas in the summer when large numbers of them shed into larger sizes. The number of traps per unit of area is high, since there is relatively little of this kind of bottom and the numbers of fishermen is at its annual high, since large numbers of part-timers with small skiffs are in the fishery in these months. Under these conditions, excluding others will increase the proportion of traps one has on the bottom, augmenting catches per trap. It will also reduce snarls. In such areas, the benefits of holding territory outweigh the costs. The benefits of maintaining territorial rights to offshore areas, where lobsters are concentrated in the winter, are far less. At this time of year the number of traps per unit of area is less. There are more square miles of offshore fishing grounds. There are fewer boats fishing at this time of year, since only those with large boats are capable of exploiting these offshore grounds, and even many with large boats choose not to fish since the weather is often very bad, trap losses are high, and the fishing is far less productive. Since traps are not crowded in offshore zones, snarling is not generally a problem, and removing other traps will not increase one's own catches much, if at all. In these offshore waters the costs of defending an area generally outweigh the benefits to be had by defending territorial claims.

There are two different types of territories at the local scale. Mainland harbors have what Acheson (1988) calls nucleated territories. That is, there is a strong sense of territoriality near the harbor where the boats are anchored, and a stranger putting traps in this area is almost certain to be retaliated against. This sense of ownership grows progressively weaker the further from the harbor one goes, and the willingness to retaliate against interlopers is less. On the periphery (i.e., three to five miles away from the harbor) there is no strong sense of territoriality. (This is not to suggest that these more distant "mixed fishing" areas are open to anyone.) If one goes far enough away from one's own harbor, one inevitably enters an area that is defended by another gang. How far one can go without incurring retaliation depends greatly on one's personal characteristics. Older, experienced fishermen from large, well-established families who have a history of fishing in the area and a lot of "friends" are accorded more leeway. They have more allies, after all.

In the middle of the twentieth century, mainland harbors maintained some control over who was permitted to join the harbor gang. Usually only people from the town were permitted to go fishing, with members of long-established fishing families given preference. These restrictions have broken down in many places. People wanting to join the gang may be harassed for a time, but most will succeed in joining if they are persistent enough and obey the conservation laws. As a result, the number of people in most of these mainland gangs has increased dramatically, which has exacerbated the problem of trap congestion....

The increases in the amount of gear finally led to a trap limit law. Many fishermen have wanted trap limits (a maximum number of traps that could be fished by a single license holder) for some thirty years. There was no coast-wide consensus on what the limit on the number of traps per license holder should be, however. What was considered an adequate limit in some areas was considered far too restrictive in others. In 1955 the Maine legislature solved this problem by passing what has become known as the zone management law, which went into effect that year. This law stipulated what the entire coast of the state was divided into zones and that each zone was to be governed by a council composed of lobster fishermen elected by the license holders of that zone. These zone councils have the power to recommend rules for their zone on the number of traps to be used (a trap limit), the times of day when fishing will be permitted, and the number of traps that can be fished on a single warp line. If these rules are passed by referendum by two thirds of the voting license holders in the zone, they are referred to the Commissioner of Marine Resources, who can make them regulations enforceable by the wardens. In fact, seven zones were established, and by 1998, all of them had passed trap limits. Six of the seven zones passed an 800–trap limit for 2000; one passed a 600–trap limit.

* * *

This research into common property regimes and to their possible expansion to deal with nagging resource-use problems raises fundamental questions about the line between private and public resource ownership. In the American mind, a clear line divides the two, and resources are thought about much differently when publicly owned rather than privately owned. Resources under common property management, however, seem to fit into neither category. Indeed, they implicitly suggest that the attempt to place land and other resources into the two categories might itself be a cause of resource misuse, or least a stumbling block to the construction of new resource regimes that take advantage of the best of both public and private ownership. In what ways does private land differ from public land, and might we conceive of land-management regimes that bridge the two? Consider the following reading:

GOODBYE TO THE PUBLIC–PRIVATE DIVIDE

Eric T. Freyfogle

in AGRARIANISM AND THE GOOD SOCIETY: LAND, CULTURE, CONFLICT AND HOPE (2007).

...

With this behind us, let us turn to the two categories of property that are familiar to us: public land and private land. They seem like different things, but how different are they? The points covered thus far help frame the answer.

Both public and private property are forms of power, meaning power that some people exercise over other people.

Both are defined by law and indeed are creatures of law.

Both forms of property, public and private, are morally problematic in that they entail the coercive restriction of individual liberty. Both therefore need justification to remain legitimate.

When we turn to the laws that govern uses of private and public lands we find that, like all other laws, such laws are rightly enacted only when lawmakers are attempting sincerely to foster the good of everyone, landowners and the landless alike. Lawmakers are supposed to legislate for the common good, not for the benefit of any faction. Property laws are no different. Property is legitimate to the extent that it fosters the shared good . . . It is simply not the case that private rights exist apart from law, or foster private interests apart from the public good, or exist as a form of private power that is independent of public power.

How then do, the public and the private differ, because surely they do?

To get at their differences, we can return to our opening scene, with our people entering their new land. As the people gaze upon the landscape, thinking about how they'll inhabit the landscape, they confront three questions.

First, *how* are they going to use these lands to foster their collective good?

Second, *who* is going to use which lands?

And third, who gets to *make the decisions*?

These are the vital questions, both for the first people who enter a place and for each generation that follows. By keeping the questions front and center we can get at the differences between public and private lands.

The biggest difference between private and public land has to do with management power over the land. Who gets to decide land uses? Decisions about *public* lands are mostly made by public decision-makers, but not completely so. Public decision-makers are often influenced by private parties who want to use the lands. Indeed, private involvement in public-lands processes is extensive, too extensive some people say. When we turn to *private* lands, the equation is flipped but again is not one-sided. Private owners have greater say in land-use decisions but lawmakers commonly play important roles; again, too important, some people say. In many settings, private lands are also subject to limits imposed by other private citizens—by a homeowners association, for instance. In both cases, then, public and private influences intermingle. So varied is this intermingling that we do not really have two categories of lands. We have a continuum, with some lands more subject to public control and some lands more subject to private control. Yet control of either type is always a matter of degree.

On the question of how the land is used, we also see a continuum or mixture of uses rather than two distinct types. On public land we have nature preserves, intensively used parks, grazing, logging, mining, office buildings, stores, and so on. On private lands we find pretty much the same, less in the way of nature reserves and more in the form of intensive land uses, particularly residential uses. Without maps or signs, though, it is often hard to tell public from private.

We get even greater overlap when we consider who actually uses the land. Private lands are used by private actors almost exclusively. But activities on public lands also involve private actors; indeed, private parties are the primary users of public lands. Logging, grazing, timber harvesting, mining, recreation—all are undertaken on public lands by private parties, usually at some private initiative. So again, in terms of land use, the differences between public and private actors are ones of degree. The public and the private overlap.

Consider, for a moment, the typical residential subdivision lot, a familiar form of private property. The owner's use of the lot is probably subject to severe limits as a result of restrictive covenants, enforceable by neighbors. Permanent easements might allow public utilities or even private entities to enter this residential lot and use it for specified purposes. Zoning laws could limit activities, or even prescribe affirmative duties such as shoveling snow, maintaining fences or keeping weeds trimmed. When we get down to it, the owner of this lot might really have only a single, narrowly defined use right in the land—a specific right to use the land for a single-family home.

Compare this carefully prescribed residential-use right with a similar right to use public land, such as a Bureau of Land Management (BLM) grazing permit or a federal oil and gas lease. Here, too, we have a private property right, and it is carefully tailored by law. So how different is the BLM grazing permit from the homeowner's use right? There are differences, to be sure, yet both are specifically tailored use rights, both are largely defined by law, and both are crafted, one hopes, so that the private activities promote the common good.

. . .

The public-private divide as an intellectual framework, as a way of thinking about our current land-use regime, is distinctly unhelpful today. It implies that some lands can be used solely for an owner's benefit while others are used for the good of everyone. Yet that division makes little sense. The public has a legitimate interest in how *all* lands are used. No land use takes place in isolation. As for public lands, many are needed to serve distinctly public purposes but most are not. Or rather, most publicly owned lands would not be needed to serve public activities if we could be confident that, when the land is placed into private hands, private uses would comport with the common good. . . .

The virtue of private ownership is that it designates particular people as land stewards, charged with looking after the land and putting it to good use. Private ownership can protect privacy, provide incentives for economic enterprise, and add ballast to civil states. Public ownership, on the other side, is better able to consider the long term and can assess land uses in broader spatial contexts. Government can resist market pressures to misuse land, and it can manage lands to provide an array of public goods that make little economic sense for individual owners. Of course, both forms of ownership can and do fall short of the ideal. Private owners are often not good stewards: their perspectives are too short, they ignore ecological ripple effects, and their isolated decisions can produce chaotic land-use patterns. Government agencies, on their side, are buffeted by political winds and have trouble saying no to powerful groups. Their decisions can be painfully slow and inefficient.

The main challenge we face today in attempting to live well on land—attempting to succeed at the "oldest task in human history"—is coming up with better ways of combining public and private on the same piece of land. The public has a legitimate interest in the way all land is used, private land very much included. In the case of private land—as our current land-use squabbles illustrate—we are having trouble finding good ways to protect that public interest without undercutting the vital benefits we all get from a scheme of widespread private ownership. How do we protect the public's interest while at the same time retaining the important benefits we get from a private property system? That is the question. We need better answers.

This need to protect the public's interest in private land is particularly vital because it goes to heart of private property's legitimacy. As noted, private property in land is not morally legitimate when it allows owners to harm the public good. After all, why should we deploy our police and courts to support private action that harms the community? That simply is not right.

No law, of course, can ever be so precise as to prescribe the exact ways that land should be used. Laws are crude tools, and they can do little more than restrict the most harmful practices. To get truly good land use, landowners have to want to conserve. They need to know the nuts and bolts of sound, conservative land use as applied to their own lands. That said, though, there is a lot of room to improve the *institutional* context of private land use so as to increase the influence of public values in private land-use decision-making. And the place to begin, in asserting this public interest, is with the basic rights that landowners possess. If plowing a hillside can lead to degradation, harming the public as well as the landowner, then why should the landowner have the legal right to plow? Why should that be a component of a landowner's bundle of entitlements created and supported by public action?

New laws could better protect the public interest. We could call these laws property laws, or we could call them regulations; it makes little difference. We could also protect the public interest using mechanisms that are less obviously public. Examples here include restrictive covenants, rules imposed by homeowners' associations, and restrictions that come through resource-management cooperatives. There is also the public involvement in private decisions that takes the form of economic incentives to used land in publicly good ways, whether funded by taxpayers or private donors.

These familiar ways of combining public and private, though, need to be understood as merely illustrations of what is possible, perhaps as precursors of more effective methods that await our courage and imagination.

Consider, for instance, a grazing arrangement, the Tilbuster Commons, that has been put together in eastern Australia. Under it, private landowners lease their private lands to a collectively managed grazing cooperative. Their combined lands are worked in concert—like open-field farms of centuries ago—with their animal herds mingled. By working jointly the grazers can employ a larger spatial perspective in their land management, thereby reducing one of the main defects of traditional private ownership. Here in the United States, we have similar examples of cooperative land management, such as the pooling and unitization schemes that govern oil fields and water-management schemes orchestrated by water conservancy districts. Safe-harbor and candidate-conservation agreements under the Endangered Species Act offer useful precedents, as do federal agencies' experiences managing grazing, timber harvesting, and mining on federal lands. The new Forest Service program involving Stewardship Contracts illustrates a willingness to try new public-private land management forms, and could prove a step in the right direction. Across the West, there is talk about connecting private and public grazing lands in ways that view them as integrated management units. Again, though, these are just hints of what is possible when we stop thinking about land as either public or private and instead look for new ways to combine public and private on all lands.

For the vast majority of lands, where we need to head (and are heading, haltingly) is toward blended landscapes, in which private actors possess use rights that are loosely tailored to protect the public interest. These use rights are forms of private property, but they bear little resemblance to the industrial, ownership-as-absolute-dominion ideal of private property that arose in the nineteenth century. Tailored use rights have existed for years on public lands. On public lands, we are likely to see an expansion of these use rights so that private holders can plan over longer time periods and can take broader responsibility for the land, subject to duties to take good care of it. These private use rights on public lands will not typically be exclusive; the land might remain open to public recreational use, for instance, and a holder of timber or grazing rights might need to defer to someone else who holds mining rights. But public recreational rights might be more limited than today; they might be limited to public hiking on defined trails, without ATVs, snowmobiles or even mountain bikes. In addition, the holder of a private use right might have the power and duty to halt destructive trespasses.

Tailored use rights could look pretty much the same when they exist on private land. For a look into the future of private-lands ownership, we might consider the case of timber harvesting in a state that is aggressive in regulating forestry to protect nature. In such a state, a forest owner today could be restricted by law from harvesting trees along waterways or near residential areas. A state forestry practices statute could require the owner to preserve the diversity of tree species and ages, while limiting harvesting methods and imposing duties to replant. Perhaps the forest owner has already sold hunting rights to a local hunting club, and perhaps an old railroad right of way or mining road is used as a public hiking trail. Perhaps there is even a conservation easement on the land. When we put all these elements together, our hypothetical private forest already might look a lot like a public forest, in terms of the legal rights that the timber company holds and the ways multiple uses of it are mixed.

As we look ahead we are likely to see new ways in which the public interest in land is identified and protected. We will rely less on distant governments and instead make greater use of novel, collective-management arrangements that are closer to the land. We are also likely to have the public interest refined and promoted by multiple levels of government that pay attention to differing spatial scales. Perhaps we will even see more arrangements that involve collaboration, cooperation, and adaptive management, undertaken by groups of people whose roles blend the public and private, groups like today's homeowner's association that are essentially private in operation but recognized by law and subject to legal constraint....

TENNESSEE ENVIRONMENTAL COUNCIL, INC. v. BRIGHT PAR 3 ASSOCIATES

2004 WL 419720 (Tenn. App. 2004).

WILLIAM H. INMAN, SR. J.

A conservation easement affecting property adjoining South Chickamauga Creek in Chattanooga was created in 1996. Property zoned for business and owned and developed by some of the Defendants is adjacent to the easement. The Plaintiffs allege that the development and construction activities of the Defendants adversely and unlawfully affect the easement. The complaint was dismissed upon a ruling that the Plaintiffs had no standing to enforce the easement, notwithstanding the language of the Conservation Easement Act, Tennessee Code Annotated § 66–9–301, et. seq., that it may be enforced by the "holder and/or beneficiaries" of the easement. The controversy centers on the meaning of the word "beneficiaries." We hold that any resident of Tennessee is a beneficiary of the easement, and thus has standing to enforce it.

I.

On May 1, 1996, the East Ridge Development Co., conveyed to the City of Chattanooga a conservation easement affecting 40 acres of land adjacent to Chickamauga Creek.

A conservation easement is a negotiated agreement between a landowner and certain nonprofit or governmental entities that are qualified to monitor and enforce the land use restrictions of the easement, all pursuant to certain federal and state regulations. There are several qualified organizations in Tennessee, most notably The Land Trust for Tennessee. The types and severity of the restrictions in conservation easements vary from agreement to agreement. If negotiations and research are carefully conducted, the restrictions should be tailored to fit both the long-term use plans of the landowner and the resource preservation goals of the qualified grantee.

The restrictions in a conservation easement generally prohibit use of the land that may adversely affect those resources that the easement intends to protect. For example, subdivision, development, significant commercial use (other than agriculture), clear-cutting of timber, strip mining, and billboard advertisements are commonly prohibited. Landowners are routinely able, however, to negotiate terms that will allow them to own, occupy, and perform a variety of activities on the property. These permitted activities may include, without limitation, residential occupancy, construction of new residential structures, construction of new agricultural structures, farming, hunting, camping, private airstrips, and equestrian activities.

Conservation easements are recorded in the public land records so as to be binding upon the then-current landowner and its successors in interest to the subject real property. That is, once a landowner has placed a conservation easement on its property, anyone purchasing or inheriting the land from that landowner will also be bound by the restrictions contained in the easement. The term of the easement is typically perpetual in nature, and the qualified grantee has no obligation to amend the restrictions should a landowner's desired use of the property be prohibited by the restrictions.

The creation of a conservation easement is authorized by Tennessee Code Annotated § 66–9–307 which provides, inter alia, and as pertinent here, that

> (c)onservation easements may be enforced by injunction or proceedings in equity by the holders and/or beneficiaries of the easement, or their bona fide representatives, heirs, or assigns.

II.

The complaint, as amended, alleges that the "Property" is owned and is being developed by the Defendants. The "Property" is alleged to be commercially zoned, and that it contains or has adjoining it wetland and conservation easement areas, protected under state and federal law, which drain directly into South Chickamauga Creek, a waterway subject to contaminant and discharge limitations under state and federal law. Further allegations are that a Wal–Mart Supercenter and adjoining strip mall are being constructed on the "Property" which would result in an illegal discharge of pollutants into South Chickamauga Creek and/or illegal alteration of the protected areas, and that site preparation has already resulted in damage to the protected areas. Irreparable harm is forecast unless the Defendants are restrained from further construction.

A temporary restraining order was issued on July 7, 2003, in accordance with the demand for relief, and scheduled for hearing on July 15, 2003. The Defendants filed motions to dissolve the temporary restraining order, alleging that the Plaintiffs cannot succeed on the merits, that there is no imminent threat of irreparable injury to the Plaintiffs or to the protected areas, and that the proposed injunction is contrary to the public interest.

At the July 15, 2003 hearing, the sole issue for resolution was whether the individual plaintiff, Ms. Kurtz, had the requisite standing to maintain this action. The Chancellor stated " ... we need to find out whether Ms. Kurtz has any injury separate and apart from that of the member of the public." Ms. Kurtz thereupon testified at length about her environmental concerns, her dedication and devotion to the preservation of the flora and fauna of the property described in the easement, that she was an independent, environment education consultant, that she serves on the Board of the Tennessee Environmental Council and related organizations. She conducts nature walks through the easement property, and generally enjoys its solace and solitude.

The Chancellor made a finding of fact that Ms. Kurtz suffered no injury "separate or different" from an injury that the public at large has sustained, and that under settled law in Tennessee she had no standing to file the action. The Chancellor further found that only the grantee, the City of Chattanooga, has standing to enforce the easement and accordingly dismissed the complaint.

The Plaintiffs appeal and present for review the issue of whether Ms. Kurtz or the organizational Plaintiffs have standing to enforce the conservation easement. We review the record *de novo*. Because the dispositive issue is one of law, there is no presumption of correctness. Our concern is focused on the dismissal of the complaint, which necessarily dissolved the temporary restraining order, in light of the language of the Conservation Easement Act, Tenn.Code Ann. § 66–9–307, that conservation easements may be enforced by the "holders and/or beneficiaries of the easement."

III.

The Chancellor held

> Paragraph 5 [of the easement].... sets out the grantee's remedies. It says this easement may be enforced by its holder or beneficiary. Grantee may bring an action for any remedies provided by Tennessee law. So the deed ... that creates the easement says the grantee, the City of Chattanooga, is the one who has the right to pursue for a remedy provided by law. The easement is created for the benefit of the citizens of Chattanooga, but they are not designated as benefi-

ciaries. They are not the grantee of the easement. The City of Chattanooga is.

We stress the language of the Act which provides that the conservation easement may be enforced by injunction or proceedings in equity by the holder and/or beneficiaries of the easement. The City of Chattanooga is the grantee, and thus the holder of the easement and obviously entitled to enforce the easement. Who are the beneficiaries?

We are bound to ascertain and give effect to the Legislative intent with no undue restriction or expansion of the statutory language. *Lavin v. Jordon,* 16 S.W.3d 362 (Tenn.2000). We think it evident that the phrase "by the holder and/or beneficiaries" means someone in addition to the grantee; otherwise, the words "and/or beneficiaries" would be utterly meaningless, and we are not at liberty to ignore this language. The word "beneficiaries" has a commonly accepted dictionary meaning: "those who benefit from the act of another." Who benefits from the act of the grantor in creating this easement? A conservation easement is "held for the benefit of the people of Tennessee." Tenn.Code Ann. § 66–9–303. We hold that any resident of Tennessee has standing to enforce it. This interpretation is consistent with the terms of the deed and the Act, both of which require a liberal construction of the word "beneficiaries." Superimposed is that the Act is a remedial one, and must be liberally construed to further and give effect to its purpose. *See, Loftin v. Langsdon,* 813 S.W.2d 475 (Tenn.Ct.App.1991). Further superimposed is the fact that the Legislature chose not to adopt the verbiage of the Uniform Act which precludes the enforcement of a conservation easement by any entity other than a governmental body, charitable corporation or association with the specific right granted in the document.

As stated, we have focused on the legal issue of standing, and express no opinion and make no findings respecting the merits of the case. The judgment of dismissal is reversed and the case is remanded for further proceedings.

We take note of the brief filed by Wal–Mart Real Estate Business Trust requesting that we consider the issue of whether the dismissal of the complaint against it was proper even if the Plaintiffs had the requisite standing. We are unable to respond for two reasons: First, the Chancellor did not rule on the specific issue, and secondly, it would be meaningless dictum for us to do so.

Notes

1. *Conservation easements and politics.* One of the challenges of promoting conservation in landscapes is to provide ways for the people living there to protect their interests. In this case, a conservation easement restricts private land, yet major commercial development was about to take place in violation of the easement terms. The easement ran in favor of the City of Chattanooga, which apparently was disinclined to enforce the valuable public property right that it held. Can we imagine why the city was

failing to act (and the kind of political clout that Wal–Mart might have had)? And what does the city's inaction say about the durability of conservation easements, particularly easements donated to government bodies? An easement is only as protective as the willingness and ability of the easement holder to enforce it. Government bodies are subject to political pressures, particularly by landowners who stand to gain economically if an easement goes unenforced. As for easements held by not-for-profit entities, the entities must have the capability to monitor compliance and seek legal enforcement, typically at their own expense. Consider the Tennessee Environmental Council, which brought this litigation to protect the public interest. The Council had no chance of receiving any monetary recovery or even recovering the costs of litigation. Enforcement, then, rests on the willingness of community-minded citizens to sacrifice in the public interest. How reliable and fair is this arrangement? In some settings, the amount of money at stake for the landowner is so high that a not-for-profit entity could stand little chance in the high-stakes game of expensive litigation.

2. *Standing for members of the public.* In this case, the court took an unusual legal tack and ruled that a member of the public who used land covered by a conservation easement could enforce the easement's terms. In many states, only the holders of easements can do so, and only government bodies or charitable organizations can hold them. The court ruled that Ms. Kurtz, the individual plaintiff, had standing as a member of the public to enforce the easement. Was it important that she was also an actual user of the land covered by the easement? What if the easement protected land that was not open to public access? Would she or anyone else have had standing to enforce the easement? Here, also, the deed conveying the easement stated that it could be enforced by the holder or a beneficiary. The beneficiaries were not identified. What if the deed had authorized enforcement only by the easement holder? Would the state statute still have authorized citizen enforcement on the ground that every citizen of the state is an implicit beneficiary of every conservation easement, regardless of easement language?

The underlying issue is when and whether members of the public have the legal ability to challenge resource-use practices that harm the public interest or that violate a law or property right. In the law of public nuisance, a citizen typically can sue to halt substantial harm to the public health, safety, and welfare only if the citizen satisfies the "special injury" standing requirement, which calls for a showing of injury different in kind from the injury suffered by members of the public generally. This standing requirement arose in the nineteenth century and was intended to do what it did: reduce significantly the ability of citizens to challenge industrial activities that caused environmental and social harm. The limitation on citizen standing meant that only government bodies could bring public nuisance actions, and government bodies (like the City of Chattanooga in this case) can sometimes prefer to let a nuisance continue.

KIDD v. JARVIS DRILLING, INC.

2006 WL 344755 (Tenn. Ct. App. 2006).

WILLIAM C. KOCH, JR.

This appeal arises from a dispute between an oil drilling company and a group of Scott County property owners regarding the company's plans to recover oil from the currently non-producing West Oneida Field. After the Tennessee Oil and Gas Board approved the company's unitization and secondary recovery plans, the property owners filed a petition in the Chancery Court for Davidson County seeking judicial review of the Board's decision....

I.

The West Oneida Field, located on the Fort Payne reservoir in Northeast Tennessee, was discovered in 1943. The first oil well was drilled in September 1969, and in 1979, the peak oil rate reached 1,720 barrels per day. By 1974, there were 51 producing oil wells and 13 natural gas wells on the field. By 1997, the number of oil wells had increased to 62, and the number of natural gas wells to 15. A majority of the producing wells were operated by Jarvis Drilling, Inc. (Jarvis Drilling), a Kentucky corporation that had possessed an ownership interest in the field since 1977.

By December 1996, the West Oneida Field had produced 1,452,355 barrels of oil or 12.9% of the estimated amount of oil originally in the field. However, production had fallen off significantly because of the release over the years of the natural gas that had provided the energy needed to extract the oil. Jarvis Drilling retained experts to assess the amount of oil remaining in the field and to recommend economically feasible alternatives for extracting the remaining oil. In December 1997, these experts reported that another 1,493,000 barrels of oil could be recovered from the West Oneida Field over twenty years using an enhanced secondary recovery process. The process recommended by the experts entailed injecting natural gas back into the field to increase the pressure in the reservoir. The experts anticipated that the re-pressurization of the field would drive the remaining oil to the downdip oil wells.

Accordingly, Jarvis Drilling set about to devise a financially viable secondary recovery plan to extract more oil from the West Oneida Field. Its plan had two key components. The first component was the unitization of the West Oneida Field.[6] The second component was the use of the field to store natural gas owned by others for a fee. This natural gas, referred to as "working gas," would aid in the re-pressurization of the

6. Unitization is an industry term for operating multiple tracts of land as a single tract for the purpose of producing oil or gas. Tenn. Comp. R. & Regs. 1040–1–1–.01 (1999) defines a "pooled unit" as "two or more tracts of land, of which their ownership may be different, that are consolidated and operated as a single tract for production of oil and/or gas, either by voluntary agreement between the owners thereof, or by exercising of the authority of the Board under the statute."

field and would be an additional source of income that would make the secondary recovery plan financially viable.

In April 2001, Jarvis Drilling filed a petition with the Tennessee Oil and Gas Board (Board) seeking the unitization of the West Oneida Field in accordance with Tenn. Comp. R. & Regs. 1040–5–1–.01 (1999). Jarvis Drilling also sought the Board's approval of its "pressure maintenance and secondary recovery project" under Tenn. Comp. R. & Regs. 1040–4–9–.03 (1999)....

The Board notified all affected persons of Jarvis Drilling's petition and of a contested case hearing set for June 10, 2002. This hearing was held in Nashville and was attended by representatives of Jarvis Drilling and several property owners and their lawyer who objected to the unitization plan. Jarvis Drilling presented a great deal of evidence regarding the technical details of its secondary recovery plan. It also presented evidence that 95.45% of the persons affected by its proposal had approved its secondary recovery project. The dissenting property owners, in turn, voiced their objections to unitization and gas storage. These objections were based on the property owners' belief that the proposed unitization plan did not compensate them adequately for their interests and that the plan, if implemented, would prevent them from obtaining natural gas from the field for personal use.[7] On November 12, 2002, the Board filed a final order approving the unitization plan as well as the pressure maintenance and secondary recovery project....

II.

.... The Board has promulgated rules defining the conditions that must be met before it will exercise its power under Tenn.Code Ann. § 60–1–202(a)(4)(M) to force unitization of a field. Unitization may be required only after the Board has determined that unitization (1) is necessary to conserve the State's natural resources, (2) will prevent waste of oil and gas and the drilling of unnecessary wells, (3) will appreciably increase the ultimate recovery of oil and gas from the affected pool, (4) is economically feasible, and (5) will protect the correlative rights of both landowners and owners of mineral rights. Tenn. Comp. R. & Regs. 1040–5–1–.01(1)(a) (1999). The Board must also see to it that the proposed unitization plan assures that the owners of the separate tracts receive their just and equitable share of the recoverable oil or gas in the unit, Tenn. Comp. R. & Regs. 1040–5–1–.01(1)(b), and that the cost of production is proportionately allocated among the separately owned tracts. Tenn. Comp. R. & Regs. 0140–5–1–.01(1)(d).

Projects involving subterranean natural gas storage must be approved by the Board following a public hearing. Tenn. Comp. R. & Regs. 1040–4–8–.01 (1999). The rules regarding subterranean natural gas

7. One property owner testified that four natural gas wells were located on her property and that she was obtaining natural gas from these wells for her private use, even though she was also connected to a private gas utility. Jarvis Drilling's witness explained that these wells would be capped for safety purposes because of the increased pressure in the field once re-pressurization began.

storage differentiate between reservoirs "capable of producing oil and gas in paying quantities" and reservoirs that cannot. With regard to reservoirs that are capable of producing oil and gas in paying quantities, the rule provides that the Board may not approve a subterranean gas storage project unless "all owners in such underground reservoir shall have agreed thereto in writing." Tenn. Comp. R. & Regs. 1040–4–8–.01(1), –01(2). . . .

III.

. . . . The property owners insist that the Board lacks authority to force unitization for the purpose of subterranean natural gas storage for two reasons. First, they argue that the Board's enabling statutes do not expressly empower the Board to require unit operations for subterranean natural gas storage. Second, they assert that, even if the Board has the authority to approve unit operations for natural gas storage, its regulations do not permit subterranean gas storage without the unanimous written approval of all owners in interest. The property owners are mistaken on both counts. . . .

B.

The Board has unquestioned statutory authority to approve and regulate secondary recovery projects. Tenn. Code Ann. § 60–1–202(a)(4)(K). While neither the statutes nor the Board's rules define "secondary recovery project," the term is commonly used in the industry to refer to the enhanced methods used to recover additional oil or to prolong the production of oil in fields where the primary production has run its course. The purpose of a secondary recovery project is to restore the pressure in the reservoir by mechanisms such as gas reinjection.

One of the Board's obligations is to prevent the waste of Tennessee's non-renewable oil and natural gas resources. Secondary recovery projects prevent waste by prolonging the economic life of older oil fields and by increasing the quantity of oil ultimately recovered from the reservoir. In a similar manner, unit operations also prevent waste by increasing the amount of oil produced in a particular field.

The Board's rules explicitly envision that field unitization may be a part of a secondary recovery project. Tenn. Comp. R. & Regs. 1040–4–9–.04 states that a unitization plan must be approved before approving a secondary recovery project when the common source of supply is not limited to a single lease. Thus, the Board's statutes and rules clearly permit the Board to impose unitization on an oil field for the purpose of operating a secondary recovery project.

The property owners assert that even if the Board has the power to approve forced unitization as part of the secondary recovery project, it does not have the power to permit the unit operator to engage in the subterranean gas storage business as part of the operation of a secondary recovery project. The enabling statutes and the rules do not support this argument.

Restoring the pressure in an oil field is accomplished by injecting natural gas back into the field. The unit operator may obtain the required natural gas in one of two ways. It may purchase the natural gas, or it may charge others to store their natural gas in the oil field. The net effect is the same whether the operator buys the natural gas or charges others to store the gas—the field is re-pressurized, and additional oil that would not otherwise be recovered is produced. Accordingly, the Board's broad statutory authority to regulate secondary recovery projects includes the authority to authorize subterranean gas storage as part of a secondary recovery project.

C.

Using a reservoir for subterranean gas storage may be part of a secondary recovery project. However, if the operator of a secondary recovery project intends to include subterranean gas storage as part of the secondary recovery project, then the operator must also comply with the Board's requirements for subterranean gas storage. The property owners insist that Jarvis Drilling cannot comply with these requirements because all the affected owners have not consented to the subterranean storage of natural gas in the West Oneida Field.

The property owners have misconstrued Tenn. Comp. R. & Regs. 1040–4–8–.01(1). This rule requires unanimous written agreement by all the owners of the underground reservoir only when the reservoir involved is "capable of producing oil and gas in paying quantities." The evidence before the Board demonstrates convincingly that the West Oneida Field is no longer capable of producing oil and gas in paying quantities. Therefore, Jarvis Drilling was not required to obtain the written consent of all owners before obtaining the Board's approval to use the West Oneida Field for subterranean gas storage....

IV.

As a final matter, the property owners assert that the Board erred by approving Jarvis Drilling's unitization plan for the West Oneida Field because (1) the proposed unitization plan is not economically feasible, (2) the proposed unitization agreement is not fair and equitable, and (3) the dissenting property owners cannot be charged for the cost of gas storage. We have determined that each of these arguments are misplaced.

Unitization plans must be economically feasible. Tenn. Comp. R. & Regs. 1040–5–1–.01(1)(a). The property owners, separating the proposed unitization plan from its gas storage component, insist that unitization of the West Oneida Field is not economically feasible because it would not be profitable without gas storage income. While the property owners are correct that the gas storage income is necessary to the economic feasibility of the project, they are incorrect when they argue that the secondary recovery project and the gas storage proposal should be considered separately. Subterranean gas storage is an integral part of the secondary recovery project because it is one of the ways that Jarvis Drilling plans to re-pressurize the West Oneida Field. Secondary recovery will not be possible without re-pressurization, and re-pressurization will necessitate injecting natural gas into the reservoir. Insofar as re-pressurization is concerned, it matters not how Jarvis Drilling obtains the natural gas. Accordingly, the Board acted properly when it considered the economic feasibility of Jarvis Drilling's unitization plan in light of the revenue Jarvis Drilling anticipated from natural gas storage.

Unitization plans must protect the correlative rights of the affected parties and must be just and equitable. Tenn. Comp. R. & Regs. 1040–5–1–.01(1)(a), (b). The property owners take issue with eight provisions in Jarvis Drilling's proposed unitization agreement and insist that the Board erred by approving the proposed agreement without separately considering the fairness of each provision in the agreement. We find no authority for requiring the Board to review each provision in a proposed unitization agreement, and, therefore, we decline to find that the Board erred by considering the entire agreement in light of the parties' testimony regarding its fairness.

An overwhelming number of affected property owners must have found the terms of the proposed unitization agreement to be just and equitable because they consented to it. In light of the overwhelming acceptance of the agreement, the dissenting property owners faced an uphill struggle to demonstrate to the Board how the proposed agreement was not just and equitable. Their evidence focused on their skepticism that they would receive any of the revenue from the secondary recovery project, their belief that they might have received more if Jarvis Drilling were required to negotiate with them individually, and their concern that they would no longer be permitted to use natural gas from the West Oneida Field for their personal use. The record reflects that the Board factored these concerns into its deliberations and then determined, based on its expertise, that the proposed unitization agreement was consistent with industry standards and that it was just and equitable. We will not second-guess the Board.

Finally, the dissenting property owners insist that the Board erred by approving a provision requiring that part of the costs of the natural gas storage portion of the secondary recovery project be deducted from their proceeds. They insist that the Board does not have the authority to require them to share in the costs of a subterranean gas storage program. We disagree because the gas storage program is an integral part of the secondary recovery project. The Board's rules expressly require affected property owners to pay their pro-rata share of the costs of the secondary recovery project.

Unit operations and secondary recovery projects are intended to benefit all affected owners by increasing the amount of oil recovered from a field. The Board's rules reflect a policy that owners who benefit from these projects must pay their fair share of the expenses reasonably incurred to extract the oil. These rules are intended to dissuade dissenting property owners from becoming "free riders."[8] They require property

8. In the parlance of economics, a "free rider" is a person who chooses to receive the benefits of a good or service without paying for it. Free riders are persons who

owners either to pay their pro-rata share of the costs of the project or to have between 150% and 350% of these costs deducted from their share of the proceeds. Tenn. Comp. R. & Regs. 1040–4–9–.07, 1040–5–1–.01(d).

The fact that Jarvis Drilling's proposal for the West Oneida Field contains a subterranean gas storage component does not transform the project into anything other than a secondary recovery project. Accordingly, Tenn. Comp. R. & Regs. 1040–4–9–.07 applies, and the Board, in its discretion, had the power to set the surcharge on dissenting property owners who declined to pay their pro-rata share of the costs of the secondary recovery project anywhere between 150% and 200% of their share of the actual costs. Based on the evidence, the Board determined that the surcharge to dissenting owners who did not contribute their pro-rata share of the production costs would be 200%. The record provides no legal or factual basis to disagree with this decision....

Notes

1. *Private condemnation IV: pooling and unitization.* From an early point in the nation's experience with oil and gas production, it became clear that landowners stood to gain if they could coordinate their exploitation activities. Fewer wells would be needed to extract the minerals from a reservoir, and carefully controlled extraction could remove more minerals overall. Coordination was even more important when it came to undertaking secondary recovery operations, which entail injecting a substance into an underground formation to lift the oil and gas or otherwise make it easier to extract. (Recall in the water law case of *Mathers v. Texaco* (chapter) the use of fossil aquifer water for this purpose.) Here, natural gas is being injected to pressurize the formation. Incidentally, the storage is valuable to the owner of the gas, who is paying for it and making the entire operation economically feasible.

Due to well-spacing and minimum drilling-size requirements many individual landowners often cannot drill because their land parcels are too small. Only if several landowners cooperate can drilling go on. The coordination of land parcels under such requirements is commonly called pooling. In many states a landowner can be compelled to engage in pooling involuntarily. Secondary and tertiary operations that cover entire fields are commonly called unitization, which in many states can also take place involuntarily. Note the standards that Tennessee law sets for the approval of involuntary unitization. The statute appears to protect landowner rights strictly, but it fails to do so in important ways. Most plainly, a landowner no longer has the right to say no; the statute effectively allows the use of private property over the landowner's objection (that is, it authorizes private condemnation). Beyond that, pooling and unitization effectively alter the rule of capture as among members of a pool or unit. The members share revenues on a correlative basis, which takes into account (but need not strictly follow) the relative acreages that people own. With production undertaken jointly,

take more than their fair share of benefits or who do not shoulder their fair share of the costs of their use of a resource.

landowners also lose control over the timing of production. Do the statutory requirements seem sufficient to protect landowner interests? Are they all necessary?

2. *Joint management.* In the case of pooling and unitization, the goals of landowners are largely the same—to maximize income from production while reducing risk. It is therefore understandable that mandatory pooling and unitization statutes gained legislative support even as they involved major revisions of private property rights as commonly understood. Petroleum pools and units also do not typically encounter anything like the kind of sharp management disagreements that we might expect in the case, for instance, of the Great Onyx Cave that was the subject of the Kentucky litigation in chapter two or with a nonnavigable lake that owners might want to use for widely varied purposes. In this regard the situation is like the lobster fisheries in Maine, where the fishers have roughly similar goals. Still, the pooling and unitization cases provide important legal precedents for compulsory resource management in the United States, sometimes on a wide spatial scale. The law in effect treats natural resources as jointly owned by the overlying landowners and authorizes the creation of private management entities to control the resource. While landowners representing a majority or supermajority of interests must support (and usually initiate) the planned pooling or unitization, minority landowners can no longer say no.

3. *Holdouts and free riders.* Forced participation in resource management makes the greatest sense in two rather similar factual settings. One case involves a resource that is effectively co-owned (like the underground storage capacity of a gas field) and that no one can use unless all owners consent. A single hold-out can halt the operation. Related to this is the situation in which expenditures to develop a resource benefit all landowners, whether or not they have contributed to it. When a well pumps oil from a shared reservoir and all overlying landowners share in the royalties, whether or not they have contributed to the costs of production, a free rider situation arises. A landowner can refuse to contribute to production costs while still enjoying the benefits—unless the law either denies the landowner the benefit or compels the landowner to contribute involuntarily. In the case of an open-access fishery, all fishers benefit from snag removal even when only a few exert the effort to perform it.

In many oil and gas settings, landowners today cannot be compelled to contribute to exploratory drilling costs even though they will participate in resulting royalties. They can stand aside as free riders. Typically, though, their shares of productions costs are subtracted from any royalties that they are owed. Also, they may be forced to pay extra costs (a double share) because they did not incur the risk of a dry hole. Holdout and free-rider problems arise frequently in natural resources law. Eminent domain has often been used to remedy these problems, though as we saw in chapter the "public use" requirement might now stand as a more formidable obstacle to its continued use.

4. *Why unanimity?* In the case of resources such as oil and gas, which are best exploited on a scale that often transcends property boundaries, why do we typically begin with the assumption that joint operations require the unanimous consent of all affected landowners? Why do we give individual

landowners the legal power to remain holdouts, thereby halting an activity supported by a majority of their neighbors?

Consider the common case of the residential subdivision with a homeowners association. The association might manage common areas that are co-owned by the residents. It might also regulate land uses, even in detail. These associations are legally valid because they are supported by restrictive covenants, which a developer imposed before the land was divided and lots sold. Under present law, covenants cannot be imposed after lots are sold unless each landowner consents to them. In the case of developer-imposed covenants, individual lot owners are deemed to have consented to an association and to its powers when they purchased their lots with knowledge of them. But how free is this consent, particularly in geographic regions in which essentially all homes are covered by them? And if buying a home is deemed consent to a homeowners' association, could we similarly say that a landowner consents merely by continuing to own a lot that is subject to a newly created association? That is, might we say that a landowner has the right to dissent from the creation of a new homeowners' association by selling her home rather than retaining ownership of it? Is the power to escape by selling an adequate level of landowner autonomy?

Consider as a further comparison the typical government body. Under many state statutes, a majority of residents in a region can create a new taxing authority empowered to acquire and operate parks or forest preserves or to perform other functions. Landowners need not support the institutions unanimously. Individual landowners can dissent only by escaping. Why might we allow for the creation of such government bodies, without unanimity, while requiring that landowners unanimously consent to restrictive covenants that create a private homeowners' association? Keep in mind, homeowners are subject to the regulatory actions of local government whether or not they consent to them. Is it an adequate response to say that government bodies are subject to constitutional limitations while private bodies such as homeowners' associations are not?

5. *Unanimity and private condemnation.* As you consider the issue of landowner unanimity, note its close similarity to the public use requirement in eminent domain law. Eminent domain is a way of dealing with holdouts. The more freely it is available the more readily we can give landowners the legal power to remain holdouts. The connection between these bodies of law–property law and public use/eminent domain–dates back for centuries.

Late in the seventeenth century various lords in England wanted to take control of (enclose) common lands, but they could often do so only by buying out users of the commons who possessed one form or another of secure use rights. Purchases took place voluntarily, but what happened when one or more users held out and refused to sell, thereby frustrating the lord's ability to enclose the commons? Was unanimous approval required, or could the holder of a super-majority of rights in the commons squeeze out the remaining users? In a 1689 ruling the English court of Chancery ruled that a super-majority of interests in a commons could take control (on the ground of "proper and natural equity") despite the opposition of "one or two humoursome tenants." Delabeere v. Beedingfield, 2 Vern 103, 23 Eng. Rep. 676 (1689). In a 1706 ruling, however, the court considered whether a supermajority could take control when the opposition included the rector of the local parish and nine other users of the commons. The court then held that "a right of common cannot be altered without the consent of all parties concerned therein." Bruges et Al' v. Curwin, 2 Vern 575, 23 Eng. Rep. 974 (1706). This ruling would have aroused great turmoil among larger landowners except that Parliament promptly stepped in and began enacting private bills that authorized particular landowners to enclose commons by paying off (often with allotments rather than cash) resistant users. The first bill apparently came before Parliament in 1710. According to historian E.P. Thompson, "once the private act of enclosure became possible, it was clear that *enclosure* might not take place unless by due parliamentary process even if one humoursome landowner dissented." E.P. Thompson, Customs in Common: Studies in Traditional Popular Culture (1993), 109. Parliament did not begin routinely enacting private bills authorizing enclosure until after 1760. As Thompson reports, "the great age of parliamentary enclosure, between 1760 and 1820, is testimony not only to the rage for improvement but also to the tenacity with which 'humoursome' or 'spiteful' fellows blocked the way to enclosure by agreement, holding out to the last for the old customary economy." *Id.*, 110. The Parliamentary bills were essentially authorizations of private condemnation, undertaken directly for the private benefit of the enclosing lords and indirectly for the economic benefit of the larger community.

SUSTAINABLE GROWTH INITIATIVE COMMITTEE v. JUMPERS, LLC

128 P.3d 452 (Nev. 2006).

Rose, C.J.

In this appeal, we address a challenge to a growth initiative adopted by the voters in Douglas County, Nevada. In 2002, the voters of Douglas County passed the Sustainable Growth Initiative (SGI), which limited the number of new dwelling units in the county to 280 per annum. The SGI was challenged as being inconsistent with the Douglas County Master Plan (Master Plan), and the parties filed competing motions for summary judgment. The district court found that the SGI conflicted with the Master Plan and held the SGI void *ab initio*. The Sustainable Growth Initiative Committee (the SGIC) appeals that decision, arguing that the SGI is in substantial compliance with the Master Plan and should not be defeated on summary judgment. We agree with the SGIC and hold that the SGI is not so inconsistent as to require us to strike down the will of the people by holding it invalid. Thus, we reverse the decision of the district court.

Facts

The SGIC was formed for the purpose of qualifying an initiative to limit residential growth in the Carson Valley and the Antelope Valley drainage basins on a sustainable, managed basis. The SGI was submitted and approved for the November 2002 ballot. The SGI read:

> Shall Douglas County adopt an ordinance amending its development code to provide that no more than 280 new dwelling units shall be built annually in Douglas County, exclusive of the area regulated by the Tahoe Regional Planning Agency (TRPA), except in a disaster emergency declared by the Board of County Commissioners?

The SGI passed with a total vote of 53.22 percent. Several parties (collectively Jumpers) immediately thereafter filed an action seeking injunctive and declaratory relief. The SGIC was permitted to intervene in the action, and following a hearing, the district court granted Jumpers' application for a temporary restraining order....

The district court heard the summary judgment motions in February 2003 and found that the SGI was inconsistent with the Douglas County Master Plan. It granted summary judgment in favor of Jumpers and Douglas County and denied the SGIC's summary judgment motion. The district court stated, "Although [the] SGI is consistent with the Master Plan's goal of establishing a growth cap, it is completely inconsistent with the Plan's methodology for doing so, and frustrates other facets of the Plan's vision for orderly growth and development." ...

Discussion

.... The appeals and cross-appeals before us today address three main issues—whether the SGI substantially complies with the Master Plan, whether the SGI is facially constitutional, and whether the SGI will require an amendment within three years of its enactment in order to implement, apply, or adopt the SGI. We have carefully considered all of the parties' arguments and conclude that only the arguments hereinafter addressed merit discussion.

The SGI's compliance with the Douglas County Master Plan

The district court granted summary judgment in favor of respondents, finding that the SGI did not substantially comply with the Master Plan. The SGIC appeals that determination, arguing first that the SGI is a new legislative policy and, therefore, is not required to substantially comply with the Master Plan. Alternatively, the SGIC argues that the district court erred by finding that the SGI does not substantially comply with the Master Plan. We disagree that the SGI is a new legislative policy, which is not required to substantially comply with the Master Plan. We agree, however, that the district court erred by finding that the SGI did not substantially comply with the Master Plan as a matter of law.

The SGI is required to substantially comply with the Master Plan

All counties with populations of 40,000 or more people must create a planning commission. The planning commission is responsible for creating and adopting a comprehensive, long-term master plan for the county's physical development. The purpose of a master plan is to provide "[a] pattern and guide for that kind of orderly physical growth and development of the ... county which will cause the least amount of natural resource impairment and will conform to the adopted population plan, where required, and ensure an adequate supply of housing, including affordable housing." The Douglas County Master Plan was approved and adopted by the Board of Commissioners (the Board) in 1996.

A county's governing body can create zoning districts in order to "regulate and restrict the erection, construction, reconstruction, alteration, repair or use of buildings, structures or land." Adopted zoning regulations must be in accordance with the master plan. When adopting zoning regulations, the governing body must give reasonable consideration "to the character of the area and its peculiar suitability for particular uses, and with a view to conserving the value of buildings and encouraging the most appropriate use of land throughout the city, county or region."

The SGIC acknowledges that zoning ordinances and variances must be in substantial compliance with the Master Plan. It argues, however, that the SGI is a new legislative policy, not a zoning ordinance, and, as such, is not required to substantially comply with the Master Plan. The SGIC cites *Garvin v. District Court* as conclusive authority that the SGI is a new legislative policy that is not subject to substantial compliance requirements. In *Garvin,* we stated that the SGI is "policy-driven, and is legislative in character. Executing this new policy will be an administrative matter."

The SGIC's reliance on *Garvin* in support for its argument is misplaced. As pointed out by Syncon, the question of the SGI's precise status in regard to substantial compliance was not the issue before us in *Garvin.* In *Garvin,* we merely addressed whether the SGI was legislative or administrative in nature, thereby either allowing a vote or precluding it from appearing on the ballot. Thus, *Garvin* is not wholly controlling.

The Nevada Constitution reserves the power of initiative to voters of a county as to all "local, special and municipal legislation of every kind in or for such county." The voters' initiative power is not without limits, however, and, indeed, the voters have only those legislative powers that the local governing body possesses.

Black's Law Dictionary defines "policy" as "general principles by which a government is guided in its management of public affairs, or the legislature in its measures." By classifying the SGI as a "policy," it would have no practical effect other than to be treated as a guideline. At the county level, legislation is adopted as ordinances. To have legal effect and achieve the desired 280–unit per annum limit, the SGI must be enacted as a zoning ordinance under the Douglas County development code. Further, the SGI states, "Shall Douglas County adopt an ordinance *amending its development code* to provide that no more than 280 new dwelling units shall be built annually in Douglas County?" (Emphasis added.) In the SGI ballot explanation, a similar statement is made that the initiative proposes to amend the development code. As a zoning ordinance, the SGI must substantially comply with the Master Plan.

Thus, the SGIC's argument that the SGI is a new policy and, therefore, not subject to substantial compliance fails.

The SGI is not substantially noncompliant as a matter of law

"[A] presumption of validity attaches to local zoning enactments and amendments." Additionally, the master plan of a community is a " 'standard that commands deference and a presumption of applicability,' " but it is not a legislative mandate from which no leave can be taken. Thus, although the SGI is entitled to a presumption of validity, the Master Plan is also entitled to deference.

In *Lesher Communications v. Walnut Creek,* the California Supreme Court announced what is known as the "consistency requirement." It said,

> A zoning ordinance that conflicts with a general plan is invalid at the time it is passed. The court does not invalidate the ordinance. It does no more than determine the existence of the conflict. It is the preemptive effect of the controlling state statute, the Planning and Zoning Law, which invalidates the ordinance.

Thus, the California Supreme Court held that zoning ordinances that conflict with the master plan are void *ab initio*. In *Nova Horizon v. City Council, Reno,* we expressed a similar "consistency requirement," noting that under NRS 278.250(2) " 'zoning regulations shall be adopted in accordance with the master plan for land use.' " We further stated that "[t]his suggests that municipal entities must adopt zoning regulations that are in substantial agreement with the master plan." We have since reiterated this requirement, but have also explained that a zoning ordinance need not be in perfect conformity with every master plan policy. The relevant inquiry is not whether there is a direct conflict between a master plan's provision and an ordinance, but whether the ordinance "is compatible with, and does not frustrate, the [master] plan's goals and policies."

In the present case, the SGIC notes that the relevant Master Plan goals are: to enhance Douglas County citizens' way of life, to ensure equal access and opportunities to all Douglas County citizens, to adopt future growth management tools to direct future growth and land use, to protect and enhance every aspect of Douglas County's natural resources, to protect the County's agricultural resources, and to ensure orderly development and limit the potential of natural hazards.

A portion of the introduction to the Master Plan reflects these goals:

> A number of common and consistent themes were evident from the public discussion. First, many residents feel strongly that Douglas County is an excellent place to live, work, and raise their children. They feel strongly that protection of this high quality of life and the particular features which make this County so attractive should be a high priority. The theme "keep our rural character" was heard many times and in many different ways from residents.

Most residents acknowledge and support continued growth, but believe that growth should be managed or directed and should occur at a pace that doesn't overwhelm or negatively impact the current attributes of the County. Most residents also indicated that the County should live within its means, both fiscally and environmentally, and not grow beyond the limits imposed by financial ability or natural resources. Finally, most residents agree that new development should pay its own way and should not be a burden on existing residents.

The SGIC appropriately notes that the argument in favor of the SGI included in the sample ballot echoes these themes by stating, "a large number of citizens of Douglas County are concerned about excessive residential growth and want to slow it down before the quality of life, property taxes, and natural resources, particularly water, are negatively impacted." The SGI clearly mirrors the policies and concerns of the Master Plan. Thus, the SGI is substantially compliant with Master Plan policies and goals. The district court, however, found that the SGI was inconsistent and incompatible with certain Master Plan goals. Although we hold that the SGI is not inconsistent with the Master Plan as a matter of law, we conclude that five purported inconsistencies merit our discussion—the building cap, conservation of natural resources, public facilities and fiscal responsibility, affordable housing, and transferable development rights and development agreements.

Building cap

The SGIC argues that the SGI is substantially consistent with the Master Plan because the Master Plan anticipated a residential building limit. We previously stated that "[t]he Douglas County Master Plan anticipated a future limitation on growth, but it did not establish one. The initiative's proponents evidently decided that the time was ripe, and chose to change the Master Plan by establishing a general building cap on residential units to regulate growth."

Under NRS 278.160(1)(g), a master plan must establish "[a]n estimate of the total population which the natural resources of the city, county or region will support on a continuing basis without unreasonable impairment."[9] The jurisdiction's related zoning ordinances must also protect the natural resources from unreasonable impairment and conform to the adopted population plan.

The Master Plan's growth management goal, Goal 9.03, states, "To accommodate new development at a pace which can be adequately served by available community facilities and services." The Master Plan also provides that "[i]n order to protect both the County's financial and natural resources, the County should adopt a building permit allocation system covering residential uses." As such, under the Master Plan, "[a] growth rate between 2 and 3.5 percent annually is suggested to attain"

9. A master plan must also be coordinated with the master plans of adjoining regions. NRS 278.170(1).

the goal of managing growth while not negatively impacting the community.

The 280–unit per annum cap reflects approximately a 2 percent increase in population from the 2000 census population figures. Respondents argue that this percentage will necessarily decrease each year as the 280 units are added to Douglas County's population base. Although this is true, the 2 percent increase is nonetheless consistent with the Master Plan. The residents of Douglas County voted specifically to control growth at the lowest level recommended by the Master Plan. We cannot say that the mere fact that the level of growth may fall below 2 percent in the future renders the SGI substantially noncompliant as a matter of law.

As respondent points out, the Master Plan states that the County's building permit allocation should be tied to both a capital improvements planning program and hydrological studies in order to protect the County's financial and natural resources. Although not tied to hydrological studies or a capital improvements planning program, the 280–unit per annum cap is tied to the Master Plan's recommended population growth. Because the SGI is tied to population growth, it is not inconsistent with the Master Plan even though not tied to hydrological studies or a capital improvements plan. There is no assurance that the SGI will continue in perpetuity, and after the three-year limitation on amending an initiative, the voters can amend or repeal the initiative. Thus, the SGI's 280–unit per annum cap is not inconsistent with the Master Plan.

Conservation, development, and utilization of natural resources

NRS 278.160(1)(b) requires a master plan to create a conservation plan for the development and utilization of natural resources, including water. The jurisdiction's related zoning ordinances also must protect the natural resources from unreasonable impairment. The Master Plan included a plan for estimated water demand through 2015. It concludes that the current underground water resources are sufficient until the population approaches 47,000 people. Thereafter, the annual recharge of the underground water supply would be insufficient to meet continuing needs, and it would be necessary to use surface water to recharge the groundwater basin and/or store the surface water to meet the population demands.

Simply because the water studies demonstrate that the water supply is adequate for 47,000 people does not require the citizens of Douglas County to allow expeditious growth until that population number is reached. In fact, the SGI's growth cap serves to conserve water, in accordance with the Master Plan. And there is nothing in the SGI that prevents the Board from otherwise creating a conservation plan for the development and utilization of natural resources.

Public facilities and fiscal responsibility

The Master Plan identifies several goals and policies establishing the County's commitment to maintaining existing levels of service within fiscal means and ensuring that growth will not take place beyond the county's financial capabilities. Douglas County argues that this makes the County's tying of a building permit allocation system to the County's capital improvement plan legally supportable. Douglas County argues that none of the capital improvement plan reports indicate that planned projects are negatively impacting the County's fiscal health. The Nevada Association of Realtors (NVAR) argues that the 280–unit cap ignores economic and public service plan considerations and circumvents Master Plan policy critical to the public welfare. The NVAR also notes a conflict with promoting future economic stability.

At issue are two general obligation bonds held by Douglas County for water and sewer projects that are secured by pledged revenues from connection fees. These fees are directly related to the number of new residences built. The bonds were issued based on sewer and water rate studies of a 3.5 percent annual growth rate. Therefore, NVAR asserts that the SGI's 280–unit cap will cause a revenue shortfall that will have to be satisfied through the general fund or increased utility rates.

Although Douglas County's fiscal health is of the utmost importance, the SGI is not so substantially noncompliant with the Master Plan as to require this court to strike it down for that reason. . . .

Affordable housing

NRS 278.160(1)(e)(8) requires that a master plan contain a housing plan that includes a provision for the development and maintenance of affordable housing. The Master Plan notes that growth control programs can cause escalation of housing prices and that empirical studies on that issue have shown mixed results. The primary Master Plan step to promote the housing goals is the set-aside provision for the building permit allocation program. Master Plan Policies 8.02.01 and 8.02.04 promote affordable housing projects and order development code revisions incorporating incentives for the development of housing to aid seniors and the disabled. Douglas County incorporated the policies into its code. Douglas County argues that the SGI overrides these provisions and enactments by creating an inflexible 280–unit cap that makes no provision to support affordable housing. Nevada Northwest agrees and argues that because the cap reduces by half the average number of permits Douglas County issues and the cap ties itself to new units rather than permits, the SGI does not ensure that there is an adequate supply of affordable housing. We do not agree.

As noted by the SGIC, if the SGI had been drafted to specify the number of building permits allocated for affordable housing versus other competing housing needs, we would have likely held it to be administrative in nature and thus an invalid initiative. Also, there is no evidence that the 280–unit cap will create an affordable housing problem, and nothing prevents Douglas County from allocating a certain number of the 280 units to affordable housing. . . .

Transferable development rights/development agreements

The SGIC argues that the district court erred by finding that the SGI violated Nevada Constitution Article 1, Section 15, which proscribes that any law impairing a contract obligation is invalid. The contracts at issue are transferable development rights[10] (TDR) and development agreements, which are permissible under the Douglas County Development Code. The SGIC asserts that NRS 278.0201(3) clearly establishes that subsequent changes in the law do not apply to preexisting development agreements. NRS 278.0201(3) states:

> This section does not prohibit the governing body from adopting new ordinances, resolutions or regulations applicable to that land which do not conflict with those ordinances, resolutions and regulations in effect at the time the agreement is made, except that any subsequent action by the governing body must not prevent the development of the land as set forth in the agreement. The governing body is not prohibited from denying or conditionally approving any other plan for development pursuant to any ordinance, resolution or regulation in effect at the time of that denial or approval.

By its plain language, NRS 278.0201(3) does not prohibit the SGI. And there is nothing to indicate that had the Board implemented a permit cap, TDRs and development agreements would have been better protected or not affected. There is also nothing to indicate that a higher building permit cap would remedy any TDR or development agreement issues that may arise. Further, the purpose of the TDR is to protect the rural lifestyle, which the SGI arguably accomplishes by limiting development. Respondents have failed to meet their burden of proving that the TDR program and development agreements are so affected by the SGI as to render it substantially noncompliant with the entire Master Plan as a matter of law.

Although we acknowledge that there are inconsistencies between the SGI and certain provisions of the Master Plan, after comparing the SGI to the Master Plan as a whole, we cannot say that as a matter of law the SGI is noncompliant to an extent that would require us to usurp the will of the people. Ultimately, the district court might strike down the SGI at trial after finding that these inconsistencies render the SGI substantially noncompliant. However, we cannot hold that, at this stage in the proceedings and with the evidence before us, respondents have met their summary judgment burden to demonstrate inconsistency as a matter of law. . . .

Amendment of the initiative

Amendment of an initiative is prohibited within the first three years of its passage. Additionally, NRS 295.180(1) states:

10. TDR is a concept that allows a private landowner to "sever his development rights in an area where development is objectionable and transfer them to an area where development is less objectionable." Andrew J. Miller, *Transferable Development Rights in the Constitutional Landscape: Has Penn Central Failed to Weather the Storm?*, 39 Nat. Resources J. 459, 465 (1999).

> When a majority of the registered voters of the county voting upon the question submitted, by their vote, approve the act or resolution, it is the law of the State, and may not be repealed, overruled, annulled, set aside or in any way made inoperative, except by a direct vote of the registered voters of that county.

The district court found that, given the brevity of the SGI, any adoption by the County through ordinance would entail amending the SGI. It noted that it might be appropriate to allocate the 280–unit permits between various types of housing, *i.e.*, affordable, single-family, and timeshares. Primarily, the court found that the conflict with the Master Plan would create the greatest need to amend the SGI after implementation. We disagree.

It must first be noted that the district court, in its amended order, determined that this issue was moot because it held the SGI void *ab initio*. In the interest of judicial economy, we exercise our power to address constitutional issues *sua sponte* to resolve this issue. There is nothing on the face of the SGI that precludes the Board from allocating the 280–unit permits between various types of housing or offering incentives to developers to create affordable housing. Such an allocation would not require amending the SGI. We have also concluded that as a matter of law, the SGI is not inconsistent with the Master Plan and, therefore, the district court's finding that inconsistencies with the Master Plan would require amendment of the SGI within three years is error.

Conclusion

Douglas County residents were concerned with maintaining, conserving, preserving and protecting their way of life and, as such, the majority of Douglas County residents voted to keep the rural character of their community. We conclude that, based upon the evidence before the district court, the SGI is substantially compliant with the Master Plan to survive summary judgment and, as such, we will not upset the will of the people by holding the SGI invalid.

Accordingly, we reverse the district court's orders granting summary judgment and remand for further proceedings.

Notes

1. *Shared governance VIII: who decides and how?* In this unfolding land-use drama, four actors play major roles. First, the *state* has required that counties undertake county-wide planning and that they adopt comprehensive, long-term master plans that meet various requirements. The plans must cover the conservation of natural resources, while providing for their development and utilization. All ordinances and other land-use actions taken by the county—including rezoning ordinances, which are legislative acts—must conform with this master plan, unless and until the plan is changed. Second, there is *Douglas County*, which has adopted a plan, apparently in conformity with state law. County leaders had their own ideas about the best

rate of residential growth. Third, there are *private citizens* who sought to control growth more firmly than did the county leaders. Under state law they proposed a voter initiative that was passed by a majority of county voters, adopting the SGI. And then there are the *courts*, including the state supreme court, which was called upon to determine whether the SGI was or was not consistent with the county master plan, and thus consistent with state statutes. Once you get the legal issues straight, consider how power is allocated among these four actors. Note that, given the outcome of the case, all four actors have options to influence future events. The trial court can still declare the SGI void as inconsistent with the county master plan. The county if it wants can change its master plan, bringing it into alignment with the SGI. The state legislature could enact a statute specifically approving the SGI, insulating it from challenge under state law (or instead striking it down). And voters could begin a new initiative to supplement the SGI, reducing its conflict with the Douglas County plan. The case is thus a vivid illustration of divided governmental power and of the practical challenges of shared governance. As you consider these actors, pay attention to their quite different ways of making decisions. Which methods of decision-making are most likely to promote the long-term welfare of the community as a whole?

2. *Planning and consistency.* Nevada law is typical of state law in requiring local governments to prepare comprehensive land-use plans and insisting that individual land-use decisions be consistent with the plans. The Nevada court on this issue cites the highly influential ruling of the California Supreme Court in *Lesher Communications v. City of Walnut Creek*, 52 Cal.3d 531, 277 Cal.Rptr. 1, 802 P.2d 317 (1990), which clarified the consistency requirement as applied to an initiated growth-control ordinance. Note how the Nevada court explains this requirement, pointing out that state law does not require "perfect conformity."

The requirement that individual zoning actions be undertaken in accordance with a comprehensive plan has been a central element of state zoning laws for nearly a century. The idea is that governments should not regulate land uses on a parcel-by-parcel basis, but should instead develop plans covering wide regions while considering communal needs comprehensively and dealing with landowners fairly. The idea sounded good when first inserted into state statutes (circa 1920) but it has proven hard to implement given changing circumstances. Local governments found themselves wanting to alter plans constantly. They also by steps shifted toward a much different model of land-use regulation based on negotiations with individual developers. Recent generations of land-use laws typically require various permits before development can take place, and permits terms are worked out on a case-by-case basis, not in accordance with clear, predictable standards. For these reasons and others, most state courts have not applied the consistency requirement with real rigor. Instead, they have looked for evidence that local governments do their best to consider larger contexts and the long-term; that they embrace processes designed to pay attention to the full range of factors, even if they cannot put together overall plans that have much binding force. As the next case illustrates, the danger of parcel-by-parcel action, treating adjacent landowners quite different, remains real.

3. *Redefining the right to develop.* In light of the SGI (assuming it remains valid), how would we best describe the right of landowners in

Douglas County to build houses? Home construction requires a building permit, and only 280 are available in the county each year. These permits are, obviously, a scarce natural resource use right, and the county board now faces the very issues that we have taken up in this course. What methods of allocation might make good sense? Will the permits be transferable and how long might they last? Presumably permits will be allocated only to owners of land that is suitable for home construction, but is this essential or even wise? If development permits are transferable, the permits themselves would have considerable economic value. If government is handing out valuable permits, why give them only to landowners? Why not allocate them based on a lottery in which all citizens have equal chances to obtain them? Or why not offer them for sale to the highest bidder? Why not give them to charities, which can then resell them?

The problem with these latter options, of course, is that they deprive landowners of all inherent development rights. So long as only owners of vacant land can gain development permits, we can assert that landowners still have a development right of sorts: they have the right to wait in line with other landowners, perhaps for decades, for their turn to get a building permit. Plainly, this development right is a faint echo of what landowners once had, back when they could develop essentially at will. Has the time come, perhaps, to address the issue of development rights more directly, and ask whether landowners should give them up entirely? Under the SGI landowners have little control (save through political clout) over the *initiation* of development. What they retain is the right to enjoy the economic benefits when and if development is finally allowed. While that economic benefit is plainly important, the economic value (in the case of vacant land) is value created by the community, not the landowner (as we saw in chapter 4). Should this idea ever gain widespread acceptance in the United States (as it has in certain other countries), landowners might finally lose even this last bit of their once vast development powers.

IN RE REALEN VALLEY FORGE GREENES ASSOCIATES

576 Pa. 115, 838 A.2d 718 (2003).

Justice Lamb.

We granted allowance of appeal to consider the validity of the agricultural zoning of a tract located in the heart of one of the most highly developed areas in the region, entirely surrounded by an urban landscape, and immediately adjacent to what is currently the world's largest shopping complex at one discrete location: the Court and the Plaza at King of Prussia. We hold that this agricultural zoning, designed to prevent development of the subject property and to "freeze" its substantially undeveloped state for over four decades in order to serve the public interest as "green space", constitutes unlawful "reverse spot zoning" beyond the municipality's proper powers. Therefore, we reverse the order of the intermediate appellate court upholding the validity of the legislation.

The subject property, located in Upper Merion Township (Township), Montgomery County, is the site of the Valley Forge Golf Club (Golf

Club), about 135 acres of landscaped links located at the confluence of the region's primary arterial highways and immediately adjacent to one of the most intensely developed commercial areas in the region. The Golf Club is owned by the Hankin Family Partnership and is the subject of a conditional agreement of sale to Realen Valley Forge Greenes Associates (Realen), Appellant herein. The Township's consulting land planner, John Rahenkamp & Associates, in an analysis of the Golf Club's zoning in June 1984, described the critical location of the property in these terms.

> There are six (6) major limited access highways that service the King of Prussia area, four (4) of them actually begin at the [Golf Club] site (Schuylkill Expressway, PA Turnpike, Route 202, County Line Expressway).... The fact that the site is uniquely accessible and is essentially at the hub of such a major road network, places an extremely heavy pressure on the site. Added to this is the reality that there is very little vacant land as a single large parcel in the adjacent Valley Forge Industrial Park, especially with the visibility of the Golf Course site.

The Golf Club opened in the 1920's, several decades before the Township enacted its first zoning regulations. In 1953 the Township created an AG–Agricultural Zoning District (AG District) and so designated a substantial portion of the Township including the Valley Forge Park, the Golf Club, and more than 1,500 acres of land surrounding the Club. Uses of land permitted by right in the AG–District, both then and now, are limited to municipal, single-family detached homes and agriculture. Upper Merion Township Zoning Ordinance § 165–10(A)—(D).

Between 1955 and 1990 the vast majority of the properties within the AG District were rezoned to permit intense commercial development. As the trial court here wrote:

> [S]ince the date of its creation, portions of the AG district have been rezoned, many to commercial uses, reducing the district to its current parameters containing the golf course and two other properties [a 7.3 acre parcel improved with Pennsylvania Turnpike Interchange No. 24 and its associated highway ramps and toll plaza and a one-half acre parcel improved with a nonconforming residential structure] previously identified. The last such change or reduction in the district's size occurred in 1985 ... with the most significant revisions taking place between 1955 and 1960, when areas including the present Valley Forge Industrial Park, King of Prussia Mall, General Electric, Acme and Valley Forge Convention Center Areas were rezoned.

Trial Ct. slip op. at 6.

The trial court described the properties surrounding the Golf Club, noting that those in the Township were all within the AG District in the early 1950's, and the current state of their zoning and development, in these terms:

> Across North Gulph Road lies an area zoned SM–Suburban Metropolitan, within which district there is located a combination of restaurant, hotel, and office uses. Beyond North Warner Road is found an area zoned C–2 Commercial, containing a Home Depot store, a bank, a gas station and a convenience store, and, below DeKalb Pike, within an AR–Administrative Research district, are located a number of office buildings. To the west, as one crosses the boundary line of Upper Merion Township, Delaware (sic) County into Tredyffrin Township, Chester County, there are to be found three different zoning districts, consisting of an HO–Hotel Office district, a P–Professional Office district and the Glenhardie Condominium situate within the OA–Office Apartment district.

Trial Ct. slip op. at 3–4.

On July 13, 1964 the Township governing body enacted Ordinance No. 64–141 which provided that:

> The Township has a general plan (here in after [sic] called General Plan) of its parks, playgrounds, recreation areas and facilities which plan has been on file at the office of the Township; and
>
> . . .
>
> There is hereby located and superimposed ... a recreation area, being all of the land and appurtenances thereon of the Valley Forge Golf Club, said located generally in the area of the Township ... the same consisting of approximately 138 acres.

R.R. 255a–256a. The purpose of Ordinance No. 64–141 can be understood only with reference to Sections 1907–1 and 1907–2 of the Act of May 1, 1933, P.L. 103, added by the Act of July 2, 1953, P.L. 354, to the Second Class Township Code, as it then was, 53 P.S. §§ 66907.1 and 66907.2, which authorized the creation of "A GENERAL PLAN OF [The township's] parks, recreation areas, and facilities, including those which may have been or may be laid out but not opened." Once such a general plan was created and filed, "[a]ll subdivisions of property thereafter made shall conform thereto." Moreover, for a maximum period of three years:

> No person shall hereafter be entitled to recover any damages for the taking for public use of any buildings or improvements of any kind which may be placed or constructed upon or within the lines of any located park or recreation area after the same shall have been located or ordained by the township supervisors.

Section 1907.2 of the Second Class Township Code, 53 P.S. § 66907.2 (repealed).

Thus, the purpose and effect of Township Ordinance 64–141 was to preclude any further development or improvement of the Golf Club or its facilities for three years. The Golf Club challenged the validity of Ordinance No. 64–141 and the enabling provisions of the Second Class Township Code by complaint in equity and the trial court, in a decision dated January 14, 1966 on the Golf Club's motion for judgment on the pleadings, reported as *Valley Forge Golf Club v. Upper Merion Township,* 39 D. & C.2d 181, 187 (Montg.Cty.1965), held Ordinance No. 64–141 unconstitutional as depriving the Golf Club without compensation of the full enjoyment of its property.

On the failure of its initial legislative action, the Township sought to create public support for a bond issue, the proceeds of which were to be used to acquire the Golf Club property. By ballot question, the Township referred to the electorate in November 1965, the issue of whether to incur $2 Million in debt "for the purpose of providing funds for and toward the acquisition of lands and buildings known as the Valley Forge Golf Club. . . ." R.R. 266a. In a brochure distributed to Township residents, the governing body made the following representations, among others, in support of the proposed acquisition.

> The Board unanimously believes it is of utmost importance that the Valley Forge Golf Course remain as a green, open area in Upper Merion Township. . . .
>
> The acquisition of the Golf Course will, by no means, benefit only those who play golf, but is a vital necessity as far as maintaining green areas before the last of our good, green areas is gobbled up. In addition, it is for the welfare of the human being to enjoy natural green areas in view of the ever-increasing jungle of cement and steel all about us . . . . .
>
> A privately-owned golf club, the course consists of 135 acres of rolling, green property including several buildings. . . . It is the last major open space, green area—not designated for any type of residential or commercial development—remaining in the 17–square mile township. The township supervisors and local planning commission never have considered the tract for development. The township comprehensive plan, a complete program for orderly community development lists the area as open, green space. Development of the land for other purposes would create a serious imbalance in the township. . . .

The governing body's campaign was successful and the bond issue was approved by the electorate. The Township created a municipal authority, denominated the Upper Merion-Valley Forge Municipal Authority, pursuant to the Municipal Authorities Act of 1945, the Act of May 2, 1945, P.L. 382, *as amended,* 53 P.S. § 301 *et seq.,* for the purpose of acquiring the Golf Club's lands and operating a public golf course thereon. By resolution of November 4, 1968, the authority resolved to initiate the condemnation. A declaration of taking was filed by the authority two days later on November 6, 1968. The Golf Club responded with the interposition of preliminary objections to the declaration of taking challenging, *inter alia,* the power of the condemnor and the sufficiency of the posted security. By opinion and order entered August 3, 1970, the trial court sustained the Golf Club's objections, set aside the declaration of taking, and ordered title to the lands revested in the Golf Club.

The Township, by its municipal authority, perfected an appeal to this Court but then, by Township Resolution No. 70–63 taken November 16, 1970, authorized the solicitor to withdraw the appeal and to "terminate all actions and activities relating to the purchase of the Golf Course by either the Upper Merion-Valley Forge Municipal Authority or the township." R.R. 280a. The following explanation of this action appears in the minutes of governing body's meeting conducted on November 16, 1970.

> In view of the cost of pursuing the acquisition to the higher courts, the recent court decision and the cost of acquisition, it would not be in the best interest of the Township. *The recent decision of the Courts enables the Board to control the use of the land for open space by zoning.*

Id. (emphasis supplied).

During this period, the Golf Club and prospective purchasers thereof initiated the first of a series of requests for a rezoning of the subject lands addressed to the Township governing body. By a "citizen's petition" filed on April 11, 1967, the Golf Club attempted to avail itself of the authority now codified at Zoning Ordinance § 165–260 under which the owners of more than fifty (50%) percent of the lands in a described area may by petition request a modification of the zoning regulations applicable to their lands. The Golf Club requested a rezoning of about sixty acres of the tract to SM–Suburban Metropolitan zoning designation in order to permit construction of a clubhouse, hotel, accessory recreational facilities, and additional parking. R.R. 267a. The request was denied by unanimous decision of the governing body made on October 9, 1967. R.R. 268a.

Subsequent requests for legislative zoning relief fared no better....

Following the final denial described above, the disappointed purchaser, with the Golf Club's consent and joinder, presented to the Township zoning hearing board a challenge to the substantive validity of the AG District designation of the tract. Twenty-three sessions of a public hearing were conducted by the board from January 1984 through July 1985 in which the Township and a citizens group opposed the challenge.

During the course of these proceedings before the board and in response to the citizens group's letter of inquiry, the supervisors' chairman prepared a memorandum to the governing body dated May 30, 1984, in which he first describes "the Board's goal of retaining the Golf Course as a Golf Course", and then discusses the Township's position with respect to the zoning ordinance validity challenge. After agreeing with the citizens group that "[t]he Golf Course issue is the single most important issue to confront the Board during 1984," the chairman represents: "[f]or myself, my goals are simple: (1) I would like to maintain the Golf Course as it is. I want to do this not only at this time but also in the future." R.R. 510a–511a.

In a report prepared during this initial validity challenge by the Township's land planner, John Rahenkamp & Associates, in June 1984, entitled "Evaluation Of Existing Agricultural Zoning District", the authors concluded that the only negative effect of the then proposed office/hotel development proposals on neighboring properties "would be the loss of the Golf Course." The planners continued:

> The impact of the present ... proposal is obvious in terms of the elimination of the open space, but not as obvious regarding infrastructure impacts. Given sufficient developer contributions and wide reaching traffic studies and plans ... the road improvements contemplated might more than outweigh the impact of increased cars.... Both the storm water and sewage impacts can be handled. The tax ratables will have a positive fiscal impact on the township. On balance the issue clearly becomes loss of the open space which is an issue of significant public impact or visual loss because so few of the area residents use the Golf Course.
>
> The bottom line is that this critical piece of remaining open space is in a concentrated area nearing if not surpassing urban intensities. The site may well be the link-pin [sic linchpin?] in a series of public decisions which must be made. The reality of the evolving urban character of the area must be dealt with thru [sic] a rational planning process....

R.R. 347a.

By decision and order dated September 5, 1985, the board denied the challenge. The purchaser then sought review of the zoning board's decision before the trial court, but the expiration of the purchaser's contractual rights required dismissal of the appeal. Despite the inability of the Township's planners in 1984 to justify municipal inaction to that point, no public action was taken with respect to the Golf Club for more than a dozen additional years until, by letter dated October 29, 1997, less than two weeks prior to the filing of the instant validity challenge, and presumably in anticipation thereof, the Township tendered a formal purchase offer.

On November 13, 1997, Realen, under contract to purchase the property, presented its zoning ordinance validity challenge to the Township zoning board. Realen's challenge included claims that the Golf Club's AG District zoning constitutes spot zoning, special legislation, and is both arbitrary and irrational....

Fourteen sessions of a public hearing were conducted by the zoning board between February 1998 and June 1999 in the matter of Realen's challenge. By decision dated August 13, 1999, the zoning board denied the challenge in every respect. In rejecting Realen's spot zoning challenge, the zoning board concluded

> The subject property is unique. The subject property has many distinguishing features that make it different from other surrounding properties. Such characteristics include its shape, road frontage,

> adjoining and existing uses as well as natural features, not to mention the shear large size of the property.

Zoning board decision at 24. Of these factors, the major arterial highways serving as the tract's perimeter were, in the board's view, the strongest zoning justification.

On further appeal, the trial court, by decision dated December 1, 2000, affirmed the zoning board's rejection of Realen's challenge as did a panel of the Commonwealth Court by decision dated June 4, 2002. We granted Realen's petition for allowance of appeal by order dated December 18, 2002. *In re Appeal of Realen Valley Forge Green Associates,* 572 Pa. 716, 813 A.2d 847 (2002)....

...

The right of landowners in this Commonwealth to use their property as they wish, unfettered by governmental interference except as necessary to protect the interests of the public and of neighboring property owners, is of ancient origin, recognized in the Magna Carta, and now memorialized in Article I, Section 1 of the Pennsylvania Constitution (protecting as an "inherent right of mankind ... acquiring, possessing and protecting property").

Property owners have a constitutionally protected right to enjoy their property....

> That right, however, may be reasonably limited by zoning ordinances that are enacted by municipalities pursuant to their police power, *i.e.,* governmental action taken to protect or preserve the public health, safety, morality, and welfare. *Cleaver [v. Board of Adjustment],* 414 Pa. 367, 200 A.2d [408] at 411–12 [(Pa.1964)] ("it is well settled that [the] constitutionally ordained right of property is and must be subject and subordinated to the Supreme Power of Government—generally known as the Police Power—to regulate or prohibit an owner's use of his property"). Where there is a particular public health, safety, morality, or welfare interest in a community, the municipality may utilize zoning measures that are substantially related to the protection and preservation of such an interest. *National Land and Investment Co. v. Easttown Township Board of Adjustment,* 419 Pa. 504, 215 A.2d 597, 607 (1966); *see also* 53 P.S. § 10603(a) (zoning ordinance should reflect the needs of the citizens and the suitability and specific nature of particular parts of the municipality).

C & M Developers, Inc. v. Bedminster Township Zoning Hearing Board, 573 Pa. 2, 820 A.2d 143, 150 (2002). The limit beyond which the power to zone in the public interest may not transcend is the protected property rights of individual landowners. Our cautionary words in *Cleaver,* 200 A.2d at 413 n. 4, are no less appropriate today:

> The natural or zealous desire of many zoning boards to protect, improve and develop their community, to plan a city or a township or a community that is both practical and beautiful, and to conserve

the property values as well as the 'tone' of that community is commendable. But they must remember that property owners have certain rights which are ordained, protected and preserved in our Constitution and which neither zeal nor worthwhile objectives can impinge upon or abolish.

Recognizing that "[u]nder the traditional standard applied when determining the validity of zoning ordinances, a zoning ordinance must be presumed constitutionally valid unless a challenging party shows that it is unreasonable, arbitrary, or not substantially related to the police power interest that the ordinance purports to serve", *C & M Developers,* 820 A.2d at 150–51, nevertheless,

> [a]mong other reasons, an ordinance will be found to be unreasonable and not substantially related to a police power purpose if it is shown to be unduly restrictive or exclusionary.... Similarly, an ordinance will be deemed to be arbitrary where it is shown that it results in disparate treatment of similar landowners without a reasonable basis for such disparate treatment.... Moreover, in reviewing an ordinance to determine its validity, courts must generally employ a substantive due process inquiry, involving a balancing of landowners' rights against the public interest sought to be protected by an exercise of the police power.

Id. Moreover,

> The substantive due process inquiry, involving a balancing of landowners' rights against the public interest sought to be protected by an exercise of the police power, must accord substantial deference to the preservation of rights of property owners, within constraints of the ancient maxim of our common law, *sic utere tuo ut alienum non laedas.* 9 Coke 59—So use your own property as not to injure your neighbors. A property owner is obliged to utilize his property in a manner that will not harm others in the use of their property, and zoning ordinances may validly protect the interests of neighboring property owners from harm.

Hopewell Township Board of Supervisors v. Golla, 499 Pa. 246, 452 A.2d 1337, 1341–42 (1982).

> Hence, the function of judicial review, when the validity of a zoning ordinance is challenged, is to engage in a meaningful inquiry into the reasonableness of the restriction on land use in light of the deprivation of landowner's freedom thereby incurred.

Id., 452 A.2d at 1342.

The Township, as a municipal entity possessing only those powers expressly delegated by the Commonwealth, derives its zoning power from the Pennsylvania Municipalities Planning Code, the Act of July 31, 1968, P.L. 805, No. 247, *as amended* ("MPC"), 53 P.S. § 10101 *et seq.* As is there mandated, the Township's zoning regulations must be designed "[t]o accommodate reasonable overall community growth, including population and employment growth and opportunities for development of a variety of residential dwelling types and nonresidential uses." MPC § 604(5), 53 P.S. § 10604(5). As regulations grounded in the delegated police power, zoning must accomplish "an average reciprocity of advantage" so-termed by Mr. Justice Holmes in *Pennsylvania Coal Co. v. Mahon,* 260 U.S. 393, 415, 43 S.Ct. 158, 67 L.Ed. 322 (1922), by which "[a]ll property owners in a designated area are placed under the same restrictions, not only for the benefit of the municipality as a whole but also for the common benefit of one another." *United Artists Theater Circuit, Inc. v. City of Philadelphia, Philadelphia Historical Commission,* 528 Pa. 12, 595 A.2d 6, 13 (1991).

Spot zoning challenges have at their conceptual core the principle that lawful zoning must be directed toward the community as a whole, concerned with the public interest generally, and justified by a balancing of community costs and benefits. These considerations have been summarized as requiring that zoning be in conformance with a comprehensive plan for the growth and development of the community. Spot zoning is the antithesis of lawful zoning in this sense. In spot zoning, the legislative focus narrows to a single property and the costs and benefits to be balanced are those of particular property owners.

In *Appeal of Mulac,* 418 Pa. 207, 210 A.2d 275, 277 (1965), we confirmed the definition of "spot zoning" described in such authorities as *Cleaver v. Board of Adjustment, Upper Darby Township Appeal,* 413 Pa. 583, 198 A.2d 538 (1964); *Glorioso Appeal,* 413 Pa. 194, 196 A.2d 668 (1964); and *Putney v. Abington Township,* 176 Pa.Super. 463, 108 A.2d 134 (1954), "as a singling out of one lot or a small area for different treatment from that accorded to similar surrounding land indistinguishable from it in character, for the economic benefit of the owner of that lot or to his economic detriment is invalid 'spot' zoning." Viewed more generally, "spot zoning ... is an arbitrary exercise of police powers that is prohibited by our Constitution." *United Artists' Theater Circuit, Inc. v. City of Philadelphia,* 535 Pa. 370, 635 A.2d 612, 620 (1993). While the size of the zoned tract is a relevant factor in a spot zoning challenge, "the most important factor in an analysis of a spot zoning question is whether the rezoned land is being treated unjustifiably different from similar surrounding land." *Schubach v. Silver,* 461 Pa. 366, 336 A.2d 328, 336 (1975).

The zoning board rejected Realen's spot zoning challenge on the ground that the difference in zoning treatment between the agriculturally designated Golf Club property and the adjoining properties, all of which are designated for intense, commercial development, is justified by the "shape, road frontage, adjoining and existing uses as well as natural features, not to mention the shear large size of the property." Zoning board decision at 24.

The trial court agreed with the zoning board's analysis and the Commonwealth Court affirmed, writing:

> the Board found that the Property is unique and distinguishable in several respects from the surrounding properties. (Board's Op.,

> Findings of Fact Nos. 40–42, at 7, 8). Two notable differences found by the Board were that the Property is considerably larger than the surrounding properties and the Property is completely surrounded by roadways. (Findings of Fact Nos. 61–62).

In re Realen Valley Forge Greenes Associates 799 A.2d 938, 944–45 (Pa.Cmwlth.2002) (footnote omitted).

The analysis of the tribunals below on this issue is seriously flawed. First, the large size of the tract is not determinative. Zoning unjustifiably discriminatory is beyond the municipality's police power and "[i]t makes no difference whether it is a 1/4 acre lot or a 50 acre industrial complex area...." *Commercial Properties, Inc. v. Peternel,* 418 Pa. 304, 211 A.2d 514, 519 (1965) (invalidating as "spot zoning" the rezoning of a tract from commercial to residential designation for the purpose of preventing a shopping center development for which the landowner had conditionally agreed to sell the property), or, we might add, a 135 acre golf course. The question is whether the lands at issue are a single, integrated unit and whether any difference in their zoning from that of adjoining properties can be justified with reference to the characteristics of the tract and its environs.

Of the land characteristics offered by the zoning board in support of its rejection of the spot zoning challenge, only the size of the tract and its location entirely bounded by arterial highways, are the subject of any discussion. There can be no question, as the zoning board found, that arterial roadways are, in many instances, an appropriate feature to be designated as the boundary between incompatible zoning districts. But the issue here is not whether *any* zoning district designation could be appropriately applied to the Golf Club's lands but whether the AG District designation can be so justified. It turns reason and land planning precepts on their head to assert, as the zoning board's decision implies, that this tract's *restricted, agricultural zoning* is justified by its ready access to the region's primary arterial roads on every hand. Apart from a bare assertion that it is so, neither the zoning board nor the courts below have offered either reason or authority to support the proposition, essential to the propriety of the decision here reviewed, that the location of these highways makes agricultural zoning appropriate for this tract while the properties on the opposite side of the same roadways are appropriately zoned and developed for intense, commercial use. Any relationship between agricultural zoning and the other tract characteristics identified in the decisions below, including the property's topography and shape, is similarly unexplored in the evidence of record, the findings of the Board, or the arguments of appellees.

On this record, no characteristic of the Golf Club's property justifies the degree of its developmental restriction by zoning as compared to the district designation and use of all of the surrounding lands both within the Township and in the adjoining municipality. This is spot zoning.

We recognize that the circumstances here presented differ factually from the spot zoning cases we have previously decided in the chronology of the municipal action creating the unjustified "island" of disparate zoning. In previous cases, the island was created by a single municipal act directed toward the property which became the disputed island; either to that property owner's benefit or detriment. Here, in contrast, the Golf Club's status as an island of agricultural zoning was the product of a series of rezonings of surrounding properties beginning in the 1950's and ending in about 1985.

Realen contends that the origin of a tract's unjustified zoning treatment as compared to adjoining properties is not decisive and we agree. It is the difference in treatment that must be justified, not its origin or chronology. Some courts have used the term "reverse spot zoning" to describe the circumstances where the unjustified difference in treatment arises from the rezoning of lands surrounding the tract at issue and this term appropriately underscores the distinction between cases like that here presented where an island is created by the rezoning of other land from the more common situation where the challenged legislation is that creating the island tract....

For these reasons, the order of the Commonwealth Court is hereby reversed and the record is remanded to the Court of Common Pleas of Montgomery County for further proceedings consistent with this opinion, our decision reported as *Casey v. Zoning Hearing Board of Warwick Township,* 459 Pa. 219, 328 A.2d 464, 469 (1974), and MPC § 1006–A (c) through (e), 53 P.S. §§ 11006–A(c) through (e), which require that Realen be afforded "definitive relief" as the successful challenger of the Township's zoning ordinance.

Notes

1. *Buying versus regulating. Realen Valley* presents a stark illustration of the problems that communities face as they become more congested and realize too late that they have failed to protect open space. Communities that act early have far more options, and can act more fairly, than communities that wait until the last minute to save bits of green. In this dispute we see the how buying land and regulating can seem like alternatives to a local government. If the land is purchased (as the community tried hard to do, both voluntarily and through eminent domain), the land can be open to public access, which is not an option available through regulation. Also, land that is purchased could be changed from a golf course into something other use–a natural area, for instance. On the other hand, regulation is far easier on the public pocket book and attractive for that reason, particularly if the community is content with the current use. Critics of regulation sometimes assert that local governments are too prone to regulate when they ought to buy, but the facts of *Realen Valley* do not illustrate this danger. The government only turned to regulation when it failed in its repeated efforts to buy the land. Still, the incentive to regulate is plainly present, and many local governments will regulate if they can thereby save money.

2. *The (un)fairness of first in time.* On the facts, there was little difference ecologically between the golf course land and surrounding land.

Nor was there evidence that development of the golf course would create a harm that was different in kind from the effects of development that had already taken place elsewhere. It was thus hard for the local government to claim that development of the golf course would violate the do-no-harm or reasonable use limit on land ownership. The government sought to protect the golf course only because too much land had already been developed. The landscape could sustain only so much development, and its development carrying capacity had been reached or exceeded.

By allowing development to take place in this manner, the local government essentially employed a first-in-time allocation system. Once development reached the limit, later development was banned. Landowners who wanted thereafter to develop were essentially too late. On the facts we see the unfairness of this system. Why were the golf course owners unable to develop when surrounding landowners were allowed to do so? The only real answer is that the surrounding landowners were prior in time to develop. In many settings we tend to view first-in-time as a fair method of allocation, but being first in time can seem like an arbitrary trait. Indeed, should we not be thanking the owners of the golf course for keeping their land open so long and benefitting public? Far from penalizing them for their delay in doing what their neighbors did, shouldn't we be honoring them for their public service? Is it enough to say that their development really should be different because other land is already developed? And could we claim, as noted above, that the high development value of the land is not a creation of the landowners, that it is due instead to the actions of the surrounding community, and thus the golf course owners have not really lost the fruits of any labor?

3. *Regulating versus redefining property rights.* A commonly accepted distinction is that land-related laws are of two types—those that define the elements of private property rights, and those that regulate the use of private rights. The distinction, as we have seen, is rather artificial and in any event difficult to apply. Nonetheless, it seems to lie at the heart of the challenge of evaluating the fairness of what lawmakers have done in a particular case. It also explains why courts such as the one here are so prone to view "spot zoning" and "reverse spot zoning" as evils and to look askance at land-use decisions affecting one or a few land parcels. Lawmakers have a legitimate role in redefining property rights over time. On the other hand, they need to respect the rights that landowners have at any time and cannot take property from them without compensation. So when has a governmental body legitimately redefined what ownership means (like the Idaho legislature did in the *Moon* case) and when has it wrongly interfered with private rights?

Surely one relevant factor, as we have noted, is whether the new law seems to ban an activity that lawmakers view as harmful or of a type contrary to the public interest. In evaluating a law on this basis it seems essential to see how many landowners are affected by it. Have lawmakers applied their judgment across the board to all landowners similarly situated, or have they instead singled out one or a few landowners for burdens not imposed on other owners? The practice of crafting rules on a parcel-by-parcel basis plainly raises suspicions of unfair treatment, and has led courts to develop the idea of spot zoning—an inherent evil. Spot zoning, it is often said, is the antithesis of zoning undertaken in accordance with a comprehensive plan.

State courts (such as the Pennsylvania court here and the Nevada court in the last case) routinely review actions by local regulators to determine whether they adequately respect private property rights. As noted earlier, many courts are more interested in the *processes* of local government decision-making–whether the local government has clearly considered the whole landscape and long-term community needs—than they are in insisting that a county have *a single written plan* and consistently stick with that plan. That is, whether a government has engaged in a legitimate act of redefining rights, rather than unfairly taking property from a landowner, may have more to do with the process used by the government than in the ultimate effect of what the government has done. Note that in *Realen Valley* there was no real argument that the local government's action amounted to an unconstitutional taking of property without just compensation. The golf course could continue operating, and it was presumably a reasonable economic use. The federal constitution, that is, offered the golf course owners no protection. It was state statutory law that invalidated the reverse spot zoning.

C. THREE DISCUSSION PROBLEMS

Set forth in this section are three discussion problems that draw together the issues throughout the book, those relating to governance as well as well as those dealing with use rights. The problems could be used in various ways: for individual review, for group discussion, for class presentation or as writing projects.

Discussion problem #1

Managing the nonnavigable lake for residences, water quality, wildlife, and recreation

Imagine that you have been asked to develop a new natural resource law regime governing nonnavigable lakes in the state, and that you have the unexpected liberty of starting from scratch. You can craft any sort of legal rights and governance regimes that you like. What would you do?

Here are some of the problems and challenges that you'll need to consider.

First, there are the potential conflicts over using the lake surface. Motorboats, sailboats, canoes, jet-skis, etc., just don't all get along. Electric motors are better than gasoline motors, in terms of noise and water pollution. As for gasoline motors, they come in widely varied sizes based on horsepower, muffling, and equipment to contain water pollution. Do not forget about safety issues.

Second, there are the ecological issues having to do with the protection of fish spawning areas and the like (which are most productive when snags and vegetation are left in the water, though what is good for fish can be bad for motorboats and people who like clean-looking lakes). If waterfowl are to nest around the lake, they need vegetation along the lakeshore where they can hide from predators, perhaps lengthy stretches of shoreline that are left relatively natural. (On the other hand, waterfowl have ways of nesting wherever they like, and their nests once constructed may need protection.) Related to these issues are matters of water quality. If landowners put chemicals on their lawns, chemical runoff will cause algae blooms that diminish the water's oxygen content and harm aquatic life (also making the lake unsightly to many). The problem can be reduced somewhat if landowners leave vegetative buffer strips along the lake shore. Of course, further chemicals can be put into the lake directly to control vegetation—if landowners agree on it and fund the operation. Other land uses can also have water-quality impacts, including septic systems, drainage practices, construction, and other land-cover changes. Nonnavigable lakes are typically connected hydrologically to other bodies of water, meaning that water pollution will inevitably spread.

Third, the levels of lakes often fluctuate naturally but can be maintained at a rather uniform level if a dam or spillway is constructed and maintained. When the lake level is kept uniform, owners can more readily keep boats attached to docks and the lake doesn't have a "bathtub" ring when the water level is down. As for the matter of docks, some people like them, some people don't, and they come in widely varied shapes and sizes. Of course large docks tend to disrupt waterfront vegetation. Docks can be big enough to serve multiple landowners, and it might well make sense to limit the number and location of docks.

Some additional points.

- Many people like lakes best when houses and other structures are kept back in the surrounding woods and not built too close to the water's edge.
- Lake management of any sort will take money and effort on a continuing basis.
- One worry of lakeside dwellers is that a government body might buy a lot on a lake and attempt to open the lake for public access.
- Whether or not the public has access to the lake surface, it will no doubt have interests in the lake's ecological condition, particularly its value as wildlife habitat and the ways that activities in and around the lake affect water quality and hydrologic cycles.
- Homeowners will of course be concerned about the resale value of their lands and structures.
- Some homeowners may not want to boat themselves, but could well have nonresident family members or friends who would be interested in doing so
- At least in some lakes people will want to swim, and may want swimming docks set up or areas cleared and protected for swimming.
- Then of course there are the questions about fishing and hunting, including the stocking of lake with native or nonnative fish species.

Discussion problem #2

Grazing, recreation, wildlife, and community building on the high plains

The hypothetical setting is the high plains of Montana, a vast expanse of some 3,000 square miles. About 1/3 of this land is owned by the federal government and managed by two agencies—the BLM and the Forest Service. The other 2/3 of the land is owned by private owners, mostly in the farm of large ranches (averaging 100,000 acres each), though with about 100 owners of smaller parcels, varying from a few acres to a few hundred acres (some crowned with "trophy homes"). The federal lands are contained in scattered blocks. As for the private ranches, they too are sometimes broken into separate tracts, and most of the ranchers have grazing rights on the federal lands. Most of the region's grazing involves cattle, though there is some sheep raising as well. The region is renowned for its wildlife—including its elk, bears, pronghorn, and (most recently) its wolves. It is a popular place for hunters as well as other recreational visitors. The elk and pronghorn are both prone to congregate in herds and to migrate long-distances over predicable routes.

This region is under various pressures that affect the resource-use practices. The wolves that have entered the region are causing problems with the grazers, especially those raising sheep, who want to control their numbers and to have some freedom to kill wolves causing problems. The same predation problem arises to a lesser extent with the bears. Environmentalists, predictably, are concerned about predator control. Waiting in the wings are hunting groups that would like soon to have hunting seasons for wolves (which already exist for the bears).

A second source of pressure comes from the outsiders moving in and building homes, often vacation homes. Long-time residents are concerned about the "sprawl" and about the changing composition and visual appearance of the landscapes. Many are concerned about houses being built in the migratory routes of animals; owners sometimes put up long fences that can block or disrupt the passage of herds.

A third problem has to do with the grazing itself, especially the cattle grazing. Many parts of the region are in poor condition ecologically. The problem is commonly termed "overgrazing," but that term is a bit misleading—or so say some grazing researchers. When bison lived in the region, they typically traveled in large herds over very wide areas. As they passed through a region they grazed it rather intensively, but then moved on, only to return much later (many months if not years later), allowing the vegetation to regrow. Cattle, on the other hand, behave differently—they tend to stay in specified places and to eat particular plants, leading in time to the near disappearance of those plants and thus to the prevalence of other, less palatable species. Cattle also degrade stream banks and riparian corridors much more than the bison did. These problems are reduced, many have concluded, when the cattle are managed so that they behave more like the bison did; that is, when they are put in large herds and then deliberately moved over large areas. Movement over large areas offers the additional benefit of allowing herders to keep the cattle away from areas that are degraded or that have received less rainfall. A few of the ranchers are taking a good hard look at the bison, and wondering whether it makes sense to bring back more bison, raising it as a meat animal and managing it so as to mimic its natural behavior patterns.

A fourth problem: the region does have several endangered species, mostly living along the riparian corridors. The problem related to these species is that the cattle tend to degrade the corridors, undercutting their habitat value for the endangered species and other wildlife forms.

Fifth, the entire region is semi-arid, and water is on the short side. Several mountain streams do have reliable water flows, sometimes high during the spring snow melts. But few reservoirs have been built to store the spring run-off, and the costs of reservoir construction would be quite high. Individual ranchers over time have developed their own water sources to serve the needs of their own animals. They are reluctant to share this water because it is not plentiful.

A sixth issue—less a pressure than an opportunity—is the growing attractiveness of the region for recreation and hunting, particularly among people who want to roam widely and to experience the sense of living in a wide-open, frontier-type landscape. Federal land managers have noted a distinct market niche for visitors who would pay good money to be able to head out for several weeks in a setting where they could wander over thousands of square miles, hunting, fishing, and just enjoying the land, without regard for boundaries. Included among these potential visitors are many wealthy foreigners. Several landowners in the region have openly wondered whether they might get together and turn their entire region into an open hunting range (no shooting of the cattle and sheep, of course!), and to charge hefty sums from people allowed to enter. Among the appeals of the region is the chance to go boating (canoeing mostly) down lengthy, uninterrupted rivers and to camp along the way—Lewis-and-Clark style.

Seventh, there are places here and there with expanses of timber that are valuable for timber harvesting. The timber is not worth much, however, when it is simply cut and shipped from the region as whole logs, for processing elsewhere (perhaps in Mexico or even Japan). It would be worth more if a timber processing plant could be built in the region. But such a facility would be possible only if it had a reliable source of timber, and didn't get outbid by outside companies who remove the timber without processing.

A few notes on the legal regime. Assume that landowners in the state possess the right to exclude hunters from their lands. Assume also that navigable waterways are open to public boating but many rivers are nonnavigable and riparian landowners can control access to them. Even in the case of navigable waterways (you should assume), boaters have no right under current law to stop along the way to cook or camp overnight unless on public land. As for the various federal lands, they are subject to detailed federal land-management statutes. But agency heads (with Congressional approval) are willing to set aside the land-management requirements on an experimental basis to try something new in the region, as a sort of test case for more bottom-up, citizen-led landscape management.

The idea that has arisen is this. Many landowners, including the federal agency managers, are interested in considering ways to coordinate resource uses over the entire 3,000 square mile region, or as much of it as possible, so as to deal with these resource issues and take advantage of the opportunities. Local government units could be involved—and might be asked to help by enacting land-use rules of one type or another. But the landowners would like to do as much as they can on their own, through privately arranged deals and with land management that is run by the private parties, not by government.

Your assignment is to come up with a detailed resource-management proposal for the region, one that takes into account where things are today in terms of legal rights and moves to a region-wide management scheme, addressing as many of the above issues as possible. As you do this, you'll need to keep in mind human nature (American style), which is to say the reluctance of people to shift completely from private property to (damn) socialism and to commit to some novel scheme over a lengthy period with no option to get out. Keep in mind, too, the small landowners and their trophy homes, who may not fit into the scheme very well, and the newcomers who want to enter the region. As for the latter, a complication not mentioned is that, while ranchers today don't like these newcomers, they do like the high prices they're willing to pay to buy some small pieces of land. At the same time, most realize that the number of people allowed to move in must be limited. As you contemplate this whole problem, you might want to consider the possibility of setting up one or more not-for-profit land trusts, that could hold conservation easements, perhaps even buying or leasing the easements using money generated in some way by the resource uses in the area. Also possible could be cooperative business ventures that operate in the region, owned and operated by some or all of the landowners. You'll need to think, too, about enforcement issues—not such a small thing, when you're talking about 3,000 square miles. You need not cover every little aspect of this problem, so long as you've set forth the main outline of your proposal and covered the biggest issues.

A final recommendation: don't be timid in exercising your imagination!

Discussion problem #3

Drainage, nonpoint pollution, wildlife, farmland protection, groundwater allocation, and tax-base enhancement in a rural Midwestern county

A rural county in the Midwest suffers from a number of problems that have made land-planning difficult. The county is relatively flat and heavily altered. It has no cities of any size, though a large city is located about 40 miles away. Four different rivers run through parts of the county, along with hundreds of miles of small streams and just as many miles of human-made drainage ditches. The county enjoys adequate rainfall although dry times during growing seasons are not unknown.

Some 90% of the county is devoted to row-crop agriculture, planted annually in corn and soybeans, with rarely any other crop. Most of the land is tilled regularly, but even land that is managed for low-till or no-till agriculture is left relatively bare during much of the year. The regular tilling of land and lack of permanent vegetation has many effects. Rainwater runs off more rapidly, soil dries out more quickly, and the land provides very wildlife habitat. Even on lands with very slight slopes the lack of vegetation leaves the land susceptible of soil erosion, which remains a serious if gradual and little-noticed problem. The problem would be less if more land were devoted to pasture, hay crops, or other relatively permanent vegetation, including forest.

The flatter areas of the county are underlain with subsurface drainage lines, which help speed the runoff of rainfall after storms. The effect of the drainage is to keep lands dry enough for farm equipment (especially in the spring) and to avoid crop losses due to saturated soils. The drainage, though, has many ecological ripple effects. The faster runoff after rains exacerbates flooding and thus streambank erosion in county rivers. Because water runs off more rapidly there is less water left to percolate slowly through soils and into rivers, with the effect that late summer water flows in rivers are artificially low—worsening water-quality problems and putting greater stress on aquatic life. Many farm drains run into drainage ditches that are maintained by special drainage districts. The districts are run by local farmers and are operated with the single-minded purpose of getting water downstream as rapidly as possible. Ditches are often "cleaned" of surrounding vegetation and dredged and straightened every decade or two to keep them visually neat and to help water flow rapidly. According to environmental critics and many civil engineers, much of the drainage work is unnecessary, and ditches could be managed to enhance their wildlife value.

Related to the drainage are the problems of runoff of pollutants, particularly farm chemicals—fertilizers (which produce nitrates in the water), herbicides, and other pesticides. Fertilizer runoff feeds aquatic plant life, leading to excessive plant growth and eutrophication, harming aquatic life. Runoff would be less if farmers left buffer strips along waterways, if they put more land in permanent cover (noted above), and if drainage districts (or even individual landowners) constructed wetlands along streams so as to slow water flows and allow the chemicals to degrade before the water moves downstream. Farm chemicals also contaminate groundwater close to the surface, and thus can harm users of shallow groundwater wells (like many individual homeowners).

Worsening the problems of polluted runoff are the many malfunctioning septic systems that homeowners operate. Few of the rural landowners are connected to sanitary sewer districts. Instead, they operate individual septic systems, with wastewater dissipated on the land through subsurface drainage fields. The drainage systems often clog or otherwise malfunction over a period of years, in ways that homeowners do not detect. The result is sewage that percolates into streams and occasionally groundwater.

As farmers in the region become more intent on producing crops consistently and with high yields more of them are buying irrigation equipment to deal with occasional dry periods. This trend could increase should, as expected, the county experience hotter, drier summers as a result of global climate change. Also, new groundwater users are entering the county—ethanol plants, which require huge quantities of water to turn corn into ethanol, and natural gas "peaker" plants, which burn natural gas to generate electricity during peak electricity-usage times, again using vast quantities of water (for cooling; the water is typically returned to nearby streams). County leaders are fearful of excessive demands on local groundwater supplies. Already a number of rural residents are finding their household wells running dry due to falling water tables.

After declining for several decades the county's population is rising due to the influx of residents who want to live in rural areas while commuting to the distant city. Houses are springing up here and there in the county, putting demands on the county's infrastructure (especially roads). Various leaders have called for county zoning that restricts residences to particular areas within the county. Compact housing would be required for homes to be served by communal wells or by small sanitary sewer systems. County leaders—many of them farmers—would like to see new houses built to add to the local tax base (which is, overall, in sad condition). At the same time, they are concerned about losses of prime farmland. They also know that a vibrant farm economy requires large portions of the county to remain in agriculture. If too much land switches to other land uses, the farm population may become too small to support essential farm services—such as equipment dealers, chemical dealers, and grain elevators—without which local farmers would be at an economic disadvantage. As for farm diversity, some farmers would consider shifting to raising cattle on pastures (with hay feeding as needed) but it is difficult to raise cattle unless a critical mass of farmers do so. Again, it is difficult for one or a few farmers to raise cattle because necessary supporting services and markets would be too far away.

Two further problems merit attention. The massive alteration of land cover and of waterways (through drainage, polluted runoff, and alteration of riparian corridors) has greatly diminished both wildlife habitat and recreational opportunities in the county. Some 90% of the natural wetlands are gone, along with 100% of native prairies. Waterways could provide wildlife habitat and valuable corridors if the vegetation along them was restored and the corridors widened. The corridors could provide greenbelts that address recreational needs, including canoeing, hiking, and birding. Enhanced recreational opportunities might also make the county more attractive for further residential development.

Your task is to develop a new resource-management scheme for the county, paying attention to governance processes as well as use rights. As for the drainage issue, you'll need to consider the timing of water flows, as well as water quality and overall drainage-ditch management (vegetation removal and dredging). Dealing with polluted runoff from farms will require attention to tillage practices and buffer strips/riparian corridors, as well as to chemical-use and drainage practices. Planning and coordinated land use will obviously be required to restore wildlife habitat and provide recreational opportunities. As you consider the options, keep in mind that landowners in the county like to keep taxes low. They also like to respect private property rights, though they do not think that landowners should engage in harmful activities and they widely support the idea of protecting prime farm lands.

D. CHALLENGES: SELECTED READINGS

The readings in this section and the following one supplement what you have already learned. This section includes readings that highlight some of the challenges posed by problems such as the three set forth above—problems that require coordinated planning and action at spatial scales well above the usual land parcel. The readings mostly focus on the management of landscapes to keep them ecologically healthy and productive, although the cultural and political problems that they address arise in a wide variety of land-use settings. The readings in the next section, E, offer more positive ideas about ways to govern the commons. Many of them deal with issues of institutional design, including ways of allocating power among levels of governance, private and public.

TRAGICALLY DIFFICULT: THE OBSTACLES TO GOVERNING THE COMMONS

Barton H. Thompson, Jr.

30 Envtl. L. 241 (2000).

In many landscapes, land-and resource-owners would benefit if they could coordinate their activities to deal with various resource-use tragedies. Yet they are often reluctant to come together to plan and agree. This article by Barton H. Thompson considers some of the psychological and sociological reasons for this resistance to beneficial collective action. It sets the stage for all that follows.

III. Understanding the Obstacles to Solving the Commons

Why has it proven so difficult to adopt solutions to these commons tragedies? Why have people who would seemingly benefit from mandated solutions often actively opposed them? It is often tempting to blame the people themselves when they are locked in a political battle over fishing, groundwater use, or global climate change. It is also tempting to believe that those who are opposing a solution are selfish, shortsighted, anti-environmental, or overly focused on immediate material gain. But most people trapped in commons dilemmas are good people who want to do what is right for their community, for society at large, and for the environment.

In *Song for a Blue Ocean*, Carl Safina goes out of his way to give readers a sense for the morality of the fishermen who are the root of the overfishing problem. Fisherman after fisherman in his book describe how they love the very fish that they are catching. These fishermen often label themselves conservationists and decry obviously destructive activities. Many of the fishermen throughout the book claim they would be among the first to stop fishing, if they thought the fish were really in trouble. Farmers say the same thing about their water resources. People worldwide say the same thing about the climatic balance that nurtures and protects them.

If you believe these resource users, the problem is not the people locked in the commons dilemmas, but the situations in which they find themselves. When put in a commons dilemma, most of us behave in a similar fashion. To help understand and overcome the difficulties involved in gaining support for commons solutions, we must turn away from attribution of blame and look to recent research conducted by psychologists, economists, sociologists, and anthropologists both in the field and in experimental simulations on why people sometimes do not behave in their best interest. . . .

A. *Framing: Losses Versus Gains*

The first point may seem obvious. The tragedy would be easy to resolve if the user of a common resource did not have to sacrifice anything to avoid the tragedy of the commons. However, my premise is not simply that the tragedy is difficult to resolve because solutions involve giving up higher consumption today in order to preserve the resource for the future. In the cases that I've discussed, many "rational" resource users should find the necessary trade-off worthwhile. The problem is that most resource users view the trade-off as requiring them to give up a current right. And most people will accept a high degree of risk to avoid giving up a current right.

Psychologists have long recognized that the framing of an action as either a gain or a loss can make a great difference. In particular, people are more risk-averse when dealing with gains (they prefer sure payoffs to gambles) and are more willing to take risks when dealing with potential losses (they will risk much to avoid an otherwise sure loss). In evaluating proposed solutions to commons dilemmas, most resource users appear to start with their historic level of resource use and ask how the solution affects that level of use. Thus they see most proposed solutions, such as caps on use, as constituting losses rather than restricted gains. These solutions, in the eyes of the resource users, require the users to give up something that they currently have. And as researchers have predicted, resource users are therefore willing to risk sizable future losses to avoid the sure immediate loss. Repeatedly, experimental simulations of commons dilemmas have found that participants have a harder time resolving the commons in a loss framework than in a gains framework. In real life, moreover, resource users believe that they have achieved their historic level of resource use through their own industry and skills, strengthening the framing effect and making the resource users more willing to risk potentially catastrophic future losses to avoid a sure cutback in their current use of the resource.

Governments make the problem worse where they recognize property rights in common access to a resource, as many states have done with groundwater. Property rights can help solve the tragedy of the commons when the rights result in the effective internalization of the cost of excessive harvesting, but property rights turn harmful when they reinforce a sense of entitlement to an unlimited harvest. Not only do such property rights reinforce the framing effect, but they also can cause resource users, as a matter of fairness, to reject out of hand even the suggestion that they should reduce their current usage. Property rights are sensible and important societal tools, but in thinking about potential solutions to the tragedy of the commons, resource users often convert property rights from practical tools into absolute moral rights that prevent them from thinking carefully about the potential benefits of averting the tragedy. Moreover, property rights may focus resource users on their individual interests rather than on total societal well being, undermining social norms of cooperation and reinforcing the very dichotomy between individual and social welfare that underlies the tragedy of the commons.

B. The Problem of Uncertainty

The second problem that prevents people from thinking "rationally" about solutions to the tragedy of the commons is uncertainty. Two types of uncertainty often plague commons dilemmas. The first is scientific uncertainty regarding the current health of the resource, the impact of human actions on the resource, and the potential future of the resource. The second is social uncertainty regarding what is a fair or proper means of allocating the burden of trying to save the commons . . .

Unfortunately, when there is scientific uncertainty, people faced with a tough solution to a commons dilemma engage in tremendous wishful thinking. If scientists estimate that there are between one thousand and thirty thousand fish in any given population, most fishermen assume that there are thirty thousand fish in that population.The fishermen find confirmation for their views in their own personal experience, no matter how unsupportable. One good day of fishing will convince them that the more cautious estimates are wrong. The fact that fish are hard to catch the rest of the year serves as evidence merely that fish are getting smarter and learning to stay away from the boats.

Scientific simulations of fishery problems duplicate this phenomenon. As uncertainty increases regarding the exact size of a pool of fish, participants in fishery simulations increasingly overestimate the likely number of fish and boost their harvesting accordingly. Uncertainty over the regeneration rate of the fish population leads to a similar jump in harvesting. According to some psychologists, mathematic misperceptions might be at work. Because people often have found in the past that mean and variance are positively correlated, they mistakenly believe that increased variance justifies an upward shift in their estimate of the size of both current and future fish populations. But a more likely explanation is that people use uncertainty to willingly fool themselves that the resource is in better shape and under less threat than it is in fact. . . .

Assuming that resource users believe there is a problem, they must determine the fair means of allocating the burden of solving the tragedy. In each of my examples, this is difficult because the tragedy is asymmetric. People contribute in different degrees to the problem, and people benefit to different degrees from a solution. In these settings, there are multiple ways to allocate the burden of reducing resource use and no generally accepted societal norms for how to choose between the various allocations . . . . .

Unfortunately, where there are multiple fairness rules, people suffer from what some psychologists have labeled "egocentric interpretations of fairness." People assume that the rule that benefits them is the fairest. As a result, agreeing on a common solution becomes difficult if not impossible. In one group of fishing simulations, for example, researchers found that most participants were able to agree on equal reductions in catches where the dilemma was symmetric so that the participants benefited equally from cooperation. If some participants balked at an equal reduction, the other participants were able to argue effectively that any approach other than an equal reduction was unfair; the dissenters quickly dropped their opposition when their position was criticized. Where the dilemma was asymmetric, however, both egocentrism and harvesting levels increased. Explaining the phenomenon to people, moreover, does not cure the problem. When told of the phenomenon, people assume that others' fairness perceptions, but not their own, suffer from an egocentric bias. The problem, moreover, is not merely theoretical. As emphasized in Part II, biased interpretations of fairness have plagued efforts to address global climate change. Developing countries argue that the developed countries should resolve the problem because they are overwhelmingly "at fault" for current greenhouse gas levels and have more resources with which to address the problem. Developed countries argue that it is only fair that all nations share in the burden because all will benefit.

The scientific and social uncertainties, when combined, also permit resource users to indulge in what some psychologists have called "self-enhancing attributional biases," or what I call a "halo effect." Because bad behavior is hard to define and determine, everyone assumes that they are more cooperative than they are in reality. In one experimental simulation of a fishery, for example, eighty-four percent of the participants thought that they had acted in a socially "cooperative" fashion, even though a review of the experiment's results showed that a majority of the participants had engaged in varying degrees of gluttonous behavior. Seventy-seven percent of the participants thought they had been "cooperative," even though they had not left sufficient fish for an optimal fishery; thirty-two percent reported they had been "cooperative" even though they took more than their proportionate share of all the fish in the fishery. . . .

C. *Intertemporal Tradeoffs*

Getting resource users to come to grips with the tragedy of the commons is also difficult because the resource users must engage in an intertemporal tradeoff: should they accept a loss today in order to avoid a bigger loss at some point distant in the future? *Homo sapiens* are better than most mammals at considering the future consequences of their current actions—but not much better. We do care about the future, including the well-being of future generations. But we suffer from a variety of temporal anomalies. In particular, individuals trapped in a commons dilemma appear to extravagantly discount the future consequences of their current actions.

I want to avoid the standard debate about whether or not private discount rates are appropriate for making intertemporal trade-offs involving environmental consequences. As others have discussed, there is tremendous disagreement as to whether market discount rates are socially proper, particularly when discounting across generations. Professor Cass Sunstein, for example, has argued that market discount rates do not fully account for effects on future generations, because future generations are not involved in the discounting decision.

My concern is that people have difficulty making any sacrifice to avoid uncertain future losses. Several factors may be at work here. First, people tend to focus myopically on current costs in evaluating the wisdom of conservation measures. In the energy crunch years of the late 1970s and early 1980s a number of economists studied people's willingness to purchase energy efficient appliances. It should have been relatively easy, one might think, for people to make rational trade-offs between the increase in the current purchase price of an appliance and the future energy savings they would enjoy by buying that appliance. Governmentally mandated labels supplied consumers with all the basic information necessary to make those trade-offs. But the studies found that people nonetheless were highly biased towards buying the cheaper, energy consumptive appliances. Depending on the particular study, the "applied discount rates"—the discount rates reflected in the actual purchases people were making—ranged from a low of 17% (a high discount rate, even for the inflation-prone 1970s) to an astronomical 243%. Because people had trouble making complex discounting decisions, they focused on the most obvious statistic confronting them: how much they could save immediately by buying the cheaper appliance. In a similar fashion, resource users confronted by a commons dilemma may decide that it is easiest to treat current harvesting decisions as if they were the last.

Second, several experiments have shown that people often tend to minimize the risk of future losses, willingly gambling on the future, where the risk is characterized by significant uncertainty and avoiding the risk would require giving up something today. Interestingly, this result is in marked contrast to the way that people generally respond to the tradeoff between current and future losses that are certain to occur. Psychologists have found that most people tend to employ lower discount rates when choosing between losses than when choosing between gains; indeed, some subjects demonstrate negative discounting when choosing between losses, preferring an immediate loss over a delayed loss of the same amount. Distant losses, in short, appear to weigh far more heavily in peoples' decision making than distant gains. But where the loss is risky and uncertain, people often act as if there's virtually no future risk to them at all. Why the reversal?

A major explanation is that, when confronted by an uncertain future, most people assume that they will be able to avoid, reduce, or ameliorate future risks. We tend to be optimists about the future, at least when taking precautionary steps today is costly. Part of the optimism is an unrealistic belief that tragedy will befall others but not ourselves. . . .

Psychological studies have found that this innate optimism about the future is even more pronounced in business settings. Business managers, who have typically advanced to their current positions because they have been successful in overcoming problems in the past, believe that they can also effectively control the odds and magnitudes of future risks. One suspects that fishermen and farmers, who have repeatedly confronted and overcome severe risks in their businesses, might be particularly prone to believe that they can avoid future risks.

We as a society have frequently reinforced resource users' natural sense of optimism by bailing out the people who take on risks and turn out to have bet wrong. Most groundwater users, if you talk to them about overdepleting their aquifer, will probably tell you "yes, it's a problem, but we don't worry too much about running out of groundwater because if we end up depleting our aquifer, the government will bail us out." Based on past experience, groundwater users believe that the government will build a project to import needed water if the farmers ultimately run out of economically withdrawable groundwater. In a similar fashion, fishermen expect that the government will provide "transition relief" if a fishery is ultimately depleted.

A final reason for expecting high discounting of the future risk of resource tragedy is people's uncanny ability either to totally ignore problems that are not immediate and visible—what Sandra Postel has called the "out-of-sight, out-of-mind syndrome"—or to see them in their rosiest light. The phenomenon here is similar, but slightly different from, people's over-optimism ..... As Sandra Postel has noted, "[w]hen looking at say, a field of golden wheat, it can be difficult to imagine why crops like that can't just go on forever." Even where resource users think about the problem, they are likely to "underimagine" the consequences of overusing the resource, placing the best face on the potential tragedy. Indeed, most resource users do not even have a past experience upon which to draw in trying to imagine the import to them of exhausting the fishery or aquifer. Resource users may find it even more difficult to imagine the full scope of the negative impact where future generations will suffer the consequences.

IN DEFENSE OF ABSOLUTES: COMBATTING THE POLITICS OF POWER IN ENVIRONMENTAL LAW

Amy Sinden

90 Iowa L. Rev. 1405 (2005).

Along with the psychological and sociological barriers that make cooperation difficult there are a variety of power imbalances that skew democratic processes. They make it particularly difficult to promote conservation goals that generate benefits widely spread in space and time. They are considered here by Amy Sinden.

III. Power Imbalance

A. *Market Failure and Political Failure*

Just as markets are only part of the decision making structure that organizes society, so is market failure only part of the story that explains the riddle of environmental degradation. While market failure is an important aspect of the problem, environmental degradation also stems in part from a kind of political failure. Environmental disputes involve asymmetries of power that consistently skew government decision making in favor of less stringent environmental regulation.

The structure of this power asymmetry is straightforward. On one side, environmental disputes commonly involve an interest that is broadly shared among individuals, non-economic in character, and often of relatively minor consequence to each one. This interest may involve, for example, breathing cleaner air, avoiding some statistical probability of contracting cancer, enjoying some pristine natural area, or knowing that a certain species has not been pushed to extinction. On the other side, the interests pitted against this set of diffuse public interests are of a very different character. First, they are usually held by a much smaller set of actors. Second, they tend to be economic in character and have the potential to directly impact each individual actor to a far larger degree. And third, the actors are typically businesses and corporations, rather than individuals.

Accordingly, it is apparent that this profile of environmental disputants contains two axes of power imbalance, both weighted in the same direction: against the interest in environmental protection. First, basic and well-accepted principles of interest-group theory predict that a group whose interests are diffuse and have less marginal impact on each individual member will have far more difficulty organizing into an effective pressure group than a smaller group in which each member suffers substantial economic harm. Second, other things being equal, corporations tend to have far more political clout than individuals, both because they tend to be wealthier and because of the privileged position they occupy in politics. As a result, environmental disputes almost always involve an asymmetry of power that weighs against environmental protection.

B. *Distortions of Government Decision Making*

This power imbalance, endemic to environmental disputes, has the potential to skew government decision making in the legislative, executive, and judicial branches. Most obviously, monied corporate interests have significant advantages in lobbying legislatures and administrative agencies. First, those with more wealth can, of course, afford to hire more and better lobbyists and to participate in more agency proceedings. Second, corporate lobbyists may also enjoy special access to government officials that those representing individual interests are denied.

The superior access and influence over government decision making enjoyed by anti-environmental interests may, in addition to simply influencing outcomes, also help shape the agenda. Thus, powerful lobbyists may exercise control over what bills are introduced in the legislature and may even write the bills. Similarly, they may have extensive input on the shape of proposed regulations or even draft them. The recent furor over Vice President Cheney's Energy Task Force, which formulated the President's energy policy in close cooperation with industry executives in dozens of closed-door meetings from which environmental groups were excluded, provides a particularly vivid example of this phenomenon.

Indeed, it has long been recognized that agency decision making has the capacity to be grossly distorted by the power imbalance between regulated industry and regulatory beneficiaries. The prevailing view is that "agencies unduly favor ... the interests of regulated or client business firms and other organized groups at the expense of diffuse, comparatively unorganized interests such as consumers, environmentalists, and the poor." In addition to the straightforward advantages in lobbying power that allow anti-environmental interests to exert more influence on agency decision making than their pro-environmental counterparts, many courts and commentators point to a phenomenon peculiar to the administrative process widely referred to as "agency capture."

Administrative law scholars point to a number of factors to explain the tendency of agencies to become "captured" or controlled by the business firms they are charged with regulating. Long-term repeat contacts with the businesses create a psychological and organizational disincentive for agency bureaucrats to adopt an adversarial posture toward the regulated firms. Bureaucracies naturally seek a kind of "routinization of administration" that requires the maintenance of an amicable relationship with the regulated firms over the long term. The incentive to compromise with and placate industry is further fueled by the disparity of resources between the agency and the firms it regulates....

Judicial review is often seen as a corrective for distortions in agency decision making caused by the undue influence of powerful private groups, and it can sometimes play such a role. Indeed, I argue in the final Part of this Article that judicial review plays an important role in counteracting the disparities of power that would otherwise distort decision making under the Endangered Species Act. Nonetheless, while lobbying and other attempts to influence judicial decisions directly are prohibited by ethical rules and thus undoubtedly play far less of a role than do similar efforts in the political branches, judicial decision making is by no means immune from the distorting effects of power.

First, because industry has more money to file court challenges than do public interest groups, the number of industry challenges seeking to block regulation in the courts far outstrips the number of public interest lawsuits seeking to spur regulation. Once in court, wealthy litigants are significantly advantaged by their ability to hire expensive expert witnesses and employ resource-intensive litigation tactics. These problems are compounded by the fact that administrative law contains built-in biases that tend to favor regulatory objects over regulatory beneficiaries. These include the presumption against review of agency inaction, the doctrine of standing, and the law's general preference for negative injunctions prohibiting regulatory action over affirmative injunctions spurring regulatory action. Finally, industry-filed litigation can become a mechanism for excluding citizen groups from important regulatory decisions when consent decrees are hammered out behind closed doors in bilateral negotiations between industry plaintiffs and agency defendants.

In addition to these kinds of relatively direct impacts on government decision making, power disparities may manifest themselves in more subtle ways as well. Power and wealth may sometimes create the capacity to shape individual preferences, when, for example, corporations promote a "taste" for certain products through advertising. Such preferences may in turn shape government decision making, either through democratic processes that may register such preferences or through agency decision making methods, like CBA, that attempt to empirically measure them....

C. Some (Tangential) Thoughts on Pluralism and Civic Republicanism

... I offer here a few preliminary thoughts on the question of how, in light of the power disparities discussed above, legislatures have been able to pass environmental-protection laws containing absolute standards. To begin with, if my claim about the existence of an endemic environmental power imbalance is accurate, then under a pluralist understanding of politics as a struggle among self-interested groups for scarce public resources, one would certainly predict that the enactment of environmental statutes imposing absolute standards would be unlikely at best. But I am inclined to look instead to civic republicanism for an explanation for the undeniably real—if rare—phenomenon of absolute standards in environmental legislation.

Civic republicanism takes the view that legislative outcomes can reflect some conception of the "public good" rather than a simple aggregation of private preferences resulting from "deals" among self-interested groups. To be sure, this ideal is often not achieved in the real world because the "problem of faction"—that is, the capture of the political process by powerful private groups promoting their self-interest at the expense of the public good—threatens to undermine the deliberative process. But civic republicanism at least holds out the possibility that every now and then, the stars align, the interest groups drown each other out or are otherwise momentarily quieted, and the elusive voice of the public good, momentarily audible above the din of power politics, carries the day. Indeed, there are occasionally legislative enactments that seem to defy a simple pluralist explanation, where the interests of the most powerful private groups are overridden in favor of some notion of the "public good." The environmental statutes of the 1970s are often cited as examples of that phenomenon.

While this republican nirvana may be reached by legislatures only rarely, it is far more likely to occur in the legislative than the administrative arena. This is so for two reasons. First, legislatures deal primarily in broad generalizations of policy and principle, while administrative agencies confront the far messier task of applying these principles to particular situations involving particular people. Arguments based on economic hardship to specific private interests at the agency-implementation level are far more likely to gain traction. Visions of the "public good," on the other hand, are far easier to maintain in broad legislative debates about basic principles. Thus, in the Halls of Congress, it is difficult to argue with the broad proposition that we should preserve the rich heritage of the earth's biodiversity by making every effort to protect species that are threatened with extinction. On the other hand, when it comes to implementation in specific instances, the argument that efforts to preserve the northern spotted owl are costing tens of thousands of jobs may be quite compelling. Second, particular applications of a statutory standard by an agency are far less likely to be subject to widespread public scrutiny than are legislative enactments. Thus, political arm twisting and back-room deals, which clearly play a role in the legislative process, can potentially play an even more prominent role in agency implementation. . . .

NO SUCCESS LIKE FAILURE: THE PLATTE RIVER COLLABORATIVE WATERSHED PLANNING PROCESS

John D. Echeverria

25 Wm. & Mary Envtl. L. & Pol'y Rev. 559 (2001).

Among the procedural options often touted for dealing with resource-use conflicts is the idea of governance by local "stake-holders," organized on the basis of a watershed or some other geological or ecological feature. Whatever the merits of this approach, it is not without dangers, particularly when processes require expertise and great investments of time and energy and when participants arrive at the table intent on protecting vested interests. The author of this article, John Echeverria, spent years working on the watershed planning process described here, which sought ways to restore the ecological functioning and habitat values of the Platte River. Overall, he concludes, the process was a failure with power allocated in the wrong way and with public interests under-represented. On the other hand, the experience generated valuable lessons for structuring governance processes.

V. Fundamental Issues/Concerns

1. Problematic Planning Unit

One fundamental problem is the choice of the Platte River Basin as the program management unit and the inclusion of the states of Nebraska, Wyoming, and Colorado as lead partners with the federal government in developing the Platte program.

From the physical perspective, there is obviously logic to attempting to approach Platte River wildlife issues by including the entire river basin in the three states. Water development projects throughout the basin have contributed to and continue to cause degradation of the riverine habitat. As a matter of law and as a matter of fairness, water users in each state have a responsibility to contribute to the solution to the problem. In addition, water users and others throughout the basin will be affected by Platte River management decisions and therefore have a legitimate interest in ensuring that their voices are heard.

However, from the political perspective, the choice of the Platte River raises a concern about whether the appropriate unit for effective environmental decision-making has been selected. In general, environmental management decisions should be made by the smallest possible unit of government to provide affected citizens the largest possible role in the decision. At the same time, when a resource management decision affects a large geographic area, decision-making authority has to be lodged at a level of government whose jurisdiction includes all those who will be affected. Thus, everything else being equal, decisions affecting migratory bird species should logically be assigned to the national government. As stated in a report by the conservative Political Economy Research Center: "when species range over territories larger than a state ... the optimal locus of governmental regulation may be regional, national, or even international."

The choice in the Cooperative Agreement to delegate a significant portion of the federal government's decision-making authority to the three basin states conflicts with the fact that Platte River management decisions have national and even international consequences. After all, the threatened and endangered bird species that use the Platte migrate across many states. The national government should logically take the lead role in developing a Platte River management program. Subordinating a portion of the national authority in favor of the basin states inevitably elevates water development interests (which are concentrated in the three basin states) relative to wildlife conservation interests (which are broadly shared across the country).

Involving the three basin states is cause for even greater concern given that the target species are basically present only in Nebraska. One can reasonably presume that Nebraska has an interest in conservation of the wildlife habitat, along with an interest in protecting its water users. But neither Wyoming nor Colorado would directly benefit from the conservation of Platte River wildlife while both states have water development projects that could be burdened by new mitigation responsibilities....

2. *Uncertain Management Standards*

A second fundamental difficulty involves confusion over the standards governing the content of the future Platte River program. On the one hand, the Cooperative Agreement calls for the development of a program that reflects "consensus" among all the parties. On the other hand, the program is supposed to ensure that project operations comply with the ESA.

The apparent hope of the DOI and some of the other parties is that the final program can satisfy both of these mandates. The odds seem strongly against it. The entire history of the Platte controversy suggests that the basin states' views about the optimal balance between development and wildlife conservation will depart significantly from what the ESA, which reflects a national policy-making perspective, will dictate. Thus, the two basic goals of the Platte River program are in serious conflict with each other. This conflict has slowed progress in developing a program, and postponed resolution of the ultimate questions about the kinds of policies which should be reflected in the program....

This raises a more fundamental question about the nature of the so-called "collaborative" watershed approach on the Platte. As discussed, if Platte River wildlife management decisions were actually guided by the preferences of the basin states, wildlife conservation would not receive equitable treatment along with development interests. The threat of direct ESA enforcement provides a powerful incentive for the states, despite their natural political preferences, to help develop a program that addresses the national interest in wildlife conservation and attempts to comply with the ESA. But if the ESA represents the ultimate legal standard for any legitimate Platte River program, what is the actual purpose of the so-called "collaborative" aspect of the program? Is the states' involvement ultimately more form than substance? On the other hand, if "collaborative" decision-making were really occurring, what would become of ESA compliance?

All these questions raise a basic question about whether the Platte River program should be viewed as a useful model for environmental decision-making. If collaborative programs such as that on the Platte are ultimately restricted by the terms of federal law, there is very little substance to this supposedly new approach. On the other hand, if there were substance to this new mode of environmental decision-making, there likely would be little left to federal law and the valuable policies federal law is designed to advance.

3. *Confused Procedural Rules*

A third concern is the lack of effective or even intelligible procedural standards to guide the development of the program. On the one hand, the commitment to a "collaborative" approach implies a good deal of highly informal negotiation among a fairly limited set of parties. On the other hand, the DOI has a legal obligation, under the National Environmental Policy Act (NEPA) and the ESA, in particular, to follow various formal procedural steps designed to improve the quality of agency decision-making. At least on the Platte, these informal and formal processes do not appear to have worked together well.

NEPA, the Magna Charta of U.S. environmental law, imposes a powerful discipline on agency decision-making. By requiring agencies to describe in writing their proposed actions and their consequences, as well as alternatives to the proposed actions and reasons for rejecting them, the NEPA process produces better decisions. Equally important, by providing several formal opportunities for public review and comment, NEPA serves to promote broad-based public participation in environmental decisions. ESA is quite different from NEPA because it contains a number of substantive standards governing the actual outcomes of agency decision-making. But the ESA also includes a number of procedural provisions designed to discipline agency decision-making and to encourage public involvement.

The procedural requirements of NEPA and the ESA cannot easily be adapted to a process that relies on informal negotiation. If compliance with NEPA and ESA procedures precedes or coincides with negotiation, the time and effort required to execute the legal procedures will likely impede the negotiation process. On the other hand, if a proposal is developed through negotiation, and NEPA and ESA procedures are applied after-the-fact to the outcome of the negotiations, there is substantial risk that compliance with the procedures will be meaningless paperwork exercises, violating the spirit if not the letter of the law....

4. Uneven Negotiating Table

Other concerns arise from the identity of the interests participating in the Platte River collaborative process, and from the fact that participation in the process imposes resource demands on conservation interests. The Platte River negotiating table tilts in favor of development interests and against conservation interests.

The composition of the Governance Committee itself is seriously unbalanced. Direct representatives of water interests outnumber direct representatives of environmental interests by three to two. More importantly, however, the three state representatives expand the support for water development interests on the Committee. The representatives of the upstream states, Wyoming and Colorado, have no natural political incentive to advocate wildlife protection measures of little or no value to their citizens. Nebraska brings somewhat more balanced incentives to the table, but has traditionally favored in-state water development interests over wildlife interests. The DOI simultaneously represents the FWS, which has an institutional interest in protecting wildlife, and the BOR, which has an institutional interest in avoiding burdensome new operating constraints on its projects.

Equally important, development interests and environmental advocates have wildly different capacities to marshal the resources to support their respective positions in the time-consuming Cooperative Agreement process. Environmental advocates working on the Platte bring an extraordinary amount of skill, energy, and passion to the issues. But compared to the environmental advocates, water-development interests are capable of deploying more lawyers, more hydrologists, more biologists, and so on. These differences matter because, after more than a decade of computer modeling and other voluminous environmental analyses, Platte River issues have taken on a mind-numbing legal, technical and scientific complexity. The complexity of the issues is compounded by the fact that current discussions assume knowledge of a long series of policy calls and political compromises over the preceding years.

... Because their constituency is so large and diffuse, conservation advocates are routinely at a disadvantage in contests with the representatives of relatively more cohesive and more easily organized economic interests. This imbalance is clearly reflected in the kinds of expertise and staffing levels the conservation interests have managed to bring to the Cooperative Agreement process. Thus, far from ensuring a fair outcome, providing conservation groups a seat at the table along with other, more powerful interest groups simply ensures that wildlife interests will continue to be disadvantaged.

COLLABORATIVE ECOSYSTEM GOVERNANCE: SCALE, COMPLEXITY, AND DYNAMISM

Bradley C. Karkkainen

21 Va. Envtl. L. J. 189 (2002).

Adding to the challenges of landscape-scale management is nature itself. Nature is inherently dynamic, and there is much about it that we do not understand. The challenges of nature are considered here by Brad Karkkainen. He describes also some of the virtues of management at the ecosystem level and of management methods that constantly monitor ecosystems and make adjustments in response to shifting conditions and understandings.

II. Three Propositions about Ecosystems

Let me begin with three propositions about ecosystems that I hope are uncontroversial.... Proposition One: the ecosystem context matters in environmental decision-making. As humans we live our lives not in an abstract, uniform, and undifferentiated space, but in the particularized physical and biological contexts of ecosystems. Ecosystems are many, varied, overlapping, and interrelated. In crucial respects no two ecosystems are quite alike; they operate by different sets of rules. As a result, the environmental consequences of our actions may also vary widely, depending upon the particular ecosystem context in which the action occurs. Now this may seem too patently obvious to mention in this age of ecological enlightenment, yet it is hardly a trivial notion. For the last thirty years, we have attempted to manage the environment largely by crafting and enforcing more-or-less uniform rules to be applied on a large-scale basis, as if the particularized ecosystem context did not matter very much. Only recently have we begun to pay more serious heed to the ecosystem-level consequences of environmental decision-making, recognizing that how we act may well need to be tailored to the needs, demands, and constraints of the particular ecological contexts within which we find ourselves.

Proposition Two: ecosystems are complex dynamic systems. This also may seem too obvious to mention, but I mean it here in a fairly specific, somewhat technical sense; the sense used by the emerging cross-disciplinary science of complexity. As complex dynamic systems, ecosystems are composed of many mutually interdependent parts operating in dynamic, co-evolutionary trajectories. They are not static, and do not necessarily tend toward equilibrium. Parts interact with other parts in rich, multiple, and often poorly understood ways, so that the arrows of causation—what action causes what effect—often point in many directions simultaneously, some in self-reinforcing chains, some held in check by others tending in the opposite direction (i.e., positive and negative feedback loops).

Like other complex dynamic systems, ecosystems exhibit nonlinearity. That is to say, the effects of many actions are discontinuous. There are numerous natural threshold effects, as well as complications caused by co-causation and synergistic interactions among multiple factors operating along multiple complex chains of causation, often incorporating both positive and negative feedback loops simultaneously. As a result, small inputs can sometimes result in large and often partially or even wholly unpredictable consequences for other parts of the system, and for the system as a whole. As with other complex systems (such as the weather), even if our understanding of the individual components and their operational principles is relatively complete, our understanding of the trajectory of the entire system qua system, and the ultimate effect that particular inputs will have on the system as a whole and its individual component parts, may be quite limited....

Proposition Three: Most ecosystems are human-influenced or human-dominated complex dynamic systems. As human beings, we interact with the ecosystems that surround us (and upon which we depend) in numerous and complex ways. There are multiple anthropogenic inputs into the ecosystem, some benign, others more pernicious to other species and the physical environment that sustains them. For starters, we are responsible for:

- multiple kinds and varying levels of air, water, and groundwater pollution;
- habitat destruction, fragmentation, or degradation through, for example, displacement of native vegetation by controlled, domesticated replacements, many of them exotics;
- resource exploitation, placing immediate pressures on populations of certain members of biotic communities, or withdrawal of critical physical components (e.g., water).

These various human-induced stressors can themselves interact in complex ways. For example, it now appears that when nutrient pollution is combined with the systematic, large-scale removal of filter-feeding shellfish such as oysters, each makes a larger contribution to algae blooms and eutrophication in the Chesapeake Bay and other estuaries than either factor would without the co-presence of the other. Indeed, at a certain point their interaction may develop into a self-reinforcing feedback loop. High nutrient concentrations lead to algae blooms and eutrophication which block sunlight and oxygen from reaching filter-feeding shellfish, reducing their populations and thereby preventing them from filtering the water in the estuary, thus reducing its buffering capacity and worsening the impact of a given level of nutrient inputs. At the same time, of course, a reduction in shellfish populations means that a given level of fishing effort puts even more pressure on the remaining population, potentially disrupting its ability to regenerate and thus indirectly reducing the estuary's buffering capacity for nutrient inputs, and so on. In this self-reinforcing cycle, everything depends on everything else, in ways that are complex and often difficult to specify, quantify, or predict....

Dynamism, Experimentalism and "Adaptive" Ecosystem Management.

We are accustomed to thinking of environmental protection in terms of centralized, top-down prescription of fixed, enforceable, uniform rules. The unstated background assumption is that an expert regulator (whether at federal or state level) will know enough to be able to identify and isolate the most important problems, and gather sufficient information about them to prescribe effective solutions with sufficient specificity to translate into legally enforceable commands. This approach assumes, in general, that there are definitive "right" and "wrong" answers to every question, and that the challenge for the regulator is to study the problem until she decides she has enough information to prescribe a fixed rule, and then make it stick.

But given what we have just said about complexity, the search for "optimal," fixed, categorical, centrally prescribed rules, or even minimally effective ones, may prove illusory. . . .

[W]e inescapably operate under a chronic information deficit with respect to a variety of factors relevant to environmental decision-making. Under the circumstances, the conventional strategy—the strategy of acting only at the point where we think we know with reasonable certainty what the effects of a particular management choice will be, and then adopting fixed rules based on our best current understanding—is a prescription for inaction and ineffectiveness, or policy failure.

An alternative strategy, therefore, commends itself. This approach emphasizes dynamic and flexible decision-making, adjusting and correcting decisions over time in light of subsequent scientific advances, new information, and the observed effects of past management efforts. In short, what is required is a "rolling rule" regime capable of relatively rapid adjustment to new learning and environmental change. Under this approach, we act on the basis of the best currently available information, yet explicitly acknowledge that the action undertaken now is necessarily provisional. As a corollary, emphasis is placed on mechanisms to continuously improve our knowledge and information base, to ensure that future rounds of decision-making are as well-informed as possible. With focused scientific effort, coupled with systematic monitoring and thoughtful experimentation, our understanding of the complex dynamics of ecosystems may improve over time. Still, at any given moment, it will necessarily remain incomplete. Yet if we make a good faith effort, we can put ourselves in a position always to know more tomorrow than we do today, and to make progressively better-informed decisions by stages.

This dynamic "rolling rule" approach is being adopted increasingly in practice in places like the Chesapeake Bay and Great Lakes Programs, and the Everglades ecosystem restoration project. These new ecosystem governance arrangements tend to place heavy emphasis on systematic monitoring of ecosystem conditions and stressors, seeking to inform policymaking with real-time (or close to real-time) data and to generate continuous information feedback so that the actual consequences of each successive round of policy adjustments can be measured. If necessary, those measures can then be modified in light of measured results which may or may not correspond to the predictive calculations upon which the decision was originally based.

A related management tool is to set specific, quantified biological and environmental objectives, as measured by carefully selected biological and physical "indicators" of (or measurable proxies for) ecosystem health. Further emphasis is placed on scientific and technical collaboration among agencies and tiers of government, as well as among academics and other independent researchers, aimed at generating a continuous stream of high-quality, policy-relevant, locally-situated ecosystem science that at each successive stage refines and challenges the scientific hypotheses, theories, and assumptions upon which previous rounds of policy-making had been based. In this process—where the baseline expectation becomes the continuous advance of science and the continuous flow of monitoring data—the monitored indicators may themselves come under challenge and need to be revised in light of subsequent learning.

Finally, and in tandem with all these developments, the last decade has witnessed widespread adoption of an "adaptive" management approach, explicitly embracing self-conscious experimentation in the design of policy measures. Under this approach, policy measures are understood as provisional and subject to modification in light of scientific advances and the results of rigorous monitoring. The net result of all these developments is the generation of a complex web of continuous information feedback loops; continuous reassessment of specific policy measures and the scientific and other assumptions upon which they are based; and ongoing readjustment and revision of policies in light of new learning. Rather than "codify[ing] existing knowledge in rules that are hard to change," the new ecosystem governance institutions seek to "foster an open-ended process of knowledge creation" on the theory that although we can never know enough at any given moment to decide what is right or best, we also cannot afford to defer decision-making until "all the information is in" for the simple and inescapable reason that all the information will never be in.

The pervasiveness of uncertainty, unpredictability, and surprise also suggests a more humble approach to ecosystem management. Increasingly, we are coming to recognize that we cannot really "manage" ecosystems in the sense of controlling them. But we may be able to constrain or influence (and in that sense "manage") human behavior in ways that will affect the whole ecosystem, even though we will not ever be entirely certain precisely what effects our management efforts will have. This, too, has led ecosystem managers to emphasize "adaptive" approaches. Rules are self-consciously provisional and experimental, not only because we recognize that new science and changing conditions as revealed in monitoring data may call into question our prior assumptions about the likely ecological consequences of a given action, but also because we recognize that human behavior is itself subject to imperfect prediction and control, so that policy measures may turn out to have very different effects on human behavior than we imagined at the outset.

The currency of exchange under all these arrangements is information, and particularly information generated through continuous feedback loops of experimentation, monitoring, learning, and, adjustment. If environmental management is chronically information-starved, then collaborative governance mechanisms may provide at least a partial solution. . . .

WHAT IS GOOD LAND USE?

Eric T. Freyfogle

in WHY CONSERVATION IS FAILING AND HOW IT CAN REGAIN GROUND (2006).

Ultimately the people making decisions about a landscape have to decide what they are trying to accomplish. They need to set a goal for their management efforts. They need to come up with a vision of land use that is good overall. What, though, are the elements of good land use, and how might it be defined? The following excerpt identifies the main components of an answer.

Conservation, ultimately, is about promoting good land uses for the benefit of people, future generations, and the land itself. But what is good land use? What are its characteristics or elements, and how do they fit together? Is the best way to identify good land use to start with the land and its ecological functioning and then add the people, tailoring their activities so as to sustain that functioning? Or should we begin instead with the people and their needs and then insert nature to the mix?

The instinct of scientists is to begin with nature; that's the aspect they know best. The instinct of economists, typically, is to begin instead with the market and with the production and exchange of goods and services and then somehow adjust the market to take better care of nature. A third approach, popular among some conservationists, is to begin with the human-nature bond in emotional terms and to ask how we might persuade people to love nature more. Here the assumption is that if people really cared about nature in their hearts, all else would largely fall into place; a more specific, ecologically based goal is apparently unneeded.

Then there are the many people who approach land-use issues in fragmented terms, one parcel at a time, rarely pausing to consider landscapes as a whole. This last approach, probably the most common one, has the considerable virtue of practicality. When a land-use problem is obvious, why not tackle the problem directly instead of viewing it as a small part of something much bigger? Tract-by-tract conservation work largely fits into this category. Preserve a piece here, buy an easement or development right there, and perhaps all will work for the best.

None of these approaches starts from what ought to be the obvious place. Inevitably, people are the ones who decide whether land use is good. The logical place to begin, then, is not with science or with nature, much less with the market or with a simple love of the wilds. It is with a direct question: What makes land use good for people?

This question, it turns out, is a fruitful one, because it is relatively easy to identify the broad factors to use in evaluating land uses. The factors fall into three basic categories. Once we identify and explore these, spreading all the factors on the table, we can appreciate the many building blocks of good land use. We are also better positioned to spot the omissions and deficiencies that afflict much of today's conservation rhetoric.

Human utility, broadly defined. Embedded as they are in nature, people necessarily depend upon the land for daily sustenance. Good land use needs to meet these basic needs—for everyone, if possible. A good life, though, entails far more than just food, clothing, and shelter. There are the beauties that a surrounding landscape can provide, in terms of both the natural and the built environment. There are the conveniences and satisfactions that come when a home territory is well laid out and arranged in ways that foster healthy social interactions. Sometimes people want to escape society; good land use would offer remote places for them to go. Many people enjoy interacting with wild creatures, whether at backyard bird feeders or in secluded locations. Good land use would make this possible as well.

Once we start enumerating the many ways that good land use benefits people, the list turns out to be quite long. And it gets longer when we go beyond the immediate direct benefits and consider the types of land uses *indirectly* required if the land is to continue supplying these direct benefits. For soil to remain fertile and productive, for instance, soil fertility cycles need to keep functioning, which in turn has implications for the protection of biological diversity. For fisheries to remain productive, rivers and lakes also need to be healthy, which means water flows that are reasonably clean and not significantly altered in physical terms. Genetic diversity—a wide range of plants and animals—needs to be respected to ensure the continued viability of species that are directly and indirectly useful to people. Natural areas also require protection, not only because they directly benefit people but so that scientists can study them and gain the lessons needed to manage lands well. Then there are the many species and natural processes that play vital roles in keeping pests and diseases in check. Human utility, in short, is complexly tied to the land's biotic composition and ecological functioning, as ecologists over the past century have so often said.

There is little need to be fully comprehensive here in listing the ways that good land use can benefit people, because the central conclusion is easy stated. *Good land use would promote overall human utility,* with utility defined broadly to include aesthetics and quality-of-life issues as well as bread-and-butter needs.

When utility is defined this way, it is clear that it extends beyond the particular resource uses that are assigned prices by the market.

Many land-use benefits lack market prices, though they are highly valuable to people, because they are never bought and sold. The market deals only in commodities and services that people can purchase and consume personally, without significantly sharing benefits with others . . . . .

Ethical considerations. Standing beside human utility is a constellation of factors that might be termed ethical. They, too, play significant roles in defining good land use. When people use ethical considerations in evaluating land-use behaviors, then the goodness of their land use will depend upon whether they have abided by these considerations. The point is a rather simple one, yet it is rarely mentioned directly and its implications are easy to overlook.

Looming large in this second, ethics category is the whole matter of future generations. The popular goal of sustainability, presumes that people living today ought to look out for their descendants. Most people agree. What this duty entails, of course, is far from clear. But whatever shape the duty takes, it plays a vital role in defining good land use. Land use is good only when it fulfills the ethical obligations that people today have to tend the land for future generations.

This component, it needs emphasizing, could prove exceptionally influential if we decide to define broadly our obligations vis-à-vis the future. If we feel obligated to protect all life forms for future generations to enjoy (a widely held ideal), then land use will be good only when it achieves this conservation result. If our duties (instead or in addition) include the maintenance of representative examples of all types of natural areas, or perhaps the protection of the land's overall natural productive capacity, then land use again will be good only if these duties are fulfilled. Land use is not good when these duties are breached.

A duty to future generations makes sense only when understood as a *collective* duty of people now living. It is implausible to think of it merely as a duty imposed upon an individual as such, to fulfill or not as the individual sees fit. Practically speaking, no individual could remotely fulfill such a duty. Here again, we stumble upon a potent reason why we cannot rely entirely upon the market to foster good land use. The market leads to land uses that benefit people living today, the landowner above all. Although the market does permit landowners to use their lands in ways that respect the future, individual owners can often accomplish little acting alone. Which individual alone can save a species, or protect the Earth's soil, or halt the degradation of unique natural areas? Any sensible expression of a duty to future generations would require planning at large spatial scales. Only with such a perspective, and thus only by means of collective action, is it possible to keep the Earth functioning in ways that leave options open for the future. If we have duties to future generations, they bear upon us collectively, as a people. To assert that individuals should make up their own minds about such matters, implementing their own ethical leanings, is to deny that such ethical duties really exist.

Aside from possible duties to future generations there are other broad bases for interjecting ethical considerations into good land use. Many people sense religious duties to tend the land with care. For them, land use is truly good only when these duties are fulfilled....

Along with future generations and religious beliefs is the claim that nature itself is intrinsically valuable, or that parts of nature have intrinsic value (rare species, for instance). Intrinsic value can be defined as all value possessed by nature that is unrelated to human utility. Philosophers vigorously debate whether nature can have such moral value on its own, independently of what people might think, or whether value instead can only arise when humans recognize it as such. For purposes here, in defining good land use, this distinction is unimportant. It is the ultimate moral vision that counts. If nature is valuable, then good land use ought to respect its value, whether the value is intrinsic or not....

Finally, in this ethical category there are the considerations related to virtuous living. What does it mean to live a virtuous life, in terms of our interactions with nature? Does wasteful or excessive consumption amount to a defect in virtue? Is it wrong, in moral terms, to wantonly or needlessly impose suffering on other life forms or carelessly to alter lands in ways that kill plants and animals? The issue here is not the "rights" that other organisms might have. It is about people, and about what it means to live the virtuous life. A land use would be bad if it deviated from widely held notions of individual virtue.

These, then, are the major categories of ethical thinking about land (or at least one way to categorize them): approaches based on duty to future generations, religious obligations, intrinsic value, and virtue. As with the category of human utility, there is no need here to dwell on the category's many variations. *Land use will be good, for a people who recognize ethical limits (which is to say, a civilized people), only when it is consistent with their chosen ethical ideals:* that is, only (1) when it adequately fulfills duties to future generations and to nature itself; (2) when it performs felt religious obligations; and (3) when it is consistent with shared ideas about virtuous living....

Ignorance and precaution. Any well-considered definition of good land use is almost certain to dwell at length on the first two categories of factors: on overall human utility and on the relevant ethical considerations. A third category also requires attention, although it is more elusive and it enters the equation from a different angle.

Human knowledge about nature is far from complete. Many of nature's parts are unknown or poorly understood; many processes and interactions are hard to evaluate and harder still to trace. Inevitably, decisions about land use and consumption are made behind veils of ecological ignorance. The more one learns about nature, it seems, the greater the recognition of that ignorance. Somehow, decision-making processes need to take into account this limited knowledge. It is dangerous to act based solely on what is known when that knowledge is obviously incomplete. It is even more dangerous to take major action based only on the few facts that can be empirically proven with high confidence, when countless other relevant facts are unproven or unknown. In scientific research it makes sense to insist on scientific proof; in real life it does not.

To fill in the gaps of our knowledge, hunches are required. Deep-seated intuition needs to be drawn upon. Wise land managers try to work with nature rather than against it, mimicking its ways and hoping to benefit from its built-in wisdom, even when not understood. Because mistakes are inevitable, it is prudent to leave room for second chances. When tinkering with a landscape, it is wise to save all the parts. Prudence is particularly essential in light of nature's inherent dynamism and unpredictability, which adds further layers to our ignorance.

These ideas are certainly familiar to readers of serious conservation literature, where the wisdom of acting cautiously appears prominently. A common version of the idea takes the form of the so-called precautionary principle. The legal mind is more inclined to phrase the same idea in terms of burdens of proof: the burden of showing harm ought to be kept reasonably low, conservationists assert, particularly when the harms that might result are grave. Would the sane person, told that he faces a 20 percent chance of getting hit by a car while crossing a street, decide to take extra precautions, or would he ignore the warning on the grounds that the chance of harm is too low or unproven? . . .

The idea of acting cautiously toward nature stimulates widely different responses. Some think the point so obviously right that debate about it seems silly. Others take a sharply opposing view, usually phrased in terms of individual liberty: people should be free to alter nature as they see fit, unless and until the evidence of harm is manifest. According to ardent defenders of liberty, the burden of proving harm should rest on those who claim that harm will occur. Some would go even further, contending that evidence of harm should take the form of scientific proof, admissible in a court of law. It is worth recalling on this point the debate about Rachel Carson's classic, *Silent Spring*. Carson's chief complaint was that we were acting recklessly in our uses of pesticides, and that greater caution was in order. Many of her attackers, however, overlooked or affirmatively ignored the issue of caution. Their critiques presumed that caution was entirely inappropriate, and that pesticides were properly used unless and until their overall harmfulness was fully shown. Because the evidence of harm was incomplete and (in their view) not fully persuasive, Rachel Carson was wrong to challenge what pesticide users were doing.

What we have, then, are alternative ways of talking about this third category of factors relating to good land use. The issue is about human ignorance and the limits of our sensory perceptions, about the recurring errors in human reason, about the wisdom of acting cautiously given our tendency to err, and about burdens of proof. At one time we freely introduced exotic species into landscapes, unconcerned about possible harmful effects. Now we are prone to hesitate; we have suffered too many instances of these introductions gone awry. That hesitation, however we phrase it, is an important component of land-use thought. Land use is good when it avoids gambles with nature that we are ill prepared to lose. Land use is good when managers refrain from charging ahead without study, reflection, and efforts to minimize unnecessary change. . . .

These three categories—overall utility, ethical considerations, and ignorance-precaution—provide a framework for thinking about good and bad land use and hence for considering conservation's aims.

Plainly, to move beyond this three-pronged framework we would need to start making policy decisions—lots of them. At every step, in each of the three categories, alternatives are available and tough choices have to be made. Some choices, though, are far wiser than others—and the three-part framework, by identifying and distinguishing the relevant characteristics, can be of value in helping us make these determinations. An approach to land use that overlooks any of these considerations—that ignores one or even two entire categories of factors, as some do—is plainly deficient and deserves to be labeled as such.

E. POSSIBILITIES: SELECTED READINGS

The readings in the previous section focused largely on challenges and ultimate needs in the land-management arena. We turn now to consider elements of answers. The readings here, like those above, are only suggestive, but they introduce central themes and raise wide-ranging possibilities.

NATURE, CULTURE, AND CIVIL SOCIETY

Julianne Lutz Newton & William C. Sullivan
1 J. Civil Society 195–209 (2005).

Ultimately, government by the people requires citizens to step forward and take interest in the landscapes that they help inhabit. Good governance, it increasingly appears, depends upon the existence of a vibrant nongovernmental sphere in which people organize, learn, speak, and act on issues of common importance. This essay highlights the importance to good land use of a vibrant civil society and identifies ways that efforts to heal land can in turn make civil society itself more healthy.

CIVIL SOCIETY AND THE NATURAL COMMONS

People are necessarily bound together and made interdependent by the forces of nature; this is a basic truth upon which we build. This interdependence, it is important to note, has nothing to do with ethnic bonds, or with national boundaries. It is not about religious membership, skin color or language, nor about anything having to do with us except in our most basic human needs. We are bound together by nature simply by virtue of inhabiting the same landscapes.

Our tendency has been to expect government to address our environmental ills. But government is limited in its ability to do so. Governments are buffeted by political winds and led along by powerful interests. Adding to the problem are our inherited ideas of property ownership, our excessive faith in the market, and our love of liberty (defined negatively and in individual terms). At bottom, our social ills and environmental problems have more to do with contemporary individualistic culture than with anything else. Unless we change that culture we are unlikely to produce landscapes that are truly healthy and pleasing.

We find ourselves, then, with several related needs. We need better designed places in which to dwell, with more nature and more wisely tended nature in them. We also need land-uses coordinated at large spatial scales to deal with a wide array of environmental problems, from urban sprawl to the protection of rare species. We need new understandings of what it means to own land privately—understandings that expect owners to use their lands in ways consistent with the common good. And we need to strengthen an array of communitarian cultural values, ones that reflect and honor our many interconnections and commonalities, particularly our natural interconnections.

This brings us, finally, to the possibilities for collective action, taking place not only through government but in the public arena. What are the prospects for this type of action, and how does it relate to civil society as now understood?

One body of scholarship relevant to this subject has to do with natural resources that are managed by groups of citizen-users as commons. Scholars of what are termed 'commonproperty regimes' have attended closely to characteristics of resource-management regimes that succeed over the long-term, compared with the many that fall apart (Ostrom, 1990). Civil society students might do well to review this important literature. It reveals how and why resource management is a difficult business, even (or particularly) in the case of a single component of nature (a lobster fishery or mountain pasture, for instance). Management success is dependent not just upon good scientific data but upon tightly knit senses of community among the users. For a group of independent users to manage a commons successfully, they need strong bonds among them, transcending mere individual economic interest. The dialectic here is clear: A strong civil society makes good resource management possible, while the landscape and its needs provide an attractive context for social interaction, thus strengthening civil society.

Also relevant to this issue are the experiences and studies of residential homeowners' associations. Here, too, we find users of landscapes coming together to manage their landscapes, for good and ill. This literature is too detailed to survey here except to note that associations work best when participants see themselves as parts of something larger—not just individual owners out to protect their land values and keep assessments low—and when decision-making processes are ones that engage people in ways that build trust and co-operation.

These examples only scratch the surface, both of what is now taking place and of what is possible by way of civic action that improves landscapes and fosters civil society....

As we have explained, the civil society we deem vital would endeavor to counter the culture of separation and the commodification of everyday life, particularly the fragmentation and commodification of nature. It would also promote the critical goals of (i) improving ecological understandings; (ii) lengthening planning horizons; and (iii) encouraging people to value local landscapes that are healthy and biologically rich. In terms of its dealings with the market, another under-studied issue for civil society scholars (Keane, 2005), our civil society would seek to correct market failings (externalities and others) and to provide what economists term public goods. We would seek to tame the market, not to tear it down as inherently evil or specifically to create islands of nonmarket interactions. Just as markets need good rules and shared values (trust and co-operation) to operate over the long term, so too they need to avoid degrading or exhausting the natural systems and biotic elements upon which all life depends. Markets need to become friendlier toward nature, more respectful of its ecological processes and mindful of generations unborn.

We do not mean to overstate the powers that local organizations might have to improve nearby nature. Local associations face severe limits in their abilities, particularly to counter the market's immense power. They are also subject to takeover by narrow interests. We agree, too, with John Ehrenberg in his observation that:

> ... categories derived from the face-to-face democracy of early nineteenth century New England towns cannot furnish a credible model for public life in a highly commodified mass society marked by unprecedented levels of economic inequality. (Ehrenberg, 1999, p. 234)

We cannot expect local organizations to do the work of government, either in terms of halting socially harmful behavior or raising money for projects that taxpayers ought to support. As for government, its roles in our mind are properly expansive, for only governments with ample power can adequately supervise the market and engage in meaningful landscape-scale planning. Again to quote Ehrenberg, democracy requires "a vibrant civil society" yet "it also requires public supervision of the market, and this necessitates sustained public action, vigorous state activity, and broad political thought" (1999, p. 248). Thus, the civic associations we endorse would be ones that are politically active, especially in pressing the state to counter the fragmentation of nature and the ills of the capitalist market....

Conclusion

We have plentiful reasons today to devote energy to citizen-led, community-based efforts to improve our landscapes, bringing nature into them and keeping that nature healthy. Difficult though the work is, civic efforts to promote nature offer considerable promise. Government-led efforts are essential but they face their own high hurdles. Aside from well-known distrust of government, it is simply not possible for government to take care of all land or to prescribe precise land-use norms. Beyond that, citizens are unlikely to value and support wise land-use plans unless they can see clearly the needs for them and benefits of them. And the needs and benefits too often are simply not understood. Private efforts are required, at local and national levels, to heighten concerns about nature and promote shifts in our dominant culture—getting people to appreciate our ignorance about nature's complex ways, to respect nature's dynamism, and to honor nature's ways.

Civic projects can provide learning opportunities that slowly chip away at the cultural origins of our environmental ills. Well-conceived projects can make lands healthier ecologically, while also making the participants themselves healthier, physically, psychologically, and emotionally. Civic efforts can help people see the ways nature makes them interrelated and interdependent. This is good work, or can be when well done.

NOTE, THE ECOCOMMONS: A PLAN FOR COMMON PROPERTY MANAGEMENT OF ECOSYSTEMS

Evan van Hook

11 Yale L. & Pol. Rev. 561 (1993).

The management of landscapes in the future, blending public and private interests in novel ways, calls for new visions of how we might define and allocate private rights over broad areas. In this excerpt, Evan van Hook offers one provocative vision, which draws upon basic principles of conservation biology in its call to preserve core nature areas.

. . . The Man and Biosphere (MAB) Program of the United Nations Educational, Scientific, and Cultural Organization (UNESCO) has developed ecosystem management programs. These programs manage ecosystems that contain both large undeveloped areas and a significant human population. Under the MAB plans, ecosystems are separated into "core" and "buffer" areas. Core areas are composed of ecologically sensitive public lands. Humans live and work within the buffer areas, but land use in these zones is strictly regulated. These regions provide a protective buffer for the highly sensitive core areas while allowing for human economic activity.

The MAB plans, however, have been impossible to implement in the United States. Ecosystems encompass both public and private lands, and the MAB plans require broader authority over private land use than our state or federal governments currently exercise. As many individuals working with the MAB program have noted, the lack of a fair and effective method of implementation is the single greatest obstacle to the creation of MAB-style ecosystem preserves in this country....

This Note presents a proposal for the implementation of MAB-style ecosystem preserves in the United States through the creation of "ecosystem commons" or "ecocommons," in which the government would create buffer zones by condemning conservation easements on the private properties surrounding ecologically sensitive public lands. Compensation would be paid for these easements not in cash, but in rights in common to the natural resources on the public lands. Ecocommons could best be created in ecosystems encompassing significant amounts of public land and in which the human economies are centered around exploiting the natural resources on those public lands. I will refer to the human communities participating in these economies as "resource-dependent communities." The ecocommons plan is premised on the hypothesis that private landowners living within resource-dependent communities would willingly alter their land use practices to protect the ecosystem in exchange for a share of the natural resources of that ecosystem. Other plans have been or are currently being developed for ecosystems that do not fit this description. For ecosystems that do, the creation of ecocommons may be the most effective and least expensive way to implement ecosystem management....

C. The Creation of Ecocommons

The ecocommons plan is a method for creating and administering MAB preserves within ecosystems containing resource-dependent communities. Under the ecocommons plan, MAB preserves would be created by condemning conservation easements on the private lands that would constitute the buffer zones. While the federal programs discussed above rely on voluntary sales of easements, easements on private lands within the buffer zones of ecocommons would be taken by eminent domain. More importantly, rather than purchasing easements with cash, compensation would be paid with rights to the natural resources on the public lands that these resource-dependent communities had already been exploiting.

There is no constitutional requirement that compensation for condemned land be paid in cash. In many areas, the value of the natural resources that could be harvested on a sustainable basis from public lands is more than adequate for this purpose. The MAB plans require reserve managers to develop additional methods of harvesting natural resources without damaging the ecosystem. Creativity in this task could enhance and diversify the availability of valuable resources through such measures as wild animal ranching; trophy hunting; sustainable harvesting of nontraditional forest resources; and research and extraction permits for new drugs. The economic potential of sustainable-yield exploitation of natural resources could also be enhanced by granting intellectual-property-right protection for new sustainable-use methods....

Within an ecocommons, private landowners in resource-dependent communities would exchange conservation easements on their property for "rights in common" to natural resources on the adjoining public lands. A right in common is "a right or privilege which several persons have to the produce of the lands or waters of another." For centuries, common ownership has been an effective strategy for managing a variety of natural resources.

Within a traditional commons, specific individuals are granted rights to harvest resources and land use is strictly regulated. Because those holding the common interests are able to exclude outsiders and therefore retain the benefits of careful management for themselves, many commons have been managed with high levels of sustainability and cooperation and with relatively low monitoring costs.

Common property regimes are most often applied to single resources, such as pasturage or fish. Rights and obligations are connected to that resource: restrictions on present fish harvests within the commons, for example, are rewarded with future fish harvests. The ecocommons plan expands on the notion of managing individual resources to create a common property management regime for complete ecosystems.

The extension of the principles of traditional commons to ecosystem management entails a complex matrix of relationships. Limitations on tree harvesting, for example, may be imposed not to protect trees, but to protect fish from river siltation. Restrictions on tree harvesting on buffer zone lands, therefore, may be compensated with rights to future fish harvests on the nearby public lands.

Ecocommons would be established through several steps: first, the government would identify ecosystems that are appropriate candidates for ecocommons. As under the MAB plans, the public lands within these ecosystems would be designated as core zones or manipulation zones depending on their ecological importance and sensitivity, and on the extractable resources they contain.

The next step would be to inventory the natural resources that could be extracted from the public lands without damaging the ecosystem. As discussed above, those completing the inventory should think creatively about the type of resources that could be extracted and about extraction methods.

In the last step, conservation easements on private lands within the buffer zone would be condemned. Specific land use restrictions would be designed for these lands. This would be similar to the creation of the Natural Resource Conservation Management Plans created for burdened properties under the Environmental Easement Program discussed above. These Plans set forth conservation measures and practices for the land subject to the easement and the commercial uses still permitted on the burdened land.

Creation of such buffer zones would not be a painless task. Private landowners may resist inclusion of their lands out of concern over the attendant regulations. Serious political opposition, however, might be avoided. Concern over the loss of biodiversity is rising and the political will seems to exist at this time to begin protecting ecosystems. Individuals living within ecosystems of vital public importance may have no choice but to reconcile themselves to the fact that they will be subject to some type of ecosystem management plan. Supporters of the ecocommons plan can point out that the adjustments required under this plan may be no more significant than those engendered by alternative plans. Also, the resources that would be exchanged for the conservation easements represent a significant payoff to the burdened landowners.

Development interests may oppose the ecocommons plans since they would not be able to purchase unburdened land within the buffer zones to convert to more profitable uses. On the other hand, development would not be precluded within these zones, and developers may find that the burdens and benefits promote creative and profitable development ideas that do not damage the surrounding ecosystem.

Compensation for the condemned easements would be paid in rights in common to a share of the natural resources of the ecosystem ("Resource Rights"). The private lands would be categorized in regions depending on the nature and extent of the easements to be imposed upon them. The number of Resource Rights that landowners received would depend on the region in which their property was located: greater restrictions would be compensated through larger Resource Right allotments.

This plan, therefore, would entail the privatization of a portion of the resources on public lands, but not the privatization of the public lands themselves. Elinor Ostrom makes a useful distinction between resource units and resource systems, explaining both the nature and the purpose of a commons. Resource units, such as fish, animals, or grazing rights, are what individuals harvest from a resource system. The resource system is the biological system that produces the stream of resource units. Subtractability characterizes resource units, while jointness characterizes the resource system. As Ostrom explains it, many boats can fish on a lake resource system, but each fish can be captured by only one person. By exchanging rights to resources on public lands for conservation easements on the surrounding private lands, the ecocommons plan would privatize public resource units, while leaving resource systems under public ownership and control.

In addition to allocating resources, Resource Rights would stipulate the conditions under which the resources could be harvested. Both the easements and the Rights would be recorded in the appropriate deeds and would become permanent benefits and burdens running with the property.

The government with jurisdiction over the public lands forming the core and manipulation zones of the ecocommons would assume management responsibility for the ecocommons. This authority would oversee resource management within the reserve and enforce the land use and harvesting regulations. In addition, the managing authority would organize research both on the biological functioning of the ecosystem and on newly discovered extractable resources or resource extraction methods.

After the initial distribution, Resource Rights would be leasable. Presumably, many of the individuals living within resource-dependent communities would choose to continue in their profession and would exercise their rights directly. However, they would not be forced to do so. Individuals or companies interested in resource extraction could lease the rights to those resources on a yearly basis. In this way, the market would help ensure that Resource Rights would flow to the individuals valuing them most highly.

Nevertheless, Resource Rights should not be alienable separately from land within the ecocommons. Property owners within the ecosystem should have a permanent stake in the health of the ecosystem in order to preserve their incentives to comply with land use regulations and to monitor the compliance of their neighbors. All property owners within the ecocommons would have, in other words, an equity interest in the ecosystem. The income stream from their Resource Rights would be positively related to the health of the ecosystem, whether or not they were personally employed in resource extraction. Although these limitations on alienability may result in some loss of efficiency in the allocation of resources, this deficit would be compensated for, in part, by increasing the monitoring incentives for the residents of the ecocommons.

Although landowners would not be able to separate the ownership of their land from the ownership of their Resource Rights, there would be no restrictions on the alienation of property within the ecocommons. The fee estate, the conservation servitude, and the Resource Rights would accompany the transfer of property and anyone from outside the community willing to share in the responsibilities of maintaining the ecosystem could purchase land within the ecocommons.

PUBLIC LANDS AND LAW REFORM: PUTTING THEORY, POLICY, AND PRACTICE IN PERSPECTIVE

Robert B. Keiter

2005 Utah L. Rev. 1127.

Particularly in parts of the country dominated by federally owned lands, future management regimes are likely to involve considerable reallocations of power over landscapes, dividing power among various levels of governance while moving much of it downward. Here, Robert Keiter discusses experiments now underway in vesting power closer to the land in ways that get local people involved while remaining responsive to the needs of broader citizen populations.

D. Devolution: Constituency-Based Governance

The traditional model of public land governance is a centralized one based on federal supremacy. As owner of the public lands, the federal government has generally used its authority to define and enforce the rules governing these lands. With authority concentrated in the land management agencies, uniform standards are ordinarily applied across the landscape, thus promoting equity among user groups and minimizing interstate discrimination problems. But central authority has also exacerbated federal, state, and local tensions over public land policy. While such conflicts are not surprising (and should even be expected in our federal system), they can create unnecessary management inefficiencies, frustrate legitimate local interests, and promote jurisdictional fragmentation. . . .

Devolution can be understood in two separate ways in our federal system. In its strongest sense, devolution means the transfer of governmental power from the federal level to the state or local levels, and either the full or partial surrender of jurisdictional authority. Proposals to transfer federal ownership of the public lands to the states as well as the concurrent jurisdictional arrangements that prevail on the federal multiple-use lands are both examples of this stronger form of devolution. In a weaker sense, devolution can be achieved by the sharing of decision responsibility, either among different levels of government or with various constituencies. These arrangements can take several forms, such as dual regulation regimes, integrated federal-state-local collaborative management arrangements, or public participation opportunities in federal decision processes.

From the beginning, local citizens and communities have played a major role in public land policy. In the years before the national government consolidated its control over the western lands, state law and local customs governed mining, water, grazing, and other activities on the public domain. Even as the federal presence grew, Congress expressly incorporated state and local legal norms into such laws as the General Mining Law of 1872 and the Desert Land Act of 1877. When Congress authorized creation of national forest reserves at the turn of the century, it did not displace state authority, but rather left federal forest officials and the states sharing concurrent jurisdiction over the new reserves. During the Forest Service's early days, Gifford Pinchot specifically instructed his new managers to heed local interests and needs in managing the new reserves. . . .

During the mid–1930s, Congress gave local constituents formal responsibility for the public rangelands. In the Taylor Grazing Act of 1934, for example, Congress created local grazing advisory boards, composed of public land ranchers, to administer the federally owned rangelands. Dubbed "democracy on the range," this experiment in local governance can appropriately be viewed as a distinctive devolutionary management model. The theory underlying the grazing advisory boards was that local livestock growers, being more familiar with range resources and conditions than anyone else, could be entrusted to protect against overuse since their own livelihoods were at stake. Because the Taylor Grazing Act also granted preferential lease rights to existing ranchers and limited participation on the advisory boards to livestock producers, this early experiment in public land democracy was actually more exclusive than inclusive. It was also clearly motivated by the ranchers' desire to avoid any federally imposed regulatory limits on the public range. The grazing advisory boards are now widely regarded as a classic example of local capture of the public land agencies.

By the 1970s, devolution had taken the form of constituency-based involvement in federal decision processes, which has become an important dimension of modern public land management. Several factors account for the greatly expanded role that public involvement now plays in natural resource policy. In the aftermath of World War II, as public confidence in government waned under the weight of a burgeoning federal bureaucracy, important administrative law reforms opened federal agency decision processes to public participation and judicial scrutiny. The Administrative Procedure Act of 1946 served as the principal vehicle for injecting this new transparency into federal policy. In the environmental arena, passage of NEPA, with its judicially enforceable procedural standards, required federal officials to solicit public comment on agency actions and assured that these concerns would be taken seriously. NEPA not only introduced environmental considerations into public land decisions, it provided interested constituents and others not previously included in these matters a vehicle to participate. The NEPA process also helped reveal that most controversial resource allocation decisions involve conflicts over values and interests as much as technical disagreements over scientific data....

Over the past three decades, the rhetoric of devolution on the public lands has periodically taken a more radical turn. Where the agencies historically dealt with a relatively homogenous constituency of ranchers, loggers, and miners, the urbanized West now presents them with an increasingly diverse constituency intent on making its various views heard over an array of issues, including livestock grazing, old-growth timber sales, and ORV policies. The traditional constituencies, finding their voice and influence challenged by a growing environmental movement, urban recreationists, and others, have responded by seeking to reassert local control over the public lands.

During the late 1970s, a disparate group of ranchers and western politicians, upset over the increasing federal regulatory limitations that accompanied the FLPMA reforms, promoted the short-lived Sagebrush Rebellion. The rebels asserted that the federal government was not legally entitled to retain the western public lands, and they urged federal officials to relinquish ownership to the states, which is the ultimate devolution policy as well as a variant on earlier disposal policies. Their ardor waned, however, once Ronald Reagan was elected President and proceeded to implement policies more attuned to their liking....

As these conflicts intensified, the constituent-based governance model in the form of collaborative processes and partnerships has emerged as a means to reduce acrimony and to promote understanding among competing interests. Recognizing that natural resource controversies often transcend traditional jurisdictional boundaries and can have far-flung ecological implications, the public land agencies began informally convening the diverse affected interests in an effort to address common concerns. Numerous ad hoc, citizen-initiated groups also sprung up as forums for discussing and resolving persistent conflicts outside traditional agency and judicial venues. Noteworthy examples include the Quincy Library Group in the northern Sierras, the Applegate Partnership in southwestern Oregon, and the Malpai Borderlands Group in southern Arizona. At a more formal level, under Secretary Bruce Babbitt's guidance, the Department of the Interior established state resource advisory councils to replace the old grazing advisory boards in setting local range policy. The regulations governing these resource advisory councils require an expanded and balanced membership that today includes environmental and wildlife advocates as well as local ranchers. The Western Governors' Association joined the chorus, too, adopting a much-publicized set of governing principles (known as Enlibra) designed to promote the local resolution of natural resource controversies on public lands. Moreover, the Bush administration has made local involvement in public land planning and resource decisions a cornerstone of its management philosophy. While none of these experiments in constituency-based democracy can yet be labeled an unqualified success, their proliferation lends credibility and relevance to this devolved management model....

[T]he collaborative process movement has made major inroads in the public lands setting, establishing itself as a force to be reckoned with. Most importantly, Congress has embraced the notion. With passage in 1998 of the Herger–Feinstein Quincy Library Group Act, Congress endorsed a locally negotiated forest management plan that covered three national forests in California's northern Sierra Nevada Mountains, setting specific timber harvest targets while also superimposing national environmental laws on the project. Although the Quincy Library Group process has been severely criticized by environmental organizations, the fact is that Congress has blessed this devolutionary experiment and funded it as a pilot project that other communities are now trying to duplicate. In 2000 the Valles Caldera trust legislation went one step further: it created a civilian board of trustees to oversee management of the newly acquired Valles Caldera lands in central New Mexico, essentially entrusting local citizens with responsibility for setting resource priorities and policies on these ecologically significant lands. In addition, the 106th Congress established an array of citizen advisory committees in several public land bills passed in the wake of President Clinton's end-of-term national monument designation frenzy. To be sure, these bills were designed as site-specific solutions to longstanding local controversies, and they should not be viewed as a universal endorsement of devolved management authority on the public lands. Yet the collective impact of these congressional actions is to legitimize such collaborative initiatives for managing the public domain, perhaps setting the stage for further federal legislation based on a devolutionary model.

The potential benefits and perils of devolved decision making on the public lands have been much debated and examined. The key question is whether such arrangements put the public interest at risk. If a local entity assumes responsibility for management decisions, parochial interests may well trump the national interest in the affected lands and resources. Even when the local role is advisory only, federal land managers may still be under intense pressure to hew the local line, regardless of countervailing national or other concerns. Congress can, however, always incorporate federal resource management standards into enabling legislation, thus ensuring that national concerns are part of any new management arrangement....

G. Place-Based and Hybrid Models

Congress has a long history of using place-based enabling legislation to establish specific management standards and responsibilities on the public domain. Beginning in 1872 with Yellowstone National Park, Congress has regularly adopted individual statutory mandates to create national parks, wildlife refuges, wilderness areas, and other protective designations. More recently, in locations as diverse as the northern Sierra Nevada and central New Mexico, Congress has adopted special place-based legislation modifying the otherwise uniform multiple-use mandates governing specified public lands. The executive branch has also long engaged in a similar pattern of place-based management and protection. The Clinton administration, as we have seen, developed prescriptive regional plans for the Pacific Northwest public lands as well as California's Sierra Nevada national forests, and it used the Antiquities Act to create an expansive set of BLM-managed national monuments. Other place-based ideas are still simmering, and yet other proposals are pending legislative or executive action. The net effect has been a restructuring of federal standards and authority on designated lands in order to address local resource conflicts and other problems. Attractive as such locally tailored and hybrid models may be, they can have a balkanizing effect on the public lands, raising concerns similar to those inherent in the devolution model.

Historically, Congress has employed site-specific enabling legislation to protect unique portions of the public domain from disposal or development, essentially carving enclaves from the larger federal estate. The various units of the national park system each owe their origins to an enabling act that not only transferred administration of the affected lands to the National Park Service, but also established specific management standards for each newly created park. Congress has used a similar legislative strategy to create national wildlife refuges, many of which are governed by site-specific enabling legislation....

More recently, Congress has utilized a similar place-based strategy to establish new hybrid management models without transferring the affected lands into the preservation system. One high-profile example is the controversial 1998 Herger–Feinstein Quincy Library Group Forest Recovery Act, which sprang from a unique collaborative process involving the timber industry, environmentalists, and local officials, who collectively negotiated a community stability proposal designed to refocus timber management on three northern Sierra national forests, reduce fire risks, and enhance environmental protection. Congress endorsed the Quincy agreement in legislation that established a five-year pilot project mandating specific harvest levels and thinning techniques while placing roadless and other areas off-limits for logging purposes. The Forest Service was charged with implementing the new strategy, and required to adhere to existing environmental laws and species protection obligations. While this arrangement has precipitated implementation problems, the project is moving forward in the context of the larger Sierra Nevada forest plan amendment process. Though not a permanent change in forest management policy, the Quincy legislation suggests Congress is amenable to revising multiple-use policy in specific locations to address significant local problems, at least where most of the affected constituencies can reach agreement on new policy directions.

Another high-profile example of an alternate management strategy is the 2000 Valles Caldera Preservation Act that governs newly acquired federal lands in central New Mexico. In this legislation, Congress agreed to purchase the 95,000 acre Baca Ranch, but only after creating an experimental public-private management arrangement to oversee this new federal landholding. Bowing to local resistance opposed to expanding the federal estate, Congress established an independent nine-person board of trustees to administer these new lands; it includes two local federal land managers and seven private citizens appointed by the President to four-year terms. The board, in conjunction with the Forest Service, manages the trust lands under a multiple-use sustainability mandate also designed to preserve ecological and historical values and to afford public recreational access to the area. Because the Valles Caldera lands strategically conjoin the Santa Fe National Forest and the Bandelier National Monument, the trust legislation provides for coordinated management efforts to promote ecosystem values. Both the trustees and the Forest Service must adhere to federal environmental laws in making planning and management decisions. Congress viewed the trust arrangement as an experiment to determine whether "new methods of public land management . . . may prove to be cost-effective and environmentally sensitive." Although this unique trust arrangement was linked directly to federal acquisition of the Baca ranchlands, it may also signal congressional receptivity to new public-private management arrangements.

The Quincy and Valles Caldera experiments are not the only examples of such hybrid management arrangements. In the Columbia River Gorge National Scenic Area Act of 1986, for example, Congress created a unique multistate commission to administer, in conjunction with the Forest Service, over 253,000 acres of national forest and private lands situated in Washington and Oregon. In the Steens Mountain Cooperative Management and Protection Area Act of 2000, seeking to "conserve, protect, and manage the [area's] long-term ecological integrity," Congress created a diverse twelve-person advisory council with which the Secretary of the Interior must consult over both the area management plan and its implementation. Not surprisingly, these hybrid management arrangements have spawned other locally inspired legislative proposals that would alter the prevailing federal land management scheme. In Utah's San Rafael Swell country, for example, local officials sought congressional designation of a joint National Heritage Area–National Conservation Area for nearby BLM public lands, with the heritage area subject to management by a local governmental entity, and the conservation area subject to local advisory council oversight. In Colorado, Moffat County commissioners have proposed creating a Northwest Colorado Working Landscape Trust that would vest a locally controlled board of trustees with management responsibility for all federally owned public lands within the county. Upon close inspection, however, many of these proposals seem little more than an attempt to displace federal authority and assert local control over the adjacent public lands. But if successful, these proposals might foretell a broader congressional move toward enabling legislation for individual national forests or BLM resource areas—a development that could undermine the legal uniformity that now prevails across the multiple-use public land systems....

Knowledgeable observers have proffered other hybrid models designed to restructure management arrangements and procedures on the public lands. One of the more provocative models is the brainchild of Daniel Kemmis, who argues that western communities should be vested with management responsibility for nearby public lands on a regional or watershed basis. Kemmis envisions a series of congressionally approved regional or water basin compacts creating a functional regional governance structure (or trust) that is responsible for overseeing the nearby federal lands. The regional trust would be subject to the requirement that the lands remain in public ownership and be managed under a sustainable ecological health standard. Exactly who would serve on the regional trust is vague, but the basic idea is for a new watershed democracy that essentially devolves or eliminates centralized federal control over the multiple-use public lands. A related proposal from the so-called Lubrecht group calls for experimentally transferring some national forests from federal control to a local collaborative group that would then manage them free from the legal mandates and traditions that bind the Forest Service bureaucracy. This proposal would test the thesis that local community groups can manage these lands more efficiently and better than the existing agency. Early on, the Bush administration floated a similar charter forest proposal, which would empower a local trust entity to administer individual national forests "outside the Forest Service structure." The basic thrust of these hybrid management proposals is to displace federal agency authority by substituting an alternate entity with local ties to oversee the public lands. Although the new watershed council or forest trust might still be governed by federal environmental laws and other standards, this does not change the devolutionary nature of these proposals. . . .

The potential advantages of these place-based or hybrid management models are apparent. A place-based approach enables Congress (or the agencies) to acknowledge and address local interests, problems, and circumstances; management standards can be tailored to the landscape itself as well as community economic and social needs. Such arrangements will ordinarily enhance local control over resource decisions and should promote greater local engagement in decision-making processes. Besides taking advantage of local knowledge, these arrangements can help foster a greater sense of community responsibility for maintaining and conserving important resource values, and perhaps even instill meaningful self-enforcement mechanisms. By treating public land policy more as a local rather than national matter, these models may also generate greater consensus over resource priorities and management strategies. . . .

The potential disadvantages of these place-based or hybrid management approaches are also very real. Most obviously, place-based legislative or administrative reforms tend to undermine the systemic qualities that now attach to the public lands. The western federal lands are managed systemically by four separate agencies as national forests, BLM public lands, national parks, and national wildlife refuges. Within each system, a relatively uniform set of laws and policies guides the administering agencies, engendering a level of stability, common purpose, and efficiency in how these lands are managed. Not only does this uniformity minimize fragmentation of the federal estate and facilitate cooperation among the agencies, it ensures equitable treatment for the states, communities, and citizens who utilize or depend upon the public lands and their resources. It also discourages the worst aspects of parochialism, the tendency of local communities to view nearby federal lands solely in terms of their own self-interest. . . .

NEW INSTITUTIONS FOR OLD NEIGHBORHOODS

Robert C. Ellickson

48 DUKE L.J. 75 (1998).

The need for new governance institutions, closer to the ground, exists in cities as well as in rural landscapes. Urban settings raise many of the same legal issues, particularly when it comes to allocating power to local groups that blend public and private. In this article Robert Ellickson offers a proposal for new management institutions created at the level of the urban city block, analogizing their creation to the unitization process in oil and gas fields. His observations would seem equally applicable to other resource settings.

INTRODUCTION

West 163rd Street crosses Washington Heights, a neighborhood near the northern tip of Manhattan. The scene there is typical of a poor section of an inner city. Drug dealers operate openly in the streets and in abandoned buildings. Graffiti and peeling paint disfigure aging facades. Rubbish accumulates in vacant lots. The sidewalks, street furniture, and street plantings are in a sorry state. The amelioration of many of these conditions would be cost-justified, but no institution is providing the collective goods and services necessary to improve the situation. What is to be done?

According to a September 1997 newspaper account, officers of the New York City Police Department (NYPD) have concluded that the residents of West 163rd Street primarily need new micro-institutions to enable them to take collective action at the block level. Leaders of the Thirty–Third Precinct of the NYPD have been encouraging the residents to form a tenant association in each apartment building, and have the eventual goal of organizing all residents into an overarching block association. Because membership in each of these associations would be voluntary, however, the NYPD officers have had to overcome residents' fears that the drug dealers who parade on the block would single out neighborhood activists for retaliation. The police officers are reported to have achieved some success in organizing the block's residents and in helping them deliver previously neglected services. But many residents are not confident that their fragile new institutions will endure when the officers of the Thirty–Third Precinct shift to other endeavors. The block's residents face a classic problem of collective action: when the provision of local public goods is voluntary, each individual may be tempted to take a free ride.

In this Article I propose a legal structure for a block-level institution that would be resistant to the free riding that threatens to undermine the NYPD's efforts on 163rd Street. I refer to this micro-institution as a Block Improvement District (BLID). My proposal builds on—but in important ways departs from—the ideas of George Liebmann and Robert Nelson, two pioneers who have striven to design new micro-institutions for old neighborhoods. The basic idea is to enable the retrofitting of the residential community association—an institution commonly found in new housing developments—to a previously subdivided block such as the one on 163rd Street in Washington Heights. Unlike a voluntary-membership tenants association of the sort that the NYPD has been pushing, in the usual instance a BLID would be mandatory-membership association of property owners. A BLID would levy assessments on its members in order to finance services supplementary to those ordinarily provided by local governments. Partly because I propose authorizing the owners of a supermajority of property to compel dissenting property owners to join a BLID, this innovation would require passage of a state enabling act to govern the formation, structure, and powers of these institutions. Legislative drafters could pattern these statutes after the ones that many states have enacted during the past decade to authorize the establishment of mandatory-membership Business Improvement Districts (BIDs). Just as BIDs have successfully revitalized many central business districts, BLIDs may be able to rejuvenate inner-city residential areas.

I. Alternative Institutions for Providing Block–Level Public Goods

Local public goods are services or physical improvements that enhance the appeal of a discrete, circumscribed territory. Some local public goods, such as a mosquito abatement program, a sewage treatment facility, or a tourism office, can benefit an entire metropolitan area. This Article focuses, however, on the provision of public goods that typically benefit only a few blocks—for example, a tot-lot, a street planter, or a block patrol officer. . . .

Sometimes property owners can succeed in providing block-level public goods even in the absence of a formal institution. For example, informally enforced social norms may induce building owners to paint facades or trim shrubbery. Property owners also may manage to coordinate by express contract, perhaps one that divides the costs of hiring a street patrol service. These decentralized systems work best when a block's owners and residents belong to a closely knit social group. Many inner-city blocks, however, lack social cohesion. When relevant owners and residents are heterogeneous and more numerous than a dozen or two, their efforts at voluntary coordination are likely to be beset by significant free rider problems. . . .

A. The Niche for Block–Level Institutions

Before exploring the theoretical advantages of the provision of services by block-level entities, I adduce evidence that participants in markets for new residential areas have been busily creating institutions that operate at that scale. What works in a new subdivision can provide clues about what might work in an old one.

1. *Lessons from the Residential Community Association.* Residential community associations (RCAs) have been greeted with resounding approval in new real estate developments. The number of RCAs in the United States increased from fewer than 1,000 in 1960 to an estimated 205,000 in 1998. By 1998 more than forty million Americans were living within the jurisdiction of an RCA.

Today a developer of a large subdivision routinely organizes a mandatory-membership RCA before selling the first unit and publicizes the RCA during the marketing period. This business strategy is sound only if most homebuyers anticipate that the value of an RCA's services will exceed the costs of assessments and other burdens it will engender. The prevalence of RCAs in new developments demonstrates that most homebuyers sense that these micro-institutions are effective providers of low-level public goods. Because members rarely vote to terminate an RCA, their initial expectations apparently tend to be fulfilled. Indeed, residents of RCAs generally report a high level of satisfaction with the operation of their associations.

Surveys have found that an average RCA includes from 40 to 160 dwelling units. This is a strong clue that micro-institutions retrofitted onto already subdivided urban lands should be scaled to the level of the block, not of the neighborhood. . . .

2. *Some Advantages of Block–Level Institutions.* Why have housing markets generated tens of thousands of RCAs that typically contain only a few dozens or hundreds of dwelling units? Small institutions may outperform larger ones for a number of reasons. First, micro-institutions seem to be efficiently scaled to produce the most localized varieties of public goods. RCAs in suburban developments commonly engage in removal of refuse, landscaping of public spaces, management of recreation facilities such as swimming pools, and administration of regulations such as architectural controls. Similarly, in an inner city, a BLID might involve itself in maintaining sidewalk planters and tot-lots, removing litter and abandoned vehicles, conducting block-watch programs, and providing other highly localized benefits.

Second, block-level institutions are better able than neighborhood institutions to cater to individuals' tastes for uncommonly provided public goods. For instance, if artists were to concentrate their studios on a particular city block, their BLID could make unusually heavy expenditures on street sculptures. Indeed, the prospect of forming a Block Improvement District might encourage artists to cluster together in the first place.

Third, support from a coterminous informal social network helps an institution flourish. A high level of solidarity generally is easier to maintain within a small group than within a large one. Heterogeneity of interests is less likely when numbers are few. Smallness also enhances the quality of internal gossip and the frequency of chance encounters. These features of a small group help its members administer informal rewards and punishments on one another. As a result, at the block level, social pressures to pull one's oar tend to be stronger than they are at the neighborhood level. Indeed, the act of creating a formal block-level organization such as a BLID might foster acquaintanceships that would then strengthen the informal social capital of the block's residents and property owners. A person who knows his neighbors is more likely, say, to keep his facade painted, to refrain from littering, and to reprimand delinquent children on the block. As Jane Jacobs has perceptively observed, the presence of informal "eyes upon the street" enhances a pedestrian's sense of security. Establishment of a BLID on a block might add to the number not only of formal block patrols, but also of informal lookouts.

Fourth and finally, block-level institutions are well scaled to strengthen members' involvement and skills in collective governance. Many commentators seek to revitalize civic life in the United States. They should welcome block organizations that might serve as incubators of local social capital. The proceedings of a block organization would provide easy opportunities for people to engage in meaningful debate, voting, office-seeking, and other forms of community participation. Candidates for office would be few. There would be little or no wait to speak at a meeting. Participants would be unlikely to be intimidated by the setting because the turf would be familiar and most of the faces known. On routine issues involving block welfare, an ordinary owner or resident would have little reason to be cowed by the views of experts....

II. The Structure and Functions of a Block Improvement District

The BLID proposal envisions authorizing the owners of a supermajority of the taxable real property in an existing block to create an organization that would have limited powers to tax and govern all taxable real property within the district's boundaries.

A. The Case for Governance by Property Owners

Hyper-egalitarian commentators tend to be hostile to RCAs and other institutions that are governed by property owners. They prefer conventional liberal democracy—that is, governance by residents who vote according to the principle of one-resident/one-vote. History, theory, and constitutional precedents, however, all cast doubt on the soundness of the hyper-egalitarians' normative position.

1. Historical Precedents. In numerous contexts American legislatures have authorized landowners to create, by less than unanimous agreement, institutions to govern already subdivided lands within a small district. The roots of this tradition—which is directly at odds with the one-resident/one-vote principle—are ancient. Prior to the American Revolution some colonial governments authorized landowners to obligate reluctant neighbors to participate in the draining of meadows and marshes. More contemporary examples also are plentiful. Some states have enacted unitization statutes that authorize a supermajority of landowners to compel the minority to participate in joint exploitation of a common field of oil and gas. By the late 1980s many states had begun authorizing urban landowners to petition to create a Business Improvement District.

Most pertinently, there are scattered precedents for the compulsory unitization of residential neighborhoods in cities. In the early twentieth century, before the Supreme Court had upheld the constitutionality of ordinary zoning, a few states authorized a majority of homeowners in a neighborhood to prohibit uses other than single-family housing provided that they compensate the property owners damaged by the restrictions. The city of Laredo, Texas, and municipalities in St. Louis County, Missouri, frequently have privatized street segments to enable abutting homeowners to set up a street association empowered to levy assessments. Many states authorize property owners to approve (or disapprove) the formation of a special assessment district (or other special district) that possesses the power to tax.

In sum, governance by property owners hardly has been exceptional in American law. Indeed, the state statutes that regulate condominium associations and other RCAs almost invariably require that an association allot voting power according to property ownership rather than according to the one-resident/one-vote principle. What could be the appeal of this system for governing a micro-territorial institution?

2. The Rationale for Voting by Property: The Capitalization of Local Benefits and Assessments into Land Values. A block-level institution's niche is the provision of public goods with territorially focused benefits. Both theory and evidence indicate that most of the benefits of a localized public good redound to the owners of real estate located within the benefitted territory. The advent of a desirable public good prompts households and firms to bid more to rent or buy the benefitted properties. As a result, the value of ownership interests in the affected real estate rises. . . .

B. Powers and Functions

> . . . Both the general enabling statute and the BLID's own articles of incorporation should routinely authorize a BLID to provide supplementary services on at least the following fronts (with examples indicated):
>
> —life safety (block patrols, crossing guards, supplementary sidewalk and street repair, emergency snowplowing);
>
> —sanitation (street cleaning, litter removal, vermin eradication);
>
> —beautification (graffiti removal, street-furniture maintenance, tree and lawn care);
>
> —culture and entertainment (parties, newsletters, research on block history); and
>
> —political activity on behalf of the block (lobbying, litigation).

In addition, a BLID routinely should have the authority to undertake a variety of capital improvements:

> —street furniture (signage, benches, light posts, waste receptacles);
>
> —landscaping of public spaces (street trees, sidewalk planters);
>
> —supplementary or ornamental repavings (sidewalks, streets); and
>
> —land purchases (community gardens, tot-lots, lots with derelict buildings (in order to eliminate them)).

Should a BLID also have regulatory powers? As Liebmann and Nelson both contend, there is a compelling case for empowering a block association to relax many of its city's zoning restrictions. Nelson plausibly anticipates that a grass-roots organization would be more likely than a municipality to bargain to lift an inefficient land use restriction, such as a legal barrier to opening a day care center. As a long-time proponent of the decentralization of land use regulation, I applaud experimentation on this front. Most zoning regulations mainly govern use allocations, building bulks, lot shapes and sizes, parking requirements, and other land uses whose spillover effects are limited. A BLID should be empowered to grant variances from these sorts of regulations, although perhaps not from the few zoning provisions (such as limits on extraordinary heights) that are aimed at preventing neighborhood-wide negative externalities.

Nelson also proposes entitling a block organization to impose new regulations within its territory. The success of RCAs, which typically have limited powers to adopt bylaws to regulate members' behavior, suggests that experiments in this vein would be worthwhile. Conferring this power might prove to be unwise, however. American law rightly is more tolerant of grass-roots deregulation than of grass-roots regulation. A BLID's regulations might irk both property owners who dissented in the referendum that established it, and also resident tenants who were not eligible to participate in that referendum. Liebmann, therefore, is wary of empowering block-level organizations to regulate. As a compromise, I urge drafters of a state enabling act to authorize formation of extraordinary Regulatory BLIDs (RBLIDs). An RBLID's articles of incorporation could include limited regulatory powers of the sort that an RCA typically possesses. The statute would deny these powers to an ordinary BLID. On the other hand, to enhance an RBLID's legitimacy and responsiveness, the enabling act also would condition the formation of an RBLID on approval by extraordinary and concurrent majorities of both its owners and residents. The statute might also require affirmative votes both from owners of three-fourths of the taxable property in the district and from two-thirds of the resident registered voters casting votes in the referendum. To further curb regulatory abuses by RBLIDs, courts could look to the well-developed body of law on judicial review of RCAs. The general point is that a governing institution such as RBLIDs warrants more and more external checks as its power grows.

IDEAS, INCENTIVES, GIFTS, AND GOVERNANCE: TOWARD CONSERVATION STEWARDSHIP OF PRIVATE LAND, IN CULTURAL AND PSYCHOLOGICAL PERSPECTIVE

Christopher S. Elmendorf

2003 U. Ill. L. Rev. 423.

Among the models that can be used to form new governance institutions are existing ones set up to perform specific development functions, such as the drainage district or irrigation district that is run by landowners for their mutual benefit. In this wide-ranging article, Christopher Elmendorf considers the many types of new institutions that might be created using this model. He explains why they might gain broader acceptance and work more effectively than traditional local governments that exercise regulatory powers.

1. The Special District Model

American farmers and ranchers have long benefited from landowner-initiated and landowner-controlled special districts, which furnish irrigation water, drain swampy lands, control pests, even seed the clouds.

There are thousands, maybe tens of thousands, of such districts across the country.

A prototypical special district enabling act begins by specifying a purpose for which landowners may create special districts, such as irrigation. It then establishes a petition process by which districts come into existence. District proponents are required to collect the signatures of a certain number or fraction of the landowners in the district they propose, whereupon the petition is heard by a county judge or county commissioners. The presiding officials make a finding as to whether the district serves the public interest, and then hear objections from any landowners who want to be excluded on the ground that they would receive no benefits from the district. After revising the proposed boundaries to exclude unbenefited landowners, the officials order the district created or, depending on the statute, hold a vote of the affected landowners. Some enabling acts give one vote to each landowner; others weigh votes by acreage or assessed property value. Many enabling acts condition special district creation on supermajoritian rather than simple majoritarian assent from the affected landowners.

Some special district statutes instruct the county court or commissioners to appoint the district directors. Others have the district landowners elect directors. Directors administer the district project, levy assessments, and issue bonds. Their discretion in distributing the costs of the district among member landowners may be sharply constrained by statute or by the courts.

Agricultural special districts commonly exercise powers of taxation and eminent domain; much less often do they employ the police power. Still, police-power districts are not without precedent. For example, liability for livestock trespass has been an object of special district regulation. And in rare cases, landowner-controlled special districts wield planning and zoning authority comparable to that of a city or county. Also, some otherwise ordinary special districts carry out their work under the guise of the police power. A police-power justification traditionally exempted these districts from certain lines of constitutional challenge. Assessments for draining and filling wetlands and channelizing rivers have been so justified.

As a way out of the private-lands predicament, landowner-controlled special districts ("special nature districts") have several virtues. They can discipline holdouts; they jibe with the political rhetoric of the mainline agricultural trade groups; and they are uniquely positioned to change the normative valence of ecological stewardship and government cooperation in rural landowner communities. Also, they powerfully establish a shared fate among member landowners.

For purposes of these arguments, let me stipulate a few features of the nature district: (1) that its existence depends on dual-supermajority support from the member landowners (a straight-up vote or petition, and one weighted by acreage or assessed value); (2) that its ordinances take effect subject to referenda approval by the member landowners, again on a dual-supermajority basis; and (3) that it is governed by elected rather than appointed commissioners. Nonlandowners would not have the right to vote in special districts elections....

IV. Nature Districts: Powers, Purposes, and Services

The workings of nature districts are readily envisioned by example. This part illustrates the possibilities by way of the desert mountains of southern Arizona and New Mexico, degraded rivers East and West, and the problematics of big game management in ranch country. My brush strokes are quick—operational details comprise a project for another paper.

A. Ecological Management on a Landscape Scale: The Malpai Group

Along the Arizona–New Mexico border, hard by Mexico, all the stars align just right for private-lands conservation. This is Malpai country, more than a million acres of desert grasslands and broken mountains, home to one of the greatest concentrations of rare species found anywhere in the continental United States. Land ownership maps of the Malpai region resemble jigsaw puzzles, unassembled. New Mexico has pieces of turf here and there. Other chunks sport the colors of the U.S. Bureau of Land Management, or the U.S. Forest Service. Arizona lays claim to a few stretches. And intermingled throughout are the holdings of the private landowners, who claim about half of the total in fee and lease the balance for grazing.

A few years ago, The Nature Conservancy bought the 325,000–acre Gray Ranch, which it intended to convey to the FWS for operation as a national wildlife refuge. Neighboring ranchers objected. It was their good fortune that one of the nearby landowners, respected locally and by the Conservancy, happened to be heir to the Anheuser–Busch fortune. He struck a deal with the Conservancy, creating a charitable foundation to hold the Gray Ranch, and helped the Conservancy and area ranchers get to know one another. The ranchers and the Conservancy turned out to have some similar goals, goals for which they needed each other: to hold at bay the subdivisions sweeping down from Tucson, and to reintroduce fire to the grasslands (which necessitated the public agencies' cooperation, which the Conservancy was well positioned to secure). There were further strokes of good fortune, antidotes to polarization. It turned out that one respected local rancher had been working with herpetologists for years to conserve one of the world's last populations of the Chiricahua leopard frog, and that another, though five generations deep into the community, was the son of an English professor and had married a microbiologist. Malpai was a land of intersecting groups, not a pocket of rural hostility to the fearful, unknown urban environmentalist.

Malpai's successes are legion and widely reported. Fire is back, the Conservancy having played go-between with the public agencies; swarming ecologists monitor just about everything; livestock management is evolving; and ranchers have bartered conservation easements on some

30,000 acres in return for grazing rights to the Gray Ranch. Less often heralded are the holdouts. Even Malpai, blessed with good fortune, must reckon with holdouts. A few ranchers want nothing to do with the environmentalists or conservation stewardship. By selling to developers they could badly disrupt the emerging management regimes. Subdivisions and fire would not mix, the population influx probably would hurt jaguar recovery, and the community would lose the desolate expanses it cherishes. With nature districts, the Malpai Group could keep the dissenters from undermining everyone else's work. The possibilities are wide open. Imagine what the Malpai Group might accomplish through one of the following districts, or some combination thereof:

- "Open-fire" (default rule) district. This district would absolve landowners of liability for bona-fide stewardship fires, intentionally set, that leap property lines and damage other property in the district. Developers beware. It would represent a modern, post-Smokey-the-Bear updating of the "no-fence" or "open-range" districts of yore, which alleviated member landowners of responsibility for fencing in their livestock.

- Open-space zoning district. If Malpai ranchers were to choose for their community a minimum lot size of, say, one square mile, few developers would come knocking. This may sound fanciful, but elsewhere in the West (in Montana) state law authorizes landowners in rural, unzoned areas to establish zoning districts in self-defined jurisdictions by supermajority petition of the affected landowners. In Jefferson County, Montana, a group of agriculturalists picked 640 acres (one square mile) as their minimum lot size.

- Subdivision "time-out" district. This district would establish a "notice" period (say, up to twelve months) for property owners who intend to subdivide land. Just as the sixty-day notice that federal environmental statutes demand of citizen plaintiffs gives the Justice Department a chance to intervene in citizen suits, a notice period for subdivision would give the neighboring ranchers, the Anheuser–Busch heirs, and the environmental groups a window to negotiate before the land gets chopped up. The time-out district might not provide the peace of mind of a very-large-lot zoning district, but it would not entail much financial sacrifice either.

- Open-space "backstop" district. The district here conceived combines time-out powers with eminent domain. Notified of a pending subdivision, the district would be positioned to condemn the landowner's development rights—insofar as the district could secure donations from members or outside conservation groups.

- Transfer-tax/ecological improvement district. This district might also be authorized to levy special assessments, or impact fees on new development. Enabling legislation would cap the tax rate. The tax would discourage the sale of land, stabilizing the community, while also furnishing a pool of money for purchasing development rights and making other conservation investments. The district might be authorized to levy general property taxes, special assessments, or impact fees instead of real estate transfer taxes, but these instruments are not likely to prove as popular among long-time ranchers.

B. Rivers, Floods, and Runoff

In the East, rivers flood too often. In the West, they flood not often enough. East and West, runoff from streamside agriculture and silviculture threatens aquatic life. East and West, riverine and riparian biota suffers for rivers' separation from their floodplains. Special districts bear no small measure of the blame.

Starting in the nineteenth century, Eastern and Midwestern farmers banded into special drainage districts to finance ditches and drains, which hurried the flow of water off their fields, out of wetlands, and into streams. Downstream riparians formed special levee districts to channelize the ever-rising rush. The federal government was an assiduous aider and abetter, subsidizing levees and insuring riparians against flood damage.

Springtime snowmelt in the mountains used to send tremendous early season torrents down Western rivers. The spring rip surged into floodplains, leaving behind slow moving backwaters that served native fish as rearing grounds, and fine silt deposits that cottonwoods need to germinate. High spring flows scoured the sediment from river-bottom cobbles, too, making them suitable for spawning fish. The twentieth century's binge of dam building—financed largely by the feds, but carried out in close cooperation with special irrigation districts—corked the seasonal floods and imperiled aquatic and riparian ecosystems across the West. In the free-flowing rivers that remain, lax permitting by the Army Corps of Engineers and weak floodplain protections under local law have created a sort of prisoner's dilemma for riparians. The Corps liberally hands out permission for landowners to protect their property against flooding with levees and riprap; each landowner who does so increases the velocity of the river as it rounds the next bend, which creates pressure on the landowner's downstream neighbor to install flood barriers; and so forth and so on. The process essentially transforms rivers into swift, precarious, and costly-to-maintain canals.

On other fronts, though, federal policy is restorative. The Bureau of Reclamation experiments with episodic springtime flushes of its Western reservoirs. The NRCS buys floodplain easements and restores the encumbered land's hydrologic function; it also pays farmers and ranchers to plant buffer strips of native vegetation along waterways, and to exclude livestock seasonally from riparian pastures. The FWS finances wetlands restoration and protection. Just as irrigation and drainage districts once worked hand-in-hand with the government to undo natural rivers, nature districts could assist in putting rivers back together again. Consider the following scenarios.

- (Physical) flood control co-management districts. To overcome the riparian prisoners' dilemma, landowners could form nature districts with permitting authority supplemental to the weak-kneed Army

Corps of Engineers. In this venture the nature district might find it profitable (financially and technically) to partner with the more conservationist FWS. FWS scientists could help district commissioners make better permitting and mitigation decisions. Broad societal benefits justify the FWS's paying the nature district for co-management rights.

• Wetland restoration assessment districts. Midwestern states once authorized drainage districts to apportion the cost of improvements between district landowners and upstream districts, on the theory that enhanced downstream drainage capacity redounds to the benefit of upstream farmers. In a modern updating of this theory, upstream districts that restore wetlands to reduce flooding in the district and downstream would be authorized to apportion the cost between district landowners and downstream vicinages. Whether such an apportionment is technically feasible or defensible is open to question, but the possibility is worth investigating.

• Floodplain reconnection districts. It is easy enough for the NRCS to breach a levee and buy a floodplain easement if the breach only affects a couple of landowners. If the floodwaters would spread out over many properties, though, the project becomes tricky. A nature district comprised of the affected landowners might help in two ways. It could signal community sentiment through a purely hortatory vote, through which landowners would express approval or disapproval of the breaching plan. Second, the district might sell to the NRCS a collective conservation easement over the member landowners' floodplain property, solving the holdout problem.

• Riparian revegetation districts. Early irrigation arrangements in the American West burdened the landowner with responsibility for constructing and maintaining the portion of the shared waterworks that traversed his land. A modern analogue would burden each riparian farmer with responsibility for maintaining streamside buffer strips of native vegetation, and each rancher with the duty to furnish a riparian fence and seasonally exclude livestock. In exchange for the district's commitment, a conservation agency would make an annual rental payment, at a price reflecting the degree of habitat protection afforded by the district's chosen regulations. Member landowners with innovative conservation or mitigation plans for their acreage could petition the contracting government agency for regulatory variances.

C. *Ranching for Wildlife*

Most Western states now sponsor "ranching for wildlife" programs. Landowners who improve habitat for wildlife are rewarded with extended hunting seasons and a guaranteed number of transferable hunting tags specific to the farm or ranch. These the landowner sells for premium prices. Ranching for wildlife can be a boon to very large landowners, and to wildlife. For small landowners the program has not worked as well—it is costly for the State to administer, and the resulting habitat improvement are scattershot rather than contiguous, and thus of modest conservation value.

Special wildlife management districts could complement and enhance ranching for wildlife programs, increasing the value of wildlife and, for midsize landowners, the viability of wildlife ranching. State fish and game departments face incentives to maximize the number of permits they sell, and hence the size and reproductive potential of wildlife herds (a sex ratio skewed toward females), rather than the value of wildlife. Landowners who sell hunting rights, by contrast, confront incentives to manage for prized "trophy" males. If landowners were empowered to establish a concurrent regulatory regime, such that hunters within the nature districts had to have permits from both the district and the State, landowners could restrict the take of males and build up a trophy herd.

Also through nature districts, small landowners could band together and act as one large landowner vis-à-vis the state fish and game agency. Thus ranching for wildlife could become viable for owners of modestly proportioned farms and ranches. Collective contracting would lower administrative costs to the State, and, more importantly, make it feasible for member landowners to coordinate their game harvests and habitat restoration projects across a large, contiguous landscape. The upshot would be better wildlife, better habitat, and better hunts—which for the landowner would translate into higher income.

NOTE, APPURTENANCY RECONCEPTUALIZED: MANAGING WATER IN AN ERA OF SCARCITY

Olivia S. Choe

113 YALE L. J. 1909 (2004).

For local institutions to function well, as we have seen, they often need to fit into larger governance structures that possess responsibilities over larger spatial scales. Scholars of common property regimes have explored many methods of nesting smaller entities into larger ones. That literature is surveyed in this article by Olivia Choe, which considers the ways that the longstanding appurtenancy rule in riparian rights law (allocating water rights to landowners appurtenant to waterways) can be viewed as a mechanism for defining membership in a common property regime. (The equally vast literature on allocating power to deal with environmental problems–the issue of environmental federalism–is thoughtfully critiqued in William W. Buzbee, *Contextual Environmental Federalism*, 14 N.Y.U. ENVTL. L. J. 108 (2005).)

2. NESTED ENTERPRISES: SOME MODELS

Numerous instances of successful nested enterprises exist. This Subsection explores four models and considers in each instance how norms of usage and conservation developed by appurtenant groups can be effectuated within a larger government system. These examples highlight the ways in which nested enterprises may yield the advantages of both the commons and the state, while mitigating the weaknesses of each.

One nested enterprise model, which we might call the reverse command-and-control model, utilizes state authority, expertise, and administrative resources to enforce usage rules developed by appurtenant groups to protect against scarcity. For example, the Maine lobster gangs have, in recent years, formed links with state government, which in turn aids them in the enforcement of their voluntary restrictions on fishing. Acheson notes that the inhabitants of Monhegan Island have "persuaded the legislature to pass a law forbidding fishing in Monhegan waters from June 25 to January 1," thereby making official a customary closed season that the islanders have observed since the early 1900s. Fishers from Swan Island likewise convinced Maine's commissioner of marine resources to enforce a self-imposed limit on the number of traps surrounding the island. A similar example comes from the Aleut community in Alaska, where the community controls access to the territories, and thus can control the level of fishing, but has also "made the state limit fishing effort in adjacent territories where the local stocks might be intercepted by outsiders."

Yet another example can be found overseas, in the state of Kumaon in India, where centralized rules create "a framework for the management of forests rather than a defining straitjacket," and at the same time establish "a domain of relatively autonomous action and rule making in which local residents and their representatives can operate." Specifically, local authorities "make rules and enforce them," "facilitate some kinds of actions . . . and restrict others," meet frequently to modify rules, and "create monitoring and sanctioning mechanisms." The state government supplements these efforts by supervising recordkeeping, coordinating harvesting, providing technical assistance, and aiding in rule enforcement. As these examples demonstrate, reverse command and control takes advantage of the greater skill of local users in developing rules of conservation, and places those rules under the enforcement authority of government.

Another nested governance model that has gained attention recently combines market-based tradable allowances with community management. Under tradable allowance schemes,

> governmental regulators in effect place an upper limit or cap on the total quantity of a given resource that is to be available for use. . . . The regulators then divide the capped total into individual allowances. Henceforth they require all resource users to purchase or trade for whatever allowances they use.

In a nested enterprise model, quotas are allocated to appurtenant communities, rather than individuals or individual entities. In Alaska, for example, some of the walleye pollock quota was allocated to native communities; similarly, New Zealand transferred forty percent of its fishery quota to the Maori. Such schemes incorporate groups of users—proximate both to each other and to the resource—into a larger regulatory market, thereby protecting community interests while maintaining the advantages of a centralized decisionmaker for setting and managing overall goals.

In these regimes, as compared to the reverse command-and-control model discussed above, the state does not undertake enforcement of specific usage restrictions developed by the user community. Instead, it grants an appurtenant group of users a block of rights that is presumably large enough to allow the group to maintain a sustainable level of withdrawal, leaving the group to implement and enforce its own conservation norms. At the same time, the tradable allowance scheme permits user groups to operate within a broader market of uses and users. The existence of a wider market in standardized rights can facilitate transfers from lower-to higher-value uses, thereby increasing the efficiency of resource usage. The creation of standardized rights can also facilitate coordination across different appurtenant groups—functioning as a kind of common language and in some instances leading to larger-scale conservation efforts.

A third model—what we might call the horizontal governance model—comes from voluntary associations of groundwater users in Southern California. These nested enterprises should be particularly persuasive not only because they involve water as opposed to fisheries or forest management, but also because they demonstrate the viability of such a model among institutional, as opposed to individual, users. The parties involved here are not members of an Indian village, or an Aleut fishing community, but include municipalities, utility companies, and private mutual corporations.

Elinor Ostrom documents the rise of "a set of institutions [established by water producers] to manage a series of groundwater basins located beneath the Los Angeles metropolitan area." Faced with the prospect of saltwater incursions, dropping aquifers, and uncertain rights, appropriators began to engage in a "pumping race," a classic example of a tragedy of the commons. During the 1940s and 1950s, many believed that the race would result in the destruction of the basins, with dire consequences for the water supply in southern California. But instead of succumbing to the tragedy, water producers entered into a series of negotiations, through which they were able to form institutional structures that combined public and private governance, to set restrictions on withdrawals, and to institute conservation measures. Nested within the public arena, private actors were able "to impose constraints on themselves."

A few features of these settlements are particularly noteworthy. First, the disputes arose among functionally appurtenant users—claimants with shared interests in the same body of water. Second, in coming up with a solution, it was important to the users that they maintain some measure of management authority; they did not want to turn decisions over to large-scale agencies, "for fear that they would lose control of the decisions being made and might end up worse off." In short, they exhibited the same desire for autonomy and self-governance as members of the common property regimes discussed above. Third, while users maintained decisionmaking control, they did so within a larger governmental regime; the institutional solution was neither deregulation nor centralization, but rather "polycentric" systems of shared private-public governance. While the first two models of nested governance are largely vertical and thus somewhat hierarchical, with the state at the top and user groups at the bottom, this model vests management authority in a more horizontal, or multipronged, manner. Fourth, the costs of monitoring and enforcement were shared by the users (two-thirds) and the state (one-third). And finally, the negotiations among parties led to a better clarification of rights, which in turn allowed a market to develop, leading to a transfer of rights to those using them at "a higher value."

The Ostrom study allows us to draw two important conclusions. First, appurtenant groups can be defined to include institutional users—here, the appurtenant groups were voluntary associations made up of both individual and institutional user-appropriators—who may prove just as capable of developing and enforcing conservation norms as individuals within a small community. Specifically, institutional appropriators restricted their water usage and monitored each other's withdrawals, just as farmers in huerta villages restricted water usage to certain parcels of land and kept an eye on their neighbors' withdrawals. Second, a nested enterprise model in which management is "polycentric" rather than centralized, and in which appurtenant groups of organized users actively participate, can produce an allocation of tradable rights that is efficient and stable, as well as conducive to conservation....

A fourth model—what we might call the umbrella model—is illustrated by local water institutions in the western United States. Mutuals and water districts are the retail distributors of most domestic water and much agricultural water in western states. Mutuals are private nonprofit corporations whose customers are also shareholders; water districts, on the other hand, are governed by elected boards, like other local government units. "Both types of institutions engage in a broad set of activities, including obtaining and storing necessary water supplies, transporting the water to their service areas, and distributing it to their members." ...

These institutions have developed into multilayered regimes, thus exemplifying a more complex, cross-scale kind of nested enterprise than the models already discussed. Mutuals and water districts may obtain their water from a larger umbrella agency acting as a wholesaler, or they may sit within larger umbrella institutions themselves. All of these institutions ultimately sit under the general authority of the legislature.

Several features of these institutions are familiar. For instance, whereas users have generally been resistant to state proposals for conservation, they have been receptive to conservation programs implemented by local institutions. These programs have been able to reconfigure groundwater rights; impose well-spacing rules; institute pump taxes and import projects to optimize use of ground and surface water; and establish loan programs, conservation rebates, and, in some cases, tiered pricing structures. In short, appurtenant groups of users have, here as elsewhere, voluntarily recognized the need to conserve, and they have advanced creative methods to meet that need, but in a way that emphasizes local control.

Thompson also describes at length the failure of state governments to facilitate voluntary transfers: "Legal restrictions on formal water transfers pose insurmountable transaction costs for many small water users...." In response, users "have employed local institutions to obtain or exchange water." Institutions provide members with "largely interchangeable water entitlements," allowing the development of standardized markets; members of institutions are also likely to be familiar with each other's needs; and many institutions have constructed extensive physical infrastructure that facilitates the transfer of water from one user to another. Finally, institutions have proved adept at allocating water during times of scarcity: They can "balance their service areas, water supplies, and storage capabilities.... [They] can also more readily calculate and enforce pro rata allocations." In the language of appurtenancy, physical, social, and functional proximity among users facilitates efficient trade and reallocation within the group.

Of course, mutuals and, to an even greater extent, districts can exhibit some of the less savory features of appurtenant communities as well. While they vary in size, and while some encompass a large geographic area and a range of users, their success seems due in part to the homogeneous—and sometimes insular—interests of their membership. Many mutuals are "enlivened with a dollop of community spirit." While such community spirit may make informal transfers between members less cumbersome than statutory transfers and encourage the adoption of stronger conservation measures than those imposed by the state, internal community norms also reflect the exclusionary tendencies and insider-outsider mentality that an appurtenant group of users can exhibit. In particular, Thompson notes the resistance of some local institutions to interjurisdictional transfers, such as "ag-urban" trades. Such resistance can often be the result of "parochical self-interest that is inconsistent with broader societal good."

REGULATING VERSUS PAYING LAND OWNERS TO PROTECT THE ENVIRONMENT

John D. Echeverria

26 J. Land Resources & Envtl. L. 1 (2005).

One of the knottiest questions that arises in any land-management regime is how to convince resource owners to use their resources in ways consistent with the common good. The two main choices appeared starkly in the final case above, Realen Valley Forge, *in which a local government vacillated between regulating a golf course and buying it. The tradeoff involves much more than merely fairness to landowners (and to taxpayers). It raises fundamental policy questions about the meaning of land ownership and about the most effective methods of achieving landscape-scale goals, as John Echeverria explains here.*

The basic problem is to induce the private landowner to conserve on his land, and no conceivable millions or billions for public land purchase can alter that fact, nor the fact that so far he hasn't done it.

Aldo Leopold

Should we protect the ecological, open space, aesthetic and many other public values of private lands by restricting uses of land through regulation? Or should we pursue these objectives by paying owners who volunteer to place restrictions on their land? Or should we use both of these approaches in tandem, perhaps to address different challenges, in different circumstances or in different locations? If the latter, how should these different approaches be coordinated to avoid potential conflicts between them and improve the overall effectiveness of U.S. protection efforts?

These rank among the most fundamental and pressing questions in U.S. land use policy. A handful of thoughtful scholars have begun to explore this difficult topic. But policymakers and advocates have largely failed to address these questions. In practice, different government officials and conservation advocates tend to embrace one approach or the other, and supporters of each approach can be seen as engaging in a kind of friendly, and sometimes not so friendly, rivalry. However, there has been little discussion among practitioners about whether one approach is superior to the other under certain circumstances, or how use of one approach might interact with the other. The primary purpose of this paper is to generate more public debate about these questions.

As the discussion that follows will show, weighing the pros and cons of these different approaches is a complex task that, so far at least, fails to produce pat answers. Nonetheless, this paper draws a cautionary conclusion about the long-term utility of the voluntary, publicly-financed approach to land protection, especially the use of conservation easements. Thus, in contrast with most of the other scholarship in this area, this paper presents a frankly skeptical perspective on what is arguably the most popular approach to land protection in the U.S. today. In particular, this paper raises the concern that widespread use of the voluntary, publicly-financed approach to conservation may undermine the viability of the regulatory approach. At worst, widespread use of the voluntary approach may have the ironic and unfortunate effect of setting back the cause of environmental protection itself by making it more difficult and expensive to protect the environment. . . .

I. The Not so Quiet Counter-Revolution in Land Use Controls

. . . The early 1970s saw the enactment of many far-reaching regulatory measures at the federal, state, and local levels. At the national level, the legislation that launched the nation's modern program of land and resource conservation, including the wetlands provision of the Clean Water Act, the Endangered Species Act, and the Coastal Zone Management Act, were primarily regulatory in nature. Similarly, at the state level, such measures as the 1973 Oregon Senate Bill 100 and the 1971 Adirondack Park Agency Act, also used the regulatory approach. All of these laws remain in place today and, generally speaking, continue to be effective in protecting significant land resources. However, contrary to widespread expectations at the time, they did not succeed in stimulating the adoption of a large number of other, equally far-reaching regulatory programs.

This reversal was the result, in significant part, of the rise of a substantial and vociferous property rights movement. The movement drew its principal intellectual inspiration from the writings of Professor Richard Epstein of the University of Chicago School of Law. In a remarkably successful "reframing" of the environmental debate, the property rights movement converted negative opposition to environmental and community protections into an affirmative campaign on behalf of personal liberties grounded in property ownership. Takings advocates have focused, with only limited success, on persuading the courts to adopt more expansive interpretations of the Takings Clause and, with somewhat greater success, on attempting to obtain enactment of legislative measures codifying the takings agenda. However, the greatest success of the property rights movement has been indirect: creating a political environment that makes it difficult to advocate for, and even more difficult to enact, meaningful new regulatory programs.

Simultaneously with the rise of the property rights movement, the 1980s and 1990s witnessed the rise of the alternative approach of paying volunteers to protect the environment. The Nature Conservancy emerged as the largest and arguably most successful national conservation group. The Land Trust Alliance and the Conservation Fund encouraged the creation of hundreds of local and regional private land trusts around the country. One of the most important catalysts in the creation of the land trust movement was the addition of new provisions to the Internal Revenue Code, made permanent in 1980, allowing land owners to take tax deductions for gifts of easements to charitable institutions. At the same, the land trust movement gained strength from the frustrations that conservationists frequently encountered in their efforts to expand, and sometimes even merely defend, regulatory programs.

The future direction of U.S. land use policy is difficult to predict. It remains to be seen whether the current, pervasive political hostility to the regulatory approach represents a long-term shift in thinking. . . .

. . .

As will become apparent from the following, it is difficult, at least at this stage of our learning, to reach definitive conclusions about whether regulations or conservation easements are most likely to maximize social welfare. There are arguments for each approach. There is no handy formula for toting up all the benefits and costs of each option in order to compare them. Furthermore, the strength of the arguments for each approach varies a good deal depending upon the character of the natural resources at issue and the specific development threat presented. Absolute answers must await another day.

A. The Advantages of Regulation

1. Addresses the Collective Action Problem

The most important advantage of the regulatory approach to land protection is its capacity to address the "collective action" problem. A well-ordered land use pattern can benefit a community and its members by maintaining critical ecosystem functions, reducing public infrastructure costs, minimizing conflicts between different land uses and producing a healthier and more livable community. But if each citizen, left to his or her own devices, can refuse to join in the common effort to maintain the community, pursuing these beneficial goals frequently will become impossible. Each citizen would benefit if he could selfishly pursue her individual self interest, and "free ride" on the contributions of others. In the absence of an external constraint allowing citizens to coordinate their efforts, the pursuit of narrow self-interests will frequently prevail over the common interest. Specifically, an individual owner within an historic district could destroy a building that is critical to the integrity of the district, build an unsightly structure in the middle of a scenic vista, or degrade the habitat of an endangered species.

Regulations address the collective action problem by creating a mechanism to ensure that individual citizens' contributions to the common welfare will be effective and not exploited by others. They also ensure that citizens' actions for the public welfare will be matched by contributions of others, generating more confidence, and more willing participation, in community protection efforts.

By contrast, voluntary conservation easements plainly confront a serious collective action problem. If the goal is to preserve the rural character of an agricultural area, the entire project could be thwarted if some owners agree to put their lands under easement but other owners do not agree. Ironically, the conservation efforts of some land owners may make other owners less inclined to restrict their lands because the restrictions may preserve scenic amenities and reduce the supply of developable land, making development of unrestricted land more profitable. Environmentalists generally decry a voluntary approach to controlling global warming or addressing air and water pollution. A voluntary approach to land conservation appears to be no more workable in many cases....

Biologists have increasingly come to recognize the importance of addressing environmental issues on a large scale and, accordingly, conservationists have turned their attention from parcel by parcel protection to conservation of larger geographical areas. Given the capacity of regulations to overcome the collective action problem, regulations are much better adapted to address conservation at the landscape level than voluntary approaches. Not surprisingly, therefore, some of the most significant and most successful landscape-level conservation efforts in the U.S., such as the programs protecting the Adirondack Park region and the New Jersey pinelands, have relied largely on the regulatory approach. By contrast, the voluntary approach is not as well suited for pursuing conservation on a landscape level. . . .

While the basic argument for regulation based on the collective action problem is initially straightforward, it turns out, upon analysis, to be somewhat more complicated. In the first place, public financing of conservation under the easement approach can be viewed as a means of overcoming the collective action problem. The tax system arguably provides an enforceable method of ensuring that all citizens contribute to the pursuit of common social objectives, including conservation. But the critical political process for conservation purposes is not the decision to collect taxes but rather the decision how to allocate tax revenues. Because of the collective action problem, one would anticipate that the conservation-minded public would have difficulty competing for public dollars with more discrete and well-organized interest groups. This prediction appears to be borne out by the relatively small amount of taxpayer dollars devoted to land conservation. On the other hand, one would anticipate that relatively well organized groups of land owners would lobby to shape conservation programs in order to maximize the financial rewards for land owners and to minimize the burdens. This too appears borne out in practice, especially in the farm conservation programs. . . .

3. Provides for Relatively Strong Enforcement

Another advantage of the regulatory approach in terms of overall efficiency is that regulatory programs typically include relatively strong enforcement mechanisms. Regulatory agencies can invoke administrative, civil, and even criminal enforcement powers to compel compliance with regulatory standards and impose penalties for non-compliance. In addition, many federal as well as state environmental laws include citizen-suit provisions allowing citizens, acting as private attorneys general, to go to court to enforce regulatory standards. Citizen suit provisions have proven quite effective in improving the level of compliance with environmental laws.

By contrast, the tools available for enforcing voluntarily negotiated conservation easements are far weaker. In many states, the only party with clear authority to sue to enforce an easement is the holder of the easement, such as a private land trust. The land trust may be reluctant to press a landowner over enforcement issues for fear of gaining a hard-nosed reputation that drives away potential future contributors of land. Smaller land trusts may lack the financial resources to mount effective enforcement actions in court. Even if it has the resources to bring an enforcement action, the land trust may face competing demands on limited financial resources, possibly leading the trust to forego enforcement to pursue other priorities. Moreover, the land trust may cease to exist at some point in the future, because of financial difficulties or other reasons.

Some, but apparently not most, easements include provisions granting back up enforcement authority to larger land conservation organizations. The state attorney general, under the authority to safeguard public charitable trusts, may have the legal authority to enforce conservation easements, but policing of private easements must compete with numerous other law enforcement priorities. In addition, the extreme variability among easements complicates the enforcement challenge, and requires extensive resources even to monitor easement compliance.

Finally, regardless of whether conservation easements are expressly authorized by state law, judicial willingness to enforce easements may founder because of the judiciary's deeply ingrained hostility to "dead hand" controls on the use of land. For all of these reasons, there is substantial reason to think that private enforcement of conservation easements, at least as they are currently designed and administered, will be less effective than public (and third party) enforcement of regulations . . .

B. The Advantages of Easements

1. Fosters Cooperative Conservation

The primary efficiency argument in favor of the voluntary, publicly-financed approach to land protection is that it rewards environmentally beneficial behavior by private land owners and thereby encourages and promotes more such behavior. By making friends with, rather than waging war on, land owners this approach encourages owners to support rather than oppose conservation programs. In addition, the argument proceeds, once they become invested in conservation, owners will develop and help implement innovative environmental protection strategies that centralized government bureaucracies would overlook.

These advantages of the voluntary, publicly-financed approach to conservation stand in sharp contrast, according to advocates of volunteerism, to the sometimes perverse incentives created by regulation. Owners are said to be encouraged by regulations to avoid coverage by environmental laws, such as by developing an area before it is placed under more restrictive zoning. One version of this argument is that owners faced with burdens imposed under the Endangered Species Act will have an incentive to "shoot, shovel and shut up." Rather than being willing, innovative partners in conservation, regulated owners will consistently resist and seek to evade engagement in conservation programs. In economic terms, according to this argument, the investment of time and effort in evading the law will produce "deadweight loses," reducing the overall efficiency of conservation efforts.

While plainly not frivolous, there are a number of responses to this argument. One general problem with relying on public financing of conservation efforts is that the government taxation needed to support such programs creates its own economic inefficiencies. According to traditional economic theory, taxes cause companies and individuals to take certain actions, or refrain from taking certain actions, simply to minimize taxes. While difficult to quantify, these costs are undoubtedly substantial. These costs counterbalance, to some indeterminate degree, the dead weight social losses associated with regulation.

A second objection to this argument is that the allegedly perverse environmental costs of the regulatory approach are probably overstated by regulation's critics. As a practical matter, numerous steep hurdles, primarily economic, stand in the way of development of natural lands. The possible additional incentive for a developer in avoiding potential future regulatory requirements (which the developer might be able to satisfy in any event) is unlikely in most cases to tip the balance in favor of immediate development. Of course, the actual impact of a potential new regulatory initiative will vary with the costs of removing different areas from regulatory jurisdiction by developing them; cutting commercial timber is one thing, filling a swamp is quite another.

The prospect that land owners might simply violate environmental laws—the so-called "shoot, shovel, and shut up" syndrome—is both more plausible and more troubling. Certain owners have an economic incentive to violate environmental laws, and in many circumstances, such as in rural areas, violations may be difficult to detect. However, it is distinctly unsettling to speak of basing public policy on the premise that companies and individuals may routinely violate the law because it is in their financial interest to do so. Perfect compliance with the law is generally unattainable and unnecessary to achieve the law's purposes. But we do not ordinarily frame policy on the assumption that citizens will consistently break the law. Or at least we normally do not do so without inquiring whether the penalties for legal violations are high enough and whether government is being sufficiently vigorous in prosecuting violators.

Third, logic and experience indicate that voluntary, publicly-financed conservation programs make it difficult to maximize conservation results and, therefore, risk expending substantial public resources for relatively modest conservation gains. It is reasonable to presume that those most likely to volunteer to accept financial incentives will be those for whom incentives are most nearly pure windfalls. In other words, land owners most likely to donate or sell an easement on their property will be the most unlikely to develop their property in the foreseeable future. On the other hand, those with specific development plans are the least likely to participate in such programs, regardless of the relative importance of their land for conservation purposes. By contrast, regulatory programs, because their implementation is under government control, can be targeted much more efficiently to protect the most threatened lands....

Finally, as Professor Federico Cheever has astutely observed, the "cooperative" spirit of conservation easements turns out to be distinctly time-bound. At the outset, a willing seller of an interest in property for conservation purposes may view the transaction as a positive event, especially if the seller who received the financial reward shares the conservation objectives of the group acquiring the interest. But as Professor Cheever explains, as years and decades pass and title to the underlying property changes hands, new owners of the underlying fee, who did not receive any direct financial reward for the easement, may view the easement as a costly encumbrance. The new owners will have a financial interest in seeking out opportunities to cancel or evade the restrictions imposed by the easement. In this respect, a successor in interest to the original conservation donor might have the same antagonistic attitude about the easement restrictions as many land owners are said to have about the Endangered Species Act. In sum, while the grant of an easement might appear to be a form of win-win, cooperative conservation, over time the enthusiasm is likely to wane considerably.

2. *Internalization of Social Costs*

A second efficiency argument for paying owners to accept restrictions voluntarily is that this approach appropriately requires the public to internalize the social costs of conservation. According to this argument, if the public is permitted to enjoy only those regulatory benefits it is actually willing to pay for, the degree of regulatory protection will tend to equilibrate at the socially optimal level. By contrast, the argument continues, regulation leads to over-restriction because regulators operate under the "fiscal illusion" that regulation is cost-free and therefore impose more restrictions than can be justified under a public welfare test.

There are a number of flaws in this argument, which is basically a variant of the basic property rights argument against regulations articulated by Professor Richard Epstein and his followers. One response is that the so-called "fiscal illusion" problem is itself largely illusory. As Professor Barton Thompson has observed, "the traditional argument—that land owners are systematically at a disadvantage in defeating regulations that are not cost justified—appears wrong both as a matter of theory and empirical evidence." Land owners and developers represent discrete, well-organized interest groups that are well equipped to defend their interests in the political arena and ensure government does not over-regulate. Even though real estate interests may be outnumbered by the general populace that benefits from strong conservation programs, the diffuse public is no match for land owners and developers in political warfare. Thus, reliance on easements cannot be justified on the ground that it avoids the risk of systematic over-restriction based on government regulations....

3. Providing Permanent Protection

According to easement advocates, another valuable feature of this tool is that it ensures "permanent" protection of the land. Indeed, land trusts typically highlight protection in "perpetuity" as the most distinctive aspect of their work. Land trust advocates routinely contrast the benefits of "permanent" easements with regulatory controls, which they characterize as being subject to elimination or modification through the political process at virtually any time.

There are a variety of responses to this argument, which raises quite complex issues. First, regulations are not nearly so impermanent as easement advocates contend. To be sure, as a theoretical matter, land use regulations can be repealed by a vote of elected officials at virtually any time. But the practical reality is quite different. A major political struggle is often required to get a new regulatory program established. Once regulations are in place, however, and especially after a few years have passed, regulatory programs often become quite impervious to change....

Furthermore, even assuming all development were essentially irreversible, permanent prohibitions against development cannot be defended as optimal in every context. Perhaps the most obvious example is presented by management of land development along the urbanizing fringe. Permanent easements are sometimes described as an antidote to the problem of "sprawl" development. But permanent restrictions on land use at the urbanizing fringe, even if they appear worthwhile in the short term, may well turn out to be ill-advised over the long term, as the demands of a growing population generate the need for more housing and other development. Even more significant, because land use restrictions along the urbanizing fringe may deflect land development pressures out from the urban center, easements ostensibly designed to curb sprawl may actually exacerbate the problem.

Another reason "permanent" easement restrictions may not necessarily be optimal is that the ecological conditions of land will change over time, making it difficult to anticipate whether it will be valuable to safeguard certain portions of the landscape from development. While dynamic change is inherent in natural systems, there is an emerging scientific consensus that global warming will produce dramatic shifts in ecological conditions across the landscape. As a result, one cannot confidently predict whether a patch of coastal wetlands, or habitat currently used by an endangered species, will have any ecological importance a hundred years from now. In the face of accelerating ecological change, a strategy focused on "permanently" locking away portions of the landscape appears both naive and wasteful.

In dealing with constantly changing ecological conditions, regulations that are expressly "temporary" have some obvious advantages. Precisely because regulations do not purport to be permanent, they are ideally suited to facilitating the gradual, orderly transformation of land on the urbanizing fringe to development uses....

One thoughtful response by easement advocates to concerns about the feasibility and desirability of "permanent" easement restrictions has been to acknowledge that the "in perpetuity" slogan of the land trust movement has been overdone. They recognize the need to establish formal standards and procedures to address the likelihood that certain conservation easements may outlive their usefulness. For example, Professor McLaughlin has argued for frank acknowledgment that easement restrictions on certain properties may no longer be justified in the future. She argues that state courts are well equipped, using the cy pres doctrine, to regulate the amendment and termination of easements, like any other charitable trust, in response to changing social needs and values. In this fashion, easement restrictions can be lifted from land where they are no longer needed, and the funds earned from developing the property can be rededicated to other conservation purposes. To help ensure conservation interests are not disadvantaged over the long-term, Professor McLaughlin has argued that the portion of a property's market value assigned to conservation purposes should be based, not on the value of the property's development rights at the time of the original donation, but based on the value of the development rights on the date of easement termination.

While the acknowledgment that easements are not necessarily permanent reflects a welcome dose of reality, proposals for reform along the lines suggested by Professor McLaughlin appear to beg the basic question of why conservationists should rely on easements at all. According to easement advocates, as discussed above, the primary problem with regulations, which easements are supposed to solve, is that they are impermanent. If it turns out that impermanence is both unavoidable and valuable, at least in certain circumstances, then a primary argument for using easements in the first place is undermined. Stated differently, if what we really need is a land management tool that permits restrictions to be modified as circumstances change, then we already have in hand a good tool for that purpose, traditional regulation.

A second potential objection to the idea of relying on legal doctrines governing the modification of charitable trusts to manage extinguishment and amendment of easement restrictions is that the courts are not well suited to making land use decisions. Judges lack the institutional competence to evaluate whether certain types of restrictions continue to serve a valuable conservation purpose, and how they might be modified to better advance conservation goals. In addition, while parties interested in potential easement terminations can seek to intervene or file friend of the court briefs, courts are not set up to manage the kind of intensive, elaborate public participation process that characterizes local land use decision making in this country. As Professor Cheever has said, judicial supervision of conservation easements does not provide a "governance structure" to manage easements over the long-term, or "a forum in which to debate changes in conditions and values."

*

Index

References are to Pages

References are to Pages

References are to Pages

†